D1716762

HOW TO BE A DIRT-SMART BUYER

OF COUNTRY PROPERTY

Curtis Seltzer

ISBN 0-7414-3443-1

Published by:

PUBLISHING.COM

1094 New DeHaven Street, Suite 100
West Conshohocken, PA 19428-2713
Info@buybooksontheweb.com
www.buybooksontheweb.com
Toll-free (877) BUY BOOK
Local Phone (610) 941-9999
Fax (610) 941-9959

Printed in the United States of America
Printed on Recycled Paper
Published May 2007

To Molly, a wonderful daughter and a good writer

ACKNOWLEDGMENTS

I've needed help and was fortunate to have gotten it.

Clif Rexrode, Appalachian Forestry Services of Waynesboro, Virginia, has been a boots-on-the-ground consulting forester for 30 years. His knowledge of forestry issues and his willingness to share it with me were invaluable. I cannot thank him adequately. I hope that I, at least, amused him with my questions as I wasted his time looking at one high-graded tract after another. He's been a true friend over the years.

Tom Arbogast, who heads the tax practice at Schnader Harrison Segal & Lewis, LLP in Pittsburgh, is both a lawyer and a CPA. His generous offer to review what I wrote on tax issues was a brilliant beacon in what always looks to me like impenetrable, unfathomable darkness.

Susan McCray, my CPA in Staunton, Virginia, reviewed drafts of Chapters 6 and 24, both dealing with tax issues. She saved me from myself many times. She prevented me from reaping in final form what I had sown in draft.

Les LaPrade, Jr., of McDowell, Virginia, rescued me from my computer ignorance. With patience and good humor, he reformatted the entire manuscript, taking out my "hard returns" line by line and justifying my right margins. Since I'm just a typewriter guy transplanted to a keyboard, I feel that Bill Gates treated me and all other old manuals pretty shabbily by ensnaring us in this hand-work booby trap. Les has a more sensible attitude toward computers than I have. He wants to understand why they do things: I just want them not to hurt me. I could not have submitted this manuscript without Les and his wife, Laura, who showed him a thing or two when he needed to be shown a thing or two.

Tom Atkeson, a retired engineer in Monterey, Virginia, drew several drawings that required a clear and steady hand, not my scritch-scratch penmanship. And even though Tom's hand is not as clear and steady as it was when he was at VMI and in Vietnam, it's still clear and steady enough to get the job done.

All errors of fact and misjudgments are mine.

I've picked up land knowledge over the years from many individuals, including Harrison Elkins, David R. Underhill, Portia and Tom Weiskel, Mike and Joy Brenneman, Charlie Taylor, Jim Loesel, Gibby Crummett, Harry Haney, Robert Barrett, Stephen W. Dorris, Sam Vansickle, M.C. Davis, Pete Johnson, Tim Linstrom, Joe Leininger, John Crites, Julia Elbon, Darrell V. McGraw, Robert W. Tufts, Robert Guerrant, Angela Blythe, John Alexander Williams, Nancy Debevoise, Thomas Taylor, John Lindsey, Mark Yanoski, Carey Dowd, Stephen J. Small, Willie Anderson, Barbara E. Smith, Helen Steele, Ann Swartz, Robert Payne, John David, Beverly Medgaus Jones and Melissa Ann Dowd.

I've also learned from Billy Shepherd, Alan Gourley, Mike McEver, Dan Girouard, Dave Mayo, Murray Gibson, Jim Woltz, Chris Bland, Huel Wheeler and Daniel McKittrick.

The first book I read about investing in real estate was formative—George Bockl, How to Use Leverage to Make Money in Local Real Estate (Englewood Cliffs, NJ: Prentice-Hall, 1965). I bought it for $1 at our library's annual book auction. It led to my first purchase of land—400 acres—with no money in the deal.

I have used masculine pronouns for lack of a gender-neutral alternative. I found using he to refer to a seller or buyer was less offensive to my ear than using she or the brain-jarring, they. My ear, of course, is now 61 years old; younger ears may find the old-fashioned masculine objectionable. For what it's worth, whenever I wrote he and him, my thoughts included she and her.

My mother, Rena C. Seltzer, helped me buy my first piece of land, and the estate of my father, Robert Seltzer, helped buy our farm. My aunt, Lucy Katz, helps me keep their memories.

My wife, Melissa Ann Dowd, didn't ask, didn't tell and didn't wonder out loud why I never seemed to be finished writing.

TABLE OF CONTENTS

INTRODUCTION

Tired of living where it's hot and flat? Want to find a cool spot in the mountains?

Need to escape the city on weekends?

Ready to bail out permanently on the close-in "burbs"?

Looking to retire to an old farmhouse with a front porch and big shade trees?

You are not alone.

We are now a nation of 300 million, up from 200 million in 1967. Population growth increases demand for property, and income growth, particularly in the urban/suburban upper middle classes, makes feasible the purchase of land and second homes in the country. In almost every rural county, farms and undeveloped land are being divided and sold to both the 75 million of us who are Boomers and to those coming after us. Although data are lacking, my guess is that urban and suburban buyers are now purchasing annually about three million parcels of country property—broadly defined. These include farmettes, ranchettes, hunting lots, farms, second homes, timberland, investment properties, waterfront properties and lots in developed and semi-developed projects. This rising demand trend, coming from urban and suburban buyers like the readers of this book, has pushed up the price of all types of rural land for the last 20 years. Country property has proved to be an excellent investment for most buyers. If global warming does indeed raise the level of coastal waters over the next century, displaced individuals and shrewd investors will be buying higher and safer ground. They will look to the countryside, taking advantage of technologies that allow them to make a living away from their city offices. If you're reading this paragraph, you've probably already come to the same conclusions.

Thousands of us buy rural property each year. Some are looking for a weekend getaway; others to relocate full-time. Some want undeveloped, or **raw**, land. Others feel more comfortable in a planned community with **infrastructure**—roads and utilities—in place. Some want a cabin at the end of a long dirt road; others want a plantation house with hot and cold running servants or a solar-powered passive-aggressive statement of environmental correctness. As America's population grows and metropolitan areas become increasingly hectic and congested, more and more of us will be looking for a place in the country.

In most of America, country property has been a wonderful investment and is appreciating at a more or less strong and healthy clip. The average acre of farmland was valued at $1,900 in 2005, up from about $600 in 1987. That reflected a 15 percent rise in value in 2005, on top of a 21 percent increase in 2004. Pasture land now averages about $1,000 per acre, while cropland is now valued, on the average, at almost $2,400 per acre. The sharpest increases are found nearest urban areas. Timberland—with and without timber that can be sold immediately—and undeveloped recreational land are appreciating at similar rates (Jilian Mincer, "Tilling a Farmland Investment," Wall Street Journal, September 9-10, 2006.). Appreciation is being driven by large institutions, wealthy individuals and people like you and me. People want land because it can generate income, build wealth and is fun to have. These are good reasons to become a dirt-smart buyer of country property.

When I bought my first rural property in 1971, I lacked even a clue about how to think about the questions that such a purchase inevitably involves. I liked the idea of woods, on a hill with a view and a site for a pond. I found a spot near Wendell Depot, Massachusetts, about a 30-minute, back-roads drive north of Amherst. The woods, it turned out, had just been timbered, which I understood more abstractly than practically. The view appeared only from the crest of a snubbed off, north-facing ridge that was sort of accessible with a 4WD Bronco for a few months each year and during Sahara-type droughts. The site for a pond turned out to be a bottomless bog, which we now call **wetlands** and value for its habitat. The deed, I discovered after purchase, never specified the number of acres. I thought we bought 100, but wiser heads put the number at 60. We owned an undeveloped right of way that swamped through the Mekong Delta before it stalled in the Central Highlands.

Over the next 15 years, we bought a small parcel that brought frontage on a state-maintained road and also contained a usable access drive into the original 60-acre island. Through little effort, the land appreciated in value ten-fold owing to its proximity to a thriving college town. It was like having a high-interest passbook savings account that doubled as a sixth-grader's hide out. At 26, with wars raging abroad and at home, I was far more interested in finding a placid hole than in projecting my annualized return on investment. Nonetheless, the possibilities of rapid appreciation of rural land were not lost, even on me. Necessity forced me to learn a little about boundaries, roads, utilities, water and timber. But, in hindsight, I didn't learn very much. The next property I bought had a farmhouse that piped its sewage behind the barn, into the creek—a fact I discovered after taking possession.

I didn't start teaching myself how to buy country property until my fourth purchase. This 400+ acres was an investment, so I approached it as a research project. Researching property is a process called, **scoping**. I began my scoping with three **investment questions**: how can I buy it without any money; can the property pay most of its own mortgage servicing through rental; and, finally, if I need to sell it after a few years, am I reasonably confident that I can make a profit? In addition to these investment questions, I developed and then scoped a series of **property questions** that bore directly on the appropriate purchase price, risks, uncertainties and the value of saleable assets, such as merchantable timber and an old farmhouse. One question led to another, and I soon discovered that I had cobbled together a methodological approach that was adaptable in general terms to other rural properties, notwithstanding differences in size, purpose, location and type. I bought the 400 acres without any money and used the pasture rent to carry about half the mortgage costs. I had taken the first step to becoming **dirt smart**.

I discovered that I liked doing dirt research. I looked into other properties for my own account. The work was practical and, unlike academic research, did not drag on endlessly. It satisfied whatever interest I ever had in doing investigative reporting, which reporters tellingly refer to as, digging. Each property presented its own combination of assets, liabilities, knowns, unknowns and unknowns that I didn't know I didn't know. If I dug deeply, I would uncover any embedded deal-breakers. I started by writing long memos analyzing each purchase. (Writing is a bad habit that I'm hoping will solve itself as I age.) The memo format forced me to think through both a **buying plan** and a **profit plan**. Investors need both. The buying plan is akin to a plan for winning a war; the profit plan is what you do once you've won.

I used these research skills in the purchase of other properties, and then began to work as a **land consultant** for investors who were interested in buying large tracts of farmland and timberland. Part of the experience of buying country land is learning how to do it knowledgeably, a process I call **becoming dirt-smart**. There's always a trial-and-error element to learning a new skill, but learning how to buy country property is a process that need not involve supplying yourself with a lifetime of ironic stories for cocktail conversations. I wrote this book to show you how to be dirt-smart about buying country property. Consider it a piggy-back ride on me. I also wrote it to make some money.

Land buying starts with dirt. Look, first, at how the land lays—its **topography**. Which directions do its slopes face? How steep are they? If the land is flat, will it drain quickly or hold water because the subsurface contains a lot of clay? The surface vegetation and the feel of the dirt in your hand will give you an initial reading. Topographically interesting land is usually more interesting to spend time on, but it's also more expensive to work with and much harder to work against.

Look, second, at your **soils**. Different soils have different characteristics and capabilities, which will determine what you can do with your property at a reasonable cost. Your first stop in **scoping property** is to pick up a copy of the county's Soil Survey at the local U.S.Department of Agriculture office. In this book, you will find maps showing soil types throughout the county as well as the virtues and liabilities of each type. County-level aerial maps and soil-survey information are available for some states and counties on the Internet at http://soils.usda.gov/survey.

Look, third, at the **location of your dirt**. Will it be hard to get to in bad weather? Is it subject to flooding, earthquakes, mudslides, windstorms, fires and prevailing weather? If you have shoreline, is the land low (bad) or high (good)? Is the shoreline eroding? Is the land facing in the right compass direction for your plans?

Finally, look at your **dirt in terms of proximity to local goods and bads**—hospital, fire station, public water and sewerage, rescue squad, floodplain, job opportunities, distance from your current residence, post office, bank, supermarket and objectionable facilities, however you care to define them.

Most buyers from the city and suburbs, including me, focus first and almost exclusively, on the country house, whether existing or planned. This comes at the expense of paying attention to the dirt on which the house stands and which surrounds it. We do this, I think, because all of us have a passing familiarity with houses. So we evaluate country property in terms of what we know rather than what we don't. There's nothing wrong with thinking about "house in the country." Just remember that this thought contains two elements: house + country. Don't fall into self-induced house hypnosis. You'll find that dirt acquires more prominence in your country life over time.

I've come to think of buying rural property in terms of analogies.

Finding country property is like finding a mate. The more you look, the more possibilities turn up. Each is different. Some candidates will be warm and inviting; others can make your head pound. Love at first sight happens, but that kind of love may not survive the practicalities of living and working together. While love may conquer all, the more it has to conquer, the harder it's going to be to both stay in love and stick it out. You can't sign a prenuptial agreement with land, which exempts you from paying future costs if things don't work out. So you have to look for a good fit on many levels, not just sex. This book is written to help buyers learn to keep their heads and use them too. The object, of course, is to find a property that you like better over time, a property that fits you financially and emotionally, a property where love has to conquer as little as possible.

This book shows you how to find and buy such a property.

Here is a second analogy.

Most people judge books by their covers, even though we know we're supposed to be smarter than that. The publishing industry spends a great deal of effort and money in cover design because we're not. Standing in a bookstore, how else can we judge a book if not by its cover? If you judged this book by its cover, the worst that can happen is that you've bought an over-priced doorstop. If, however, you buy rural property on the basis of a once-over glance at its cover, you may find yourself selling over-priced doorstops to a village of tent dwellers.

As with any other large purchase, large mistakes can be made on country real estate. The most common are **under-scoping, overpaying and "poor fitting".** The first can lead to unexpected, burdensome, aggravating and expensive surprises that affect your use, enjoyment and pocketbook. The second makes it harder for a buyer to carry the property, sell it and make a profit. Under-scoping leads to overpaying. "Poor fitting" refers to a buyer finding his property ill-suited to his evolving needs. This often results from an initial purchase of too much house and too little land, or land that is all one type, such as nothing but open, flat ground or all steeply sloped wooded land facing north. It's difficult for a new country buyer to anticipate what he might want to do with property five or ten years in the future. Consequently, I would advise such a buyer to buy more land and less house if a choice has to be made between the two, and buy a property that contains more rather than fewer types of soils and land—pasture, field, wooded, flat, hilly and bottom.

First-impression buying puts at risk not only thousands of your dollars but the hard work and love you will inevitably invest in your purchase. To prevent first-impression buying, you must learn to read the cover of a property enough to know whether it merits scoping effort. This initial process, called **screening,** requires that a buyer have a pretty firm idea of both what he seeks and what he doesn't want. Screening is a first-cut selection process that involves knowing how to **screen out properties** that have unfixable negatives or expensive problems (such as a pre-Revolution house whose historically correct reconstruction will cost no less than two launches of the space shuttle) and **screen in** those properties that can be cleaned up with reasonable investments of time, effort and money. Screening uses the same questions and research techniques found in scoping. The difference between them lies in the depth and breadth of the investigation. Neither process is long in absolute terms—screening should take minutes, scoping several days or weeks, at most. The more you look at properties analytically using the methods I describe, the faster and more confident you will become at making both screening and scoping decisions.

Screening is the same process of preliminary research as that which an investigative reporter does when he gets wind of a story. The tip is checked enough to decide whether to pursue it or forget it. Screening—and later, scoping—is rational and analytical. It is not a matter of "falling in love." A property, like a good investigative story, has to stand on its merits during both processes. Otherwise, it should be rejected.

First-cut screening is the opposite in principle and practice to first-impression buying. First-cut screening is not a decision to buy; it's a decision to investigate further. It's based on the more or less systematic acquisition of enough knowledge to decide between stopping and going further.

You can screen property quickly if you know the questions to ask and the level of information you need to make a decision. I am now usually able to screen investment properties in or out with a five- to ten-minute phone call to the owner or his real-estate agent. I bring to that conversation a general idea of current land values in the area and learn the seller's asking price. If this is your first time in an area, you can get a quick-and-dirty notion of market land values by subtracting ten to 20 percent from asking prices found in real-estate listings. Subtract another five percent if the seller is marketing with a real-estate agent whose commission will range between six and ten percent. (A rural-land **appraisal** determines the **fair market value [FMV]** of the property being sold by comparing it with three or four recent sales of comparable properties—called, **comps**—in the area, after adjusting for differences.) My shake-and-bake method gives a buyer enough sense of fair market value to get started.

My first investment screen is **price per acre ($/A)**. I eliminate property priced way above what I think its FMV is. I screen in property priced at, close to and below market. With property priced *some* above what I think its FMV is, I might pull it in for further study if it has some feature that makes it especially valuable or I think the seller's price is soft. Just keep in mind that you cannot count on selling land that you bought above market for an above-market price in the near future.

My next screens focus on size, location, improvements, current use and ratio of wooded land to open. Looking at property for investment rather than a personal residence, I avoid listings that are house-heavy and land-short. A $700,000 house standing on one country acre must be resold as a unit; profit in such a deal usually comes only from long-term appreciation. I screen in properties that are a mix of assets, some of which can be turned into cash quickly and easily. I also screen in properties that generate annual cash from production or rental that will cover at least 30 percent of an expected mortgage payment. I usually screen out properties where the minerals won't convey with the surface, where the timber has been reserved by the seller for his future benefit, where some regulatory condition devalues the property (such as a tobacco farm that has lost its tobacco subsidy, or land that can't be divided because of zoning restrictions), where a conservation easement is in place that limits profit potential, or where some property-specific factor hampers my plan for the property. The latter might include dirt that is unsuitable for septic systems, lack of sufficient sight distance on a state-maintained road that eliminates a proposed entrance, lack of legal or feasible access, road-building costs that are prohibitive, the presence of a protected species or its habitat, and the presence of expensive-to-settle boundary disputes. One or two unacceptable facts are usually enough for me to scratch a candidate.

Buyers who are less interested in rural property for its investment potential and more interested in its second-home or recreational values will develop a set of screens that are more personal. Total price, rather than price per acre, may be the money screen such a buyer uses. FMV may be a less important screen than a buyer requirement that cannot be added on later, such as a particular view or specific location. A second-home buyer may want to screen in properties with obvious, even hideously expensive, problems if it has unique virtues and the buyer's pocketbook matches his remedial plans. Many property-related problems can be fixed by throwing money at them. But some are impervious even to cash. If your dream farm is located next to an airport, you cannot buy your way free from over-flight noise. You cannot create a ridge-top view from a flat Iowa cornfield. You can, however, build a lake if you want one and replant large trees if you want shade.

Visiting and scoping property takes time, so it is productive to eliminate non-promising properties by phone or on the basis of a package of materials the seller sends to you. Screening is not kicking tires. You are a legitimate buyer, not an endless looker.

Screening is the first step in doing dirt-smart scoping, which is your deep research into a promising property you've screened in. You might screen out 25 properties to find one worth a visit, visit five before you scope one, and scope three before you buy. There are no formulas to determine the amount of effort you need to put into screening and scoping before buying. Scoping is a process with a purpose; it is not a game played for the benefits of playing. Take comfort, however, in knowing that each scoping goes faster with experience. You don't need to own a property for 20 years before you know it well enough to buy it. A buyer will never acquire an equivalent level of intimacy when scoping a potential purchase. What you need to make a dirt-smart purchase is knowledge, not intimacy. This book will show you how to learn enough to know whether to buy and at what price.

The information in this book will save you money and make you money.

Inexperienced land buyers have two fears: paying too much and looking foolish. Fears like these can be self-protective when they are converted into rational analysis. That's what screening and scoping do. Fear can be made useful, but, left on its own, it can lead to paralysis or impulsive decisions. Buying rural land is not risky as long as you do your research. A buyer strips risk from a land purchase by acquiring specific information. You now have in your hand the way to get what you need to know.

If you don't like reading advice, put this book down now. This is a how-to book. Its purpose is to provide information on which the reader can base his own actions for his own benefit. The advice given is based on actual successes and disasters, including my own. I wrote this book, wishing that I had had one like it during the last 35 years.

CHAPTER 1: THREE WRITERS SHOW HOW NOT TO DO IT

Without being too didactic about it, my position is that there is a more-or-less right way to buy any rural property and several more or less not-so-right ways. If you approach buying more rationally and analytically than not, you will in most cases be more satisfied with your purchase. If you allow yourself to be emotionally stampeded into a purchase, or stampede yourself into one, you lower your odds for good results. A property that you fall in love with at first sight should not be exempt from rational analysis and the identification of lurking problems. I offer three illustrations of self-induced emotional stampeding.

Michael Korda, editor-in-chief of Simon & Schuster and prominent author, wrote Country Matters: The Pleasures and Tribulations of Moving from a Big City to an Old Country Farmhouse (New York: HarperCollins, 2001). His story is a self-deprecating celebration of his adventures with a house built in 1785 that he and his wife, Margaret, purchased on 20 acres in Dutchess County, New York in 1980. In a sequel, Horse People: Scenes from the Riding Life (New York: HarperCollins, 2003), he notes that their country house came with "...numerous problems.., literally enough to fill a book..," Country Matters. (Horse People, p. 347.)

The Kordas met while riding in Manhattan's Central Park. One snaffle led to another, and soon they were looking for a second home in the country where they might spend time with their horses. Margaret discovers their country place and shows it to her husband on a day, he writes, that

> could hardly have been less promising. Sheets of rain poured down...[with] heavy fog.... The house, when we got to it, was hard to see, being surrounded by huge old maple trees looming out of the fog. There was so much water that it was erupting out of the culverts [tops of the downspouts] like Old Faithful and cascading over the sides of the gutters. I glimpsed two barns, which looked as if they might need a bit of work...some run-down outbuildings. ...the path to the house was made of huge stones...which were lethally slippery with rain and moss. (Country Matters, pp. 10-11.)

The house had wide-plank floors, old windows, four fireplaces and hand-made hinges—in Korda's word, "character." "Less than an hour after we got there we had shaken hands on a deal," he writes.

In less than an hour, in a rain storm and without looking at the farm's land, the Kordas agreed to buy a country place for $250,000 (1980 dollars). Neither seems to have looked at the fields where horses would graze, fences built and water lines buried six feet deep. The land initially seems to have represented nothing more than distance between the charming house and the neighbors, charming and otherwise. When they later decided to use their land, the Kordas discovered that in the country, dirt counts. The fields were rocky and covered in scrub growth, both of which were costly and difficult to overcome.

He wrote, "...we did not...know it at the time, [that] no amount of hard work or money was going to turn *these* acres into the kind of grassy, rolling fields dotted with galloping foals and mares that appear in television commercials for banks and insurance companies every year about the time of the Kentucky Derby." (Horse People, p. 182.) As you read Dirt-Smart, you will learn how to acquire this very information in advance.

It was no secret in 1980 that "Dutchess County is just close enough to New England to qualify as rock country—plowing, even raking, merely brings up the next layer of loose rocks, and the soil is spread thinly over layers of solid rock." (*Id.*) It had not been a secret for more than 300 years. Not looking and not knowing are proven ways of ending up not happy. Had the Kordas done a little dirt research, they might have reoriented their property prospecting to an area better suited to a horse operation. Had the Kordas followed one all-purpose country buyer's gnome—**buy good dirt that can support multiple uses**—they would have saved themselves thousands of dollars in quarreling with rocks and whacking "scrubbish."

Korda applied only one faculty in buying country property—his heart. Am I instantly and hopelessly in love with this place no matter what? If so, let me give you my money. This method—to continue an analogy—is no different than a fellow marrying a woman only moments after glimpsing her once across a dark and crowded disco. The romantics and odds-makers among my readers will say, even some marriages of that sort work out. True, some do. It helps when the thunderstruck buyer has sufficient money to make a hasty and ill-matched union workable enough. Country Matters is the story of the consequences and costs of buying rural property using only your heart.

How exactly does one go about buying land in this fashion? Korda never left the charming house during his visit. He never walked his road frontage. Had he done so, he would have discovered that it was used as a community trash dump.

He never even realized where he was and where he wasn't. He tells his readers that the house with character was located on "the 'wrong' side of the Taconic [State Parkway]." He had inadvertently purchased west of the Taconic. His friends were east of the Parkway, where "excess scarcely even raises eyebrows," with showpiece barns made of "...rare paneled woods, crystal chandeliers [and] tack rooms that look as if Ralph Lauren had designed them." (Horse People, p. 164.) I will assume that my readers know how to read a common road map.

Korda did not look very hard at what he was buying and does not appear to have understood the implications of what he did see. Before submitting his purchase-offer contract, he never walked his boundaries or viewed prospective neighbors. One turned out to be a trailer-bound commune. Another was a "huge family with many snarling dogs and no-neck teenage children living in the middle of a kind of mini wrecking yard of worn-out snowmobiles and pickup trucks in a ramshackle house from which the toilet emptied onto the lawn without the benefit of a septic system." One neighbor "...had a son who, when he wasn't in and out of one of the many local psychiatric institutions, sometimes rode across our property bareback on a farm horse, grinning maniacally." (Horse People, p. 164.) If I can read between his lines, the Kordas never became tight as ticks with any of these souls. Neighbors who are genuine nuisances will spoil the best view or the most character-laden house so it's best to check out who shares your property line before making an offer.

The outbuildings at a distance looked to Korda as if they could use a nail here and a shingle there. If only farms were so accommodating. Outbuildings that look run down from a distance through the scrim of a monsoon will look worse on a sunny day up close. Wood buildings are usually old and have often had little maintenance. Foundations and roofs tend to go first. It is impossible to evaluate such needs without inspecting them, inside out. Big, old, swaggy barns smell richly of old hay and departed livestock. They creak pleasingly. Their amazing mortise-and-tenon framing will appeal to anyone who appreciates simple solutions to complex problems. They can be expensive to repair. Older barns are often not well suited to contemporary needs. A barn hayloft, for example, that was originally designed to store loose hay or 50-

pound "square" bales stacked to the rafters, can rarely be adapted to hold an equivalent volume of modern 800-pound "round" bales.

A neglected barn may indicate that the farm's land is too poor to make a go of the type of farming the barn was supposed to support. Farmers invested in the building and upkeep of their barns because of their central importance to the economic viability of their farm enterprise. A barn in structural trouble signals extended neglect, which may or may not be localized to the building. The Kordas lucked out twice. First, the barn was sound enough to be rehabbed and reconfigured to their horse needs, and, second, they found someone to do a good job for them.

When Korda did see a red flag, he seemed to note it as an observed idiosyncrasy—"culverts [sic] erupting like Old Faithful..," cascading over the gutters. A roof-and-drainage system that creates cataracts over its gutters is always a bad sign. It's likely to mean water-damaged walls and water-rotted sills. Systems that don't work properly may be charming when they belong to someone else, but not when they're yours.

Did it not occur to the Kordas that the lethally slick flagstone path leading to the house would soon be endangering their lives?

Would anyone buy a used car this way? No matter how much you loved its paint job and hood ornament, would you not crank the engine? Would you not sit in the driver's seat and work the controls? Would you not take it for a test drive? How many of us buy property with less consumer research than we would routinely apply to a 1980 Chevy showing 500,000 odometer miles whose owner claims it "runs like new"? The fewer of us, the better, I believe.

The only thing Korda did right on his first visit—and that inadvertently—was to arrive on a butt-ugly day. If a property's promise shines through the rain, you'll like the place even better when it's nice. Bad weather also gives you an opportunity to see how the property handles weather-related stress. Does the roof leak? Is the basement wet? Does water "pond up" in a low spot? Does the septic system backup when the ground is saturated? Is the entry road unusable in wet or icy conditions? In drought, does the spring, well, creek or stock pond dry up?

What Korda did wrong was that he failed to prepare himself for buying a house and land in the country. He didn't learn how to look at property; how to evaluate the dirt, outbuildings and house; how to read the property's subtle signals as well as its big red flags waving through the rain. Former UCLA basketball coach, John Wooten, put this situation into the aphorism: He who fails to prepare, prepares to fail. That's observed wisdom, trite though it is.

The predictable result was Korda's annual Brinks delivery of cash to local folks to do, maintain, rebuild and adapt.

Country Matters reads as if Korda spent the next two decades hiring every blue collar on his side of the Taconic to do something for him or his farm. From time to time, he employs a cook, housekeeper, garden person, barn lady, barn-lady helper, fix-everything man and non-resident excavation person who "adopts" the Kordas, along with practitioners of every trade and craft related to house maintenance, horses and vehicles. These people—"...the loyal, hardworking peasantry"—were essential to this area's horsey pseudo-feudalism in which the gentry were now more dependent on the "help" than the other way around. (Horse People, p. 171.)

Korda manages in these circumstances, because he says that he was "...pretty good at writing checks, a basic skill without which nothing gets done, though it seldom gets much in the way of attention or praise." (*Ibid.*, p. 166.)

Check writing is, indeed, one way of getting stuff done around the farm. (Another way is to hope the chore will go away if it's ignored long enough.)

You don't need to be Harry Homeowner to manage a second home in the country. You don't need to be skilled, strong or handy—though all three are useful country attributes. But you should be willing to prepare yourself to do a few basic things—light a pilot, drain water pipes, replace a fuse, flip a breaker, remove creosote from a chimney by tossing in a few tablespoons of creosote remover every couple of weeks, shut off the water into the house, make a fire in a woodstove and clean a filter. If you refuse to learn these most basic tasks of house mechanics, you will be completely dependent on local folks. Some will help you for free now and then because you're so pitiful or because you make such good copy down at the feed store. Most, however, you will have to pay—and should pay—to do the simplest and easiest bit of work regardless of your local comedic news value.

While local labor prospered from frequent visits to the Kordas' open vault, other locals appeared unbeckoned. Immediately upon taking possession, Korda more or less allowed himself to be bullied and guilt-tripped into allowing organized snowmobilers, pheasant hunters and the local fox hunt, among others, to have free run of his place in return for keeping off the unorganized riff-raff. Then, he feels put upon by his own posses, and, finally, bounces the fox hunters.

I reluctantly offer this bit of hard counsel: **the only way to keep folks off your land is to say no to everyone right from the start**. This will spare you accidents involving gun-shot pets, livestock stuck with arrows, strangers doing both familiar and unfamiliar things under your nose as well as fleets of ATVs, pick-up trucks, dirt bikes and snowmobiles disturbing you in their seasons. If you say yes to every request at the start of your ownership as Korda did, you will be overrun as he was. After some years of just saying no, you can make exceptions.

Had Korda done even minimal scoping, he would have had a ballpark notion of what his "going-in" fix-up expenses were going to be. Then, he might have used these cost estimates to help himself in negotiating a purchase price that took them into account. Instead, Korda negotiated as if he were buying a "cream puff"—a property that's turnkey perfect. This amounts to blindfolding yourself just prior to jumping off your own gangplank.

Despite my pokes at Korda's ways, I really have no objection to spending money on country property. Doing so, is, in fact, one of life's pleasures. It's fun to plan and execute improvements to property that you appreciate and enjoy. It satisfies something in us that goes back to both childhood and caves. It gives us an opportunity to mark our passage in a way that's different from making a profit or writing a book. Decisions about scale and style of how country property will be changed during your ownership are up to you. My concern is to protect a buyer from having to spend money to solve a problem that comes as a post-purchase surprise.

It's one thing to be inexperienced and not savvy about buying country property; that's nothing to be ashamed of and is, presumably, why you bought this book. It is, however, quite another, to be either intentionally blasé about basic self-protective consumer behavior or so incredibly wealthy that ignoring one's own self interest is no more than one of life's petty details.

Whether you're Bill Gates or Humble Pie, no good reason exists to buy rural property without scoping it first. I'm not arguing against buying an old country house with character. Rather, I'm arguing that any such purchase be made after you unemotionally and analytically add your initial purchase cost to those you estimate you will incur in required fix up. The total gives you a reasonably accurate idea of what your country place will cost. With the Korda place, almost every one of the basic house systems—roof, gutters, siding, fireplaces, wiring, plumbing, windows, heating, septic and water—had to be substantially repaired or totally replaced. A competent house inspector should have flagged every one of these problems—and perhaps the inspector Korda hired did. The cumulative weight of across-the-board repairs such as these is large in terms of time, emotional energy, inconvenience and money. If the seller is not asked to discount his asking price or make some repairs, the full weight of remedy, or lack of remedy, falls on the new owner. Even if you are fortunate enough to be able to say, "This is what I want. Money is neither object nor subject," you should consider your non-dollar costs—time, inconvenience and emotional energy—that will be involved for every improvement you plan and implement.

The Kordas bought without choosing to get an idea of what lay in store because the house's character trumped all. Certain properties are immediately pleasing, because of their overall effect. Character is quality construction and design that carries its age well. Be careful to distinguish between genuine character and imitation. Faux character is achieved through fake beams and windows with plastic pane inserts, and modern components made to look like old materials, such as flooring, cabinets and hardware. Be forewarned: true house character costs a lot upfront and is also expensive to maintain. Such places sing to us the way vintage steam locomotives do, with their bells and smells and chugga-chuggas. They too burn cash by the ton. Imagine shoveling your dollars into a roaring furnace. Still, if you want character, you have to buy it at a price that the market determines.

Often, buyers with limited cash to spend on a country second home face the choice between buying a cash-burning charmer and a less charming but cheaper and more practical alternative. One way of making that decision is to determine whether genuine character—wide-plank floors, hand-made hinges, hand-hewn ceiling beams, leaded glass—can be worked into the cheaper alternative without creating a composite freak. There are limits to your ability to add true character. You can't turn a 1950s bungalow into a four-story *ante-bellum* mansion by tacking up a couple of oversized white columns. Still, the buyer faced with such a choice should evaluate the possibilities of blending character piecemeal into the more plebian alternative. That approach is likely to prove more feasible than having to redo the basic systems in a house built more than 100 years ago. For instance, hand-made hinges—both old and new—are readily available if you think your doors need them and could wear them without shouting: "Look at my hinges!" Any reputable finish carpenter can hang them so that they squeak and stick.

Korda's place is what I call a "**look farm**," a spot in the country owned by someone who wants a country place that produces, not food or fiber, but the right look for themselves and their guests. People buy rural property for many, varied reasons. Some I endorse, others I don't. Look farms don't bother me. I want our farm to look the way I want it to look, which, I suppose, in its slightly run-down way reflects my own slightly run-down ways. If you want to own a look farm, you'll have to decide whether you're better off buying as much of the right look as you can afford at the outset or adding it as you go along. I added.

The Kordas had three audiences in mind for their look farm: their neighbors, their guests and themselves. They raised a couple of pet pigs to show to their weekend guests. The Kordas thought the pigs also proved to their neighbors that they were "not just another city couple with aspirations to play at being gentry with more money than is good for them, and not your typical city-bred weekenders…." It's not clear whether the neighbors were convinced; I wasn't.

5

To achieve the right look for their guests and themselves, the Kordas resculpt their front yard to imitate an English manor lawn. Here we find a situation where the Kordas are trying to prove to their down-at-their-heels neighbors that they were not gentry by raising a couple of Wilburs while trying to prove to their friends through strategically placed boxwoods and rocks of the right sort that they were.

Finally, there is the question of we-are-what-we-drive farm look. To that end, Korda buys a red Porsche 942, Ferrari 308 GTS, Honda 600 Nighthawk, Harley-Davidson Fat Boy, three tractors, two ATVs, two horse trailers, Chevy Blazer and one "seriously big" Ford pick-up truck. "If there is one thing I do enjoy doing," he writes, "it is buying motor vehicles of any kind." (Horse People, p. 206.)

Remember my analogy about finding land and finding a mate. Korda chose a property based solely on an intense emotional reaction to the look and feel of the house. The analytical skills he uses as an editor were never brought to bear. He was charmed by the house's character, but, practically speaking, this place got his nose open like a 16-year-old boy about to lose his virginity in the backseat.

The Kordas bought on impulse. There's no sensible reason to buy country property this way. If you fear that you will lose the property if you don't act quickly, you can submit a purchase contract with **results-acceptable-to-the-buyer contingencies** that will give you time to scope and allow you to back out of the deal without penalty. Impulse buying is not the same as **moving quickly**, which is what dirt-smart buyers do when their scoping indicates a good deal.

I urge readers to read Country Matters, though I would have re-titled it, Country Natters. Or Country Dirt Matters.

Michael Korda is not alone in his views. A cottage industry—a small industry working out of very large cottages—has emerged from writers who produce travelogues about their encampments in the American countryside, often within a two-hour drive of Times Square.

Laura Shaine Cunningham has written an honest and moving autobiography, A Place in the Country (New York: Riverhead Books, 2000). This is the second installment of her memoirs, which began with Sleeping Arrangements (New York: Knopf: 1989), the story of not knowing her father, her mother's early death and a make-shift upbringing involving two bachelor uncles who subsisted largely on popcorn and tuna croquettes, hot and cold. Orphaned at eight, she subsequently made it to large country estates, first at Tuxedo Park, and then to the Frederick Law Olmstead-designed Willowby Park in the Catskills. Her home there came complete with a genuine English Lord and Lady. She has lived there for more than 20 years.

Cunningham is a writer whose work I admire. I also admire her perseverance in the face of a tragic childhood, then divorce and cancer. Still, her normative observations to would-be country buyers are dumb beyond belief:

> The love of city people for the country is a mad love; it feeds on impulse and pays no attention to fact. We, the buyers of country places, don't really want to know too much about them before we take possession. We don't want our joy deflated by such details as E. coli counts, carpenter ants, and logging rights-of-way. Often, in the heat of purchase, we don't even want to know the actual location of the country house or how long it will really take to get there from the city. We never dwell on the nasty mathematics of cost or hear the

'mort' in 'mortgage.' We want that house, that plot of land, and we are as unstoppable as the blade of city grass that cracks through concrete.... (Place, pp. *iii-iv*.)

Perhaps only gifted writers like Michael Korda and Laura Cunningham are afflicted with this way of buying country property.

Following her own advice, Cunningham was smote by a 20-room place in Willowby Park on her first date. It was called, The Inn. She and her then husband did nothing to research the property once under what she calls a "trance of desire." (*Ibid.*, p. 112.) She writes: "There were, of course, flaws [in the house], but I saw these defects only as endearing traits. The bathrooms seemed weird, added in 1840.... At the front of the house, there were twin toilets that looked as if they had been sliced in half: I had to ease in sideways to view them." (*Ibid.*, p. 113.) If you feel yourself coming down with a trance of desire, or a trance of anything else, go home and get a good sleep. Don't look at property when you are buying under the influence.

This is where Cunningham's intoxication led her:

- Every year she is expected to pay her share of the upkeep for the Olmstead-designed gravel drive, "which is so expensive to maintain for cars. Every spring, the lord sets down costly gravel; every winter, the snowplow shovels it up." (*Ibid.*, p. *xvi.*). The road fees surprised her.

- "It's always beautiful to be here on the farm; it isn't often easy. ...even as I write, my hands stiffen from the cold, and I hear the roar of my generator, hooked up this dawn, at the start of one of the frequent power failures that afflict my dream place." (*Ibid.*, p. *xvii.*) "Am I deluded in insisting this lifestyle of medieval inconvenience has some charm?" (*Ibid.*, *xviii.*)

- A diagonal boundary line along the property's front puzzled her when the lord first pointed it out: "I wondered why the line was cut in such an odd way, but I was afraid to appear critical, and so didn't say anything. Seventeen years would pass before I knew the reason for that diagonal cut. [It had to do with the lord wanting ownership of a line of sight.] By then [with a new neighbor], the property line would be of crucial interest to me, and I would spend thousands in legal fees to determine my right to prevent a threat from the 'other side.' [The threat came from followers of the late Swami Vivikenanda who wanted to build a shrine trail near the common property line.] But, of course, I knew nothing of the future on this spring day, and I chose not to give the triangular design of my front lawn any further thought." (*Ibid.*, pp. 116-117.)

- At the time of purchase, she and her husband had been vaguely aware that there had been British renters [of the rear portion of their house, The Innlet] on weekends, but "...we'd been told that they had returned to England. In any case, according to our deed, their lease would be up in ninety days—then they would be gone forever. But without telling us, the outgoing tenant had sublet The Innlet to this new couple, who were now demanding that we turn on the hot water so that they could shower. And so my dream of privacy ended, and my true role of homeowner, that of custodian, began." (*Ibid.*, p. 118.)

Within days, the original British tenants 'in the back' returned and took up residence in The Innlet. "They arrived with two children, two hairy dachsunds, and a parrot that spoke with an English accent. They had lots of friends on or around the estate, and when I arrived for my next weekend, I saw them playing tennis on 'my' court, while eleven guests (I counted them) lounged on the Adirondack furniture and drank gin." (*Ibid.*, p. 128.)

The lord, not the Cunninghams, collected the rent from the tenants who were charged "'for wear on the sheets.'" (*Ibid.*, p. 142.)

- Cunningham, like Korda, had not bothered to check out her neighbors prior to purchase.

  "As I watched in horror [on her first owner's night], I also became aware of a strange glow in the sky. The sun had set, but a blood-red aura appeared across the fields, emanating from a site half a mile away. I knew that there was a commuter college somewhere over there, known as 'UCK' or 'Ugly College' officially, Ulster County Community College, and as the evening descended, the school's system of anticrime lights flared into phosphorescence [*sic*]. Atmospheric conditions stained the light red, and the college glowed like a Martian heliport. ...not only that, I was soon to discover, UCK was not silent. UCK would emit what Lord Hodgson called 'noxious noises,' rock concerts, football rallies." (*Ibid.*, pp. 118-119.)

- With respect to maintenance expenses:

  "On our first morning in residence, we woke to several surprises. The workmen began to arrive, an invading army of pickup trucks and vans. While the sugar maples that lined the [graveled entrance] Avenue looked lush and healthy, [Arthur] Woodcock [their new tree man said:] 'They all have crotch or butt rot.' ...the projected medical bill—ten thousand dollars to treat their distress and chain their sick limbs together." (*Ibid.*, p. 122.)

Had the Cunninghams spent a few hours using their urban intellects in property scoping, they could have identified most of the elements of medieval misery that would later torment them. In some cases, they could have prevented their plagues; at the very least, they could have priced the cost of surgical repair into their purchase negotiations.

Country property need not be a source of existential agony and a self-imposed scheme for redistributing your wealth. You can buy a place here at an affordable price and enjoy it too! Here are some ways the Cunninghams could have improved their purchase.

When the lord told the Cunninghams that they would be expected to pay their share of the maintenance, all they had to do was ask to see what those expenses had been in the past and what the lord projected them to be over the next year or two. That would have eliminated the surprise of a first-day $10,000 tree bill. If the lord failed to volunteer this information, nothing prevented the Cunninghams from asking: Who pays for upkeep, repairs and snow removal on the entrance Avenue and other common areas? If the Cunninghams' deed and other purchase documents failed to provide for sharing of such expenses and they had no knowledge of a cost-sharing obligation at the time of purchase, they had a strong legal position for refusing to pay. Cost-sharing on common facilities is typically written into one or more of the purchase documents. The lord of a manor may have had a medieval right to impose such "taxes" on his peasants, but that is one feudal misery that the Cunninghams should have resisted.

Buyers can always include language in their purchase-offer contracts that states: Seller shall disclose any condition, situation or defect in the property that would adversely affect Buyer's possession, use and enjoyment, or lead to unanticipated expenses by Buyer arising from the failure of Seller to disclose such defects.

The boundary issue that Ms. Cunningham faced when her new neighbor wanted to erect the Swami's shrine trail near their common line could have been addressed 18 years earlier by arranging a mutual no-development, set-back easement on both sides of their common boundary. Such an easement would bind both property owners and their successors to keep that strip open. The easement would not have prevented the Swami's followers from meditating next to Cunningham's boundary line, but it might have stopped them from erecting shrines.

The Cunninghams have no one but themselves to blame for not reading the lord's rental lease with the tenants in the house they just purchased. The terms of this lease, like many others, lasts for its specified term regardless of any change in ownership. Apartment-dwelling New Yorkers know that the length of their leases is not affected by the sale of their buildings. Could the Cunninghams have thought that rent-paying tenants would evaporate for their convenience?

Similarly, how much sympathy should a reader muster for the Cunninghams' failure to notice UCK's presence even though they knew that it was just a half-mile away. A quick drive around Willowby Park would have revealed their neighbors, UCKy and otherwise. Buyers need to be alert to both the obvious and not-so-obvious annoyances that turn up on neighboring property. College students—their noise and their lighting—surely fall into the category of probable annoyances. Were both Cunninghams blinded by a trance of desire? Or was it a coma of deliberate witlessness?

And lest you think I am picking on New Yorkers, I offer a third example of a writer throwing urban brains to the rural winds. Jeanne Marie Laskas, a then-Pittsburgher, offers Fifty Acres and a Poodle: A Story of Love, Livestock, and Finding Myself on a Farm (New York: Bantam Books, 2000). Her sequel, The Exact Same Moon: Fifty Acres and a Family (New York: Bantam Books, 2003), recounts her adventures on a Virginia farm where she and Alex, her husband, moved following their first farm and farm book.

Laskas and Alex—self-described "country-wannabes"—found a house that sat on a hilly tract about a 50-minute drive south of Pittsburgh. She falls in love with the house at first sight because it is a "house with an identity crisis... something like a chalet stuck onto a trailer. ...this house needs me." (Fifty Acres, p. 34.) She is describing a large one-room artist studio recently appended to an older conventional residence. She is also smitten with a view from a hilltop and the fact that the property comes with free gas associated with an on-site gas well. On their first visit, she sees a pond, "...blooming with lilies a la Monet. We see a barn, a crooked old thing, baking in the sun a la Wyeth." (Ibid., p. 32.) She sees the look of the place, not what it can and cannot do, not how it does and does not function, not what work it will and will not demand of its owners.

Though she walked through its fields, she failed to see that the "farm" is covered in multiflora rose, a fast-spreading, nearly indestructible shrub that must be bulldozed out of the ground in the winter at $50 per hour. A neighbor enlightens Laskas. She says to Alex, her then fiancé: "'We are stupid.' And this multiflora is a symbol of our stupidity. We bought fifty acres of thorns. Thorns we can't get rid of. Thorny weeds that attract both wild animals and bloodthirsty hunters." (Ibid., p. 93.)

She also doesn't see that the Wyeth barn needs to be rebuilt or that the "farm," as it stood, was not a farm in an operational sense because it was incapable of supporting anything more than a couple of dogs and cats. This is seeing without comprehension.

Not knowing the difference between grass and hay or what a bushhog is, she and Alex keep "processing" the decision to buy the farm.

'We don't know the first thing about farming,' he said last night at City Grill, a South Side restaurant with excellent grilled shrimp. 'True,' I said. Then I said, 'How hard can it be?' (*Ibid.*, p. 39.).

No real farming occurs on Laskas's "farm," which in no way diminishes the experience of living on what she calls a "farm." Farming is very hard—physically, intellectually and financially. But living in the country on land that is not farmable is no harder than maintaining a suburban house. It can, however, be different.

In considering an offer, she and Alex reflect on the question of purchase money.

'Where in the hell are we going to get the money?' he said. 'Well, I don't know,' I said. We are, neither of us, moneybags. We are normal working stiffs. But hey, we have good credit ratings. And we both have some investments we can cash in. Not only that, but we both have equity in our houses. We'll pool our resources, make it work. Whatever. I mean, if I have learned anything about money in my thirty-seven years of living, it is to ignore it. It just scares you. Never, ever add numbers up. It just makes the numbers bigger and scarier. '...okay,' he said. 'So where are we going to get the money?' 'I have no idea.' Then I changed the subject. Because, well, that's another way of dealing with money. (*Ibid.*, pp. 40-41.)

If, as it seems, Laskas is recommending this method of farm purchase, I recommend that you pay no attention to her. Alex, at least, has enough sense to make an offer 25 percent below the seller's asking price. Still, it also seems, this "method" of costing out a purchase worked for her. They even had money left to buy a $13,000 tractor, found for them by a helpful neighbor.

Laskas comes to realize that doing farming is what she calls three-dimensional while wanting a place in the country is two-dimensional.

Alex and I have been talking a lot about what to do with fifty acres. How, for instance, do you mow fifty acres? We learned that you mow fifty acres with the brush hog, which turns out to be the low flat thing that you attach to the back of the tractor. It's the mower attachment. [Not exactly. The bushhog is a device that's suitable for rough-cutting weeds and high grass. A separate mower attachment is available to keep large areas cut as grass. And a different type of attachment—a sickle-bar mower—is used to cut hay for baling.] See, now, I never knew tractors even *had* attachments. I mean, I never really thought about it. To me, a farm tractor is a thing you see in the distance when you are on the [Pennsylvania] Turnpike going somewhere, and it is out there on those fields doing very important farm things. That the farm tractor is made up of parts—attachments and levers and hydraulic-powered thises and thats—was not in my consciousness. Why should it have been in my consciousness? This is one example of a much larger principle I am dealing with, ever since we closed on the farm. Because, fifty acres. [*sic*] Fifty acres in a place called Scenery Hill. Fifty acres of gorgeous scenery. Scenery. We bought scenery. We bought a postcard. We bought green hills and a pond blooming with lilies *a la* Monet. We bought a creaky old barn leaning in the wind *a la* Wyeth. We bought the most beautiful picture we could possibly find. We bought 2-D. Not 3-D. It did not enter my consciousness that the three-dimensional version of this thing was included with the package. Because how could it be in my consciousness? When would it have had the opportunity to get in? Chaos never announces itself, never advertises. Who would buy chaos? (*Ibid.*, p. 68.)

That's a fair self-analysis. I started out the same way, seeing the two-dimensional postcard and not the three-dimensional reality. Dirt-Smart should help to prepare its readers for anticipating three-dimensional country life on the property of their choice.

A book of a different color is Mark Phillips's, My Father's Cabin (Guilford, CT: The Lyons Press, 2001), which describes the need of a welder in an old coal-fired power plant to buy a weekend escape in the Allegheny Mountains near Buffalo, New York. There's nothing impulsive about Jim Phillips's dream to free himself from his job, its dusts and fumes. He plans for years, as he works overtime to save the purchase price dollar by dollar. As the weekend searches progress, the screens he uses—price, size, water source, hunting potential, mix of open and woods—are refined. When he locks onto the right 42 acres, he buys quickly—$100 per acre in the late 1960s. The ice-cold spring turned the deal: "You can plant trees," he writes, "but you can't plant water." He pays immediately for the construction of the spring-fed trout pond. (Another property was rejected, because of a weak spring.) His primitive cabin—no electricity, no indoor plumbing—takes five years, time squeezed from a heavy workload and completed with the help of his son, Mark, and his father. When Jim Phillips dies young of prostate cancer, Mark inherits the cabin and upgrades it for year-round use. His book is about the importance of land to his father and later to him.

One lesson from My Father's Cabin is that you don't need to be rich to buy rural land. A buyer can substitute planning, work and clear objectives for cash. You will need some money and some cash flow, but you can adapt your needs and wants to fit your savings and your projected income.

A second lesson is to start "improving" the property slowly. Jim Phillips starts with a trout pond, not a house. Had the pond been made by damming a creek, it would probably have been washed out; spring-fed ponds are more permanent than ponds in waterways. The cabin takes shape weekend by weekend. Lack of money and lack of time set the pace, which, in turn, allows the Phillipses to fit the construction project to their finances and the land.

A third lesson is to start small and add incrementally rather than in Maoist giant leaps. Small steps taken slowly usually mean small mistakes that are not that hard to correct. Large steps taken quickly can mean the opposite.

Finally, ask around. Jim Phillips came to his 42 acres by asking the owner of a general store if he knew of any FSBO land in the immediate area. The owner didn't, but one of the store's bench sitters suggested that he talk to a local who had "...been saying for years he's gonna break up the farm and sell. ...worth a try, Brown is." (Cabin, p. 120.) The jury hanging around Cookie's store were not keen on another fellow from Buffalo buying land in their neighborhood, but Jim Phillips apparently looked okay enough for one of them to feed him a lead. It's important for outside buyers to look and act okay enough.

Maybe I'm missing a subtle point that Korda, Cunningham and Laskas are making. Is it possible that certain city buyers want to be country fools, because they think that's part of the move-to-the-country experience? Is there urban status to having a country place fall down around your ears the day you move in? Do writers feel they deserve to endure these miseries for reasons of class or culture? Do they feel that the money they pay for unanticipated repairs is penance for having money in the first place? Are only writers so afflicted? I hope so.

I confess to being blind to cachet of this sort. I can't see how my interests are advanced by being deliberately obtuse about buying land, or anything else. Making a large purchase is hard enough when you're trying to be smart about it. If you find a logic in reading <u>Consumer Reports</u> before buying a $20,000 car, you'll see the same logic in reading <u>Dirt-Smart</u> before buying a $200,000 farm. If, on the other hand, you want to rely on the kindness of sellers, stop reading now.

The lesson from the Kordas and Cunningham is that large, old country houses with plenty of curb appeal can be made to function through large and regular cash transfusions. Such places will always be burdensome second homes since something or other will always be breaking down unless you are prepared to replace every system. This is not an argument for the bomb-proof brick rambler. It is, instead, an argument for country romance leavened with one eye on your wallet and the other on your tolerance for living the next decade in the anarchy of serial remodelings.

My point is simple: there's no need to be miserable in a country second home, despite Cunningham's endorsement. Nor is there a need to spend hundreds of thousands of dollars unnecessarily. The only reason for doing so is to acquire first-hand material for another book of this genre, <u>Why I Paid $500,000 for a Pint of Wild Blueberries and a Family of Mice in My Country Bedroom</u>.

Here are a few basic ideas that these three good writers should have kept in mind when searching for country property:

1. Ask questions.

Do your research, so that you can ask sensible, informed questions. Don't be snotty or nerdy in this. You're not trying to show how smart you are. You are trying to learn what you don't know, as well as what you don't know you don't know.

2. If something looks funny, figure it out before you submit a purchase offer.

If you stumble upon a non-working toilet, do not assume that it will be fixed on its own before you close. (I'm speaking both about toilets and metaphorically.)

If the house furnace looks like it heated a Roman bath in the days of Caesar, determine the cost of replacement. If you don't see ductwork, you will have to install it if you want whole-house air-conditioning. This can be a real mess on old houses with solid walls. If the electricity in the barn doesn't work, ask why?

If the pond is dry in July, ask about it. If you see a creek, ask how often it floods and how extensive the flooding has been. If you find a sump pump in the house basement, find out why water is entering. A rule of thumb applicable everywhere is this: basements should be dry.

3. If you can't see how something works, ask about it.

Ask where all solid and liquid house wastes go. If you are told they go into a septic system, get a copy of the permit to find out its capacity and design. Ask how the seller maintained the system? Were the solids in the settling tank emptied regularly; if so, check with the company that did the cleaning. Don't be surprised if grey water (from the laundry and kitchen sink) does not go to the same place as black water (toilet water). Country houses may pipe grey water into a hole or creek rather than a septic system. Your new country house may be grandfathered, but, if it isn't, you might be expected to build a modern septic system that takes both waste streams—an expense that can total anywhere from $3,000 to $30,000 or more.

If there's a motor in the sale, ask to see it operate and find out who has repaired it; check the repair record. Run all motors, including the furnace, AC, water pump, ventilating fans, freezer, washer/dryer, refrigerator, sewage pumps and everything used for agricultural work.

If the seller says the walls are insulated, take off the faceplate of electrical receptacles and look. As an alternative, ask your house inspector to check for insulation.

Examine the roof if you can. Look for signs of deterioration. Use a mirror to look up a chimney: you should see sky past the damper. Cheap cosmetic compacts work fine. If there's a crawlspace, crawl into it with a flashlight. Look for deterioration in the foundation, sills and floor joists. Look for evidence that critters are chewing on your wiring. Look for leaks in water and waste lines.

4. Talk to your neighbors before you buy.

Ask them about themselves, and then the target property. Does it have a history of flooding? Do its springs go dry? Ask about fences. How is fence ownership apportioned? Are there any boundary disputes or grievances? Do any neighbors feel they have a claim to own anything or use anything on the property you're about to buy? Look around for activities that could disturb your use and enjoyment of your new property. Barking dogs are obvious, as are shooting ranges, extra-bright outdoor lights, teenagers with jacked-up trucks, poultry houses, hog farms, manure lagoons and close-by fields that are fertilized with green (fresh) manure. Less obvious are lots where bawling, just-weaned calves are kept for a week, barrels and pits for weekly trash fires upwind of you, and individuals with alcohol or drug problems. More often than not, a helpful neighbor will take newcomers under his wing to protect them from the worst errors they might otherwise make. See if you can establish this protectorate status with at least one neighbor from the start by doing what you can to extend your own genuine friendship.

5. Get expert advice when you don't know something.

You may need a surveyor to check boundaries, forester to determine the value of the timber, lawyer to advise you on a title problem or zoning issue, insurance agent to give you a quote for a farm policy, civil engineer to give you a rough cost for a new septic system or bridge, architect, landscape planner, agriculturalist, well-driller, excavator and house contractor.

When you're out on a pretty fall Sunday afternoon with the sun warm and the sky clear, and you happen upon a rural place that jellies your knees, STOP! Take a deep breath. Say nothing. Keep your pen in your pocket along with your wallet. If you happen to be with a real-estate agent, mumble something like, "Very nice, but it sure is a long drive from home." This indicates cautious interest, which at this point is all you want to indicate both to the agent and to yourself. "Let's take a better look here before we go to the next place." A little caginess should be part of your property-hunting kit.

This book will show you how to take that better look. With the information you assemble from your scoping, you can submit a written offer within a week or two. The point of resisting impulse is not delay for its own sake or the building of your character through self-denial.

The point of scoping is to couple speed with security. **Scoping is, in other words, the vehicle that allows you to move fast by stripping risk out of the purchase.** Don't dawdle. Good deals on good properties don't last long.

Buyers must learn to use their eyes and brains to make **dirt-smart decisions**. Some individuals may be born with this talent, but anyone can learn how to do it. I know people who have a knack for buying property and others who find a dollar wherever they turn. I'm not one of either kind. When I've made money in real estate, it was directly related to thorough scoping, which, in turn, led to buying at the right price. The one time I lost, it was directly related to inadequate scoping. If you're looking for country property for your personal use and enjoyment, you may want to pay more for the right place than an appraisal says it's worth. If you're looking at an investment, the dirt-smart decision is always to buy at a price that guarantees a future profit. You must let the facts lead you to that decision. Your job as a dirt-smart buyer is not to rig your analysis to confirm what you want. Don't argue yourself into a deal. If your head and your pencil tell you to walk, don't let your heart buy it. Your decision is the product of work that you will do after your first look. Be prepared to work. Your scoping—the information gathering and analysis and evaluation—begins the moment you say to yourself, "I like this place."

CHAPTER 2: WHAT AM I LOOKING FOR AND WHY AM I LOOKING FOR IT

Few of us *need* a second home in the country or a patch of woods, though many of us want one or the other. Wants are often perceived as compelling as needs. Fulfilling a need is pedestrian, an obligation done because it's required. Satisfying a want, on the other hand, makes us feel good, successful and in control.

The first thing, then, is to interrogate yourself, Want or Need? There's nothing immoral about wanting country property just because you want it. My only caution is to make sure that you can afford this want over the life of your country mortgage without impinging on some future need. This chapter discusses how to think about your wants and needs in country property before you ever answer an ad or call a realtor.

My opinions are the product of my own experience, the limits of which I acknowledge and to which I alert each reader. I have not purchased property in most of our 50 states, though I've looked at and/or scoped land in more than 20. I have, for example, never had to understand western water rights as a practical matter, value a tract in Humboldt County, California where the big Coastal timber grows, or size up a cattle-and-corn operation along the North Skunk in Jasper County, Iowa. On the other hand, I've been asked to scope investment properties ranging from a couple of hundred acres to more than one million. I was once asked to screen—not scope—600,000 acres in Ontario in one afternoon. I was able to learn enough to advise my client to pass it up. Anyone can learn enough to avoid bad properties and buy good ones.

What I am sure of is that buying land is always local. A generic understanding of how to scope and buy property—which is what you get in this book—will always help as long as you adapt the generic to the particular, to the local. **Scoping is tract-specific** because each property has its own set of virtues, drawbacks and uncertainties, all of which are set in a context of state law, local zoning rules, market conditions and the personalities of the owner, neighbors, brokers, lawyers and lenders. Scoping, as a process, can be applied broadly whatever the specifics. I think my own experiences with sellers reflect common practices. Still, certain things I write or beliefs I pass on may not apply to your target tract, because of local conditions with which I have no experience.

The point I have held to in writing this book is not to tell you to buy a certain type of rural property but to show you how to approach buying any such property in a way that maximizes your chance for success and minimizes your chance for unpleasant surprises.

<u>Dirt-Smart</u> is a how-to manual on buying country property. Since my manual is based in part on my own errors and successes during the past 35 years, keep in mind that many ways exist to perform a particular task. My how-to approach may be different than yours or that of another author. When you find something that I've written doesn't square with your own experience, test both hard. I am not fool-proof. I will be pleased if my effort to help you become knowledgeable gives you the tools to turn up my errors and any you might make before you make them.

KNOW THYSELF

Most Americans who live in cities or suburbs can live full, satisfying lives without buying a country home or undeveloped rural land. I say this without any empirical proof, but I'm pretty sure it's true. Or at least true enough for most everyone.

Consider for the moment an urban buyer who comes to the decision one morning that he **needs** a place in the country. Perhaps you are such a buyer.

To me, a need is non-negotiable. Food, water, shelter—or the means to get them—those are needs. Affection and companionship could be added to the list without much of a quarrel. Looking for and buying a country place is usually not a need. It is usually a choice that is discretionary rather than coerced—a want.

A search for recreational land or a second home should never be conducted under the same pressure to find "something" that a buyer often feels with a job transfer. Buyers feeling desperate to find their place should bench themselves for a bit since desperation leads to decisions that can be bad and are usually costly. Buyers who are able to shift their thinking from needing to buy a country place to wanting to buy one make life easier for themselves.

If you find that you've been looking for the **one right place** without success, you have chosen to search for a lone needle in a field of haystacks. You may argue that every field of haystacks probably contains at least one needle. This may be true in your profession. It is always true in argument.

Since this is a book about country property, I feel obliged to reveal that farmers no longer make haystacks. The metaphor loses its lyrical punch when updated to "like finding a needle in a round bale." I've never found a needle in any hay, stacked or baled, through I have found snakes, nails, rusty horseshoes, pieces of balers and nests of bees.

The search for the one right place leads most often to ceaseless searching. As frustration builds, it can also lead to either the dreaded impulse purchase or buying a place because you're fed up with looking.

Few places will strike you as practically perfect in every way. But many spots can be made perfect enough with vision and money. Michael Korda demonstrated that **thrown money** can solve most country problems. I don't recommend his approach, because it may involve the hideous expenses of turning a sow's ear into a silk purse. (I also have no experience in actually implementing his approach, but I would certainly like to be able to try it some day.) Start with something closer to a silk purse and you spare yourself headaches and expense. Screen in properties that can be made into what you want within a sensible time-and-money budget. Don't screen in a place that has one or more absolutely unfixable feature that you hate. Don't screen out a place that has a few things that you dislike if they can be fixed within reasonable limits.

A viciously rational individual can calculate the costs and benefits of buying a country place and arrive at a startling though sensible conclusion: most of what people like to do on second properties in the country can be done without owning second properties in the country. What might these things be? Hunting and fishing. Hiking. Riding. Camping. Driving motorized vehicles (4WD vehicles, ATVs, snowmobiles, motorcycles) through the woods. Wildlife watching. Nature communing. Vacationing on a lake. Spending the summer in a beach house. Skiing at a resort. Puttering. Relaxing. Staying on working farms. Activities like these do not require owning any property.

Most of these recreational activities are available on state or federal lands that can be visited by the day or week. Public land provides variety, challenge, relaxation, wilderness, near wilderness and fully developed, multi-dimensioned recreation. State parks rent cabins—rustic to modern—at reasonable prices in all manner of rural settings. Fully equipped cabins are available within a few hours drive of most Americans that offer various packages of developed recreation—boating, swimming, horseback riding, nature education, restaurants and so on. And if you don't like public facilities, you can rent every type of rural property that interests you from private owners, in whatever form and setting pleases you. Vacations—working or not—are available on real farms. No farmer turns down volunteer labor, no matter how unskilled and klutzy. Dude ranches have made a living for more than century by providing pseudo-cowboy experiences. It's not hard to find any of these opportunities.

It's not the same, you say. I know. You're right. You can't invest your labor and your heart into a public campground.

It's emotional investment, not money, that drives much of the second-property market in rural areas. Despite the fact that most Americans now live in cities or suburbs, many of us feel a need for land of our own where we can sink roots. This is particularly powerful, I think, if your principal urban home is an apartment, townhouse development, planned community or suburban house. Each of those housing choices is efficient and practical, but also thoroughly regulated and tightly scripted. Having once lived in Washington, D.C., both in an apartment and my own house, I know the feeling of being penned up and incomplete. I wanted out, but I also needed to be in to make a living. Finding a permanent place in the country that would always be "home" regardless of the vagaries of career was how my thinking took shape. I was looking for a second home in the country, a sanctuary, an axis around which I would spin, a place to plant fruit trees, have a barn, rattle around in an old truck on warm fall afternoons, sleep in a hammock and sow wildflowers. Familiar?

I bailed out on Washington more than 20 years ago. My new wife and I moved to a 73-acre grazing farm in a mountain county with 2,500 people, perhaps the least populated county east of the Mississippi River. I argued that I "could continue to make a living off Washington from almost five hours away." Wrong. I argued that "we can always make a living from the farm." Wrong. I argued that we can "make a clean break, without going through the second home stage and without knowing how we'll make a living out there." Wrong. Our decision to buy and move was more impulse and less planned than I realized at the time. Owing to that, it has taken years of financial struggle to adapt ourselves to making a living in a beautiful place that has no need for my doctorate in international relations and her masters in public-sector labor relations. We discovered that small-scale cattle farming, no matter how efficient, never produced much net income even in the occasional good year. We ended up making her into a dirt lawyer and me into the writer of this book among other things.

Since you are reading this book, I will presume that similar thoughts are now floating in your mental ether. I offer this caution: certain city people should not think seriously about developing their "inner hick." There is no hard-and-fast set of characteristics that define those who will be better off staying on the urban side of the line, but here are some that I have seen that cause the most problems with new owners of country property:

1. Cash-strapped. Don't stretch your wallet to buy a country want. Wait until your fortunes improve and your cash pile is higher. Selling a country place can take time and cost money; don't assume that you can dump your second place quickly if you are unexpectedly RIFed and find yourself carrying two mortgages while unemployed.

2. Handy. If you're not at least below-average handy, you can either try to learn to be or pay others to fill in. If both options are unappealing, rural housing is not a good fit. Entropy is a fact of every second home's life. Everything breaks, wears out or needs to be replaced. If you are one of those few individuals who literally can't hammer a nail, stick with apartments that have friendly and competent supers. Even bare land will ask you to do something that involves having your brain instruct your hands to do something, like use a chainsaw, dig a trench, fix a fence or nail up a "posted" sign.

Rural property sooner or later entails internal combustion engines (ICEs)—a 4WD pick-up truck, tractor, gas-powered electric generator and chainsaw are a common quartet. If you know nothing about ICEs and can think of nothing so unpleasant as to learn a few basic remedies and preventives, don't buy rural land or a farm. ICEs are just the tip of the country berg—there can be hand tools, pumps, compressed air, diesels, hydraulics, vacuums, electrical gizmos, gravity-feeds and a whole bunch of other stuff that will cause you angst.

3. Discomfort. If your idea of permanent nirvana is a frisky game of tennis followed by ten hours of serious spa stewing, don't exchange netter's togs for bib overalls. Rural property always involves work. Sometimes the work is demanded at inconvenient hours and when you need to be in two places at once. Sometimes, rural property demands that you anticipate a problem and solve it before it becomes a disaster. If you want to enjoy a rural experience but don't really want to invest effort in the furtherance of your own enjoyment, visiting, not owning, a country place is for you.

4. Fear. If you do not like being around people who are not like you, if you fear the unknown, if you will not investigate a strange odor and if you will consciously ignore a weird sound coming from the basement, you now have four good reasons to rethink owning country land.

5. Exposure. If you detest the idea of your new neighbors knowing a lot about you, think again about buying a place in the country. There is no privacy here. Whether or not you are doing one thing or another, sooner or later someone is likely to tell someone else that you are. Gossip is common, since we mainly have each other as grist for our mental mills. Your words, manners and style will be noted. If you drive a new Mercedes convertible down a country road, you will inevitably get it stuck and have to ask a yup-and-nope guy with a tractor to pull you out. He may strike you as taciturn, even slow, but be aware that his powers of social observation are acute. So think twice before acting like even more of an idiot. He's the guy with common country sense, not you.

MAKE A REVOCABLE LIST

Before you start looking at the newspaper ads or riding the back roads on pleasant Sunday afternoons, make a **Revocable List** of those things you think you're looking for in rural land.

I stress the revocable quality of this list. Your ideas will and should change as you acquire knowledge of what's available, and more importantly, as you refine your needs, wants and the sense of your own capabilities. The last of these—your new capabilities—is important to track. A country place is likely to ask you to do things you haven't done before—hang a 14-foot-long farm gate, drive a tractor, build a bridge or inject antibiotics into the eyelid of a steer with pinkeye. Everyone does something for the first time. I learned from scratch how to do each of these tasks and many others. If you have no experience with a task, take little bites, one at a time. Be patient with yourself. You probably won't get something new right on the first try. Don't start a 10,000-square-foot dream house as your first hammer-and-saw project since making a broom holder in seventh-grade woodshop. The Revocable List should change as you find your needs and wants changing.

A buyer will use a Revocable List <u>after</u> he's screened in a property over the phone or through material sent to him. The completed List should give the buyer enough information to decide whether the property appears to meet enough of his criteria to justify the next bit of time and money that initial scoping requires.

I've provided the start of a generic Revocable List. This should be taken as a way to get you moving on developing your own List. I've set up four categories for you to work with: **Needs, Wants, Don't Wants and Possibilities.** I've further sub-categorized Needs and Wants into things you need or want now, that is, immediately; things you need or want within five years; and things you project you will need or want after your first five years of owning the property.

The more cash you have to spend, the more of your needs and wants you should be able to satisfy upfront. The choice the cash-heavy buyer may face is between a more expensive property that requires little additional work and one where a great deal of time and a hard-to-forecast amount of cash is needed to obtain the same result. There's no always-right formula for deciding between these choices. If you value convenience more than money, buy the ready-to-go place. If, on the other hand, interest rates are high and you think your future cash flow will increase, take the cheaper alternative and put up with the sawdust. Every buyer should calculate his upfront purchase costs together with those improvements projected in the foreseeable future to avoid buying more than he can afford. When doing this calculation, add in at least 25 percent more than your projected improvement costs, and one-third if you're feeling skittish about the accuracy of your projections. If you follow Laskas's advice and ignore money, you may find yourself cash squeezed and land poor. It makes no sense to buy land whose debt and expenses keep you cashless. Thomas Jefferson resolved being chronically land poor by dying.

I would begin filling in your Revocable List with your Don't Wants. You might have a clearer vision of the negatives you want to avoid than the positives you believe you either need or desire. Your Don't Wants might be a house next to a busy highway; or property adjoining a commercial dairy or hog farm; or house near airport; or all flat acreage; or house in floodplain; or property more than 100 miles from current residence. When you start filling in Needs and Wants, be very specific about items about which you feel strongly. These intensely felt considerations are not likely to change during your search. Each √ check represents the intensity of your feelings. Don't limit yourself to physical attributes of property. Include financial considerations, community infrastructure (church of your choice; condition of roads; proximity of fire department, rescue squad, medical clinic and so on), appreciation potential and tax-benefit opportunities.

You will undoubtedly have needs and wants that you can articulate generally but not with specificity. For example, you might write a Need as "pretty spot." That's fine, since many combinations of different physical components can add up to a "pretty spot," and its determination is always in the eye of the beholder. As you look at property, continue to turn generalities into specific, articulated wants and needs.

The danger in using generalities instead of specifics can be illustrated by the Need for privacy. Let's say you find a house in the middle of a 40-acre square. That puts you less than one-half mile from each of your four neighbors. Let's assume that the house is surrounded by deciduous trees along with an occasional pine. Is that privacy? It depends on your neighbors. If the adjoining property is uninhabited, it's privacy until a new second home is built on the adjoining property. Then you won't have privacy from unwanted sights (in the winter), sounds and smells, owing to changed circumstances beyond your control. If gunshots bother you, you'll need a far greater distance between you and the shooter. Privacy cannot be perfectly achieved, even with thousands of acres. Airplanes fly over; neighbors abut; trespassers come on. It will be helpful if you can break down "Privacy" into more articulated concerns, such as out-of-sound of neighbors and barking dogs (current and projected), no regular odor invasions, out-of-sight of neighbors, house is isolated from passing headlights, house cannot be seen from public road in all seasons. This set of criteria, I should add, would screen in a property on which you heard gun shots and smelled seasonal farm odors. Over the years, I've settled for operational privacy where intrusions are known, predictable and tolerable.

As you work through the Revocable List, you will soon get a feel for your **Hard Needs, Wants and Don't Wants** as against your **Soft Needs, Wants and Don't Wants**. The Hard items are those that you can articulate with unambiguous clarity and fervor; your Softs are less clear or less intensely held, but present and now accounted for. Hards are those that you do not want to negotiate with yourself; softs are those that can be compromised, adapted, fixed, ignored, sold or tolerated to a degree that you determine.

You can further indicate the intensity of your current feeling about each item by using a three-check system. One √ check indicates your preference; two √√ checks indicate high priority; and three √√√ checks indicate absolute requirement.

Like any other research, the search for property benefits from organization. Your first file folder is labeled Revocable Lists. Keep it stocked with blanks, as well as each dated iteration you do. As you become more knowledgeable, you should revise your Revocable List, even though the changes are slight. Anticipate both the wholesale revision and a lot of fine-tuning. Don't box yourself into a never-buy-anything corner by loading your List with impossibly specific requirements, such as access road built to state specifications or four sugar maples in front yard, each at least 75 feet tall. When listing your Needs-Now, exercise care that you don't overload this category, which will be the hardest to satisfy. Use the List's different time horizons to build flexibility into your plan while spreading costs over future years.

Possibles give you the chance to be flexible with the combinations of actual assets and liabilities you find in the field. For example, you might have listed that you Need Now not more than 100 acres, but have fallen for a farm of 250 acres with the perfect house. The Possible here that can make this work is for you to consider buying the larger farm and selling 150 surplus acres immediately after your purchase. As you look at properties, increase your ability to create Possibles in them. An orphan tract, down the road and removed from the main tract you like, is a saleable asset rather than a liability. A falling down barn may have significant old-lumber salvage value. An ugly, 100-foot-long, two-story turkey house can be converted into a convenient and efficient barn for feeding 60 steer calves through the winter. An old outbuilding might be remodeled into a homeoffice.

One question that can drive where you place Needs and Wants is whether you plan to live in a country house full-time or use it as a second home. How you answer that question in turn depends on how you tolerate make-shift conditions. Some buyers assume that a second home in the country will be—even should be—primitive, or at least, subject to old-fashioned quirkiness. Other buyers can live with a full-time construction project in their permanent residence, but want their country place to be a sanctuary of simplicity and reliability.

My experience is that all houses require maintenance; older houses require more than newer ones; and second homes that are not visited often tend to suffer problems that escalate or build on each other. A small roof leak, for example, in your permanent residence will be immediately obvious and simple to repair. The same leak in a second home can rot out a ceiling, floor and even cause an electrical fire before you discover it. With second homes that stand uninhabited for weeks, even months, at a time, you need to list as Needs items related to the dependability of various house systems, heat and water in particular. Second homes should be easy to open when you roll in late on Friday night and easy to close down. Water systems should have a single drain at their lowest point. Radiators should have an antifreeze solution in them, not water. Heating systems should have reliable thermostats with programmable timers, if possible. It's far more pleasant to pull into a warm house on a cold night rather than one where you have to start a fire while hauling in groceries and turning on crawl-space water systems. These types of considerations can be thought of as Wants rather than Needs, because they usually can be added after purchase. But don't assume too much. If there's no water in your rustic cabin at 4,000 feet elevation, it may be related to a lack of feasible water and not the lifestyle preferences of the current owner.

Here is a starting list of things to consider:

Generic Revocable List

	Needs			Wants			Don't	Possibles	Unknowns/Uncertainties
	Now	<5 Yr.	5 Yr.>	Now	<5 Yr.	5Yr. >	Wants		

Acreage
    <10
    10-25
    25-100
    100 +

2WD access
    All year
    Good weather only

4WD access
    All year
    Good weather only

Open Land (___%)

Woods (___%)

Special Facilities
    Horse layout
    Crop land
    Ag. buildings
    Garage
    Kennel

House

    New
    Modern
    Old
    Needs work
    Systems dependability
    View from
    Tree shade
    Garden spot
    Home orchard
    Approved septic
    Well/spring/public water

Amenities

    Rental unit
    Home office
    Pool
    Other assets
    Wetlands
    Year-round stream/river
    Pond/lake
    Land suitable for hunting

Features

    Minimum elevation
    Soil type
    Water quality/quantity
    School district
    Proximity to
            certain church
            airport
            town
            doctor
            hospital

Security

    Police
    Fire protection
    Break-in potential if
      used for weekends
    Medical providers
    Rescue services

Money

        Property asking price,
                less than $_____
        Anticipated closing costs,
                less than $_____
        Interest rate, ___% or lower
        Monthly payment, $_____
                or less
        Seller financing
        Income from property
        Timber worth ___% of
                total purchase price

Legal

        General Warranty Deed
        No boundary disputes
        Acceptable easements
        Minerals convey
        Right to water (if appropriate)
        No reservations of interest

When you get your Revocable List completed, consider screening in properties for additional thought but not full scoping that have at least, say, 80, percent of your checked Needs, 50± percent of your checked Wants and at least 95± percent of your Don't Wants. If you reject every property that does not satisfy 100 percent of your Needs and Don't Wants, you'll exclude some that you may be able to work with. Be willing to consider properties that can have your Needs met within five years. You're looking for a package, a property that fits you as a whole. It makes no sense, to me at least, to exclude an otherwise terrific property because it doesn't have one of your Needs Now, such as a mature home orchard. Put up with purchased fruit and plant your own trees, which will bear within five years.

Your Revocable List is one important defense against the **hot-flush buying** of Korda, Cunningham and Laskas. The listing process forces you to evaluate property analytically rather than emotionally. At the same time, it doesn't force you into a numerical straitjacket in which you buy only when 92 percent of your immediate needs are met.

You should, of course, use the List to help you make decisions about which properties deserve to be scoped and at what level of seriousness. It's unlikely that you will be able to complete a Revocable List on your first visit. But you may be able to learn enough to screen the property in or out for scoping.

When you make a note under Unknowns/Uncertainties, make sure to clear it up. Nothing feels dumber than getting burned by an Unknown you identified and then ignored. Staple whatever free-hand notes on the property you've made to your Revocable List. Throw no note out, ever.

Your Revocable List file is one of the first that you start in your **Search Kit**. I've found it easiest to organize a Search Kit by county. The Search Kit is a collection of documents, information, maps, plans and notes that profile the county's land and resources. In each Kit, a buyer should include notes on properties he's screened in and out, along with any Revocable Lists and scoping results on individual target properties.

The Kit's **county-specific** documents include:

Soil Survey, from the local USDA's Natural Resources Conservation Service or USDA Farm Service Agency

Road Map showing all roads, available from state highway department in each county. A buyer should "drive the county" to determine which sections he likes more than others. That familiarity will focus the search and provide the buyer with knowledge of local resources and landmarks.

Topographical map, state topographical maps are available in book form from DeLorme, P.O. Box 298, Yarmouth, Maine, 04096; 207-846-7000; www.delorme.com. These 11" x 16" books are available in bookstores. Their maps are scaled at 1 to 150,000, or 1" equals 2.37 miles. This provides sufficient detail to get you started. Maps with greater detail are available from the U.S. Geological Service (USGS) and are generally available at book stores and local surveyors. At nominal cost, a surveyor will print out a 1"-to-300' topographical map that shows waterways, woods, elevations and roads. Using the deed's description of the property, he can draw the boundaries on the map.

Local weekly and daily newspaper, subscribe to both; clip relevant articles

Telephone books for relevant communities in and around county

Zoning Ordinance, relevant portions, including division and subdivision. The ordinance book may be purchased at the county's zoning office. The Zoning Ordinance will set forth what can and can't be done in each type of land classification, e.g., residential, agricultural, conservation etc.

Real-Estate Guide, this is the monthly publication put out by local real-estate brokers that includes all current listings. Local papers also carry listings. Most real-estate agencies now have websites where additional information is provided.

County Economic Development Plan, which shows areas where residential and industrial growth are planned.

Local ordinances and regulations, such as an ordinance prohibiting the installation of wood-burning fireplaces; or one that regulates outdoor lighting; or one that requires a minimum number of square feet for new construction; or one that imposes limits on non-agricultural uses of agricultural property, etc.

Property tax information. Counties and other jurisdictions calculate property tax based on the assessed value of the land and a tax rate, e.g., so many cents of tax due per each $100 of assessed value. These formulas differ from place to place. You can find these formulas for each type of land in the office of the county tax assessor. Determine whether the county has adopted **land-use valuation**, which is a tax break for agricultural land. **Greenbelt** status is a conservation-oriented tax break that seeks to keep undeveloped land undeveloped. An owner who changes such a status is usually expected to pay **rollback taxes**.

Other types of public information, such as maps showing floodplains, maps of federal and state lands, county-level geological information related to subsurface minerals (oil and gas, coal, stone, etc.), rules pertaining to any areas designated historic districts, plans for any public lands near your target property, hunting regulations and seasons.

Comparables, is information that you gather on current asking prices and current selling prices for properties that fit your search profile. You want to get a sense for how much land of each type (timberland, open farmland, pasture) is selling for in various size ranges, expressed in **dollars per acre ($/A)**.

Information on current asking prices will come from a brokerage-published Real-Estate Guide, newspaper ads, bulletin ads, **For Sale By Owner (FSBO)** information, websites and word of mouth.

Information on current selling prices is available in the county courthouse where deeds are recorded and/or tax records kept. Sale records—deeds, mortgages—will often provide the selling price, show the transaction tax on the sale from which you can calculate the selling price, or provide information on the financing of the sale from which you can infer a likely selling price.

The next step in your Search Kit is to set up a Resources file that will include the names, addresses, phone numbers, fax numbers, websites and e-mail addresses of individuals and service providers that you are likely to need, including:

Lawyers with real-estate expertise

Accountants, who are experienced in handling farm and timberland taxation issues

Lenders—banks, mortgage companies, federal sources (Farm Service Agency/Farm Credit Administration), credit unions

Surveyors, licensed in the state where the property is

Consulting foresters, names are available from the Association of Consulting Foresters (ACF) and state forestry agencies

Certified soils engineers, who may be needed to locate soil on the property where a septic system can be installed

Physical Engineer (PE), if the property requires a constructed septic system, which is installed where the dirt is unsuitable for a conventional system

Testing laboratories, where you can send samples of water and materials for analysis. The county's extension agent will be able to tell you where to send soil samples.

Title insurance companies, if you want or need title insurance

Farm-related businesses, such as local stockyard where farm livestock is sold, farm supply stores, fence-builders

Insurance agencies, to provide a Farmowner's Policy

Utility companies

Excavation contractors for road building, foundations, septic systems

Architects

Building contractors for new construction

Carpenters/remodelers, and other tradesmen (plumbers, electricians, roofers, painters)

Home inspectors, to evaluate existing residences prior to purchase

Building supply/hardware companies

Well drillers

Consultants: environmental (testing for hazardous materials, wetlands, endangered species); historic preservation; farm-business evaluation; appraiser; mortgage broker; landscape architect, etc.

Government Offices

<u>**Local**</u>
Sanitarian or Health Department
Zoning Office
Building Inspector
Planning Office
County Clerk, where deed books are kept
County Assessor, where tax information and tax maps are kept
Water and conservation districts

<u>**State**</u>
Local office of state forestry department
Local office of state fish and wildlife department
Local office of state environmental protection agency
      Surface-water division (streams, lakes, coasts)
      Underground-water division
      Solid-waste disposal division
Local office of state highway/road department
State Office of Natural Heritage Resources, the state agency that is responsible for the management of state-listed endangered, threatened and sensitive species.
County extension agent, an employee of a state university that offers agricultural graduate programs

Federal
U.S. Army Corps of Engineers
Federal Emergency Management Agency (FEMA), if your property is in a floodplain
Regional office of U.S. Environmental Protection Agency (USEPA),
Regional office of U.S .Fish and Wildlife Service, if you suspect the presence of a **federally listed endangered, threatened or sensitive (ETS) species**. Ask if any portion of the target property is included in a **habitat-management plan**; this designation severely limits what an owner can do with his property.
District office of National Forest or National Park, if you share a boundary
Other federal offices that may be relevant in a particular area, such as Bureau of Land management or the Office of Surface Mining

I'll explain in other parts of this book how these resources are useful to you in scoping property. You won't need to contact all these information sources on every property. But the more scoping you do, the more likely you will need such services. Whenever you have special needs, such as for specialized medical care or a particular type of school, you will need to narrow your property search to areas that are convenient driving distance to those facilities. Long drives, particularly long daily drives, become increasingly less palatable as you get older.

The last item in your Search Kit is a **separate file for each target property that you scope**. Properties that you've visited but not thought worthy of scoping can be gathered and clipped together. These are your **non-starters**, which provide useful pricing information, even though you were not interested in a purchase. You can group your non-starters into a separate file.

Every property that you scope should be organized into a **Scoping File**. Each property-specific Scoping File will contain these types of materials:

Maps and other location documents
Road map showing general location of property
Topographic map (s) of property with boundaries
Tax map
Survey of target property if available. May also need surveys of adjoining properties.
Aerial photograph, available from local USDA office
Photographs
Google Earth map

Deed of current owner. May also need earlier deeds if boundary **calls** (compass directions and linear measurements) are incorporated in current deed by reference to earlier deeds.

Other documents of record, such as access easements, conservation easements (which limit what the owner can do with the land), liens, mortgage documents, leases, contracts, water rights and agreements, utility rights of way, etc. that affect the property. ("**Of record**" means that the document is publicly recorded, i.e., on file, in the office—county or city—where such documents are kept. The time and day of entry is logged on the document. "**Recording**" a deed, easement or other legal document refers to this process.)

Property tax information—current assessment value and property tax for land, improvements and minerals on target property are available in one or more county offices, usually in an annual **Land Book**, Tax Roll or a computer-accessible database.

Permits running with the property—approved septic permits; building permits, variances and conditional uses permits; mining permits; water permits, etc.

Timber cruise—if the property has timber with substantial present (**merchantable**) value, you should hire a consulting forester to work up a cruise that estimates timber volumes and dollar values. In many cases, a forester will be able to estimate merchantable timber value with a simple **walk-through** rather than the more elaborate and expensive cruise.

Current income produced by property—property-based business (e.g., farm), hunting leases, rent, mineral royalties, agricultural subsidies, conservation-practice payments.

Information on improvements—house inspection report; notes or cost estimates you've received from contractors; sketch of house floor plan; your notes on house and outbuildings.

Notes on seller—the more information you have on the seller—his motivation for selling, financial resources, personality, plans for the money received from the sale, willingness to self-finance—the better you will be at negotiating with him

Notes on Problems, Unknowns and Uncertainties—jot down whatever you're not sure about. Put a big star next to things that are problems that will require your money or time.

Names and Contact Information for all adjoining neighbors.

Kitchen Sink—include scraps and tidbits of information that might possibly come in handy, such as the name and number of a fellow who knows old apples and might do some grafting for you; names of neighbors and their out-of-town children; livestock prices; current rental rates for pasture; delivered hay prices; and your likes and dislikes about different areas in the county.

The last package of materials that you should take on your property visits is a **Personal Kit**, which, for starters, might include:

Hard-back clipboard with note pad

Pen (water-proof pens eventually prove their worth)

Compass

Sunglasses, hat, bug dope, water-proof matches, long-sleeve shirt and long pants

Hiking-type shoes or boots. (Do not appear in Gucci heels; this goes for women too.) If you're looking at land, anticipate getting your boots muddy and wet; if you're looking at a farm, don't wrinkle your nose at manure.

Unobtrusive camera

Decent flashlight (something more than a pen-type but less than a deer spotter. You'll use it in attics, crawlspaces and far corners.)

Duct tape (If you're going on land where ticks, chiggers and the like crawl up legs, you'll need to seal your cuffs tight with tape.)

Snake boots or leggings if you will be walking on their turf

Emergency car stuff kept in car—spare and jack, tire-inflation aerosol, tow strap or chain

Light-weight rain parka

Small backpack

Cell phone (it may work)

Hiking stick—helps with balance; good for whacking brush out of your path, probing impenetrable brush for snakes and flicking branches off trails

Water-filled bottle; hard candy or chocolate, fruit or trail mix

Think of your Search Kit as a pyramiding process. You start by building a very wide and solid base of information on which each higher and increasingly focused level of information and analysis rests. The point of the pyramid is the purchase of one of the properties that you've scoped. Properties that you've screened out or rejected after scoping to one degree or another are the surplus building materials that all pyramid builders end up with.

Let me summarize the organization of your Search Kit:

Generic Revocable List (blanks)

County Documents File

Resources File

Property-specific Scoping File

Completed Revocable List

Other materials

Non-starter File

Personal Kit

Two questions that buyers typically ask of themselves are: Will I ever find the right place? and How long will it take? Both questions are understandable. Both also depend on what the buyer means by "the *right* place."

It's hard but not impossible to find the one needle in a field of haystacks. It's easier and a lot more practical to find a place that is mostly right. Whatever gap you find between perfect and mostly right ought to be either closeable over time or of not much significance. You want to set your sights high, but not impossibly high; you want to settle pretty close to what you want. The saddest buyers I see are those who spend years looking for the one spot that is absolutely perfect. I'm not of that school; life goes by too quickly.

I advise buyers to settle for a place whose aesthetics feel right, a place that can be adapted to their goals and one that can be bought within the buyer's budget. The last point must be balanced with the first two. It is important for buyers to come to a property search with a definite and disciplined idea of the amount they can spend—in upfront cash, monthly mortgage payment, carrying costs (local taxes and fees, insurance, utilities) and immediate repairs following purchase. Buyers need not spend up to their **budget cap** to achieve their objectives, nor should they consider only properties they consider "deals" because they are less than their budget cap. If a property exceeds the buyer's budget, I would not buy, except in circumstances where some marginal asset of the property can be quickly sold and the buyer's purchase exposure brought back in line with his financial capability. "Stretch" is a concept that should apply to minds and Spandex, not to dirt-smart land purchasing.

The length of a search depends largely on the buyer's capabilities and pickiness. Industriousness shortens the length of a buyer's search. Putting together a Search Kit saves time. As you become increasingly familiar with a target county, you will be able to screen out properties that appear to have promise with your own first-hand knowledge. You can also shorten your search by adapting your wants and needs to the local property supply. Don't, for example, insist on finding a Swiss chalet in south Florida or an adobe ranch in Franconia, New Hampshire.

Macro-economic forces, such as interest rates, can affect when you search. Since most hunts for country property involve discretionary spending, it makes superficial sense to search only when interest rates are low. Low rates help buyers by reducing the cost of financing a purchase over time. The longer the term of a mortgage, the more interest the borrower pays on a given amount of money. Borrowing $100,000 at 6 percent for 10 years involves a monthly payment of principal and interest of $1,110.21, or 120 payments totaling $133,225.20, of which $33,225.20 is interest. Borrowing the same for 30 years involves a monthly payment of $599.56, or $215,841.60 in all, of which $115,841.60 is interest. Borrowing $100,000 at 10 percent for 30 years involves a monthly payment of principal and interest of $877.58, or 360 payments totaling $315,928.80, of which $215,928.80 is interest. The lesson is obvious: borrow at the lowest interest rate possible and pay off the debt as soon as you can. Buyers help themselves by amortizing a loan over a long period of time—which brings down their monthly payment—but accelerating the pay back of principal to minimize total interest paid. You can follow this tactic only when your mortgage document allows for early payment of principal without penalty.

Be aware, however, that low interest rates can work against buyers to the extent they heat up the real-estate market. More buyers appear, and asking prices can rise as mortgage money becomes cheaper. On the other hand, high interest rates can hammer asking prices, and persuade desperate sellers to self-finance purchases at below-market rates. Seller financing can be used as a bridge to a low-interest-rate environment in the future. Sellers in a high-interest-rate environment are pressured to deal with any buyer who looks half serious; with lower interest rates, you risk becoming a supernumerary buyer in a cast of dozens. Every buyer knows that it's to his advantage to be the only game in the seller's town. If a seller is trying to move his property when interest rates are high, the buyer should investigate the seller's motivations. Chances are he needs to sell quickly, which is leverage for the buyer.

Assuming a buyer is comfortable with the available interest rate, he should be able to find a suitable rural property within 18 months, and often much sooner.

The exception to that seat-of-my-pants generalization is the buyer who wants a property that is idiosyncratic in his target county. Examples of such idiosyncrasy are the buyer who demands a 4,000-acre wooded tract in a county that is mostly open farmland divided into parcels of fewer than 500 acres, or the buyer who needs a private air strip in a mountainous county where flat land does not occur naturally. Such properties are hard to find in the target counties of these buyers, but not elsewhere. The good news for a buyer is that out-of-the-ordinary properties can be even harder to sell than they are to find. Buyers will probably do best by looking for a type of property in a county where many such properties of that type occur.

If you're looking to buy a needle, don't look for it in a haystack; look in a pin cushion. Shape your expectations—Needs, Wants and Don't Wants—to the types of properties that are available where you are looking. Within those types, there will be enough variety to suit most buyers.

Renting can be used to test-drive a farm property for possible purchase.

You might consider a **rent-with-the-option-to-buy approach (lease-purchase option [LPO])**, for a target property that you can't quite afford at the present time. In this format, you rent the target farm/land for a fixed period, say one to three years. You agree on the future purchase price and terms as part of the deal. If you decide this farm is not for you, you can walk away from the property at the end of the rental period. An LPO usually requires that you agree to pay the full rental value for the full term. In this case, your contract should allow you to sub-lease the property and/or buy your way out of agreement for a specified sum. Some LPOs are negotiated in a way that allows a portion of rent paid to be credited against purchase price. You might also find it advantageous to agree, for example, to pay $700 per month rent for three years for a farm that both parties agree should rent for no more than $500 per month in return for a $400 deduction (not $200) in purchase price for each month of rent you pay during the term.

If an LPO seems to you to be more of a commitment that you're ready to make, consider renting a house in a small rural town from which you can scope properties on weekends. And if that seems to be a stretch, share the rent with another couple with whom you alternate country weekends.

TYPES OF PROPERTIES.

A place in the country means different things to different readers of this book. In the next section of chapters, I'll organize this discussion of property types in the following way:

Farmland
Undeveloped (Raw) Land
    For Hunting
    For Second Home
    For Investment
Developed Land for Second Home
    Full-package Developments
    Half-package Developments
The Flip
Land with Existing House
Owner-built House in the Country

CHAPTER 3: FARMLAND AND FARM DIRT

Dozens of types of farmland can be found in the United States. They range from western deserts and dairy pastures in Wisconsin to Iowa cornfields and trout ponds in New York's Adirondack Mountains; from row crops like soybeans, cotton, wheat and tobacco to orchards, vineyards and Christmas trees; from intensive, industrial-type poultry and hog operations to hardscrabble mountain plots where Old MacDonald would feel right at home. Operating farms range from hundreds of thousands of acres to just a handful.

Farmland begins with dirt. The type of dirt and its qualities have determined what's been done in the past and what you can do with it in the future.

Louis Agassiz, the famed Harvard naturalist, would give his students a fish and expect them to figure out its evolutionary history from sustained, concentrated observation. Superficial student analyses were met with Agassiz's instruction: "Look at your fish!"

Land buyers: Look at your dirt!

Farm buyers: Look at your dirt harder!

You are looking at its **topography**, as well as what it's best suited to do, what it's not well-suited to do, what it might be adapted to and how it should be cared for. Some dirt has been so neglected or abused that a fortune is needed to reclaim it.

Your first task when looking at land, including farmland, is to get oriented in several senses.

First, take out your compass and determine how the land lies in terms of directions. Estimate how much of the total acreage faces each way. Certain crops, such as native grass and hardwood timber, grow more vigorously on north-facing slopes, which are cooler and wetter than south-facing slopes.

Second, classify the land into rough topographic categories—essentially flat (wooded and open), rolling, steep slope, river bottom, swamp/wetlands, frontage on a public road and so on. Use the topographic map you've sagely brought with you to match what you see on the map with what you see on the ground. Locate boundaries to the extent you can, using the **topo**, a survey if one is available, a tax map (where a survey is lacking) and the **legal description** of the property's boundaries found in the deedwork. (Subsequent chapters explain how to do all of these things.) Note any problems, such as eroded hillsides and gullies, floodplains, overhead power lines crossing the property, bare spots, reclaimed strip-mine acreage, landslide area, wetlands/bogs/swamps, atypically dry areas, evidence of fire damage in the woods, garbage dumps, among others.

Third, determine which way the weather usually comes from. On a house, paint will peel first and worst on the side that takes the brunt of prevailing wind and rain. Trees lean away from strong winds. Other things being equal, you probably want to orient new buildings with their long sides in line with prevailing weather.

Your first eyeball survey will give you an idea of how the farm is internally distributed among **land types**: crop land (relatively flat and fertile), grazing areas (ranging from planted pasture to arid land to steep mountainsides), hay fields (planted crops, such as alfalfa, to native grasses), woodland (usually at the back of the farm) and agriculturally non-productive areas (gullies, wetlands, rocky areas, steep slopes, etc.) The same eyeball survey will tell you how the seller has worked with the dirt on each section of the farm. Look for the logic and balance in what you see. The seller might be grazing three acres for every acre in hayfield and every acre in corn. If he's running a self-sufficient farm with few purchased inputs, his land allocation may tell you that he can produce enough grass, hay and corn to feed the number of cattle he's carrying each year. You will see crops or crop residues on crop land. Livestock and their droppings indicate active pasture—or possibly a new breach in the seller's fence. Hayfields can be waist-high grass prior to cutting, uniformly short grass just after cutting, somewhere in between, or livestock pasture after haying is completed. Fenced land is used for pasture and hay; cropland, too, may be fenced. The seller, or his agent, can give you the acreage breakdown for each current use. Most farmland is also tracked by use categories by the local Farm Service Agency (FSA) office of the U. S. Department of Agriculture (USDA). Farmland that is no longer being farmed will have grown up in brush, weeds and trees—the mixture of which depends on how long ago farming was abandoned.

As you walk through the farm, look at the dirt in each area. What's growing on it? Vegetation will tell you a lot about the dirt quality under your feet. Good dirt, with sufficient natural precipitation or irrigation, grows healthy plants owing to its fertility, chemical composition, drainage and other factors. Bad dirt generally tends to grow good things poorly, but thistles, teasels and other weeds do just fine. If you are clueless about which plants indicate good dirt and which the opposite, talk to the **county extension agent** or a local farmer about the local species that indicate one or the other. A field guide to wildflowers, like The Audubon Society Field Guide to North American Wildflowers, Eastern and Western editions, will describe preferred habitats. Plants growing on bad dirt (for agricultural purposes) will be described as being found on waste areas, barrens, roadsides, damp open ground and the like. If you are unsure about a plant in the field, take a specimen home and check it against a field guide from the local library or www.enature.com, where you click on native plant guide and then click on wildflowers, grasses, grass-like plants or shrubs.

What type of dirt is under your feet? Sandy? Clayey? Rocky? Shaley? Is the topsoil thin or deep? How far below the surface is rock or hard pan—the seller will know. Get down on your knees and look at it carefully. Is it hard packed, cracked and dry? Gummy and wet? What color is it? Dig down about 12 inches. Does it look rich, with grass roots, worms and life in it? Does it smell rich? Pick up a handful in each field. Compress it. Does it ball up into a spongy wad? Or does it crumble for lack of moisture and tilth? Better dirt has a deeper color, ranging from black to red, than poorer dirts, though color alone won't tell you all that you need to know. Poor dirt will grow vegetation that's adapted to what it provides, and that vegetation can support livestock as long as many acres are available for each animal. It may take 20 or 30 acres to graze a steer in parts of the arid West compared with one acre in fertile Mississippi. What you will learn from your dirt will depend, in part, on when you visit during the year and recent local weather so adjust your opinion for those factors. Don't count on grabbing a handful of dirt from a frozen field in the middle of January: a winter visit will rely on farm records and the local Soil Survey for information on dirt qualities. County Soil Surveys are discussed below.

Start learning about the properties of soil, and how soil quality can be maintained and improved. Visit the National Sustainable Agricultural Information Service's website at: http://attra.ncat.org. Click on to soils management, which provides information on soil testing; manure, compost and green manure (tilling a cover crop into the ground); pasture soils; soil and water quality; and links to other sites. This website also covers other aspects of sustainable (organic) agriculture. This information is worth reading whether or not you see yourself producing organic farm products. ATTRA is the acronym for Appropriate Technology Transfer for Rural Areas. The USDA funds numerous programs to improve and protect agricultural and rural soil. Access these through http://www.nrcs.usda.gov/programs.

The single handiest dirt book is the target county's **Soil Survey**, available through the local office of the USDA's Farm Service Agency (FSA). It shows the soil type on every acre in your county. The Survey locates each type of soil on **soil maps**, which are aerial photographs with the soil-type boundaries drawn on. Your target property may have a dozen or more soils. The Survey explains what each soil type is both suited and unsuited for in terms of agriculture (crops, pasture, hay), tree production, recreational uses such as hunting and wildlife habitat, construction purposes (dirt has to be sufficiently stable and firm to support the weight of a house) and waste disposal using a conventional septic-tank system. The tests used to determine whether dirt will support a conventional septic system are often called "**perc tests**," pronounced, perk, which assess a soil's absorption capacity by timing how long it takes water to drain from a hole. **Dirt-color analysis** is also used for this purpose. Many types of dirt won't pass a septic-system test, and some soils won't support house construction. If you are looking at a county whose soil has not been surveyed, talk to the local FSA official or a USDA soils specialist in the closest county where a survey has been completed. The chances are very good that you will get a reasonably accurate read on your farm's dirt based on the same types of topography and dirt found in a nearby county survey. You can find out about soil surveys, county-by-county, by accessing the USDA's Natural Resources Conservation Service's (NRCS) website at: http://soils.usda.gov/survey/printed_surveys/. Additional information on soil surveying is available from NRCS's National Cartography and Geospatial Center (NCGC) in Fort Worth, Texas. **Soil tests**, where you sample the dirt in each field and send it off for lab analysis, are described below. The NRCS now has soil-survey maps online at http://soils.usda.gov/survey.

I would reject property that had unsuitable dirt—soils that are lacking in fundamentals (workability, sufficient top soil, organic matter, productivity, "percablity," etc.)—for the type of use I had in mind. I would not reject property with bad dirt if my only "uses" for acreage were to look at it and keep distance between me and my neighbors. If you want land area for these reasons alone, consider buying bad dirt cheap. I would be inclined to reject property whose dirt is limited to one or two types, each of which is seriously unbalanced in terms of acidity or are disproportionately clay, sand or rock. You can balance and build soils, but it takes time and money. In my area, I've come to appreciate the difference between soils based on limestone and those based on shale. The latter are less productive for crops and trees, difficult to perc and tend to have problems with water quality. You cannot escape the characteristics of your dirt in your country property if you intend to make any use of the dirt. For that reason, I tend to screen out property with unsuitable dirt, look skeptically at property with uniformly bad dirt and celebrate property with a variety of soils, most of which are pretty good. I look for farmland dirt that can support multiple uses with reasonable efficiency.

Farms that have pastured cattle and sheep should be screened for overgrazing and eroded land. In my mountainous area, steep hillsides were cleared for pasture. Grass, however, can't absorb rainwater on a slope as well as forest. Some of these slopes have lost all their topsoil as a result. Overgrazed slopes tend toward landslides under heavy rain. When the soil on these hillsides reaches the limit of its capacity to absorb water, the rain will slide off them in sheets. Flooding results. If you see bare dirt and weeds, pastures are overgrazed. Thin soil and erosion are other signs of too many animals spending too much time on that pasture. Overgrazing and the environmental impacts that follow are common patterns on western ranches. Overgrazed pasture can be brought back by grazing fewer head or installing a rotational grazing system. You may need to fence livestock out of some areas. You may need to plant soil-building and water-holding vegetation in other spots. Remediation requires work and money.

As you drive and walk over a prospective property, look for trouble spots in the ground. Every farm is likely to have a couple of soft places where the tractor gets stuck every spring. These spots can be caused by a seasonal spring or a layer of impermeable subsurface clay that keeps the topsoil saturated with water. There are two places on my farm that are too slick in wet conditions for me to drive uphill in my 2WD tractor; there's a steep spot at a gate where it's impossible to stop coming downhill on wet grass without sliding. My wife refers to my learning efforts in these areas as "Mr. Toad's Wild Rides." Ask the seller to tell you where his land's little quirks lie. While on the subject of vehicles, ask the seller which hillsides are too steep for sideways driving. (You can drive safely straight up or down a slope whose steepness would cause a rollover in a truck or tractor if you were to try to drive across it.) Don't test yourself on steep slopes: rollovers kill.

Ask how the seller manages his land and works with its assets and trouble spots. What is each field used for? Where does he stop plowing because of wet ground? Is there a hidden rock in a hayfield that has to be skirted? Are there sinkholes to avoid? Which hillside meadows are too steep for hay-making? Which fields require what inputs of manure, chemical fertilizer, lime, weed control and pesticides for the use he made of each one? Ask the seller to rank his fields in terms of their best use, production and **productivity**. The latter—a measure of input efficiency in terms of output, not gross production—will be expressed as a ratio, such as pounds/bushels/bales/tons produced per acre, or number of acres required to carry one grazing animal for either a year or the spring-to-fall season. (Grazing ratios may be expressed in terms of a cow-calf unit or animal unit, so make sure that you understand the local definitions of "unit" as well as their equivalencies, that is, one unit equals so many steers each weighing so many pounds. A cow-calf unit might weigh 1,200 pounds together at spring turn out, so, roughly speaking, three 400-pound steers would equal one cow-calf unit. Keep in mind that as animals put on weight, they will be consuming more grass.) Ask the usual date when cattle can be turned out on spring grass. Are there any hot spots in the pastures where concentrated clover or alfalfa might cause bloat in newly turned out livestock? Find out the usual dates of the last spring frost and first autumn frost, because, together, they determine planting and harvesting schedules.

The farm and land will provide the buyer with climate clues. Snow fences indicate a pattern of deep drifts. Windmills indicate regular winds. Trees broken in their main stems usually indicate strong wind or ice storms. A cistern indicates the need to store water. You can find out current county-level climate information from the local **weather station**, which collects primary data on precipitation, temperature, wind speed, etc. The County's local chamber of commerce should have basic information regarding annual rainfall and temperature ranges. Most counties have several weather stations. You can identify the whereabouts of these stations in each county at http://lwf.ncdc.noaa.gov/oa/climate/stationlocator.html. Extensive data from each station can be purchased through this website.

Dirt needs moisture to grow vegetation. Is the farm located in an area where rainfall is sufficient and regular to grow crops without irrigation? I suggest looking at the target county's **annual precipitation map**. An example of such a map for Napa County, California can be viewed at http://www.ca.nrcs.usda.gov/mlrao2/napa/figure1.html. Rainfall and other weather conditions can vary significantly within a county owing to elevation, topography and other factors. Buyers are interested in the **micro-climate** of their target property, one clue to which is found on the annual precipitation map. The seller and his neighbors are first-hand sources of information on the farm's micro-climate. Don't ask the seller about his farm's micro-climate. Ask how many times during the last ten years his crops have been affected by drought. Or how many times he's had to sell calves early due to lack of grass growth, which is another way of measuring rainfall. Frame this question so that it is sensibly answered, not laughed at.

Do you see evidence of irrigation systems? Irrigation is usually accomplished by watering the surface either through long tubes mounted on large wheels or center-pivot sprays. Drip systems use buried water lines and porous tubing. All irrigation systems involve both upfront costs for equipment and continuing costs. The latter may include the cost of purchasing water, which is often sold as dollars per acre foot (43,650 square feet by 12 inches deep, or 43,650 cubic feet). Irrigation is not environmentally neutral. Continued draw downs can dry up a river, or a body of water as large as the 24,500-square-mile Aral Sea or your local **aquifer**, which is your subterranean strata of water-bearing rock. Aquifer depletion is a factor to weigh in purchasing land in the American Southwest, parts of California and in the southern Great Plains. (Lester R. Brown, "Dry, With a Chance of a Grain Shortage," <u>Washington Post</u>, December 14, 2003.) Where irrigated water is applied, it can deposit salts and minerals on the land. These can build up over time. If you are looking at an irrigated farm, I would advise retaining a local agricultural consultant to help you understand its requirements and implications.

As you walk the farm's dirt, notice ponds, springs and creeks, particularly in late summer. It is very important to learn whether ponds, creeks and springs go dry—never, rarely or routinely. I know of houses in my end of our county that are without household water when their springs dry up during droughts. This has happened several times during the last two decades. If the farm's water supply weakens during drought, how does the farm make it through? Does water have to be trucked in? How was agricultural production affected in the past?

If your target farm is east of the Mississippi River, you should generally have sufficient precipitation to grow area-appropriate crops. Even so, certain areas tend to summer drought if they lie just east of a line of mountains that catches rain as weather moves from west to east. Our farm lies east of the Allegheny Front, a line of 4,000-foot-high ridges running southwest to northeast. On our side of the Front, you find lots of Dry Creeks, Dry Forks, Dry Branches and Dry Runs. Such places were named for that important characteristic. Inasmuch as precipitation is always iffy, some farms in Southeast states have installed irrigation systems to guarantee a steady supply of water to their crops, even though irrigation may not be needed in most years. Drought can ruin a crop and shorten a livestock grazing season—both of which cost farmers money. Protracted drought that lasts for several years or more can lead to farm bankruptcy. The further west you are beyond the central Midwest corn belt, the more precipitation, underground water and irrigation determine your agricultural choices. In dry areas, you need to get detailed information from the seller and others about where the farm's water comes from, how much is needed, its quality, how it is accessed, its reliability in dry years, restrictions and constraints on its use and its cost. You must make sure that you have a legal right to the quantity of water the farm needs as part of your purchase.

The wildcard in scoping local climates is the impact of changes in global climate patterns, particularly temperature. Local trends over the last ten or 15 years may be more of a predictor of trends over the next ten to 15 years than averages derived from a 50- or 75-year sample. If you're buying property in an area that's borne drought for the last five or six years, I would make a call to a university-based or federal climatologist to discuss temperature and precipitation forecasts.

I've been discussing some of the elementary considerations of buying farmland. My reason for doing so is that much of the rural land that I've seen for sale during the last three decades was once, or is currently, being farmed in one way or another. Much of the wooded land that is now being sold in the East was once cleared for pasture or crops. Abandoned farmland continues to have potential for certain agricultural purposes, but the buyer should recognize the risks and limits of "re-agriculturalizing" land dismissed as uneconomical. Small pieces of such farms might be reworked as modern commercial agriculture under intensive management for high-profit, niche crops. Buying a 200-acre mountain farm with 25 acres of good bottomland might be a good *farming* buy if your idea is to convert the bottom to trout ponds and a large patch of specialty garlic. Such a place will not work economically as a traditional farm raising traditional crops in the traditional way; the market has already made that judgment. So don't count on making a profit from running cattle on its overgrown or overgrazed pastures, or planting corn on hillsides so steep that the seller's grandfather had to prop up each growing stalk with a rock. In such a case, the buyer is only interested in the dirt qualities of the 25 acres for a new use—trout ponds and garlic. The remaining 175 acres could be evaluated for timber production, recreation and woodland aesthetics—another new use. Old farms that are no longer economical cannot be made economical doing old farming the old way with new ownership. When you find a seller who has reached the end of this particular rope, you might find a very good deal. But don't take up where he left off.

It is also common for non-farm buyers to find grazing farms and dairy farms beyond the suburbs being marketed to them more as second homes and less as agricultural businesses. The 42 acres that Jim Phillips bought in the late 1960s were part of a working dairy farm whose owner was old and tired and ready to parcel out his land to fund his retirement. Such places obviously have dirt that is suitable for pasture, hay, row crops and woodland. What is equally obvious—to their sellers, at least—is that this dirt is far more valuable as second homes than as the type of working farms their sellers operated. Where dirt becomes economically marginal for one purpose, it may find a new and higher value with another purpose. The existing farm with such dirt is not competitive and provides a modest income, at best. The owner is finally forced to make a cold business choice between continuing to struggle for $20,000 a year as a farmer on one hand and the sale of his farm and its capital stock for 25 times that on the other. From the buyer's perspective, however, you should not pay a developer's price for this farm if your intent is to keep it in agriculture. You need to find a farm whose price is not inflated by a new or "higher" use.

The point here is that a buyer should evaluate the agricultural qualities of the dirt on farms of this sort in terms of both their current agricultural use and the buyer's projected use, agricultural and otherwise. Once that is done, the buyer should evaluate the value of this target for his projected use. The buyer wants to reach a price with the seller based on its value to the buyer, not on the seller's notions about the land's highest and best use. The buyer can sometimes turn this difference in market values to his advantage by bargaining with the seller on the basis of the land's value in its current use, which is likely to be lower than its highest-value use (i.e., second-home property sold to the likes of Mr. Korda), and lower than its value for the buyer's new use.

FARMS AND MONEY

I will assume that most readers are not interested in buying working farms as the first step to becoming full-time working farmers. This assumption, if true, shows good sense on your part. Still, many readers will be intrigued with this idea, and many more will like the idea of having a working farm as a second home. I offer these observations.

Working farms run by full-time working farmers who make a respectable living are a subset of American farm operations that novices have a very small chance of joining upon the acquisition of such places. It is very hard for real farmers to make a respectable living, particularly those working on comparatively small acreages and those producing basic commodity crops, like grain and beef cattle. On farms of fewer than 200 acres in the mid-Atlantic and New England states, it is next to impossible both to make a living and retire a farm's mortgage from full-time conventional commodity production. The value of these farms often lies not in what they can produce but in where they sit. Thus, the seller wants the buyer to pay a premium for location.

Family farms that are financially successful generally involve large acreages (much of which may be leased), huge investments in capital stock and manageable debt. The individuals who in my experience survive at conventional farming have been farm-raised, trained in agriculture, operate on a sufficiently large scale and are blessed with a cash cushion to ride out the inevitable bad years. I have not come across a successful farmer who started from scratch, borrowing for land and equipment. Most full-time farmers made their learning-curve mistakes on someone else's nickel (often their parents') or squeaked past their errors when times were more forgiving. Many got their start from their parents: it's a lot easier to make a living from a farm "when it was give to ya" free and clear of a mortgage. They have survived by figuring out farm-specific resilience strategies, including what to do and how to do it when most everything goes wrong at the same time. Many also seem to have made shrewd acquisitions of land and timber over the years, the equally shrewd sales of which have provided income subject to a favorable capital-gains rate. Farming's ever-present danger is debt. When farm debt—mortgage, equipment and operating expenses—exceeds farm income, its servicing can consume farm profit, cash reserves, other assets and non-farm income. The farmer ends up living to pay down his debt.

Making a living from full-time, conventional farming is so experience-dependent, capital-intensive, complicated, weather-dependent and risky that any reader who contemplates a career change would be well-advised to begin burning $100 bills in preparation. Better yet, burn your money after working a 12-hour day, half of which was spent pleading with a banker not to call a note, and the other half shoveling manure as self-imposed penance for wanting to produce food or fiber.

I should add that I've run into several examples of inexperienced newcomers who succeed after buying working farms. All of these exceptions involve individuals who have a lot of money from some non-farm source that is used to buy and then subsidize large farms. I have not seen these farms work out as businesses. I have seen them work as long-term investments when land appreciation creates profit taxed at the capital-gains rate or otherwise discounted through sophisticated tax strategies. The individuals who do this type of farming have a lot of fun being farmers.

The other group of non-farm buyers interested in farms are those who like the idea of farming and are free of the burden of having to support themselves through that type of work. These folks buy modest places, not the large showpieces. Some relocate to the farm, particularly if they have early retirement. They find a job off the farm or make one up to generate the cash they need. I've seen one member of a couple continue city-based employment on a four-day work week while the spouse lives full-time on the farm. These non-farm farmers started with a money cushion—either cash in a pile or cash flow—that muddles them through their farming errors and spells of rural underemployment. Trust funds, savings, inheritance, non-farm employment and pension benefits are the most common cushions I've seen. It is foolhardy to move to a working farm if you do not have either cash in a pile or cash flow—and preferably both—from non-farm work or investments. Buyers of this sort need to be confident about the long-term sustainability of their cushion. Financial circumstances change, and not necessarily for the better.

Most American farmers don't make a living from farming. The USDA reported that in 1993, the most recent year for which survey data were available, the average farm operator household income was just over $40,000, of which only 12 percent came from farm income. (See www.usda.gov/news/pubs/factbook/003e.pdf.) The rest came from wages and salaries (46 percent), off-farm business income (17 percent), other off-farm income (18 percent) and interest and dividends (7 percent). Of the slightly more than 2.03 million farm operator households that year, almost 152,000 reported a negative income, averaging $28,526. Forty-five percent of all farm households earned less than $25,000, and all of these households earned most of their income off the farm. Households reporting income of between $50,000 and $249,999 that year, derived an average of $14,590 in farm income and $26,718 in off-farm income. Only when income exceeded $250,000 did farm operator households average more income from farming than from off-farm sources. USDA projections for 2003 forecasted average farm operator household income at $68,900, with only $5,250—7.6 percent—from farming. (See http://www.ers.usda.gov/publications/agoutlook/aotables/oct2003/aotab31.xls.)

Rather than non-farm income supplementing farm income, it appears to me that most farmers, except for the very wealthiest, are supplementing their non-farm income with farm income. Why, then have a working farm? For most farm households, the farm generates a little spending income and a lot of depreciation, deductions, tax breaks, credits, subsidies, cost sharing, loss and income taxed at the capital-gains rate from the sale of land and timber. This pattern can be a wonderful fit for a buyer in the highest tax brackets with most of his cash flow in salary and taxed as current income. Such a buyer is helped by the deductions, depreciation and losses that farms generate. Renting out your farm keeps most of these benefits in your pocket, though you get more tax goodies if you operate the farm yourself. Chapter 6 discusses farm-taxation issues.

The relationship between farm income, farm size and federal policies, particularly crop subsidies, was the subject of a series of articles in the Washington Post at the end of 2006 (See www.washingtonpost.com/harvestingcash). Large farms—with revenue of more than $250,000 per year—produce almost 60 percent of all agricultural production but account for only seven percent of farms. These large farms get more than 54 percent of federal subsidies—and their share is increasing. The average farm size has doubled to 441 acres during the last decade, but the sector employs fewer farmers. Subsidies have encouraged these trends. (Gilbert M. Gaul, Sarah Cohen and Dan Morgan, "Federal Subsidies Turn Farms into Big Business," Washington Post, December 21, 2006.)

To those few readers who are sitting in a city office still thinking about earning a living from farming. I urge you to invest your time and money in self-education before buying. Take a degree—or at least college-level courses—in the agricultural specialty of your choice before you put dollar one into that type of farm. Apprentice yourself to a farmer you want to emulate during your next summer vacation. Approach your move-to-a-farm idea as a long-term business plan, not a lifestyle choice. Being broke, or farm-poor, is not a fun-filled lifestyle. It's fine to aspire to produce healthful, organic produce in a way that allows you to live on a healthful, organic farm. But doing so can lead to bankruptcy if you lack a non-farm source of cash or a feasible business plan along with the management skills and experience to make the plan work over time. Making a subsistence income year after year in the service of higher values wears thin. Test your plan. Send various drafts to extension professors for comments. Talk it out with real farmers who are doing similar ventures. Make your mistakes on paper, not on the ground. Don't be shy about adding 25 percent to your most inflated cost calculations to represent the unexpected that almost always breaks against the novice. Force your farm to make a profit on an unforgiving sheet of paper before you ever try it in a merciless field.

When we bought our farm in 1983, I confidently told my trusting wife that "we could always make a living off the farm if the economy went into the tank." This was one of those opinions that I routinely express based on nothing more than the rumored fact that one male ancestor clad in animal skins got lucky one morning and spotted a mammoth just as it was having a fatal heart attack outside his cave. This ancestor then boasted to his spouse that rational thinking and analytical planning lay behind his successful hunt. All future opinions, he informed her, would be similarly based, and, therefore, not to be questioned. Using reason and analysis, he then left her the job of butchering 8,000 pounds of fresh mammoth before it spoiled. I've often wondered where my pre-purchase wisdom about "living off the farm" came from. At first, I blamed a book whose cover I may have glimpsed. Now I blame my ancestral crock in which such opinions still occasionally ferment.

About six months after purchase, I received a nice little analysis from Virginia Tech in response to my sending along our farm's particulars. The crunched numbers showed I couldn't hope to break even on running 35 spring stocker steers as had always been done in the past. Loss was programmed. What did they know, I said. I invested in a **rotational grazing system**, which allowed me to double the number of animals and add each pound of gain as cost-efficiently as possible. The farm now produces about 75 percent more pounds per year than it did before I installed this system. But after ten years of trying every which way to make money from our small grazing farm in a pretty place, I gave up and began renting it for seasonal pasture. There's no risk in renting as long as the cash is paid upfront. The annual income—$3,000—turned out to be about what I would net from running the steers myself, with no risk and less work.

Producing basic product is the hardest and riskiest end of the agricultural business. The risk-taking, investment and work of basic production supports layer upon layer of businesses above it. Market forces have divided producers of agricultural commodities into two groups: 1) full-time producers who have achieved a level of efficiency, scale and capital to farm at a profit, and 2) part-time (marginal) producers who don't have to be efficient because they consider their farm income as a supplement to non-farm earnings. Producers whose operations fall between these groups don't last. A novice farmer reading these words should consider joining the second group, not the first.

While it's easy to enter farming, it's not easy to make it pay. If you want to try conventional production farming because you want to be outside, work with your hands, produce something of value and live in a clean environment, look for some other occupational vehicle. These are fine goals and farming meets them. But those goals get submerged in farming by the inherent, depleting hassles of operating a farm as a business—debt management, unpredictable weather, low prices, increasing input costs and genuine catastrophes. No prospective farm buyer, especially one who has not done much farming, should ever enter a barnyard romancing the seller's dirt. If you insist on thinking about farming as a livelihood, approach it as capitalism at its least forgiving...and you will be in the right frame of mind. The odds are that you will find yourself an entrepreneur who feels like a 19th Century "immiserated" industrial worker whom Marx predicted would rebel against the hopeless degradation free-market capitalism imposed. Perhaps the farm revolution will be led by an individual who comes into farming from outside the system and soon asks: Why does anyone put up with this?

In the fall and winter of 2003, a bit of luck fell to the one million American farmers—about half of the total—who run either beef cattle or dairy cattle. Together, cattle are America's single largest agricultural sector in terms of gross revenue. The prices paid for feedlot-ready cattle spiked due to a combination of unforeseen events—principally, a U.S. embargo on Canadian beef imports after one cow had been confirmed with bovine spongiform encephalopathy (BSE, or mad-cow disease) and the popularity of high-protein, low-carbohydrate, weight-loss diets that encourage the consumption of beef. Beef producers had been squeezed for more than two decades by oversupply, softening demand and stagnant prices. Suddenly, cattle farmers were getting $100 more per head sold than ever before. Normally, they might net $25-$50 per head. Blaine Harden, a <u>Washington Post</u> reporter, talked with ranchers in Montana:

Ranchers here have taken out larger-than-normal operating loans in recent years, owing to the drought, smaller herds and depressed beef prices. 'We are trying to make up for losses we suffered for five straight years,' said Rick Kuntz, 53, who raises cattle on 20,000 acres south of Dillon [Montana]. During that period, drought and lack of range grass forced him to cut his herd by more than 30 percent, to 450 head from 690. He said he has had to borrow more and more money just to keep the ranch operating. At the same time, he said, he has not been able to spare any cash for mending fences, painting his barns or buying new equipment. His 30-year-old tractors and haying machines, he said, are held together with 'spit and chewing gum.' The hurt, though, seems to be ending. (Blaine Harden, "Protein Diet Craze, Thin Supply of Cattle Fatten Ranchers' Wallets," Washington Post, December 22, 2003.)

The market, it seemed, had finally thrown cattle farmers a life line. And then, a few days later, an old "downer" (non-ambulatory) cow from Canada that had presumably been fed feed containing infected cattle tissue was found in Washington state and diagnosed with BSE. Fifty countries banned U.S. beef imports within a month, affecting about 10 percent, or 2.6 billion pounds, of total U.S. beef production. (Scott Kilman, "Farm Economy Seems to Absorb Impact of First Mad-Cow Case," Wall Street Journal, January 21, 2004.) Cattle prices plunged 20 percent, and then recovered about half. To the extent that export is slowed in the future, U.S. farmers will be producing more beef than the domestic market wants. This will reduce cattle prices paid to farmers. Since much range and cattle pasture are not well-suited for alternative uses, this production capacity is likely to hang on. "Cattle keep the fields mowed" is an oft-expressed opinion by farmers who know they net little from "running some beeves" every year. The long-term, structural impact on U.S. cattle farmers from changes in beef imports and exports is hard to predict. The temporary life line may have looped itself into a noose. Good times for American cattle producers had lasted about three months. In July, 2005, beef imports from Canada resumed, whether or not Canadian beef represents a BSE threat. U.S. beef packers expect lower cattle prices, hence more demand for their finished product. Cattle farmers are expecting to be paid these lower prices as supply increases.

And in March, 2006, another cow—this one in Alabama—was diagnosed with BSE. Cattle producers sought comfort in that all three U.S. cows found carrying the disease were likely infected prior to August, 1997 when both the U.S. and Canada more or less prohibited their feed industries from using rendered cattle remains that are contaminated with BSE. USDA announced that it would reduce BSE testing, which had screened 650,000 brain samples since June 2004. (Scott Kilman and Janet Adamy, "Mad-Cow Diagnosis is Confirmed," Wall Street Journal, March 14, 2006.)

The BSE episode is the tip of an iceberg of questions about the safety of beef. The high-protein diets that I've seen don't address such safety issues. Consumers of conventional beef have no way of knowing what their hamburger ate, how it was medicated and what growth hormones, if any, were implanted.

The World Health Organization (WHO) recommended in 2003 that all nations ban the routine use of low-levels of antibiotics as growth stimulators. (Marc Kaufman, "WHO Urges End to Use of Antibiotics for Animal Growth," Washington Post, August 13, 2003.) About one-half of animal antibiotic use worldwide goes for growth stimulation, not treatment of disease. WHO, and others, are concerned that such levels of antibiotic use are leading to resistant bacteria, which some scientists believe are decreasing the effectiveness of antibiotics in humans. Resistant bacteria can get into meat products in the slaughtering process; they also get into the environment from farm runoff. (Margaret Webb Pressler, "9 Steps to Safer Beef: Much of What Advocates Propose, Cattlemen and Government Oppose," Washington Post, January 18, 2004.) Denmark imposed a ban on growth-oriented antibiotics in 1998, and McDonald's told its suppliers to cut back. Apart from antibiotics, animal products are still used in animal feeds. Cattle blood is processed into a milk substitute for calves, and cattle byproducts are fed to chickens and hogs.

As of October, 2005, it was still permitted to feed cattle poultry litter (protein-rich manure, urine and whatever else is cleaned from a poultry house); I did this for several years in the late 1980s. In January, 2004, the federal Food and Drug Administration proposed to end the practice of including high-risk meat and bone meal derived from cattle in animal feed, prohibit using mammalian and avian meat and bone meal in ruminant feed, and stop using materials from disabled and dead cattle in animal feed. The FDA's proposed rules would not end feeding litter to cattle. In slaughterhouses, Federal inspectors do not inspect each carcass, and testing for pathogens like the deadly *E coli* Q157:H7 is inadequate.

My feeling is that the American beef and meat industries would do far better in the long run to embrace product safety fully rather than reluctantly and piecemeal. Each scare—mad-cow, *E-coli* deaths from contaminated hamburger, the January 2004 recall of Giordano ready-to-eat deli meats due to *Listeria monoctyogene* contamination, hormone implants, resistant bacteria—softens demand and price, making it harder for farmers to make a living from raising cattle. (Food recalls can be accessed at the USDA's Food Safety and Inspection Service's website: http://www.fsis.usda.gov; click on Food Recalls and Alerts. Most meat and poultry recalls involve contamination that occurs at the processing plants, but mad-cow and concerns over hormones and resistant bacteria would need to be regulated on the farm.) If you are looking to buy a small cattle farm, the bottom line is something like this: count on cattle to keep your pasture cropped, your farm qualified for IRS farm treatment and a source of Christmas money

What the mad-cow episode blurs is the fundamental problem in agricultural commodity production, beef and otherwise, namely **chronic overcapacity**. Too much production capacity leads to overproduction and low producer prices. America has the capacity—land and other resources—to increase the supply of most row crops by 25 percent in a year or two with no increase in productivity. Meat and milk products would take additional time. In a real pinch, some crops might be increased by 50 to 100 percent by planting marginal land, crop shifting and other strategies. The marginal capacity—land, capital, labor—for each crop is not cost-efficient and is normally used for activities that make more financial sense. But this capacity can be swung from one use to another when the cold winds of January bring the scent of higher fall prices. The relative ease of having farmers of most kinds being able to increase output quickly undercuts producer prices permanently. Farmers are selling many commodity crops and products at roughly the same prices today as 20 years ago, despite inflation. Oligopolistic processors encourage overcapacity and excess supply, because they profit from cheap farm commodities. Many farmers find themselves in a permanent economic squeeze manufactured by the constricting triangle of excess capacity, oversupply and weak prices.

The other factor that is now contributing to excess capacity is the increasing flow of agricultural imports into the United States from cheaper foreign producers. Cheap imports discourage marginal domestic producers who might move their land into familiar harbors, such as corn and soybeans, thus contributing to their oversupply. The North American Free Trade Agreement and other similar arrangements have encouraged U.S. consumption of foreign agricultural products—winter tomatoes from Mexico, farm-raised salmon from Chile, garlic and apples from China, for example—whose cheapness is based on cheap labor and inadequate safety and environmental regulations. (Gannett News Service, "Farmers eye trade deals with both fear, optimism," January 27, 2004.) Those American agricultural sectors such as corn, soybeans and wheat where labor is not a significant cost factor in production will probably benefit from "free trade" of this type. Where labor is significant, American producers will not be able to export and may lose much of their domestic market. If these trends develop in this way, American agriculture will be further divided between crops that can be kept price competitive through increasing productivity based on technology and highly articulated specialty crops that serve particular domestic and foreign niches. A farm buyer should approach labor-dependent farm operations with much caution.

Farming works best these days for farmers who don't need to extract a living from their farming. At the macro level, these farmers bolster their sector's overcapacity. Their supply contributes to low prices for their product. But at the individual's level, voluntary marginal farming is perfectly sensible, particularly for absentee owners and those who are not farming to make a living. My advice, then, is to think of marginal farming as a secondary vehicle for getting you into a second-home farm. Marginal farming will not pay for your farmstead. The primary vehicle for purchasing a farm must be cash from some other source. Assume that farm production will never pay for the farm's purchase—until you sell it.

The books by Jeanne Marie Laskas and Michael Korda illustrate the absolute necessity of financing and subsidizing marginal farms externally. The more marginal the farm, the more this rule applies. With both Laskas and Korda, it appears to me that their "farms" never produced a dollar in net farm income, and possibly not many more in gross farm income. These farms are farms in the sense that work is done there and money is spent on agriculture, broadly, very broadly, defined. Such places are farms for life pleasure and, perhaps, the IRS. "Farming" the tax code and federal agricultural-support programs has become as important a farm skill as driving a tractor in a straight line. Like it or not. For better or worse.

SUBSIDIES

While trying to work a farm for a profit is a chancy proposition, buying a working farm is not as long as it is not expected to pay for itself. Working farms bought for second homes usually require that they continue to be operated as farms of some type, even if not the type that was being worked when they were bought. Otherwise, they revert to weeds and woods. Continuation in one form or another also makes sense in terms of the owner getting a farm discount on local property taxes as well as numerous federal tax breaks.

Apart from tax benefits, readers should know that the federal government continues to subsidize certain farm products and farm (conservation-enhancing) practices. USDA subsidies amounted to about $12.2 billion in 2002, $8.8 billion of which went for commodity subsidies, about $2 billion for conservation practices and the rest for disaster relief. (See http://www.ewg.org/farm/regionsummary.php?fips=00000.) Most subsidy money goes to the very largest corporate farm operations. The top ten percent of the 2.8 million individuals and companies that received subsidies in 2002 took in 65 percent of the $12.2 billion total. (See http://www.ewg.org/farm/findings.php.) Crops with the largest subsidies are corn, wheat, soybeans, cotton and rice. Annual subsidy to an individual farmer is supposed to be capped at $360,000, but there are loopholes that allow higher payments.

You can identify individual subsidy recipients by city, county or zip code since 1995 through the Environmental Working Group (EWG) Farm Subsidy Database 2.0 (http://www.ewg.org/farm/). This site allows you to track the recent "**subsidy history**" for any target farm property you're scoping. It provides the dollar amount of subsidy for each year, divided into three categories—commodity, conservation and disaster. Ownership information and farm location are also provided. Absentee farmowners receiving subsidies for their farm operations are found everywhere. You will find subsidized farmowners in Beverly Hills, California like Mary Ann Mobley as well as in Washington, D.C. and New York City. Most subsidy money goes to corporate farmers and trusts, because they own the largest farms and produce the most of whatever crop is receiving the subsidy. Nonetheless, small farmers are equally eligible and receive payments according to their output. If you operate or rent your new farm, you are eligible for whatever commodity subsidies may apply. The farm is also eligible for conservation programs.

Some readers may want to immerse themselves in the vat of ethical quandaries commodity programs stir. Most Americans don't get paid to not produce the product of their job. Most Americans don't have a price guarantee for the work product they produce. Subsidies maintain the overhang of excess capacity and oversupply. The EWG subsidy data show the lopsidedness of American subsidies in practice: the biggest producers, who need help the least, get most of the subsidy; the struggling small farmer gets a pittance, which helps to keep him in a game that he can't win. Subsidies help maintain marginal farmers— the politically mythic small, family farmer—whose continued presence legitimizes continued payments to the largest producers.

To the extent that our subsidized crops compete in foreign markets, "rich" American farmers as a group are making a living at the expense of poor Third World farmers who generally can produce whatever cheaper because their standard of living is so low and labor, including themselves, is paid a few dollars a day. (Most developed countries retain subsidies of one sort or another for at least some of their farm products, which is a chronic and contentious "globalization" issue.) Eliminate commodity subsidies and production shifts to the lowest-cost producers. American production will be squeezed out of foreign markets. If the American market is open to cheaper foreign crops (themselves, often aided by their governments), American farm products will lose domestic market share as well. This has happened to textiles, shoes, steel, cars, electronics, shipbuilding and even some services. If it keeps happening, sector by sector, some Third World living standards will rise marginally as living standards for large numbers of ordinary Americans decline. Eliminate agricultural subsidies and many marginal producers—small, inefficient (even family) farmers—will be forced to either produce something that earns them a profit in the marketplace or turn their land to some other activity. None of these paths are lined with rose petals. (The social and political consequences of nation-state agricultural policies have been apparent since the 1600s, if not earlier. The consequences of how Europe and America organized the production of quinine, sugar, tea, cotton, coca and the potato are discussed in Henry Hobhouse, Seeds of Change: *Six* Plants *That* Transformed Mankind [UK: Macmillan, 1999].)

Every American farmer has a right to avail himself of crop subsidies in the same way that every taxpayer has a right to avail himself of every tax break. As a buyer, you need to factor subsidies into your scoping as have thousands of absentee farmowners who receive their checks at home in America's cities and suburbs. You should also perform some rudimentary risk analysis to determine the probability of your target-farm's crop subsidy continuing in the future at existing levels. National policy has backed out subsidy to some products, such as tobacco, through buyouts. If you are the type who tries to align his behavior with ethical standards that involve national economic policy and global justice, you probably want to think through accepting crop subsidies. I don't think such a person would have any problem accepting federal subsidy for conservation practices or disaster assistance.

My own preference is to not get hooked on subsidized crops, more for reasons of economics than ethics, though the latter clinches it for me. I think the political and economic undertow of our increasing debt is pulling against crop subsidies over time. A marginal farm counting on a subsidy payment to squeak by is a vulnerable investment. A farm whose equipment and buildings are customized to produce one or two subsidized crops may not be readily adaptable to other crops. If corn, for example, were to have its subsidy withdrawn tomorrow, some marginal producers with thousands of dollars of specialized corn-only equipment and storage facilities would exit the market. If you're planning to grow tomatoes on former corn land, you will have to remodel the farm's infrastructure and obtain different harvesting equipment. A new buyer needs to consider both current and alternative uses of a farm's resources. In terms of subsidies, a buyer must determine whether non-subsidized production of the previously subsidized crop still suits his overall financial needs; it very well may. If you are a buyer who is basically looking for the tax benefits from a farm investment coupled with long-term appreciation of the land, the prospect of losing a crop subsidy payment may not deter a purchase. Less farm income, in other words, might mean more farm loss available to offset non-farm income. If, however, you are looking to buy a farm that you plan to farm, concentrate on land with facilities that allow you to produce different crops each year and make substitutions from year to year without a whole lot of additional investment. Farmers these days need to be nimble, flexible and adaptable.

On the day I was proofreading this chapter, I took a break when the Wall Street Journal arrived. On the front page I read the top-right headline: "In Fight Against Farm Subsidies, Even Farmers Are Joining Forces." Here are relevant excerpts regarding the record $23 billion paid to farmers in 2005:

A movement to uproot crop subsidies, which have been worth nearly 600 billion to U.S. farmers over the decades, is gaining ground in some unlikely places—including down on the farm.

[A Republican running for Iowa's state agriculture secretary]…told a room full of farmers recently that federal payments spur overproduction, which depresses prices for poor growers overseas.

…any significant change in the payment formula would rock the farm economy. Federal money could shift between regions, possibly at the expense of Southern farmers who are subsidized to such a degree currently that no new system would likely maintain their level of payments. The price of land, which is tied to the income it generates, would likely fall, denting farmers' biggest source of wealth and collateral.

…the gluts spurred by production-based subsidies are a key reason the U.S. enjoys some of the world's lowest food prices.

…nor do subsidies do much for rural economic development. Most rural people are no longer engaged in farming and two-thirds of those who farm are growing nonsubsidized crops such as fruits and vegetables.

The Bush Administration, which pushed through a huge five-year $150 billion farm bill in 2002, criticized farm subsidies in 2006 inasmuch as they "'hurt countries that could benefit from exporting these commodities to the United States,'" in the words of the White House Council of Economic Advisers, "Economic Report of the President" of February, 2006. (Scott Kilman and Roger Thurow, "In Fight Against Farm Subsidies, Even Farmers Are Joining Foes," Wall Street Journal, March 14, 2006.)

I anticipate some cherry-picking-type reforms of the farm-subsidy framework in the near future. One likely change would be to lower the annual subsidy cap from $360,000 per individual per year to $250,000 while continuing obscure loopholes. Or a buy-out program might be set up for one or more particular crops, similar to the one crafted for tobacco. But it would not surprise me to see farm bills continue to pump increasing amounts of money into agriculture, if not as crop subsidies, then as tax credits and price guarantees for production of biomass feedstocks used as petroleum substitutes. Given that every state has an agricultural sector and two U.S. senators, I'd anticipate continued payments to agriculture with some continuing reconfiguration of how the money is spent to show "reform of the subsidy system."

RENT WITH AN OPTION TO OPERATE

The least risky and most sensible way of making a transition from an urban non-farm person to the owner of a farm operation is to **rent out the farm soon after purchase.**

Farming is not simple in practice, and often not in theory. While it may look easy enough to have 50 head of calm cattle munching your grass for six months, the novice cattle farmer will be expected to be able to apply a world of skills including knowing how and where to buy cattle, selecting medications and applying them properly, identifying illnesses as they arise, knowing how to fix old fence and build new fence, disposing of those animals who "up and die" and choosing a marketing strategy. All such tasks are not beyond your abilities if you read the literature, ask questions and watch your neighbors. "Running" several dozen cattle is easy farming compared with other types of farming that depend even more on judgment and experience.

As a first step in getting your feet dirty, I recommend renting your newly purchased farm to a local farmer who is patient with having you around and is willing to answer your questions. Keep notes on what your tenant does, how he does it, when he does it, and then ask why he did it the way he did. He may be out of date and out of step with the latest advice from the ag school experts. Still, old fashion has a lot to teach you about the tricks of your ground and what has worked in the past, whether or not it is now state of the art. I learned about thrift in farming when I saw my neighbor, then in his late 60s, bend down in the heat of the afternoon to gather small clumps of hay that the baler had missed and place them in the next windrow. Maybe it amounted to a half a bale altogether, of the 300 we made that day. This was my hay that he was saving for my cattle.

Consider renting out your newly purchased farm for two or three years before trying to run the farm as a business on your own. I write as one who did not follow this advice, and spent many hours in self-taught crash courses involving the injection of antibiotics into the eyelids of sick cattle as well as trying to herd blind steers through open gates. Calling this on-the-job training a "crash course" is apt since my 700-pound ingrates spent a good deal of our moments together mashing me into the boards of my barn like demented hockey players.

The seller can recommend likely renters. You can also advertise in the local paper. One or more neighbors will probably approach you about renting your place. You need to step carefully with the choice of tenant. The neighbor who offers you the most money may or may not be the best match for your land. You may want to take a little less rent from a farmer who sees you less as a rich dope and more as a kind of farm-literacy project.

Some potential tenants may be controversial among your neighbors who will be acutely attuned to the "business" alliances you make—or seem to make—during your first year or two. You may not know the implications of what will appear to you to be a simple choice to rent your land for a year to Neighbor Y rather than Neighbor X. Your neighbors know that Neighbor Y comes with a history of crooked dealing, which your decision has accepted, if not endorsed. (You, of course, are blissfully unaware of Neighbor Y's baggage. He was the first farmer to approach you, so you took the first money because it was easiest.) If Neighbor Y rents your place out from under Neighbor X who's rented it for the last three years, rest assured that most of X's family will never be friendly since you are now aligned with the hated Y. If you know no one in your new community, ask your lawyer and the seller for guidance. Be aware, of course, that each of these individuals has his own relations with both the Xs and the Ys. If you ask these questions often enough—To whom, should I rent and why? To whom, should I not rent and why? Who will be miffed if I rent to this individual and why? Am I making a good renter choice if I choose this person?—you're likely to pick up the dimensions of the local alliance networks. Ignorance of these networks will not serve as a defense. Your neighbors—Xs, Ys and Zs—will read more into your choice of renter than you mean to invest. Try your best to make an informed choice.

If you rent your land, you will be entering your new country neighborhood with a second financial step, the first being what you paid for your new farm. The details of your purchase are likely to become common knowledge as will be the seller's opinion of how you comported yourself in the negotiations with him. The selling price is often available from the deed documents recorded in the county at the time of purchase or in the tax records. Assume, for this discussion, that you have overpaid for your farm in the eyes of your new neighbors (but not in your eyes and not objectively in terms of comparable properties). Your rental candidates will assume that since you overpaid for your farm, you will accept something less than fair market rental value for your land. If these potential renters pay fair market rental, they may fear they will be seen as fools by the boys down at the Home-Cooked, Slow-Speed Interface Grille who scrutinize such matters.

A new owner can approach this rental problem in one of two ways. First, you can use **neutral third-party authority** to establish a fair rental rate. Your "neutral" authorities might be drawn from the local banker, county extension agent, real-estate brokers, stockyard owner, grain merchants, buyers of your farm product, Farm Bureau representatives, the local lawyer who handled your purchase and the local CPA who will advise you on farm taxes. Ask such folks what the going rate is for your type of land, even for your particular farm. Use that information to establish a fair rental value. Then use the generic "they say" to inform your prospective tenant of what you expect: "They [local, objective authorities] say my farm should rent for $X per acre. I've checked around on this number, and there's a consensus." You should plead in your own ignorance on this subject and rely solely on the impartial, uninterested and never named authorities you've consulted. If really pressed by the renter on this point, say something like, I've talked to several farmers, bankers, lawyers and CPAs in the county. This method should get you pretty close to a fair rental number, if not dead on. Don't inflate the consensus number; that type of behavior will backfire. If the seller rented the farm a year or two before you bought it, use that number as your own.

The second method relies on the same research from local authorities, but you use it to **market your farm rental outside your neighborhood**. You might offend all your new neighbors if you choose to not rent your land locally, but you will probably spare yourself making long-term neighbor enemies if you stiff everyone a little, equally. (At least, you can't be accused of playing favorites.) The exception to this small-offense-to-everyone tactic is the case where a neighbor has rented your land for a number of years and has come to depend on it, psychologically and/or financially. Make your best effort to continue with this person. If he's been paying less-than-market rental, it's fair for you to show him your consensus per-acre rental number, which he can meet or not at his choice. If you back him out of a long-standing arrangement or if he backs himself out because he's unwilling to pay market value, assume that relations between the two of you (and his alliance network) will be stiff for at least a decade or two. Make sure to consider the non-dollar benefits from continuing a below-market rental with a neighbor. You can agree to continue the discounted rental if he's willing to help you in other ways. If, on the other hand, the negotiations descend to a point where he's threatening you with one thing or another if you don't do what he wants, don't start with him. Extortion feeds on itself.

Non-local rental works best when the property has not previously been rented to a neighbor. It buys you a couple of years to learn the folks in your new neighborhood and how each relates to you and you to them. Once you have a sense of the **alliance networks** in your neighborhood, you can choose to join or stay out. These networks are often based on family connections (and disconnections), church, club memberships, work relationships and assorted historic squabbles, loyalties and sleights that will never be forgotten or forgiven. It will take you years to discover all the layers, ties and crossed circuits within and among these networks. Do not be surprised to find 60-year-old grievances recounted as if they are current. Do not be surprised if you are held partially responsible for a dispute that happened 50 years earlier where your predecessor in title did something that offended a neighboring family. If a fence line you now own was built on your neighbor's property three owners back, you will be partially blamed for that transgression—and you should fix it the next time new fence is built. The trick is not to step too deeply into too many of these holes; give yourself time to learn where they are and how deep each is.

You can find a non-local renter by advertising in both local and non-local papers. Non-local farmers read your local paper for just this reason. The ad should be placed at least two months before the renter will need the property, and certain types of farming will require their farmers to plan as much as a year in advance. The advance time is needed to integrate the new rental property into the farmer's other lands, figure out schedules, labor and financing. Some farmland is easier to rent to non-local farmers than others. Grazing land is readily rented, both locally and non-locally, since cattle and sheep are easily transported and can be bought at spring sales for six-month, spring-to-fall grazing leases. Rental may become more difficult when large pieces of equipment have to be trucked from a distance. There are farmers who are set up to manage equipment rotation, but they may want a discounted rental price owing to their additional logistical expense.

If, incidentally, no local farmer expresses an interest in renting the farmable portion of your new property, it's reasonable to assume that they know something that you didn't and don't—at least, until you're able to prove otherwise. I would not attribute the absence of local renters to shyness. Had the Laskases tried to rent their 50 acres of thorns, local cattle farmers would have probably passed it up, even at a discount. Fences would have had to have been repaired. Dense multiflora rose will scratch the eyes of cattle, increasing the likelihood of pinkeye. Renters do not want to "get up" their livestock through pasture clogged with blackberry brambles and thorn groves. The hassle of making use of that type of pasture would discourage most renters. The same hilly acreage, reasonably clean and clear, should find a ready pasture market.

Inasmuch as this is your second "public" piece of local business, treat everyone involved with respect and care, especially those who propose terms to you that are so nonsensically one-sided that you want to laugh. Try to pick a tenant who you feel will take some responsibility for your land and who comes across as a rational problem-solver. Avoid the candidates who tend to personalize business relationships, those who talk about how they got the better of someone in some past deal, the man who tells you how the world of "them" is arrayed against him, the man who can see only his way to accomplish any particular task, and the man who sees every transaction as a zero-sum game and is uncomfortable with the idea of win-win. Look for someone you can count on to live up to the terms of your agreement. Look for someone with a history of successful farm rentals in your area. If you have doubts about an individual, ask for and then check several local references.

Rent payment is a matter of how much but also of when. Many farmers borrow to get their crop in during the early spring and repay after the fall harvest. They will want to pay their rent at the end of the season when they have money, not in the spring when they may have to borrow it. If you agree to an end-of-the-season payment you risk not getting paid the full rental owing to any of a dozen bad breaks that befell your tenant—none of which are your fault. You will certainly lose the use of or interest on money paid at the beginning of the lease. I recommend against end-of-season rental payments because the renter has nothing to lose by trying to reduce the rent when it's due. If he chooses to short you $500 or $1,000 because of drought, low prices or any other reason, it may not be worth suing for full payment. **I recommend getting all farm rental money upfront in a lump sum**. In most situations, you will not have to discount the rental sum for full payment at the start of the tenancy. If you agree to a two-step payment schedule—half at the beginning of the lease, half at the end—make sure that the second payment occurs before the renter has left with his equipment, livestock and harvest.

Rent is usually paid in cash. Part of the rental can be worked out as in-kind labor, materials or equipment. Keep in mind that you will have to treat in-kind rental "income" no differently than you treat cash for tax purposes.

I advise inexperienced farmowners against renting their property on the basis of a division of anticipated crop income unless they made their fortune by consistently beating the house in Las Vegas. This is generally referred to as "**shares**," whereby the landlord (you) and the tenant divide either the gross income or the net income according to percentages agreed to at the time the rental agreement is negotiated. While a shares format may entice you with penciled-in upsides, the reality of farming may teach you the many downsides of playing in this crapshoot. Apart from the risks from natural phenomena—rain, drought, flood, lightning, disease, pests, hail, freezes, etc.—you are vulnerable to dishonest dealing by your tenant in the sale of his crop. Never do shares with someone who knows more than you know about what he's doing unless you have solid reasons to trust him. A shares format can work for an inexperienced, absentee farmowner, but it requires a thoroughly conscientious and ethical tenant. Such folks exist. I've run into them, but I've also run into their lesser relations.

You, a landlord now in the literal sense, should have a **written lease** with your tenant that spells out the terms of your arrangement. You will want to believe that a handshake will do. It probably will in the sense that you will allow your land to be used and your tenant will pay you the agreed-on amount, according to the payment schedule. What a handshake leaves out are all the details of a contract concerning the allocation of liability, things you want to prohibit, how disagreements or contract breaches are to be resolved and so on. While oral business contracts are binding on both parties (oral "contracts" are not binding when they involve the sale of real estate with a few exceptions), oral terms are easily forgotten or misconstrued whether or not a disagreement has arisen. It's easy enough for written contracts to have different interpretations. Oral agreements are difficult to enforce if only because it's so hard for the disputing parties to agree on what they had agreed. Before you (or your lawyer) write a farm lease, talk to your tenant at length about the terms that will be mutually acceptable. Work out as much as possible orally and then commit those understandings to paper. Don't blindside your new tenant with a full-dress lawyer's contract whose liability exclusions, waivers and except-thats are designed to flummox the U.S. Supreme Court.

While your new neighbors will stamp you as an incorrigible urban intellectual for insisting on a written farm lease, the alternatives are worse and can lead to more troublesome disputes than any you might foment in negotiating a written contract. "Paper people" like me tend to trust paper more than people while "non-paper people" tend to distrust both paper and paper people. If you are a college-educated paper person—i.e., someone who makes a middle-class living manipulating words and numbers—who is renting to a farmer unlike yourself, you should be prepared to overlay your written contract with a full discussion of what you think the written language means. In other words, get your contract down and understood, both in writing and face to face. You are not doing this because your tenant is dumb; he is far smarter than you are about renting your land. You are doing this because you are getting into a business and legal relationship that is both familiar and unfamiliar to both you and your tenant. It's important for you to

explain yourself, eye to eye, because your tenant will understand a lease for your farm from the dirt up while you will understand it from the words down. The **oral overlay** will benefit both parties by clarifying intentions in light of on-the-ground reality. As landlord, you have to work with the tenant "within the four corners of the lease," and working with the tenant demands frank discussion before problems emerge. When you find your tenant objecting to something you've proposed in writing, work it out then and there. Leaving ambiguity or disagreement hovering in the background buys nothing but trouble in some future foreground. Finally, don't surprise your tenant with a new "demand" after you've reached an agreement. Make sure to live up to your obligations. Act toward your tenant as you want him to act toward you, so to speak. If the tenant is a neighbor, a lease provides you with another channel to introduce yourself to your new community. Hissy-fits over pennies may be your preferred negotiating tactic in the urban jungle, but don't use it with your new country neighbor.

Farm/land leases will vary with the type of land and type of farming operation. Local lawyers will be experienced with rental terms appropriate for your new farm. State agricultural universities, which you can access directly or through the **county extension agent**, will usually have model contracts for different types of agricultural operations. Agricultural and forestry faculty at land-grant universities who are associated with the state's **Cooperative Extension Service** make themselves available to the public by phone, letter and e-mail as well as through seminars. Many extension publications are available on the Internet. They should be available on each state's extension service's website, e.g., Virginia's is www.ext.vt.edu/pubs with "vt" standing for Virginia Tech. Virginia's site links to other states. These publications provide an introduction to their subjects, but vary greatly in their depth and detail. Many agricultural counties have extension offices with one or more agents. Some extension agents specialize in one or more crops of local interest. Sample leases and other agricultural documents of a legal nature are available from the extension service in many states. I would review any generic legal document from any source with my local counsel. If you are working with organic agriculture, environmental practices and non-conventional ideas, you will have to dig deeper for lease language than the extension service's forms. You can work up this language yourself and have your lawyer review it. You can also contact advocacy organizations, such as your state's association of organic farmers, for help in drafting specific language.

The minimum components of your lease agreement are:

- **parties** to the agreement. (Is the tenant an individual or a corporation? Who is bound by the agreement?)

- **mailing address, phone and fax numbers of both parties**

- **duration** of the lease

- **description of the land** that is subject to the lease

- **description of land and facilities** that are outside the lease or exceptions to it. (specify land and/or buildings reserved by the landlord for his exclusive use; or woodlands to be used for grazing but not for harvesting timber)

- **definition of what is being rented** (all land and all agricultural buildings and facilities; all land, but just some facilities; water rights; federal subsidy payments or crop allotments; capital equipment; livestock)

- **post-lease**; what happens if tenant's livestock, crop or equipment are still on the land after the lease expires. (grace period; penalty for late removal?)

- **rental payment schedule**

- **storage rights**, if any, in landlord's barns, silos, buildings

- **allocation of maintenance responsibilities** between landlord and tenant for rented buildings, facilities, fences, etc. (Have some idea of what normal wear and tear means. Who fixes fence holes? Who chases fugitive cattle?)

- **practices permitted and prohibited** (Spell out which agricultural practices you will permit/prohibit under the lease. Specify, if necessary, where each practice will occur. If you are renting grazing rights, specify the type of animals you want pastured. Steers, for example, are less trouble than cows and heifers who attract fence-wrecking bulls. Spayed heifers are usually ignored. Steers are also easier to manage than a bull running with a herd of cows and calves. Stallions are far more trouble than geldings, which are stallions lite.)

- **specify place/entrance of tenant access**

- **times of tenant access** (If you don't want to see your tenant early, late or on certain days, put those conditions in the lease with an except-in-emergency clause.)

- **limits/reservations on tenant's use of non-farmland** (Tenancy does/does not convey hunting rights, for example. If you do not specifically exclude hunting, fishing and firewood harvesting, you may find your tenant doing all three on your land.)

- **use of agricultural chemicals** (If you are renting land to be farmed organically, you should get in touch with your state organic-agriculture association and one or more national organizations to determine the specific practices allowed and prohibited. If you are not organic but want to impose some constraints on the tenant's chemical use, you will have to become knowledgeable about the chemicals, their applications, duration and environmental consequences. Conventional tenants will want as few constraints on their farming practices as possible, whether or not you can "prove" that less chemical application will produce greater profit. The lease should state that tenant shall dispose of chemicals, chemical residues and their containers in accordance with applicable state and federal regulations. If disposal will take place on your land, you will need to spell out exactly where and under what conditions. Landlord should be released from liability in the event that tenant's chemical use produces environmental harm or violates regulations.)

- **how will sick livestock be cared for**; who will do what and when. (Tenant should be expected to treat/medicate livestock in timely manner to prevent spread of illness in his own herd and to neighboring farms. Your cattle-raising neighbors will not like a herd of cattle oozing with contagious infection next to their healthy cattle.)

- **how will dead livestock be handled;** who will dispose of them, where and when. There may be a local ordinance requiring burial or incineration. Otherwise, the carcass needs to be dragged to a spot where its natural decomposition will not offend you or your neighbors.

- **landlord is not responsible for accidents** on his premises involving tenant, his laborers, family or bystanders arising from tenant use of landlord's land.

- **landlord usually inserts lack of liability** for tenant losses due to theft, vandalism and accident. (If the landlord is negligent, however, tenant may be able to win a suit against him. If, for example, the landlord left a bucket of antifreeze in a field where tenant's cattle could drink it, landlord would probably be responsible for any loss. Open gates are a not uncommon source of dispute. If the landlord left a gate open that should have been closed and the tenant's prized stallion wandered into the road and died after being hit by a truck, the landlord may be liable for damages to both tenant and truck driver.)

- **landlord waiver of liability for loss arising from natural conditions**. (Landlord bears no responsibility or financial liability for natural conditions such as, but not limited to, drought, snow, rain, hail, windstorm, insects, disease, flood and lightning that may adversely affect the tenant's farming efforts and property.)

- **landlord retains right of entry** to leased property; right to repair leased facilities; to use and enjoy these premises in any way that doesn't interfere with tenant's business.

- **who is responsible for injury/accident involving tenant's livestock escaping from landlord's farm**. (This will depend on who is responsible for fence maintenance and also state law regarding livestock in the road and on property other than the landlord's.)

- **landlord bears no liability for tenant's crop and farming practices adversely affecting neighbor's property and livestock.** (Tenant should be held responsible for damage done by his practices to landlord's neighbors. If tenant's pesticide application poisons neighbor's livestock, it's the tenant not the landlord who should make things right with the neighbor.)

- **how is the tenant expected to leave the land** at the end of the lease. (How are crop areas to be left? If tenant is expected to plant a cover crop for the winter, the particulars should be spelled out.)

- **how are disputes to be resolved**

- **tenant may sublet** only with advance written permission of landlord

- **specify the state** whose laws are to govern the lease when two states are involved

- **premises will be subject to lease** even if landlord sells or transfer ownership

- **provide emergency (backup) phone numbers for both parties**

- **when does the lease come into effect** (Usually it's the date of second party's signature or a date specified in the contract itself.)

- **what happens if the lease is breached or in default** (What happens to rent already paid? What obligation does landlord have to minimize his income loss?)

- **who pays the property taxes on the farm** (It should be the landlord.)

- **tenant is expected to comply with all applicable local, state and federal laws** and engage in no illegal activity

- **no partnership or joint venture is created** by the lease. Neither party has the authority to obligate the other without written consent.

- **tenant's leasehold is subject to, subordinate to and inferior to any lien or encumbrance placed on premises by landlord**.

- **indemnification of landlord** for claims arising from tenant's negligence.

- **if either party fails to perform** once the lease comes into effect, the other has full claim to all damages incurred.

- **notarized signature is/is not required** for contract to become effective.

I've presented these contract components in a general form because farm/land leases are drawn up and interpreted in light of the laws of each state. I'd advise against using a sample lease that you find in a book of legal forms. Such forms can get you started thinking about issues to address, but generic lease language needs to be adapted and customized to your particular farm. It's worth paying a local lawyer to draw up your first land lease. You can then modify the lease in succeeding years on your own if you feel confident in doing so.

FARM LEASES AND CROP GENETICS

If you're leasing your land to a tenant who wants to use **genetically modified (GM) seed,** you, as the owner/landlord, have another set of issues to consider. Genetically engineered crops are grown in the U.S. on about 100 million acres compared with less than one million acres in organic crops. (The U.S. has about one billion acres of all types of farmland.) About 35 percent of our corn and 55 percent of our soybeans are grown from GM seed. The majority of U.S. crop acreage is planted in crops that are not genetically modified as I write this, but the GM fraction has been growing as a share of the whole. (Environmental Working Group, www.ewg.org, June, 2000; Justin Gillis, "Debate Grows Over Biotech Food," Washington Post, November 30, 2003.) All food crops have been genetically changed over the centuries to enhance their size, taste, nutritional value, color, quantity and other attributes. The genetic modifications that are now at issue in the GM crops are those that arise from the insertion of genes from other species to achieve either specific characteristics or new "behaviors" in the host species.

Some GM seed contains a gene that causes each plant cell to produce its own pesticide, often ***Bacillus thuringiensis (Bt)****,* a bacterium that controls budworms, caterpillars, beetles, the European corn borer and moths. Organic farmers use *Bt* as a spray on an as-needed basis, as do landowners protecting trees against gypsy moth. GM seed with a *Bt*-gene will lead to *Bt*-resistant pests if it is used exclusively, just as herbicides create their own survivor weeds. Another practice is to engineer into a crop plant the ability to survive the application of an herbicide like Roundup. This makes weed control simpler and possibly cheaper. If your conventional-farming tenant does not use GM corn, he will use more chemicals to bring in his crop. If he does plant GM corn, he will use fewer chemicals, but may suffer a price discount depending on the market for his crop.

If GM corn is planted fence line to fence line for a number of years, you can expect to see resistant pests. This is bad farming practice. Your lease with your tenant should require planting of conventional (non-GM) corn on at least 20 percent of your corn acreage to prevent resistance. Twenty percent is the U.S. Environmental Protection Agency's standard, but the Agency has survey evidence that at least one-third of farmers violated that standard in 2000. (Washington Post, "EPA Calls Biotech Corn No Threat," October 17, 2001.) The 20-percent requirement provides "habitat" for a sufficient number of non-resistant corn borers, for example, to reproduce with resistant borers so that resistance is minimized in succeeding generations. Corn-raising tenants can also vary their planting practices by using new GM seed (if it's available), or non-GM seed with pesticides, or crop rotation (growing a non-corn crop that is unaffected by the resistant corn pests who may disappear for lack of food). *Bt* corn appears to have no significant effect on monarch butterflies. National Academy of Sciences' researchers estimated that at most "...500 in a million caterpillar larvae would die from eating corn pollen deposited on the milkweed," which is their food. (Id.) GM corn, canola and other crops have accidentally mixed with conventional plantings through cross-pollination, a situation likely to upset neighbors and lead to disputes.

A majority of food products available in the U.S. market contain GM commodities; most products of this type are not available in Europe. (Gillis, "Debate.") A particular GM corn—StarLink—has not been approved for human consumption at the time of this writing owing to questions about its theoretical potential to cause allergic reactions. Approved GM corn does not appear to have been linked to such reactions after a decade of consumption. Hundreds of recalls occurred when StarLink corn became mixed with non-StarLink corn and found its way into food products that carried no warning of possible allergic reactions. An EPA panel reported in July, 2001 that since its investigation was not able to rule out the possibility of allergic reactions, the ban on even trace amounts of StarLink in human food should be continued. The Agency's green light given to *Bt* corn in October, 2001 did not extend to StarLink.

Genetic engineering is also working with insects (pests like the pink bollworm that ruin cotton, honeybees and silkworms, among others) to modify their DNA either to control the pest or increase the ability of good insects to resist disease. The dangers, critics point out, lie in creating resistant pests or accidental crossbreedings that weaken good insects. (Marc Kaufman, "A Glowing Achievement or a Can of Worms? Proposed Field Test of Gene-Altered Pest Worries Some," Washington Post, April 25, 2001.) Critics are also concerned with "gene flow," the transfer of modified traits to non-GM-modified species with unpredictable results for that species, other species and the wider ecosystem. Much of the battle is currently being fought over whether GM crops and insects will perform exactly as predicted and whether the process of altering one or two genes out of 50,000 is exempt from the "law" of unintended consequences.

New farmowners should keep in mind that modern agriculture has depended for years on crossbreeding and genetic manipulation to encourage or discourage one or more traits in both animals and plants. Our food supply, including what we call organic agriculture, does not use species as they existed before Columbus. (Kaufman, "Alter Genes, Risk an Ecosystem?" Washington Post, June 4, 2001.) The choice that faces the conventional farmer is between choosing a GM-modified stock that holds the promise of greater yields and more disease protection (less chemical use) but carries the prospect of unknown environmental consequences and possible price discount on one hand and sticking with established products with familiar upsides and downsides.

I would advise every new farmowner to go slowly and cautiously. Don't be the first to allow a tenant to use a GM product; approach genetic engineering the way you might evaluate buying a new but promising brand of automobile from a country relatively new to the market. Give GM products enough time for field reports to generate more reliability data and analysis. It seems at this time that the problems that may appear with GM crops are less those associated with the consumption of the end food products and more those that can appear on the farms where they are grown.

Ask the farm seller whether any GM seed was used in the past and then talk to your tenant about his preferences. The tenant will like GM seed because it's a cheaper input than the normal non-GM seed plus pesticides, and he doesn't have to apply as much pesticide—an awful job. On the other hand, his GM crop may have a limited market and a price discount owing to the controversy now swirling around GM seed. The tenant may offer to pay more rent if he can use a GM seed. As the property owner, you have to weigh both short-term and long-term ecological and financial considerations. There is no easy or obvious answer to this situation. You can try to have your tenant rotate crops if that's an option, so that the same crop is not planted in the same field year after year. This is good practice on its own, and staggers pesticide and GM use. Perhaps you can work in a livestock component and a hay crop into your multi-year, rotational land-use plan with the tenant. If your tenant is likely to rent for no more than a year or two, assume he will try to get as much crop/livestock gain as he can without much concern for your land's long-term condition. This may have unacceptable consequences for your land or your long-term plans, and if it does, you have to establish the ground rules in the first lease. If you object to both pesticides and GM seed, your choices narrow to using the land for livestock (which has its own set of environmental and ethical issues), planted grass/hay or doing nothing.

An organic tenant is not likely to be found for conventionally farmed land, except, possibly, on a lease that runs substantially longer than five years. I have not heard of any examples of organic farmers renting conventional land. If you can find one, expect that he will pay below-market rental since your land is worth little until he brings it into compliance with organic standards. That process demands a lot of work on his part and at least three years.

CHAPTER 4: FIRST-TIME FARMERS

Some readers will disregard all of the sound advice I've offered about the pitfalls of buying a farm and farming it themselves. I, myself, dumb and innocent, fell into this very curriculum for acquiring the sound advice I now offer. Once again, I advise that you seriously consider renting out your newly acquired farm for a year or two while you get your feet dirty observing. (The object of your observation is not your feet getting dirty.)

Before you start thinking about farming your new farm, you need to perform an existential and practical self-analysis of what exactly you have just purchased. Many readers will have purchased what real-estate brokers call, "**pleasure farms**," which are long on providing an opportunity to play farmer and short on being able to support a family doing farming. The Laskas's thorn patch with the pretty view and the Kordas' scrub with its nice house are **non-farm farms of the pleasure type**. Often such places were once active farmsteads. Their current agricultural value is usually minimal owing to a lack of maintenance, outdated infrastructure or a scale problem (usually that the farm is too small to produce its traditional product efficiently and at a reasonable profit).

There's nothing wrong—and many things right—with buying a non-farm farm for pleasure. You will, however, run into considerable expense and aggravation in trying to resuscitate it as a profit-making operation, which it might have once been. A pleasure farm is intended to be fun whether it's a second home or a full-time residence. You can have fun bringing back some barnyard attributes to such a place—a cluck-cluck here and a moo-moo there. You can acquire stuff that goes with farming—noisy, dangerous stuff like chainsaws, tractors and ATVs. I know of pleasure farms that revolve around the raising of token numbers of sheep, cattle, buffalo, horses, dogs and semi-exotic livestock such as llamas and Asian pigs. These operations are mainly about lifestyle and don't support themselves as farms. If they qualify as a farm for IRS purposes, so much the better for their owners. You can view an intriguing effort to raise alpacas in a way that qualifies as a farm-business within IRS guidelines at www.alpacas.com. This site shows how to incorporate tax planning into a small farm operation based on breeding niche livestock.

It is possible to take a pleasure farm and convert it to a different agricultural purpose. **Farm conversions** can work if the new farmer has thoroughly scoped the idea and understands its requirements and risks. For instance, you might buy 100 acres of grown-up cattle pasture but only intensively farm five acres of high-profit lavender that you package and sell over the Internet. You might then plant trees on the remainder with the help of federal and state programs. To be successful, you would have to have developed a business plan for the growing, drying, packaging, marketing, financing and distribution of lavender. The tree-planting component of this farm might be divided between fast-growing pines and slow-growing hardwoods. The pines can be thinned about halfway through their scheduled growth cycle and completely harvested when they get to 20 to 30 years old. If you had replanted in pine at the end of the first cycle, you would have taken four pine cuts over 60 years and would then be close to harvesting the hardwoods.

If you are intending to purchase a **full-time working farm** as an absentee owner who is available part-time for farm work, you might consider a small operation that is less than 300 acres and within a couple of hours drive of your principal residence. It's possible that you could carry this off if you had extremely reliable local help who didn't need much management from you. Your help is likely to know far more than you about what you are trying to do and when and how you are supposed to do it. Pay this person fairly and treat him well, because your operation needs his skill and time. A neighbor might be willing to do this work for you, but don't expect him and his family to work for free. Managing a farm for you is likely to be a principal source of your manager's income. Farm size always increases the number of things to do as well as their cost. The further you are from the farm, the harder it will be to be a hands-on manager. Small places can be run from a distance with part-time local help, but at some point size and distance will lead you to hire a full-time manager.

CONVENTIONAL FARMING

Most full-time, commercially viable farm operations are capital intensive and use chemical inputs. I'll call these **conventional farms** in contrast to **organic farms**, discussed below. Conventional farms will come with barns, machine sheds, storage facilities (like silos and grain tanks) and require expensive and often highly specialized equipment. You can obtain background information on different types of conventional farming by reading the literature that is available through your library and on the Internet.

Land-grant universities in each state conduct research and produce publications on every aspect of conventional farming—production, inputs, financing, marketing, disease/pest control, equipment, design of buildings and facilities, handling of agricultural chemicals and so on. These "extension" universities have faculty specialists in the state's principal agricultural products (crops, livestock, fish, timber) whose job is to teach, publish and educate the state's farmers. I have had positive experiences with such faculty over the years; they were accessible, knowledgeable and patient. The county extension agent can get you started on informational materials, which are available for free or at low cost, and provide university contacts. If you are thinking about doing something out of the ordinary—say, grow organic cotton and raise tropical birds on Alaska's North Slope—you will have to go beyond the extension service, which is oriented to the conventional and ordinary. Extension services in other states may be able to help.

Each conventional crop and type of livestock has at least one trade or producers' organization (e.g., National Cattlemen's Beef Association) that should be able to link you to sources of information. Since conventional farming has both a local/state aspect (weather, site-specific conditions, local markets and costs) and a national/international aspect (interest rates, international demand, trade restrictions, national supply-and-demand factors, transportation costs, prices and federal policies), you have to check into both in evaluating how they intersect on the specific farm operation you have in mind. A directory of the major trade/producers' organizations can be found at www.reeusda.gov/agsysapp/farmorgs.htm.

The voice of production-oriented, conventional agriculture is the American Farm Bureau Federation (www.fb.com). The Farm Bureau and its state affiliates provide lobbying, information, links, education, market news, insurance and other membership benefits. It lobbies for government policies that help agriculture directly and indirectly. It favors subsidies, tax breaks, more farm exports and less regulation. It is broadly supported in the farming community for its conservative political positions. www.FarmPage.com provides additional information on conventional agriculture. http://directory.google.com/Top/Science/ Agriculture/Publications/Journals displays agricultural journals.

Conventional agriculture is intimately wrapped up with a wide variety of federal assistance and credit programs, national and international marketing efforts, environmental and safety regulations, research and tax policies. Each product sector is organized to promote its interests, and umbrella organizations represent agriculture as a single industry. A farm buyer needs to become aware of the specific benefits (crop subsidies, research, technical help) that are available for the products his farm produces as well as the general benefits that are available to farm operators (tax breaks, financing, loans, cost-share programs and assorted assistance such as payments through the Agricultural Market Transition Act

[AMTA] and Loan Deficiency Payments [LDPs]). The scope of federal agricultural policy can be best gleaned by scrolling through the **Farm Security and Rural Investment Act of 2002 (PL 107-171)**, the most recent omnibus farm legislation. (See http://www.fsa.usda.gov/dam/BUD/PL107-171.pdf.) The farm bill was renamed the "Farm Security Act" after September 11, 2001 and signed on May 13, 2002. The extension agent in the target county and the local CPA you plan to use for farm taxes can get you up to speed quickly on USDA programs that match your needs. It is also useful to note that federal money runs parallel with federal farm regulation on matters of air and water pollution, food safety and issues of land use.

  Agricultural benefit programs through the USDA are numerous, and a number of them involve huge sums. In addition to crop subsidies, the Federal Money Retriever (http://www.fedmoney.com/grants/f0000000.htm) groups current USDA programs into seven categories: resource conservation and development; production and operation; marketing; stabilization and conservation service; forestry; research and development; and technical assistance and information. Programs are often found in more than one category. Individual farmers (new and old alike) would be interested in farm-operating loans ($2.90 billion); loan-interest assistance ($903 million in loans); livestock assistance ($189 million in grants); crop-disaster programs ($1.299 billion in grants); emergency loans ($572 million); crop insurance ($3.31 billion in grants); commodity loans and Loan Deficiency Payments ($661 million in loans and grants); production-flexibility payments for contract commodities ($5.01 billion); farmownership loans ($1.15 billion); temporary assistance for needy farmers ($19.08 billion); and forest-incentives program ($10.5 million).

  USDA through its county-level **Farm Service Agency** (FSA) offices provides these loan and loan-guarantee programs to individual farmers to purchase farmland and finance production. These functions were formerly performed by the USDA's Farmers Home Administration (FMHA). Borrowers must meet a set of eligibility criteria, one of which is that they are unable to obtain private commercial credit. Most of the loan programs provide favorable amortization schedules and below-market interest rates. Federal credit, however, is "supervised credit." Borrowers can expect FSA planning and oversight. These USDA farmownership and production programs are separate from the farm loans that are available through the **Federal Land Bank**, an independent, non-USDA agency that is a borrower-owned lender. The USDA programs may be limited to farmers at risk, that is, loans the Federal Land Bank and other commercial lenders would turn down. When the farmer is no longer at risk, FSA expects the borrower to refinance with a commercial lender. General information on these programs can be obtained from the local FSA office, which will provide Fact Sheets and a pamphlet, "Producer's Guide to FSA Loan Programs." Specific information on FSA loans can be had from the USDA FSA Loan-Making Division, 1400 Independence Ave., S.W., STOP 0522, Washington, D.C., 20250-0522; 202-720-1632; and at www.fsa.usda.gov. Novice farmers may not find the USDA loan programs available to them if their financial profile is strong. Some programs require the borrower to have three years of farm-operation experience as a precondition, but the three years need not be immediately prior to applying for the FSA loan. Federal Land Bank financing is open to novice farmers for the purchase and equipping of farms.

  In addition to the loan and loan-guarantee programs, USDA's FSA administers other programs that seek to stabilize farm income, encourage farmers to conserve water and land resources, and provide assistance in the event of disasters. The county FSA offices provide information on these programs, which are available to farmers regardless of their financial strength. The 1996 farm bill recast some of the price-support programs by establishing "**production flexibility contract payments**," a set of seven annual fixed-but-declining payments that were independent of commodity prices and production. A one-time sign up was held in 1996. The program was supposed to liquidate itself in 2002.

The 2002 Farm Security Act, above, extended these crop-support payments, but renamed them, **direct payments**. In addition to the seven 1996 crops—wheat, corn, grain sorghum, barley, oats, upland cotton and rice—that were renewed, Washington added soybeans, other oilseeds and peanuts to the crop-subsidy list. The payment is limited to $40,000 per person, per crop year. A farmer need not plant the crop for which he is receiving a payment. If the farm is not currently enrolled, you will probably have to wait until the next sign-up period. A farm buyer should check with the local FSA office to determine whether the farm he's interested in buying is signed up and the scope of the payments it has received. Additional information on this program can be found at http://www.ers.usda.gov/Features/farmbill/analysis/DirectPayments2002act.htm. Federal deficits are putting pressure on Washington to reduce crop-support programs.

FSA offers **commodity loans** for wheat, rice, corn, grain sorghum, barley, oats, oilseeds, tobacco, peanuts, cotton and sugar where the expected crop is the borrower's collateral. Certain dairy products will be purchased directly to support the farmer's price of milk. If you need more information about these programs (as well as the disaster assistance and conservation enhancement) than the local FSA office provides, contact the USDA's FSA Public Affairs Office in Washington at the address above, STOP 0506; 202-720-5237.

The first-time farmer should look particularly at the various **conservation programs** that provide money in several forms—payments, cost shares and rents. These funds help farmers who agree to stop producing on highly erodible land (HEL) and other sensitive areas, or agree to develop water for livestock, invest in fencing for rotational grazing systems, implement nutrient (manure) management systems and so on. Such practices help the farmer's land and benefit the public as well.

The **Environmental Quality Incentives Program (EQIP)**, for example, provides technical and financial assistance to farmers/ranchers in complying with state and federal environmental laws, including those related to HEL and wetlands. EQIP requires that the landowner apply a conservation plan for a period of five to ten years. The plan involves various conservation-enhancing practices, many of which bring a 75 percent cost-share from the government. EQIP, like other farm programs, uses a "concentrated" sign-up period, often in the spring. Your chances of getting funded are better if you apply during the relevant window of opportunity. The **Conservation Reserve Program (CRP)** provides money to farmers for practices that promote conservation of soil resources. The **Conservation Reserve Enhancement Program (CREP)** provides "enhanced" (more) funds for "enhanced" CRP-type practices, including removal of certain lands from agricultural use. The USDA paid farmers about $2 billion in 2006 to leave fallow about 37 million acres of marginal farmland. (Bill Tomson, "U.S. Sees High Retention Rate of Idled Farmland," Wall Street Journal, November 20, 2006.) The local FSA office is the point of landowner contact, but each conservation plan is drawn up by the local agent of the **Natural Resources Conservation Service (NRCS)** with the landowner. The proposed plan is then reviewed and judged by the local **soil conservation district** and the FSA's county committee

Farmers have the benefit of federally subsidized, cheap crop-insurance programs to protect against risks. Various plans are available for different crops in different states, including alfalfa, almonds, apples, apricots, avocados, barley, beans, blueberries, cabbage, canola, carambola trees, cherries, chili peppers, citrus, clams, corn, cotton, cranberries, cucumbers, figs, flax, forage, grain sorghum, grapefruit, grapes, table grapes, lemons, lemon trees, lime trees, macadamia nuts/trees, mandarins, mango trees, millet, mint, mustard, fresh nectarines, nursery, oats, onions, oranges, peaches, peanuts, pears, peas, pecans, peppers, plums, popcorn, potatoes, prunes, raisins, rangeland, raspberry/blackberry, rice, cultivated wild rice, rye, safflower, soybeans, stonefruit, strawberries, sugar beets, sugar cane, sunflowers, sweet potatoes, tangelos, tobacco, tomatoes, walnuts, wheat and winter squash. The six basic programs insure against natural hazards, low prices and low yields. The insurance is written through private companies; premiums are the same regardless of the provider. An overview of these offerings is available from **National Crop Insurance Services (NCIS)**, 7201 West 129th Street, Suite 200, Overland Park, Kansas, 66213; 913-685-2767; http://www.ag~risk.org.

Along with federal benefits and assistance come the systems of overview, direction, constraints, costs and regulations that are imposed on particular crops as well as farm operations generally. During the last 80 years, farming has moved from being essentially unregulated to an increasingly regulated industry. These programs/regulations affect production, environmental protection, marketing, processing, financing, workplace safety and health, labor standards, taxation, land use, R&D and disaster relief. The scope and depth of agricultural regulation is likely to increase in the future. The most probable areas of increased farm regulation are air and water quality, food safety and aesthetics.

The last-named in my opinion is increasingly invoked as more non-farmers move to the country and are offended by some of what they find. (These folks drive the "offending" farmers nuts. It's useful for the newcomer to draw a distinction between the normal sights, smells and noises of normal farm operations in that area and those associated with large dairy farms and **concentrated animal feeding operations [CAFOs]**—cattle feedlots and confined operations for hogs and poultry.)

Agriculture can expect increased environmental regulation, because it is the pollution-generating sector that has been least regulated relatively speaking. I expect that such regulations will be applied to smaller and smaller farms over time. The USEPA, for example, proposed new water-protection regulations for agriculture since an estimated 50 percent of "**nonpoint source**" pollution in surface water comes from agricultural runoff of nutrients (such as nitrogen), agricultural chemicals, manure and sediment. (A point-source of pollution is a discharge pipe into a river; nonpoint sources, like runoff, are general in nature.) **Agricultural runoff** has been linked to about 60 percent of all river pollution. (Small Flows Quarterly, "EPA Proposes New Controls To Reduce Water Pollution from Large Livestock Operations," Spring, 2001, Vol. 2, Number 2.) The point sources—municipal and industrial waste pipes—were the principal targets of the early regulatory rounds insofar as they were readily identified and measured. The next set of water regulations was targeted at the 39,000 CAFOs, each of which is, by definition, an operation feeding 1,000 or more cattle or equivalent "animal units." CAFOs are large—often huge—industrial-type production operations; readers of this book are not likely to be buying one of them. The EPA proposed in 2001 to define a CAFO in such a way as to include smaller operations and require Clean Water Act permits for more than the estimated 2,500 CAFOs operating with permits in 2000. The next level of regulation will undoubtedly involve farm operations that are smaller than CAFOs.

Buyers of operating farms should expect to work within a tighter regulatory framework in the future. Sooner or later, even small farmers will be swept into more and more of it. My guess is that most farms will eventually be expected to fence livestock out of surface waters (ponds, creeks, rivers) and use troughs instead; leave vegetative buffer strips between fields and waterways; abandon erosive practices on steep pasture; implement a nutrient (manure) management plan covering all animal wastes, whether deposited naturally or mechanically; further limit the use of chemicals; keep records related to livestock purchase and sale, livestock medication, seed used, production and crop practices; and follow certain soil-conservation practices that heretofore have been voluntary, such as crop rotation, contour strip planting and no-till/low-till planting methods. Each new requirement will probably be accompanied by a cost-share program that will ease the burden of the initial investment. "Homeland security" may be used to justify the scrutiny. If you hate the idea of civil servants involving themselves in what you do, farming will become an ever less comfortable sandbox.

The best way to scratch-start your education is to contact local federal agricultural offices—USDA

Farm Service Agency, USDA Natural Resources Conservation Service and the cooperative extension agent in the county where your target farm is located. Ask for both general and crop-specific information about how their programs have been applied to the target farm in the past and which programs could be applicable in the future. You can then sift through the information to find what's relevant to your goals and situation. Every agricultural sector has its own trade group, and that is your next contact. Each group has a detailed understanding of how the crop-specific and general agricultural-benefit programs apply to its sector. These sources will also provide some information on regulatory constraints, enough to start getting you acclimated.

Environmental regulations involve state and federal environmental-protection agencies, wildlife agencies, natural-heritage agencies, soil-conservation agencies, U.S. Army Corps of Engineers, state forestry departments and local offices (planning commission, zoning board, etc.). Other regulatory constraints materialize if you intend to process agricultural products, either on your farm or at a separate location. You may, in that case, become involved with compliance regulations involving records, reports, inspections and enforcement actions with the Food and Drug Administration, USDA inspectorates and occupational safety and health agencies. If you employ farm labor—full-time, part-time, seasonal or migrant—another set of public agencies appear in your life. Certain benefit programs (money) are available only if you agree to come under certain regulatory programs.

One of the first portals for information about environmental requirements affecting farming is the USEPA's **National Agriculture Compliance Assistance Center** (901 North 5th Street, Kansas City, Kansas, 66101; 1-888-663-2155; http://es.epa.gov/oeca/ag/). The Center provides advice and publications on a wide range of topics, including air and climate, animals, compliance, drinking water and wells, emergency planning and response, fertilizers, facilities, health and safety, heating and cooling, land use, pesticides, surface groundwater, tanks, toxics, vehicles, waste and risk management. The Center's advice covers the ten federal laws USEPA enforces that affect agriculture: Clean Air Act (CAA); Clean Water Act (CWA); Coastal Zone Management Act (CZMA); Comprehensive Environmental Response; Compensation and Liability Act (CERCLA) and Superfund; Emergency Planning and Community Right-To-Know Act (EPCRA); Federal Insecticide, Fungicide and Rodenticide Act (FIFRA); Oil Pollution Act (OPA); Resource Conservation and Recovery Act (RCRA); Safe Drinking Water Act (SDWA); and Toxic Substances Control Act (TSCA). There are other environmental regulations that apply to agriculture as well. The Center is also able to provide county-level environmental maps on its Website.

Most new farmowners are likely to be "**small farmers**" in one sense or another—acreage, production, net revenue, amount of time devoted to farming, portion of farmer's net income derived from farming, etc. No matter how the term is defined, small farms have an outsized political voice if only because they represent the vast majority of farm operations and farm-based voters. There are, in other words, more small farmers than large farmers though the latter are much more central to agricultural production. USDA programs benefit large farm operations disproportionately, because federal crop subsidies and other assistance are linked to the scale of production or the scale of need. USDA also offers assistance to small farms specifically in the form of publications, counsel and money in various forms. The USDA site includes links to more than 150 small-farm websites. (http://www.reeusda.gov/agsys/smallfarm/guide/webs.htm#VIRTUAL.)

Agriculture speaks with many voices politically, sometimes in unison when faced with a common threat, sometimes against each other on the basis of region, product or size. Two voices singing discordantly at times amid the Farm Bureau's chorus on behalf of conventional agriculture are the **National Farmers Union (NFU)** and **National Farmers Organization (NFO)**. The NFU's constituency is mainly agricultural cooperatives and small farmers, two groups that do not necessarily and always share the same financial and political interests. (See http://www.nfu.org.) NFO is a producer-owned marketing organization that applies principles of collective bargaining to agricultural production. It finds buyers for its members' products and also offers a price-hedging service. (NFO, 2505 Elwood Dr., Ames, Iowa, 50010-2000; 515-292-2000; 515-292-7106 FAX; e-mail: NFO@info.org; website: http://www.nfo.org.)

Conventional farming is the first step in a stairway of conventionally organized food and fiber production and consumption. Most sectors of conventional agriculture are set up primarily to work with large producers. The little guys can sell in these markets, but, as individual producers, they have no leverage on price and other matters. The smaller you are in the production of a plentiful commodity like beef or corn, the harder you will find it to make a living selling your product into the conventional markets. It follows that the number of small farmers making a living at it has declined steadily. My guess is that most of these withdrawals were farmers who produced conventional crops in the conventional way and sold them through conventional channels into conventional markets. While the farmers themselves were forced out, their land—at least, the best of it—probably stayed in production. Investors, large (local) farmers and large agri-businesses have probably taken ownership or control. Most of our food is now produced by corporate farms, not Old MacDonald and his horizontally integrated, diversified barnyard.

My county may be an instructive example of larger patterns in farm communities. We are overwhelmingly rural and agricultural—cattle and sheep. Yet, I can't buy locally grown beef or lamb in any local grocery. Our one small slaughterhouse closed in the late 1980s, owing to the high cost of regulatory compliance. Our store-based food supply is far inferior to that available in any suburban supermarket, and we eat less well and less healthily. We have a dozen or so poultry growers in the county, but all of their output is dedicated to vertically integrated processors who supply the chicks. We have one farm-based shop that sells some local food products and a couple of farmers who sell lambs to individuals that they then arrange to have slaughtered. We have one company that produces trout which it sells to individuals at their facility, though most of their product is shipped out. Locally produced maple syrup is available locally. A farmer's market was started several years ago to encourage small-scale production of agricultural goods and local consumption. An effort is underway to determine the feasibility of starting a slaughterhouse. With modest exceptions, my county is as dependent on the national corporate food chain as the most urban neighborhood.

In many agricultural sectors, a small number of buyers/processors structure the market and price for a large number of producers. More and more production—hogs and poultry are familiar examples—is vertically integrated so that the farmer becomes a contract producer who is paid a fixed rate per pound of gain. The contracts that establish these arrangements require the producer to build facilities and accept the price the buyer/processor chooses to pay. The latter may terminate the contract, leaving the farmer holding the bag of debt. This arrangement echoes the "furnish-and-shares" format that was the heart of Southern tenant farming. Tenants did not fare very well under that system.

One view of how modern farmer-to-consumer agriculture works is found in Eric Schlosser's, Fast Food Nation: The Dark Side of the All-American Meal (Boston: Houghton Mifflin Company, 2001). He discusses how the enormous business of fast food has changed the business of producing food, tracing the processor-led restructuring of how we produce potatoes (for French fries), beef and chicken. My experience confirms Schlosser's analysis, which is that it's next to impossible to make a living producing conventional farm commodities on a small scale for sale in the established markets. You can try, as many do, for which you will be rewarded at tax time. Avoid buying the producing farms that are the bottom of the integrated corporate ladder; you will be indentured to your debt and the self-interested decisions of your processor. Don't think you can hustle the system because you're smarter; smarter counts, but your kind of smarter doesn't count for as much as you think down on your conventional farm.

CHAPTER 5: NON-CONVENTIONAL FARMING

ORGANICS

Organic farming is less a subset of conventional commercial agriculture than a different worldview of ideas and practices that are expressed in lifestyle and often business. While conventional agriculture, as I've been using the term, has borrowed a few practices from the organic-farming community, the transfer has not been great. Organic farming must be carried out in accordance with very specific and rigorous dos and don'ts farm-wide. Organic products must meet rigid standards that establish how the item is and is not to be produced. A certification process, periodic inspections and controls enforce these standards. Farm products that carry the word "organic" should only apply to items that have been grown on farms that embrace the totality of this way of doing things.

Organic standards and practices are a matter of continuing discussion. The USDA operates the National Organic Program (NOP) through its Agricultural Marketing Service, which has developed standards and practices for the organic farming industry (www.ams.usda/nop/). Although these continue to be a work in progress, it's reasonably safe to assume that a food product that carries an **organic certification label** is about as unadulterated as a general consumer can expect. Words like "natural," "free-range," "chemical-free," "hormone-free," "pure," "veggie," "meatless" and "farm-fresh" can mean almost anything as well as not much of anything. Such products probably fall short of official organic standards, though they may be nutritious and perfectly safe to eat. The "USDA organic" label means that at least 95 percent of a product is farmed without chemicals, hormones, pesticides or environmentally harmful methods. "Natural" now means   no artificial ingredients or food coloring; it does not mean "organic" (Kylene Kiang, Cox News Service, "Is the Organic Food Label Being Corrupted?," Richmond Times-Dispatch, September 10, 2006).

I have backed into a discussion about organic farming by way of talking about its products. Operating a certified organic farm involves having your facilities and practices inspected and approved. Organic farming associations and **certifiers** are organized state-by-state, regionally and nationally. Since the term "organic" has become a vernacular term that is often used to describe a wide assortment of farm practices and products, it's best to define "organic" as those farms and products that are certified by an appropriate association of organic producers. Certification separates those who are organic farmers from those who are not.

As a new farmowner, you may be taken with the idea of growing organic crops and livestock. Your definition of what you mean by organic may not be the same as the relevant certifying agency. You may want to consider working up to certified-farm status over a period of years. You can incorporate some "organic" ideas immediately, in whole or part. You can, for example, decide to not implant cattle with hormonal growth stimulators and confine your wormer to organic-approved products. You can also use techniques for raising crops that require fewer chemicals to control weeds and pests. The only thing wrong with being sort-of organic is that you can't sell your product in the premium-priced organic market. The markets for conventional agriculture either don't value your efforts or actively discount your products for various reasons, often appearance. A one-step-at-a-time transition is a conservative way of trying on organic farming to see whether it fits you and your farm. It may not. I couldn't make it work on my farm, because I couldn't find a reliable supply of organic calves or a reliable market for the finished cattle. While the farmer gets a higher price for organic farm products, he bears more risks and does more work for the money. If you're comparing operating your farm conventionally as against organic, compare your projected net income, labor requirement and risk under both scenarios.

Several national organizations provide services and information about organic agriculture. The **Organic Crop Improvement Association** (OCIA, 1101 Y St., Suite B, Lincoln, Nebraska 68508-1172; 402-477-2323; 477-4325 FAX; e-mail: info@ocia.org; www.ocia.org) is the source on certification and standards. The **Organic Farmers Marketing Association** (OFMA, POB 2407, Fairfield, IA 52556; 515-472-3272; e-mail: erorganic@aol.com; ripplebrook@aol.com; www.iquest/net/ofma/) provides marketing information, news updates, prices, land-for-sale ads and links. Research information is available from the **Organic Farming Research Foundation** (OFRF, POB 440, Santa Cruz, California 95061; 831-426-6606; 831-426-6670 FAX; e-mail: research@ofrf.org; www.ofrf.org. OFRF has published a National Directory of Certifiers and a summary, "State of the States," of the organic farming research at America's 67 public land-grant agricultural schools. The research found that of the 886,000 research acres at these schools, not surprisingly only 151 acres were certified organic. The Rodale Institute is a long-standing source of information on organic gardening and farming (Rodale Institute, 611 Siegfriedale Rd., Kutztown, Pennsylvania, 19530; 1-800-832-6285; 610-683-1400; 610-683-8548 FAX; 610-683-6009 bookstore; e-mail: info@rodaleinst.org; e-mail: ribooks@fast.net; www.rodaleinst.org. A good starting point for information links is www.ibibio.org/farming-connection/links/organic.htm. A useful overview is Nicolas Lampkin's, Organic Farming (UK: Farming Press Books, 1992; distributed in North America by Diamond Farm Enterprises, Box 537, Alexandria Bay, New York, 13607.).

Sustainable agriculture is a fuzzier label than certified organic. It is a set of farm-level practices that share certain approaches and objectives with organic agriculture. It differs in that it is not a process judged by a certifying agency and product standards. A lot of farmers can feel comfortable in describing their operations as implementing sustainable agriculture principles, though they would never qualify as organic. A comprehensive list of organizations involved in sustainable agriculture is available on the Internet from **Appropriate Technology Transfer for Rural Areas** (ATTRA, POB 3657, Fayetteville, Arkansas, 72702; 1-800-346-9140; 501-442-9842 FAX; www.attra.org/attra-rl/susaorg.html.) The ATTRA list includes national and state organizations and sources of published information. A second hub site is the Factory Farm Project, sponsored by the Global Resources Action Center for the Environment (GRACE) at The Johns Hopkins University, through David Brubaker, 410-502-7577; 410-502-7579 FAX; www.factoryfarm.org.

Agricultural books—both conventional and organic—are available through the large Internet booksellers like www.amazon.com and www.barnesandnoble.com and specialty sites, such as www.books@agribook.com. (See Fertile Ground Books, 3912 Vale Ave., Oakland, California, 94619; 530-297-7879; 530-298-2060 FAX.)

If you are looking to buy an operating organic farm, the seller should be able to show you its certification papers and production records. Do not buy an "organic farm" without certification papers from the organization whose standards and practices you intend to follow. Do not take the seller's word that his farm is "organic" without confirming its certification history. The seller's notion of "organic farming" may or may not fit the organizational definitions with which you are intending to comply. If, for example, certain chemicals have been applied to the farm within the last several years prior to its sale to you, it will take you several years of non-chemical farming before even being eligible to apply for organic certification. Ask to see annual production records, showing all inputs, control measures, yields, buyers of products and correspondence with the certifying agency. (This, of course, is in addition to the normal farm financials and tax schedules that you want to examine.) If the seller says he is organic, but he's selling to a conventional market, be suspicious. He may be sort-of organic, but not rigorously so and certified. He's also not getting market value for his harder-to-raise product. The buyer should also check with the farm's certifying organization to make sure the target farm is in full compliance. Ask for inspection reports and records of violations or complaints. Talk to the certifier.

If you think you are buying an organic farm and intend to farm organically and market as a certified organic operation, you should write an **organic contingency clause** into your purchase contract on the order of:

> **Buyer's offer is contingent on obtaining full satisfaction that Seller's farm is currently a certified organic operation according to the rules established by the _____.**

> **Buyer's offer is further contingent on satisfying himself that the farm is currently in full compliance with organic farming standards and practices set forth by the _____.**

> **Seller warrants that the farm has been certified organic according to the standards of the organization (s) referred to above and has been in full compliance with those standards for at least _____ consecutive years, beginning in _____.**

> **Buyer may void this contract without penalty if he is unable to obtain information and results acceptable to him**

Organic sellers will not object to such a contingency clause because they know that the financial viability and market value of their farm depends on their certification and being in continuing compliance. Organic certification is worth a premium to an organic buyer who values that certification and wishes to continue the organic status of the property. Organic certification is not worth a premium to a buyer who is uninterested in organic status.

Buyers should exercise much caution and apply a great deal of research effort before buying a conventional farm with the idea of taking it organic. The process of conversion can take five years of exclusive organic practice before organic certification eligibility is reached. Conventional farming equipment that comes with the farm may need to be supplemented. Storage facilities will need to be cleaned in certain ways. The first years of converting from conventional to organic methods will be the riskiest and toughest. Organic soil takes time to build.

A buyer considering conversion should hire a consultant, if only another farmer in the area who is doing successfully what you want to do, to develop a **conversion plan**. If the buyer is truly dirt-smart, he will get a preliminary conversion plan in his hands before submitting a purchase offer to the seller. The plan should address the feasibility of conversion; the types of transition products, markets and prices envisioned; needed inputs; suggested measures for soil and water development; strategies for controlling weeds, disease and pests; livestock medication plans; timing issues, required investments; expected yields; expected gross revenues; expected net profit; risk analysis; and financing sources. You may find on the last of these points that conventional lenders may be a reluctant to lend for a non-conventional operation. A conversion plan should also include a human-capital component. How do you propose to get smart enough fast enough to prevent you and your organic butt ending up in bankruptcy? If you are going to need farm help, where are you going to get it; who's going to train and manage it; what regulations will apply to your farm; and what is the projected cost of the labor you will need?

Plan on planning. Organic farming is not like military battle where The Plan is changed as soon as first contact is made with the enemy. Your plan should include contingency tactics for possible adverse events, such as infestations and disease. Develop your plan through reading, going to conferences, talking to organic farmers who are raising your intended crops and retaining a consultant if necessary. Your plan should include a **time line**, which is a schedule that indicates when things—planting, weeding, thinning, application of control measures, harvesting—need to be done. Where possible, start the conversion slowly to minimize disaster and maintain cash flow. Plan for changes based on feedback and experimentation. The conversion process will take at least five years if you're starting with conventional dirt. Soil needs at least that long to clear out years of chemical inputs and be rebuilt with organic inputs. Anticipate trial and error in figuring out the best way to control pests and disease in the micro-environment of your fields. Yields may never be as high as before conversion, but input costs could be lower and product prices (when sold to organic outlets) should be higher. You can consider phasing in organic farming by starting with livestock as a source of both cash and manure, assuming you can find a suitable market.

Part of your marketing plan should be to determine the feasibility of **direct marketing to consumers**, a strategy that should generate higher returns than selling organic commodities to an organic processor or wholesaler. The more you can process the organic products you raise, the more money you should net. Farm-based marketing works best when your farm is within a reasonably convenient drive of a city or town. Proximity to college towns and communities devoted to second-home recreation and retirement would be ideal. The more distant your farm is to its consumer markets, the harder you will find it to build a local customer base. You can, alternatively, develop an order-and-delivery operation to overcome distance, but it will require a lot more management and expense on your end. You can also market over the Internet after complying with state and federal regulations and inspections.

If you are looking to convert a conventional farm to organic, seek out land that maximizes your chance of success and has capabilities that lend themselves to your goal. That should be self-evident, but I've seen heads bloodied against the wall of unsuitable ground. Avoid trying to rescue "reclaimed" strip mines, eroded lands, shale banks and arid, overgrazed areas unless you are both a missionary about organic techniques...and wealthy. "Conventional" farms differ among themselves in the intensity of their conventionality. The less invested in conventional agriculture the farm has been, the easier it's likely to be to make the switch. A farm that's been abandoned may be a better choice for conversion than one that's actively producing through conventional methods, assuming the soils are what you're looking for.

It's hard, labor-intensive, sustained work to bring a conventional farm into organic compliance. I would look for a conventional farm that has some of the makings for a conversion rather than fight the problems of converting a hard-shell heathen. Many farms have scaled back on chemicals, and some have adopted soil-saving and soil-building methods. I would look for a place that meets as many of the following basic criteria as possible:

- sufficient, regular rainfall appropriate to your purpose

- fields that have been treated with as few (type) and as little (quantity) chemicals for at least a couple of years

- land that is not subject to second-hand chemical exposure from neighbors or upstream farms

- appropriate soils for your purpose (find out the pH, mineral and other needs of your target crops)

- sufficient topsoil—dirt depth for your target crop (thin soils will require the addition of a lot of organic material, which takes money, labor and time)

- local sources and costs of *acceptable* inputs (manures, lime, hay, mulch, wood chips, crop wastes, leaves, compost, etc; the inputs have to meet organic standards)

- land capable of being grazed intensively on a rotating basis, which, with additional fencing, adds lot of manure to fields and pasture (the livestock need to have been medicated and fed in an acceptable way); sufficient water sources to allow rotational grazing in paddocks

- acceptable perimeter fencing to get started

- weather-tight storage (facilities will have to be cleaned and brought up to organic standards)

- community of organic farmers ("organic neighbors" will be the source of practical wisdom and sources of information about where to get acceptable inputs locally)

If you are looking at a farm that grazes livestock, you should investigate the practice of **intensive rotational grazing**. The idea of rotational grazing is to graze a small paddock intensively for a couple of days then shift the entire herd into the next paddock with fresh pasture for another couple of days, and so on. The number of paddocks, number of animals and the size of the paddocks should be designed to allow sufficient grass growth in the first paddock by the time the last paddock has been grazed. The grazing cycle will depend on your farm's location and the time of year. The cycle is shortest when grass growth is fastest. Rotational grazing allows the farmer to produce more pounds of gain per acre (though each animal may not gain as much as it would have with a lower stocking ratio of animals per acre), use his grass as efficiently as possible, improve the pastures by forcing the stock to eat the less palatable vegetation and increase soil fertility through higher rates of manure deposit. Since livestock is being changed into fresh grass every few days, internal parasites are less of a problem. Using cattle in a rotational grazing system will load manure onto a field five or six times each grazing season without compacting the soil or having the grass eaten down to the dirt. Five years of rotational grazing on conventional fields will go a long way toward preparing them for organic crops.

Rotational grazing requires investment in fencing and water. Large fields need to be cross-fenced, permanently or with portable electric wire, into paddocks of two to ten acres each. Water needs to be available to, if not in, each paddock. Design of such a system can use a hub model whereby the hub is the water source surrounded by a number of paddocks. Any corridor and area around a water source will be subject to heavy livestock traffic. This can lead to compaction and erosion. I've used rotational grazing for 20 years and am completely sold. I run almost one head of cattle (one head = one animal) per acre, which is twice the stocking ratio of comparable farms as well as this farm prior to installing the rotational system. I get almost the same gain per head as when the farm was carrying half the number of cattle. Federal conservation cost-share money is available to help with the costs of installing fencing and water systems.

Much material has been written on rotational grazing, especially during the last 20 years. Three books helped me: Andre Voisin, Grass Productivity; Bill Murphy, Green Pastures on Your Side of the Fence; and Allan Nation, Grass Farmers. Nation edits The Stockman Grass Farmer, a magazine devoted to providing farmers with information about efficient and profitable grazing methods (SGF, 282 Commerce Park Drive, Ridgeland, Mississippi, 39157; 1-800-748-9808; 601-853-1861; 601-853-8087 FAX; e-mail: sgf@stockmangrassfarmer.com; www.stockmangrassfarmer.com). SGF sells books, videos and holds conferences. See also: www.grassfarmer.com.

A farm buyer should have a **soils test** and, where appropriate, a **forage test** done on the target property's fields and pastures whether or not he is interested in organic farming. These tests should be done as part of your pre-purchase scoping. Both tests are available through state cooperative extension services for a modest cost; the county extension agent can provide sampling information. Proper sampling procedures are critical for each test. The test kits come with instructions; containers are usually plastic or paper bags, not metal. An organic farm is likely to require more extensive soils testing.

A soils test will indicate the sample's **pH**, which is the symbol for the logarithm of the reciprocal of hydrogen-ion concentration in gram atoms per liter of solution. pH, standing for the "potential of hydrogen," expresses the level of acidity or alkalinity on a scale of 0-14, where 7 is neutral, less than 7 is increasing acidity and more than 7 is increasing alkalinity. The pH scale is logarithmic, such that each numerical step away from 7 represents a multiple increase in the level of intensity. A pH of 4.3 is, for example, ten times more acidic than a pH of 5.3 while 3.3 is 100 times more acidic than 5.3. Farmers may call acidic soils "sour" and alkaline soils "sweet." Pasture should have a pH of at least 5.8, with closer to 7 being better. Each plant (grass, legume, tree and crop) does best in a specific pH range, which can be adjusted by adding lime and other inputs. Be careful with the kind of lime you apply to lower acidity. Most lime is high in magnesium, which is generally okay, but not always. Some lime—burnt or "hydrated"— helps for a season because it releases quickly, but must be reapplied. pH also indicates acidity in surface waters, notably trout streams. A stream with high acidity, i.e., low pH, stops being trout habitat. Acidic precipitation, caused by emissions from power plants and other sources, has been linked to forest decline in Germany's Black Forest, the northern Appalachians and other areas. The soils test will also indicate the sample's levels of Nitrogen (N), Phosphorus (P), Potassium (K), Calcium (Ca), Magnesium (Mg); and trace elements such as Zinc (Z), Manganese (Mn), Copper (Cu), Iron (Fe) and Boron (B). The **forage sample** analyzes hay and other livestock feeds, indicating levels of protein, energy, phosphorus, calcium, potassium and magnesium.

"Alternative" farmers criticize the conventional soils tests because they recommend conventional remedies, usually more N, P or K, from conventional, chemical-fertilizer suppliers. Application of such fertilizer year after year can leave the land burned out and ill-suited for growing much of anything without its annual fertilizer goosing. The soil tests available through your state's land-grant university's extension service will not recommend more carbon, organic material, manure or compost because those materials are not in the conventional box (though manure and compost, of course, have been in farmers' boxes for thousands of years).

A conventional soils test will tell you what your soils have and what they need, but it will not explain the alternatives available for adding needed elements. If your soils test reveals that every field in the target property lacks a lot of many elements, you will need to get a feel for the cost and amount of time needed to build the dirt up to what you want. Every input will cost you money, time and labor, and organic inputs may involve even more investment, take longer and cost more. The best strategy is to work with the land's existing constituents as much as possible rather than trying to grow crops in land badly suited for them.

If you find yourself attracted to organic, alternative farming, hire a soils consultant from the alternative farming community to test your soils, evaluate your farm's capabilities and needs and recommend a long-term soils-building plan. Farming begins with dirt, so things you do to build the dirt give you more farming flexibility. Organic farmers build their soils by applying manure (naturally through rotational grazing or mechanically), planting organic cover crops and turning them into the ground, alternating crops to supply soil nutrients and "dressing" fields with compost and other organic materials, such as wood chips (exclude artificially colored mulch and chemically treated woods), spoiled hay, saw dust and other products. Naturally occurring sources of fertilizer encourage soil bacteria and earthworms. Though I do not operate an organic farm, I once built **worm bordellos** in each of my pasture paddocks. I stocked them with hundreds of purchased guests who I hoped would engage in a lot of carrying on. Worms aerate soil, and their castings (manure) enrich it.

Building farm soil organically is a basic building-block subject in its own right, and the interested reader might look at Allan Savory with Jody Butterfield, Holistic Management: A New Framework for Decision-Making (Washington, D.C.: Island Press, 1999); Andre Voisin, Grass Productivity (Washington, D.C.: Island Press, 1988); and Joel Salatin, You Can Farm: The Entrepreneur's Guide to Start and Succeed in a Farming Enterprise (Swoope, Virginia: Polyface, Inc., 1998, especially pages 233-324. Available from author at Rt 1, Box 281, Swoope, Virginia, 24479; 540-885-3590.). See also The Savory Center, 1010 Tijeras NW, Albuquerque, NM 87102; 505-842-5252; 505-843-7900 FAX; http://www.holisticmanagement.org.

If you are planning to farm your target property, you should include a **soils-test contingency in your purchase offer** when pH and other constituents are critical factors for operational success. Here is one version of such a contingency:

> **Buyer at his expense shall be permitted to take soil samples from the property's fields and pastures and have them analyzed at his expense. The sampling and analysis shall be completed within ___ days of the date on which this Contract takes effect.**
>
> **Buyer may terminate this offer without penalty and with the full return of his deposit if the test results are unsatisfactory for his intended purposes.**

This is an unusual contingency, and it should only be used when a specific soil constituent (s) is essential to your plan and remediation would be costly. The buyer should know prior to submitting his offer the acceptable range of soil-test results for his intended agricultural uses. I recommend, however, against putting this range into the contingency language. Soil-test results can vary according to the places in a particular field where the samples are dug. A seller could easily perform his own soil test simultaneously with the buyer's. If the seller's results fall within the range and the buyer's don't, the dispute could end up in court. Soil-test results should not be a deal-killer if you plan to use the farm as it has been used in the past. Results are likely to show that the soils need additional inputs, but that should be expected.

This contingency is intended to protect you against extremes—too little of something and too much of something else—in terms of your intended use. If, for example, your pH results show high acidity and your planned use requires a pH of no less than 7, you will be fighting your dirt every year. I would summarily reject a farm whose dirt is obviously unsuited to my agricultural plans. While chemical and organic fertilizers are available to correct soil deficiencies, it's always better to start with dirt that is close to what you want. A **long-term soils-building plan** should be part of your farm planning. You will adopt certain practices (and reject others), grow certain crops (and not others) and add certain inputs (but not others) in accord with your long-term goals for soil building. A soils-consultant's expertise is a wise investment.

One other farm-related issue a buyer should investigate is the **occupational safety and health aspects of the type of farming** he plans to do. Conventional farmers are routinely exposed to toxic materials on their skin and through their inhalation of dusts, fumes, bacteria and other substances. Farmers are in and around manures, soiled bedding, waste litter, disease-carrying domestic livestock and dead animals. Lifting causes back problems as anyone who has pitched 300 hay bales on an August afternoon can attest. Repetitive-motion injuries are not uncommon on farms. Farm equipment—particularly tractors, PTOs, augers, conveyors, and other machines that handle and process raw materials—is dangerous. Children are especially vulnerable to farm accidents.

Farming is dangerous work. I know of two young farmers whose hands were mangled in harvesting equipment. I know of three farmers who killed themselves in tractor accidents. I have had my tractor pop out of gear when going downhill with a loaded hay wagon behind. I have had my tractor's front end rear up like the Lone Ranger's "Silver" when a log I was skidding caught on an unseen stump that held the tractor in place as its spinning back wheels lifted its front.

Farm-related occupational health and safety is not liberal hand-wringing. The National Institute of Occupational Safety and Health (NIOSH) has eight agricultural centers in the United States, each of which provides information and counsel on agricultural health and safety issues. NIOSH is headquartered in the Hubert H. Humphrey Building, 200 Independence Ave., S.W., Washington, D.C., 20201; 1-800-356-4674; e-mail: pubstaff@cdc.gov.

I have used my region's center, New York Center for Agricultural Medicine & Health, 1 Atwell Road, Cooperstown, New York, 13326; 1-800-343-7527; e-mail: nycamh@lakenet.org; www.nycamh.com. My question was whether broiler (poultry) litter, which is mixed with corn and fed to beef cattle as part of a winter feeding program, posed any health hazard to me when I was exposed to its voluminous dust. Litter is the cheap bedding-type material—usually sawdust or peanut hulls in my area—that is spread on the floor of a poultry house. When the grown-out birds are removed, the litter contains feces, urine, spilled food, residues from medications and whatever the poultry shed during their confinement. Litter is high in protein and cheap, which explains its use as cattle food. The poultry grower cleans out the litter and piles it in a covered shed where it generates enough heat to kill bacteria. The resulting material is a nitrogen-rich field fertilizer, and certain types are fed to cattle. The Center did a literature search whose results prompted me to begin wearing an $800 full-face, self-contained respirator. The next year, I stopped feeding litter altogether. While litter has many advantages as a cattle feed, the Virginia Tech professors who were advocating its use had not done sufficient research in my opinion on the health hazards to farmers handling this material or to consumers eating this beef.

In January, 2004, the US Food and Drug Administration seemed to ban farmers from using poultry litter in cattle feed. FDA's concern was that feed given to poultry contained beef products that could contain tissues where BSE (mad-cow disease) is found. Spilled chicken feed went into the litter and then was fed back to beef cattle. Poultry litter as cattle feed certainly fit the conventional farming mode. Whether it is safe for the farmer to handle and its beef safe for human consumption is a matter of debate. My first-hand experience with the dusty, ammonia-smelling stuff for three years—feeding eight wheelbarrows a day for about 150 days each winter—was enough to raise doubts. As of October, 2005, poultry litter as cattle feed was still allowed. Surely, we can do better than feed shit and sawdust to animals we eat.

The photograph below shows a 1950s-style two-story poultry house that I converted to a cattle-feeding facility in the mid-1980s. The grain-tank on the left holds corn that is carried through an auger into the top of the building and unloaded through tubes into swinging trays on the ground floor. The trays are chained to the floor joists above them. The top floor can store square bales of hay as well as about 30 tons of grain at each end. The hay is fed through drop holes along the back wall into a long rack, capable of handling 60 head. The plywood doors on the front wall open outward; grain can be put into reinforced storage rooms at each end with a front-end loader or wheel-mounted auger. These buildings are readily converted to other agricultural purposes, but they cannot be converted to organic agriculture without a lot of cleaning and resurfacing with 1/4"-thick plywood.

PHOTOGRAPH 5-1

An Unphotogenic Barn

If you are intending to have animals on your new farm, you should invest in the latest edition of The Merck Veterinary Manual: A Handbook of Diagnosis, Therapy, and Disease Prevention and Control for the Veterinarian (Rahway, New Jersey: Merck & Co.). The Manual is comprehensive, covering all diseases of pets, livestock and exotica. It offers conventional drug therapies for conventional farming.

Organic farmers use certain naturally occurring substances to prevent livestock disease. Their emphasis is on minimizing illness through clean farm-management practices, like rotational grazing and no large-scale confinement of animals. Since true organic programs prohibit antibiotics in the product, organic livestock growers have to invest in prevention through management. Organic standards do not rule out all vaccines and all "drugs." The certifying organization is the source of what is currently permitted and prohibited. **Herbal remedies** are favored. Homeopathic treatments may also be permitted. **Homeopathy** treats disease and symptoms with highly diluted solutions of active ingredients (possibly a poison) and bacteria of the disease that is being prevented. Homeopathy, unlike vaccines, does not produce antibodies; its intent is to raise the resistance level of the whole animal. **Probiotics** is a bacterial treatment that stimulates an animal's gut flora and "outcompetes" harmful bacteria. If you are operating a certified organic farm, you will be expected to make sure that your medications, wormers, feed and mineral salt are approved under the group's rules.

Different farmers hold different beliefs about medicating animals. Some do only the most rudimentary preventive vaccinations and worming. Most, if not all, feed mineral salt to livestock. Opinion differs about clipping, filing teeth, dehorning, debeaking, castrating, spaying, using growth hormones, docking tails, delousing and a dozen other practices of that type. Some farmers invest in rigorous proactive regimens of what they believe are cost-effective, profit-enhancing medications to control worms, parasites, flies, pinkeye, disease and the like. They believe that each dollar invested pays for itself at the very least. Concerns about resistant bacteria and pests are rarely part of this common dollar-and-cents calculation. If many animals show symptoms of illness, you will need to treat them to avoid a disaster regardless of your preferences. If one animal has something that is not infectious, you will need to weigh the cost of paying for a vet visit against the risk of doing nothing or playing vet your self. Sometimes, the cost of care is more than the value of the animal. Do not be surprised if a neighbor advises you to let a sick animal go without treating it; I've both taken and given that advice. Each case presents its own choices about dollars and ethics. Animals that look and act really sick generally are, and a vet is unlikely to be much help by that time. I have medicated a sick calf because I thought it was the right thing to do, only to prolong its sick life for a week or two. Although each sick calf is its own call, I'm more inclined now to allow a calf without much chance to die. (Recall, if you will, its ultimate fate is the slaughterhouse.) Each of you who raise animals for profit will have to make such decisions.

Many farmers accept the loss of an ordinary animal rather than spend the money on a vet call. Most will do what they can themselves, though a few I know are from the swim-or-sink school. Farmers do not see farm animals raised for market as pets; they see them as economic objects with certain subjective attributes. Farm kids who hand-raise lambs and calves for 4-H livestock auctions learn early that farms raise livestock to make money, not friends. Do not expect that your barnyard will have Charlotte spinning "Some Pig" to save Wilbur's life and your conscience.

CHAPTER 6: FARMING THE TAX CODE, SOWING AND REAPING

Buyers of country property need to inform themselves of the **tax benefits and tax consequences** of owning a working farm, rural second home or unimproved rural property before making an offer. Each of these types of land involves a different set of tax implications. The more you think about buying properties like these **as an investment or business**, the more opportunities you will have to take advantage of federal programs and state and federal tax benefits. Federal tax law is found in the U.S. Code, Title 26, online at www.law.cornell.edu/uscode/html/uscode26. The Internal Revenue Code (IRC) should be read together with Revenue Rulings, case law, IRS letters of opinion and instructional booklets. Farm-tax policy is summarized in **IRS Publication 225, Farmer's Tax Guide**, at www.irs.gov; or 1-800-829-1040 or 1-800-829-3676. Another site with farm-tax information is www.irs.gov/business/small/farmers/index.html.

Real-estate investment has much to recommend it. It lends itself to **leveraged buying**, where a small amount of cash can start the acquisition of a much larger asset. While markets fluctuate and track interest rates, property generally **appreciates in value** over time. As the owner pays off the property, he builds **equity**—cash value—in it. Interest on investment and business real estate is generally deductible dollar for dollar from the taxpayer's gross income, but exceptions exist. If the real estate has buildings and other improvements used to produce income or in a business, their cost can be **depreciated**—a tax benefit that is not available to alternative investments such as stocks, bonds and CDs. Depreciation amortizes the cost of an asset like a barn or a tractor over a certain number of years, allowing the taxpayer to reduce his taxable income during that time. (See IRC, Sections 167 and 168.) Any depreciation allowed or allowable to the taxpayer over the years is subject to **recapture** in the year of the asset's sale. That portion of the depreciation recaptured is taxed at the taxpayer's ordinary-income rate, with exception for residential or nonresidential property.

There are other advantages. If real estate is held for more than a year, any taxable gain on its sale qualifies for the **capital-gains rate**, which in most cases should be lower than the taxpayer's rate on ordinary income. Income taxed as a capital gain would be at 15 percent compared with a rate of more than 30 percent on ordinary income for higher-income taxpayers. If the real estate is held in a self-directed Roth IRA, the taxpayer can have the trustee sell the asset in his retirement tax free. If the taxpayer does not need to capture immediate profit when he sells his real estate, he can do a tax-deferred **1031 exchange for another like-kind real-estate asset** by which he sells his business property and acquires a new one without receiving either income or profit from the sale. Since the 1031 taxpayer has realized no taxable gain through the exchange, he owes no tax at the time the exchange is made. (See Chapter 33 for more on 1031 exchanges.)

In my opinion, real estate is far easier for a layperson to research and understand than any publicly traded stock. To that extent, the investor who does his homework on real estate buys into a less risky investment than the investor who must depend on the financial statements corporations release about themselves. Most real estate is not illiquid, though it may not sell quickly at the price you want. It also carries several kinds of loss potential: you can lose real estate to your lender if you fail to make payments on your mortgage debt; you can suffer a loss to the property from natural events; and you can lose money when you are forced to sell in a down market. Investing in rural real estate shares these benefits and risks. It also involves other financial benefits that I discuss in later chapters. And, of course, you can enjoy country property for itself.

A **farm business** combines real-estate qualities, such as long-term appreciation in land value, with business treatment from a tax perspective. If you are living on a farm that is a business operated for profit, you should qualify for farm treatment. This will allow you to either deduct ordinary and necessary expenses from gross income in the year you incurred them or amortize them as a capital expense over several years. A farm loss can be used against off-farm income, subject to certain limitations. Farm tax benefits are fewer if you do not materially participate in the farm business, or if the farm you own is not operated as a profit-oriented business, or if you rent the farm rather than operate it yourself. The ability of a taxpayer to use farm loss against ordinary income from other sources is limited by IRC Section 469, **passive activity losses** and credits (referred to as PAL) and Section 465, deductions limited to amount at risk (referred to as **at-risk rules**).

From a tax perspective, I would advise buyers to look for rural property that can be operated as and qualify as a **farm business** rather than either recreational land or a for-personal-use-only second home. Even if you do nothing but rent your farm acreage to your neighbor, you will be eligible to deduct some farm-related expenses and get other benefits. Similarly, I would advise a buyer to buy woodland and build a cabin rather than a five-acre country home in a development. The woodland can be managed for timber production—a legitimate business. I would also advise buyers to favor property with an existing home, because it can be a source of rental income and a variety of tax benefits, the extent of which depends on how much the taxpayer occupies the house for personal use. A second home also gives the taxpayer the opportunity to live in it as a principal residence for two years and gain the benefit of excluding as much as $250,000 (single taxpayer) to $500,000 (married taxpayers, filing jointly) of taxable gain (net profit) upon its sale.

From a tax perspective, the optimum investment would be a working farm, with a habitable farm house, with usable outbuildings, with some equipment thrown into the deal, with some immediately **severable assets** (such as, unneeded land that could be quickly sold), with a tenant house that could be sold or rented, with crop land that is currently receiving some production subsidy, with some land that is eligible for a conservation easement, and, finally, with as much land containing **merchantable timber** (trees with immediate sale value) as a buyer can find. These qualities have an income or a tax benefit, or both, depending on how the taxpayer uses each one.

From a tax perspective, I would not buy a property that carries a **conservation easement,** because a prior owner has captured the associated state and federal tax benefits, leaving me with the restrictions in perpetuity. Lacking one or more rights in the property, most of these tracts will always appreciate at a discounted rate, possibly sharply discounted. Adjoining properties, however, may appreciate at an inflated rate, now that they will always be next to land that's not developed or never timbered. I often look for land that is suitable for a conservation easement because of these benefits in circumstances where the land with the easement will continue to appreciate at near-market rates. (Conservation easements are discussed in Chapter 33.)

I would advise against buying land that has been recently clearcut unless you get it very cheap, want it for hunting or plan to put it in a self-directed IRA. It will appreciate, but it will take at least seven to ten years for the logging detritus to disappear and another ten for the 20-year-old trees to gain "treely" presence and shade out the dense new-growth underbrush in the areas opened to the sun by logging. Clearcuts can be good buys for hunters whose game prefers thick brush and young growth, and who are looking to sell at some point in the long-term future.

When looking for farms—and rural land generally—look for property containing **merchantable** timber—standing trees the landowner can sell immediately. Income from the timber sale held soon after closing can be used to buy the property. If you sell the timber for an amount less than or equal to its value at the time you purchased the property, no taxable gain is realized and you will pay no tax on that sale. The timber sale will reduce your **basis** in the overall property, thus increasing your likely taxable gain when the property as a whole is sold. Timber sales and taxation are discussed in Chapters 21-24. Farms often come with woodland at the back of the property where merchantable timber may or may not exist.

I prefer to buy property that is conveyed in **fee simple**, that is, with all mineral rights running with the surface rights. If you own your mineral rights, you can lease them to a mineral developer. Mineral leasing produces rental income and, if minerals are produced, royalty income. Royalty owners can deduct a portion of their annual payment for **depletion**. State taxes on minerals and royalties can also be deducted. As an alternative, mineral owners may be able to get tax benefits from placing a conservation easement on their minerals by forgoing development. A farm whose mineral rights are severed may find a new gas well operating 200 feet from its front porch.

I look for a farm that has a couple of **immediately severable assets**—a second house, land across or down the road that can be divided into second-home lots, merchantable timber—that could be sold without substantially affecting my interest in and enjoyment of the core property. Cash from the sale of severable assets can be used to pay down acquisition debt or for any other purpose. I discuss the **purchase strategy using severable assets** in Chapter 33.

Taxpayers report farm income and expenses on either **Schedule F, Profit or Loss from Farming** (if the seller himself is actively farming) or **Form 4835** where the taxpayer receives crop or livestock shares, but no cash. **Schedule E** is used by a taxpayer who receives income from the rental of his farm. **Schedule F** is used for a farm business and permits the taxpayer to charge all farm expenses against farm income. A taxpayer who is renting his farm is allowed to charge only those farm-related expenses that are necessary to the rental of the farm. Do not claim a farm business using a Schedule C or combine farm profit and expenses into one of your other farm-based businesses, such as consulting, antiques or B&B. **IRS Publication 225, Farmer's Tax Guide** is your starting point for understanding this subject.

Farms are eligible for a wide range of public price supports, cost-share programs, emergency relief and the like—all of which have tax implications.

Genuine farm-business operations are eligible to take farm-related losses against current income from other sources, such as wages and salaries. (This is why taxpayers with high incomes want to own farms.) The most loss benefit can be claimed by a taxpayer who is a "**material participant**" in the farm business, which requires under Section 469 PAL rules that he, for example, spend more than 500 hours doing farm-business work during the tax year. Other options to qualify as a material participant might include taxpayer's participation in the activity substantially constituted all material participation in the tax year; participation exceeded 100 hours and no other individual participated more; aggregate participation in all of the significant participation activities exceeded 100 hours; material participation has occurred in the activity for any five of the preceding ten tax years; and taken as a whole, the taxpayer's participation was done on a regular, continuous and substantial basis for at least 100 hours during the tax year while no other individual participated more and a paid manager was not employed. The at-risk rules in Section 465 limit the amount of loss the taxpayer can claim from farming to the amount of money the taxpayer has at risk in the farm operation. Despite these restrictions, farm-business loss can help many taxpayers.

Capital improvements (farm buildings, bridges, big fencing projects, etc.) and equipment purchases used in farming (tractor, ATV, pick-up truck, hydraulic log splitter, trailer, etc.) are **depreciated**, which allows the taxpayer to write off a portion of each asset's beginning cost (called, "**basis**") every year for a certain number of years according to one of several IRS depreciation formulas. Expenses related to ordinary and necessary farm supplies, fuels, feed, labor, professional fees, insurance, animal medications and other farm-related costs can be charged against current farm income. Interest on the farm's mortgage and loans for farm equipment, livestock, improvements and crops is deductible. Certain capital expenditures may be deducted rather than depreciated when they are **Section 1245 (a) (3) assets** that are acquired for use in an active business. This is called **Section 179 property**, and a qualifying taxpayer may deduct up to $108,000 in 2006 worth of tangible, depreciable property that is "acquired by purchase for use in the active conduct of a trade or business." If you buy a farm that you then rent out, you are not actively engaged in farming, so the 179 tax break is not available. Section 179 property can include breeding stock, pick-up trucks and certain SUVs (the vehicle must have a loaded gross vehicle weight exceeding 6,000 pounds; a $25,000 expensing cap applies)—as long as they are used in a trade or business. If you buy a big vehicle for $20,000 and use it 80 percent for business, you can deduct $16,000 from your gross income in the year of purchase. You can get the same deduction if you borrow the money to buy the vehicle. A taxable-income limitation on Section 179 deduction expensing exists as well.

A taxpayer can set up a **home office** in his new farm as long as it meets the IRS criteria set forth in **Publication 587, Business Use of Your Home and Section 280A**. The home office must be the taxpayer's principal place of business, and it must be used regularly and exclusively for business purposes. The home office, of course, cannot be in the taxpayer's second home, because that residence is not the taxpayer's principal residence. If you move to your farm, look into setting up a home office. A taxpayer who owns an operating farm with a farmhouse on it should not have a problem qualifying that portion of the farmhouse used exclusively for running the farm business as a business expense. This arrangement is not a home office; it is the farm business's business office. A taxpayer with a farm-business business office of this type should not file a home-office form, unless he operates another type of business from it.

Part of your pre-offer scoping of any target farm is obtaining the advice of a farm-savvy, tax-preparing CPA. He can review the farm's financial performance and assets from the perspectives of both income and tax benefits. The time to think through a farm's tax strategy and ownership structure is prior to purchase; I go a step further, think it through before submitting a purchase offer. Planning in advance of purchase will make post-purchase accounting and tax preparation easier and more productive. I recommend the buyer hire a CPA in the target county who prepares a fair number of local farm returns. He will have a good sense about the financial performance of similar farms. He's also likely to have been involved in IRS audits of local farmers. Your local CPA can coordinate his advice with your regular tax preparer to give you a blended opinion as to how the new farm business will alter your tax situation. After purchase, you should consider having this CPA do the farm part of your return if your tax preparer is not experienced. Don't attempt to prepare a farm schedule on your own, particularly the first return where you have to allocate **basis** among different assets, select depreciation schedules and make decisions with future tax consequences.

CPA tax advice is even more important if a buyer is considering rural property that the IRS might consider a **hobby farm** or **tax shelter**. The buyer will be in a little stronger position if the seller operated the property as a farm business, but the IRS will make its determination on your operation, not your predecessor's. Farms, especially those that might look a little fishy to the IRS, should be set up as a business separate from the taxpayer's other income streams. To help establish your farm-business purpose, you can name the farm, set up a separate checking account for the farm alone and transact farm business in the farm's name. You should also write/assemble a set of business-planning documents, beginning with copies of key documents you collect during your pre-purchase scoping. The taxpayer should orient the farm around making a profit from its farming activities. Your accountant can help you think through the tax implications of different farmownership formats and different agricultural products.

You should have your CPA review the seller's farm records and IRS farm returns to help you in evaluating the income performance of the property. The seller has priced his farm as an income-producing business, not as a pretty place for a second home. Your CPA will help you project expected income and tax benefits if you continue running the farm as the seller has. He can also project estimates of future income, net profit, costs, deductions and depreciation for different farming scenarios you might have in mind. (The extension service in your target property's state may also be able to run farm-operation financial scenarios for you; the more conventional your scenario, the more likely that the extension service will have a forecasting program that fits.) Your CPA's estimated projections will fall into a fairly large ballpark inasmuch as each is subject to your management skill, macro-economic factors such as interest rates and commodity prices and risk factors like weather.

You can ask your CPA to work into his projections several **discount rates to account for your farm-business risk**, say 15, 30 and 50 percent. The resulting lower projections will give you a pretty good idea of your possible down sides. The more "alternative" your farm plan is, the greater your down-side risk in my opinion, particularly if you haven't done it before and you're doing it without mentors. You should understand that it's possible that you will produce less farm revenue than your most steeply discounted projection anticipated. The probability of disaster decreases in step with careful, knowledgeable planning and prudent implementation of your plan. Starting small keeps your beginning mistakes small. Your farm plan is not a roll of the dice or in for a dime in for a dollar. It's a conservative business plan, using conservative assumptions and conservative expectations.

Remember that non-farm income represents the majority of household income in most farm households. That's where you probably want to be. Successful farm-business households of this type lose money on paper for tax purposes. Unsuccessful ones lose cash out of pocket. As long as you see the farm as supplementing your non-farm income and providing some tax-sheltering loss and other tax benefits, the financial down side of your farm's business should fall into an acceptable range.

When a farm property meets IRS criteria for a farm business, **active farm losses can offset active income from non-farm sources.** That is why the eyes of big-city CPAs light up when one of their high-income clients says he's looking at farms. But be very careful about buying a farm mainly for its anticipated **tax-loss benefits.** If, for example, you want to find about $50,000 in farm loss to reduce your gross income by that amount, you will probably have to break even on the sale of the farm's output and pick up most of your loss from depreciation and the deduction for interest payments. Assume for illustration that you would need to purchase about $500,000 (or more) worth of farm to produce that $50,000 in paper loss each year while breaking even on cash. The subtraction of $50,000 from your gross income might save you $17,500 in annual tax. The annual principal-and-interest payment on borrowing $500,000 at 7 percent is $39,919 amortized over 30 years. Of that payment, about $400 is principal in the first year, leaving interest at about $39,519. (The interest portion of your annual mortgage payment slowly declines each year, making it slowly ever harder to find your $50,000 loss.) The remaining tax loss of $10,500 that you are seeking would be found in depreciation (a paper loss) and in farm-related expenses that exceed income (cash out of pocket). If your depreciation is $10,000, you are spending $40,000 in interest payment and cash expenses to save $17,500 in taxes at the 35 percent tax rate. All of that $40,000 is deductible. You are also using that money to buy the farm, which generates cash and is an asset that should appreciate while giving you pleasure and aesthetic value.

You might also be able to pick up some non-loss tax advantages through a conservation easement and tax credits for conservation practices. Various types of tax credits and exemptions are available in every state, ranging from a family-farm credit, to a homestead property-tax exemption and a beginning-farmer credit. State tax-credit information as of 2003 can be found at www.ctahr.hawaii.edu/awg/workshops.asp. Federal credits are available for certain conservation actions and reforestation (a ten percent credit up to $10,000). A typical Iowa county—Mills—lists nine credits/exemptions available to farmers beyond a homestead tax credit, military tax exemption and family-farm credit, including forest reserve, fruit tree reservation, wetlands, native prairie, wildlife habitat, water-impoundment structures, pollution control, cattle facilities and historic property. (See www.millscoia.us/ assessor/ assessor2.html.) The county's assessor will have information on local property-tax breaks. The tax benefits of farmownership are substantial compared with other investments, but I would not take on a farm for that reason alone.

If you're mainly looking for farm-based tax-loss benefits, consider investing in a *large* farm with other similarly situated investors. The group can set up its own investment-ownership structure—e.g., as a limited liability company (LLC), tenants-in-common (TIC) or limited partnership—which then buys the farm and either hires farm management or works out a share-the-crop arrangement with the tenant. Investment advisers in farm areas know of properties for sale and will take care of the management for a fee. If you are a passive investor in the farm, you will get fewer tax-loss benefits compared with an active participant in the investment.

Another way of investing in farmland is to buy shares in a Real Estate Investment Trust (REIT) that concentrates in farm properties. Other REITS concentrate in timberland. (See www.nareit.com and www.inrealty.com. Real-estate books on agriculture can be found at the latter site by clicking on "timberland" and then clicking on "books.")

While farming continues to offer tax benefits of many kinds, investors should not look at farms primarily as a tax shelter, but as a multi-faceted investment that produces income, loss and long-term appreciation of the property. The tax-shelter aspects of farming are of less importance today than they were 20 years ago when marginal income tax rates were much higher and exclusions, deductions and credits more numerous. The passive-activity-loss rules begun then limited the ability of high-income taxpayers from sheltering this income through farm losses.

It's worth a quick look to see how farming has been affected by federal tax policy. The USDA's Economic Research Service found that federal income, estate and gift-tax policies together supported growth in very small and very large farms. As discussed above, a relatively large number of small farms tend to be unprofitable while the relatively few number of very large ones are. Federal tax policies also worked to inflate farmland value; concentrated farmland ownership with high-income taxpayers, both farmers and non-farmers; and encouraged increased supply and lower prices for some farm commodities, such as cattle. **Those taxpayers with substantial farm income—the top ten percent, in particular—had "significantly lower federal income tax burdens compared with all other taxpayers."** (See USDA, ERS, "Effects of Federal Tax Policy on Agriculture—Conclusions," May 1, 2001 at www.mindfully.org/Farm/Tax~Policy~Agriculture~USDA.htm.) My guess is that these taxpayers with high farm incomes were not considered passive participants in the farm enterprise, thus allowing them to offset non-farm income with farm losses.

Looking at these USDA conclusions from the perspective of advice to a prospective farm buyer, I draw three suggestions. First, the larger the farm operation, the larger the tax benefits of all types.

Second, while farm operators of all sizes have access to tax benefits, the current set of policies mainly benefits those with the largest farm incomes. Third, federal tax policies taken as a whole over time have helped rich farmers stay rich while most of the rest get by with not much help from their friends in Washington.

BUSINESS AND HOBBIES

Properties that are operated as **farm businesses** offer the most opportunities for tax benefits as well as the federal subsidies discussed earlier. The IRS does not require that a farm business meet a certain acreage threshold, though more acreage would probably help the taxpayer make a stronger case that he's operating a farm business. An organic garden on just a few acres that sold its vegetables should qualify as a farm business consistent with a profit-making intent. So would a livestock breeding farm that contained no more than one registered stallion on five acres. Both farm businesses would generate income from the sale of products or service, and both are run to make money regardless of whether or not they net very much. The taxpayer's intentions and manner of operation are very important in persuading the IRS to accept a farm as a business operated to make a profit. The more conventional a farm looks on its return and the more conventional an operation looks in the field, the less likely the IRS will be to question the taxpayer's farm business. I base this opinion on the image of the slippery slope that constitutional lawyers are always invoking. In this case, if the IRS disallows a non-profitable conventional farm, it will have to apply its reasoning to all other similarly situated farms. That's the politically slippery slope—so it's best not to take the first step down it. Don't get cocky or greedy. The pleasant, farmy places that Laskas and Korda purchased would not qualify as farm businesses at the time of purchase in an IRS audit, because they don't appear to have been operated to make a profit if they were farmed at all. Korda's horse operation could qualify if it goes beyond a hobby. Showing a little net income each year is not enough to prove that you are trying to run a for-profit farm business.

The IRS is trying to catch—and weed out—high-income taxpayers who are **using their farming losses to shelter non-farm income** and are not genuinely trying to operate a farm business. The other type of farm-taxpayer that the IRS will disallow is the "**hobby farm**," discussed below. The IRS's distinction between qualified farm businesses on one hand and non-qualifying tax-shelters and hobby farms on the other can make a huge difference in your annual tax payment. As an active participant in a farm business, you can deduct expenses, count farm losses against non-farm income and depreciate farm assets, all of which reduce your tax payment. It may go without saying but I will anyway, **the dirt-smart buyer wants to operate a farm business that will qualify as such if the IRS chooses to perform an audit.** It follows that a dirt-smart buyer prefers to buy rural properties that lend themselves to operating as a farm business.

The IRS's official position in **Section 183 (Hobby Loss rule**) is that a farm business must earn a profit three years out of five (3/5 rule) to qualify as a farm for tax purposes and allow the taxpayer to deduct expenses above income in succeeding years. (Horse farms have to show profit in two of seven years.) If the IRS determines that the farm business failed to hit these profit goals, the taxpayer will be able to deduct expenses in the future up to, but not in excess of, income. (You can read the IRS's audit guidelines at www.dese.state.mo.us/divcareered/ ag_helpful_webblinks.htm; click on IRS Hobby Farm Audit Guidelines.) You want to be able to deduct expenses in excess of income, because that excess represents loss that you can deduct from non-farm income.

Cattle and horses are two of the most common farm activities. If you are thinking about them, read through IRC Section 183: Farm Hobby Losses with Cattle Operations and Horse Activities, 2001 at www.ors.gov/pub/irs-mssp/a1farms.pdf. This is the manual that the IRS instructs its auditors to use. It shows taxpayers what the auditors look for, such as gross farm income not exceeding deductions; LUQ items (large, unusual, or questionable deductions); taxpayers with other substantial income sources who are sustaining financial farm losses to offset other substantial income; and the presence of fancy buildings, barns and expensive fence.

While Section 183 sets forth the 3/5 profit rule, my experience and sense is that the IRS does not apply this rule either rigidly or rigorously in practice. Why? For one thing, profit from farming is such a manipulable number that it can be achieved, if necessary, simply by not counting expenses. Anecdotal evidence is that a lot of part-time farmers deliberately underreport expenses to make sure their Schedule Fs show a profit on paper.

More important, I think that the IRS recognizes that a large number of America's small and part-time farms are incapable of ever making a profit in any authentic sense. If the IRS were to apply its 3/5 rule scrupulously, Congress would be visited by waves of tax-clobbered, newly-disqualified farmers looking to reinstate the status quo *ante*.

The IRS acknowledges that the 3/5 rule is not the only criterion it uses to determine whether a farm is a genuine business. If an audited farmer/taxpayer does not meet the 3/5 rule, he then has the burden of showing that his farm activity is motivated by profit. The IRS has developed a set of nine criteria to apply in this situation:

1. Does the taxpayer operate the farm in a business-like manner?

2. Does the amount of time and effort the taxpayer spends on the farm business demonstrate that he intends to make a profit?

3. Does the taxpayer depend on farming income for his livelihood?

4. Are the taxpayer's losses due to circumstances beyond his control? Are the losses normal for the start-up phase of the taxpayer's farm business?

5. Has the taxpayer changed his methods of farm operations in an effort to improve profitability?

6. Do the taxpayer and his advisers have sufficient knowledge to implement the taxpayer's farm business successfully?

7. Has the taxpayer made a profit from farming of a similar type in the past?

8. Can the taxpayer document profit from farming in other years? How much profit was made in each of those years?

9. Can the taxpayer anticipate a profit in the future from the appreciation of his farm business's assets?

A first-time farmer can ask for a grace period from the 3/5 rule. A first-timer who does not have three years of profitable farming in his past can file a Form 5213, which postpones for five years any IRS eyeballing of his farm business. Before filing a 5213, consult with your CPA who can advise you as to whether your audit chances increase if you use it.

My opinion is that the IRS mainly looks for the farmer-taxpayer's effort and commitment toward making money, rather than successful results. But I also suspect it also depends on who you are financially. A couple with $10-per-hour, off-the-farm jobs is likely to have a part-time, cattle operation scrutinized less than a CEO with the identical farm profile. Ironically, the CEO may be able to substantiate his farm business on paper far better than the couple, owing to his CPA's counsel to make the farm look like a business and his own "paper skills." And if both these hunches are true, it would confirm my other notion that the IRS mainly looks for egregious examples of hobby farming and high-income tax sheltering. *Absentee farmowners, particularly those with high salaries and incomes, should expect a close inspection of their farm business.* Full-time farm residents should have a better starting point with the auditor than an absentee. But plenty of absentee farm operators have no trouble with the IRS just as plenty of full-time farm residents—like the Kordas—whose farms are mainly a lifestyle get disallowed. I do not know, of course, whether absentee farm operators are classifying themselves as active or passive participants. Full-time farmers will be given a presumption of operating a farm business, whether or not they show any profit, ever. Taxpayers with part-time farm operations, whether absentee or in residence, must show that the part-time farm business is aimed at and operated to make a profit. The expenses and losses the farming generates must have some reasonable relationship to revenues generated or expected in the future. A $400,000-a-year, big-city doctor should not expect to shelter his salary by purchasing a 20-acre weekend farmette on which he runs two potbelly pigs, one of which he sells for more than he paid. Doc will end up with an audit, back taxes and a lonely pig.

I cannot determine whether the IRS screens Schedule F returns for possible **hobby farms**, but if a taxpayer with a farm is one of the randomly selected audits his operation is likely to be scrutinized, as mine was. Your job will be to show (not tell) the IRS auditor that you are trying to make as much money from your farm as your farm is capable of making. Don't wax eloquent about either the spiritual side of your hideously expensive llama or the Zen of watching worms eat the apples on your three organic dwarf trees that you've called a working orchard. Talk about wanting to make money! If you have trouble doing this, have your CPA do as much of the talking as possible.

The presence of farm animals and farm equipment does not make a farm business. (See http://www.irs.ustreas.gov/pub/irs-mssp/alfarmls.pdf or IRS, "Farm Hobby Losses with Cattle Operations and Horse Activities.")

You cannot establish that you are a farm business by showing that you have a lot of farm-related expenses—all of which you deducted or depreciated—or by displaying a lot of manure on your boots—all of which you've left on when you met your auditor.

A hobby farm can use its expenses and deductions only against the income the hobby activity generates and only up to the amount of that income. A farm business, in contrast, can use its expenses, deductions and loss against non-farm income and these write offs can exceed the amount of farm-business income. The difference can amount to thousands of dollars each year in tax paid or tax saved.

If you think your operation might look like a hobby farm, make sure that you do all of the following: 1) consult a tax-and-farm savvy CPA in the set up phase; 2) write a five-year business plan with profit shown by at least the third or fourth year; 3) periodically adapt and amend your original business plan to show that the plan is a working part of your business and you are incorporating feedback lessons; 4) take some university and extension courses related to your farm plan; 5) buy appropriate books and subscribe to journals; 6) join the appropriate crop/livestock associations; 7) go to some agricultural meetings (the travel and other expenses are deductible); 8) track and record everything—your time, expenses, travel, planting and animal histories; 9) look like a business—name your farm, set up a farm-exclusive checking account, put up a farm website describing what you do, have a phone and/or fax/and or e-mail in the farm's name; 10) keep a set of farm books (not a shoebox with receipts); 11) set up your farm as an LLC or other appropriate legal structure (since land appreciates in value, the rule of thumb is to not put real estate into a corporation); and 12) try to show gross sales of at least $10,000 in farm products; the more gross you can sell, the less net, I think, you'll have to generate.

You want to be an **active farm-business operator**. An active farm operator is one who is sufficiently involved in the farm business to qualify as "active" for the IRS. A passive farm investor or operator is one who is insufficiently involved to qualify as an active participant. The reason that you want to be, and qualify as, an active operator is that you are then eligible to offset active income from non-farm sources with losses from the farm. Keeping a **time log**—date, time spent, purpose—can help substantiate your claim of active farm participation.

You want your Schedule F to raise as few flags as possible. The most common flag I've seen occurs when the new, high-income owner buys thousands of dollars of farm toys—tractors, ATVs, trucks, wagons, equipment and new barn—to support a dozen pet sheep and a wild burro that can't be ridden. Expenditures way out of proportion to farm revenue cast a very dark shadow on a farm business. Let me put this a different way: **a great big loss is a redder flag than real small income**.

The IRS has no problem with a taxpayer working full-time off the farm and operating a farm business after work as long as the **part-time farming** is intended to make a profit. This part-time farm is considered a genuine business whereas a full-time hobby farm is not. If you are audited, the IRS will judge whether your part-time farm is a farm business based on your records, your motives as indicated by what you say and show to the auditor and your farm's annual **profit-and-loss statements**. The more business-like your paperwork is, the easier it will be for the IRS to endorse your farm business.

Most farms in America are **small**, measured either in number of acres or net income. The IRS, in practice, does not seem to expect that small farms will ever achieve genuine, sustained profitability, despite its own *pro forma* requirement of profit three years out of five. If it did, it would have to disallow about half of all farm operator households—about one million altogether—who earned less than $25,000 in income, most of which was made off the farm. The Agency seems to judge a small farm only in terms of itself—Is it run for profit, with levels of investment, time, production and loss in some reasonable relationship to gross revenues? The IRS auditor I had understood that my part-time, cattle business would never show net income owing to legitimate farm-business expenses, such as mortgage interest; depreciation; loan interest for livestock and equipment; purchase of non-depreciable supplies; and chronically low selling prices at market time.

Apart from spending two days watching the auditor comb through three years of receipts—all of which I had combed through in advance of the audit—I had no problem establishing that I was operating our 73-acre farm residence as a part-time farm business, with a B&B business in two bedrooms and two baths, and a home office in another room. Expenses exceeded income for the farm and the B&B, but they were proportional and in line with other Schedule Fs and Schedule Cs for the same levels of business activity. My receipts were well organized. The errors found were mainly those in adding long columns of receipts; some were in my favor, others were not. I walked the auditor through the house showing the B&B rooms, the B&B license, brochure, advertising and labeled spots in the refrigerator and pantry where we kept B&B supplies separate from our own food. I also walked the auditor around the farm, showing her the profit-based rationale for installing a rotational-grazing system (lots of fencing and gates) and winter-feeding barn. It was obvious that I was trying to crank out every dollar from the farm that I could. Showing worked.

There are three common IRS-ethics situations that you should consider before getting into any of them.

First, farming presents opportunities to not report income. Farmers can sell manure, hay, seasonal grazing rights, water, supplies, livestock, equipment and labor without leaving a paper trail. Not reporting cash income reduces gross income, hence taxable gain, hence tax owed. If you get caught doing this, expect no mercy. It's a deliberate cheating strategy.

Second, farming also presents opportunities to inflate expenditures. No one will know whether you paid your neighbor $1,000 or $1,500 for some hay, except your neighbor. If you claim $500 of phony hay cost, it will save you at most $175 in tax. The auditor will probably not pick this up from your records if you forge a receipt. Maybe your neighbor will cover for you, if the auditor asks. But do you really want to be a tax cheat, a forger and at the mercy of your neighbor? I think not.

Third, some individuals whom you hire for farm work or from whom you buy something for the farm will ask to be paid in cash. You might infer that they want cash so that no paper trail will establish that they received income. Cash payments, it might be further inferred, may not be reported to the IRS by those who receive them. A cash payment is usually made without the payer—that is, you—obtaining a receipt. If these payments are for legitimate business or farm expenses keep some record of them and write them off. If an auditor asks why you have no receipt, simply say that you paid in cash. If the auditor wants further confirmation of the expense, try to get a receipt. Don't be surprised if that turns out to be harder to obtain than it should be. I would not advise shorting yourself on legitimate deductions for business expenses because the vendor wants cash. What he does with your cash payment and his 1040 is his affair, not yours.

BASIS

The IRS taxes **ordinary income**, such as wages and salaries, on a sliding scale that imposes higher rates on higher incomes. The highest rate on ordinary income for 2006 was 35 percent for single filers, married joint filers and heads of households earning $336,550 or more in taxable income. In descending order, the tax rates are 33 percent, 28 percent, 25 percent, 15 percent and ten percent. (www.bankrate.com/brm/itax/2005taxrates.asp) The IRS has a two-step sliding scale for most **long-term capital gains**, which is the net profit on the sale of capital assets held for more than one year. Depending on the taxpayer's income, the current scale for long-term capital gains is ten percent or 15 percent. (See discussion in Chapter 31.) Farming can provide income of both kinds. The tax-wise farmer in the high tax brackets wants as much of his income classified as capital gains as possible.

If capital assets are sold after one year of ownership, they qualify for the IRS's **long-term capital-gains rate**, which is commonly shortened to, the capital-gains rate. Sale of tangible or intangible business property is not technically a "capital asset" sale although the gain may be taxed as "capital gains." Rather, it's a gain or loss on the sale of a **Section 1231 asset**, which is property used in a trade or business. The gain on a 1231 asset is capital, but the loss is ordinary—the best of both worlds. The highest capital-gains rate is now 15 percent which is applied against the taxpayer's **taxable gain**, i.e., net gain on the sale of the capital asset. Only capital assets, such as land, property, buildings, rental units, big pieces of equipment, depreciated items, vehicles, timber and minerals, qualify for the capital-gains rate. Sale of livestock or crops will be taxed as ordinary income, even if you hold them for longer than one year. They are not considered capital assets.

To figure your taxable gain, you must first calculate what your **adjusted basis** is in the asset. **Basis** is an IRS term that refers to the dollars the taxpayer has "in" the asset. You need to understand basis and its adjustments, because **adjusted basis** is the number that is subtracted from net sale revenue to produce your **taxable gain**. Your tax obligation will be determined by multiplying your taxable gain by the appropriate tax rate. Some expenditures the taxpayer makes increase his basis, and other expenses have no affect because they are deducted against current income. Depreciation decreases a taxpayer's basis in the asset that he's depreciating. **Adjusted basis**, then is, the taxpayer's net basis left in the asset after all permissible additions and subtractions to his beginning basis—the original cost of acquisition—are made.

Adjusted Basis = Original purchase cost of the asset

+ Permissible expenses related to purchase
+ Capital improvements made to the asset
- Depreciation (if any)
- Previous sale of part of the asset (if any)

Adjusted basis starts with the taxpayer's **beginning basis**, that is, the cost of acquisition. Beginning basis in property will include the amount of money you pay to the seller, plus routine acquisition-related expenses—attorney fees, escrow fees, recording costs, broker or finder's fee, appraisal cost, survey cost, title search, title insurance, cost of acquiring outstanding leases, inspection fees and other miscellaneous expenses. Farmowners will do things over time that change their beginning basis, often significantly. All expenditures that prolong the capital asset's useful life or add to its value are added into its basis, dollar for dollar. Such expenditures include construction and/or reconstruction, other improvements, certain special assessments, casualty losses and demolition losses. The sale of a portion of an asset, such as selling timber from the land asset or selling a five-acre lot from a 100-acre farm, decreases basis in the root asset, in these examples, the land and the farm. With certain assets, such as minerals and timber, your CPA may set them up independently, each with its own basis that is adjusted over time.

It is the taxpayer's adjusted basis, not his beginning or original basis, that is used to figure taxable gain when the asset is sold. **Taxable gain** on the sale of a capital asset is figured this way:

Taxable Gain = Gross sales income to the taxpayer/seller
-Permissible expenses related to sale
-Adjusted Basis

Taxable gain is considered a **long-term capital gain** if the taxpayer holds a capital asset, such as land or a tractor, for more than one year from the date of purchase. Sold within one year of acquisition, the taxpayer will pay on the capital asset's taxable gain at his **ordinary income** rate. Most readers will probably fall into the higher tax brackets for ordinary income, which means you will benefit from treating income as capital gains and paying a 15 percent tax where possible. (Capital-gains are taxed at different rates depending on how long the asset is held, taxpayer income, the type of asset and what type of account it is held in. I'm using 15 percent as a short-hand, because it is the highest and most likely rate.) Other things being equal, owners will net more from an asset sale after taxes if their gain qualifies as a long-term capital gain. It follows that where a taxpayer has a choice between selling an asset for a profit within his first year of ownership or sometime after the 365th day, he'll choose the latter because of the lower tax hit.

A buyer should start thinking about basis with his CPA prior to purchasing a farm. Your tax-preparing CPA can allocate total purchase basis among various component assets—land, depreciable buildings and structures, timber, minerals, equipment and so on. Basis in the components cannot exceed the property's total acquisition basis. You will need to have the basis allocation and depreciation schedules set up, beginning in the tax year that you bought the farm. All future adjustments are made to the basis values assigned in this first-year allocation. If you're planning to sell a component asset soon after buying the farm, it may be in your interest to allocate as much basis to this asset as you can. Ask your CPA for his suggestions about basis allocation in light of your plan. He will know the minimum basis value that he must assign to each asset. If you have managed to find a farm with a lot of immediate timber value, assign as much basis to your timber as you can so that you pay as little tax as possible when you sell it a few weeks after closing.

SEVERABLE ASSETS

Think of a farm purchase as a bundle of assets—a farmhouse, crop land, pasture, farm buildings, equipment, timber, minerals, rights and so on. Every buyer will consider most of his farm's assets as **core assets**, things he doesn't want to part with. Other items he might consider as **severable assets**, something that can be sold without materially detracting from the core farm assets that he wants to keep together as a unit. The larger the farm, the more severable assets the new owner is likely to find.

Selling a **severable asset** after a year of ownership is a handy **buying tactic** for farm properties that contain such assets. When you are formulating your offer to the seller, you can factor into your calculations the anticipated sale of one or more such assets after a year. In negotiating with a farm seller, be open to buying severable assets—throw ins—that you can sell after a year with only a 15 percent capital-gains hit. It's often more advantageous to hold that asset for a year and pay 15 percent on your gain than to flip immediately after purchase and pay as much as 35 percent. If your ordinary rate is 15 percent, then, of course, you would do better to flip rather than hold. Taxpayers in the 25-to-35 percent brackets are probably better holding, but it depends on the individual circumstances. The capital-gains rate helps a taxpayer who has little basis in an asset and sells for a lot of taxable gain. The sale of a severable asset can help to pay down the cost of buying the core property.

To minimize your tax payment on the sale of a severable asset, you need to do two things.

First, **obtain an appraisal of the individual severable asset's value prior to purchasing the property**. This valuation will help you in negotiating with the seller, and it will also establish your **beginning cost basis** in each asset that you plan to sell. (An appraisal of the entire property will not, as a general rule, provide values for each asset that in combination make up the target property.) The asset's appraisal is a neutral, third-party's estimate of its FMV. This appraisal should satisfy the IRS as to the severable asset's market value at the time you bought the whole property. Insofar as you plan to sell the severable asset, **you want the appraisal of any severable asset to come in as high as possible**. This will keep your tax liability as low as possible to the extent that it increases its basis and thus decreases your taxable gain on its sale whenever that occurs. Don't be shy about explaining your strategy to the appraiser. You should share with him as much information and evidence as you have to support your high valuation. A high appraisal may also help you sell the asset for a higher price. While it's true that you want to establish as high a basis in your severable asset as you can, you don't want to put money into the asset for the sole purpose of increasing your basis if a buyer will not pay you a proportionately higher price to make your additional investment worth your while. The tax tail should not wag the profit dog. Still, the idea is that the higher your basis in the severable asset you sell, the lower your taxable gain; the lower your taxable gain because of high basis, the lower your tax hit on the sale of the asset.

The severable asset's basis may increase or decrease between the day you buy the whole property (and establish your beginning basis) and the day you sell the asset. Basis will be adjusted according to what you do with the asset. A business-related asset like a barn will be depreciated, which decreases its basis over its depreciation-recovery period. If you add three stalls and a water system to the barn, you will have increased your basis. Basis does not increase on its own like land appreciation. Once your CPA sets up a depreciation schedule, basis in an asset will decrease each year. If you're selling soon after purchase, your asset's basis is not likely to have changed much in normal circumstances. When you sell timber, your basis in the timber asset will decrease; where sale income equals or exceeds your basis, it will vanish.

The net effect of additions and subtractions is your **adjusted basis**—what you have in the asset at the time of sale. Adjusted basis is subtracted from net sale income to arrive at taxable gain on the asset's sale. You then apply the appropriate tax rate to your taxable gain to determine the amount of tax you pay on the sale. If you sell your severable asset for the amount of its adjusted basis, you have no taxable gain, hence you will pay no tax on that gain at that point. If you sell your asset for more than its adjusted basis, you will pay either at a capital-gains rate or your ordinary income rate depending on the timing of the sale. The selling of timber from land you continue to own will reduce your basis in your timber, which will have the effect of increasing your taxable gain when you sell the land itself. The tax consequence of the timber sale will in most cases be deferred until you sell the land on which the sold timber stood. If the timbered land is passed on as part of your estate, there may never be any tax liability at all to anyone, depending on the size of your estate and how much estate value federal tax policy allows to be free of estate tax in the year of your death.

With the quick sale of a severable asset, is it possible that you can show a loss? Let's say you buy 100 acres for a total of $100,000. Your pre-purchase timber cruise indicated fair market value of $50,000 for the merchantable timber. Your CPA allocated your basis in the property as $50,000 in land and $50,000 in merchantable timber. When you sold the timber a month after closing, you only received $40,000 from the highest bidder in a competitively bid sale. You can take a loss of $10,000 on that sale of your merchantable timber. Or you might want to reallocate your basis between land and timber so that timber has a starting basis of $40,000, which produces no taxable gain on your sale.

Second, **you may want to determine the most efficient ways to increase both the value and the tax benefits of the severable asset before you sell it**. This is not a simple exercise, and you will need a CPA's advice on the tax angles for your individual circumstances.

Consider the following example. You buy 150 acres, of which your core keeper asset is 130 acres with a farm house and farm buildings. At the far end of the property, there is a smaller residence that the seller rented out. You decide during your scoping that you want to sell the rental house and 20 acres. You pay $400,000 for the 150 acres, and your appraisal for the rental house is $50,000. Your CPA allocates your beginning basis in the entire property as follows:

Small rental house basis	$50,000
Residence basis	100,000
Farm buildings basis	25,000
Land, 150 acres @ $1,500/A basis	225,000
Total Original Basis	$400,000

(I'm simplifying your beginning basis by not adjusting for purchase expenses that increase your basis.) Let's further assume that you borrow the entire purchase price of $400,000. (I'm simplifying again, by not considering borrowing expenses, such as fees and points.)

Your plan is to sell the smaller house and 20 acres in which you have a beginning basis of $50,000 in the house and $30,000 in the land (20 acres x $1,500/A = $30,000), for a total beginning basis of $80,000 in the asset that you want to sell. If you do nothing to the property over your first year of ownership and then sell it for $80,000 against $80,000 in basis, there is no taxable gain in this deal. (I'm simplifying again by not reducing your basis in the rental house by one year's depreciation or paying the 25 percent tax on recaptured depreciation at the time of its sale.) This means you have $80,000 in your hand deferred of tax, and possibly free of it depending on other things that you do and don't do.

If you sell the smaller house and the land for $100,000 after one year of ownership, you will have a capital gain of $20,000. If you pay a capital-gains rate of 15 percent on your taxable gain, you will owe the IRS $3,000 (.15 x $20,000 = $3,000), for an after-tax net profit of $17,000. You will have made a $20,000 gross profit and a $17,000 after-tax net profit by repackaging the two assets—rental house and a little land—into one, then scheduling the sale for a year and a day after you bought the entire property.

Your strategy in buying the original property was a simple variation of "**buy all of it wholesale; sell some of it retail**." The twist in this example is that you divided the property into pieces and then combined two pieces to make a marketable sale property. Smaller acreages always fetch a higher per acre price than larger acreages of the same type. You might have made even more by packaging the rental house with five acres and then dividing the remaining 15 acres into three five-acre lots. Your strategy rested on having an FMV appraisal of the rental house in hand prior to your purchase. If the house appraisal was on the high side, that would lower your taxable gain. Allocation-of-basis decisions may be made by your CPA at the time of your purchase. Your CPA might help you by allocating more basis to the rental unit and proportionately less to the residence that you're keeping and putting into your estate. The CPA's allocation cannot be arbitrary or unreasonable, but within those guidelines, judgment can be exercised.

You can consider adding value to this house prior to its sale in two ways, each of which has different tax consequences.

First, you can make **maintenance-related repairs and upkeep** whose costs you write off against your income in the year they are incurred. "**Write off**" means subtract from gross income; a **deduction** is a write off. For tax purposes, consider this house a rental unit whether or not you rent it out during the year that you own it. Maintenance costs might include exterior and interior painting, fixing broken windows, replacing a broken toilet, refinishing a floor and patching a roof. Together, these maintenance costs amount to $10,000 and bring you an additional $10,000 in sales income above what the house would have brought without the repairs. (More often than not, cosmetic repairs of this type more than pay for themselves by working together to create an overall favorable impression of a property cared for and in good order.) You can also write off the $10,000 in repairs if you use the entire house during that year exclusively for some business purpose—such as a farm office; a storage facility for farm and business records, farm equipment and supplies; or a business library and conference area. If you are not using the house for business and are simply sprucing up an investment for sale, you can deduct maintenance expenses in the year you incur them. Money a taxpayer puts into maintenance repairs and upkeep—whether a rental unit or not—does not increase his basis in the asset.

Your sales price of $110,000 is now $30,000 more than your $80,000 beginning basis in the house and 20 acres. You've not put any money into a property improvement that would significantly increase the house's value or extend its life—that type of expenditure would increase your basis. After one year, that $30,000 is a long-term capital gain on which you pay 15 percent, or $4,500, in tax. (Had you sold the rental house and 20 acres within your first year of ownership, your taxable gain would have been taxed at your ordinary rate.) The $10,000 in maintenance repairs that you've made reduces your gross income in the ownership year by $10,000. At the 35 percent tax rate on ordinary income, this write off would save you $3,500 in income tax on your return filed for the year you incurred these costs. By waiting a year, you will pay $1,500 in capital-gains tax on the extra $10,000 in sales income. If you had flipped the property during your first ownership year for $10,000 more after the repairs, you would have saved $3,500 in tax against your gross income but paid $3,500 as tax at your ordinary rate on the extra taxable gain of $10,000. If you hold for more than a year, you get the $3,500 in deductions for the repair year and a tax hit of $1,500 on the $10,000 in taxable gain. Your total capital-gains tax is $4,500 (.15 x $30,000 taxable capital gain = $4,500). But you've saved $3,500 in overall tax payment in the first year by writing off the $10,000 in maintenance repairs against your gross income.

Your net tax situation looks like this:

Capital Gains Tax on $30,000	= $4,500	($110,000 income -$80,000 basis)
Tax savings from $10,000 write off	- 3,500	
Net Tax	$1,000 on sale of house and 20 acres	

While you make a tax payment of $1,500 on the additional $10,000 in capital-gains income you've made from the $10,000 in maintenance, it really only costs you $1,000 in tax when your total tax obligation is netted out over two years. If you did not actually rent out your rental house during the year you were off-and-on repairing it, you can still take deductions for maintenance and upkeep on Schedule E as long as it was available for rent during the year. Remember: maintenance repairs and upkeep are expensed against income in the year your incur them and do not increase your basis.

Second, you can add value to rental houses and business-related structures by making **capital improvements**. Improvements include room additions or replacement of a major system, such as plumbing, HVAC, roof or foundation. This type of expense is defined as one that extends the life of the asset or adds significant value to it. Unlike maintenance repairs and upkeep, the costs you incur for capital improvements must be **depreciated**, about which more below. The money that you invest in a capital improvement cannot be deducted in the year that you incur the cost, but it will be added to your basis, which helps you when you sell.

Let's say you add a second full bathroom to the small rental house that you want to sell. It costs $10,000, and you receive $10,000 more in house-sale income than you would have without it. The $10,000 improvement boosts your starting basis in the property by $10,000. You sell the improved property for $110,000, but your basis has now increased to $90,000 instead of $80,000. So your taxable gain is $20,000 ($110,000 in sales income -$90,000 in adjusted basis = $20,000), on which you pay the 15 percent capital-gains rate, or $3,000.

In this example, you would be better off to add value through maintenance repairs than through a capital improvement, because you would pay only $1,000 in net tax over two years instead of $3,000 in capital-gains tax during your second ownership year. Talk over adding-value options with your CPA to determine which are the most tax efficient in light of your selling plans and individual circumstances.

As a general rule, maintenance-type repairs and cosmetic brightening will generate more sales revenue than they cost. If you can combine these deductible expenses with classifying the income as a capital gain, you should come out ahead in net-after-tax income compared with putting the same number of dollars into a capital improvement prior to sale. Capital improvements—roof replacements, rewiring, replumbing, bathrooms, swimming pools and kitchens—do not generally pay for themselves dollar for dollar, though the degree of discount varies from improvement to improvement. The worst situation—at least in a theoretical sense—is to make a capital improvement and then flip the rental house in your first ownership year, thus paying tax on your sale gain at your ordinary rate. These relationships change internally depending on your tax bracket. The carrying costs of mortgage interest and property taxes should also be factored into your calculations.

Let me continue with the idea of selling your new farm's small rental house in light of **depreciation**, which is a tax-accounting process that occurs on your returns whether or not it occurs in the condition of the house itself. The common occurrence, of course, is for an improvement like a rental house to depreciate in value on paper for tax purposes while appreciating in value on the ground.

The general depreciation rule set forth in **Section 167** is that a reasonable allowance for exhaustion, wear and tear, and obsolescence can be taken on property used in the taxpayer's trade or business, or property held for the production of income. The taxpayer's original cost—basis—in an income-producing property is recovered over time by taking a portion of it each year in the form of a depreciation deduction. Rental property, which is held for income production, is depreciated. The house and its new bathroom in this example can be depreciated even if it did not yield any rental income since rental-income production was your intention and the house was capable of being rented.

Depreciation reduces your gross income and lowers your tax liability each year that a portion of an asset's cost is deducted. Different types of assets have different depreciation schedules (recovery periods), ranging from three years for a race horse more than two years old at the time it's placed in service, to five years for a pick-up truck, to ten years for a single purpose agricultural structure to 27.5 years for residential rental property. Commercial property and commercial rental property are currently depreciated over 39 years. Buildings and improvements have much longer depreciation periods than equipment. Generally, a shorter depreciation schedule will be more tax-advantageous to most taxpayers, though the total amount the taxpayer can depreciate is determined by original basis. Basis in the property or asset is decreased each year in equal steps, according to whichever recovery period applies.

The IRS provides several depreciation formulas, each with its own rules. These and related information are found in Section 167 (a), Depreciation—General Rule; Section 168, Accelerated cost recovery system; and Section 179, Election to expense certain depreciable business assets. Revenue Ruling 69-229, 1969-1 CB 86 sets forth the principles that distinguish capital expenditures taken as depreciation from maintenance expenses deductible as ordinary and necessary business expenses.

When thinking about depreciating a new asset, you also need to consider the potential applicability of the **Section 179 deduction** when you acquire what are called **1245 (a)(3) assets** that are used in business. Qualifying business equipment bought and placed into service in 2006 could have up to $108,000 of the cost deducted in the purchase year, instead of depreciated over seven years. A taxpayer can choose to take a Section 179 deduction for the full cost of a qualifying asset, or depreciate the full cost, or take some of the cost as a deduction and the rest as depreciation. Qualifying 1245 property, new and used, must be tangible, depreciable under Section 168 and acquired by purchase for use in the active conduct of a trade or business. Office furniture, telephones, appliances, books, fax machines and farm-related equipment used for a farm business qualify. Business vehicles with a gross vehicle weight of more than three tons—like a big SUV or pick-up truck—can be deducted up to $25,000 if they are used at least 50 percent for business in the first year. Equipment used in a rental property would not qualify unless your business is operating rental properties. If you rent out your new farm, you cannot deduct the cost of your new tractor under Section 179, but you can depreciate it. The IRS would not consider a taxpayer who rents his farm actively engaged in a farm business so the newly purchased tractor would not fit within Section 179, but it would if you were actively operating a farm business. The maximum Section 179 deduction will be adjusted for inflation annually through 2009 when it falls to $25,000 in 2010. Financing has no effect on the 179 deduction. There are other limits on using Section 179 involving a cap on the cost of the property and setting the amount of the expensed property as no more than the total amount of taxable income derived from the active conduct of the trade or business. Current Section 179 terms may or may not be changed, so you need to check with your CPA in the year you are thinking of making such a purchase to determine what level of deduction, if any, is available.

Your personal residence cannot be depreciated and neither can land. Any property or asset that a taxpayer holds for personal use—vehicle, ATV, boat, shop equipment, computer—cannot be depreciated. You cannot depreciate a second home unless it qualifies as either a rental property or as a business property.

The IRS has four ways of categorizing second homes, which have different levels of tax benefits. All second homes qualify for deducting mortgage interest and property taxes. The four categories sort themselves by the amount of time the taxpayer spends in the second home.

Category 1: Fewer than 14 days of annual rental. The taxpayer can deduct mortgage interest, property taxes and uninsured casualty loss, but not insurance, maintenance and depreciation. The taxpayer does not need to report this rental income.

Category 2: Taxpayer uses second home either more than 14 days or ten percent of rental days, which are days rented over 14. The taxpayer can deduct mortgage interest, property taxes, uninsured casualty loss, loss expenses, operating expenses, insurance, maintenance, repairs and depreciation. When these expenses exceed rental income, the taxpayer cannot apply that excess loss to his other income. But he can suspend these losses and take them in the future. The taxpayer must take expenses in the order listed above.

Category 3: Taxpayer uses second home less than either 15 days or ten percent of rental days. In both cases, the taxpayer has no limit as to how much tax loss he can take against ordinary income, subject to the $25,000 passive-loss cap for taxpayers with adjusted gross income of $100,000 or less for 2005. This taxpayer, in other words, can take up to $25,000 of qualifying loss, including depreciation, against other income. Loss in excess of $25,000 is suspended and carried into the future. To take passive-activity loss from a second home rental, you must "**materially participate**" in managing it. Material participation requires at least a ten percent ownership interest, and the rental property cannot be part of a rental pool that others manage. There are other tests as well.

When a taxpayer materially participates on a regular, continuous and substantial basis, he can deduct losses in full from his trade or business. Both his losses and income are treated as nonpassive (active) and are deductible. A taxpayer who rents out his second home is considered to be engaged in a passive activity. If he "materially participates" in his passive activity, he can take losses. The IRS has seven tests to establish material participation, with the taxpayer having to meet only one of the seven. These are:

1. He participates in the activity for more than 500 hours during the tax year.

2. His participation amounts to all of the participation in the activity of all individuals— owners and non-owners—for the tax year.

3. He participates in the activity for more than 100 hours during the tax year, and he participates no less than any other person.

4. The activity is classified as a significant participation activity, which your CPA needs to explain to you.

5. He materially participated in the activity for any five of the immediately preceding ten tax years.

6. The activity is a personal service activity, and he materially participated for any three tax years preceding the tax year.

7. He participated in the activity on a regular, continuous and substantial basis during the tax year, for more than 100 hours. (See IRS Temporary Regulation, Section 1.469-5T.)

Category 4: Taxpayer doesn't use second home, except for a few days of repair time. Every expense is deductible as long as the property was either rented or available for rent. A reasonable amount of travel expenses to inspect or repair the property may also be deducted. (See Robert Bruss, "Real Estate Newsletter," February, 2006.)

The tax benefits of a second home by themselves would not justify the expense of acquiring one. Where, however, loss can be taken against ordinary income and the second home is appreciating on the ground, a second home is a helpful investment.

Loss has a different benefit for each tax bracket. A taxpayer in the 15 percent bracket pays $150 on every $1,000 in taxable income. If he has a $100 second home loss per $1,000 in taxable income, he reduces his taxable income to $900 and his tax is lowered by $15 ($900 x 15% = $135.) A taxpayer in the 35 percent bracket pays $350 per $1,000 in taxable income. A $100 second home loss for him reduces his taxable income to $900, on which he would pay $315 in tax ($900 x 35% = $315). He saves $35 in tax. For the same level of loss, the 35%-taxpayer saves more than twice as much as the 15-percent taxpayer. In both cases, taxpayers want their out-of-pocket, second-home expenses—mortgage interest, property tax, maintenance, insurance—covered by their rental income, and the tax loss to be generated by depreciation as much as possible.

Depreciation is complicated, and I would advise against trying to figure it out with no more than a high IQ and a Ph.D. in logic.

Depreciation of a capital asset is an obvious tax benefit that owners of farms, businesses and rental properties use. But depreciation comes with two costs of its own. First, depreciation of rental property, business property, equipment and improvements used in an income-producing operation (like a farm) lowers the taxpayer's basis in that asset, which in typical circumstances will increase the taxable gain at the time of its sale. Second, when you sell depreciated real estate, you will pay a 25 percent tax on the amount of money you depreciated. This is called the **depreciation recapture rate**. When figuring your total tax due on the sale of real property after one year, the 25 percent recapture tax is applied to the depreciated amount and paid at your ordinary-income rate; remaining tax liability is taxed at your appropriate capital-gains rate. Recapture can burn you. If you were to buy a country rental house for $100,000 when the market was high and sold it for $100,000 five years later when the market was soft, you would end up netting no income on the sale but owing the IRS several thousand dollars in recapture tax on the five years of depreciation you took.

Remember my example of the small residential rental house at the back of the farm? Instead of considering it a residential rental, you might want to think of it as a non-residential rental property that you intend to rent to a self-employed individual or business. This house might appeal to a writer, artist, contractor, craftsperson, consultant, telecommuter and so on. In this circumstance, you can take a **50 percent depreciation bonus** write off for certain types of improvements in your first year, subject to 1) the improvement is made or pursuant to a lease, 2) the portion of the building where the improvements are made is exclusively tenant occupied, and 3) the improvement must be placed in service more than three years after the building itself was put into service. Certain types of improvements do not qualify for the 50 percent depreciation bonus—enlarging the building, elevators, a structural component that benefits a common area and work on the building's internal structure. Qualifying improvements include electrical and plumbing systems, permanent lighting fixtures, heating and air-conditioning systems, security systems, and non-maintenance recarpeting, retiling and repainting. Non-real estate assets that qualify for the 50 percent first-year depreciation bonus include trucks, trailers, business furniture, business machines, computers and most software. You might find a situation where the numbers work in favor of having you rent the small house for three years, then redo it as a rental office for a lease-holding tenant, after which you sell it and 20 acres to the tenant. The maximum amount you can expense under the 50 percent bonus in the first year is $100,000. This 50 percent bonus was enacted in 2003. A property to qualify must have been acquired after May 5, 2003 and before January 1, 2005. It must have been placed in service before January 1, 2005. Like all other tax breaks, this one is subject to change.

Related to tax issues is how you take ownership of your newly purchased farm or farmland. You, your CPA and your lawyer should choose the **most advantageous ownership structure for your farm in light of at least seven generic needs: 1) estate planning, 2) minimize annual income tax, 3) minimize tax when you sell or otherwise dispose of the farm and its component assets, 4) privacy, 5) protection from creditors, 6) liability and 7) control of property**. I discuss ownership considerations in later chapters. This is an important decision, so make sure your CPA and lawyer have experience in evaluating alternative farmownership structures.

92

ESTATE TAXES

Most farm operations don't make much net profit, though they do keep money flowing through the farm economy. It's hard for small and mid-size operations to squeeze savings and capital out of their cash flow. Therefore, the common pattern is for farmers to build wealth through the long-term appreciation of their farm operations and land. Their heirs get most of the benefit. The less tax their estates pay, the higher the pass through.

Many farmers complained to their political representatives in the 1990s that the **federal estate tax** fell with particular harshness on them, owing to their common plight of being land wealthy and cash poor. They wanted the elimination of this so-called "**death tax**," referring to the federal estate tax that applied when the decedent's taxable estate exceeded the tax-exempt amount. Heirs—family farmers—said they were forced to sell the decedent's farm to pay this tax.

This was infrequently the case from what I can determine, though undoubtedly it occurred. Most estates paid no federal estate tax at all, because they either fell beneath the taxable estate cap (the exemption amount was $675,000 in 2001 with a top rate of 56 percent), or they were passed on tax-free to a surviving spouse, heirs and/or charity. Only two percent (48,000) of all U.S. estates paid any federal tax in 1998, and only 1,200 of those were made up primarily of farms and small businesses. (Jane Bryant Quinn, "Winners, Whiners and the Estate Tax," Washington Post, August 13, 2000.) A Congressional Budget Office study in 2005 found that estate returns filed by farmers and small business owners in 1999 and 2000 confirmed that only a small number of such estates were too cash poor to pay their tax. Only 1,659 farm estates had taxes due in 2000, and only 138 of those reported inadequate liquid assets to cover their liability. At the 2005 exemption of $1,500,000, only 300 farm estates would have owed any tax, and only 27 of that number would have been pinched. By 2009, when the exempt amount rises to $3,500,000, only 65 farm estates would owe taxes, of whom only 13 would be cash-strapped. (Washington Post, "Estate Tax Myths," July 24, 2005.) Overall, of the 2.3 million individuals who died in 2004, only 30,276 estate tax returns were filed; 3,500 estates were greater than $5 million—and they paid about two-thirds of all estate taxes. (Christopher Swann, "Estate tax repeal is on its last legs," Financial Times, June 13, 2006, quoting Joanne Johnson, wealth adviser at JP Morgan Private Bank.) Swann reported no evidence that family farms were being sold because of the "death tax."

While the tax rates on estates exceeding the exemption cap ranged from 37 to 55 percent in 1996, an IRS study found that the average tax on estates of $600,000 to $1 million in that year was only six percent. The higher rates fell on the very wealthy and/or those who did no estate planning. A federal estate tax return had to be filed only if the decedent's cumulative gifts and estate value exceeded the exemption amount. Thus under the old rules, 98 percent of estates never had to file a federal estate return. Under the old rules, every individual estate was entitled to a federal unified credit that amounted to an exemption of $675,000 on the decedent's taxable estate in 2001. **Taxable estate** represents the gross value of the estate, less allowable deductions. The taxable estate is always less than the gross estate.

Here is a summary of exclusion amounts and tax rates between 2001 and 2011.

New Tax Law, 2001

Individual

YEAR	Old Exclusion Amount	New Exclusion Amount	New Highest Marginal Rate Above Exclusion Amount
2001	$675,000	$ 675,000	55%
2002	700,000	1,000,000	50
2003	700,000	1,000,000	49
2004	850,000	1,500,000	48
2005	950,000	1,500,000	47
2006	1,000,000	2,000,000	46
2007	1,000,000	2,000,000	45
2008	1,000,000	2,000,000	45
2009	1,000,000	3,500,000	45
2010	1,000,000	Repealed (no cap)	Repealed
2011	675,000	675,000	55

The new rules under the 2001 tax-cut legislation provided for an annual increase in the exemption cap to $3,500,000 and a gradual reduction to a 45 percent top rate in 2009. Exemption means the estate is not required to pay any federal tax on taxable amounts less than the cap. In 2010, the exemption is repealed under the 2001 legislation, which means that wealthy individuals with strong family values should schedule their estates for that year. In 2011, the $675,000 exemption cap and top rate of 55 percent (the 2001 rules) are reimposed. It's difficult to imagine that this death lottery will not be modified before taking effect since it makes absolutely no sense. As I write in the summer of 2005, Congress is again debating whether to abolish the estate tax entirely, recast the truly nutty rules for 2010 and 2011, impose a flat 15 percent rate or increase the tax burden on the very richest estates. My bet is that only the largest estates—farm and otherwise—will pay federal tax in the future, which was the case even before the 2001 legislation was enacted.

Individuals whose estates are likely to be subject to the estate tax are usually smart enough to have their CPA and lawyer develop an estate plan that reduces their taxable estate so as to lower the anticipated tax bite. This involves transfers of wealth to others, charitable donations and gifts, along with different ways of structuring the ownership and control of assets. Many ways are available for individuals to give or transfer assets and income streams to family, beneficiaries or trusts to reduce their estates.

Many farmers—and others—avoid federal estate taxes by using the full tax-free exemption and then leaving everything above the cap to the surviving spouse, which is known as the **unlimited marital deduction**. A tax burden then falls on the spouse's estate when it exceeds the joint cap.

The current rules do contain a clinker for the tax conscious. Under the old rules, a beneficiary would inherit assets whose value was determined at the time of death. The gain in an asset's value, between its cost at time of purchase (beginning basis) and its value at time of death, was put into the taxable estate on which the estate tax was figured. The asset's value at time of death is called the **stepped-up basis**. The estate might pay a tax on the gain, but the beneficiary did not since he was being given the asset with the tax already figured against and paid by the estate. Once the beneficiary possessed the inherited asset, his gain over the succeeding years was figured against the stepped-up basis at the time of inheritance rather than the original cost paid by the decedent. Under the new law in 2010, the beneficiary receives the asset on a **carry-over basis,** which is the original basis not the stepped-up basis. There exists an "allocation" with carry-over basis whereby the carry-over basis is usually higher than the original basis. The 2001 law shifts the tax burden from the estate to the beneficiary. On assets that have greatly appreciated, this will produce significant tax hits even at a 15 percent capital-gains rate. Eliminating the "death tax" will mean that heirs will pay a capital-gains tax on inherited real estate—like farms and timberland, going back to the original basis in the property.

When the estate tax is repealed in 2010 under current law, many estates will end up paying more in taxes, not less. Allan Sloan wrote:

> under the 2009 rules, estates of up to $3.5 million ($7 million for a married couple) would be exempt from federal estate tax. The tax rate on assets above that level would be 45 percent. Inheritors would be able to step up the basis of $3.5 million (or $7 million) of inherited assets to their value the day they inherit them. Flash forward to 2010, when the estate tax is repealed. ...heirs would be able to step up only $1.3 million in assets to their value on the day of death. ...assets above $1.3 million would be valued for tax purposes at carry-over basis—their cost (for income-tax purposes) for the person who died. So any estate with $1.3 million to $3.5 million in assets ($2.6 million to $7 million for a married couple) is worse off under full repeal in 2010 than it would be in 2009. Inheritors in the $1.3 million-to-$3.5 million range would face higher taxes if they sold inherited assets than they would under the 2009 rules. ...but if you're dealing with an estate of $3.5 billion, you'd be far better off inheriting in 2010. (Allan Sloan, "Doing a Big Favor for the 'Small Rich,'" Newsweek, June 19, 2006.)

A study by the Congressional Joint Committee on Taxation projected that 7,500 estates would pay the federal estate tax in 2009, none would pay in 2010 and 63,900 estates would be worse off in 2010 than in 2009. The wealthiest estates benefit from repeal; the least wealthy wealthy are hit harder; the vast majority of estates are unaffected. Most farmers who would be ensnared in an estate tax would be the small rich, not the big rich.

In June of 2006, the Senate rejected President Bush's effort to repeal the estate tax permanently. A few weeks later, House Republicans introduced legislation that would retain a reduced estate tax on the wealthiest estates and eliminate it for estates less than $5 million, beginning in 2010.

The tax rate for estates worth between $5 million and less than $25 million would be the capital-gains rate, now 15 percent, compared with 2006's 46% estate-tax rate. Estates above $25 million would be taxed at twice the capital-gains rate, a cut of 16 percent. (Brody Mullins, "House Republicans May Settle for a Muted Estate-Tax Reduction," Wall Street Journal, June 20, 2006.)

The 2001 law did not repeal the **gift tax**. The exemption amounts that continue to be in effect until 2010 **unify** the gift exemption and the estate exemption. You can get a tax benefit by gifting an asset but the value of that gift is added into your estate on which you may pay a tax if the estate's value exceeds the exemption amount. In 2010, the top gift tax rate will be reduced to 35 percent, the top individual rate. The gift tax will survive repeal of the estate tax, as I write.

Farmers, rather than sad-sack victims of jack-booted IRS thugs, were—and still are—better situated than most individuals to protect their assets from estate taxes. Much of a farmer's estate is tied up in land, improvements and equipment rather than easily valued and easily sold mutual funds and stocks. The executor need only open a book to determine the value of the decedent's three-year-old sedan, but the value of a barn, or a lot, or subsurface minerals, or a stand of timber are matters of judgment. On such farm items, the cash value can be typically discounted by as much as 50 percent. The degree of discount for a farmowner like you depends, of course, on the degree of anticipated scrutiny.

Another common discount tactic is to use **property-tax valuations** to assign a fair market value to the farm's land, structures and minerals. Despite periodic reappraisals, these assessed values frequently underestimate fair market value. Valuing with property-tax assessments can lower the value of most estates with a land asset, but it helps most those estates, like farms, whose assets are disproportionately concentrated in taxed property. It appears to me to be the case that rural property assessments always lag current fair market values. In this fashion, the estate of the land-rich, cash-poor farmowner from Blue Grass, Virginia is advantaged over the cash-rich, land-poor investment banker from Wall Street. This is one more reason why both bulls and bears like to buy and operate farms.

Farm estates can also benefit from inherent difficulties in placing a fair market value on **fractional ownership interests**. When, as is usually the case with large farms, the property ownership is organized either as a family corporation or a closely held entity (e.g., corporation, partnership, limited liability company, family limited liability corporation, limited partnership), the decedent's fractional share will usually be discounted owing to its lack of broad marketability and minority. The same discounting can occur when a farm is operated as a "non-organized" business (sole proprietorship without any additional legal structure). In this case, it is not fractional ownership that is hard to value, but the assets and profitability of the farm itself. Judgment, once again, can be applied to discount the estate's farm value.

The IRS does not have a fixed set of rules for valuing a business or a farm business. The Agency looks at certain "factors," including the nature of the business, its financial history, the economic outlook for the type of business, book value of stock, current financials, future earning capacity, dividend history, stock sales and comparables. If the heirs sell the farm soon after the decedent's death, the IRS will value the farm at the net sale price. If there is an agreement among the owners on a value for each interest prior to any death, that value could be presumed to represent fair market value since all the owners are both willing to buy and sell at that price.

The estates of farmers and woodland owners can also be discounted when the present value of the estate's merchantable timber is not determined through a consulting forester's **cruise**. A cruise is a sampling technique by which the forester estimates the volume of timber and projects its current dollar value. Timber that has immediate sale value is referred to as "**merchantable timber**." (Timber cruises and related issues are discussed in Chapters 18-24.) Without a current cruise, wooded land in an estate would usually be assigned a **default value**, typically the off-the-shelf, property-tax valuation for generic woodland in the county. Where the woodland has recently been timbered, the property-tax assessed value will overestimate fair market value of the acreage, since the tract will not produce another crop of trees for 20 to 80 years, depending on the land and the tree species. In that situation, the estate should hire a forester to cruise the recent cutover land to get an appraisal value that's more realistic, i.e., lower, than the property-tax valuation.

Consider the opposite situation. An estate finds itself with woodland that contains a substantial amount of merchantable timber. Here, the estate will want to use the property-tax valuation, which can easily be $1,000 to $1,500 per acre lower than the timberland's true fair market value. Estates containing a lot of merchantable timber can be worth two or even three times more than the property-tax value. Undervaluation of this type of asset benefits the estate at the expense of the tax collector. The estate, obviously, should not sell the timber, because that act would accurately establish its value. The better strategy is to convey the woodland to the heirs as is. The heirs should have a cruise done immediately to establish the value of the timber, which will be their **timber basis** for tax purposes. The heirs can then sell the timber with little, if any, taxable gain inasmuch as they are selling the timber for what the forester determined was its value at the time of their inheritance.

Charles Davenport, a tax specialist at the Rutgers School of Law and former assistant director for tax analysis in the Congressional Budget Office, argued that a farm couple under the old 2001 rules who planned properly could pass about $8 million in assets to the next generation free of federal estate taxation. That's $6,650,000 more than the $1,350,000 joint exemption in effect before the 2001 legislation. The first step in organizing a farm to achieve this end would have been to establish a **limited liability company (LLC)** in which the farmowner and his spouse each held 49 percent ownership. Each principal is considered a minority interest, and such interests are difficult to value given the lack of marketability. The residual two percent could be held in Professor Davenport's words by "almost anybody, including one of the street homeless if there is no other deserving person." (Charles Davenport, e-mail to Curtis Seltzer, May 17, 2001.) The farm interest is now a minority interest that passes to a trust when the first spouse dies. By passing the first estate to the trust, it is not aggregated with the estate of the surviving spouse. The joint farm asset worth $8 million is divided into two equal 49 percent shares, each of which is worth $3.92 million. Owing to the lack of marketability and other discount factors, each spouse's estate would be valued at a 50 percent discount, that is, $1.96 million apiece. From that sum, $750,000—the unified credit—is deducted from each estate. Where land is a large part of each estate, it is possible to get all of the $750,000, Professor Davenport says. Subtracting $750,000 from $1.96 million leaves $1.21 million, which was less than the unified credit and the small business deduction of Section 2057 together under the old rules. This farm-owning couple armed with an LLC, a trust and tax planning that set up the farm as a small business could have protected most if not all of $8 million in joint assets from estate tax. The higher exemption caps would under the new rules, presumably, allow an even larger farm estate to be free of an estate tax. The cost of setting up the LLC and the trust might be $2,000 to $3,000, depending on an area's hourly rates for lawyers and CPAs. Farm-owning estates that exceed the exemption would do well to consider structuring their assets in light of Professor Davenport's observations. Using limited liability companies and trusts provide other tax benefits, liability protection and privacy apart from estate considerations.

If your estate is likely to be $2 million or more, you should talk with your CPA about setting up a **family limited partnership (FLIP)**. Under a limited partnership, a general partner runs the enterprise though he may own as little as one percent of the partnership's assets. Parents set up the FLIP with themselves as both general and limited partners. Then they gift to their children their limited partnership interests, 99 percent of the partnership's assets, but retain the one percent of the assets that is owned by the general partner. The parents continue to control the partnership and its assets, but they have given their kids 99 percent of the ownership. Accordingly, 99 percent of the partnership's assets are now removed from the parents' estates. Appreciation of the partnership's assets is out of the parents' estates as well. There is also a discounting process of about 40 percent that applies to the gift of the limited partnership interests, because ownership of these interests does not bring control. Farms are just the type of asset that are put into FLIPs. (See Jeff Schnepper, "Protect your family with a partnership," http://moneycentral.msn.com/content/ Taxes/ Taxshelters/P33545.asp; February 29, 2004.)

Lifetime gifts together with donations to charity are often used to whittle estates. As of 2006, an individual could give away as much as $12,000 a year to any person without incurring any taxation. The allowed annual gift exclusion is not counted against the unified credit and does not reduce the exemption cap. The 2001 tax act did **not** reduce or repeal federal gift taxes.

If the couple has set up a trust and transferred title to some or all of their farm assets into it **during their lifetimes**, estate sheltering becomes even more reliable and less dependent on Professor Davenport's 50 percent discount rate. **Lifetime asset transfer** is critical to keeping large estates, farms and others, under the cap. Spreading ownership of and income from your assets increases the family's spending income by reducing taxes. New taxpayers are created (who pay taxes at lower rates), and income is leveled, thus reducing the aggregate tax on the family. You can reduce the size of your estate without losing control of your assets or any of their benefits by creating one or more **trusts** to accept the transfer of your assets.

Trusts may be part of a comprehensive farmownership and farm-estate plan, depending on the amount and type of your assets. A **living trust** (which is different from a living will) is one way to hold real-estate title that avoids the delays and costs of probate. A **joint living trust** is a common choice that spouses make, which allows either to make decisions in the event of incapacity of the other without the expense of becoming a court-appointed guardian or conservator. Once created, you transfer assets and retitle them to the living trust which you can continue to control in your role as trustee. A co-trustee whom you name will assume control quickly and without complications in the event of your death or incapacity. A living trust can be **revocable**, that is, you can change or cancel it if you, the trustee, find it is not to your liking.

A living trust, standing alone, does not reduce an individual's estate taxes. For that reason, a second trust or other ownership structure (s) is needed whose purpose is to hold assets or pass them on with as few tax bites as possible. This can be done by placing assets in other types of trusts—**generation-skipping trust, charitable remainder trust, charitable lead trust, bypass trust and credit shelter trust, among others**—in conjunction with the living trust. You may also want to consider using life insurance to offset the bite of anticipated estate taxes and setting up a life insurance trust for further tax benefit.

Establishing the right farmownership structure and estate plan for a farm is not a do-it-yourself job over one weekend. Many ownership options exist, as do many estate-management structures. They intersect where estate-planning needs require certain ownership structures during your lifetime. The tax implications of various ownership structures and estate-plan components are both immediate and long-term. Trust laws differ from state to state, as do state inheritance and gift tax policies. Each state has its own set of rules for setting up corporations, partnerships and other entities. Whether or not you like lawyers and accountants, you should ask for their help in planning your farmownership, for both current tax benefits and as shelter for your estate.

The 2001 tax act does not free farmers and others from the need for tax and estate planning, especially since it's not certain whether the law will stand unchanged (which leaves the 2010 and 2011 crapshoots in place) or be modified. If your estate exceeds the rising exemption caps, I would advise you to have your CPA and estate lawyer work up a structure and a plan reasonably soon.

You can inform yourself of the general ideas involved in farmownership structures and estates through reviewing citations found at the **American Agricultural Law Association's** (AALA) website (http://www.aglaw-assn.org/biblio/), the section (#33) on Organizational Forms for Agriculture. Citations are provided on family farm corporations, S corporations, limited liability companies, partnerships and individual ownership. Experienced lawyers in farming communities should be knowledgeable about these ownership structures. AALA has more than 40 subject bibliographies relating to all aspects of farming. It's located at the Robert A. Leflar Law Center, University of Arkansas, Fayetteville, AR 72701; 501-575-7389; 501-575-5830 FAX; e-mail: bbabione@uark.edu. A selected bibliography on agricultural law in 2000 was published in the Spring, 2001, 54 Arkansas Law Review, by Sally J. Kelley *et al.* (earlier bibliographies go back to the mid-1980s). That document provides references on air quality, alternative agriculture, animal law, antitrust, aquaculture, bankruptcy, biotechnology, business organizations, commodity futures, cooperatives, credit and finance, endangered species and wildlife protection, energy, environmental issues, farm programs, food, food safety, forestry, general farm issues, intellectual property, international trade, invasive species, labeling, labor, land use, liability and insurance, marketing and sales, pesticides and herbicides, production contracts, property law, public lands, recreational use, soil conservation, taxation and estate planning, water quality, water rights and wetlands. All of the bibliographies are available through the **National Center for Agricultural Law** (NCAL) website at http://law.uark.edu/arklaw/aglaw (University of Arkansas, School of Law, Fayetteville, AR 72701; 501-7646; 501-575-5830 FAX; e-mail: awinfred@uark.edu).

The process of choosing from among these options and integrating your financial, legal and personal elements into a plan for current and estate purposes is too complicated and arcane for the layperson to do on his own. It's certainly too complicated and arcane for someone like me to offer advice. The interface between current ownership structures, tax minimization and estate planning is not a problem with a one-size-fits-all solution. Read a couple of background books so that you have a basic sense of what trusts do and how ownership structures can benefit both current and future tax obligations. Among those I found useful were: Martin M. Shenkman, The Complete Book of Trusts (New York: John Wiley & Sons, Inc., 1993, or most recent edition); Denis Clifford, Make Your Own Living Trust, 7th ed. (Berkeley: Nolo Press, 2005); and Kathleen Adams and Robert Brosterman, The Complete Estate Planning Guide (New York: New American Library, 1998, or most recent edition). Books on ownership entities are readily available. A local law school library will have vanilla forms along with detailed information that is given to lawyers at their Continuing Legal Education (CLE) seminars. Nothing, however, substitutes for competent CPA and legal assistance.

Two other considerations might be relevant in planning the best way to own land. If you have pre-college kids, you may want to think about how your ownership options affect each child's ability to qualify for financial aid if assistance might be required. Transfer of farm or landownership into your child's name or a trust with a child as the beneficiary may disqualify him from eligibility.

A second factor is providing for your own long-term elder care. If, for example, you are not likely to be able to self-finance such care and will need to rely on Medicaid to pay for nursing home costs, the current rules require that you spend almost 100 percent of your assets paying for your own care before you become eligible for the federal program. The Medicaid rules can be a huge bite out of your potential estate and can swallow all of it. This "tax" falls heaviest on the middle class whose members have some assets but not enough to finance long-term care. The poor qualify for Medicaid because they are poor and have few assets to spend down; the rich can afford to buy care on their own without liquidating their estates. To protect your assets, you have to structure or restructure their ownership in advance of when you would otherwise need to spend them down to finance your care. Consequently, it's best to think through the question of farmownership structure at the time of acquisition with a lawyer and an accountant in light of all your short-term and long-term needs.

As a rule, I would not hold ownership of either land or a farm operation in my name and my wife's name in light of the seven needs I outlined above and repeat below. If your estate is modest, however, ownership in your own name is certainly workable. I cannot recommend a one-type-fits-all ownership structure that can be applied to every individual situation. The optimum ownership structure for your land or farm is part of a plan you should have for meeting seven needs: 1) estate planning, 2) minimizing annual income tax; 3) minimizing taxes when selling farm/land; 4) privacy; 5) protection from creditors; 6) liability; and 7) control of property. While all property-owning taxpayers share these needs, each plan requires a custom fitting. There is no substitute for getting CPA and legal help.

CHAPTER 7: MANURE BELONGS ON YOUR BOOTS, NOT IN YOUR RAP

"IS THERE ANYBODY LEFT TO WALK THAT MUDDY MILE?"
Eric Andersen, "Plains of Nebrasky-O," <u>Today is the Highway</u>, Vanguard, 196?

Farms are getting bigger as their number steadily declines. Conventional agricultural production requires scale economies. High-cost farmers are being squeezed out, and the more profitable farm operations are picking up the best agricultural lands, hence the steady increase in average farm size. Farms that disappear may be converted into housing, commercial developments or non-farm second homes. The lesson in the size trend is that whether or not larger farms are more efficient than smaller ones, larger and fewer is the trend.

Small farms, consequently, are no longer valued as full-time farming operations because, with some exceptions, full-time farmers can't make a living from them. In my rural county, no one is able to make a living from operating livestock farms of less than 200 or even 300 acres. Where such small farms were family-supporting as late as the 1950s, today they are not. In some places, this has led to large farmers buying small farms as part of their own land-accretion process. In my area, small farms are generally owned either by natives who work full-time off the farm and operate the farm in their spare time or city folks using them as retirement residences or second homes. Most of the first group inherited their farm residences in one way or another. They are not farm buyers. The market for small farms comes almost entirely from the second group. A small farm in a place like mine can be a good investment for a buyer who understands the many hurdles in trying to make small farms pay their own way and is willing to allow long-term ownership make his profit through appreciation of property value.

The more conventional your agricultural operation, the more full-time farming is about managing debt and scrounging cash. Most farmers have to borrow. Farm debt consists of business-related loans that finance land, equipment and crops. Not infrequently, land is mortgaged to buy equipment and pay for improvements. Federal programs are a central player in the system of farm debt. This house of cards is sustained by the underlying appreciation in land value, which is the lender's security in the debt. Since farming yields relatively little net income for most farmowners, farmers have a hard time piling up cash over the years after servicing their debt. Consequently, they are always borrowing and repaying to keep the farm going.

Debt can slowly crush the life out of you as you eke out each month's payment. Live on the edge long enough, and inevitably you slide over. That's what foreclosure auctions are about: farmers going splat. As a rule, you will do best by keeping yourself off the hamster wheel of farm debt as much as possible. You do this by containing both your annual input costs and your investment in capital stock. Look for cheaper ways to do a job consistent with getting it done reasonably right. Invest labor (both mental and physical) instead of cash. Manage more rather than invest more. Follow the principle that's incorporated in the time-honored tactic of buying cheap stocker steers in the spring that might be upgraded for fall sale through care and good grass rather than the best quality at the highest price. Figure out your marketing strategy before you buy or plant: test it small at first, increasing your production in step with your feedback. Consider ways of achieving predictable cash flow at the sacrifice of upside potential. In other words: hedge don't gamble. Take satisfaction in making a little money, not in driving up your dirt road on a new, $50,000 tractor.

Farmers, historically, have tended to be **land poor**, that is, rich in land but poor in cash because farming and landownership consume so much of their income in debt service and operating costs. Virginia plantation owners, like Jefferson, were poster boys for this predicament which resulted from their continuing need to buy additional land to replace that which their farming practices wore out. Non-farmer buyers like you can become land poor just like everyone else if you don't have reliable non-farm income sufficient to cover the farm's mortgage (if necessary) and your expenses. Prudently run farms can contribute to a non-farmer's net worth and an estate protected from federal taxation. A farm can provide you with yearly tax benefits that help build wealth. It can provide income, even some net income. But farming is a risky venture at best. A non-farmer buyer can fold a farm into his asset base and lifestyle, but it must be planned properly and effected cautiously.

A first-time small farmer must choose between producing conventional commodity crops—many of which enjoy price supports—and less-conventional alternatives. The smaller your farm, the more a full-time farmer has to find his way within the less-conventional group. I would not try to make a living that includes a mortgage payment from a small farm that produces conventional crops. Your choice, I think, will come down to a few conventional alternatives that might work on small acreage (such as a specialty orchard, vineyard or niche crop) or a less-conventional alternative, (such as organic crops, pick-your-own fruit/berries, exotic livestock breeding, specialty products and farm-added-value products.) I don't think you can beat the conventional system if you're small; you must go around it.

All farming is hard, constant and dangerous work. Even hobby farming is like this, though there's less of it. You might begin your farm work by reading Bryan Jones's, The Farming Game (Lincoln, Nebraska: University of Nebraska Press, 1982; reprint 1995), which has the farm experience dead right, though some specifics are now out of date. You can obtain books and other information on all aspects of farming from these websites: www.onthefarmradio.com; www.reviewcentre.com; www.farmingbooksandvideos.com; www.streetSmartfarmer.com; www.freeplants.com; www.keepmedia.com; and www.draftresource.com.

You might also want to read Joel Salatin's, You Can Farm: The Entrepreneur's Guide to Start and $ucceed in a Farming Enterprise (Swoope, Virginia.: Polyface, Inc., 1998; available from Stockman Grass Farmer, 1-800-748-9808 and Acres USA, 1-800-355-5313; or Rt 1, Box 281, Swoope, Virginia, 24479; 540-885-3590). Salatin's book is written for the individual who wants to make a living from full-time livestock farming and who has little experience doing so. His approach is to fly under the radar of conventional agriculture, looking for labor-intensive but not capital-intensive, value-added, *organic* farm products that can be sold directly to consumers. The book touches on many sensible ideas and experience-based insights.

Like all missionaries, Salatin is selling a total package of beliefs, liturgy and practices. You need not buy the package to appreciate and apply particular bits of insight. His objective is to find a way to make his inherited farm provide a living for his family. He's quite right to avoid conventional agriculture, and stress thrift, direct marketing to nearby population centers, soil improvement, flexibility, diversity, pastured chickens ("free-range" is the menu-preferred adjective), rotational grazing, record-keeping and environmentally enhancing agriculture. The key to his success is having a farm located within a two-hour drive of several Virginia cities, which allows direct marketing of higher-priced organic beef, pork, chicken, turkey, rabbit and eggs to upper-middle-class consumers and regular deliveries to fancy local restaurants. Customers contract for the meat they want and are then assigned a pick-up day. His marketing pitch is based on raising organic livestock in the field and processing it on a small, even backyard, scale. For a look at the conventional alternative, visit www.factoryfarming.com. Salatin has been operating his farm for about 20 years. In itself, this is proof of success even though he does not provide the numbers that would allow a reader to judge the farm as a business. Salatin's farm business is undoubtedly helped by sales of his field-tested farm books and his other promotional activities.

Farms are great second homes, great places for kids and great ways to make connections of many kinds—to the past, to the land, to the future, to values that are often obscured. Our farm gives our lives a balance between doing and thinking that I had a hard time finding in a city. You can get that balance even on a weekend farm. But the key to balance is…balance. Do a little bit of farming, then maybe a little more. But keep it balanced—less than half—of your life.

BUYING AND SELLING TO YOUR FRIENDS AND NEIGHBORS

Farming is not a gentleman's business. As I think about that sentence, I realize that I can't come up with any example of a gentleman's business.

Let me start again. Farming is self-employment where your costs tend to rise faster than your revenues. If you're a small farm producing conventional products, you will often find yourself less in competition against fellow producers and more in the same slowly sinking boat with them. Price competition—that is, cutting your price to keep yourself afloat—often results in a quicker trip to the bottom. You will find moments when the price of your farm's product is set by supply-and-demand interactions that can be seen and are understandable, and moments when the price you receive makes little sense in light of what is visible and comprehensible. Buyers tend to be large and oligopolistic while producers tend to be small and many. You, the new farmer, will be one of the small and many.

You will find, as a farmer or rural landowner, that you will need to buy from and, occasionally sell into a local market. The cost of purchasing locally produced farm-related products, labor and services can be substantial, but each purchase is often in the $250 to $5,000 range. Purchased items and services might include excavation work, fence-building, custom farm work (haying, harvesting), materials (stone, fertilizer, manure, fencing, firewood), used equipment, livestock, hauling and labor, both skilled and unskilled. These purchases and your local sales can be freighted with community scrutiny, and you will do well to realize that your approach to buying and selling can be published on the front page of your community's oral newspaper.

Few experienced farmers—your supply-side competitors—will give you—a new farmer—much of a break because of your inexperience. Why should they? Some will try to take advantage of you before you smarten up. Others won't. A couple will help you out. Obviously, it's important for you to learn who is in each camp. It's also important to keep your opinions about who's who to yourself. You won't know enough yet to know who is related to whom, who can keep your confidence and who likes to stir up pots in which you are the one being boiled.

If a knowledgeable neighbor takes you under his wing, consider yourself blessed. This individual is a treasure. Don't expect, however, that he will provide Farming 101 on demand. His advice is not likely to be offered as: "You should do it this way." Advice came to me something like this: "A man could think about it this way if a man was going to think about this at all, which a man might not do because there's not enough time to do everything that needs doing and too much thinking is like driving your vehicle into thicker and thicker mud, which sooner or later, stops you dead…if a man was foolish enough to drive through a mud hole in the first place. But if a man had a mind to try something, a man might think about it this way." Listen for the "**local subjunctive**," since it's offered for your benefit. I was fortunate enough to have a couple of neighbors like this. They let me bloody my own nose with flawed cattle decisions that they knew were limited enough to teach me a lesson while preventing me from knocking myself out. They assumed that I would learn and profit from these mistakes. I appreciated their efforts to contain my exuberance...and losses.

Fellow local producers have no incentive, no reason, to help you learn their business. They don't benefit by you becoming smarter from their hard-won wisdom. You wouldn't open your Rollodex to the fellow who opened a business like yours down the street, so don't expect your neighbors to share their survival skills with you because you need them. Nonetheless, several will, mainly because they're decent people and know what it feels like to lose money. Try to ask as few questions as possible. It's better to learn through unobtrusive observation, which is the way a lot of farm kids pick up things. Limit your requests for free advice since the knowledge you seek was acquired at a cost. You should offer to pay for continuing advice just as you would pay a consultant. Neighbors should—but probably won't—take your money, but you've done the right thing by valuing their expertise. While their information has great value to you, it is not similarly valued by those of your neighbors who have it; they consider such information common knowledge.

You might handle this situation by hiring the neighbor whose advice you want to do some "real work" for you, and while you are working together introduce your questions. Since you are paying for his time at that moment, both of you should feel comfortable with the arrangement. When neighborly advice is given without compensation, provide something of value in return to keep things square. Make available your urban skills, advice and contacts as a kind of standing swap for farm wisdom. Any expertise you have in filling out forms, taxes, law, medical insurance, college applications, financial aid, estate planning, finding doctors and lawyers, understanding consumer protection, haggling with creditors, evaluating business plans, interpreting rules and regulations and finding information on the Internet can be worth something in a swap.

The farming efforts of newcomers are watched microscopically, and both innovations and mistakes are likely to be the subject of hours of café dissection. (Diners need fresh material, having already exhausted each other's mistakes—about which you will only learn later. Live somewhere long enough and you may be accorded visitor seating, from where you can offer your opinions about the latest newcomer who is doing strange things.) What you do with your new land—which has probably been the seller's for a while and is, in any case, somebody's homeplace—is a matter of public interest. Get used to it. Fresh paint, orderliness, mowed yard grass and tended fences will reflect well on you. Large changes and flashy remodelings will raise eyebrows. Be neighborly.

Farmers buy and sell certain things from one another—livestock, equipment, supplies and occasionally land. You will find that some farmer-sellers have a price for whatever it is they're selling and will not budge. These folks are easy to deal with: you either meet their price if you want it badly enough or don't. Most sellers, however, anticipate, even look forward to, a little horse-trading negotiation with buyers, particularly the likes of you. If you are an urban professional, some sellers, not all, will consider you smarter than they are about certain things, which gives them just a bit more reason to make you pay a little more than you should for things they know about and are selling. This seller's intention is not to gouge you, but to come out just a bit more up than he thinks he should be...at your expense. This is not about money. It's often about self-image as well as evening self-perceived class, educational and cultural differences that are never really evened. The seller's self-image is involved, and you will do well to understand this in advance. The meta-issue from his perspective is who he is sociologically and who you are sociologically. It may not make any difference to you whether you pay $48 for a metal gate at the store or $52 from your neighbor, just as long as you get the thing hung before dark. But you will do better in the long run to bargain a little over the $4 so that you can both win at $50...or even $51. You won't need the store down the road as much as you are likely to need something from that neighbor. You should consider the little bit extra he tacks on as a kind of political contribution that buys you access and goodwill. It's best, I think, to buy from this neighbor-seller a time or two, using your friendliest bazaar-style negotiating skills. Don't walk away from his gate over a couple of bucks. Down the road, you will find he'll start treating you the same as everyone else. More importantly, by bargaining and buying, you've entered into the local economy and presumably did good enough. More than good enough is not what you want.

You will undoubtedly run into at least one local seller who is willing to sell you whatever you are dumb enough to buy, regardless of how dangerous it is and whether or not it runs. (Any time a seller tells me that "it runs good," I'm wary.) You have two ways of protecting yourself in these situations. First, when you have no experience buying what you have decided that you want to buy, pay a knowledgeable individual to go with you. Busy the seller while your expert checks out the goods. He'll tell you whether or not to make an offer and what it should be. Don't lay off the buy/no-buy decision onto your helper, because that will cause bad blood between him and the seller. Take responsibility and ownership of a no-buy decision: "It's more than I can afford"; "It's not quite what I was looking for."

If you are buying on your own and you're not sure after a first inspection, walk away from it. Come back for a second look. Don't be rushed into a purchase. When the seller says that there's another buyer begging to buy it for twice the money you've offered, quietly suggest that he should consider making that deal. Your deal at close to your price is likely to be available a couple of days later. Be especially careful when buying farm equipment and livestock on your own. Greenhorn buyers bring out the worst in a few sellers.

A newcomer will inevitably pay too much for some country goods, but he makes up for it when hiring local labor, which is always priced below city and suburban rates for equivalent skills. Do not gloat over or take advantage of this situation. Pay a dollar or two more than the going hourly rate for certain jobs to get quality work. You will still get the job done for half what you would otherwise pay.

Most sellers will judge you by **how you horse-trade**. Horse-trading is not like finding a price on the stock exchange floor where sellers and buyers make instant deals. Horse-trading is much more like having sex between consenting adults. It should be done with self-deprecating humor, creativity, concern for the other person and reasonableness. Expect some veil dancing. Neither side should make take-it-or-leave-it offers. Everyone should feel good the morning after. If the seller's price is outrageous and he does not seem inclined to budge, it's best not to move into horse-trading with him because you will wind up with either a bad deal or no deal—and everyone frazzled by the experience. Horse-trading, in other words, is a process that you enter after you've scoped out enough of the seller to know that he is receptive to dickering. If the seller is a horse-trader, don't pay his first asking price. Slip into the process that he offers and be creative. Horse-trades are often swung by using "throw ins" that are not part of the original negotiation. You come out okay in horse-trading when you know the going price for what you are selling and what you are buying. Never horse-trade without knowing both numbers.

If you're trying to horse-trade on the price of land and get stuck, throw in something you think the buyer values more than you do: offer free hunting and fishing rights for a couple of years; or use of all or part of the property for agricultural purposes for a transition time; or hay-making rights; or free storage in the barn for a year; or some professional assistance or skill that the seller might need that you can offer. It's easier to trade horses when saddles, bridles and hoof picks are available to help make the swap. In return

105

for the cash and "throw ins" you offer for land, you might ask the seller for return considerations, such as building fence with materials you provide or dipping out a stock pond with the backhoe he has, or including a functioning tractor in the farm purchase. Horse-trading should be done with an eye cocked to establishing a functional relationship in the future with the other person. You may find yourself relating to the seller in many ways over the coming years. And if not him, his parents, siblings, children or friends.

While most service vendors in your new farm community will treat you fairly and expect to be treated the same, you should not be surprised to find a few who use a **two-tier pricing system: a lower price for locals and a higher price for newcomers**. Advertised prices, of course, apply uniformly to everyone. But prices for local services—house painting, roofing, excavation, fencing and other trades— lend themselves to tiering. (Lest you are starting to think that newcomers are virtuous and locals are not, I can report that I've seen new farmowners bargain with needy locals like they were parting with their Uncle Scrooge's first dollar and then demand a discount when it came time to pay.)

If the two-tier vendor appears to be your only choice, then you may have to work with him though I would keep asking around. The best response is to walk away from any deal that turns you into a knowing patsy. If you discover after the deal has been struck that your vendor charges a different rate to others for the same service, you can choose to confront him or forget about it. Confrontation usually leads to the vendor's explanation that different jobs require different things, which explains different hourly rates. (See?) If you've agreed to his terms, you should pay the bill and learn from the experience. If you're dickering over terms, I'd forget about hiring the vendor whom you've just accused of cheating. If you go ahead with him, the work will not be done well.

The virtue in rising above this situation is that hard feelings can last forever in rural places, and grudges complicate life far beyond the dollars at stake in the initial dispute. It doesn't matter that you may be "right"; what matters in the long run is that you have asserted your rightness in a way that reveals the vendor to be less than honorable. In the normal course of urban life, you would not think twice about pitching a fit over two-tier pricing. In your new rural neighborhood, you will be judged over the accusation you make, not whether you are objectively right. And in the event of a dispute over money, you should know that the vendor's communications network is far more extensive than yours. It is his side of the dispute that will become common currency, not yours.

Having been in these situations, I believe it is best to continue to shop your work rather than confront the vendor in hope of trying to shame him into fairness. Where you are looking for a vendor in a not-very-competitive market, you may find it hard to locate an alternative. Try nonetheless, since it is better for your long-term relations with your new community to avoid this type of dispute than to prevail. Only in the most desperate circumstances should you pay the inflated non-local price. When I've done so, I've found that the vendor does a bad job despite the premium, or perhaps because of it. The element of mutual respect is at the center of all successful rural buy-sell deals. When the vendor forces you into the non-local price, he's forced you to lose respect in his eyes, which, in turn, enables him to do shoddy work because he thinks you won't know the difference, or don't care, or won't do anything about it. When you do stick up for yourself with a vendor like this, he will be affronted that you've questioned his ethics and work quality—both of which are likely to stink for you, regardless of his reputation with others.

I suggest invoking the Golden Rule in horse-trading. You can back into it by saying that you want to bargain with the other person the way you want him to bargain with you. Backing in is more acceptable than demanding adherence as your opening gambit. Make sure that you live up to your end of your offer.

In all dealings, it is critical for you to remember that you are interacting with an individual, not a sociological group. If a person treats you fairly or unfairly, it is that person—not his family, his neighbors or his community—that did so. It's easy to fall into a habit of thought that says everyone of such and such a group thinks this way and behaves that way. That habit is just plain wrong. The "other" group is just as varied as "your" group. Your new community is made up of individuals whose responses to you will be individual. If you start thinking in terms of them and us, you're destined to end up in that unfortunate place.

Price is the rural platform on which stand both respect and effort. When you negotiate a price that both sides regard as fair enough, then you have the standing to expect quality work. Don't be a fool just because you can afford to be, except where you will gain over the long term by accommodating the vendor's insecurities in the short term. On the other hand, don't feel that you need to show you're no city fool by squeezing pennies out of the vendor's wallet. While he needs your cash, he's gotten along without it until then. You are likely to need him more than he needs your dollars. Don't count on being able to bully a guy into a deal; bullying seldom works. I've seen rural vendors walk away from fair offers proposed by newcomers for no reason other than the source of the offer.

I've run into a few local guys who are so existentially angry over the influx of outsiders and their own inability to prosper that they try to skunk every non-local and newcomer they run into. Avoid these people; nothing is to be gained from dealing with them—win, lose or draw. You should also be aware that your behavior in these affairs will be judged locally by a different standard than locals judge themselves. While you might see a price squabble with farmer Jones as a price squabble between you and farmer Jones, some of your new neighbors—fortunately, a minority—will see it as a fight between farmer Jones, who is one of them, and you, who is not. It will not matter to such folks that they too have squabbled with farmer Jones or that he is notorious for slippery behavior when it comes to money. Most of the time, your new neighbors will judge you on your own merits as you should judge them.

Newcomers should be aware of a **second-bite tactic that arises on fixed-price contracts.** Some vendors, not all, do not see a fixed-price agreement as involving a fixed price. They will want more money at the end of the job, because it took them longer to do the work. It's fair to both ask and pay if the vendor ran into problems that he could not have anticipated. It's also fair to refuse additional payment if you feel you're in a stick up. Don't pay a portion of the demand if you are *absolutely* convinced that the claim is groundless.

The main local **sell-buy relationship** you will have is with the purchaser of your farm products. Depending on the product, this buyer can be a multinational corporation, local cooperative, individual or the general public. When dealing with a "big" buyer, whether an institution or individual, the new farmer needs to remember that the buyer is not his friend. You should assume that most commodity buyers approach your deal as a zero-sum game in which every penny you make is a penny they lose. Don't expect them to help you out in a bad year when they can buy your product below your production cost. There's no sympathy for a novice in the agricultural marketplace.

If you are a conventional producer of a common commodity, you will soon learn that buyers of your product usually get the longer end of your stick. Such buyers are more liquid as a rule than individual sellers. They also have more precise information than you do about what your product will bring at the next step. If the buyer has a locked-in price for your product, you'll never know what it is. In contrast, you, the farm producer, are trying to determine your range of feasible selling prices using incomplete local data, your costs which you know all too well, hearsay, misinformation and macro-level price data at the state and national levels. Even when you, the small-guy producer, sell for a profit, it does not mean that the buyer has not won his little game with you. Since the buyer knows where the product is going and, usually, at what price, he knows in advance how much money he will make at each price for your product. As long as such a buyer has alternative sources of your product, he'll pay you as little as he can. You can do a little better when he needs your product to fill out a shipment. A farm producer almost always does best when several buyers are competing for his product.

Economics for small farmers boils down to a "**bottom analysis**," that is, net profit is what's left at the bottom of the producer's purse after he pays for everything off the top. When there's something left on the bottom, it's rarely because the farmer is a sharpie who got the better of the commodity buyer. It's usually the result of an increase in wholesale prices based on macro supply-and-demand factors.

Cattle are a common farm product and one which new farmers often try. In my part of Virginia, we have two usual ways of selling cattle. The first is to run your animals through a stockyard sale where they are weighed, graded and grouped for auction. The stockyard imposes predictable charges and certain risks. The farmer pays the stockyard a per-head fee for selling. If your cattle truck must wait three hours before unloading your steers before the sale, you can anticipate that each animal will lose five to ten pounds in the truck as additional **shrink** before it is weighed. Shrink is the loss of weight (feces and urine) in farm-to-sale transit; producers want to keep shrink as low as possible, while buyers benefit from more shrink. With 50 head in a truck and a six-pound-per-head shrink due to a jam at the dock, the farmer has "lost" 300 pounds, possibly $300, before he even gets his livestock into the auction ring. Moreover, the farmer has no control over which frame category the state graders assign each head of his stock. The difference between an 800-pound steer being classed as a "Medium-1" frame as against a "Number 3" can easily swing the selling price by $100. And, finally, the farmer's sales revenue will be directly affected by the number and motivation of the bidders. Most local stockyards are now connected by phone to distant feedlot buyers who are often the best money.

Some farmers avoid the stockyard's risks and fees in favor of dealing directly with independent cattle buyers who come to the farm, estimate the weight and quality of the stock in the field, and then offer a straight-through dollar-per-pound price for the scale weight. These buyers estimate scale weights of cattle herds every day. The good ones can project herd-wide average scale weight in the field to within ten pounds or less. These dealers will know before they step out of their fancy trucks what they can sell your cattle for and the cost of delivery. The buyer will generally offer you a penny-per-pound (or dollars per hundredweight) price that you think you might get at the stock market. You then figure that you'll save the stockyard's charges—as much as $10 per head—and avoid the risk of a truck jam, downgrading on frame size and poor bidder turnout. Then the buyer allows that he believes your cattle weigh a little more than you figure. You do the arithmetic in your head: cents per pound times more pounds than you thought, which puts more money in your pocket than the stockyard sale. So you make the deal. Lo and behold...when you get to the scales, you find your cattle weigh less than what the dealer believed and even less than what you thought they'd weigh. So you end up with a little less than you thought you'd get. On a trailer load of cattle—48,000 pounds—the $500 you lost on this deal is cash in your buyer's pocket. The safest method of working with these field buyers is to have at least three bid in a competition for your cattle.

Selling directly to a feedlot is likely to be more profitable, though it's difficult for a small seller to arrange. You will need to have a trailer load. A professional grader can be secured to field grade your stock. An identification system will be used to make sure the cattle bought are the cattle shipped. The seller will figure in a shrink factor.

Whether you will come out ahead at the stockyard or with the field buyer is always unknowable. In dealing with field buyers, I've done best—though not particularly well—by getting two or more bidding against each other and never accepting a price-per-pound offer when it is presented in the field. Give the field buyer a decision in a day or two after shopping your cattle to other buyers. It's useful to get a knowledgeable cattle person to look at your cattle before the buyers do, to give you an impartial idea of average field weight and the distribution of frames. Remember to subtract shrink from your average weight to account for hauling from field to scale.

If you're fooling with cattle as a novice, spend time at the stockyard in an effort to develop a cattleman's eye for judging weight and frame in the field. You should assume that a field buyer will play a couple of games with you to get your cattle for a price that he figures is a little lower than what he would pay at the auction. This keeps money in his pocket that could be in yours. The most common game I've seen involves the buyer inflating the field weight to induce the seller to accept a lower per-pound price. Another game manipulates a **price slide**, which is a device that should be used in field weighing to protect both buyer and seller equally.

A price slide starts with the price per pound that the buyer and seller have negotiated in the field based on an agreed average weight per head. If the average scale weight varies from the agreed field weight by five to ten pounds, the field price remains unchanged. If the average scale weight exceeds the no-change range, then the price per pound is reduced by a specified number of cents. If the average scale weight falls below the no-change range, the price per pound is increased by the same number of cents. A seller gets taken when the slide uses big changes in price per pound and the dealer forces an agreed field weight on the seller that he knows is higher than what the weight will be at the scale. This technique gives the dealer-buyer your herd at a much lower price per pound than is fair. Field buyers are much smarter than novice sellers about slides. A seller can protect himself against an unscrupulous buyer by having a professional grader provide him with an average field weight just prior to the buyer's visit. The seller must then subtract farm-to-scale shrink from the field weight. The net weight is what the seller will be paid for. If the seller accepts the buyer's weight estimate and the buyer's slide formula, he is opening himself to losing money on the deal.

If you are a person who will stew all winter over the loss of $500 in the selling of $40,000 worth of cattle in October, sell your cattle in the most conventional way open to you. Otherwise, you will turn into one of those individuals who nurse small grievances over lifetimes, which is not a good way to spend yours.

Increasingly, the end-buyers of agricultural products, such as poultry and hog processors, integrate vertically by turning individual farm producers into captive contractors who are paid for their captive production at a price the end-buyer sets. This is an updated version of sharecropping that rarely works to the benefit of the guy producing the crop. Farmers enter these contracts because they promise more or less predictable cash flow and the prospect of being able to make a living from farming. Sharecropping worked enough to last a long time, and contract farming works enough to last too.

Depending on your location and your product, farmers will have developed marketing venues and tactics that may or may not work for you. Certain agricultural sectors still use middlemen, such as an independent livestock sale, to bring sellers and buyers together in an auction. Livestock is often sold this way. Other crops—grains and milk—are sold through, or to, cooperatives. Cooperative commodity selling maximizes suppliers' market power. Some farms have the ability to time their sales by having on-farm storage. Some producers use financial tools to hedge their price exposure or sell on a forward contract at a fixed price. New owners of farms should consider ways to make their revenue predictable, though it means less up side. Many things can distort expected farm revenue every year. For the first-time farmer, I advise choosing ways of getting cash in hand rather than playing in future craps games. Many farmers I know do not try to improve their marketing. They sell the same way every year, because they have concluded that they can't beat the system. They're probably right about that.

START NEW THINGS SLOWLY; MAKE SMALL MISTAKES

As part of a pre-purchase farm plan, the dirt-smart buyer will have thought about a marketing plan for both the products the farm is producing and those it could produce. I urge caution on new uses. A new farmer with a new plan is at risk on both counts. Be careful about plunking a book model down in your new field, or assuming that you will make money because money looks like it can be made on paper.

When we first moved to Blue Grass in 1983, I had a notion to graze hogs instead of cattle on our pasture. Sometimes a great notion is best left alone. While our grass would have fattened hogs, everything else was wrong. All perimeter fences, including those of my neighbors, would have had to have been seriously upgraded or electrified. Concrete water troughs that fit cattle are too high for hogs. Stock-handling facilities would have had to have been rebuilt. The investment was too great to have made it pay. Further, I would have had to have found a reliable market for grass-finished hogs, or, alternatively, finish them myself with purchased grain. Finally, I couldn't find a steady supply of several hundred spring pigs ready for pasture. My pig idea was impractical on too many fronts. Our local county extension agent sagely told me as much. Twenty years later, however, a consumer market has emerged for this product. The farm's infrastructure, however, remains all wrong.

It is too easy for folks who are used to thinking analytically to design a theoretically better way of making money from a farm that they've never actually farmed. Puff pieces in agricultural magazines about the guy 400 miles away doing something that you think you can make work too are bait for people with too many degrees and a wide open mouth. Farming is at the mercy of forces beyond your control. Farmers must be gamblers, because they control so little of what affects them.

Most farmers, I think, assume that the mean will always occur; others try to protect themselves against the atypical through insurance, hedging, diversifying and adding redundancy to their operations. A person new to farming a new piece of land has no dirt-experience with managing the atypical. So a theoretical plan to change a farm's use assumes that the new owner knows the mean, as well as the range of variation. Such assumptions are fragile. The mean rarely occurs, though one can always be found in the longitudinal data on rainfall and temperature.

There is only one way to avoid the potentially disastrous consequences of your enthusiasm to create your own farm immediately. Don't do it. Be patient. **A new dirt-smart farmer learns his land before he starts substantially changing how it is used**. Land-learning is a huge step beyond the pre-purchase scoping that a buyer does. It takes several years—at least five, preferably more—for a novice to have sufficient experience to understand what his land can do, can't do and might do in specific circumstances. Your ability to produce an agricultural product is totally dependent on local factors—weather, water, soils, topography—and how each works with the others in a given year. You have to be on land over a sufficient period of time to see how various combinations occur and what their effect is on farm produce. There are few short cuts to time-tested, site-specific knowledge. While a piece of flat land may look to the inexperienced eye like any other piece of flat land, the farmer who preceded you will know that it has water-bearing clay soil six inches below the surface which makes it unsuitable for certain crops, particularly the Iranian elephant garlic that has captured your imagination. Change slowly.

Having said all of that, I don't mean to discourage you from thinking outside the conventional box when it comes to revising your farm's uses. You should be collecting research and new ideas, and keeping your ear tuned to *long-term* shifts in consumer tastes. Think about ways to add value to farm products and market them directly to retail consumers. Diversifying your product mix helps to insulate your cash flow from short-term events that often clobber conventional producers of one conventional commodity. Federal crop supports and insurance programs are intended to manage risk, though I think they encourage dependency and discourage innovation. Small, intensive production systems for specialty products can be explored, because they may be less subject to some of farming's risk factors. Rather than dedicate your new 20 acres to garlic consider building a couple of greenhouses to grow both garlic and salad greens all year long. The cautionary homily—"Don't put all your eggs in one basket."—came from farms where families knew first hand about both eggs and baskets.

It is critical to any new marketing plan to know where you can sell your new product and to understand that market's pricing and supply-and-demand balance. Don't become the tenth producer of organic spinach selling in a Saturday morning farmer's market in a town of 10,000—unless you have a trust fund. Don't start raising Kobe beef on a hardscrabble patch of glacial till in northern Maine because you've heard the Japanese pay a high price for it. You'll never be able to get a competitively priced product to Tokyo. Hearing something is not a marketing plan. Don't covert your 640 acres of cornfield to pick-your-own blueberries when the closest city is 200 miles away and the dirt couldn't grow a blueberry if Little Sal herself planted and watered each bush. Specialty products and direct marketing are excellent ways to make farming profitable, but the production has to fit the many features of your land, and you must be able to access a market that is ready and able to buy your products.

Many farm products are easier to produce than they are to sell at a profit. New farmers are often attracted to fads, exotic crops or livestock that are hot for a year or two. I've often seen new farmers fasten themselves to farm ideas that sacrifice trying to make money from their farm to promoting other values and aesthetics. While it may be neat to have five Polish longhorn steers on your farm, you cannot make any profit from this investment. (Steers, unlike bulls, cannot reproduce, and this breed, while now valued in Europe because it is outside the circle of beef animals that consumers fear carry mad cow disease, have no market in this country.) Resist investing heavily into crop-specific or livestock-specific infrastructure to take advantage of the latest agricultural tulip frenzy. You're likely to be too late to catch the really high prices, and you may find yourself with a locked-in and exclusionary infrastructure that can only produce a faddish product that is fading fast.

It's far better to build flexibility into your farm infrastructure, diversify your products and be able to sell into more than one market. You will always be in a good position if you keep improving your dirt. Unfortunately, failure is the mother of knowledge. Try not to be the farmer who fails gloriously so that others benefit.

CHAPTER 8: FARM EQUIPMENT: STUFF IS US

Farms are nice places to live and have as a second home. They provide opportunities to do simple, straight-forward labor. (Endless opportunities, I should add.) Such work provides a balance for people who spend most of their time in urban offices pushing paper, numbers and people. Real farm work is also hard, often boring, and ranges from highly skilled to endlessly unskilled. Most farmers could step into most Fortune 500 companies and do a passable job as the CEO because they are used to doing many tasks of many different kinds all at once and in sequence. Very few CEOs could switch places with one of these farmers and do anything except lose their shirts.

Farm work also provides opportunities to play in the dirt with big sandbox toys. Equipment and machinery is intended to enable an individual to accomplish more for a given amount of time and effort. Modern farmers, organic and conventional, need such tools to produce the quantities we require at a competitive cost. As farming systems were engineered to require less and less labor, more and more money had to be invested in the necessary "labor-saving" capital stock to maintain and increase output. Today, there is no escaping the need for large investments in equipment and machinery on large conventional farms.

For a new farmowner who is eyeing these unknown waters, I advise against doing a cannonball into the near bottomless pool of farm equipment. Buy equipment with the same careful research methods you've applied to buying land. Never buy anything without knowing its approximate value before negotiating, and the prices being asked by other sellers.

If your new place comes with no equipment, ask yourself whether you can do what you want without any equipment at all. Ask your neighbors whether it's possible to hire machinery work, such as fence-post driving, tractor work and baling. Felix Dennis, the British publisher, offers this sound advice on buying stuff: "If it flies, floats, or fornicates, always rent it. It's cheaper in the long run." (How to Get Rich: The Distilled Wisdom of One of Britain's Wealthiest Self-made Entrepreneurs, quoted in Stephan Stern, "Confessions of a Self-Made Multimillionaire," Financial Times, August 23, 2006.)

You may want to consider renting your agricultural land, rather than buying equipment and doing it yourself. Some products—cattle, sheep and hay—can be produced with the owner owning no equipment as long as hired machinery is available. When trucks and other equipment are needed, hire a neighbor to help out. It's relatively easy to hire most machinery work as needed, though you have to make sure that hired harvesting comes to your place at the right time. If you are cash short after purchasing your land, you will need to do without equipment, or hire what you need, or buy used or some combination of these choices.

When you have determined that you need to buy equipment, you face a number of decisions about each piece:

new or used

bigger or smaller (more power or less)

more complicated or less complicated

well-known brand or lesser known brand (often foreign made)

newer or older

more easy to use or less easy to use (newer tractors have hitch systems that are much easier to use than older tractors)

buy from dealer or buy from individual

more expensive or less expensive

more safe or less safe (older tractors and machinery have fewer safety features engineered into their design than newer models)

harder to service and maintain or easier to service and maintain

more fuel efficient or less fuel efficient

more comfortable to operate or less comfortable

If you see yourself as a part-time farmer or a weekend user of a farm second home, the only reason to load up on expensive new equipment is in the case where the tax benefits make sense in your circumstances. New equipment is hideously expensive. A basic small tractor runs $10,000 to $20,000 in 2006, and cost can easily rise to $20,000 to $30,000 or more with attachments and implements. If you're dollar conscious, I suggest going with multi-task/flexible equipment rather than one-task/specialized machinery, used rather than new, newer rather than older, simple rather than complicated, reliable rather than temperamental, common rather than exotic, smaller rather than larger, and functioning rather than beat to hell. You can upgrade your combination of equipment as you better understand your changing needs.

As a some-time farmer or non-resident landowner, you don't need to own the most efficient piece of equipment, nor do you have to perform any particular task with cutting-edge efficiency. Your goal is not to be as efficient as is technologically possible; your goal is to produce your product and do your land work at the mix of cost and efficiency that allows you to reap a reasonable—not maximum—return for your effort. For those who are farming full-time, you will learn that buying production efficiency at the expense of net income can ruin you. The last increments of productivity are expensive and often unnecessary.

To take a simplistic example: it will undoubtedly be more efficient to work a 50-acre field with a 100-horsepower tractor than one that only has 20. It will also take you less time. But if you only have one field to work, the smaller tractor will do the job at a fraction of the capital cost. A $50,000 tractor is "too much tractor" in terms of your bottom line for work that a $5,000 one can do, almost as well.

Full-time conventional farms have to be capital intensive, substituting mechanical energy for human labor wherever possible. Productive and cost-efficient agriculture now requires constant investment in new capital stock—newer and bigger machinery, different infrastructure and production systems; upgraded facilities, computer controls and so on. That is one reason why full-time farmers are so knowledgeable about **debt-management tactics**. Each full-time farmer will have evolved his own set of choices about buying equipment, new and used. If they're making a profit, they'll buy big and new; if not, it's finding used with low hours.

This chapter discusses **buying new and used tractors** as a way of walking through the broader topic of buying farming equipment. The information comes from my own seat-of-my-pants experience along with what I've culled from tractor-savvy friends, mechanics, articles and old-timers who've sat on steel seats for hour upon hour.

TRACTORS: NEW AND USED

I operated a 73-acre cattle farm without a tractor for five years. I put the money I could have spent on a tractor into building fence for a rotational grazing system. That investment allowed me to almost double my farm's carrying capacity, from about 30-35 head to about 65-70 head, depending on the size (weight) of the cattle I was grazing. I didn't need to own a tractor to do this type of farming. When I wanted to make hay, I worked out a shares deal with a neighbor.

When I did buy a tractor, I bought a '57 Ford with a front-end loader, bushhog, scoop and scraper blade for about $4,000. I could have bought new equipment for four times that sum, but it would have done no more work than the old stuff, though it would have been easier to operate and required less maintenance. I also could have bought newer used equipment, but the additional cost would not have yielded any increment in productivity that I needed. In other words, a 1977 tractor in the same horsepower (hp) class as the 1957 Ford would have done the same work in essentially the same way for at least twice the initial cost. My ability to raise cattle efficiently was not increased by having a tractor, either old or new. But a tractor is handy and makes many tasks easier, particularly lifting, loading, pulling, skidding logs, scraping, moving materials, building fence and mowing.

Some ten years after buying the farm, I bought a 1980 4WD Toyota pick-up truck with about 250,000 miles on the still-working odometer for $1,000. It's a "FARM USE" truck—unlicensed, uninspected and restricted. It's perfect for hauling materials around the farm, and its nimbleness is especially good for working in the woods. As much as I like having this vehicle, I did not need it to produce cattle, hay or timber. I could have made do with a $300 trailer behind my street pick-up truck and saved the $1,000. At the level of $1,000, gaining work and time efficiency at the expense of cost efficiency is not of great concern. At many multiples of $1,000, it is. You will observe that most farmers have something similar to my old beat-to-hell Toyota that they use for farm work. It saves wear and tear on their good vehicles.

To perform the same tractor and farm-truck work, I could have easily spent $40,000, rather than $5,000. If money were no object, maybe I should have done so. However, I've never found that money is never an object.

If you're cheap, or even a little thrifty, you'll start with a used tractor, probably a bit smaller than what you might like. Working with it will teach you which equipment upgrades you think are worth the additional investment. In my case, I'd like a slightly more powerful tractor with 4WD, more comfortable seat, better rollover-protection, an exhaust pipe that doesn't blow back in my face and an easier rear hitch. I could buy a better seat. The roll bar that I had fabricated is the best that I can get given the tractor's pre-safety frame and configuration. The exhaust now vents in front because the front-end loader I added required the removal of the down-and-under system. I cannot economically retrofit more hp, 4WD or an easier hitch. To get a better tractor package means buying a newer and more expensive tractor—a $10,000 to $20,000 shift. It's not worth that money for the 50 hours a year I use it.

The most obvious first step is to determine what you want your tractor to do and where. The work you need done will determine tractor size, attachments, implements and other features. The work you need done is what you have to do regularly or normally. It excludes jobs that you might need to have done every ten years. Such work is more economically done on a hired basis. If you try to size for every eventuality, you wind up with too much tractor at far too high a cost. The exception to this rule might be where you have to dig a 3,000-foot-long water line to your new farm house and the cost of the backhoe attachment would be less than the cost of hiring out the job.

The "topography" of your tractor work is a major screening factor. Smaller tractors are more maneuverable and have tighter turning radii than bigger ones. The tighter the radius, the handier your tractor. A lot of cleaning out barn stalls with a front-end loader will skew your decision toward nimbleness rather than horsepower. That type of work will also lead you to power steering. Tractors with a wider wheelbase are more stable than narrower models. On hilly terrain, I'd look for lower, wider models. Stumps, groundhog holes and 18"-deep gullies can roll a tractor if you hit them wrong. Don't be afraid to ask "stability" questions of the seller, particularly the degree of angle at which the model you're looking at will roll. If you will be doing a lot of inside-the-barn work, ask about emissions and emission controls. Breathing either gas or diesel exhaust (particulates in particular) for several hours at a time is not advised.

Despite my scrimp-and-save advice, there will be readers who want to buy a **big, new tractor**, whether or not it is needed. I will now stop berating these readers for wanting all things bright and shiny, as well as something they probably don't need. Here are some considerations for buying a new tractor.

You want to size a tractor to the work you want it to do. Size is mostly judged by **horsepower (hp)**. The heavier the stuff is that you want the tractor to pull and operate through its **power take-off (PTO)** and **hydraulics**, the more horsepower you need. PTO refers to an engageable, rotating shaft at the back of the tractor that can run both stationary and mobile attachments like grain elevators, generators, hay balers, bushhogs, winches and crop machinery. Look between the rear wheels for a splined shaft sticking out of the rear end of the engine—that's the PTO. A nearby lever engages it. It rotates at the speed of the tractor's motor. Both PTO and hydraulics are discussed below.

If you undersize a tractor for its work, you will use it up; if you oversize, you will be wasting your money, in both purchase and maintenance. A safe rule is to get sufficient power for all your foreseeable tasks with maybe a little extra for what you might need in the future. The previous farmowner—the seller—is an excellent source of information on tractor sizing for the farm work he did. And you may want to package your farm purchase with his equipment, assuming it checks out.

When sizing the tractor to the job, you also have to size the implements to the tractor and the work. An implement too big for its tractor will not do what you want it to do, and the undersized tractor will not last long trying to do it.

"The Little Engine That Could" might make a candy run over the mountain once or twice, but it would soon collapse from repeated efforts of that magnitude. You can ask your tractor to do more than it's sized for every so often, but that practice catches up with it eventually in blown thises and stripped thats.

Horsepower is a unit of power measurement. One hp was fixed by James Watt, the modern steam engine's inventor, as equal to doing 33,000 foot-pounds of work in one minute. (A "foot-pound" is the work done by the force of one pound moving through a one-foot distance in the direction of the force.) Since horses were the standard engines of work at the time Watt was tinkering, "horsepower" has been our way of rating engine power for more than 150 years. One hp is equal to 745.7 watts, named after James.

Tractors have different horsepower ratings at different points in their mechanical anatomy. **Gross engine horsepower, or indicated horsepower**, is the power the manufacturer estimates is produced at the cylinders. This is usually the type of horsepower that is used to rank tractors, even though it is a theoretical rather than an actual rating. It is theoretical, because as power is transmitted mechanically through shafts and gears, gross horsepower is lost. Some manufacturers publish a **net engine horsepower** rating, which is generally three or four "horses" lower than gross. You may also find tractor engines rated according to **kW.** (One kilowatt equals 1,000 watts; a watt measures the amount of energy the tractor's engine consumes at a certain speed.) The kW rating will be about 75 percent of the horsepower rating.

You will also find tractors rated according to **PTO horsepower or shaft horsepower**, which is the power available to do work at the PTO shaft when the tractor is stationary. PTO horsepower will be less—a lower number—than engine horsepower, somewhere between 85 to 90 percent of gross horsepower.

The third type of horsepower is **drawbar horsepower or effective horsepower**, which is the power available at the drawbar when the tractor is moving forward. The drawbar is a horizontal steel bar at the back of the tractor where implements and trailers/wagons are hooked on. Drawbars are discussed below. Drawbar horsepower represents the power that's left to pull or power equipment. There's roughly a ten to 15 percent horsepower loss between each rating step—gross, net and drawbar. Manufacturers' sales literature usually gives gross/indicated engine and PTO horsepower ratings. A 20 hp (gross) tractor will be underpowered when hooked to an implement that requires 20 hp at the drawbar.

You may also find reference to **brake horsepower**. This rating is the maximum horsepower available from an engine as measured by a dynamometer. A tractor engine's brake horsepower should exceed its expected normal operating load. An engine should not be run in excess of 80 percent of its brake horsepower—those red areas on the rpm (revolutions per minute) gauge where you want to be as little of the time as possible.

You will also hear some other "enginey" terms that you may or may not need to understand. **Displacement**, measured in cubic inches or "cubes," is the total volume of space that the engine's pistons move through on a single stroke. Bigger engines have more cubes. More displacement in a given engine size means that it won't work as hard to generate the same amount of horsepower and will operate at a slower engine speed, which is good for fuel consumption and service life. **Cylinders** are the spaces inside the engine's block in which the pistons move and where the fuel is combusted. Today's smaller tractors will have three cylinders and the bigger ones, four. **Lugging power** is the ability of an engine to continue to pull hard while the engine's rpms fall, which happens when the engine is under load. The more **torque** (the engine's ability to turn its central shaft under load), the more lugging power and overall power a tractor will have. **Engine speed** is measured in rpms; lower engine speeds are easier on the machine as well as on your ears. Other things being equal, a 25 hp tractor with a rated rpm of 2,600 will wear longer than the same horsepower tractor with a rated rpm of 2,800.

Smallish tractors were widely used after WWII, and the common ones are readily available in farming areas. Today, small tractors, called "**compacts**," are available in three gross horsepower classes: 1) 18 to 25 hp +/-; 2) 25-35 hp +/-; and 3) 35-45 hp +/-. A 25- to 35-hp (engine hp) tractor should be able to handle the work of most small farms with power to spare. While some compacts can be rigged for front-end loading, backhoe work, log skidding and other heavy-duty tasks, you will do better in the long run to hire a bigger machine and its skilled operator to do the occasional big, tricky or dangerous job. (Follow this advice and you may continue to have a long run.) New compacts are now priced between $10,000 and $25,000. Newsweek reported that Americans bought 900,000 garden tractors in 2005, and that hobby farmers, who make less than $500 annually from agricultural sales, made up 55% of these compact-tractor sales. (Karen Springen, "Let the Good Times Roll," <u>Newsweek</u>, March 13, 2006.) The next category of tractors are those in the 45-50 hp to 65-70 hp range. The largest tractors exceed 70 hp. A helpful article is Bryan Welch's "Discover Versatile Compact Tractors," <u>Mother Earth News</u>, April/May, 2006.

Here's a list of things you will probably get with a new tractor:

1.. Roll-Over Protection System (ROPS). Manufacturers began installing a ROPS (at the very least a rollbar) as a standard feature about 1985. Do not buy a new tractor without one. **A seatbelt must be used with a ROPS**, but if you are using an old tractor without a ROPS, do not use a seatbelt. Tractor rollovers (sideways) and flips (front end over backwards) are the most frequent cause of farm fatalities. Several U.S. manufacturers are encouraging their dealers to retrofit ROPS/seatbelts at cost—about $600, plus freight and labor—on older models. Make sure that your tractor with a ROPS will fit into the building where you will park it. Bigger tractors have cabs that include rollover protection. On old tractors, you may be able to get a local welder to fabricate a rollbar out 3" tubular steel that he bolts to the frame.

2. Earmuffs. Buy good-quality ear protection to protect your hearing. Noise reduction rating should be 25, or more. You may look like Michael Dukakis riding a tank, but you will be able to hear your kids ask for tuition when you are 50.

3. Four-Wheel Drive (4WD). It costs about $1,000 to $3,000 or more to add this feature. Take this option, and you will bless me at least twice a year. If you pay me no heed, buy a set of **wheel weights** for the back tires. You might also consider a set of chains. Buy the 4WD, and call it an investment in your safety—which it is.

4. Category 1, Three-Point Hitch. This rigging at the back of the tractor allows you to hook up and lift/lower common implements. Thus, you can lift a bushhog over a rock or raise a plow when you need to cross a road. Category 1 is the size that will work with most tractors under 50 hp. Your tractor hitch will need an adjustable **toplink** that has sockets at both ends; you hitch one to the tractor and the other to the implement. Toplinks are readily available at farm-supply and tractor stores. The other two "points" on the three-point hitch are sockets at the end of hydraulically operated **lift arms**, or rocker shafts. Each implement will have two cylindrical stubs that slip through these sockets. The stubs are secured with locking pins. Never substitute a chain for a toplink on an old tractor without a ROPS, because you risk having the implement swivel on the lift arms and come over on top of you. Old tractors may only have a pin hitch and a PTO. Lacking a hydraulic hitch, these tractors are limited to activities like pulling wagons and running a hay baler. Tractors made in the late 1950s and thereafter are almost always rigged for a hydraulic hitch. Avoid tractors that require brand-specific implements rather than Category 1's universality. Older models of Allis-Chalmers, Farmall and others used a **proprietary hitch**, which would only accept same-brand implements. The mid-50s Fords and Fergusons came with what became the standard Category 1 hitch. The 8N Fords from that era are still widely used because they are relatively cheap, reliable, parts friendly and can handle all the Category 1 implements. Category 0 ("ought") refers to a smaller hitch design; Category 2 refers to the larger hitch you find on 50 hp+ tractors.

5. Power Take-Off. Don't buy any tractor (new or old) without an independently engageable PTO, that is, a **live power take-off**. A live PTO allows you to operate stationary machinery at the rear of the tractor when the tractor is standing still and in neutral. You can run a hay and grain elevator, concrete mixer, electric generator, posthole auger, winch, arc welder, air compressor and pump from a stationary tractor with a live PTO. New tractors should have this. Make sure the exposed, six-spline shaft at the rear is protected by a **heavy metal shield** that is welded or bolted onto the tractor. The PTO shaft itself should be covered when not in use by a **protective plastic sleeve**. Never step on the bare PTO shaft, either at rest (which will wear down the splines) or when turning (which will wear you down quickly and badly). Keep yourself and your clothing clear of this spinning shaft.

6. Power Steering and Hydrostatic Transmission. Life is easier with both. Old tractors have neither. A tractor with a full front-end loader that does not have power steering is your upper-body work-out machine. Older tractors did not have synchronized transmissions, which means you, like me, have to come to a dead stop to shift into each gear. New tractors have synchronized transmissions and some have a hydrostatic transmission that allows you to slip from forward to reverse without coming to a dead stop and provides many speeds. If you have to do a lot of tight work, "backing and forthing"—shuttling material from one spot to another—the hydrostatic transmission at an extra $1,000 will be well-spent.

7. Hydraulics. Hydraulics refers to a tractor-mounted system that pumps fluid (oil) under pressure to operate attachments and implements, such as the front-end loader, three-point hitch, log-splitter and post-driver. Bigger tractors will have **live hydraulics** at the rear and possibly in the mid-section of the tractor (in addition to the loader controls) that allow you to operate an attachment like a post-driver from the ground. You need at least about 25 hp to operate these type of attachments. Live hydraulics is not a farm necessity, but it allows you to do more work with less effort. There's a cheap kind and a more expensive kind of hydraulic oil. You can use the cheap kind in the tractor's rear differential but not in the other hydraulic systems. Make sure you use the right kind of oil for each system. Better to use the expensive kind throughout. Try to keep dirt out of the system by cleaning/replacing breather filters and using clean funnels when adding hydraulic fluid. Do not put yourself under a raised loader or other attachment. If a hose were to choose that moment to blow out, you will learn that gravity pulling down heavy metal moves faster than you do. If you must be underneath, block up the load.

8. Friendly Ergonomics. Easy Mounting. You will be getting on and off your tractor a lot—to open and shut gates, hook and unhook stuff, fix stuff that you've just fixed, etc. Make sure that you can get on and off easily and safely. If you lose your footing getting off, what will your head hit? Also check for **visibility** in the front—a sloped front provides better visibility. Most new tractors and recent models have a sloped front. Favor a model where the **exhaust** is vented under or behind the driver's seat rather than in a stack sticking up in front of you—unless you get off on fumes. Exhaust smoke is unpleasant and bad for you, particularly in semi-enclosed spaces. The front stacks also tend to snag tree branches. The bigger tractors use the front stacks; many of the compacts vent behind. If the tractor has an enclosed cab, you can live with a front stack.

Check for **easy access** to dipsticks, liquid containers and grease fittings (which are little nipples that you attach your grease gun to and pump grease into; failure to grease your tractor results in large repair bills).

Check **hitch ease.** If you've never connected an implement to a three-point hitch or a PTO, do it on the dealer's lot. The design should let you attach stuff with as little lifting, leveraging, pushing and grunting as possible. If you start sweating on a fall day, look at other brands.

9. Front-End Loader. This is a hydraulically operated bucket at the front of the tractor that scoops, lifts and dumps. Bigger tractors have bigger buckets, higher lifts and more capacity. Very handy. Have your local machine shop or mechanic weld a couple of self-locking **grab hooks** onto the loader's frame (not the bucket itself) so you can pull and lift things with a chain. Some models have a quick coupling arrangement that allows you to install or uninstall the loader in a few minutes. These quick couples give you the opportunity to save fuel and tractor wear and tear by making it easy to take off the loader when you don't need it.

If an older tractor does not have a front-end loader, you may be able to find one that fits. I found a Dearborn loader in a cornfield that could be matched up with my old Ford. I discovered after the job was done that I could mount the tractor only by climbing into the seat from the rear. This meant navigating a jungle gym every time I got on and off. The Dearborn's seller knew that I would lose the safety and ease of side mounting with this old design. I didn't know enough to ask, and he knew enough not to tell.

10. Forks. If the bucket on the front-end loader does not slip onto a set of forks, have your local welder add forks to the loader's frame. This will allow you to remove the bucket and use the forks. I use the forks far more than the bucket. Weld grab hooks onto the fork frame. Forks are far more useful than the one-prong **spikes** you can buy for round hay bales.

11. Stuff.

   a. Drawbar. This is a thick piece of steel with holes through it that attaches between the two lift arms of your three-point hitch when you are running without rear implements. It is the metal bar from which pulling power (hp) is measured. Make sure the cylindrical stubs of your drawbar match up with the size of your lift-arm sockets. You'll probably need some type of **stabilizer device**, which is one or two metal arms that keep the drawbar or implements from swaying back and forth as you drive. You hook wagons and other wheeled machinery to the drawbar with a thick metal pin.

   b. Bushhog. These are field/brush mowers used for rough cutting jobs, such as thistle whacking. The Category 1 models are four-to six-feet wide, and they're configured with one or more blades, or a bat-wing-style blade. New models have clutches to protect their joints and shafts when a rock or hidden stump stops the blade dead. They are usually powered off the rear PTO, though some have their own gas engines. **Bush Hog** is a brand of mower, though it has become the vernacular name. (See www.bushhog.com.) Get a **mounted model** that you can raise and lower using your three-point hitch, not a pull type.

c. Finish Mower. Optional. If you have a big lawn, get one.

d. Adjustable Blade. Allows you to scrape dirt, rock, gravel, manure and snow going forward or push it going backward. Get the heaviest blade your tractor can handle; the lighter ones bounce more than they grade. Make sure the blade is as wide as the outside distance between your rear wheels.

e. Trailer. Get a single-axle, four-sided cart for hauling firewood, rocks, hay bales, gravel, heavy stuff, supplies, manure and kids. Saves wear and tear on your new $35,000 pick-up truck. Used trailer carts are always available. Unless you're suited to the task, don't try to make your own. Hook to the tractor's drawbar using a pin or ball hitch with safety chains.

f. Hay Wagon. Optional. Four-wheeled, open-sided wagon with end rack. Handy for hay bales, both square and round. Also lumber and fence stakes. Get a couple of mechanical binders/tie-down ratchets to use with chains.

g. Manure-spreader. Optional. If you have to clean out a barn (poultry, horses, cattle, etc.), the spreader allows you to haul the manure to a field where it then kicks it up and out as you drive forward. Operates from rear PTO or is ground-driven.

h. If you did not get a front-end loader, consider buying a heavy-duty three-point **lifting boom** and a heavy-duty **three-point platform lift**. Both attach to the three-point hitch at the back of the tractor. The boom allows you to lift something heavy several feet in the air. The lift is a platform, either open-sided or boxed in. If you are intending to put a lot of weight on the rear end, get a set of **ballast weights** that attach to the tractor's front end, otherwise your tractor will rear up and paw the air.

i. Posthole Auger. These work well in some soils, but are useless in others. For stony soils, you will need a **hydraulically operated post driver** that pounds the post/stake like a pile driver. Neighbors will have such drivers, and will know how to operate them safely. Posts, incidentally, are stouter than stakes. They are used in corners and for hanging gates. In my neighborhood, good posts are eight-feet long and at least 8" in diameter. Stakes are the same length, but split from logs. Yellow locust is the preferred wood. Unless you intend to spend a lot of time and money building fence, I'd advise against buying a post driver for your tractor. It's usually more economical to hire fence builders.

j. Plow and disc (harrow). A plow turns ground over as a first-step in planting row crops or a garden. A disc harrow breaks up dry clumps of dirt left after plowing. Harrows come in different sizes and need to be matched to the size of your tractor. A heavy-duty, walk-behind tiller can handle a garden of an acre or two. More than that, you should consider an appropriately sized plow and disc.

k. Low-boy trailer. What happens when your tractor breaks down? You have three choices: 1) field repair, using yourself, a skilled neighbor or a mechanic who makes house calls; 2) pay someone to haul the recalcitrant beast to a shop; or 3) haul it on a low-boy trailer that you hitch to a big-enough pick-up truck or SUV. Low boys are handy for other hauling chores. You will need to figure out how to get the dead tractor onto the low boy. Make sure the low boys's hitch matches the hitch arrangement on the pulling vehicle. Generally, buying a low-boy is an unnecessary expense; someone around you will have one for hire or rent.

l. Seat. You should fit comfortably. As you're sitting on it, turn and look behind you at an imaginary bushhog. You will be spending hours in a tractor seat looking behind you. Make sure the seat allows you to do this comfortably. Swivel seats are a great improvement. Old tractors have uncushioned steel seats bolted to a spring. The seat bottoms out hard when the tractor rolls over a bump. You always wanted to know why old farmers walk funny; this has to be one reason. It's why I walk funny.

12. Grease Gun. You'll need a grease gun whose nozzle head matches the ball-shaped fittings on your tractor and attachments. Use it. Put the cartridge into the gun with its opened end facing away from you unless you yourself are in need of lubrication.

13. Chains. Get at least two 3/8" x 14' log/tow chains with **grab hooks** on each end. This size chain gives you 2,600 pounds of capacity. Half-inch chain provides 4,500 pounds of capacity, but weighs 38 pounds vs. 19 pounds for the 3/8". High-test towing chain provides more capacity at roughly the same cost with just a little bit more weight. Do not put slip hooks at the end of these chains.

14. Diesel or Gasoline Engine? You will need to choose. A diesel engine is more expensive to buy and maintain, and can be cranky in the cold. It gives more power per unit of fuel input, and is simpler (no spark plugs). Gas engines are more familiar to first-timers. Some manufacturers, such as New Holland, use diesels exclusively in their compact tractors. New Holland's line of compacts is called, "Boomers," which says a lot about who's buying small, expensive farm equipment these days.

15. Rear Tires. Three kinds are available. The first type is referred to as R1, Agricultural or General. This tire is what you think of when you imagine a tractor tire. It has V-style grooves and is good in fields. Driving a lot on paved roads wears its tread. The second type is R 3, Turf or All-Weather. It has a flat tread that is designed to work on grass without tearing it up. It is used on lawns, but not fields, mud, woods or snow. The third type is R4, Industrial, which is intended for light industrial work. It's a variation on the R 1. Pavement won't wear R4 treads as fast as R1. The same tread designs are available for front tires on 4WDs. Have the dealer or a mechanic fill rear tires 50 to 75 percent full with the proper mixture of water and calcium chloride for better traction. This solution prevents freezing down to -60 degrees F. If you're buying a used tractor with worn rear tires, buy a new set. Otherwise, you will spend a lot of time spinning your back tires in place on mud and in snow.

16. Tricycle or Wide-Front Tire Configuration. Almost all new tractors are wide fronts. Stay away from the old tricycles because they are more "rolly" on slopes and don't bite into slick surfaces when turning. Consider a tricycle if you are only interested in row-crop agriculture on relatively flat land.

17. Hand tools and odds and ends.

a. Come-a-long (power puller). Get a big one (four-ton) and a small one (one-ton).

b. Heavy-duty jack. High-lift, upscale, bumper-jack model—7,000 pound capacity. Can also be used with a chain at either end as a winch in a pinch. You should also get a screw-type jack that raises the tractor from underneath.

c. Tire-inflator. It works off the cigarette-lighter in your car. Front-tires of tractors pick up punctures from nails, fence staples and locust thorns. Unlike human beings, tractor tires pick up stuff more easily as they get older. You can now get an electric battery-charger and tire-inflator in one unit that you need to charge every so often.

d. Drawbar hook, which is a grab hook for chains that pins through the drawbar, and a **drawbar clevis**, which is a u-shaped connector used to attach things that are being pulled.

e. Miscellaneous. Screwdriver, locking pliers, electrical tape, tire gauge, extra **drawpins or hitchpins** that are used to connect pulled implements and extra **locking lynch pins** that are used to connect the three-point hitch. Your tractor should have a little toolbox for this kit. You'll also need hydraulic fluid, funnel, gear oil, engine oil, grease cartridges and shop towels.

f. Fire-extinguisher—you won't laugh the one time you're out in drought-beset woods and an electrical short causes a fire. Attach the extinguisher to your tractor, using bungee cords.

18. Slow Sign. A red safety triangle should be fastened somewhere—on the ROPS or rear fender—facing traffic behind you.

19. Tractor Bunnies. Compact tractors are not designed to transport passengers. I will sleep better if I write that without qualification. Make your significant other and kids walk. Tractors are tools, not toys. While farm kids learn how to drive tractors and stick shifts when they're eight or nine, I would not let kids run farm vehicles until I had confidence in their maturity. Kids should not be driving 35 hp tractors—kids of any age.

And so inevitably we come to the subject of **used tractors**, a favorite topic in America's countryside. Tractors are worked hard on real farms. Little old ladies don't buy them to drive to church. (I know of only one little old lady who's bought a new tractor, and she's a retired lawyer. She drives to church in an SUV and used to drive sports cars.) "Used" usually means worked hard if it's been owned by a hard-working farmer.

I'd start thinking about a used tractor by finding out why the owner wants to sell it. Good reasons are: 1) he needs something bigger; and 2) he's leaving farming. You can get reasonably priced tractors in good condition in both situations. Buying from a tractor dealer can be a safer option, though you will pay more for the same tractor. Dealers take in trade used tractors that are in fair condition and better. They avoid the basket cases because there's not much profit on their resale and the buyer will soon be complaining and asking for free repairs. The basket cases are sold by FSBOs who can't do a trade in. Look for a dealer-owned used tractor with as few hours as possible, less than a 1,000 might be your target. Ask to test drive it at your farm for a week, with haulage at your expense. If the dealer refuses, ask for a 30-day money-back return agreement or, failing that, a 30-day parts-and-labor warranty. If the dealer refuses, give the tractor a hard workout on the lot, preferably on muddy ground going uphill and down.

There's no substitute for field testing a tractor. Driving around the dealer's paved and level lot in third gear is not a field test. Drive it through all of its gears, under load if possible. Hook it to a loaded hay wagon. Drag a log uphill. How much traction do your front wheels lose when skidding a log? Does the tractor slip out of gear under load? Is the steering tight? Does it feel tippy when you are traveling across a slope? Do you have pulling traction on mud, ice and slick ground? Can you brake coming down a hill with weight behind you? Drive with a loaded front-end bucket—how's your visibility ahead of you?; how hard is it to steer?

Farm liquidations often auction farm equipment, including tractors and farm trucks. If you can field-test these machines a day or two before the auction with a knowledgeable individual, you can buy with reasonable confidence. Simply hearing the engine run on auction day is not good enough. I've found that auctions often get above-market prices for tractors, but I've seen the opposite on occasion. Auctions are snapshots of a local market at a specific moment. As a rule, you will do best at equipment auctions when farm commodity prices are down and interest rates are high. But you can never know the hammer price in advance. Just keep in mind that auction tractors are bought "as is" with no guarantees and limited disclosures.

There are a lot of bad reasons to buy a tractor from a farmer FSBO, especially if this is your maiden tractor purchase. Most bad buying reasons involve a low "get-in" price, which is the first step into every quagmire, and a new paint job. Tractors, like every thing built and operated on a farm, are entropic. They start falling apart and wearing out from their first hour of use. Who better to know when a tractor's general entropy has passed the point of economic repair than its owner? Nonetheless, there are several recurring rationalizations that have run through my head on at least one occasion, including: 1) it's knocked to shit, but it's cheap; 2) it leaks oil, but...; 3) it smokes bad, but...; 4) it slips out of gear, but...; 5) it ain't got no power no more, but...; 6) the PTO slips out of engagement under load, but...; 8) it needs rings, seals, bearings, new electrics or "just a clutch," but.... Do you see the common noose in these lines of argument?

When you face a used tractor in a farmer's front yard, it will have been cleaned up. You will find yourself judging what you can't see by what you can. In these circumstances, you may be weighing a known—below-market price—against the unknowable future costs of repairing the tractor's interior woes. If you pick up one big reason not to buy, you probably should assume that a lot of little reasons are present though not obvious. Of course, "good deals" exist, which is why impulsive bargain hunters trick themselves into believing that their act of purchase inoculates the tractor from future distress.

If you ever hear a FSBO use any form of the word "rebuild" as in, "You might want to rebuild the binglebanger before you....," RUN HOME! Rebuild means a big, expensive job, which can approach a year at Harvard. Rebuilding the binglebanger may lead to rebuilding other parts that it is tied into or dependent on. The deeper into the engine the owner's whispered reference to rebuilding is directed, the faster you want to run home.

If you are new to tractors, you will discover that many farmers are intensely brand loyal and proselytizers to boot. It's helpful to get such an individual to go with you to evaluate a used model of *his* brand. He'll give you an honest opinion, as long as you agree that his brand, when hooked end to end, will pull every other brand all over the lot. But it may not be useful to have a brand-loyal man help you scope other brands, none of which, in his opinion, are worth anything by definition. It is, on the other hand, extremely helpful to have a general-practice farm mechanic or a brand-neutral farmer help you evaluate used tractors. Pay this person fairly—his normal hourly rate plus—for his consulting time, especially if he consents to go looking with you. If he hauls equipment, pay him to haul your beast home. Buy him a good breakfast and a big lunch.

The Yesterday's Tractors website (www.yesterdaystractors.com) posts a large number of useful articles dealing with the infirmities of older tractors. In "Buying your first tractor: Choosing the right one," the anonymous author assumes you are buying used. Here's his checklist in abbreviated form:

> Does it start easily? Make sure that you try a cold start.
>
> Does it run well when hot? Run it under drawbar/hydraulic load.
>
> Do the brakes work well? Do they stop the tractor?
>
> Does it smoke? (The author is referring to exhalation, not inhalation.)
>
> Does it make clunking noises from inside the engine?
>
> Is the oil foamy, filmy (with water) or so black and thick that you could cut it into brownies?
>
> Is there engine head seepage?
>
> Is the clutch good?
>
> Does the electrical system charge?
>
> Do the hydraulics and PTO work?
>
> Are there cracks in the metal castings—engine, transmission housing, etc.?

Here are my additions to this check list: Be alert for engine roughness, dripping leaks (fuel, engine oil, hydraulic fluid, antifreeze, brake fluid), slow-moving hydraulics, electricals that don't work, six-volt battery rather than the preferred 12 volt, welds or metal patches on crankcase, blistered paint (fire!), evidence of roll-over damage, odd noises, fresh paint, new tires and fresh paint, gear slipping into neutral while under load, PTO slipping under load, hydraulics slipping (Lift a loaded bucket, turn the engine off. The bucket should stay up.), dreadful ergonomics, tires with little tread (rear tires are expensive), hard to shift gears, no grease in fittings, low liquid in differentials, outside parking (lots of rust) and, finally, not running.

Don't buy a **not-running tractor** at any price—especially a not-runner whose oil-filler cap has been lost thus allowing rain, dust and mice to get into the engine. A not-runner may be described as one of the "up boys"—**froze or locked**. This gang of two hangs out inside the tractor where a lack of lubrication, broken parts or rust prohibits the normal turning of shafts and gears. Nothing involving the up boys comes cheap. Cousins to the up boys are a couple of girls who never get asked to dance. They are always described as having a little something wrong with them—"Her ignition switch give out." or "Oh, she's just got her a blowed gasket." It stands to reason that a seller would make a minor repair to get a girl up and running before introducing her to a suitor. This no-runner is likely to have more wrong with her than a switch and a gasket. The lamest excuse for not running is a dead battery. If a seller is too lazy to charge a battery or get a new one, what greater evils has his poor character wrought? You don't want to buy this answer. In short, here is the best used-tractor advice I ever received: "If it don't run good, don't buy it."

I'd also be careful with buying a tractor that the seller claims "was running when I parked it." Every tractor was running before it wasn't, including the up boys. Sitting tractors can be either totally non-operational or victims of disinterest. In either case, "**sitters**" become homes for wasps and playgrounds for rodents who like to gnaw on electrical wire insulation. Gasoline left in a fuel tank and carburetor turns to a gunk that must be cleaned out before the engine will run. Moisture can build in an unused hydraulic system. Tires weaken when they stay in one position for a long time. Still, short-time sitters can be real bargains if the owner purchased a replacement and just never got around to selling the old one. Sooner or later, he'll want the parking spot in his shop or barn for something else. His wife may be on his back to "get rid of that old thing." When a seller is tired of looking at a tractor, that's a good time to see whether it's worth buying. And don't forget to dicker for some throw-ins—implements, grease gun, shop manual, PTO connector shaft (which has a universal joint at each end) and spare parts.

"Knocked to shit" is another type of tractor you should avoid. You know this fellow when you see him. He sort of runs, a kind of semi-functioning survivor of hard, long use and deferred maintenance. He looks like he just came out of fight. You'll find dents and welds, maybe even wire holding something in place. Certain farmers are cheap this way; I am sort of cheap this way. You want to leave to these farmers the spoils of their convictions. New paint is a frequent tip off that there's not much life left in this veteran.

Having said all of the above, I will also say that tractors carrying decades of age can be run another 20 years or more. The length of their future depends on what they've been used for, how many hours they carry, how well they've been kept up and how roughly or gently they've been handled. Tractors are designed to pull loads and run equipment. That work won't wear them out prematurely, but thousands of hours of that work inevitably will. What shortens a tractor's longevity is abuse—running it over stumps and rough ground, yanking rear loads out of jams, operating at high rpms, jamming gears, riding the clutch and failing to keep it oiled and lubed. Age alone is a factor, but not one that calls a third strike. Good deals can be found on old tractors whose owners no longer need them.

If a usable tractor from the 40s or 50s appears in your life, it may come with a rigid drawbar between its rear wheels and no three-point hitch system. You can either live within this limitation or consider a three-point retrofit. Kits are available to add a hydraulic hitch, and a skilled farm-implement mechanic may be able to fabricate one. (Before authorizing someone to jigger a hitch together, ask the jiggerer if he's performed this operation before and with what degree of success.) If your old tractor has no hydraulics, this will be a big-dollar retrofit. All things being equal, it's better to buy an old tractor with an operating Category 1 hitch rather than a cheaper old tractor that you plan to retrofit.

As a general rule, gasoline engines should be overhauled (big deal and costly) at 3,000 hours; diesels at 5,000 hours (bigger and costlier for same horsepower). Check the hours on the tractor; ask for rebuild records; don't be shy about this. Tractors built after the mid-1950s should have meters that record hours of full power on the engine. Ask how many rebuilds have been done? Talk to the mechanic if you can; he'll know the tractor as well as the owner. Ford 8Ns and 9Ns from the 1950s are common and may be in reasonable shape even without a functioning hour meter. Ask what the tractor has been used for. Don't buy a tractor that's been used for a lot of heavy logging: it's too rough a job for smaller farm tractors. Older, lighter tractors that have been fitted with a front-end loader will have front-end problems sooner or later if they have been used regularly for lifting heavy stuff (like wet manure) in tight spots that require a lot of turning. I'd recommend sticking with gas engines on older tractors, particularly if you're looking at one built before 1970.

I've included a photograph of my old Ford to illustrate a few points to keep in mind. The front-end bucket can be slipped off, leaving two forks for lifting logs, round bales and items that don't fit in the bucket such as woodstoves, water tanks and pianos. The forks are inserted from the rear into sleeves inside the bucket. The shop-made rollbar carries a warning sign and a fire extinguisher. The rear wheels on this 2WD tractor have new tires, which makes a huge difference in mud and in the woods. The wheels have been "turned inside out" to widen the rear wheel base and decrease roll-over risk. The three-point hitch is carrying a scraper blade, which can be turned so that it pushes material when the tractor's in reverse. The blade has been extended by about 12 inches on each side so that it is about as wide as the wheels, outside to outside. Heavier blades work better than lighter ones, though they're harder to wrestle on. The PTO shaft at the rear (under the hitch) is guarded by a metal shield. The two most objectionable features to this old rig are its front-mounted exhaust stack which inevitably forces me to share the engine's pollution, and, second, the necessity of climbing through the mess at the back to reach the seat. Small tractors of this vintage do not have 4WD, power-steering and rear hydraulics—all of which are handy.

PHOTOGRAPH 8-1

An Old-But-Still-Useful Tractor

It is possible that you are enough of a mechanic that you can do your own tractor repairs. If so, consider yourself one of Heaven's blessed. Working on a tractor is not like working on a 1967 VW bug. You'll need big wrenches and 1/2-inch drive sockets, and sooner or later a cutting torch and welder. Farm shops are heavy duty. Servicing a tractor is work that you will need to do, but working on one is not for the innocent.

If you are condemned, like me, to "lacking the aptitude," as my high school guidance counselor put it, find the nearest reliable tractor/farm equipment repair shop to your target property **before** you buy any farm that needs such machines. If the closest good mechanic likes to work on Fords, be disposed to buy a Ford. Don't assume that he will work on a foreign-made tractor, particularly one of the new entries. My experience is that local tractor mechanics like to do jobs they've done before on familiar brands. You want these mechanics to be your friends and welcome your business. Throw them nice big fat pitches, not screwballs. Ask the local mechanic what he thinks of the tractor you're about to buy.

Dealers charge labor rates that are almost always higher than rates charged by independent shops. Dealers may or may not work on brands other than their own. If the nearest tractor mechanic is a Kubota dealer, I'd look to buy a Kubota tractor, new or used. His rate will be higher, but convenience is worth money too.

My preferred mechanic would be an experienced independent, close by, who treats you and your tractor's woes with patience and humor. If he'll make house calls in desperate situations, you're set. When this wise man speaks, listen and obey.

Here are a few simple used-tractor tests.

A test for poor compression is to warm the engine and take off the oil filler cap. (This is where you put in motor oil; it is not the dipstick cylinder.) If oil or oily mist comes out, you have **blowby**, which indicates weak compression. If nothing oily comes out of the oil-fill tube, good.

On diesels, look for black jelly gunk coming out of where the engine block (bottom) and the engine head (top) meet. This fuel-and-oil mess will ooze out after the engine is warm and you turn it off. It means something is cracked inside.

On gas engines, look for antifreeze on the engine block. Start the engine and remove the radiator cap (remove slowly, using a mitt or towel to protect your hand). If you see air bubbles in the radiator liquid, there is a crack in the engine's block or head—both bad.

Smoke location and color are important. If smoke is coming off the engine as well as out of the stack or exhaust pipe, the tractor is leaking liquid and then burning it off. Could be a big repair. On gas engines, exhaust smoke should be white when you start and then clear. Blue smoke or black smoke indicates engine wear, usually a ring job, valve job, or both. If you find a lot of soot or oily mess at the end of the exhaust stack/pipe, oil is being burned—which is bad. On diesels though, black smoke is good when you're running with the throttle open; white smoke is a sign of burning oil.

Operate everything twice: once when cold (go on a miserable, rainy, freezing day); then when the engine's warmed.

Make sure the gauges, choke, levers, lights and hydraulics work. On older models, check the hand clutch and belt wheel.

On tractors with hand (gas) throttles, make sure the throttle handle engages fully and sticks in all positions. Throttle teeth tend to get rounded off in the most-used positions. If you find yourself with one hand having to hold the throttle in position and your other hand having to hold the gear shift in third, you have no hands left to steer. This can get hairy, especially when you're coming down a hill and you get a leg cramp.

Knock-out considerations. I would not buy a pre-1960 tractor for small farm needs if it had any one of the following shortcomings:

1. No live PTO.

2. No Category 1 three-point hitch.

3. No hydraulics capability.

4. Not running; froze up; locked up.

5. Loud internal clunking.

6. Smoking, indicating oil being burned or other liquids in wrong places.

7. Slipping of gears (transmission, PTO) under load.

8. Incapable of being retrofitted with ROPS.

9. An exotic brand or a model made by a now-defunct manufacturer. If you stick with familiar brands—Deere, Case, Ford, Massey Ferguson, IH—you'll be able to find parts and knowledgeable mechanics for the older machines. The more obscure American brands and foreign makes will be harder to service.

10. Too small to handle a front-end loader.

11. Anything that can be considered restorable as an antique.

12. Unless you like to do this work, leave the pre-1950s' stuff for the buffs. This includes everything with steel wheels.

Current prices for tractors are available in the most recent edition of Intertec's Used Tractor Price Guide (POB 12901, Overland Park, Kansas, 66212) or similar publications, available at any rural library and bank. Know your make (brand), model (year), model number, gas or diesel, number of engine cylinders, engine (indicated) horsepower, number of forward and reverse speeds and 4WD or 2WD. Increase value if it has a front-end loader, full hydraulics, good rear rubber and throw ins like a bushhog.

Parts is a subject in which you will become versed, well and otherwise. Before you buy an old tractor, check locally to see whether the nearest dealer can get parts for you. Sample his ability to get parts by asking if he can turn up a fuel filter, carburetor kit, clutch, rear differential, steering linkage, hydraulic seals and a radiator. Ask around to see how others with older tractors like the dealer's service. I try to avoid obscure brands for parts, though I might just be blindly prejudiced. Sometimes, you don't have a choice about where the part comes from and its price.

Check on the Internet for parts suppliers who handle your brand and model. Start with Yesterday's Tractors, www.ytmag.com, which posts shop manuals, recent used tractor values, links and specific information on Allis Chalmers, Case, Cockshutt, Farmall (IH), Ford, Ferguson, John Deere, Massey, Minneapolis-Moline, Oliver and others. The articles can be found at www.ytmag.com/articles/artint.htm. Use the Google search engine to look for brand-specific, tractor-parts suppliers, e.g., "antique Ford tractor parts." "Antique" sort of refers to pre-1970s models. You'll also find websites, newsletters and small magazines devoted to individual tractor brands. Common parts, for both old and new tractors, are available from Valu-Bilt, 3915 Delaware, POB 3330, Des Moines, Iowa, 50316; 1-888-828-3276; 1-800-433-1209 FAX. You can get buyer guides for different brands and shop manuals for the major brands from Valu-Bilt.

Once you have the tractor home, follow a few simple practices. Lubricate. Change the oil and various filters. Replace worn hydraulic hoses. Routine preventive maintenance on large and/or new tractors will save money over time. Other steps to take include storage out of the weather, periodic tune-ups, oil testing and not modifying the tractor's engine. (See Robert Grisso, "Five Strategies for Extending Machinery Life," Publication Number: 441-451, Virginia Cooperative Extension Service, January, 2002; www.ext.vt.edu/pubs/bse/442-451.html.) Run the tractor at least once every week or two, if only to keep the battery up. Pay attention to unfamiliar noises, wet spots and smoke. Do work slowly and gently; tractors are not dirt bikes. The more you ask your tractor to do what the tractor is not sized to do, the sooner you will be doing nothing at all.

Read up on tractors before you take your first look and test drive: "Compact Tractors: The Horseowner's Sports Car," Horse Journal, Vol. 8, Number 11, November 2001; Farm Journal editors, The Tractor Sourcebook 2002 from www.agweb.com/sig_home.asp?sigcat=farmjournal; Yesterday's Tractors at www.ytmag.com/articles/artint.htm; Chris Pratt, "Buying an Older Tractor," www.kountrylife.com/articles/art4.htm; Melody A. Snider, "Vintage Tractors: A guide to finding a used machine with years of work left in it," Country Journal, September/October, 1990. Get the appropriate owner's book and shop manual. Manuals and books on tractors/machinery, as well as other aspects of farm life, are available at www.diamondfarm.com; click on, general store, and then a specific category.

Tractors are not fun in the way sports cars are. They are useful, and, to that extent, provide satisfaction when they allow you to do a job properly. They've always served as markers of rural status and prosperity. You can buy one for $5,000 to $10,000 that will perform the same work as one costing two or three times that much. It will not be as shiny or as cool looking. If you buy a $30,000 tractor when a $5,000 tractor would do, your new neighbors will admire your tractor but maybe not you.

CHAPTER 9: UNDEVELOPED PROPERTY FOR HUNTING

Undeveloped property in the country is land on which there are no improvements, such as homes, barns and other structures, that carry an assessed value for tax purposes. Undeveloped land can be open or wooded, flat or hilly, dry or wet. When land is advertised as "undeveloped," it should mean that it contains no usable structures, no functioning utilities and no infrastructure to speak of. In practice, "undeveloped" land may contain functional improvements broadly construed such as a barely habitable house and a utility building or two.

When looking at undeveloped land, you should evaluate its possibilities for different levels of future development. Future potential directly affects the price you pay, whether or not you ever improve the property. Developing undeveloped property might mean anything from bulldozing a road to a cleared house site, to building a second home, to dividing 100 acres into 15-acre lots complete with paved roads, buried utilities and houses.

The value of undeveloped land is enhanced when utilities are either already installed or near *and* accessible. Not all nearby utilities are accessible. Neighbors may not be willing to agree to an easement, and the cost of bringing the service to where you want it may be high. It's easiest and usually cheapest to develop utilities on land where they have already been extended to the property. Land that contains **frontage** on a publicly maintained road usually has access to electricity. Frontage is valuable, because it gives property legal and physical access, except in cases where the latter is topographically impossible. If you have no plans to build a house or set up a mobile home, you need not look for undeveloped land with an eye toward a septic system, spring/well and electricity. But land that lends itself to the cheapest versions of these "utilities" has more uses down the road, should be easier to market and will bring a higher price than undeveloped land that lacks the possibility of development.

Undeveloped land is enhanced in economic value and usability to the degree that it is accessible, physically and legally, from a publicly maintained road. Though there are those with just the opposite opinion, I believe that undeveloped land benefits from **internal accessibility**, that is, a system of roads, creek crossings, culverts and trails that allow the owner to get around the property on most days of the year without getting his 4WD stuck. Hiking, horseback riding, fire protection, recreation and firewood-collection benefit from 12-foot-wide roads.

There are five main types of buyers for undeveloped land. Developers buy large tracts, divide them and then retail the resulting lots, which they may call "**farmettes**" in the East and "**ranchettes**" in the West. Second, individual buyers look for tracts of, say, 100 acres or less, for building a second home. The third type is an investor who tries to buy undeveloped land cheap and then sell it for an appreciated price in the future. Fourth, sawmills and timberland investors buy wooded tracts, mainly for their timber value. They may hold the tract or resell quickly after logging. These investors look for higher-and-better use (HBU) potential, which allows them to resell at a much higher price. Finally, there are buyers who are looking for a combination of open and wooded land for hunting. The second-home buyer tends to be the most willing to buy at the highest price per acre. Hunters are generally happy with larger tracts of cheap land as long as it provides habitat for the species they hunt.

HUNTING HUNTING LAND

If you're looking for a couple of hundred of acres of undeveloped woodland to use for hunting and fishing, you will save yourself the purchase cost if you can satisfy your needs on state lands and national forests, which provide game for the price of a license. The hitch is that you may find yourself sharing this space with others similarly inclined. That could be your best friend or a dozen obnoxious strangers. The closer your favorite public hunting or fishing spot is to a public road, the more likely it is that you will be sharing it just when you don't want to. Private ownership conveys the right to keep other hunters off. Privacy has a dollar value; people pay for it. And, assuming, that a particular tract produces only one ten-point buck a year, the hunter-owner wants to make sure that that buck comes within his gun's sights. For that reason, then, a hunter in my area will pay $1,000 per acre and more for scrub woods and old fields. This investment gets him into his woods on weekends—running a chainsaw, improving old logging roads, dozing out a couple of small ponds near his tree stands and putting in feed plots. What the hunter gets for his purchase is 1) the expectation that others won't hunt out his land when he's not there, and 2) steady appreciation in land value.

Serious hunters believe that having their own land is a *need*, not a want. The need is emotional and comes from their belief that hunting is a central axis in their lives and defines much of who they are. A cost-benefit analysis is misapplied to matters of identity and faith. If money, however, is an issue with you—in those moments when your field boots are drying and your wife is waving bills in your face—then allow me to present a few reasonable alternatives that can keep you hunting for a lot less than the cost of buying 100 acres.

Hunters can arrange a **hunting lease** with private landowners. The renter gets exclusive use of the land for a finite and reasonable amount of money. The renter does not bother with any of the hassles of ownership—taxes, insurance, fencing, insect infestations, flood repair and so on. The renter will need to arrange for accommodations during overnight visits. Some leases allow the renter to pitch a tent or set up a camper; others don't. You may be able to camp on nearby public land during hunting season. I've rented some of our property to hunters with good results all around.

The best version of a hunting lease is one that involves no money, that is, **free permission to hunt**. Farmers and absentee landowners are sometimes willing to give hunters permission to take fish and game from their land with no compensation. The landowner sees himself receiving benefit from reducing the number of wild creatures he considers nuisance "varmints," such as groundhog, rabbit, fox, coyote, skunk and deer. Certain game birds are hunted in harvested fields during the fall and have no value to a farmer's farming. As the deer population explodes, woodland owners who want to encourage tree regeneration may look kindly on hunters who reduce the whitetail population; I do.

Permission-hunters make arrangements in person with the landowner and often keep a connection for many years. If no money is paid for permission to hunt, the hunter should provide the landowner with something of value in return. The landowner may be interested in a portion of any edible game taken from his land. Or the hunter may bring the landowner a treat from his home town. Vermont hunters might give a gallon of maple syrup to a rancher in Idaho who lets them hunt fall birds. Or a hunter may swap some of his labor for permission. Lawyers, financial planners and auto dealers can offer advice or a discounted price in return for hunting privileges. Hunters discover permission tracts from their friends and from taking out ads in local papers. The key to a continuing relationship is for hunters to act responsibly. This means they agree to the landowner's ground rules about what and where to hunt, leaving gates open or closed exactly as found, cleaning up after themselves, shooting game (not cows, dogs, horses, hay balers and overalls hanging on a line) and paying for any accidental damage to same.

Landowners have some responsibility toward their hunter/tenants to notify them of concealed dangers (such as quicksand) and remove certain hazards (or provide warning where a hazard cannot be removed). Landowner liability increases if the landowner has done something willfully or grossly negligent that creates a hazard that results in injury. State law governs liability and responsibilities for both landowner and renter. Some states have a recreational-use statute that exempts landowners from the obligation to provide warnings or keep their property safe for individuals with permission to use the property for recreation. Where there is a fee- or rent-charging lease, however, the landowner may lose this protection. The hunting lease I provide for tenants places full liability on the tenant for property damage and injury that he either causes or sustains. If you lease hunting property as either a landlord or tenant, you should put the terms of the agreement in writing and have your local lawyer review it before signing.

Hunting leases are typically written to allow the lease holder access to the leased property for a calendar year. Different game species have different seasons. Wild turkey, for example, may be hunted in both the spring and fall in some states. Fall deer hunting may start with bow-and-arrow hunting, followed by black-powder hunting and then by a rifle season where bucks may be taken on any day but doe only on the last day. Game laws differ among the states, so the lease may have to be tailored to a particular state and even a particular county. Depending on the hunting schedules in a particular state, hunting leases may be expanded to allow non-hunting access during non-hunting times of the year. Woods-loving hikers or trail-riding horseback riders might share the cost of leasing land if it gives them access during non-hunting periods. Low-impact, off-season uses should present no problem to the landowner as long as he knows in advance who may appear in his woods. High-impact, off-season uses—four-wheeling, motorcycles, snowmobiles and the like—should never be done without advance permission from the landowner. If a renter's use produces road rutting and erosion the lease should require the tenant to repair the damage at the end of the use period.

The cost to lease hunting land depends on the type of land being rented, how often the hunters intend to be on it, the type of game that will be hunted, the degree of impact and other factors. Run-of-the-mill land might be rented for $5-$7 per acre/year, or more. Or the landlord may simply charge whatever his annual property tax is. Land for duck hunting and field birds is more expensive. Land and timber companies usually lease their land to hunters. Woods that have been recently timbered provide more game forage than mature woodland, so hunters will want to rent such land.

If a hunter persists in feeling the need to have his own hunting ground, he can consider buying into a **hunt club**. These are like-minded individuals who pool their money to buy a large tract. A club can also lease land in lieu of purchase. An individual may be able to buy a membership in an established club; otherwise, he will have to form a group from scratch and then look for land. Land-owning clubs can be organized as limited liability companies, corporations, partnerships, non-profits, trusts or other forms of joint ownership. Each type of ownership carries its own set of benefits, liabilities and tax consequences.

Buying a membership or a share in a hunt club is a commercial transaction that may put your future wallet in play for improvements to the club's land, facilities or future expansion. Where a club is governed either by majority rule or elected leaders, a member may be obligated for expenditures that he opposes.

As a member, you may also be entitled to a share in future revenue from the club's land. Club revenue can be generated from the development of minerals, the sale of timber or land. Clubs distribute current revenue to members or hold it in a club account for use in improving facilities and services, or a bit of both. It's important for a prospective member to have a clear idea of how the by-laws provide for future financial obligations, benefits, decision-making and leaving the club.

Your tax situation can also be affected by the structure of the club's organization. If you are buying an interest in the club's property and the club is set up as a business (anticipating revenues from timber sales and memberships), you will probably need to look at it as a business investment so that you obtain the appropriate tax benefits. A club membership, on the other hand, whereby you pay an entrance fee and dues is not an investment, though you may be able to consider it a business-related expense in some circumstances. Before buying into a hunt club, make sure that you understand the legal and financial implications of its organizational structure for your cash flow and tax obligations. If you're not sure how membership will affect your tax status, pay an accountant who does taxes (not all do) to review your finances and the club's structure.

Hunting clubs often buy back-country land that individuals interested in second homes reject because it's too rugged or too remote. Clubs are chiefly interested in good habitat for game species and sufficient size to provide good opportunities for all members. If you are thinking about forming a hunt club in anticipation of buying such land, you should plan for the estimated revenue the timber is likely to provide the next time it is cut and how your club members want that money handled. The kind of game the club focuses on will determine the kind of land it buys. Deer hunters, for example, value a mix of rough terrain with thickets, young woodlands, scattered openings/fields, and the tree species that provide fall mast and winter fodder. Views are unimportant, and electricity, telephone, soil productivity, timber quality and road frontage may be of less importance. Woods that have little timber value due to poor tree quality can produce abundant game forage. Hunters and hunt clubs can lower their acquisition expense by targeting land that has little value to second-home buyers who are seeking country aesthetics like big views and bold streams. Cost-conscious hunters should concentrate on finding tracts that combine the habitat of their game species with features repugnant to second-home buyers, such as remoteness, 4WD-only access, recent timbering, steep slopes, wetlands, lack of perimeter fencing and a seriously run-down house, which is good enough for hunters during deer season but not good enough to entertain the boss for a weekend. Hunting land should be cheaper than second-home land on a per-acre basis, unless it is also valued for timber resources or location.

In particular, hunters and hunt clubs should look for recently timbered tracts—**cutovers**—that should sell for a discounted price. A cutover discount should be twice applied: first, the seller has removed the timber's present value, and second, even in the best of circumstances, he has left the next owner a visual mess of tree tops that will last for at least five or six years. If the trees left standing are low-value species or worthless because of poor form, the buyer should add a third discount into his negotiations. A timber tract **high-graded** in this fashion impedes the regeneration of well-formed, high-value species on cutover land. It reduces the future value of the next timber cut.

From a hunter's perspective, cutover land provides better habitat for certain game species like deer and turkey than mature forest and pasture. Logging creates openings in the leaf canopy that allow sunlight to penetrate to the ground. This stimulates the growth of palatable vegetation and provides thick underbrush. Shade-loving vegetation is replaced by young, sun-loving plants such as tree sprouts, grass, high weeds and brambles. Logging also leaves **slash**, tree tops left on the ground after the logs are cut from the stem and taken to the mill. Slash provides cover for game and helps tree seedlings get established by protecting them from browsers. Slash is a big, ugly mess until it breaks down. Hardwood tops may have commercial value as pulp, chips or firewood, but loggers often find it not worth their time to work with it.

A **clearcut** removes all standing timber. Left in place are stumps and slash, which might be piled and burned. A **selective cut** removes some trees, usually determined by their diameter size and/or species. It leaves stumps, slash and standing timber. The more trees the seller has taken down in a selective cut, the worse the tract will look and the deeper the discount the hunter-buyer should propose. Both types of cutover may be called **raw land**, which is land lacking improvements, or **bare land**, which is land lacking both improvements and present timber value. Timbering turns raw land into bare land. When negotiating for cutover tracts, buyers should always refer to it as bare land to help lower the seller's sense of value. The value of bare land rests on its location, views, water resources, utilities, topography, subsurface minerals, access and other virtues. Cutover land is stripped bare when its owner wants to establish a tree plantation, which requires brush clearing and the application of herbicide to control unwanted vegetation. Woods with intermittent ten-to-20-acre clearcuts provide good habitat for many game species.

The concept of **bare-land value** does not refer necessarily to land that is physically bare. In my experience, rather, it refers to the fair market worth of cutover after the seller has removed or optioned whatever timber he could sell. Bare land, in other words, could have trees up to 14" in diameter and larger (where culls are left standing). Hunter-buyers should determine the current bare-land value of cutover land and use that number as the axis for their negotiations. Bare-land value on cutover tracts will increase over time as a result of timber regeneration and background appreciation. Typically, a hunter-buyer of a recent selectively cut tract should expect to pay about half the per-acre price the land would have brought with the timber in place. If the selective cut is severe, pay less than half. Clearcut land might be about one-third the price.

If the clearcut land has been replanted as a pine plantation, it will be valued at the cost of the replanting effort plus something for the dirt itself. Replanting cost—which involves preparing the site and planting the trees—varies with location, terrain, type of tree and its stocking density. Loblolly pine, a common fast-growing species, planted at 600 to 700 seedlings per acre might be valued in its first year at $600 to $700 per acre in many areas. An owner adds value to replanted pine by applying herbicide in a few years to suppress competition. Planted pine acreage is currently selling for between $1,000 and $3,500 per acre, depending on age and location. High prices are paid for tracts where the pine is ready to be cut. If the tract has residential development value (HBU), it will be priced above its timber value and above what a hunter should pay for hunting ground.

I have found in recent years a few selective cutovers priced at what I might offer for the land with all the timber in place. Their owners know the value of cutover to hunters and are pitching their property specifically to the cash-heavy urban hunter. These properties are located in areas where land is appreciating for reasons unrelated to hunting or timbering. In such cases, the buyer is usually paying for location. If the hunter-buyer's goal is simply to have a place to hunt, appreciating location is not a factor in his reasoning. Better to buy remote and cheap than near and dear. But if the hunter-buyer is looking at his purchase as an investment that offers hunting as a recreational benefit, a higher-priced cutover can work. Certainly within ten years, the cutover will look clean and have recaptured then-current, full market value.

A hunter will also value cutover tracts because they will have a network of 4WD-capable interior logging roads—called **skid roads**—that facilitate access throughout the property. These ten- to 12-foot-wide roads make it easy for hunters to get to their stands and then haul the field-dressed game out of the woods with a minimum of dragging and humping. Loggers bulldoze roads through the woods to allow them to pull out a half-dozen logs at a time using a large rubber-tired machine called a **skidder**, which usually has a dozer blade in front and a cable winch in the rear. A common plan is to have a main haulage way with spurs off to either side. On slopes, loggers may have the main road take most of the pitch, using switchbacks where necessary, with spur roads branching off along level contours. Skidders or dozers will drag a just-cut log from where it was felled to a place where it can be chained up with several others and dragged to the **landing**, or **deck**, for loading onto a truck. Landings are level spots of an acre or less near the entrance to the property. There, newly cut logs are sorted by species and quality, cut to length and then trucked to the log yard or sawmill. Some skid roads, left alone, are suitable for hiking or trail-riding on horseback, but they can be too steep for a tractor or too tightly curved for a truck. Still, the main skid-road network along with many spurs can usually be made truck capable with some dozer work.

Loggers want to build as little road as possible owing to the construction expense and the cost of applicable state reclamation standards. In some states, loggers are now expected to leave their logging roads with **waterbars** in place. Waterbars are dozed-out ditches that run diagonally across the road's width whose function is to funnel surface water off to the side where it is absorbed. They can be five feet wide and three feet deep. Waterbars minimize road erosion, but when they are too steep-sided or too deep they prevent subsequent vehicle use. In that event, the landowner has to rework them by hand or machine to make them passable. His purpose is not to fill them in. It is rather to keep an erosion-control channel in place, though in a broader, shallower form that allows traffic.

The logger should smooth a road disturbed by skidding or hauling before leaving. This is followed by seeding it with grass, which holds the dirt in place. The landowner will almost always need to tidy these post-logging roads by hand. Rocks and small tree branches need to be pitched aside and holes need to be filled. Some bulldozer work may be required to realign roads that are too steep or tightly switch-backed. Culverts and drainage ditches can be installed. While the hunter-buyer may object to redoing what the logger should have done, it is far cheaper to a new owner to upgrade existing roads—even ones left in poor condition—than to pay a dozer operator to cut new roads through a forest. A typical 50-acre hardwood tract that's just been logged and reclaimed might require a day or even two of bulldozer time to get the roads ready for vehicles, and then another couple of hours of hand work per ten acres to get them safe for travel by foot, hoof and tire.

With this level of effort, a hunter-buyer can improve most logging roads enough for near year-round 4WD use. Sufficiently deep snow or spring mud, of course, can bog a Hummer. If you use anything other than a 4WD vehicle on skid roads in the woods, expect to get stuck. Spruced-up skid roads are **not** suitable for year-round second-home access in wet and/or mountainous terrain. If you're looking to build a second home on a wooded tract that's been logged, you can start with a skid road but anticipate widening, ditching, regrading and adding culverts and stone/gravel if you're planning to bring in trucks loaded with cement, block and building materials. You may want to bury utility lines next to the roadbed when you're doing this work. Bridges are expensive and should be engineered to carry your heaviest load, plus 50 percent more for safety. Hauling base rock—about the size of a softball—and gravel to your road site can quickly involve a lot of money, because soft ground can eat up an enormous volume of rock. Where possible, work the road around wet spots rather than through them. Spots that are usually wet because of subsurface water may have to be dug out and filled in with rip-rap rock then topped with base rock and gravel. Water needs to be channeled out from under the road. Otherwise, the perma-mud will suspend rock and gravel like bits of sausage in gravy, and you've gained nothing for your expense.

As a hunter-buyer, you will save yourself time by asking the seller a few questions in your initial telephone conversation. First, you want to know the type of logging that's been completed—clearcut, selective cut or a combination of the two. The more cutting, the more open area and slash you will find. A hunter often prefers a combination of the two, which provides newly cleared areas within a selectively cut forest. If you are told it has been selectively cut, you need to pinpoint the date of the cutting and the selection criteria used to govern the timbering. The larger (wider) the diameter threshold, the more standing timber you will find when you arrive. A selective-cut threshold of 20" diameter and larger will leave much more timber in place than a 12"-diameter cut, that is, all the trees with diameters 12 inches and larger.

Timber size in the field is usually measured as **diameter at breast height (DBH**, which is taken at 4.5 feet above the ground.) Thus, a hardwood tract that was cut "18 and better" usually means that all the valuable 18" and larger DBH **hardwood sawtimber** was removed. You would find this cutover with stems smaller than 18" DBH, which is a stand with sizeable trees and future timber value within ten to 20 years. A heavier cut—using a smaller diameter threshold—usually benefits hunting because it creates more openings and edge in the remaining woods, but it lengthens the time needed for the remaining trees to add the diameter girth to make them merchantable.

The hunter also needs to ask whether all "18 and better" stems were taken, or just the high-value, hardwood sawtimber. If all stems—sawtimber and **culls**—were cut, the woods will be far more open than if the valuable sawtimber alone was cut. Culls are low-value species and trees that have no timber value for various reasons. Culls may have value as pulp, but not sawtimber. Hunting habitat will usually be better when both types of timber are cut. Dropping the culls also improves the woods in terms of future timber value, because the high-value trees left standing will have more access to nutrients and sunlight. From a hunting perspective alone, leaving the pulp logs in the slash will provide more wildlife forage and cover than if they're removed.

Be careful to pin down the seller's terminology. A seller telling you the timber was cut "18 and better" may be telling you either that the loggers took all sawtimber hardwood 18" and larger or all trees—hardwood and pulp—18" and larger. In addition, he may be saying either that all the trees were 18" and better **DBH** or 18" and better **at the stump**. In the latter case, the 18" diameter is measured at ground level, not 4.5 feet up the trunk. A stump cut of 18" and better can drop trees as small as 12" DBH, as long as the stump measures 18" across. The difference between 18" DBH and 18" at the stump will normally mean a huge difference in the number of trees cut and, accordingly, the number of trees left. The more timber removed, the deeper the price discount you should expect.

Hunter-buyers will also find timber tracts involving **planted pine**. Typically, these tracts are a mix of native hardwood that has been left along the water courses ("in the drains") for protection and even-age pine plantings. Where an entire stand of pine has been removed, hardwood and naturally occurring conifers will reestablish themselves. This provides food for wildlife, but not much cover until several years have passed. From an investment perspective, pine value comes in two "lifts": the first is a thinning cut that is taken at about 12 years, plus or minus, depending on local conditions; the second is the harvesting of the mature pine 12 to 15 years later. The cheapest price on pine-plantation land is just after a clearcut and before any replanting has occurred. Your next best price will be when the planted pine is less than ten years old, younger being cheaper. Pine land will be priced higher if hardwood growth has been suppressed by herbicides, which has the effect of increasing pine yield. Some pine is now being planted at 400+/- seedlings per acre with only a sawtimber cut planned.

Paper companies have been active sellers of this type of land since the 1990s. Typically, tracts of 20,000 to 100,000 acres or more will be divested to parties who then break them into smaller parcels of 5,000 to 20,000 acres which are then sold in 1,000- to 5,000-acre tracts that are then sold retail in lots of a 100 to 1,000 acres. At each step, the per-acre price is boosted by $50 to $200.

On mixed-species tracts, ask the seller what he thinks the most prevalent tree species is. This is usually framed in my neighborhood as, "What's it (run) heavy to?" You can then ask the seller for his opinion about the percentage distribution among species. If you're looking for deer habitat, you want the tract to run heavy to mast-bearing trees like oaks. These species allow deer to fatten in the fall, increasing their chances of surviving the winter and producing healthy offspring. You're also interested in young growth for winter feeding and a species like striped maple (moosewood) for browse. The County's Soil Survey provides soil maps with information ranking each soil's suitability for various wildlife habitats. Locate the seller's land on the soils maps and then refer to the table that sets forth habitat suitability. A hunter does not want to buy woodland whose standing trees won't provide good habitat for his preferred game. The question the hunter asks of cutover woods is: How productive is this cutover habitat for my game species?

The last information the hunter-buyer needs to find out in his first conversation with the seller concerns the tract's hunting history. The buyer needs to listen for what's not being said, as well as for what is. Most sellers of woodland will say, with varying degrees of honesty, "The hunting's great." Hunting for which game species? A deer hunter doesn't much care if the land is brimming with rabbits. How does the seller define "great"—by the number of trophy bucks or the number of deer taken each year? How hard has the land been hunted for the last five years? Are there too many deer for the land? Has he hunted the land himself recently? For what game? Does he get his legal limit each year? Is the land currently posted for hunting? (Yes is good; no could mean it's considered a public hunting ground.) Do neighbors and local residents hunt it? (Yes is bad; no is good.) Is it accessed by a locked gate? (Yes, means it has history as off-limits; no could mean anything.)

Do his relatives and buddies—R&Bs—also hunt the place? (If so, you may find the R&Bs showing up next hunting season. The seller, they will say, gave them permission to hunt before he sold to you, which is news to you. You can prevent this by including language in your purchase contract that requires disclosure of such an agreement.) If the buyer gets wind of R&Bs during negotiations, he must insist that the seller put the word out that the new owner will not grant hunting rights or recognize any claim to post-sale hunting rights. This might be accomplished by a newspaper ad. In years past, the seller may have given his R&Bs his personal permission to hunt. In the law, this is called a **license**, and it expires with the sale of the property. The buyer must be firm with both the seller and the R&Bs, otherwise the potential exists for continuing conflict during hunting season.

While cutover land can be a bargain for hunters, it can also work for thrifty non-hunters who are willing to live with unsightliness for a few years. A woodland buyer looking at cutover will find everything from land looking like it has just been bombed to land that has been roughed up but is essentially intact. Logging, no matter how careful, doesn't improve the immediate visual aesthetics of woodland. The day after a logging crew leaves, you can expect to find muddy skid roads, trees that have had their ground-level bark skinned off by logs being skidded out, trees with top branches broken by falling timber, slash everywhere and a general aftermath of recent mayhem. Don't be discouraged by slash. See it as an opportunity. It's easily gotten firewood. It rots pretty quickly and adds nutrients to the forest's soil. You don't want a spic-and-span forest floor free of debris if you're interested in healthy trees. In ten years, slash disappears completely in most environments on its own through Nature's recycling system.

I had a client who was selling about 500 acres in a very desirable, very pretty part of western Pennsylvania. The property had been a girl scout camp. My client had cut about 15,000 trees and put in about 15 gas wells. The camp—with all of its buildings, kitchens, pools and developed infrastructure—was untouched and in good repair. The timber sale and the gas development would almost pay for my client's purchase and then more over time. He was willing to let the surface go for a steeply discounted price, because he had no use for it. If a buyer could see seven or eight years out, he could acquire appreciating land and improvements at about 25 percent of their real value.

Bad logging jobs usually look worse than good ones. Bad logging is done as fast as possible, which generally maximizes the visual damage. These loggers drop trees with little concern for protecting those they're not taking. This leaves a lot of bashed up trees, leaning trees that will soon fall and widowmakers—broken branches hanging above the ground that fall without warning. A bad logging job looks ragged and messy. The skid roads are rutted, rocky and subject to erosion. You might find slash dropped across roads as a cheaper and faster alterative to waterbars. You might find tree tops in stream channels and straddling fence lines. The buyer needs to be able to distinguish between the roughed up look of a good logging job and the look of a bad logging job. A typical hardwood tract might take six to eight years for slash to rot to the point where it is no longer obtrusive. That process can be accelerated by wet conditions and some chainsaw work that lops the tops so that the wood lies closer to the ground. A bad logging job takes longer to heal. The battered trees are weakened and may never recover. Buyers should not equate immediate post-logging looks with future timber value, or roughed up aesthetics with environmental health. Cutover land can contain much future timber value and be environmentally healthy and productive as well. Hunters can make great buys on wooded tracts that have been severely cut and left a dreadful mess as long as they are willing to hold the land for at least 15 years. These opportunities allow the hunter to buy cheap and sell dear, after the land has healed.

My final point on aesthetics is that you can, as I have done, measurably improve a cutover's looks with a chainsaw, mattock, shovel and rock bar. Improvement does, however, take time and hand labor. Slash decomposes fastest where as much of each tree top lies as close to the ground as possible. You hasten decomposition by lopping and bucking up the tops, cutting the branches from the main stems and cutting the stems into five- to ten-foot-long chunks. This allows both the top stem and the branches to settle. The combination of snow, rain, wildlife and bugs will get rid of the wood. After three to five years on the ground, most wood, with exceptions like yellow locust, gets punky and loses its value as firewood. By the third or fourth year, you will not see much of the slash in the summer as pioneer plants spring up in the open spaces. By the seventh or eighth year, most slash left to itself will be inoffensive. The best time to buy this type of land for an investor with a longer term horizon is immediately after logging when it looks its worst. Every year that passes improves cutover appearance and increases the land's value. A hunter should aim his buying at cutover and not clear its slash, except from roads.

If you want to accelerate slash decomposition, work a deal with a couple of local guys to take away all the slash firewood they want. In the best of circumstances, this work is hard and dangerous. It should not be attempted by inexperienced chainsaw users. If you wage this war yourself, wear protective chaps, gloves, steel-toed logger's boots, and helmet with hearing protection and a screen face mask. Cutting firewood out of tops is light on your cutover land, requiring nothing more than a pick-up truck and basic woods tools—chainsaw with extra blade and chains, splitting maul, logging chains, sledge hammer and a couple of wedges, peavey and a tie-pick. The last of these is an ax with its blade ground and sharpened to a point. It's used to pick up chunks of wood without bending. In addition to the aesthetic benefit of making your woods look better, the firewood boys will get your roads in shape for 4WD traffic. That means they'll help clear them of rocks and logging debris and remove anything that threatens their tires and exhaust systems. These folks are doing you a favor; don't charge them for the wood they remove and treat them well.

The first property I bought was a new cutover that was dirt cheap. I was too dumb-young to know how bad it looked or how bad a job the logger had done. But I did know that $5,000 for 60 acres 30 minutes from Amherst, Massachusetts wasn't likely to prove to be a risky investment in 1971.

Selectively cut hardwood tracts bought cheap will reward you financially in relation to the number of years you carry them. The longer you can hold a hardwood timber tract, the more value it produces. Depending on the individual characteristics of the site and the timbering job you've inherited, you should be able to take another selective cut 15 to 30 years down the road. And if you hunt the land every year—your main purpose, of course—you will have won three times.

CHAPTER 10: INFRASTRUCTURE—LAND, PROPERTY AND SITE

INFRASTRUCTURE PACKAGES

Many buyers are looking for second-home possibilities on undeveloped or semi-developed rural land. A second home can be anything from a mansion to a wilderness cabin. It is usually thought of as having a fixed foundation, but it may also be a mobile home or even a more-or-less permanently parked recreational vehicle. Mobile homes and RVs held by absentee owners are generally associated in my area with "hunt camps," places that are used a few weeks and a dozen or so weekends every year for hunting. Hunt camps, however, come in all sizes, ranging from a much-used trailer to a sumptuous lodge complete with servants. Hunters may or may not be concerned with a house site and house-related amenities.

The land buyers I discuss below are looking to have a second home on their land. This can take the form of buying a lot in a second-home development where the seller/developer is also the house builder, or land where the landowner needs to procure a **general contractor** to build the house, or a spot where the landowner wants to do the construction himself. The alternative is to buy land with an existing house. Each of these second-home options will involve you in the question of **infrastructure**—roads, utilities and so on—which is discussed in this chapter.

Second-home buyers in the country in my experience tend to be either folks in their 30s or 40s who are looking to build a weekend/summer place within a two- or three-hour drive of their principal residence or folks in their late 40s and 50s who are thinking about relocating in anticipation of retirement. The latter are looking for a low-stress rural environment where their pensions will stretch farther. In other areas, younger families with high incomes are in the second-home market. Individuals from each group differ in finances, time horizon and priorities, but they share the problems of evaluating an existing second-home house or building one from scratch.

Younger second-home buyers are looking for recreation and physical activity. Building their own house on unimproved land may become part of their lifestyle choices. Other buyers may be looking for a rural development of second homes, where they do nothing more strenuous than pick the model, write the checks and unlimber their woods and irons. These are the ends of the hands-on continuum, and they are very far apart.

Whether you buy rural land on your own or as part of a development, you should be concerned with both the level of existing infrastructure and the level that you might want in the future. As you age, the ease and convenience of your second-home infrastructure will become increasingly important to your ability to use your property.

Land infrastructure refers to roads, water, sewerage, utilities and the like that serve the land or development lot you're investigating. Land infrastructure is, around, near to or adjoining your target property.

Property infrastructure refers to these same components to the extent they are currently **on** your target property. While "on" is better than "planned" or "accessible," you may still not be able to get electricity, for example, from a pole at the front corner of a 200-acre property to its back boundary where you want to put a cabin. It may be physically impossible to build or bury a line to your spot, or the cost of doing so may be prohibitive. You will need to assess the feasibility and cost of putting in or upgrading property infrastructure according to your second-home plans.

Site infrastructure refers to the type and level of infrastructure you need and want **at** the spot where you are intending to build a house.

Most rural property has some degree of land infrastructure, though it may be no more than a primitive road. If you buy land that has been divided for resale or as a lot in a development, the level of property and site infrastructure will range from zero to fully developed, complete with amenities. Where you are intending to build a house, you will need to scope property and site infrastructure. Your beginning questions are: What kind of site infrastructure is feasible at my house site? and How much will each component of feasible infrastructure cost?

You may want no infrastructure of any type, because you intend to use your new land only for walk-in tenting. Even if you have no immediate plans for building a house, you should still consider the feasibility and cost of all three types of infrastructure. The easier and cheaper it is to put infrastructure in place, the more marketable your new property is and the more valuable it will be if you want to sell. I would avoid buying property that is deficient in infrastructure unless a wilderness-type use is what you and your heirs want. When a target property's infrastructure is deficient, I would use that projected expense to work down the seller's asking price. The cost of putting in infrastructure tracks inflation at the very least, and my guess is that it gets more expensive relative to other rural costs over time.

The first step a developer usually takes with a second-home project on a large, undeveloped tract is to propose a purchase contract with a contingency that makes the sale dependent on the developer securing whatever permits and zoning clearances he requires for division. This process can take a few months to several years, depending on the project's size, location and complexity; the site's topography and features such as wetlands, trout streams and endangered species; and the degree of administrative challenge and/or litigation. Sales should start once all regulatory hurdles are cleared, but sometimes lots are reserved or marketed before this happens on a contingent basis.

Permitting and project success is also directly affected by local opinion. Political opposition to building houses on farmland and woods can limit a project's size and design—and kill it in some cases. A buyer should be wary if he hears the project he's considering is bad-mouthed locally and has yet to be fully permitted. Such a buyer cannot be assured that the project's infrastructure will be developed and completed as the developer promises. One who buys a lot in a less than fully permitted project is assuming risk in return for no benefit. If you find yourself buying in advance, propose to the developer that he give you a discount for your willingness to buy early, which lends credibility and financial underpinning to his project. If the developer refuses, wait at least until he's fully permitted before buying. You can also propose **buying an option to buy a particular lot**, contingent on the developer getting all permits and/or putting in all infrastructure as promised. You are purchasing the right to buy the lot at a certain price at some future point; if you don't follow through with the purchase once the developer has satisfied your concerns, you lose your option money.

Permits and plans do not guarantee the project will be completed as presented. The risk of partial completion hovers over many developments; lack of cash being the most common problem. Projects done by large, well-capitalized developers with a track record are usually less risky than those done by local independents. But the buyer should check the record of any developer from whom he's considering buying a lot. Ask, in particular, whether the developer completed all the infrastructure that he promised.

The buyer who fears taking on the A-to-Z tasks in building a home on land with no infrastructure should look for a lot in developments that offer a **full package of infrastructure**—survey, all utilities (electricity, water, sewerage, phone, among others), surface-water drainage system and roads. (Sidewalks and street lights may or may not be part of the infrastructure a country second-home development needs.) Buyers benefit from fully developed lots, because they are purchasing property and site infrastructure at a group rate. The developer should be able to get this work done more cheaply by bundling it, scaling it efficiently and using competitively bid contracts or his own crew. The developer can pass along some of these savings to lot buyers. Of greater ultimate value, I think, is that you don't have to spend time and money finding, vetting and negotiating with infrastructure contractors; scheduling and sequencing their work; securing permits; getting materials to the site; and inspecting the finished job.

The alternative to a full-package development is one that offers a **partial package of infrastructure**. At the minimum, a developer will have clear title to the land, platted it into lots and put in enough of a road system to make each lot reasonably accessible to buyers like you. House construction may or may not be something the developer offers. The less infrastructure the developer has installed, the less likely it is that he will be building houses owing to the logistical hassles involved. The level of infrastructure in a partial package can be nothing more than a logging road into the property. Whatever property infrastructure the developer does not put in falls to the lot buyers either as individuals or as a group. If the buyers are of like mind and pocketbooks, they can organize and do the level of work they desire. When, however, buyers are dissimilar, making group decisions is difficult and often contentious. For that reason, I would avoid partial-package developments where the developer has punted property infrastructure decisions into both the future and the laps of lot buyers.

Partial packages offer cheaper lots than full packages. If the buyer is looking for 4WD-access, rough-and-tumble land, a development with nothing more than a dirt road can be a perfect fit. If, on the other hand, you and other lot buyers are likely to need more property infrastructure than the developer is putting in, then you must investigate feasibility and costs *with your new neighbors*. One reason why a developer may not offer a fuller property infrastructure could involve a cost that is prohibitive. If you don't find electricity service to each lot, for example, the explanation may lie in the upfront cost of installing it. Some steep, rocky or wet conditions can make certain typical infrastructure improvements too costly to be practical. When a lot buyer has infrastructure expectations that are higher than what he is purchasing, he is asking for future headaches.

A buyer approaching a partial-package development should keep in mind a few cautions about **surveys** the developer provides for both the lot you want to purchase and the tract from which it has been carved. (See Chapter 17 for a discussion of surveys.) Surveying costs can involve a considerable upfront cash outlay when the perimeter boundary is unmarked, in dispute, or requires the surveyor to dig out the "calls" (for metes and bounds) from the chain of title and possibly the chains of title in deeds of adjoining property owners. A developer looking to save dollars may not try to clear up boundary disputes before "lotting out" the tract. Some surveyors will not mark boundaries on the ground unless they are paid extra. The surveyor may or may not note a potential dispute on the survey he prepares. Even where nothing tricky is intended, ten surveyors may not come up with the same line owing to flaws, mistakes and typographical errors in the chain of title, though in most cases they will. A surveyor may or may not note on his survey that he suspects an adjoining neighbor may have a prescriptive easement over a developer's lot. Similarly, not all surveyors will indicate on their surveys where an existing fence line is not on the surveyed boundary line.

Buyers should be aware that even when they purchase a parcel of land with a current survey, that survey may not be accepted by adjoining neighbors who may have surveys or claims of their own. In a few cases, a new survey will create the very disputes the buyer hopes it has settled. A buyer should personally visit each adjoining neighbor outside the development before signing a purchase contract. Provide the neighbor with a copy of the developer's plat with your lot and the common line highlighted. Ask if he has any problem with the joint boundary as shown. The copy of the plat you provide will give the neighbor a chance to review it with his own surveyor. Your neighbors inside the development will be working off the new internal division lines, and there should be no dispute between you and them. If the developer offers lots in a division where the boundaries have not been recently surveyed, it is even more important for the buyer to check with the outside landowners adjoining his lot.

I ran into a situation in 2002 where a speculator had purchased an option to buy a 4,800-acre tract, 4,000 acres of which was wooded mountain land with various access problems and disputes. The remaining 800 acres was a 15-year-old clearcut and scrubby pasture. The tract had about 30 miles of perimeter boundary. A surveyor who was working for the option-holder said he estimated there were about 75 adjoining landowners, and most were going to have line disputes with any division the speculator/divider proposed based on the seller's 1908 survey. The surveyor estimated the cost of running a boundary survey around the 4,800 acres at about $125,000. The owner had shrewdly chosen not to do a survey; the less-shrewd speculator had optioned it without knowing that the 1908 survey boundaries were unreliable. The speculator's strategy was to divide the acreage into four or five chunks and sell them to hunting clubs with whatever boundary he had purchased. There's nothing illegal about this. It simply passes through to the next buyer a likely dispute and predictable expense. In my opinion, the shaky survey and boundary was a "defect" that a seller should disclose to a buyer. This seller had not disclosed it to the option-buyer who lost his option deposit when he failed to proceed with the deal. Had you bought a lot from the option-buyer in these circumstances, it's quite possible that you would have faced one or more lawsuits over boundaries and ended up with significantly less acreage than you had purchased.

Second-home developments often feature infrastructure and amenities (common community and recreation facilities) that may or may not be built at the moment you are asked to sign a purchase contract. In this situation, the buyer should assume the developer is well-intentioned and wants to build out everything shown in his plans. If you get the feeling that he is not well-intentioned, don't buy. The buyer should also assume that if you don't see things in place, they may not get there regardless of the developer's intentions and promises. The price of the lot you're buying should include the cost of building out all infrastructure and planned amenities. However, developers run out of money every so often, a situation that will cancel work promised. When a developer runs short of cash, individuals who have bought lots in the project may either abandon the developer's vision or complete it in full or in part. Where the buyers pool their resources to build a promised common facility, they will be paying twice for getting what was promised. When a group of buyers is left with a half-completed project, they will either spend time and money working out an acceptable solution or descend into feuding and paralysis. These experiences are not pleasant. When a buyer is looking to sign a purchase contract based mainly on plans and promises, he needs to coldly assess the probability that all the developer's promises will be fulfilled. Check the developer's track record—as reliable a guarantee as any. The buyer should grill—and I do mean **grill**—the developer and other knowledgeable locals on the project's finances (particularly sales and cash flow), break-even point (in terms of number of lots sold), scheduling for construction of common facilities and so on. If you feel you are standing on mush, jump away. Or put another way, if the meat smells bad, don't eat it.

Buyers should be especially careful when buying cheap land in the country that they've never seen.

Why anyone would do this is beyond me, but it is not uncommon. My father bought two lots in a Florida development in the late 1950s, sight unseen. And he never found time to look before he died, more than 20 years later. They were barely developed and did not appreciate for 45 years. Many of these current "deals" involve antiquated subdivisions just like the one my father bought into that lack water, sewerage, paved roads and perhaps utilities. They might be sited on land that would now be considered unsuited for construction owing to slope, soil stability, floodplain and other factors. Some of these projects are marketed through companies headquartered in California, including National Recreational Properties, Inc. (NRPIPI), Land Disposition Company, Real Estate Disposal Corporation and LandAuction.com (aka NRLL). All are owned by Jeffrey Frieden and Robert Friedman in Orange County, California. Project names include, among others, Moon Valley Ranch (near Termo, California), California (Cal) Pines in Modoc County, Lehigh Acres (east of Fort Myers, Florida in Lee County), Palm Coast and Port Charlotte (both in Florida), Concho Lakeland (Apache County, Arizona), Hawaiian Ocean View Estates (Island of Hawaii), Shelter Cove (Humboldt County, California) and Deming Ranchettes (Luna County, New Mexico). These lots are sold "as is" and can be financed through the seller on installment contracts. Some—marketed by Eric Estrada, the television actor—are pitched toward Spanish-speaking buyers. Never buy property sight unseen. (See Brian Melley, Associated Press, "Buyers beware: Many in California, Florida regret purchasing land in left for dead" and "For one couple, land looked good on paper, not in reality," Richmond Times-Dispatch, January 9, 2005.)

It is clearly much safer for you to buy into a fully completed project. The problem, of course, is that buyers coming in when the infrastructure is complete and most lots sold have only those lots available for purchase that all previous buyers have rejected. The last lots are not usually the most expensive or most desirable. More often, they are the least costly and have some factor discounting their appeal—an overhead power line, odd shape, poor site or uninspiring view. A smart buyer can make very good buys on these last lots, because the developer by that time has usually recovered his project costs and wants to move to the next deal. See if there's a way you can mitigate the offending feature by moving dirt, planting fast-growing trees or revising a house design. As an investment, the cheapest lot in a development may appreciate a bit faster than its pricier neighbors.

Second-home projects should be—but rarely are—marketed with all the project's infrastructure (however that is defined) complete and operational. Developers always begin marketing as soon as their plans are approved. Where the full infrastructure package is not complete, the buyer should insist on a specific itemization of infrastructure the developer promises to complete as part of the purchase contract he signs for his lot. The developer should not balk at giving you an itemized list of what's already in place and what he intends to do beyond what he has already done.

The next step is a bit harder: getting the developer to carry out the remainder of his infrastructure plan. When a project is slow to sell and the developer starts getting short on cash, promised infrastructure is the first place he'll look to cut costs. A lot-buyer's itemization should take the form of a promise in contract form that the missing elements will be completed. What happens, then, if the developer fails to complete the promised improvements? You can sue for performance. If the developer has assets, this might work. You can ask that the developer take on a performance bond for the value of the remaining work, though I would not count on this happening. You can also ask the developer to put a price on each infrastructure item in terms of your lot's share of the whole. He should be able to provide you with an average per-lot or per-acre infrastructure cost, because he has been projecting and refining these calculations since before the first spade of earth was turned. If the infrastructure does not get built, you will, at least, have a starting point for your claim for monetary damages against him. There may also be some tax benefits from this situation. I suggest bringing a real-estate lawyer in to help you think through the "what-if" scenarios.

Information on **land infrastructure** will be available from the agencies and companies that provide each service. You can find information on the road leading to the property from the state/county road department. You want to ask about road maintenance issues. Is the road plowed during the winter? Some properties are so remote or lacking in population that their roads receive little maintenance. What level of priority does the public road have for maintenance, such as snow clearance? Does the road have a flooding history? Does it need to be widened? Are accidents frequent? If so, where? Does the school bus serve road residents? If so, where would the closest stop to your property be? (School-bus service may be of no concern to you, but it does increase the value and marketability of your lot.) You will need to check with local utilities (electric, water, sewerage, telephone, cable TV, Internet, etc.) to determine the proximity of each service to the property and the cost of bringing it to your house site. And remember that you will need to obtain an easement (consent from the owner) to have your line cross another's property.

Your developer will have certain information on land infrastructure available on his property's **site plans**, which are used principally to set forth the infrastructure design for the property. Site plans are blueprint-type, technical drawings that show the location, specifications and design of all physical infrastructure on a developed property. The developer will probably have simplified drawings of the site plan, along with some dimensions and specifications, prepared as handouts. Ask to see the site plans, particularly as they affect the lot you're investigating. The site plans will include individual drawings for all planned excavations, roads, drainage of storm water and surface water, water pipes, sewerage, utilities, walkways, finished site grading and possibly landscaping. (Keep in mind that different second-home projects offer different levels of infrastructure.) You will be able to locate how and where each of the offered infrastructure components will service your particular lot. Make photocopies of the site plans that interest you and get a copy of the **specifications**, or **specs**, for each infrastructure component. These set forth the size, material and application of each component. If a civil or physical engineer (CE or PE) has drawn the plans, you should be reasonably confident that he has applied the standard formulas for sizing and materials. If you have doubts about the size of a culvert that will drain water from your lot, pay an engineer to review the plan. Roads, water and sewerage systems are expensive to rip out and do over, so you want to feel reasonably confident that the developer has not cut corners you can't see.

Installing and/or maintaining land infrastructure often involves coordinating and spending money with neighbors. Even where you own land outside a development, you can find yourself sharing an access road or a spring. Within a development, you will usually find that all lot owners will be expected to pay for infrastructure maintenance and upgrades. If you are philosophically opposed to such arrangements, make sure that your second home in the country is on land that is completely free of these obligations.

On a practical level, these sharing schemes range from well-functioning to disasters of various dimensions. The critical variable that I've seen is the degree of care, planning and thought that is invested in the documents the developer prepares for the **homeowners' association** he sets up that will take over the project's infrastructure management. A homeowners' association is a private neighborhood government whose board of directors is elected from among those who own a unit of property in the project. While homeowner associations are found mainly in metropolitan areas, an increasing number of the more than 50 million Americans who now live in projects whose house designs, aesthetics and governance are managed in this fashion are found in rural areas. (John Tierney, "The Mansion Wars," New York Times, November 15, 2005. A study by Amanda Agan and Alexander Tabarrok of George Mason University found that a home in the northern Virginia suburbs of Washington, D.C. that was in a private community with a homeowners' association sold for a five percent premium). About 275,000 community associations (homeowners' associations, condominiums and cooperatives) now exist in the United States.

Association documents are often long and complicated; sometimes, they are badly conceived and written clumsily. Nonetheless, you must understand them because they are the rules by which you must live as part of that community. Make sure you understand any house style and materials standards, provisions for pets, maintenance (what you're obligated to pay for; what your dues pay for), fees (both routine and special) and the governance system. An individual's buyer best protection against finding himself a neighbor to a stubborn fool is a rational, reasonable structure of decision-making that you've both agreed to at the time of purchase. Sharing the burdens of a common infrastructure requires everyone to be neighborly, especially when disagreements occur. If the developer tanks or has done a bad job in drafting the homeowners' association documents, you and the other owners will have to agree on many procedural and substantive issues involving taste, time and money. Agreeing on a method of how to agree is in itself a difficult boat to launch, particularly in a sea of hurt feelings and lost money. But where the documents are sound, a group of strangers can save their sinking ship.

The worst situation is when the developer drops out before completing the project and leaves a mess, both in the paperwork and on the ground. It is easy for me to write that folks in a nightmare should act rationally and reasonably. It is terribly hard to do. Nonetheless, reason and rational behavior should prevail sooner or later if only because no lot-owner has more power than any other. A problem-solving attitude will hopefully contain the anger that all feel. The goal should be to spread analytical reasonableness through the entire group.

Rural living rarely allows for the anonymity and isolation that you can find in a city or suburb. When you move to the country, you are forced to live with the culture and habits of mind of your immediate neighbors. These may not be to your liking, and yours may not be to theirs. A project with a homeowners' association provides a constitution of rules, procedures and structure for maintaining the development and handling neighborhood disagreements. It provides a common set of cultural and procedural assumptions that are intended to override personality quirks. Without an association, you're on your own with neighbors, the last resort of which is the local court to resolve country-type spats, such as fence fights and the nuisance of barking dogs. Court rulings may decide a dispute between neighbors without settling much of anything. Grudges can arise in other matters. In a developed project, you will inevitably find yourself solving common problems with your neighbors through channels that everyone understands. While forced neighborliness has its downside, the homeowners' association is a model that works, despite all the times it doesn't satisfy every individual.

The chances are greater, I think, for a country newcomer to discover neighbors who do not want to solve problems as he does when he buys outside of a development, especially one marketed toward a specific group of buyers who share cultural and income demographics. Do not assume that neighbors outside of a development will see a problem where you see one or engage in problem-solving in the manner you propose. It is unlikely that you will be able to organize them to solve your problem, which may be the way your neighbors have done things all their lives. They won't cooperate with your efforts to change them for your benefit—even for their own benefit. You are likely to build a problem-solving relationship if you can help to solve a problem that your neighbors have defined as a problem. As anywhere, you will run into individuals who go out of their way to be helpful and neighborly, as well as a few who go out of their way to be the opposite. In the country, you have to work with neighbors from time to time, and the format used for these interchanges is one of the more important choices you make when deciding between a second-home development with a homeowners' association and a stand-alone property. Whether or not you are in a development, you will be in a "neighbor process" with those on your boundaries. No matter how large your property, everyone has neighbors. Whether you're looking at property in a development or not, finding neighbors with whom you can work on common infrastructure issues is as important to your future happiness as any other consideration.

PROPERTY AND SITE INFRASTRUCTURE

For **roads**, you want to know their location in relation to your lot/land and house site. Important design elements are the width of the finished roadway (which is the portion that traffic normally uses), width of the gravel apron on each side, thickness of the rock base, composition of its substructure (type and thickness of various layers), whether geotechnic fabric was used as underlayment, and the type and thickness of surfacing material (gravel, concrete, asphalt, tar and chip). **Geotechnic fabric** is used under roads where the water table is high. It creates an impenetrable barrier between the subgrade beneath the road and the groundwater. The fabric prevents water from being "pumped" (i.e., drawn up) into the road's base rock by the traffic above. If pumping is not prevented, the road will eventually break up. The better the road—wider, thicker and surfaced—the more it has cost the developer, a cost he needs to pass on proportionally to each buyer. If you get the sense that he's put a lot of money into a rock base and below-ground drainage systems, it's reasonable to assume that he's tried to do a good job throughout. If site plans are not available, look for culverts, drainage ditches, hillside roads pitched slightly to the downhill side to encourage rapid runoff—all of which will give you an idea of whether the developer has tried to do a good job.

A project's road plan will show top-down and cross-section drawings of the road's design, along with dimensions and specs. Ask whether the project's roads are to be built to the **state's standards**. Ask which roads in particular will meet state standards. Then ask the state's local road department whether the state has agreed to incorporate the project's roads into the state system—which gives you a guarantee about the quality of the road and future maintenance. The more rural the second-home development, the less likely that its roads will be built to state standards. Perfectly usable roads can be built below these standards, depending on conditions and traffic loads. State-standard roads are not appropriate for undeveloped land that is "backup there"; they're too big, polished and expensive. Where a road system will not be built to state standards, make sure that you understand which standards will not be met—and then ask the state road engineer whether those shortfalls will have any practical significance. If the project's roads are to remain a private road system owned by the lot owners, they will have to pay for and manage its maintenance.

When you drive the public/private road to your lot or land, check for steepness, tight turns, floodplain, blind curves, narrow spots, hidden driveway entrances, improper pitch, washboarding (on dirt/gravel), clearance from trees and protruding rocks, turnarounds and adequate drainage. Imagine the property's road in bad weather. Do you anticipate problems? If a developer's road plan shows a 20-foot-wide, asphalt-surfaced roadway with a two-foot-wide gravel apron on each side and you find yourself driving on an 18-foot-wide gravel road with no aprons, you should presume that the developer is running out of money and/or has cut more corners than the two you've just discovered.

Public roads in the country range from paved to dirt. The further back you go, the narrower and rougher the roads will be. The least usable are a bit more than one-lane wide with wide outs and backup spots every so often. Dirt-and-gravel roads can be used year-round where they have a decent rock base, and are ditched, drained and periodically graded and graveled. But the fewer residents and vehicles on these roads, the less maintenance they get. I've driven over public country roads that were eroded, studded with rocks the size of gallon jugs and too narrow and steep for safe driving. The more inhospitable the road that services your property, the more *regular* inconvenience and expense you will have getting people, vehicles, material-loaded trucks, fire engines and rescue-squad ambulances in and out. Imagine the road to and on your property at night, then with snow and ice, then during a wet spring. Do not count on being able to persuade the local branch of the state road department to upgrade their road that you are now using. Assume that what is, is what will be, particularly if the county is poor or has a small population. Any road that you judge to be less than safe and usable in all conditions is just that. In some situations, local government may get a developer to upgrade a portion of a public road to accommodate traffic from his project. I've not seen this happen very often with out-of-the-way, second-home developments.

When you look at a development's **water plan**, your concerns are for quality, quantity, pressure and fire protection. Rural second-home developments usually have one of three types of water systems: 1) each lot owner installs his own system, usually a well; 2) centralized private system that serves houses in the project; or 3) a hook up to an existing public water system. If your lot is getting water from a central source, find out the details and the type of treatment it's subject to. Determine whether current users have experienced problems with **potability** (drinkability) or pressure. The developer's plan should show the project's water mainlines ("mains") configured in a loop, which keeps water moving through the system and prevents dead ends where bacteria can build. If yours is the house furthest from the source of water or highest in elevation, ask the developer to measure the water pressure in your presence. The comfortable range will be between 60 and 100 pounds per square inch (psi). Stepping down the pressure at your house with an in-line regulator is a far more desirable problem than insufficient pressure in the system. On level ground, you will need a minimum of 45 psi; on hills, a minimum of between 60 and 75 psi. Inadequate pressure will lead to, among other things, continuing frustration and the possibility of contamination.

In central-source water systems, the feeder water line to your house—called a **lateral**—from the main line should be no less than one inch wide (inside diameter), and 1 1/4" inside diameter is usually more reliable over time. Water-supply design details can be found in Ernest Brater and Horace King, Handbook of Hydraulics, 6th ed., (New York; McGraw-Hill, 1976).

A fire hydrant should be within 500 feet of your house if you're buying into a second-home development with that level of infrastructure. Homeowner insurance rates are higher for residences that are not close to a hydrant and higher still where no hydrant is available. Insurance companies look favorably on ponds close to rural houses not served by hydrants. If you have a pond on your property or close by, it is worth making sure that your local VFD pumper truck can get to it easily in bad weather. Another idea, assuming it's practical, is to bury a **standpipe** from the pond to a nearby all-weather road. The standpipe has a fitting that allows the pumper to connect at the road, a much more reliable procedure than getting to and away from a pond in ice and snow. The local VFD may help with the standpipe's cost, and make sure the pipe is sized correctly and the fittings match up. The standpipe's access fitting should be located to minimize the amount of vertical lift a pumper will have to provide.

Many rural second-home developments will not have their own water system or access to an existing public system. Each lot-owner then is expected to figure out a site-specific water solution—carry-in, cistern, spring, surface water (such as a pond or stream), dug well or drilled well. Talk to other lot-owners about what they know, or think they know, about water on your site. Talk to adjoining neighbors about their first-hand experience in drilling wells, particularly about cost, flow, depth, potability, contaminants and drilling contractors. Your neighbor will probably have had a water sample from his spring or well tested and should be willing to share the results. Ask about water sources during drought.

Flow during drought will indicate the strength of the source at its most stressed condition. It's important to find out whether there's enough water underground to support the number of houses planned for the surface. Ask neighbors about sources of pollution that might affect the aquifer from which you both will tap. Determine whether a neighbor's septic system is likely to contaminate the water source that you want to use. The county sanitarian will be able to tell you the minimum required distance between septic field and well. In areas of porous rock, you may need to leave more distance than the minimum. Where karst topography underlies the surface, pollution can travel long distances through hollowed-out limestone.

In primitive situations you can use a gravity system to supply your house where the water source is higher than the tap; the higher the source, the more pressure up to a point. More common than a central water supply or gravity system in rural homes is to have a pump in or at the source (spring, well), or between the source and your tap. Pumps can be powered by electricity, gasoline, photovoltaic cells (solar energy), hand and the force of falling water itself. The latter is called a **hydraulic ram** and is used in circumstances where power is not available. (See www.pumpsandtanks.com; www.RamPumps.com; and www.theramcompany.com.) If you find flow or pressure is uncertain, you may want to install a reserve tank that holds a reservoir of water from which the house draws. A reserve tank is often used where supply is uncertain—and sized accordingly. In cold climates, you have to bury most water pipes below the frost line and put pumps in places that don't freeze. No one likes to dig up frozen pipes in frozen ground.

With municipal or project **sewerage systems**, your concern is that the pipes be sized sufficiently (have a wide enough diameter) to handle the expected load from your house and all the others on the line. Undersized pipes can lead to sewage backups in your house, a condition best avoided. An in-line butterfly-type valve at your house connection can prevent such backups. (When this valve is shut because of a backup on the mainline side, your own wastewater will backup after a few flushes.) The lateral sewer line from your house to the main sewer line should be no less than four inches in diameter, and the main line should be sized according to the maximum number of houses it will be servicing. I know it is obvious but I will write it anyway: your sewer pipe should run downhill from the lowest point in your household drain line. If your house is lower than the stub where your line connects to the main sewerage line, you will need to pump your sewage into the system. This is doable, but a sewage pump adds to your system a machine that will fail sooner or later. Gravity flow is what you want. The developer's sewerage plan will show the elevation of your house, the elevation of the sewer lines and the pitch from house to main. Lest it is not obvious, the plan should show the pitch of your lateral sewer line running downhill from your house; a level line will not work. If you run a water line and a sewer line in the same trench, the water line should be above, usually by a distance set by code. You might also ask to see any **as-built drawings** of the water and sewerage systems on your lot, which represent what's actually underground rather than what was envisaged.

Buyers should be cautious about buying undeveloped lots that lack either a municipal/package sewerage system in place or a septic (**percolation**, or "**perc**") permit. If you are considering an undeveloped lot that has neither a system nor a permit, consult the county official—the public health officer or the sanitarian—about the septic regulations that will apply to your house. Ask him whether other recent home builders on similar soils in that part of the county have been required to employ systems beyond the conventional septic tank and drainfield. You want a lot with soils that will "perc," that is, soils in place that will pass the sanitarian's percolation test and allow the use of a conventional gravity-flow septic tank and drainfield at a current installed cost of $3,500 to $5,000. Alternatives to a conventional septic system using sand or imported soil are three to four times as expensive and involve higher maintenance costs and requirements if they use pumps.

A buyer's interest is served when he finds a developer who has gone to the trouble and expense of obtaining a **septic permit** from the county for the specific lot or parcel the buyer wants. In many places, developers are required to get permits before being allowed to sell lots. That is not the case in my county, however. As percolation standards are made stricter, you may find even large lots—particularly mountain top and sloping lots—without a site that will be approved. Where there is a septic permit, read it carefully. Make sure the permit is specifically for your lot or land before signing a purchase contract! The permit will indicate the type of system the sanitarian has approved for a particular spot. It should also show the size of the system being permitted, often expressed in terms of the number of bedrooms. Make sure that your house floorplan conforms to the size of the system for which a permit has been granted. If you are planning a house that has more bedrooms than the developer's permit allows, you will not be allowed to build it without increasing the septic system's capacity. If you want to do something unusual with your system—such as hooking in a bathroom from another building, or running a B&B or home-based commercial enterprise, or use more water than might be normally expected—you will probably need to get additional approvals. Apart from permitting, if you overload a septic system with more liquid than it's designed to handle, it will fail.

On both lots and non-development land, I recommend that you put a **septic approval contingency in your purchase-offer contract.** This allows you to determine whether the parcel you are considering has an acceptable perc site near your house site. If an acceptable site can't be found, you will soon get an idea of the cost of installing an alternative system. Where there is an existing system, a septic contingency will allow you to have it examined to determine its condition. Where the results of your contingency inspections are not satisfactory, this contract language allows you to either back out of the contract or negotiate the issue with the seller. Having a perc test done usually involves about $500 to $1,500 in expenses, paid to: 1) the county for a fee, 2) a certified, buyer-hired soils engineer for locating possible septic-system sites, managing the test and reporting the results, and 3) a backhoe excavator for digging the test holes.

If the test indicates a conventional septic system will not be approved, the soils engineer can propose an alternative system, which is usually based on constructing a septic drainfield in good dirt placed on top of the bad dirt. The switch raises the cost to the lot buyer from, say, $4,000 for a conventional system to as much as $20,000 or more for the acceptable alternative. (Other systems, such as, digesters, composters and chemical toilets, may or may not comply with local requirements.)

A buyer faces other issues when a septic system is already installed on property he's interested in buying. The system should come with an approval or permit on file with the county health department that indicates its capacity, design, age and location on the property. An old system may be in need of repair or replacement.

Electricity and other utilities may or may not be part of your target property's infrastructure. Where electricity is not on the property you're buying, you may not be able to get conventional pole-strung power. Adjoining landowners may not be willing to work out an easement for you to cross their property. Or they may insist on burying the line where it crosses at additional expense.

Electricity and telephone lines are usually run on the same poles or in the same trench. If your house site is within 1,000 feet of an existing pole, your cost to run a new line is minimal and may be divided into 60 equal installment payments that you pay during your first five years of service. Each utility has its own way of calculating these costs and having you pay for them. The five things a buyer should be concerned about are: 1) the location of the nearest pole to his house site, 2) whether or not that pole is on the target property (if not, you have to obtain an easement), 3) the distance from the nearest available pole to the site,

4) the type of topography the line must cross and 5) the means the utility will use to suppress tree growth and underbrush under the line. Negotiating a utility easement with a neighbor can be easy or very sticky. He is not legally obligated to give you an easement, so you are asking for a favor. The two power companies with which I've worked have very reasonable cost-and-payment plans for distances of less than a couple of thousand feet; after that, the per-foot cost of a new line increases by a factor of five or more. Sites that cannot be economically served by conventional electricity are not uncommon.

A final thought about infrastructure is this: visit the property and your choices of house sites on a bad-weather day. Some developers and sellers may do just enough roadwork to get buyers to the site on a dry afternoon. If you can use the project's dirt road during and after a heavy rain, your confidence should build. If you see washouts and undersized culverts, you will live with these problems until you fix them. If you feel washboard as you drive in, it will be there until it's graded out. (Washboard is one of life's many problems that does not solve itself through deliberate indifference.) A wet or snowy day will also test your ability to access lots located on steep, winding roads. If your vehicle doesn't make it to your site when the road is wet or icy, plan on paying for roadwork, buying a more suitable vehicle, or both. If you are buying exposed ground or mountain land, ask about wind—frequency, velocity and prevailing direction. The higher your property is, the more you should think about wind as both a hazard and an energy source. You may be interested in leasing your land for large (400-foot-tall) wind turbines, and, if not, your neighbors may lease theirs. You may also need to consider a government "taking" of your wind site at fair market value through eminent domain for use by private wind-energy developers. Some land buyers object to wind-farm projects near their property; other's won't.

With each land-infrastructure component, you need to determine how close it is to your target property; its level of usability, reliability and safety; what is involved in gaining access to it from your property (easement, application, permit); and, finally, the work and cost involved in bringing each component to your property. And, then, you will need to go through the same set of questions when you want to bring each component to your house site. On large and remote properties, you may be able to get an infrastructure component to your property, but not to your first choice of house site. Where it is too costly or infeasible to hook into existing land infrastructure, you will then have to devise either a site-specific solution *that complies with local ordinances* or do without.

INFRASTRUCTURE COSTS

From your perspective, there's nothing necessarily wrong with buying a lot in a subdivision where the developer has put in little, if any, infrastructure. A lot of rural land is bought by "**flippers**" who purchase large, undeveloped parcels at a wholesale price, put in the least amount of infrastructure they can, divide and then sell the lots retail. With any division, you need to understand what infrastructure you're getting for your money, what it will cost to obtain whatever additions you want, and how decisions that involve all lot owners will be made.

If you—*and the other lot owners*—want no more infrastructure than what's in place at the time of purchase, then you've found the right spot. You will be buying land "as is, where is," and no more infrastructure will be forthcoming from the seller. Some dividers and developers can connect lot buyers with infrastructure contractors. The lot seller may have a commercial relationship with these contractors. You can ask other lot buyers about the practices of the recommended contractors. If there are troubles, you will undoubtedly hear about them. If you are the first purchaser in the development, you may be treated royally in hope that you will talk up the project to those who follow. Other things being equal, the developer and his contractors have more incentive to act decently with the first buyers than with the last.

Infrastructure costs vary from place to place and rise over time. The costs in the following example were representative in my area in the early 2000s. Assume that you are scoping 100 acres of undeveloped mountain woodland that has been carved out of a 1,000-acre tract. You've yet to offer a purchase contract to the seller. You're taking your first run at determining infrastructure costs. Your lot fronts a public road with electricity and telephone, but neither water nor sewer lines. The best house site on your 100 acres is about 500 feet in from the public road. An old logging road goes back that way. It crosses an intermittent creek and goes through a couple of wet spots. The site itself is a natural bench on a slope, which faces southeast. The seller's asking price is $2,000 per acre, for which you get the land and a survey of the lot's boundaries. Here is a quick-and-dirty cost estimate to get your infrastructure in place:

Road: $35,000

> Widen existing logging road to 12 feet along its length. Cut trees along the side as needed. Put in one turnaround about half way and widen in three spots to allow vehicle passing. Install two 16"-diameter, 16-foot-long culverts. Ditch uphill side where necessary. Grade road so that it sheds water to downhill side. Dig out two wet spots around culverts and fill in with rip-rap, stone and gravel as needed. Haul and emplace rock in four other spots. Install two or three 8"-diameter culverts. Widen entrance at public road, install rock and gate. Includes no finish surface material like gravel (with two exceptions) or asphalt.   **$30,000**

> Creek is crossed using a low-water bridge consisting of three 20-foot-long, 24"-diameter steel culverts embedded in concrete.   **$5,000**

Drilled water well @ $20 per foot, est. 250 feet: **$5,000**

> Includes pump and 2" line to the house from well. 100 foot-long trench, 36" deep. **$1,500**

Site preparation: $3,000

> Clear 1/2 acre (about 22,000 square feet) of trees and debris into burn pile. Level site; stockpile any usable top soil. Bring in needed rock and gravel for parking area. (Does not include foundation work or finish grading after construction is completed.)

Septic system: $22,000

> Soil won't pass perc test. Design and installation of **constructed sand filter**. Includes cost of test, engineering and permit fees.

Utilities: $3,000, prorated over 60 months for above-ground service .

The total infrastructure costs in this example total **$69,500**.

The road costs assume a road that's capable of carrying a cement truck and other heavy vehicles related to house construction. The amount of work involved in clearing trees and the quantity of rock hauled to fill in the soft spots are cost variables driven by site-specific conditions. Graveling or asphalting the entire entrance road adds additional cost. Infrastructure costs are charged in several different ways—by the job, by the foot in the case of entrenching a water line or stringing above-ground electric service, by the ton for buying rock, by the hour for operating excavating machines (a mid-size bulldozer and operator now cost about $70-$100 p/h) and by the hour/day for labor.

At this point, the buyer should ask: What other properties are available for $269,500 that also suit my needs and wants? One answer might be a smaller lot with infrastructure in place. A second answer might be a smaller parcel with a usable house and basic infrastructure. A third answer might be to buy the 100 acres and use an RV or camper, both of which can be driven in and out in dry weather on a road that's less developed than one suited for heavy, house-building related trucks. A fourth answer might be a similar property, but with lower infrastructure costs.

A final possibility is to take higher-than-expected infrastructure cost estimates to the seller with a discounted offer for the land. Append the estimates to your contract. This shows that you're a seriously interested buyer and want to make a deal. Most developers who sell lots without much infrastructure want to sell out quickly. If you're one of the first buyers, you probably won't get much discount, because the seller doesn't want to set a precedent. If you're buying close to the end of the project, you may have some success. Don't inflate the estimates. The developer is likely to have as accurate an idea of these costs as you do, which is why he didn't do the infrastructure work himself. (Developers know that buyers like you balk at paying for infrastructure that they put in and you can't see.) You can make the point in your price negotiations that roughly equivalent properties—that are acceptable to you—are for sale nearby. FSBOs (For Sale By Owners) of semi-developed rural land may not add in to their asking price the value of a half-good interior road and electric service; they've taken both for granted for years. This attitude can allow you to buy more of what you want from a FSBO than the Flipper who expects you to do all the property infrastructure and site work. If nothing else, FSBO properties give you bargaining leverage with a developer.

You should also tell the developer that the bank you want to use is willing to lend only 80 percent of the land's selling price, which means that you will have to come up with both $40,000 in cash down payment and $69,500 to get the property ready for a house. Not a house, you emphasize, just ready for a house. Ask the seller to consider lowering the land price by the amount you think is beyond what was expected or what a reasonable person would consider reasonable. You could propose as well that the seller do part of the infrastructure work, or that you pay for the labor and fuel and he pays for the equipment time. You can get additional leverage in this negotiation by digging out the selling prices of other lots in this development and their infrastructure costs. In most cases, lots further from a public road will be cheaper per acre than lots with frontage, though I've seen just the opposite when the "far" lots had the best view. It's fair for you to ask for cost-sharing from the developer when unexpectedly high infrastructure costs appear, but you won't get anywhere with a developer who sold you an undeveloped lot or one "as is."

Each buyer has to assess whether the property's infrastructure meets his goals and his capability of getting this work done on his own. If, for example, you are 65 with a family history of heart attacks, I would not buy 100 acres of mountain land whose only infrastructure is a long, logging road to your planned full-time residence. If you try to build without putting in an all-weather road, you will precipitate another coronary. If you organize the infrastructure work through an assortment of specialized contractors, assume at least six stressful months of coordinating, haggling, redoing and inconvenience. If you think you can still drop trees and shovel dirt for eight hours straight the way you did one summer in high school, I hope you are not wrong.

If you try to make this 100 acres work by putting in the least amount of infrastructure you can live with, you will find yourself living with a hazard that regularly collapses when you most need it not to. I've had a marginal bridge that I hoped would suffice disappear during a thunder-storm flood, leaving an empty cement truck on the wrong side, at night, in the downpour; a loaded dump truck break a rear axle on a too-tight, sloped turn; and many episodes of sliding off, bogging down and hanging up. I now get the road right first. Heavy snow and other extreme conditions become harder to deal with as you age. Getting stuck on chancy roads shifts from an adventure in your 20s to an annoyance in your 40s to a nightmare in your late 60s. The easier a home in the country is to get to, maintain and live in, the longer you will be able to live there, despite the infirmities of age. I advise land buyers in their 50s and 60s to look for properties with owner-friendly infrastructure for this reason.

PROPERTY AND SITE INFRASTRUCTURE CHECK LIST

As you investigate the **land infrastructure** that services the target property, you will also be asking and answering questions related to the **property's infrastructure** (what's already in place and usable) and the **site infrastructure** needed where a house is planned. Again, you will be looking at road work, electricity, other utilities and options for water and sewerage.

The list below combines the principal property- and site-infrastructure issues within a broader analysis of the target property's attributes, both natural and man-made. The target property's physical features directly shape the type and cost of property and site infrastructure that can be installed. A buyer has to think about infrastructure in terms of terrain, distance, impediments and cost. As you walk through and come to be familiar with a target property, use the list below to assemble a picture of the land's suitability for your plans and the infrastructure they will require.

Property and Site Analysis for Infrastructure

A. Natural features

1. Compass orientation of land and specific house site

2. Land types—open/wooded; crop, pasture, hayfield, irrigated, range

3. Topography—elevation, slope, drainage patterns

4. Sheds—viewshed, windshed (look for tree sculpts), watershed, "odorshed"

5. House site—southern exposure, prevailing wind/weather, shade/sun

6. Surface water—floodplain, wetlands, creeks, springs, ponds

7. Walk the boundaries with a topographical map with boundaries drawn and/or survey and/or deed with boundary calls (compass directions and distance). Look for corners—metal stakes; described trees; three slash marks or ribbons; and marked lines—ribbons, paint, slashes; boundary fences/lines not coincident with surveyed boundaries; areas that possibly have overlapping claims; internal roads that appear to be in current use by others; check for boundary line congruence between deed calls/survey and ground reality; look for congruence of "Posted" signs with boundary lines

8. Walk/drive all drivable roads on property—they will lead somewhere, perhaps to

a trash dump or spring

9. Neighbors—who joins the target property and what do they use their land for?

10. How much of the land is inaccessible by various types of vehicles?

11. Other factors, such as climate, rainfall, soil instability (landslides), ground instability (earthquake) and erosion

B. Soil analysis

1. Take copy of property's soil map (from <u>Soil Survey</u>) on your walk-around. Get a sense of where soils change and how soil change affects land use and capability; soil type can determine where you put a septic system and the type of house foundation you use

2. Take soil sample for analysis from crop fields

3. Observe vegetation—look for marker species that indicate dirt quality

C. Overview of woodland and timber

1. Get a sense for the extent of woodland, diameter size of timber and species distribution

2. Are woods accessible by usable roads?

3. How many trees need to be cut to clear a house site and gain road access to it?

4. Do you think there's enough merchantable timber to justify hiring a consulting forester to do a walk-through or cruise?

D. Land use

1. Rough percentage distribution among different land types/uses—such as woodland, pasture, cropland, wetlands, unusable land

2. Is property being sold with access to adjoining private or public lands? Is a state or federal land lease involved?

3. Does property have deeded use of adjoining property? If so, what for and what are the terms?

4. What percentage of property is unusable due to steepness, wetness, lack of water and so on? Draw these areas on your topographical map. Do these areas benefit the property in some way that is not connected to your intended uses, such as wildlife habitat, buffers from neighbors, or visibility screen from road?

5. Are there areas that have some obvious conservation/environmental value, such as wetlands, lakes, rare habitat, etc? You may want to determine whether the property in whole or part lends itself to a conservation easement.

6. Note land characteristics, such as stoniness, rock ledges, types of plants growing in different areas, eroded spots, floodplain—all of these characteristics will affect your infrastructure plans.

E. Access

1. Does your target property have physical and legal access?

2. Entrance road to property

Does your target property have frontage on public road or on developer's private road? Is its entrance road located on this frontage? If not, where is the entrance? Can the frontage be used to access your house site?

If property has frontage but no entrance road exists, is there 500 feet of sight in both directions on the public road from where you would put in a new entrance? Check with state road department to determine sight-clearance-distance requirements for new entrance roads.

If there is no frontage, how far is the target property from the nearest publicly-maintained or private four-season road?

Are there any physical features on the entrance road that might be a safety hazard—ford, steep drop off, eroding cliff, undrained wet spot, tree leaning steeply over road, turn that is too steep or tight, slippery surface?

Do you find evidence that others are using the target property's entrance road? Who and by what authority?

Is year-round use of this entrance road feasible as is? Can a fire truck get to the house site in winter? (Ask someone in the local VFD if you're not sure.)

Who is expected to maintain the entrance road?

3. Crossing others

If the entrance road to the target property crosses intervening land (public or private), what are the features of that entrance road? Length, width, condition, locked gates?

What is the legal basis for the target property using this entrance road? Does the property's seller have a deeded right of way or ingress/egress easement? If not, has the owner legally established an easement by prescription or necessity? Is the owner using the entrance road by permission of the property owner who is being crossed? (In that case, the permission can be withdrawn.) Is there a dispute about using this entrance road?

Is the entrance road that is being used the same as the one described in recorded documents? You may find that your legal entrance road is not the one that is being used, in which case the target property may have no legal right to use it.

Is the entrance road that is being used physically located where it is shown on the survey?

Who maintains your entrance road where it crosses another property? To what standard? Is the road currently in good shape? If not, determine with the seller who pays for which repairs.

F. Utility analysis

1. Electricity—closest pole to property; closest pole to house site

How far must an electric line be run to serve property/site? Cost and cost formula used by local power company? Feasibility/cost of running line underground versus above ground? Must service line cross others? If so, what are the prospects of getting easements?

Feasibility of alternative sources of electric power at house site—windmill, photovoltaic cells, low-head hydro, fossil-fuel-powered generator, other.

2. Sewerage system

Possible hook up to established central system. Cost.

Site for conventional septic system. Cost of non-conventional, alternative systems if conventional system won't comply with local requirements. Prospects for passing percolation test—check soil map in <u>Soil Survey</u> and with county sanitarian.

Site for non-conventional waste-disposal system. Feasibility, cost, maintenance issues, reliability. Does local ordinance permit this type of system? Can you find an excavator to install non-conventional system? Will it comply with local ordinance?

3. Water

Possible hook up to established central system

Natural sources close to house site—location of spring or creek

Well-drilling prospects. Cost.

Quality considerations—pollution potential; take water sample.

Quantity considerations—flow during drought

Fire-protection pond—possibility of building pond near house

Is water being purchased for irrigation or other uses? Source, cost, reliability, degree of target property's dependency.

4. Other utilities

Telephone, cable tv and other lines may be hung on same poles

Check reception for dish tv, cell phones, radio

Internet options

Possible hook up to established natural gas line. Some residences are entitled to free gas where a property has a gas well. Can a propane or fuel-oil truck make deliveries year-round?

G. Subsurface and Above-surface factors

1. Are subsurface minerals owned by the seller of the surface?

2. Evidence of past, present, or future mineral development?

3. Is property crossed by natural gas or oil pipeline, or overhead high-voltage power lines? Is there a pumping station or transformer on property? Pipelines and power lines will have recorded easements.

4. Is property/site adversely affected by nearby tower, wind turbine, structure or natural feature?

H. Constraints

1. Legal constraints on property and/or infrastructure

Restrictive covenants—are certain types/sizes of structures prohibited?

Conservation easement—limit on number, size or location of houses and structures; limit on timbering or grazing; limit on division.

Life estate—is property owner retaining a life estate in the occupation or use of some portion of the property?

Retained interest—is the owner retaining some interest or profit in the property?

Zoning restrictions

Limits on uses of property

Prohibitions on structures on property, e.g., towers, dishes

Prohibition/restrictions on division

Setback requirements

Minimum house requirements, e.g., square foot requirement; fixed foundation

Restrictions on height of structure

Architectural style requirements

Road construction standards

Regulatory/Environmental restrictions on property/infrastructure

Wetlands

Threatened, endangered or sensitive species, on state or federal lists.

Floodplains

Archeological resources on property

Caves and karst geology

Earthquake zone

Hurricane hazard; storm-related flooding hazard

Historic structures

Restrictions on surface water access/use e.g., right to draw, right to fish

Wildlife restrictions—no hunting rules

Water quality—activities that affect surface waters, e.g., mining, point-sources of pollution in a high-quality stream

Air quality—restrictions on certain activities, e.g., uses that create dust, sulfur oxides, nitrogen oxides, particulate

Nuisance species on property that limit property uses, e.g., multiflora rose, coyotes (decimate sheep), Africanized bees, fire ants, termites, starlings and house pests (winter flies, ladybugs, termites, ants)

2. Physical constraints on infrastructure

Steepness

Soil not suited to buildings; can't find sewage-disposal site; soil won't hold pond; soil too rocky, etc.; insufficient nutrients

Access too narrow, too steep, to tightly cornered, too slippery etc.

Inadequate water quantity or quality

Land lays in the wrong direction, e.g., artists prefer light coming into their studios from the north

Too rainy, too cold, too dry to support plans

3. Encroachments that adversely affect use of property or its infrastructure

Adverse possession (someone is occupying the target property without permission, which may or may not be legal)

Adverse use (someone is using property/infrastructure without permission, which may or may not be legal)

Common situations of adverse possession and adverse use involve fences that are not on the property line; the property's road being used by individuals without a right to do so; a neighbor tapping a spring on the target property; a neighbor's antenna mounted on the target property; unauthorized individuals hunting or otherwise recreating on the property without permission; a neighbor's building or structure on the target property;

I. Neighbors' uses affecting property or its infrastructure

1. Pollution—air, water

2. Noise—barking dogs, gunfire, equipment

3. Smell—poultry, hogs, dairy cows, feedlot

4. Bright night-time lighting

5. Visual offense—junk cars, etc.

6. Adjoining public land—trespass

These issues are discussed in detail in other sections of this book. Use this list during your walk-through as a way to organize your observations in terms of the property's current and needed infrastructure.

FLIP, FLIPPERS, FLIPPING

Flippers are land dividers rather than developers. They are interested in a quick turn-around profit on large undeveloped tracts that they divide with as little investment in infrastructure as possible. Flips are simple to understand: The Flipper buys 200 acres for $1,000,000, or $5,000 per acre, surveys it into 25-acre lots (farmettes), gets the division approved and then sells the lots for $10,000 per acre. A variation is to buy a timber tract, cut the timber or reserve it, and then go through the division-and-sale process. The timber variation demands that the Flipper project two paths to profit: a buy-divide-flip approach or the buy-divide-timber-flip approach where the timber harvest generates income but the land is discounted. The Flipper's form of capitalist enterprise is no different than that practiced on the Lower East Side in 1900: buy a yard of cloth for $1, divide and sell nine handkerchiefs from the pushcart for two bits each.

Since a considerable amount of rural property is being sold and resold in this manner, you should become familiar with the process and its pressure points. The Flipper must make his profit on the spread between buying something big wholesale and selling it fast in small pieces retail. Flippers add only the amount of work and value that is needed to effect the Flip. Flippers have a good eye for marketable property with features that lot buyers want—views, water frontage, a few decorative big trees. There's nothing wrong in buying from a Flipper. Just keep in mind that the property's lack of infrastructure will become the lot-buyers' collective problem once the Flip is sold out. I've also noticed that Flippers often price their lots above FMV for similar properties, which leaves room for negotiation. Some buyers like the Flipper's offerings because the lot is appealing and their hunt for property can stop. The buyer's work in "developing" the flipped property and lot, however, has just begun.

Flippers obtain property in different ways. Some buy land outright. Others buy a **purchase option** from the seller. This is a contract between the Flipper and the land seller that gives the Flipper the right to purchase the property at a certain price at a point in the future, typically three months to a year from when the option takes effect. The Flipper buys the option to purchase for one or two percent of the purchase price. This cash, often called **option money**, is forfeited to the seller if the Flipper fails to complete the purchase. A purchase option gives the Flipper the right to buy, but not the obligation to buy. If the Flipper does not exercise his option, he loses his option money but incurs no lawsuit or penalty. The Flipper uses his option time to market the property to buyers like you. He will divide the property on paper (and maybe on the ground too) and offer a sales contract to you that is contingent on completing his purchase with the seller. If he does not exercise his option, there is no sale to you. Any deposit you placed in escrow for this contingent sale should be returned to you; do not give a deposit directly to the Flipper. Flippers count on knowing the market price for their divided parcels.

The option's advantages to the Flipper are that he can bring a large property under control with very little cash in a way that gives him an opportunity to make a lot of money fast and without much work. But every option holder runs the risk of losing his option money if he is unable to flip the pieces. Options appeal to gamblers. A Flipper working an option wins when he sells the property without ever buying it. Option Flippers do not want to take title to the property since that would mean they have to come up with the full purchase price.

If you find yourself negotiating with a Flipper with or without an option, you may be able to work a very good deal depending on how far along in the selling process he is. The closer you are to the front end, the more resistance you will find to having him lower his asking price significantly. Flippers start their price at a level that allows them to make a concession so that the buyer thinks he did a good job negotiating. He'll cut an asking price meaningfully after he's paid for the property from previous sales and is marketing his profit. The last couple of lots in a Flip should be good buys, as long as they're not the dogs of the deal. You can do very well with an Option Flipper whose option time is running out. There's no risk to you in low-balling a Flipper: he knows this game better than you do.

You can also play chicken with a Flipper (who's flipping an entirety without dividing it) if you're convinced that you're his "best-money" buyer. If he doesn't meet your low-ball price, "sit with him in the waiting room." Watch for sweat. Time is working on him. He'll lose his option money if he doesn't make the deal with you. That's fine. It leaves you free to negotiate directly with the landowner once the Flipper slinks off. But games of chicken can lead to wrecks, yours included. The Flipper may turn up an acceptable buyer at the last minute. Or the seller may have an alternative to you in mind in the form of a **backup contract** once the Flipper loses his option.

This gaming of the Flipper raises questions of etiquette and ethics. Flippers with an option fear a buyer **backdooring** them in various ways, one of which is waiting them out. Another is for a buyer to approach the land seller directly while the option is still in effect. If the buyer offers the owner more than the option's purchase price, the owner has an incentive to "squirrel up" the Flipper's deal if he can. The buyer then wins the property at the Flipper's expense. I recommend against backdooring, because it diminishes the buyer. There's an honorable way to play these real-estate games, as well as other ways.

Here is an example of a real flip. The landowner advertised a 400-acre+/-property for $350,000. I looked at the property five days after the newspaper advertisement. A Flipper had already signed a deal with the owner to purchase, not option, for $300,000. The Flipper had a local surveyor divide the wooded property into three lots. The local zoning ordinance prohibited further division. One lot included a usable but bedraggled farmhouse that served as a hunt camp. The landowner had made several ten-acre clearcuts to provide better habitat for deer. About 50 percent of the land had been selectively timbered, and maybe ten percent had been clearcut. I estimated that a selective cut on the remaining timber would yield about $75,000 to the new owner. The Flipper immediately sold the remaining timber for an unknown sum and advertised the three parcels without mentioning the timber had been sold. Here is an edited version of the ad that appeared about three months following the purchase:

COUNTRY HOME/LODGE

85 ACRES

$159,990

Old Country Home/Lodge on 85 ACRES adjoining the 14,000 ACRE STATE PUBLIC GAME AND FISHING LANDS in _____ County. This large 1935 Home is livable but needs tender love and care. It has water and electric heat, bathroom, four bedrooms, three fireplaces plus several small outbuildings. This 85 Acre Tract is bounded on the East Side by State Route ___ and has extensive frontage on the west side of the Game Lands. The house is situated on a manicured knoll with a rushing trout stream traversing the back yard and running most of the entire length of the property. There is a large meadow behind the house through which the stream runs, and there is a small garden on the south side. A few hundred feet south of the first meadow through a Sherwood Forest type setting there is another another larger, hidden meadow with a few old apple and pear trees. This wildflower meadow is loaded with game and fowl. There is yet another meadow further up the Valley. It is smaller, but even more protected, with unparalleled views of the Mountains in the distance and the Valley below. The balance of the property that leads up to_____

Mountain is level and wooded. The timber has been select cut, and there are numerous old trails and paths throughout this area from which you have fantastic views of the _____ Valley below. Adjoining this Tract are two other tracts of 160 Acres @ $129,990 and 147 @ $149,990.

Sounds interesting, doesn't it? A little scoping added useful information.

The "meadows" referred to were clearcuts whose stumps had been bulldozed off to one side. The resulting open space had been seeded for wildlife forage, though the dozing had skimmed off the topsoil cover and reduced the land's fertility. The ad makes no mention of any clearcuts.

The "livable house" was a two-story farmhouse that hadn't been lived in, save during hunting season, for many years. The "manicured knoll" was, in fact, quite lovely. It referred to the spot where grass was cut around the house.

The "old trails and paths" were old skid roads used by loggers to take out the timber, which the owner kept mowed to facilitate hunting.

The "select cut" referred to the timbering that had taken place in the past during the seller's ownership. No mention was made of the Flipper's timber reservation. The Flipper told me that he had sold the valuable sawtimber 14" DBH and larger when I asked him about it directly, but no cutting had yet to occur. Land buyers would see the property with all trees standing.

One other point. The Flipper's survey showed that he only had 392 acres to sell, not 400. The "+/-" covered him.

After seven months of trying to peddle a $300,000 property, less its merchantable timber, for almost $440,000, the Flipper hadn't flipped anything. So he "cut" his price to about $410,000: 1) 85 acres plus house, $159,990; 2) 159+ acres, $90,000; 3) 147 acres, $159,900. All the price reduction was taken out of the 159-acre tract of woods that had been "select cut," clearcut and was about to be cut again.

The property was worth $300,000 with the merchantable timber, maybe $225,000 with the timber sold. At the lowered price of $410,000, the Flipper was still looking to gross $185,000 if he could find three full-price buyers. The only value the Flipper had added was to have a surveyor run interior division lines (from which the correct total acreage was derived). Still, seven months into the Flip, ads were still summing the three parcels as 407 acres, despite the fact that they totaled only 391-392 acres.

The Flipper, I think, was having trouble selling land with the timber reserved. Land buyers knew enough to know that they would be left with a mess. He was also pricing the Flip at roughly $950 to $1,000 per acre, which was $200 to $300 above comparables for recent cutover land. The Flipper ran his ads in the big metropolitan Sunday papers, but not in the local weekly where local buyers would know the current value of this land.

One possible reason for the Flipper pricing the three lots above market would be to delay any resale for one year following acquisition so that the profit would be taxed as a long-term capital gain and not as current income. On a $100,000 gross profit, the difference at that time between the two tax rates would be $15,000 or more. The Flipper could afford to wait the year, because he had about $75,000 in hand from the timber sale.

The other reason this Flipper was waiting for his price had to do with the fact that the Flipper was actually two individuals, one of whom fronted the purchase price to the other at 20 percent interest. (The details of their arrangement were available in the courthouse records.) The lender was doing just fine getting 20 percent from his partner who had to hold out for a high price so that he made something too.

I felt they could have gotten close to $400,000 for the three parcels pretty quickly had they not sold the timber. Had I been flipping it, that's how I would have done it. Eventually, of course, everything sold, and each parcel is now worth about twice its purchase price. Rapid appreciation makes every one of these games a win-win.

I had the chance to watch another Flipper at close range. He bought a three-month option from a big paper company for $300,000 on about 40,000 acres of mountain woodland, some of which had been clearcut and planted in pine. The purchase price was $500 per acre (p/A), or $20 million. While valuable timber could be found here and there, I estimated that the timber was worth in the $250-$300 p/A range, straight through. But the timber value was concentrated rather than spread evenly across the tract. The Flipper was an older, country-boy-type who had wiggled through deals like this many times before. But he had mistakenly relied on the seller's outdated timber inventory to project the timber's market value. It didn't take him long to figure out that his option price was too high to flip to local buyers. His strategy from the first was to flip the entire property to another Flipper who would do the division and resale. He sold about 4,000 acres to adjoining landowners in "small" pieces for prices at and above $650 p/A. Then he sold 6,000 acres to an out-of-state Flipper who held an even more inflated idea of the timber's value. By this time, he had extended his option for another $300,000. With time and money running out, he dropped the asking price on the remaining 30,000 acres from $650 p/A to $535 p/A and found an entirety buyer—a former prominent Congressman—at the last minute for $525 p/A. And that buyer—a Flipper—has been trying to sell it for $1,000+ p/A without quick success. If I had a retail client in this game, I would have advised paying no more than $450 p/A for a large chunk of this 40,000 acres and no more than $550 p/A in small lifts. Other comparable property was available at those prices and less.

A buyer can benefit from understanding the Flipper's immediate circumstances. He's more likely to sell below his asking price if he's already paid for the deal from earlier sales. You can bargain better by determining the Flipper's purchase price for the root property and the selling prices he's received from prior sales. These prices can be found or calculated from deeds recorded in the Courthouse. You gain leverage by "knowing his numbers." Option contracts are not likely to be recorded. You'll have to put your ear to the local ground to listen for the Flipper's option price, his deadline and whether or not he can extend. It never hurts to ask the seller about the option price.

Buyers can assume that the Flipper is looking to make at least a 50 percent gross profit for his effort, and 100 percent is not unusual. When a tract has both good and bad sections, the Flipper may mark up the good sections proportionately more than the bad ones. The latter might be bought for not much more than what Flipper has in it. Bargain hunters may find a "bad" piece that perfectly fits their needs. If, for example, you're looking for hunting habitat, you should consider buying the "bad" lot with the recently clearcut areas; the more ugly slash, the better.

Flippers divide their property and sell the parts according to state law and local ordinance. Where those frameworks are lax, you will get less protection than where they are not. You should assume that a Flipper will disappear after the Flip. Any problem that emerges will be yours to fix. You should not rely on oral promises. Written statements bind real-estate transactions.

Rural residential developments, like any other business, have their share of people from whom you don't want to buy either the Brooklyn Bridge or a hillside lot that reminds the salesman of those "million-dollar cliff-hangers in California." Outright and intentional land frauds and swindles are harder to pull off today because of federal and state laws—and are, therefore, probably of less concern than they were before the era of regulation and consumer protection. Buyers still get taken, and it doesn't do you much good to have your developer jailed for mail fraud as you sit on Lot #31 on the top of a mountain with only a mile of goat trail to get you there.

One Flip that you want to avoid is the outright fraud. The clue here is that you, the buyer, find yourself negotiating with a "seller" who "has" a contract with the landowner that hasn't closed. In and of itself this is not a fraudulent situation. Most real-estate contracts allow the buyer to "assign" or sell his interest in it. The seller pumps the value of the property to you to make it appear that it's worth much more than the contract price, which he discloses. He can do this in several ways. The seller pays a compliant appraiser to provide an inflated value, or obtains a bogus cruise on the timber value (See Chapter 31), or links up with a pliant mortgage lender who agrees to lend you the inflated value. Your best protection is to scope the property thoroughly to determine its real market value. (A similar urban scam was described by Benny L. Kass, "Housing Counsel: Beware of Fraud in 'Flipping' Schemes," Washington Post, October 20, 2001. Kass, a lawyer, writes an excellent column on housing issues and will consider questions from readers; Benny L. Kass, Suite 1100, 1050 17th St., N.W., Washington, D.C., 20036.)

Some readers may be interested in learning how to flip property. Take a look at William Bronchick and Robert Dahlstrom, Flipping Properties (Chicago: Dearborn-Kaplan Publishing Co., 2001) and Bradley K. Haynes, How You Can Grow Rich Through Rural Land—Starting from Scratch (Front Royal, Virginia: Greatland Publishing Co., 1979). Mr. Haynes operates a real-estate brokerage in the north end of Virginia's Shenandoah Valley and runs ads in the Washington Post that offer a free report, "50 Ways to Buy Land With Little or No Money Down." He can be reached at B.K. Haynes Land Brokers, www.bkhaynes.com or e-mail: bkhaynes@shentel.net; Since the Haynes book was published, many rural counties have tightened their subdivision ordinances, making flipping harder, more expensive and more responsible than in the past.

CHAPTER 11: SECOND HOMES: DEVELOPERS AND DEVELOPMENTS

BUILDING A SECOND HOME OUT HERE

Whether you're building your own or buying a house off a developer's rack, it's worth doing background reading before you sit down with architects, excavators, contractors, developers or just the back of your own envelope. I've found these general books to be helpful: Alan and Denise Fields, Your New House: The Alert Consumer's Guide to Buying and Building a Quality Home, 3rd ed. (Boulder, CO: Windsor Peak Press, 1999); Myron E. Ferguson, Build It Right!: What to Look for in Your New Home (Salem, OR: Home User Press, 1997) and Better Houses, Better Living: What to Look for When Buying, Building or Remodeling (Salem, OR: Home User Press, 2004); Gary W. Eldred, The Complete Guide to Second Homes for Vacations, Retirement, and Investment (New York: John Wiley & Sons, Inc., 2000); Bob Johnson, Houses are Designed by Geniuses and Built by Gorillas: An Insider's Guide to Designing and Building a Home (Lenexa, KS: Addax Publishing, 1998); Dennis Wedlick with Philip Langdon, The Good Home: Interiors and Exteriors (New York: Hearst Books International, 2001); Janice Papolos, The Virgin Homeowner: The Essential Guide to Owning, Maintaining, and Servicing Your Home (New York: Penguin Books, 1999); and Katherine Salant, The Brand-New House Book (New York: Three Rivers Press-Random House, 2001). Robert J. Bruss, the knowledgeable and always helpful real-estate columnist. described the content of Salant's book as "superb" though its readability due to font choice and layout led him to write: "I have never encountered a book as hard to read as this one." Ferguson can be contacted at the Home User press, 1939 Woodhaven St., NW, Salem, OR, 97304; 503-391-8106, 1-800-530-5105, 503-375-2939 FAX; e-mail: info@betterhousebetterliving.com.

You will help yourself if you take the time to become familiar with the basic components of house construction. I recommend buying a comprehensive how-to book with a large index and glossary. The one I used in studying for my Virginia Class A residential-contractor's exam was John L. Feirer, Gilbert R. Hutchings and Mark D. Feirer, Carpentry and Building Construction, 5th ed. (Glencoe/McGraw Hill: New York, 1997), $59.95. Look for the most recent edition of this book or another of the same type and format. A simple and comprehensive discussion is found in Francis D.K. Ching and Cassandra Adams, Building Construction Illustrated, Third Edition (New York: John Wiley & Sons, 2001). Such volumes do not lobby for one type of house over others. Rather, they discuss the variety of *conventional* materials, practices (how stuff should go together) and design choices available to the trade. They provide common standards that should be applied, e.g., at a certain load, how much clear span can be designed for a floor with 2x8 joists spaced on 16" centers. Books like this are a handy generic reference when construction contractors start asking you to make decisions. The simpler the design and the more conventional the materials, the cheaper the square-foot construction cost—that's the rule of thumb that you will discover. Books devoted to specific building concerns—log cabins, passive-solar construction, stone work and so on—are available in bookstores, libraries and through the Internet. More exotic construction materials and practices will not be found in the conventional-building literature.

Reliable house-construction books and information are available from The Taunton Press and The Journal of Light Construction, 186 Allen Brook Lane, Williston, Vt., 05495; 802-879-3335. Fine Homebuilding (www.taunton.com; e-mail: fh@taunton.com) and The Journal of Light Construction (www.jlconline.com) are superb monthly magazines written for the trade that can be understood by semi-knowledgeable and half-handy prospective homeowners. (If you are not now semi-knowledgeable and are planning to build or have a house built for you, becoming semi-knowledgeable will pay for itself many times over.) While "book knowledge" has many limits, it's a very big first step toward being able to make sensible, cost-effective decisions in consultation with architects, excavators and contractors. Both magazines have been publishing for a number of years, and their back issues will have articles on specific subjects of interest. These collections are an amazingly rich source of trustworthy information, current as of the publication date. It is certainly possible for a non-knowledgeable urbanite to pay a contractor to build a second home in the country without ever asking a question, reading a book or learning the difference between a jamb and a joist. But when you are thinking of spending $100,000 or more in principal and (mainly) interest over the next 20 or 30 years, doesn't it make sense to spend $100 on books and magazines and $300 in fees for talking to an architect?

Certain residential-building practices and requirements will be set forth in the **local building code**. If you're hiring an architect or contractor, you won't have to know anything about these codes, unless the building inspector finds a problem. If you're being your own general contractor or doing the work yourself, you will need to know and follow the code requirements. If you violate the code, ignorance is not a defense.

Codes establish minimum practices governing residential design and construction, electrical work and plumbing. Until recently, no single national residential building code existed. In the late 1990s, the three regional code-writing organizations agreed on a single comprehensive code, 2000 International Residential Code (IRC), which provides standards for one- and two-family dwellings. The IRC also includes building standards for high-wind and high-seismic areas, as well as energy-efficiency standards. If you want a copy, contact the Building Officials and Code Administrators International, Inc. (BCOAI), 4051 W. Flossmoor Rd., Country Club Hills, Il., 60478; 708-799-2300; order from 1-800-214-4321, Ext. 777; www.bocai.org; e-mail: info@bocai.org. Request the most recent edition. The IRC is being adopted throughout the country, though localities choose which codes they want to use. If you do not want to become an instant expert on the IRC but want to have some idea of these standards, refer to the following books by Redwood Kardon from The Taunton Press: Code Check Electrical Revised Ed., 2nd ed.; A Field Guide to Wiring a Safe House; Code Check Plumbing; and Code Check Revised Ed., 3rd ed.: A Field Guide to Building a Safe Home. (The Taunton Press, publisher of Fine Homebuilding and building-related books is at 63 S. Main Street, POB 5506, Newtown, Ct. 06470; 1-800-283-7252.)

You may also hear reference to the National Electrical Code (NEC), or "The Code," which should be taken to mean whichever electrical code is used locally. Less technical books on electrical wiring and plumbing are available from Home Depot, Time-Life Books and Ortho. These are stocked at building-supply stores, online vendors, bookstores and libraries. If your house project is in a cold climate, you might also read Joseph Lstiburek's, Builder's Guide to Cold Climates from The Taunton Press. Make sure to use the most recent edition of codes and building books.

The local building inspector can tell you which code he applies. If the locality is not using the IRC, the inspector may be able to identify those sections of the local code that differ from the IRC and make recommendations for upgrades where he thinks they're a good idea. Nothing prevents an owner or his contractor from building "above" the code, for example, using stouter materials than the local code requires. Clear any upgrade with the local building inspector before you tell your contractor to do it. Make sure your architect, if you are using one, has designed to the local code. If you are using purchased house plans or developer plans, ask the local inspector to check them for code compliance before you build from them.

The local inspector can be counted on to know and enforce the local code, which may be customized to suit local conditions. Your house needs to comply with local standards. Areas prone to windstorms may—and should—require stouter roof designs. Earthquake areas have higher and different foundation standards. If you insist on building in a floodplain—some folks just have to have their fishing cabin a fly cast away from their trout stream—ask your architect, contractor and inspector what options you have, consistent with the local code, to protect your new house from the inevitable flooding. I have seen river-side houses perched on stout posts 14 feet above ground level. The code will provide the specifics on post height, dimensions and foundation.

Code inspections by the local building inspector are scheduled at different points in the construction process—typically before the footer is laid, when the foundation is complete, after the building is framed and when the electrical and plumbing are "roughed in" (that is, open for visual inspection). A code violation may imply a very small repair or thousands of dollars of new materials and rebuilding. Your contract with the developer and/or contractor should state that all work done on your behalf shall comply with local codes and that any instances of non-compliance will be corrected without additional expense to the owner (you). The local building inspector will only look for code violations; he will not inspect for things your architect and contractor have done that are impractical, stupid, wasteful and shoddy. If you have an architect working for you, he should keep an eye on your contractor. The architect's overview is limited to the times he visits the house, and some mistakes cannot be corrected once work proceeds beyond them. If you're not on the scene, you might hire a retired individual with some construction sense to visit the site every day as your representative. An arrangement of this sort is likely to keep down the number and size of mistakes and miscommunications. This "**clerk of the works**" should pay for himself in preventing costly errors.

Rural land buyers have four main ways of getting a house built: 1) buy into a second-home development where the developer also handles the building; 2) hire an independent, handle-everything **general contractor** who builds the house you want from plans you like either on a development's lot or on non-development land; 3) act as your own general contractor by hiring and coordinating other contractors to do the work; and 4) do the work yourself.

BUYING A SECOND HOME IN A FULL-PACKAGE DEVELOPMENT

Owners have several ready alternatives to buying undeveloped rural property and developing it on their own. You can find a **full-package second-home development** where everything—roads, utilities, house, community amenities—is in place or there for the buying. The advantage of a full-package deal is that you can see exactly what you're getting for your money, and you can talk to those who've already jumped in. Such developments usually come with a set of house-construction guidelines, such as minimum number of square feet, that every lot-owner follows. The full-package developer also handles house construction for each lot buyer, either acting as a general contractor or through an arrangement with one or more general contractors. The developer will usually set up a **homeowners' association** to manage the development after he's done.

Where a developer is also the contractor for the project's house construction, one or more models may be available for inspection. *Before signing a purchase contract for land and house*, ask the developer for a set of house plans and materials to review. Then hire an architect to check them. Buy two or three hours of his time, no more. Architects are trained to imagine two-dimensional drawings as they will be in three dimensions. They will know the standard formulas that house designs should incorporate, from the proper width of "elder" hallways to the height of counters. Ask him to scan the plan/materials for corner-cutting and point out both the good and bad features he sees. A common way for a developer or contractor to cut corners on a house is to skimp on the things you can't see. This can take the form of underinsulating (e.g., using insulation with a too-low R-factor; not insulating the ground floor; not installing whole-house insulation wrap); using plastic water pipe not copper; skimping on structural materials (e.g., using 1/2"-thick plywood as a roof underlayment rather than 5/8", or thicker; using 2x4 wall studs instead of 2x6s in climates where six inches of wall insulation is much better than four; not using treated lumber for sills); using cheap windows, doors, fixtures and cabinets, and so on. Stock second-home designs tend to provide as many square feet as possible and short the buyer on structural stoutness and quality materials.

Where the developer has built similar second homes in developments, ask owners for their opinions. A poorly constructed house will usually turn up problems soon after it has been occupied and certainly within five years. Ask the owners what they like and dislike about the design and materials, and what they'd change. Ask about roof problems and leaks around windows and doors; windows that don't work well; doors that have warped; cracks in masonry; plumbing problems; degradation of siding and interior surfaces; undersized heating and air-conditioning units; insufficient phone jacks and outlets; cheap appliances.

Take this information to the architect whom you have asked to suggest changes and upgrades in the developer's house plan. Remind the architect that you are looking for suggestions appropriate to the house the developer is planning to build. (If the architect tells you to bail out of this developer, do so.) The architect's review will cover the house plan's structural integrity, materials, design functionality (how well the design fits your needs) and quality. He can make *modest* floor-plan revisions to provide more efficient use of horizontal and vertical space. He can also propose more substantial revisions to fit your individual needs, subject to the developer's willingness to incorporate them. Make sure the architect understands the scope of what you're asking him to do; you are *not* asking him to redesign the entire house. If you find the architect you have chosen for this limited work is recommending wholesale changes with which you agree, you may want to walk away from the developer's project. The alternative would be to buy land outside a development, hire the architect and find a general contractor to build the house you want.

The architect's review is also a chance for you to evaluate the architect. You may want to reconsider the architect if you sense that his "vision" of your house is grander than or stylistically incompatible with yours. If you get stuck, hire a house carpenter or contractor to review the developer's plans. Not all carpenters and contractors can provide this kind of review. Some may be reluctant to act as an "outside" consultant, because they have business relationships with the developer. Regardless of the title or professional status of the individual you use, you're looking for a combination of hands-on experience and the intellectual ability to judge how systems will work together in practice on your site. The actual review-and-comment time should take no more than a couple of hours. The suggestions you get will pay for themselves many times over.

Despite my cautions, I believe that a second-home buyer gets substantial advantages from a full-package-infrastructure-plus-house development. First, most—but not all—of both the work and worries of house-building are done by those you hire. In the best of circumstances, you will still have to find the money to pay for things, make choices that involve taste and expense and do the final inspection and acceptance before making your last payment. (You might want to take your outside consultant on this last inspection.) Still, the thousands of decisions required of an individual building his own second home are not yours. You are also spared the hundreds of decisions required when you act as your own contractor.

You cannot avoid several dozen decisions—most of which can be made over the phone and during a half-dozen, scheduled site visits. Buying a full package minimizes the stress and time you will spend getting your second home done. Convenience and simplicity have both psychic and monetary value.

Second, you will be choosing from developer-offered designs that have been conceived to be simple enough for run-of-the-mill crews and **subcontractors**, referred to as **subs**, to complete well enough. The crews building your developer house are not Old World craftsmen who lovingly hand plane each floor board and carve your likeness into your walnut fireplace mantle after hours and on their own nickel. They are for the most part adequate at what they do; and at least one—hopefully, the crew chief—can read a blueprint and has built your model before. The more times a crew has built a house design, the better job they are likely to do. They will have discovered design errors and made their mistakes on the earlier structures. As a later buyer, you will benefit from the crew's rise on the construction learning curve. The developer will offer house plans that he knows his crews are capable of building. Developer-contractors will offer you options on basic plans, but not the option of building anything you want. Since developers are in business to make money, the more you deviate from the package of options, the more uncertainty and time the developer will take on and the more it will cost you. Every customization and change order you make will involve extra cost, because each one inevitably requires extra work, time and risk of not getting it right.

Finally, if the house the developer builds fails to meet the terms of your contract or customary standards of workmanship, it will be far easier for you to get him to resolve the dispute—before your final payment—than it would be for you to chase down a general contractor and his subs. House building is sausage-making insofar as it turns raw land and thousands pieces of stuff into a functioning structure. It is hard, messy and, often, distasteful work. Houses built by developers must be put up quickly, efficiently and for a fixed price. Labor, a major cost component, is contained by using materials that can be put up fast, working off familiar designs and substituting cheap labor for skilled, expensive labor wherever possible. Mistakes are inevitable. Still, every developer depends for future sales on good word of mouth from buyers who have gone before. Both profit and customer satisfaction depend on making sausage simply, using the same basic recipe. This allows the developer to have confidence in his product, and he should stand behind it, making good whatever might turn up not quite right. An absentee owner will have a far harder time getting the average independent general contractor to right the same wrongs. It will be especially hard on one-of-a-kind houses and those with a lot of custom work. You will have little chance to resolve the dispute outside of court if you've given him his last payment.

When a house is built from scratch, you should expect to find some construction mistakes and defects. Before you accept your new house, you should inspect the house and fill out a **punch list** of items you think should be corrected. You might want to do this **walk-through** with your architect/consultant, home inspector, or even a friend with house-building experience. A completed house conceals most structural mistakes under exterior and interior finishes, siding, drywall, paneling and the like. You can catch these errors only if you or your **clerk of the works** is on the scene when they are still visible and correctable. Your final payment is contingent on the punch-list items being corrected. Most contractors guarantee their workmanship for one year. The head of one national real-estate engineering firm estimated that "…nationwide as many as 15 percent of new residences have serious defects.., the most common involve roofs and water intrusion in windows and doors." (John Handley, Chicago Tribune, "Welcome to Your Imperfect Dream Home," Washington Post, May 8, 2004, quoting Alan Mooney, president of Criterium Engineers of Portland, Maine.) Defects, Mooney said, are caused by house-building materials, weather and poor construction techniques. Cost-pinching builders can scrimp on nails, screws, caulking and vapor barriers—with major consequences. The temperature when concrete is poured and asphalt shingles are applied will affect job quality. Among other commonly observed defects are inadequate caulking, missing or unbolted anchor bolts that connect the foundation to the house frame, lack of flashing above windows and doors, unsealed seams on ductwork, nail and screw pops and foundation cracks. Lawsuits over construction defects now have put the cost of builder insurance at about $6,000 for the average new house. A lot of new houses will have a lot of little things not quite right. Your interest is in not buying a new second home with big things wrong.

If you are flexible about your house plans and schedule, consider buying the developer's model. You should expect a price discount in proportion to the amount of money you pay in advance of possession. If, for instance, the developer wants to use his model for one year and you are willing to give him cash a year in advance of his exit, you should be able to reduce the purchase price on the model considerably. He needs your cash more now (to pay his bills and debt service) than he will in a year, when the last sales revenue is profit. Be mindful of your tax consequences in working this tactic. Models tend to be loaded with options, built and maintained carefully, and located at the front of the project. They can be a great buy, as long as you're comfortable with a front-of-the-development location.

It's possible that you believe that you can save money by buying undeveloped land and hiring a contractor to build a house for you from plans you provide instead of buying into a full-package development. Possibly. Developers-contractors have salaried crews who must work efficiently if they are to retain their employment. They are able to purchase materials at the **contractor's price** where one is offered, usually two to ten percent below retail. They may be able to negotiate a quantity discount on top of the contractor's price. The contractor you hire on your own may or may not get the contractor's price, may or may not pass along any savings to you, and may or may not mark up materials to the point where you would have been ahead to buy materials retail. Developers should be skilled in using cost-estimator computer programs and should have **take offs** (price quotes that are good for fixed period of time, e.g., 90 days) from suppliers and prices from subs before they quote you. Certainly after building the first couple of project houses, the developer will know what his actual costs are and can price subsequent houses with some confidence.

If you are using a general contractor to build your house, he will get a contractor's discount on materials (where they are offered) and then mark up the cost of materials by ten percent or more to cover overhead and profit. Some contractors earn their markup by shopping around among suppliers for the lowest price. Others will simply buy all materials from a single supplier, making their lives easier but your bill higher. I once asked a general contractor working for me why he didn't get materials from the lowest-priced supplier, which I had researched for him, instead of using one supplier exclusively. He replied that his supplier would be "no more than ten percent higher on any item on my list than the cheapest guy." I pointed out to him that since he was getting a 20 percent mark up on materials he purchased, this could result in spending as much as $10,000 more on a $100,000 materials purchase, along with 60 percent more profit for him. (The math worked like this: $100,000 materials cost + 20 percent markup = $120,000 cost of materials to owner; $100,000 materials cost + 10 percent added for higher price = $110,000 + 20 percent markup = $132,000 cost of materials to owner; $12,000/$20,000 = 60 percent more profit on the materials mark up from a 10 percent higher price.) He agreed, but argued that there was a "convenience factor" that I should consider (his convenience, that was). This particular supplier, he added, always took back materials, he, the contractor, wrongly ordered or were wrongly sent. (Don't use a supplier who refuses returns.) With a fixed mark up over cost, neither the supplier nor my general contractor had any incentive or reason to hold down my cost of materials—and, of course, they didn't. With the project running over budget, I began ordering some supplies myself from low-cost suppliers and to save the contractor's mark up. He and I parted ways, though not soon enough in my opinion.

Shopping suppliers can save you five percent on a project's total cost. But you will spend a lot of time making comparisons and coordinating the delivery of stuff from different suppliers. I think the best way to handle this situation is to establish relations with no more than three multi-purpose building suppliers, buying from whichever offers the best price for the quality. You will have to purchase enough either to make a truck load or pick up materials yourself. You will learn from the take offs each of your suppliers prepares who is the cheapest on each type of material—framing lumber, windows, doors, blocks, hardware, drywall, paints, siding, roofing and so on. You will have to weigh price against other factors, such as whether you will need to store materials under cover or inside, and for how long. It's common to buy most materials from the overall low-cost supplier with specific items from others, as needed.

Some contractors will work out a sweetheart deal with a supplier, and others will treat you properly. It's fair for a general contractor to mark up materials cost when he is shopping for you, coordinating deliveries and hassling with returns. Doing these jobs well takes time and a good head for details. A conscientious contractor will save you money on materials and know which suppliers to avoid regardless of their prices. He'll also know when the low price reflects low quality. His time in managing materials will increase if he's building at a remote location where he has to drive a ways into town each time he finds he's short the proper nail.

I think the best way to handle this owner-contractor-supplier triangle is to have frank talks with your preferred contractor and various suppliers before you sign a construction contract. Your preferred contractor may want to work with one supplier more than others, and there may be good reasons to follow his advice. If you want to buy and manage materials yourself, make sure that your contractor understands this. Materials are usually about 50 percent of total new-house cost, so if you're taking this mark up away from a contractor, he needs to know this in advance and price his work accordingly. You should expect that a contractor will build in overhead and profit to whatever work he does on your project. Don't quibble over pennies, but, at the same time, be clear with each other over how you are being charged. Don't be rigid about insisting that the contractor always use the lowest-cost supplier, because other factors can weigh on this decision. A supplier who slips in low-quality, unusable materials is more trouble than the cost "savings" are worth. (I've seen roof framing stop dead when the last two rafters in the supplier's package contained defects that prevented them from being used safely.) Follow your contractor's advice when he gives you specific examples of a particular supplier delivering shoddy materials, or dumping a load out in the rain without covering it, or unloading in a way that damaged merchandise or consistently botching up orders.

Also make sure that either you or your contractor always pays suppliers in time to get any fast-payment discount offered. Suppliers will offer, as a rule, **10/1 Net 30** or **10/2 Net 30 discounts**, which mean that the purchaser can deduct either one or two percent from the bill if payment is received within ten days of the billing date, otherwise the full bill—the net—is due within 30 days of the billing date.

You can get a reasonably accurate idea of the cost of doing any piece of new house construction work by consulting **annual pricing guides** that are available in libraries and at major bookstores. (Remodeling work is harder to estimate, because conditions vary.) New construction work can be costed out in different ways: by the **square foot**; or as **unit cost** (one brick costs $1 x 5,000 bricks needed to build a wall; a unit might also be laying 100 linear feet of brick); or by the **item** (one free-standing fireplace with 24 feet of 12"-diameter insulated flue pipe costs $x.) R.S. Means Company, Inc., publishes Contractor's Pricing Guide: Residential Square Foot Costs, each year. (R.S. Means Company, Inc., 100 Construction Plaza, POB 800, Kingston, MA 02364-0800; 617 585-7880; 1-800-334-3509). This is an easily understood cost compendium of every new construction component and system that allows you to cost out a specific house in a specific geographic region in a given year. Much of the data is broken down so that you can find the cost of materials (which includes a ten percent mark up for profit) and cost of installation (labor plus contractor's overhead and profit) for everything from putting in a driveway to installing a skylight. Basic house types in economy, average and custom versions are costed out by the square foot along with the cost of common upgrades and modifications. The Means Company also publishes a cost guide for those who are thinking of remodeling: Repair and Remodeling Cost Data, annual edition. Another cost guideline that I've used is Marshall & Swift, Dodge Unit Cost Book, annual edition (Marshall & Swift [McGraw Hill], POB 26307, Los Angeles, CA 90026-0307; 213-683-9000; 1-800-526-2756).

These books will give you a reasonable estimate of average construction costs in your location. You should, of course, anticipate variation from these average estimates, depending on site-specific conditions, local labor costs and the always changing price of materials. If you're building a high-end second home, you should expect to pay a bit more per unit than if you're building a two-bedroom, one-bath ranch. Your budget for labor rates and profit will be larger, and your contractor will know that. These books cannot factor in site-specific variations from the norm—bad soils that require a more expensive foundation footer or a ledge that takes an extra-big backhoe to remove. As a rule, overall building costs are cheaper in the country than in urban areas, but not in the rural pockets of wealth like Aspen, Colorado or Jackson, Wyoming. Labor costs are usually cheaper in rural areas, but standard materials can be a bit more expensive. Locally produced materials—stone, native lumber for finish work—should be cheaper and, often better, than their nationally marketed counterparts.

If you are at the point where you have an architect-drawn house plan or a set of similarly detailed plans, take them to various building-supply companies near your site and ask them to prepare a **take off**. These companies can calculate your materials need from a set of detailed house plans. Better still, your plans may come with an itemized list of materials, quantities and specifications (including brands and model numbers; dimensions, wood species and special features, e.g., plywood with tongue-and-groove edge rather than the more common butt-edged type). A supplier's take off represents a quoted price to you of the materials listed on the company's response to your plans or list. Quoted prices are good for at least 30 days, with 90 days being common. When comparing take-off estimates, be alert to substitutions of what the supplier is able to provide with what your plans specify. Costs vary with the quality of materials used, and it's easy to become the low-bidder by substituting lower-quality materials for those that are speced. Suppliers will quote a take-off price to those owners buying materials for a general contractor in their employ or an owner-built project.

A developer-contractor will usually offer to build a house for you using a **fixed-price contract**. This will specify the work to be done (and imply what's not done) along with a schedule of payments. The developer will offer to build his house plan for you for a lump sum (fixed price). He may offer to finance the land, construction, or both. Contractors are usually paid in several lifts during construction, the last occurring after you've approved and accepted the house. You will not know either his cost of materials or labor. You can get a rough idea of his building costs by consulting the Means or Dodge estimating guides, described above. If you change the scope of work during construction, called a **change order**, you will negotiate its cost separately. The developer will incorporate into his fixed price all of his known costs, plus his estimate of unknown expenses, delays and risk—all of which may amount to as much as 30 percent above his hard projections of expenses and materials. He then may add in overhead if that factor has not been included in labor and materials. Finally, he'll add profit onto that number. This may sound like a formula for excessive charges, but keep in mind that his package must be priced competitively against all other new housing in the local market and to a lesser degree against the owner who acts as his own general contractor on land outside a development.

A developer-builder must price his houses competitively, because second homes are almost always discretionary purchases and buyers have alternatives. He must also keep to his quoted construction price unlike an independent contractor being paid on the basis of time and materials. Apart from cost certainty, the developer-builder offers an absentee owner convenience and security, which may seem like abstract and marginal benefits as you're reading this book but take on major significance when you're in the middle of construction 150 miles from where you live.

You will inevitably ask whether the same house can be built for less money working through your own general contractor on land outside a development or by doing some or all of the construction yourself. On paper, you will find yourself saving money. But you will rarely, if ever, be comparing one apple of a specific size, weight and quality to another with identical characteristics. Of course, you can save money if you do a lot of the work yourself—and have the time to spend doing it. You save money if you count your time and labor for free. That may or may not be a fair calculation, depending on your individual circumstances. I would count owner labor in for something, if only a fraction of current labor rates. You should assume that it will take you longer to do each task than the developer's work crew, particularly if you're working by yourself. Putting on a shingle roof might be estimated at six person days for a three-person crew; I'd increase the time by at least 50 percent to do it myself to account for a slower work pace, more care in doing the work and adding more nails than the crew would use. If you're older, count on taking more time to do a task than it would have taken you to do when you were not older. The solo builder is less efficient in performing a unit of this type of work, and he's also responsible for getting the materials to the site and humping them up the ladder. And if you're not an experienced builder, add in time for lack of familiarity with local vendors, forgetfulness, visitors and errors only an idiot like you and me would make. If you're taking time off from work in a manner that's forgoing a unit in your pay to not pay a dollar to a builder, you're probably netting a loss on a do-it-yourself. Don't forget to count in time that you spend fussing with house headaches by long-distance phone when you should be concentrating on your day job, as well as worry, stress and marital strain. There are, in other words, excellent reasons for an absentee buyer to build a second home through a full-package developer-builder when you can find one whose package meets all of your needs, most of your wants, a majority of your aesthetics and the available part of your pocketbook.

If you are inexperienced about house-building and wish to remain so, you should confine your search for a new second home in the country to full-package developments. You will still have to choose from among developments, and within a particular development you will have the ability to change the developer's house plans consistent with options he presents and the thickness of your wallet. The trouble with choosing among full-package developments is that you may not like the house designs or the prices. All things considered, the full-package second home is a safer and more reliable path than other new-construction options generally available to an absentee owner interested in a simple entry into country living. If, however, you hate faux 1890s farmhouses and places that look like someone stuck corks in their ears and shoved an air hose up their back door, you can jump in and look for non-development land and a general contractor, or limit your search to **improved land**, that is, country property with an existing house.

A typical **semi-developed project—a partial infrastructure package**—will offer a buyer sufficient infrastructure to allow him to place or build a dwelling of some sort on his new lot. (In rural second-home developments, a lot can be any size. Lots tend to be larger where the infrastructure investment is smaller.) Semi-developed infrastructure may be nothing more than interior dirt roads. The buyer must understand that he and other lot owners must add the remaining property infrastructure on their own or do without. Each buyer is then responsible for his own site infrastructure and house-building.

A common rural second-home development is one where the developer has purchased a large undeveloped tract and then divided it into lots in compliance with the local zoning ordinance. A developer might stop his capital investment at that point, proceeding directly to sell the newly surveyed parcels with nothing more than a marked-out road right of way. The developer might handle lot sales or run them through either a real-estate broker or an auction. This is The Flip described in Chapter 10; Flips do not offer a house-building package.

If you are looking to buy a house from a developer of any kind, never sign a purchase contract without first scoping the project, the lot and the house choices. Don't sign a purchase contract without having your local lawyer review it. Your lawyer should pick out your legal risks, but some risks will reveal themselves only through your own diligent scoping. Where a house is being purchased along with a lot, you may have a separate construction contract. Both standard developer-supplied contracts will favor the developer. Consider submitting your purchase offer for the land and house on a contract that you and your lawyer draft, using the standard contracts where they are fair to both sides. You are not required to use the developer's contract to buy his land or his house, though he's likely to resist using your version. If nothing else, your contract alternative will reveal those portions of the developer's contract (s) that he doesn't want to give up. That can give you a lot of information. If your lawyer tells you the developer's basic contract is acceptable from your point of view, then go with it and propose revised language where he recommends. I also recommend having your lawyer with you when you negotiate price for land/house and options with the developer or his sales personnel. This evens the sides, and gives you an excuse to leave the bargaining table for a private strategy caucus with your lawyer. If you feel inept or uncomfortable bargaining on your own behalf, have your lawyer take the lead.

The best-intentioned developers fail in whole or in part. Their failures can drag buyers into a protracted mess that costs money, time and emotional energy. These train wrecks occur when the developer runs out of money; train wrecks will change your journey. Less infrastructure and fewer amenities are installed. Another developer with a different plan might take over. The project design is changed, e.g., increasing the number of units or decreasing the size of unsold lots so as to have more to sell. House options may be narrowed; house prices are likely to be increased. The developer's investment in the project can be scaled back in many ways. Bankruptcy may be taken or the developer takes a one-way night flight to a beach near the Equator. Even where the developer sticks with a troubled project, a buyer can find that a problem condition is not disclosed or an oral promise is not kept (e.g., a promise that the State has agreed to take over ownership and maintenance of the project's roads when the State has made no such commitment). Financial shakiness can affect any development, no matter size or location. A big jump in interest rates over a couple of years can strangle the most well-planned development. Buyers must assume the responsibility for protecting themselves. It is impossible to eliminate all risks from buying in a development, but scoping and question-asking can minimize them.

The 1968 Federal Interstate Land Sales Full Disclosure Act covers projects of 25 or more undeveloped lots that are marketed through the mail or in interstate advertising. Various states have enacted laws regulating developments that are organized with homeowners' associations (also referred to as, "lot associations"). Make sure that the second-home developer gives you a copy of association regulations. In the absence of a homeowners' association, ask very detailed questions about how you and your fellow lot owners will manage infrastructure maintenance once the developer leaves.

You, as a development buyer, can also find some security in local building regulations. Counties may have ordinances that impose infrastructure and house standards that determine the number of houses on a particular project site and control the type and size of housing that can be built on its lots. House design may also come under the purview of a local county committee charged with reviewing the appearance and style of new housing. There's less regulatory framework in less-developed, second-home counties, and a great deal in highly developed areas. You should have confidence in a developer who has given the county a **performance bond** for the purpose of assuring completion of the project.

You, as a buyer, must do everything you can before buying into a development to assay the background risk of developer failure. Building contractors, as well, can fail unexpectedly. A useful exercise is to anticipate what you would do were the developer or the general contractor you've hired disappear the day after you sign your contract and hand over your check. You can't prevent the failure of others, but you can use your scoping and question-asking to measure the risk you will assume. Nothing beats direct questions from you to the developer prior to signing a contract: What happens if you run out of money before the project is completed? What happens if sales do not proceed as anticipated? What guarantee does he offer that he will build out all of his promises? What protection do you as a buyer have if he doesn't? What happens if he runs out of money with your house half built? If his answers smell off, don't hold your nose while signing the contract. Find another place.

Buying rural property can be one of your major life commitments. This is especially true when the property is a second home and carries with it ever more layers of family memories. "On Golden Pond" is not fictive in this regard. The second home can easily become a family's primary emotional residence. The process of acquiring such places becomes one of the family's foundation legends. Apart from the very sensible idea of spending your money wisely, it's far better to step into these places with positive feelings and a sense that you've managed the acquisition and construction well rather than stumbling in, feeling pummeled and ripped off. Bad start-up vibes reverberate for a long time, and, in my experience, never really go away. Good vibes are what we want. And good vibes will result from research, research, research and knowing increasingly what you want.

BUILDING A SECOND HOME WITH A GENERAL CONTRACTOR

A general contractor coordinates, arranges, schedules, secures, directs and carries out. He is responsible for getting each sub-task in the construction process done in the proper sequence, using either his own crew or subcontractors. The general contractor is responsible to you for the quality of any subcontracted work. General contractors will have house plans for you to select and should be willing to work from plans that you provide. Your plans can be purchased from a supplier or drawn by an architect. You hire a general contractor, but he is not your employee. You should do no building without a written contract with your general contractor.

When you pay others to build a second home, you spare yourself the physical labor of construction, but you will still bear certain responsibilities and associated stress of coordinating the process; finding, vetting and paying a contractor; and possibly getting property rezoned and various permits, obtaining certain materials and accepting finished work. If an architect is involved, he can help with these tasks, but he adds another level of owner coordination. Lest I sound that building a house in the country is a choice between worse and worst, it's obvious that it is a job that is done all the time by people just like you. Start this journey with cautious enthusiasm. Become knowledgeable about the implications of choices and realistic about the amounts of time, money and emotional energy that will be required. Talk to those who've gone down this road before. Do not expect a road without bumps, but you can expect a road without wrecks.

If you are unsure, inexperienced or in search of wise counsel about the multi-layered, quasi-existential experience of dealing with residential building contractors, take a look at the following: Duncan C. Stephens, The Unofficial Guide to Hiring Contractors (New York: Macmillan, 1999); Tom Philbin, How to Hire a Home Improvement Contractor Without Getting Chiseled, rev. ed., (New York: St. Martin's Griffin, 1996); and Alan and Denise Fields, Your New House: The Alert Consumer's Guide to Buying and Building a Quality Home, 2nd ed., (Boulder: Windsor Peak Press, 1996 [1-800-888-0385]). Tracy Kidder's classic, House, describes a wonderful architect, a dedicated general contractor and a talented construction crew. To hit three for three is, in my experience, improbable.

The absentee buyer must be prepared for a great deal of long-distance consultation and a number of site visits when he retains a local general contractor. Building a house requires many on-the-spot decisions that the owner will want to decide in consultation with his contractor. Cell phones and laptops with e-mail enable you to stay closely in touch. If you find a general contractor who seems reluctant to talk with you, keep looking. By "talk" I mean two things at the minimum: return your calls in a reasonable amount of time and genuinely communicate. I've had nothing but bad experiences with contractors who don't talk to their customers. For your part, don't be a pest and don't share your agonies. Be a professional customer even when you're a first-time amateur.

General contractors will build a "**turnkey**" house for you, but you should not assume that your involvement is limited to signing checks and turning the key in the finished product. Some general contractors handle everything from site work to landscaping, while others will expect the owner to arrange for certain permits, utilities and site work. You need to have a very clear understanding from the start with your contractor as to what "turnkey" includes and does not include. It's best to stay in regular touch with the contractor even when the house plans are detailed and he's built from them before. Every owner changes a plan. Any change you make in an off-the-shelf plan is likely to lead to other changes, about which you want to be consulted. Something as simple as the location of light switches is a decision that you should make, because you will be living with its consequences.

Each owner has to establish a functional relationship with his contractor. You have to be decisive when a decision is required. An owner who keeps changing his mind about a design will find his project costs skyrocketing. You have to be involved, but you should not be meddlesome, obsessive and constantly micro-managing. If you exceed the contractor's patience for this behavior, you may find yourself without a contractor.

It's hard work to find the right balance with someone you don't know very well, whose judgment you are forced to trust, who may see you as another rich and dumb outsider, and to whom you are paying a lot of money for something you may not know much about. If you get the feeling that a contractor will be hard for you to work with, get out before you get in. You don't want someone who is insecure, inflexible, dismissive, ill-humored, unreachable, too busy for you, stupid or dishonest. The process of an absentee owner working with a general contractor is fraught with opportunities for disagreement and misunderstanding even when personalities mesh. You need not find a friend in a contractor, but you do need to find someone who can work with you in a friendly, problem-solving manner for mutual benefit. You don't want a contractor who personalizes differences of opinions. If you don't feel comfortable talking with a general contractor in your first discussion or two, I'd look for someone with whom you have a better chemistry. But before you burn through every contractor in a four-state area, make sure you are coming across as patient, reasonable and rational. While you are obviously invested in the outcome of each problem as it arises, remember that your contractor is a large part of any solution.

The general contractor will handle getting all of the construction work done. Other things being equal, you will want him to manage all of the **pre-construction house infrastructure** as well. Site-grading, excavating, road building, hauling infrastructure materials, coordinating the installation of utilities, putting in a septic tank and well and doing the final grading—is a huge headache if you're trying to find and coordinate individual specialist contractors, especially from a distance. Infrastructure must be planned, coordinated, designed, secured and installed correctly prior to construction. Permits and inspections from the local building officer are required. Other permits involving a septic system, erosion control and water may be required. If an endangered species is in on your land, you may not be able to build anything at all if construction destroys needed habitat. Getting the site infrastructure in place usually involves surveying (set-backs may be involved; you will need to have elevations "shot" on sloping sites so that you know how deep to dig your foundation footer), obtaining permits (which may require elevations and other drawings), road work, electrical service, other utilities (gas, telephone, cable TV, internet service), site clearing and preparation, surface-water drainage, soil stability under the house foundation (a civil engineer tests the soil; you want soil that compacts and stays in place; if the soil doesn't pass the test you may want to move to a different site or cut out the bad dirt and replace it with rock and good dirt), potable (drinkable) water (tying in to an existing line or developing a source on site) and wastewater (sewerage) system.

Having your general contractor take responsibility for arranging all of this work is money wisely spent. I also think it usually works out best when your general contractor does the site infrastructure himself. The next best arrangement is for your general contractor to "sub out" the work that he doesn't do to specialists with whom he's worked before. The least preferable approach is for your general contractor to coordinate among contractors that you find for him to work with. Your general contractor should know which subs to pull into your project based on cost and competence. Any sub used should be expected to guarantee the quality of his work to the standards of his trade. Ask your general who he plans to have do the infrastructure work. Run those names through your growing network of local contacts. If you have chosen your general well, you should have confidence in his choices and his ability to coordinate and implement tasks in the proper sequence. This takes experience and communication skills. Keep in mind that all local building and ground-disturbance approvals must be secured prior to doing that type of work.

A general contractor hired to do your project, in whole or in part, should be state-licensed and approved to handle the dollar scale of your work. A **residential contractor's license** indicates that the individual has at some point complied with whatever requirements were then imposed for that particular type of license. In Virginia, residential building contractors can obtain one of three levels of licensure, "A," "B" or "C," which require different levels of experience and financial worth, and allow the holder to build projects of increasing value. Most of the Virginia contractors I've worked with were grandfathered into their licenses, because they were working as contractors when the licensure standards were established. Some "A" contractors who are allowed to build residences of any type and with no dollar ceiling could not in my opinion pass the written test that is now the sole gate controlling access to their trade. These older contractors are not comfortable with book-knowledge tests, but are perfectly capable of doing a good job in the field based on experience. The license categories are not awarded on the basis of demonstrated competence. Many licensure applicants now enroll in multi-day preparation classes to increase their chances of passing. The B and C contractors I've used have been more competent and honest than the As, who tend to be wealthier and better at the business side of contracting. The B and Cs have low overhead and work by themselves or with one or two others at most, always on small projects falling under the dollar ceiling of their license. If you were building an entire house in Virginia, you would probably have to work with an A, because he alone is allowed to build projects involving more than $70,000. Each state has its own licensing system with an oversight/regulatory board. The board can send you a list of contractors who have been disciplined over their business practices. You may be able to learn whether the contractor you are considering has complaints pending against him.

You, as an absentee buyer, will have to select a contractor and then work with him. Your choice should be based on feel (personal chemistry), intellectual compatibility and your interview findings with each contractor's recent customers. Get references, and check out the houses he's built. Try to fit your project to the contractor's usual construction profile. A contractor who builds nothing other than bungalows for $75,000 should not be hired to build a $600,000 architect-designed, three-story oval home with a conical roof. Ask other absentee owners about their level of comfort in working with him.

If you're feeling overwhelmed by the prospect of jumping into the unknown, consider ordering the Home Building Manual (www.HomeBuildingManual.com), which breaks down a building project into the tasks that you undertake with your contractor.

Conventional building contractors like to stick to conventional materials and designs. They are comfortable with basic frame construction using materials available from the local supplier, the "lumber yard." The farther your design and materials are from convention, the harder your road in finding a contractor to build it. In most rural areas—with some prominent exceptions—you will have a very difficult time finding a contractor willing to build a **green house with green materials**. Building green is a continuum of methods and materials that incorporate an environmental ethic. The materials continuum includes everything from rock construction to building with rammed earth, straw bales and timber that is certified as having been harvested in a certain way from forests managed in a certain way. (See www.greenhomebuilding.com for a one-stop overview and resource guide; also www.buildinggreen.com.) Two editors of Environmental Building News put out Green Building Products (Canada: New Society Publishers, 2005), which lists more than 1,400 green products. Alex Wilson, one of the editors, suggests that a new home have has its highest priorities energy-efficient windows, heavy insulation, high-efficiency furnace/air conditioning-system and materials that have low or no emissions of volatile organic chemicals (VOCs), such as formaldehyde in particleboard cabinets. Individuals sensitive to VOCs can find low-emission products at www.greenguard.org. Some areas in New England, Colorado, California and the like support green contractors; Blue Grass, Virginia does not. (Contact the U.S. Green Building Council, www.usgbc.org for a list of members who are architects, contractors and suppliers.) Where green construction has not taken root, you will probably have to build a green second home yourself.

Another type of home offered in rural areas is the **log house**, almost always built from a kit. Plans and discussions of log homes are available from the North American Log Homes Council, part of the National Home Builders Association, 1201 15th St., N.W., Washington, D.C., 20005; 1-800-365-5242; www.loghomes.org. The advantage of a kit home is that it will go up faster than a stick-built house—and probably with fewer hassles and mistakes. Kits won't be problem free, but they have been tested in the field before you buy yours. Some log kits have a construction crew option, which further reduces buyer risk. Before buying a particular kit, I would examine at least one in the field and talk with its owner. A kit buyer needs to be confident that the logs being used have been treated with preservatives to protect against insects and rot without affecting the health of the people who will live within its walls. Logs should not emit gasses. If the logs are untreated, carefully check the manufacturer's instructions regarding owner-applied sealants and other protections.

I once had a very small hand in building a log home from scratch, starting with cutting trees and encouraging a mule to drag logs to the site. It should have come as no surprise that this work is out of the 18th Century—hard and slow. The house was finished eventually, and the house finished the marriage. For every chink put in one, a chink fell out of the other.

Modular construction is a quick-house option that brings the efficiencies of assembly-line construction to housing. Modular housing is factory-built in units (modules) that are assembled on your site. (Panelized construction puts together factory-built walls on your site; pre-cut construction is another name for kits. Manufactured housing is now the official name for what had been called mobile homes.) An excellent collection of articles on modular housing is available from the National Association of Realtors, www.realtor.org/libweb.nsf/pages/fg321. See also www.modularhomeusa.com.

YOUR CONTRACT WITH YOUR CONTRACTOR

General contractors are in business to make money by building houses for the likes of you. If the general is experienced and familiar with your house plans, he should be willing to agree to a **fixed-price contract** for your house. His price will be based on his estimate of his costs, plus additional money to cover the inevitable unexpected events, plus a profit, which ranges between ten and 20 percent of the total. A fixed-price contract allows you to change plans during construction with attendant adjustments in cost. It's best to change as little as possible once you've started. You may want to include a provision that allows you to delete without penalty features, such as a deck, stand-alone garage or finish work (attic, basement) if your pile of construction money vanishes faster than expected. The more unusual and intricate your design, the harder it will be for a contractor to estimate his costs. He will have to bid high to cover his risk. While you want a fixed price to make your final cost predictable, you should expect to live up to that figure as well when your money tightens. A fixed price imposes obligations and discipline on both parties.

A residential contractor—often, himself and a crew of two or three—working for you with a set of plans that he's never used before will have a hard time costing out your project, particularly the labor. He will be able to get a firm materials cost from suppliers. But owing to the difficulty in estimating labor time, he will have to pad any fixed-price quote to cover himself. This can still lead to the uncomfortable experience of negotiating fixed-price contracts with contractors who then ask for additional money at the end of the job. (I've also had contractors live up to a fixed price even when it pinched them.) As a general rule, I think both sides should live up to the letter of the contract. Where performance has been good, I would add money where the contractor ran into a problem that he could not reasonably have been expected to foresee. I've also run into situations where the contractor's cultural perspective is that he sticks to a fixed price when it works for him and asks for more money when it doesn't. My best advice in dealing with contractors, particularly those you don't know, is to have a frank conversation before you sign a contract as to what you mean by fixed price. This discussion should be conducted after he has given you his fixed price, so that he doesn't immediately add 15 percent for his own comfort.

The other way to pay a contractor is to reimburse him on the basis of his **time and materials (TAM), plus profit**. The time cost will be calculated according to the hours each member of his crew works and their hourly rates. Where your general contractor uses subs, he will bill their cost to you, usually with some agreed mark up. It's fair for a general contractor to add overhead to his charges, but you need to determine whether his labor rates include overhead. If they do, he should not tack on overhead a second time. If his labor rates do not include overhead, he may add it as a percentage of his TAM costs. Profit can be added in different ways. It may be a fixed, agreed-in-advance number, or a percentage of total TAM cost, or a percentage of total TAM and overhead cost.

A TAM format does not give a contractor an incentive to work efficiently. The longer a TAM project takes, the more money the contractor makes. Many independent contractors prefer to work on a

TAM basis because they are not skilled at estimating jobs and fear losing money on fixed-price contracts. TAM formats also encourage slow work and, for lack of a better term, "standing around"—which may involve more sitting than standing. It's fair for construction crews to take a couple of breaks and 30 minutes for lunch. These typically add up to about an hour a day. You need to agree in advance whether you will be paying for this time. A four-person crew on a 40-hour week will spend four hours a day, 20 hours total each week, on break. At $15 per hour, that's $300 a week, or $7,500 on a 26-week building job. It may be local practice for contractors to bill for break time, for which they may or may not pay their crews. My experience is that contractors bill for break time and will routinely bill you for 40-hour weeks, save where weather cancels work.

Since you are building a second home in a rural, possibly remote, small-population area, you should assume that you won't have a wide range of choice among local contractors. Most will bill and contract in the same way, whatever that is. Demand for building services will probably exceed supply. Weather may limit the building window. In these conditions, it's next to impossible to force TAM contractors to be efficient and competitive. You may find one contractor billing his labor at a lower rate than another, which can lead you to think that the whole job will cost less. His crew, however, may be less skilled and less efficient than those of his competitors. My experience is that it's best to find a general contractor whose crews are expected to work hard and efficiently, because that's the way the contractor is. You may pay higher labor rates, but you are likely to get faster and better work. The difference between hard-working, productive crews and their opposites is readily apparent to an experienced eye. Your architect consultant may be able to direct you to the best local contractor. The local lawyer you are working with may also be able to narrow your search. When you get references from each contractor you interview, ask them how they felt about the crew's effort and efficiency and the contractor's billing practices. I would try to avoid TAM contracts, particularly if you are an absentee owner. The fixed-price contract may "look" high, but it does force a contractor to work within its parameters, forgiving though they will be. Of course, you may have no choice in the matter where all local builders refuse to work on fixed-price contracts.

The worst experience I had with a contractor involved a deal where I paid him for time and materials plus 20 percent profit over the total cost. His overhead was built into his labor rates. This was an overly generous arrangement by local standards, but I had no choice in the matter—always a rotten position to be in. Predictably, vulnerability was exploited. The contractor would not agree to a written contract, or a time frame or a cost. I knew going in that this payment format provided no reason for the work to be done efficiently or costs controlled. The contractor did not like me, the design, the architect or the work. Being reasonable and generous with him did not produce reasonable work and efficiency. He refused to shop suppliers and buy materials for the lowest price. He insisted, instead, on buying everything from one supplier. I grew to suspect this arrangement. "Bad attitude" infected the work. The crew was packed with redundant labor when work on other houses was short. I once found him using six men to put up roof rafters—one cut, a second lifted the rafter to the second floor where four men installed it, two on either end. This is work that four men could have done. I never received an accurate bill; some were off by a few dollars, one was in error by $2,000, in his favor. I finally gave up and fired him, which he seemed to be expecting. In contrast, the excavation contractor on this job was a confident, competent individual whose tasks were difficult and required great skill. He was comfortable working on a fixed-price contract. His judgment was flawless, and his crew knew, without being told, how to incorporate effort and efficiency. I liked and trusted the excavation contractor from the time I first met him; I never had this feeling with the house contractor who lacked confidence in working with architects and me. This contractor might have done a better job had the work been more conventional, but I think the problem went deeper than that.

The lesson I drew from this mess will probably be applicable to your second home: **you have to**

feel comfortable with contractors to be able to work well with them. This involves the ability to communicate, but more than that, it's the ability to solve problems without personalizing disagreements. It also involves the mutual feeling that fairness, honesty and reasonableness should be governing both parties. Most contractors with whom I've worked over 35 years produced work that was acceptable to good, and billed reasonably—and in each and every case they were individuals with whom I felt comfortable.

If you have reason to trust a contractor and trust his work habits and integrity, payment on an hourly basis or on TAM can work fairly for both sides. The more conventional your project is, the more TAM costs are predictable. Where construction is unconventional and/or involves a lot of custom work, hourly billing is a better payment format than a fixed price. In such circumstances, the contractor will have to set a very high price to cover time that he can't estimate very well. If you have to contract with a contractor you're not quite sure about in a locale where it would be difficult to find a replacement, I'd advise working very hard to get a fixed-price contract. If you agree to a TAM contract, you should insist that the general contractor be on the job every day. Lack of supervision creates too many opportunities for poor work and bad work habits.

On conventional construction, you can use a recent edition of a **cost-estimator book** and **supplier take offs** to project costs on which you can negotiate a fixed price. Or, you can hire a professional estimator or an architect to work up the numbers and help negotiate with the contractor. Your goal is fairness, not beating a contractor into the lowest price that he will accept. That tactic will backfire in poor quality and things not done that should be done. Every fixed-price contract will—and should—include some padding to cover what can't be projected with reasonable certainty. Your interest lies in containing padding, not eliminating it. Don't be self-righteous about paying five to ten percent over hard cost projections to cover the contractor's risk. Your concern over cost is legitimate, but it needs to be balanced with your concerns to employ a contractor who will work on schedule with acceptable quality, who does the things that make your house better without being told to, who makes an authentic effort to do a workman-like job and who you get along with. Your interest does not lie in haggling over padding, nor does it lie in being opened like a spigot.

ARCHITECTS, CONTRACTORS AND YOU

You don't need an architect to build many types of houses. Plans are readily available in magazines and on the Internet, e.g., www.natalieplans.com, www.homeplans.com, www.dreamhousessource.com, www.AreaPlans.com. and www.house-floor-plans.com, among others. One set of off-the-shelf plans costs between $150 to $500 or so, depending on the number of square feet and complexity. Make sure you are buying complete plans, including drawings for electrical, plumbing and heating/cooling systems, along with drawings of details where components fit together (doors, windows, counters, roofing, etc.). If the plan involves a large or complicated house, you might have an architect review it. And before you start, make sure your contractor is thoroughly comfortable with building from them. If he has questions or alternative ideas, you may want to get him together with an architect who can, if necessary, provide supplemental drawings.

Courses are also available for about $1,000 to help individuals learn the basics of house design and construction. (See www.yestermorrow.org and www.heartwoodschool.com.) Workshops are available on conventional construction techniques as well as alternative/green methods and materials. The Heartwood School, for instance, specializes in timber-framing construction.

You can, of course, hire an architect to draw plans for a custom, one-of-a-kind house. With this in mind, you can approach an architect with ideas of your own in whatever form they might be—vague notions to drawings to scale. Alternatively, you can have a general discussion with the architect and then ask him to prepare some **rough concept drawings**. The more certain you are about particulars—one-floor or two, maximum cost, heating system, number of bedrooms, number of square feet, finished basement or attic, number of bathrooms, type of foundation, roofing material, style, etc.—the better the architect's first drawings will be. Your final cost will be determined, in part, by the degree of expense you want to incur for finished interiors and kitchen/bathroom fixtures. A 200-square-foot kitchen can be outfitted for $10,000 with standard appliances from Sears or $100,000 in restaurant-type appliances, coupled with expensive counters, cabinets, flooring and lighting.

Where your contractor will be working with an architect you've hired to draw plans and oversee the project, get them together as soon as possible to get a feel for their ability to work together. Often, a buyer acquires an architect and his drawings before he decides on a contractor. In that case, both you and the architect need to agree on the contractor. Another way is to search for an architect and a contractor who have worked compatibly before; the architect can point you in the right direction. You can also ask your architect to help you find a contractor where neither of you have any leads.

Contractors in rural areas may have little, if any, experience working with architects. They may be suspicious of architects and their plans, which promise to be harder than what they've built before. Some contractors can rise above these doubts and self-doubts; others cannot. You will probably find a tendency for architects and contractors to blame the other for screw ups. If this gets out of hand, it poisons the project. Neither can be a diva. They have to learn to function together.

While my next statement may strike you as dumb beyond the extraordinary, I state it anyway: **make sure the contractor you hire can read and understand the plans your architect draws**. I once had to have an architect make a balsa wood model of a roof system because my contractor could not figure out how it was supposed to go together from the drawings. Lack of understanding is not a contractor monopoly. I heard this architect say to this contractor, "Certain parts of these plans were not supposed to be taken literally." How else was the contractor to take them? I asked. Plans, unless otherwise noted, *are* to be taken literally rather than as suggested guidelines. Your contractor is your last line of defense against architect mistakes. If you find a contractor coming to you regularly with plan errors, you will need to ask the architect to review the drawings with a fresh, proofreader's eye.

The addition of an architect creates a triangle with you and the contractor. Both are working for you, but you may find yourself mediating between them. This triangle is shaped by personality as well as the contracts you sign with each. Architects have a standard, complicated contract they use with owners that is provided by the American Institute of Architects (AIA; 1-800-365-ARCH). This is not a client-friendly contract, and you need to adapt it to your circumstances. Make sure your architect's contract specifies how often or at what stages he will inspect the contractor's work; the level of responsibility he agrees to bear for any errors in design and construction; and how disputes will be settled. You must have all your wants and understandings clearly stated in writing with both contractor and architect soon after your first conversation with each. I urge you to communicate wants and understandings in writing, which forces you to be as clear as you can and notices those working for you about what you expect. Make sure to keep a file of all written correspondence and field notes. Don't let vagueness snowball into conflict. It is your responsibility for establishing the highest level of forthrightness in these discussions. Plow into the most uncomfortable topics as soon as they arise because they will become increasingly uncomfortable and harder to resolve the longer they are unaddressed.

There is another problem with plans that I should point out. When an architect revises a drawing, he will slip it into his roll of plans and assume that the contractor is now working off the revised drawing that he has given him. The architect assumes that the contractor has understood the revision and has started incorporating the changes immediately. Future revisions will be based on past revisions. This sounds simple enough. In the field, contractors want to work from one, never-to-be-changed, set of plans. They mark up plans, and it is often hard for them to work off both an original and one or more revisions. A roll of plans might start out with 15 blueprints and end up with 30 or more, owing to revisions and change orders. Try to get the original set as perfect as possible. One contractor I once used tended to ignore revisions, because they complicated his work.

I've backed into the subject of **architects** on the backs of contractors. My experience with architects has been mixed and, occasionally, lousy. But I don't think my experience is the rule because it's limited to academics who took fee work on the side. Having spent time in college and universities, I knew that professors live in odd environments that are insulated from the give and take of market economics. But I knew little about modern architecture design, particularly the pervasive intellectual grip of the hard, spareness tracing back to Wright and Johnson. I have seen glass-and-steel office buildings that look like Orwell's vision of political asylums as well ones that look like Dali on acid. That's not what I wanted. I wanted to build people-friendly cottages, reasonably priced and easy to maintain. I liked the architects I hired and connected with them on most levels, but I found myself stuck with their Wright-like, people-unfriendly designs that were only partially suited to my customers, people in their 50s and 60s. I had told them clearly and repeatedly what I wanted; they simply chose do it their way. I then discovered that I was being forced to sell against the design. Good things don't follow when you have to apologize for your product.

Architects should "ride for your brand," that is, they should help you think through what you want to do and then fit their design to your objectives. I'm not recommending that they abdicate giving you advice; obviously, they know more than you do about fitting all parts of a house together. I am recommending that any architect you hire not have a professional or style agenda other than helping you conceptualize and build the best place for your needs. This excludes "making statements within the profession" and "building his vision for you"—using your money. If you want a state-of-the-profession statement, turn a professor or architect loose. If you want a conventional look and feel, find plans in the house-plan books that are close to your objective. Show these plans to the architect and tell him what you like and what changes you think you want. Don't use the plan as a straitjacket; use it as a reference point. If you get the feeling that you are dumbing down his genius, by all means, dumb it down: it's your money, and you will be living in what your money builds.

There are three things you must state clearly when dealing with your architect. (By "clearly," I mean make them look into your eyes like a three year old so that you know they are focused on your words.)

First, be explicit in what you want and don't want. If you want big closets and many of them, don't settle for two broom closets. If you want to maximize usable floor space, don't let them use atriums that take away half of your second floor. If you want a house that's friendly to a 60 year old, don't accept a second floor and bathrooms the size of a laundry chute. Being explicit requires that you develop a basic knowledge and vocabulary of construction materials and designs. Books can give you this. You will also need to go through houses whose looks you like to determine whether you like the inside feel. Get a sense of what materials and floor space cost in your area. Take notes on your reading and observations. Consolidate your research into a **written memo**. Give this Memo #1 to all architects you interview. This will be the first of several written memos you will give to the architect you choose, copies of which you keep in a loose-leaf binder or file. Give them time to read your memo. If an architect talks down to you, get up and leave. If he's arguing you out of your thoughts, consider his arguments carefully. Valid ones are those pertaining to safety, feasibility, cost, practicality, zoning codes, historic-preservation guidelines, future marketability and the like. Others dealing with matters of taste, look, materials and design may be equally valid. Or there may simply be a conflict between what the architect likes to do and what you want.

Second, be clear about style. If you want a traditional look, don't go along with 24-foot-high walls of unwashable windows mounted in stainless steel. Give your architect pictures of houses and details that you like. Show features that suggest the style you want. If you like sharp angles and the "industrial" look that win design awards, don't okay drawings for the country cottage of the Seven Dwarfs. Size—floor space and volume—determine cost, but style decisions involving materials, quality standards and workmanship also drive cost. Stuff that's standard is cheaper than stuff that has to be ordered or custom-made. Materials that go together quickly and as a unit (like a 4x8 sheet of plywood) are cheaper than materials that do the same job but have to be applied board by board or by a skilled worker. Slate roofing is more expensive than rolled roofing; vinyl siding is cheaper than brick; brick is cheaper than natural stone (which takes more time because it has to be shaped and fitted); imported kitchen tile is more expensive than formica. If your architect finds your taste and preferred style beneath him, find a more compatible architect.

Third, tell the architect the exact total of what you want to spend, from buying the lot to the last seed of grass. Estimate with him the pre-construction costs—lot purchase (include cost of loan, legal, etc.), excavation and infrastructure (water, sewer, utilities, road-building) work and landscaping. He should have a computer program and books that provide accurate cost estimates for each task. If your non-construction, infrastructure costs come to 25 percent of your total budget, assign construction 65-70 percent of your budget and assume that the unassigned five to ten percent will be spent on things unforeseen.

Once you have determined the dollar figure for construction, say these words: **"I want you to design a completely finished house, including everything, that can be built on my lot for not a dollar more than $____. I understand that any change orders I approve during construction that involve additional materials and/or labor will cost extra."** I would go so far as to put the dollar number into the contract you sign with the architect, as in, "The parties agree that _____, architect, will design and provide other architectural services to _____, client, for the construction of a _____ square-foot-house on the client's lot to cost no more than $_____." If nothing else, a proposed sentence of this sort will focus the architect's attention on one of your objectives and remind him that you are serious about it. The process of construction tends in every aspect to go over budget. Your architect is both a cost cop and your proxy profligate. It's always more fun to upgrade materials or to design in more luxury than you can afford. If you have a finite number of dollars to spend, make sure that your architect designs below that figure, maybe by five percent. That gives you dollars to spend on upgrades and amenities. When your project goes over budget, you will be the one responsible for paying the difference.

Architects are skilled in imagining in three dimensions. Most of their clients don't have that ability. If you're like me, you will look at blueprints and see component views but not the true scale of the structure or how the components create interior space. Your architect should have a computer program that projects two-dimensional drawings in three dimensions. These **CADD (computer-aided architectural design) programs** allow you to "be" inside as well as see the finished design built to the blueprints. If your architect is not CADD-capable, have him arrange with a colleague a CADD display. You wouldn't buy a $30,000 car, or even a $5,000 car, without getting inside and seeing how it feels. Don't build a house without doing the same. I once used two prominent architects who insisted on drawing by hand and not using CADD technology. I liked the old paper-and-pencil approach until I discovered I was locked into building a house that created great volumes of vertical space at the expense of usable floor space. Had the design been put into a CADD, I might have been able to stop their visionary inefficiency before building it.

If you have a lot of money, patience and are building a "statement" second home, get an architect you like, review his work to make sure you're on the same beam (or planet) and be patient about choosing a contractor. You'll need one who is willing to put up with a demanding owner and his architect. If, on the other hand, you are comfortable with one of the hundreds of stock plans for second homes that are available, first pick a contractor who can build that house. Then, if necessary, bring in an architect for revisions. Many contractors are experienced enough to make their own drawings or even build a room or two without them. An off-the-shelf plan is a cheaper and safer way to build a second home, but a statement always has the last word, good or bad.

OWNER-BUILT SECOND HOME

Building a second home on your own demands that you become your own **general contractor, plus carpenter, materials gofer and anything else that you don't hire on a subcontract**. Among other things, you will arrange for everything—land purchase, site infrastructure, permits, house design, materials, finding/negotiating/supervising subs, scheduling work in proper sequence, inspections and compliance with local ordinance and code, securing the financing and paying the bills. Banging nails is the fun part of this job.

You will save the mark up and profit you would pay to a general contractor, but you will be spending your own time in his place. Every component of your project will take you longer to do than a general contractor unless you are almost a pro yourself. There are, of course, intangible satisfactions of doing a house yourself. Like writing, I've found it more fun to have built than to be building.

As your own general contractor, you will be responsible for buying materials and getting them to your site. Building supply houses will take your design or your list of materials and provide you with a time-limited quote, a take-off price. Some suppliers give owner-builders a **contractor's price**, and some don't. Some suppliers will give a contractor's price to an owner-builder routinely; others give the discount only if asked. You lose nothing by asking. You don't need a contractor's license when owner-building in the states with which I'm familiar.

When comparing take-off prices from suppliers, make sure that the suppliers are quoting prices for the items that you speced. They routinely substitute what they have or can easily get for anything in your materials list that they don't have and can't get easily. The more exotic the item you spec, the more likely it is that suppliers will throw in an off-the-shelf substitute. Suppliers in my experience do not work hard to get owner-builders what they want. Windows, doors, fixtures, hardware, cabinets, garage doors and roofing are items that are often substituted, varying by brand, quality and price. Substitutes may be as good as what you speced, but often are not. Lumber, for example, comes in different grades, which affect its strength and price. An architect or general contractor can give you some help in determining whether one brand or grade is equal to or better than another. It is often difficult to know whether a "utility-grade" 2x4 stud from Supplier A is the same as the "construction-grade" 2x4 from Supplier B and the "standard" from Supplier C. Your comparisons of price should take quality into consideration, which can only be determined by going to each supplier and examining the materials they are proposing to sell you. If you are building from an architect's plan, make sure that any substitution of the materials he speced is done with his approval. And remember to compare take-off prices from suppliers on a **delivered basis.** It is often more efficient to interview several suppliers before you work up your materials list; get their product literature; then develop your list based on what you know they have.

You can build the house yourself with whatever wives, children and friends you can conscript into the project's labor force. An **owner-built home** is an exercise in patience, character, skill and optimism. It stresses the builder, spouses and kids. It's hard, often frustrating, work. It requires time, money, knowledge, head skills, hand skills, friends, strength, perseverance and a tolerance for your own mistakes and amazing stupidity. It is a humbling experience; I speak with more first-hand knowledge than is necessary to make that statement. A sense of humor and irony is as useful as a level. Plan on doing some dumb thing (s) more than once, and you won't be disappointed. Errors in construction usually involve tearing something down or out, and doing it over. Foundation mistakes are particularly irksome. The killer owner-builts are the idiosyncratic designs that use unconventional materials and require inordinate amounts of hand work. Many of us can throw up a quick 1,200-square-foot ranch by ourselves; nobody can build the Taj Mahal single-handed, though some still try.

If you want to start thinking about an owner-built house on rural land, you should get in touch with the **Owner Builder Center**, 4777 Sunrise Blvd., Suite A, Fair Oaks, CA, 95628; www.ownerbuildercenter.com; e-mail: questions@ownerbuildercenter.com ; 1-800-233-4838; 916-961-2453. The Center provides classes, construction loans and answers to questions. A very good book is Myron F. Ferguson's, Build It Right! What to Look For in Your New Home, which can be ordered from the Home User Press, 1939 Woodhaven St., N.W., Salem, OR, 97304; www.userfriendlyhome.com; 1-800-530-5105; The Home User Press also sells a New Home Check List; the book and the list together are less than $25. Architect Dennis Wedlick designed the "Dream House" in 1995 for Life magazine. It is a flexible, 2,300-square-foot floor plan with ganged windows, lots of light and a dramatic roofline. You can view the model and floor plans at www.lifemag.com/Life/dreamhouse/wdlick/wedlick.html.

Lots of books have been written for non-professionals about how to build one type of house or another. But I've yet to find one that offers a story that fully recounts all of the things that actually go on. House, by Tracy Kidder, is wonderful reporting about the multi-level interactions over time among an architect, contractor and owner. First-person narratives of the same process are lacking. If I were to write a first-hand account of my owner-built efforts, the story would be that I was always hurt most by the things I didn't know I didn't know. This seems to be one of Life's Big Lessons, which responsible parents try to teach to their children—with mostly modest success. I was also done in by things I thought I knew and didn't, along with things that I thought I could fix later and couldn't.

The place to start thinking about owner-building is with a dispassionate assessment of your motivations, character, skills and tendency to become overwhelmed by a seemingly endless, overwhelming task. Saving money is often cited as the primary motivation for being your own builder. If you dollar-value your time at zero, you will "save" money in the sense of substituting your own time for purchased labor. You will save a contractor's mark up on purchased materials and his add-on profit. You will, of course, spend more of your time doing the work than it would take the contractor. The quality of the work may or may not be better. If you dollar-value your time spent building at or above the rate you pay purchased labor, you won't save money. If you're retired or between jobs, then building it yourself will save you money, though you might want to ask whether that's the best use of your time.

"Building your own space" is another common reason advanced for erecting your own house. I've used this one myself. It was very persuasive when I was 30. It has lost oomph over the years just the way I have. The virtue and romance of making your own space can be sustained through some houses, but in others I've seen where owner labor is substituted for expensive machine work, the project turns into a protracted, mind-numbing test of character. Solace can be found, at least abstractly, in knowing that all house-construction tasks are finite—none go on forever, though it can seem that way. As an owner-builder, you have to be prepared to live with the quality of your own work. If you're inclined to cut corners and say "good enough" short of good enough, you will find the space you've built is a permanent, unflattering mirror. Occasionally, building is fun, but most of the time it's hard work. A buyer needs to provide himself with an honest answer as to how much hard labor over how long a time does he want to do. This is apart from the question of how much you are physically able to do. If your main country objective is to relax, nap, read, eat and enjoy the sunsets, you want to avoid the pressure and effort of house-building. No second home is without the need for some owner maintenance, but installing screens is nothing compared to putting in a house footer by wheel-barrowing ten cubic yards of concrete up a hill. How do you really want to spend your time? If you don't want to spend hour upon hour doing mindless, repetitive tasks, you don't want to build a house from scratch. You will be much happier having resisted the romance of being an owner-builder than jumping in and failing badly.

You can also consider building a portion of your second home, depending on your time and skills. If you have no experience, I'd hire out foundation work. Rough framing, however, is something that a novice can do with a hammer, power saw, tape and level as long as he can read a blueprint. I would not advise an inexperienced individual to try finish carpentry, drywalling and certain roofing (metal, slate) with only book knowledge. A skilled person can contract out the rough work and then finish the interior as time permits. Inexperienced owners can do interior and exterior painting, decks and landscaping.

Apart from physical labor, owner-builders take on a highly charged, multi-dimensional emotional load when building a house on their own. Having undertaken several such projects on limited budgets, I offer the observation that they come to dominate your life and are hard on marriages, especially shaky ones. If you are trying to get a project done within budget and within an inflexible time window, you are asking for miseries.

Even if you enjoy all of that's involved in home construction, are good at it, have all the tools, can get extra hands when you need them, don't have competing demands on your time, have plenty of cash and don't mind dealing with pouting kids and grumbling spouses, yes, even when everything lines up, you will still spend a year or more of stressful physical and mental labor building your place by yourself. In places with six-month winters, a house-construction project can spread over two or three years. House construction that occurs only on weekends can stretch beyond that. For every 1,000 square feet of constructed space—from first free-hand drawing to last stroke of paint—I'd assume the need for 100 to 150 owner-built days invested in the project, counting everything, both onsite and off. If you're building single-handed or doing a lot of custom work, the time will lengthen. The same size house can be completed in much less time where an experienced crew is building to standard dimensions, e.g., a Habitat for Humanity home.

You can contain your effort and expense by building something small and simple, from which additions can be constructed. The virtue of something small and simple is that you can get it done reasonably well and within a reasonably short period of time. Owner-built second homes are often constructed in stages, starting with infrastructure and a core building. Bedrooms, studies, second floors, bathrooms, porches and decks are readily added as time and cash permit. It is also wiser to start educating yourself as house builder with a small and simple project. Your first house should not be an owner-conceived, no-blueprint, 13-sided structure that hangs over a cliff on cables of native weeds reinforced with silk from recycled pajamas. You want to start within your range of skill, cash, time and patience. If you build Monticello, you will never finish and end up broke just like Jefferson.

The best part of building a house is the advance dreaming, all of which stops when the backhoe dips out the first bucket of dirt for the footer… and bounces off granite 12 inches below the surface and 400 feet thick. If the dreaming and sketching weren't so much fun, I'm not sure any novice would want to build a house.

CHAPTER 12: COUNTRY HOUSES AND THE SECOND HOME

The easiest way to establish a second home in the country is to buy land with a house. Consider the merits of this approach before developer packages, contractors and owner-building. If you want a house in the country, buying an existing one gets you there faster and usually cheaper than other ways. Beware, however, of ending up with more house than you want and less land than you will ultimately need.

The advantages of buying a standing house are numerous.

First, you are spared the inconvenience and expense of installing the property and site infrastructure from scratch, though you may need to upgrade each. This factor is particularly important where the house is located in a remote area and at a distance from a public road and utilities. A road and an electric line that may have cost a few hundred dollars in 1940 might cost $50,000 today. The seller will not price in to his asking price $50,000 for the road and electric service. In this sense, the seller will discount the value of existing "background infrastructure assets," which benefits the buyer. Even where a seller gets an appraisal of his property as part of his marketing strategy, it's been my experience that appraisers do not value a dirt road, utilities, septic and well at their current replacement costs, which are the costs a buyer would pay to put them in. Appraisers, however, should and will lower their appraised value for any country house that doesn't have these background systems in place.

A buyer should have more confidence in infrastructure that a seller has installed for his own use and benefit than infrastructure quickly dropped in to make the property more marketable. You can *probably* assume that the seller did not short himself by using shoddy materials or by under-designing a system. Honesty, however, requires that I confess to having seen examples that belie this assumption. Most of these involved old systems where, for example, an undersized three-inch diameter pipe led from the house to the septic tank or a water line used too-small 3/4-inch pipe. I also once looked at an owner-built house that was constructed on a wooded slope with a parking area so small that it took me five minutes to turn my truck around. The owner apparently tired of digging rock from his cut into the bank. Left as it was, this parking strip would have been a daily nuisance. The best way to detect unforced errors of this sort is to test every system in the house/land you are scoping. An owner won't deliberately shoot himself in his infrastructure foot, but feet get shot through ignorance or penny-saved-pound-foolish choices.

Second, an existing house allows you to begin using your property immediately without additional investment. While it may not be the house of your dreams, it's probably functional enough to get started. It gives you a base from which to work, a place to store stuff. At the very least, you have a place to come to and get out of the rain once you're there.

Third, an existing house offers room for visitors who are valued for their company and labor. Scoff not.

WRECKS

These advantages apply to a "semi-functional house," and better. You will find houses in the country that don't rise to that standard. These are various versions of what is commonly known as, **A**

Wreck. These structures appeal to men who want to resuscitate the dead after the autopsy has been completed. (I'm exaggerating a little, but not by much.) Prudence suggests that you don't invest your dreams, time and money in wrecks. Still, throw enough money at a building and you can make it work better than when it was new—because you are constructing a new, updated building in most respects. Wrecks can be brought back with a lot of money, time, patience, determination and emotional energy. If the place is more of a wreck than you thought, it can leave you spent and regretting your good deed. Even when a buyer has both time and money, consider the **opportunity cost** of pitching a life into a bottom-to-top reclamation project. What will you forgo by spending your resources on a basket case? What will reclaiming the wreck cost you emotionally and personally? Ground-up projects tend to grind up people.

I have seen wrecks take three and four times as much time and money as the owners originally projected. I have seen them skewer marriages and stub off careers. The "right" basket case can turn into your very own gulag on which you slave and spend without respite. The romance of these projects wears off quickly even when you are not doing the actual work yourself. THE HOUSE turns into an endurance contest that tests your cash and character, one nail at a time. New houses and additions can be built fairly quickly. But extensive reclamation of old houses is always a long, surprise-filled trip into construction psychedelia where nothing much is square, plumb, level or consistently dimensioned.

Most buyers, even the incurable romantics with advanced degrees who look for land only on sunny Sunday afternoons, can recognize a real wreck when they see one. Recognition requires sharpening your analytical eyeballs and turning down your emotions. Look for signs that indicate more of a problem than the sign itself—a leak in a ceiling, green stuff growing on inside walls, spongy floor boards, funny smells, structural woodwork that crumbles at your touch, a bouquet of extension cords and multiple receptacles sprouting from a wall outlet, water stains around windows, amphibians mating in the basement wetlands, blackened structural beams, ceilings and doorways that are too short for you and a setting whose unfixable flaws you hate. When you are shown this fixer-downer, do not be swayed by a front-porch swing and a couple of hanging plants. You do not want to be fixed up with this one.

Home inspectors say that water in the wrong place is the most common threat to the integrity of a house. (See Judy Rose, Knight Ridder Newspapers, "Water, water everywhere: Inspectors list moisture as No. 1 house threat," Richmond Times-Dispatch, January 4, 2004.) This means water-saturated ground around a foundation because of improper grading; plugged gutters and overflowing downspouts; water penetrating roofs and exteriors through deteriorated flashing and caulking; and a faulty chimney cap. Old wiring and badly installed wiring are the second most common threat. Deteriorating heating systems with poor exhausts, old pipes, gas leaks around old appliances and inadequate ventilation in highly insulated homes are also on their list. In homes built before 1950, you're likely to find galvanized plumbing and sand-cast metal waste lines, both of which will be wearing out. Homes from the 50s have energy-efficiency issues, particularly steel-casement and single-pane windows. Homes from the 60s may still have aluminum wiring (banned in 1973), which can arc behind walls and cause a fire. (You can install an AFCI—arcing fault circuit interrupter—to detect arcing and shut down the system.) Homes from the 70s and 80s used cheaper lumber products and cheap windows; they were insulated but may not have been adequately ventilated. Composite sidings made of pressed wood were used in the 1990s and may now be rotting, particularly in damp climates. (Fiber-cement sidings are durable.) In my opinion, defects such as these that cannot be readily observed should be considered "latent" and, accordingly, disclosed to buyers. When you buy a property "as is," the seller is still expected to disclose the presence of such defects; the "as is" only gets him out of paying for their repair.

Any time a real-estate agent takes you to an advertised "fixer-upper" or "handyman special," you are being put on notice. Real-estate brokers don't advertise "Basket Case: only really big fools should buy this." Properties that are the true bargains—those that need cheap cosmetics and new doors on their kitchen cabinets—are often snapped up by agents themselves for resale. Further, country wrecks are likely to be worse than the city/suburban wrecks with which you may be familiar. The country version will, if nothing else, have less usable infrastructure. Its building quality can also be lower. Cheap materials might have been used, and the house may have been built by not-so-skilled owner-builders. One marker of material quality is windows. If they look and feel flimsy, if they don't work very well, you may reasonably assume the builder used low-end materials throughout. It's also the case that building codes, which set construction standards, came to rural counties late. This explains why the living-room floor of our 1916 farmhouse bounced like a trampoline when I jumped on it during my first visit. Soon after purchase, I slithered into a 16"-high crawl space littered with cat poop to prop up its joists, which were spaced on two-foot centers and had no bridging between them.

If your goal is to putter happily on the occasional sun-dappled weekend, avoid buying a wreck. Happy puttering is the last thing you will be doing. Wrecks require system replacement not puttering, upgrades and remodeling. It's the difference between an afternoon excursion on a friend's sailboat and doing a single-handed circumnavigation. Heartbreak wrecks are only for those who love doing—or paying for—this type of soup-to-nuts rebuilding—and maybe not even for them.

In my area, I've found two types of wrecks. The first and far more common is old farmhouses that sheltered cash-poor farmers poorly. They weren't much when they were new and have not improved with age. They are almost always found on marginal farmland. The two run together, of course, sorry ground, cheap housing. Tenant dwellings often fall in this category, though some tenancies are exceptionally well-built.

The second type of wreck is the idiosyncratic, owner-built house from the 60s and 70s when some of my generation "went back to the land," building south-facing structures that were abandoned after the divorce. I know of three of these, one of which I spent a year building, losing a marriage and a best friend in the process. These efforts have both the virtues and liabilities of being built by well-intentioned nincompoops. Even the well-built failures have, shall I say, off vibes, arising from both their failure to work out and the broader alienation that underpinned them. Most houses are built with hope and optimism, and all wrecks are sad. But the hippie wrecks seem the most forlorn.

A step above the wreck is the **marginal project**, a house that's been long neglected and which requires some structural rehabilitation and/or a lot of modernizing. You can start learning about how to evaluate these houses by reading Rex Cauldwell's, Inspecting a House, from the Taunton Press. The first level of decision is whether the place fits more comfortably in the wreck category or qualifies as a marginal project. If you have to totally replace four or more major systems—roof, foundation, exterior, plumbing, heating, window/doors, electrical, kitchen, all bathrooms—call it a wreck. In contrast, repairs like gutters, painting, floor refinishing and remodeling qualify a house as marginal. If you find a place where three major systems need to be fully replaced and everything else needs work, I'd consider it closer to a wreck than a project. To get into this amount of work, the house needs to have a lot of something else going for it.

If you think the place is a possible project, your next decision is whether its rehabilitation is financially, practically and emotionally doable. Use nothing other than gimlet-eyed analysis and the sharpest pencil you have. Do not make this decision with your heart; do not make it on the spur of the moment based on a "gut reaction"; do not make it on your first visit; do not make it on a cheerful day; do not make it while you are holding hands other than your own; do not make it while a real-estate agent is chirping out the charms of the old place ("Look at that native stone chimney!" cries the agent, turning your head with both of his hands. The chimney was built before fire-safe flue liners were available and, you might infer, that it's the cause of the charred remains through which you are stepping.) Do not make this decision without consulting at least one local contractor/carpenter who has been recommended by at least two or three knowledgeable people in the community, such as the county building inspector and the local lawyer you plan to use. A contractor/carpenter can give you a quick ballpark estimate of the time and cost required to do what needs to be done and the other things you want. Make sure to tell your contractor where you want to do specific activities. For instance, if you plan to put a four-person spa on an old farmhouse floor, you will need to reinforce the framing, redo the surface with impermeable materials, install an appropriate electrical receptacle, vent the moisture and figure out how to drain the thing without messing up your septic system.

You should also consider hiring a **consulting house inspector**. For a fee of several hundred dollars, an inspector will examine a house and provide you with a *written report of what he can see during the visit*. Inspectors are listed under "Home Inspection Service" in my Yellow Pages, or try the website of the American Society of Home Inspectors at www.ashi.com; National Association of Home Inspectors (www.nahi.org); and The National Association of Certified Home Inspectors (www.nachi.org). You may have to bring in an inspector from an adjoining county or work with a local contractor when your target property is located in a low-population area.

A house inspection is not a one-stop, fail-safe guarantee of anything. The inspector and his inspection report guarantees the buyer nothing. The inspector simply reports his observations and the results of whatever minor inspection-related tests he might perform, such as looking up a chimney flue with a mirror to check for creosote blockage. If something is concealed, the inspector may not pick it up. For instance, fire damage to floor joists and wall studs could be covered by new drywall and fresh paint. If the floor parts company with the wall two days after you move in, you can't sue. Inspectors may specifically exclude from their reports investigations for termites, indoor air quality, mold, water quality and radon gas among others. These may require specialists. You can get a mold inspection from a member of the National Association of Mold Professionals, www.moldpro.org. A professional inspection does not obviate the need for you to insert into your purchase-offer contract clear language requiring the seller to disclose all material defects in the house and property.

An inspector will report what he finds. Your question, however, is: What needs to be done to get this house to where I want it? This means you want two types of analysis: the inspector-type inventory of current conditions that will flag obvious things needing repair or replacement, and, second, a contractor/carpenter's estimate of the feasibility, time and cost of doing that work plus the work involved in whatever changes and upgrades you also want done. The first cost estimate will cover work that should probably be done before you move in, or soon thereafter. The second estimate is money that you can spend immediately, in the future or not at all. Both estimates can be helpful in negotiating price with the seller. A familiar example comes to mind. Old country houses often have old bathrooms, patched in decades earlier and never modernized. The fixtures still work, but even the seller will concede that they are ready for replacement. Move the cost of redoing the bathroom from your list of future upgrades to your list of immediately needed repairs—if only for the purpose of negotiations.

Pay for the contractor/carpenter to put together an itemized plan of work tasks with cost estimates for each one. To be safe, add another 25 to 50 percent to these preliminary estimates to take into account both what can't be anticipated and changes that you will undoubtedly want to make when you become

192

aware of their availability.

If the house was well built but has been neglected and lacks modernity, it can be a project worth taking on **at the right purchase price**. You will determine the right price in light of the list of things that need to be done and their cost. If, on the other hand, the place was ill-conceived and badly put together when it was put up and has been subsequently "remuddled," then it becomes more of a wreck to avoid and less of a project to take on.

I can think of several project houses whose marginality I weighed with great seriousness. One was a two-story brick farmhouse from the 1760s that had been defaced with a new cathedral-style dining room (which had collapsed) about ten years earlier and further deformed by a second-floor apartment with outside stairs (also collapsed). Nothing could be salvaged from this mess save the original roof and walls. Somebody—me, in this case—would have to spend six months just pulling stuff down, ripping stuff out and hauling stuff away. After the collapsed "additions" had been subtracted, the advertised floor area would be cut by about half, leaving only the original two-story shell. The house came with a few acres, a very nice spot in an upscale farm suburb of a Shenandoah Valley town.

I figured it would take 18 months of my labor to bring this house back to family-habitable condition. I would be spending our savings during that time and not generating income. My wife, young daughter and I would have had to rent while I worked on the house or try camping inside the demolition and rebuilding. Neither choice was good. Having done some of this before, I knew this project would dominate my life across the board. The money—at least $75,000-$100,000 for demolition and rehab on top of the $80,000 purchase price—would yield a house with about 1,600 usable square feet. In that time and place, that amount of money could buy a whole lot more house than that, with no work at all. It took a few visits and some sober thinking, but it wasn't hard to affirm my first-impression conclusion that this old house was beyond my emotional and financial means.

A few years later, I evaluated another old farmhouse as part of a small land flip that I thought might work. This home sat in the middle of about 200 acres on the side of a mountain, at the end of a rocky, rutted farm road. It was frame construction with a familiar two-story, four-over-four floorplan. The virtue of the land and the farmhouse was its beautiful, long mountain views in an area known for pretty views. After drinking in the view, I nibbled around the wreck. I noted that water had been supplied by a now non-working hand pump bolted next to the sink and the pump was hooked to a collapsing cistern; the one non-functioning bathroom was located in an add-on shed next to the non-functioning kitchen; wiring dated from the 1930s; two unlined stone chimneys provided heat; a new roof was needed; the foundation had come apart at its seams; everything needed to be painted, repaired or replaced. It appeared that routine house maintenance had stopped about 50 years before—and those were only first impressions. Beyond that, all of the basics were wrong: the floorplan was impossible to reconfigure; ceilings were too low for Baby Boomers and their protein-pumped offspring; the entire stone foundation would have to be relaid (assuming someone could be found to do such work); the roof work would probably involve replacing roofboards and rafters. Like a ball of string, tug on any loose end and the whole thing would come undone. Most of the outbuildings were just a hair on either side of ramshackle, and several were dead center. Almost every section of fence that ran with this property needed replacement, not repair. I valued the house and the outbuildings at zero; none were in acceptable shape, and most needed to be demolished. Still, because I am sometimes given to being an idiot, I asked a carpenter friend to spend an hour with me looking it over. His dispassionate verdict was the same as mine: great spot, but don't try to bring the house back to what it never was.

I offered the seller $125,000 instead of the $200,000 they were asking because the "improvements" had so little worth, almost all of the site infrastructure had to be put in and the fencing alone was likely to be $10,000. I valued the house at zero, and I could not assume that anyone I might sell it to would value it more than I had. My plan was to divide the land into four or five parcels for immediate resale, so I offered what I thought the land alone was worth as an entirety. The owner, who knew the shape of his things better than I did, wanted $150,000. The $25,000 difference was the money I was budgeting for closing costs, carrying charges on the purchase, surveying, marketing, a little road work and one thing or another. I didn't want to pay the asking price, so I told the seller that I was not his best money. We both thought that the best buyer was someone who wanted to keep the 200 acres together and had a lot of discretionary cash for monkeying with the house. In effect, I was saying look for a buyer who hadn't read this book. Eventually, they found him, at full price no less. After the sale, I ran into the new owner and his wife; they were bubbly with the house project in front of them. I mentioned that I had looked at it and thought it would take a lot of work. "No," he said, "just some paint and a few things like that." Never correct a new owner who's made an obvious mistake that's not yet obvious to him: he'll blame you for what comes next. I wished him good luck. They painted and piddled and "did like that" for a year or so, then lost interest.

These stories are about two different "old" farmhouses, the first an 18th-Century place that probably had historic—but not certified historic—significance; the other a typical wood structure built in the late 19th Century. The first had been constructed stoutly and honestly, but had been degraded by cheap and inappropriate remodeling. It could have been restored, but was not worth the effort to me. The other could have been restored too with heroic effort. The degree of effort in both cases qualified them as wrecks in terms of my emotional and financial resources.

Wood-frame farmhouses built between 1865 and 1930 are fairly common throughout the countryside. They range from simple five- or six-room designs bordering on humble to big, rambly two-and three-story affairs. They usually have had at least one bathroom added. Their simple materials and architecture allow you to do a lot with them as long as their basic structure is sound. Wood framing allows motivated, semi-skilled Harry and Harriet Homeowners to do at least some of the work themselves. Wiring and plumbing must be done by—or at the very least checked by—professionals. Finish carpentry such as bookcases, molding and stairs are worth contracting out if you're not skilled. (Skilled is a lot more than being handy.)

One job that you should be careful in taking on is stripping old paint. The paint may contain lead, and the stripper chemicals can be harmful. If you need to strip more than one room or do a room that you suspect has lead paint, buy a professional quality full-face, filtered-air, breathing apparatus to protect from both fumes and dust. (Good-quality, industrial respirators are the opposite of a disposable paper dust mask. They are not cheap, but neither is being sick. The apparatus I've used for dust and chemical fumes is made by Racal Health & Safety [a division of 3M], 7305 Executive Way, Frederick, MD., 21701; 1-800-682-9500; www.3M.com/occsafety; e-mail: occsafety@mmm.com; 1-800-896-4223).

You should also be careful with older outside decks, stairs and playground equipment made from lumber treated with chromated copper arsenate (CCA). A phase out began in early 2002, which arose from lawsuits against retailers and manufacturers about health risks in situations where bare skin or food came in contact with this wood. Decks and other structures built before 2003 with treated lumber used the now-banned CCA product. Don't walk barefoot on this material, and don't put a sandwich on a CCA railing. The new treatment uses alkaline copper quaternary (ACQ) or copper boron azole (CBA), which make wood resistant to rot and termites. These materials too require care—dust masks and gloves when handling; hand washing when done; don't use them for mulch, burn them or put them where animals might chew them. They also require special new hardware that resists corrosion. Do not use aluminum flashing or old galvanized hardware with ACQ. If the new treated lumber is used with old hardware a new deck will collapse. The new lumber is more expensive than the CCA, and plastic/vinyl substitutes are twice the cost of treated wood. One country alternative might be locally available resistant woods, such as yellow locust or cedar, that a local mill can saw into lumber. Both old and new treated lumber are best sealed with solid stains; the other stains don't do much. Don't clean the old lumber with a deck wash or sand before sealing. (See www.ewg.org; Eric Pianin, "Use of Arsenic in Wood Products to End," Washington Post, February 13, 2002; Matthew Robb, "Deck Lumber, Hardware Present Risks," www.washingtonpost.com, May 1, 2004; Gene Austin, "Do-It-Yourself," Knight Ridder, Washington Post, May 15, 2004.)

KEEPERS

A big step above the marginal project is the **keeper**. This is the country house that can be restored and modernized without making it into an architectural clown, and at a sensible cost in terms of your budget and the final result. Older houses can be great buys when their structure is sound and they can be modernized without doing much structural work. You can update plumbing and electrical systems without changing the house's structure. You can usually add a fireplace onto an exterior wall without much change in existing structure, but you cannot add the same fireplace in the middle of the house without doing structural work at every level, from ground through roof. Older houses are sturdier than contemporary structures in some ways and flimsier in others. Finish flooring, for example, in old frame houses was usually at least 3/4-inch thick. (Flooring gets thinner with each sanding/refinishing cycle.) Today, new hardwood flooring may be as thin as $5/16^{th}$. New tongue-and-groove thickness ranges between 1/2-inch and $25/32^{nds}$. Thicker flooring is better than thinner. Old wall studs were often fully dimensioned 2x4s whereas modern studs are nominally 2x4s but are actually only 1 1/2 x 3 1/2. On the other hand, the fully dimensioned, oak floor joists in my WWI-era farmhouse are spaced too far apart (24 inches) and their clear spans are too long. (When looking at the seller's farmhouse, jump up and down in each room to see whether you spring like Tigger. Pay no attention to nasty looks; you are being careful, not rude. You generally have to do a lot of work to beef up floors and ceilings.) Old houses tend to be under-insulated and energy inefficient (leaky, single-pane windows; uncaulked doors, windows and other openings). Electrical and plumbing systems are undersized for modern needs. Kitchens may be large, but poorly laid out. (Ours has seven doors and about one-third the counter space we need.) Old farmhouse kitchens did not plan for refrigerators, freezers and dishwashers. Bathrooms tend to be small.

HOUSE INSPECTION CHECK LIST

To find a keeper, *take a slow walk* through the seller's house. Go by yourself or with a local contractor/carpenter. Don't do this with a real-estate agent or the seller; agents, in particular, like quick trips through old houses. Use a table like the following to organize your first look and a follow-up inspection.

TABLE 12-1: House Inspection: What to Look for

	System	Type	Condition	Comments

A. Site Infrastructure

1. Access
2. Driveway
3. Turnaround/parking
4. Drainage
5. Landscaping
6. View
7. Compass orientation
8. Shade, windiness
9. Privacy
10. Proximity of mailbox
11. School pick up—distance to house
12. Outbuildings
    a. Type
        1. Workshop
        2. Spring house
        3. Barn (s)
        4. Chicken/pig/wood
        5. Horse facilities
        6. Misc. storage
        7. Detached garage; single/double door
            a. Remote-control
    b. Virtues to look for
        1. Concrete floor
        2. Water outlet in barn/shop
        3. 220-volt outlets
        4. Shop
            a. Heat
            b. Lighting
            c. Ventilation
            d. Counters/shelves
13. Closest fire hydrant
14. Yards, front and back
    a. Condition
    b. Features
    c. Mowability
15. Trees around the house
    a. Shade providers
    b. Too close/gutter clogs
    c. Need to be trimmed

     d. Are the planted species of the type
       that break foundations and invade
       water/sewerage lines, e.g., willow, maples
16. Safety/ Security
     a. Lighting for safe night access
     b. Are pathways good for foot traffic?
     c. Condition of steps
17. Convenience
     a. Can big furniture be driven close to the house
     b. Is the most frequently used entrance other than
       the front door. (Old houses are often entered
       through the kitchen.)
18. Amenities—pool, garden, orchard

B. House Structure—exterior

1. Foundation
     a. Look for big cracks
     b. Look for missing mortar
    in brick and stone work
     c. Sagging corners/shifting
     d. Look for termite tunnels
     e. Look for rot in log
       sills and wood plates
     f. Ventilation
2. Roof
     a. Type and condition
3. Gutters/downspouts
4. Exterior wall materials
     a. Types and condition
5. Exterior Doors
     a. Quality/fit
     b. Screens
6. Windows
     a. Cracks/glazing
     b. Screens
     c. Insulation (double/triple glazing)
       or storm windows
     d. Caulk, where frame of
       window meets house siding
7. Steps or ground-level access
8. Chimney/flashing
9. Entrance weather protection
     a. Porches
       1. Front
       2. Back
     b. If no porch, is there some overhead covering?

       c. Does entrance face away from
          prevailing weather
            1. Front/back
   10. Deck
   11. Electrical outlets
   12. Water spigots/freeze protection
   13. Exterior access to basement/crawlspace
   14. Lighting—entrances
   15. Examine surfaces that face prevailing weather
       a. Which, if any, need repair or painting

C. Structure—interior
   1. Basement/crawlspace
       a. Height/access
       b. Finished/unfinished
       c. Evidence of termites or wood rot
       d. Wetness or evidence of past wetness
       e. Mold
       f. Insulation
   2 . Kitchen
       a. Size/layout
       b. Island
       c. Space for freezer (upright or chest)
       d. Dining area
       e. At least ten linear feet of counter top
       f. Wall cabinets—at least 12 feet for
          1,400 sf house
       g. Base cabinets—at least nine feet
          for 1,400 sf house
       h. Built-in dishwasher/portable
       i. Icemaker waterline hookup
       j. Disposer
       k. GFI outlets*
       l. Lighting
       m. Exhaust fan
       n. Flooring
   3. Utility room/area
       a. Washer
       b. Dryer
       c. Sink
       d. Cabinet/shelves
       e. Storage for vacuum
          cleaner/broom/supplies
       f. Space to work/iron
   4. Living area
       a. Windows
          1. Do they work/seal?

      2. Sufficient light/ventilation
    b. Compatibility with your furniture
    c. Usable wall space
    d. Bookcases
    e. Floor material
    f. Size—area/height
5. Dining Room
    a. Size—area/height
6. Front Entrance
    a. Adequate closet for outdoor wear
7. Mud room/back entrance
    a. Space for winterwear/boots
8. Bedrooms
    a. Number
    b. Area/height
    c. Groundfloor/upper floors
    d. Dedicated bathrooms/shared bath
    e. Closets
9. Special areas
    a. Fitness
    b. Home office
        1. Computer/phone/fax capability
        2. Outlets/jacks
            a. Number; separate computer circuit
        3. Internet capability
10. Closets
    a. Per bedroom/walk-in/size
    b. Linen closet—available?
    c. Junk closet—available?
11. Attic
    a. Usable area (48"+ height)
    b. Access—permanent/pulldown/ease
    c. Ventilation/windows
    d. Finished/unfinished
12. Bathrooms
    a. Number and location
    b. Features
    c. Fixtures—vanity/cabinet
    d. GFI

D. Mechanical Systems
1. Electrical
    a. 200-amp breaker panel minimum
        1. Are heavy electricity users—e.g., baseboard heaters, dryer, spa, range, hot water heater—each on its own dedicated circuit?
    b. Signs of aluminum wiring? Aluminum is cheaper than copper and was used in the early 1960s, but has been banned for many years.

Look in a switch or receptacle. Flickering lights and TV static are clues. Should be replaced. In very old houses, look for fabric-wrapped wiring and even wires run on insulated knobs. The fabric-insulation wire should be replaced eventually; the knob system immediately.

    c. Receptacles—modern wiring uses three-hole design; old two-holers require adapters and are less safe
      Old houses tend to be "under-receptacled"

    d. Computer areas with dedicated circuit.
      Need phone jack in computer area.
      Whole-house surge protection can be added.

    e. Smoke alarms—wired or battery. Wired is better

    f. How often does power go out? Is there a need for emergency generator?

    g. Fixtures—how ghastly are they? Light fixtures can be very expensive.

    h. Timers and thermostats reduce electricity usage

    i. Ground-Fault Interrupters (GFIs) protect individuals from electrical shock. Should be in wet areas—baths, kitchen.

2. Phone—number of jacks/placement
    a. Internet provider/cost/reliability

3. TV—cable/dish/local reception
    a. Location of hookups inside

4. Heating/Ventilation/AC
    a. Source of heat
    b. Age/type/condition of furnace
    c. AC/windows
    d. Fireplace/woodstove
    e. Are space heaters used?
    d. Radiator/forced air/
      electric baseboard
    e. Insulation
      1. Location—groundfloor/wall/roof
      2. Type/estimated R value
    f. Location of heat source
      1. Accessibility
      2. Odors/leaks
    g. Estimated monthly cost
    h. Miscellaneous
      1. Heat pump
      2. Whole-house humidifier
      3. Air purifier
      4. Whole-house ventilation fan
      5. Heat recovery ventilator**
      6. Thermostats—number/placement
      7. Sited for passive solar benefit
    i. Fire-extinguishers in place?

          j. Energy efficiency of heating/cooling systems

    5. Plumbing

          a. Bathrooms—number/features/GFIs

          b. Pressure when all faucets
             open/toilet flushing

          c. Hot water heater—energy/capacity

          d. Where does wastewater go?

          e. Source of water supply

          f. Adequate stack venting—do you smell
             sewage in bathrooms?

          g. Evidence of toilet backup

          h. Bathing

             1. Are shower stalls big enough?

             2. Grab bars

             3. Ventilation to outside—mechanical

    6. Security and Safety

          a. What level do you think you will need?

          b. Lights, locks and alarms

          c. Safety

             1. Stairs—treads, railings, steepness, construction, width

             2. Bathrooms—footing, heating, electrical

             3. Fire protection—chimney inspection;
                nearest fire department

E. Environmental concerns in and around house

    1. Asbestos—pipe/furnace insulation, disintegrating
       floor tile, exterior siding/shingles; popcorn-type ceiling tiles

    2. Lead pipe in water supply lines; lead poisoning danger

    3. Urea formaldehyde foam insulation in walls

    4. Lead paint inside

    5. Radon gas in air; radon in water

    6. Carbon monoxide—unvented fuel-burning
       appliances; very tight houses

    7. Mold in basement or other areas—look for sump pump,
       damp smell, evidence of seepage in block work,
       basement should have a drain

    8. Infestations—ants, bugs, traps, bait, smell,
       corpses, little piles of fine sawdust, rotted wood,
       tunnels on outside walls, etc.

F. Overall impression

    1. Total square footage

    2. Room size

    3. Obvious repairs needed

          a. Leaks

          b. Breaks

          c. Peeling paint

      d. Roof

      e. Treatment for infestations

      f. Other

   4. Hard/expensive to retrofit missing pieces

      a. Masonry fireplace (woodstove is easy)

      b. Integrated garage (depends)

      c. Front entrance closet

      d. Whole-house AC/forced air heating

      e. Relocate stairs to second story

   5. Common can-do remodels

      a. Finish attic/basement

      b. Upgrade/add bathroom

      c. Convert bedroom to other function

      d. Add garage, particularly detached

      e. Modernize kitchen

      f. Replace windows

   6. Things that you want to replace/do

     before moving in

      a. Kitchen remodel—$15,000 and up, and up

      b. Add bathroom—$5,000 and up

      c. Finish attic—$7,500 and up

      d. Rewire whole house—$5,000

      e. Replumb whole house—$7,500 and up

      f. New furnace—$5,000 and up

      g. Add deck—$2,500 and up

   7. Maintenance level—general impression

      a. Compulsively neat and kept up

      b. Pretty good

      c. OK

      d. Not so good

      e. Everything's bad

      f. Acceptable—about the level you do at home

   8. List anything that looks like

      a. Added on—e.g., room

      b. Recently repaired, upgraded, replaced or painted

         Determine whether this was done for

         marketing or functional improvement

*GFI, Ground Fault Interruptor, is a type of electrical receptacle that is typically installed in "wet" areas to reduce the chance of shock. It breaks the circuit when there is a short.

**Heat Recovery Ventilator is a device that removes dust and fumes from inside air while recovering most of its heat for reuse.

    After working up this table, I found an even more comprehensive inspection check list in Robert Irwin, Home Buyer's Checklist (New York: McGraw-Hill, 2001). In his review, Robert J. Bruss of Tribune Media Services describes Irwin's book as "...the ultra-complete list of questions buyers should answer before purchasing a house." (<u>Richmond Times-Dispatch</u>, December 16, 2001, J3.)

Notice that almost everything on my list is substantive and structural. Stuff that is of little concern to a buyer are the cosmetics, which sellers routinely touch up to help market the property. If substance and structure are sound, don't worry about exterior details and the pile of junk farm equipment next to the barn. Where the house is structurally sound and can be readily adapted to your purposes, you, in fact, want to find a few easy-to-fix, obvious blemishes to use for leverage on price negotiations.

You can use this table format for screening properties, but its level of detail better fits a second-tour, take-your-time scoping. These types of questions at a general level, of course, help you to screen in a property that deserves a second, in-depth look. This format forces a buyer to look systematically and analytically at a house in all dimensions, both functional and aesthetic. Even more important, it forces you to *look slowly and deeply at the important stuff.* How many of us have bought a house based on a quickie visit or two? Have you noticed a seller or his agent marching steadily through the house, maintaining eye contact with you as much as possible. Why do you think that is?

It is important for you to **focus on individual house components**. Your brain is sabotaging this effort by running movies of the house and land as a whole and then packaging them with emotional previews of coming attractions. A disaggregating, analytical format forces you to identify what can be observed and then organize that information in a way that gives you useful evaluations. It flags items where a professional eye might be needed. A house inspector, specialist or contractor can fill in your blanks. Focusing on components is even more difficult when a real-estate agent is playing "Look at that vintage overhead light bulb!" just as you notice a hole in the floor. You don't need to be an expert on construction or a professional inspector to understand house components. But you will need to do reading in proportion to your existing knowledge. If you don't know some of the terms I've used in TABLE 12-1, buy a house construction book, such as the one I've recommended (Feirer, *et al*, <u>Carpentry</u>, latest edition, or Ching and Adams, <u>Building Construction Illustrated</u>, Third Edition). Terms are explained simply and illustrations show what makes up a component system and how these systems fit together. Understanding house basics is within everyone's ability. If you've lived in a house of your own, you will have a feel for how structures are built and what goes wrong.

Use the table format as an excuse to be microscopic. You are not observing the seller's house as you would admire a passing parade. You are there to use your wits. You need to be looking in a question-asking, data-gathering mode. This is business, not personal. Carry a hard-backed pad of paper for writing. Make drawings. Write out your specific questions so that you don't forget them. Note things that stick out, both good and bad. One trick that you can use with this format is to write your answers with a two-color (red/black) pen that can be switched back and forth. Use red for negatives and question marks; black for positives. Major stuff can be written in CAPS; minor stuff in lower-case letters. At the end of a tour, if you see a lot of capitalized words in red ink, you will know that you don't know a lot and/or a lot of costly work needs to be done. Take a camera with at least two rolls of 24 color exposures or the equivalent. At the house site, take a picture looking out from the structure North, East, South and West. Take at least one picture of every outbuilding, inside every room of the house, kitchen appliances, bathroom fixtures, furnace, problems and things you like. If you are thinking about upgrading or reworking some part of the seller's house, you can use one of the remodeling estimator guides, like the latest edition of Means, <u>Repair and Remodeling Cost Data,</u> to factor these expenditures into any purchase offer.

In most cases, the seller or his agent will accompany you through the house the first time you see it. That's fine. You're just trying to screen properties in or out on this walk-through. If you screen the property in as a possible candidate, then you need to schedule a second tour, which is when you unlimber your note pad and inventory table. Your second tour is often complicated by a house being lived in and the need for you to step over headless Barbies in the presence of the seller's family. You want to be cordial and respectful to those in attendance, but your uppermost thought is to visualize this house buck naked, and then use your x-ray vision to see its bones and organs. When you talk to the seller or the agent, concentrate on talking. Don't try to scope the house and schmooze at the same time.

One way of softening the intrusiveness of your inspection is to notify the seller in advance that you want a chance to look closely at the property on a second tour. Tell him that this will take a couple of hours, and you will try to be unobtrusive as you can. But make clear that you will be taking a long, serious look. The seller should be cooperative, since your level of effort shows him that you are not there to kick tires. If you hire a professional house inspector, the seller may want to be present during the inspection. You may not be able to avoid the seller walking around with the inspector, but you should insist that the agent not do the same. New York, in fact, prohibits agents from accompanying house inspectors.

Houses for sale can be thought of as a package of component systems and appliances. The systems are the exterior skin, roof, structure, heat, plumbing (water and waste), ventilation and so forth. Items sometimes thought to be **appliances** can be considered to be part of a system, as is the case with a garbage disposal (part of the plumbing system), electric baseboard heater (heating system) or roof fan (ventilation system). When such items are integrated permanently into a system, they are considered **fixtures**. As such, they always convey with the purchase, because they are thought to be permanently attached. Often, appliances that are not fixtures stand alone as is the case with a range, washer/dryer and refrigerator. Stand-alone appliances are the seller's **personal property**. The seller may or may not include items of personal property with the house he's selling. Some items, if not all, may be negotiable if you want them, such as a wood stove, shop tools, portable dishwasher, movable hot tub, window air conditioner and the like. Items/appliances that are attached to the house or one of its systems by something more than a plug and/or detachable water hoses should convey with the property without elaboration, e.g., a garbage disposal, furnace-attached humidifier, smoke alarms (wired certainly, maybe battery), antenna, water pump and hot-water heater. Misunderstandings can crop up around items like mounted mirrors, blinds, curtain rods, curtains, adjustable screen inserts (but not screens that come with windows), TV dish, outside wood-burning furnace, porch swing and a roadside mail box. When you write a purchase offer, list every item that you expect to convey and might want. You can reduce your offer in step with those things from your list the buyer wants to exclude from the sale.

Each system, each component of each system and each appliance has an effective **life expectancy** during which investing in repair makes sense and after which a new unit is the more cost-effective choice. Most common appliances—dishwashers, clothes dryers, ranges, refrigerators, washing machines—cross the repair/replacement line at about seven years, according to Consumer Reports (Sandra Fleishman, "To Fix or Not to Fix," Los Angeles Times/Washington Post News Service, Richmond Times-Dispatch, February 10, 2002.). Furnaces and central air-conditioning units generally last 20 years or more, and new models are expensive. When valuing the seller's basic house systems and appliances, estimate their age to get a rough sense of when each will need to be replaced. Warranties should show the date of purchase. Appliances that are older than seven or eight years should be valued at zero, because they have crossed the repair/replacement line. If you do have an interest in buying the seller's personal property/appliances, you can fold your estimate of their value to you into your offer for the house, or make a separate offer. There are negotiating advantages and disadvantages to both approaches.

Do not take oral statements as facts or oral promises as legally binding. With real property (land, minerals, houses, etc.) sales, only written statements and written contracts are legally enforceable. (Certain states may have exceptions to this rule, but you will do best to act as if no exceptions exist.) You need to verify "facts" that the seller relates. If you're told the farmhouse has a septic system, ask to be shown where the tank and the drainfield are. You should find a cement lid over the tank itself, or at least a capped pipe where a clean-out hose can be inserted for emptying solids. If you are told that the county has approved the septic system for four bedrooms, you can make your purchase offer contingent on the seller providing a copy of the permit. Or, you can go to the health department in the county seat and ask to see the permit. If you are told the washing machine works just fine, run it through a cycle to see for yourself, preferably loaded with dirty jeans. All oral statements of facts must be confirmed, or put in the form of a written seller promise. A contingency that makes purchase dependent on the "house being in good repair with all systems and included personal property to be conveyed in good working order two days before closing" protects your interests. When your pre-closing walk-through turns up a problem, this contingency allows you to void your offer without penalty. This late in the game, however, it's more likely you'll work something out with the seller.

Sellers have developed many tactics for improving the cosmetics of a house. They want to draw your attention toward what looks pretty and away from what they don't want you to see. Since most buyers have been, or will be, sellers, you should become familiar with **seller house-selling tactics.** The basic strategy that sellers use is making the property *look* fresh, clean, flawless and ready to go. Removing trash, mowing grass, painting the front door, shampooing the carpet, tacking up a drooping gutter—are the type of low-cost, pre-sale investments that are intended to draw the buyer's eye away from those features of the house that cannot be readily seen. Sellers are counseled to focus their pre-sale spruce-up dollars on what's most visible. (See Steve Berges, 101 Cost-Effective Ways to Increase the Value of Your Home [Chicago, Ill.: Dearborn Trade Publishing, 2004]).

Sellers go beyond tying pretty ribbons around house exteriors. Other tricks include using wall mirrors to make small rooms appear larger; increasing wattage in certain light bulbs to "brighten" a room; using softer lights in the spot where the seller steers the buyer to negotiate; having a fire going in the fireplace to provide a "homey" feel; using odor-killing additives in humidifers to mask mildew, lingering tobacco smoke and other unpleasantness; decluttering closets so that they look one-third empty, hence big; taking one piece of furniture out of each room for the same optical effect; removing family pictures so that the buyer can imagine his family in the space; adding live plants to hide flaws and provide atmosphere; cleaning off kitchen counters to make the amount of counter space appear bigger; buying new slip covers to make the room look brighter; discarding shabby drapes; washing windows if they reveal a view, otherwise keeping them covered; sanding floors to make them appear larger; having freshly baked cookies (not boiled cabbage) wafting from the kitchen; setting fresh flowers out on the dining room table; placing candles in candlesticks to lure the buyer into imagining their soft, beneficial effects; and on and on. (Berges, 101 Cost-Effective Ways; and Nancy Dunnan, "Sell Your Home in 60 Days," MSN House & Home," July 15, 2004.) I've been given the gingerbread-in-the-oven version, and I can report that it worked before I knew I was eating my own lunch so to speak. The tactics don't work once you're clued in to them.

Selling a farmhouse presents additional tactical opportunities, such as throwing copper sulfate into the pond to clear up the algae (temporarily); hanging a hammock between a couple of shade trees; chaining a tire swing from a tree limb to invoke barefoot boys with cheeks of tan; installing a faux antique weather vain on the barn roof; purchasing a couple of no-good, paint-peeling chests for $25 from a neighbor (who's had mice and birds antiquing them for ten years out in his long abandoned chicken house) that the seller "throws in" to make the deal work for you (because you are pretty sure that you've seen these exact chests appraised for $10,000 each on the "Antiques Roadshow"). Dirt-smart buyers should know the difference between a sweetener that makes a pot and one that makes your teeth hurt.

Here are some recent books that either coach sellers on, or alert buyers to, seller tactics: Terry Eilers, How to Sell Your Home Fast for the Highest Price in Any Market (New York: Hyperion, 1997); Gary W. Eldred, The Complete Guide to Second Homes for Vacations, Retirement, and Investment (New York: John Wiley & Sons, Inc, 2000); Carolyn Janik, How to Sell Your Home in the '90s' With Less Stress and More Profit (New York: Penguin Books, 1991); Gregory D. Lerch, How to Sell Your Home When Homes Aren't Selling (White Hall, VA: Betterway Publications, 1991); and Eric Tyson and Ray Brown, Home Buying for Dummies (New York: Hungry Minds, Inc., 1996).

CHOICES

The vernacular farmhouse in good shape is usually priced in the middle of the spectrum of local housing choices. Style, size, condition and neighbors shift a specific property's asking price one way or the other. Manufactured housing (mobile homes) are usually among the least expensive options, along with small, older houses of fewer than 1,000 square feet. One-story houses from the 1940s-1960s and smallish, one-to two-story frame houses are found in the middle of the local price range. If you like their style, these houses can be good buys as long as they can be upgraded and enlarged to fit your needs. They tend to have small rooms and a chopped-up floorplan. But the rooms can be readily combined into larger living areas by taking down a non-load-bearing wall or two. The bottom half of the housing market tends to serve local buyers with local paychecks more than second-home buyers who are backed by inflated Big City incomes.

Certain second-home buyers are looking for what my wife calls, "**the big shack in the country**." She's referring to one of four kinds of big shacks: 1) *ante-bellum* "Taras" with white columns (the taller and thicker, the better); 2) "Englishy" brick/stone country houses that combine grandness with the feel of a cottage; 3) one-story ranch houses that sprawl like J.R.'s "Dallas" spread; and 4) pumped up, puffed out, over-fenestrated, exposed beamers with garage-sized closets that were built after 1970.

New big-shack owners tend to start making their places bigger and better right away. I urge a cooling-off period between the time you buy and the time you start to redo. Give yourself a chance to learn how the house works with your family in it. The Taras are the most difficult to remodel well, because their original materials are no longer used much, and craftsmen who can do period work are rare. These houses don't lend themselves readily to modern systems, such as forced-air heating and air conditioning; in-wall electrical wiring and plumbing; and insulation. They are hard to enlarge with stylistic integrity, because additions look like additions. The English country houses seem to appreciate with or without upgrades. Unlike the Taras, they were originally built with electricity, plumbing and central heating. Their structural framing allows modernization without tearing into floors, walls and ceilings. They can be added to without spoiling their style. The Dallas houses—basically bungalows on steroids—can be adapted and enlarged without damage to their architectural integrity since sprawl is their style. They're the easiest to upgrade/remodel because they have one-story floorplans and nothing tricky about their designs. The modern beamers are still in style, so you won't have trouble finding crews to work on them.

Each of these big-shack styles deserves consistency and maybe even fidelity from new owners wanting to make improvements. Remodeling should be in keeping with what is being retained. Otherwise, you end up with a **remuddle**.

The worst remuddling I've seen was a one-car garage made of T-111 (exterior plywood) stubbed out of an 1840s-era, three-story, white-columned Tara mansion. The owner boasted that he had been able to "game" the local zoning board into granting him a variance to house his sports car. He wanted an attached garage, so he attached one, by gum! Had his Tara grown a wart that size, it would have looked better.

The second worst remuddle I've come across involved a big, two-story country house in a pretty part of West Virginia that came with about 700 acres. The owner's children lived in three of the 15 rooms during the winter where I found them huddled next to a $150 woodstove. The exterior style and condition were good, and the setting was lovely, but the interior had been totally mish-mashed. The largest room on the first floor—what was once a grand dining hall—had been converted into a utility area where I found two elephant-sized, forced-air furnaces from the 1940s side by side, both non-functioning. Metal ducts sprouted from them and ran around the house's solid interior walls like a berserk hydra. Bathrooms had been clubbed into hallways and bedrooms, along with an elevator. Still, enough money and time could rescue this mess, because the basic structure was in good shape.

The older the house style, the more expensive faithful additions will be. Older houses require better trades people, costlier materials and more time. If you fall in love with a Tara, pick up one of the many coffee-table books on the history of Jefferson's Monticello, which looks better now than it did when he had it. Jefferson died broke. The causes were several but a main one was the ruinous expense of a 30-year, big-shack building/redoing project. It has taken years and millions of dollars to turn Jefferson's fantasy into what appears today to be an effortless reality where everything works (even without the slaves) while being stylistically honest and consistent. If a big shack is a stretch for your pocketbook, don't put yourself on that rack.

Second-home buyers often find nice big shacks being sold on postage stamps. The mansions have been severed from the land that originally supported them to pay debt or generate cash. You may find these houses surrounded by farmettes with modern homes. If you want a second home in the country without the country, a house-heavy/land-light package can work. I would, however, insist on getting at least ten acres. The long-term appreciation of a house like this depends as much on what happens around it as what the owner does with it.

Be careful when you are considering the odd duck on the local pond. They tend to not appreciate as fast as the rest of flock and are harder to sell. Conventional advice is to find the cheapest property in the most expensive neighborhood. In rural areas this type of buying advice is not that relevant, because the concept of neighborhood is a lot less defined in the country. The housing mix around any particular country house is likely to be a hodge-podge of ages, styles and values—the direct opposite of suburban neighborhoods which tend toward homogeneity. I would feel safe buying a country house that is one of a local type or one of a cluster. I would steer away from a one-of-a-kind unless it comes with enough land to make it a stand-alone property that is independent of, and shielded from, those surrounding it. You cannot change the look or the value of your neighbors' properties. The expensive country house is judged by the company it keeps. I know of two cases where owners of big shacks have been driven to distraction by the proximity of less sightly property—and eventually bought them to get rid of them.

Two common country houses are the **mobile home** and the **one-story rambler or bungalow**. Mobile homes have virtues and not-virtues, but their essential feature is that they can be moved. If you find a piece of land that you like, you can sell the mobile home that comes with it and start from scratch, using its well, septic system and utilities. The mobile home can also function as a base that you can use while building a new house. If the unit is in decent condition, you may want to consider donating it to a tax-exempt charitable organization for pass through to a family in need of housing. If you can't sell it or donate it, give it away. You can also offer the seller a contract for the land less the mobile home, which gives him an opportunity to sell it for more than what he valued it as a package with his land. Mobile homes are generally not what urban buyers are looking for when they envision their second home in the country. My advice, however, is not to reject land summarily because you don't like the mobile home that's on it. Resolving a mobile-home presence is much easier than you think.

Since WWII, the one-story ranch/rambler/bungalow design has become the country vernacular. One version of this style is the doublewide mobile home, which is often set atop a fixed block foundation (thus making it immobile). Doublewides provide more than 1,000 square feet relatively inexpensively and quickly. Newer models are designed to look stick-built. Ramblers and modulars are the preferred fixed-foundation options in my area. They range from small and cheap to large and not cheap. The ramblers are often owner-built or a Jim Walters-type, stick-built package. If the house comes with 50 acres or more and you don't like the house, consider buying the land without the house, or carving off one or two acres with the house for immediate resale. (When doing this, make to sure to retain an access right of way and utility easement if you need them for your own house site located deeper in the property.) With the right configuration of land and house, you will be able to recoup a substantial portion of the original purchase price. An alternative that I've also seen is for the new owner to build a new house elsewhere on the property and then convert the existing house into a rental unit, guest house or office.

Another option is to build or buy the two-story, faux farmhouses that look like the originals on the outside (and always have a covered porch) and contain modern, efficient floorplans. Faux farmhouse plans are widely available and not hard to build. If you're considering buying one that's been built, check the insulation, window and door quality and whether it has a mud-room entrance.

Second homes involving waterfront (beach, lake or river) location involve a special set of considerations. Many waterfront properties are in developments where the "ruralness" of the locale has been upgraded by project infrastructure. In these places, you can evaluate houses in much the same way you would suburban residences. Certain features will be different, such as a southern beach house's lack of central heating or insulation. Where tidal surges or flooding is a threat, you will need to establish that the house is outside or above the danger zone. Otherwise, anticipate water damage and knock down the seller's asking price. Such hazards increase your insurance rates, and, in some cases, may make it difficult for you to buy affordable homeowner insurance or prevent existing insurance from being cancelled. Ask to see the seller's insurance policy; if that doesn't work, ask for the name of his insurance agent, who should tell you approximately what the coverage is and its cost. More and more, water frontage is subject to local zoning and state/federal environmental regulations. Make sure you have a complete understanding of how these constraints will affect your plans. If you buy on the waterline, get flood insurance that will cover water damage from hurricanes and storm-caused water surges. Call the local building inspector and state environmental agency as first steps. Talk to neighboring landowners and folks active in the homeowners' associations. You will be unhappy if you buy a wonderful ocean-front house at half what you expected to pay and later discover that you are not allowed to protect your house from wave damage and beach erosion, both of which are coming at you with open jaws.

On developed waterfront property, you should be especially concerned about the density of development, current and future, which affects traffic, water quality and noise, among other quality-of-life factors. Check to see whether the developer is selling with covenants that restrict certain recreational uses on the water. Are there references in the seller's deed to local restrictions? If you like a lot of people and activity on your waterfront, you won't mind high-density development. But some types of water recreation may start to annoy, particularly noisy ones and those that you don't do yourself. Waterskiing, jet skis and loud motor boats grate on those who confine their water sports to sailing and paddling. Watercraft restrictions are common on lake property, especially small lakes. These can mean a horsepower limit on gasoline engines or no gasoline engines at all.

Two important considerations with waterfront housing are water and sewerage systems. Lakes are particularly susceptible to contamination and overloading from waterfront septic systems. I've rented summer property in New Hampshire on two lakes where every charming older house had its septic system near the water and every house drew its drinking water from the lake. One place prohibited putting toilet paper down the toilet. (I found this out only after I arrived.) The closer the house is to the water and the older it is, the more you should check out the septic/drinking water systems. It is not uncommon to find two pumps at work in these houses: one pumping sewage away from the house to a septic system, and a second pumping water to the house for domestic use. Empty water bottles on the back porch tell you that the tap water is not fit to drink.

A final factor to consider when thinking about buying a country house relates to **your likely use pattern**. If you expect to visit the place a half-dozen weekends a year and maybe a week in the summer, you can save money by purchasing a house smaller than you might otherwise want. I know this is abundantly obvious put that way, but I've watched many second-home buyers purchase much more house than they need. They tend to think of their second home in terms of their principal residence, and they don't want to downsize. Most folks don't need as much space in a second home, particularly one used sparingly, as they have in their full-time residence. Moreover, as kids move out, less space becomes increasingly appealing. A second-home buyer is often better off in the long run buying less house and more land if his finances force a choice. Self-denial, of course, applies only to those who need to budget dollars or are inveterately thrifty.

Existing country houses often present themselves to buyers who have evolving space needs as a choice between spending money upfront (for something newer or bigger) and spending time and money down the road (for additions and remodeling). If you are planning to use the country place as a second home until you can either move there full time or retire to it, the size-money question takes a different spin. You have to project your future space needs in light of future income. As a retiree or an empty-nester, your space needs are likely to be different than before. You may want to use the move to your country place as an excuse to cut back on the stuff you've accumulated. And it's probably cheaper to store the drag-along things in a rental unit than to buy a house large enough to function as your archives. Of course, the advantage of buying farms with barns and outbuildings is that you have even more space to fill. (Don't fill them with valuable furniture and papers.)

Average new-house size for retirees fluctuates year to year according to taste and fashion. Recently, it's been in the 2,000- to 2,500-square-foot range. (This provides at least two or three bedrooms/study/work-out room/home office, two full bathrooms, good closets/storage, utility room and a kitchen-dining-living area.) My guess is that a couple who retires to a farm property can get along with 1,800 to 2,200 square feet, and additional space can be found in an outbuilding or rental storage unit. In 2006, you might assume typical new-house construction cost of at least $125 per square foot and new outbuilding construction cost at half that, or less. Buying an existing outbuilding for storage of durable items as part of a farm/second home is even cheaper.

If you are watching your dollars, you might want to buy a smaller second place and then add area if, and when, you need it as full-time residents. Finishing an attic or a stand-up basement is cheap space compared with building from scratch. Reworking a roof can also give you extra space for transients like children and grandchildren. Remodeling an outbuilding is another possible source of space as long as the building is worth the investment.

There's another time-money issue that relates to your anticipated use of the second home. Money buys convenience and reliability in a country place. A second home with a modern, whole-house, heating system is a welcome sight when you pull up at 11 pm on December 24th, braving a wind-chill factor of minus 5. Your cranky, sleepy family does not want to shiver for an hour while you start a fire in the woodstove. So the choice you face is spending $5,000-$10,000 for a heating system or having an impatient spouse, whiney kids and grimly cheerful guests pray that your last match ignites a frozen log. The same type of time-money dynamic plays out with water and sewerage systems, kitchens and driveways. Weaker and cheaper involves hassle and breakdown sooner or later. And the less frequent your visits to a second home, the more likely that problems materialize in weak, cheap systems. If you can't afford to go first class everywhere at once, you can add a few things that will make your comings and goings easier. For heating, install a few baseboard electric heaters that will warm a room quickly. For water, bring a couple of gallon jugs with you so that you don't have to crawl under the house first thing to get the pump working. Any water line or outlet that can be protected from freezing, should be. Install a spigot at the lowest point in the house's water system to allow you to drain all pipes with a few quick turns. Drain your system before you go home in the winter. Frozen water pipes are not how you want your ski weekend to begin. You can protect water traps (the U-shaped thing under your sink) by draining the system, then putting non-freeze windshield cleaner or non-toxic antifreeze in them.) Having lived in a country farmhouse for 23 years that I've had to shut down and open up periodically in below-freezing conditions, I would put scarce dollars first into reliable second-home systems at the expense of space if a choice had to be made.

If you're planning to retire to a country house, think through how you might want to adapt the structure to age-related needs. **Elder-friendly adaptations** can involve a lot of money or none at all, depending on what is being done. (For an overview/links, see www.infinitec.org; and www.design.ncsu.edu/cud/univ_design/princ_overview.htm for an explanation of "universal design" principles, which rethink housing so that it better fits everyone.) Elder-friendly changes may involve grade-level access, ground-floor bedroom, thermostat-controlled heating system, covered porch, lever-style handles rather than door knobs, dual hand rails on stairs, additional lighting (stairs, entrances), grab bars, slip-resistant floors (throw away throw rugs), wider doorways, ramps, and Personal Emergency Response System (PERS).

Buying a functioning country house as a second home makes the most sense to me for many buyers. The house has to be functioning at a level acceptable to you, which I hope now excludes wrecks and the more marginal projects. I would buy a setting (which I can't change) with a small house over a house I like better with a setting that doesn't suit. Small can always be enlarged; outdated can always be modernized, but the unchangeable will be with you always.

CHAPTER 13: ENVIRONMENTAL ISSUES

OVERVIEW

Buying rural property involves environmental issues in four basic ways.

First, how is the target property affected by environmental factors arising beyond the property's boundaries? These factors can be as global as long-range atmospheric transportation of acidic, fossil-fuel combustion products that are harming trees on the property and increasing the acidity in its lake, or as local as a neighbor dumping his dirty truck oil in the creek upstream.

Second, what adverse environmental impacts, if any, does the target property generate from its current uses? These impacts can be on the target property, as well as on adjoining properties.

Third, what environmental liabilities, if any, does the property contain? These can range from an insect infestation that limits the property's production of a particular crop to an abandoned underground mine that is leaking acid-enriched water.

Finally, what legal responsibilities and restrictions of an environmental nature come with the property? Restrictions can limit current uses and future plans.

The buyer must look at a target property with Superman's x-ray vision. To think about the land's environmental pluses and minuses, the buyer must look behind, through, under, around, above and into the property. It's easy to spot a 5,000-gallon, above-ground oil tank with a squirting leak. It is far more difficult to identify concealed problems unless you are looking for them and know what they are when you see them. It can be impossible to identify a federally listed endangered snail and its habitat, either of which can stop a second home from being built, unless you research the issue. Don't assume that you can dump clean sand in a bog or fill in that mosquito-breeding wet spot near the seller's house: you may be prosecuted for destroying wetlands.

The larger the tract, the more likely it is that buyers will discover one or more environmental issues in their pre-purchase scoping. But even small lots, located on ocean front or high-quality inland waters, can be affected. I advise asking the seller and his agent in your purchase offer to disclose *any* environmental condition of which they are aware that could affect your use and enjoyment of the property. You may also want to incorporate an environmental contingency in the contract that allows you to back out of the offer if you turn up any unacceptable environmental condition during, say, a 45-day study period.

On properties where you suspect an environmental issue—typically a restriction related to endangered species, wetlands, property adjoining water or water pollution—I recommend that you hire an **environmental consultant** to inspect the property and place a results-acceptable-to-the-buyer contingency in the contract. The consultant, who may be an engineer or a degree-holder in environmental studies, inspects the property for environmental problems just as a house inspector examines a building. The consultant should be broadly knowledgeable about environmental issues and be alert to a property's environmental values and benefits as well as its liabilities. Obviously, a lot of rural land can be—and is—purchased without an environmental inspection and without any resulting dire consequence. I simply submit the equally obvious response: state and federal restrictions on private property arising from environmental concerns are a fact of modern life, an increasingly prominent fact. Property-rights groups describe one horror story after another on their web sites about innocent individuals finding themselves ensnared over activities that appear to be harmless and minor.

A buyer cannot expect to become an overnight expert on the implications of environmental law for owners of rural land. But you should have a general overview of what these laws cover and a rudimentary checklist to go through. The U.S. Environmental Protection Agency (USEPA, or EPA) administers the following major laws that may be delegated to individual states for enforcement:

1. Clean Air Act (CAA)
2. Clean Water Act (CWA)
   a. Section 404 protects wetlands and designates permitting to the U.S. Army Corps of Engineers
3. Safe Drinking Water Act (SDWA)
4. Comprehensive Environmental Response, Compensation and Liability Act (CERCLA)
   a. Superfund Amendments and Reauthorization Act of l986 (SARA)
5. Resource Conservation and Recovery Act (RCRA)
6. Federal Insecticide, Fungicide and Rodenticide Act (FIFRA)
7. Toxic Substance Control Act (TSCA)
8. Marine Protection Research and Sanctuaries Act (MPRSA)
9. Uranium Mill Tailings Radiation Control Act (UMTRCA)
10. Hazardous Solid Waste Act (HSWA)
11. Endangered Species Act of 1973 (ESA)

Most of these acts regulate the pollution of air, land or water. Rural property can be the source of pollution or its victim, or both. Section 404, the Endangered Species Act and various coastal-preservation laws protect habitat and certain types of land from human activities that would harm them. This means that a landowner cannot use his in a way that has a detrimental effect on the habitat of a protected species. Good reasons exist for this restriction, but it also imposes costs and restraints on affected landowners.

COMMON ENVIRONMENTAL PROBLEMS, BROADLY CONSTRUED

Before discussing some of the land-buying concerns these federal laws raise, here are several unregulated "environmental" problems that are fairly common in the country.

Take **man-made light**, for example. If you look at rural property when most buyers do, you will be there during the day. Since you will be spending a good part of your time at your new country property in various degrees of darkness, it's sensible to know how things look from there at night. Sodium-vapor and other high-intensity lights on nearby properties can be intrusive and offensive. Remember how Laura Shaine Cunningham was shocked to discover that her country house was next door to a local community college whose anti-crime lights "glowed like a Martian heliport." (I'm not sure how an observant writer, even one besotted by big-shack ethers, could have missed a detail of this magnitude in broad daylight.) Look for neighboring (unlighted) light fixtures during your daytime visits. Big, modern-looking globes, often attached to barns and houses, are the ones that can disturb a neighbor. You will have no luck in asking their owners to turn off these monsters, which they've installed for security and safety, both valid concerns. You will lose a nuisance suit; the lights were there before you were. Even if they're installed

212

after you join the neighborhood, you'll probably lose, because the lights are likely to be unexceptional and "in keeping" with community standards. Keep your eyes open, in addition for, blinking lights on nearby towers, tanks and silos. Another startling source of light is industrial-type poultry/hog housing. These long, one-story structures glow all night, and there might be five or six clustered together. If you can see a neighbor when trees have shed their leaves, **light pollution** may be a problem for you regardless of whether it bothers anyone else in the neighborhood.

Another type of annoyance is the practice of folks using your driveway entrance as a turnaround, particularly at night when their **vehicle lights** shine directly into your living room or bedroom. A turnaround habit can be long-standing, and you will be seen as a kill-joy crank if you object to that which has been visited on the previous owner. You should also determine whether the house catches headlights from the passing road. Houses situated at corners and curves are especially vulnerable.

Noise, constant or intermittent, can be a nagging bother. Teenage boys on big dirt bikes (motorcycles) are not the preferred peace-and-quiet neighbors. If you see a nearby neighbor with a big truck parked in his driveway, you should assume that you will hear its engine being cranked at five in the morning. If you don't like the sound of sirens, you don't want to buy close to a volunteer fire department. If you don't like the sound of bloodlust baying, avoid buying next to a kennel of hunting dogs. You can assume that you will hear gunshots in the country. Your neighbors—and maybe you too—will find it necessary every so often to shoot a rabid animal, snapping turtle or garden-ravishing groundhog. Some enthusiasts like to fire away at targets off their back porches. Gunfire noise can travel a fair distance, depending mainly on the gun's caliber (size). If gunfire bothers you, ask the seller and his neighbors whether this should be a concern, and don't buy next to a gun club or shooting range. You should expect to hear gunfire during hunting seasons, which vary from state to state and by game species. You may also want to avoid property situated near sawmills, wind-turbine farms (the towers are 400 feet high and impossible to ignore), oil or gas pumping stations, mines and quarries, dumpsters (green boxes) and small-engine repair shops.

Farms generate noise. Calves bawl for three or four days when they are weaned. When cattle are doctored, they protest loudly and often with justification. Sheep bleat. Donkeys bray. Roosters crow. And so on. Tractors and other types of equipment are noisy, but are generally not intrusive. If your property is next to a mechanized barn, you may hear the clank and rattle of a silo unloader and feed line. Farmers use all-terrain vehicles (ATVs) for farm-related tasks, such as herding cattle.

Normal farm noises are part of living in a farm community. Normal is usually defined as what is or what is typical, not what a newcomer would prefer. If you will find the routine of farm noise offensive, it's best not to buy around working farms. You don't have much of a right to tell a neighbor not to do what he was doing when you bought the property. The law of nuisance provides some protection against new noises and noises that exceed what a reasonable person might judge to be within the range of acceptability and typical by community standards, but local judges will be reluctant to tell farmers they can't farm—which is how the issue will be framed. States that adopted **right-to-farm legislation** will protect farmers in these circumstances.

You should anticipate **agricultural odors** in agricultural areas. If you're next to a dairy operation, you will smell fresh manure when the dairyman spreads it on his fields. A single dairy cow produces about 120 pounds of manure each day; a typical herd of 200 cows produces 8,760,000 pounds per year—all of which, in most cases, is used as field fertilizer. Farms gather liquid/slurry-type manure in open structures— concrete storage containers, earthen pits (lagoons or ponds)—and dry manure in sheds or piles. The closer you are to these gathering spots, the more you will notice the odor. When manure is applied to fields, the same rule of nose applies. Farm fields have manure/litter applied to them several times a year and smell bad for several days each time. Manuring pasture and crop land is a sensible agricultural practice that recycles nutrients, but you may want to avoid buying a property whose house lies close to such fields.

The no-buy rule should apply without exception to property within smelling range of **feedlots**. The stench of thousands of tons of cattle manure, especially when its wet, is unforgettable. (In dry weather, you get less odor but more dust.) Many Midwestern counties—where feedlots are common—have enacted zoning regulations to control odors. While property might be cheap downwind from a feedlot, it's not likely to prove to be a pleasing place to live. These odors don't stop on the weekend.

Factory farms are large operations that raise or handle livestock in concentrated areas, such as a feedlot or a building. Factory farms go by the official name, **Concentrated Animal Feeding Operations (CAFOs)**, and are now subject to EPA regulation through individual states. A buyer of land adjacent to a CAFO should assume that his nose will confront smells. EPA now requires that CAFOs obtain a pollutant-discharge permit and implement a nutrient-management plan by 2006 to protect surface waters. Nutrients, in this context, refers to manure's constituents—nitrogen, phosphorous and potassium; management refers to gathering, storage, handling and use of manure. EPA's CAFO regulations can be found at www.cfpub.epa.gov/npdes/afo/cafofinalrule.cfm.

Some folks are not bothered by farm odors, just as some folks are not bothered by the smell coming from plants that manufacture chemicals and paper. They are used to those smells and don't find them to be anything but routine. If, on the other hand, you have not been acclimated to CAFO odors, my advice is simple: Do Not Buy property near a CAFO or in an area where they exist. Certainly, the larger the farm or CAFO operation, the more potential for odor problems. But odor also depends on how it is stored and how manure is spread on fields. Certain types of applications—such as the injection technique where manure is inserted mechanically below the surface of the field and aerial spraying where the smelliest components of the manure are not the main part of the spray mixture—produce little odor. Composted manure also is inoffensive. Where fresh liquid/slurry manure or poultry litter is spread on fields, the odor is strong for several days.

A recent news story reported on a law suit in Nebraska where 11 residents living within two miles of a hog-raising CAFO won damages against Progressive Swine Technologies, because the stench forced them "…to stay inside and prevents them from eating food from their gardens or hanging clothes out to dry." A state Court of Appeals ordered the damages to be paid, and a trial court will determine their amount." (Kari Lydersen, "For Neighbors of Nebraska Farms The Days of Swine Aren't Rosy," Washington Post, June 20, 2004.) My impression is that it's next to impossible for a new resident to win smell-suits against farmers, and out of the ordinary to win against CAFOs.

I would ask whether any neighbors are planning on, or might be agreeable to, CAFOs or poultry houses, which tend to be located within a 90-minute truck drive of a processing plant. If you're driving down a pretty country highway and notice white feathers in the roadside weeds, you're in an area where large-scale poultry operations exist. The feathers originate with the fowl as they are being trucked to the processing plant. Local and national environmental and animal-rights organizations track these industries and can inform you of possible developments in your locale. (Start with the Environmental News Service, http://www.ens.lycos.com.) Trade associations and state cooperative extension services provide information from the producers' point of view. Urban/suburban buyers should distinguish between farm odors from small farms (which should be acceptable and accepted) and those of a CAFO, which are a different scale and intensity (and should be avoided).

CAFOs are to be shunned for another reason as well: high concentrations of nitrates and phosphorous from manure can easily contaminate both surface and underground water. The farmer's nutrient-management plan—which governs the storage, handling and distribution of manure—is supposed to prevent this.

You might also keep your eyes, ears and nose open for **sludge operations** near a target property. Municipal organic waste is treated and then transported to farms to be spread on fields as fertilizer. I like the idea in theory. Living next door to a farm that accepts sludge may be less likeable. It would depend on how it's managed.

Most, if not all states, have now adopted "**right-to-farm**" statutes that protect farmers from nuisance-type suits. These laws appeared in the 1980s for the most part as a result of successful suits that shut down some farms or forced their relocation. Owners of newly built suburbs in farming areas were winning complaints against farm operations about which the new buyers should reasonably have known. The buyer can protect his interest by inserting into his purchase offer a requirement that the **seller disclose any condition around the property that constitutes an annoyance and might limit the buyer's use and enjoyment. Annoyance would include conditions such as noise, odor, excessively bright/strong lights and dust**. California now requires such disclosure. For more on neighbor law, check out www.nolo.com and search for FAQs on noise, boundaries, fences, trees, views, water damage, rural neighbors and the right to farm.

Roadside trash is a common irritation to urban buyers. Drive along many country roads and you will see aluminum cans, glass and plastic bottles, potato chip bags and styrofoam fast-food containers. You may run across a slope that has been used as a community dump before the days of scheduled trash pick up and dumpsters. Despite anti-littering laws, lifetime habits die hard, and, often, not at all. You may find the property you're investigating has a do-it-yourself dump, active or inactive. I once owned land along a remote road that someone insisted on using as a mortuary for his dead lambs every spring. In the fall, I would find butchered deer carcasses thrown over the fence. I had a couple of suspects in mind, but I never caught anyone in *flagrante delicto*. The gravel entrance to woods I own about one mile from my farmhouse attracts an evening parker every so often who leaves me a beer can or two for recycling and an occasional soiled diaper.

Roadside trash may upset country newcomers more than the trash they routinely see on urban streets and during their commutes to work. Newcomers, I think, expect things to be tidier in the country, because the country is prettier. But there's not much an individual can do to prevent littering, except clean it up and hope that others take note of a good example. (It's also therapeutic to grumble in self-righteous pique over every beer can.) Local families and community groups in Virginia adopt sections of road for regular clean up—and their effort shows amazing results.

It's easy for a newcomer to slip into a them-and-me perspective over littering which attributes a beer can thrown from a car to "their" culture (or lack thereof), "breeding" (or lack thereof) and ignorance. I urge you not to do go there, because it gets you stuck in unhelpful generalizations about your neighbors that are both unfair and inaccurate. "They" did not litter; one thoughtless jerk littered. If you or a group won't pick up the trash that bothers you, the best advice I can give is learn to live with it before it drives you crazy. Once a year, I walk my road frontage on trash patrol and feel virtuous afterward. (I've been unable to persuade anyone else in my family to share this virtue.) However, I would not move into a country place and on my first afternoon start picking up roadside trash. That's a statement about your neighborhood, even though it may not have been intended to be anything but a good deed.

With roadside dumps on your just-purchased property, erect several bold "No Dumping! Violators will be prosecuted" signs. This is fair notice that you don't want to be dumped on, despite local history and mores. A sign will usually be taken as a reasonable assertion of your property rights by most reasonable people. Violators, of course, will see you as an arrogant curmudgeon. Signs may be taken as an affront, which encourages more dumping just to show you. The best way of dealing with illegal dumping is to make a friend or two in the neighborhood, and then ask them to put the word out that you would really appreciate an end to the dumping.

Other types of **visual "pollution"** can mar a viewshed. A frequently complained about example is a sign or billboard that you see every time you enter or leave your driveway. Another is a sore-thumb house that doesn't fit into its setting or the neighborhood. It might be five times bigger than any other house in the county, or it might be the only hacienda in a school of Cape Cods. Wind turbines startle me by their out-of-scale size. A big water tank, a decrepit house, a fleet of junked cars on blocks—anything that snags your eye the first time you see it may or may not fade into the background if you have to see it everyday. Some things you will get used to, and other things are constant saddle burrs.

Country houses and barnyards attract **pests** of different kinds. Our farmhouse was infested with winter flies when we bought it, and has since become infested with the Asian lady beetle, which likes to winter in bright, sunny walls. Many houses in my county are similarly burdened. The flies emerge on warm days in cold seasons, buzz around the warm windows, then die in the cold night. (Unlike houseflies, they pay no attention to people, though they will get entangled in your hair, inadvertently.) The beetles eat aphids, which is good, but can stain stuff and cause allergic reactions in some individuals, which is bad. They smell, leave spots and bite. They are found in the South and Midwest, from the Gulf Coast to Canada. (The USDA released them in the 1980s to control aphids on pecan groves in Georgia and other places; the rest is history. Felicity Barringer, "Asian Cousin of Ladybug Is a Most Unwelcome Guest," New York Times, November 15, 2005.) Termites, carpenter ants and powder-post beetles can damage woodwork. Wasps often nest in a farmhouse attic or under an eave. Snapping turtles like farm ponds; snakes hang out under things; groundhogs burrow under buildings; rats and mice like barns, as do bats and some birds. Other critters you may face include skunks, raccoons, squirrels, deer, opossums, starlings, foxes, weasels, beaver, porcupines, feral cats and dogs, venomous spiders, coyotes, bears, mountain lions, javelinas and wolves. Alligators can be a dangerous nuisance.

Do not feed wildlife, including birds. (Other creatures, including bears, will raid your bird feeders.) A "fed bear is a dead bear" can be applied to other wild creatures, because they can't distinguish between when you want to feed them and when they want to eat the food they know you have. They become a pest to you and then to others. Sooner or later, a guy with a rifle gets fed up. Be neat and clean with food left for livestock and pets. Don't leave pet food on your porch at night unless you want to share. If you don't want a critter around, remove the habitat that lets him make a living there. Having shot or otherwise killed some of the aforementioned visitors, I can report that their descendants continue to journey through my habitat because it's theirs too. Passage is fine with me; residency is not. If wild creatures give you the willies, think again about buying a country place. They come with the territory. Country living will change your idea about the meaning of cohabitation.

The other category of pest is unwanted plants, insects, diseases and animals in the property's forest, fields and water. Often, these species are non-native, and, for that reason, have no local predators to control them. Trees have been greatly affected by invasive and non-native insects and diseases. Both hardwoods and pines are susceptible. Oaks, ash, maples, hemlock and pine, among others, are at risk. The best way to determine whether woods and valuable timber trees are being, or are likely to be, impacted, is to hire a consulting forester to walk through the target property's woodland before you submit an offer. He will be knowledgeable about prominent local pests. Don't assume that your target property is exempt. The county extension agent will be able to give you a first-cut opinion about the type of pests that affect local crops. Pests, broadly construed, can inflict serious economic damage to valuable trees and agricultural products.

Human visitors are not usually considered an environmental problem, but they are to the extent that unwanted ones negatively affect the use and enjoyment of your land. Properties bordering national forest land can be overrun during hunting season. Even where you clearly post your common boundary with a clearly marked national forest line, certain properties are routinely invaded by hunters and sometimes their packs of dogs. Hunters have the right to retrieve their dogs from posted land; if your land is properly posted they have no right to kill game on your land. The law of trespass is, shall I say, not always followed to the letter in the field. Ask the seller about this. He may be reluctant to reveal the extent of hunting-season trespass.

If your property borders a fishing stream, you can count on finding fishermen in your section of stream. Landowners normally hold **riparian rights** to waters in a river, stream, pond or lake flowing through or joining their property. If the waterway is considered **navigable**, the landowner owns land to the water's edge with the state owning the land under the water. Navigable waters are considered to be the same as public highways, allowing the public—that is, fishermen and boaters—to "travel" and use the navigable water without restriction. If the waterway is considered **unnavigable**, the landowner owns the land under the water to the centerline of the waterway. Landowners can prohibit fisherman access to unnavigable waterways, but not to navigable waterways. The legal definition of navigable can be broader than you think. Fishing access may also be controlled by special state provisions. A well-known trout stream near me, for instance, is off-limits to public fishing even though it is considered navigable because the original grant of lands from the English King specifically stated that the fish belonged to the holder of the grant, and by extension to all successors in title. The owner of a fishing right can give, rent or sell it to another. The **common of piscary** is a rarely used legal phrase that means the right to fish in waters belonging to another, which I once heard a trespassing lawyer in waders cite to a farmer in muck boots. The farmer said something like, "I don't give a damn about your piss, common or otherwise; get out of my fishing hole." When a buyer finds himself evaluating property with water running through it or adjoining it, he should determine whether it is considered navigable or unnavigable, because that fact will usually control what rights, if any, he has to restrict public access. This information can be obtained from the state's game and wildlife department, county sheriff or local game warden. The U.S. Army Corps of Engineers may also have to be consulted. Exceptions and unusual circumstances regarding fishing rights can be found in deeds and by asking state game and wildlife officials about local laws.

You may also find visitors checking out a well-known berry patch, fruit or nut tree, rock quarry, cave, picnic spot, spring, sand pit, bird's nest, mushroom spot, ginseng stand, snake den, swimming hole or dump on your newly purchased property. This is in addition to hunters, four-wheelers, motorcyclists and hikers who may also turn up. Yellow posted signs help spread the word that you do not want uninvited visitors, as do advertisements in the local paper. It should not take long for the word to get around the neighborhood that you do not welcome visitors unless they are invited or secure permission in advance.

Having said all that, I can report finding a birder's car parked in the middle of my woods driveway, not 15 feet from a No-Trespassing sign posted at eye level at the entrance with my name and address on it.

I had left my gate open the evening before, and he pulled into my property rather than park on the roadside—something readily done and safe enough. I considered having him arrested. I considered having a sarcastic conversation about his level of literacy and eyesight. I considered scraping his SUV with my woods truck, which bears scrapes, dents and scratches with no ill will. I considered kicking his ass down the road. I was in high dudgeon over my violated property rights. But I knew I didn't have the right to harm his person or property. The cooler part of my head prevailed, so I simply growled at him to get his car out of my driveway. Other enforcement choices involve time and possibly money. Still, had he asked permission, he could have parked on the land and walked its trails all afternoon. Trespass often becomes a highly charged issue for country newcomers, especially when reasonable and rational efforts don't prevent recurrences.

My inclusion above of a swimming hole may seem petty to a reader sitting in his secure living room contemplating a wonderful life in the country. A recorded agreement to access another's swimming hole is rare. But your enjoyment of this swimming hole will diminish as soon as you discover that it has been used by at least seven generations of local kids as a matter of custom. Whether current kids have any legal right to use this hole is a matter of state law, and the answer is probably not. If you insist on ending or limiting their visits, you have fallen into a bad way to introduce yourself to the neighborhood. To learn about such water usages in advance, your purchase contract can ask the seller to **disclose any uses of the property and its resources that occur outside of a recorded easement.**

Laugh! Swimming holes have been the subject of disputes between new owners and "old" users in Crystal Springs, Florida; High Falls, New York; and Ben Lomond, California to name a few places. (Winnie Hu, "Locked Out," Richmond Times-Dispatch, July 29, 2001, p. A-2.) Landowners are subject to a lawsuit if an uninvited guest gets hurt in their hole, and they have not taken adequate precautions and erected adequate signs to prevent its use. The **doctrine of attractive nuisance** can pin liability on the landowner who did not do enough to prevent trespassers from using his swimming hole. If you are buying a swimming hole, check with a local lawyer to determine exactly what you need to do to satisfy your obligations under state law to keep out unwanted swimmers. On well-known swimming holes, you will need to do more than post a no-trespassing sign or put the word out. You may have to choose between becoming the new ogre for telling everyone to stay out or the community patsy by putting up with a dozen kids traipsing across your fields on hot afternoons. If you value privacy, become the ogre. If you let folks use your hole, you should carry liability insurance and have them sign a liability waiver. I'm serious.

Sooner or later, the new owner of rural land will have a run in with trespassers on his property. I quote below an extended account of one such incident in a part of West Virginia not far from where I live. It was written by non-resident-owner, Chris Bolgiano, in The Appalachian Forest:

> …we arrived for a visit years ago. A new road greeted us, a narrow track up a vertical slope, with the forest floor churned into powder. Rain would soon turn it into a gully. We knew right off it was OHVs [Off-Highway Vehicles, or All-Terrain Vehicles (ATVs)]. We raced up the new road, cursing, yelling ideas back and forth about how to fell logs across the road and stud them with case-hardened nails. We felt righteous with ownership, passionate with protectiveness. The road continued up to the barbed wire fence that marked our boundary. The wire had been cut, and the track crossed our border to join an old path along the ridge. We had explored that path and then forgotten it, forgotten that our property was linked into a generations-old network of trails.

> As I planned how to cunningly angle the nails, we heard the chugging of motors. A

caravan of four OHVs came into view just below, moving toward us up the hill. Ralph [her husband] raised his arms and walked toward them down the middle of the new track, palms out, fingers spread, like an evangelist at a camp meeting. For a few seconds I thought that the vehicles might swerve clean around him and keep going. But they stopped. Ralph stood beside the first one while I walked up and straddled the front wheel, leaned into it, put one hand on the handlebars. I hadn't studied mountain manners all these years for nothing. There was going to be no doubt about who had rights here.

The lead vehicle was decked out like an Amish buggy: a square of thick black vinyl stretched over a pipe frame welded to the body of the OHV, with plastic windows zippered into the front and sides. Later we heard that the driver had black lung from a lifetime spent mining coal and couldn't tolerate wind in his face. From his creases and the texture of his skin, I guessed that he was in his sixties. His hair was still dark, and his eyes were the darkest, most solid brown I've ever seen. They were shaped like almonds, slightly tilted.

'I own this property,' Ralph began, 'and I'm just real surprised to find this road here.' His voice was calm and twangy with the mountain drawl we had picked up and slipped into years earlier, at first unconsciously, for protective coloration.

'We're just going to our hunting place to put this stuff out for the deer,' the man in the first OHV said. Near his feet, apples bulged, round and red through plastic mesh bags. 'It's legal,' he added quickly. 'Baiting's all legal except for bear.'

I had been looking for guns without even realizing it, scanning the rears of the OHVs and glancing at shoulders for rifles slung there as carelessly as sacks of apples. We almost always brought a gun with us when we camped here. Mainly we used it to answer when shots sounded too close for comfort—a rural dialogue to announce our presence. Now, I realized that this was one of the few times when we could expect not to see guns. Hunters, accustoming their prey to being fed in certain places, were too easily accused of poaching if guns were in sight. It was a reassuring thought.

'Well, I don't know who put this road in, but it's eroding on that steep place there and I don't much like that,' Ralph said. 'And whoever put it in cut my fence.'

'We never cut no fence,' the man said. 'We started riding through here after we saw the road. I thought the preacher owned it yet. If I'd of knowed how to get in touch with you, I'd of asked you.'

Well, now, no one could demand more than that. Grateful to him for the face-saving he was offering, we eased a bit. 'He used to,' Ralph said, meaning the preacher. 'We bought it fifteen years ago, and this is the most people we've seen in all these years.' I was pleased that the man seemed surprised. I kept looking for a power fulcrum, a way to show that we weren't total strangers here, people from the city who didn't know spotlighting [hunting deer at night with high-powered lights, which cause the deer to freeze, making them easy targets] from a Sunday drive.

The three young men who were driving the other OHVs got off. We all stood around for some time, kicking our toes into clumps of grass and shielding our eyes from the sun as we talked in brief spurts between bouts of silence. The state did not provide a registration procedure for OHVs, they explained, and it was illegal to run unregistered vehicles on state roads. So they had to stay off-road or get a stiff fine. We walked around looking for a better place on our slope to put a road, but there wasn't any. In the meantime, three more OHVs and then two motorbikes drove up and stopped at a distance, waiting for the crowd to clear out. A regular wilderness road had developed across our place.

'Tell you what,' the man said. 'You give me and my boys permission to come through here to hunt, and we'll build you gates. We'll put one down below where we come on, and one up there where we go off. We'll do it and mail you the keys.'

It was an honorable solution, and without a doubt the best we could hope for under the circumstances. Ralph got out some paper and wrote Jesse Hoover's name down, followed by six sons. 'I knew you wasn't a hard kind of feller,' Jesse said, slapping his knee. Who could blame him for using the road, once he had noticed it? With locked gates, we could at least limit the damage to the forest. And by giving Jesse proprietary rights, we would make an ally and give him incentive to look out for our interests. Maybe this would prove to be the tie to the larger community we had been trying for years to make. Maybe it wasn't, as it seemed at first, the end of a dream, our outdated vision of serenity and isolation. We all shook hands, and a month later, two keys arrived in the mail. Jesse and his caravan pulled away, and Ralph walked down to the next group.

'I don't know who put this road in,' he began again, 'but it's tearing up...'

'You know Jesse Hoover?' one of the drivers interrupted him. 'He put it in.' (Chris Bolgiano, The Appalachian Forest: A Search for Roots and Renewal (Mechanicsburg, Pennsylvania: Stackpole Books, 1998, pp. 168-170.)

The result of this conversation is that the land's owners gave their oral permission to allow Mr. Hoover—an individual who had trespassed, destroyed their property (fence), eroded their ground, cut a road across their land that they did not want and lied to their faces—exclusive right to continue his activities in return for installing two gates to keep out his hunting rivals. This is not a face-saving or honorable solution. This was a shakedown. Ms. Bolgiano and her husband got nothing. While it is true that an absentee owner cannot keep determined intruders off his distant property, every owner should resist being maneuvered into accepting something that he feels is unacceptable. Don't start playing the patsy in an extortion racket; it will never end.

The choices an owner has concerning access are these: 1) let everyone in for approved purposes, 2) let some people in for approved purposes, and 3) let no one in for any purpose. If you choose the first option, you give away control of your property. You will be unhappy with the result. If you choose the second, you may make enemies of everyone you exclude. In the case of the Bolgianos, they thought they made the best of a trespass problem by authorizing its continuance. If you choose the third, your lack of exception will ruffle some feathers. At different times and in different places, I've tried all three, and now mainly use the third.

Enforcing a no-trespassing rule can be difficult for an absentee owner. I am, for example, half-owner of a West Virginia property that is about a 45-minute drive from my home. This is mountain woodland that we bought as a timber investment. We don't use it for hunting or recreation. Its few posted signs are not honored and a locked cable was cut during hunting season soon after I put it up. I deal with this trespass situation in the most reasonable fashion available to me in the circumstances: I neither think about it nor worry over it. While I would prefer that the land not be subject to trespass, we didn't care much about it. When I began to lease the property for hunting, I took out an ad in the local paper to notice readers that trespassing was prohibited. I also talked personally to a neighbor about the new arrangement. The word got around.

When an absentee owner *does* want to prevent trespass, he can take the following steps:

1. **Tack up posted signs**, according to state requirements.

2. **Place an ad in local paper before hunting season**. Property owned by _____ on _____ Road is posted. Trespassing is illegal, and trespassers will be prosecuted. We do not trespass on the land of others, and we expect others to respect our property rights.

3. **Talk to your neighbors**. Establish a rapport, or at least, give them your name, address and phone numbers. Put the word out that you do not want trespassing because.... Among other reasons, you may not want your land to be considered open access to the public; you do not want the **liability exposure** that can arise from visitors having accidents or injuries on your property; you do not want others using your land without permission because that unwanted usage over time can give rise to a legal right to use your property; you do not want your land to be degraded by individuals who do not share your environmental values; you don't want visitors if you have a second home and/or personal property on the land; you don't want visitors taking down trees for firewood; you do not want hunting, fishing or ATV use for whatever your reasons are; you do not want your property to be exposed to fire hazards from camping and cigarettes. If all else fails, say that you don't want your land to become a place of beer-drinking teenagers and all the trouble that entails.

4. **Erect a gate across your entrance**. Install a very heavy-duty chain lock. Give a key to your local volunteer fire department along with an annual donation.

5. **Talk to the local sheriff and game warden**. Tell them that you'd appreciate it if they kept an eye on your land and put the word out.

6. **Be prepared to prosecute trespassers**.

If I had discovered a road on my property and then an ATV convoy using it as the Bolgianos did, I would have told the intruders that I wanted no trespassing, that the road was an act of trespass and destruction of property and that I was fully prepared to prosecute trespassers and property destroyers. (I would have been in a stronger position had the property been posted before the encounter, which the Bolgianos' apparently wasn't.) I would also ask them for their names and addresses. Mr. Hoover, it should be remembered, could have easily found out who owned the Bolgianos' property by looking up the tract in the tax records at the county courthouse, something I would bet my farm he knew how to do. He was knowingly trespassing and then knowingly lying about what he had done. The last thing I would give him and his offspring is a license to do exactly what I didn't want done.

It is my experience that trespassers and hunters who trespass believe they have a right to do what they please with your land. They don't see how their use harms the owner. Most "locals" are not like this, and most hunters I know respect the rights of other property owners. Dealing with the exceptions can only be done by being firm, reasonable and consistent. In almost 30 years of living and owning property in the middle of Appalachia, I have never heard of a single incident of violence of any kind arising from a property owner asking a trespasser, hunter or birdwatcher to leave. I'm sure, however, such things have happened. Unarmed, I have asked groups of armed strangers to leave, and they have complied. The trick with armed men is to stay low-key and not get personal. Explain your reasons for posting; don't get self-righteous about the glories of private property and your civic virtuousness. Don't be surprised if a hunter claims that he did not see your signs. I once discovered a trespassing bird hunter in a friend's bog, aiming a loaded shotgun out of season, not more than 12 inches away from a posted sign at eye level. He said he never saw the sign. It's hard to prevent customary trespass, but you can make it clear through signage and ads—and mainly by word of mouth—that your land is not open. It will take several years for the word to spread. If you do not make this effort, you will find ATVs, hunters, birders and others visiting you whenever they like. You may live in fear of gunfire and will be deprived of the use and enjoyment of the property that you've purchased. The Bolgianos gave away their privacy because they were unable to say, "Please leave and do not come back."

COMMON ISSUES

Certain environmental situations can involve the property owner in regulatory and administrative law, which can be either federal or state, or both. Among the most commonly encountered are:

1. Wetlands

2. Floodplain

3. Endangered, Threatened and Sensitive (ETS) Species

4. Polychlorinated Biphenyls (PCBs)

5. Underground storage tanks (USTs)

6. Waste disposal on site/dumps

7. Animal waste

8. Oil/gas wells and coal mines

9. Asbestos

10. Wood smoke

11. Carbon monoxide

12. Radon

13. Chemical and hazardous exposures and wastes

14. Air-borne pollution

1. Wetlands are more or less permanently wet areas that fall within certain federal regulatory definitions, particularly Section 404 of the 1972 Clean Water Act as interpreted by the U.S. Army Corps of Engineers' regulations, the courts and the Act's 1977 Amendments. Wetlands are currently defined according to the Corps' 1987 Manual for Delineation of Wetlands, though this scheme is subject to continuing debate within the government and between the government and non-government interests, both private and public. Wetlands are coastal and inland areas between land and water. (See http://h2osparc.wq.ncsu.edu/info/wetlands.html.)

A wetland can be identified as land having groundwater (i.e., underground water) near to, at or over its surface for much of the year, or land that supports aquatic vegetation. Look for marshy, swampy, boggy areas and land with vegetation that indicates saturated soils, such as ironweed, Joe Pie weed and skunk cabbage, among others. These plants are "hydrophytes" and are found in "hydric" soils associated with wetlands. Bottom land and floodplains contain wetlands. Wetlands were historically places to be avoided or converted by drainage into usable property. Today, we know they provide important wildlife habitat and a reservoir-like function for gathering storm runoff for slower release. We now construct new wetlands for just such flood-mitigation purposes. Additional information can be obtained by logging on to http://wetlands.fws.gov, which leads to the U.S. Fish and Wildlife Service's National Wetlands Inventory Center.

A buyer may consider the presence of wetlands on a property either an asset or a liability, depending on what he wants to do. The general rule of regulatory thumb that now seems to be applied is that there should be no net loss of wetlands. If your plan is to alter a wetlands area by adding fill, drainage or other excavation, you will probably need to construct at least an equivalent wetlands area on your site or obtain an equivalent credit from a wetlands mitigation bank. Very small wetlands areas are exempt from these requirements. The Army Corps of Engineers administers the permitting, inspection and management of wetlands activity. The Corps' authority covers navigable waters, which have been defined to include any waters that have the capability of affecting interstate commerce. The commerce clause has been stretched to include headwaters where water flow is intermittent and often non-existent. A navigable waterway need not be navigable to be classified as navigable.

The US Supreme Court weakened the scope of wetlands protection in June, 2006 when a divided bench ruled that the Corps had exceeded its power under the Clean Water Act by defining almost any place that might have water as falling within the category of "waters of the United States." If a wetlands is not connected to water under Corps jurisdiction, it is not likely to be protected in the future, but the exact definition of how that is to be determined is likely to be settled case by case. The current Court is leaning toward narrowing wetlands protection, but a buyer should not count on any change until new interpretations are settled. (Jess Bravin, "Split Supreme Court Narrows Use of Wetlands Act," Wall Street Journal, June 20, 2006 and Patti Waldmeir, "Landowners baffled as court splits on wetlands protection," Financial Times, June 20, 2006, both referring to *Rapanos v. U.S.; Carabell v. U.S. Army Corps of Engineers.*).

On major wetlands-disturbing projects, including those involving federal land, the Corps must prepare an **Environmental Impact Statement (EIS)** that assesses the full range of environmental impacts projected to arise from the applicant's wetlands-changing proposal. (The draining of less than one acre may need only a Corps on-site inspection and go-ahead.) The applicant pays the cost of preparing an EIS, which can be enormously expensive as well as contentious, depending on the size of the project, location, type of wetlands and the projected impacts.

An urban buyer looking for a country property does *not* want to get entangled in the wetlands regulatory process. No second-home buyer wants to prepare an EIS or a lesser impact analysis, and go through that type of regulatory review. As long as you do nothing to change an existing wetlands, you should not be entangled in these regulations. Site your new house or barn on higher ground rather than in a floodplain or wet spot (that requires fill and/or underground drain pipes). If you have a farm plan for the target property, run it by the Corps' local office to determine in advance whether the farm has wetlands and, if so, whether your plan will change them. If the seller is currently grazing stock on wetlands, which is fairly common, a new owner can continue this practice or fence them out. Work around the wetlands, because they benefit the property's wildlife and drainage.

I once had to dry out less than two-thirds of an acre of wet land on which I was building houses. It was permanently wet because the uphill neighbor gathered the runoff from his uphill land and piped it onto mine. These pipes had been installed years before. My ground was an impermeable, water-bearing clay, which was why it was wet land. Much of my ground had to be cut out, the hole filled in with rip-rap-size rock and smaller rock; drainage pipes had to be laid under the rock, and fabric had to be installed in certain spots to help with channeling the new underground water system. It was a very expensive job, and I would never willingly enter this quicksand again. Had there been any other way to install the road, I would have taken it. The Corps official was quite helpful in not subjecting this wet land to wetlands review. A lot of wetlands was drained before protective legislation was enacted, and these pipes and ditches remain in various states of repair. Check with the Corps before purchasing any farm property with these systems in place. Determine what you will and will not be allowed to do without review and permit.

If you find yourself unavoidably having to develop wetlands acreage, you should first look to construct the same type of wetlands in a similar location on your property, using the same kind of dirt, vegetation and water. If that cannot be done, the Corps representative can put you in touch with a **wetlands mitigation bank**, which has constructed wetlands from which you can "withdraw" an equivalent parcel in various ways, including paying for it. Banks are operated by both public- and private-sector organizations. The property may also be eligible for a **conservation easement**, by which the owner donates the right to develop or use the wetlands in certain ways in return for tax benefits. Local land trusts or conservation groups accept the donation of such easements and hold them in perpetuity, unless the owner imposes a time limit. The higher the appraised value of the easement given away, the greater the tax benefit.

The presence of wetlands on a target property may not affect a buyer's plans at all. Once scoping finds wetlands, however, the buyer can use their presence to work down the seller's price, owing to the restrictions they impose on use. Wetlands lower asking price in my experience, except where they are integral to hunting. The seller may know something about wetlands on his property, but more likely than not he's simply cursed those "bad spots" and driven the tractor around them, hoping not to get stuck. Any wet area, whether official wetlands or not, should tip off a prospective buyer to the possibilities of a spring, seep or clay-rich soils that won't drain well. Wet soils are usually not suitable for road building, construction or septic fields. An excavator must remove them and then replace them with rock and good fill—all of which is expensive.

If you find yourself evaluating a target property that you suspect has a wetlands presence that is relevant to your plans, you can place a contingency in your offer that gives you enough time to have a Corps' representative visit the property and hire an environmental consultant.

Buyer's offer is contingent on obtaining a preliminary determination and assessment from the U.S. Army Corps of Engineers regarding any wetlands on said property, whose results shall be judged by Buyer to be acceptable or unacceptable for his purposes.

Buyer shall have the right to investigate any wetlands on the property to determine their relevance to his future use and enjoyment. This may involve agents of Buyer taking soil samples, borings and other tests. Buyer will restore the land wherever it is disturbed by these activities.

Buyer shall complete this work within ___ days of this Contract taking effect.

If Buyer determines the results of these investigations are unacceptable for his purposes, he may void his offer without penalty and all security deposits shall be returned to him in a timely manner.

A contingency also gives the buyer the opportunity to recast his offer at a lower price where his wetlands investigations indicate future expense or the need to modify his plans for the property.

One last point is worth mentioning. Those buyers who are considering eliminating wetlands or cutting old-growth forest in the process of building a trophy home, run a risk, albeit small, of being targeted by arsonists, some of whom claim to be associated with the Earth Liberation Front (ELF). Homes in subdivisions that drained wetlands near Seattle were targeted in 2004. A high-profile construction project in an environmentally contentious area may be subject to attack. (See http://seattletimes.nwsource.com/html/localnews/2001954671_elf1m.html

2. Floodplains are found where low land lies next to a waterway, lake or ocean (where storm surges cause coastal flooding). Floodplains are usually dry, though they may contain wetlands. We generally associate a floodplain with a low-lying, level area. It is, however, any area that becomes inundated with floodwater. In steeply sided, V-shaped stream valleys, the "floodplain" can extend 30 feet up each leg of the V. In such places, it is not unusual to find houses built on pilings.

As a buyer with dozens of property choices, I would encourage you to avoid those where buildings are in a floodplain. This property will be flooded eventually. Even where no improvements are involved, floodplain properties will sustain damage that you will have to repair. Fences crossing the floodplain and gates will be damaged or destroyed; flood debris will need to be removed, possibly off site; toppled trees will have to be cut up or burned; fill or topsoil may have to be hauled in; septic systems may have to be repaired; roads and culverts will need work, and on and on. Sometimes, federal money will be available to defray some flood costs, but this is not certain and won't cover all your expenses. Federal money has been available on some flooding occasions to restore the bank of our stream to its original shape, but it was not available to remove rock from the channel or build up the bank to keep future floods in place. When you add improvements and personal property—houses, barns, vehicles, storage tanks—to a floodplain, the clean-up costs increase. Despite these warnings, many readers buy floodplain for the obvious reason: it puts them right on the water.

Flooding frequency is expressed in terms of either how often a flood of a particular size occurs or the probability of flooding each year. A 100-year flood can represent either a very large flood or a one percent chance of a flood occurrence. The volume of a 100-year flood will fill a 100-year floodplain. The **Federal Emergency Management Agency (FEMA)** tries to mitigate flood damage proactively, manages post-flooding clean up and provides insurance for floodplain property.

FEMA is charged by the Federal Emergency Management Act with identifying all natural flood areas and developing plans to minimize loss. Accordingly, FEMA's Flood Insurance Administration has developed **flood-hazard maps** for most known floodplains in the United States. The maps show boundary lines of a 100-year flood. The local FEMA office and/or the local or state office that has responsibility for flooding issues can provide these maps for your county where they are available. Even where the map has not been finished, one or more of these offices may be willing to show you the work in progress. The local zoning office or building inspector should also be able to provide both anecdotal flooding histories and additional information. The local U.S. Department of Agriculture office, now called the Natural Resources Conservation Service, or the state's Soil and Water Conservation District office should have information on the flooding history and any record of publicly funded flood clean-up assistance for individual farms. Finally, ask the seller if he carries flood insurance; if he does, ask about the claims he's filed in the past and the premium costs.

FEMA administers the **National Flood Insurance Program (NFIP)**, which subsidizes insurance to property owners in floodplains. The typical **homeowner or farmowner's insurance policy** does not cover flood loss. Private insurance carriers, however, sell and issue NFIP insurance to individuals for a 31.8 percent commission and a fee of 3.3 percent of any claim amounts. NFIP is the taxpayer's pot of money that pays these claims. With rare exceptions, NFIP will pay insurance losses no matter how many times a floodplain property is damaged. While "repetitive flood-loss properties" account for about two percent of the policy holders, they amount to nearly 40 percent of the NFIP-paid claims. This insurance program encourages development in floodplains, though some construction is discouraged through community land-use controls that are a condition of the insurance. NFIP insurance is necessary to secure a bank mortgage for new construction on land that will predictably flood. FEMA's schizophrenia is the result of the cross-cutting pressures at work: individuals want to build in floodplains; individuals want cheap insurance; insurance companies want big commissions with no risk; politicians find a way to help constituents by spreading the cost.

While FEMA tries both to mitigate loss and compensate property owners as soon as flood loss occurs, more and more communities are restricting, or even banning, floodplain construction through **floodplain district zoning**. Beyond the economic loss argument, proponents of restriction show that the more building there is in a floodplain, the more a flood spreads its area of damage to the extent that buildings occupy space (in the sense of volume) that would have otherwise been partially filled with water. Floodplain zoning ordinances differ. Some prohibit construction of any new structure in designated floodplains; some prohibit residential use of such property; some prohibit damming and filling activities. Opponents argue that such ordinances constitute a government **taking** of value from their property without compensation because the property owner is denied all reasonable uses. The trend appears to be toward more building-and-use restrictions on inland floodplains and in coastal areas.

Floods are frightening events that cause enormous damage. When the waters recede, the landowner is left with a dispiriting and often expensive clean up. I've been through four 100-year floods in the intermittent creek in our back field between 1983 and 2007. I have seen these floods wreck buildings and take lives in my neighborhood. I have spent several thousand dollars cleaning up fences and fields, and building a levee. It never occurred to me to ask the seller of this farm in 1983 about flooding, and even had I asked, the truthful answer was the creek had never flooded before. I don't think I would have walked away from this farm because of flooding, but I would have planted an acre of walnuts on higher ground instead of in the bottom where they've been clobbered repeatedly.

Coastal flooding from hurricanes is a factor that any beach-oriented buyer should consider. Following Katrina, insurers are dropping homeowners' policies from Texas to Rhode Island. Allstate dumped 27,000 customers in New York's coastal counties and 120,000 in Florida in 2006. (Liam Pleven, "Hurricane Losses Prompt Allstate to Pursue New Path," Wall Street Journal, November 24, 2006.) In addition to "hundreds of thousands of policyholders...being dropped by their insurers," a larger number have had to "...swallow double-, even triple-digit increases in premiums and deductibles." Average losses are now running about $17 billion annually. (Karen Breslau, "The Insurance Climate Change," Newsweek, January 29, 2007.) More than half of Americans live within 50 miles of a coast. If climate change increases the number and intensity of coastal storms, prudent buyers will move inland to places where they can obtain insurance. Beaches may become nice to visit, but impossible for residences and second homes.

3. A typical buyer will not be able to "see" **endangered, threatened or sensitive (ETS) plant and/or animal species** unless he knows what to look for and is looking for them. The federal Endangered Species Act protects the habitat of selected flora and fauna whose survival is deemed threatened. More than 1,300 species were protected as of 2005; ten species have been recovered to the point of being delisted. The Act is administered primarily by the U.S. Department of Interior's Fish and Wildlife Service (FWS) and the Department of Commerce's Marine Fisheries Service, depending on the habitat location of the species. ETS species not on the coasts fall under the Endangered Species Office of the Fish and Wildlife Service at http://www.endangered.fws.gov. The EPA's Office of Pesticide Programs (OPP) becomes involved when farmers apply pesticides on their farms that are also ETS habitat or near such habitat. (See http://www.epa.gov/espp/how-to.htm.) Both FWS and OPP can provide maps showing ETS species locations, and OPP can provide a list of pesticides that are limited in such areas. Buyers should be aware that individual states may publish state-specific ETS lists. Properties that have unusual topographic features—high elevations, remote/isolated locales, swamps, marshes, caves, remote running water, unusual trees and atypical ecologies—are the most likely places to find rare species. You can obtain a summary of each state's law, policies and programs related to **biodiversity** at http://ipl.unm.edu/cwl/statbio/.

The presence of an ETS species or its habitat can limit, or even prohibit, a buyer from implementing farming, construction and development plans for newly purchased property. The US Fish and Wildlife Service estimates that about seven million acres of private land is regulated under the 1973 ESA. Woods on the property may not be timbered or a field cleared for agricultural purposes where a highly protected species or a "**critical habitat**" is found. The Service found that "…the cost of critical habitat designation to range from an average $77,000 to protect the San Bernandino Mountains bladderpod, a kind of herb, to $915 million over 20 years for the California coastal gnat-catcher, a tiny bird." (Jenny Johnson, "Fight to save 'species over people' law that infuriates developers," Financial Times, April 21, 2006.) Land and water areas can be assigned a no-disturbance status. Fire-prone brush may not be cleared if it shelters a protected species. Building may be prohibited. Assume, until learning otherwise, that you won't be able to do much of anything with private land that is identified as habitat for a federally listed endangered species. This is too harsh an assumption, but it puts you into the proper state of alert. If a federally listed species is present, you must check with the appropriate federal FWS office for advice on what you can and cannot do with the land you are considering buying. Most states have an **office of natural heritage resources** that has maps showing ETS locations and likely habitats. Some of this mapping is based on field research, but much appears to be based on extrapolating from models that predict the probability of certain species being found in certain conditions.

If you have reason to believe that ETS species may be found on a target property, place a contingency clause in your offer that allows you to back out of the contract without penalty if the results of further study are not satisfactory. Sellers can be expected to balk at accepting such contingency clauses since any finding of ETS species or habitat on their property will generally inhibit their ability to sell it. The market for ETS properties may be limited to individual preservationists and conservation groups. Many buyers will view ETS presence and the limitations imposed as liabilities and a price-discount factor. They will, accordingly, pay less for such properties than what might be otherwise expected.

And to every generalization, the exception must be appended. A waterfront farm can likely fetch a higher price because of the nesting bald eagles in the old snag. If a buyer has no plans to build a house, dock or barn near the snag, the eagles add value. If a house, dock and barn already exist, you may be able to watch the eagles from your front porch. As always, the buyer must take responsibility for sorting this out prior to submitting an offer, to the extent he can. For more information look at The Endangered Species Act of 1973, http://endangered/fws/gov/esa.html.

Property rights advocates see the application of the Act as imposing unreasonable, nonsensical and sometimes dangerous restrictions on landowners. Advocates see the Act as a wise conservation measure whose ultimate benefits are still to be reckoned. A program to compensate landowners for being prohibited from using that portion of their property defined as habitat makes sense to me. I endorse buying habitat to protect species and have been involved in several such purchases.

At the end of 2005, Congress was considering various amendments to the 1973 legislation that would either modify or eliminate some provisions that restrict certain human activities in areas designated as critical habitats. These changes would make permitting for logging and construction shorter and less burdensome. The government would under some proposals be expected to compensate landowners when they suffer economic loss from restrictions on the use of their land arising from the Act. (Eric Bontrager, "In Senate, Endangered Species Act Faces an Overhaul," Wall Street Journal, December 27, 2005.) Land buyers need to review their plans against current laws and regulations as part of their pre-purchase scoping.

4. Polychlorinated biphenyls (PCBs) are a class of up to 209 chlorinated organic compounds that were manufactured by Monsanto in the United States between the 1930s and late 1970s. About two to three billion pounds were made, of which about one percent is estimated to remain as an air and water contaminant. They are odorless oily liquids or solids that are clear to light yellow. They were used as coolants and lubricants in electrical equipment because they don't burn. The major sources of PCB pollution are dump sites where it was manufactured or places where it was handled. Old appliances and old fluorescent lighting may contain them.

On country property, I'd be concerned about PCBs in two distinct areas. If the property is on a river (Hudson) or lake (Great Lakes) that has been identified as a PCB carrier, you need to be careful in using the water or eating fish. PCB-polluted waterways are well-known. The other spot I'd look for is a place behind the barn where used hydraulic oil and other waste liquids were dumped on the ground. Kids, in particular, should stay away. PCB exposure is associated with acne-type rashes in adults and more serious impacts in children. (See www.atsdr.cdc.gov/tfacts17.html and www.epagov/opptintr/pub/.) In 2003, EPA decided that private property contaminated with PCBs could be sold. Known PCB sites will be disclosed as part of the seller's legal obligations. But the "backyard" PCB sites, like the behind-the-barn example, will not be disclosed because the seller does not recognize it to be such.

5. Underground storage tanks (USTs) that hold motor fuels may be found on farms. The federal Resource Conservation and Recovery Act (RCRA) governs USTs, as well as solid and hazardous wastes. Farm-sited underground tanks holding motor fuels and heating oil of 1,100 gallons or less in capacity are exempt from federal regulations. Individual states may, however, impose regulations on such tanks. Federal UST regulations (promulgated in 1988, 40 CFR Parts 280 and 281) also do not apply to: tanks of 110 gallons or less capacity, whether or not sited on farms; tanks storing heating oil used where stored; tanks on or above the floor of underground areas; septic tanks, and storm and wastewater systems. All other USTs larger than 110 gallons are federally regulated if they are not found on farms. You are not likely to find an 1,100-gallon plus UST on a farm, other than the very largest.

USTs of 500 gallons or less, however, were reasonably common, because bulk buying of motor fuel and heating oil saved money. These metal tanks leak, sooner or later, and there will be spills and splashes in the refueling area. Removing a UST requires excavating it and all contaminated soil, then disposing of both properly. New, above-ground tanks employ a concrete containment vessel beneath the tank. Removing an old, leaky tank is expensive when done properly and a potential nightmare when environmental agencies become involved. Trucking contaminated dirt and an old tank to a certified disposal site can be very costly. Most farmers abandon a leaking UST rather than remove it when they become aware of the leak. Federal regulations allow this. For that reason, if no other, the amount of contamination is usually limited to the time between when the leak starts, its discovery and when it's drained. The distance petroleum pollution travels in soil is determined by the amount of the contaminant and the characteristics of the soil and ground where the leak occurs. If the tank site is higher in elevation than a water source that people and livestock use, the water should be tested. The more permeable the soil and the rock beneath it, the more area the contaminant plume will affect. Above-ground bulk fuel tanks offer farmowners convenience and savings, but their containment vessels can deteriorate over time too. Disaster strikes when the metal tank leaks into a cracked containment vessel.

It is possible, though unlikely, that you will find a property with an old UST containing one of RCRA's listed Extremely Hazardous Substances (EHS). Some of these EHSs could have been used in farming operations or on rural property used for various industrial purposes. (For information on hazardous substances, see Code of Federal Regulations, CFR Part 302.4; also Federal Register, Vol. 52, Number 77, April 22, 1987.) The owners of a single tank containing any of EHS is subject to federal regulation. Profiles of these chemicals are available on the Chemical Abstract Service (CAS) Registry, which assigns a number to each substance and provides basic information on its nature, uses, hazards and safe usage. Information on the CAS Registry's 23 million organic and inorganic substances can be accessed at www.cas.org/EO/regsys.html#q9. Databases on scientific information and journals, including agricultural science, are available at www.cas.org/casdb.html. EHSs are more likely to be found in dumps than in USTs whose main farm use was for gasoline, diesel fuel and heating oil, though some may have contained farm chemicals and home-made, wood-preservative brews (dirty motor oil, creosote, insecticides etc.; such brews were an early form of recycling). Regulations on toxic and hazardous materials have been and continue to be far less strict for individual farmers than on other businesses. Creosote, a familiar wood preservative, is still available to farmers for farm applications, though it's been otherwise prohibited. Cattle pens and chutes may show the tell-tale black color, even if the odor has worn off. Working farmers appreciate the regulatory leniency, but working buyers need to avoid acquiring a pollution problem created by barnyard chemistry.

Nearly all of the 714,000 active, federally regulated USTs contain petroleum products, not hazardous substances. It is unlikely that any rural land or farm that you scope will have EHSs in old buried tanks. Still, it's worth asking the seller to disclose his knowledge of any USTs or EHSs (just call them chemicals and hazardous substances in your contract) as part of your purchase offer. An old UST with a lot of old petroleum in it is a situation that should be addressed; it is a "defect" in the property that should be disclosed.

Buyers should have water tested for petroleum products and other chemicals where the seller discloses a UST or where the size of the tract suggests that bulk fuels and chemicals may have been purchased. If a tank is contaminating underground and/or surface water, you, as the new owner, may find yourself with some financial liability for the clean up under state law, even though no federal liability exists. Clean-up costs can be very expensive, and you don't want to buy a clean-up site. Old rural gas stations are especially to be avoided. I know of a remodeled station that a buyer bought to be used to process locally raised organic food products. The buyer found himself with a UST in his front-yard parking area, and the projected cost of removal helped to strangle the project. If you find a leaking tank, get the mess sorted out before you submit a purchase contract. Otherwise, use the appropriate adaptation of a contingency clause like this:

Seller warrants to the best of his knowledge and belief that said property contains no underground storage tanks. If such tanks are found subsequently, Seller agrees to bear the full cost of remediation.

If Seller knows of or has belief of underground storage tanks on the property, he agrees to identify these tanks and disclose these sites to Buyer. Buyer then has ___ days to study these conditions. If the results of his investigation are not satisfactory, he may void this offer without penalty and have his security deposit returned in full and in a timely manner.

Buyer may choose at his expense to determine whether these tanks are polluting surface or groundwater resources, as well as obtain estimates of clean-up costs.

Buyer's offer to Seller is based on the assumption that the property contains no such tanks. Buyer is under no obligation to submit a revised offer in light of the presence of underground tanks and their remediation costs.

6. Waste disposal on site/dumps. Many farm properties I know contain abandoned or active dumps that are principally filled with household garbage, old appliances, farm junk, rolls of rusty wire, unusable buckets, odd pieces of this and that, cans, plastic, scrap wood and a cracked toilet. Waste petroleum products and agricultural chemicals may have been included in past years. In my mountainous area, trash was often thrown into a stream, or dumped down a hill or used as fill in a sinkhole—all environmentally bad practices. Dumping from a public road over the side of a hill was also popular. Whatever contaminants were present when they were dumped have probably leached into the soil and aquifer long ago. Active dumps, of course, can be actively polluting. Farm dumps are of more concern to a buyer if trash has been dumped into flowing water, particularly if containers of hazardous substances are present and still leaking. On the other hand, you should not throw a Greenpeace hissy fit at the sight of a rusted oil can in a creek bed. In that case, the odds are that the contaminants have long done whatever harm they're going to do. When you are worried, have a water sample analyzed.

These common farm trash piles can be left alone, removed, possibly burned or buried. While a farm-variety trash dump is visually repugnant, remember that ordinary rubbish is not a Superfund site. You won't die from it. You might ask the seller to clean it up as part of your purchase offer, but don't hold your breath. The buyer might expect a seller to do a *small* amount of such work, though no one likes to clean up his own mess after being made to feel funny about it. A house should be conveyed to the buyer "broom-clean"; the same standard applied to farm trash is defensible. Where the dump is substantial and you have reason to worry about it, get estimates of clean-up costs from local excavators and disposal companies. If it's just rubbish, it can be machine-loaded and hauled off. If there's asbestos or some other hazardous material, removal becomes more complicated and costly. Burying the mess may make sense with some types of rubbish. In most cases, your best option will probably be to do nothing if the pile presents only visual annoyance. Farm dumps may present an environmental danger where they contain significant quantities of petroleum or hazardous substances. Typical farm garbage is not subject to federal regulation, but local or state laws may prohibit current open dumping. Buyers should not let the presence of a small rubbish dump kill a deal, particularly an old dump that is no longer used. Consider it a trove, awaiting excavation by a future archeologist—perhaps one of your own children. If you get self-righteous and snotty about the seller's dump, you may have the door of your deal slammed in your face.

As part of your scoping, make sure to find out how trash is collected. Certain types of junk—wire fencing, wood, appliances, chemical containers—may have to be hauled to a central facility where you pay a fee. Some counties use open roadside collection dumpsters, and some require proof of local residency for use of their central gathering facilities. Public home-by-home trash collection may be the local practice, or private fee-for-service collectors may operate.

Federal "waste" laws (toxic substances, solid waste, FIFRA and CERCLA/Superfund) rarely bear on the type of farms and other rural land that most readers want to purchase. They can, however, be a factor when hazardous materials in significant amounts have been used or disposed of on the site. Under CERCLA, for example, a current landowner could be held responsible for the cost of cleaning up contamination when there has been a release or a threat of release of a hazardous substance from his newly acquired property. Liability under this law is strict, joint and several, and retroactive—and is determined case by case. Strict liability means the owner is responsible for damages without excuse. Joint and several liability means every owner is personally responsible for damages in whole, with the deepest pocket paying the most. Retroactive liability means former owners can be liable as well. Liability is extended without regard to individual fault. Offsetting this blanket of exposure and liability is SARA's (Superfund Amendments and Reauthorization Act of 1986) provision for **innocent landowner immunity**, which exempts from liability those landowners in the chain of title who were innocent of wrongdoing, where the contamination was caused by another, where the landowner had no knowledge of the hazard, where the landowner came to own the property after the contamination had occurred, where the landowner had used "due care" to determine whether the property he was purchasing contained a hazard, and where the landowner exercised reasonable precautions in exercising his ownership rights. Scoping is one protection for the buyer; the other is a **disclosure clause** in the purchase offer by which the seller warrants that no such waste-disposal sites exist on the property.

I recently sent for information on a 9,000-acre property in West Virginia that featured active coal mining, royalty-producing gas wells and merchantable timber. This type of property can throw off a good bit of cash, and sale of the merchantable timber could do a lot to pay down the mortgage immediately. When I looked at the owner-supplied survey, I noticed the following note in fine print: "3.0-acre +/-soil-covered dump unknown contents." The seller's prospectus contained these statements:

While the information contained herein is believed to be accurate to the best of Seller's knowledge, the Seller expressly disclaims any and all liabilities for representations or warranties, if any, express or implied, contained in, or omitted from this Offering Memorandum or any other written or oral communication transmitted or made available to you as a prospective bidder. This includes but is not limited to any representations as to possible yields in terms of coal, oil, gas, timber or other mineral products, which are solely estimates.

All properties will be conveyed "AS IS, WHERE IS, WITH ALL FAULTS" regarding any conditions affecting the properties with no representations or warranties whatsoever expressed or implied.

This language is a very big, very red flag. There's no telling what's in the three-acre dump, for example, and whether contaminants are affecting neighboring houses. The seller is clearly trying to exempt himself from all liability, which means he was trying to shift it to the buyer. This seller, I thought, knew or suspected something that he didn't want to disclose. His written warning amounted to a statement: "I ain't tellin' you nothin'. Take it or leave it." I also discovered that the timber volumes were inflated, and the coal was marginal. What I couldn't determine was what was in the dump. Since the tract joined an industrial/chemical area, I assumed the worst. Had the other assets proved up, an offer might have made sense for the tract less the three acres of dump. Or an escrow could have been set up to fund a dump investigation and resolution. As a rule, I advise buyers to stay away from property where the seller is standing in front of it waving a red flag. I told my client to forget this one, which he did.

7. Livestock create waste. Inevitably. Managing manure can range from mucking out a one-horse stall every couple of weeks and giving the stuff to neighbors for their gardens to operating a computer-run, mechanized system to gather and then treat the daily waste of 5,000 hogs. Where livestock grazes on pasture that permits access to running surface water, pollution will appear downstream. You may find algae, aquatic plant growth, suspended solids and higher-than-normal amounts of manure-related substances, including pathogens, nitrogen and phosphorous. The degree of pollution will depend on the amount of "loading" that goes on upstream, the characteristics of the stream itself and your distance from the source. Watersheds (surface waters) would undoubtedly be cleaner were livestock fenced out of running water, but farmers generally oppose doing this owing to its expense (fencing, gates, installation of water tanks), costs (less pasture to graze), maintenance and inconvenience.

Where livestock production is concentrated in factory-like buildings ("houses"), huge amounts of manure are gathered, stored and eventually applied to fields in one or another manner. Manure's potassium, nitrogen and phosphorous substitute for purchased chemical fertilizer. Farmers are expected to manage these nutrients so as to keep them from polluting waterways. The farmer is expected to apply the manure to his fields at a time and rate appropriate to conditions to prevent pollution. The primary problem in this system is its potential to pollute surface waters, though underground waters can also become contaminated. Much depends on how and when the farmer spreads manure. Nutrient-management plans certainly help prevent water pollution, but the continuing presence of polluted waterways suggest that unregulated, "non-point sources" of pollution, such as manured fields, are still a source of pollution.

8. Oil and gas wells involve environmental hazards in getting the resource out of the ground and transporting it away from the well. The typical pattern is for a driller to work on a pad of an acre or less. The drilling occurs in a small area that is circumscribed by an earthen berm high enough to contain spills. Drilling excavates material that can be contaminated with lubricants and other substances. This is generally not a problem, unless severe weather causes a breach in the berm thus allowing the contamination to get into surface waters. An all-weather road needs to be constructed to the drilling site to provide access for heavy service vehicles. Once the drilling is done, a working well has a "Christmas tree" of pipes left in place. Gas is piped from the wellhead to larger lines, usually underground, for transmission. When oil comes up with natural gas, it is separated at the well and collected in large metal tanks. Gas wells and lines, both above-and below-ground, present explosion hazards, though these rarely occur. Where oil pipelines are above ground, they can be a spaghetti of ugliness and may leak. Pumping stations are noisy. Trucks that pick up oil are heavy and often rut up roads and weaken bridges on property where their tanks and lines are located. Property with oil wells are more environmentally burdened than those with gas-only wells. Abandoned oil tanks and pipes may be left on the property to rot. Old leases allow mineral lessees (developers) to do pretty much what they want with the surface, consistent with current state law. A lease you (lessor/owner of minerals) sign with a lessee can include restrictions on surface use.

Coal is mined from Pennsylvania to Alabama, Ohio to the Midwest, Texas and into the Rockies. Abandoned underground (deep) mines can present problems of surface subsidence, fractured water tables and acid (sulfuric) drainage into surface waters, among other things. Underground fires can burn in these old works for years. Old piles of discarded mine wastes are unsightly, can burn and can be unstable when used to impound water. Prior to federal surface-mining regulation in the late 1970s, abandoned surface mines often left high walls winding around a mountain and unstable banks on the down slope where rock and dirt (overburden) had been dumped. Federal law and regulation now require restoring such surface mines to their approximate original contour and controlling water pollution from active mines. Reclamation involves revegetation to control erosion. Flooding has been a major problem in some areas where mountain-top-removal surface mining has occurred.

Active underground and surface mining continue to create contentious environmental situations—flooding, blasting noise, collateral damage, dust, noise, traffic, road damage, water pollution, among others—in areas next to and around the operations. For that reason, I would be very cautious about buying property near an active mine or quarry.

9. Inhalation of air-borne, invisible **asbestos** fibers causes asbestosis (a disease that causes increasing amounts of scar tissue to form in the lungs), mesothelioma (a cancer in the lining of the lungs) and other cancers of the lung, stomach, large intestine, kidneys, larynx and rectum. The more fibers inhaled, the greater the risk of disease. Easily crumpled (friable), disintegrating asbestos is highly dangerous; asbestos that is not friable and disintegrating is not immediately dangerous, because fibers are not being released.

Homes built before 1981 might contain asbestos in the form of pipe or boiler insulation, external shingles, vinyl floor tile, acoustical ceilings ("cottage-cheese" ceilings), plasterboard, cement (glue), fireproofing insulation, roofing insulation (Zonolite is the brand name of the W.R. Grace Company product) or as safety boards shielding walls and floors from woodstoves and fireplaces. Asbestos should be taken seriously. Homeowners are put at risk when asbestos products are disturbed or are disintegrating, thus releasing fibers that are then inhaled. As of 2001, there were between 150,000 and 200,000 lawsuits pending against companies that produced, sold or installed asbestos products, and 300,000 others have been resolved. (Sabrina Jones, "Grace under Pressure," Washington Post, March 19, 2001.) Twenty-six companies have had to seek bankruptcy protection, and claimants were awarded about $20 billion between 1981 and 2001. Six class actions and more than 121,000 claims have been filed against W.R. Grace alone arising from its Zonolite attic insulation. In 2006, class-action lawyers continue to advertise for clients who have suffered asbestos injury. Some of these many asbestos claims are without merit, but many are legitimate.

If the asbestos product is not releasing fibers, you are not in immediate danger. If you suspect disintegrating tile floor, it is probably better to lay a new floor over the old one than to remove the tile, which would release fibers. Similarly, encasing intact asbestos pipe insulation with a sandwich wrap of heavy plastic and duct tape should stabilize the situation and prevent fiber release. If, on the other hand, you find floor tile or pipe insulation actively disintegrating, crumbling, or flaking, then it will have to be removed by a specialist. If you suspect a house has asbestos attic insulation, you may be able to have a specialist contain it in place. You want to avoid any activity—attic fans, human movement, air infiltration—that stirs the insulation, releasing fibers. Any removal work must contain and remove all the fibers released in the removal, a process that involves specialized equipment and training. Both the material and all released (invisible) fibers have to be taken out and disposed of properly. If you suspect asbestos, carefully cut off a small piece of the material (then place it in a plastic bag) and have it tested at a lab. If you find yourself facing a large asbestos-removal problem, get a couple of cost estimates and then determine how to proceed with the contract.

The seller may or may not know he has an asbestos problem. You can certainly ask him to disclose any asbestos as part of your purchase-offer contract. Don't be surprised if he is miffed by your inquiries and sampling. Be especially vigilant on properties being sold as is.

In addition to asbestos in older rural houses, you might look for it in older, insulated farm buildings, shops where asbestos sheets were used as pads for hot metal, around water pipes and furnaces in old poultry houses and trash dumps where you might find a pile of deteriorating house shingles.

10. One country smell that is both pleasant and dangerous is **wood smoke**. Many rural homes, both old and new, burn wood for heat as I do. Fireplaces continue to be a popular feature in new-home construction. The heat from woodstoves and fireplaces is direct, and many individuals, including my wife, prefer it to other forms. The smoke and combustion products from burning wood, however, present health hazards to users, neighbors and communities that shouldn't be ignored. Wood-burning results in smoke that contains over 200 chemicals and chemical-compound groups. These include substances that have been shown to cause various cancers, which occur more often in individuals exposed to wood smoke. The air-borne particulate matter in wood smoke ranges from invisible particles that penetrate into the bottom of the human lung where oxygen is exchanged for carbon dioxide to larger particles that can cause respiratory problems in the nose and upper respiratory tract. The dust that you find on your book shelves and television in a house burning wood may be of less concern than the smaller particles. Each time you open the door of a woodstove, a bit of smoke is released into the room, especially if the flue is not drawing well. Old stoves tend to be leaky and not air-tight. If the house you are looking at is tightly caulked, well insulated, with modern windows, you may not have sufficient exchange of outside air for inside air. Smoke particulate will hang around. The dust generated from cleaning out wood ash, flue pipes and chimneys (creosote, tars, etc.) contains concentrations of toxic chemicals; don't mix stove ash into your garden soil. Burning plastics and other household trash exposes the homeowner and his neighbors to additional harmful substances.

Wood smoke can create problems in a neighborhood. Smoke from a neighbor's fireplace, indoor woodstove or outdoor woodstove can infiltrate your non-wood-smoke-burning house, leading to the same kind of harmful exposure. The worst wood smoke generators in my experience are the large **outdoor wood-burning stoves** that are scaled up to supply a house with hot water (for heat and personal use) and operate year round. Unlike an indoor wood stove or fireplace, the tops of their flues are relatively close to the ground. When their smoke is blown around, it can hang low as it visits your house. Outdoor stoves can put out a fair amount of smoke, depending, of course, on the type of wood being burned, intensity of the fire and the design of the stove. Look for a shed with a metal flue near the house; the seller will know whether neighbors use these furnaces.

Local communities in a number of states now regulate the quantity of wood smoke by banning wood-burning devices other than pellet stoves or woodstoves certified by EPA as low-emission and efficient, and requiring gas-burning rather than wood-burning fireplaces. When choosing a heating system, consider that a wood-burning fireplace emits 50 grams/hour of particulate; conventional woodstove, 30 grams/hour; certified woodstove, 7.5 grams/hour; pellet heater, 1 gram/hour; gas fireplace, 0.07 grams/hour. (See "Reducing Wood Smoke Pollution," Bay Area Monitor, March/April 1999; http://bayareamonitor.org/mar99/woodsmok.html.) For all the bad news, go to: Burning Issues/Clean Air Revival, Inc., P.O. Box 1045, Point Arena, California, 95468; 707-882-3601; 707-882-3602 FAX; e-mail: PM10Mary@mcn.org; http://www.burningissues.org.

I have used non-certified woodstoves for years as our primary heat source. As I type these words, my old Vermont Castings Defiant is burning yellow locust in our living room as it has since 1984. Newer stoves are cleaner and more efficient. I think there's enough credible evidence to choose a different, cleaner heating system even though wood is the cheapest heating fuel available to most farms. (Cheapness assumes you already own a pick-up truck, chainsaw, personal equipment and logging stuff.) If you must heat with wood, you can reduce wood-smoke particulate inside your home by using a certified stove; maintaining its seals, gaskets and catalytic converter; burning seasoned high-Btu hardwoods (locust, hickory, sugar maple and oaks, not pine); burning hot fires rather than smoldering, dampered ones; and using a good-quality air-purification unit to remove particulate. The older the stove, the more pollution it will generate for a given quantity of wood.

I think the evidence is that wood-burning as your primary heat source raises your chances of various diseases and respiratory impairments, and adversely impacts your neighbors and community. You will not drop dead from a crackling fire in your fireplace, but the risk-to-benefit calculation is not any different from smoking cigarettes—and some evidence suggests that it's worse. Since wood-burning rural houses are more dispersed, wood smoke health risks from air pollution are greater in more densely populated areas, particularly those that are located in topographical bowls or where there's limited wind. If you're looking for a summer and occasional weekend retreat from the city, you're probably no worse off in front of a country fireplace than you are in your urban apartment breathing diesel fumes from buses and trucks. I write that sentence with regret.

11. Carbon monoxide is an odorless, invisible, tasteless, highly flammable gas that is a combustion product of burning hydrocarbons. Everyone knows not to sit in a closed garage with the car engine running because of the danger of being poisoned by carbon monoxide. The combination of unvented or badly adjusted fuel-burning appliances and tightly insulated and sealed (with caulk) houses can produce illness (dizziness, fainting, nausea, headaches, shortness of breath) or death. About 1,500 Americans die and about 10,000 become ill from CO poisoning annually. Old houses, in the country even those that have had their insulation upgraded, usually exchange air sufficiently to keep CO from building up inside. Be careful, however, in basements and farm shops. If you find yourself with a seller who boasts of the tightness of his recently constructed home, I would be concerned about CO if the house featured fuel-burning space heaters, unvented appliances or woodstoves. If you buy such a place, you should install CO monitors as a precaution and consider changing the heating plan. Combustion of gas, fuel oil, coal and wood creates CO; the less efficient the combustion, the more CO is generated. Wood and coal when burned directly in a stove are the worst of the lot per unit of energy.

12. House buyers often test for **radon,** an invisible, odorless gas that can be both airborne and in the water. Indoor radon is the second-leading cause of lung cancer and high levels are found in nearly one of every 15 U.S. homes. (See www.epa.gov/radon/; National Radon Information Line, 1-800-767-7236; and Radon FIX-IT Program, 1-800-644-6999.) A sampling test kit and analysis can be purchased for $9.95 at 1-800-557-2366. Hardware stores have them as well. Take the sample in the basement where gas is most likely to concentrate.

Radon gas is present in areas where underlying minerals and rock, such as shale, granite and phosphate, contain small amounts of uranium that decay to radium which produces radon. Radon is associated with specific locations around the country—including the eastern divide of the Rocky Mountains, Upper Midwest, Pacific Northwest, eastern Appalachians and most of the East Coast from New Orleans to Maine. The radon risk is higher in air-tight houses. Older houses that are not tight allow an exchange of air, outside for inside. This dilutes and flushes radon-rich inside air. New houses, particularly those with basements that are "wrapped," insulated and caulked, don't leak as much, which is good for heat and bad for radon. If the sample indicates a high concentration, the solution is to ventilate the basement/crawlspace better, either passively through additional vents or mechanically with fans. The buyer can use a high sample result to negotiate a better price with a seller who understands that radon is a real hazard; the buyer is not likely to get much of anywhere with a seller who thinks radon gas is a bunch of foolishness because he's lived in the house for umpteen years and hasn't died of lung cancer, yet. Give the radon results to the seller and tell him that he should disclose them to every buyer who comes after you inasmuch as radon is a latent, material defect in his property.

I once considered buying a very large ante-bellum house. I asked the owner, himself ante-bellum in his attitude toward environmental regulation, to allow me to place two radon samplers in his basement for 24 hours. Since I lived some distance from this property, he reluctantly agreed to send in the samples with the pre-posted containers I provided. He never did. This individual also objected to a home inspection and was offended when his pipe insulation turned out to contain asbestos. I doubted that radon would be a problem, given the limestone geology in the area. The asbestos could have been wrapped and sealed. While I waited for the radon results, he signed another contract. I was miffed that he had not sent in the samples as agreed, but I was thankful in the end that I did not buy a house that cost $2,000 a month to heat in the winter.

In urban and suburban areas, environmental testing and home inspections are routine. They have been less routine in small towns and the countryside, but, I think, they are becoming increasingly so. Many sellers will get fed up with 15 or 20 hazard-related tests; I would too. If a buyer insists on testing for everything, it's likely that a seller will do the sale with the buyer who probes the least and is willing to buy more or less, as is. Each buyer must gauge the level of tolerance a seller has for being inspected and analyzed. If you know from your research that radon is not likely to be found, you can consider not testing for it. The line I'm proposing is finely drawn: test enough to find out what you need to know, but not so much as to kill your own deal.

13. Working farms typically generate a variety of **chemical and hazardous exposures and wastes** in the normal course of raising livestock and crops in conventional ways. The exact substances will vary with the type of farming. Conventional farmers are routinely exposed to a variety of harmful substances from tractor-generated diesel fumes (particulates), dusts and pesticides to disease-carrying livestock and too much sunshine on their skin. Farmers show higher than expected rates of certain cancers and respiratory problems. As a buyer, you will have exposure to various farming-related substances if you do the farm work yourself. Whether you do this work or hire it out, you should read the health and safety literature that comes with each product regarding handling, application and personal protective gear. You can also obtain the appropriate **Materials Safety Data Sheet (MSDS)** from the U.S. Department of Labor's Office of Safety and Health Administration (OSHA). Individual manufacturers also provide MSDSs on chemicals they make. www.ec.gc.ca/science/sandejean99/current_e.html and www.rtpnc.epa.gov/naaqsfin/pmhealth.html are two comprehensive sites for MSDS information. The sheets spell out the personal and occupational hazards of each chemical.

Most field chemicals that are now sprayed or dusted break down into their constituent elements over time. If a buyer is concerned about possible pollution of this type, he should make a list of the chemicals he believes were used in recent years and investigate the break-down times. A water sample can be analyzed for specific chemicals and substances that might be of concern from chemical use. You should ask the seller where agricultural chemical containers were dumped on the farm and how he got rid of extra chemicals that he didn't need or were somehow contaminated. Farms that are cattle/grazing/hay operations generally have had few chemical inputs, though a crop like corn may have been routinely sprayed. Animal medications and insecticidal waste products are generally tossed into the household trash; that's what I did in any case. Conventionally farmed row crops and orchards always use chemicals to control weeds, pests and disease. The seller should know what chemicals were applied, frequency and method of application, quantity used in a typical application, what was done with containers and where the equipment wash up took place. The most common chemicals and substances involve petroleum products, paints, solvents, wood preservatives, livestock de-licer, pesticides, insecticides, fungicides and fertilizers.

14. Rural air-borne pollution comes in several versions. Dust from mining and quarrying operations is a common problem. Long-range atmospheric transport of pollutants—mainly flowing west to east—produces adverse effects on both human beings and the environment. Coal-fired electric generating plants in the Ohio River Basin, for example, are linked to tree mortality and acidification of lakes and streams in the Mid-Atlantic states and Northeast.

The USEPA announced in December, 2004 that 224 counties in 20 states don't meet clean-air standards for fine particulates, or soot, 2.5 microns or less in diameter. This type of pollution is associated with emissions from power plants, gasoline and diesel engines, wood-burning stoves and the like. Much of Southern California, the New Haven to Washington, D.C. corridor, the Cleveland to Pittsburgh area, cities along the Ohio River and counties around Atlanta, Birmingham, Chicago, Detroit and St. Louis are among those affected. Particles this size penetrate into the lower part of the lung where oxygen and carbon dioxide are exchanged. Premature death, bronchitis and other diseases are associated with particulates. Federal standards are expected to be met in these counties by 2010, but five-year extensions are available. (Associated Press, "EPA says 224 counties fail to meet clean air standards," Staunton News-Leader, December 18, 2004.) While air pollution is concentrated in metropolitan areas, the downwind countryside may also have higher levels than you would assume to be the case. County-level air-pollution data are available from the USEPA.

The Associated Press assembled a map of the United States showing risk intensity from industrial air pollution by Census blocks. (The Associated Press, "Unhealthy air casts shadow on blacks, poor," Staunton News-Leader, December 14, 2005.) Poor and minority neighborhoods tended to have higher risk than white, affluent areas. Map 13-1 shows the AP's findings. What intrigued me was the large number of high-risk neighborhoods—indicated by darker shadings—in rural areas where intuition would not expect them. My guess is that these hot spots are related to the presence of smelters, refineries, paper-making plants, coal- or oil-fired generation plants and the like.

MAP 13-1
U.S. Industrial Air Pollution, 2000

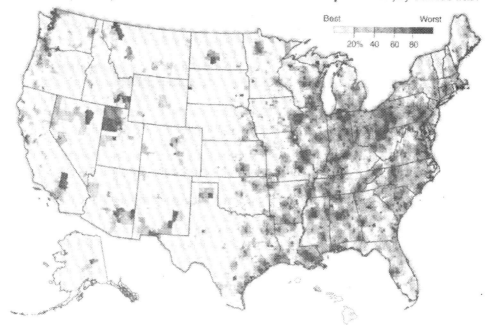

Industrial air pollution hot spots

T he Associated Press combined government industrial air pollution data with Census figures to map areas with the highest risk to human health and compared their demographics.

Relative per capita health risk from industrial air pollution, by Census tract

Every country property that I have looked at during the last 15 years has involved at least one of the environmental issues discussed above. The degree of seriousness, however, ranged from obvious deal-killers to ignore and proceed. I no longer assume rural property is environmentally "clean" just because it looks that way. When my initial screening turns up a property that I consider for purchase, I might work up a short environmental history of the property as part of my scoping. I explore the environmental issues I've outlined in this chapter, and then keep my eyes open for other snags. Talk to the seller and the broker to determine what they know, don't know and what they might allow.

You can also include a broad-brush **environmental-disclosure provision** in your purchase contract:

> **Seller warrants that he has disclosed to Buyer in writing all conditions in, on, under, around or otherwise affecting the property of an environmental nature that could adversely impact the Buyer's full use, possession and enjoyment of this Property.**

You can talk through your list of environmental concerns and even hand the seller a yes-no disclosure sheet for him to complete. A provision of this type protects both seller and buyer. The seller protects himself by disclosing what he knows; the buyer is protected to the extent that he is informed. The real-estate agent is also protected. (I am assuming that most states now have an **environmental-disclosure statement** that a seller signs with a listing agent since even Virginia now requires one.) If a seller balks at negotiating a purchase because of this disclosure requirement, I'd find out why. Environmental defects can be dangerous and hugely expensive in the worst case. Their consequences make inquiry worth the effort, even when you feel that you are pushing the seller's envelope of patience.

WATER HAZARDS

Water is usually the venue of most environmental concerns in rural property. Surface water is found in lakes, ponds, streams and wetlands. Underground water is tapped from springs (at or near the surface) and aquifers, which are subterranean water-bearing rock formations. Springs are a common source of rural water for households and livestock alike. They occur where a surface opening allows underground water to escape. Springs and surface water (both ponds and waterways) are readily seen on topographical maps using a 1"=300' scale, where a contour line is drawn at every 40-foot elevation interval. A local surveyor can provide a map of this sort for your target property or you can lift it for free from www.topozone.com. (Less detailed topographical maps are available from the U.S. Geological Service, and are often sold at local sporting goods stores and bookstores.) The topographical map will not show wet-weather springs that only appear in the rainy season. Continuous springs produce anywhere from a couple of hundred gallons per day to thousands. A spring is "good" if it keeps flowing during dry weather, even though the volume is less than normal. Wells, dug or drilled, provide about 80 percent of rural water, usually through the use of pumps.

Chapter 14 discusses water as a resource and the legal framework that has developed to resolve water-related disputes. Water-pollution issues can be governed by state or federal laws, or both. Chapter 14 looks at alternative ways that states govern water and certain pollution issues within their borders.

Rural water—both surface and underground—can be contaminated with many different **pollutants**, both natural and man-made. One of the first "looks" a buyer should cast is at the property "above" the target property, because water flows downhill along the path of least resistance. Do not assume that water flows south; water flowing downhill may be heading north as is the case with the upper reaches of the Potomac River watershed. Property "above you" is land higher in elevation, as well as land that drains upstream of you.

Natural and synthetic chemicals used on upstream farms can contaminate downstream water through storm-water runoff that gets into surface waters. If your uphill/upstream neighbor is applying fertilizer or chemicals in quantities beyond the ability of his land to absorb or break them down, some will end up downhill and downstream. It is harder for chemicals to work their way into underground aquifers than it is for them to contaminate surface waters. Property in intensively worked agricultural areas should have drinking water tested for nitrates and other chemicals associated with natural and chemical fertilizers, pesticides and petroleum compounds. Chemical pollutants can contaminate underground water supplies, particularly in areas underlain by porous rock such as limestone.

In thinking about the purity of the underground water supply in a rural area, the buyer needs to determine what substances are being used on and around the target property that might be a pollution hazard. It will probably be easier to find out what's being used than to figure out if they are being used in safe amounts. Since the agricultural practices of individual farmers are rarely monitored and the water-borne pollution from individual farms is not measured, a buyer in such an area is really looking for a pollutant that turns up at the tap or in some other obvious way.

The buyer might begin by asking the seller and the **county extension agent** what chemical substances have been typically used on the target property and adjoining properties. The extension agent should be able to identify commonly used fertilizers and chemicals in the area of the property, and direct you to publications and resources for more information.

The county extension service is associated in each state with a public university whose faculty is available to residents for advice as part of their appointments. In Virginia, for example, the county extension system is associated with Virginia Polytechnic Institute and State University (Virginia Tech), and each agent is a local Tech representative. The agent will have access to publications and research, much of which is available at little cost through the U.S. Superintendent of Documents or directly from extension-based universities around the country. Extension faculty often post their research on the Internet. Buyers should be aware that many agricultural academics are advocates of conventional, production-oriented agricultural and may deemphasize certain environmental hazards associated with conventional farming operations. Certain faculty may be paid consultants to agricultural-producer groups. I have seen faculty experts on beef cattle and poultry production marginalize environmental problems that might constrain production. Faculty specializing in environmental science may be more helpful on agricultural hazards. State organic agriculture associations will be able to direct a buyer to literature on the hazards of various agricultural chemicals.

If a large-scale agricultural operation drains onto your target property, you must ask questions about the neighbor's farming practices in a tactful, non-accusatory manner. Since both surface and underground water can be polluted by agricultural and non-agricultural activities higher in the **watershed (drainage)** than your target property, the buyer should become knowledgeable about likely sources of pollution upstream. The county sanitarian and/or the local public health official are reliable sources of information about known water-borne pollutants affecting drinking water in the general area, if not on your target property. They will know about nitrate pollution if it has materialized as a health concern. You can also call a couple of local water-treatment companies and ask if they have installed water-purification systems in your property's neighborhood. If they have, ask about the nature of the problem, what pollutants are causing it, what kind of systems have been installed to protect water supplies, and their cost. When you are walking through the house, examine the place where the water-supply line enters. If you see equipment other than a water pump, holding tank and water heater, find out what it is, what it does and why it's needed. If it's on the floor, it's probably a sump pump to drain a chronically wet basement. If it's in line, it could be something as simple as a fiber filter to catch suspended solids, such as dirt and grit. Or it could be a purification unit, which may involve ultra-violet rays, chlorination or other means. Systems designed to control bacteria do nothing to remove or neutralize chemical pollutants.

Nitrate pollution of groundwater is a human-health hazard usually arising in farm areas from the practice of ground disposal of animal manure and poultry-house litter. Nitrate concentrations are related to the amount of urea (ammonia) in the waste. Nitrogen is a beneficial fertilizer, but high concentrations of nitrate (nitrogen/oxygen compound) in the water can hurt adults and cause potentially fatal methelmoglobinemia (blue-baby disease) in infants. A farmer who is regularly applying poultry litter or manure to his fields in the dead of winter (when the land's absorption capacity is lowest) may be applying too much. Excess nitrogen, phosphate and potassium will run into both surface waters and groundwater.

If you find yourself considering property "below" a dairy farm, poultry operation or CAFO, get in touch with the county's **soil conservation officer** who is usually found through the local office of the U.S. Department of Agriculture's Farm Service Agency and the local **water-conservation district official**. Many counties now require such farms and operations to develop and follow a farm-specific **nutrient-management plan** that sets forth when, how and how much waste/litter/manure may be spread on their fields. These individuals may know of water contamination from such operations on or around your target property. The soil conservation official will be able to tell you about the geology and soil types in the area, which will suggest whether underground water sources are likely to be polluted and how far the pollution plume may spread. The water-conservation officer may be the issuer/designer of nutrient management plans; he may also be involved in monitoring runoff and enforcement actions as well. Unless there is some compelling—and I mean *really* compelling—reason to buy a property in the midst of these types of farms, I urge non-farm buyers to avoid them. You will not like the noise, smell and pollution they generate, and you will be able to do little about any of that.

Potable water is safe to drink. Your water supply in the country should be reasonably clear, free of man-made chemicals, free of harmful bacteria, taste good and not smell bad. In the best of circumstances, you will be able to draw water from a spring or well without doing much, if anything, to it. We've drunk spring water for more than 22 years, sometimes using a fabric filter and sometimes not. The bacteria count is probably higher than it should probably be, but neither we nor any guest has become ill from it. You want to avoid circumstances where you have to create your own little municipal water-treatment system at the end of which you end up with chlorinated water, no different than the most urban municipal supply.

The most common farm-based contaminant that affects potability is *e. coliform* **bacteria.** High levels of this bacteria, which is associated with mammalian waste, can cause dysentery and typhoid fever, among other unpleasantries. Sometimes, you can remove the source of pollution by fencing livestock further away from the spring or well. The problem is harder to solve if its source is a neighbor fertilizing his field with manure. In that event, the cheapest way of dealing with the bacteria is to treat the water before it comes out of your tap. You might find that the farmhouse draws from a spring that is being polluted by the farmhouse's own waste system. The solution is to replace or relocate this system, develop a new water source, or treat the incoming water. The first two solutions can range from $2,500 to $20,000; the third is less than $1,000 spent on a purification unit.

If the source is a neighbor spreading manure or litter on his fields just upslope of your spring, it is not likely that he will want to change his practice. Before you say bad things that will instantly create trench warfare between you and your new neighbor, consider that the local judge is not likely to side with your complaint since the practice preceded your ownership. Rise above your anger as you write a check for $1,000 to install a treatment system. If your neighbor agrees to not spread above your spring, consider yourself blessed and show him your appreciation. Offer him the cost of the treatment system in reimbursement and hope that he takes it. Then you're square, which is where you want to be in the country.

E. coliform is the common indicator for contaminated water. Several water-borne diseases are associated with contamination from sewage, human or animal waste. *E. coli* 0157:H7, one strain of Escherichia coli, is found on some cattle farms. When infected cattle are processed, it can be incorporated into hamburger. Live cattle can infect water where you swim or from which you drink. **Giardiasis** is a diarrheal illness that is caused by a one-celled parasite, *Giardia intestinalis*, which lives in the intestines of people and animals and is released in feces. It contaminates surface waters, such as lakes, streams, rivers, pools and springs as well as hot tubs and swimming pools. It can turn up in very remote places. Cryptosporidium is a germ that causes diarrhea and cramps, and Shigellosis is caused by Shigella, a bacteria that produces similar intestinal distress. All of these illnesses can be picked up in country surface waters that are used for drinking, washing utensils and swimming. For more information, see www.cdc.gov/ncidod/dpd/parasites/listing.htm.

Bacteria can be controlled with a home-chorination unit, radiation, ultraviolet rays and other methods. An elevated count can sometimes be cheaply fixed by regular **"shocking"** of the water system. Add a gallon of bleach at the water source, such as a spring box or well. Open the taps in the house and allow the highly treated water to flush through the system: Do NOT drink or use this water! When the tap water no longer smells and tastes of bleach, take another sample. The count should test out at an acceptable level. Most spring systems should be shocked every year or two; it's easy, cheap and effective.

Water-purification systems for the home differ in cost, complexity and objectionable qualities. Where the problem cannot be fixed at the source, the owner has no better choice. Be careful with lakefront properties where the shoreline is heavily developed with homes using septic-tanks and drinking water is pumped directly from the lake.

As a rule, the deeper the water source, the cleaner the water. Deep wells, on the other hand, are expensive to drill and can be a maintenance bother. Water from a drilled well should not be contaminated with bacteria since the earth between surface and aquifer should stop the bacteria from reaching the water. Some dirt and rock are better at filtering pollution than others. Property-owners on limestone karst should be aware that a plume of bacteria can travel a mile or more underground through this porous, cave-riddled rock. Limestone that is less porous provides good drinking water. If you see sinkholes on the surface, ask about karst on and around your property.

A **water sample** and laboratory analysis can usually be performed within two or three weeks. Any result that exceeds federally established levels, which both your lab and local officials (sanitarian and/or public health officer) will know, would be reason for concern. The lab you use will provide the sample kit (s) you will need and sampling instructions. Make sure to sterilize the tap by putting sufficient flame to it, and then fill the sample bottle and send it to the lab. Ask the lab to test for common substances, such as **total hardness, nitrate, iron, chloride, sodium, pH, fluoride, copper, corrosion index, sulfate, manganese, total dissolved solids, total coliform and *e. coliform* bacteria.** Testing for these 14 substances costs about $150. Test for **lead** if you suspect the supply line, and **petroleum products** if you suspect that. Make sure to inform the lab whether the sample is treated (chlorinated, filtered for particulates, etc.) or direct from the source. You should test the water with and without treatment.

Public water systems must monitor for and control contaminants. The Safe Drinking Water Act (SWDA) and the SWDA Amendments set forth the requirements and establish procedures these systems must meet. Rural public systems draw from reservoirs, lakes, rivers, springs and wells. Each water-treatment plant must publish an annual water quality report, explaining the water's sources, what it contains and how it compares to regulatory standards. SWDA requires water-treatment plants to test for **microbial contaminants** (viruses and bacteria) and turbidity that come from sewage, septic systems, livestock and wildlife; **inorganic contaminants** (salts and metals, including fluoride, copper and lead) that can either occur naturally or result from wastewater discharges, oil and gas production, mining, farming and runoff from urban and residential areas; **pesticides and herbicides** that come from agriculture, urban and residential sources; **organic chemical contaminants** (synthetic and volatile organic chemicals) that are by-products of industrial processes, petroleum production, gas stations, septic systems and urban runoff; **radioactive contaminants** that either are naturally occurring or the result of mining and oil and gas production. Certain contaminants, including sodium and sulfate, are unregulated but are often tested anyway. If you are moving to an individual residence or small town in a rural area and are concerned about drinking water, read the water-treatment plant's last three annual reports. If you have concern about a particular chemical or contaminant, talk to the plant manager providing your water, or call the state office that monitors the plant. (You can call the EPA's Safe Drinking Water Hotline, 1-800-426-4791, to obtain more information on contaminants, standards and procedures.)

Very old homes may still rely on **lead pipes** to bring water from a source to the house. The danger of **lead poisoning** from such pipe is especially acute among young children, but lead in drinking water can also harm adults. Some historians pin the decline of the Roman Empire to its leaders poisoning themselves in this fashion. Ask the seller about the age of the water system he uses and what type of pipes are underground. Make sure to have the water lab test for lead whenever an older property relies on its own installed water supply. Lead pipe is now more likely to be found between the water source and the house than inside the house. Old lead pipe often snakes around and may have bulbous joints. Look at the pipe that comes into the basement from the ground. Lead pipe is soft, grey and silvery when you scratch it. Galvanized pipe is silvery, and iron pipe is hard. Lead leaches into water. Houses built before 1930 are most likely to have lead pipes, and those built before 1988 probably used lead-based solder on copper pipe fittings. Brass faucets and fittings made before 1986 are likely to have a lead content higher than eight percent, which is the threshold imposed by the SDWA amendments. Wells can be the source of lead where brass or bronze pumps are used, or lead shot or lead "wool" was used to keep sand out of the water. In-house lead filters are available. See www.propex.com/C_f_env_leadpip.htm and www.checnet.org/healthhouse/education/articles-detail.asp?Main_ID=147. Washington, D.C. decided in 2004 to replace 23,000 lead service lines by 2010 at a cost of $350 million owing to elevated lead levels in household taps.

Rural home-water supplies may also taste of **iron** or **sulfur**, making them unpalatable or unusable. This is a problem in the source of the water and is often difficult to eliminate. Look for iron's tell-tale redness in a toilet bowl and around sink drains. You will smell sulfur-rich water as rotten eggs. Both minerals can be controlled, but the equipment is expensive.

Groundwater can also be **hard** or **soft**, both of which present use problems. Calcium and magnesium cause water hardness which, in sufficient quantities, affects washing and cooking. Soft water is hard to lather and wash with; you never feel rinsed off. Both hard and soft water can be treated.

Spring and well water will also invariably contain bits of one thing or another—"suspended solids," such as particles of dirt, rock and sand. A fabric-type filter cartridge installed in line between the water source and the tap will trap most of this stuff. You will need to change the filter every couple of months; if your water pressure begins to fall at the shower head upstairs, one problem may be a severely dirty filter. Washing machines usually have tiny brass screens in the couplings that connect their flexible hoses to hot and cold taps. These cone-shaped screens keep grit from getting into the wash. Every so often, you should unscrew the couplings and clean the screens. As the crud builds up, the water flow into the washing machine will diminish. This lesson cost me $50 for a Sears house call years ago after I could not figure out why we had good water pressure and flow at our kitchen sink but only a trickle coming into our nearby washing machine. Whatever you find in your washing-machine screen will be in your drinking water as well, unless you have one or more filters.

Harmless water-borne **minerals** also build up in metal pipes and heating radiators. Older farmhouses may still have galvanized steel piping (a metallic grey-silvery color) that, over time, clogs like an artery. Calcium compounds, in particular, drop out of the water chemically and mechanically, and build up inside pipes. I have replaced 3/4-inch galvanized water pipe whose functioning diameter had been reduced to no more than 1/4 inch—thus explaining the lack of water pressure and flow in our second-floor shower. Galvanized pipe should be replaced when it's causing diminished flow and pressure owing to mineral build up. Replacing internal water pipes to and from sinks, toilets, showers and radiators can involve a significant amount of money, particularly where floors, walls and ceilings have to be ripped out and replaced.

Buyers should remember that underground water is an open system, subject to whatever gets into it. Sometimes it defies our best efforts to make assumptions. A neighbor of mine built a new house and drilled a well into a limestone karst formation 15 years ago. The water was plentiful and potable. Ten years later, heavy rains and a large flood recast the underground water flows through much of the valley where we both live. The flow in the aquifer that he tapped was subsequently polluted by the manure of livestock grazing at a higher elevation, a practice that had not affected his water previously. The same flooding reduced the flows to two springs on our farm, which we discovered in subsequent droughts.

A buyer may find a **cistern** for drinking water in dry areas. Cisterns are large, (usually) covered containers that collect rainwater from roofs. They can be as simple as a metal holding tank or an underground, concrete vault. Unfiltered cistern water will be no cleaner than the rain itself, the roof that catches the rain and the container in which it is held. Roofs will also contribute bird droppings, grit, paint flecks, twigs, insects and so on. Sometimes a buyer will find a sand-type filter on the line going into the cistern and other filters on the line coming out of the cistern to the house. Cisterns usually indicate one of two things: a lack of rainfall that forces the property owner to use rainwater or a problem with water in the ground. Virgin Gorda in the British Virgin Islands has a state-of-the-art desalinization plant that uses reverse-osmosis technology, but because the resulting water is then chlorinated some residents prefer to continue drawing drinking water from their cisterns. These cisterns were built to solve the problem of scant rainfall in a near-desert environment, and now solve an unanticipated "taste" problem. Cisterns may also suggest a problem with water quality—iron or sulfur contamination, for instance. In some places, cisterns were used because they were a cheaper way to provide a house with potable water than the alternatives. I've seen cisterns used on ridge tops where the owner could not afford to pump water from a spring down slope, or electricity was not available when the house was built. Properties located in remote areas are more secure for having a large cistern for fire protection. If a cistern supplies drinking water, it must be tested and the system inspected by someone who knows what to look for—cracks/leaks in the container, odors, visible contaminants and colonies of flora and fauna. Crayfish and salamanders are especially fond of these man-made habitats. If you find yourself with the unenviable task of having to clean a cistern, use extreme caution with bleach in closed or limited-air environments. Make sure there is adequate ventilation, and, if there isn't, don't enter without a self-contained, air-supply apparatus. Never clean a closed cistern by yourself.

When you walk through the seller's house, you should test for **water pressure** and **flow volume** by opening four or five taps at the same time. Pressure refers to the force with which water emerges from the tap; flow volume is the amount of water that emerges. They are not the same, though we tend to think of them that way. If you open the tap for ten minutes, you may find a steady volume with weak pressure or weakening pressure over time with concomitant reduction in volume. You want to find steady volume under good, steady pressure. Make sure to check the tap at the end of the line (farthest from the pump) with intermediary taps open. If the last tap still shows good flow and pressure, the system is good. Weakening flow suggests a problem in the pump or supply into the house rather than a clog. Poor pressure and volume can be caused by clogged internal pipes, pump problems, clogged/undersized pipeline from water source to the house, or problems at the source, such as low water levels due to drought or a salamander stuck in the pipe at the spring box. The buyer finding a simple problem—not much pressure at the kitchen tap—may be seeing a symptom of a major illness. In this event, the best thing to do is discuss the problem with the owner, put a plumbing-inspection contingency in the purchase offer and have a local plumber take a look.

Assume that each adult will need at least 50-80 gallons of water per day (gpd) for all household purposes, though it's not that hard to get by with less. If you have seven kids and are buying an old farmhouse from a retired couple who say with quiet confidence that they've always had plenty of water from their spring, make an effort to determine whether their supply as is will meet your much higher demand. And if you plan to water livestock from the same spring the house draws from, figure in 35 gallons per day for each milk cow, 20 gpd for each beef cow, 12 gpd for each horse, four gpd for each hog, two gpd for each sheep and at least one gpd for each dog. The spring system should be designed so that the household is served first, then the livestock. The household pipe at the spring should be lowest in the spring box so that it draws first.

If a buyer determines the need to replace the **water supply line** from the source to the house, its cost will be determined mainly by the excavation requirements—length of the run and depth of the trench. A two-inch-diameter flexible plastic pipe is more than adequate to supply a household and barn; most excavators will recommend one inch to inch-and-a-quarter pipe instead. The extra cost of the larger diameter pipe is small and provides a margin of protection against long-term silt build up. No owner wants to replace this line more than once in a lifetime; actually no owner wants to replace this line ever. Replacing a water line will mean digging a trench from source to house that may cross roads, other buried lines and lawns. The excavation scar will take months to fade. The most complicated part of doing this work is getting the new water line into your basement, which involves exposing the outside basement wall and possibly enlarging the existing entrance hole.

Water lines must be buried below the frost line, which in some northern or high-elevation areas can be as deep as 40 inches underground. The deeper the trench, the more it will cost to excavate. A spring-fed line that contains an open overflow outlet will resist freezing. A plastic water line should not be buried deeper than just below the frost line. A farmer I know who over-engineers all things he builds buried his new plastic line eight feet deep on the theory that if four was recommended eight had to be better. Not so; the extra weight crushed the pipe, which led to every farmer's nightmare—repair the repair you just repaired. Soft dirt, gravel or sand should be hand-shoveled around the new pipe so that when the backhoe refills the trench, sharp, heavy rocks don't puncture the line.

If you're working with a gravity-flow system or one with a pump located at the source, you would do well to install a two-inch-diameter stub line about 50 feet before the line enters the house. Fit the vertical stub with a brass fitting that matches the threads of the local fire department's hoses. This will help a little, but a pumper could easily overload the spring's capacity to supply volume. Still, a **fire stub** is cheap, easy to install and may help a bit. Ponds that are developed for fire protection typically use a four-inch-diameter or larger, L-shaped pipe located about three feet below the water's surface. The vertical section of this pipe appears next to a spot in the road where the fire department can get its pumpers.

If a buyer comes to believe that improving the seller's water system is a necessity, he should gather the proof and present it to the owner as part of the purchase offer. The buyer is not likely to get a seller to replace a functioning, non-hazardous system because it's not functioning to the buyer's higher standard. Buyers must exercise cautious judgment when criticizing a water system the owner has used for years with no apparent problems or ill effects. A seller will interpret nerdy nit-picking as being rooted in the buyer's cultural arrogance or stupidity. A lead problem is not frivolous; a crayfish found in the spring is.

The easiest way to evaluate potential problems is to include a **water contingency** in any purchase offer. It might be worded this way:

> **The Parties agree that the sale of this property is contingent on Buyer obtaining at his expense water-sample results in the house taps that he deems satisfactory.**

> **Seller agrees to allow Buyer access at a mutually agreeable time to both household tap water and water sources for the purpose of drawing samples. Buyer agrees to take samples within _____ business days of the date on which this Contract between the Parties becomes effective.**

> **Buyer agrees to notify Seller of sample results within __ days of their receipt.**

> **The Buyer shall invoke this contingency or remove it within ___ business days of receiving laboratory results.**

> **The Buyer may void this offer without penalty and all deposits shall be returned to him in a timely manner if the results are unsatisfactory and the Parties cannot agree on a mutually satisfactory remedy.**

If you suspect one or more water problems may emerge from your contingency, you should give yourself enough time to evaluate the problems and determine the feasibility and cost of appropriate remedies. That could mean a window of as much as six to eight weeks during the contract's escrow period if redeveloping a spring and installing a new pipeline to the house are involved.

Some water-quality problems can be solved with a couple of hundred dollars; others—such as nitrate contamination—may require $1,000 or more in treatment equipment. The buyer should remember that a particular symptom may be caused by one problem or more than one. Low or irregular water flow at the tap can arise from clogged pipes <u>inside</u> the house, a clogged or leaky supply pipe from source to house, or troubles at the source. A high coliform count may suggest contamination of the source, infiltration of polluted water into the supply line, or contamination in the house system, such as bacteria build up in a holding tank. Repair costs will depend on which problem, or combination, is causing the symptom.

Clean water in; dirty water out. The "out" part of a rural water system involves **sewage**—human waste and water dirtied by human activity. The seller's **sewerage system** is largely hidden from the buyer's view even if the old farmhouse is still piping raw sewage directly into a creek behind the barn. I once owned a small farm in West Virginia whose farmhouse had a full set of indoor fixtures—sinks, bath/shower and toilet. An old outhouse was situated below the house, near the corner of a shed. I asked whether the outhouse was still used. The owner laughed and shook her head, no. Only after buying the farm did I discover that a four-inch pipe drained the farmhouse wastewater into the creek, just below the abandoned outhouse. Later, having smartened up a good bit I thought, I asked the owner of another farm whether the house had "an approved septic system" in place. I spoke the words—approved septic system in place—clearly and slowly. She said yes indeed. I later learned that the house used a three-inch metal pipe to drain sewage into a hand-dug hole that was lined with concrete block, with spaces left between each one. This "system"—a cesspool—to my knowledge had worked problem-free for at least 60 years, its waste load mixing with that of the cattle grazing above it. Such "systems" are not approved septic systems. They are still being used in rural areas, as are outhouses. In the right conditions, neither will adversely impact water supplies.

All new septic systems require a permit from the local health department/sanitarian. Buyers can best determine whether a target property has an "**approved septic system**" by asking the county's health department to show you the application and permit. The permit should include a description and schematic of the septic system, its location on the property and its capacity. If you are planning to add a fourth bedroom to a house with a three-bedroom septic permit, your plan will probably require enlarging the septic system if possible and replacing it if not.

A **septic system** is a means for disposing of human waste and household liquids in an environmentally safe manner. The system is composed of a settling (holding) tank—usually a cast-concrete box holding 1,000 gallons or more—that feeds more or less clear liquid into perforated drain lines as the solids settle out. The three or four drain lines are buried in a drainfield. Each line is laid in a trench and embedded in gravel. The design of the drain lines resembles the tines of a pitchfork with the settling tank at the throat where the metal fork is joined to the handle. The liquid disperses through the perforated pipes and seeps into the trenches and then into the underlying earth. The settled solids in the holding tank eventually build up to the point where they have to be removed. (Hire a professional to do this work; it is not something to do with a shovel between halves on a fall Sunday afternoon.) The critical element in septic systems is the type of dirt available in the septic field. Soil types differ in their ability to **percolate** ("perc") liquid, a process that filters and purifies the liquid before it reaches water-bearing rock. Heavy clays won't "perc" because they hold liquid in place, which creates a bacteria-rich marsh with the characteristic odor of septic waste. Other soils perc too quickly, which means that bacteria is not trapped in the ground before it reaches underground water supplies.

A buyer considering an unimproved property will need to think about finding a site for his septic field near his house site. The septic-field dirt must meet the local percolation standard. The county health department will provide an application for a septic system. (The application may also cover a well permit.) The applicant indicates the location and dimensions of the proposed septic field. The field itself will vary in area, i.e., number of square feet, depending on local requirements. Often, the area of the field is pegged to the number of bedrooms or the number of square feet in the house it serves. A 10,000-square-foot drain field—a little less than one-quarter of an acre—is typical.

Testing the drainfield site to see if the soil percs involves either a soils test or a water-percolation test. The object of both tests in most locales is to find a minimum of 36 inches of approvable soil underlying the proposed septic field.

In a **soil test**, the applicant digs three or four holes, each 36 inches deep, usually with a backhoe. The county sanitarian or a private soils consultant (who must be state-certified or state-licensed) will judge the soil's percolation characteristics by the dirt's color, look and feel. Ground that is steep is hard to approve. If lines are pitched too steeply, liquid will "bunch up" at the end of the lines or in the low turn, preventing proper diffusion. On hilly ground, the best chance for a conventional septic field lies with siting it on a reasonably level bench or protruding brow. A common **water-percolation test** uses a power auger at least four inches in diameter to bore four holes, each 36 inches deep. The holes are filled with water. The tester waits for four hours then fills them again and times how long it takes them to drain. A buyer needs to use the specific perc test required by the county's health department. If a private soils consultant is used, you will face a cost of $500 to several thousand dollars for this individual to prepare a permit application. Sanitarians in some counties still do a soils test of some sort for free.

Where a **conventional system**—septic tank and drainfield—cannot be used because the soils won't perc, an **alternative system** must be devised and approved. Alternatives usually involve some form of constructed drainfields, constructed wetlands that filter effluent, aerobic treatment or filtration through an approved medium, such as peat. Where an alternative involves constructing a drainfield over non-percing dirt, the 36-inch depth requirement may be reduced. Buying, hauling and emplacing such dirt or sand can be expensive. A sand-filter system runs between $15,000 and $22,000 to engineer and construct in my low-cost area in 2005. Alternative systems always require retaining a professional engineer to choose the most appropriate option and provide a site-specific design to be submitted for approval. Each state has its own set of approved practices and standards for conventional and alternative systems that counties administer. These practices are posted on the Internet, either through the state's department of health or department of environmental protection (water). Key words to look for are "onsite" and "GMPs," which stands for General Management Practices. The local health official or sanitarian should be able to provide an information booklet on conventional septic systems and the local percolation-test procedures. Information on alternative systems may or may not be available locally.

A great deal of information on conventional and alternative systems is available from the USEPA-established **National Small Flows Clearinghouse** (NSFC), West Virginia University, POB 6064, Morgantown, West Virginia, 26506-6064; 1-800-624-8301; 304-293-4191; 304-293-3161 FAX; www.estd.wvu/nsfc/nsfc. NSFC publishes the "Small Flows Quarterly," which discusses research and septic applications for individual houses and small communities.

If a buyer is so unfortunate as to have his house sited below his drainfield, he will find it necessary to pump waste water uphill into the settling tank. Pumps are expensive and can be cranky; repair is expensive and inconvenient. In this situation, you must be sure that the source of drinking water is located uphill of the septic field with at least 100 feet between them, the more distance the better. Local well and septic standards will guide the buyer as to the minimum separation distance for new homes. Old houses with old systems, however, may not comply with current regulations and persist by virtue of being grandfathered.

Buyers of a country house who seek to upgrade bathrooms, add a bedroom, start a B&B or otherwise find themselves seeking a permit from the county's health department or building administrator, may open themselves to having to install either a new well or new septic system, or both, to serve their projected improvements. Therefore, *before submitting a purchase offer*, the buyer should discuss any such plan with these officials to determine whether the current well and septic systems are county-approved and are capable of handling the increased use anticipated from the buyer's improvements. The other way to handle this is to write a **septic-approval contingency** into your purchase contract:

The Parties agree that Buyer's performance on this Contract is contingent on Buyer receiving a satisfactory review of his water and sewerage plans from the appropriate local building and health officials.

Buyer may void this Contract without penalty if any such official does not provide a review that Buyer deems acceptable for his purposes.

If the review suggests you will need to upgrade the well or septic infrastructure, have the official put something to that effect in writing and take it to your seller for negotiation. He is likely to say that any improvements you make for your benefit are on your dime, but if he is a motivated seller, he may help you. Use this time to nail down the cost and time involved in any required well and septic upgrades.

Composting toilets and chemical toilets are alternative systems that may or may not be permitted in a particular county. Do not assume that either type of self-contained toilet will be approved as a substitute for either a conventional septic system or an alternative septic system. Even where non-flush toilets are an acceptable option for handling **black water** (toilet sewage), local rules may still require that the residence have a full-sized functioning septic system for the house's **grey water**—the waste coming from sinks, washing machines and showers. Hunt camps and seasonal residences may not have to meet the same requirements as full-time residences.

Septic-system requirements are getting more stringent rather than less, particularly in populated watersheds with chronically high bacterial pollution. Even the most rural communities and those highest in the watersheds are now tightening their standards, which raises the cost of new residential construction. Buyers who tempt fate by proposing alternatives to conventional septic systems will frequently run into state and local regulations and local officials who will not be sympathetic or flexible. It can be a maddening experience. The rule a buyer should follow is this: learn the regulatory handles before submitting a purchase offer and, at worst, figure the highest cost alternative on top of your purchase price.

Common septic-system problems arise from design, construction and use. Older systems may have been installed on marginal soils, not pitched correctly, or not designed with sufficiently long drainage lines or a sufficiently large absorption area. The perforated pipes may have become clogged with solid material over the years, causing backups. If household water use has increased beyond what the original system was designed to handle, too much wastewater will be flushed into the tank and the drainfield will not be able to disperse fluid fast enough. These conditions can produce a system backup that will be noticed in the house.

Do not drain hot tubs and indoor pools into septic systems because their volume can overload the system and their treated waters—with anti-bacterial agents such as chlorine, sulfur compounds and anti-algae chemicals—will kill the bacteria that help septic systems break down solid waste. Water from gutters should not be directed into the septic system. Inexpensive septic-tank treatments add bacteria to a system; two quarts flushed into a toilet typically treat a 1,000-gallon tank once a year. If the septic drainfield is located in a topographical depression or floodplain, heavy rains or floods will saturate it, fill the drain pipes and settling tank, and prevent waste water from leaving the house. A buyer should look for evidence of water damage and staining on bathroom floors around the bases of toilets located on the ground floor. The seller may disclose a backup problem, or a local plumber looking for future business may flag a backup history for the buyer. Cleaning—"dipping out"—a system's settling tank of accumulated solids may be all that is necessary to make it operational. Cleaning ought to be done prophylactically for obvious reasons. Ask the seller to tell you when his tank was last "dipped" and who did it; check the system's history with this vendor. He should be able to determine whether the seller's tank needs to be dipped and how often you should schedule such work.

CHAPTER 14: RESOURCES—MINERALS AND WATER

DISCRETE ASSETS

Rural land is usually a package of discrete assets that has both a break-up value and an entirety value. It's important for you to know both. The break-up value of a country property should always exceed its entirety value, which, in one sense, is the price you negotiate with the seller.

In their pre-purchase scoping, buyers determine the sale value of each asset that can be leased, rented or sold. The sale of an asset can involve parting with a piece of the surface property or the right to excavate a subsurface mineral. In certain areas, a property will be valuable simply for its access to prized water or land. Air rights may have market value in windy areas. And rights to develop a special property, timber it, mine its minerals and so forth can be sold or donated as easements to conservation organizations.

It's helpful to value all assets in a property whether or not you plan to turn any into cash. Each has future value to you and buyers down the road. When you sell rural property, you will under-price it if you don't value each asset separately and show the proof of these values to potential buyers. Smart land sellers add the separate values of the property's assets—bare land, minerals, timber, water, air rights, aesthetics, improvements, income production, wildlife, crop entitlements, etc.—in justifying asking price. Where a seller can show fair and honest valuations of each asset summed into one asking price, buyers will have a harder time working it down. The flip side, of course is to buy a multi-asset property for a below-market price and then sell one or more of its severable assets for market value. Done shrewdly, the buyer can part out some of the property and pay for much, if not all, of the original acquisition cost. I've done this, and I'm less shrewd than most.

You should look for properties where one or two discrete assets can be readily sold with little degradation of the core assets that attracted you in the first place. Buyers of timberland are always looking for the fully self-financing purchase in which the property is paid for through the quick sale of its merchantable timber.

Buyers and sellers will not always agree on what is an asset and what is a liability. A 20-acre wetlands to a working farmer who is prohibited from draining it and producing crop revenue is a liability; to an environmentalist buyer looking to preserve wetlands for its habitat value, the 20 acres is an asset that may also have a tax-benefit value if it qualifies for a conservation easement. The farmer will value the wetlands low; the environmentalist buyer will value it high…to himself. In negotiating price, the buyer can emphasize the liability aspects of the swamp. On the other hand, the farmer may assign a $20,000 value to a fully-equipped but small and outdated dairy barn, which the vegan environmentalist will consider a demerit of the first rank. The farmer may stick on his $20,000 dairy valuation, because he knows the equipment alone will fetch that.

First-time buyers tend to think of each rural property they visit as a whole, with value determined principally by the size of the tract, condition of the improvements and aesthetics, such as ponds and views. The dirt-smart buyer should also value each asset that can be sold, leased, rented, exchanged, given or swapped. **The three assets that are often misunderstood by inexperienced buyers are minerals, water and timber.**

Typically, a property owner will own both the land's surface and the subsurface, which includes underground solid and liquid resources. The surface owner will also own certain air rights above his property. Air rights can be valuable as a source of solar energy (in which the surface owner wants nothing—like a neighbor's building—to impede direct sunlight) or as the right to air flowing over his property if he wants to lease the surface for wind turbines, which I once saw written as "wind turbans." (Air rights are often modified by zoning ordinances that limit the height of buildings and towers; a surface owner does not have the right to restrict aircraft from flying over.) When the seller owns all resources and the complete bundle of rights in his property, he is said to own the property in **fee simple**, or **in fee**, for short. Dirt-smart buyers always prefer properties that are conveyed in fee simple. Sellers should disclose when they are not selling in fee simple, but this does not always happen. The buyer-paid **title search** should turn up any limitations on fee simple ownership of record. There is, of course, the atypical situation where a property is not being conveyed in fee simple and the severance of some right is not recorded.

Ownership of land can be thought of as owning a layer cake of assets—above, at and below the land's surface—and the right to use, sell, lease, exchange or donate each one. Assets—goods and resources—may have market value. A "good" is often an aesthetic value—the pleasantness of the house site, a partially shaded swimming hole—that has cash value only in context. An asset may also be game habitat that the new owner can lease for hunting, a high spot that's suitable for a communications tower or a trail system that you might want to rent to snowmobilers. Many of the cake's layers can be pulled out legally for sale or rent. Legal separation of one layer from the others is often called, **severance**, or **split estates**.

MINERALS

Subsurface minerals are obvious assets that can be legally separated from the surface. In many areas of the United States, property owners severed some or all of their subsurface minerals—oil, gas, coal, rock, and clay—from surface ownership years ago through sale. Severed subsurface resources do not convey to a buyer of the surface. Subsurface owners have rights to develop and extract them, subject to state and federal laws providing for protection of the surface. Pennsylvania, for example, requires surface owner consent before the owner of the minerals can extract them by mining the surface.

Where a fee-simple owner/seller wants to **retain ownership** of some mineral resource, he is pulling that layer out of his sale to you. Retained ownership is also referred to as a "reservation from the sale." A seller can also retain ownership of a property's timber and water as well as reserve a right to use part of the property you're buying. I would be very cautious about purchasing such properties. The odds are that the seller will do something with the retained resource that you won't like.

Subsurface minerals can be owned by the owner of the surface who lives on the land or an absentee owner 3,000 miles away. Minerals can be produced (extracted) by their owners or by a company who leases the minerals from their owners. With the exception of large minerals-owning corporations, most individual owners of minerals lease them directly to producing companies or to companies who lease them to producing companies. Mineral owners can sell outright, the minerals beneath the surface, in which case, the surface owner has no role in their development. The involvement of the surface when minerals are severed are then subject to lease provisions, if any, and state and federal laws

Mineral rights are commonly severed. Their owners may then sell these rights or lease the minerals to mineral-development companies through agreements of record that typically run for five to ten years and are renewable at the leaseholder's choice. Rights to subsurface minerals are controlled by: 1) mineral deed, where the title to the minerals is sold; 2) reservation, where an owner retains the minerals while selling the surface; 3) lease, where the owner of the minerals sells through a lease agreement the exclusive right to extract the mineral, which he continues to own; and 4) option, where a mineral buyer pays the owner a sum that gives him the right to explore, purchase or lease the minerals for agreed terms by a certain future date. (Frank Gibson, James Karp and Elliot Klayman, Real Estate Law, 3rd ed. [Chicago: Real Estate Education Company, 1992], pp. 29-30.)

With smaller tracts, a surface buyer will often find that the mineral owner has leased the minerals he owns to a company capable of extracting them. A mineral lease allows the leaseholder to explore, develop and extract the last gram of these resources. The lease may set forth restrictions and conditions on his use of the surface, and state and federal law also set forth certain restrictions and reclamation expectations. The empty layer, the hole left by the mineral extraction, stays with the surface owner. Even after a portion of the mineral has been removed, the leaseholder may keep the lease active. New techniques may be developed to access deeper deposits. And natural gas can be stored underground in worked-out gas deposits for sale during the winter. A mineral lease may include all minerals, or only one. The most recent oil and gas (o&g) lease submitted to me amounted to an assignment of these rights in perpetuity with an annual rental of $5 per acre that would never change.

Not a good offer.

The holder of the lease (**lessee**) pays the owner (**lessor**) of the minerals an annual **lease fee (rental)** plus a **royalty** on every unit of production extracted. If the lessee produces nothing, the lessor still gets the annual lease fee but no production royalty. Lease terms are set forth in the **mineral lease** the parties sign. A **lease fee**, or **lease rent**, is usually a modest fixed dollar amount per acre that gives the lessee the right to explore, develop and extract the mineral. The surface acreage is usually the basis of this calculation. An annual lease fee might be $5 to $15 per acre for natural gas and a dollar or two per acre for coal east of the Mississippi River. A **production royalty** is based on an agreed dollar rate per unit of production, which may be a ton (coal, rock), barrel (oil), 1,000 cubic feet (natural gas), gallon, pound, or acre-foot of water. (Natural gas might also use a rate of so many dollars per million Btus produced.) Remember a surface owner who does not own these subsurface resources gets neither lease fee nor production royalty.

Mineral leases are written in small print usually by the **lessee**, the party that is leasing the resource. In the usual landlord-tenant relationship, it is the landlord/owner(**lessor**) who prepares the lease. Landlord-tenant agreements, written by the landlord, not surprisingly favor the landlord. The situation is usually reversed with mineral leases, so a lessor like you (the landlord/owner of the minerals) must do what he can to protect his interests in a "tenant-drafted" agreement. With small o&g leases, the lessor/owner rarely finds himself in a market where two or more potential lessees are bidding for his mineral rights. More often, the owner is approached by the only lease-buyer working his area and is handed a boilerplate contract. Where the mineral owner has a sufficiently large deposit, he may be able to create competitive bidding and negotiate better terms with a lessee. Owners of very large, desirable deposits have bargaining power that owners of a couple hundred of acres and less are denied. You can view a Texas o&g lease at www.landman.org/files/Forms/Texas_Form_659-85.pdf. This site is that of the American Association of Professional Landmen (AAPL) who are mainly involved in the o&g industry. The site provides a contact-information directory for every courthouse in the country along with step-by-step instruction on how to research a deed at https://www.courthousedirect.com/AAPL/Main.asp.

If you are the owner of a small amount of mineral resource, you can still try to wheedle better terms than the boilerplate offered. Unfortunately, most mineral leases in any given locale will be pretty much the same, so shopping around may or may not do any good. If you object to a provision in the lessee's contract, cross it out and write in substitute language. Don't be bashful about doing this. You have nothing to lose. If the lessee objects, a fresh contract will be produced. Before you sign is the only time that you will be in position to bargain over lease terms unless the lease includes a reopener clause, which most don't. Lessees are not likely to budge on the rental fee or royalty payment with small lessors, but you may be able to negotiate important limits and reclamation provisions regarding the surface.

Lessors should pay attention to the specific terms proposed regarding:

- **duration**—how long does the lease run? The lease may say that it runs for a five-year term, but in perpetuity is more likely given the ease of meeting the renewal hurdles.

- **resource definition**—coal leases usually include all seams regardless of depth; a single lease usually covers both oil and gas; a lease could cover all subsurface minerals and non-mineral resources; an area of possible confusion exists regarding whether methane embedded in a coal seam is covered by a coal lease or a gas lease.

- **area covered by lease**—the lease will usually cover every acre underground that you have in surface ownership, i.e., if you own 100 acres of surface, the lease will cover 100 acres directly underneath; some surface areas, however, should be exempt and protected from impacts, such as the acre or more around a house.

- **number and location of o&g wells** and other surface facilities that the lessee may drill and build; the small surface owner's interest generally lies in having as little surface activity and disturbance as possible to protect his property's value. The surface owner benefits most from signing an o&g lease that prohibits wells and other surface facilities on his land.

- **area and siting of mine and excavation**—underground mines involve a relatively small amount of surface in proportion to their size beneath the surface; surface mines, open-pit mines and quarries affect all surface acreage where they operate; locate surface facilities and determine their size in advance.

- **area and siting of any waste products**—how and where does the lessee propose to store or dispose of mine tailings, waste products, drilling muds, etc?

- **renewal**—what does the lessee have to do to be allowed to renew the lease; the answer is usually not much.

- **lease rental**—is the rental fee fixed at a specific dollar figure, regardless of the number of renewals; the lessor benefits from a royalty that increases over time. The lessor can propose that the royalty be adjusted every five years to reflect current market rental rates that the lessee is paying for new leaseholds.

- **royalty**—is the royalty a percentage of gross revenue or gross less expenses and other items, such as taxes, undefined "allowances" and expenses?

- **royalty**—is the royalty figured on gross output produced or net production sold; gross coal output, for example, right out of a mine may be scaled at 100, but after being cleaned and processed, only 85 might be sold.

- **royalty**—how is production measured? How can the lessor confirm the accuracy of the lessee's production data on which the royalty is calculated?

- **royalty**—how is lessee's revenue calculated? What is the definition of sale income for the purpose of calculating royalty? How can the lessor confirm the accuracy of the lessee's sale/income data?

- **payment in production**—does the lease allow lessee to pay lessor the royalty in actual production? (Here is actual language: "Lessee agrees to deliver to the credit of Lessor, free of cost, into the pipeline or storage tanks to which the well may be connected, the actual one-eighth (1/8) part of all produced and saved from the Land, or, from time to time the market price at the wells of such one-eighth (1/8) part of all oil produced and saved from the Land." Since the market price fluctuates, this lessor needs to make sure that he will not be getting product credit primarily during market dips.

- **surface**—what restrictions, if any, does the lessee agree to regarding
  - lessee's structures—type(s), height and location?
  - road location and design.
  - protection of special areas.
  - tanks, size, type, number and location; visual buffers.
  - transportation lines—all buried vs. on-surface pipelines, size and location.
  - frequency of vehicle usage for maintenance.
  - extent of exploration activity—type, location.
  - setbacks from residence—200 feet is typical, but I'd advise 1,000 or more.
  - excluded areas—areas excluded by local, state or federal regulations (e.g., wetlands or endangered species habitat, buffer strips along streams).
  - excluded areas—areas excluded by agreement between lessor and lessee, such as certain fields, woodlands, aesthetically valuable areas, viewsheds.
  - utility lines—size, location.
  - security measures—fences, gates, locks.
  - **no surface occupancy (NSO)**—small owners (lessors) may be able to negotiate an NSO provision in their lease in circumstances where the lessee can extract the resource by placing a well on an adjoining property.
  - **limited surface occupancy (LSO)**—the owner restricts the lessee to certain areas of the surface, or limits the type of surface structures the lessee is allowed to erect (e.g., no compressors).

- **"nuisance-type" facilities**—things like compressors, towers and storage tanks; they lower the value of surface property; if they're going to be put on your surface, you should negotiate over location and access roads. Ask for vegetative screens.

- **setbacks**—what setbacks in linear feet are included that govern the location of wells and other lessee facilities; setbacks should be applied to waterways, houses, other structures, orchards, roads, other similarly sensitive sites.

- **responsibility**—lessee's plan for spills and other clean-ups.

- **abandonment**—what are the types and level of reclamation that the lessee is expected to do when the lease expires or is released?

- **facilities**—is the lessee expected to dismantle and remove all surface facilities after production ends—he should be, if you can get it.

- **liability**—what liability, if any, does the lessee accept for accidents, environmental damage, damage to surface property, etc.

When leasing solid resources—such as coal, hard-rock minerals, dirt, stone, clay, etc.—make sure that you understand the volumetric base on which your dollar royalty is to be calculated. For example, **run-of-the-mine coal** includes coal plus whatever rock, slate and other impurities are also extracted in the mining process. **Washed coal**, or **"prepped" (prepared) coal**, has been run through a plant that removes the incombustible rock, washes away some impurities and grinds the coal to the size each customer wants. Depending on the intensity of this process and the characteristics of the run-of-the-mine product, prepped coal might be five to 20 percent less in volume than run-of-the-mine. It will make many dollars of difference to the royalty holder whether he is to be paid $1 per run-of-the-mine ton, $1 per washed ton, or $1 per ton washed and prepped. Coal royalties may also take into account the coal's qualities—hence, its market value. A ton of Wyoming's subbituminous coal has about half the heat (Btu) value of eastern coals, but also contains far less pollution-causing sulfur. Eastern coals, themselves, vary by how much sulfur they contain. The best coals for combustion (to make steam to turn a turbine to make electricity) have a high heat value and a low sulfur content. As a result, royalties are sometimes determined not only by volume but also by Btus and/or sulfur content. Royalty on western low-Btu coal will be lower than the higher Btu eastern coal, because the latter sells at a higher price. The royalty owner might also want to know the details of the coal's weighing. It is not unheard of for royalties to not be paid on full production. Another factor to be aware of in estimating the royalty value of underground resources is that each mineral deposit will be extracted at its own **recovery rate**, depending on local conditions and extraction techniques. The recovery rate of natural gas can approach 100 percent, while small, inefficient mines might be satisfied with a recovery rate of 75 percent of the coal in place.

Royalties can amount to very large sums over the years, depending on the quantity produced and the per-unit payment formula. An acre of eastern coal seam that is four-feet thick is usually thought to contain about 4,800 tons of coal; a royalty of $1 per ton over 100 acres of this one seam generates $480,000 in royalty to the owner, assuming 100 percent recovery. It doesn't take much time to mine that acreage, so all of that royalty might come in one or two annual payments. A gas well that produced only 100 million cubic feet over its lifetime at an average price of $4 per 1,000 cubic feet (mcf) would generate $400,000 in gross revenues during its producing life of 15 or 20 years. Gas and oil flows are typically strongest in the first few years and then taper off. The annual revenue from a well is usually split 7/8ths to the company producing the gas and 1/8th (12.5 percent) to the owner of the mineral rights who has leased the gas to the producing company. The life-time royalty from this gas well would be $50,000, assuming a 1/8th royalty payment figured against gross revenues. New gas wells produce much more than this example, and the current well-head price is more than $10 mcf.

It is important to the owner of the mineral rights to understand whether the lease gives you 1/8th of the gross revenue realized from the well's production or 1/8th of the gross revenue, "less a proportionate part of the costs incurred by Lessee [leaseholder] in delivery or otherwise making such gas or oil merchantable, including a proportionate part of all excise, depletion, privilege and production taxes now or hereafter levied or assessed or charged on oil or gas produced from the land." If you are leasing minerals, you want a 1/8th royalty based on gross revenues, not gross less expenses, taxes and undefined items.

States impose different requirements regarding the intensity of o&g development (expressed in number of acres needed per well) and minimum distance between wells. This is often expressed as no more than one oil or gas well on each **drilling unit**. Typically, oil wells will involve a 40-to 80-acre drilling unit while a natural gas unit might be 640 acres (one square mile). If the property contains both oil and natural gas, a new 640-acre gas unit could be developed to have one gas well and as many as 16 oil wells. Surface land may have more than the state's allowable number of wells if they were drilled before current unit rules were enacted. In that case, the existing surface facilities were grandfathered. State rules differ on drilling-unit size, so you need to check locally about how many wells can be drilled on a fixed amount of surface acreage.

Lease rental fees are based on acreage, usually so many dollars per acre per year. O&g royalty income is usually figured against the owner's proportional share in the drilling unit's acreage. In the o&g lease, you will find the developer's right to put together a drilling unit referred to as "**pooling**." If Joe owns 256 of the 640 acres in a gas unit (pool) and Bill owns the rest, Joe will receive 40 percent of the 12.5 percent production royalty taken against gross income and Bill, 60 percent.

If Joe, however, refuses to lease his 256 acres to the company that is organizing Bill's drilling unit, the company may be able to drain Joe's oil and gas without paying him a dime in lease fee or royalty. As long as the drill hole is located on Bill's land and does not slant under Joe, the law has traditionally allowed Joe's oil and gas to be taken without compensating him. In part, this is due to the fact that there's no way to keep the underground oil and gas under Joe from being drawn to Bill's well. The person whose well extracts the oil or gas becomes its operational owner regardless of its origin. This is referred to as **the rule of capture**, and it applies to resources that can migrate underground regardless of which ownership theory of minerals a state follows. (The rule of capture may also apply to underground water resources, allowing one landowner to pump dry the water beneath his surface as well as take water from beneath his neighbors. The rule of capture may or may not be softened by reasonable-use limitations.) If the mineral under Bill was a solid, the mining company under his land could not extract Joe's deposit without his agreement. Joe's refusal to sign an o&g lease will probably cost him his proportional share in the lease fee and royalty from the production of his minerals, but, in turn, he makes sure that no exploration activity, road construction, production or storage facilities mar his surface. While the producing life of a well may be no more than 15 years, surface use and facilities may continue for as long as the leaseholder pays the lease fee and meets the other "use" conditions of the agreement. The rule of capture is well-established law, but some states may be moving toward modifying it as it pertains to oil and gas royalties.

Where Joe highly values protecting his surface, he might either refuse to lease his minerals or lease them subject to surface restrictions. The most rigorous restriction is **No Surface Occupancy (NSO)**, which prohibits a producing company from placing facilities on the surface but permits the extraction of the resource. An NSO would normally include no road construction and no exploration activity as well. Surface-occupancy rules can be written broadly or narrowly, according to the needs of the owner and the producing company. Surface restrictions can exclude certain surface areas from having a well, or confine wells to a particular surface area, or prohibit all transmission facilities, or exclude/limit above-ground tanks and pipelines, or stipulate where access roads may be located and how they're to be constructed and maintained, or limit the types of exploration activities that are permitted. It is unlikely that the owner who severed minerals under the target property sold or leased them with surface restrictions. It's very difficult for the surface owner to persuade a mineral developer to accept surface restrictions beyond what his lease and the law requires.

While mineral developers obviously prefer as few restrictions on their development rights as possible, Joe, the owner of both surface and minerals, may have some leverage regarding surface restrictions on his land when Bill, who has 60 percent of their pooled drilling unit, is willing to give the developer full surface rights. In those circumstances, it's entirely possible that the leaseholder can agree to surface restrictions on Joe, because they may not affect his plans at all. It pays to ask for what you want, and it always helps to have your lawyer in the room when discussions with the mineral developer turn into negotiations.

When dealing with mineral leases and mineral-production companies, it's advisable to keep in mind the words of the late J. Paul Getty, who made his money in oil: The meek may inherit the earth, but not its mineral rights.

Mineral activity can have enormous visual, economic and environmental impacts on the property's surface. Exploration can involve seismic tests whereby dynamite charges are set off just below the surface and their reverberations measured. Less intrusive methods are available. Leases usually give production companies broad rights to explore, construct and maintain roads, drill, lay pipe lines (both above and below the surface), and construct tanks and storage structures. States may impose **set-back requirements** to protect residences, water wells and property lines. The mineral-owning surface owner has an opportunity to negotiate additional restrictions with whomever is buying or leasing his minerals. The fewer surface facilities that mineral developers install, the more protected is the economic value of the surface itself. The exception to this rule is undeveloped land that might benefit from a road network.

Natural gas wells are relatively modest affairs, involving a small "Christmas tree" of pipes and valves, possibly a tank for collecting associated oil, and sometimes a small building and a surface pipeline. The well pad will be serviced by a heavy-duty, all-weather access road that will be wide enough to accommodate well-drilling rigs and trucks. The level well pad is rarely more than one acre, a square approximately 209 feet on a side. Oil well pads are about the same size, but feature a moving pump and possibly several large collection tanks that tanker trucks empty as needed. Both oil wells and gas wells may be hooked directly into their respective pipelines. Pumps and compressors can be intrusively noisy. The possibility of a tank rupture or a gas explosion is always present, but the probabilities are not high. If you, as a surface owner, own the minerals, your lease should specify that all structures, facilities and materials (wells, tanks, pipes, lines, buildings, etc.) associated with mineral production should be removed once production ends or the lease terminates. If the leaseholder intends to use the depleted field for storage, this proposed language is likely to flush out that intention. The life of a well may be a few decades; the life of a storage field is likely to be forever. If surface aesthetics are important to you make sure that you negotiate language prohibiting surface pipe lines to the extent possible. Otherwise, you may find orange plastic or metal pipelines running haywire over your property. I've looked at a number of otherwise pretty properties in West Virginia that are disfigured by this clutter. Gas and oil companies vary with respect to how much cleaning up they're willing to do on both abandoned locations and active ones. The way a buyer determines what a lessee's policy is to ask in writing, either personally or through his lawyer. Your lawyer will also help you determine what level of clean up you might be able to force on a reluctant lessee, given the existing lease terms and state law. This question-asking should take place as part of your pre-purchase scoping, not after you buy the property.

Where the property seller is selling only the surface, you, the surface-only buyer, should expect to pay less for that land for three reasons. First, the seller is selling something less than the full package of land rights and assets. Second, the surface owner may have to put up with all surface activity and uses the mineral lease allows. Third, the surface owner will bear the full loss of discounted property value from the degradation of the surface environment. This can amount to a discount of 50 percent or more from a property's fair market value.

Modern oil-and-gas operations are less offensive than older fields, which, when left in place, can fairly be described in my wife's words as a "big fat mess." The best way to understand how a new mineral lease might affect surface property is to visit a nearby operating field operated by the company that wants to extract your target-property's minerals. Make this visit *before* you buy surface-only property.

A severed coal right presents serious issues to the surface-only buyer. The resource is mined by both underground and surface methods, depending on the seam depths and other geologic factors. It is not uncommon in Appalachia to find a property capable of being mined both ways. Underground mining uses either a vertical shaft excavated down to the seam of coal or a tunnel into a hillside. These mines can involve as few as a half-dozen miners and a couple of surface facilities to several hundred miners and a multi-acre complex of surface facilities, including a washing/preparation plant, settling ponds, refuse heaps, parking lots, bath houses (where miners change clothes), coal piles, loading facilities, power facilities, exhaust fans, equipment sheds and so on. The coal can be taken away from the mine by truck, overland conveyor belt, rail or barge.

Mining companies try to extract as much coal from a seam as is feasible. When deep coal is extracted, the surface can subside as the earth collapses into the open space. **Surface subsidence** can wreck buildings, crack foundations, rechannel underground water and springs, and ruin roads and bridges. Coal companies are now generally held liable for surface damage, but the cost and hassle of getting payment and effecting repairs can be high. Abandoned underground mines can catch fire and smolder for years. These mines can, alternatively, become flooded and leak sulfur-rich water that ruins streams.

Surface mining of coal and other minerals creates obvious impacts on a property's appearance. Surface-mining techniques range from contour stripping that cuts a bench into a mountain slope to access a seam to huge open-pit operations. In Appalachia, **mountain-top-removal mining** is a controversy-generating system that pushes the top of a mountain into the adjacent valley, thereby exposing the mountain's coal seam. This technique is also called **valley fill**, and it used to be called **mountain-top decapitation**. It ends up replacing a ridge-and-valley topography with a plateau amid the ridges and valleys. The 1977 federal Surface Mining Control and Reclamation Act (SMCRA) regulates the various forms of surface-mine operations and their reclamation. The law requires that surface miners regrade mountainside benches to their "approximate original contour." Valley fills are not required to restore ridgelines. There's nothing gentle-on-the-land about surface mining. Post-mining land will not look like the original. With the best reclamation in the world, the surface owner will not have the same piece of land after being surface mined. In some ways, however, it can be better than the original. Reclaimed surface-mined land can have economic value where flat land is rare or where it can grow trees or function as pasture.

I generally recommend against buying surface-only property in coal-mining areas. The surface-impact issues from mining are usually substantial, and your surface property can even be adversely affected by mining on adjoining property. If, however, you are looking for a rough-and-tumble recreation property that lends itself to off-road vehicles and hunting, worked out surface mines and other mining properties can be good buys.

Leases and state laws vary with respect to the rights of surface owners *vis-à-vis* underground and surface mining. The older the lease, the more freedom it grants to the mineral developer. Where coal rights were sold under no-longer-used, anything-goes deeds in eastern mining regions, the surface owner could not even get compensated for damage and loss until the 1960s and, in Kentucky, until the 1990s. These deeds and leases were entered into before surface mining was used. Underground mining—with its more limited surface impacts—was the basic method for extracting coal until after WWII, with the exception of some mines in the Midwest and West. The surface owners could not have anticipated the surface consequences these deeds allowed. A huge amount of "externalized costs" was foisted on surface owners until grass-roots rebellions forced state and then federal legislators to regulate surface mining.

Where minerals have been severed from the surface ownership, the surface buyer must determine whether the state where the property is found has a **surface-owner-consent requirement**, which may force the owner of the minerals to obtain the surface owner's agreement before mining/drilling occurs. Policies differ from state to state, and from mineral to mineral within states. The laws that I've read appear to have a number of "except thats," which restrict surface-owner protection. If you find yourself in this situation, ask your local lawyer to review the state's surface-owner-consent rules (if any) for any mineral that might be beneath the surface you're buying. The rule might be found by looking up "right of entry" if it's not listed under surface-owner consent.

It's interesting to me that I can drive virtually every Interstate mile in West Virginia and see almost no physical evidence of coal mining. These highways largely skirt the coalfields and where they don't, surface mining went on mainly out of sight, behind the ridge. The picture changes on the state's own roads, and the farther back you go, the more you see. A small-plane ride is the only way to understand the size and scope of surface mining. Had surface mining been done in areas more visible to the public, I think it would have been regulated sooner. Today, most surface-mining companies mainly comply with federal reclamation requirements. Erosion should be controlled. The sites will be regraded and seeded. Reclamation has hugely improved the aesthetics of post-mining land. But if you're buying land that is about to be mined, be prepared for a much different topographical look than what you see on the date you take possession.

If the seller cannot or will not convey all mineral rights to the property, you should discover this fact—if, for some reason, your scoping has missed it—when you present your purchase contract to him. You should write that your offer is for **fee-simple ownership**, that is, all surface and all underground rights, including ownership of all minerals and other resources.

You should, of course, get a sense of the degree of his ownership before you ever get to a contract. First, ask the seller and his agent whether the seller owns all rights in the property. Be careful with an answer that goes like this: the seller will convey all the mineral rights he owns. I have found that statement to mean that the owner does not own all the mineral rights, though he will give you title to whatever he has.

A related answer is: "I don't know." In mineral country when a seller gives me an "I don't know" about minerals, I assume first, he does know, and second that he doesn't own them. I'm willing to be proved wrong, of course. Second, it's easy enough to look up his deed in the county courthouse and see what he bought and whether he's sold or leased the minerals since then. If you find words in the deed into the seller or an earlier deed in the chain of title like **"excepting minerals,"** your seller only owns the surface and that's all he can sell to you. You may then have to track down the **mineral deed** in records that are separate from the land deeds. If the minerals have been leased, that document will also be recorded. The lease may be active or expired. In the latter case, a **release** may or may not have been recorded. When you have the title searched as part of your contract, if not before, make sure that your lawyer determines the degree of mineral ownership that will be conveyed to you and whether there are current leases.

You may also encounter a property where the minerals have been worked in the past, but no mining is currently being done and none appears to be contemplated. The seller of the surface may own the minerals or they may have been severed. If he still owns his minerals, make sure that they are conveyed to you. New mining and drilling technologies become available that allow the extraction of deeper or more difficult deposits that were impractical or uneconomic to work earlier. Some coal deposits now lend themselves to *in situ* gasification or tapping the methane while leaving the coal in place. Higher energy prices make formerly uneconomic resources newly valuable. Minerals can easily have value in the future, though they have none presently. If you don't own the minerals, you may find yourself facing unanticipated and unwanted mineral activity affecting your land at some point in the future. This is unwelcome.

Regardless of who owns the minerals, it's useful to determine whether the property has ever been worked for subsurface minerals for reasons of personal safety and environmental considerations. In the Appalachian coalfields, it was common for small landowners to punch do-it-yourself mines into their hillsides to extract house coal. Now long abandoned, these tunnels are unsafe and may be leaking acidic water. The seller, his neighbors and local surveyors may know the property's mineral history, both official and unofficial.

Some counties may have maps showing the location of worked-out mines. Some topographical maps indicate surface-mined areas and/or known underground mines (using a pickax symbol). You can quickly access such maps at www.topozone.com; use the 1:25,000 scale. You can also check out the **state's geological survey** and/or the state's geology office. Take a look at the **geological map** of the area; it will indicate known mineral resources. These maps are available from the state's geology office. The U.S. Geological Survey (USGS) is another source of mineral/geological maps. The USGS published state surveys in the 1920s and 1930s that contain county-level and sub-county-level information. Local libraries will have them, as will the state geology office and university libraries. Keep in mind that mineral maps show *known* deposits; a future discovery of a new deposit will not appear. Then check with the **state's division of mining** and its **oil and gas division**. Both offices will have maps, records of drilling and exploration, geological information indicating coal seams and o&g formations. In West Virginia, for instance, you can access well-by-well data—including production and ownership—on the state's o&g-division website.

The ground itself may still reveal its early mineral-development history. Look for openings and indentations in hill sides to indicate old coal-mining tunnels; rusting pipes and tanks signal old o&g activity. The Mineral Policy Center estimated in 1993 that the United States had almost 560,000 abandoned hard-rock mines on private, state and federal lands. Hundreds of thousands of abandoned coal mines, both surface and underground, also exist on the estimated 1.1 million acres of abandoned coal lands. Unreclaimed coal shafts, tunnels and high walls left from strip mining claim about 30 lives every year, according to the U.S. Mine Safety and Health Administration. And acid drainage from these old mines has polluted about 9,000 miles of streams, primarily in the eastern United States. Mining companies are no longer allowed to abandon mines without complying with reclamation requirements.

Each mineral has its own system for evaluating the extent of underground deposits. In general terms, a **reserve** is the least proved, most-iffy category; a **resource** is more confirmed. **Inferred resources** are less sure than **demonstrated** which are less sure than **proved**, which have been estimated on the basis of core drillings and/or other tests. Inferring a resource's existence is based on the recovery experience in similar geology and other information. **Economically recoverable resources** should provide a profit at current prices. "Current," however, may not mean contemporary; it may mean the date when the resource was valued. If prices are now higher than before, more resources will be considered economically recoverable. Each mineral has its own nomenclature. USGS and the U.S. Department of Energy classify coal as measured, indicated, demonstrated (measured plus indicated) and inferred. One million tons of a measured economically recoverable coal seam can be readily valued by determining the current market price for coal of that quality in that area. (It can, however, take two years for a mine to be planned and permitted, so the economics of extracting a deposit that is currently feasible may change.) One million tons of inferred coal resource may or may not be there, and if it is, may or may not be worth something. It can be proved up by drilling for samples. As energy prices rise, marginal deposits become economically feasible to develop. Economically recoverable coal is not growing as a result of new discoveries, but by demand-driven price increases.

I've touched on the monetary benefits of mineral development, the risks and costs to surface property and some of the issues that a land buyer needs to consider when minerals are involved. If your pre-offer scoping reveals the presence of minerals, I advise that you hire a local **minerals consultant** to help you evaluate the implications of purchasing this particular property. Your local lawyer is a source of consultant referrals as is the state's office of mines and minerals. This consultant can give you an educated estimated of what's there, its current and potential economic value, the methods that would be most appropriate for its extraction and the likely surface impacts.

It is relatively common in regions with coal and o&g to find surface property being sold without the minerals. These will have been sold, leased or retained by a previous owner. The seller of the surface may be trying to unload his land just prior to a mine being opened on his property. If the mining plan is in its formative stage, you may not be able to discover it. But if it's close, you may be able to learn of these plans by checking with the appropriate state agency that issues **mining permits** for coal, solid minerals and rock, and **drilling permits** for non-solids such as oil, gas and geothermal resources. The mineral developer will have filed a plan with the agency as part of his permit application, which will show the location and extent of the project, descriptive details and, possibly, a proposed reclamation plan. These plans and permits are public documents, and some proposals are subject to public hearings and comments. Ask the agency whether any mining or drilling permit is current or proposed for the property you're scoping. If a permit exists, request a copy of both the plan and the permit. Ask if the property has ever been permitted in the past and get copies of the relevant documents.

The state may have an **environmental agency** that issues permits in addition to the mining agency. These agencies are looking to see how the developer intends to manage the environmental impacts, especially on water resources, of mining or drilling, and how the site will be reclaimed once the mineral has been extracted. Mining generally involves surface waters and the construction of ponds for various purposes. The county's planning office, building administrator and the clerk's office may also know about pending mineral development. Ask these officials if they know of any plans—mining, drilling, development (residential, commercial or industrial), power lines, dams, road construction, public park or other facilities, and the like—that involve or are likely to affect your target property. Finally, call the biggest mining company and biggest drilling company in the area. Ask if they know of any plans that would affect the property you're scoping. Ask enough questions of enough people to make it highly probable that you'll pick up a trail if one exists.

Your right to the seller's full disclosure regarding minerals is not fully established everywhere. Severance of minerals is not what state judges would consider a "material defect" in the seller's property; the law doesn't consider it a defect. Therefore, while many states require the seller to disclose material defects, you can't count on that requirement to give you information on minerals. If the seller is conveying something less than fee-simple ownership, a local court would probably put the burden of this discovery on the buyer and his pre-purchase title search. The seller can, of course, always say that he told you about not owning the minerals, and then it's your word against his. You may face even less disclosure with FSBOs than with brokers, but anything's possible.

A Maryland real-estate agent called me a few years ago to look at a property that was very pretty and had some timber with commercial value. He did not inform me that the property was about to be deep-mined, a fact I subsequently learned from asking around. I also learned that he knew about the impending mining when he called me. Did he have a legal obligation to tell me what he knew: that the minerals had been severed and mining was about to commence? Probably not, given that he was representing the seller. When I asked about mineral ownership, he said he didn't know whether the seller owned the minerals. I took his "don't know" as a signal to go to the courthouse and find out. The deed showed that the seller didn't own the minerals, and a call to a local coal company with mines in the area told me of their plans. I've learned over the years that when a seller or a real-estate agent says, "I don't know," it often means either "I don't want to know" or "I don't want to tell."

Do not count on a seller's real-estate agent to know anything about minerals, though some know a great deal. Do not count on the seller's agent to disclose anything about minerals, unless you ask. If the minerals have been severed, they are not part of the surface property that is for sale, so the agent and the owner may have no legal obligation to alert you to this fact. Some states, such as Colorado, now require that real-estate agents for the seller disclose to potential buyers the ownership of subsurface oil, gas and mineral rights. Colorado contracts now include language that informs the buyer that purchasing land doesn't necessarily mean the buyer is also purchasing underground resources, such as oil and gas, minerals, water and geothermal energy. This provision is buried in five lines in the standard six-page purchase contract. In the event of a future dispute, a mineral developer will point to that very small print as having provided very large notice of possible severance to the buyer who purchased the surface anyway.

Definitive knowledge of a property's mineral ownership will be found in documents recorded in the county courthouse. I have never found a property where the minerals had been severed from the surface without a recorded document, though it's possible that a mineral buyer failed to record for one or another reason. If the buyer did not record his purchase, the mineral seller's recorded deed, or earlier deeds (his chain of title), should show the severance. It's possible that both buyer and seller did not record, in which case you won't find a document showing severance in the courthouse. This is highly improbable. Your backup protection is to have a section in your purchase-offer contract that provides:

Seller warrants that he is conveying the Property in fee-simple ownership with all rights to all resources, both surface and subsurface.

Seller agrees to disclose to Buyer any severance or reservation of interest in the

Property's natural resources within five calendar days of this Contract taking effect.

Buyer may void this Contract without penalty if Seller is unable to convey the Property in fee-simple ownership or, alternatively, in a way that is acceptable to the Buyer.

If the seller knows of an unrecorded severance and proceeds with the sale, you will have grounds to be compensated for damages since the seller promised you that he was selling in fee. (You will also need your contract to provide that all seller warranties survive the contract, that is, the escrow period during which the contract exists between buyer and seller.) If the seller does not know of an unrecorded severance and a mining company shows up on your doorstep ready to dig, get a lawyer. Unrecorded mineral deeds are possible, though rare. Some states do not recognize property conveyances unless they are recorded, so your legal situation would be determined by the facts and state law where the property is located. It is unlikely that a mineral developer will try to get a permit without a recorded lease or deed in hand.

With the vast majority of properties, mineral severance will be recorded. But you may not find any mention of either minerals or severance in the seller's deed, which is the most recent one recorded. The seller's deed may be something as vague as "All that property known as the River Place, situated on the east side of Big Bend Road in the Samsom Magisterial District of Blue Ridge County, containing 100 acres as described in earlier conveyances." A deed as poorly drafted as this doesn't tell you whether the seller does or does not own the subsurface minerals. Some deeds will specify that the property does or does not include ownership of subsurface minerals; others won't. Where the seller's deed says something like "all mineral rights included" or "minerals run with the land," you can feel confident that the surface acreage you are buying includes the subsurface rights. Where the seller's deed says nothing about minerals, you or your lawyer need to backtrack the seller's deed to find out whether or not the minerals have been severed.

Mineral leases may be recorded in a set of **grantor/grantee indices and books** that are separate from the grantor/grantee indices and books that reference all other real property. Both types of records will be found in a county office, such as that of the county clerk or land records. A **grantor index** lists alphabetically those persons giving or selling property in one column and to whom the property was given or sold in the next. The index will reveal the date of the transaction and the **deed book (DB) number** and **page number (PN)** where the deed of gift or deed of sale will be found. Remember mineral deeds may not be indexed in the same index as land where mineral ownership has a separate recording system. A **grantee index** provides the same information except that the persons listed alphabetically in the first column are those who acquired ownership through gift or purchase from those in the second column. Mineral deeds and leases are usually indexed and found in their own separate books, but you have to ask the clerk. You may find a twist or two, though the basic system is the same across the country. Ask the clerk for assistance; you will get the hang of deed-researching quickly. Older deeds may or may not be in the county's computer system. Make sure that you check both sets of indices—the first for real property, which can include both surface and subsurface ownership, and the second for minerals alone—so that you don't end up buying surface property without its underlying minerals.

If you are having a lawyer do a **preliminary title search**, which backtracks the chain of title to determine whether the seller is the legal owner of what he is selling (and you are buying), make sure to have him check title for mineral ownership as well even in counties where minerals are not currently being produced. It is worth paying him to find out whether or not you are buying in fee simple. I've known lawyers who do not routinely check for mineral ownership/severance in their title searches. In some places, back-checking should look specifically for severance, leasing and other types of qualifications on the property's water rights as well. The title search will also turn up other *recorded* agreements that affect the property, such as life estates, reservations of interest, conservation easements, leases, rights to water for irrigation and so on.

Once legally severed, subsurface mineral rights can be bought, sold, traded, given away and leased regardless of the surface owner's desires. I've found two common patterns of severance. First, the mineral rights will have been sold to a large corporation that may or may not be a mineral developer. Mineral owners can also be land companies private investors or railroads (which own millions of acres in both the Appalachian coalfields and the West). The other pattern is for the mineral rights to have been severed but retained by a previous fee-simple owner. Where minerals rights have been passed down, several dozen individuals may each own a fraction of the whole. The buyer of surface only will have a next-to-impossible time in acquiring the severed minerals from either type of owner. If all underground resources have been depleted, the mineral rights have been liquidated and revert to the surface owner. But do not assume that because some gas has been tapped and some mining has occurred that the mineral rights are now joined back with the surface. The U.S. Supreme Court ruled in 1982 that mineral rights that were unused for 20 years could revert to the surface owner, but your definition of unused and the definition of use within the lease may not be the same.

When large companies no longer want a mineral lease, they will generally allow it to expire without further communication with the surface owner. Some companies will routinely record a **notice of release** in the courthouse, stating that the owner of the mineral rights of record has abandoned all claim to and interest in the mineral rights on the subject property. A **partial release** would give notice that the mineral owner no longer claims an interest in, say, the property's coal but retains his interest in all other minerals. If a mineral lease has expired and no release has been recorded, you should ask the seller as part of your purchase offer to have the minerals owner record such a notice. The only way that you can be absolutely certain that the last recorded owner of the mineral rights has abandoned his interest is to find a recorded release. The release document itself is boilerplate with the deed particulars filled in. A person representing the leaseholder—usually a local lawyer—records the release by giving it to the clerk, who then notes the time and date and places the document in the appropriate book for mineral deeds and leases.

If the owner of an expired mineral lease is unwilling to respond to a request from you—at the moment, only an interested potential buyer of the surface—a letter to the seller of the target property might produce what you want. This letter to the target property's seller might look like the following:

> As you know, I am considering buying your property. In researching the deed, I discovered that the subsurface minerals were leased to XYZ Corporation some years ago. The lease seems to have expired, but no release was recorded. I have found no record of renewal. It appears that you own the minerals.
>
> I would appreciate a clarification of the minerals situation before I submit an offer. I am, therefore, asking that you request that XYZ record a minerals release before I submit my offer.
>
> I want to buy your property in fee simple, with all minerals and rights included. I will offer less if XYZ refuses to record a release and may not submit any offer depending on XYZ's plans. The same would be true if you want to retain mineral ownership and sell me surface only.
>
> The release should resemble the following:

XYZ Corporation of _____, ____ (state) which is the last recorded owner of the mineral rights for the following property, _____ acres whose surface is owned by _____, recorded in Deed Book __, Page __, in _____County, State of _____, under a lease recorded in said county and found in Minerals Book ___, Page__, of same _____ County sets forth that its mineral lease expired as of _____, ____.

XYZ, Inc. claims no reservation of interest or profit of any kind in either the subsurface mineral rights or surface property.

XYZ, Inc. agrees that all mineral rights, in whatever condition, are released and have reverted to _____, the owner of the surface property.

I'd like to talk with you about this situation at your convenience.

XYZ Corporation will know what a release is and does not need to be educated as to its language. The point of the letter is to let the seller understand the nature of a release and put both the release and mineral ownership on the negotiating table.

Where a mineral leaseholder has done nothing under his lease to use the minerals—and "use" is generally construed to mean minimum leaseholder activity—a state may provide that the severed mineral rights revert to the surface owner after the passing of a certain number of non-use years set by statute, typically 20 or 30. A buyer should never assume that mineral rights have reverted to the seller where no drilling or mining has occurred once the statutory time period is met. The mineral owner and/or leaseholder may have met the state's minimum requirements without doing anything that is obvious to you. To find out how the mineral owner and/or the leaseholder feel about mineral rights, you must talk with them, starting with the leaseholder.

The buyer may find himself in a situation where current or past mineral production has left certain environmental and/or legal problems on the land. These may include mine-waste dumps, tailings, unreclaimed surface-mined land, ponds for retaining surface water, ponds for settling out waste (which may include toxic substances), leach fields, miscellaneous dumps of this and that, barrels of waste, etc. Ownership—hence, liability for clean up—varies according to the law and what the problem residue is. (See Chapter 13.)

Certain mineral-related things left are considered **personal property**, rather than real property. Personal property does not convey with the sale of real property, unless specifically included in the contract. A seam of coal is real property, but a heap of mined coal sitting on the ground and a heap of coal-mine waste sitting next to it is the personal property of either the mineral developer or the owner of the mineral rights. Whoever is the owner is likely to take the coal (that is, sell it before or after the property conveys) and is just as likely to leave the waste heap. While real property can be abandoned, it is difficult to do so with certain personal property. On big environmental hazards, federal law governs the ownership and liability questions. On small hazards, the surface buyer may end up with the former mineral leaseholder's personal property, such as a non-hazardous dump. In this situation, the buyer should try to make sure that someone—the surface owner, mineral owner or mineral leaseholder—accepts ownership and responsibility for surface-deposited mineral wastes before submitting a contract offer. Ownership of other minerals-related problems—abandoned tanks and pipes, sources of pollution, wetlands fills and so on—should be similarly flagged and resolved where possible before making an offer. If a small problem is inoffensive, it will stay in place and convey with the land. My understanding of the law is that most courts now hold that the generator/originator of the waste remains liable for any damage that is not covered by applicable federal or state environmental statutes. The buyer will need to determine the extent of any such minerals-related problems, whether they fall under the jurisdiction of a federal or state statute, what potential for damage they present, who is liable for any damage they cause and who will do the clean up.

States differ in how much say a surface owner has over how privately owned subsurface minerals can be extracted and what rights an adjoining landowner has for protecting his property and getting compensated for damage. In the late 1800s, coal companies purchased millions of acres of subsurface mineral rights and billions of tons of coal using deeds that allowed them to use or affect whatever portion of the surface they wanted. Such deeds were upheld for many years even after new techniques—surface mining (using open pits, augers and contour stripping)—appeared which damaged the surface in ways that could not have been foreseen when the contracts were signed. These early deeds and leases allowed coal operators to use the surface without additional permission or compensation for damage. Before such deeds were modified by state laws, hundreds of thousands of acres were left in ruins. In the 1970s, I saw houses, barns and churches damaged when strip mines, operating above them, pushed rock and dirt—called "overburden"—down the hill. I saw stream channels completely filled with this material, to the extent that the water was running over the top of a bridge's planks. Federal regulation forced mining companies into more responsible, protective behavior in the late 1970s. Since **surface-rights** law differs from state to state and mineral to mineral, the buyer must check locally to determine what rights, he, as the surface-only owner, would have with respect to mineral development on his property and around him.

Surface conflicts over mining damage can occur both when the mineral rights are severed and when they are not. Adjoining owners are still impacted by the noise, vibrations, debris, dust, erosion and blasting of surface mines and quarries, though less overall than before the federal legislation was enacted. Mountain-top-removal surface mining has been implicated in flooding, with the loss of 12 lives between 2000 and 2006. When coal is exposed, the heavy metals it contains—mercury, arsenic, lead, barium, beryllium, among others—can get into local water supplies. (See Diana Nelson Jones, "Almost flat, West Virginia," Pittsburgh Post-Gazette, February 26, 2006.)

State and particularly federal agencies, such as the U.S. Forest Service and Bureau of Land Management, own millions of acres of surface and minerals throughout the country. Some federal- and state-owned minerals lie beneath privately held surface. It appears to me that the surface owner enjoys a better set of rights with federal resources under his feet than with privately held minerals. (Opinions differ on this point, I'm sure.) Where the federal government owns land beneath private owners, the energy companies that have leased the federal minerals may be able to drill for oil and gas or mine for coal simply by posting a modest bond. This situation has come to a point in Wyoming where the mineral rights under about 48 percent of private surface is owned by the federal government, often the Bureau of Land Management. Pressure to produce energy on **split estates** has led to conflict between landowners, energy companies and public agencies.

Land buyers in the West may find themselves buying privately held surface only, with the minerals in federal hands or under lease to private interests. The federal government does not mine its own minerals. Large corporations are the principal owners and lessees of federal mineral rights. Federal reservations of mineral rights are called **patents** (deeds) and are recorded in **patents books** in the county courthouse. A moratorium on patenting federal land has been in effect since 1994, which means that the federal government is no longer passing title to a claimant, making the land private. Mining of minerals may still take place on federal land without a mineral patent. Lisa Takeuchi Cullen, "Bittersweet Boom," Time, September 11, 2006.

Federal agencies may agree to a **reconveyance** of the mineral rights if you, the surface owner, can show either that no mineral value exists in the federal mineral rights or that federal ownership interferes with or precludes appropriate development of the surface. The surface owner will have to pay for geological tests to prove no mineral value and may have to pay for the rights themselves. Each reconveyance determination is site-specific, and reconveyance is not a guaranteed outcome. Reuniting surface and minerals, however, adds value to the surface property by removing the possibility of unwanted mineral development from surface ownership and allowing the property to be mortgaged at its full value. Each federal agency has its own procedures, forms and expenses for reconveyance. Agencies will provide pamphlets explaining the process, and you can dig out the procedures by looking at that portion of the Code of Federal Regulations (CFR) that governs the agency. The CFR is available on the Internet and in law libraries. Agencies should provide the relevant documents, and, if all else fails, ask your Congressional representative for help.

The place to begin learning about a target property's minerals is in the county courthouse with the seller's deed and his chain of title. If you find in his chain that the minerals have been severed, look up that deed of sale and any subsequent lease. Limitations, if any, on surface usage will be included in the lease. You will probably find a boilerplate deed of sale and the same type of lease. In that case, check with a local lawyer and state mining/drilling officials to determine statutory and case-law protections that apply to surface ownership. You may end up calling the general counsel's office in the state's mining/drilling agency and talking to a staff lawyer. Ask about restrictions that limit the developer's use of your surface, liability for damages to the surface and its improvements, the surface owner's right to notice, environmental protections that impose setbacks from streams and lakes, and the developer's track record.

The buyer who purchases the surface only cannot void an "active" mineral lease, but the leaseholder (lessee) may be willing to offer some concessions and accommodations for goodwill. It certainly doesn't hurt to establish a personal relationship with the lessee's management as well as any of its crew that appear. In some circumstances, the surface owner may be able to buy back oil and gas rights if the leaseholder can tap the resource from adjoining property or when the leaseholder is persuaded that he's removed all of the resource. My experience is that mineral leaseholders are reluctant to sell their lease rights to surface owners, though it's worth asking.

States tax subsurface minerals differently.

Some apply a **severance tax** that is owed by the owner of the mineral rights as the mineral is produced. (The producer of the minerals may actually be the party that pays the tax, depending on the terms of the lease agreement.) The owner of the surface, whose mineral rights have been severed, owes no severance tax on the minerals produced beneath his land. The severance tax is a state-level tax with some portion usually being repatriated to the county of production. Counties, of course, may impose their own severance tax, sometimes called a **yield tax**, on mineral (or timber) production. Such taxes are either calculated on a measurable production unit, such as a ton of coal or a barrel of crude oil, or levied against the gross sales revenue of the product at its point of origin.

Severance and yield taxes are a marginal factor in deciding whether or not to buy land with mineral resources. I think tax burdens might come into play when the buyer has a choice between mineral properties in different states, one low tax and the other high. In what might be considered high-coal-tax states, such as Wyoming, West Virginia and Kentucky (with its tax on unmined coal and a severance tax), I've seen no backing out of coal ownership or production. Pennsylvania, Virginia, Illinois, Indiana and Texas do not have a coal severance tax.

States change their severance tax rates from time to time; some, like Wyoming, fairly frequently. It makes sense for a buyer of land with minerals to determine what its current tax burden is and keep in mind that politics and public needs will change that burden in the future. On the other hand, I would not worry that a state will tax minerals excessively. States generally try to keep their tax burdens competitive with neighboring states that produce the same mineral so as not to disadvantage their own producers.

A severance tax does not diminish mineral lease rent (fee) paid to the owner of the mineral rights. The lease rent/fee is paid to the mineral owner whether or not production occurs. The amount of rent is not reduced by any tax increases on unmined mineral resources, because that rent payment is established in the lease agreement. The payment of a severance tax should not reduce production royalties as long as the royalty is figured on gross sales or gross production. Royalty would be reduced by state/local taxes if the royalty is figured against after-tax (net) revenue. Mineral owners should not agree to royalty formulas based on production less expenses and taxes.

Unmined minerals may or may not be taxed separately from the **property tax** imposed on the surface. (You might find the local property tax referred to as an *ad valorem* **tax**, that is, a tax based on the market value of the property.)

States, as a rule, do not tax real property, preferring to raise revenue from fees, and taxes on sales and income. Some states, however, do impose a property-type tax on certain unmined minerals, which may also be referred to as a **reserve tax**.

Counties and other sub-state jurisdictions are the principal taxers of property, both real (land, improvements, minerals) and personal (vehicles, boats, equipment). **Real property** is land and the structures attached to it, along with the rights, interests and benefits that come with the ownership of the land. **Personal property** is assets owned by an individual apart from real property. Personal property can be on the land but not attached to it. Planted crops are personal property, standing trees are not.

Counties impose a **property tax** on real property that is calculated on its tax-assessed value multiplied by the local tax rate for the particular type of real property. The tax rate is expressed as so many dollars per $100 of assessed value. You might see a rate shown as, $.85/100, which is eighty-five cents of tax per $100 of assessed value. (A tract of undeveloped land that has been appraised by the county at $100,000 FMV would be taxed at $850 per year.) Tax-assessed values for land (surface) and improvements are based on a county-wide, property-by-property **reassessment** that takes place every few years. Appraisers are hired to do this work.

States use different formulas for valuing unmined minerals. Mineral valuations may or may not be part of the periodic reassessment process that values surface land and improvements. Counties may apply a generic formula, where, for example, it is assumed that so many dollars of mineral value goes with each subsurface acre. Minerals-owning companies are often asked to provide tax authorities with an estimate of the amount of minerals they own, from which their tax payment is calculated.

Each county will have its own way of taxing minerals. In my county, minerals are taxed at the same rate as other real property, but their valuation is no more than token. The county has no practical way of determining how much gas is underground. And the value of that gas, whatever its extent, depends entirely on a field being developed with an associated transportation system. Lacking that investment, the mineral deposit is worth nothing. In counties where minerals are a significant resource, unlike mine, they will be valued separately. You may also find counties where worked out mineral deposits are taxed the same as minerals that are still untouched. Unmined minerals may be taxed at a different rate from surface land, and different tax rates may be applied to different minerals. When all is said and done, minerals are not taxed highly.

Information on local mineral tax rates, assessed valuations and recent tax payments will be found in the property-tax records at the county courthouse in the **Land Book**, or its equivalent. The Land Book is the county's database for all property-tax information. It is generally organized by sub-county jurisdictions, listing owners alphabetically. It shows current tax-assessed values for each parcel of property, divided among land (surface), improvements and minerals. Each parcel of land has a **tax number**, and each parcel is available as a **tax map** in the county's **tax book**. The tax book is a compilation of tax maps showing every tax parcel in the county; the Land Book shows the tax data for every tax parcel. The amount of tax owed is figured against each parcel's tax-assessed values for land, improvements and minerals. Ask the assessor whether the tax-assessed value for land and improvements represents 100 percent of current fair market value (FMV) or some percentage. (Land values in West Virginia, for example, are carried at 60 percent of FMV.) Different types of surface property—farmland, timberland, urban residences, commercial land, etc.—will be taxed at different rates. The Land Book shows the amount of tax owed in each asset category as well as the total. Minerals are unlikely to be carried at 100 percent of FMV. The Land Book gives you the assessed valuation of the target property's minerals for tax purposes alone. This valuation has not much to do with the actual worth of the minerals in place and even less to do with the actual worth of those minerals once invested capital makes them capable of being extracted.

Counties give tax breaks to certain classes of real property. Farmland, for example, may benefit from a **"farm use"** designation, which can cut its property tax by 75 percent or more. Farm use is a tax tool that counties adopt to encourage farming and preserve farmland. It shifts the county's tax burden to non-farm property owners.

Unmined minerals are generally taxed low, whatever the taxing format.

The biggest mineral tax break occurs at the federal level, in the form of the **percentage depletion allowance**. This allows the producers of some 70 minerals to take off a fixed percentage, ranging from ten to 22 percent, of their annual gross revenues against their taxable incomes. The total deduction from the percentage depletion allowance can, and typically does, wind up exceeding the amount of invested capital. Clay, sand and gravel have a ten percent allowance, while lead, sulfur and uranium are at 22 percent.

Minerals in the ground can be valuable or worthless. The presence of a mineral deposit does not necessarily translate into income for its owner. It may not be economically recoverable owing to its size, quality, geological situation, location and a dozen other factors. If it's not economically recoverable, it may be worth something down the road, but it's usually not worth much right now. And it's anyone's guess as to how long the road will be until the deposit acquires value. Dozens of "deals" are around that ask investors to buy into old gold mines, iron-ore deposits, oil-and-gas projects and the like. All of them promise amazing profits. Some involve the purchase of the minerals; others offer participation in the development of a resource. All of these "deals" carry high risk for inexperienced buyers, and I encourage you to stay out of them unless you truly know what you're doing. I'll give one example of the many I could cite.

A group of individuals bought an iron-ore deposit in New York about 30 years ago when its underground mining operation shut down. Depending on which geologist's opinion I wanted to believe, the deposit contained 20 million to as much as 60 million tons of high-grade ore. The mineral rights to whatever was there were priced at $300,000—a steal, given that the royalty on that amount of ore would run into the millions. Two problems, however, became apparent when I scoped it. First, the owner of the minerals owned no surface property. A big, deep mine needs 50 to 100 acres on the surface for its facilities. Perhaps that problem could have been solved. Second, however, was the unfortunate fact that this ore—good as it was—lay deep underground in fractured seams and could only be extracted by expensive, labor-intensive, underground mining methods. No iron-ore company could mine that deposit profitably when surface-mined ore would always be produced at a fraction of the cost. Almost every mineral "deal" that I've looked into has something wrong with it, something big enough to kill it.

Buying land for its minerals and buying mineral rights are not games for amateurs. Investing in minerals is a different book for another author. My concern for an inexperienced buyer of rural land is to make sure that you understand minerals can be a financial asset, a financial zero, a financial loss and an aesthetic/environmental liability. I advise against buying surface only when economically recoverable minerals exist below unless your uses of the land are compatible with the potential surface impacts that mineral development can impose.

WATER AS A FINANCIAL ASSET

Chapter 13 discusses the environmental considerations of **rural water** as they can bear on a buyer. In addition to being a source of life and a vehicle for pollution, water is a natural resource that often has a dollar value. Its flow can be affected by natural and man-made events, which can negatively impact both your land and your pocketbook. As population and development continue to increase, the quantity and quality of rural water is likely to become an ever more prominent issue of law and policy. Drought and global warming affect local water supplies. Metropolitan areas, irrigated agriculture and rural residential developments will lay ever-heavier demands on these supplies. When rural water supply is made into a market, the highest dollar bid will prevail. That fact will change the availability of local supply in rural areas, because the highest money will not be local.

I foresee more reservoirs and pipelines being built from water-supplying rural areas to populated, water-needing areas. I assume that the trend toward **privatization** of municipal water systems will involve the buying of water from distant watersheds. If water is developed like Arabian oil in the 1930s, maybe we "country Saudis" will get rich from this arrangement. But I doubt that will be the way water entrepreneurs will proceed. My guess is that water for export will be "developed" in America's rural areas by water-development companies that lease rights much as domestic oil and gas is now leased. They will store it in large impoundments and ship it to needy areas through a system of pipelines. Counties where water is leased and stored will receive some modest tax benefits. The local property owner might get free water for domestic purposes just as a gas lease usually provides one residence with free gas. It would not surprise me if after the commercially recoverable reserves of Appalachia's coal, oil and gas are mostly gone, the region continues to function as an exporter of natural resources—renewables, such as water, timber and wind-generated electricity.

Whether or not rural water resources are sold and shipped in the future, a land buyer should give thought to a target property's water needs and supply to determine whether they are currently in balance. This is an elementary scoping question both in the arid West and non-arid places where water is valued both on and off site. Water-surplus regions in the future will find both a local and regional market for what can be sold. Even East of the Mississippi River where water supply is generally not the principal factor in a land purchase, I urge readers to think a bit about it. Does the target property have a surplus of water, and, if so, will that continue in the future if you and the neighbors increase your draw? Is there a way to maintain your supply given the water law in the state where the property is located? (See discussion below.) Does the target property's surplus water currently have market value and, if so, what is it? What might be the value of the property's water at various future points?

Surface waters can be thought of in several ways: intermittent or permanent; standing or flowing; navigable or unnavigable. The same stream can share contrary characteristics, depending on the time of year and recent precipitation. These categories have legal and policy implications.

A landowner's rights and obligations to surface water can vary with its category or type. **Intermittent surface water** is linked to precipitation, which recharges underground reserves. Such water can become a legal issue when a landowner does something to capture it or concentrate it, thus affecting the quantity or quality of water flowing onto his neighbors. **Flowing water** (streams, rivers, creeks) is surface water that has value to a landowner for economic purposes, farming (irrigation), livestock, recreation and aesthetics. (Flowing water—even channels that are dry almost all year—is also a potential liability, because it can flood during high-volume precipitations.)

Where precipitation is scarce and surface-water flow uncertain, the right to surface water (both intermittent and permanent) takes on great importance and substantial economic value. Any buyer looking at arid or irrigated land should investigate what legally established rights to water, if any, the seller is also conveying with the land. Do these rights provide a sufficient volume for your purposes? Is the source of irrigated water being reduced upstream by natural factors or man-made reasons? If supply changes gradually from snow pack (stored water) to rain, how will that affect your property? Protracted drought can ruin river-irrigated crops. Ask about the regularity and volume of summer rainfall, especially if you have in mind growing something that hasn't been done successfully before. (Success means crops sold for a profit over a period of time.)

If you are buying irrigated property that depends exclusively on drilled wells or have plans that require drilling a large-volume well, hire a consulting engineer for testing and advice before you purchase. You want his opinion about the feasibility and cost of your plan. You can include a **test-results-acceptable-to-buyer contingency** in your purchase contract. Also, check out the water uses (both actual and potential) above you in the watershed. You may discover a use or planned use above you that will substantially change the amount of surface water available to you. In places where water is always an issue in land sales, discuss things with a local lawyer before you submit a contract. Your ability to use surface waters in the quantity you want may be the single most important factor in selecting among properties.

On certain waterways, you may have to determine whether flowing water on or bordering the target property has been deemed **navigable** or **unnavigable**. Your landowner rights are greater with unnavigable streams; with navigable waters, your water rights are limited to those that do not interfere with public needs and uses. **Navigable** is defined as a waterway that is designated as navigable on a federal survey map that is available from the U.S. Geological Survey. And for regulatory purposes under federal clean-water legislation, navigable has been interpreted to include any waters that have the capability of affecting interstate commerce. Navigable, consequently, includes some watercourses that no one can navigate, including the local ducks. The creek in my backfield is classified as navigable despite being dry at least nine months of the year; a skilled and foolhardy kayacker might paddle a few yards in it about seven days a year. It is "navigable," because it is part of the Potomac River watershed. The current definition of navigable allows federal agencies to control what happens in this non-navigable navigable creek. Court cases are challenging this broad definition, which underlies the extended federal reach. If, for instance, federal water-pollution regulations are amended to require fencing livestock out of waterways, those amendments will be based on the federal government's authority to manage navigable water.

With exceptions, the general rule is that the landowner who borders a navigable stream owns to the low-water line, which allows public use of the water between these lines. The area between the high-water and low-water lines on each side of a waterway is known as **flat land**, with the public holding a right to its use superior to that of the bordering landowner. A fisherman or boater has no right to cross your land to get to a navigable stream, but once there, he may enjoy use of the water even if your enjoyment is reduced. With an **unnavigable** waterway, the bordering landowner owns to its centerline. Both navigable and unnavigable waterways can rework their channels from floods and other natural forces. The boundary lines of bordering owners can change with the gradual, natural shifts of streambeds and the erosion and accretion of land in and around them. Floods, on the other hand, generally do not change boundary lines. Where a deed says something like "the boundary runs with the centerline of the stream channel," the boundary line can change.

Surface-water ownership and usage operate under two legal theories. In most of the eastern United States, states mainly follow the theory of **riparian rights**. **Riparian land** is land over which water flows and land that borders and extends away from a stream. It is land that is owned by a person whose property fronts the flowing water. Not all of a watershed or drainage is considered riparian land, just that which has water frontage. Riparian rights are also used in some non-eastern states, such as Louisiana, Arkansas and Minnesota. Riparian rights run with the land, but they can be severed from its surface through sale, lease or reservation. A large piece of riparian land can be divided in such a way that some parcels continue to border the water and continue to have riparian rights but other parcels lose these rights unless they are specifically reserved in the deed to the buyer. (**Littoral land** borders an ocean, sea, and, in some states, lakes. Littoral rights are like riparian rights, except that littoral owners own to the high-water line, not to the water, with the state owning between that line and the low-water line.)

Riparian theory sets forth that ownership of riparian land establishes an equal right to water use. The riparian owner does not own the water, but he has the same right to use it as every other riparian owner. Each riparian owner loses "control" of the water once it passes his land.

What right does the downstream riparian owner have in the upstream water? There are two doctrines that address this question within riparian theory. Under the **natural flow doctrine**, a downstream owner can limit the upstream owner where the upstream owner interferes with the natural flow of the stream. The doctrine has been modified over time. Maine, New Jersey, Pennsylvania, West Virginia, Georgia, Mississippi, Missouri and South Dakota provide that each riparian owner must do nothing to diminish or impede the natural flow of water downstream.

The second doctrine—**reasonable use**—posits that each riparian owner is allowed to make reasonable use of surface water as it flows by his property. The upstream riparian owner may reduce the flowing water for a reasonable use in a way that does not unreasonably injure down-stream riparian owners. Consider, then, what you, a downstream owner might accept as a reasonable injury? The upstream reasonable use should be for ordinary or domestic purposes (including watering livestock) and is sometimes capped at a specific volume. In the case where an upstream owner is using his water in such a way that it is affecting the quality of the water as it passes the downstream owner, a court would have to decide whether the upstream owner is using the water reasonably and whether the harm suffered by the downstream neighbor is unreasonable in the circumstances. Reasonable use does not guarantee that everyone downstream will have all the water that is wanted or needed; nor does it guarantee the quality that downstream users want or need. An upstream user, however, probably could not get away with making downstream water unusable. An upstream owner would be able to use all the water in a stream or make it unusable where a court determined that his use was reasonable in the circumstances. It depends on how "reasonable" is defined. Riparian-law states apply the reasonable-use doctrine more than the natural-flow doctrine.

The other theory of surface-water rights in the United States is called "**prior appropriation**," which is the basis of water-rights law in the drier states of the West. Some states use both theories. Prior appropriation gives to the person who first uses surface water for an economic or beneficial purpose a superior right to those who follow in time. Colorado rejects riparian rights completely, while California combines the two theories. If the upstream owner was the first to draw water from a Colorado stream for irrigation, his right to take what he wants is stronger than those downstream who established their irrigation uses later. All beneficial uses are not equal; they are usually ranked in a hierarchy of user claims with domestic use at the top. That highest-ranking claimant need not be a riparian landowner. Nine states— California, Kansas, Nebraska, North Dakota, Oklahoma, Oregon, South Dakota, Texas and Washington— follow the California doctrine that gives priority to riparian user-owners over those who are non-adjacent appropriators. The other nine western states—Alaska, Arizona, Colorado, Idaho, Montana, Nevada, New Mexico, Utah and Wyoming—follow prior appropriation doctrine strictly. (See Les and Carol Scher, Finding and Buying Your Place in the Country, 5th Edition [Chicago: Dearborn, 2000.])

I had occasion to scope a ranch southeast of Cody, Wyoming that contained about 9,000 deeded acres and about 45,000 acres under lease from the state and the Bureau of Land Management. Of the deeded acres, almost 1,200 were irrigated hayfields that had first-draw rights from the Greybull River. This ranch had established its first-draw right because it was first in time under the prior-appropriation doctrine. The ranch's irrigated land and its river bottom land were the most valuable acreage in the parcel, both types being valued at between $4,000 to $5,000 per acre. The rest of the property was valued at between $350 and about $600 per acre. Water is money.

The right to use surface and underground waters is crucial to property value in the arid West. A dirt-smart buyer there must also become water-smart. The seller may have rights to surface water by deed, lease, prescription or permit. **Water-appropriation permits** are used in prior-appropriation states (except Montana). They set forth the parameters for the permit holder to take (divert) water, including the location of where the water is to be diverted, amount (cubic feet per day or acre-feet per year), seasonal timing, purpose of the diversion, methods to be used, among other items. A buyer in a prior-appropriation state must check into use patterns on permit waterways through public records and the sophisticated survey-research technique called, "asking around." Permit research may or may not indicate what will happen in the future—or even what actually happened in the past if there was night-time bootlegging. Asking around may prevent the new buyer from finding his stream bone dry when he needs water most.

From a legal perspective, surface water is conceptualized differently than underground water. Surface water is more thought of as a *resource*, particularly lakes and rivers. But it is a resource with a downside.

Snow and rain supply surface waters, mainly through **runoff,** which is also referred to as diffused surface water and storm-water runoff. When surface water appears in a quantity that overwhelms the ability of the land to absorb it, flooding, soil erosion and sediment build-up occur.

Twelve of the 50 states allow a landowner to take any measures to protect himself from runoff and flooding, even those measures that increase the risk and damage to his neighbors. (The 12 are Arizona, Arkansas, Hawaii, Indiana, Missouri, Nebraska, New York, North Dakota, Oklahoma, Virginia, West Virginia and Wisconsin.) All follow the "**common-enemy doctrine**," which allows a landowner any manner of self-defense. This doctrine would allow me to excavate a large drainage ditch in my creek bottom that would channel a flood into my downstream neighbor's backyard. Upstream landowners have, in addition, no obligation to do anything to protect their downstream neighbors. Uphill neighbors may install drainage pipes to capture runoff and direct it onto their adjoining, downhill neighbors. I encountered the reality of the common-enemy doctrine several years ago when I had to install a complicated and expensive drainage system to capture the directed runoff from an uphill neighbor who had installed underground drain tiles that emptied onto my land at our common property line.

In the other 38 states, a landowner may protect his own land from runoff and flooding only if his measures are reasonable and impose minimal harm to adjoining landowners. Eight of the 38—Alabama, California, Georgia, Illinois, Kansas, Kentucky, Pennsylvania and Tennessee—prohibit a landowner from interfering or affecting surface water flow, even where he is harmed by his inaction. These states, following the **natural flow doctrine**, embrace a concept of responsibility that is opposite of the 12 common-enemy states. Either doctrine can directly impact you if you buy property that floods. Look for floodplain, streams, coves, and then evidence of flooding, such as loose rocks on top of bottom land, creek beds filled with rock, vegetation hung on fence lines and household debris festooning creek-side trees.

Underground water resources are classified as either **percolating waters** or **underground streams**. Percolating water is precipitation migrating through the soil, or water from a stream that has seeped out of its bed and is no longer part of the flow. The concept includes veins of water that are not discoverable from the surface, underground lakes and artesian basins. If water is flowing underground, it is an underground stream, not percolating water. The underlying legal rule for percolating waters is that the owner of the land owns them absolutely and may use them without regard to others. This English common law root has been modified by the substitution of the reasonable-use idea, whereby each surface owner has a right to use these waters for his reasonable needs on his land. California rejects both ideas, and says that landowners must share percolating waters in proportion to the surface area each owns. California's theory is called **correlative rights**. Underground streams are difficult to identify from the surface and are, inevitably, connected with percolating water. Where an underground stream is identified, surface water law is usually applied.

In sum, there are four main ideas that make up state water-rights law on ownership and usage: 1) absolute ownership, 2) reasonable use, 3) prior application and 4) correlative rights. While federal environmental laws and regulations control most water-pollution issues, you can find yourself in a situation where the individual state's water doctrine controls the ownership of your property's water, what you and your neighbors can do with it, and how those uses may affect its quantity and quality downstream. Since a state may combine some of these ideas and then have state-specific judicial and legislative interpretations to boot, you will need to consult with a local lawyer who has done water cases to know where you stand on any given question that your scoping identifies.

Water in the East is not generally considered a discrete asset that can be leased or sold independently, though I think that will change as metropolitan demand for water increases. When you buy land in the East, you are usually safe in assuming that you are buying the subsurface (and surface) waters as well, without restrictions. (If constraints other than those imposed by state water law exist, they will appear in the deed or other document of record.) A purchase-offer contract that incorporates the phrase "**fee** simple" or "**in fee**" means that the buyer is making an offer for the property's full bundle of rights and assets. If the seller doesn't own the land's water in fee, he can't convey it to you. Your incorporation of that phrase in your contract forces the seller to disclose any diminution of his rights and ownership. It's fair to assume that the surface owner will have reasonable use rights to the subsurface water beneath the property. "Reasonable use," however, can easily mean reduced water for the next neighbor, which is you in relation to the higher neighbor. Check, therefore, how uphill neighbors use their water. Large farming operations may be tapping into an aquifer to a degree that reduces supply to your target property. Before you submit an offer, consider how any water-using plans you have might affect your neighbors, and vice versa.

It is always possible that you will find a property where a deed has conveyed away a water right that would normally run with the land or otherwise diminished the seller's usage right. This might be a sale that allows a neighbor to draw water from your spring. It might be a right to fish in a pond, or even a life-estate to let a particular family swim there. (A life-estate terminates with the death of the individual holding it.) Any recorded water restriction will bind you as the next owner.

It's not unusual to discover one party using water, such as a spring, located on another's property without any recorded agreement. This is a ticklish situation for both parties. The user may be able to establish a legal right to have his pipe in your spring despite your opposition by invoking some form of **adverse possession** (ownership) or (adverse) **prescription** (right to use) under state law. If he says that the seller gave him permission to put in a pipe, that permission (**license**) expires with the sale of the property or the death of the individual who gave it. If the user has no legal right to use the water from your spring, you then have three choices: put up with his usage, end it, or impose restrictions or conditions. If you put up with his usage despite being against it, he will be able to claim an adverse right after a certain number of years as long as his use meets all the other tests under state law. If you put up with it by giving him permission, then you can revoke permission if and when it suits you. The user acquires no independent and superior right to the spring over time beyond your permission. If you choose to sell the property and know of this spring encroachment, you should reveal it to your buyer before he submits an offer. When all is said and done, the user is taking spring water that did not belong to him when he first started taking it and should not belong to him now, though he may have a valid adverse claim to it. You may need this water, and he may depend on it. This is a problem that needs to be solved, not ignored. Check with your local lawyer as to the user's legal rights and then proceed carefully. This kind of dispute can generate recurring squabbles for many years.

The seller's deed may show that his water originates from a spring on a neighbor's property. This is a "**spring right**," which entitles its holder to draw water from the spring on another. The wording might even specify the diameter of your seller's out-take pipe and its location in the neighbor's spring box. It is not uncommon for a single spring to serve more than one property. We, for example, draw household water by deed from a developed spring on a neighbor's farm located on the other side of a state-maintained road. At another spot, we share a developed water trough that is situated 50-50 in a boundary line fence that is supplied by our spring. (The vernacular way of putting this is, "the spring is on me.") At another place, one neighbor draws water from another neighbor's spring through a pipe laid in a stream that's on me. Only the first of these spring "arrangements" shows up in a title search.

The owner of a spring can sell a permanent right to spring water, rent access to it, or simply grant a use right to a neighbor. The owner cannot, however, void a neighbor's deeded spring right. The owner might be allowed to "reasonably use" his land in such a way that it reduces or even eliminates the spring serving the neighbor. You might ask your local lawyer his opinion were you to drill a well above a shared spring.

The common practice when developing a shared spring is to put the springowner's out-take pipe lowest in the spring box and other users above the owner according to their order of right. In this fashion, the owner reserves to himself the first draw of water in the box. This protects the owner's water supply from the draws of other users, all of whom get water only if the supply in the box comes up to the level of their pipes. Your water supply is at most risk when your out-take pipe in a shared spring is highest in the box and smallest in diameter.

A buyer must check all of the following with developed springs:

- Is the seller's residence served by a spring on the seller's property? If not, on whose property is the spring located? Does the seller have a deeded right to tap this spring? If not, what is the basis, in law and otherwise, for the seller's use of this spring?

- How reliable is the spring during droughts? Measuring flow during a rainy period will not give you a reliable answer. You have to talk to the seller and his neighbors.

- Is the spring subject to either natural or man-made events that might affect its flow? Has the flow been affected by such events—flooding, drought, landslide, earthquake, new wells, etc.—in recent memory?

- Has the spring served the seller's property adequately for at least the last ten years? If you are going to use significantly more water than the seller, do you anticipate a shortage? On what do you base your opinion?

- How does water get from the spring to the house? Is the pipe old? Is it corroding? What is it made of? Will it need to be replaced soon?

- How is the water held at the house? Is the tank big enough for your purposes?

- Where does the spring overflow from the house go? If the house takes more, will there be enough supply for these secondary purposes?

- Have you tested the tap in the seller's house for common contaminants? If not, do you need to insert a contingency in your purchase contract for this purpose?

- Is the source of the seller's household water a shared spring? If so, which out-take pipe inside the spring box is the seller's?

- What is the position of the seller's pipe in the spring box with respect to other pipes? What is its internal diameter? Is there a screen over it to keep out dirt and critters? Is the pipe solid and without corrosion? When do you think the pipe will need to be replaced?

- Who is responsible for routine cleaning/maintenance of the spring box, spring house, pump, electricity, underground pipes, etc.?

- How are costs to be divided among the users when the spring has to be repaired or replaced?

- Does the spring box need to be cleaned or repaired?

- Is a neighbor tapping any spring on the seller's property? If so, what is the legal foundation of that neighbor's usage? Does this arrangement negatively affect your plans?

- Does the seller's property have a backup source of household water if the spring were to go dry?

Be very cautious about buying any land whose water and water rights are in any way not being fully conveyed to you as part of the land purchase. You protect yourself in three ways: 1) writing your purchase contract in a way that describes the land that you want to buy and will be conveyed to you as the property in fee (or fee simple), including all waters and water rights; 2) being alert for deeds that reserve a water right for a neighbor, third-party or the seller; and 3) scoping out unrecorded uses. You will need to determine exactly what water rights the owner holds and is conveying, just as you checked the title for mineral rights.

Depending on the particulars of a target property's water situation, you may need to write specific water guarantees into your purchase contract. One objective of doing so is to determine exactly the scope and validity of the seller's ownership of these resources under his signature. If he doesn't own them, you might pay for them but he can't convey them—a situation that you want to avoid. You can only own what the seller owns, even though he may want you to buy what he doesn't own.

Contract writing is discussed in Chapters 29 and 30, but the general requirements are worth summarizing here insofar as they bear on minerals, water, timber and other issues under review.

Your purchase contract should always include language that says your offer is for the seller's property with **a general warranty deed, marketable title and in fee**. The general warranty deed (sometimes referred to as a "**warranty deed**" or "**full-covenant deed**") conveys the property to the buyer with the maximum amount of seller promises regarding his ownership and clear title. General warranty deeds include five warranties, or seller promises, that are called the **covenants of title.** Among the promises in a warranty deed, is one where the seller promises the buyer that the only encumbrances—debt secured by a lien on the property—on the title are those that are found in the deed. A general warranty deed also means that the seller is offering these promises not only for the time that he's owned the property, but also for the time under previous owners. Other types of deeds may be offered, but they are not as good as a general warranty deed. A **special warranty deed** offers seller promises only for the period under the seller's ownership; it may also be referred to as a **limited warranty deed**. A **bargain-and-sale deed**, which is used in some states, provides fewer promises than a general warranty deed, but should protect the buyer against encumbrances and lack of seller ownership. A **grant deed** provides fewer promises and less protection than a general warranty deed. A **quitclaim deed** provides no promises and no protection, since the owner is selling only his interest in the property, whatever that interest is, which may be none at all.

Any encumbrance, severance or reservation on the owner's water or minerals should be recorded, but you may find something that is off the books. These arrangements may or may not be legal. Consult with your lawyer before submitting a purchase offer.

A **marketable title** is one where no question exists as to who the owner is. When a seller agrees to convey property to a buyer with a marketable title, he is saying that he has good, or clear, title to that which he is conveying. A marketable title should have no defects and should not open the buyer to litigation over ownership. A buyer can reasonably expect that a property conveyed to him with a marketable title can be sold or mortgaged. Buyers want sellers to provide them with marketable title to all land, minerals, water and associated rights where possible. Land can be conveyed without a marketable title if the buyer does not specify marketable title in his purchase contract.

Finally, the buyer wants the seller to convey the property **in fee**, which may also be referred to as fee simple title or fee estate. This level of conveyance gives the buyer complete ownership of all the rights and assets of the land, including minerals and water, with the power to sell, lease, give or encumber them at his discretion, subject to a lender's note or mortgage. To make sure that there is no misunderstanding as to what in fee means, you can provide in your contract that the "**seller agrees to convey to buyer by general warranty deed marketable title to the subject property in fee simple, including all surface and underground minerals, waters and all other resources and rights**." If the seller's ownership is hinky or he owns less than a full set of assets and rights in the property, this language should smoke him out. In the worst case—where the seller signs your contract with this language and you discover after the purchase that his title is flawed or the minerals did not convey—these words in your purchase contract are the foundation of your suit against the seller. He promised you certain things when he signed your contract and could not/did not deliver.

CHAPTER 15: MATCHMAKING

FINDING

How do you find rural property?

The Internet now has several websites that provide such information, including www.landandfarm.com, www.landwatch.com, www.elandusa.com, www.land-fsbo.com, www.land.net, www.fsbo.com, www.landsofamerica.com, www.ebay.com, www.landlister.com, www.forestlandmls.com, www.eaglestar.net, www.unitedcountry.com, RLi@realtors.org, www.owners.com and www.forsalebyowner.com, among others. These sites host sellers looking for buyers, and in some cases, buyers looking for property. Ebay auctions land; the bidding is often on the amount of deposit. Wood-products companies, such as paper manufacturers and sawmills, sell undeveloped land in tracts of all sizes and can generally be accessed through corporate websites. You can find woodland for sale through the websites of timber investment management companies and consulting foresters, such as www.fountainforestry.com and www.landvest.com. Land is also sold by companies whose business is to buy large tracts, divide them and flip them as quickly as possible. These large tracts are bought wholesale and, after division, sold retail. These companies will advertise every week in the Sunday editions of large metropolitan newspapers, usually with toll-free numbers. These parcels are directed toward retail consumers willing to pay full market price for convenience shopping.

The traditional buyer approach is to contact a real-estate broker in the target area and look at properties that are shown to you. The broker in this arrangement is usually working for the seller. Properties on which the broker has the listing will be shown first, because the agency's own listings produce the most money for the broker and his agents when they're sold.

You can take out a **Land-Wanted ad** in the local paper. This strategy is primarily prospecting for a FSBO, though brokers may respond. Ads work best when you are already familiar with the county and have a reasonably clear idea as to what you want and don't want. Make your ad specific in terms of preferred location, acreage, house (or no house) and whatever features you consider necessities. I recommend that you ask sellers to respond to your ad by sending their property information to a local post office box, addressed to "Property Buyer." You might describe yourself and your purpose in the ad, e.g., "family of three looking for old farm property." I would not include a phone number and an address that might lead a seller to infer that you are "rich." Pick up your mail on a Friday afternoon or Saturday morning and look that weekend at the responses with the most promise. The ad should ask the seller to send you a copy of the property's tax map or survey, a road map that locates the property with access marked and a brief description. The seller should also be asked to send his name, mailing address, phone, fax and e-mail address. If you ask for more than this, you will discourage replies. After you've become familiar with your target county, this is sufficient information to allow you to screen a property in or out for further scoping. The cost of local want-ad advertising is small. While an advertising "campaign" may save you time, you should want to spend a certain amount of time "wasted" in looking at properties that don't fit your needs. Each rejected property will teach you a bit more about fitting your search to what's available and what your dollar buys. Looking at properties you don't want is a necessary part of dragging yourself up the local learning curve; you just don't want to drag yourself up the same curve over and over again.

I would not have the ad state either the per-acre price or overall price you are willing to pay. Let the seller propose a price. If you state an able-and-willing price, you will get FSBOs calling to sell you over-priced properties that meet it. The advertising buyer should expect responses from some owners wanting to sell over-priced properties as well as from sellers of something-wrong-with-them properties. These are "fishing" replies cast in your direction. Smart fish pass on hooks, particularly baited ones.

The best approach to finding property is to develop a friendship with a local contact or two who will let you know when a property that fits your search criteria is about to come to the market. This allows you to take advantage of local word-of-mouth information. The local contacts will screen properties on your behalf. Make sure to arrange to pay these contacts a consultant's fee for your purchase. Two or three percent of the gross selling price is a fair finder's fee. You, the buyer, should initiate the proposal for this type of consulting service.

Word-of-mouth leads can come to you in other ways as well. As you go through a target county, ask about property that might be for sale. The individuals you might ask are those you're working with (lawyer, surveyor, forester) and folks you run into—the motel owner where you stay, the restaurant owner where you like to eat, the banker you've talked to about a mortgage, county extension agent, state forester, building and excavation contractors, and the local building inspector. Word-of-mouth finds are often very attractive purchases when a buyer approaches a seller at just the right moment with a simple, cash offer. The seller's asking price is more than likely set without an appraisal or a comparables analysis. On the other hand, buyers should be aware that some sellers like to "float their property" in this manner to test a high asking price, and others shop their property this way to screen in certain types of buyers and screen out other types.

Most rural property is sold either by **owners themselves (For Sale By Owners,** or **FSBOs)** or through **state-licensed, real-estate brokers** (and their **agents**). Property can also be sold by a bank that repossesses it, at auctions of various types or through an attorney handling an estate.

A variation on the usual broker listing is a property that's for sale through a broker but not advertised. This arrangement allows the broker to select "qualified" buyers and match them with particular properties and owners. It spares the seller the publicity of being a seller. The practice may be officially prohibited, because it lends itself to discrimination. From the buyer's perspective, a listing that has not been publicized (yet) can be either a good deal or a set up. My impression is that "off-the-books" listings are sometimes used to steer certain urban clients (who are perceived to be wealthy) to properties that are priced above market value. This often happens just before a broker officially gets or processes a listing. The farm I bought in Blue Grass in 1983 was not advertised by the broker who had the listing, though the neighbors knew it was for sale. I was willing to pay more than the local buyers, so the tactic worked for the seller.

Private auctions are also used to sell rural property, usually as part of settling an estate or when the owner is pinched by debt and needs to raise cash. Auctions are also used by lenders to dispose of **foreclosure properties**, which is real estate that the lender has taken over because the borrower/owner has fallen delinquent in his debt repayment. I discuss auctions below. Foreclosure auctions are rare in my area, and I don't have any first-hand experience with them. In more densely populated rural areas, foreclosures are more common. Two books that cover this topic are George Achenbach, Goldmining in Foreclosure Properties, 3rd ed. (New York: John Wiley & Sons, Inc., 1994), and Ted Thomas, Big Money in Real Estate Foreclosures (New York: John Wiley & Sons, Inc., 1992).

Another matchmaking technique is the **sale of tax-delinquent property**. It's rare that a non-local buyer is able to find the right property through a tax sale, but it's possible. Investors work these sales to make money, not to find a second-home property. Tax sales are announced in the local paper. They are properties whose owners have either chosen not to pay property taxes because the property isn't worth it to them or lost the ability to pay the tax. The sale's trustee—usually a local lawyer—will not provide much information to buyers about the property, and these properties are sold "as is." Owners have redemption rights in most places, which allow them to get their property back by paying the tax bill plus interest to the buyer holding the delinquency within a certain period of time. There's nothing wrong with buying at a tax sale; just remember that the original owner may reclaim his property in states that provide for redemption. You won't lose money in a redemption state, but you may waste time and opportunity.

Buyers need to know the state's rules for purchasing tax-delinquent property before getting involved. Contact the local agency, often the county sheriff's office, to obtain information; then call the state office for further information. (You can get the state office by asking the local official.) Go to a tax-delinquent sale before you are a bidder yourself. Talk to one or two of the regulars; they may be inclined to be helpful if you say you're only looking at one parcel. Make sure you understand the redemption provision and whether the property is burdened by a mortgage or other type of lien—which will have to be settled in one fashion or another. Tax-delinquent properties may also bear other sorrows—such as a questionable access—which led the owner to stop paying the property tax. You shouldn't buy tax-delinquent properties just because they appear to be cheap: they may be cheap because they're worthless. You need to scope them thoroughly. While it is possible to obtain land for back taxes, it's often more complicated and more costly than that. You can acquire information by searching the Internet under "**tax liens**," by state.

Property finders are generally people who primarily do other things in and around real estate. Depending on their position, they may or may not be able to accept a buyer-paid fee. An excavation contractor who gives you a call with a lead should get a **finder's fee**, a banker with the same tip should not. Finders work in various industries, though they are discouraged from working in real estate by state laws that protect the business interests of licensed brokers. A buyer can always contract with an unlicensed individual, acting as a consultant not a broker, to help him find rural land and pay this person a fee for his successful service. The consultant, of course, cannot provide brokerage services. The fee paid to the consultant would vary with the amount of work he performs for you. One to three percent of your gross purchase price would be fair for providing you with a lead that results in a purchase. Where the buyer wants the consultant to scope a property, it's fair to either pay a higher percentage or a lower percentage plus an hourly rate for billed time. On small-dollar properties of, say, $100,000 or less, you might arrange to pay a flat fee and shift the time-risk to the consultant. Small properties often involve as much time-work as large ones. You can also buy a fixed number of hours at an agreed rate, the last eight of which will be used to prepare a report of the consultant's findings. If you work with a consultant, I would advise that you make sure that he is working exclusively for you. Avoid an arrangement where a finder is getting paid by both buyer and seller, because the finder is then working primarily for his own interest in getting the sale done, whether or not it's good for you. A finder-consultant should reveal to a buyer whether or not he expects payment from any other party in the deal.

States differ in allowing a non-broker to act as a **finder**. Nothing prevents a buyer from hiring a consultant-finder to identify and scope a likely property for him. Some states regulate "finding" when it also entails introducing a buyer to a seller. My sense of this is that a finder who does nothing but find (identify) and scope does not run afoul of state laws, but the finder who acts as a **middleman** may, depending on the state. A middleman, unlike a finder, introduces buyer to seller and may facilitate the negotiation and purchase in various ways. That's what a broker does, and that's what states prohibit unlicensed individuals from doing. Some states allow anyone to serve as a middleman, charging one or both parties a fee for the service; other states allow none but licensed real-estate brokers to charge an introduction fee. Brokers in some states are also prohibited from sharing real-estate commissions with unlicensed finders. States that prohibit non-brokers from introducing a buyer to a seller may allow a lawyer in the course of his legal work to perform this function and charge a fee.

Land consultants, who are not licensed brokers, are rare. You probably won't find one in the phone book. Consultants I've met on timberland deals don't advertise and are not interested in working on small purchases. It is not a profession in the sense of having entrance requirements and licenses. A buyer's best chance of finding a knowledgeable local contact who can provide this service is to ask his local lawyer, forester and surveyor. The buyer wants to find an individual who knows local real estate and can bring analytical skills to property evaluation. A land consultant who is a licensed broker and works exclusively for the buyer is a **buyer's broker**.

Even where states do not allow a middleman to charge a fee, a buyer can hire a **land consultant** to bird-dog properties for him and pay for the service. The nature of the consultant's work for each buyer is up to the parties themselves and is subject to state law. Consultants should not be employed to provide legal advice or brokerage services. A consultant can offer an opinion about a boundary encroachment or an access problem, but the buyer needs to keep in mind that the non-lawyer consultant is not offering competent legal advice. In consulting contracts I sign with clients, I always include language where the buyer acknowledges that he understands that he alone is responsible for performing **due diligence**, evaluating any information provided and making the decision to purchase or not. The consultant should be expected to give opinions, framed between his best experience-based judgment and the best interest of his client. Consultants, like stockbrokers and investment advisers, can fail to learn something about an investment or err in calculating benefits. A court would ultimately decide whether the consultant should have reasonably known the fact that led to the buyer's harm. Consultants who deliberately steer clients into bad deals should not be held harmless.

You will get a sense of a consultant's reliability and thoroughness through close examination of any scoping work and written analysis he does on your nickel. If he projects timber values, for instance, he should state clearly the origins and timeliness of the species prices he used in his projections. If you read a consultant's report that is filled with general statements and unsupported assumptions, it's probably a hurry-up job. Property-evaluation reports should be fact-based, logical, transparent and documented. Where assumptions are made, they should be both identified and justified. You want to know how the consultant got to his bottom line, not just what his bottom-line recommendation is. If you get a feeling that the consultant is pushing you toward a buy, back away; he's working for a fee, not his client. Pay attention to what the facts and numbers tell you on their own. Since a land consultant's loyalty and duty are to the buyer (his client), I believe buyers are better served by having a land consultant on their side than by working with a broker who is obliged to represent the seller's interests. Brokers will quarrel with that opinion.

REAL-ESTATE BROKERS: THE SELLER'S AGENT

Buyers typically begin prospecting for rural property by phoning several real-estate **brokers** in their target area. A broker is a private-sector businessperson who has passed several levels of examination and is licensed by the state where he operates. A broker can buy, sell, lease or exchange property for a commission or fee charged to the seller or buyer, or both. He will typically have **agents** (and perhaps other licensed brokers) working for his brokerage **on commission**, that is, for a share of the fees they generate from sales. A commission is usually a percentage of the gross sales price. The typical commission charged by a broker to a seller is five to six percent, though that percentage falls on larger properties. A fee is usually a fixed charge. The terms are often used interchangeably.

The broker and seller sign a contract whereby the broker markets the seller's property for a commission. The seller's property is **listed** with this broker for either a fixed period of time (e.g., six-months, one year) or on an open-ended basis. The seller's contract with the broker is called a **listing agreement**, and it spells out the property to be sold, duration of the listing, commission owed to the broker and other contract terms. Such a broker is the **listing broker**. If another broker finds a buyer for the listing-broker, he is a **cooperating broker**. A real-estate agent who works for the listing broker and who brought the listing to the brokerage is the **listing agent**. An agent from another brokerage who brings a buyer to a listed property is a **cooperating agent**. **All of these individuals represent the seller and his interests, not the buyer and his interests**. The seller's broker/agent (s) has a **fiduciary** responsibility to, and relationship with, the seller, arising from the listing agreement. The broker/agent owes the seller the duties of care, obedience, accounting, loyalty and disclosure (of information or material facts that the agent knows or should have reasonably been expected to know). As a group, I'll refer to the seller's side—his agents and brokers—as the **seller's agent** or the **seller's side**.

The seller's side gets paid its commission when the seller sells the property to a buyer that the seller's side has produced. The commission is paid from the seller's funds at closing by the escrow agent. The commission appears on the **settlement statement** as a debit to the seller's proceeds. Commissions for all real estate averaged a bit over five percent of the gross sales price in recent years, though property in my rural area often bears a ten percent commission.

The seller-paid commission is split among whichever brokers and agents were involved on the seller's side, a number that typically ranges between one and four. A real-estate broker makes the most money on a sale when he is both the listing agent and the individual who sells the property; in that case, he gets 100 percent of the commission. A listing broker will split a commission with a cooperating broker, and each in turn will split his share with any agent who was involved in the sale. This commission structure explains why agents who drive you around take you to their personal listings and the listings of their broker first. If nothing interests you, they will show you listings from other brokers with whom they will become cooperating agents in the event of a sale.

When a buyer is driven around looking at properties with a seller's agent, he is in the company of an individual who is legally obliged to represent only the seller's interest in the sale. No matter how friendly you become, no matter how many cups of coffee you share, *this agent is not working for you*. This should not mean that the seller's agent will lie to you, though this happens. It often means that the agent does not share certain information with you that would put a sale—and the agent's commission—at risk. This behavior can harm a buyer who does not know the right questions to ask with the right words. Agents usually know some of their brokerage's listings better than others. An agent may give a buyer false or misleading information for lack of familiarity, or from being informed erroneously, or from not wanting to know a particular fact, or from making an assumption that turns out to be false. Even where an agent tells a buyer the truth as he genuinely believes it to be, the buyer can be misled if the agent is mistaken.

A seller's agent should not give a buyer information that advantages the buyer at the expense of his client—the seller. This can be a tricky act of judgment for an agent when he is in the vortex of conflicting interests. His client's interest—that is, the seller's—lies in getting his property sold at an acceptable price, as quickly and cleanly as possible, with no post-sale complications. The buyer's interest lies in purchasing some property—if not this seller's, then another's—that fits his goals, at an acceptable price, and free of post-sale surprises or complications. The seller's agent's interest lies in getting a deal done with the least amount of time, work and money invested in the process of matching seller and buyer. The longer a listing stays unsold, the more likely it is that the price will be cut, which in turn lowers his percentage commission. Stale listings may also produce a seller's request that the listing broker lower his commission to allow the seller to lower his asking price. When the listing expires, the disgruntled seller can move the listing to another broker or try to sell it himself. If the agent's listing does not produce a sale, the agent and his brokerage receive nothing for their marketing efforts and expenses. Thus, an ethical line exists between a seller's agent working both seller and buyer toward a mutually acceptable deal and this agent working both seller and buyer toward a deal that's not quite right for either party. You—the buyer—can assume that the seller's agent cares little whether the deal is good for you; remember his fiduciary duty is to the seller. When the seller's agent crosses the line by working for the sale despite his client's best interests, these deals can have **snakes at both ends** in the sense that the seller or the buyer, or both, find themselves bitten after the purchase. Agents must police themselves against pushing a deal that's more for their own benefit than for the seller's. It's fair for a seller's agent to work toward a deal, but it's a red flag for the buyer when he senses that the seller's agent is nudging both sides toward a purchase that the seller's not quite committed to. If an agent is prepared to push his client, the seller, over the edge, consider what he's willing to do to the buyer

I was recently mailed a promotional flyer from a broker in the Southeast who markets mountain property of 20 to 1,000 acres. This seller's agent advises buyers whom he's trying to attract to show his sellers that they "mean business." How does this seller's agent suggest that you show his sellers that you're serious. First, the buyer should put his offer in writing. Absolutely; any other offer is worthless. Second, he advises that the buyer should make his offer as "clean" as possible. What's that mean? Offer the highest price you are willing to pay with no contingencies, he writes. Omit language that gives you, the buyer, a way out. Third, the buyer should offer more earnest money deposit than might normally be expected. Finally, offer to close the deal in a short period of time. Well, well. This behavior will certainly help his clients. Admittedly, occasions exist when a prudent buyer can take one or more of these steps as long as he has scoped sufficiently. But buyers can open themselves to great harm if they follow this path in most circumstances.

I have found sellers' agents to range widely in their knowledge and honesty. I have been shown timberland by agents who could not distinguish one tree species from another and who had no idea about how to value timber on the stump. This did not stop them from advertising tracts as "containing valuable timber" when the tracts didn't or as advertising themselves as "specialists in timber tracts and farms" when they weren't. I have seen brokers advertise woodland property as containing "standing timber," which, I'm sure, is better than the alternative. "Standing timber" is a meaningless phrase in terms of whether or not the trees have commercial value. Very large trees can be absolutely worthless, standing or not. I have also seen agents advertise woodland properties as "pre-cut," as if a buyer receives some benefit from having the kindly seller remove the merchantable timber before selling it. I have had sellers' agents lie to my face, distract me from a defect, mislead me, plead lack of knowledge when they knew what I wanted to know, offer opinions about zoning and regulatory matters that were dead wrong, suggest that I do things that would harm me, advise me to make a full-price offer in order to get a full-price offer with no contingencies from another buyer, and provide false information about the seller. I have seen some agents routinely violate their legal responsibilities to their own clients to get a sale. There are two stereotypical real-estate agents—the ditzy, middle-aged woman and the sleazy guy. I've met them both—and so will you if you're persistent. But I've also had dealings with honest, hard-working, decent sellers' agents who played fair with buyers and their own clients. You have to determine where on the spectrum the seller's agent falls as part of your approach to any property. And remember that you can run into an agent who is both ditzy and sleazy.

Several times a seller's agent has told me that the seller would accept an offer below the listing price, or asking price. What to make of that? If the statement is made without the seller's consent, it strikes me that it's an ethical breach. It may be a ploy to get me to offer the agent-recommended price that is below the asking price when that price is actually higher than what the seller would really accept. Then it's a tactic to get me to pay more, which is fine with both the seller and his agent. Sometimes, however, it is an honest effort to get to a consensus price, sparing each side discordant bargaining that might produce nothing more than deadlock. Your price should be the price you're willing to pay after scoping the property's values and liabilities. If your price is below the seller's bottom, don't go up just because he's come down.

Buyers must be alert to the possibility that one or more of dozens of traps can be waiting for those who do not scope and get accurate answers. An agent once showed me a pretty tract of woods and pasture, but failed to tell me that he knew an underground coal mine was about to start operations beneath the entire acreage. I knew that Garrett County in western Maryland had mining—both surface and underground—in its southern half. And I also knew that an underground mine was active on the other side of a hill—out of sight and sound of the target property—a couple of miles away. Since the seller was only selling the surface rights, I checked into both the ownership of the subsurface minerals and whether plans were afoot to mine them. I did not want to buy the surface and then discover that I was facing subsidence or water problems. A call to the local office of the Maryland Department of Mines found an underground-mining plan on file that projected moving up to the property line. And, finally, a call to the mining company confirmed that it had leased the coal rights and was about to file a plan revision and start mining under my target property within the next couple of months. When I asked this agent—a "land specialist"—whether he had known of the mining plans, he shrugged and said that he thought I was interested in the timber and the pasture—both statements being true. Did he know the possible consequences of luring a buyer into this situation? Undoubtedly, he did. Sleazy.

Another broker once discouraged me from contacting the local electric-utility company to get an estimate of the costs involved in running a new line from the closest existing power pole onto a target property with no electricity. Several thousand feet of new line appeared to be needed. I knew that each power company has its own formula for determining the cost of new lines and spreading them over a period of years. He said, he thought it might come to a "couple of thousand," based on what he had seen on other properties with this utility. The important thing, he said, was for me "to get this 300 acres bought before that rich doctor from Washington buys it out from under you." (Rich doctors, I have found, are always about to buy the places I'm looking at, according to the agents. In my local area, the rich doctor is either from Richmond or Washington, D.C. When I looked for property in Wyoming, he was a Denver surgeon.) I called the utility. The cost estimate came to more than $80,000. It included a warning that in the utility's opinion the adjoining landowner might refuse to grant a utility easement over his property. In that case, the connection would have to be made at an alternative pole on another neighbor with an even higher cost. It became apparent from talking with the utility representative that he had tried to get an easement from the closest neighbor before—without success. I backed away and hoped that all rich doctors diagnosed this property as I did, the cost of which was the price of a phone call. Was this broker being dishonest with me? Absolutely. But he couched his estimate as being based on what he had seen in other circumstances, not on what he knew first hand. Had I accepted his opinion at face value, I would have bought 300 acres—and soon after that a bunch of candles. If a target property does not have an electric pole on it, don't make an offer until you have a cost estimate in hand.

One broker told me that a target property whose listing he had contained 347 acres, more or less. He advertised it so. He knew, however, that it was short, because he had access to an unrecorded survey done by a mineral company who had leased the minerals years earlier and then let the lease expire. When I proposed as part of my offer that we adjust the per-acre price, up or down, depending on what a survey that I paid for showed, he declined. "It's the same money," he said, "whatever the acreage." My surveyor found that the property lacked 27 acres. In his defense, the broker never said that the property contained 347 acres. He said it contained 347 acres, more or less. It's also true that he never volunteered information about the old survey's findings. I had asked my surveyor to run the deed's calls through his computer program to determine acreage before I made my offer. He did, and then told me it was probably seven acres short. The other 20 acres disappeared, it seems, as a result of "bad calls," which showed 20 acres in the deed, but not on the ground. Or something like that.

I was once shown a perfectly nice house and small acreage along a major two-lane highway on a sunny Saturday morning. At the property's back line was a dense stand of large pine trees. An unpaved public road bordered one side of the property about 75 yards from the house. No vehicle turned from the highway onto this unpaved road during the hour or so I was looking around. The broker never told me that a major sawmill lay behind the pine buffer. Since I didn't know the area, I didn't know enough to ask and wasn't smart enough to look. The broker didn't think it was necessary to volunteer that information. Had I visited on a weekday, the mill's activity would have been obvious. This broker didn't tell me something that he knew and I didn't, and he knew I didn't. When I stumbled by chance on this bit of information a few days later, I should have stopped looking with this broker. From that experience, I learned to look and ask about neighbors as part of my scoping.

Had I purchased the property and then learned of the mill, I would have been a fool to take the broker to court. His defense: "Your honor that sawmill's been there for 50 years. Logging trucks go in and out of there every day of the week. Anyone in the neighborhood could have told him about the mill. It's his responsibility to do his own due diligence. The mill is not a legal nuisance, and, to my knowledge, the people who owned this house before never complained. Ours is a rural community that depends on logging. I don't consider this mill, which employs 20 individuals and is the county's third largest employer, a liability or a defect in the property the buyer purchased. I am not required to disclose the presence of neighbors. This is not analogous to a house with termites, which I am obliged to disclose."

My argument would have been: "This broker was told specifically that I only wanted to buy quiet property. He knew that I would not have considered this house had I known of the sawmill. The omission of relevant information constitutes fraud. While the broker represents the seller in this transaction, surely he has a duty to disclose information that he knows I would consider relevant to a purchase decision. I now have a contract to purchase a house I do not want. But for the broker's failure to inform me of the mill's concealed presence, I would not have signed this contract. Therefore, the contract should be voided."

The judge, I think, would have sided with the broker. It is the buyer's responsibility to investigate what he's buying. While the trees concealed the mill and no road sign indicated its presence, it was my duty to understand the property. Since the mill was not a nuisance and since it could not be construed as a defect in the sale property itself, the contract is valid. The judge would say that the buyer did not take reasonable measures to inform himself about neighboring property and nothing prevented him from so doing. The seller's broker has no obligation to do this work for the buyer.

I encourage a buyer to ditch a seller's agent who deliberately puts a buyer in this position. This broker knew that I would have rejected this property out of hand without looking at it. If a broker is willing to pull something like this on one property, he's likely to pull something else on the next. Lawsuits are a bad way to move into a community. Forfeited deposits and purchasing unwanted property are other entrances to avoid.

Everyone who buys and sells real estate has stories about both getting nicked and surviving the near misses.

On the other hand, I've worked with several sellers' agents who went above and beyond their obligations to help me determine whether a property would work for what I had in mind. One spent a day with me and a soils technician taking soil samples with a hand auger as we looked unsuccessfully for a couple of acceptable percolation spots for septic systems. He even did a market analysis to determine whether a modest subdivision might be feasible, given the bad percolation results and the local ordinance. Another helped me think through financing strategies that involved the current owner and the previous owner, an absentee grand dame, who retained an interest in the property by virtue of a note, secured by the property, that she held with the current owner. Another said, after a long conversation that showed he had a two-decades knowledge of a large tract in up-state New York, that it would not fit my client's interest for second-home development. That saved a trip. The usual pattern, in contrast, is for the seller's agent to encourage buyers to come for a visit regardless of whether the property suits the buyer's search criteria.

If you don't like the seller's agent who shows you a property, find another. Let the seller's side work out the commission split in the event of a purchase. Buyers, however, should not be petty or arbitrary in rejecting agents.

If a buyer finds himself working with an agent he has come to distrust, he could stick with the "devil he knows" instead of starting from scratch. Perhaps, you will not be harmed as long as you scope diligently and validate every statement. Nonetheless, it's hard to imagine working productively with such an agent.

The seller's agent that I recommend bailing on immediately is the one who you come to believe will get in the way of your deal. This agent may be inept, manipulative, too shrewd by half or just intellectually clumsy. Don't make a scene; just stop visiting properties with that agent.

I have observed that buyers tend to connect most easily with sellers and agents with whom they share class, education or cultural backgrounds. Buyers would be silly, however, to refuse to work with an agent unlike themselves. To the extent that buyers and those on the selling side share such demographics, they will have a common vocabulary and shared perspectives whether or not their current political and cultural opinions are compatible. Negotiating is easier when both sides have the same style of bargaining.

When a buyer finds he is working with an agent whose opinions and manners he actively dislikes and with whom he feels awkward, he should look for another. I often see ardent, tofu-eating, urban, liberal environmentalists driving around with a broker who hates them sociologically. It's hard for me to imagine how these buyers will succeed with this broker. I once came across a broker who was forthrightly and routinely anti-Semitic, exercising no self-censorship in advising buyers, including Jews, to "Jew down" his own clients. Older Southerners often use "Jew down" and "Jew boy," without, it appears, pointed, personal malice; younger Southerners don't. Kinky Friedman turned those phrases on their heads. When he ran in 2006, he promised, as the first Jewish governor of Texas, that he would lower the state's speed limit to

"54.95." Verbs like "gyp" and "welsh" are rooted in ethnic prejudice, but most people who use them don't mean to invoke historical slurs. Whether "queering (spoiling) a deal" reflects homophobic prejudice probably depends on the individual and the context; "queer" carries definitions unrelated to sexual orientation. I have not heard "colored" or "Nigras" from real-estate agents for a long time, though I've heard "black" used as a slightly scrubbed-up replacement. "White trash," and "hillbilly" used synonymously, speak for themselves. I would avoid agents whose vocabulary I find objectionable. A buyer should feel intellectually and culturally comfortable with the seller's agent with whom he's working. It's more productive to negotiate through an agent who is culturally neutral and professional; it's harder with one who is not, though not impossible.

I prefer full-time sellers' agents who are smart, knowledgeable, rational, hard-working and fair-playing. Differences in class, culture, race and religion don't matter to me, but they come into play sometimes when negotiating. Experienced agents are better able to anticipate potential problems, having stumbled into them before. I try to avoid part-time agents who may be smart but tend to be less knowledgeable. I avoid ditzy agents who seem incapable of ever getting anything straight but their commissions. I am very wary of good-old-boy wheeler-dealers whose way is to screw in all directions. You can't trust these guys when they're on your side (because they are mainly working for their own interest at your expense), and certainly not when they're on the seller's side.

I have found that the seller's agent will treat you according to how he perceives you. If he sees you as a rich, dirt-dumb buyer, you are likely to be plucked. The same is often true of those who are urban arrogant or neurotically compulsive about details. Every country boy likes to get the better of a city fancy pants. Don't come across as too smart about land-buying. I have found agents who don't want to work with smart land investors. Perhaps they think that such investors will approach a property with a sharp eye and a sharper pencil. Investors, however, offer the seller's agent a lot of saved time since they know what they need to find in a property and won't waste the agent's time. If you are a dirt-smart buyer, keep this light under a bushel and don't stare too hard at it.

The buyer cannot expect the seller's agent to do his scoping, but it is fair to expect the agent to provide the data on his **listing sheet** as well as assistance about what additional information may be available from various sources, including the seller. Listing-sheet information ranges from perfunctory to detailed. The listing agent should provide you with the basics: acreage; asking price; percent of land in woods, wetlands, pasture, fields, woods, etc.; type and size of buildings; access; whether or not a survey exists; tax-assessed value; annual property tax; whether the owner is selling in fee; tax map; deed book and page number of the seller's deed; type of deed—general warranty deed being the best; recorded easements; whether the seller is carrying a mortgage secured by the property; when woods were timbered last; who the neighbors are; schools; fire protection; and local contact information. Most, if not every seller's agent I've ever dealt with, does not have this information in his file, or does not choose to provide it, or is too lazy to get it. The rule of thumb appears to be that the less a buyer knows, the better for the seller.

The agent may or may not tell a buyer the seller's purchase price, which the buyer himself can usually gather from the seller's deed. Some will give you a **competitive market analysis (CMA)**, which is the recent selling prices of a group of similar properties in the area of your target property. But such an analysis may be more than a small, independent rural broker can, or is willing to, do. You should expect to have a seller's agent produce a CMA that justifies the seller's asking price. A refusal to provide such an analysis to a buyer may suggest the target property is priced above market. Most agents will be quick to tell you if they think the property is priced below FMV. Don't expect to hear any say that the seller's price is over market. Also don't expect a seller's agent to give you information that is beyond his competence.

Don't ask him to produce a timber cruise or a minerals analysis. He will not search the seller's chain of title for you. He will, however, pass on documents—an appraisal, timber cruise, legal opinion—that are favorable to the seller's interests.

One trick that I've seen is for a seller's agent to provide a CMA of a part of the seller's property, the most valuable part. This is not dishonest; it's just misleading. A Wyoming agent had a listing for a large ranch that was about ten percent irrigated bottom land and 90 percent dry range. The agent correctly valued the most valuable acreage using recent sales of properties of similar size and characteristics. He gave this work to me. He didn't provide a similar analysis for the remainder of the property—the 90 percent that was barren scrub. On a per-acre basis, the good land was worth at least ten times the rest. But there wasn't enough of the high-value land to justify the straight-through per-acre price for the entire property. A CMA, or comparables analysis, has to be based on a property in its entirety compared with other entireties that are similar in size, location and features.

Sellers' agents in my experience prefer to keep buyers thinking about property as an experiential whole, not the sum of discrete parts that are subject to analysis. Many provide just enough information to get a buyer to visit. But a few agents believe that buyers are worked more efficiently when they have information to process prior to on-site visits. When a buyer finds himself working with an agent who plays hide the ball on basic, readily obtained information, the buyer can anticipate other problems with this individual. If the agent is not minimally helpful, find another.

ALTERNATIVES: BUYER'S BROKER

One way for an out-of-town or inexperienced buyer to acquire a paid ally is to retain a **buyer's broker**. A buyer's broker, or buyer's agent, works for, and has a fiduciary relationship exclusively with, the buyer. Such an agent is sometimes paid his commission out of the seller's funds that are part of the commission paid to the listing broker. While the buyer broker's money is coming from the seller, he should, under this arrangement, be working for the buyer. A buyer can also arrange to pay a buyer broker from his own funds in which case the buyer's broker forgoes any interest in the listing broker's commission. For his money, the buyer's broker should help find the best property for the buyer and shepherd him through the entire process. The buyer looks at properties with his own broker, not the seller's. A true buyer broker is paid exclusively by the buyer; when a "buyer broker" splits the listing agent's commission, he is subject to dual-loyalty pressures.

In most real-estate purchases, the buyer is out there by himself. I like the idea of a buyer having a knowledgeable advocate in his corner, from beginning to end. The problem that can arise with a buyer's broker is that he has a set of permanent business relationships with those on the seller's side that, taken as a whole, can be more important than any single buyer-paid commission. I would avoid working with a buyer's broker who also works as a listing broker. The buyer may not get what he's paying for. A buyer's broker who works exclusively for buyers is a far better option, but such brokers have not been welcomed in many areas and you may have difficulty finding one.

A broker can draw a commission from both the seller and the buyer as long as he discloses his **dual agency** to each party before each signs a contract and obtains consent from both. I see little advantage to the buyer in using a dual broker, but neither do I necessarily see harm. Mainly, the dual broker makes more money for himself.

DISCLOSURES, PUFFING and FRAUD

Matchmaking succeeds for a buyer when he has acquired as much as information as he needs to make an analysis-based purchase. Analysis depends on quality information. A buyer always needs to evaluate information coming from the seller's side.

Many, if not all, states now require that the seller's broker fully disclose all information of which he knows about a property's condition. If the broker doesn't know something, or chooses not to know, a buyer will probably have a hard time proving that the broker should have reasonably known about it. FSBOs are probably held to a lower standard of disclosure in practice. Compliance with disclosure in my experience is followed more rigorously on houses than on raw land, though certain states require disclosure regarding water and other salient land factors.

More often than not, the law reasons that buyers can see for themselves major defects in land when they're on the property. Sellers have a duty to disclose a **latent defect** in a structure or the land itself that an ordinary inspection would not find. One example might be a grassed-over area covering unstable fill—not a place to build a house. Another might be a lake with elevated mercury levels—not a good place to fish for tonight's supper. A third might be a violation of the local building or zoning ordinance. A fourth could be an encroachment of which the seller is aware that results in harm to the buyer, such as the seller's driveway being located on a neighbor's land and which the seller knows the buyer will have to abandon. (See Fillmore W. Galaty, Wellington J. Allaway and Robert C. Kyle, Modern Real Estate Practice, 13th ed. [Chicago: Real Estate Education Company, 1994], p. 45.)

Legal opinion will divide, of course, as to whether a buyer can reasonably be expected to know a defect when it's in front of his nose. A defect in front of one buyer can be no more than an assumed risk in front of another. If, for example, a buyer purchases ten level acres on both sides of a trout stream with a charming old fishing lodge just a cast away from the coldest hole in three counties, the local judge is not likely to be sympathetic to the new buyer's suit against the seller after he discovers four feet of cold water in his living room the following spring. The seller will argue that the property was obvious floodplain—it could be nothing else. And the long-standing house was built way before restrictions were imposed on floodplain dwellings. The seller concealed nothing and certainly disclosed the juxtaposition of the house to the stream. That was, in fact, why the buyer bought it. This defect, latent or otherwise, is also the property's virtue, which is not the usual foundation of a successful lawsuit. The buyer assumed the risk of flooding to get the benefit of trout fishing from his porch. If the buyer had financed the purchase through a lending institution, he would have probably been expected to obtain and maintain federal flood insurance since the property securing the debt was in a special flood-hazard area. In that case, he couldn't claim that he didn't know about a flood risk when he bought the place.

A buyer might win a suit against this seller if he could prove that the seller knowingly misstated the land's flooding history. The buyer is not likely to win on the basis of the following seller representations: "I've owned the property for 15 years, and I've never seen the creek overflow its banks," or "I don't think you'll have a problem with flooding back there." The first statement is factually accurate, and the second is simply an opinion, not a promise or guarantee of future events. To the extent that flooding history and floodplain knowledge are available, the buyer's case is weakened.

The buyer may find better legal footing in the case where this property has flooded every year for the 15 years of the seller's ownership, and the seller said nothing about that pattern to the buyer. In my lay opinion, the gravity of this latent defect—15 years of flooding—requires disclosure, but contrary opinion would argue that 15 years of flooding has disclosed itself.

The legal recourse the buyer has in these disputes is to sue the seller and his agent (if one is involved) for **misrepresentation**. The highest form of misrepresentation is **fraud**, in which the seller intentionally misrepresents a material fact (the property's flooding history) and that misrepresentation leads the buyer to purchase the seller's land to the buyer's detriment. If the buyer never asked about the flooding history, the seller did not intentionally misrepresent anything unless that history was so notorious that the seller had an obvious duty to disclose it. The seller can defend by arguing that the flooding "defect" was open, obvious, knowable, and neither latent nor concealed. The seller loses if he lied, saying that the property did not flood when it regularly did. If the seller says nothing about flooding and the buyer asks nothing, my guess is the seller wins.

Actual fraud (misrepresentation) is intentional deception, and usually involves misstating, lying about or concealing a material fact. (**Constructive fraud** occurs when one party violates the trust or confidence of another party, as when a lawyer breaches a fiduciary duty to a client.) A long history of repeated, severe flooding would be a material fact; a history of one flood 20 years ago would probably not be. A buyer does not want to contribute to his own harm by failing to make reasonable inquiries. I would not expect a local judge to be very sympathetic to a buyer arguing that he should be made whole for a lack of reasonable effort on his own behalf. My back field has flooded four times since we bought it in 1983, though no one recalls this creek flooding before 1985. Were I to sell this farm, I would disclose that history to a buyer, because I think it's a material defect in the property. I've excavated a very large diked channel as a flood-control measure, but I do not assume that an inexperienced buyer would understand its function without explanation. The mortgage holder does not require flood insurance, however, since no improvements are threatened.

When the buyer can prove he was deceived and harmed by misrepresentation, courts will generally provide a remedy to cover the actual damages the buyer experienced. Part of any compensation award will depend on whether the court finds intentional misrepresentation. Intent to deceive is called, **scienter**, which takes place when the seller knowingly makes a misrepresentation (e.g., false statement) or even asserts that something is true or false without actual knowledge of truth or falsehood. **Innocent misrepresentation** would be the unintentional misrepresentation of the flooding history, leading to the buyer's purchase of the property. When an error is unintentional, it is a **mistake,** or an honest misrepresentation. An aggrieved buyer can rescind a contract made on the basis of a mistake of fact supplied to him by the seller's side. Where parties find themselves in a contract that was made under a mistaken belief of a material fact shared by both, either party can rescind the agreement. The better the buyer's proof that the seller knowingly and intentionally tricked him into buying a lemon, the greater are his chances that the court will find in his favor. Intent can be hard to prove, and sellers usually defend by invoking innocent mistake.

Puffing is not considered fraud. Puffing is the expression of an opinion, usually an exaggeration of the property's virtues. Here is an example: "You [the buyer] have nothing to worry about. The seller built this house, and it's probably the best-built house in town. And that timber on the back of the place. I bet it's worth $700 or $800 an acre if it's worth a nickel." Puffing is not fraud, and it's legal. Sellers and sellers' agents do it all the time. As long as the statement is expressed as an opinion rather than a fact, the law finds no fraud insofar as the person offering the opinion is not trying to deceive the buyer. A buyer trying to prove that the opinions above were expressed to deceive him will have a very hard time, despite the obvious truth that the agent is puffing to lure the buyer into a purchase.

The line between puffing—expressed opinion—and misstatement of fact is not always as obvious as a buyer might assume. A FSBO's statement about his drilled well, which would be protected as puffing, might be: "It's a fine well. The water runs good. It's the best well around here; I know that for a fact." The first two statements are opinions, but a pseudo-fact is embedded: the well "runs good." Since neither the seller nor the buyer clarified what "runs good" means, the seller is protected against fraud even if the well runs good only in comparison with other wells that always run bad. I doubt that a court would find either a fact statement in "runs good" or an intent to deceive. The third sentence could be factually true, but it's highly unlikely that every well in the county has been flow tested and even more unlikely that pollution data are available on every well and the seller has reviewed them. This statement is presented to the buyer as fact, and to the extent that it is false, it is fraudulent. But a judge might rule that "I know that for a fact" is nothing more than a vernacular expression and should not construed as establishing a verifiable fact. The seller would probably protect himself against fraud if he had said: "My well has the greatest flow and lowest e. coli count of all the wells I know." Since the seller knows of only one well's flow and count—his own—puffing has probably covered him. A fraudulent statement would be: "My well has the greatest flow and lowest e. coli count of any in the county," unless, of course, the seller has reviewed flow data and e.coli counts on every well in the county, both of which support his assertion.

Consider this five-part FSBO statement to a buyer: "It's a good well [though it's just an average well compared with others]; I've never known it to run dry [a factually correct statement that does not disclose the well always runs weakly in August and September]; you shouldn't have any problem with it [more of an opinion than a prediction]; the water's sweet [sounds good, may taste good too, but what does it mean exactly]; and we've never gotten sick from it [chronic diarrhea, however, seems to run in the seller's family]." These statements individually and collectively are puffing, not fraud. If the buyer is forced to drill a new well, I doubt that a court would make the seller pay for it based on these words. After all, a judge will reason the seller made do with the well during his years of ownership. The seller's words, therefore, were his opinion based on the well's performance judged against his standards, whatever they might be. Accordingly, the buyer's new well, which he had drilled during his first August, is more of a discretionary purchase than a necessity resulting from misrepresentation in the opinion of this court.

Seller-commissioned timber cruises are often given to a buyer, and these cruises can inflate the true merchantable value of the timber by 50 percent or more. Chapter 22 discusses all the ways that cruises can be puffed. Here's a quick example. A seller says to you: "The cruise I commissioned estimates two million board feet of sawtimber stumpage on my 5,000 acres. That volume of timber at current local prices projects to a value of $400,000." Sounds good! You didn't think the scrubby pine and hardwood were worth much of anything. It's a windfall! The seller is being truthful. He did commission a cruise, and it did project two million board feet of sawtimber, which his forester valued at $400,000. Both the seller's statements and the cruise are factually correct in a sense, and are, therefore, not fraudulent—despite being big, fat lies. The seller's cruise does indeed estimate two million board feet of sawtimber on the tract and does in fact project a value of $400,000 at current local prices. But none of this projected sawtimber value is realizable in the real world. How can this be? What is lacking from the seller's statement is the fact that 750,000 board feet of the two million are found on 80-degree slopes that are too steep for timber operations. That's why it's never been cut. Another 250,000 board feet are so far back on the property and the trees are of such poor quality that no logger will pay to cut them. The other one million board feet are in trees so widely scattered that loggers would find it uneconomical to build the skid roads to get to them. While 2,000,000 board feet of sawtimber exist, none are economical or feasible to cut and for that reason the new owner won't realize $400,000 in a timber sale. But the seller's statement is not fraud, though it is certainly misleading.

Courts have increasingly considered the context of statements, narrowing the puffing defense a bit.

In specific circumstances, oral and written statements have been found fraudulent, along with actions, failure to act, failure to disclose, concealment and silence. Cases involving seller silence are the hardest for a buyer to win. As a rule, contract law does not require a seller to disclose a fact that is detrimental to the agreement, except when his silence may physically harm a person using the property, or limit the buyer's planned use of the property which is known to the seller, among other exceptions. Half-truths that induce a buy and which then harm the buyer can be the basis for fraud. In fraud cases, the buyer, in addition, must show reliance (that is, he bought the seller's property because he relied on the misrepresentation) and the materiality of the misrepresentation (that is, the fact that was misrepresented must be important and critical to the sale). If reliance was based on puffing, the buyer loses, because puffing is allowed. The remedies to a buyer successful in proving fraud can be upholding his refusal to perform on the purchase, rescinding of the contract, or collection of damages where monetary loss is proved. Punitive damages can be awarded in fraud cases where the buyer proves that he suffered actual monetary loss and that the fraudulent act was gross, oppressive and committed with ill will. If a buyer discovers fraud and does nothing about it, he waives his right to remedy. A seller and his agent do not shield themselves from a misrepresentation suit when a purchase contract contains the boilerplate language that the buyer has not relied on any representations made to him by either the seller or his agent. (See Gibson *et al.*, Real Estate Law, 3rd ed., Chapter 14.)

Lawsuits are aggravating, draining and time-consuming—even when you win. A newcomer does not want to announce joining a rural community by suing an established member, the seller. It will not matter much that the former owner is universally regarded by his former neighbors as a crook. The suit will be interpreted as a shot across the community's bow. Fellowship will not follow from your pursuit of what you see as your stand on the high moral ground. The other factor to keep in mind is that the routine puffing and fraud sellers commit may only involve small amounts of money. It is often wiser to take a small hit and move along than to sue and win, which can be the first successful battle in a losing war. Your own diligent scoping will prevent you from being taken in by either fraud or puffing.

Property involved with estates—especially estates with a number of heirs—is often sold to generate cash. The executor will arrange the sale with the help of a broker, or do it himself, or work through the estate's lawyer. Consequently, local lawyers are sources of early information on estate property. Local papers will eventually carry announcements of estate auctions involving land and personal property. Where heirs cannot agree on the disposition of their shared inheritance, one or more may file a **partition suit**, which forces the sale of the property at auction. These, too, are announced and advertised in the local paper. Such properties often produce above-market prices when family members are bidding against each other.

I phoned a lawyer early in 2006 who was advertising an auction for "approximately 400 acres" that included timber and minerals. I suspected that it was a partition suit since the majority owner was a land company and the minority owner was a set of heirs. I asked the lawyer about the merchantable timber value. "About $200,000," he said. I then asked him a set of forestry-related questions to determine how the number was calculated. In exasperation, he gave me the phone of the forester who had been hired. The forester was honest. He told me that he had done a walk-through and figured a landowner could count on getting $100,000 in a timber sale. Of course, someone might value the timber at $200,000. The 400 acres turned out to be 361.5, which is "approximately" 400. Puffing is a part of real-estate sales. I know of no other profession where puffing is a legitimate sales tactic.

AUCTION BUYING

Rural property is frequently **sold at auction**. One of the virtues of an auction from the seller's viewpoint is that the property is sold quickly, without the protracted wait that often accompanies listing with a broker. Auctions solve the major investment drawback of real estate—lack of liquidity. If the seller finds himself in debt with monthly payments eating him alive—a situation I've been in and did not like—the auction will produce a chunk of money that will pay down, if not retire, the debt. By assembling a crowd of motivated buyers, auctions can generate a price higher than what a seller might net either through listing or selling on his own. The risk to the seller, however, is that the sale is limited to whomever shows up and bids on that one day. Auction sellers can be an individual; public agency (the county selling tax-delinquent land; the IRS selling seized land); U.S. Bankruptcy Court which authorizes the sale to raise cash to pay debt; lending institutions such as a bank; estates; and business entities such as partnerships, non-profits, corporations and limited liability companies.

Auctions are conducted as either **absolute** or **with reserve**. An absolute auction is one where the seller and auctioneer promise the buyers that the property will be sold that day for the highest bid, no matter how low. An **absolute auction above minimum opening bid**, a variation of the absolute auction, becomes absolute as soon as the advertised minimum opening price is met. The seller cannot withdraw his property from the auction process once the minimum opening bid is met, and he cannot bid himself or through a proxy. Absolute auctions encourage buyers to come because they know the property will be sold even if it brings a sum far below fair market value. Sellers who are extremely confident in their knowledge of the value of the property or sellers who are desperate to raise cash use the absolute auction. Buyers are guaranteed that the property will be sold, but the seller has no guarantee as to what he will receive from the sale. Auctioneers prefer absolute auctions, because they will make a sale and get their commission plus expenses. An absolute auction is also known as an **auction without reserve.**

An **auction with reserve** is a contingent sale, subject either to a minimum selling price the seller has set with the auctioneer in advance or a minimum price that a lender imposes on the seller before it will release the property from its note. Also known as an **auction subject to confirmation**, these auctions allow the seller to accept or reject all bids, or withdraw the property from the sale before the auction is completed, depending on how the reserve is structured. Usually, a reserve price is set, and the seller is guaranteed either a minimum amount of gross sale revenue or no sale at all. Buyers are guaranteed nothing. The seller whose property is not bid up to the reserve price must still cover the auctioneer's expenses and fees. When an auction with reserve does not meet the reserve, the seller may choose to let the property go for the high bid anyway or declare the auction sale null and void. A **seller-set reserve price** is one between the seller and the auctioneer; a **bank-set reserve price** is imposed on both auctioneer and seller

Where there is bank debt on a property, the buyer at an auction with reserve may find himself being asked to raise his offer after the auction ends if the **hammer price** at the auction's close is less than the lender's pre-auction imposed reserve. The hammer price is the final high bid, signaled by the auctioneer striking his hammer and announcing, "Sold to Bidder X." When a buyer finds himself with the final bid below the reserve price, the bank will ask him to put more money into the purchase or else lose the property. If the bank fails to release the property, the seller retains the property and continues to owe the bank the amount of the debt. The seller, however, is now poorer by the amount he's paid to the auctioneer. The bank does not want to take possession of the property, so the high bidder has some bargaining leverage. The bidder can wash his hands entirely of the purchase without penalty or come up with more money to meet the lender's reserve. If the seller has personally guaranteed the note to the bank (which is rarely the case on mortgage debt), the bank may sell to the bidder and leave the shortfall on the seller's indebtedness. Buyers in this situation should keep in mind that the bank does not really want to take possession of the property, which will have to go through another sale. This creates good conditions for negotiation, particularly if the buyer is willing to finance the purchase through the bank. For the buyer to gain from this negotiation with the lender, he must be willing to walk away from the property. The bank will call a bluff. The buyer might as part of a negotiation go up one tick and then stop for good. This will either work or not. If the bank senses that you have the resources and motivation to go higher, rest assured that you will be escorted there. I've seen a bank shake out another 33 percent from a motivated high bidder before releasing a property auctioned with a reserve price.

Where the property at auction is only part of the collateral securing the seller's note with a bank, the buyer will want the bank to **release the property** from the seller's note for his bid price, whether or not the reserve was met. This is referred to as a **partial release**. The seller's remaining collateral continues to secure the residual debt. The buyer gets title to that portion of the seller's property he's purchased that has been released from the seller's note.

An auction with reserve provides more certainty for the seller about revenue (because the sale is contingent on the reserve being met), but less certainty about whether or not a sale will take place. Reserves are set to get at least a minimally acceptable price, which is usually below market. A seller-set reserve price provides him with protection against a catastrophically bad auction where the best bid is ridiculously low. Where the best bid approaches the reserve, the seller, in attendance, can signal the auctioneer to accept it. With a bank-set reserve, the bank cannot unilaterally lower its reserve price without agreement from the seller; if the seller does not agree, the sale does not go through.

Auctioneers recommend that the reserve price not be revealed to bidders; they think concealment encourages attendance and bidding action. A buyer who learns the reserve price is advantaged because he knows the price at which the lock is taken off the sale. That is the point where the auction with reserve converts automatically to an absolute auction even when this change is not announced to the auction bidders. The reserve price gives the buyer a good sense of FMV since the lender will set the reserve close to, but usually under, FMV.

Lacking inside information, a buyer can piece together an estimate of a reserve price within a likely range. The bottom of the range would be the 100 percent fair market value that is used for tax-assessment purposes. The top of the range would be the property's FMV as determined by a comparables analysis. This bottom is likely to be too low and this top too high. Therefore, you may have to narrow the range by adding to the bottom number and subtracting from the top. A real-estate agent can give you a quick idea of how much to add and subtract. Professional appraisers and real-estate brokers can provide comparables analysis to establish FMV, for which you should expect too pay. In fact, that may be the method by which the bank sets its reserve price. A bank reserve price, in addition, can be set to cover the seller's debt and costs of collection. If you can find out from the mortgage documents in the courthouse records the amount of the mortgage and its terms, you can estimate the remaining principal owed using an amortization table. Figure in that the bank will be owed some delinquent interest as well. The bank's mortgage paper is usually recorded immediately after the deed and follows it in the deed book. A bank reserve will usually be the amount of principal remaining on the seller's note and the auctioneer's expenses. Depending on local markets, the bank may try to get some portion of its delinquent interest too. Banks, generally, do not make money on the sale of foreclosed property.

Auctioneers believe that a reserve-price format discourages bidding, but I've been unable to find evidence other than their opinions to support that belief. It may be impossible to substantiate it empirically since a property auction on a given day can only be run once either absolute or with reserve. It's impossible to run the same auction on the same day in front of the same bidders in both formats. If auctioneers are right in believing that absolute auctions achieve a higher price, the buyer should expect to pay more for a property auctioned absolute than bid with a reserve. But, an absolute auction always holds out the prospect to a buyer of buying property at a steep discount, even pennies on a dollar of fair value.

When you see an auction ad in the newspaper, it will have the word "absolute" prominently featured if it is such a sale. In Virginia, at least, all auctions by law are with reserve unless specifically advertised and conducted as an absolute sale. If the ad does not say "absolute," buyers here should know it is with a reserve even where it does not say reserve. At the sale itself, the auctioneer will announce the auction's format, absolute or with reserve, in a way that will be plain and unambiguous. Auctions are now videotaped in case a dispute arises.

Auctioneers will usually mail out a **bidder's packet** before the sale. Information provided at the sale just prior to the bidding supersedes all earlier information, both oral and written. Listen carefully to the **auctioneer's announcements** before the bidding begins for changes in what is being sold and how.

The bidder's packet is a set of documents and information pertaining to the property and the auction's rules. Each auctioneer approaches a packet in his own way, some include more property information, others, the minimum. The packet can include copies of some, or all, of the following:

- recorded deed the seller holds and will convey
- easements that run with the land both for and against the benefit of the owner of the sale property
- reservations from the sale (such as the owner excluding—"reserving"—his interest in the current lease; severance of minerals)
- survey or plat (shows the location and boundary dimensions of the property)
- professional appraisal or comparables analysis
- valuations of specific property assets, such as timber, house, equipment
- documents regarding farm income, rent, subsidy payments, royalties, etc.
- property tax data—assessed value, amount of current tax
- other tax information—e.g., rates on personal property, trash tax, surcharges and fees for various purposes
- tax map (showing property location and boundaries) if no survey exists
- permits and letters from regulatory agencies if relevant
- zoning and division ordinances (zoning classification determines what can be done on the property; setbacks for buildings; types of construction permitted, etc.)
- school district and school information
- information related to the property's sewerage and water systems, and other utilities
- percolation-test results (make sure the test was taken near the spot on which you want to build) if relevant
- water-sample results from existing house

- well-drilling information/costs
- utility rates and new-line costs
- road-building cost estimates
- liens filed or pending against the property
- proximity of police and fire-protection services
- location of health-care facilities
- termite inspection if required
- **terms-of-the-sale sheet**

This packet should be in your possession before the auction as part of your own scoping effort. Most of this material will be publicly available. Unrecorded easements and seller reservations will not be public record.

Read carefully the **terms-of-the-sale sheet**, which sets forth the rules and requirements by which the auctioneer will conduct the auction, subject to his announcements prior to the bidding. The sheet will state whether the auction is absolute or reserve. It may include language that allows the auctioneer to bid on behalf of the seller. The terms will tell you how much you are expected to deposit as the winning bidder and in what form. Some auctioneers insist on certified checks or cash. The terms will state your liability in the event that you back out of a winning bid. The sheet will state when closing is scheduled, usually within 30 days of the auction day.

Pre-auction advertising and the terms-of-the-sale information will include what you need to know about becoming a **qualified bidder** if the auctioneer requires that bidders qualify financially at registration. An auctioneer will require personal identification at a minimum. When large amounts of money are involved, expect to present evidence that you are good for the sum you bid. If you do not qualify, you cannot bid. The auctioneer will tell you in advance what materials you need to bring to the auction—or provide beforehand—to establish your credentials. The auctioneer qualifies bidders because he does not want to wind up with a high bidder who can't pay his bid price.

Auctioneers generally charge the seller a ten percent commission on the gross selling price, plus reimbursement for advertising and promotion work. Lower commission rates may be applied to high-dollar properties. Some auctioneers charge as seller-reimbursed expenses all of the costs of conducting the auction, including charges for auctioneering personnel and overhead. The cost to the seller is almost always higher selling through an auctioneer than paying a straight five-to-ten percent commission to a broker if the auctioneer does not sell with a **buyer's premium**, explained below. Auctioneers should spend a lot of (the seller's) money on advertising and promotion to generate interest and bidding for what is a one-day, make-or-break sale. Auctioneers differ in their marketing skills, and these differences can substantially affect the results. Some auctioneers will buy mailing lists, others won't. Some have good in-house mailing lists that can be targeted to likely buyers.

Many auctioneers approach the seller as a goose to be plucked. This is particularly true with sellers in desperate circumstances who are forced into an auction as a way to produce cash quickly. Such auctioneers may refuse to take a seller unless he agrees to an absolute format. They are also likely to insist that the seller do certain things at the seller's expense to improve the value of the property prior to auction, such as obtain septic permits and install gravel roads on undeveloped land, provide a new survey or fix the house. The auctioneer is trying to make the property as cosmetically appealing as possible, to make buying easy and get the highest bid price. Buyers need to look beneath any recently applied make up.

A **buyer's premium** is a percentage fee the high bidder pays in addition to the amount of his winning bid. The premium helps the seller pay for the cost of the auction. Some auctioneers believe a buyer's premium discourages bidding and produces lower net results than an auction free of a buyer's premium. Again, empirical evidence for this belief is hard to find. I don't think a buyer's premium of five percent or less has any depressive effect on bid prices. Most buyers will have adjusted their bidding to take any premium into account. I believe that most buyers will discount their bid by the amount of a premium so that the net bid price is likely to be the same with or without the premium. Buyers should set a cap on their highest bid price before the auctioneer starts his call. That cap should incorporate the buyer's premium and any other associated costs. The cap should also reflect your scoping as to what the property is worth to you.

An auctioneer with whom I worked charged me a ten percent commission on the gross selling price, which was, the winning bid price plus the ten percent buyer's premium. With a bid price of $100,000, the buyer's premium would add $10,000, making a gross selling price of $110,000, on which I paid the auctioneer a ten percent commission, or $11,000, of which $10,000—91 percent—came from the buyer. This format is sometimes referred to as the "**ten-ten system**," a plan whereby the auctioneer is paid 11 percent of the sale price rather than the nominal ten percent. A buyer's premium helps a cash-desperate seller if it doesn't depress bidding. Careless buyers who don't calculate the effect of the buyer's premium can be caught paying more than they planned.

Country people are comfortable with buying and selling through auctions. Livestock is typically sold this way, and farm-dispersal auctions are common. If you are an inexperienced country-auction buyer, you need to get your feet wet before you chance getting soaked. Attend a land auction held by the auctioneer who's scheduled to sell the property you've targeted. You can learn his schedule by logging on to his website or calling his office. Learn his rules. Listen to his calls so that you can understand his numbers. Observe how he closes the bidding: some close quickly, others will suspend everything for 30 minutes and then close it out. Strike up conversations with non-bidders. Try to learn as much as you can about how auctions are managed in your target area.

Auctioneers are licensed by the state in which the auction is being held. Call the state's auction-licensing board to confirm that the auctioneer is licensed and inquire about complaints or board sanctions (disciplines). Auctioneer licenses are usually handled by the state's real-estate office or the board that issues professional licenses. Complaints may or may not tell you something useful about an auctioneer. They can be nothing more than sour grapes from an unsuccessful or unsophisticated bidder. You should ask the auctioneer whether the sale will follow a particular code of professional ethics, and, if so, which one. The **National Auctioneers Association** (NAA, 8880 Ballantine, Overland Park, KS, 66214; 913-541-8084; FAX, 913-894-5281; www.auctioneers.org) has developed the "Standards of Practice of the Certified Auctioneers Institute" and the "Code of Professional Ethics, Certified Auctioneers Institute" that set forth rules for members in dealing with both clients (sellers) and buyers. Not all auctioneers are NAA members. These documents are also found in Stephen J. Martin and Thomas E. Battle, III, Sold! The Professional's Guide to Real Estate Auctions (Chicago: Real Estate Education Company, 1991).

And then there was the "auctioneer" who wasn't. He—a land company—had an office, stationery, business cards and secretary. He appears to have been a real-estate broker who advertised that he performed "auction services." I became suspicious, because he did not include his Virginia auction-license number on his sale notices or business cards. This fellow, it turned out, did everything that an auctioneer did, save call the sale. He hired a licensed auctioneer to perform that task. When I asked him if he had an auctioneer's license, he ducked. When I pressed, he admitted that he did not and explained his way of doing auction services using a hired auctioneer. As long as he was a broker, he could do the sale, and I never pursued why he didn't have an auctioneer's license. I didn't see anything wrong with his auction-services approach, but I would have been more comfortable with it had he been forthright. This quirk was the first of many. The guy always left me with a headache. After weeks of negotiating, it became clear that he would do my auction only as an absolute sale, which I had told him at each of our meetings I did not want. To sellers: if an auctioneer gives you either a headache or the willies, find one who doesn't.

The buyer needs to learn the auctioneer's **bidding system**. The system may or may not be described in the bidder's packet. Auctioneers may vary their system from sale to sale, depending on which format they feel will yield the most money. The simplest system is bidding dollars for the whole property, that is, the buyer's bid represents his price for the **entirety**. In this system, a buyer bidding $100,000 is offering that sum for all of the property's acreage and improvements. The auctioneer will probably call out, "100," to represent $100,000. The most common alternative to entirety bidding is the **dollars-per-acre format**, where the bid price is expressed as dollars for just one acre. The number "100" in this format represents $100 per acre multiplied by the number of acres in the entirety.

To keep your wits about you during the heat of the auction, you need to prepare a **crib sheet** beforehand so that you will know instantaneously what any per-acre bid means multiplied out with the buyer's premium added. The crib sheet below shows a tract of 153 acres and a seven percent buyer's premium.

Dirt-Smart Buyer's Land-Auction Crib Sheet

$ Bid Per Acre	Total Bid Price	Total Price to be Paid with 7% Buyer's Premium
500	$76,500	$81,855
525	80,325	85,948
550	84,150	90,041

I've included three dollar-per-acre bid prices for illustration. Your actual crib sheet will include a wider range, from just below the lowest price you think is possible to just above what you think is possible. In this example, my actual crib sheet might range from $350 per acre (p/A) to $700. Do not scrimp on cribbing! I would also stop my cribbing at my **cap price**, which is the dollar point where I stop bidding. You can fine-tune prices within your projected range by using smaller dollar increments, say $10 per-acre jumps instead of $25. From your crib sheet, you can also calculate that each dollar bid per acre will cost you $163.71 when you write your check to the auctioneer for the entire 153-acre tract. Acreage (153) x $1 = $153 + $10.71 (buyer's premium: .07 x $153 = $10.71); total is $163.71 per dollar bid.

CIRCLE IN RED INK your cap-price, dollar-per-acre bid, which you've dutifully underlined. Now underline it again in RED INK. DO NOT GO ABOVE THAT PRICE. That cap price is the result of your analytical research into the property being sold and reflects your cold-eyed financial assessment. Going above your red-line price moves you backward, from being smart to being impulsive. The auction is designed to pull you into a competitive fray where your emotions rule your head. Resist. Don't be stampeded into a higher price.

I recommend bringing a **helper** along to a land auction, preferably someone who is observant and calm. Both you and the helper should get to the auction site early to look at the pass-out materials from the auctioneer and mingle with the crowd, picking up what you can. Talk to neighbors of the property. Ask the auctioneer's associates who they think will be the likely bidders and why. Look at the auctioneer's registration list for clues as to the types of buyers at the sale. Once the auction begins, the helper should watch the bidders and get a read for who they are and the intensity of their interest. Do not assume that the city person who pulls up in a Hummer wearing his brand-new Orvis outfit has a deeper pocket for this property than the guy in the back spitting tobacco juice into a styrofoam cup. The helper should try to sense when each bidder is reaching his upper limit and give this information to his buyer. The helper should work the calculator for the buyer and warn him when the bidding approaches the buyer's top price, even though both can see that it is circled and underlined in red ink on their crib sheets.

Readers may ask: "Why in the world would the helper need to warn his friend that the red-circle price is close?" That's an excellent question posed by a person who is sitting calmly in the quiet of his own home reading a book. Auctions are designed to be intense, emotional and fast. They want to overload the buyers' sensory systems. They're loud and a little confusing on purpose. Your helper must be a rock in this storm, preferably a rock whose head stays above the chop. I have seen otherwise rational human beings forget their red-circle price in the heat of the moment; I've done it myself.

The bidder should concentrate on listening to the calls and maintaining eye contact with either the auctioneer or one of his ringmen who will acknowledge and confirm each buyer's bid with a whooped "Yup!" or "Yeah!" When your bid is on the floor, you need to know that. I've seen bidders try to up their own bids. I've also seen bidders fail, because they thought the final high bid was theirs when it wasn't. When in doubt, ask the auctioneer to confirm that your bid is high. Better to look like a fool than to be one.

Auctioneers will often do a **combination bidding system** when a property involves sub-parcels. Each sub-parcel is bid separately, on either a dollars-per-acre basis or as a sub-entirety. When all sub-parcels have been bid out to a price, the prices are chalked on the auction board. Then the auctioneer begins auctioning sub-parcels combined in different ways. The combining of sub-parcels may be initiated by individual bidders or proposed by the auctioneer. The auctioneer may impose a $1,000 premium to combine a group of sub-parcels, that is, the bid for the group has to be $1,000 more to start than the chalk-board price of the sub-parcels taken together. The auctioneer's object with combination bidding is to boost the total price the auction achieves. The theory is the more times bidders are run at the entirety from different angles, the higher the ultimate selling price.

A variation on combination bidding is a system that involves a lot of on-the-spot deal-making among buyers who may have to form coalitions with other buyers to buy and defend what they want to buy. The bidding is dollars per acre, with the winner of each round granted his choice of sub-parcel (s), any or all, at that price. The first round winner could take all sub-parcels. In that event, the auctioneer would place the entirety for bid with a premium to start it off. The entirety premium might be $10,000. If no bidder or coalition of bidders come in, the first round winner takes the entirety at his bid price with no premium.

If you wanted three parcels of a ten-parcel entirety, and you were successful in being the first-round high bidder on two of the three you wanted, you can in the second round propose a three-parcel combination by paying the premium. The first-round winner of the third parcel will have to defend. He can bid against you for the three parcels; he can let you have your three and then pull out one or two parcels as his own combination; he can form a rival coalition; he can package his parcel with a fourth, forcing you to bid on a four-parcel group if you want three. You might then resell the parcel you didn't want. When this system works, you find yourself in a three-dimensional chess game. My experience with combination bidding is that its complexity discourages participation. At some point in this maze, some bidders stop playing because of the maze, not the money. I've seen this too-clever-by-half system fail miserably three times.

A buyer can't change the auctioneer's bidding system. The buyer's protection against these sophisticated hustles is the red-circled number on his crib sheet. Never bid above the number in the red circle.

If you find yourself at an auction where the auctioneer is jumping the bidding in large increments, say $5,000 to $10,000, bid a half increment by indicating to him that you want to raise the high bid the auctioneer has (from someone else) by half the increment he's asking for. You do this by sliding your hand horizontally from left to right, or up to down in a chopping motion. If the auctioneer acknowledges that you are the high bid but at the increment he wanted rather than what you indicated, you will have to call out the bid price you wanted to make sure that he understands your number. Do not be shy. It is your money that he's trying to spend.

Most land is auctioned, "AS IS, WHERE IS," which means with all faults included, whether or not any are stated explicitly, which they should be. "AS IS" should be interpreted to refer to the condition of what you can see. It also should mean there's no reservation on the timber or pending sale of a part of the tract. It means that the seller is unwilling to spend any time or money to fix up anything. "WHERE IS" may or may not be of importance. If, for example, the seller's description of his property is actually short 25 acres and you discover—later—that the deedwork really gives you a claim to 25 acres that a neighbor has fenced in as his, you will probably find yourself stuck with the original acreage since you bought what it was, where its observable boundaries were. You can feel confident in the boundaries and acreage when the auctioneer is working from a reasonably current plat or survey. Auctioneers prefer that sellers have surveys to avoid post-auction bidder backouts over disputed acreage. A survey lends credibility to other less-substantiated features of a property.

When the auctioneer announces that the property will be sold "AS IS, WHERE IS," you are within your rights as a bidder to ask him a **general-disclosure-and-endorsement question**: whether either he or the seller knows of any defect, easement or condition in the chain of title, boundaries, physical environment, subsurface and property itself that would negatively affect a bidder's possession, use or enjoyment of the property. If you feel uncomfortable asking this question in public, write it out and hand it to the auctioneer before he starts. Bidders may or may not have a legal right to be given all such information, but how the auctioneer handles your question—forthright answer, no answer, refusal to answer, non-answer answer, weasel answer, hostility at being questioned, wrong answer, misleading answer—will provide you with more information than you had before. If you know of some defect that you can live with or overcome, asking an open-ended question like this is a tactic you can use to scare off marginal bidders. Auctioneers videotape their auctions to have an incontrovertible record of the auction's rules, announcements and conduct in the event of a dispute. False or misleading answers can get them into trouble with the state-licensing board if a bidder goes to the trouble of pursuing a complaint.

A variation on the general-disclosure-and-endorsement question is one about a specific fact whose answer you already know. This tactic can be used to alert other bidders that there's a problem whose repair cost is high or which presents a great deal of uncertainty. For example, a bidder might ask: Can you give me an estimate of how much it will cost to repair the seller's fences? Am I correct in my belief that the deed's calls do not close, and that this property is likely to be about 10 acres short of the 90 advertised?

Does the owner have a clear, marketable title to all that he's selling? If a buyer is simply trying to "game" the auction, to knock down the price with his questions, the other bidders will figure this out in a country minute, which is faster than any in New York. Such questions, however, are more than fair when a buyer wants to pin down the auctioneer and seller on critical information before getting into the bidding. If you can't get an answer in your pre-auction scoping, then ask it at the auction, either privately or publicly. It's fair to insist on getting straight answers; it's not fair to deliberately squirrel up a sale.

It is not uncommon for an auctioneer to have a **bogus bidder**, or **shill**, in the crowd who gets the bidding going when starting is hard. Whether or not this practice is legal depends on the auction's ground-rules and the shill's intentions and financial capabilities. In an auction with reserve, the bogus bidder is trying to get the sale price up to the reserve price so that the auction can be completed. The shill will bid in and drop out soon, since his job is to get the ball rolling and not to buy the property. The shill will almost always drop out just before the reserve price. If the shill inadvertently "wins" a parcel, the auctioneer will be on the phone the day after the auction trying to sell it to a genuine buyer, starting with the other successful bidders. In an absolute auction, however, an auctioneer's shill is acting illegally, because the seller and the auctioneer have announced that they will sell the property for the highest bid with no reserve or minimum price. A shill's bid effects a minimum price in an absolute auction and would be grounds to contest the sale. But shilling is hard to prove beyond a reasonable doubt. The auctioneer's uncle may be a shill, but he may be nothing more than a bidder.

If you think the auctioneer has a shill, ask him when he is finished with his announcements whether he or anyone associated with him or the seller will be bidding. Anticipate that the auctioneer and the seller will be miffed, because you are asking a question that clouds the auction. Land auctioneers want sunny skies, both meteorologically and metaphysically. The auctioneer's proper response should be to thank you for your question and tell you the truth. At an absolute auction, shilling should not occur. At a reserve auction, the bogus bidder must drop out at the reserve price. At that point, some auctioneers announce that the reserve has been met, and the auction is being converted to an absolute sale. If you ask these questions prior to the auction in private and are not satisfied with the answers, you have no choice but to ask them in public. It's a difficult role to be the dog in the manger, but it's your money at stake. I advise against asking questions, these or any others, for the simple purpose of depressing bidding by raising doubts among the bidders. Besmirching an auction for your own benefit is tawdry and reflects badly on a newcomer. Self-protection is another matter.

Auction results are not predictable from either the seller or the buyers' points of view. If the crowd sits on its hands, the auctioneer will scramble to get a bid on the board. If the crowd is motivated, things can get wild. Suspicion and uncertainty always attend an event where money is in play. Bidders should avoid trying to control an auction by engaging in **collusion**, which is the practice of agreeing amongst themselves to depress competition or otherwise fix prices. Such bidders are known as a "**ring**." The most common form is for the ring members to agree not to bid against each other, letting one of their number win, and then dividing the property according to a pre-bidding deal. This practice is either illegal or pretty close. If the auctioneer or seller gets wind of it, a suit is likely to follow. On the other side, bidders may not know when an auctioneer or the seller is using a shill to run up the price or even calling a **phantom bid** from a phantom bidder. Phantom bidding, also called **trotting**, is illegal. For all of the ways to rig an auction, my impression is that they are at least as clean as conventional buying and selling through a real-estate broker, which speaks for both.

Buyers can get great deals at land auctions that are busts for the seller. They can also find themselves in a frenzied bidding war that produces nonsensically high prices. I have found myself in situations where the auctioneer sweats to get even a below-market price for a wonderful property. I've also seen price jumps in $5,000 increments as fast as bidders can tug their ears for a property that fetched twice its real value. Often, one or two bidders are personally interested in a property owing to a family connection or because they share its boundary. These highly motivated bidders can run up an auction price. Do not assume that because some fool is willing to pay the price he just bid that he must know what he's doing, and therefore you can go him one better and still be in the FMV ballpark. If he's a bidder with an emotional interest in the property, he will bid above where reason and self-interest tell him to stop. So find out before the auction whether family and neighbors will be bidding. Know these people and do not be dragged into a bidding war with them unless you, too, are willing pay whatever you need to pay to win the property. It's best to approach auctions as an investor, not a second-home buyer. Be unemotional and rational. Let your scoping determine your red-circle price, not your heart. Do not exceed what your calculator and brain have decided for you the night before. Don't be swept into the auction's rhythm and momentum. Bid with confident strength, as if you are the deepest pocket in the house. (Of course, if you are the deepest pocket, don't act like it.)

You may run into a bidder who starts the bidding at a price that is equal to or even above where the auctioneer begins. This is a tactic to drive off every other bidder before the bidding starts. If the bid price is below your red-circle number, take him up one notch. The odds are you will win, because that bidder is afraid of an auction and has only one price to play, win or lose.

I've had two bizarre things happen to me at rural auctions, neither of which involved land. When we first bought our farm, the owners auctioned many personal items. I was bidding for an old bureau against a non-local fellow (I later learned he was a Richmond stockbroker), and the price was going up quickly. Suddenly, a casually well-dressed woman yanked my arm as I was bidding, pulling me in her direction and behind a tree in the front yard. She began firing questions at me about the farm and my background. I had been totally buried in the bidding, and then was abruptly disinterred. I tried to answer her out of residual politeness and also get my hand back into the bidding. Her husband, by then, had won the piece. I've never seen this trick pulled again, but it certainly worked on me. It turned out that the broker and his wife had a second home about a mile from me, and I would see them on the weekends when I jogged by. She always disappeared into the house, and he exchanged pleasantries with obvious discomfort. I used to make protracted conversation just to see him squirm.

I was at a house auction with my five-year-old daughter when her eye landed on a tourist trinket box from Niagara Falls. She needed that box, she said. I bid 50 cents, about three times what it was worth. I was the only bidder. The auctioneer's ringman then upped me a quarter, and we were off. I ended up paying $4.50 and was burning mad. The ringman came over and said he was bidding so that the little girl could have it. It is difficult for me to believe that he didn't know I was the little girl's father inasmuch as she's a dead ringer and was sitting on my shoulders at the time.

Auction rules vary from state to state. Auctioneers, their associates and ringmen, are usually allowed to bid if they are genuine buyers, which often they are, or theoretically could be. I have seen the owner of a sale barn bid for livestock at his own auction where he was holding buy orders from individuals who were not in attendance—the effect of which was to run up the price for whomever "won." Bidding ringmen and auctioneer confederates can be bogus bidders whose only goal is to run up the price. In a reserve auction (in Virginia, at least) this is acceptable as long as the bogus bidder drops out at the reserve price. In an absolute auction, bogus bidding is illegal—and I've never seen it happen.

At auction's end, the high bidder will sign an **auctioneer's sales contract—your purchase**

contract—with the auctioneer who is representing the seller. The buyer gives the auctioneer a deposit, which is usually ten percent of the gross selling price. The auctioneer prefers that deposits take the form of cash or certified checks, though the seller may authorize personal checks from individuals he knows. I've seen buyers bid without getting qualified regardless of pre-auction instructions and then offer a non-local check. It's better to play by the rules. Land auctions do not require full payment on auction day, though auctions for personal property, machinery and livestock do. Determine how much deposit money and in what form the auctioneer requires, and make sure that you have exactly what is needed. Closing is usually scheduled for 15 to 30 calendar—not business—days after the auction date. Bring your appointment book to the auction and schedule the closing date and place with the auctioneer when you sign the contract.

Auctioneer sales contracts are not standard, boilerplate agreements that you can get from any real-estate agent or local brokers' association. They are shorter, simpler and even less protective of the buyer. They do not, as a rule, include the common state-required inspections and warranties that broker contracts use. They are almost always drawn up by the auctioneer and his lawyer. They are designed to make sure the buyer performs, the auctioneer gets his commission and the auctioneer is protected from liability to the seller in the event of bidder non-performance. In auctions, it is up to the buyer to do all due diligence prior to bidding. Unlike a purchase contract, the buyer at auction is not submitting an offer to the buyer for his consideration; he is buying the property for the price he bid, subject only to satisfying any reserve price imposed by the seller or his lender. If you refuse to sign the auctioneer's sales contract after being high bidder, you should assume the auctioneer and the seller will sue to compel you to buy the property at your bid price. If you sign the sales contract and then decide that you do not want to go through with it, you should anticipate losing your auction-day deposit at the very least.

Once the auction concludes, the high bidder will be expected to sign the auctioneer's sales contract. To avoid surprises, you should secure a sample contract from the auctioneer before the auction. You can review its terms and conditions with your lawyer. High bidders sign previously unread auction contracts all the time. Since the buyer has bought "AS IS, WHERE IS" at auction, post-auction inspections do the buyer no good, except to identify problems. The auctioneer will not allow you to add contingencies to his contract. Buyer failure to find financing or an acceptable septic-system site will not void an auction contract. Where a buyer quickly learns of a dreadful, costly defect in the property, a lawsuit might get the buyer off the hook if the seller and the auctioneer concealed it in some fashion. As a rule, however, the "AS IS, WHERE IS" format of the auction will likely trump most buyer claims. But the cost of defending and the negative publicity may persuade a seller to negotiate with the buyer to avoid a trial. To put the matter as simply as I can: when you buy "AS IS" at an auction, you buy the property's assets and liabilities more or less without any recourse. The exception involves a buyer's ability to prove that 1) either the auctioneer or seller, or both, committed fraud whereby the buyer was intentionally misled, and 2) actual harm resulted from the deception. These points are hard to prove.

The only bit of leverage the winning buyer has in this process occurs between the time the hammer falls and the moment he signs the auctioneer's contract. You will get nowhere by demanding the seller repair an "AS IS" property. But you might be able to resolve an uncertainty, such as writing into the contract that the seller record the survey as it was publicized on auction day without change; or that the seller agree to convey good title to the property (free, for example, of the rumored life estate of his sainted great aunt). You can also ask the seller to help you with non-money details, such as showing you which sections of fence run with the property (but you should have learned this before bidding); or asking the seller to put the word out that you are a hunter and do not want to find other hunters on your new place during hunting season.

If you have not read the contract before the auction, take your time and read it carefully before signing. The auctioneer and seller will be standing there, hovering, wanting a quick signature. TAKE YOUR TIME. READ EVERY SENTENCE. Scratch your ear. Get up and stretch. Ask to consult in private with your spouse. Ask questions and write down the auctioneer's answer. It does not hurt to negotiate then and there on secondary points, but do not expect to get big concessions, such as a financing contingency. PUT EVERYTHING IN WRITING.

Two buyer protections should be included in these contracts, and you are within your rights to insist on both. First, where a house or improvements are involved, the contract should provide that the seller maintain **insurance** until closing for **full-replacement value**. If the contract does not say this explicitly, you may have trouble convincing a judge that full-replacement value was implied in the event of fire. If you are buying woodland with substantial merchantable timber value, you should ask the seller to obtain an insurance binder to cover the timber's value for the 30 days between the auction and closing. If the seller refuses, ask that you be allowed to void the contract if the timber value is substantially damaged, stolen or otherwise diminished. You can probably arrange to insure the timber value on your own, but it will be expensive.

The other language that you should have in an auction contract is a **48-hour, walk-around inspection**, which gives you the right to inspect the property within 48 hours of closing. This should be linked to the seller's agreement that the property will be **conveyed in the same condition** as existed on the date of the auction. "AS IS" should protect the buyer from intentional seller rip offs, such as a last-minute timber cut before closing or the removal of all farm gates. But language that you add to the sales contract makes the point sharper: you expect to have the seller convey exactly what was on the property on auction day. Take photos of the property on auction day and again on walk-around day as a way of making your point, if the need arises.

If tenants are involved in an auction property, the contract should state how their lease (or tenancy without a lease) will be managed. Tenants have the right to stay in the property to the end of their lease, unless otherwise provided. Auction sales typically provide that the sale is subject to the terms of any lease—occupancy, hunting, mineral rights, etc. Landlord-tenant law is community-specific. Even where an occupancy lease has expired, it will take time for an owner to evict a tenant who refuses to move. The seller may dump the eviction process into the buyer's lap despite his responsibilities. Whenever a lease is involved in a property sale, learn its terms before submitting a contract or buying at auction. Certain leases—such as for minerals—are usually recorded; occupancy and hunting leases usually are not and must be supplied by the seller. The pattern common in my area is to **prorate income** from all leases. The seller gets rent up to closing; the buyer, thereafter. Property tax is also prorated.

Property that has been foreclosed—**foreclosures**—is usually sold at auction, which are called **trustee sales** or **trust-deed auctions**. Foreclosures are properties that banks and other lenders have acquired after the owner has defaulted on his mortgage payment or deed of trust. Lenders have no interest in, or capability of, managing property so they use auctions to get rid of foreclosed properties quickly. Large lenders may have a department that does nothing but handle such properties, often referred to as **real estate owned**, or **REOs**. Lenders are willing to sell REOs before incurring carrying and auction costs. Rural lenders do not like the spotlight that finds them when they must foreclose on a customer's land. A quiet, back-door sale can be the preferred alternative. Everyone—lender, owner and even the buyer—gets roughed up in a foreclosure.

In response to a young buyer's question about the pros and cons of buying foreclosures, Robert J.

Bruss, the real-estate columnist, provided succinct advice:

> Buying homes that are in the foreclosure process usually isn't a good idea for beginners because of possible complications. There are three foreclosure acquisition opportunities: (1) buy from the defaulting homeowner and cure the default to reinstate the mortgage; (2) purchase at the foreclosure auction for cash; or (3) if there were no auction bidders, buy after the sale from the foreclosing lender that took title to the home.
>
> Foreclosure buyers purchase 'subject to' senior liens, such as unpaid property taxes. If you buy direct from the defaulting borrower before the auction, you also must pay any junior liens, such as a second mortgage. The foreclosure cash sale wipes out junior liens, but not senior liens.
>
> Buying from the foreclosing lender after the auction, if there were no foreclosure sale bidders, often results in easy financing.
>
> However, most lenders usually mark the price up to full market value. (Washington Post, August 28, 2004.)

Lenders will usually set a reserve price in a foreclosure auction, based on what is owed and what the market price is thought to be. The local banker may even openly bid for the property. Remember: the lender does not want to win the bidding. The bank will drop out below the FMV, because its loan was probably for no more than 70 to 90 percent of the property's value at the time the loan was made. The lender, in other words, does not need to get full FMV for its debt to be repaid. Most property is only collateralized by itself, but sometimes the owner's personal guarantee of the debt is involved. In that situation, the bank may not put a reserve on the property since the seller remains personally liable for all residual debt. Buyers may get such a property at a steep discount.

BEEN-HERES AND COME-HERES

Making the match is the first step to making a marriage between you and the right property. The marriage is a longer process than the matchmaking, and its success depends, in part, on how you came into the matchmaking.

When out-of-towners buy rural land and enter a new place the sale affects the local community on many different levels. You, the newcomer, are the new, unknown factor, the disturbance in the neighborhood's equilibrium. How you enter—your manner, interests, your behavior with the seller—will be observed and judged. There is no anonymity in the country.

Behind your purchase and entrance are market factors that have led many others just like you to buy their own country place. This process is shifting the demographic, sociological and economic balance in rural communities. To a greater or lesser extent, the process transforms a place from one of long-established been-heres to a mix of been-heres and come-heres like you. The phenomena of "outsiders moving in" is familiar across the United States—in rural New England, the pretty parts of Appalachia, upstate New York, coastal communities, farmland around college towns, small towns that cater to retirees and recreational destinations such as Jackson, Wyoming. About 445,000 second homes were sold in 2003, according to the National Association of Realtors, and 125,000 are expected to be added to the stock each year during the next decade. (Kristen Gerencher, "A vacation home: to buy or not to buy," Richmond

<u>Times-Dispatch</u>, Knight Ridder, August 8, 2004.) These data do not count undeveloped land or sales by FSBOs. The majority of these sales involve newcomers to a community.

Your new rural community will, consequently, have experience with "outsiders" moving in whether or not you have any experience as an outsider moving in. The rural been-heres who are your seller and new neighbors have a right to be angry at the market process that prices them out of buying that which becomes available. Since it is much harder for individuals to pile up cash in rural areas than in urban areas, been-heres sell their principal asset—their land—for a price above what their neighbors can pay. They then find themselves down-sized in the housing market. Rural kids often leave, because jobs and opportunities are in other places. Those who stay may find themselves servicing the come-heres and priced out of property ownership. Resentment is generalized and can be focused against a particular newcomer through no fault of his own. Each newcomer is often seen as representing all newcomers, though each newcomer sees himself only as an individual.

While newcomers enjoy the basic civic rights of all citizens, you will do well to think of yourself at times as a guest resident in another's home—a guest with rights to be there. Admittedly, this is complicated and often maddening. Some will see you in this light, fair or not. Newcomers may be subjected to certain testing behaviors from a few been-heres who are insecure enough to act rudely, boorishly, hostilely or stupidly toward you, but this is not the prevailing attitude in my experience If you roughed up the seller during your purchase, you will be tested. You will be judged locally by your test responses, fair or not. Your scores will get around, far in advance of your meeting those who hear them. Some will look for faults, but most will judge you on how you relate to them as individuals.

Buyers, therefore, should come into the marriage lightly. Buy softly: don't act like a jerk. Don't gloat over a seller's misfortune. Don't boast about how cheaply you bought the seller's family farm. The ordinary work-day personality you use at the corporate office may be too brusque, too business-like for your new neighbors. Be prepared to pass the time at the expense of getting some chore crossed off your list. Passing time glues a lot together in the country. I'm not advising you to become a faux native, which will be seen as phony and condescending. I am suggesting you consider a slow, low-profile, quiet entrance. You are a small piece of a very large demographic and economic change that is rearranging your new community. It's important to remember that the pebble you drop in this pond ripples out and also ripples back.

CHAPTER 16: NEGOTIATING

COMMUNICATION CHANNELS

Dozens of books are available on negotiating, many advocating a particular approach and system. Here are some that I've found to be helpful: Max H. Bazerman and Margaret A. Neale, Negotiating Rationally (New York: The Free Press, 1992); Michael C. Donaldson and Mimi Donaldson, Negotiating for Dummies (Foster City, CA: IDG Books, 1996); Roger Fisher and William Ury, Getting to Yes, Negotiating Agreement Without Giving In (New York: Penguin, 1985); George Fuller, The Negotiator's Handbook (Englewood Cliffs, NJ: Prentice Hall, 1991); Robert Irwin, Tips & Traps When Negotiating Real Estate (New York: McGraw-Hill, 1995); Gary Karrass, Negotiate To Close: How to Make More Successful Deals (New York: Simon & Schuster, 1985); John McDonald, Strategy in Poker Business & War (New York: Norton, 1989); Peter G. Miller and Douglas M. Bregman, Successful Real Estate Negotiation: How Buyers, Sellers and Brokers Can Get Their Share—and More—at the Bargaining Table, rev. ed., (New York: HarperPerennial, 1987); Peter B. Stark, It's Negotiable: The How-To Handbook of Win/Win Tactics (Amsterdam: Pfeiffer, 1994); William Ury, Getting Past No: Negotiating Your Way From Confrontation to Cooperation (New York: Bantam, 1993); and George F. Donohue, Real Estate Dealmaking: A Property Investor's Guide to Negotiating (Chicago: Dearborn Trade Publishing, 2005).

My guess is that some systems work some of the time, none work all of the time and all work every now and then.

Property negotiations work best when at least one of the parties, and preferably both, are operating under pressure to do a deal. The pressure may not be to do your deal, but, rather, to do *a* deal sooner rather than later. The greater the pressure, the harder that party will work to reach a deal. You will benefit from narrowing the seller's generalized pressure to do *some* deal into a focus on doing *your* deal by negotiating reasonably and doing what you can to help him get to where you want him to be.

Buyers should not buy country property under pressure, internal or external. Internal pressure can be the love-at-first-glimpse type that leads to impulse buying. External pressure is a relocation requirement or a deadline. When a buyer feels more pressure to buy than the seller feels to sell, the seller will sense it and the buyer is negotiating at a disadvantage. If you are an externally pressured buyer, conceal it. If you are putting yourself under pressure, stop it.

The first rule of real-estate negotiations is to learn as much about the seller as you can. Does he feel pressure to sell this particular piece of property? If so, what's the nature of that pressure? Is there a clock ticking? Is he in a cash crunch? Is his lender hounding him for missed mortgage payments? What are the consequences of not selling? What are his consequences of not selling to you? Does he need to get a certain price to pay off a mortgage or other debt? If he does not need to sell, why, then, is he selling? Can you estimate his adjusted basis in the property? (If you can estimate his adjusted basis, you can project his after-tax profit at any selling price.) How will his taxable income from the sale be treated for tax purposes— taxed as regular income (a high rate) or capital gains (a low rate)? (You and the seller will have more room to bargain if he will be paying the lower capital-gains rate that kicks in after a year of ownership.) Is there some particular aspect of the property that the seller might want to retain, such as a hunting right or use of a barn? (Such concessions can sweeten your offer and save you money.)

Each seller is part of a socio-economic group. Ethnicity, race, religion, culture, age, gender, education, regional identity, style, vocabulary, manners—all contribute to defining sellers and buyers as individuals. Individuals bargain as individuals, but their style and way of sending messages can be shaped by these characteristics. If you don't understand the bargaining culture of the seller, you can easily submit an inappropriate first offer in the wrong way and then get your counter-offer signals crossed up. I once witnessed a very shrewd mergers-and-acquisitions guy kill his own property purchase by telling the seller that his offer was, "Take it or leave it." In the wheeling-dealing world of the buyer, take-it-or-leave-it meant "we're getting close"; in the wheeling-dealing world of the seller, take-it-or-leave-it was an ultimatum that was to be rejected on principle. It's important for a buyer to understand who the seller is in sociological terms, because those factors shape how he sees you and how he bargains.

A buyer has to develop a **negotiating channel** that works sociologically with the seller, as he is and where he is. A negotiating channel is an approach, a style, that is understood by the seller and accepted as common ground. Part of finding a negotiating channel is to first find those characteristics of the seller that you can relate to outside of negotiating. It could be anything shared. Perhaps you're both fathers of high school basketball players; or vets; or divorced and single; or Methodists; or barbeque lovers, or NASCAR fans; or stock-market victims; or daughters of policemen.

I have found it helpful on occasion to make a channel into a party by bringing in on my side a friend/business colleague who has more connections to that party than I have. When I was trying to bring a client's summer-camp property to the attention of the Mennonite church, I partnered with a Mennonite friend who made the contact.

Another part of finding a negotiating channel is to determine how the seller uses words in relation to how you use words. Some people—by habit or profession—are very precise with what they say and how they say it. Others talk in generalities, often attributing one fact or another to an undefined "they." These channels don't match up well, often leading to messes styled as "miscommunication." The buyer should assume responsibility for learning how best to communicate with the seller and then choose the best negotiating channel.

If the buyer can't find this channel with a seller, he will have to rely on a middleman—a seller's broker if the property's listed; a buyer's broker if the buyer is using one; or a local lawyer who can communicate with the seller—to present the buyer's case. If you choose to bargain through the seller's agent, you must be circumspect in what you reveal. The seller's agent is working for the seller's best interest, not the buyer's. The seller's agent may or may not urge his seller to make a deal with you, depending on what other offers he thinks are in the works. He will also give the seller a frank assessment of the intensity of your interest as well as your financial ability to make a full-price offer. Anything you tell a seller's agent will be used for the seller's benefit.

A more buyer-friendly alternative is to use a local lawyer to bargain on your behalf. This is a less risky way for a newcomer to negotiate the purchase of rural land if he lacks confidence, experience and the ability to develop his own channel. This approach will cost you a very small amount in legal time. All you need to do is tell your lawyer the amount you want to pay and the top amount you will pay.

A second rule is for the buyer to establish negotiating objectives that reflect his own needs and capabilities. A buyer wants to buy for a certain price because that's what his scoping has established is what the property is worth to him. Whether that price is high or low in the local market, whether that price is what the seller is asking or far below it, is immaterial. A buyer's best price should be based only on what it's worth to him.

A buyer's capability to pay for a purchase changes over time. Unanticipated events—death, long unemployment, divorce, illness, job changes—will affect a buyer's capability, but it's hard to anticipate these events and their magnitude at the time you're buying. Since second homes and rural property are almost always discretionary purchases, their cost should never stretch a buyer's current budget or his foreseeable cash flow. Much of life is subject to events individuals cannot control, so every big buy takes place within some lamentable degree of uncertainty. A buyer's margin of financial safety might be defined as something like the ability to carry payments on the rural property for at least 12 months in the absence of all earned income. That year will give you time to sell the property if it becomes necessary. The worth of a property to a buyer should also take into consideration how **liquid** the property is if circumstances change and the buyer needs to sell. A property that can be sold quickly at FMV should be worth more to a buyer than properties that have problems or appeal to a narrow segment of the buyers' market.

In negotiating price with the seller, you can at some point reveal that the offering price now on the table is your "best money," given your financial capabilities. Once you say that, don't budge an inch. This is not a take-it-or-leave-it proposition in tone; it's a this-is-all-I-can-do fact of life. You've now shifted away from negotiating on price to asking the seller whether he wants to sell at your best money. You should not bring more money to the table once you've told the seller that you have no more. That destroys your credibility and creates a hurdle for the seller that he may not want to jump. You can, of course, negotiate on non-price issues to help the seller accept your best money.

A third rule is that buyers must understand that they rarely *need* a particular property. You will like it, even love it, but there will be other properties that you can and will like, even love. Buyers who recognize this about themselves gain bargaining power. Buyers who understand that a want is not a need gain bargaining leverage. Once a seller senses that a buyer's emotions are invested in acquiring his property, the buyer is at a disadvantage. Buyers need to approach any negotiation with the notion that if the target property cannot be purchased for the available money, there are other properties with equivalent virtues that can.

What, then, does a buyer do when he finds himself needing a particular property? First, don't say that you're smitten. Second, don't show it. Third, compliment the seller on individual features of his property, to show interest in and appreciation of the property's most obvious virtues. Fourth, raise some yellow-light issues that you know the seller can address. Finally, don't play around; make a reasonable offer that will be easy for the seller to accept.

The trick, I think, to negotiating astutely for real estate is to use only those tactics that reflect well on you. If the seller asks you a direct question, I would give him a direct answer if you can. If you don't want to reveal an answer, the best thing to do is say that you don't feel comfortable answering that question at this time. That's far better than the alternatives: lying, providing a half-truthful answer and ducking. The straighter the buyer is with the seller, the straighter the buyer should expect the seller to be with him. Straightness should start with the seller, but often doesn't. A seller may not know a fact or two that your scoping has turned up, but a seller should know his property's many features better than you do. And while the seller has a duty to disclose a material defect, not-so-material defects may or may not be disclosed. Property negotiations also have a way of highlighting recent positions that are inconsistent with earlier statements. Owing to that, consistency rewards itself. You can change the terms of an offer, from one to the next, without being inconsistent as long as you explain the reasons for the change. And you can alter the terms of an offer in response to a seller's counter proposal. But you want to avoid promising one thing and then backing away from the promise when it becomes inconvenient. Changing the terms of an offer is part of negotiating; backing off your word spoils the trust that you need to make negotiations work.

If you want to get as much information as possible out of a seller, start by giving him a straight story about yourself and your intentions (if asked). It is, of course, possible that your intentions violate the seller's wishes. He may, for example, object to your plan to tear down his family's crumbling 200-year-old home or carve 20-acre lots out of the back 100 acres. If you lie and conceal your intentions, you will enter your new community with that hanging over your head. Certain intentions cannot be concealed from sellers, because the buyer will have to make his purchase contingent on obtaining a permit from the local zoning agency. If you know the seller is likely to object to a particular idea, I think it's better to talk out with him why you want to do it and let his interest in getting the property sold help you. This doesn't work with sellers who don't need to sell their properties. A seller who can hold indefinitely and pick the buyer that he "likes" won't negotiate in the traditional way because he feels no pressure to make a deal. Try to get this type of seller to like you first and then lead him to negotiate.

NON-PRICE ISSUES

A useful way to approach price with a seller is to back into it as you "front in" all the other issues you want to discuss with him. The most common types of **non-price issues** are:

- important things that you want the seller to do to the property prior to, and as a condition of, your purchase;

- things the buyer introduces into the negotiations that are not important to the buyer and, therefore, are intended to function as buyer concessions;

- things that the buyer can do to help the seller make the deal;

- things that are property liabilities or questions that only the seller can clear up;

- liabilities that can be approached in such a way that both buyer and seller fix a portion of the problem;

- issues that the buyer can, and is willing to, resolve in return for the seller doing other things to facilitate the deal; and

- uncertainties of three kinds: genuine, marginal and tactical (the last of these is one that the buyer knows is less uncertain than the seller believes to be the case).

Non-price issues often involve dickering over money, but not over the selling price of the property.

No single correct way exists to put non-price issues onto the negotiating table. I've found that raising these issues conversationally with the seller (or his agent) prior to submitting an offer and then including language in the offer that addresses the significant ones often works. The buyer does not want to surprise the seller with the terms of his written offer. A buyer should prepare the seller for his offer through whatever preliminary communication channels are open—face-to-face meetings, letters asking for information, letters raising issues of buyer concern, information the buyer has discovered and copies of buyer-paid consultant reports on the property (e.g., unfavorable radon results with an estimate of the cost of remediation or the consultant's report indicating the failure to find soils suitable for a septic system). Preliminary communication flags buyer concerns and begins adding **non-price complexity** to price-only negotiations. The idea behind complexity is not to complicate negotiations or introduce deal-killer issues that can't be resolved. Rather, it is to raise valid (mainly) issues and give the parties opportunities to solve them. The more issues the parties resolve, the more negotiating foundation they will have jointly built. The habit of solving problems will be developed. It is then easier to negotiate price as the last step in a march through a lot of successful negotiating on other matters.

Many non-price issues involve a dollar cost to resolve. If the seller wants the buyer to absorb all these costs, the buyer needs to point out that the property will cost much more than the seller's asking price. In certain circumstances, a buyer can offer to pay the seller full-price *if* the seller fixes the list of buyer-identified problems at the seller's expense. The buyer helps to develop a negotiating rhythm and record of success by conceding the "throw-away" non-price issues he introduced for that purpose and by good-faith bargaining on the genuine ones.

The buyer will get a feel for how the seller negotiates money when they are trying to settle an issue involving cost. The seller may prefer to resolve money issues in one of several ways: split costs 50-50; let's split the difference between your (last) number and my (last) number; buyer puts the money in while seller contributes labor and/or machine time; I'll meet you half way between your (objective, third-party) cost estimate and my (objective, third-party) cost estimate; among others. If a buyer can "read" a seller's preferred way of settling money differences, he can frame the subsequent property price negotiations in advantageous terms. If, for example, a buyer is dealing with a seller who likes to split the difference between the last numbers on the table, the buyer must negotiate up with the same dollar increment as the seller negotiates down—and then split the difference. If the buyer concedes more than the seller, a split the difference proposal ends up with the buyer having given up more than the seller. I think a buyer who offers to meet the seller half way between the asking price and the buyer's offer claims the high ground. If, of course, the buyer has submitted an obvious low-ball price, any offer to meet half way will be a self-evident trick that is likely to anger the seller rather than get him to compromise

I've found it to be easier to engage in give-and-take bargaining orally than in writing. I think this is especially true in buying rural land where the country seller's cultural bargaining style is far more oral than written. But I am a better bargainer on paper than in person. So I try to convert the bargaining to writing as soon as I can. Be forewarned: written bargainers are usually at a disadvantage negotiating orally with oral bargainers. I find this to be true, because written bargainers tend to be more careful with words and draw distinctions between them while oral bargainers are less careful with their words, but not in what they believe these words were intended to mean. It's in the buyer's interest to have his written offer reflect precisely the oral meeting of the minds that's been reached during pre-offer negotiations.

If all issues save price have been settled, then offer your price, clean of contingencies and other issues if you can, packaged with a letter to the seller explaining exactly why you believe this price is both fair to him and reflects the property's FMV considering everything. To the extent the buyer can arrange it, the subsequent price negotiation should revolve around objective valuation of price fairness. Your scoping results establish your talking points. If you inadvertently back the seller into a corner: "This is my price whether or not you [the seller] think it's fair," you have not been negotiating; you've been arguing. Winning an argument with a seller rarely results in purchasing his property at a favorable price. Successful negotiators help the other side get to where they want them to go with facts, logic, third-party opinions, concessions, donations of something new or unexpected, patience, reciprocity and talk. A buyer never wants to push a seller into a take-it-or-leave-it position. When a buyer's head hits a stone wall, the best tactic is to stop hurting himself. Take a time-out for a couple of days. The seller may be so totally fed up with the buyer's persistence that he refuses any additional bargaining. But if your preliminary foundation is in place, the time-out can allow each side to reevaluate its position and then give bargaining one last, best shot.

Sellers want all-cash, full-price contracts with no contingencies or complications. The buyer's job is to build a case for any offer less than that. The best way to build such a case is to insert non-price complexity into the negotiations and use bargaining to resolve each non-price issue as a foundation-building exercise in preparation for price. The non-price issues, of course, are mainly genuine concerns. If preliminary negotiations cannot resolve them, the buyer needs to incorporate them into his written contract offer as contingencies or items requiring additional investigation.

The buyer must strike the right balance between raising issues of property liabilities and overwhelming the seller with complications to the point where he terminates negotiations. If you've introduced throw-away, non-price issues, you can negotiate with yourself and eliminate them. That is, raise the issue and at some subsequent point concede that you will handle it at your expense. You may in some cases be able to get a seller concession for giving up on a throw-away issue. This leaves only the genuine matters of concern for the parties to negotiate. It has also indicated your willingness to compromise for the sake of the deal.

In most situations, the buyer gets one bite—sometimes, a bite and a half—at getting a seller to concede something in return for the buyer accepting a jointly recognized liability. Sellers who refuse to work with a buyer on a jointly recognized liability are betting that the buyer is highly motivated. The buyer has been too enthusiastic, too forthcoming. When a seller replaces give-and-take bargaining with take-and-take, it is time for the buyer to cool the negotiations. The buyer might mention other properties that have fewer liabilities, different virtues and are below the seller's price. A deal is possible, the buyer says, but the buyer says he needs the seller to help him solve their shared problem. Don't burn your bridge to this seller, but remind him that you have alternatives if he doesn't do his share in helping you get across his. If you don't think you have alternatives, you will have them as soon as you begin looking again.

Non-price issues that emerge during a buyer's scoping can include anything, from boundary disputes and unrecorded easements to snakes under the back porch and an old chimney that you suspect needs to be rebuilt. Addressing rural property problems requires time, patience, skill, experience and money in different combinations. Often, it is the time-and-hassle factor of repairs rather than their cost that is the real incentive for a buyer to have a seller get the work done as part of the sale. In this regard, buyers should be extremely cautious about accepting the burden of a particular task, chore or repair without knowing what's really involved.

For example. The seller's farm has livestock fence all around its border. Ownership is either divided between adjoining neighbors section by section or shared jointly. (There are exceptions, e.g., where one side has livestock and the other has none and does not care if the neighbor's livestock visits at will. In that case, for instance, all fence may be owned by the livestock side.) Whatever the case, the owner of this farm will eventually have to "make fence" or hire out the job. If you acquire the seller's farm with seller-owned "bad" fence, the responsibility falls on you. "Making a section of fence" sounds simple enough, but around my place it involves a big tractor or dozer with a hydraulic post-driving attachment; some form of front-end loader to lift and move old wire and posts; dump truck to haul away the refuse; specialized fencing tools, dozens to hundreds of stakes, posts and braces; wire and fence staples; gates and hinge pins; cable for constructing water gaps; and labor that is both skilled and stout. Making fence is expensive and miserable work. No first-time farmer should attempt it on his own. If the buyer can get the seller to repair or replace those sections of the fence that are needy, his first decade of farmownership will be free of the inevitable phone call at 9:30 p.m. on Sunday night: "Is this you? Your cows are out."

The fence example also illustrates the need for a buyer to be very specific with a seller who agrees to fix a non-price item as part of the sale. Your definition of repair or "make fence" and his can be substantially different. With fencing, you need to specify in writing the type of fence (rolled wire comes in different gauges, hole size and width [that is, height]; high-tensile wire is put up with or without electrification and the number of strands must be agreed to, because a five-strand high-tensile fence is far less effective than a nine-strand fence; type of stakes and posts [material, length, width]; placement distance between each stake [every ten feet is stouter than every 16 feet]; bracing standards [location, type, number]; placement and size of gates [material, type of hinges]; depth to which stakes should be driven [at least 30 inches]; style and construction of water gaps [where the fence crosses a stream]; and disposal plan for the old fence [no plan means the old wire will be left in your field]). Many states specify in their Codes what constitutes a "**lawful fence**," which means any fence built to a lesser standard is not lawful. Such a fence may open a landowner to liability in the event straying livestock cause damage to a neighbor's crops or a road accident. If you are totally ignorant of fences, talk with the county extension agent about which type is best for your purposes. One way of handling the need to repair/rebuild a seller's fence is for the buyer to provide or pay for the materials and the seller to provide the labor and necessary machine time.

If you think I am being a paranoid about fences, I offer the following real-life experiences. I once purchased 200 sharpened locust stakes from a fellow advertising in the local paper. I was careful to make sure they would be delivered sharpened. They were. Each was seven feet long, a foot shorter than the local standard. Each was as thin as the vendor could contrive. About 25 were so lacking in stoutness that I cut them into kindling. My fault: I didn't specify eight feet and stout. Another time, a fence builder drove hillside stakes only 12 inches into the ground because his tractor couldn't maneuver on the steep slope and he didn't want to spend time driving them deeper by hand, even though I was paying him by the hour. He didn't tell me about this adjustment when I paid him. My fault again: I paid in full before inspecting the job. I had to hire another fence contractor the next year and have a second row of new stakes driven in the same fence line between the wobbly ones. The 12-inch fence builder also failed to construct a water gap behind a dense, roadside thicket, which allowed our cattle to liberate themselves onto a public highway. I had quickly inspected this section from both sides before paying, but the thicket concealed the absence of the water gap. I discovered the problem after the third jail break. I've also had to repair two long sections of fence made by a seller who failed to hammer enough staples on each stake. This high-tensile wire should have one staple emplaced wherever it crosses a stake, otherwise livestock wiggle through it. This fence had one staple per wire every three or four stakes. This little trick saved the seller time and money, but forced me to redo part of his job. I've also replaced seller-built fence that was inadequately braced at the corners and turns, facts that became apparent when the tension in the high-tensile wire winched the end posts out of the ground.

If fence repair or rebuilding is part of your negotiations, make sure that your offer refers to "lawful fence" and sets out the details.

PRICE

Some sellers set their asking price unreasonably beyond what they believe is an approximation of fair market value. They may do this in anticipation of giving the buyer steep price cuts in negotiation that end with a price at, or just above, market value. Or they may have no urgent need to sell and will wait for their price. In both cases, the buyer must show the seller evidence of what fair market value is for his property. This can involve comparables research and even an appraisal. The first type of over-priced seller can be brought down to FMV and even, occasionally, below. The second seller may be unmovable, although I've seen simple, all-cash offers work.

Most sellers in a competitive market set their asking price about 20 percent higher than what they hope to net, expecting to concede ten percent in negotiations and spend the rest for commission and expenses. This is not a rule of real-estate sales, but it is often more or less true. Buyers can get a sense for those sellers who are asking about 20 percent more than FMV and those asking much more than that by looking at recent sales of similar properties and the prices of currently listed comparables. Market-priced properties sell within six months in normal markets; over-priced properties can linger for years. Buyers should avoid over-priced properties, because you will have better alternatives, if not immediately, then in time.

Buyers should look for motivated sellers who for reason of cash shortage, emergency, divorce, relocation, lender pressure, college expenses, family squabbles or ill-health, among other reasons, must sell their property quickly. If these sellers need to get a certain price to meet their obligations, they will be willing to help a buyer with non-price issues, particularly those that require labor and not cash. When distressed sellers need to get money out of their property, they may sell for less than market value to a buyer with a simple cash offer. When the seller is a number of heirs who no longer have an emotional interest in the family's property, offer a number that divides out to a round number—$50,000, $100,000— per heir.

When a buyer finds a property priced ten percent or more below what he has determined to be its approximate FMV, it's usually a sign of one of three conditions: 1) the property has a big, easily discovered liability that can't be readily resolved; 2) the seller is in distress and needs to raise cash immediately; or 3) the seller has underestimated the true value of his property, which can happen with FSBOs. The first of these conditions is a yellow light bordering on red; the second and third are high-intensity green lights for buyers. Listed real estate is priced below market either when the owner insists that he needs a quick sale or, more rarely, when the true value of the property has not been ascertained. With under-priced property, the buyer should negotiate quickly. Driving a bargain harder than necessary may be a buyer's style when dealing with a wounded seller, but I advise against it. Piling on is never admired, and it's a bad way to move into a new place. I've seen greedy buyers lose under-priced property when they forgot that a speedy deal was their goal, not squeezing the last nickel out of a bleeding seller.

Fair market value should be the axis around which the buyer wants negotiations to spin. Whether FMV is established as a single dollar figure or a range, it has a hardness and concreteness that gives the buyer an objective platform of fact and analysis from which to negotiate. With sellers who are having trouble budging from their asking price, the buyer's FMV analysis may draw down the seller if reduction is in the cards. An FMV approach won't win the day in and of itself, but it has the effect of setting a reasonable, market-based cap **for the buyer**. To the extent that a seller insists on demanding an above-market price, he is not being market-based, hence he's being "unreasonable." The more the buyer can orient negotiations around establishing an FMV through comparables, appraisals, tax-assessed valuations and so on, the more he can shift negotiating to a rational comparison of numbers and number-based conclusions.

The persuasive power of a buyer-supplied FMV in negotiations depends on its market integrity. Any buyer who deliberately deflates a target property's FMV by selective use of comparable properties, or small arithmetic mistakes or paying for a low-ball appraisal is no better than the seller who misrepresents his property to a good-faith buyer. If a seller figures out that a buyer is peddling false information, the seller should terminate additional talks.

An FMV looks hard and sounds hard, but it can be a spongy number on rural properties, particularly those that are out of the ordinary, remote or feature an idiosyncratic structure. (FMV analysis is far more accurate in a city where the seller is marketing a three-bedroom apartment in a building that contains 50 identical units, five of which have sold within the last six months.) FMV depends on looking backward and assuming forward. FMV for most real estate is determined by finding the selling prices of recently sold similar properties in the general area of the target property. Once that is done, it is then assumed that the same market will exist in the near future. That assumption gets progressively weaker as time passes from the date when the FMV of a property is calculated and the physical distance increases between the target property and its comparables. **Comparables analysis** adjusts prices to account for differences in similar properties, given that no set of properties are likely to be identical in size, attributes and improvements. Buyers should remember that an FMV analysis gives an approximate value based on sales of other properties, not based on the target property itself. Don't get trapped into insisting on paying no more than the FMV based on comparables analysis. In real life, your target property's estimated FMV may be less than its real value if it has special features that are hard to compare with recent sales or the available comparables are not really comparable. Comparable analysis for undeveloped woodland has limited utility when the commercial value of the timber is not fairly evaluated for all properties in the set. If woodland is selling for $1,000 an acre, regardless of timber value, FMV is $1,000 an acre, regardless of the fact that your target property contains $2,000 an acre in merchantable timber value.

A buyer can readily compare the **tax-assessed values of similar properties** in relation to their recent sales prices to establish FMV for the target property. If, for instance, seven comparable properties have sold for 125-135 percent of their tax-assessed values, it's reasonable to project that the FMV of your target property is about 130 percent of its tax-assessed value as long as general market conditions have not changed. The buyer can also check to see whether the pre-sale tax-assessed values of the seven properties were roughly the same as the target property's value on a per-acre basis. They should be: that's one of the guidelines a buyer can use to establish comparability. Remember, however, that tax-assessed values can have little direct relationship to actual land value when dealing with timberland, because appraisers for the county do not determine timber value when assigning value to woodland. It is, therefore, possible to find a property with a lot of timber value that is under-priced in relation to its comparables using tax-assessed values. Similarly, crop land will differ in fertility and wetness, while pasture will differ in the amount of forage it produces owing to aspect, weeds, wetness, grass-type and elevation. A buyer can judge when per-acre comparables help his side of the negotiations. More often than not, taxed-assessed valuations of country property are lower—often substantially lower—than current FMV.

Professional appraisers are paid to determine fair market value for buyers, sellers and institutional lenders. Both buyers and sellers can commission an appraisal to frame negotiations and offer an objective, third-party opinion about a property's value. An appraiser's FMV should be more accurate than the tax-assessed property values that necessarily use some generic values and, in any case, are less current. Sellers want high appraisals from appraisers they hire; buyers want low numbers (until, of course, they become owners).

Buyers are often required to pay for an appraisal once they sign a contract to purchase with the seller. This appraisal is submitted to the institutional lender who will then lend 80 to 90 percent of either the purchase price or the appraised value, *whichever is less.* If, for instance, a buyer agrees with a seller to pay $200,000 for unimproved land, he is usually hoping that the appraisal will come in at more than $200,000. Were the appraisal's FMV to be $150,000, the bank would lend this buyer 80 percent of the appraised value, that is, only $120,000. This buyer is left with the job of coming up with $80,000 to make the purchase. In contrast a selling-price appraisal of $200,000 would require him to find only $40,000, which is, 20 percent of both the purchase price and the appraised value. The buyer, faced with a low-end appraisal, should reconsider buying the property at the price he negotiated. He can back out of the contract for this reason only if he put a contingency in his purchase contract that allows him to void the offer if the lender's appraisal comes in at less than the agreed price. If the buyer wants to complete the purchase in spite of a low appraisal, he can increase his cash investment or ask the seller to "take back" a second mortgage for $30,000, or more.

Buyers can protect themselves against low appraisals by inserting a contingency such as the following:

Buyer reserves the right to void this purchase contract without penalty if the appraisal required for lender financing does not meet or exceed at least 100 percent of the agreed purchase price. (You can insert a number less than or more than 100 percent if the circumstances warrant it.)

An appraisal contingency can shape your negotiations. It tends to deflate over-priced sellers, and it's worth something to the seller to have a buyer agree to not include it. If the buyer has already procured an appraisal, he can bargain away this contingency without risking anything. The buyer and seller can also agree that in the event of a below-purchase-price appraisal, the seller will finance some or all of the additional cash needed by the buyer at terms written into the contract offer.

Since most institutional lenders require a buyer-paid appraisal as part of their lending process, I recommend buyers get one done *before* offering a purchase contract on any property that is under serious consideration. Buyers should not commission appraisals frivolously since they cost several hundred dollars each. If the buyer-commissioned appraisal comes in below the seller's asking price, the appraisal figure is FMV and should be the buyer's target price in negotiations. If the appraisal comes in at the seller's asking price, the buyer should not introduce the appraisal into negotiations, because it will not help him. He can still provide it to his lender as part of his mortgage application. If the appraisal is higher than the asking price, the buyer should keep that to himself. Buyers have no obligation to inform competent sellers of their property's appraisal value.

A buyer should not dismiss a property that he cannot buy for his appraiser's FMV or below. I would consider buying at as much as ten percent above FMV if the cash difference wasn't that important to me, and I liked the property.

Most sellers do not commission appraisals as part of marketing their property, at least in my experience. The reason for this is unknowable, but it would not surprise me to learn that these sellers believe that a professional appraisal would not confirm their asking price. During negotiations, either buyer or seller can propose that the final purchase price be determined by a neutral appraisal, the cost of which is to be shared equally between the parties. If a buyer has an appraisal in hand, he might propose this with a high-degree of confidence in the outcome. The same is true for a seller holding an appraisal. Where a buyer and seller agree on a jointly sponsored appraisal, they should also agree to direct the appraiser to use the **"market approach"** for finding FMV. This is the typical methodology for land and most non-commercial real estate. It looks at the prices of three recently sold comparable properties, adjusts for differences in acreage and other factors, and then sets the FMV for the subject property in relation to the comps. The appraiser uses his judgment to adjust the selling price of each comparable in direct comparison with his subjective evaluation of the subject property. Once the three comparables prices are tweaked as the appraiser feels it necessary, the three can be averaged to come up with the FMV for the target property. Two other appraisal techniques—"**replacement cost**" and "**income**"—are generally not appropriate for most rural land, with the exception of the income approach for a full-time farm business.

A not uncommon technique for investment partners, heirs or spouses trying to divide jointly held property is to commission three appraisals, the deal price to be the average of the three. The appraisers should be told explicitly that the cost of the appraisal will be divided equally and the appraisal is for both sides. If one appraisal comes in significantly higher or lower than the other two, the parties should talk with the appraisers to determine the reason. Using the same appraisal approach, appraisers should arrive at three FMVs that are within at least ten, if not five, percent of each other in the majority of situations.

When using appraisals to set an FMV on rural woodland, it is important to keep in mind that real-estate appraisers do *not* appraise the tract's timber value. Appraisers using the "market approach" will simply find other recently sold wooded tracts. They are comparing wooded land but not the value of the merchantable timber on each tract, which can obviously drive real value up or down. Therefore, when a buyer wants to obtain complete information about a wooded property's value, he needs to purchase both an appraisal and a timber evaluation. Other consultant opinions may be necessary if minerals, water and farm income are involved.

Appraisers work in gross, not net. What I mean by that is that they compare properties by their large dimensions—such as number of acres and square feet in a house—rather than looking at the quality of the component assets. Two houses can each contain 3,000 square feet, four bedrooms, two baths, two-car garage and have been built in the same year. Yet one might be fairly valued at $150 per square foot, and the other at $100. Similarly, two 100-acre parcels of open land may differ markedly in their soil and water quality, which directly affects their agricultural value. Appraisals may not value rural land for their soil qualities, fencing and topography although each contributes or detracts from value. The appraiser will mainly compare on the basis of size, location and general type, e.g., open land to open land, same size house to same size house, especially in low-population areas where he needs to scrape the barrel's bottom to come up with three recent sales that are even remotely similar. Appraisals should take into consideration water supply and quality where they are important factors.

Appraisers may or may not include the value of subsurface minerals in their appraisals. If a "market approach" is used, the appraiser may not increase the value of a subject property whose owner has, for example, leased its oil and gas rights for $500 a year and has received an average of $1,000 royalty annually for the last five years. A conscientious appraiser will include a note about the mineral lease and royalties when he knows about them. Known minerals can multiply the value of an unimproved tract many times over. Appraisers, in my experience, may not do a title search as part of their appraisal, so buyers cannot count on the appraiser to flag land that does not convey with its subsurface. Another possible asset that may be of interest is a tract's potential for siting a wind-turbine farm. Such enterprises are increasingly proposed and becoming more common along Appalachian ridgelines, parts of the West and along coasts.

Buyers should remember that every FMV is an estimate based on both "hard" numbers (actual selling prices) and the appraiser's judgment. The buyer should see the appraiser's FMV number as the middle of a range of defensible market values. Buyers can use a single FMV number in their negotiations, but they will help themselves by thinking of FMV as a range on either side of that amount. Buyers will be harming themselves if they refuse to pay a penny over the appraised FMV, because "it is above market."

Appraisals are used by sellers to justify a higher asking price and by sellers to justify a lower offering price. If the seller has an appraisal, a buyer should get his own appraisal; otherwise, the buyer is entering the bargaining arena unarmed. If the seller does not have an appraisal, the buyer should seriously consider getting his own as a means of reorienting the seller's expectations around the buyer's FMV number. When a seller has an appraisal that the buyer hasn't seen and he says that he will sell the property for its "appraisal price," the buyer is being suckered into paying a price that in all probability is higher than the property's objective FMV. Beware a seller's appraisal.

Critical to the buyer's success in negotiations is "helping" the seller move negotiations toward "What's a defensible and fair price based on recent comparable sales?" and away from "This is what I want; take it or leave it." Conversely, the buyer is rarely advantaged by making a single offer that he will not change. Both sides in negotiation feel psychologically better about an agreement when there's been some give-and-take bargaining. Deals are often made on the basis of a buyer's final offer that is still subject to some last-minute changes. By inserting the concept of fair market value into the negotiations, the buyer is structuring the negotiations around real numbers—actual selling prices of properties the seller is likely to know. FMV negotiations edge into a give and take that compares the assets and liabilities of recent sales relative to the seller's property rather than a personalized buyer-seller tug of war that is experienced as winning and losing. The buyer should become familiar enough with the properties used for comparison as is necessary to have this conversation.

A buyer starts searching for a fair and reasonable purchase price for a particular property by working two sides of the same street.

First, the buyer does what he can to determine analytically the objective value of the target property using an appraisal, tax-assessed valuations, selling prices of comparable properties, asking prices of currently listed comparable properties (available in the local real-estate guide), timber cruises and other information in whatever combination he thinks is appropriate for the target property. The purpose of the buyer's effort is to come at the yet unknown FMV from various known points. This is the buyer's FMV—his most accurate and honest evaluation of the target property's current market value. It may be a number the buyer keeps to himself or shares with the seller.

Second, the buyer begins testing the seller's perception of fair market value by feeling for the bottom of the seller's range of acceptable selling prices. One way to do this is to find out what prices the seller has recently rejected. If the asking price is $350,000 and the seller rejected a contract for $300,000 two months ago, the buyer knows the seller's bottom was between the two at that time. But the buyer should remember that the same price can net different amounts to a seller. A $300,000 offer that was replete with a seller-financing contingency and a demand that the seller fix the roof is not as high as a no-contingency, all-cash offer of $300,000. If $300,000 is the FMV that the buyer has established, the buyer can offer it with a clean contract after laying the proper foundation with the seller. If the seller rejects a clean-contract, all-cash offer of $300,000, then his bottom is higher than your FMV at this time. (Six months later, he may have reduced his bottom number to $300,000.)

The buyer might look for the seller's bottom with a first offer that is five to ten percent or more below what the buyer's FMV is. This tactic is intended to end up with a deal price around the buyer's FMV number. Some sellers set an asking price (above what they think FMV is) and then tell the buyer what they'll accept. That number is often a false bottom, but it will take work to loosen the seller's grip on it.

I've also run into sellers who set an asking price, then the price they'll take, and allow me to work them off this false-bottom price—and their real bottom is still above the objective FMV.

Sellers usually have their own objective FMV in mind. That number may come from their listing broker's competitive market analysis used to set the asking price, which is likely to be 15 to 20 percent higher to allow for costs and negotiation. Or it may come from nothing more than a seller's intuitive sense of what his property is worth in the market based on what he knows and has heard. In both cases, circumstances may force a seller to accept a price below his FMV and, in rare cases, below his bottom price. Negotiations will lead a buyer to that seller hell hole, but the seller gets there because of pressure unrelated to your skill as a negotiator. It behooves a buyer to know the difference between his bargaining talents and serendipitous good fortune. Where a buyer has not determined his own objective FMV, he can offer 30 to 35 percent below the seller's asking price in hope of discounting it by 20 percent.

I have in front of me two properties that are over-priced. One is 220 acres of woods on a mountain top in western Maryland. It's surface only, and there are strip mines on two sides. It is not accessible year-round. The FSBO owners—Mom and her five kids—are asking $1.2 million, or about $5,450 per acre. The other is about 310 acres in a not-very-desirable spot in a West Virginia county that borders Virginia. This one has a 1960s ranch house, some river-bottom land (that floods) and steep woodland. It's priced at about $2,990 per acre. In both counties, there are properties of this size that have sold for such prices, but neither of these merit their prices. The Maryland property is worth about $1,500 per acre. The West Virginia tract is in the $1,600-to-$2,000-per-acre range. With the Maryland FSBO, I would offer $1,200 per acre and move up to $1,500. The sellers know their asking price is crazy, so if a realistic offer doesn't work, I'd just skip it. On the West Virginia parcel, I would be interested in buying the wooded part, leaving the floodplain and the house for another buyer. I might offer $600 to $800 per acre for the woods, depending on the timber value. That's a huge discount, but I think it's justified in so far as the 250 acres I want are steep and not easily accessed. I'm leaving the prime assets in the seller's hand. If there's no timber value, I won't make an offer. Even as little as $20,000 in immediate timber-sale income would be enough to pay the interest for a year, giving me that amount of time to resell the property as a capital gain. In both examples, the sellers will make a huge profit on their sales even at my price since the tracts were bought in the late 1940s for a few thousand each and have no mortgage. This is windfall money, and the sellers know it. Both properties would be bought for investment, and I need neither one. My feelings won't be hurt if the sellers reject my offers. In both cases, I would make all-cash, no-contingency offers to show that my offer is real even though it's far below what the seller has asked. A buyer loses nothing in making a low offer for over-priced property.

Any offer that lowers the asking price significantly should be accompanied by a letter or personal buyer-to-seller conversation that lays out the buyer's factual basis for what otherwise will be considered an insulting and not serious **low-ball offer**. No seller will be inclined to accept a low-ball offer, but some sellers will end up agreeing to about the same money if the buyer can show that figure represents an honest FMV. I don't suggest offering a low-ball price as a bargaining tactic, but I would always offer a low price that is based on objective FMV analysis. The buyer should do what he can to lift a low-ball offer out of that category in the seller's mind. No seller wants to give up genuine fair value for his property. (Giving up an inflated asking price is to be expected.) A seller maintains his self-respect if he sells for FMV as long as he can resist thinking that he's giving it away to a low-ball buyer. The buyer can sweeten a low-money offer by doing other things for the seller, such as allowing him to retain hunting rights for a certain number of years or granting him a life-time estate over a small piece of the property. A buyer helps his cause when he can show that his FMV offer reflects a fair price in the current market and his low offer is not simply a bargaining tactic. The easiest way to communicate this to the seller is for the buyer to say to the seller, "I know my offer is a lot lower than your asking price, but it's exactly what I've determined to be objective fair market value at this time—and here's the evidence that I've used."

A common low ball is to offer the **tax-assessed value** of the property, assuming, of course, that the tax value is substantially lower than the objective FMV. Farms and other rural land are commonly appraised and assessed for tax purposes at less than their FMV. Cash-pinched rural landowners are helped by below-market tax valuations and the resulting low property taxes. The current tax-assessed value of county property can be several years out of date, which usually puts it below market. Nonetheless, the tax-assessed value of a property—updated where need be—arguably represents 100 percent of an objective FMV. A buyer starting at 100 percent of tax-assessed value has grabbed a reasonable bargaining position. The seller is forced to show why and how the county's tax-assessed value differs from FMV when they're supposed to be the same. Where comps support the tax-assessed FMV, show them to the seller.

A low-ball offer, as a tactic, works occasionally for those who are discretionary buyers, such as investors who are only looking for property as a vehicle for making money. These individuals know that a purchase below market value strips much of the risk out of trying to make a profit.

If you are considering using a low-ball tactic, you must think through your next step after the seller rejects it—and perhaps rejects you too—if you are interested in the property as anything other than a take-it-or-leave-it deal. A buyer can "allow himself" to be persuaded by the seller's objections and arguments on behalf of his property to raise his low-ball offer. This disingenuousness grants both sides enough face-saving to go forward. The seller may feel some psychological edge in having worked a buyer up from a ridiculously low starting point, just as a buyer may feel the same sense of victory after working a seller down from a ridiculous high. The low-ball buyer, however, should be willing to come up a bit (which places him well below FMV). The question for this buyer is whether to come up to his final number in one jump or be stepped up in a series of concessions. I think the step-up approach is more psychologically rewarding to the seller and improves the climate of the deal.

If you are more interested in a property than just looking for a steal, I advise starting with a below-market offer that you justify to the seller as best you can. That starting price should not be insultingly low, but it can be 20 percent or more below FMV and, in some cases, even 30 to 40 percent below an over-priced asking price.

I bought a wooded tract of 116 acres some years ago from a college-educated professional who I thought would be persuaded by numbers. He had priced the property at $100,000, a number too round to have any credibility with me. A professional forester did a timber cruise and placed the current value of the merchantable timber at just under $80,000. That meant we had good reason to believe that we could sell the timber to a sawmill within a month or so of buying the land for about 80 percent of the seller's asking price. I went to the courthouse to dig a bit. I discovered that the seller had bought the property for $55,000 a few years before and had about $45,000 remaining on his note. Since I knew that tax-assessed valuations never value the timber on woodlands, I found a representative sample of about a dozen nearby woodland properties of similar size and noted their tax-assessed values. I converted these property values to dollar-per-acre numbers, which averaged $560. I then wrote the seller a letter outlining the method by which I had derived an estimate of FMV for his tract. I included all the information I found, identifying each parcel by Deed Book and Page number, owner, location, acreage and tax-assessed value. I ended this analysis by multiplying his acreage (116 acres) by the average tax-assessed per-acre value of comparable woodlands ($560), to come up with an FMV-based offer of $64,960. I included a purchase contract for that amount with the letter. I made the contract as simple as I could—no contingencies of any kind, all cash and a 30-

day closing. The seller figured that he would pay off his note and have $10,000 in his pocket before paying capital-gains tax. He accepted the offer after his over-priced, fancy lawyer in Washington asked for a few unimportant language changes that I made without complaint. The seller informed me that he knew the timber had no value, an opinion I acknowledged hearing without agreeing. The timber was sold two years later for $128,000 when stumpage prices were at the top of their fairly predictable cycle. I did not, of course, share the cruise results with the seller, and he never thought it necessary to spend $500 to have a cruise done before he put his property up for sale.

My offer was 35 percent below the seller's asking price but was deeply and impeccably grounded in hard, verifiable numbers. Indeed, $560/acre *was* a fair market value for all wooded land in this area at that time. And it was $85/acre more than the seller paid for it a few years earlier. The seller didn't argue against the numbers and knew that $100,000 had no local foundation. I don't think the seller saw my $64,960 offer as a low ball, because he knew that he had set his asking price unreasonably high in relation to comparables. In this fashion, a buyer can sometimes work a seller's own over-pricing tactic against him. It helped, of course, that the seller had on his own acquired the opinion that his timber had no value.

I draw a distinction between a low-ball offer and what I did on this timber tract. I was a highly motivated buyer since I knew the value of the timber and the seller did not. But I was motivated only up to $80,000, the value of the merchantable timber. The seller stalled for a couple of weeks, looking for other buyers, but never made a counter proposal. I told him that I would withdraw the offer if he wasn't prepared to respond. Second, I was not making an offer that would produce a loss to this seller, only less profit than he would get at a higher price. This distinction is very important in negotiations. Often, the difference between a real loss and less profit is only a few thousand dollars, and there's no sensible reason for a buyer to insist on forcing a loss. Third, I knew that the seller had paid more for the property than he should have based on comparables sold at the time, and I figured that he knew that too. I assumed that he would reason something like this: "If I had been smart and paid $44,000 rather than $54,000, I would make $20,000 on Seltzer's offer, instead of $10,000. It's my own fault. His offer is not that low; it's just that I paid too much." Fourth, this seller was a FSBO who was figuring that he would keep the ten percent broker's commission in his pocket. Fifth, I detected that the seller's emotional investment in the property had waned. He had planned to build a second home on a 4,000-foot ridge, a plan that proved to be impractical. Finally, I think he was persuaded by the transparency of the numbers and reasoning I used. The analytical framework and the vocabulary were familiar to him as they would be to any high-income professional. I also made the deal as simple and easy for him as I could, so that he wouldn't have to take time from his lucrative practice. I supplied the purchase contract, which saved him some legal fees. This approach can work with busy college-educated, absentee owners whose profit from the sale is not central to their financial well-being. It does not work with individuals who "want their price" and are willing to hold a property until they get it.

The buyer may find little budge in a seller's price. The buyer needs to determine whether the seller's rigidity is a matter of choice or lack of choice. Where a seller is forced into a sale to raise cash to meet debt or unanticipated expenses, he may be both desperate to sell and unable to move off his price. A buyer should try to work this type of seller on non-price concessions. The buyer can also shift the negotiations from talking about price to talking about the terms of the purchase, including seller financing, seller sweetening the pot by throwing in farm equipment or building new fence, and seller agreeing to pay transaction costs, such as a tax or lender points. If a seller takes the negotiating position of always saying no and refusing to move on any issue, including price, the buyer faces a take-it-or-leave-it situation. If the seller's price is fair and you can live with the non-price issues, take it. If, as is usually the case, such a seller has also priced his property above market, walk away while offering to talk things over again at the seller's convenience. If you haven't heard from the seller in a couple of weeks, find another property. If you submit to a stick up, you may never feel quite right about the place. If money is no object and you can afford to be robbed, put up your hands.

How the seller feels about a negotiation can play a role in price bargaining. A client was aiming at a large tract that was mainly water, woods and a very large white elephant of a recording studio. The seller had built a custom structure and then lost interest. He probably had $10 or $11 million in the property as a whole. That, at least, was the appraisal value based on replacement cost. The seller listed at $6.25 million. My client did not want to pay over $5.25. Price was the only issue between them. I thought $5.25 was the seller's bottom. My client started with a bit over $5 million, which I thought was the right place for credibility. The seller eventually came down to $5.35 million. My client came up, but not to $5.25 million. Then they stalled. The seller in my opinion did not need the money from this sale, but he did need to extract some psychological positive out of a situation where he knew he was losing a lot of money. I advised my client to couch his last offer in terms of "That's all folks—the seller has gotten my last available nickel. I am stretched to the limit." This allowed the seller to shift his thinking away from the enormity of his loss (which he really didn't care that much about) to the idea that he was squeezing every last penny out of the buyer—and therefore winning. The deal got done at $5.2 million when the seller could feel that he was at least not losing the negotiations with the buyer regardless of the fact that the buyer was winning the deal over the property. Each side got what it wanted.

HORSE-TRADING

The fact-and-numbers approach I used with the absentee owner above is not the way most rural sellers are accustomed to bargaining. A lot of price bargaining occurs in rural areas between individuals, and its style is usually described as old-fashioned **horse-trading**.

Horse-trading is not something I learned at my father's knee. In fact, I never saw either parent negotiate anything of a commercial nature, though I'm sure they did so in the course of operating a small business. I never learned anything remotely relevant to negotiating in college or graduate school, though I studied negotiated settlements in international politics and the deal-making of domestic politics. Growing up in a suburban Pittsburgh neighborhood, I had no experience in thinking about commodities, let alone pricing and trading them. People who grow up in rural areas and, particularly, on farms, learn to understand their immediate world in terms of commodities that are valued and sold as cents per pound, dollars per pound of gain, dollars per acre and dollars per thousand board feet. Any farmer who buys stocker cattle in the spring at the livestock auction must calculate the present cost and the future projected values of different grades of cattle priced in pennies per pound multiplied by thousands of projected pounds where weight gain can vary by 25 percent depending on an animal's genetics, health and the weather. Buying and selling rural commodities involves on-the-spot, face-to-face negotiations where give and take is expected. It's worked for farm animals, crops, trees and land for centuries. The idea of trading seems to be known in all cultures.

Horse-trading in its most elementary form is swapping one thing for a like thing, this horse for that one. It requires that each party understand the value of what he has and the virtues and liabilities of what he wants from the other. Horse-trading in this form involves no cash, though it might involve "**boot**," which is something extra—possibly cash—to even the swap. The essence of swapping is equivalence, that is, both sides benefit when the outcome is, as kids say, "even-steven." Each trader is trying to better his position, and neither would turn down the chance to get the better of the swap. Swapping generates risk when one side fails to know a defect in the other's horse—and horses are the perfect example of goods with hidden defects. Sellers are not expected to disclose defects in their horses; it's strictly, "protect yourself at all times."

Horse-trading has come to mean a negotiating technique rather than the process of swapping one like thing for another. As a technique I have seen it used during several decades of residing in a farming community. It refers to a mutually agreed process of bid and counter bid in search of a price and terms that both sides can live with. The buyer wants the seller to set the asking price. The seller expects the buyer's first bid to be too low, and the buyer knows that he will have to come up. These negotiations often take place over the hood of a pick-up truck parked under a shade tree. The more formal sessions take place around the seller's kitchen table. Nothing is put in writing until there is agreement on price and terms. Participants are expected to hold to their word. Oral contracts are enforceable in court, *except those* involving real estate. Still, a lot of rural real estate seems to bargained orally as a first step and then put in writing. A party who starts to "crawdaddy" away, backing off from his oral commitment, is not playing by the rules. Writing up an oral agreement is sometimes referred to where I live as "doing up a paper." The written agreement should not contain surprises or zingers. I have seen horse-trading work well among people who share the same values, background and vocabulary. I've also seen a university professor and his wife walk away from an oral agreement when a better offer came along.

Face-to-face horse-trading has the potential to work badly, or not at all, between individuals from different community cultures, typically a rural seller experienced with oral horse-trading in that place and an urban buyer who is more comfortable with words on paper and a different style of oral negotiations. Typically, the choice of negotiating frameworks is the buyer's since he must make an offer. Where a real-estate broker is involved, the bargaining should always be paper-based.

An urban/suburban buyer may find himself in an awkward situation where a rural seller, especially a FSBO, is unfamiliar with his negotiating framework. Sellers of this type fear being tricked by a city slicker's paper, while buyers fear they will be skunked by a crafty seller in overalls. I have seen very smart buyers—high SATs in verbal and math—negotiate very badly with honest rural people when they are not comfortable with face-to-face negotiating and don't like the give and take the seller assumes is normal. If you don't feel comfortable horse-trading with a FSBO, ask your local lawyer to do it for you, subject to your confirmation. If you try it yourself, raise your offer slowly, always getting something equivalent in return and don't exceed your scoping-based top offering price. Take your time; digress when you don't have a response; and never say, "Take it or leave it." If horse-trading doesn't lead to a deal, walk away on friendly terms. Horse-traded deals have a way of working out. Horse-trading is a skill that most people get better at with practice. Horse-trading survives on the pennant-draped lots of auto dealers and in the tourist markets of the Caribbean. And if you're a friend of Rick, the seller always has a special price.

There are two other pitfalls I will point out in horse-trading across class cultures. People who work with words—writers, lawyers, economists, scientists and the like—use hedge verbs, conditionals and qualifiers as a matter of routine. Such a person is comfortable with this sentence: "I would not think it impossible to consider $125,000 were we to agree on everything today." The vernacular seller does not hear in the subjunctive: he hears $125,000 hard and the conditional context soft. It's easy to see how the seller will feel the buyer is sliding around if one or more of the buyer's conditions—included in "everything"—isn't met. The buyer should not be obscure, and he should hold the seller to the same standard of clarity. Rural sellers may speak in generalities that are clear to them, but not to you. In that situation, you need to get it straight with the seller when he says something when he says it, not later.

The second pitfall involves the fine print in the purchase offer contract. All real-estate contracts contain fine print, some of which can be monumentally important. Phrases like: Time is of the essence; Warranties do or do not survive the Contract; Buyer's purchase is subject to the Seller's mortgage; Property to convey As Is as of the day when this Contract takes effect or As Is on the day of Closing—can make or break deals and result in one side or the other bearing unexpected expenses. If you and your lawyer are preparing a contract for the seller to sign, make sure that you explain each and every sentence of significant fine print that you want to include at the end of your oral negotiations. You do not want the written contract to surprise the seller. I have advised sellers to have their lawyer look over a contract before they sign so as to avoid future fine-print misunderstandings. If the seller's lawyer fails to explain the meaning of the contract's words to the seller, he is to blame, not you.

If you're horse-trading, you must make sure that you understand the seller's vocabulary and intent, and he yours. A constant source of amusement are conversations between an owner and an "outside" buyer that run like this:

Buyer: Where's the back property line?

Seller: Oh you go up there to where the big sugar is. Then you follow it out. You can't miss the pin. Then you head out on up the ridge. Just go along the chops. Then come back around. (These "directions" will make perfect sense once the buyer is on the ground and is oriented, but they are worthless for the purpose of helping an urban buyer who has no idea what is meant by a "big sugar" or a "chop.")

A similar conversation can occur over the conveyance of farm equipment in the property sale:

Seller: We're planning an auction to clear out the place before you move in.

Buyer: Good.

Seller: Sure. We'll get rid of all that junk out in the barn for you.

Buyer: I thought I bought all that under "farm equipment."

Seller: Now son, you did buy the "farm equipment." That means the *mechanical* equipment—the tractor, bushhog, grain elevator—things that have moving parts and do some machine work. Hell, I'll even throw in a hay wagon. (The buyer assumed he had already purchased all four of the seller's hay wagons, worth about $1,000 each.)

Buyer: What about the five new farm gates, the four rolls of fence wire and the board fencing stacked out back?

Seller: Those are supplies, not equipment. You're free to buy all of that stuff at the auction.

Buyer: But the gates and wire were in the barn when you took me around.

Seller: "Equipment" doesn't mean hay in the barn, or tools, or any of that other stuff you want 'cause you're going to need it. There's no free lunch on a farm.

The only defense against oral misunderstanding is for the buyer to take responsibility for being unambiguous and specific, and insist that the seller explain what his words mean. Spoken words mean what they mean, and then they also mean something more or something less, and sometimes, something different. If you're going to horse-trade land with a horse-trader, you better know exactly what he means when he says something such as "all one money." Your definition of "all" should match his definition of "all," item for item.

Horse-trading over land has its own peculiarities. While horse-trading always revolves around price, terms of the purchase are not usually on the table at the same time. But terms in real-estate sales can be equally critical, as expressed in the old saw: "I'll pay your price [$1,000,000], if you agree to my terms [$1.00 per year for one million years]." Horse-trading tends to disadvantage a buyer because it skews the bargaining toward price first. If a seller insists on talking price first, the buyer must immediately raise all the other issues and leave them hovering with the warning that price can't be concluded apart from all the other issues. If a buyer does not do this at the outset, the seller will be righteously indignant when the buyer starts backing away from a price. Horse-trading tends to neglect discussion about contingencies that protect the buyer. Buyers, therefore, must set out terms and contingencies along with price so that the seller has a complete view of the buyer's agenda. Inexperienced horse-traders should be careful not to get caught agreeing to a thing in isolation from other things that are related. If you feel that horse-trading has thrown you before you've ever started, submit a written offer; don't start what you don't think you can finish.

Being specific and detailed in horse-trading also avoids the problem of a seller feeling he has a certain residual claim to stuff left on the property after closing. I have seen bad feelings generated when a seller takes lumber left in the barn that he felt was his "personal property" and just hadn't had a chance to haul it off. The buyer rightly assumed anything left on the property after closing was his unless prior arrangement was made. A new owner does not want to bring a court case against the seller since all of his new neighbors will think him to be grabby and litigious. The new owner swallows his sense of violation but doesn't forget.

A variation on this post-closing last bite occurs when a neighbor informs the new owner of an obligation made by the seller that he feels "runs with the land." The neighbor built a section of fence for the seller 15 years ago, but was never paid. The neighbor informs the new owner of this fact along with the additional information that the former owner gave him the right to cut 20 sawtimber trees in lieu of payment. The seller, of course, never informed the buyer of any claim. The new owner has no legal obligation to live up to a claim of this sort even if it's genuine. The new owner needs to navigate this strait with care since he has to live with the neighbor, not the seller. The best defense is to ask the seller during negotiations whether he has knowledge of any such claims. And if the buyer is still suspicious, he can insert a clause in his purchase offer:

> **Seller warrants that to the best of his knowledge, neither he nor any of his neighbors have outstanding claims against each other that would adversely affect the Buyer's title, ownership, use and enjoyment of the subject property, its rights, assets and goods as conveyed and/or found on the property at closing.**

The biggest problem with the horse-trading style of negotiation for land is that it is entirely oral. **Oral agreements to buy and sell real estate do not bind the parties and are not enforceable until they are put into writing and signed by all parties.** (The Statute of Frauds requires that a real-estate contract must be supported by a written document that is signed by the party against whom the other party is seeking enforcement. But a memo or a letter of understanding can take the place of a formal contract; and several documents can constitute a contract. Moreover, if one party partially performs on a real-estate contract, a court may find that a valid contract exists even if it's oral. Partial performance to establish a contract might be found in possession by the buyer, payment and possession, or possession and improvement of the property.) If you start a real-estate purchase by horse-trading, you need to convert it to writing to avoid legal wrangles.

Horse-trading tends to focus on the big items—price, closing date, possibly seller financing, contingencies. A dozen smaller-but-still-important items are likely never to be discussed. If they are talked about, some may never be nailed flush. Certain "small" items can be deal-killers. If, for instance, the buyer is assuming that the seller is conveying title in fee simple with a General Warranty Deed and it then turns out when the purchase offer contract is written that the seller can do neither, the buyer has no obligation to go through with what amounted to an oral agreement on some things and not on others. A seller of real estate, similarly, has no obligation to go through with an oral agreement on some or even all terms until he has signed a contract and accepted the buyer's earnest money.

If a buyer finds himself horse-trading with a horse-trader, he should bring to their face-to-face oral negotiation a written draft purchase-offer contract that the parties complete in writing as each item is negotiated orally. The written contract provides structure to the final oral negotiations, and the buyer is assured at each step on the way that he and the seller are in an agreement that binds them both. A buyer and seller leave much too much to chance if they don't use their last face-to-face meeting to convert their oral understandings to writing. Once the terms of the contract are roughed in, both sides should initial and date the draft contract with a copy to each. The final, clean copy can then be produced by either side. The buyer submits his deposit money to an escrow agent when he signs the finished contract and hands it to the seller. The buyer should not give his deposit to the seller. If you are inexperienced in buying rural land, make sure to have your lawyer with you when you are negotiating and filling in a contract.

Buyers who prefer paper-based bargaining must be careful not to fall victim to their own preferences. While paper-based, back-and-forth bargaining may be the buyer's preference, standard real-estate contracts used by broker/agents are written to favor the seller (who is the listing broker's client). Such contracts are almost always filled in with the "help" of the real-estate broker/agent representing the seller, leaving the buyer on his own. They are rarely reviewed prior to submission to the seller by a lawyer representing the buyer. The burden of thinking up legal language to protect the buyer's interests falls totally on the buyer in a pressured situation orchestrated by a broker/agent representing the seller. Even experienced buyers are likely to forget to think of inserting both a **survival** clause in the offer, which obligates the seller to stand by the promises he makes in the purchase contract after the purchase is completed, and a **liquidated-damages** clause, which limits the buyer's financial exposure to his deposit in the event he won't or can't perform on the contract after the contingencies are removed.

Paper-based negotiation should always be the format when a seller lists his property with a real-estate broker. All offers and counter-offers are made in writing and channeled through the broker/agent. The broker/agent in this case can involve any one, or a combination, of the following individuals: listing broker, listing agent, cooperating broker and cooperating agent. The commission the seller pays can go to one person (listing broker who shows the property to buyer), two individuals (listing broker and listing agent, associated with his brokerage, who shows property to buyer), three individuals (listing broker, listing agent and cooperating broker who shows property) or four (listing broker, listing agent, cooperating broker and cooperating agent who shows property). The more individuals working the deal on the seller's side, the more opportunities are created for miscommunication in interpreting the paper. Buyers should pick a single negotiating channel to the seller, using the most reliable and precise person representing the seller. I am no longer shy about asking the seller's side to let me work through the one of their number who I feel is my best communication channel. I have seen agents who are intellectually sloppy screw up communications and the deal itself. Never let one of the seller's side professionals negotiate on your behalf.

Direct negotiation between buyer and seller generally does not occur when broker/agents are involved, except possibly in the final stages when details or a small price difference needs to be resolved. Broker/agents discourage buyers from direct contact with sellers in part because they want to manage the negotiations and in part because they want to limit the opportunities for volatile personality conflicts to mess up the deal. I usually try to talk directly with the seller, because I find it helpful to hear him answer questions; get a sense of his needs, resources, opinions; and how he weighs the various assets of the property. Most important, the seller knows the property better than anyone else. I always find it better to talk directly with a seller when my wife is present. She is a dirt lawyer and is, therefore, familiar with real-estate contracts. But more valuable for negotiations, she has a softer, friendlier way about her. (If your spouse thinks he is Donald Trump or comes across as a banshee on speed, better dicker with the seller on your own.) A buyer should expect brokers and agents to resist allowing him direct access to the seller—and sometimes for good reason. A buyer can do himself more harm than good if he is clumsy in his approach. Sellers may balk at dealing with buyers; after all, part of their rationale for paying the broker/agent a commission is to have him do all of the property's marketing, including the "management" of individual buyers and their inquiring ways. The buyer should push for direct contact *only when* he thinks it will help make the deal.

Inept real-estate agents can foul up a buyer's purchase and, thereby, work their perverse magic against their client, the seller. Property is listed in such a way that it can be co-brokered, which means that a cooperating agent who never met the seller is writing the buyer's purchase contract. Though these agents are working for the seller, they don't know his financial needs and which elements of a sale are most important to him. This leaves a buyer flying into an offer on the wings of a blind bird, apart from the question of whether this particular bird starts his flight ten feathers short a wing. Some cooperating agents have never been on the property itself. Contract offers in these circumstances are necessarily generic. They serve neither the seller nor the buyer very well. They make it difficult for the buyer's offer to be credible and predispose the seller toward rejection.

I once lost a buyer who offered me a very good price that I would have taken, but he took a cooperating agent's advice and packaged it in such a way that acceptance was next to impossible. Had the agent touched based with me or my listing agents, a possibility existed—considering the agent, I think it was at best a small possibility—that my objections could have been anticipated or even worked out prior to submitting the contract. Instead, the agent advised the buyer to put me under the gun. The buyer then became invested in one-sided terms that were deal-killers, terms that were marginal to him but important to me. One was a 48-hour response time. The offer was dropped off at my wife's law office about noon on the first of my two days. I didn't see it until late that night. We didn't have a chance to think about it because of previous commitments. I could have requested an extension, but I was not inclined to negotiate through an agent who could not help getting in his own way. He believed in bullying sellers when he could. This agent—who was legally representing me! as a cooperating listing agent—told the buyer that we were distressed sellers and would, therefore, accept a "hardball" offer. In distress I was, but I had a backup plan and did not need to accept the buyer's too-clever-by-half offer.

If you—as either buyer or seller—feel pressure to make the deal, resist unless your next best alternative is worse. A large part of successful real-estate investing and negotiation is the ability of one party to generate an acceptable alternative to his one best and preferred outcome.

I find it useful in negotiations to have the seller know to whom he is selling, but I have also seen that knowledge work against me. It depends on the seller's attitudes toward buyers like (or unlike) himself and the various uses to which the sold property might be put. Without direct contact, the seller will have only the broker/agent's thumbnail profile of you, such as "He's a rich doctor and drives a Mercedes" or "They're tree-huggers from the city." If a buyer believes his personality and ability to connect will help his offer, push for direct contact through the broker.

Buyers need to be aware of how they come across in negotiations. Even after living for the better part of 30 years in rural West Virginia and even more rural Virginia, I still look like a college professor and talk like a Yankee, despite blue jeans, boots, pick-up truck and the ability to mumble passably about cattle. Sometimes my Yankee speech and odd ways work against me. I don't try to disguise that I'm "not from around here." Generally, but not always, I can get beyond such handicaps by emphasizing shared interests in working a sale. It helps to have a wife from the South who talks like it. (The fact that she brought home a Yankee husband is one of her character deficiencies that her family has accepted but don't talk about too much when I'm around.) A buyer who feels that he might find himself similarly misaligned with a seller needs to do a quick cost-benefit analysis regarding whether he will help or hurt his chances with the seller through a personal meeting. When the buyer is absolutely convinced that the real-estate professionals on the seller's side are clunking things up, he should initiate contact with the seller. Getting a good deal done is more important to a buyer than following protocol—and a personal visit in no way diminishes the commission due the seller's agent.

As a seller, I prefer face-to-face contact with a buyer brought to my property by a real-estate broker/agent. I don't insist on doing this, but I believe I am the best source of information and, therefore, more persuasive than an agent who knows my property superficially. The same risks of personality and style are present when I am the seller. I've had buyers appear who are angry that I've priced a property higher than they want to pay and blame it on who I am or how I look; that I'm "not from around here"; and that I've written covenants to run with divided land. Since each of us can not change, or even disguise very well, who we are, I advise both sellers and buyers to be friendly, straight-forward, helpful and flexible. That is, I think, the best way to encourage reciprocal behavior. If you have firm opinions about politics, religion, ethnic and racial groups, no need exists for you to share them in negotiations over land. If you are in the habit of using expressions like "Jew down," "gyp," "nigger-rigged," "welsh on a deal," "Indian giver" and the like, adopt a new habit for negotiating, if not permanently. It's interesting to note how many of these expressions relate to the trans-cultural process of bargaining over goods and money. Sellers, in addition, may make themselves vulnerable to suit if they discriminate against a buyer from a legally protected minority. Words and expressed opinions will be evidence in such a suit.

Buyer-initiated contact with the seller works best when the buyer has no interest in altering the seller's property. A different dynamic can occur when a buyer wants to divide the property or recast it as something else, especially where a seller is emotionally involved in the property. Here, a buyer needs to make a choice between being open about his possibly alienating intentions and not. Where a buyer needs rezoning or other permitting before dividing or using land for a different purpose, he will have to make his offer contingent on acquiring all necessary approvals and permits—hence, you can't conceal plans of this type from a seller. If a buyer does not make his purchase contingent on obtaining these "papers," he will have to go through with the deal and then hope that his plans are approved. This is a chancy perch on which a buyer should not rest.

Sellers who truly want to preserve their property following its sale, will write deed covenants to that effect or impose conservation easements—and accept a price discount. Sellers often want full FMV for their property *and* some lingering control over the use of "their" land after sale to the buyer. When a buyer finds himself about to be whipsawed like this, I suggest he say to the seller: "You've listed the property at this price without restrictive covenants or easements. That means you are retaining no interest in or control over the property after you sell it to me. I will base my offer to you on the property's value as it is for sale today. If you want to curtail what I do with the property after I buy it, I will lower my offer proportionately or move on to the next property. And remember every future use that you restrict means the property is worth less on today's market, to me and every other buyer." Most sellers doused with this dose of reality will opt for the money. But where a seller feels no pressure to sell a property he's put up for sale, he's likely to be financially indifferent about burdening the property with restrictions. This is a take-it-or-leave-it seller who is better left.

In negotiating over land, cash rules. Some sellers—those who are facing a huge tax hit—may prefer a structured schedule of payments, spread over a period of years. But most sellers want an all-cash, right-now deal, even though some would net more in the end if they considered how to soften their tax hit. Cash, in the form of fresh $100 bills, is also the best way of negotiating land-related side bars, such as an access casement. Cash (folding) works in kitchen-table negotiations. The obverse rule is this: when a buyer spreads new bills on your table, make sure you are absolutely certain of the value of what you're selling *to this buyer* before you grab them.

A paper-oriented buyer may look for ways to use written language to his advantage when a listing forces a conversation-oriented rural seller to negotiate through the exchange of written offers. In this case, I advise a seller to hire a lawyer to help with deciphering the legal implications of the buyer's proposals. Agents/brokers are rarely lawyers and should not be relied on for legal advice. The buyer in this situation, however, should avoid being too smart for his own good. It's easy to slide language traps into contracts, shift liability and make the contract too one-sided. The contract offer is an opportunity to promote and protect the buyer's interests but it also should be straight and transparent. Buyer efforts to design a contract with curves banked to slide a seller into a ditch is sleazy and counter-productive. Don't buy rural land through word tricks.

Occasions, however, may arise where the seller and his agent may not understand the legal implications of something a buyer has proposed even when the buyer has stated it clearly and simply. At such a point, the buyer needs to ask himself: Is it fair and reasonable to expect *this* seller to understand the offer and its implications? Sellers differ in their analytical capacities as well as in their ability to hire expert help. An 85-year-old widow with an eighth-grade education who's never traveled farther than 20 miles from her 200 acres has a far lower level of capacity and ability than a seller who, for example, is an experienced accountant. Savvy buyers should not take advantage of aged, impaired or unsophisticated sellers who are susceptible to cash and lawyerly legerdemain. I know professional land buyers who prey on such individuals. I know a couple of scoundrels who comb the rural obituaries looking for recent widows with farms. With an able seller, however, I don't believe a buyer has any responsibility to protect him from his own failure to be informed about his own property.

A buyer will occasionally stumble into a situation where a seller is desperate to sell and cash-strapped to boot. A buyer who forces this individual into swallowing a ridiculously low price is playing too hard for my taste. The last dollars of concession are not worth wringing out, because they will cost the buyer a lot in terms of self-image, reputation and future dealings. I'm sure some readers think that statement is hilariously wimpy or economically inefficient, or both. So be it. I've heard buyers boast of deals where they "gave him the boots." I would caution the prosperous non-rural buyer in particular to not stomp the distressed rural seller into the dirt unless he cares little for the consequences of being a thug.

MUSHY BOTTOMS AND HARD FRAMEWORKS

A buyer should try to identify the seller's **acceptable price range**. That range will have no top, but it may not have a hard bottom either. Sellers usually start out with a rock-bottom price in mind, but my experience is that a rock-bottom price often softens over time and also gains elasticity when the buyer offers seller-friendly terms. Where the seller's price is unmovable, the buyer may consider offering that price packaged with adverse terms that substantially ease the buyer's burden. A buyer gets a sense of the seller's acceptable price range through suggesting different hypothetical price-and-terms offers with the seller.

Buyers are looking to find a terms-flexible seller with a mushy bottom. A mushy bottom price is one on which the seller is willing to negotiate if the buyer offers him favorable terms, the best of which include all cash at closing, no contingencies and a short escrow period. Sellers should value the absence of requests for seller financing and seller-provided repairs. Sellers understand that there is a **time cost** in holding mortgaged property, which includes monthly principal and interest, property taxes, other maintenance charges (insurance, upkeep) and risk of loss. This time cost increases the longer the seller holds his property beyond when he could have sold it to you. Time has a money value, and where time piles up without a proportional financial gain, it becomes an **opportunity cost**—lost money—to the seller. The time-cost factor stops working on behalf of your offer where the seller has a backup buyer in the wings who is able and willing to step in at or above your price or where the seller's carrying costs are minimal (no mortgage, low property taxes, no maintenance needed).

A buyer can also point out to the seller that an immediate sale has a **time value** to the seller. He can use the sale income to earn money, and every day that the buyer's money is not used by the seller is a day of lost opportunity to put that money to work. If the seller ends up selling his property eight months after he rejects your offer for the same money, he has lost that time value of his net from the forgone sale to you, and it has cost money to carry it for the extra months. Time cost and time value are two sides of the same coin. If property values are appreciating at a high rate, then time usually works against the buyer's argument about time value. In a slow market, however, time cost can be persuasive.

Buyers may find a FSBO who advertises a property without an asking price. "Make me an offer," this seller will say. I've read real-estate gurus who counsel buyers not to do this since they believe "he who puts a number on the table first, loses the negotiation." This is nonsense. Where a seller insists that *his* only negotiating format is for the buyer to move first, the buyer can either walk or start the game. With such a FSBO, the buyer must be up to speed on comparables and know, after scoping, both the property's FMV as well as what it's worth to him. Start with an offer that's at least 50 percent lower than your absolute best money. Peg it, if you can, to the property's tax-assessed value, which is often lower than FMV. This type of seller may either be scared that he will under-price his property or hope that Santa Claus will drop down his chimney with a buyer's bag of cash. Simple, all-cash offers packaged with an evidence-based discount price can work with these sellers. The buyer should remember that the Make-Me-An-Offer crowd feels at home in the give and take of oral horse-trading.

Some sellers try to signal their bottom price by including "**firm**" in their advertisements. "Firm" should mean that the stated price is the only price the seller will accept. This may or may not be the case. With land, "firm" can mean hard bargaining ahead. It can mean a seller under no pressure. It can mean a high starting point. It can mean nothing more than a bluff. It can mean a seller who's scared to death of negotiating; it's a preemptive defense against give and take. It is also a way for a seller to ascertain the financial capabilities of the buyer by forcing a buyer to reveal that he can pay the "firm" price. A buyer need only test how firm "firm" is by making a hypothetical reasonable offer just slightly below the firm price the buyer would pay. "What would you do if I were to offer you $x less than your price?" Don't be surprised if firm in theory means mushy in practice.

A buyer's first offering price is important insofar as it establishes his minimum bid, at which, or above which, negotiations will occur. The buyer's first offer is his direct response to the seller's asking price. It reflects all of the buyer's scoping efforts to determine the value of the seller's property to him. It also establishes the range of prices in which the negotiation occurs. The seller now knows that this buyer can afford at least his first offer and probably more. No rule of thumb exists that says a buyer's first offer should be x percent of the seller's asking price. I have bought properties with my first offer at the full asking price as well as less than 65 percent of it, and at points in between. Each first offer depends on where the seller's asking price is in relation to the value of the property in the market and to the buyer. Where a seller has under-priced his property, I would advise the buyer to not fool around with low offers: put a clean and simple purchase contract in front of the seller as soon as possible and reasonably close to the undervalued asking price. The only argument for not making such a first offer to an under-priced seller is one where the buyer does not want to create a case of price remorse in the seller. Where the seller has set his asking price at more than you can afford, offer close to your top money and inform the seller that you can do a little better, but not much, if he can help you on one or two items. Where the seller sets his asking price at an objective FMV, the buyer must decide whether or not FMV equals the value of the property to him. If the value to the buyer is less than FMV/asking price, offer less; otherwise make the deal. Buyers need to keep in mind that a FSBO can stick with his asking price, reduce it or even raise it in response to a buyer's offer. I've seen FSBOs set low asking prices and then raise them in response to an offer. A buyer with a *listed* property may stick with or reduce his asking price; if he rejects a clean, full-price offer he may find himself having to pay a commission without a sale. If he rejects and raises his asking price, the same commission obligation may kick in unless he is the lucky beneficiary of offers above his asking price. A seller is not legally obliged to accept a full-price offer with contingencies on a listed property.

A buyer must never submit a first offer without first testing the seller to see if he will reveal the low end of his price range, what other issues might be important to him and what amount of negotiating he will accept. You can feel around for the seller's low end—and maybe even find his rock-bottom price—by asking him how he went about setting his asking price. Was it based on an appraisal? Was it based on a comparables analysis he did himself or a competitive market analysis (CMA, similar idea) done by the listing agent? Which comparables did he use and how did he adjust his property's price in relation to them? How much of the asking price does he need right away? The buyer says, "I can come up with __ dollars [70 to 90 percent of the asking price] in cash at closing, but because of the work I need to do on the place, I can't do much better than that. And I can't borrow any more, given my cash flow." The last statement, of course, is the one that may get the seller to begin to show his low end; the others are useful but essentially diversions. The percentage figure that you use to calculate the dollar figure in that question will depend on your assessment of the seller's circumstances (pressure to sell; ability to carry) and his asking price in relation to FMV and your determination of what the property is worth to you.

If the seller replies, "I know what land is bringing around here and my asking price is just what it's worth," the buyer has the opportunity to move his own numbers into the seller's field of vision. The buyer will eventually discern the degree of attachment the seller has to his asking price during pre-offer discussions and negotiations. The seller may tell the buyer that he just came up with an asking price and later in the negotiations begin introducing comparables and other facts that suggest the price is based on the same type of research the buyer's done. This doesn't happen very often. Sellers tend to be impatient in getting to a deal so buyers usually learn what the seller wants to reveal toward the front end of the negotiations.

The buyer with hard, research-based numbers should time their introduction to get the maximum impact. I once monkeyed around for months with an individual who could be either a seller of his interests in a property or a buyer of mine. Nine months passed without a serious discussion of price, because he refused to meet with me. Instead, he had his big-shot lawyer—a blow-hard who brought absolute ignorance of the property in question to his work—spend a lot of his money on baseless challenges. Finally, his lawyer called and asked me for a price on my interests. I said the number. He exploded. I replied, "Do you know what the property is worth?" My client, he declaimed, knows every square inch of it. [In fact, his client hadn't been on the property for 30 years, which is why his client didn't know its value.] "Let me fax you some information," I said, "and then we can talk again." I then faxed an honest timber cruise done by a reputable forester whom his client trusted. The cruise placed the value of the timber at several hundred thousand dollars above the other party's most optimistic guess. I sold my interest to him in a couple of days. It appeared to me that he needed to go through a bunch of bullying and legal huffing and puffing to get to the point where reality would fall on receptive ears.

If negotiations can be moved toward more of a **hard framework**—where tax-assessed value, appraisals, consultant reports, comparables analysis and recent asking prices increasingly supplant "I WANT THIS PRICE BECAUSE."—the bargaining advantage should swing to the party who is better researched and more reality-based. It may not work that way in every negotiation, but if you take this approach you are doing what you can to help yourself. The buyer's insertion of a harder framework into the bargaining should be done gently. Don't dismiss the seller's price as arbitrary rubbish or pie in the sky. Put facts on the table in the spirit of sharing (publicly) available information. Don't quarrel with the seller or make it personal. Just keep introducing one little fact after another to support your position. Let the facts accumulate their own weight on the other side. The buyer must be careful to distinguish between a seller rejecting his hard framework of negotiation and a seller rejecting negotiations. A seller who knows that he will be disadvantaged by facts will dismiss a fact framework out of hand. Just keep working them in patiently and without a triumphant gloat.

Framing negotiations is a process intended to get the seller to come around to his best price and terms for you. That may take five minutes or five months. It may produce a split-the-difference deal. The buyer needs to have his finger on the pulse of the process. There comes a **tipping point in land negotiations** where the seller feels the momentum of his position shift toward making the deal with you rather than holding on to the property in hope of a better deal. When you sense the seller has tipped, both sides can anticipate flexibility and accommodations. A firm price may become less firm if you can help the seller on something else. Introducing a hard, researched-based framework is intended to get the seller to his tipping point in an agreeable frame of mind. The facts are hard, but the approach is soft. Buyers should use hard evidence to erode a seller's asking price—never, to diminish the seller personally. Facts should be offered with tact, diplomacy, friendliness and in the spirit of mutual problem-solving.

The buyer's first offer seeks negotiation, not necessarily acceptance—though acceptance might happen. Rejection is fine as long as it's accompanied with a seller counter. A counter signals that the seller is willing to negotiate. If your first offer is a low ball, it should be a **soft low ball**, that is, packaged with other things that the seller will like. A **hard low ball** amounts to a take-it-or-leave-it proposal, which is the opposite of the negotiations that usually benefit buyers. A deal is killed on the first offer when a seller rejects the buyer's offer to negotiate. A hard low ball may insult a desperate-but-proud seller or convince a seller than any alternative is likely to be better than bargaining with you.

The price and terms of your first offer reflects your reading of the seller's position and his alternatives to negotiating a deal with you. Part of a buyer's pre-offer scoping is to determine the nature of his competition. Where a property has been on the market for more than six months, a buyer may assume the seller is antsy, perhaps desperate. But you also need to be alert for another buyer showing up at the same time you do—at which point the seller will start a three-way negotiation that works against both buyers. Every seller wants to be in the middle of a bidding war. Savvy sellers often tell a buyer that he is in a competitive situation. I now anticipate a certain type of rural seller or agent informing me as a matter of course that a highly motivated buyer—usually a rich doctor from Washington—just left the property or is expected to arrive as soon as I leave. I now joke about it with the seller: "That guy has been following me around for years." If it's true—which it can be—the buyer must bring his negotiations to a head quickly. Some buyers may have to bail out of a truly competitive situation, especially when a "**big money buyer**" is on the scene. Big money almost always wins competitive contests, because chips don't mean as much to him, and he has more in his pile than the other players. Sometimes, you can out-think Big Money by raising doubts about the property based on your research, but you can't outbid him.

Some buyers try to scope a seller's low end by using a tactic where they ask the seller who has set an asking price, "**Well, what'll you take for it?**" In effect, the buyer is asking the seller to bargain with himself, to lower his asking price without the buyer offering anything at all in any form. This buyer is asking the seller to name his bottom price in the form of a first offer to himself on the buyer's behalf. A smart seller will *never* bite at this invitation to lower his price on his own initiative; never. I am insulted when the tactic is used against me, and tend to dismiss such buyers as tire-kickers. The seller must make a judgment as to the buyer's *bona fides* after asking the seller to reduce his price to get things started. If the seller believes the buyer is genuine, the seller might repeat his asking price in a friendly fashion and remind the buyer that only written offers with signatures are binding in the sale of real estate. Alternatively, the seller can say, "I'll take my asking price, or something reasonably close if there are terms that help me. Why don't you put an offer in writing?" Undoubtedly, the what-would-you-take tactic works with some sellers. Where a seller has blatantly over-priced his property and you are a genuine buyer, I suppose it's worth a try.

How does a buyer know how much a seller has padded his asking price above where he is willing to settle? There's no rule that sellers are advised to follow. And sellers may have in mind a price at which they want to settle and then end up settling at a lower price, the one they're willing to take. A buyer should begin with the assumption that all sellers are willing to reduce their asking price by at least by five to ten percent as anticipated bargaining concessions. Some others can and will cut their asking price more deeply. For a buyer to gauge the seller's bargaining margins, he has to research the seller's financial circumstances, motives for selling, other commitments that will pressure the seller toward a deal (such as a purchase of his own contingent on selling this land) and time pressures, such as moving to a new job by a certain date. If you think you've determined his padding, offer five percent or more below that and see what happens.

A buyer can test a padding factor with sellers who have sold other properties by learning about these transactions. Ask the buyers of these properties how much the seller came off the asking price to make the deal. You can also search the records. Take, for example, a seller who has sold five tracts during the last seven years. The buyer can find out the selling price for each of these tracts from the recorded deeds. He can then go back in local newspaper files to dig out the advertised asking price for each property. The spreads between asking price and selling price may indicate a pattern. If the newspaper records are not available, the buyer can ask the agent with whom he's working to do some asking around. I would also ask the local lawyer you're working with to give you a sense of how the seller is likely to bargain.

It is always beneficial for a buyer to design his offer to help a seller with federal income taxes. Where a seller is selling his principal residence and his profit is less than the current exemption—now $500,000 for a jointly filing married couple and $250,000 for an individual—all profit up to those caps is tax free. A tax-smart offer won't help a buyer with a seller whose profit is fully sheltered by these caps. But many sellers of rural land—and, of course, all rural property not used as the taxpayer's principal residence, such as pasture, farmland and woods—will not be able to take advantage of this break. Sellers who should be most approachable with a tax-smart offer are: 1) those who have owned the property for less than a year and are thus obliged to pay tax on the sale at their ordinary rate (i.e., probably in the 30 percent plus range), 2) those who have a low basis in the property, hence a large taxable gain on which they will probably owe 15 percent capital-gains tax and 3) those whose profit from the sale will bump them into a higher tax bracket in the sale year.

The buyer can help a seller's tax situation in several ways. First, payment can be structured so that a relatively small sum is paid at closing and the balance paid after a year has passed, which allows the seller who's doing a flip to treat the big balance of his profit as a capital gain (lower rate) rather than as current income (higher rate). Second, payment can be structured over a period of years, which spreads the seller's profit. This can help a seller stay out of a higher tax bracket in the sale year. Third, there may be some ways that the seller can increase his basis in the property prior to the sale. Finally, the seller may want to consider a 1031 like-kind exchange that allows him to defer all profit on investment property until such time as he sells and cashes out (which may be never). It's worth the effort for a buyer to think of ways that his offer can be structured to maximize the seller's **after-tax net income**, which is his real bottom line.

Every seller has only so much **give** in his asking price, whether the give is set by circumstances or the seller's arbitrary bottom line. The amount of give available to the typical seller is the difference between his asking price and what he needs to net after taxes. A seller may wind up giving all of his give, none of it or some of it. The give in a seller's price is directly related to his circumstances and degree of motivation. If the buyer can roughly determine what the seller needs to net immediately, he can structure his offer accordingly. It's worth getting help from a tax accountant to prepare a tax-friendly offer.

Certain sellers are not highly motivated to get their property sold. Such sellers may be rich by way of effort or inheritance, and the property that interests the buyer is on the market to simplify the seller's life or generate some cash for no particular current purpose. The unmotivated seller may have a heaping plate of negotiating give—and not part with a morsel. Such sellers can set a price and wait without worry. This seller presents a buyer with a take-it-or-leave-it deal. If a buyer finds himself in the dreadful position of needing this property, he takes it. But few buyers of rural property are ever objectively in this position, and buyers should not brainwash themselves into thinking that they must have a particular property. It is the rare parcel that is both absolutely perfect for the buyer of a rural second home, hunting camp or timber investment—and priced right. Next-best alternative properties will work for most buyers.

The worst example of a seller being uninterested in selling involved about 14,000 acres in New York's Adirondack Park owned by a wealthy individual in his early 80s. He had been rich his entire life, from a fortune made 150 years earlier. When approached with a more-than-fair $6 million offer, he asked, "What am I going to do with another $6 million?"

One way of edging a reluctant seller into negotiating is to agree to his price, packaged with buyer-friendly terms. Nothing guarantees that you will succeed, but you lose nothing in the attempt. If, for example, your seller can wait for his price, he can wait for his money. It may be in his interest to spread the purchase price over several years for tax reasons, and he may be willing to give you that time cheaply—after all you did meet his price. A common buyer technique used in this situation—and others—is to ask the seller to finance a portion of the purchase price at a below-market interest rate, say one half the local bank's 30-year, fixed mortgage rate or one half the bank's prime rate. Or you might borrow from the seller with interest paid at the end of a multi-year period rather than yearly. You're not trying to trick the seller with this type of financing; you're simply trying to get him to bargain with you on terms if not on price. Of course, you want to keep in mind that one little agreement can lead to another. The buyer has to figure both his yearly costs and his total costs for each possible financing arrangement to determine how his own benefits and obligations would be affected. The buyer is looking for a win-win arrangement, one that benefits both sides.

A seller getting his full asking price may be surprisingly flexible about agreeing to below-market rates for seller-financing. You can always start by proposing that you pay the current passbook interest rate—the interest rate the seller would receive from a bank were he to put the sum being financed into a savings account. Then, if necessary, move up to one half of the bank's 30-year, fixed mortgage rate or one half prime. Your individual situation may also benefit tax-wise from having the interest be paid in different ways, such as paying the loan's entire interest in one lump sum at a particular time or paying a lower rate on the first couple of payments and a higher rate on the declining balance. Seller financing also saves the buyer money that would otherwise go to lender's points, fees and other transaction costs—which can add five percent or more to a loan's face value.

If the full asking price is $100,000, the buyer can propose paying $55,000 on closing and the next $45,000 over three years. If the buyer were to borrow that $45,000 at closing from a bank for three years at ten percent, each of his 36 principal-and-interest payments would be $1,452.03. The buyer would end up paying $7,273.08 in interest on top of the $45,000 in principal. Assume the bank charges two percent of the loan principal for points and fees, the buyer eventually pays $9,273.08 in interest and lender charges, which is 20.6 percent of the $45,000 borrowed. The buyer ultimately pays the bank $54,273.08 for the use of $45,000 over three years. Instead, borrowing the same $45,000 from the seller at four percent passbook rate paid in two 18-month installments would look like this:

Day 0 to Day 540	Due on 540th day
4 % interest due on $45,000	$1,800
Principal due	22,500

Day 541 to Day 1,080	
4 % interest due on $22,500	900
Principal due	22,500
	$47,700

With the break in interest, no upfront points and a two-payment schedule, the buyer has saved himself $6,573.08 and still paid the seller's full price. The cost to the seller of working with the buyer in this fashion is that he has probably received a lower return on his $45,000 than he would have from an alternative investment during the debt's term. If the seller compares the buyer's offer with what $45,000 might bring in the stock market, the rate of return becomes entirely hypothetical given the market's short-term volatility and the vagaries of picking stocks. The buyer should not quarrel with a seller's assertion that over a long period the Dow Jones Industrial Average or any broad basket of stocks like an index fund appreciates more than many investments. The buyer need only point out that three years is not the time period when this "rule" has held true historically. Inherent in any stock purchase is the possibility the investor will either earn a return lower than the passbook rate or even lose principal. Every stock investor knows that dogs bite. I have teeth marks to prove it.

A variation on seller financing is a **land contract** or **installment sale**, which allows the seller to retain title (deed) to the property until all scheduled payments are made. Seller financing and a land contract allow the seller to be taxed only on the proportional amount of gain (profit and interest) he receives each year from the sale. The seller is allowed to report a certain percentage of each payment (after subtracting interest) as installment sale income. This is called gross profit percentage, and it is calculated by dividing the seller's gross profit from the sale by the contract price. If the seller's contract price is $5,000 and his gross profit is $2,500, his gross profit percentage is 50 percent. After subtracting interest, the seller reports 50 percent of each payment, including the down payment, as installment sale income from the sale for the tax year in which he receives it. The balance of each payment is tax-free inasmuch as it represents the seller's proportional share of his adjusted basis in the property. (See http://www.irs.gov/publication/p537/ar02.html#d0e455.) A land contract is a risky proposition to both seller and buyer. It can, on the other hand, give the seller a full asking price and tax benefits as well as providing the buyer with a 100-percent-financed purchase. DO NOT PROPOSE A LAND CONTRACT WITHOUT FULLY UNDERSTANDING THE LEGAL AND TAX IMPLICATIONS FOR BOTH YOU AND THE SELLER.

The ultimate sweeteners a buyer offers the seller in return for financing are that the debt is secured by the seller's own property and the seller usually gets a big chunk of cash upfront that he keeps if the buyer defaults. (Some buyers try to substitute other collateral, a gimmick that is often intended to put sellers at risk.) If the buyer in the $100,000 sale example above fails to make either of the two scheduled 18-month payments, the seller can declare the note in default, keep the $55,000 and remove the buyer's claim against his property. The buyer generally loses the $55,000 in such a default, but it may take some lawyer time to make it stick depending on the note's language. It is essential for the parties to have a written note that spells out in unambiguous terms the degree of exposure the buyer faces in the event of default, how the default will be determined (default occurs when payment is ____ calendar/business days past due; seller must provide written notice of default) and who pays the cost of collection. If the buyer doubts his ability to make the payments, he should not propose seller financing. But a seller who doubts the buyer's ability may sniff an opportunity for a double profit.

Be flexible and creative with a seller who won't budge. Take him to supper. Send him a book that he'll like. Find common ground beyond your interest in his property.

The buyer can also try shifting from participating in the first-person to **negotiating from a third-person perspective**. Third-person allows the buyer to participate as a kind of facilitating consultant to both parties where the outcome is no longer a matter of self-interest. The third-person-negotiator persona the buyer adopts on his own behalf is designed to get the seller thinking and acting as if he were negotiating. The buyer's objective is to get the seller to budge—on anything. It is the budging, not the "anything," that is important. The first budge is emotionally and intellectually the hardest for a seller fixed on his asking price. Once this seller takes a first step—no matter how tiny—he's taken *his* largest step. Take a slightly larger one back toward him. Don't look at your feet. Smile at your partner. You're dancing!

Off-angle ideas can stimulate discussion, with a chance of carrying you to a deal. You might suggest that you're really just interested in a piece of his property instead of the whole—the house and ten acres, or just the woods, or the back pasture with an access easement. Propose different combinations of his property's components to get him moving. Throw in stuff. Offer some service the seller values. Buy him ten hours of financial advice from the planner of his choice. Or provide a paint job for his new house. Or underwrite a Christmas vacation to the Caribbean. Or tutor his grandchild on how to take SATs.

A buyer who has completed his scoping and is faced with a set-in-concrete seller might pose an offer orally and hypothetically: "If I can arrange to offer you an all-cash deal at _____ dollars [start with 10 percent less than the asking price] with no more than two contingencies—financing and a 30-day study period with results acceptable to the buyer, can we work a deal?" The buyer in this case has communicated that he's willing to *try* to pay 90 percent of the asking price, but he's not promising that he can arrange it. Note, however, that this oral and hypothetical "offer" obligates the buyer to buy nothing at all were the seller to respond, "It's a deal." Real-estate "deals" made orally are not deals until they are written and signed. Hypothetical offers are not genuine offers. A smart seller will tell such a buyer to put his offer in writing and stop playing games.

The buyer might stick with his tactic and offer 95 percent of the asking price in this form: "Would you take $1,000 per acre?" The buyer has moved no closer to making a genuine offer, but he appears to be making both a concession and a firmer proposal. The buyer is not offering $1,000 per acre when he asks, "Would you take...?" He is just testing the seller and trying to get him to negotiate. Smart sellers **never** bargain with themselves. The seller's best response is simple: "I only consider written offers."

I don't recommend these two buyer ploys, because they can end up with no deal and a lot of hard feelings. But I have seen them work. When a seller does respond, the buyer needs to convert the oral discussion to paper as soon as possible.

A classic seller trick is to agree over the phone to one price only to increase it when the buyer appears in person able and willing to sign at that price. It is especially suited to a buyer defined as "wealthy" by the seller, and who has to travel some distance to get to the property's location. The first time this was pulled on me, I fell for it. The seller had agreed to sell the night before over the phone at a certain price. When I arrived at the property the next day after a five-hour drive, the seller insisted that the agreed price was $5,000 above the phone figure. (Remember: an oral agreement on real estate binds no one.) Maybe, I had misheard the seller's statement, I thought. Maybe, the seller was hard of hearing. Maybe, my mind was playing a trick on me. Actually, the seller had "read me" perfectly. I was highly motivated to get the deal done. We settled between the phone figure and the higher one. This seller, I later learned, was not unfamiliar with this type of bargaining.

Faced with a "misunderstanding" ploy, a highly motivated buyer should not challenge the seller's integrity. The buyer should announce that he is able and willing to buy at the phone/oral price, but not higher. The buyer can then hand a signed purchase contract to the seller at that price, with a 24-hour signing window—and leave on friendly terms. The odds are that a bad-faith seller will either sign or continue to negotiate. The second time I faced this trick I was at least smart enough to recognize it. The seller—a woman of self-proclaimed sophistication and wealth—jumped the price by $100,000 over what her son, a lawyer, quoted over the Internet. I didn't much like her property after I saw it, and had no inclination to negotiate with her. A month later, the son tried to get the deal going again. The third time I saw this used was when I was accompanying a client who thought he was looking at 45,000 acres of timberland and a sawmill. The acreage turned out to be 12,000 and the price of the mill jumped $4 million when we walked into the mill's office. If a buyer is highly motivated to make a deal with such a seller, he can respond by ignoring the changed price and remembering several items of his own that the seller should keep in mind, such as, the buyer needs 100 percent seller financing at one percent interest over 40 years, for starters. When a seller wants to reopen price, the buyer wants to reopen everything else. This tactic can reorient the bargaining or collapse it altogether.

When a buyer finds himself bargaining with a seller who is richer than he is, the buyer may go into the negotiations thinking that he is at a disadvantage. The buyer has a tendency to come up more than he should. Very rich people have gotten very rich by selling something. They may have more ability to hang on to a property until their price arrives, but they want to get rid of the property quickly—and don't want to go through negotiating pressure. You can get good deals just as often from a rich seller as a poor one.

In buying real estate, a buyer has no way to force a seller to come down on his price and offer favorable terms. A buyer can approach a seller as if negotiation is expected and do what he can to stimulate that process. Most sellers expect to negotiate as do most buyers, though either side can adopt a take-it-or-leave-it position. If you are faced with a a seller who insists on a price that is higher than you can afford or one that exceeds what the property is worth to you, keep looking.

Sellers tend to think that buyers have the advantage in negotiations, and buyers think the opposite. I think it's important for a buyer to show confidence in his scoping-based facts and information, but I think it's counter-productive to feel that you thereby have the seller at a disadvantage. The seller will pick up the buyer's attitude and run the other way. The attitude that I think does help the buyer is one of **patient problem-solving and professed reluctance about doing the deal**. The more the buyer comes toward—not at—the seller with this approach, the more the seller is encouraged to embrace it himself.

Negotiating is not about getting the better of the other side. It's about getting a deal that works for you.

CHAPTER 17: PROPERTY LOCATION—SURVEYS AND SUCH

Every land buyer must ask and answer at least three "physical" questions about every property he's scoping for purchase:

1. Where is the acreage located?

2. How much acreage will be conveyed by the seller to the buyer?

3. Are the boundaries, as marked on the ground, legally accurate and free of dispute?

I am constantly surprised by how often buyers do not ask these questions and, when asked, fail to obtain accurate answers.

You want a property about which you can say: "It contains X.00 acreage. I know this because I had the boundaries in the deed checked against the boundaries on the ground. I know where it is located in relation to adjoining properties. The property is being conveyed to me in fee, with all rights, free of boundary disputes, claims, unrecorded easements and encumbrances of various sorts that would diminish its value to me."

The knowledge on which each of these statements is based is not a matter of intuition, gut-feelings or faith. It is, rather, based on facts you gather before you submit a purchase offer by scoping the target property. This chapter discusses how to think about these questions and gather these facts.

LOCATION

Land involves two types of location: 1) legal location, as described in deed and/or drawn in a survey, and 2) physical location, that is, on the ground, in relation to the legal and physical location of adjoining properties. Your scoping task is to make sure, first, that the legal location is correct, and, second, that it matches the property's boundaries on the ground.

We use three principal systems of legally describing real-estate boundaries and establishing acreage: 1) rectangular (or, government) survey, 2) subdivision and lot and 3) metes and bounds. The last of these is the system that is used with rural property in most of the East. I occasionally run into large-lot, rural subdivisions that have been developed to one degree or another. Metes and bounds is the oldest of the three, and from my experience, it's the system most likely to contain acreage and boundary errors.

The **rectangular-survey system**, or **government system**, covers most of the United States, excepting the original 13 colonies (and Kentucky, Tennessee, Vermont, parts of Maine and West Virginia), Texas and a piece of Ohio. This system began in 1785 when land ceded to the new United States by Britain was surveyed into a grid using **north-south meridian** lines and **east-west baselines**. This grid allows property to be divided into smaller and smaller squares, starting with a **township** (six miles on each side, 36 square miles), **section** (one mile on each side, 640 acres) and then descending fractions of sections. A township contains 36 sections.

Townships north and south of a given baseline are laid out in **tiers**, such that township-one-south (T1S) would lie in the first tier of townships south of the baseline with the township's north boundary being the baseline. Township-two-south (T2S) would be directly below T1S. Several dozen township tiers can be laid out both north and south of a baseline. T20S, for instance, would be the twentieth township tier south of a baseline.

Principal meridians, running north-south, intersect with baselines and are used to locate townships east-west of themselves. Six miles east and west of every principal meridian is a **range line**, which forms the east or west boundary of the township. Townships are laid out in rows, east to west, and tiers, north to south. Thus, a township will be described both in its north-south location, say T1S, and along its east-west dimension, say R1E (range-one-east). This township lies immediately southeast of the intersection of the baseline and the principal meridian; it is the township closest to that intersection in the southeast quarter that intersection forms.

Once the township is described, property within it is described as a particular fraction of a particular 640-acre section of that township. The township's 36 sections are numbered, 1-36. Sections are laid out in a 36-cell grid in each township with Section 1 situated in the northeast corner of the township. Figure 17-1 shows the conventional numbering system for Township X.

FIGURE 17-1

Township X

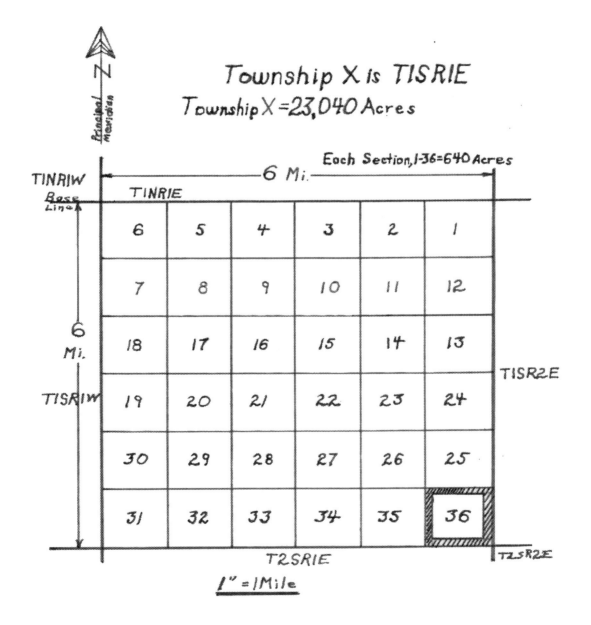

A deed description might read: SW 1/4 NE 1/4 NE 1/4 N 1/2 of Section 36 T1S R1E. This is code for ten acres in Section 36 of the Township that lies in the first tier south of the baseline (T1S) and one row east (R1E) of the principal meridian. The ten acres lies in the 320 acres of the northern half of Section 36 (N1/2), in the 160 acres representing the northeast quarter (NE 1/4) of that one half section. In the northeast quarter (NE 1/4) of that northeast quarter lies 40 acres. This ten acres is the southwest one quarter (SW 1/4) of the northeast one quarter (NE 1/4) of the northeast one quarter (NE 1/4) of the north half (N1/2) of Section 36. You have to work backward in the description, from the township to the section to the half section to the quarter section to the fraction of the quarter section. The decoding process is akin to narrowing your frame of vision and then focusing so that only the land in question appears in your mind's eye.

A 100-foot by 50-foot lot within this ten acres can be fixed by continuing the same process, then locating the given point of beginning in feet and inches on a north-south or east-west line of the smallest referenced section fraction. Figure 17-2, the shaded area, shows the location of this ten-acre property in Section 36 of Township X.

FIGURE 17-2

Township X, Section 36

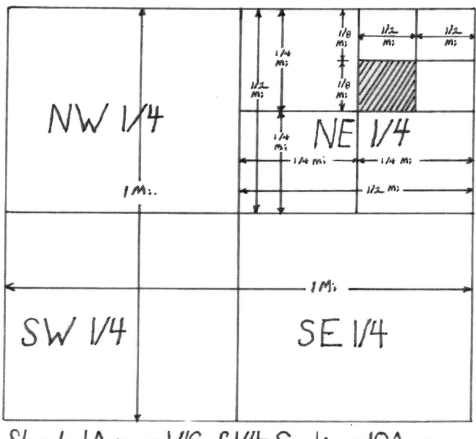

These simplified examples illustrate the basic concepts underlying the rectangular survey system. It is complicated in practice by various corrections and adjustments. You may run into an acreage uncertainty where townships join or where original surveys, done by different teams, connect. If you find yourself bewildered in a courthouse that uses this system, don't panic. Look pitiful and politely ask the clerk to help you. Tell the clerk you have a Ph.D. in nuclear physics to get especially patient treatment.

Subdivision and lot is based on a surveyed **plat**, or **plat map,** which shows the precise, surveyed dimensions of each lot within the subdivision. The plat will also show the location and dimensions of roads, utility easements, common areas and other subdivision features. The location of the subdivision as a whole will be shown on the plat in terms of known streets, roads, intersections, waterways and the relevant jurisdiction. Where a field-surveyed plat of an entire subdivision exists and has been recorded, you should feel confident that the lot you are buying contains the indicated acreage and no boundary uncertainties exist. **You should be wary of subdivision drawings that either are not based on field work and/or have not been approved by local zoning authorities**. A plat that has not gone through the zoning process is not binding on anyone. It is no more than a seller's "concept drawing." A buyer can feel safe with a subdivision plat when the zoning office says that the plat in his hand has been approved.

I should note a special case. Auctions are sometimes used to sell land that's been projected into lots. Five hundred acres might be drawn conceptually as five 100-acre lots. This proposed division can be done by computer and then flagged on the ground. The division may or may not be recorded prior to the auction. Presumably, the unrecorded concept division has been done in accord with local zoning rules. A buyer should determine whether the concept division has been given preliminary approval by the appropriate zoning official. If the auction produces separate buyers for each lot, the seller records the plat prior to closing with these individuals. If one individual buys all five lots, it is then his choice as to whether he wants the 500 acres recorded as five 100-acre lots or left as is. No harm arises from this **hypothetical division**, except where it would not comply with the local division regulations. I've seen hypothetical divisions of this sort work with no complications for buyers.

While neither a surveyed plat nor recordation of a survey establishes clear title, a developer whose lot titles will be searched for each sale is likely to have made sure he has good title to the entire tract and each of its lots. If the seller has good title, he will convey good title to the buyer. Aside from the special case of an auction, do not buy a lot in a division whose plat with your lot shown is not approved by the appropriate local authority and recorded. You're likely to find title problems in a lot that lacks these two building blocks of good title. Don't buy a "concept" lot from a developer; make him produce a **recorded, marked-on-the-ground survey**.

Subdivision and lot is no longer confined to suburbs; I increasingly find **large-lot subdivisions** in rural areas where each lot can be hundreds of acres, though 20 acres is more common. They are often described in marketing materials as hunting or recreational lots. Corporate land dividers are often behind this type of development. They scout for properties that have second-home and recreational appeal, survey for division, obtain approval, do the required infrastructure work and market the lots in nearby metropolitan areas. They may do a limited high-grade, timber cut—called a **"residential cut"**—before selling lots. This approach removes a relatively small number of the highest-value trees. Corporate subdividers now know enough to play by the zoning rules.

Since some counties still do not manage land division through zoning and approval by a public board (zoning/planning commission), you cannot assume that all rural division plats you are shown have been legally established, based solely on the drawing in front of you. Look for some notice of official approval, usually signed and dated, on the plat. In non-zoning counties, division rules may be non-existent or insufficiently protective of the lot-buyer's interests. In the latter instance, a lot buyer may find that he has purchased a lot with an access problem, ambiguous water right or impracticalities owing to the absence of infrastructure. If the county has a subdivision ordinance and the plat the buyer holds has gone through the approval process, a buyer can be confident in each lot's location, boundary lines and acreage. A phone call to the zoning office will determine whether the developer's plat is approved.

In **planned unit developments (PUDs)**, land is divided and developed intensively. Multi-unit residences, such as townhouses, and high-density projects are often involved. PUDs commonly use a condominium form of organization. The approved PUD plat may even show where house **footprints** will be located. You may run into a rural PUD, though the land unit for sale is likely to be small. A 1,000-acre PUD, might be marketing 100 one-acre lots, townhouses on 150 acres, with 750 acres held as common land that is available to all owners. PUDs devoted to recreation, such as skiing or lake sports, and second homes in rural communities are in increasing evidence. I would have confidence in a PUD's unit acreage; its plat will have been prepared by a licensed surveyor and have gone through zoning approval prior to marketing.

Subdivisions are designed to comply with local zoning ordinances that establish rules and specifications regarding lot size, roads, density and other features. In jurisdictions with zoning, a subdivision must go through a process of design, review by appropriate local officials, public hearing and approval. The developer will submit a detailed surveyor-drawn plat, along with engineering plans for water, sewerage, storm-water drainage, roads and utilities. The larger the rural subdivision, the more expensive its homes and the closer it is to a town, the more paper—drawings, impact studies, reports—and infrastructure are likely to be required. Local officials will review preliminary plans and both suggest and require changes if necessary. In such divisions, it's safe to assume the acreage contained in each lot is accurate and so are its boundaries, both in the deed and on the ground.

Every division and lot survey should carry the **surveyor's state seal and license number**, as well as a date. If you don't see these items on the developer's drawings, ask for an explanation and listen with a skeptical ear. You can hire a surveyor to verify boundary lines and acreage on the ground and in the deed, but I would be very suspicious of a lot in a division where that double-checking precaution is necessary.

Recordation of a document—survey, plat, deed, lease, or note—provides public (constructive) notice that the document exists and, where appropriate, is in place between its parties. An unrecorded document—deed or note—has no legal authority, except between the parties who made it. An unrecorded plat or survey may be no more than a "representational drawing," preliminary sketch, concept or marketing idea.

If you find yourself interested in purchasing a lot whose *bona fides* don't quite smell right, you need to have a surveyor and, perhaps a lawyer, check the legal location on the ground and in the deed's chain of title. If you decide to purchase this lot, make sure to include your own survey and/or verified legal description as part of your purchase offer. Submitting a purchase contract for "Lot A in Mr. Developer's Muddied Waters project" won't protect you.

If you can't verify location and acreage during your scoping, you can insert a **survey contingency** in your purchase contract. The contingency can take one of two forms. First, you can insist that the seller provide a survey acceptable to you as a condition of purchase. This survey, of course, should be prepared by a licensed surveyor. Second, you can make the purchase contingent on having a surveyor of your choice and at your expense prepare a survey whose results must be acceptable to you. A proper, accurate survey is a cost that a buyer should expect a land divider or developer to bear.

Many jurisdictions now require that most divisions of land involving multiple lots meet local subdivision standards. Exceptions may be made for off-conveyances to family members or for no more than one or two sales. Some rural counties, like mine, continue to draw a distinction in their zoning ordinance between a subdivision, which must meet all requirements, and a **non-subdivision division** that does not. Location, lot size, density (number of houses per acre) and road access distinguish one from the other. A non-subdivision division has to meet less rigorous standards. A non-subdivision division can be perfectly trustworthy in terms of lot boundaries and acreage. I've sold both non-subdivision land and subdivision land using the same licensed land surveyor and his same standards of precision in each case. Nonetheless, a buyer should approach a non-subdivision division cautiously. Zoning codes also provide for **variances** and **conditional uses**, which allow subdivisions to go forward even when they don't meet the established standards. In these cases, a lot buyer should determine the nature of the exception and figure out how it might affect him before making an offer.

Metes and bounds is the oldest system of deed description and the one I've found to be susceptible to acreage discrepancies and boundary peculiarities. **Metes** refer to linear measures of distance, the most common being feet and inches, links (7.92 inches each), rods (16.5 feet each), pole or perch (one rod or 25 links), chains (one Gunter chain is 66 feet or 100 links) and miles. You may also find metes in metrics, though I haven't. Regional metes can include the *vara* (33 inches, a measure you might find in California and the Southwest) and the Texas *vara* (33.5 inches, beginning in 1919). While the acre is the most common area unit of rural land, you may also run across the rood, which is .25 acre (10,890 square feet) and the arpent (approximately .85 acre, which was used in grants from the French King). **Bounds** are the compass directions (headings) and landmarks that, with the metes, establish a property's boundaries. Landmarks include natural features, such as waterways and trees, and man-made reference points, such as roads and iron pins. Document 17-1 is excerpts from the first two pages of my farm deed, which uses a metes (poles)-and-bounds description of the boundary lines.

DOCUMENT 17-1

Metes and Bounds Deed

That for an in consideration of the sum of TEN ($10.00) DOLLARS, cash in hand paid to the parties of the first part, and for other good and valuable considerations, the receipt of which is hereby acknowledged, the said parties of the first part do hereby grant, bargain, sell and convey, with GENERAL WARRANTY of Title, unto the said Curtis I. Seltzer, all those four certain adjoining tracts or parcels of land, with all buildings and improvements thereon and all appurtenances thereto belonging, situate about one and one-half miles north of Blue Grass, Blue Grass Magisterial District, Highland County, Virginia, adjacent to and on the west side of Route 640, adjoining the lands of William C. Will and others, containing 33 acres, 23.562 acres, 16.812 acres and .154 acre for a total of 73.528 acres, more or less, this, however, being a sale in gross and not by the acre and intended to include all the land that Russell T. Andrews and his wife acquired from W. Lurty Arbogast and wife and all the land which the said Russell T. Andrews and Eva Ruth Andrews, his wife,

owned in Highland County, Virginia. The 33 acre tract is bounded and described as follows:

BEGINNING at a set stone on the west edge of the right of way of the said highway, a common corner with the 21.186 acre tract, this being the new division corner, and with the new division line of the 21.186 acre tract, N. 38 degrees W. 34.48 poles to a set stone; thence N. 54 degrees W. 67.20 poles to a set stone on the old line, and with the same N. 20 degrees E. 49 1/2 poles to a locust; thence S. 61 1/2 degrees E. 95 poles to a rock near a chestnut stump; thence S. 15 1/2 degrees W. 36 poles to a rock between the barn and the shed; thence S 61 1/2 degrees E. 2.64 poles to the said highway, and with the same, S. 29 degrees W. 29.44 poles to the beginning, containing 33 acres, more or less.

Metes and bounds, which are also referred to as the **deed's calls**, start at the surveyor's **point of beginning (POB)**. The tract's boundary line follows the distance and direction calls from the POB and ends there as well. The distance north should equal the distance south, and the distance west should equal the distance east. Surveyors refer to this balancing from the POB as "mathematical closure." When all boundary sides balance, as they should, the **calls are said to close** (at the POB). When a property's calls don't close, you may find the reason in an error in the deed's description (e.g., a typo), or an error the surveyor made in his survey, or several types of error in combination. When calls do close, the acreage said to be contained within them should be accurate. Anyone with a surveyor's computer program can check both closure and acreage. The process of "**plotting the calls**" involves typing in the metes and bounds from a deed or survey, and then directing the program to draw them to scale and calculate the acreage contained.

When calls do not close, the acreage may still be reasonably accurate if the explanation for the failure is something minor and acceptable. Old surveys, which relied on relatively unsophisticated transits and steel tapes, often contain small errors that prevent perfect closure. In such cases, the "more or less" that follows the deeded acreage is a useful and legitimate fix. On the other hand, I've seen calls that don't close because of a 100-acre screw up on a 300-acre tract.

Metes and bounds were a clear improvement over a description like "that pasture lying east of John's meadow," but many opportunities exist for errors. Old metes-and-bounds descriptions are only as good as the equipment the surveyor used, his linear units (the smallest unit being presumptively more accurate than the largest), his competence and the meticulousness of those who copied the original calls each time the property was sold.

SURVEYS 101

"**Survey**," as a verb, is the process by which a surveyor determines the location of property boundaries on the ground, from which its area and location on the earth can be fixed. "Survey" can also refer to either this process or the finished drawing the surveyor makes from his ground measurements. Surveyors can also determine and map out the height and contours of the ground's surface in relation to some known, fixed height, usually sea level. **Elevations** refer to distances above or below a fixed point. House construction on slopes or tricky road excavations require a surveyor to "shoot" elevations so that foundations and road beds are dug to the correct depths, thus allowing the finished construction to top out at the right height.

"Plotting," or **deed mapping**, refers to the process and finished product of drawing a deed's calls—distances and bearings—on paper. Plotting is now done by readily available computer programs, though it can still be done by hand using graph paper, ruler and compass. The surveyor enters the calls, and the program draws the boundary lines in two dimensions and calculates the acreage contained within them. Calls can be drawn on plain paper or imposed on **a topographical map (topo)**, discussed below. A **plot** of this sort is not a field-tested survey. It is only as good as the calls inputted. It may or may not line up with how boundary lines are marked on the ground.

Plotting is the method by which you begin to verify the seller's boundaries and acreage. The advantage of hiring a surveyor to draw boundaries on a topo for you is that he can check the deed's calls for closure and acreage. A survey's calls used for plotting should be more reliable than those from a deed, though the deed's can be, and should be, accurate.

If a seller gives you a topo with boundaries, it may or may not be accurate. Ask the seller to tell you who drew the boundaries and from what data. Sellers have handed me topos with boundaries drawn by a surveyor, their real-estate agent, their auctioneer, their friend "who's good with a pencil" and themselves. In one case, a seller drew boundaries on a topo that included a 400-acre parcel he didn't own. In another case, a helpful real-estate agent, relying on what he later described as "artistic license," drew boundaries with a 15-acre mistake in a 50-acre property. His defense was: "I drew it the way the seller said his Granddaddy always said it lay." Granddaddy was wrong, to the seller's benefit.

Buyers should understand that a plot is as accurate as the inputted calls. If something is wrong with the calls, the lines won't close. A plot may close, but its acreage can still be wrong in the sense that it includes more or less land than the owner is entitled to. At that point, the surveyor will have to go into the field and/or the courthouse to dig out the error. A buyer has no guarantee that a survey will be 100 percent accurate, and a survey does not guarantee legal ownership of all land shown within the boundaries.

Some Americans in the East and mid-South still own the land that was conveyed to their ancestors from an English King, or a land company with a royal charter or as a grant for war service. The first land documents emerging from these origins were based on approximate surveys of huge tracts, such as those George Washington did in the 1750s. They incorporated easily found topographic features, such as ridgelines and waterways. These surveys might refer to all the land between this ridge and the branch of that river. The first generation or two of surveys could be almost as rough. Early deeds might use descriptions such as "being the land of Jones" or "the Dry Fork bottom of Bates, joining Smith on the North, Brown on the South, the run of Dry Fork on the East and Grayson on the West."

The following excerpt is a 1685 survey description of land that is now part of Washington, D.C., but then known as Port Royal in the Maryland colony: "Land called port Royall lying in Charles County in the freshes of the potomoke River near the head of a Creek called Broad Creek [Tiber Creek] beginning at a marked white oak within half a mile of the head of said Creek and running east by north for the length of 500 p. to a bounded hickory then for the length of 160 p. to marked red oak then west by south for the length of 500 p. to a marked white oak then with a straight line to the first bounded tree." (Michael Farquhar, "The Past is Present," Washington Post Magazine, March 23, 2003.) Such descriptions were good enough for frontier legal work when all concerned understood and agreed with how these descriptions fit ground-level reality, but they were not good enough when disputes arose, land changed hands and time passed.

While descriptions gained specificity as land was divided and surveying improved, landowners, as taxpayers, had a financial incentive to undercount the acreage in their holdings. I've found land with old calls that contained an **acreage undercount** in the deed on which property tax assessments were based. (The periodic property-tax reassessments that update valuations of each parcel of land in the country do not check acreage as carried in the county's records.) Old-fashioned tax avoidance may explain why these properties have more land in the field than on paper. You might find an **acreage overcount**—where the deed shows more land than what exists on the ground. An acreage overcount in the deedwork means the buyer will pay for more than he's actually getting. An overcount can arise from unrecorded off-conveyances; gifts to family members; errors by clerks, lawyers, owner-dividers or surveyors; long-ago chicanery; unrecorded resolutions of disputes; and simple self-interest, where, for example, an owner knows that his acreage is undercounted in his deed but the cost of correction was greater than the tax savings. Acreage overcounts benefit sellers who appear to be selling more than they really are. Acreage undercounts benefit buyers because you get more land than you're paying for.

As land moved out of the families with the original deeds, the ground-level knowledge on which those deed descriptions were made faded. Trees used as points of deed reference, or **corners**, disappeared. In working with one 110-year-old survey, I found some corner trees still standing (though in bad shape) and others gone without a trace. As time air-brushed communal memory and removed points of reference, oral versions of reality could acquire validity in the minds of their speakers. I know of several examples where a seller sold land that had been in his family for generations after walking the boundaries—as he believed them to be—with the buyer. The seller would say words to the effect, "This is how the deeded acres lay." The buyer would assume the seller knew the boundaries and never bothered to verify the deed's calls and acreage. Later, the buyer—now owner—learned that the seller's idea of the boundaries was wrong.

As the original large tracts in the East were divided and sold repeatedly, deed descriptions and acreage numbers got better. Nonetheless, it is common to buy land in rural areas using deeds that rely on calls that are more than 100 years old, have never been verified and have been hand-copied as the parcel changed hands. Sellers, in my experience, rarely make the effort to clean up a deed's calls and verify acreage prior to putting their property up for sale. The burden of verification falls on the buyer. Since land can be sold without a survey, the buyer has to nail down boundaries and acreage on any tract lacking a survey, with an old survey, and where he finds a discrepancy between acreage on the tax map and the deeded acreage. Occasionally, you might find a property that is being sold without an acreage figure in the deed. In that event, you will have to be extra careful in determining the acreage contained in the legal description and then make sure that boundaries are not in dispute.

Owing to the messy origins of both deed descriptions and title, a land buyer is required to go back 60 or so years in his **title search** in determining whether the seller's title is sound. Each state sets how far back the title search must be taken to **certify good title**. It is often a good practice, however, for a title search on rural property to be taken back more years than any statutory requirement if the property has not been sold for a long time or the deedwork reveals a problem in acreage or ownership. A title search determines whether the owner can sell a piece of land by confirming his **ownership through a chain of title**.

A title search does not guarantee that what is being sold actually contains the acreage or boundaries claimed. Title searches verify ownership of a parcel, but not necessarily its acreage. In other words, your lawyer can back-track the 100 acres that you want to buy for 100 years through a half-dozen sales, and you can still end up with acreage being short of 100 acres legally and on the ground because of an error made 125 years ago. In each subsequent sale, the land was referred to in the deed as 100 acres; no one bothered to check whether it was true legally and on the ground. Acreage on the ground may have been changed from acreage in the deed by adverse possession, force, mutual consent, theft or trickery. **Title insurance**, which protects against certain defects in title, may not make up the difference if the policy excludes acreage discrepancies that an accurate survey would disclose. If you can prove an acreage shortage is the result of fraud, forgery, lack of legal competence, incapacity or impersonation, then title insurance should make you whole.

Discrepancies between deeded acreage and on-the-ground acreage are caught when someone does the work necessary to verify acreage. This can involve one of more of the following techniques: 1) survey; 2) computer mapping of the deed's calls which are then field checked; and 3) researching the deed's antecedents, including, if necessary, the deeds of adjoining neighbors, to resolve an acreage discrepancy.

A quick way for a buyer to alert himself to a possible significant acreage discrepancy is to apply a **planogrid** to a scaled topographical map with the property's boundaries drawn. The transparent planogrid provides a rough approximation of acreage. (See discussion below.)

Various problems can arise with the acreage and location of country property. Before you submit a purchase offer, you want to ask and answer the following questions:

1. **What are the physical dimensions of the property in linear distance and compass bearings, as described in the deed ?**

   The three common formats of property description—rectangular/government survey, subdivision and lot, and metes and bounds—provide these dimensions in narrative and drawings. (I'll use "calls" to refer to the linear measurements and compass bearings in all three systems.)

2. **Can the deed's reference points—corners, rock piles, iron pipes and trees—be found on the ground?**

   The POB, corners and significant angles are the most important points. They should match up exactly with the calls in the deed and/or survey. For exact checking, you'll need to have a surveyor shoot the lines; for acceptable checking, a surveyor or forester can walk the boundaries. With a compass and a set of calls, you should be able to walk the boundaries and find the most important corners.

   If you acquire a property that is missing crucial ground points, you will need a surveyor to reset them if you plan to divide it or a boundary line is in dispute.

3. **Are the boundary lines on the ground identical with those in the deed and/or survey?**

   Do not be surprised to find that the deed calls say one thing and you find something else in the field. A familiar example is a boundary fence being "off" from where the calls fix the boundary. Fence lines have a way of being adjusted, with and without mutual agreement, over time. Roads also have a way of taking the easiest path, whether or not a recorded access easement exists.

4. **Do the calls close?**

   Sometimes, this is called "closure of the land" or the "balance" of the calls. Whatever the terminology, the buyer wants the calls in the deed to produce a closed boundary line. When the calls close, it should mean that the calls are accurate and correct. However, exceptions to that generalization may exist. A frustrated surveyor 150 years ago might have jiggered the calls to get them to close when those taken from his field notes would not. Rather than go back and find the error, he "adjusted" his numbers.

If the calls do not close, how big is the problem? Some "failure-to-close" problems are the result of nothing more than a transcribing error where, for example, a "3" was written or typed as an "8," a "1" became a "7" or a bearing "N 45 degrees W" was copied as "W 45 degrees N." If easy explanations can't be found, a surveyor will have to go into the field and figure it out.

5. **When the calls close, you then need to ask three other questions.**

First, does the acreage contained within the checked calls match the acreage stated in the deed and/or survey? It should. A discrepancy between the acreage figured by running the calls through a computer program and the acreage in the deed needs to be resolved before submitting a purchase offer.

Second, does the acreage in the deed's checked calls and/or survey match the acreage contained within the boundaries on the ground? It should. You won't need a full-fledged survey to determine whether they match; a walk-around will do.

Third, is the acreage located where it's supposed to be? It's possible that the calls close and the acreage is right, but the entire tract is actually a number of feet to one side or another of where the deed places it. A property boundary may be found in the field on the west side of a creek (thus enclosing the creek) rather than on the east side (thus excluding it) where the deed puts it. "Misplacements" of this sort can work for or against a buyer. In either case, you want to know about one before you submit a purchase offer.

The discussion that follows shows how you can answer these questions and what to do when you find different answers to the same question.

SURVEYS 102

Old surveys are often unreliable; and the older the survey, the more this is likely to be true. Old surveyor instruments were far less accurate than those used today. This affected linear measurements, angles and compass bearings. Modern instruments are adjusted for barometric pressure and ambient temperature; the older ones were not. The still-used basic instruments are a **transit**, which can measure horizontal and vertical angles and show compass readings in magnetic degrees, and a **steel tape** for linear measurements. In addition to **transits**, surveyors now use a **theodolite**, which is a souped-up transit, or a **total station**, one model of which employs laser-pulse technology to determine distance and can measure electronically up to 4,000 meters to within 5 mm +/-. Old transits could be fussy to adjust and were not as precise as a total station. Distance measured horizontally with a steel tape was subject to error from sag. If this were not enough, an error can creep into calculations from survey to survey as magnetic north itself shifts. Field surveying done even with the most modern devices is not perfectly exact. Normally, rural land surveying can get by with an **error of closure** of one foot in every 5,000 feet. Boundaries that close within the error of closure are fine.

Where an original survey from the 17th or 18th Century was vague, it may have been easier for later surveyors to either avoid or finesse ambiguities than fix them. Repeated for a long enough time, small fictions can become large facts. Unreliability can also result from human error in the field, conditions on the ground (ranging from weather to the disappearance of reference points (**corners**), human error in writing and copying deeds and drawings, misinterpretation, illegibility and a dozen other factors.

Where an old survey established a boundary line in a waterway, it's likely that you will find a note that the line "**runs with the meander**" of the stream. This language can appear in either a deed or on a survey drawing, or both. Absent further information, such a line could run down the centerline of the stream or along either bank. It can also mean: 1) no calls were taken for the meander; or 2) calls were taken, or 3) the surveyor "straightened" the meander by imposing an arbitrary line. Confirming the line of a meander may also involve the inconvenient fact that the channel of the creek has changed since the survey's date as floods cut new channels. Don't count on the functioning fence line to reflect the true boundary line in a meander mess. Locating a true boundary in a meander can be extremely important where, for instance, the stream is the only source of livestock water and your neighbor's fence is on your bank thus fencing you out, or where the stream's channel has changed leaving you with bottom land less rich than was intended in the initial division. One way to resolve the first type of dispute is for the neighbors to agree to run the fence line on one bank for a stretch and then the other, giving livestock of both parties adequate water access. A section of fence, called a **watergap**, must be constructed across the water at a right angle to its flow to keep livestock properly separated. The flap-like watergap is hung from a stout cable, allowing surging water to push the gap up and then close when the water resides. Watergaps are not hard to build, but they are a nuisance to maintain, particularly when high water is common.

Where a deed or survey says the boundary line **runs with the channel of a waterway**, I would take that to mean the waterway's centerline. Remember that waterways change their channels, which means the centerline/boundary line will change too unless the original channel centerline was surveyed and incorporated into the deed. When a waterway works *gradual* changes in the land—giving some to one landowner, taking from another—the parties are expected to accept the **accretion** of land or its **dereliction**. Changes of a catastrophic nature, such as those from a flood or earthquake, do not change settled boundaries

Surveyors, themselves, have become better trained and more skilled over the years. Many states did not impose licensing standards until the 20th Century; some states did not require **land surveyors** to be licensed until the 1950s. Even today's best surveyor can make a mistake or fail to note something that is relevant. There are, in addition, occasions where two equally competent surveyors will look at the same facts and reach different conclusions. And there is always a chance that another party has a legal claim to own or use land belonging to your seller even though the boundary line is perfectly accurate. In such cases, a survey does not establish ownership. Adverse possession and related ideas are discussed in Chapter 26.

You may find a parcel of land that is **orphaned** in terms of a survey, or a chain of title, or on the ground. Either no one claims the orphan parcel, or no one's claim is definitive. Sometimes a parcel is orphaned because surveyors made a mistake. The Monongahela National Forest in West Virginia includes a small orphan tract of genuine virgin timber whose existence is due to just such an error. Orphan tracts are uncommon. If your seller claims that he owns an orphan tract, your scoping will have to determine the basis and strength of his claim in light of other claimants. As a rule, I would avoid tracts whose legal ownership the seller can't persuasively establish. If the orphan is a survey problem, a surveyor may be able to fix it; if it's a chain of title issue, both a surveyor and a lawyer may be needed.

Other acreage errors arise from the messy origins of land distribution in the original colonies and their westward claims. Various systems of granting land succeeded each other—royal, colonial, state and federal—and each were burdened by exceptions, overlaps, conflicting claims and, of course, squatters. Early deeded **grants** (also called **patents**) went to individuals and companies following a survey. (See www.ultranet.com/~deeds/landref.htm for a discussion of the origins of landownership east of the Mississippi River.) The surveys on which these grants were based were subject to all of the problems noted above. Later surveys should have resolved uncertainties, but you cannot assume this to be the case. My own rule for buyers is to plot the calls of every target property, no matter how recent the survey. If the computer plotting shows something amiss or a field inspection turns up a mismatch, then you have a problem in need of solution.

You cannot protect yourself with 100 percent certainty against errors in a survey, though there are steps you can take to reduce your exposure. When hiring a surveyor to double-check the seller's survey, I think it's good practice to find a local individual who's done considerable work in the county—even the area of the county—where your target property is. Such an individual will have acquired a feel for those surveyors who've worked this land before. He may even have access to some of their archives. An out-of-town surveyor will not have this sense for ancestral habits and quirks, such as how one individual in the mid-1800s printed his "1s" and "4s" to look like "7s" when they came in the middle of a number.

A second qualification that I recommend is that the surveyor you choose be "good in the courthouse." He should be both skilled and dogged in digging out land history. Some surveyors are competent at shooting boundary lines, but not at solving problems, particularly those involving words and law. You'll need to plumb local opinion as to which surveyors are good both in the field and with the books. Local lawyers are probably the best reference.

Third, you generally want to avoid a surveyor who is doing, or will be doing, business with the seller. You want exclusive loyalty. You may not be able to avoid hiring an individual who's worked for the seller in the past. This is not cause for alarm in and of itself. Ask those whom you interview whether or not they can work for you free and clear of any ties to the seller. In sparsely populated areas you will always find that a lot of professionals live with open conflicts of interests, arising from the inherent problem of a small number of individuals having to wear many local hats. It is not uncommon for a surveyor to work for both a seller and a buyer; the same is true for lawyers and real-estate brokers in small communities. I've seen these situations managed ethically and without harm to either party; I've also seen the opposite. As a newcomer, you should anticipate that local professionals may have history with your seller. When that history has been good, you can assume that they have a default protectiveness for the seller's interests. The seller may also have family who employs the professional from time to time. You must, therefore, screen a surveyor—and other professionals—for dual allegiances. You have a right to expect fairness, impartiality and loyalty, even from those who are friends of the seller. As a first-time buyer in a community, I would avoid arrangements where one professional works for both seller and buyer. I would also avoid using any local professional who is related by blood or marriage to the seller, a member of the same fraternal order or church, or a close friend.

Finally, I'd ask each surveyor you're thinking of hiring to show you a couple of recent surveys he's done on similarly sized properties. If you feel awkward about doing this, go into the land records office in the county courthouse and work backward through the deed books. Surveys are often recorded with deeds, usually immediately following. I have, however, also found surveys kept in a separate book. Compare the work of different surveyors. Some include more detail than others; I've always found detail handy in the field, particularly the location of prominent features, such as roads, 4WD "roads," utility easements and watercourses. You may also find notes of boundary uncertainties, possible overlaps, acreage discrepancies and potential claims both for and against the current property owner. Don't be a minimalist when it comes to surveys: more information is better.

A survey refers to both a drawing and a physical marking of boundaries in the field. It is obviously essential that the measurements on the ground match those on the drawing, both of which match those found in the deed. A three-layer coincidence is what a buyer wants. And even with such a match, an error could be embedded or an adverse claim not noted.

A survey (drawing) is a two-dimensional picture of a property's boundaries, expressed in units of length and compass bearings. Every point where the line changes bearing (direction), no matter how slight, is usually referred to as a **corner** in deed descriptions. Major corners, such as the four in a rectangle, will be well-marked on the ground by an iron rod, paint, ribbons, a chevron of slashes in a corner tree, rock piles or, on occasion, an implanted car axle. Boundary lines are projected on a plane, both in the field and on flat paper; a drawn survey is an exercise in **planimetry**. Illustration 17-1 is a typical field survey, expressed in metes and bounds.

ILLUSTRATION 17-1
Survey

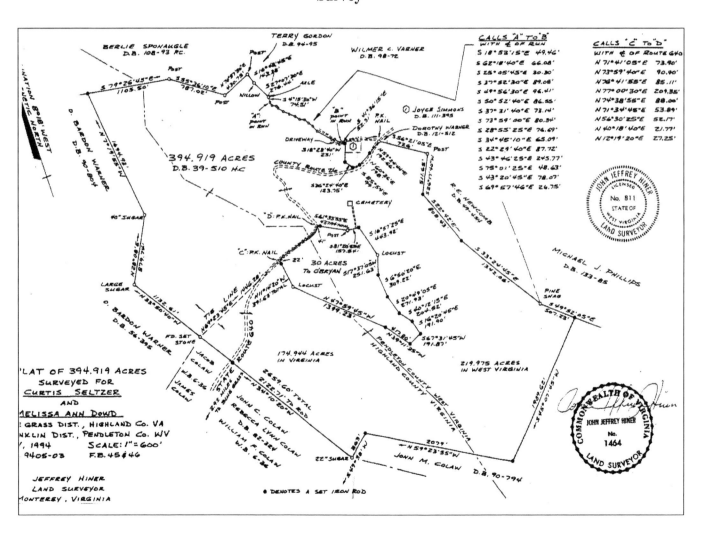

Remember that land boundaries drawn on a plane are measured horizontally on the ground and do not run with the land's topography. A 1,000-foot surveyed boundary line between points A and B on paper is a straight horizontal line of exactly 1,000 feet in length in the field. In Illustration 17-2 you can see the difference between a surveyor's 1,000 feet of boundary line, A-B, and the actual linear distance of that boundary, 1,450 feet, as it runs on a parcel of land with its own topography, a-i.

ILLUSTRATION 17-2

Linear Distance and Topographical Distance

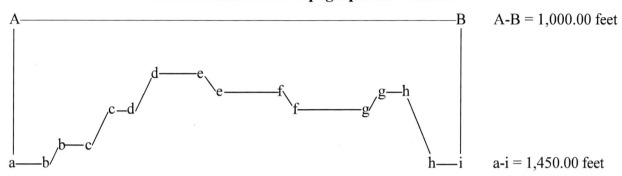

Non-flat land always contains more acreage on the ground than the calculated acreage a survey shows as enclosed within its boundaries. The more irregular the land's surface, the more acreage above the surveyed amount there will be. If you were to flatten mountains, like smoothing out a rumpled bedspread, 100 surveyed acres (contained within the horizontally measured boundaries) would increase as you pulled the corners and sides to their limits. In contrast, 100 surveyed acres of Iowa cornfield that is as level as a championship billiard table will contain 100 acres.

A surveyor should always **mark his lines on the ground** when he's doing a survey for a landowner. Make sure that you and the surveyor are agreed on ground marking; he may charge more for it.

A surveyor can draw an accurate, field-based survey without ever actually walking—or marking— *all* the boundary lines. This is done through basic geometry. The transit is set up within the property's boundaries where the surveyor can "shoot" two points (corners) in a boundary line. He will know the three angles and the length of two legs of the triangle that vee-out from his transit. From that information, he can then calculate the length of the third leg without ever having walked between its two points. This technique is called **triangulation**. There's nothing wrong in using triangulation in certain circumstances. A buyer, however, will want his new boundary lines well-marked on the ground. Some surveyors triangulate when they don't want to negotiate a laurel thicket, briar patch or swamp through which a boundary line runs. It's fair for a surveyor to use triangulation when the land is impassable, but not when the surveyor is just lazy. I've seen a new owner have to hire a surveyor to mark lines that the seller's surveyor had triangulated just a few weeks earlier prior to the sale.

When you are handed a seller's survey, routinely ask whether *all* the boundaries are marked on the ground. If you run into a triangulated seller survey, you might ask the seller as part of your offer to have his surveyor mark the lines. Lay off as much surveying cost on the seller as you can. When you are hiring a surveyor to "do a survey" for your own property, make sure his quoted linear-foot price includes ground marking. If you plan to sell the timber from your property, the boundary line should be clearly marked with bright ribbon, paint and/or slashes at the time your forester sends out his timber-sale packet so that the buyers know where your property and timber end.

When walking a boundary line through woods, do not confuse a **blaze**, which is a removal of bark two or three inches wide by four-to six-inches long and often painted, with a surveyor's **slash marks**, or **chops**, which are two or three machete hacks into the bark, parallel to the ground, a couple of inches apart.

353

A painted blaze is used to show a boundary line; the U.S. Forest Service and certain paper companies do so. Hiking trails are often marked with painted blazes. Surveyors I know who are marking a line for an individual landowner use slashes. A double chop is a surveyor's mark for a boundary line, and a triple chop represents an important corner in the line. A tree marked by a surveyor is called a "**line tree**." It is owned jointly by the adjoining landowners. Do not cut down a line tree.

As your surveyor marks your boundaries, any place where the surveyed boundary line and the functional boundary line, such as a fence, are non-congruent will be immediately obvious. Ask your forester or surveyor to tell you about any such areas; if you don't give the surveyor this instruction, you may not be told. Boundary misalignments can be minor or significant, so you should determine their cause and importance as part of your due diligence during scoping. I have found misalignments involving a few acres to several hundred. I've discovered a 75-acre error on a tract advertised as 300.

Boundary lines can be drawn on a **topographic** map, which shows land in a third dimension—elevation. **Topos** portray the lay of the land's surface features. They do this by using elevation lines—or, **contour lines**—to indicate height in relation to sea level and each other. Each elevation line might, for example, represent a 40-foot change in height, up or down from the next closest line. Lines closer together show steepness; further apart, flatness. With a little practice, you'll be able to recognize valleys, knobs, ridges, cliffs and benches. Woods are colored green or shaded; open land is white. You can read a topo in the field to determine your approximate location by fixing yourself in relation to surface land features that you can see.

Boundary lines found on topographic maps are measured horizontally. A 1,000-foot-long line drawn on a topo by a computer program is 1,000 feet long on an imaginary level plane though it may be 1,400 feet long walking over the ups and downs of the ground itself. When boundaries from a survey are imposed on a topographic map, they are drawn to the map's scale. Be careful to check the scale of any topographical map you use. Some now express height in meters rather than feet: the conversion is one meter equals 3.3 feet.

When a forester or surveyor draws boundaries on a topo, the calls are usually left off. You can judge distance in the field using the topo's scale and a small ruler (which is often built into a plastic compass that you should be carrying). Bearings can be taken off the drawn lines using the same see-through plastic compass laid atop the topo. With a bit of practice, you will get a feel for how a given distance, say 500 feet, walks out in various field conditions. If you want to step up the preciseness of your own measurements, you will need to use a compass and a 100-foot-long tape (fiberglass or steel). You can temporarily mark lines and corners with plastic "flagging" ribbon. Help in using a compass can be found at www.learn-orienteering.org.

So far, you have two or three documents in your effort to confirm boundaries and acreage: 1) the calls from the deed, 2) survey, if available, and 3) topo with plotted boundary lines produced by a surveyor or forester using the calls. You may also have acquired a fourth document—the property's **tax map showing boundaries**. Tax-map boundary lines and acreage figures may not be accurate, and they are not legally binding. Use a tax map in the field if you have nothing else to suggest boundaries. Tax maps are discussed below.

Boundaries drawn on a topo also give you several ways to estimate acreage quickly and cheaply.

The first method involves a **planimeter**—an expensive, pencil-like, digital instrument that physically rolls along a map's boundary line and calculates acreage according to the topo's scale. Most land surveyors and US Forest Service district offices have planimeters and can estimate your acreage in a few minutes. You need to bring a topo with the property's calls drawn to scale. Planimeters are accurate to about one acre in 100, depending on the steadiness of your hand as you roll it over your topo.

A second method is to use a **surveyor's transparency**, which is a see-through grid divided into ten-acre squares each of which is divided into 1/10th-acre squares. You have to match the scale of the transparency to the scale of the topo. By counting squares, you can closely approximate acreage contained within boundary lines.

A third approach is to use a **planogrid**, a transparency with dots that you lay over the topo. Each dot represents a certain number of acres. The planogrid will have dot-acreage formulas for ten or so common scales. By counting dots within the boundary lines, you can approximate acreage. A planogrid is inexpensive and good enough to get started.

None of these substitute for determining acreage through computer plotting, using a program such as DeedPlotter Plus, available from Z-Law Software, Inc., POB 40602, Providence, RI, 02940-0602; 1-800-526-5588; e-mail: info@z-law.com. There's no reason for a land buyer to invest in a plotting program, however. A surveyor or forester can do this work for you for a nominal sum.

Topographical maps are usually available in each county at a retail outlet—surveyor's office, sporting goods store or stationery supply. You can order the U.S. Geological Survey's (USGS) 7.5 Minute Topographic Quadrangle Series, commonly called a "topo quad" or just a "quad," from the U.S. Department of the Interior, U.S. Geological Survey, Reston, Virginia 22092; map sales at 1-800-435-7627; map information at 1-888-275-8747; www.usgs.gov (click on "topographic maps"). Their scale is 1:24,000 (1 inch equals 2,000 feet; 2.6 inches roughly equals 1 mile; 1 square inch equals roughly 90 acres) with 20-foot contour-interval lines. While other map scales are available, quads cover a good bit of area and are convenient to use for broadly understanding a general area's topography. A topo with boundaries for a target property should be drawn with a smaller scale than the quad's. For a 100-acre parcel, a topo scaled 1 inch = 200 feet is easily read, and 1:400 is readily used. Quads are updated periodically using aerial photography to show physical changes such as new buildings and surface mines. USGS also supplies digital topographic maps, and maps of areas prone to earthquakes and landslides. Individual states may also supply topographic maps. (Bureau of Land Management [BLM] shows topography as well as federal, state and private ownership.) You can download your own topographic maps of a target property for free from www.topozone.com at different scales. The www.topozone.com maps average about 20 years old. The scales are consistent among themselves, but the printed copy is affected by the size of your computer monitor. The USGS maps are scanned at 250 dots per inch (one inch = 24,000 inches = 2,000 feet = 250 pixels). Owing to the translation problem, the printed map you hold may not replicate the scaled topo map you've downloaded. Other GIS and geospatial maps are available from www.maptech.com and www.data.geocomm.com/catalog/US; some are free, others carry a fee. www.googleearth.com is available for those with high-speed Internet access. National Forest maps are available from www.edcdaac.usgs.gov/dataproducts.html.

Map 17-1 shows a topo at 1:50,000 scale (one inch = 50,000 inches in the original) with boundary lines drawn for 95 acres my wife and I own on the border of Virginia (South and West) and West Virginia. Green represents forest; white, open land—in this case, pasture. Blue represents water. Small black squares are houses or agricultural structures. The bolder contour lines are spaced every 200 feet in elevation, with the lighter lines drawn at 40-foot intervals. Flat areas are found where contour lines are widely set; the closer together the lines, the steeper the land.

Map 17-2 shows the same property in 1:25,000 scale. This scale is readily used for walking boundaries, though even a 1:50,000 can be used in a pinch.

Map 17-3 is a topo with boundaries drawn for us by a local surveyor. I have added additional detail, including the location of roads and a sugar house built in the mid-1990s.

MAP 17-1

Topographical Map with Boundary Lines, 1:50,000

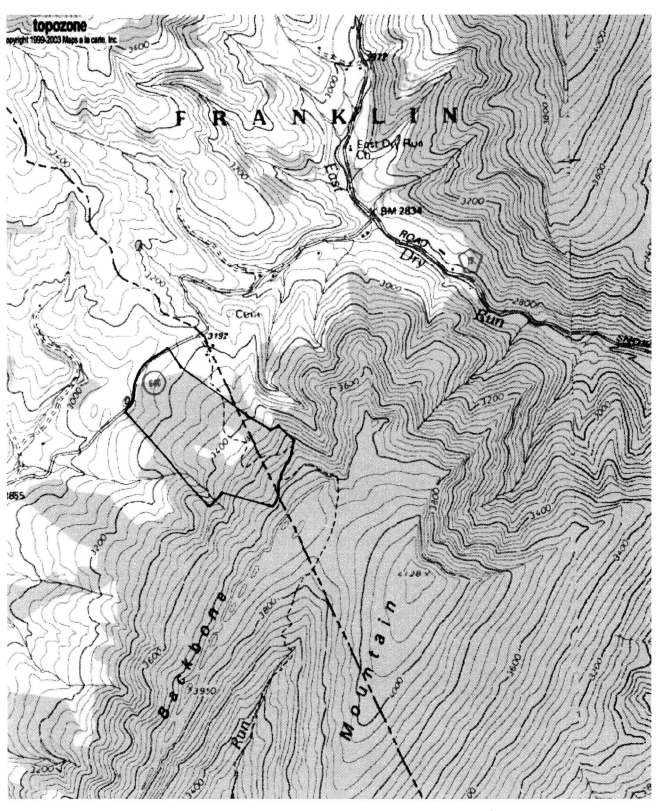

Source: www.topozone.com

MAP 17-2

Topographical Map with Boundary Lines, 1:25,000

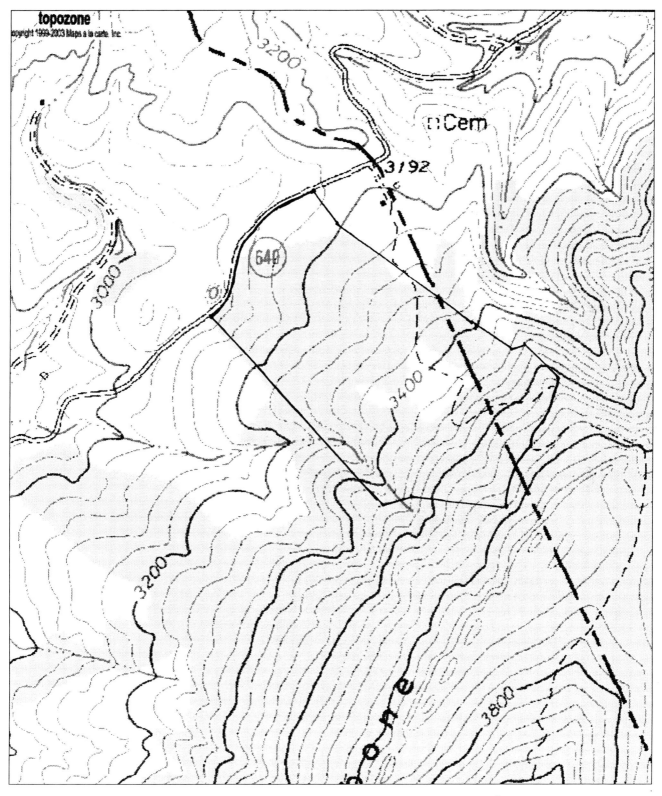

MAP 17-3

Topographical Map, with Surveyor-drawn Boundaries

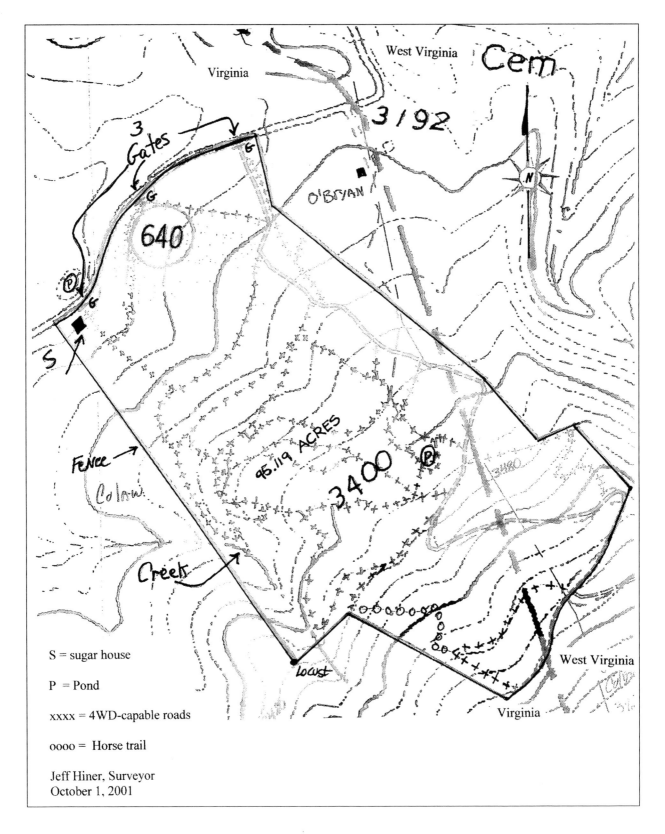

S = sugar house

P = Pond

xxxx = 4WD-capable roads

oooo = Horse trail

Jeff Hiner, Surveyor
October 1, 2001

358

A buyer can use a topo like Map 17-2 or Map 17-3 to understand the lay of a target property before setting foot on its dirt. Such maps show you likely road locations, existing watercourses and potential building sites—relatively flat spots that might perc. They give a buyer a sense of how topographic features exist spatially in relation to each other and in relation to compass points.

DeLorme Atlas & Gazetteers are available for the 50 states for $19.95 each, excepting Texas at $24.95. The DeLorme topos are scaled 1:150,000, which are usable, but are not sufficiently detailed for boundary walking. I use DeLorme Atlas and Gazetteers to get a first-cut sense of a property's features and its location relative to nearby "goods and bads," such as public land, surface water, mines and buildings. DeLormes are available in book stores and at www.delorme.com; 207-846-7000.

While on the subject of maps, I'll mention several other orientation tools that are often useful in buying land.

Aerial photographs are available through the county's USDA's Farm Service Agency, which will provide the map number for the target property. That photographic map can be ordered from: USDA-FSA, Aerial Photography Field Office, 2222 West 2300 South, Salt Lake City, Utah, 84119-2020 or POB 30010, Salt Lake City, Utah, 84130-0010; 801-975-3500. Aerial maps are easy to understand and show functional boundaries, but they're not good for calculating acreage. The ones I've used were done in the 1960s. When the photos are shot in the winter, it's easy to distinguish between conifers (evergreens) and deciduous trees. Remember large crowns do **not** necessarily indicate timber value. A hardwood tract that's been repeatedly high-graded will show largely worthless trees with very broad crowns. Big, old, wide-crown trees standing by themselves in open fields rarely have much timber value owing to internal flaws, rot and poor formation. Aerial photos help a land buyer visualize the property's topography, land uses and the spatial relationships between various land features.

A number of Internet sites offer aerial photographs for a fee. www.topozone.com offers a simple version of these photographs for free. You can also check out http://kh.google.com; www.globexplorer.com; http://edc.usgs.gov/products/aerial/napp.html; www.MYTopo.com; and www.terrafly.com.

Another useful map, available from federal agencies, shows land in and around **national forests, wildlife refuges, national parks and the Bureau of Land Management**. These maps can be purchased from facilities in the field and through the agency. I've used national forest maps a lot since I often look at land that is near two national forests, the Monongahela (primarily in West Virginia) and Virginia's George Washington-Jefferson. The scale on the Monongahela's map is one inch equals two miles, which is easy to use. It shows all the National Forest's (NF) holdings in dark green and privately owned land in white. Privately owned land within a national forest is called an "**in-holding**." These parcels can carry a price premium for private buyers and, when appropriations allow, may be sold to the federal forest after an FMV appraisal. Many rural land buyers, particularly hunters, like to "border national forest," because it gives them private access to public land. I've found NF maps to be detailed and accurate. Individual states may also issue maps. New York, for example, provides maps of the Adirondack Park that show private and public holdings, which is helpful to a land buyer.

Do not be surprised if a seller hands you a **tax map**, rather than a survey or a topo with boundaries. Each county has a set of tax maps that, together, show all of its taxed land represented as **tax parcels**. A tax map is a two-dimensional drawing that looks like a survey but displays no bearings or measurements. Each map shows the division of a certain portion of the county into coded tax-map parcels. A tax-map parcel is land that is known for tax purposes. Privately owned property is taxed, parcel by parcel; non-profit and public property are not taxed. Your target property may consist of one tax-map parcel or a dozen. You will find a **tax-parcel number** for each parcel owned, which is used for administering county tax records. (The tax map may also show an acreage number.) The tax-parcel number is not the same as the **tax-map number**. The tax-map number (s) of the seller's property will be the number referenced in the tax-maps index. Map 17-4 shows the Highland County (Virginia) Tax Map 10-A, with the four parcels—tax-map numbers 10-A-42, 10-A-47, 10-A-48 and 10-A-50—of our farm residence outlined.

MAP 17-4

Tax Map, Section 10-A

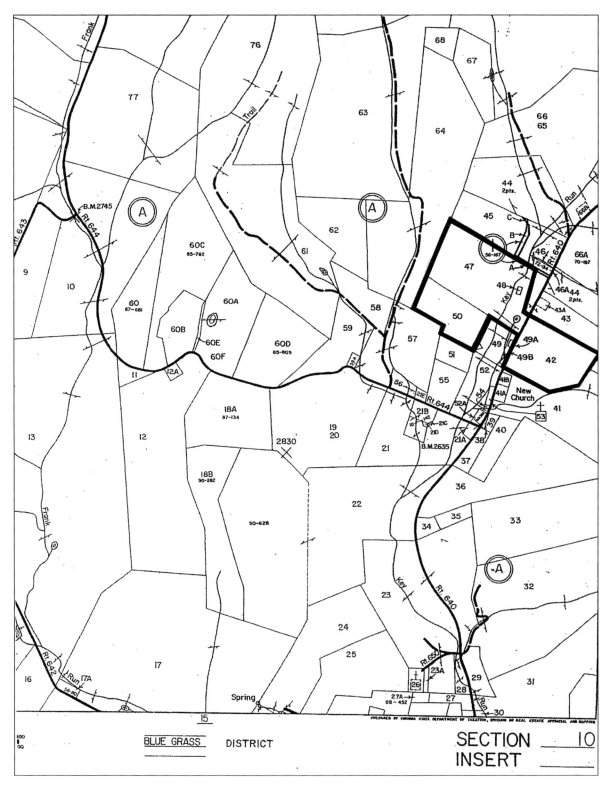

The set of tax maps and its index is usually found in the office of the county tax assessor. The index provides a tax-map number for each land parcel on each map, along with acreage and ownership information. This acreage number is the one used for taxing the parcel; it may or may not be accurate in terms of what the seller owns and will convey to a buyer. The tax map will also show the *approximate* boundary lines and some physical features such as roads, cemeteries and waterways. Document 17-2 is the tax map legend for real property in Highland County, Virginia.

DOCUMENT 17-2

Tax Map Legend

REAL PROPERTY
IDENTIFICATION MAP
OF
HIGHLAND
COUNTY
VIRGINIA

~LEGEND~

STATE LINE		SMALL STREAMS	
COUNTY LINE		RIVERS	
DISTRICT LINE		SCHOOLS	
PROPERTY LINE		CHURCHES	
QUESTIONABLE PROPERTY LINE		CEMETERIES	
DOUBLE O'S OR SUBDIVISION BOUNDARIES		AREA MAPPED AT 200' SCALE	INSERT 3A
RAILROADS		PROPERTY IDENTIFICATION	7
IMPROVED ROADS 1"=600'		PROPERTY CROSSES BARRIER	
IMPROVED ROADS BY PLAT 1"=600'		PROPERTY DIVIDED BUT UNDER ONE MAP NUMBER	
UNIMPROVED ROADS 1"=600'			
IMPROVED ROADS 1"=200'		PROPERTY TOO SMALL FOR NO.	8
IMPROVED ROADS BY PLAT 1"=200'		CITY CORPORATE LIMITS	
UNIMPROVED ROADS 1"=200'		LAKES - PONDS - BAYS	
TRAILS			

~SCALE~
BASE MAPS 1"=600'
CONGESTED AREAS 1"=200'

361

You can back your way into the tax maps by starting with the county's **Land Book**, copies of which will be, at minimum, in the offices where deeds are recorded and taxes are handled. The Land Books I've used are organized by sub-county areas; in my area these are magisterial districts. Once you're in the right sub-county district, look up the seller's name. The Land Book lists owners alphabetically. The seller may go by his first initials, or a business entity or hold the property jointly with his wife. The Land Book will provide the tax-map number of each parcel, along with the owner's address; deedbook and page number where the owner's deed is recorded; acreage, as established for tax purposes; jurisdiction; assessed valuations for improvements, land and minerals; tax rate information by land type (class); whether the land is in "land use" if a county has adopted it; and finally, the amount of current property tax levied. Document 17-3 is an excerpt from the 2004 Highland County Land for two parcels my wife and I own:

DOCUMENT 17-3

Land Book

```
VALUE OF TRACTS OF LAND, LOTS IN THE COUNTY STANDING TIMBER, TREES, BUILDINGS
AND IMPROVEMENTS AND COUNTY LEVIES ASSESSED THEREON FOR THE TAX YEAR 2004
IN THE COUNTY OF HIGHLAND BY Bobbie J. Griffin COMMISSIONER OF THE REVENUE
              Tax Rate on Every $100 = 0.67 ALL DISTRICTS AND TOWNS COMBINED
                        ---------ASSESSED VALUES---------
MAP NUMBER/
NAME AND ADDRESS            DESCRIPTION      LAND    IMPS    TOTAL   CLASS   TOTAL TAX
```

MAP NUMBER / NAME AND ADDRESS	DESCRIPTION	LAND	IMPS	TOTAL	CLASS	TOTAL TAX	
11(A)6 SELTZER, CURTIS & MELISSA ANN DOWD HCR-02, BOX 20 BLUE GRASS, VA 24413	DB117-671 63.976 ACRES	51,800 51,800	2,400 2,400	54,200 54,200	5	363.14 363.14	BLUE GRASS DISTRICT
10(A)42 SELTZER, CURTIS I. ETUX HCR-02, BOX 20 BLUE GRASS, VA 24413	DB73-523 23.562 ACRES	18,900 18,900	100 100	19,000 19,000	5	127.30 127.30	BLUE GRASS DISTRICT
PAGE TOTALS		443,000 443,000	63,500 63,500	506,500 506,500		3,393.55 3,393.55	

CLASS-1	CLASS-2	CLASS-3	CLASS-4	CLASS-5	CLASS-6	CLASS-7	CLASS-8	CLASS-9	
	64,300			129,200	313,000				1

Once you have tax-parcel numbers from the Land Book, you can go to the assessor's office and look up the appropriate tax map in the index. Then go to the set of tax maps to find the target property. Make a photocopy for your property file.

Using the Land Book and the tax maps is easy enough once you've done it. If you need help getting started, ask the clerk to walk you through the system. Once you've made a photocopy of the seller's tax-map parcel, highlight the seller's boundaries. This can be tricky, so don't hesitate to ask the clerk for assistance. You can then compare the shape of the seller's property as shown on the tax map with the shape drawn from the deed calls that are mapped on a topo. They should be identical, but are often not, usually owing to tax-map errors. Tax maps are useful to a buyer, because they provide a general idea of where the seller's property is located, its relation to adjoining properties and acreage. But they are unreliable on all three counts, and you should never assume they carry the authority of a survey.

Newer tax maps are based on high-quality aerial photographs that may or may not be verified through other sources. Older tax maps, which you often find in small rural counties, may be based on out-of-date aerial photos. Boundary lines may have been located from the functional boundary lines visible from the air. These may or may not have been checked against other records. Corrections may or may not have been made as surveys were done in later years. **Boundary lines and acreage figures from tax maps are not legally binding on anyone**. You should use a tax map for preliminary scoping and getting oriented, but it is no substitute for a survey or a surveyor-drawn boundary line on a topographical map. Never pick a fight with a seller or his neighbors based solely on a tax map.

As I write, hand-held **Global Positioning Systems (GPS)** are available for $200 to $400 that will help you navigate into and out of unfamiliar terrain. The Garmin models, for example, allow you to load topographic data from a three-CD ROM set onto a PC and then to the compatible GPS receiver. If you like gadgetry, you can rig yourself out, but a GPS capability is an unnecessary expense for a land buyer. Most properties that a typical buyer will scope are neither so big nor so remote that they require GPS technology for safety in the field. A see-through compass and a topographical map are good enough for most properties. Such compasses can be purchased for between $10 and $20. If you can't get the hang of a compass and a map, you will find a GPS outfit even more bewildering.

You can find all of these items—planimeter, planogrid, compass and GPS—at The Forestry Suppliers Catalog, PO Box 8397, Jackson, MS, 39284-8397; 1-800-647-5368; 1-800-543-4203 FAX; www.forestry-suppliers.com.

As you walk the property with topo in hand, make sure its boundary lines coincide with where you find boundaries marked on the ground.

Keep in mind that boundaries on the ground can be of two kinds: **marked and functional**. A marked line is one that carries a surveyor's marks. The functional boundary line—a fence, waterway, road, etc.—is the one that divides landowners in practice. The best case, of course, is to find a boundary line that is consistent with the deed's calls and which is both marked and functional. That combination gives you, the buyer, the best hope for a boundary line that is free of disputes.

All the paper boundary lines—deed calls, survey and surveyor-drawn boundary lines on a topo—should line up with each other, and all the paper lines should line up with both the marked and functional boundary lines in the field. If you find a functional boundary in a place other than on the boundary line as set forth in the deed or survey, something ain't right.

A marked line shows physical signs of having been deliberately designated a boundary. Markings typically include plastic ribbon on trees, paint on trees, surveyor slashes (chops) into trees, iron rods (rebar), old pipes, car axles, wood stakes in the ground, fence lines with ribbons, marked corner trees, piles of rock, a set stone and the like. When looking for a boundary line in the field, you hope to find markings that are unambiguous, recent, frequent and aligned with the deed calls, survey and/or lines drawn on a topo. Be skeptical: don't trick yourself into thinking that a crack in a tree's bark is a surveyor's chop. Surveyors almost always use two parallel slashes about breast height to mark a boundary line and three on an important corner; a single slash is not a surveyor's boundary mark. If you find what you think is a boundary mark by itself and obviously off the marked lined you've been following, chances are that it is not a line mark.

The coincidence of marked and functional lines signals, at the very least, that the boundary lines are where the seller and his neighbors think they are supposed to be. To be certain that the seller's lines are dispute free, you must question both the seller and every neighbor. The absence of pending litigation does not mean that everyone agrees on everything. If a long-standing boundary grievance exists, the buyer may inherit it. At the very least, you should be on record with the neighbors that you asked the seller to fix such disputes as part of your negotiations. You do not want to inherit the seller's position in a grudge and then be expected by your new neighbors to solve it at your expense, though this is often the case.

CHAPTER 18: THINKING ABOUT WOODLAND

OVERVIEW

I'm a guy who believes that you can't beat tree shade. Life is good in a hammock stretched between two broad-limbed maples, looking up into an Impressionist's hundred shades of shimmering green. The grass is cut. The dog's asleep in the Saturday sun, paws twitching. Such moments are often worth a three-hour Long March through Friday-evening traffic.

I know these house trees. I've had them trimmed twice, the first time badly. I rake their leaves each fall. I worry that their roots will invade my water line. I lost one of their kind in the back yard. They're family.

People like me tend to anthropomorphize trees in relationship, I think, to how scarce they are in our everyday lives. Work in a city-canyon office building 50 hours a week, and it's easy to see trees at home as friends, children or Zen pillars of serenity. The affection felt for the individual trees around our houses is readily expanded to trees *en masse*, to all woods.

A lot of people feel a kinship with a young woman's vigil to spare all redwoods from logging by nesting in the top of one magnificent tree for more than a year. Her appeal would not have had the same resonance had she camped in a coal mine (to protect miners), or "squattered" at the top of an off-shore oil rig (to protect clams) or perched at the top of a 40-foot-tall loblolly pine in the middle of a 1,000-acre, even-aged plantation destined for newsprint. As a buyer and then owner of woodland, you may find it useful to examine your use of wood products and your attitudes toward trees. This chapter and the next discuss ways to think about woods and trees, as well as your objectives in relation to them.

Trees, unlike hydrocarbon fuels, are living creatures, big living creatures with crowns/heads, branches/limbs, roots/feet, bark/skin, blood/sap and even children—as in, "Giant oaks from little acorns grow." Felling a tree usually kills it, though its roots may shoot up sprouts from the stump. A chainsaw is noisy, smelly and dangerous. It is yang, not yin. The felling process is risky—the cutter can be hurt by his own tools or have the score evened by his victim. Each tree falls with a great cracking, rush and thump. A large opening appears, like a Soviet-style erasure of a liquidated Politburo member or the disappearance of the World Trade Center towers from the Manhattan skyline. Stumps bleed. When we limit cutting in the woodlot to the culls, there is an uneasy eugenic queasiness about eliminating only those that are diseased and deformed. Some feel there exists an absolute right to life across all species. Others object to the taking of tree lives for financial benefit. Each of us can agree, I think, that human life would be very different, very diminished, were all of us to stop using forest products—newsprint, paper, cardboard, flooring, kitchen cabinets, salad bowls, toilet paper. I admit, however, that the bundle of issues and viewpoints about trees, habitat and use is a prism, not a pane.

For whatever reasons, some of us don't see cut trees as we see cut flowers, cut grass or harvested corn. When we weed our garden and thin the lettuce, most of us don't consider that as killing some to allow others to grow more efficiently. If there is a moral difference between cutting ten acres of suburban grass, ten acres of hay and ten acres of planted woods, it is not large enough for me to appreciate. All regenerate after being cut. If we carve out an exception for crops we plant—the exception being, it's ethically okay to take the life we give—then there should be no difference between harvesting peanuts on a Georgia peanut plantation and harvesting loblolly pine on a Georgia pine plantation.

A distinction can be drawn between cutting wild trees in a natural forest and planted trees in a "man-made" forest. Most of us probably feel that a crop of plants has a lesser claim on life than a redwood forest, though both are fated to die because both are living. I feel this way. My reason to allow some trees to live and die naturally while taking others, both domesticated and wild, is that those I would spare have value beyond their human utility. These can include values related to environmental health, aesthetics, genetics, wildlife preservation and endangered species. While I can see cutting some redwoods for commercial gain, I certainly wouldn't cut all redwoods for that reason. Mine is not a philosophy of stewardship that imposes preservation of what is as a trump value. I favor preserving some and using others of the same kind.

Killing and using species other than our own is necessary to our lives, just as the killing of species other than their own and using resources is necessary to the life of all other species. Trees themselves engage in a no-quarter-given struggle for life, each trying its selfish best to crowd out all others from sunlight and nutrients. So much the better when a close-at-hand neighbor is starved to death. The ethical aspect of our necessity to use other life forms requires that we be prudent and conservative, that we balance our needs against those of other life forms, that we husband our resources and theirs, and use what we take efficiently and for good reason. While nature tends to balance itself, we must enforce balance on ourselves. The alternative to self-imposed balance is a level of consumption that leads to catastrophe.

Trees in a "wild" forest can have a trump value when the forest as a system has an overriding value to itself and many species, including our own. Reasonable individuals can disagree as to what "old growth" forest is. "Old growth" has come to mean much more than virgin forest, of which very little remains in the continental United States. Land buyers reading this book are not likely to find virgin forest despite what the real-estate ad says. And those patches of woods that I've seen that have "never been cut" are almost always located on dirt so poor that the trees are stunted and barely able to survive, thus explaining their pristine condition. In my experience of actively looking at eastern timberland, I've not seen a *tract* of privately-owned woodland that's much older than 100 years, though I've seen plenty of trees with more age than that. These older trees are either singles that are off by themselves or unwanted culls left standing in woods that have been timbered a couple of times. Protecting virgin forest and not cutting old-growth forests are choices not likely to face most land buyers. If you find a wooded tract with merchantable timber, it's likely to have been cut at least once, twice or three times within the last 100 years, depending on where it is and which tree species grow there.

If you're looking at hardwood forests, it's quite probable that you will find the tract has been **high-graded** more than once. High-grading is a timbering practice in which the logger cuts only the large-diameter, high-value **sawtimber** and leaves standing low-value species and all culls. Sawtimber is good-quality wood that's used for lumber; high-value species—walnut, cherry, sugar maple, certain oaks—bring premium prices. (Veneer-quality trees are even more valuable than sawtimber, and I know several smart investors who, when they can, take only veneer to pay for a timberland purchase, leaving the sawtimber for future profit.) The result of repeated sawtimber high-grading is the long-term degradation of a forest's commercial value as the low-value tree species and culls mature and reproduce at the expense of the high-value species. A tract of cherry, sugar maple and northern red oak might be transformed by high-grading over 100 years into a tract of striped maple, black birch, hickory and low-value oaks. Had the tract been timbered with the future in mind (taking out the culls along with the sawtimber), it would be worth today five times or more its current value. Hardwood tracts are high-graded, because it takes less time, costs the

365

logger less and is the most productive use of the logger's resources. High-grading's future economic loss is shifted to the landowner who usually is happy to see big trees—culls and low-value species—still standing.

A recently timbered tract is called a **cutover**; the term can refer to an intensity scale ranging from very selective harvesting (where, for example, just the veneer-quality trees are removed) to a **clearcut** that removes every tree no matter how small. The tell-tale signs of recent timbering are fresh-looking stumps, treetops (**slash**) scattered on the ground, roughed-up roads, dense and weedy underbrush (blackberries, ferns and sunlight-loving weeds like stinging nettle) and a landing (or deck) where logs were trimmed and loaded. A recently high-graded tract will "look" better than one where low-value species and culls have been taken for pulp or just dropped. High-grading takes fewer trees and, therefore, leaves less residual mess. A properly conceived logging job on a hardwood tract should leave some large trees, including several high-value seed trees and old den trees.

When looking at woods that have not been recently cut, you may see a lot of large-diameter trees that have no commercial—**merchantable**—value, because they are the survivors of several earlier high-grading jobs. High-graded woods will still embody the non-commercial values of forests—wildlife habitat, recreation and aesthetics—that land buyers seek. If you want to preserve "as is" a high-graded tract that is certainly your right as a private landowner, but it's not in your financial interest to do so. That decision will benefit the existing mix of species. It will not benefit species that would take advantage of a different mix of trees. There is always both a value in and an opportunity cost of doing nothing. Do not be fooled by a seller or his real-estate agent assuring you that the tract's only been "**select cut**." High-grading is the most common type of selective cut. A high-graded tract will have little, if any, present merchantable value, and its future merchantable value will have been reduced. In any case, it's advisable to hire a **consulting forester** to evaluate any significant patch of woods that you're thinking of buying. You will be helped in your price negotiations if you know the current value of the property's timber. If your forester's **timber cruise**—an estimated inventory of species, volumes and commercial value—shows little merchantable timber value, give that report to the seller, "Your woods are nice to look at, but they have little commercial value. Here's the cruise that shows that." If the cruise shows a great deal of value, you can keep that fact to yourself. A buyer is in a stronger negotiating position if he has a neutral forester showing that the seller's high-graded woods are worth little than if he offers that opinion on his own say-so.

All privately-owned woodland I've seen has been timbered several times or more. Much aboriginal woodland was converted into open farms and then allowed to grow back into forest when the farms could no longer support the farmers. You can find these woods all over New England and the mountainous sections of the mid-Atlantic states. The charming rock fences that I found in north-central Massachusetts in the late 1960s told me that the woods I was standing in had once been cleared pasture. And that land had been timbered at least once since being allowed to revert to trees. Repeated high-grading and heavy cutting can leave woodland dominated by low-value species and scrubby-looking trees. In the trade, heavy timbering is referred to as "hammering." Trees that pioneer newly open spots in hardwood forests are often the less commercially desirable species, such as striped maple, locust and birch. If you are interested in woods for their non-commercial values and don't care about their economic value, none of this matters with one exception: don't pay a timberland price for woods that have no timber value.

In my part of western Virginia, American chestnut was the dominant species in the hardwood forests colonials explored. The huge chestnuts resisted rot, which made them good for split-rail fences. The wood was easy to mill and work, which made it valuable for timber-framing and construction. The chestnuts were cut along with everything else to transform the forest into cropland and pasture. They thrived until the 1930s when a blight killed them. Chestnut saplings will still grow to a three- or four-inch diameter, occasionally more, and then die. Oaks and maples have taken chestnut's place. Most tree species are subject to diseases and insects. About 60 percent of my hemlock died in 2003 and 2004 from a tiny white creature, the woolly adelgid. I have timbered my woods twice between 1994 and 2004, taking non-sugar maple species and culls the first time and then the large sugar maples. The woods in my area that have been successively high-graded tend toward a mix of low-value pine, oaks, maples and assorted low-value hardwoods. This mix is good wildlife habitat. I try to manage my woods to encourage high-value species, such as sugar maple, red oak, black cherry and ash. I cut culls for firewood. While the species composition of this type of woodland has changed significantly since the 1700s, deer, bear and coyotes have adapted.

Woodland, of course, varies with region, topography and climate. Mixed hardwood forests of different types are common in the upper South, Mississippi Valley, upper Midwest, Appalachia and Northeast. Conifers may or not be mixed in. Land buyers will find these types of woodlands as well as land that has been converted to tree plantations, usually a species of fast-growing pine.

Where a pine plantation has been recently clearcut and not replanted, the buyer will be able to buy the property for its true **bare-dirt value**, the cheapest it's likely to be. It will naturally regenerate into native hardwoods and conifers. It will be thick with underbrush until trees become large enough to provide shade. Buying planted pine land gives the owner cash from a thinning cut and then from the final clearcut. Buying land that's just been selectively cut can also be a cost-effective purchase strategy, because, presumably, the owner has captured all of the present merchantable timber value and is selling the land in its least attractive condition.

Controversy over forestry practices focuses on four issues: 1) clearcutting, which removes all trees; 2) establishing even-age, one-species plantations, which are very efficient at growing trees but lack diversity; 3) cutting "old-growth" forests; and 4) timbering publicly owned land. Aside from possibly buying and clearcutting land, readers of this book are not likely to face these issues with respect to the purchase of woodland.

About one third—728 million acres—of America's 2.271 billion acres is forested land. About 483 million acres of that 728 million is commercial forest; the rest is considered noncommercial woods. Of the commercial forest land (483 million acres), federal agencies (principally the U.S. Forest Service) own 97 million acres; states, 26.7 million acres; other public jurisdictions, 7.0 million acres; and Native Americans 5.6 million acres—a total of 28 percent. Private farmers own about 97 million acres, and other private, non-industrial owners—like you, potentially—own 179.4 million acres—57 percent. Most of these private, non-industrial holdings are smaller than 500 acres. The remaining 70.6 million acres is considered private, industrial forest land. The four issues of controversy mainly center on the 28 percent of commercial forest land in public ownership and the 15 percent in private industrial (corporate) ownership. The interesting fact, however, is that about half the wood harvested comes from private non-industrial land like mine. As more public land is backed out of timbering through roadless areas, wilderness designation and environmental restrictions, an increasing share of production will fall on private U.S. landowners and foreign suppliers.

Federal forest land is managed through elaborate systems of planning, public comment, regulation and pressure politics. Each national forest has its own publicly available **management plan** that describes the activities that may occur in each geographic forest sub-area. The first-time reader may have difficulty deciphering a forest plan, but it will provide a newcomer with a useful set of concepts and vocabulary for thinking about managing different types of land.

If you are interested in national and industrial forest issues, you might read the following, which include a range of perspectives: Alston Chase, In a Dark Wood: The Fight over Forests and the Rising Tyranny of Ecology (New York: Houghton Mifflin, 1995); Bill Devall, ed., Clearcut: The Tragedy of Industrial Forestry (San Francisco: Sierra Club Books and Earth Island Press, 1993); Alan Drengson and Duncan Taylor, Ecoforestry: The Art and Science of Sustainable Forest Use (New Haven: New Society Publishers, 1997); Charles E. Little, The Dying of the Trees: The Pandemic in America's Forests (New York: Viking, 1995); Richard N. Jordan, Trees & People: Forestland Ecosystems and Our Future (Washington, D.C.: Regnery Publishing, Inc., 1994); Ray Raphael, Tree Talk: The People and Politics of Timber (Washington, D.C.: Island Press, 1981); Gordon Robinson, The Forest and the Trees: A Guide to Excellent Forestry (Washington, D.C.: Island Press, 1988); Laurence C. Walker, The North American Forests: Geography, Ecology, and Silviculture (Boca Raton, Florida: CRC Press, 1998); and Jerry Mander, Eco-Forestry: The Art and Science of Sustainable Forest Use (New Haven: New Society Publishers, 1997).

Forestry-management publications can be found at www.ForestryIndex.net, which provides links to a wide range of websites and extension publications related to management, estate planning, timber taxation, environmental/conservation regulations and so on. Many periodicals are available, including: American Forests, American Tree Farmer, Canadian Journal of Forestry, Conservation Biology, European Journal of Forest Pathology, Forest Farmer, Forest Land Review, Forest Science, Forest Products Journal, Journal of Forest History, Journal of Forestry, Journal of Wildlife Management, Natural Areas Journal, Northern Journal of Applied Forestry, Oecologia and Southern Lumberman.

Forestry is a subject that is extensively researched at the U.S. Department of Agriculture's Forest Service and state land-grant universities. This literature is usually free or nominally priced. As a result of the Resources Planning Act, USDA is required to publish an assessment of America's renewable resources every ten years. The 2000 RPA Timber Assessment was published in December, 2001 and is available at www.fs.fed.us/pnw/sev/rpa/haynes_files. (e-mail: rhaynes@fs.fed.us or 503-808-2002.) The Assessment sets forth aggregated data and trends on timber inventory, harvesting, products, prices and an implication analysis

Industrial owners control about 15 percent of the forestland total. G-P (Georgia-Pacific) and Weyerhaeuser are the two largest owners, followed by Kimberly Clark, Stone Container, Mead/Westvaco, Scott, Champion, James River, Boise Cascade, Willamette, L-P (Louisiana-Pacific), Bowater and Potlatch. These forest owners have traditionally managed their large holdings to serve their needs for sawtimber and/or fiber. As a group, they are increasingly selling their land base to raise cash. International Paper sold all of its seven million acres in 2006. Most of this collective land base continues to be managed for timber production after being sold, but the maintenance costs and taxes are shifted to the new owners. These land sales can be packaged in parcels as small as 20 acres up to more than one million. If you are looking to buy woodland, these sales can be a good opportunity, especially if you are looking for hunting properties.

Timber Investment Management Organizations (TIMOS) are private companies—GMO, Pope & Talbot, and The Forestland Group, among others—that manage production from about $7 billion worth of woodland on behalf of pension funds, endowments and private investors. TIMOs provide their individual and institutional clients with financial evaluations of forestland and property-management services for millions of acres. **Real Estate Investment Trusts (REITs)**, like Rayonier and Plum Creek, also manage timberland.

FOREST PLANNING

Since each wooded property you investigate will have different features, you will inevitably find yourself thinking about what you might want to do and not do with each possible property. These thoughts are the precursor of a **management plan**, which, of course, may be nothing more than to walk through the woods three or four times a year admiring what you experience. The two basic questions that you need to answer as you think about the appropriate management plan are:

Which objective (s) do I want to promote through my management plan?

Common objectives include financial return (immediate, mid-term, long-term); wildlife enhancement (birds; non-game wildlife; game by species); biological diversity (more than currently exists or less); no human intervention/do nothing; improve property's interior accessibility with foot trails, horse trails or roads; control erosion; non-hunting recreation; etc.

Which management methods do I feel comfortable using and which do I reject?

Depending on your values and objectives, available methods can include cutting trees (all, some or a few; removing some species; removing trees larger than a certain diameter); using fire ("prescribed burns") to clear underbrush and promote wildlife; using chemicals and/or introduced species to suppress invasive vegetation or combat insects; allowing naturally occurring fire to burn or not burn; opening the woods to engines (chainsaws) and/or vehicles; hunting; making habitat more hospitable to some wildlife and less to others; building or maintaining roads for vehicles; planting trees; among others.

Consider such questions with an open mind.

You may find that your set of answers to these questions varies with the unique characteristics of each property you screen even as some answers to each question are consistent across the board.

If you see yourself as a card-carrying tree-hugger, ask yourself whether absolute non-intervention leads to your objectives. It may or may not. Leaving woods—as you now find them—uncut in perpetuity is not a zero-change guarantee for the property or a zero-cost choice for you. (You can achieve either absolute or less-than-absolute non-intervention by placing a conservation easement on the property that spells out how you want the woods managed forever.) Non-intervention may not benefit the health of your trees, biological diversity or the conservation of the land's soil resources. Tree-hugging may get in the way of your other objectives, such as fire control, usability or promotion of a particular species. Leaving (cutover) woods uncut in perpetuity is often not the best approach even for the ecology of a specific site. Remember the ecology that you find in today's woodland is not untouched by human beings. What you see is the ecology left after the most recent human intervention, which, itself, is the successor to earlier interventions. If your objective is to manage the woods back to some earlier ecology, you probably will have to remove and suppress some of what's there so that your preferred species can become dominant. It's not uncommon to find that you have to intervene with a saw to alter the consequences of earlier interventions with saws. If you want to let what is evolve however what is evolves, there's really no telling how your woods will look and function at any particular point in the future. Woods can be significantly damaged—even decimated—by fire, hurricane, ice storm, drought, windstorm, flooding, disease and insects—all of which change what is.

Land buyers are usually appalled at what a clearcut looks like on the day the logger leaves. I am, too. I'm also disturbed at seeing the residue of selective cutting—huge tree crowns left in the woods, heads decapitated at the neck. It's easy to make the connection that if something in man-affected nature "looks bad," it is bad—morally and environmentally. It's hard for an individual who's not familiar with forestry ecology and logging practices to distinguish among timbering that increases future timber value, timbering that promotes game, timbering that encourages both game and other wildlife, timbering that was done to remove scrub and allow the woods to regenerate naturally, timbering that was done to squeeze every penny out of the woods, timbering that high-graded a site, timbering that has done environmental harm and timbering that has done environmental good.

A site that "looks good" in the sense that only a few trees have been cut on each acre could be nothing more than the most recent round of serial high-grading. This site will keep its recreation and aesthetic values, but have little future timber value. If you do not know what to look for, your eyes may trick your brain by focusing on what *looks* bad at the expense of what really *is* bad from an environmental or timber-management perspective. A patch of woods that is too clean, can lack the old snags, downed trees, rotting logs and standing dead trees that are necessary for wildlife and a healthy forest. A clean look at ground level often comes from cattle grazing, a practice that reduces the nutrient cycling on which trees depend, compacts soil and limits the ability of seedlings to establish themselves. Cattle also rub the bark off saplings and trample out grass around the trees they prefer for shade, exposing and damaging roots. But they *do* keep the woods cleaner-looking.

A last word about logging and its look: the worst every logging job looks occurs on the day timbering ends. Time improves visual aesthetics, slowly at first and then more quickly. Even the most severe clearcut looks entirely different and better ten years later. In 20 years, dominant trees will have appeared, shading the ground beneath them. Shade clears out the thickets and brush, which look bad but are good for wildlife.

Timbering can be destructive to many values, particularly in the short term. When woods are hammered, it means that too many small-diameter trees were removed in an effort to squeeze the last dollar out of the current timber sale. This leaves a tract with a much-elongated timber-cutting cycle and a more roughed-up appearance. Cutting smaller diameter hardwoods can double the time required needed until the next cycle of selective timbering can begin—from 25 years or so to 50. The marginal dollar gain that the current owner captures from cutting the smaller-diameter trees is overshadowed by the amount of future lost income. Hammered tracts are often put up for sale. Timbering to maximize current dollars can also harm wildlife and reduce game species. For example, a cut that takes out all the acorn-producing oaks and other nut-bearing trees leaves poor habitat for deer and won't provide squirrels the food that, in part, reseeds these species.

Much harm can befall land when badly conceived and implemented timbering decisions aggregate over time. No better proof of this is our own land-use history that leveled forest after forest without much thought toward the future. Injury was added by overgrazing, deep tilling and plowing, repeated burnings and introducing non-native pests and diseases. Badly timbered land erodes and returns less productively than before. The legacy of our past mistakes and ignorance can be remedied today by applying knowledge and management techniques sensibly.

Some readers undoubtedly feel that the only proper response to past abuse of forestland is to do nothing to the patch they own. I don't oppose that position if hands-off preservation is your only objective. If, on the other hand, you have multiple objectives and a time frame that's longer than today, cutting trees in one way or another can help you get there. A personal no-cut policy should be coupled by a no-wood-use policy. Otherwise, you are simply shifting the environmental costs of your consumption to some other landowner. I don't think that's a defensible position, especially if the shift involves timbering Third World forests in Third World ways for our benefit.

I advise caution, patience and conservative decisions. Don't make big decisions until you've been on the property for at least three or four years. It's far easier to live with bad consequences from a small decision. If you're unsure about cutting timber, try it out on five or ten acres, not 300. Then wait five or six years. By then, you'll have an idea of what you get from timbering and how long the logged-over look lasts.

It goes without saying that our species has a responsibility to conserve other species and do what we can to maintain enough habitat for healthy, viable populations. The elimination of any species weakens an ecosystem that has evolved with it. Successor ecosystems may or may not be better environmentally, but they will be different. That timber cutting reduces the population of some species and increases those of others in an ecosystem does not mean, in my opinion, that we should refrain from every logging activity that can be judged to adversely affect the current species mix. If you cut 15 large red oaks on 100 acres— that is, every red oak on the property larger than 20 inches in diameter, you will adversely affect the red oak population while benefiting both other trees standing close to those now-removed oaks as well as those species that pioneer the new patch of sunlight on the forest floor. While Nature advances and eliminates species, we should be properly reluctant to step into that role. We have changed ecosystems quickly, profoundly and unalterably—and we do not know all the ways those losses of habitat and species affect everything else, including us. Might the dodo have been the source of a generic cancer cure? Might the snail darter yet be that source? Might the loss of either lead to the loss of another species that is the source? The line I'm drawing is one between an absolutist position that says no harm to any species anywhere at any time for any reason and a position that allows some harm to most species in most places at most times for defensible reasons. Fortunately, you will not have to make decisions about how many spotted owls or red-cockaded woodpeckers there should be. If you have endangered species on your property, they and their habitat are currently protected.

Where one draws the line that balances the needs of some species against the needs of others should always be a matter of debate. If your position is that all logging is harmful because it harms some species and therefore no tree should ever be cut, then you have excluded the reasonable and careful use of a renewable, sustainable resource. If your position accepts that resources, such as trees, can be used in an ethically and environmentally defensible manner, then consider the commercial timber potential of whatever woods you may purchase.

My feeling is simple: as long as I use wood products, such as newspapers, plywood and paper products, I should be prepared to cut my own trees to provide in a theoretical and ethical sense some of that supply. If you won't allow some of your trees to be cut, how much of a moral right do you have to continue using these products at will? And if you want to back out wood products, what materials might replace them—oil-based plastics, genetically modified crops? Every material we produce comes with a cost, and each has a net environmental balance.

Some environmentalists are undoubtedly appalled at the notion of landowners cutting their trees, let alone cutting them to make money. If I saw something wrong with cutting trees properly, I would agree with that position. Since I don't, I have no problem making money from doing something that I feel alright about.

371

Much effort has been devoted to reconciling forest welfare and economic interests. No forester or logger I know, no forest products company I know, would admit that they do not have the welfare of forests foremost in mind. I do not doubt the sincerity of those expressions, but some practices, even when done properly, can have harmful consequences when scaled up. Environmental advocates claim the same interest in forest welfare when they oppose all interventions. Neither side has a monopoly on truth. Both have valid arguments—as well as some that aren't so valid. **Sustainable forestry** is the term that now refers to the idea of using forests—and the timber they produce—in an environmentally sound manner that balances various interests. It can be taken to mean cutting no more wood than the cutover land can regenerate over a certain period of time. Sustainable forestry can be stretched to cover opposite viewpoints.

If you're interested in sustainable forestry in its various meanings, start with the National Network of Forest Practitioners, 305 Main Street, Providence, Rhode Island, 02903; 401-273-6507; 401-273-6508 FAX; www.nnfp.org. The NNFP website provides links to state and individual contacts and other providers of services, information and technical assistance. These contacts can refer you to foresters in your area who can help you manage your woodland according to your own definition of sustainable forestry. You can do a www.google.com search for "sustainable forestry" by state and find additional organizations and contacts. Forest-related databases are available at www.forestworld.com; Forestworld, POB 426, 161 Austin Drive, #7, Burlington, Vermont, 05402; 802-865-1111; 802-863-4344 FAX. Other contacts related to a broad view of sustainability are the Forest Stewards Guild, POB 519 Santa Fe, New Mexico, 87504; 505-983-8992; 505-986-0798 FAX; www.foreststewardsguild.com; and Forest Stewardship Council, POB 10, Waterbury, Vermont, 05676; 802-244-6257; 802-244-6258 FAX; www.certifiedproducts.org.

This has been a long-winded way of encouraging new landowners to keep an open and inquiring mind about cutting trees in your new woods. Certain types of cutting can make your woods healthier, more productive in terms of supporting more species, more interesting and more useful. Timbering need not be done harmfully. If you have a steep slope that's easily eroded, cut somewhere else. You can improve the look of timbered land with time and a chainsaw. It's hard and dangerous work, but it's doable with time and diligence. Timbering has many facets—getting the best money from the trees you sell, enhancing your woodlot for future timber value, improving wildlife habitat, creating access where access is wanted, handling the visual mess and protecting the land and its waterways. Each facet can be done well, badly and at all stops in between.

CHAPTER 19: ONE PATCH OF WOODS

GETTING ORIENTED TOWARD TIMBER

The more time I spend on 95 acres of mixed Appalachian hardwoods where I live the more I understand how they change on their own and how I've changed them.

Seasonal change with **deciduous** trees—broad-leaf species that lose their leaves in the fall and are called **hardwoods**—is easy to track. Green switches to bright autumn colors within a few weeks; sight lines through the woods lengthen; leaf mass moves from overhead to underfoot; and the relative quiet of walking through a summer woods is replaced by the crash of dry leaves and the crunch of snow.

More profound—but far less noticeable—is the change in the trees themselves, which, in turn, alters the nature of the woods. The trees grow in height and width each year. As they do, some species crowd out others—the site-specific process is called **succession**. Cutting (or not cutting) trees shapes what the woods become as a community according to which trees are cut, their age, location and species. Succession occurs naturally and all the time. I can see succession in its various stages. Where a large tree has fallen, ferns, weeds and blackberries take hold. A few maple and locust saplings lay their claim. If mature sugar maples stand close to a new opening that's still shaded, I'll find a couple of one-inch-thick sugar saplings in a year or two; they grow fast and desperately straight. All of this new patch occurs among many others, each in various stages, each a bit different, depending on soil, sunlight, water and **aspect** (the compass direction of the slope). I have to make myself look hard at different spots to notice the dimensions of slow, cumulative change.

Before I bought this land, I hired a self-employed, **consulting forester** to **cruise** the tract to estimate the volume of merchantable timber and its dollar value. **Merchantable** refers to the dollars that I, as a landowner, would be likely to receive from, in my case, a **marked sale**, in which my forester marks with paint every tree that I'm selling. That inventory is then sent to local sawmills and loggers in a competitive bid. His inventory disaggregated the hardwood sawtimber by species and two-inch diameter classes. He expressed the estimated sawtimber volume in **board feet (bf)**. (One board foot equals a volume of wood that is 12" x 12" x 1".) **Sawtimber** is a tree of sufficient diameter, length and quality to be milled into lumber. Poor quality trees of the same size do not have lumber potential. They and low-value species have value as **pulp** or firewood. Sometimes, trees—even though they're large—have no value at all. Better timbering jobs drop these unmerchantable trees, whether or not, they are removed. A high-value species, such as a 22-inch-diameter cherry, may have no merchantable value if stout branches are found in its butt log.

I was selling **timber on the stump**, or selling **stumpage**. Buyers confined their bids to the marked trees. Prior to the bid, the forester gave me his cruise inventory along with his best estimate of what local buyers were paying for each species of hardwood sawtimber, expressed as **dollars per thousand board feet ($/mbf)**. The dollar number at the bottom of his inventory told me what he thought the marked stumpage was currently worth. Once he marked the sale, he gave me and the bidders a tree-by-tree (actually a log by log tally) count of the volume that I was selling organized by species. He only counted and painted trees 16 inches in diameter and larger.

Put crassly, I needed to know how much money I could net from the sale of the land's merchantable timber immediately after purchase. That number would figure into whether I could swing the deal. I also needed to limit the amount of mortgage debt I was going to assume. I had in mind cutting and selling the non-sugar-maple species and leaving the sugars in place to develop a sugar bush. Beyond that, I didn't know enough about woods to think knowledgeably about other woods-related objectives. Nor did I have the ability to think very much about how this timbering decision would change the appearance of the woods or its internal dynamics. Fortunately, I had stumbled into a consulting forester who knew what he was doing.

At that time, the woods consisted of 135 acres of northwest-facing slope at between 2,800 and 4,000 feet elevation. The soils were primarily limestone-based, with some patches of a poorer quality shale. The ground was rocky, mostly limestone cobble from the size of a coffee cup to that of a big-screen television. The trees were big—that much I knew—and the forest floor was pretty clean, owing to the presence of cattle who wandered in and out from adjacent pasture that also came with the purchase. A few old logging roads were in place, the main one wound up the mountain with three level spurs branching off and dead-ending at the property line. The woods had not been logged since the early 1960s. That high-grading harvest probably concentrated on red oak, cherry and sugar maple—the money trees—16 or 18 inches and larger. I figured that at least four inches of diameter had been added to trees left standing in the ensuing 32 years. That last harvest also felled the owner's ancient Reo flatbed logging truck, which sat at an intersection growing saplings out of its cab. Shed parts lay next to the carcass, along with an abandoned wood stove and miscellany of the type known as, *dumpus trashus*. Huge, waist-high chestnut stumps were scattered through the woods. The chestnuts had been cut in the 1920s and 1930s. Neighbors said that 40 timber rattlers had been killed the last time loggers ventured in. The woods were pretty.

From the cruise, I learned that the lower 55-acres had an estimated 1,200 sugar maple trees 10"+ **DBH**, each of which was capable of handling at least one tap. DBH is **diameter at breast height**, about 4.5 feet above the ground. The sugar maple 16"+ DBH had about $30,000 in sawtimber value as of that time, 1994. This acreage also had stumpage value in non-sugar species and several hundred pulp trees, both of which I wanted to remove to allow the sugars to develop. On the higher and steeper acreage, the cruise estimated about $47,000 in hardwood sawtimber stumpage, mainly oaks, cherry and sugar maple. More than 95 percent of the value in both tracts lay in the sawtimber. We decided to cut the sawtimber stumpage 16" DBH and larger, except for the sugars on the lower end. This was a **selective cut** in the sense that we were taking out trees that exceeded a diameter threshold as well as trees of certain species. The forester also marked for cutting a lot of pulp culls.

My objectives, then, were to raise cash from the sale of the non-sugar-maple sawtimber stumpage, remove culls and leave the site clean enough to install plastic tubing lines that would carry liquid sugar water from individual trees to a central collection tank at the lowest spot on the property. Some would call this type of cutting a **timber stand improvement (TSI)**, even though I was not trying to upgrade the species mix for future timber sales. What I was trying to do was to turn the woods into a source of both quick cash and annual income. The highest bid was right where the forester had predicted. After I built a collection house and invested in equipment, the sap-collection idea did not pan out for reasons having nothing to do with either the idea or the trees themselves.

This first intervention left the woods with a valuable stand of large, sawtimber-quality sugar maples along with some uncut culls and smaller diameter trees. The logger dragged most of the tops into big **slash piles** so that tubing could be run from tree to tree and then into the main lines that led downhill. Loggers leave slash in place as a rule, because dragging it into piles takes time. The logger left about 100 marked culls in place, because the cost of cutting and hauling them wasn't worth the effort. They were the logger's trees at that point, having paid for them. I wanted them cut and taken, and, if not that, dropped for firewood or forest nutrition. While most of the large-diameter, non-sugars had been cut, all of the large diameter sugars on the lower end remained along with all trees of high-value species smaller than 16" DBH. After the logging, the woods looked thinned, but not spare. The sugar maples spread their crowns into the canopy openings during the next few years. The woods did not look all that much different since we left a lot of standing volume—the 16s and smaller and most of the large sugars. I dressed up the logging roads—clearing them of rock, filling in holes—so that they were safe for trucks, tractor, horses and foot traffic. I left slash undisturbed on the steep upper half of the property where it offended my eye for the next four or five years until it decomposed. I mowed the skid roads a couple of times each summer. My wife and I walked them about eight months a year. The woods provided firewood and good company. I noticed more deer, who liked the new openings and the thick underbrush that came in during the first year.

Eight years later, in August, 2001, I faced a desperate need to pay down debt from a housing project that had crashed, miserably and overwhelmingly. Hard decisions insisted on being made. We sold 40 acres at the top of the mountain to a neighbor. I asked our forester to mark a sale on our remaining 95 acres. His cruise estimated about 231,000 bf of hardwood sawtimber 16" + DBH. Of that, about 151,000 bf, 65 percent, was the sugar maple we had left in place. Other volumes included about 27,500 bf of red oak, 21,500 bf of red maple, 13,000 bf of ash, 9,500 bf of cherry and 8,000 bf of chestnut oak. He estimated about 53,500 bf of the total of 231,000 bf were trees in the 16-18" DBH class with a stumpage value at that time of about $19,000. He recommended leaving these trees in place and cutting only sawtimber 18" DBH and larger. He also suggested focusing the sale on sugar maple and limiting it to the lower 55 acres. We included a little cherry but no white ash owing to its low price at the time. He was trying to maximize sale dollars while conserving about 100,000 bf of our timber base 16" + for the future. He estimated a sale value on the entire 231,000 bf of about $89,000, using conservative species-price multipliers.

We agreed with this strategy. He then marked for sale about 136,500 bf, confined to the lower 55 acres. About 90 percent, 123,500 bf, of that sale inventory was sugar maple, some of it veneer quality. The 1994 cutting had released them from competition. They had gained in diameter and gross volume. Some of the 14s and 16s had moved up in diameter class, which foresters call, **ingrowth**. The change from 14 to 16" diameter is significant, because mills in my area and, probably many others, pay a higher price for stumpage 16"+ than for stumpage less than 16" in diameter. The eight or ten years it takes a sugar maple to increase from the 14" DBH category (which means diameters between 14 inches through not quite 16 inches) to the 16" DBH category (which means diameters between 16 inches and not quite 18 inches) can mean a doubling, or more, of its board-foot stumpage price. The smaller diameter logs don't mill into lumber as efficiently as 16s and larger. Twelves and 14s in cherry and walnut might be cut and milled without a price discount because of their very high value, but other species in smaller diameters would generally be left or, if taken, discounted. It's far more sensible economically to let the 12s and 14s grow into 16"+ stumpage and sell them for sawtimber than sell them at a discount or at a pulp price. Our forester focused the sale on sugar maple sawtimber, because it was fetching a high price and a good portion of that was **veneer quality**, which brings an even higher price per board foot than sawtimber.

About 400 trees were painted stump and butt, and their volumes grouped by species and two-inch diameter class. The sale notice was sent out to every potential buyer within a three-hour truck haul. This is the format for a **competitively bid sale**; the alternative is a **negotiated sale**, between the forester and one buyer. Competition among buyers almost always produces a higher price for the landowner. We sweated the month-long wait.

Ten buyers submitted bids, the highest of which was a sawmill at $79,900. Two other sawmills made offers in the $70s while the independent loggers bid in the low $40s. Three bids were tightly clustered around $65,000. Owing to our forester's skill in designing a buyer-friendly, market-oriented sale, we received about $650 mbf for the sugar maple rather than the $400 mbf he had used as his cruise multiplier. And we still had 100,000 bf of 16-18s left untouched in our woodland savings account. Our forester charged 10 percent of the gross sale revenue for painting the 400 trees, marketing and managing the sale, preparing the contract and checking the actual timbering. Had we done **50-50 shares** with an independent logger, my guess is that we would have netted $30,000 to $40,000 instead of almost $72,000.

At the end of October 2002, I blew out my right knee a few weeks before the logging was to start. Following Halloween surgery, I spent the next two months on my back. While I knew that logging was going on, that was about all I knew in my drug-befuddled daze. When I hobbled into the woods in the spring, the first thing I noticed was how changed the logged areas appeared and how unchanged was the rest. This cut was far more noticeable than the first since the sugar maples were clustered in five or six areas of about five to eight acres each. These areas were now open, with a scattering of smaller-diameter sugars and a few ash and hemlock. The ground was piled high with slash; the logger had not been asked or paid to drag the slash into piles. The roads were rough, though I expected that. I was surprised, however, by the amount of slash left on the roads themselves, despite contract language that required them to be left free of slash and in good repair. I spent a lot of time that summer clearing the roads of rock and slash. I spent the next two years cutting up the slash from about 400 tree tops, two or three tops at a time, which I describe below. Photograph 19-1 shows one tree top dropped on top of another, making for dangerous footing and a tangled cutting environment.

PHOTOGRAPH 19-1

Slash

Photograph 19-2 shows one top on the ground, a much easier and safer lopping environment.

PHOTOGRAPH 19-2

Slash

Over the last decade, I've found my woods-related objectives changing as my needs changed and as the woods themselves changed. The two timber sales provided money when that was needed. As important, the woods provided quiet and tranquility, even when they looked their post-logging worst. I got two years of hard exercise lopping slash and cutting firewood, which I came to view as the penance of hard labor for making a debt-ballooning business investment based on emotion rather than analysis. The deer prospered from the flush of fresh undergrowth, and their presence may be the reason why only two rattlesnakes have been spotted in more than ten years. The deer are now acclimated to my truck and tractor. They run from our Labs, Lucy and Sophie, but both chase and flight seem perfunctory. The deer don't seem to mind a short, monotony-breaking sprint a couple of afternoons a week. They never ran from the late Briggs who, I think, wisely realized, that pursuing the uncatchable was beneath him. Two years after this second timbering, deer became so numerous that I let a neighbor hunt our woods in hope of giving the maple sprouts a chance to establish themselves.

After several months of work, the roads were clear. I then hired a bulldozer to cut in some new roads, and I've added others by hand, clearing slash, digging out rocks and filling holes. The dozer is faster; the hand-work is harder but leaves a lighter touch. The roads are kept safe for walking, horseback riding and driving. The slash is lopped to within two feet of the ground, as shown in Photograph 19-3. It is invisible in the summer and inoffensive when it is visible. I've pulled out three years of firewood—about 20 cords—and will probably be able to take one more year's worth before the downed wood loses its firewood quality. Since the woods are only a five-minute drive from our house, I spend a lot of late afternoons up there—working, thinking, arguing, revisiting life mistakes, wincing over stupid things I've done and said, what-ifing and watching the forest's paint dry.

PHOTOGRAPH 19-3

Lopped Slash

One recurring item on my agenda is asking myself whether I would have cut the timber had I not needed the money. A point comes in the life of every tree when its quality for lumber begins to decline with increasing age. If trees are to be cut, they should be taken before that point. The sawtimber trees I cut were between 75 and 100 years old. They would have gained a great deal of value had I let them alone for 20 to 40 more years, $500,000 or more. The woods would have had during that time a park-like appearance—big shady trees, not much underbrush. Had I let them be forever, they would have succumbed to breakage, blowdown, insects and disease. Had I cut them 40 years down the road, the woods would have been left with even more extensive openings. My answer, I think, is that I would have cut them later, perhaps 20 years after I bought the land to help with retirement. But the longer you know your woods, the harder it is to cut the trees. Necessity, both fortunately and unfortunately, trumps choice.

When rain softens the ground, wind—especially when it blows in opposite from its prevailing direction—will topple large, shallow-rooted hardwoods. These trees are especially vulnerable to **windthrow** after logging has thinned the stand around them. Breakage from wind and ice tends to affect older, crown-heavy trees too. Several large-diameter hickories—more than 30 inches—either broke at about 40 feet or blew over in the winter of 2004-2005. Then our little share of Hurricane Frances toppled a gun-barrel-straight 30-inch ash, which took down three smaller maples standing like a row of dominoes. Blowdowns are a major mess to clean up. When several are involved, their tops get tangled. The crown at one end and the root ball at the other creates a bind on the underside of the tree being cut that locks up the chainsaw's bar even when you know what's going to happen and try to prevent it. Wading into a mass of green, tangled tops is as hazardous a cutting job as I've done. Apart from the satisfaction of surviving these chores, the only pleasure in cleaning up blowdowns occurs when you cut an uprooted tree at the stump and the freed root pad plops right back into its hole, perfectly.

The more I know this forest, the more trees I know. Like a college class, what started as hundreds in an audience are now individuals, many of whom I've encountered personally. There's one black birch, for example, that grows on the edge of a road; if I'm not paying attention, I'll side-swipe it with my truck mirror. There are stumps with stories. One reminds me of the time I hung a big locust in the branches of a neighbor, requiring a heroic effort to get it down safely. Another I cut flush to the ground to improve a road. There's one maple with a big, exposed root on which the tractor always slips in the spring. Two maples and one huge chestnut oak have structural problems, so I try to remember to eye them carefully before I pass under. They're too hinky for me to drop. I don't know why our wind storms have taken healthy trees and not these weakened ones.

When my wife and I walk the trails, I carry a whippy, green locust branch. I use this "**flickstick**" to fillip small branches to the side without bending. It's the size and stoutness of a light-weight walking stick, but it needs to be springy to flick properly. My wife feels no compulsion to flick trails, though she and her horse like that I do it. Clear roads make walking safer and protect the soft underbellies of my vehicles. When the roads are flicked, I have a base line that alerts me to the extent of routine twig-and-branch shedding from adjacent trees. I now tend to look both up and down when woods-walking, up for **widowmakers**—broken limbs that will eventually fall—and down so that I don't trip over the fallen. I also try to be mindful of loose rock, uneven ground, holes and concealed limbs. Spend enough time tramping over rough, wooded ground, and these snares will eventually put you on your face or butt.

I try to understand what I see. A few years ago, gypsy moth infestation was in our area. I learned to recognized their egg sacs on trees and know them in flight. Before then, moths were moths to me. This species defoliated and killed oaks in the mid-Atlantic region, but we survived without loss. Three years later, I noticed that the hemlock were losing their needles. The white crud on the underside of their needles was the woolly adelgid. I note new woodpecker holes in trees I thought were sound, and fungus growing on big locust indicates internal rot. I cheer on every wiry little cherry sapling and boo the striped maples that seem to pop up overnight. For every one small thing I've come to understand, I assume there are another 100 still to learn.

I now see the familiar woods not as a forest, but as distinct patches with their own micro-communities of vegetation, trees and maybe creatures. One, for example, is a dark hemlock grove that surrounded the wreck of the Reo, whose steady disintegration I consider performance art. That area is now filled with sunlight and dead hemlock. I'm waiting to see who falls first and then who springs up. Another is a small spot where several weak-looking butternuts hang on in the middle of some huge, decrepit yellow locust. Another is an oak stand on a shaley South-facing slope where deer and turkey generally find food in the shadow of a rotting tree stand about 25 feet up. Ever observant, I noticed the stand a couple of years after I noticed the oaks. Sugar maple saplings grab space where dense slash shielded them from browsing deer and rampaging ferns. But to be honest about it, I mainly notice these triumphant maples when they're an inch-thick and ten feet tall. I do notice when a familiar view or roadway is reduced by **heliotropic** branches racing as fast as they can toward sunlight. I trim them away from the roads every couple of years. I look for evidence of bears—overturned rocks that concealed insects, grubbed out stumps, scat in the trails, a scratching tree. I even see bears themselves once in a while. I like the idea that black bears can make part of their living off me. We share the blackberries in August. (A good bear book is, Benjamin

379

Kilham and Ed Gray, <u>Among the Bears: Raising Orphan Cubs in the Wild</u> [New York: Henry Holt, 2002].) I also patrol for **multiflora rose** clumps, which I spray with herbicide to keep them from taking over. I search maple stumps for sprouts, but the deer have gotten every one. I used to cheer for the deer, now I root for the stumps.

While logging creates a volume of openness in the woods, it also creates a visual and aesthetic mess on the ground. The visitor may notice freshly cut stumps after a logging job. They are low to the ground and not offensive to my eye. You will notice the thick clump of **stump sprouts** sent up the year after cutting if deer don't browse them. Most of the visual offense comes from the crowns left after the usable logs have been cut and removed. Collectively, the crowns are referred to as, **tops** or **slash**. (See Photographs 19-1 and 19-2.)

I've seen crowns on the ground 20 feet high, even with one side mashed down by the force of the fall. Weeds and brambles thrive in the slash. By the sixth or seventh summer in my four-season area, slash is still noticeable but no longer visually offensive. Each year that it lies on the ground, gravity and hungry bugs work it down. You can accelerate the rotting and measurably improve post-logging aesthetics by lopping the slash so that as much of it as possible is on the ground. (See Photograph 19-3.) This clean-up cutting shortens the time that precipitation, vegetation and creatures need to decompose the wood. Slash makes good firewood for several years, but after that it becomes punky.

While slash is unsightly, it is environmentally beneficial, providing good wildlife habitat, fodder and nutrients for remaining trees and saplings. It looks bad, but it isn't. From an environmental view, it's probably better to let Nature rot slash slowly. Wildlife benefits from the prolonged thick cover, and the tangle allows new trees to take root. It is, however, more aesthetically disturbing than I can stand. So I cut it up. With slash lopped to three feet above the ground, there's still enough mess to protect seedlings from deer looking for an easy meal. You want to protect seedlings by leaving slash where it is. This leads to the subject of chainsaws. If you buy country property with trees on it, you will around to chainsaws pretty quick.

WOODS WORK

I ran my first chainsaw more than 35 years ago. It was a McCulloch that refused to start most of the time. The next was a Homelite that quit running without good reason half-way into every job. I now use a Stihl MS 390 with an 18" bar and a 3/8-inch chain pitch. This is a level of saw that is more than you will need for weekend work in trees with diameters smaller than 16 inches. It has been the right saw for **lopping** (cutting limbs from main stems) and **bucking** (cutting stems into logs and 20-inch-long firewood) the slash from 400 trees. For this work, I moved up from a Stihl 025C, which I found adequate for lighter use. I use the chainsaw to make length-wise cuts about two-thirds through in thick or gnarly firewood rounds, which makes splitting easy. If you do a lot of this length-wise cutting, you'll need a saw with adequate power, a bar that's long enough and a sharp chain. The dealer who sold me the Stihl said Husqvarnas were better. He had sold and repaired both, and I trust his judgment. But I've had good luck with recent Stihls and <u>Consumer Reports</u> likes them. I'd also consider the Husqvarna 350 and the 55 Rancher. (See http://forestry.about.com/library/reviews/aabyb-chainsaws.htm for reviews.)

Whatever brand and size you use, you must understand that you are working with a tool that can hurt you in the blink of an eye in an environment where a dozen things can go wrong even faster. I would not buy an older chainsaw that lacked an anti-kickback brake and other safety features of the newer ones. I would also suggest reading about safe chainsaw use before ever using one. (See http://forestry.about.com/od/chainsaws/.)

DO NOT USE A CHAINSAW WITHOUT WEARING: 1) HARDHAT WITH 2) ATTACHED HEARING-PROTECTION MUFFS AND 3) SCREEN FACE SHIELD ALONG WITH 4) KEVLAR-TYPE FULL-LEG CHAPS, 5) STEEL-TOED LOGGER'S BOOTS AND 6) NON-SLIP WORK GLOVES. One chip in your eye will convince you of the value of full-face protection; one was enough to convince me. I have nicks in my chaps to show where my chainsaw would have bitten me. When I was younger and more stupid, I would cut without chaps, without eye-protection other than my eyeglasses and without heavy boots. No more. A good book on this subject is Frank Philbrick and Stephen Philbrick, The Backyard Lumberjack: The Ultimate Guide to Felling, Bucking, Splitting & Stacking (North Adams, MA: Storey Publishing, 2006.)

The most dangerous cutting I've done is cleaning up slash right after a logging job. While felling trees causes the most logging injuries, lopping slash feels to me to be even more hazardous owing to the uncertain footing, tight quarters, impaired vision from high ground vegetation and the tangle of the material. Loggers don't like to do this work, because it's unprofitable, unsafe and goes slowly. DO NOT DO THIS WORK UNLESS YOU ARE OUTFITTED PROPERLY AND EXPERIENCED WITH A CHAINSAW. I advise waiting at least a year before moving into slash. That gives the compressed branches time to lose most of their spring. Bent branches can break your leg when cutting releases them. You will get into situations where the slash is on all sides, above you and under your feet. Stop, take stock. Take your time. Don't try to buzz your way out. Make sure your feet are on something firm and you're squared up to the cut. Don't straddle limbs that are still connected. It's easy to lose your balance with a running saw in slash jumbles. It's also easy to get the saw bound up in a cut. (Keep an extra blade and chain with you. Unbolt the saw from the stuck blade and attach the extra bar and chain. Then free the original blade and chain without getting bound up again. My rule is: anyone can get stuck in a cut once, but only a fool allows himself to be caught twice in the same jam.) When you get tired cutting, quit. You will hurt yourself if you continue. Take frequent rest breaks and drink water. Beer is not water. Keep your chain sharp. It takes me about 90 minutes—or one load of gas—to lop three or four tops. If I'm feeling frisky, I'll do two loads. But at 61, I'm okay with one. Don't take chances with a chainsaw; injury is too easy to come by.

Since we walk the roads and Melissa rides her horse over them, I try to keep them free of loose stones and pointy, embedded rocks. I pitch them downhill; if I toss them on the uphill side, they end up back in the road. Roly-poly stones are a danger to ankles and hooves; the pointy ones ruin tires. The dirt in these old skid roads is wet and soft enough in the spring to dig out the new crop of offenders. I can kick free the smaller ones with the sole, toe or heel of my logger boots. On the bigger ones, I use a heavy **mattock**, which has a curved blade on one side of its head and a point on the other. The big, buried stones require a **rock bar**, a solid steel shaft about six-feet long with a narrow blade, to pry them out. Some, of course, are so big and deep that I can't budge them. I may batter down an offending point or ledge with a short-handled sledge hammer or fill around them with dirt. I bash down any sharp edges. These big guys are now as familiar to me as the street corners I avoided in the seventh grade where the big-kid bullies gathered. Whenever I remove a rock from a foot trail or road, I *always* fill in the hole to make a safe, level surface. Where the road passes over a section of rock cobble, I'll remove the loose stuff and throw dirt over the surface. I don't like the feel of walking on ball-bearings. The **foot test**—how it feels to walk on a road's surface—is what I use to determine whether or not I need to do more. I don't try to groom these roads like the horse trails at expensive resorts. That level of investment and maintenance is unnecessary. I aim for safe use by people, horses and vehicles.

The roads you find in woods are usually old logging roads, or **skid trails**. Older roads of this sort were not designed to protect streams and control erosion. They tend to run in straight lines, often straight up a slope. They also run too close to streams, or even in stream beds. Newer logging roads are expected to meet environmental-protection standards called, **Best Management Practices (BMPs)**. If you're bulldozing roads from scratch, you should conform to the state's forestry BMPs. If you're working on a road by hand, try to gain elevation gradually and wind the road upslope. Where a slope is too steep to drive across, you'll need to bulldoze a level bench-road into it. This involves pushing the dirt and rock from the L-shaped cut downslope. Make these cuts a couple of feet wider than your widest vehicle for safety, even though more dirt will be dug out. Throw grass seed on both the road and downslope to stabilize the dirt. Loggers should grass-seed skid roads before they leave a site, presumably after they clear the roads of major slash and rocks. Some states require such work; others recommend it. You might find it useful to throw out some seed in the spring following logging, particularly shade-tolerant grass where trees arch over an uphill straight-away. Steep, shady, dry, bad-dirt spots on roads are likely to erode.

Logging is rough work, and you should expect a roughed up appearance—slash and roads primarily. The other anti-aesthetic legacy loggers leave are broken branches in standing trees and **leaners**, trees that have been knocked partially over by falling timber. In dense stands, it may be impossible to prevent this. Your forester can minimize this by anticipating how a logger will cut a tree. Rather than leave trees broken or leaning, the logger should take them down. This will leave a safer and more pleasing woodlot. Careful loggers try to minimize this type of damage and take pride in leaving a clean site. Bad loggers don't give a flip how they leave your land. Provisions can be written into your **timber-sale contract** to encourage loggers to minimize this type of collateral damage. (A sample contract—between a landowner and a timber buyer/logger—is found in Chapter 23.) On the 55 acres I timbered in 2002, I've since had to drop no more than ten top-broke saplings and a couple of leaners.

Small-woodlot logging involves heavy motorized equipment and the dragging—**skidding**—of hundreds of large, heavy logs over make-shift roads through the woods. (Logging on level ground disturbs the ground less than on slopes, and some types of logging use less skidding than others.) Skidders and bulldozers churn up rocks and debris. They also can leave roads with deep ruts if not smoothed up once the logging is complete. That last touch up work must be done when the ground is relatively dry to be effective. Erosion-control measures are graded in at that time.

The damage I find most offensive from skidding are the bark-skinned trees left along the edges of the skid roads. These wounds are caused by a bundle of long logs fishtailing as the skidder or dozer drags them from the woods to the landing where they are sorted and loaded. The skinning wound is found on the first four or five feet of tree trunk. This is the butt log, the most commercially valuable part of the tree. Apart from lost future value, these wounds are unsightly and take a long time to heal, if ever. My eye is drawn to them. I'm offended by the waste and carelessness. I'd guess that on my three miles of skid roads, there might be 100 bark-skinned trees. Most have been bumped twice in 12 years. None of these trees have died, though I've noticed peeling bark above the wounds in some. A number of trees have tried to close their wound, but none have totally succeeded.

A logger could minimize tree skinning by skidding out fewer logs in each gang or cutting them shorter. This would minimize the fishtailing and its impact. But these practices would increase the logger's investment of time and expense, so don't plan on having him skid logs one at a time in eight-foot lengths unless you pay him dearly. And even then, it would slow him down to the point of driving him nuts. I've thought of cutting old tires and stacking them like bangle bracelets five or six deep around a vulnerable trunk. Loggers and foresters will laugh at this idea. It might work; it also might be more work than it's worth. Getting a sufficient number of tires to a logging site and placing them on each skid-road tree is a big, dirty, sweaty job. But it might be practical to protect one or two trees when I do my own little back-yard logging.

Horse-logging skids out only a few logs at a time and is a much slower and softer process than conventional logging using dozers and skidders. Horses create much less collateral environmental damage, because they require less road-building and pull fewer logs in each hitch and at a slower speed. But a landowner will receive less money from his timber sale from a horse logger, because it is a more costly method per unit of timber removed. It obviously costs a lot less to maintain a team of draft horses than a $75,000 skidder, but it takes the horse-logger many times longer to do the same work. A horse logger may have to forgo cutting good timber on slopes where his horses would have difficulty. Still, horse logging on small tracts or where fewer than 100 trees are involved might be a competitive option, particularly if financial return is not your sole objective. (Horse logging leaves the same amount of slash as conventional methods, but the roads will be less disturbed.) The cost economics look even better if you're limiting the logging to a small number of high-value, dispersed, veneer-quality and sawtimber logs. It's arguable that horse-skidding will better protect their value than the rough and tumble of high-speed skidding. On such jobs, you might seek out a horse logger or an old-timer who logs single-handed with a smaller-than-typical skidder and dozer. With such timber, you don't want an outfit that rolls in with a million dollars in new-from-the-factory machines cowboyed around by 20 year olds wearing NASCAR caps.

After the first logging, I put in connecting trails to turn a tree-and-branch road design into a very rough grid with the outside loop tracking the property's perimeter. The connector trails link the ends of the level branch spurs. I wiggled the connectors through openings that offered the fewest trees, rocks and wet places. Most connectors run between spurs at different elevations. I try to use serpentine lines on slopes, because they're less noticeable, easier on the environment and more interesting. Making roads by hand is a matter of sawing out debris and dragging it out of the way. I also had to dig rocks and fill holes with dirt hauled by truck in five-gallon buckets. A dozer cut in the steeper sections. These connectors are mainly for Melissa's trail riding and getting around in my small pick-up truck. They're not wide and straight enough for skidding logs. (See MAP 17-3.)

I don't find woods roads offensive, but I know people who do. If you don't like the idea of vehicle-capable roads in your woods, you might consider threading in a system of hiking trails. Take a look at Robert C. Birkby, Lightly on the Land: The SCA Trail Building and Maintenance Manual (Seattle: Mountaineer Books, 1996) for information.

Vegetation will eventually become established on dirt roads whether or not they are grass seeded. Opportunistic weeds and brambles come in first, then trees. If the roadway is not mowed, it will soon become impassable. To prevent this, roads should be mowed twice a year at least if you want to use them safely. The easiest way to do this is to hire a neighbor who has a tractor and a bushhog. This can be a tax-deductible expense for woodland set up as a farm, business or investment. Hiring out this work is a sensible approach, particularly if you don't have the money to buy a tractor or are skittish around big things that smoke and roar. Your land may allow you to buy a mowing rig smaller than a tractor. Four-wheel ATVs can have drag-behind mowing attachments. You'll probably need a 4WD ATV with a good bit of horsepower—not a cheap mowing option. Self-propelled, heavy-duty sitting or walk-behind mowers might work, but I think they would be unwieldy on steep or rocky trails. Suburban-type riding mowers can be used if the trails are reasonably rock-free. But these mowers are not rugged enough for woods trails in my opinion. Finally, you could keep a road clear with a weed-whacker, though this would prove increasingly

less appealing with increasing road length. If you decide to apply herbicide to the grassed road, you will lose the benefit of grass holding dirt in place. If that's your choice, it's better to hire your neighbor.

You may find yourself thinking about buying a tractor and a bushhog. (I've discussed tractors in Chapter 8.) For trail mowing, you can get by with a small tractor—called a "compact"—and a four-foot-wide bushhog, though a bigger tractor and a wider bushhog will make the work easier and faster. The tractor should have a hydraulic **three-point hitch** that will allow you to raise and lower the bushhog over rocks. You won't need 4WD, a front-end loader, quick couplers, elaborate hydraulics or a lot of horsepower—all of which are handy, of course. Power steering is always useful on uneven ground. You can still find an older 20-30 hp tractor and bushhog for $3,000 to $4,000. The new ones cost three to five times that amount.

Most of my woods roads are just wide enough to accommodate my 1957 Ford 8N tractor with its 60-inch-wide bushhog mower. I need to make two passes to mow the main roads, while one does fine on the connectors where the rear wheels mash down another 12 inches on each side. The Ford's rear wheels are reversed on the axle to set them wider for extra stability. This set up prevents me from mowing the full width of the tires. A wider bushhog would, I fear, be too much for my tractor.

Mowing woods roads requires a basic **utility tractor** (not a general purpose tractor, which is generally bigger, designed for row crops, and generally carries its implements under its belly between front and rear wheels) with at least the following features, which are explained in detail in Chapter 8:

- **20 to 30 horsepower**

- **Power Take-Off (PTO).** This is a shaft that sticks out of the rear of the tractor, which can be engaged to the engine. When engaged, it turns. Through a coupling, shaft and differential, the PTO shaft turns the bushhog blade. **Live PTO** allows you to control the engagement of the tractor's engine to the bushhog. You want live PTO because it lets you run attachments while the tractor is standing still. When checking PTO operation, make sure that the engaging gears are not worn; otherwise, you will find your bushhog slipping out of gear when it hits a clump of dirt. Replacing this gear mechanism is expensive. This will make you angry. ALWAYS DISENGAGE YOUR BUSHHOG WHEN YOU ARE DISMOUNTING THE TRACTOR.

- **Three-point hitch.** This is a hydraulic arrangement at the back of your tractor that lets you raise and lower whatever is attached. When mowing trails or anything else, you will have a frequent need to raise and lower the bushhog to adapt to the contours of the ground and avoid protruding rocks. A fixed-position mower would take a beating with each use. Tractors come in various sizes and have different-sized hitch arrangements. Make sure that you know which hitch Category (O, 1 or 2) your tractor features so that you match your PTO equipment with your hitch. Category 1 is big enough for this type of mowing.

- **Bushhog (aka, brushog or rotary cutter).** This is a mower that is either driven by your tractor's PTO or its own engine. It will have a "crazy wheel" (or tailwheel) made of segmented rubber to support its outby end. This wheel rotates 360 degrees and supports the bushhog. Make sure that your tractor size (horsepower) is sufficient to operate and lift the bushhog you get. You will want to get a bushhog that's between four and six feet wide for trail mowing with a Category 1 hitch. You want a heavy-duty bushhog with a steel deck at least 3/16-inch thick.

Some bushhogs use a clutch to protect their blades when they hit an immovable object. The clutch disengages the PTO motion from the blade when the object is hit, thus sparing various shafts and mechanical parts. Older bushhogs use a three-piece blade, with the two end pieces attached to the center piece by pin pivots. This bat-wing blade allows the end pieces to hit a rock without transferring the force to the bushhog's mechanics. If you have a clutch bushhog, you won't need a three piece blade. Most bushhogs come with a shearpin in the power train, which is supposed to break before a differential or shaft when the blade whacks the unseen Gibraltar. Carry an extra shearpin or appropriately sized bolt in your tractor's toolbox or tape it to the bushhog itself.

The bushhog's gearbox changes the PTO shaft rotation from horizontal to vertical and turns the blade horizontally. Its differential is concealed in the gearbox's metal housing on top of the bushhog. The housing should have a little screw-in plug where you put in gearbox lubricant (not motor oil). Gearboxes are sized according to your tractor's horsepower. A mismatch between tractor size and bushhog size will eventually harm the smaller component. A bushhog is not a finish mower, which is appropriate for big lawns. Blades should be sharpened, advice that I don't follow very much. A sharp blade cuts neatly, a dull blade cuts raggedy. On a woods road, where the blade gets nicked a little every time you mow, you don't care that the grass is not like a putting green. Your bushhog will last longer if you don't run it over saplings, multiflora rose, embedded rocks, old fence posts and odd pieces of metal that your farm truck has decided it no longer needs.

- **Rollbar.** Tractors roll over, both sideways and end over end. Sideways rollovers are the most common. They occur when the tractor is being driven across a slope and the pitch steepens; or, when you are driving across a slope and your uphill rear tire rides up on a rock or stump. Rollovers happen in a split-second so your best protection is to avoid getting yourself into these dicey situations. Nothing is worth a rollover—no last log that you want to pull out, no last section of trail mowing, no step you want to avoid walking. You should wear a seatbelt with a rollbar.

You can also adapt your tractor for protection. You can protect yourself, first, by extending your wheel-base width-wise. Various ways exist to do this, including reversing the rear wheel rims on the axle hubs so that the wheel wells stick out rather than in, thus widening the wheelbase by the width of your rims. You can also extend the front axle on each side to widen the wheelbase. A tractor mechanic should do this work because the wheel adjustments front and back must be kept proportional to each other. The front wheel toe in also needs to be adjusted when extending the front axles. This is a cheap way to make your tractor safer.

You can also install a roll-over protection system (ROPS) and seatbelt. These have been standard for several years. Most smaller tractors prior to the 1980s don't have them. A ROPS can be a roll bar or a bar with a steel canopy that provides shade.

- **Ear Protection.** I always wear hearing protectors, muffs rather than plugs. You may be the only "fool" in the neighborhood who wears them, and a new fool in the neighborhood to boot, but you will be the one fool who will be able to hear the snide comments.

Aside from trail mowing, you may play with the idea of **using your farm tractor for logging your woods**, occasionally or otherwise. I pull out about ten logs a year, which is plenty for me. I use my 50-year-old 2WD Ford, even though it is not suited for this work inasmuch as it lacks power steering, front weights (for traction) and 4WD. I drag logs out of the woods to a spot where I can saw and split them into firewood and load them into a truck. I look for a place in a road that's shaded, where the footing is good, and the ground is level and open. The more rocks underfoot, the more dancing with a chainsaw, and the higher your risk of getting hurt. If you're cutting wood on stony ground, sooner or later you will "**rock your saw.**" This precipitates serious self-cursing and an extensive amount of chain sharpening. If you're splitting with an ax or a maul, you want enough clearance so that you can swing through vertically with an overhead, straight-down shot. I pick a place where I can park my truck immediately parallel to the firewood to make loading easy. I load the firewood with a **tie-pick**, an ax-like tool with a sharpened point instead of a blade. A tie-pick spares my back from bending over and lifting. If the truck is hitched to a haulage cart or hydraulic splitter, I make sure that I can either drive out going straight ahead or get turned around without a problem.

Before taking my tractor off a maintained woods road, I clear a "roadway" back to the tree, making it as straight and clean as I can. I'll remove downed limbs, rocks and sticks protruding from the ground. I try to avoid or remove impediments like stumps that will catch a dragged log and imperil me and the tractor. When a stump stops a dragged log, the tractor's front end lifts up and back. In that event, you need to cut the power damn quickly or the tractor can pull itself over backwards. The 30 minutes I devote to clearing the temporary roadway usually prevents getting stuck, hung up or broke down. The idea is to baby the tractor and eliminate opportunities for things going wrong.

Before hitching a chain or cable to a log, I trim all of its branches flush to prevent snagging. Skidding is easier and safer if the log is dragged butt-end first. The closer you can chain up the log to the back of the tractor, the better. I usually hitch the log onto a grab hook welded to the bushhog or scraper blade. I use the hitch hydraulics to lift the butt off the ground, which decreases the log's drag by reducing the amount of log surface touching the ground. A log hitched this way changes the tractor's balance, however. The heavier the log, the less weight there will be on the front wheels. This reduces the traction available for turning and makes dragging uphill riskier. A tractor can pull a lot more log weight on level ground than on an uphill slope. If the ground is wet or soft from earlier rain, the tractor's woods work just waits. Safety requires dry, level, clear and slow. Though I usually do this work myself, it's always safer when there's a helper around.

Farm tractors lack the **armor** for woods work. If you want to use a farm tractor for this type of work more than very occasionally, you will do well to weld a skid plate along its underside, along with metal guards in front of the radiator, headlights, exhaust stack (if possible) and engine's sides. You should also put metal protection on the four tire rims to protect valve stems. I'd also recommend a canopy-type roll-over protection system and wheel weights all around. Woods work is hard on tires when the ground is rocky, stumpy and thick with slash. Power steering, 4WD, three-point hitch and a front-end loader (outfitted with forks, not a bucket) are very handy in this environment. Farm tractors should be used sparingly for dragging logs in the woods.

I advise against doing daily logging with a farm tractor. However, I have seen large tractors—60 hp+ with 4WD, armored and outfitted with either a **logging winch** or a **grapple loader**—used this way. The winch mounts on the three-point hitch and runs off the PTO. It lifts the butt ends of a gang of logs off the ground and puts heavy steel plate between the logs and the back end of the tractor. A grapple loader grabs, then lifts a log onto a truck or trailer. You might find this loader referred to as a **knuckle boom**, and see one on a logging truck. A tractor logging winch costs up to $5,000 and a loader can be twice that. An excellent article, complete with information on manufacturers and techniques, is Robert M. Shaffer, "Farm Tractor Logging for Woodlot Owners" Virginia Cooperative Extension, Publication Number 420-090, April, 1998; also at www.ext.vt.edu/pubs/forestry/420-090.html. Every state's extension service publishes state-specific articles that are available at a nominal price, or free on the website of the coordinating land-grant university. Since logging techniques differ from region to region, the extension service and forestry agency are good starting places for acquiring information. Logging is hard, dangerous, skilled work. Logging is not cutting up six-inch-diameter firewood on a couple of sunny fall afternoons. I advise inexperienced landowners to leave serious logging to the pros.

Tractors are dangerous helpmates in woods. You can do without tractor logging. Not so, without a **woods truck**. Well, you actually can live without a woods truck, but they are incredibly handy. Where land is set up as a business, investment or farm, its cost is deductible or depreciable.

Every rural landowner has **truck stories**. You, too, will acquire yours. (But first, you need the hero.) Generally, they are getting-stuck sagas, exotic breakdowns, ingenious field repairs using spit and electrician's tape, wild rides resulting from brake failures, runaways dragging owners (who didn't set the emergency brake), downhill slides through mud as slick as snot (as the saying goes) and legendary loads—of which songs should be sung. Many truck stories involve innocent others.

One morning years ago up a holler remote by even West Virginia's standards, a young, good-looking, recently divorced woman of my casual-and-completely-innocent acquaintance nursed her extremely expensive, extremely low-slung Italian sports car up my muddy, pot-holed road. This car no more belonged on my farm dirt than the Hope Diamond belonged in a pig wallow. My best friend—young, single and charming—and I admired this mile-long feat of determined off-road driving in silence. The convertible, we sensed, was highly motivated. It stopped in front of my run-down, sheet-tin barn, a refuge that it would refuse to enter in a hurricane. Mud dripped from its polished flanks. Its beast-like motor wheezed. The driver slowly unlimbered her limbs and other charms from behind the hand-rubbed, walnut steering wheel. Real jewels flashed, danced and jangled. Legs shimmered in pants from Paris. She wasn't wearing sunglasses. "I need some work on my tailpipe," she announced with no visible distress, looking David square in his eye. Not wanting to be churlish, I did not point out that between her fancy house in fancy South Hills and the mud hole in which her Papagallos were now standing, 50 miles away, there were at least 25 auto-repair shops capable of fixing any exhaust system built since 1903. Nor did I mention that David and I had been about to start work. It occurred to me that I was not even present for all of her intents and purposes. So we jacked up the rear end, and I left, as the two of them wiggled under for a look. David appeared several days later, saying only that "additional alignment" had been needed. I know this is not a truck story, but it does involve a vehicle…in the country. It was the 70s, after all.

Woods truck. You will use one to get around the property and haul stuff/people in and out. It will carry you, other humans, dogs, firewood, tree seedlings, gravel (called "gravels" around here), game, water, culverts, five-gallon cans of gasoline, fencing materials, leaves, grass seed, lumber, building supplies, tree branches, dirt, posted signs, wood-cutting paraphernalia, tools, picnic supplies, guns and a pup tent with hot dogs for your kid's first sleep out.

My preference is a **farm-use truck** that does not require a license and inspection, but should be good enough to pass inspection if it were inspected which it will not be. (Check local standards before assuming the truth of my preceding statement.) A farm-use truck should be dinged up and more at home on a logging road than an Interstate. It may be necessary, however, to find a truck that is both fully licensed as well as being suitable for working in the woods and around the farm. The newer and more expensive your truck, the more slowly you want to drive it in the woods and the better you want your dirt roads to be.

Although I've driven a number of pick-ups over the years, only two were notable, and only one of these was truly woods-worthy. The unworthy was a red 1946 International with steel as thick as tank plates. Although it was a conventional 2WD, it had enough weight and balance to move through light mud and rough ground. I bought it for $100 in the early 1970s from a fellow who claimed it would "do a hunderd," and did I want to see? I doubt that I ever drove it over 40 mph, and that was pushing its engine. It proved to be feeble and spent a lot of time in the hospital getting transplants. (I had a 1972 International Scout at that time, which soured me on American cars. Its only reliable feature was that it could not be counted on, ever.) Getting parts for a truck pushing 30 was sometimes like securing an organ donation from my enemies. Yet, it had a simple, WWII-era straight-forwardness that I loved. The front window cranked out. It had overhead wipers and a couple of white stripes running from its hood back across its doors. It smelled trucky—old parts under the seat, oily rags, a hint of hay and candy bars from the late 1940s. I named him, "Phillip, Da Truck."

Phillip could carry a lot of weight very slowly. I mainly asked him to bring firewood home over pretty good dirt roads. But he and I once met a Ringling Brothers train in Charleston, West Virginia so that I could shovel out a load of fresh elephant manure for our garden. I drove him home, reeking, through the unsuspecting down-town lunch crowd of bored lawyers and bankers in what passed for his "bulldog first." Phillip's presence was not universally applauded by those to whom I waved. (I was young and unemployed at the time, which may explain, but does not excuse, my behavior. It was the 70s, after all.) I think Phillip was embarrassed and felt used. He was always willing though only intermittently able. I treasure those few crisp, fall afternoons when I gently drove him home loaded above his gunwales with sour-smelling split oak as I puffed on a cigar. Phillip was a self-indulgence. If you need a working truck, don't buy an antique no matter how cool.

For ten years now, I've had "The Cheetah," a 4WD truck both notable and woodsy as a fox. It has no style, no nostalgia, no cool. Some of the body is yellow—hence its name—but most of it is rust. It runs, but it has no jump. It could chase down a parked Impala. Its windows bear stickers from Brown and Harvard. In any context other than mine, it would be buried in the woods like the Reo. But it suits me perfectly. It's cheap, reliable and forgiving. I expect it will survive me.

Officially, the Cheetah is a short-wheelbase, 1980 Toyota 4WD pick-up with a four-speed manual transmission whose clutch survived my daughter's first driving lessons. It has no power anything, and is the opposite of "loaded." The engine is simple, something an Australopithecine or even a Ph.D. like me can work on. It's been a farm-use truck since 1993 and now shows about 260,000 miles. The Cheetah has about 12 inches of ground clearance and a functioning 4WD system. Newer 4WDs are better, because they shift power to wheels having traction. The Cheetah's first gear in Low Range is what I prefer to use in the woods, because it allows me to crawl down slopes without much brake. It's well balanced, and I've never gotten it stuck. It's good enough in mud, but won't go uphill through deep snow over ice. The bed is small, which means I can only haul small loads, which means I don't strain my back. No Cheetah was ever meant to be a beast of burden.

The Cheetah is beat to hell. It sheds parts like an overheated winter hiker—so far, mud flaps, a molded plastic thing, the rubber foot plate on its gas pedal, rear-view mirror, side mirror, a front wheel, exhaust system components, leaf spring and unidentifiable miscellany. The bed contains a number of ground-viewing holes—like a glass-bottomed boat—that make cleaning a breeze. The Cheetah is not an antique—and never will be. It can't be restored. I do maintain it, because it's a working truck.

I've rigged the Cheetah for work in the woods and around the farm. I've strengthened the frame, which was about to rust in half. I carry the spare tire above the cab's roof so that I have extra room in the bed. It's mounted on a horizontal V that is welded to the rollbar. This black beret sets him apart from other big cats in the neighborhood. There's a tow hook bolted onto the front frame and a very heavy-duty, shop-made bumper that can handle either a ball hitch or towing pin. (This was accomplished by welding to the four-inch diameter, steel-pipe bumper a half-moon plate of 1/2-inch-thick steel with a hole drilled through it to accommodate either one.) Two grab hooks are welded at either end of the bumper for dragging or pulling with chains. A welder fabricated a roll bar out of tube steel. Then he welded onto the top bar a series of paired horseshoes to carry an ax, cant hook, shovel, sledge hammer, tie-pick, maul and mattock. Also welded to the rollbar are four steel rectangles, about one inch in height. They are slots for carrying splitting wedges. I throw the rock bar and chainsaw into the bed, along with the dogs. On the passenger side's floor, I keep an extra cutting bar and chains, spark plug, safety chaps, gloves and a helmet with face mask/muffs.

The Cheetah, because of its condition, is the kind of truck you want for woodsying around, though its not good enough for much highway driving. It's easy to maneuver despite the lack of power steering, doesn't get stuck, can pull a cart or a log, could care less about dings and scrapes and forgives a mechanical nincompoop like me. It's dependable on inclines, both up and down, and doesn't overheat with a load. It features an operational horn and headlights; functioning heater and wipers; and a radio that has been known to pick up oldies when the stars are right. It has an occasional sense of humor. One time both doors jammed with me inside. I was forced to squeeze out through the driver's-side window. A neighbor was amused. A truck like The Cheetah would be good to have at your place in the country, but it could not be used for commuting between home and there. For that job, you can stick with your day car.

I'm no expert on pick-ups, but I have no trouble recommending the stubby 4WD Toyotas from 1978-1985 as a knock-about, all-purpose vehicle for your country property. They're cheap to buy and cheap to maintain. They're reliable even with a lot of miles and are known for their lack of temperament. They start; this is important. If you're looking for a farm/woods truck, avoid buying a fully-loaded anything as well as all trucks owned by teenage boys, defined as males under 50.

A fellow could, of course, plop down $35,000 for a new truck so that he can bring home half a cord of wood at Thanksgiving that he cut from his newly purchased land. Some portion of our Nation's economy depends on men making such decisions. You may think your new truck will be "like a rock" no matter how many tons of steel are dumped on it. If you treat a truck like the New York advertising agencies do, you will be looking for a replacement vehicle in short order.

If you're a first-timer with trucks and land, look for a well-used, light-weight, short-bed 4WD with power steering and a stick shift. Larger trucks can haul more, but they are less nimble and the older ones tend to swamp around in mud and snow. My neighbors like big, sprawly Fords and Chevys from the 1970s, but they won't get in an out of the tight spots the Cheetah slips through without a trace. You don't need a flatbed or a dump truck for most work. A friend from West Virginia, Claude Pauley, once described his late 1960s full-size GMC pick-up as the "haulin'est truck" he ever saw, which it was. But it was so wide, long and low that it would have run aground under load in the woods or, at least, dropped a few undergarments. Resist the old Dodge power wagons despite their neat looks. They are very heavy and are more truck than you will need in almost every situation. They're also very expensive to maintain. Hummers may be able to go anywhere, but they don't go through trees. They're too wide for scooting along most woods roads. Why spend $50,000 to $100,000 to haul home $50 worth of firewood? Hummers are fun to watch—at a curb, and on paper where they depreciate rapidly for tax purposes. Still, it will take applied intelligence, not just simple negligence, to get one stuck.

If I had a very large place that required a lot of work and if I had a lot of money, I would buy a Mercedes-Benz Unimog with a lot of attachments. A Unimog starts out as a combination tractor and truck, which can then be rigged to do almost anything, including, perhaps, bearing children.

Every so often, you will ask your truck to do more than it's supposed to do under fair-use rules. Things like: getting you off a steep slope with a full load; or getting you home with half its cylinders firing; or getting you out of a jam created by your own bad judgment. When you find yourself asking your truck for a favor, it's good to be on a first-name basis. You get there by paying attention to its needs on a regular basis so it will feel just slightly indebted to you. Laugh all you want. Spend enough time in the field with a truck, and I promise you will find yourself in a relationship.

The main lesson I think I've learned from all this road work and sawing is that trees can take care of much of themselves over time even with my mucking around. The logging and my other interventions will fade. Slash and stumps rot. New trees come up. The old chestnut stumps from the 1930s will undoubtedly be there when I'm gone. About four-feet high—the comfortable working height for a two-man crosscut saw—they are soft red rot inside hard grey shells. Ax marks are still visible on some, forgotten the day they were made. I honor both the stump and the unknown axman. Some of these stumps are more than five-feet wide. But even they will disappear into the woods in time. And that is the lesson, I guess: forested land works with what it has, changing some but staying forested. It's forgiving and adaptive. It can be used without being hurt, but it can be hurt.

This chapter describes my own approach to **small woodlot management**. I recommend James R. Fazio, The Woodland Steward: A Practical Guide to the Management of Small Private Forests, 2nd ed., (Moscow, Idaho: The Woodland Press, 1987) and Richard M. Brett, The Country Journal Woodlot Primer: The Right Way to Manage Your Woodland (Brattleboro, Vermont: Country Journal Publishing Company, 1983) for further reading. Fazio is especially helpful.

CHAPTER 20: THINKING ABOUT TIMBER

LANDOWNER'S OBJECTIVES FOR WOODLAND

In looking at woodland for possible purchase, it is critical for you to view each target with an eye toward a property-specific **set of objectives**, one of which may be selling (and cutting) its timber. Your starting objectives will lead to a **forest-management plan**, even if you want to do nothing at all. A plan can be as simple as a mental note to never do anything, but most plans involve active intervention to promote owner objectives.

I urge buyers to think about multiple objectives and how they interact. Setting objectives involves determining the scope and type of things you think you might do with the woods if you purchase them as well as ranking these objectives in terms of their importance. It's likely that you will find yourself listing multiple objectives, some of which conflict with each other. A **consulting forester**, discussed below, can help you think through a plan's objectives. Your objectives and plan may also need to involve a civil engineer (if major road and bridges are anticipated) and environmental specialists. TABLE 20-1 gets an inexperienced land buyer started in thinking about common woodland-management objectives over three time periods.

TABLE 20-1

Buyer's Woodland-Management Objectives

	Immediate	1-10 Years	10 + Years

Possible Objectives

1. Money
 a. Maximize immediate
   timber-sale income (TSI)
 b. Some immediate
   TSI; Maximize TSI for
   __ years forward
 c. No immediate TSI; Improve
   stand for __ years forward
 d. Annual revenue
   1. Firewood/chips from culls
   2. Tap sugar maples
   3. Christmas trees
   4. Ginseng
   5. Nuts, mushrooms, berries—
     other food and/or seedling stock
   6. Other

e. Rental lease for
  1. Hunting/fishing
  2. Birding
  3. Hiking/camping
  4. ATVs/snowmobiles
  5. Horses—trail riding
  6. Cross-country skiing
  7. Mountain biking
  8. Other
f. Mineral/energy leases
  1. Oil & gas
  2. Non-Energy minerals
    a. Surface
    b. Underground
  3. Energy resources (coal,
      oil shale, biomass)
    a. Surface
    b. Underground
  4. Geothermal
  5. Wind
  6. Hydro

2. Aesthetics
a. Preserve—untouched
b. Management for
      specific aesthetic goals, e.g.
  1. Visual neatness
  2. Quiet
  3. Unmanaged look
  4. Other

3. Flora and fauna
a. Enhance habitat for particular game species
b. Enhance habitat for non-game species
  1. Birds
  2. Flora
  3. Fish
  4. Other
c. Protect ETS species
d. Emphasize diversity of flora and/or fauna

4. Water Resources
a. Preserve existing
      watercourses/wetlands
  1. Improve fish habitat
  2. Minimize erosion
b. Add ponds

         1. Improve wildlife habitat
         2. Fire protection
      c. Protect/create wetlands
      d. Sell/use water
      e. Improve water quality

5. Recreation
      a. Non-hunting
         1. No roads/trails
         2. Improve roads/trails
      b. Hunting
      c. Vehicle recreation—develop roads
      d. Horseback riding

6. Timber stand
      a. Up-grade mix of tree
            species to improve
            long-term financial value
      b. Change species mix
            to help particular wildlife
            species
      c. Change species mix
            for aesthetics/recreation
            objectives
      d. Remove diseased/dead
            standing trees
      e. Reduce fire potential
      f. Plant seedlings to increase
            future value
      g. Other

7. Fire protection
      a. Develop road network
      b. Remove standing deadwood
      c. Develop ponds
      d. Lop slash to hasten
            decomposition

8. Develop second home/camp
      a. Pick site; coordinate building
            plans with other objectives

TABLE 20-1 can also be used to reflect the **intensity** with which you think you want to pursue each objective. With "0" representing no interest and "5" representing an objective that you are most interested in achieving, you can rank their importance within each time period.

The objectives I've included above are a typical range, but your objectives will be specific to you and your site. The ones I've included are illustrative, not exhaustive. A consulting forester can help you develop objectives and alert you to conflicts between and among them. You can't, for example, maximize immediate TSI and also maximize TSI ten years down the road, though you may be able to produce timber income at both points. (In this case, you might reframe the objective to be, produce maximum timber-sale income over ten years, with so many dollars immediately.)

The management plan you draft as a buyer is likely to change if you become the property's owner. Dirt-level experience will lead to some new objectives and some re-ranking. While you should understand that change is part of every plan, some decisions in forestry have long-term consequences. Once your land has been clearcut, you can't change your mind and decide, instead, on a selective cut. Unless you need to sell timber immediately upon purchase, I'd advise to not make any significant cutting decisions until you've owned the property for at least several years. Your management plan may never amount to anything more than an immutable decision to never do anything. (In this case, you may want to investigate the tax benefits of a conservation easement based on no surface disturbance, no development and no logging.) Your plan may involve a few general ideas, or take formal shape as a highly detailed, time-sequenced written document that guides you for many years and even takes the form of a legal covenant. To receive state tax benefits for managing your wooded property as timberland, you will need a management plan drawn up by a state-approved forester.

Woodland provides many benefits that need to be considered when thinking about your specific objectives. Forested land absorbs water, which controls the runoff that leads to flooding, erosion and sediment build up in waterways. Woodland is a sponge, bare land is much less so. As water percolates through forest duff, soil and rock, it is cleaned. Trees build dirt as leaves are shed and fallen wood decomposes. Woods provide habitat for plants and animals. Trees remove carbon dioxide from the air and give off oxygen, a process on which all of us depend. They affect surface temperature. They provide the feedstock for every wood product we use—from paper and telephone poles to furniture and ice-cream sticks. Woodlands provide high aesthetic values and diverse recreation opportunities. They can also supply food and medicine. These functions are connected and depend on each other. A major change in one function reverberates with the others. Accordingly, the landowner's objectives should be broader than finding the fastest dollar in his woods. And if that is your only objective, a consulting forester can help you get that dollar with the least harm done to everything else.

If you involve a consulting forester in your scoping, discuss your preliminary forest objectives with him. He can help you evaluate them in terms of **feasibility, time-frame, interdependence, compatibility, financial costs and benefits, opportunity costs (things you can't do because of what you do) and environmental benefits and impacts.** Some objectives may be unsuited to the type of land or soil on the target property. Certain financial objectives for the timber may not be very compatible with your preferred recreational and environmental goals. A clearcut does not fit well with scenic Sunday horseback rides, at least for the ten or 15 years after the logging. Foresters are trained to think in terms of forest-management plans over time so yours will know how to identify incompatibilities and objectives that are dependent on others.

You should do some reading and investigation to develop your thoughts about ranking objectives. The books below will help you know what you know, what you want to know and some of the things you don't know. I would not, however, advise developing objectives and a plan based on books alone. Your forester's insight and experience will produce a plan that brings benefits and prevents errors far into the future. Among the books you might consult, are Mollie Beattie, Charles Thompson and Lynn Levine, Working With Your Woodland: A Landowner's Guide (Hanover and London: University Press of New England, 1983); Country Journal Woodlot Primer: The Right Way to Manage Your Woodland (New York:

W.W. Norton & Company, 1983); Stewart Hilts, *et al.*, The Woodlot Management Handbook: Making the Most of Your Wooded Property for Conservation, Income or Both (Buffalo, New York: Firefly Books, 1999); Dave Johnson, The Good Woodcutter's Guide: Chain Saws, Woodlots and Sawmills (White River Junction, Vermont: Chelsea Green Publishing Company, 1998); Thom J. McEvoy, Legal Aspects of Owning and Managing Woodlands (Washington, D.C.: Island Press, 1998); Leon S. Minckler, Woodland Ecology: Environmental Forestry for the Small Owner, 2nd ed., (Syracuse, New York: Syracuse University Press, 1980); Laurence C. Walker, Farming the Small Forest: A Guide for the Landowner (San Francisco: Miller Freeman Publications, 1988); and Rick A. Hamilton, Forest*A*Syst: A Self-Assessment Guide for Managing Your Forest for Timber Production, Wildlife, Recreation, Aesthetics and Water Quality (Raleigh, NC: North Carolina State University, undated) and A Family Forest: A Planning Guide to Protect, Enhance and Manage Private Forestland (Raleigh, North Carolina: NC Division of Forest Resources, 2002), both available from Rick A. Hamilton, Extension Forestry Specialist, Department of Forestry, North Carolina State University, Campus Box 8003, Room 3028D Biltmore Hall, Raleigh, North Carolina, 27695-8003; 919-515-5574; e-mail at: rick_hamilton@ncsu.edu.

Valuing timber in the field involves estimating both the volume of **merchantable** trees—those which a timber buyer will pay for—and its likely price. Some experienced individuals can do these calculations as they walk through a wooded property. The systematic way of determining volume and value is to have a consulting forester undertake a **timber cruise**, which is a field-based sampling of standing timber volume that he couples with his estimate of current stumpage prices. Cruises generally limit themselves to inventorying the merchantable timber. I'll introduce you to the basic vocabulary and concepts and then take you through an analysis of a sample cruise in Chapter 21.

Broadly speaking, American timber is divided into **hardwood (HW)** species, which are **broadleaf deciduous** trees such as oak, cherry, maple, hickory, birch, beech and walnut, and **needleleaf evergreen (softwood or coniferous)** species, such as pine, spruce, cedar and hemlock. American deciduous trees lose their leaves in the fall; evergreens retain their needles.

With exceptions, hardwood species grow more slowly than evergreens. Most HW species in average natural conditions take at least 50 years to reach a diameter of 16 inches; this growth time can double on poor sites with weak soils and not much precipitation. Hardwoods are generally harvested from naturally-growing, rather than planted, stands. In the East and Midwest, a natural stand of mixed hardwood species is what a land buyer is likely to encounter. In the South and New England, you will find natural stands of mixed hardwoods and evergreens.

Conifers are cut both in the wild and from managed even-age, one-species plantations. Fast-growing pine species, such as loblolly, have been planted throughout the South. They are cultivated for both sawtimber and pulp. The initial planting is usually thinned after about a dozen years and then clearcut about ten to 15 years later. This strategy maximizes volume production and financial return.

Commercially valuable trees have two different markets, speaking broadly. Both HW and conifers of sufficient size and quality are sold for **sawtimber**, which is milled into lumber, flooring and the like. A specialty sub-market for some species of sawtimber is veneer. **Veneer-quality** logs are the best grade of sawtimber, because they are free of imperfections. Veneer is a thin sheet of wood that is used to face furniture and cabinetry. It is glued over a cheaper wood. Cherry, oak, walnut, birch and maple are the hardwood species that are used for veneer. The second major market for both hardwoods and conifers values them as a source of fiber, either as a **pulp** feedstock for making paper or as **chips** for composition products. The fiber market puts no value on a tree's suitability for lumber. Sawtimber is generally more valuable on the stump than **pulpwood**, which I will use generically to mean bulk wood that is not milled for lumber. Merchantable timber also includes trees that are used for telephone and utility poles, railroad ties, pallets and other products. Pine, not hardwood, is used for poles that are treated with preservative. Pole-size or pole timber refers to either hardwood or softwood of eight to ten-inches DBH. Low-quality hardwood sawtimber is used for ties and pallets. You may find a reference to chip-and-saw timber, or C&S. This refers to small-diameter pine sawtimber that is first run through a chipping head that squares off two sides of a log and then goes through a gang saw for ripping into products, like 2x4s. For simplicity, I have grouped all non-sawtimber wood as "pulp." Every region will show a hierarchy of pulp prices, depending on what products local buyers produce. Hardwood pulp and pine pulp have different prices. Hardwood is sold for both sawtimber and pulp, as is softwood.

My experience mainly involves Appalachian hardwoods, with some knowledge of New England forests and southern pine plantations. This discussion, accordingly, is based on my experience. Be prepared for different terms and methods in other parts of the country, even though the basic approach should be similar to the one I describe. I'll focus on valuing hardwood sawtimber **stumpage**, which is merchantable trees standing in the field. A **merchantable tree** is one that a stumpage buyer will pay a landowner for; there will be many trees on a landowner's property that are not merchantable because they are too small, or defective in one way or another, or of little commercial value, or located where they can't be cut profitably. Hardwood sawtimber is trickier to value than planted evergreen, because quality and size figure into HW value, and each HW species is priced individually. It's much easier to determine the stumpage value of 100 acres of 17-year-old loblolly pine than 100 acres of mixed hardwoods with volume distributed among two dozen species of different ages, sizes and quality.

Sawtimber is cut into logs that are milled into dimensioned boards for flooring, furniture and construction. These logs are graded according to their quality. Sawtimber stumpage (volume or weight) is estimated in the field. Sawtimber stumpage should only include those trees that are merchantable, i.e., that is, only those that a stumpage buyer will pay for. It is not uncommon, however, for a land seller to provide a buyer with a stumpage cruise that includes non-merchantable volume and, hence, unrealizable value. These bogus cruises are discussed in Chapter 22.

Sawtimber stumpage is expressed either in volume—**board feet (bf)**, usually in units of **1,000 board feet (mbf)** or in green weight—tons. Better-quality sawtimber is shown in board feet. You may see a cruise where better sawtimber is expressed in board feet and the remainder in tons.

To determine the amount of merchantable stumpage and its dollar value, a forester conducts a representative sampling of the land's merchantable trees. This is called a **timber cruise**. A sawtimber cruise should not count as sawtimber any trees that are not of sawtimber quality and diameter, as determined by the local market. Such trees should be counted as pulp or firewood, if at all. A sawtimber cruise should also not include good trees that are located on **inoperable acreage**, such as inaccessible steep slopes or impenetrable swamp. While those trees qualify as sawtimber, they cannot be logged in a cost-effective way. Therefore, a stumpage buyer would place no value on them in his bid; they are not merchantable.

The forester superimposes a grid on the hardwood property. He walks into each cell in this grid. Cell size varies with the size of the property being cruised. The larger the property, the larger each cell. A 100-acre HW tract might use cells that are five acres each, or smaller. A 50,000-acre tract might use cells of 50 or 100 acres, depending on the consistency of the timber stand. In each cell, the forester takes a sample—called a **plot**—of the standing trees. Plots are typically 1/10th to 1/5th of an acre. The forester counts the merchantable trees in each plot, and groups them by species and diameter class. Typically, HW sawtimber is grouped into two-inch diameter classes, e.g., all merchantable trees in the plot between ten and 12 inches DBH are grouped into one class, usually referred to as 10s; between 12 and 14 inches DBH are 12s and so on. Trees in the plot that are smaller in diameter than the cruise's operating definition of merchantability are not counted. In the case of a deformed or damaged tree that meets the diameter threshold, the forester counts only that volume that is log-length and of acceptable quality.

The forester then estimates the board feet (or tons) in each of the merchantable trees—and the merchantable portion of defective trees—in the plot. He starts by determining diameter, which he measures as **diameter at breast height (DBH), or 4.5 feet above the ground's surface**. Definitions of diameter merchantability vary, according to the type of timber being cruised, its likely market and the owner's objectives. For a HW clearcut, merchantability might be defined as all trees 4" DBH and larger. A **selective cut** in a HW stand might define the diameter threshold as everything larger (wider) than 18" DBH. On trees of sufficient diameter in the plot, the forester estimates the number of eight- to 16-foot-long logs in each merchantable tree. The stumpage volume for each tree is found by consulting a chart, called a **log scale**, which provides the number of board feet in each log length for a given diameter. Tonnage is calculated similarly. Methods can vary from region to region, depending on species and market factors.

Stumpage prices change over time with market conditions. Lumber markets have cycles that tend to track new home construction. Each HW species has its own price range in every local market. These prices rise and fall with supply and demand for that species. As species go in and out of consumer favor, their prices—both as finished lumber and on the stump—rise and fall. Appalachian green/air-dried 4/4 (one-inch thick) red oak lumber, for example, fell from almost $600/mbf in 2004 to about $450 in mid-2005 as furniture buyers swung to sugar (hard) maple and red (soft) maple, whose prices rose. Stumpage prices shadow retail lumber prices.

In addition, each stumpage buyer determines his bid price for each species in light of the supply he has and the demand for his milled product. One stumpage buyer, for instance, might bid $450 mbf for northern red oak because his log yard is empty and he has orders that he can't fill, while the mill buyer down the road bids only $300 mbf because his yard is stacked with red oak logs and he has few orders. Within a species, stumpage price bids will vary according to quality. The difference between published stumpage prices and those that pertain to a particular tract are discussed below.

The forester tries to determine a representative current stumpage price for each species by talking with likely stumpage buyers. He uses the most likely price for the landowner's timber, given location and quality, as his **price multiplier**. If, for example, a property contains a cruise-estimated 100,000 bf of sugar maple with a price multiplier of $.75/bf, the forester would project the stumpage value of the merchantable timber for the landowner at $75,000. (This can be expressed as 100 mbf of HM @ $75/mbf = $75,000, with HM meaning hard [sugar] maple.) Most sawtimber stumpage is fully priced in the 16" DBH and larger diameter classes, though a few high-value species will fetch the full price even for 12s and 14s. Smaller-diameter sawtimber stumpage usually carries a discounted price. The smaller diameters are not discounted in a sale going for pulp or chips.

A board foot on the stump is fully dimensioned at 12" x 12" x 1". A rough-sawn board foot as it comes green directly from a saw blade is also fully dimensioned. But a board foot of lumber that is sold retail after being kiln-dried and surfaced (dressed) is only 12" (L) x 11 1/4" (W) x 3/4" (T). Milled lumber is expressed in its **nominal—not actual—dimensions**. When you buy an eight-foot-long 2 x 4, it is eight feet long but only 1 1/2" wide and 3/4" thick.

Pulpwood stumpage is counted in green tons, cubic feet or cords. (A cord is a measure of volume, not weight, that is 8' L x 4' H x 4' W. One cord equals 128 cubic feet, or 1,536 board feet. A cord's weight varies according to the species and its water content.)

Wood weight is greatly affected by moisture content, diameter size and tree species. A forester's cruise of a tract's tonnage is based on just-cut **green wood**, which contains a great deal of water weight. A cubic foot of green oak at 85 percent moisture content, for example, contains about 3.5 gallons of water (about 28 pounds), about half its total weight. The same cubic foot dried to a 12 percent moisture content contains about .5 gallons, or about four pounds of water. Smaller-diameter trees weigh more per cubic foot than larger-diameter trees because less of their mass is found in the dry, non-living heartwood and more of it is the outside sapwood that transports sap (water) from roots to leaves. Outside wood is heavier than heartwood, and the smaller diameter trees have proportionally more sapwood to heartwood than the larger diameter trees. Ten cubic feet of 8" DBH red oak may weigh 25 percent more than ten cubic feet of 22" DBH red oak.

Each tree species has its own green weight per unit of volume. One cubic foot of generic oak can weigh 50 pounds. A 2,000-pound ton of this oak, therefore, would equal 20 cubic feet, about 16 percent of one cord. One of these cords would equal 3.2 tons, or 6,400 pounds. The next time you order a cord of green oak for the fireplace, you now know about what it weighs. Your back should instruct your brain to pay the firewood vendor for the trouble of stacking it where you want. Dried, or seasoned, firewood, of course, weighs less than green. It is also considerably easier to burn, more efficient and produces less creosote. It also costs more, as it should.

A forester's cruise may show a tract containing both merchantable sawtimber and pulpwood. The sawtimber is found in the sawtimber logs. Pulp is found in the smaller diameters, cull trees that don't qualify as sawtimber and in the tops of the sawtimber trees. The heart of a sawtimber cruise is to disaggregate the sampled volume by species and diameter class to determine its fair market value. In contrast, a pulpwood tract is cruised to include and aggregate as much merchantable fiber as possible. With pulp, all trees are pitched into the same pot. Volume matters, not quality.

When the forester completes his fieldwork, he tallies all the plot volumes for sawtimber by species and in diameter classes at and exceeding his merchantability definition. He then multiplies each merchantable volume by the appropriate species price. When totaled, this provides a projected dollar value of the merchantable sawtimber volume for the landowner from a competitive sale.

The forester might also value separately the smaller-diameter sawtimber, which is called **premerchantable timber**, or just "**premerch**." Stumpage buyers are not interested in premerch unless a clearcut is planned, in which case, the forester would typically estimate the volume of everything that can be sold. The forester can project the volumes of merchantable timber by species currently in the premerch at various future points. This helps the landowner figure what timber he will have available for sale down the road. The cruise may also separately estimate the market value of pulp or firewood.

For tax purposes, the value of the merchantable timber (of all types) at the time a buyer like you acquires the property is referred to as the **timber base**. This value shapes the taxpayer's **basis in the timber**. If the merchantable timber value equals the purchase price of the property, you still have to allocate your basis between land and timber. Total basis will equal the buyer's gross purchase price plus other allowable expenses. Basis is adjusted over time in both land and timber, according to what the taxpayer does and does not do.

Merchantable timber value can also be thought of as the property's **present timber value (PTV)**. The tract's premerch represents its **future timber value (FTV)**. Determining PTV, also referred to as merchantable timber value, is discussed in the following chapter.

CONSULTING FORESTERS

If you are thinking about purchasing wooded property, you should hire a **consulting forester** to develop information about the timber's value, both present and future. This is a necessary part of pre-purchase scoping of timber-bearing property. The forester may need to do no more than a quick walk-through to determine whether a cruise is warranted.

Consulting foresters are independent, private-sector consultants, most of whom hold four-year forestry degrees and participate in continuing-education seminars. As independent contractors, they may provide services to both timber sellers and buyers (though not at the same time in the same deal without mutual consent). Foresters may be sole practitioners or organized into consulting practices.

There are two national professional societies in the United States: Association of Consulting Foresters (ACF) and the Society of American Foresters (SAF). SAF admits non-foresters and is the larger of the two. SAF produces several publications and can be reached at 5400 Grosvenor Lane, Bethesda, MD, 20814; 1-866-897-8720; 301-897-3690 FAX; www.safnet.org. To locate a SAF forester, go to the SAF website, click on "Certified Forester," then click on "Search Online Find a Certified Forester in Your Area." My impression is that the ACF is primarily boots-on-the-ground foresters, either self-employed or in small group practices. SAF foresters seem to handle the larger tracts and work with the larger clients. My experience with ACF foresters has been generally positive. I would advise an owner of a small tract (less than 500 acres) to look for a full-time, experienced sole practitioner with a four-year degree who has an active practice in the area of your target property. You can find an ACF forester through its website, www.acf-foresters.com, or at the Association of Consulting Foresters of America, Inc., 732 North Washington Street, Suite 4-A, Alexandria, Virginia, 22314-1921; 703-548-0990; 703-548-6395 FAX; e-mail: director@acf-foresters.com. The ACF's Code of Ethics is available on its web site. Information on selecting a consulting forester is available from A Consumer's Guide to Consulting Foresters at www.ces.ncsu.edu/nreos/forest/woodland/won-06.html; Questions About Forestry and Forestland? Ask a Consulting Forester at www.wvu.edu/~agexten/forestry/forest.htm; and Selecting the Right Professional Forester at www.wvu.edu/~exten/depts/af/ahc/select.pdf.

Finding a private consulting forester is not difficult, though finding one who is a good fit for you may be a bit harder.

Private foresters may be found in the phone book's Yellow Pages under foresters—consulting, foresters, forestry consultants or possibly timber management. You will not find forestry consultants under "tree service," because they are not tree surgeons, tree removers or stump grinders. Forestry consultants work with timber on woodlands; arborists work with individual or small groups of trees. In my area at least most working field foresters/consultants do not advertise in the phone book because they get too many calls for tree work. You can also get referrals from local real-estate agents, bankers, lawyers and surveyors. As with all other references, ask your source the context in which he has worked with the recommended forester.

Public foresters can recommend private foresters. The **National Association of State Foresters (NASF)** represents the directors of state forestry agencies from all 50 states and America's eight territories. These agencies—which call themselves "state foresters"—provide advice and financial assistance to the ten million non-industrial private forest landowners (NIPFs) who provide more than 70 percent of the country's wood supply. The NASF website (www.stateforesters.org) provides links to all the departments or divisions of state government responsible for public forestry and the regulation of private forestry. Call the forestry department/division listed in the phone book in the county where your target property is found to find out what services are available to a buyer as well as owners. Most states now have on their sites a list of approved private consulting foresters, including areas of expertise and contact information. Contact several foresters who do cruises and timber appraisals in your target county.

The NASF website provides a state-by-state directory, including a contact person, address, phone and fax. (See NASF, 444 North Capitol Street, N.W., Suite 540, Washington, D.C., 2001; 202-624-5415; 202-624-5407 FAX; e-mail: nasf@sso.org). Program information is available for NIPFs from NASF on forest health management, fire protection and cooperative forestry, such as the Forest Stewardship Program and Stewardship Incentives Program described below. Publications are available, and forestry links are provided.

The state forester in your target county—who is called the **county forester**—will talk to buyers about local stumpage prices and timber characteristics in the area of the target property. If the local forester knows the target property, he may share some of that knowledge. Buyers should not treat a state forester as a free, on-demand consulting service. But you can certainly ask timber-orientation questions without violating the privacy of the owner of the target property. If the seller has a forest-management plan with the state, you should ask the seller for a copy.

Among the points of information that would be appropriate for you to ask a county forester are those like the following:

- Provide a list of private foresters who work in the target-property's general area

- A list of local timber buyers and loggers (Perhaps you can get him to tell you which buyers and loggers to avoid.)

- Local stumpage price data for private sales. (Public sales have a different cost structure than private sales, so stumpage prices on national forest land, for instance, are not comparable to private sales.) If he has no data, ask what his sense is of local species prices. Many states collect and tabulate stumpage prices. Type in "stumpage prices, state" in an Internet search engine.

- Local price cycles

- Forest health issues in the area

- State timber-taxation policies

- Landowner obligations under the state's Best Management Practices (BMPs)

- Public programs available to private forest landowners (see below)

Come to the county forester's office with at least a tax map, which shows very approximate boundaries and acreage. Better than a tax map is an aerial photo and/or topographical map with inscribed boundaries. The aerial photo with boundaries should be available through the local office of the USDA's Farm Service Agency. If you don't have a professionally done topo with boundaries, you can work up a very rough approximation using the deed's legal description, tax map and a downloaded topo from www.topozone.com or a USGS topo map. Remember you're a buyer, not a landowner; don't wear out your welcome. I have found that four of five county foresters whom I've called as an out-of-state buyer have been reasonably helpful; two of five have provided me with sufficient information to let me screen out properties; one of five was uncooperative.

I would add one cautionary note about advice. Be aware that a recommendation for a private consulting forester coming from a county (state) forester in your target area may be biased toward those of his colleagues who have recently retired from the state forestry agency, particularly the office shared with the person with whom you're now talking. I have encountered this pattern three times in three states. This doesn't mean that the recommended forester is bad. It does usually mean that he has less experience as a private consultant in the rough and tumble of getting his clients the best price for their timber. I resist "steering" of this sort. My preference would be a consultant who has made his living for a number of years in the private sector doing walk-throughs, cruises, forest-management plans and sales for individual landowners. I would favor a consultant with this profile over a retired public forester because the latter will have less hands-on experience with actual timber markets and local players. I also appreciate a forester who is knowledgeable about timber taxation. You can ask the county forester for referrals to consultants whose careers have been principally spent with private clients.

In Virginia, the Department of Forestry (VADOF) provides the following services to *landowners* (not buyers) at no charge:

- prepares a forest-management plan (includes a resource inventory—a cruise plus—of tree species, composition, age, merchantability, growth rate and wildlife habitat conditions)

- prepares map showing location of various timber types (**stands**), land uses and natural features

- advises on what timber to sell and when to sell it

- provides list of consulting (fee-for-service) private foresters

- provides list of timber buyers

- advises on timber-sale contracts

- assists on tree planting

- advises on erosion-control practices

- recommends Best Management Practices to landowner (and loggers) related to preserving streamside buffer zones, skid-road layout, wetlands protection and the like

- advises on Seed Tree Law requirements (Virginia law requires leaving uncut a certain number of cone-bearing trees when certain conifers comprise ten percent or more of an acre's trees; other provisions as well)

- advises and coordinates with public cost-share/assistance programs

- provides technical assistance on managing natural resources—fish and wildlife habitat, soil and water, recreation and forestry

This is the official scope of the VADOF's "free" advice to forest landowners. The agency does not provide timber cruises for sales purposes or manage timber sales for private landowners.

As a buyer, I've asked my state forester for price information from time to time as well as his opinion about timber quality in a particular area where a target property was located. As a forest landowner, I've asked him to visit my property for the purpose of giving me advice about controlling ferns that were preventing hardwood regeneration and controlling road erosion.

Apart from these county foresters, you can check with the county extension agent or an **extension forester** who is employed in the forestry department at the state's land-grant university. Call the county extension agent—often listed in the phone book as (state name) Cooperative Extension—to obtain a recommendation and further leads. Extension foresters may be familiar with private consulting foresters in your area. The forestry professors who teach in these universities often conduct seminars and produce research that is of interest to private timberland owners.

Your local public/county forester will not give you, a buyer, a written evaluation of the target property's timber or do a cruise. If a management plan is in place for the property as part of a conservation or tax-relief program, he may provide that document to a buyer with the owner's permission. These plans generally include a base-line cruise at the time the property is enrolled. In my case, a phone chat with the county forester is a good, free first stop for a buyer. If you buy the land without having done a cruise, the county forester will do a walk-through of your property and give you a rough sense of its stumpage and current value.

Virginia has begun the Forest Mentor Network, which is a state-wide listing of experienced forest landowners who are willing to provide less-experienced owners with information and advice (www.cnr.vt.edu/forestupdate). Other states may have similar networks that a buyer/landowner can access. Faculty in the forestry department in the land-grant university are also available to the general public for short consultations and question-asking.

More than 30 states have a privately organized association of non-industrial, private forestland owners, which provides information and represents the group's interests on landowner rights, forestry practices, taxation, environmental policies and related policy concerns. A state's **forest landowner association** (which works with the state's cooperative extension service) might provide a reference for a private consultant, among other services. The national umbrella group for these state associations is the **National Woodland Owners Association** (374 Maple Ave. East, Suite 310, Vienna, Virginia, 22180; 703-255-2700; www.nationalwoodlands.org). In aggregate, the roughly eight million small private forestland owners account for almost 60 percent (about 288 million acres) of U.S. timberland, according to NWOA President Keith Argow. NWOA membership entitles a landowner to an "introductory visit from a consulting forester through the **National Forestry Association (NFA)**, a national professional forester referral program for private forestland owners. The NWOA's consulting assistance would not be available to you as a buyer when you are scoping a target property, but referrals would be.

A buyer needs to be aware that there are two other types of foresters who are available to provide opinions about the value of a property's timber. Both the **independent timber buyer** and the **industrial forester** are always looking for timberlands.

The independent timber buyer has been buying and selling timber and timberland for a long time. He's probably been a logger and may have run a sawmill at some point. These individuals are **skilled eyeballers,** and they have often made a living by being able to walk through a parcel of land, estimate its merchantable timber value and negotiate a purchase for a price that allows them to sell the timber and some or all of the cutover land for a profit. You can learn an enormous amount of dirt knowledge from them, but you must keep in mind that they are as a rule looking to make their own deals, not helping you make yours.

Do not take one of these guys on a target property to help you scope its timber. The reason not to do walk-throughs with local eyeballers is not for their lack of expertise but because of it. If the deal is good, they will have a purchase offer in front of the seller before you arrive home on Sunday evening. For the same reason, I would advise against hiring a friendly, independent logger to help you evaluate your target property. The temptation to **"backdoor you"** is too great.

You may also encounter an **industrial forester** who is employed by a sawmill or wood-products corporation. The sawmill forester will be looking to buy timberland or just timber on the stump. Don't fold him into your scoping. The wood-products forester is looking to enroll timberland in his company's stewardship program. Most large wood-products companies will provide a landowner with a complete, updated forestry plan for his property according to the owner's objectives. In return for doing periodic cruises and other management services, the corporation has first rights—sometimes exclusive rights—over a long term to cut that portion of the timber scheduled for cutting in line with the plan. The company may have a "matching clause" in the landowner's contract that allows it to take the timber as long as it equals any other genuine offer. (Your sister, a student of 1960s' pharmacology in the East Village, the one with the purple hair, can give you a bid of $100,000 for your $25,000 timber tract, but don't expect the Georgia-Pacific crewcuts to match it.) If you're interested in working with a private company on a stewardship plan, I would approach them as a landowner, not as a buyer. You will get "free" management services and a guaranteed market from the industrial forester, but you may find yourself locked into a plan that does not suit your objectives and does not get you the most money for your timber. If you decide as a landowner to enroll in an industrial forestry program, read the discussion of the pros and cons in Beattie *et al.*, Working with Your Woodland, pp. 88-92, which includes a sample contract.

In addition to providing a market for his timber, a landowner should expect an industrial program to perform most, if not all, of the following tasks: timber cruise every ten to 20 years, periodic plan revisions, help with obtaining cost-share assistance from public agencies, boundary identification (which may include a survey and on-the-ground marking), plantings, timber stand improvements, road development (including culverts/bridge if warranted), stand protection (spraying), thinning to enhance future timber value, tax advice, etc. If you, as a buyer, become interested in land that is enrolled in an industrial forestry program, make sure to review the owner's contract. If the contract "runs with the land" for a certain number of years, you, as the new owner, will be stuck with it until it expires.

Independent consulting foresters travel, so don't be afraid to cast your net within a three- or four-hour drive of the property. On large tracts, foresters will drive a day each way—on your nickel. With three or four names in hand, interview each forester, preferably in person. (This is not wasted time; this is "quality" time. You will learn an enormous amount. You're looking to establish a long-term relationship with a forester who will help you manage your woodland.)

As a buyer, you will want a forester to do either a **walk-through** or a **timber cruise** of a target property that looks to you as if it has big trees and is ten acres or more. The forester you're interviewing may already know the property that you're scoping and can give you a thumbnail sketch of its timbering history and current prospects. A walk-through will give you the forester's informed impression of timber volume, species mix and quality. A walk-through will determine whether the expense of a cruise is justified.

In screening foresters to help you scope a target property, I would ask questions of the following type:

- Education—four-year forestry degree, two-year forestry degree; continuing education seminars on timber taxation?

- Experience
  - how long on his own as a consultant? before that?
  - types of work he does (cruises for owners/buyers; negotiated sales; competitively bid sales; plan development; management)
  - types of timber he usually sells (hardwood sawtimber; pine sawtimber; veneer; hardwood pulp; pine pulp; other)
  - has he worked with private owners who had objectives like yours?
  - how many (roughly) timber sales has he managed for private clients during the last year, last five years?
  - smallest, biggest, average dollar value of these sales?
  - how often does he manage timber sales in the area (county) of the target property

- Conflicts—does he have any personal or professional conflicts with conducting a cruise for you on this particular target property?

- Fees—how much does he charge for a walk-through; a cruise?

- References—references of several clients like you with whom he has worked during the last three years

It is very important for you to get a fix on the **forester's ethics**. The forester that you hire must be loyal to you and your interests. He must "ride for your brand." While he will have continuing relations with stumpage buyers, he must put your interests above his own. The forester you want will have forthright and familiar relations with buyers, but not "sweetheart" arrangements or anything that smacks of "steering" sales to a particular stumpage buyer. Do not agree to any arrangement where your consultant will also be paid by the stumpage buyer, particularly when a consultant says that it will "save you money on my fee." Stumpage (or timber) buyers are permanent members of your consultant's professional community while you may be a one-time visitor. Any arrangement that dilutes your consultant's loyalty to you will, in my opinion, work against you.

Ask the forester whether he has any conflicts of interest in working for you on this particular job. Don't be shy about this. He may have worked for the land seller in the past; he may even have done a cruise on the target property for the land seller. You must have complete confidence in the forester's ethics and loyalty to you. Scratch a name if you sense a forester sliding around. Ask his references whether his cruise value was roughly what they received from the sale. (When a sale occurs within a couple of months of a cruise, the cruise prices should be about the same as the actual sales prices, allowing for changes in market conditions.) If a significant divergence occurred, ask both the reference and the forester for an explanation. Avoid foresters who consistently value stumpage higher than their sales bring; this can bruise a buyer badly. I know several foresters whose cruises overestimate actual merchantable value fairly consistently. Sellers like to hand their cruises to gullible buyers.

Your forester's job for your scoping is to give you an accurate estimate of the merchantable timber value on a target property and alert you to issues that might complicate either a quick timber sale or longer-term management plan. This means that he has to think like a timber buyer, evaluating the standing timber as buyers will when they cruise the tract. When you retain him to manage your timber sale for you, his job is to package the timber in a way that gets the most money for you consistent with your other management objectives. No other interest should be allowed to confuse that simple obligation. When a consultant is helping you scope a property in advance of submitting a purchase offer, he should give you a good-faith and reasonably accurate estimate of the tract's timber volumes, species mix and likely (current) stumpage prices. Don't nickel-and-dime the consultant on his travel time or hourly rate. Don't cloud his fidelity to your interests. Authorize him to "put in enough plots" to give him full confidence in his sample-based estimates. Make sure that he understands that you don't want his choice of methods to inflate his estimates of volumes and prices. If anything, you want his timber cruise to be conservative about volumes and values so that your offer for the property is in line with the money you would net from a quick sale of the merchantable timber. Surprise in timber sales should always fall on the upside.

Tell your forester to cruise the target property using the same **log scale and cruise methodology** that are used by the stumpage buyers he will be contacting on your behalf. A log scale, or log rule, is a matrix that provides an estimate of the number of board feet (volume) in trees of various diameters (DBH) and heights (length of sawtimber logs that can be cut from each tree). Similar formulas are used to estimate green tonnage by species. You want to avoid a situation where your forester prepares a cruise for you prior to purchase that applies the International Scale (which finds more volume in certain diameter classes) while local stumpage buyers cruise with either the Doyle Scale (which finds less volume) or a local/regional scale. A tract that scales out $100,000 in stumpage value on the International Scale may sell $75,000 worth of stumpage, or less, to buyers using the Doyle Scale.

Ask the foresters you interview for their hourly rates and fee schedules. These will apply to time spent on your behalf—providing telephone consultations, walk-throughs, cruises, courthouse research, marking boundaries and the like. You should also expect to pay a mileage charge and reimburse for food and lodging expenses. Hourly rates vary by region and by consultant, with the larger firms charging higher rates. In my area, hourly rates are in the $50 range. On large jobs—say, more than 1,000 acres—an individual consultant will often team up with one or more subcontractors to get the work done in a timely manner. Since cruising is a highly site-specific process—where the time involved depends on the number of plots put in, difficulty of the terrain and reliability of the boundaries—you will probably not find consultants offering a flat cruise fee or one based on the number of acres. You might, however, find a consultant who bases his cruise fee on the number of plots he puts in. In general, it's reasonable to assume that a forester can cruise 100-200 acres in eight hours on the site. (That generalization is tossed out if he has to spend three or four hours trying to establish boundary lines.) He will also spend several hours in advance of the field cruise, plotting boundaries on a topographical map using the calls from a survey or deed and, if needed, checking boundary descriptions in the deedwork. The forester must make sure that he is not cruising—and selling—trees on neighboring property. This requires that he has confidence in the written description of the property's boundaries and that he is able to establish these boundaries on the ground. (As part of a timber sale, the consultant will flag the boundaries so that the logger does not take trees from the neighbors.) He will also spend several more hours after the field work tallying his volumes, determining current prices, drawing a map of the property that locates different stands and preparing his report. A 100-200-acre cruise on moderate topography with unambiguous boundaries would typically involve about two to four consultant days. (See, also, Fees and Services of Consulting Foresters in Mississippi at www.ext.msstate.edu/anr/forestry/forestinfo/mtn13c.html. Check with the county extension service in your state for state or regional publications on consultant fees.)

A walk-through and a cruise are paid on an hourly basis with expenses. If you choose to have the forester manage a timber sale for you, he will typically charge a percentage of your gross sale income. The percentage fluctuates according to the type of sale he conducts. A **marked sale**—where every tree to be sold is painted and its merchantable volume tallied tree by tree, not estimated—involves a timber-owner-paid fee of ten percent in my region. An unmarked sale where, for example, all trees 18" DBH and larger are being sold (but they're not marked) should cost the landowner less, because the forester has much less time involved. Your forester will recommend a timber-sale strategy based on the type of timber you have and local market practices. I've seen foresters paid so many cents per ton and so many cents per cord as well. I've always done well paying my forester a ten percent fee to conduct a competitively bid marked sale for hardwood sawtimber.

If you have little experience with forestry and logging and you're looking at tracts with substantial timber, you might want to hire a forester for a day to show you some of his recent jobs as well as ones that were cut five and ten years ago. You'll want to get an idea of what's involved during a logging job as well as the look of one that has some age on it. Ask to see a job whose objectives were similar to yours. If you're willing to spend $75,000 or more on rural property, you will be well-served to spend a small amount on a consulting forester in advance of making an offer. You will learn an enormous amount by walking through woods with a forester.

A cruise, in my unprofessional opinion, must be done on the ground when dealing with HW tracts smaller than 2,000 acres. Estimates based on aerial or satellite photos may be able to give you a general estimate of timber volume, but neither can provide a reasonable idea of the quality of the volume, which is what determines financial value of HW sawtimber. Global Positioning System (GPS) technology is now capable of generating volume estimates by species. In some circumstances—winter conditions in a deciduous forest, for example—a buyer might feel comfortable borrowing a large sum based on the results of this technology. I'm not there yet for two reasons: first, I want a forester's on-the-ground, site-specific judgment, the more specific and detailed the better; and second, I don't see any cost advantage at this time (early 2000s) on tracts of 1,000 acres or less. A third reason I suppose is that I am old enough to be suspicious of labor-saving technology. While satellite photography can produce photographs that accurately display things no bigger than a wastebasket, I don't feel confident that it can reveal the **quality indicators** that would be immediately apparent to a forester. Quality indicators are often tiny—an egg mass of the gypsy moth is the size of a finger joint; a vertical structural flaw in a tree's bole can halve the value of a butt log; a small opening at the base of a large chestnut oak is often a sign of hollowness. I doubt that current technology can distinguish among a 20" DBH veneer-quality black cherry worth $4 per board foot, a 20" DBH cherry that is sawtimber quality at $1.50 per board foot and a 20" DBH cherry with black sap disease, which in serious cases may make the tree not worth the expense to cut it. Foresters on the ground are trained to catch these differences. Given the relative inexpensiveness of getting a highly qualified and experienced forester to cruise a property, I see no reason at the present time to substitute technological wizardry for human judgment. The satellite techniques are more suited to tracts of several thousand acres and more, particularly one-species tracts.

As a buyer, you may or may not have a written contract with a consultant you've hired to provide advice and a cruise as part of your scoping. If you become the owner and decide that you want the forester to work up a management plan and/or conduct a timber sale as your agent, you'll need a written consultant contract, a sample of which appears in Chapter 23.

You will want the consultant contract to spell out the tasks you want him to do, the work products (if any) that he produces at the end of each task, method of payment and schedule, time-frame and deadlines. Another sample contract between owner and consultant is found in Beattie *et al.*, Working With Your Woodland, pp. 84-88. This owner-consultant contract is not a **timber-sale contract**, which is the contract between you, the owner of the land, and the buyer of your stumpage. (When screening consultants, ask to see the timber-sale contract he will want you to sign as a timber-selling client. Compare it with the sample timber-sale contract in Chapter 23.)

The buyer who is employing a consulting forester to scope the timber value of a target property should discuss with him the tasks that they agree will be needed to accomplish his objectives. The consultant will have a good idea of what you need even if you, as an inexperienced timberland buyer, are a little vague. Working together, develop a set of tasks that are appropriate for the particular property you're researching. These may include some or all of the following:

- **confirm to the extent possible the tract's boundaries in the deedwork and on the ground.** In the best case, you will have the owner's deed with an accurate boundary description, recorded survey and marked boundary lines. Often, you will have none of these. The forester should be able to dig out of the deedwork enough of a usable deed description to do a cruise. If he finds a big uncertainty, he'll tell you; you may have to get a surveyor involved. Once the forester has the deed description, often referred to as "the calls," he can put them into his computer program and print them out as boundary lines on a topographical map. Using that map, he should be able to locate with reasonable certainty the boundary lines on the ground.

- **alert the buyer to any problem (s) found in the boundary research**, such as lack of usable description; vague calls (a line running "from here to the top of Jones's hill"); nonexistent corners (the big red oak has disappeared), or corners that can't be found; lack of congruence between the deed descriptions and what is found on the ground (this can mean your target property is encroaching on a neighbor, or vice versa); a "bad" call (e.g., a directional call that is clearly wrong, often due to a typographical error such as NE written in the deed as SE, or a numerical transposition such as 1,345.56 feet written as 1,453.56 feet).

- **alert the buyer when boundary lines cannot be imposed on a topographical map because the deed's calls fail to close (see below)**

- **provide the buyer with a timber cruise** that disaggregates volumes by two-inch DBH classes and species on tracts where hardwood sawtimber is present, and by tons or cords where those measures are appropriate for the local market. (The forester will tell you the most appropriate way for organizing the cruise.) The forester may advise a walk-through to determine whether a cruise is warranted.

- **alert the buyer to any problems affecting health and quality of the timber stand**, such as infestations, disease and damage from fire, ice or wind, that will discount selling price

- **use the log scale that is used by likely timber buyers** (The consultant will know which log scale is most appropriate for the timber on the target property.)

- **put in a sufficient number of plots to provide a reasonably accurate sampling of the tract's timber**

- **separate sawtimber volume from pulp volume** if that separation is appropriate for the tract and/or the local market

- **exclude** from his estimates of timber volumes and calculation of values all timber that is found on **inoperable acreage**, such as steep slopes, wetlands, streamside buffer zones and other acreage that is inaccessible, economically unfeasible or limited by law.

- **prepare a topographical map** showing tract boundaries and areas within the tract (stands) where he's cruised merchantable timber.

- **gather sufficient information on local timber prices** to allow the consultant to make reasonably accurate projections of likely timber-sale revenue as of the cruise date.

- **identify any problems** that an owner should anticipate in marketing his timber (such as, no deeded right of way; need to cross a stream; need to build bridge; need to improve access road; overlapping claims to a portion of the property; environmentally sensitive areas, and so on

- **suggest a time-frame** for selling the tract's timber

- **provide a general opinion about future timber value**, based on the forester's projections of volume growth, ingrowth and price trends

- **alert buyer to any administrative or regulatory factors** that would constrain timbering or prohibit it from occurring in certain places on the property

- **inform buyer if he's expected to secure timbering-related permits**

- **write summary report of findings and recommendations**

I've worked up this generic list of tasks to help the reader understand what a forester will be doing rather than to help a consulting forester do his job. Your forester will know what to do for you even if you're not quite sure. You may want to formalize your understanding with your forester in a contract, but that may not be necessary. You should, however, have a reasonable idea of the level of detail and amount of work you will get for your money.

Consulting foresters need to be able to establish the **boundaries** of your target property on the ground. If boundary lines cannot be established with reasonable certainty, the forester may cruise acreage that the seller does not own or exclude valuable wooded acreage that he does. Foresters know how to do basic deed research and then apply a deed description to a topographical map. With that done, they should be able to locate boundaries in the field, whether they are well marked or not. Foresters now use a computer program, such as, Forest and Resource Management System Software (Farms), to draw deed boundaries on a topographical map. Older foresters can do this by hand. If you are inclined, you can obtain a topographical map and, using the deed's calls, mark boundaries with a transparent mapping compass and a set of engineering scales in feet, rods (1 rod = 16.5 feet) and chains (1 surveyor or Gunter's chain = 66 feet; 1 engineer's chain = 100 feet). Linear boundary measurements are usually given in feet, but old deeds often used rods, perches and chains. (The compass and scales together cost less than $50. You will want to use this compass in the woods if you're locating boundaries with the map.)

The forester's program will also reveal whether the property's **calls close**, that is, the deed's compass directions and linear measurements begin and end at the same point. If the calls close, the program can then easily determine the acreage within them. When calls don't close, you may or may not be facing a major problem. Sometimes the error is simply typographical, and the boundaries on the ground are correct as they stand. The error may be so minor that it falls within the acceptable margin of error. In other cases, a failure to close can mean the property is short of the advertised acreage. These surveying issues are discussed fully in Chapter 17.

If your forester identifies a boundary problem that works against your interest and is too much for him to resolve, you could hire a surveyor to give you an opinion as part of your scoping. Alternatively, you could put a **boundary contingency** in your purchase offer. This can take several forms. One version looks like this:

> **Buyer's offer is contingent on having a licensed surveyor or other qualified professional acceptable to Buyer confirm though methods accepted in the surveying profession Seller's acreage to be conveyed. Buyer shall arrange and pay for this work.**
>
> **Buyer will have _____ calendar/business days to complete this work. If the acreage cannot be confirmed, or is less than than the acreage referred to in this purchase offer, or is in any other way unacceptable to Buyer, he may withdraw his offer without penalty and his deposit shall be returned in full within five calendar days.**

This contingency can involve the expense of a survey in the worst case, so I would insert it as a last resort. The surveyor is often able to narrow the problem to a particular line or even a particular part of a line, so his field work is limited to that section. If you have not had a forester or surveyor run the calls through his program prior to your offer, use this contingency to allow this to be done after the contract has been signed. It protects you from your lack of due diligence. The better practice, of course, is get the acreage figured out prior to submitting an offer. A boundary contingency is usually paid by the buyer. You can, of course, propose cost-sharing. Sellers are, as a rule, reluctant to help pay for this work. In most cases, I've found that a survey is not needed to reach the level of certainty, or lack thereof, sufficient for me to decide whether or not to proceed with a purchase.

A word or two about **stumpage prices**. A buyer depends on his consulting forester to estimate both the merchantable timber volume on the target tract and the current prices stumpage buyers are paying for these species. The forester's estimate of current stumpage prices for a target tract are shaped by factors unique to the timber there as well as market conditions operating on each stumpage buyer, locally and beyond. You should be aware that stumpages prices also are adjusted seasonally for hardwoods, so that a price that was good in September may be lower in March, even with demand and interest rates unchanged. Price bids will also be affected by any restrictions you impose on the logging. If, for instance, you insist that the logger lop all slash to minimize visual impact, you can expect steeply discounted bids. Most timber sales are entirely local, but certain types of timber fetch a higher price if marketed to exporters. Veneer logs often find their best price in the export market as does a specialty wood, paulowinia (or princess tree), used in Japan. In such cases, the forester may segregate export-oriented trees and market them separately.

A forester's **price multiplier** for each species is an amalgam of the prices he's been able to gather through a telephone survey of likely buyers. Some mills are more forthcoming about their price list than others. In his research, the forester may discover that a particular species is bringing record highs while another is markedly below a fair price. This information may shape his sale strategy: the high-priced species will be sold, but the other will be withheld for a future sale. He needs to package enough volume to encourage competitive bids. He may or may not decide to include low-value species in his high-value sale. The alternative might be to have sequential sales: the first for the high-value species, the second for everything else that you want cut. His strategy depends on what his research reveals. And that research is based on years of developing contacts and conducting sales. Track record means a lot when a forester calls a stumpage-buying mill and asks about prices. You can get a feel for recent stumpage prices from your forester before he starts his research, but he should update his price information when he calculates stumpage values for your cruise.

Thirty-six states report stumpage prices, and some of this information is free to the public. Information on stumpage prices is available at www.rtp.srs.fs.fed.us/econ/data/prices/sources.htm, a site that has links to the individual in each state who tracks these prices. (Contacts for this website are: Dr. Barry N. Rosen, Zicklin School of Business, Baruch College, The City University of New York, New York, New York, 10010, 212-802-6493; and Dr. H. Fred Kaiser, Staff Director, Resource Valuation and Use Research, USDA-Forest Service, 201 14th St., N.W., Washington, D.C., 20250, 202-205-1032.) Private services also offer stumpage prices, which are generally regional. In the South/Southeast, for example, you can buy reports from Timber Mart-South, The University of Georgia's Daniel B. Warnell School of Forest Resources, Athens, Georgia, 30602-2152; 706-542-4756; FAX 706-542-1670; e-mail: tmart@uga.cc.uga.edu; and Forest2Market, 15720 John J. Delaney Drive, Suite 300, Charlotte, North Carolina, 28277; 704-357-0110; www.forest2market.com. Timber Mart-South posts its recent newsletters and stumpage prices on its website, www.tmart-south.com. Forest2Market provides some price data on its website. In the South, for example, Timber Mart-South reported that Second Quarter, 2004 stumpage prices averaged $37.04 p/ton for pine sawtimber, $22.69 p/ton for pine chip-n-saw, $6.35 p/ton for pine pulpwood, $18.91 p/ton for hardwood sawtimber, and $5.43 p/ton for hardwood pulpwood.

Stumpage price data are aggregated for states and sub-state regions. For that reason, this information will get you in the right ballpark but will not zero in on the likely bid prices for your target property's package of merchantable timber in its local market. Published stumpage prices are an average, which reflect a range of quality. The New York state "Stumpage Price Report" for Summer, 2005 in area F, one of 12 price-and-reporting areas in the state, showed an average price for black cherry sawtimber (including veneer) on the International 1/4" Scale of $770/mbf, with reported prices ranging from $100/mbf to $1,400/mbf. The 1/4" in this scale refers to the presumed width, or kerf, of the saw blade; a thinner blade yields more lumber.

The forester's job is to determine the likeliest price species by species for the target property's merchantable timber, given that local buyers can vary by 50 percent or more on their prices and bids. Aggregated-and-averaged published stumpage-price data are useful as recent background, but neither you nor your forester should use this average price in scoping the value of a tract's HW sawtimber. You can use published state or sub-regional data with more confidence when valuing HW pulp and pine pulp, because the price of these feedstocks are not dependent on individual species and variations in quality. Prices for pulp stumpage rise and fall with the mix of supply and demand for the products for which they are used. Your consultant is your best source of current local prices in relation to a specific target property's timber.

Pricing stumpage is not a do-it-yourself job; stumpage buyers may or may not tell a landowner their current prices, may or may not tell them their true prices and may or may not give prices that fit the timber on the target property. It's easy for a buyer to quote you a high price on the phone and then offer you a low price when you bring your logs to his mill, because of "quality issues." If you call out of the blue, stumpage buyers will try to work their own deal for any timber you have in your sights.

You may find reference to prices for "**logs [by species] on the landing**." This is what a log buyer will pay once the trees are cut, skidded and sorted on the landowner's landing—a place where logging trucks can be safely loaded. It may or may not include loading onto the log buyer's trucks. Landing price is higher than stumpage price, because it must cover the logger's expenses. A landing price assumes that the landowner will work a deal with a logger whereby the logger is paid a percentage of the landing sales, or on a time basis, or so much per ton or one thousand board feet sold. Loggers will be far smarter than you about how to work such deals to favor their pocketbook. Don't sell stumpage this way, unless you have a consulting forester managing the process for you. It's possible to make more money selling timber as logs on a landing (grouped by species and quality) than from a lump-sum sale, but an inexperienced landowner will not have the resources and the knowledge necessary to organize the cutting and marketing to make this work.

You may find data that refers to **delivered price**. Stumpage price is the amount a timber buyer pays a landowner (timber seller) for standing trees. Delivered price is the amount a timber buyer/consumer (sawmill, paper plant, log yard) pays an independent timber-cutting logger for logs delivered to his facility. Delivered price will always be higher than stumpage price. You can roughly approximate stumpage price from delivered price by subtracting the approximate cost of cutting, hauling and profit from the latter. A state forester can estimate an average local cut-and-haul cost for this calculation. In late 2004, my local cut-and-haul cost ran about $22-$25 p/ton, including profit. But that figure varies with each logger according to his individual expenses, profit rate, equipment efficiency, fuel and labor costs, haulage distance (from logging site to mill), among other factors. If all else fails, cut the delivered price in half and that should get you in the stumpage-price ballpark for a mill.

Where an independent logger is buying stumpage, he may suggest to the timber seller—you—that his payment to you be based on **shares** (a percentage) of the price he obtains on delivery of your logs to the customer of his choosing. If his delivered price is $1,000, a 60-40 (him-you) shares format would give you $400, which, according to my ballpark rule of thumb is $100 less than the likely stumpage payment if sold to a sawmill. As general rules, I advise against working shares with a logger and also allowing timber-sale income to be based on delivered price. Avoid these arrangements. Too many things can work against the landowner in these formats.

The research done to date as well as my own experience suggest that a HW sawtimber seller like you or me nets the most through a **consultant-managed, competitively bid marked sale**, even after paying his fee. Your consultant could market your sale by sending out his cruise inventory, which, as you will recall, is a projected volume *estimate* based on systematic, impartial sampling. With HW sawtimber in a selective cut, the better method I've found is to conduct a **marked sale**, which is a tree-by-tree (actually a log-by-log tally, tree by tree) inventory of sale volume. A marked sale does not estimate volume as a forester does in a cruise. A marked sale's tally is as accurate a count of timber volume on the stump as there is. With a marked sale, the landowner knows exactly what he is selling. In a marked sale, the forester paints stump and butt every tree that is being sold. When a stumpage buyer goes through your property during the inspection period prior to bidding, he may do a simple walk-through, or a cruise, or a tree-by-tree tally to confirm your forester's numbers. The buyer's tally should be very close to your forester's.

A competitively bid marked sale on HW sawtimber should generate the most money for timber sellers sale in and sale out, though it is impossible to know how the results of a **sole-source negotiated sale** or **splitting revenue (shares) from delivered logs with a logger** would net from the same tract. If you believe that competition among buyers usually pushes price up, have your consultant conduct a competitively bid marked sale for hardwoods. The skill your forester brings to marking your timber—what he excludes and includes—into a sale package is well worth his fee. (See Ian A. Munn and E.C. Franklin, "Do Consultants Really Generate Higher Timber Prices," Research Notes Series, 1995, Number 84, Woodlot Forestry R&D Program, N.C. State University.) The National Woodland Owners Association states that "less than a quarter of all landowners use a forester when selling their timber." These non-users are in my opinion netting less as a group than they would had they used a forestry consultant to manage their sales. (See NationalForestry.Net, "Top Ten Issues," October 1, 2001; www.nationalwoodlands.org/ nwoa/topten.asp.)

When you're scoping a target property with timber, a forester's **walk-through** is enough to determine whether the expense of a cruise is justified. A walk-through will give him a quick impression of the tract's timber resources in the context of what he already knows of the area and its markets. His walk-through should be more involved than a quick look from an ATV, though I've seen a forester do an accurate job on 3,000 acres of mixed hardwoods in one day from an ATV. The forester needs to get off the property's roads every so often to see the timber between the roads, hidden in coves or beyond eyeball range. The best timber on a tract is often furthest in and hardest to get to. Foresters see more than you will, because they know what to look for. They'll note the age, size and species of stumps to determine when the last cutting was done. They will know the timber-growing productivity of the soils. The mix of species and the size and condition of the large-diameter trees will give them an idea of how much high-grading, if any, has occurred. Foresters tend to spend their careers in one area and tend to specialize in certain types of timber. One forester, for example, works primarily in mixed Appalachian hardwoods; another works mainly in pine. The forester you hire is likely to know a good bit about the timber characteristics of your property based on his experience conducting similar sales in the area. A forester's walk-through usually involves a day of his time and some expense money. It's a cost-effective scoping investment.

SELF-HELP

You will do a walk-through before your forester does. It's your judgment of the timber that will determine whether you ask him to do his walk-through.

You should have a topographical map with boundaries if at all possible. This will allow you to find the boundary lines. Carry a compass and learn how to use it. Carry a **tree (dendrology) book** with you so that you can identify the dominant species. Train yourself to be able to eyeball a 16" DBH. (I took my wife's sewing tape into the woods so that I could measure diameters. After a while, your eye can tell the difference between four-inch diameter classes, and later down to two inches.) Or measure 16" from the tip of your middle finger toward your elbow: most trees that are 16" and wider at chest height will have timber value, unless they are the culls left from earlier high-grading. Trees 16" and larger in the local high-value hardwood species are what you are looking for. If you find yourself noting a lot of large-diameter trees that are poorly formed (crooked/bent stems; big branches in the butt log) or otherwise defective, you are looking at timber that's been high-graded at least once. These big trees don't have merchantable value. Don't hire a forester to do a walk-through if what you see are high-value species 14" DBH and smaller and large cull trees of all species. That good timber isn't ready to cut. Pay particular attention to the first 12 to 16 feet of tree stem up from the stump. This **butt log** should be straight and free of big branches, rot, holes, barbed wire, nicks and other damage. Every so often stop and count the high-value species 16" DBH and larger trees within a a 100-foot-diameter circle. If you count five or more of these merchantable trees each time, it's worth calling in a forester for a walk-through. Wooded property with at least 2,500 bf per acre in merchantable HW sawtimber 16" DBH and larger can be cut immediately, and that, for the roughest of estimates, is about 12 to 25 merchantable trees per acre. (The actual number of board feet will depend on diameter, defect and the number of logs that can be cut from each tree. The more board feet per acre in merchantable sawtimber in high-value species, the more timber value.)

The **county soil's survey** should be part of your timber scoping kit. It's a free publication from the county's USDA's Farm Service Agency (FSA) and provides accurate information on what the county's soils are best suited for. If no copies are available, photocopy the **soils map** for your target property from the survey in the FSA's office or local library. Take the soils map with you onto the target property, because you will be able to see how the soils change from type to type on the ground. You should also copy the table—it's called something like Woodland Management and Productivity—that explains tree productivity for each soil type.

Tree productivity is expressed in a **site index (SI)** for each soil type and location. This number indicates the predicted height of a particular species, referred to as a "common tree," after a fixed number of growth years given its soil, topography and **aspect**. The last of these, "aspect," refers to the compass direction toward which a slope faces. Aspect is an important determinant of tree productivity. In HW stands, the highest SIs are found on north aspects because they are typically the coolest and wettest. The SI time period used for Appalachian hardwoods is usually 50 years; for pine, 20 years. A site index of 60 means that the marker hardwood species on that type of soil and location would be 60 feet tall in 50 years. This is a so-so site for hardwood; an SI of 85 is much better and represents a 25-foot taller tree for the same 50-year growing period. If you find an 85-foot-tall red oak on an SI of 85 when you do your walk-through, you could anticipate three mature cuts from its root system during the next 100 years, beginning immediately and assuming a stump sprout grows after each timbering. A site like this would provide money to pay down the cost of acquisition in your 30s, retirement income in your early 80s and income to your children when they're nearing retirement.

Each species will have its own SI for each soil type and location. The soil survey provides the SIs for three to five commonly found trees on each one. These are marker trees you should look for and find on each soil type. Since most properties are a patchwork of soil types, you will find the same species growing at different rates in different spots. A valuable species like northern red oak might have a site index of 45 on steep, shaley land facing south (which is the warmest and driest aspect) and an index of 85 on nearby limestone/sandstone soils in a wet cove on a north-facing slope. Two oaks of exactly the same diameter could have an age difference of 40 years. The younger tree on the SI 85 is likely to be taller, straighter and better quality. Put another way, a 50-year-old, 80-foot-tall red oak will have far more volume than its 50-foot-tall cousin, because it should have both a larger DBH and more merchantable logs in its longer stem. And, as a rule, the faster a hardwood gets to a merchantable DBH of 16 or 18, the less it's exposed to disease, insects and other natural conditions that can diminish its quality.

If you look at enough property, you'll soon develop an eye for soil types that will indicate the quality of the site for growing timber. Certain trees and plants typically grow on certain soils. Even where a county does not have a survey, you can use the soil classifications and site indices provided for a nearby county to gauge the timber-growing productivity of a target site by matching the target property's soils to the soil evaluations in the other county's survey. If you are unable to recognize a general soil type in the field by identifying aspect, common trees, stoniness and other factors, your consulting forester can do this on a walk-through. Both your consulting forester and the county (state) forester should be able to give you a general notion of SIs just by looking at a topographical map in light of their knowledge of timber-growing patterns in the area.

The information you are hiring a forester to produce is for your benefit, not the seller's. You have no obligation to share the forester's opinion or cruise numbers with the seller. There are occasions, however, when this information should be shared. If, for instance, your forester's cruise shows little merchantable timber value and the seller's opinion is the opposite, the insertion of an expert opinion may help you negotiate a mutually workable price. If the seller challenges the objectivity of your forester, you can suggest that he hire his own to do the work again. The seller's forester may be able to confirm your forester's work simply by checking the format and parameters of his cruise. If the seller's forester uses the same format and parameters as your forester, the results of his cruise should be about the same.

A different but related issue is whether or not to ask the owner for permission to have your forester do a walk-through or cruise of his property. You may not want to advertise that you are actively scoping the seller's timber, particularly if he thinks it's not worth much. The best rule, I think, is to provide notice to the seller that you want to have a more experienced person help you out; put it this way: "I'm interested in buying your property. Since a pretty good portion of it is woods, do you mind if I have someone else visit your property before I submit an offer?" I would always get permission if the seller lives near the target property. If the seller is absentee, it's probably immaterial to him. Some foresters may want explicit permission from the owner so as not to trespass, but that seems to me to be the exception. My experience has been that sellers rarely care about what buyers do on their own nickels to scope properties prior to submitting an offer. If a seller refuses permission for your forester to visit the property prior to submitting an offer, you might reasonably infer that the seller has puffed the merchantable value of his timber and doesn't want your forester to reveal it to you. If you feel that a seller is reluctant to have non-buyers on his property, you can suggest that you'd like to take another look, this time with a potential partner.

If you find a seller asking you to respect his privacy and do nothing to bring publicity to his property, be careful. A seller once insisted that I refrain from bringing attention to his property—a large tract that was not listed with a broker and which he thought might contain anywhere from about 30 to 60 million board feet of high-value stumpage. I did some poking around. The tract contained eight to nine million board feet of merchantable timber. Its quality—hence, stumpage price—was substantially less than the seller's estimate owing to quality issues. But most important, the entire tract was categorized as a "conservation zone." While timbering was a theoretical possibility in this land classification, Hawaii had not issued a permit for logging in a conservation zone for at least ten years. When I talked to the official in the state agency who issued timbering permits, he told me that a permit was unlikely to be granted even after a well-done, environmental-impact statement. There might have been $20 to $30 million worth of stumpage on the tract, but it could not be turned into a single dollar. I now knew why the seller wanted to discourage me from scoping the property on behalf of my client. The seller had not told me an untruth; he just didn't tell me the truth about the truths he told me.

Another way to handle such a seller is to offer a purchase contract that includes a **timber-cruise contingency**. This allows you to have a forester of your choice and at your expense visit and evaluate the property once a contract is in place. Your offer is contingent on cruise results that are acceptable to you. If the price you've offered is not warranted by the cruise results, withdraw your offer and then submit a replacement. The language of the contingency is simple enough:

> **Buyer's offer is contingent on being permitted to have a forester of his choice and at his expense perform a walk-through or timber cruise, and that the results of said walk-through or cruise be acceptable to the Buyer.**

> **Parties agree that this work will be accomplished within ____ calendar/business days of the date of Seller's signed acceptance of this offer, weather permitting. If weather or other unforeseen circumstances arise, Parties agree to extend the deadline for this work by another ____ calendar/business days.**

> **If the results of this work are not acceptable to Buyer, he may withdraw his offer without penalty, and his deposit shall be returned in full within five calendar days.**

Make sure to ask your forester how much time he will need to get this work done prior to submitting your offer with its time-sensitive deadline. The cruise may take only a couple of days, but the forester of your choice may not be able to schedule your work for two months.

A buyer does not want to reveal the results of his forester's cruise when it shows a substantial amount of merchantable timber value, say 50 percent or more of the seller's asking price. Disclosure may result in the seller rejecting your offer even if it's full asking price if your timber cruise shows him that he's under-priced his property. If an under-priced property is listed with a broker, your offer must be close to full price and without a lot of "drag"—contingencies, complicated language, warranties, etc.—to position the seller to accept it without reflection. Any lesser offer gives the seller an excuse to reject it without penalty. If the seller rejects a full-price offer that's free of contingencies, which is his right, he will probably owe the broker a commission. If an under-priced property is being sold by an FSBO, the seller can reject any offer you submit. There may be circumstances where a buyer finds advantage in showing the seller the buyer's cruise value of the seller's timber, but they occur infrequently.

Woodland, even trees without any present timber value, can provide certain collateral financial benefits. To qualify as an investment for tax purposes, standing trees do not have to meet rigorous criteria, much beyond standing. The same property considered as an investment is more advantageous tax-wise to the tax-paying owner than when it is considered personal recreation property. Wooded land may be eligible for certain local property-tax breaks if it is enrolled in a state management program. (These programs start with a cruise and a set of management recommendations that are, in my experience, voluntary rather than mandatory.) The state programs are implemented at the option of each county, so you may or may not be able to enroll any particular tract. Your county assessor will know whether the county participates in **land-use programs** that benefit timber owners and agriculture interests. Conservation easements can be applied to wooded land that restrict development or timbering in return for tax benefits.

You may also be able to benefit financially by managing your timber in a way that qualifies for an environmental endorsement from one or another organization through a process called, "**certification**." A growing market exists among some public agencies and private retailers, such as Home Depot, Lowe's and IKEA, for lumber that carries a "green" certification. Several organizations inspect and certify timberland properties that meet their standards, including, among others, the Forest Stewardship Council (www.fsc.org/fsc) and the American Tree Farm System (www.treefarmsystem.org/). Certified wood costs the consumer more, about $25 extra for 1,000 bf (187 8' 2x4s). It also costs the forest landowner several thousand dollars to become certified by a group like the Forest Stewardship Council. *If* stumpage buyers exist in your area who are looking for certified standing timber, the landowner can expect a premium for his efforts. If not, being a green forest landowner may cost you money. Principle, of course, takes on meaning when it comes out of your wallet.

If you intend to manage your new property as timberland, several state and federal programs provide assistance that you should have in mind during your scoping. Public programs involve **cash subsidies** (cost-share programs) to encourage certain conservation and forestry practices, **tax incentives** and **deductions**. Some of the government cost-share dollars count as ordinary income on your 1040, while you may exclude others, partially or totally, from your income. Costs can be deducted when income is not excludable. This federal money is distributed and managed through USDA and state agencies. As of the early 2000s, they included:

>**Forest Health Protection Program (FHP)**—USDA-funded effort to survey forests for insect and disease epidemics and provide technical and financial assistance to private landowners through state agencies for management, disease prevention and intervention.

Federal and Tribal lands are also covered. About 70 million acres of public and private land are at various levels of risk from 26 insects and diseases. Risk status can change quickly. www.fs.fed.us/foresthealth/risk_maps/riskmort.pdf provides maps of forest type and disease risk.

Forestry Incentives Program (FIP)—a USDA-funded, cost-share program principally directed at reforestation and timber management, such as improving existing tree stands through selective thinning of premerchantable trees. The NIPF landowner must own no less than ten or more than 1,000 acres. Reimburses up to 65 percent of approved costs, not to exceed $10,000 per year per owner. May not be available in certain geographic areas. The owner must agree to a minimum of ten years of maintenance to the practices funded. Administered through the USDA's Natural Resource Conservation Service (NRCS), which, if you're confused about government agencies, you can find through the USDA's Farm Service Agency (FSA) or the state's forestry agency. Limited federal funding. FIP money could be excluded from income.

Environmental Quality Incentive Program (EQIP)—a federally funded program of cost-share payments to reduce the cost to a forest landowner of adopting certain forest and wildlife-habitat-enhancement practices that have environmental benefit. Assistance includes education, technical help and money. Land with special environmental features, sensitivity or threat are targeted. Improvement of forest stands, natural regeneration site preparation and tree planting may be assisted. Contact local offices of NRCS or FSA.

Forest Stewardship Program (FSP)—a federally funded program between the US Forest Service and state foresters that gives assistance to a landowner to develop a detailed management plan for all natural resources. The FSP's management plan leads to a certificate that makes the landowner eligible for additional programs

Stewardship Incentive Program (SIP)—a US Forest Service cost-share program that must be preceded by the landowner's having an FSP plan and certificate. SIP provides technical assistance and money to NIPF owners to implement their FSP. SIP funds common forest-management practices, including timber stand improvement, reforestation (tree planting) of pine and hardwoods; forest improvement; enhancement of wildlife habitat; hedge row (windbreak) establishment; wetland protection; fish stream improvement; threatened and endangered species protection; forest recreation enhancement; and soil stabilization and erosion control. The idea is to keep timberland productive and healthy. Cost-share rates range from 25 to 75 percent by practice, not to exceed 100 percent of actual costs. Payments are limited to $10,000 per person per year. The landowner must own no less than ten acres or more than 1,000. Certain circumstances, however, allow a landowner with up to 5,000 acres to participate. The owner must agree to maintain the practice for ten years. SIP funding was phased out in 2000, but was revived in 2002. SIP money could be excluded from taxable income.

Conservation Reserve Program (CRP)—a Farm Service Agency program based on acreage that pays a landowner to remove highly erodible land from agricultural production and plant grass/trees as permanent vegetative cover. Reimbursement of 50 percent of tree-planting cost, plus an annual payment for ten years. NCRS administers. CRP cost-share dollars count as ordinary income for tax purposes.

Small Watershed Management (PL-566)—federally funded assistance through the state's forester to help landowners in certain watersheds develop an FSP with emphasis on erosion control and protection of critical wildlife.

Federal Income Tax Incentives—a tax credit of up to ten percent of the cost of forest regeneration up to a $1,000 credit on the first $10,000 in total reforestation expenses in the year incurred under the Reforestation Tax Credit and Amortization (RTCA). Ninety-five percent of total cost may be partially deducted or amortized over a seven-year period. Together, the package allows a landowner to get back most reforestation costs, such as planting and seeding, over eight tax years. The amortization schedule is 1/14 in the first year, 1/7 for years two through seven and 1/14 in the eighth year. If you include payments as income and include payments with unreimbursed expenses that qualify for the RTCA deductions, you may be able to maximize tax benefits. Timber taxation is discussed in Chapter 24. Tax rules change, so make sure you get current information from a CPA who regularly prepares returns for timber-owning landowners.

State programs—vary, but can include tax breaks for tree planting/growing; rental payments for eligible lands devoted to agroforestry; cost-sharing to reforest timberland with specific species; tree seedling sales; autumn nut purchases; payments to plant trees on erodible crop or pasture land in addition to benefits from other programs; industry match of seedling purchases by landowner in return for right to buy; aerial spraying and other methods of controlling pests at below-market cost. (Some states may refer to their efforts as the BMP Cost-Share Program.)

The priorities, terms and funding levels of these programs change. Those interested in them must obtain *current* program information from the USDA or state forester's office where the target property is located. Information on the Conservation Reserve Program, Forestry Incentives Program and Stewardship Incentive Program can be accessed on line at www.nrcs.usda.gov/NRCSProg.html, which also provides links to all USDA's farm-related conservation programs. The Resource Conservation and Development office of the USDA Natural Resources Conservation Service is located at 14th and Independence Avenue, SW, Room 6103-s, Washington, D.C., 20013; 202-720-2241; 202-690-4205 FAX. Additional information is at USDA Forest Service Cooperative Forestry, POB 96090, Washington, DC, 20090; 202-205-1385; and www.forestry.auburn.edu/sfnmc/class/dewitt.html.

The **Forest Stewardship Program (FSP)** is the gateway for much federal/state assistance related to forestry. The FSP's plan involves several types of expert assessment, including a forester's cruise of the land's timber. The emphasis is on developing an integrated approach to all of the property's resources in light of the owner's set of objectives and those of the agency. Some forestry practices—such as planting, conservation, and pre-commercial thinning—may be eligible for cost-share programs whether or not your property is enrolled in the FSP. Information on all of these programs can be obtained from the nearest state forester's office. If a target property is already enrolled in an FSP, you will need to ascertain whether the obligations run with the land.

Read carefully the landowner's obligations under each federal/state program that you anticipate joining. In return for advice and monetary assistance, you will be committing yourself and your land to following a set of guidelines that may constrain you in the future. When, for example, you begin a forest stewardship plan, you are asked to choose a primary and secondary resource-management objective from the following: fish and wildlife; recreation and environmental; soil and water; and forest products. If your thinking changes, you may find yourself locked into practices that you no longer want. (You will certainly be locked in to what you've promised to do and then done during the first ten years.) You may decide that public dollars and advice are not worth the bother of either doing things the government's way or the forfeiture of doing as you please when it suits you. Before enrolling in these programs, be sure that you understand exactly how the various payments will affect both your current tax obligations and your tax status if you sell or otherwise dispose of the land. Government assistance of this type is generally classified as regular income, but some cost-share payments are excludable. Tax laws and regulations are subject to change, so it's necessary to check with a farm-knowledgeable CPA to keep current.

As I write at the end of 2005, federal tax policies could change dramatically in line with the Mack Commission's recommendations that would limit or reduce mortgage-interest deductibility, eliminate mortgage-interest deductibility on second homes and eliminate many deductions, among other things. Timber-tax policy and cost-share programs may well change in the near future. Prior to buying timberland, a buyer must check with a knowledgeable CPA to gain an understanding of current state and federal tax policies and then shape his purchase strategy accordingly.

CHAPTER 21: SCOPING TIMBER VALUE

VOCABULARY

Woodland has many values—aesthetic, environmental, recreational and economic. Each of the first three has an economic value as well.

The dollar value of woodland aesthetics is found in the lay of the land, its features and how it looks, feels, smells and sits with the owner and an eventual buyer. Woodland aesthetics, including a house site with a view, are a large part of what buyers want and are willing to pay for. The environmental values in woods—wildlife, water resources and so on—can also have economic value. Hunters and fishermen, birders, off-roaders, horse riders, cross-country skiers—all place an economic value on their recreational interests that translates into possible rental income and possible sharing of road-maintenance costs. While woodland may be the source of other economically valuable products such as maple sap, nuts and ginseng, its principal economic value is as merchantable timber.

This discussion builds on the forestry concepts introduced in the preceding chapter. It shows a buyer what a typical hardwood sawtimber cruise looks like and how to think about its findings.

Whether or not you want to cut timber on the woodland that you are interested in buying, you should learn how to think about its dollar values, present and future. At one level or another, the seller has included a dollar value for his timber in his asking price. Therefore, the timber's value (or lack of it) will be part of your negotiations. The seller usually assigns a current value to the timber that can be sold immediately and none to future timber value.

One exception to that statement may be a seller who informs the buyer about the abundance of **"young timber"** on the property. Young timber has no immediate value and, depending on its age, quality and species, may not have any value for decades. Further, a tract of young, low-value hardwood species will have far less future value than the same tract of high-value hardwood species. Whenever I hear a seller start talking about his "young hardwood timber," I assume that the property has been recently timbered—and probably hard.

"Young timber" has a completely different meaning when applied to an even-age pine plantation. In this case, the young planted trees—**premerch**—have both a current value and a predictable future value. Planted trees have an identifiable value, because it costs the owner to prepare the site, plant trees and manage the tract to promote health and growth. With hardwoods, most landowners rely on natural regeneration. Very young hardwood, 15 years and younger, would in most cases not have a discrete value in a land sale. Above that, it depends on whether the young timber is located on ground with high site indices—which means faster marketability and better quality—and contains a lot of high-value species. I've looked at timberland tracts where young timber—even as large as 12 to 14" DBH—had little value, given the low site indices and species mix. Even at that size, it would take too many years for the young timber to grow to 18" DBH and once there the species involved would not bring much money. On the other hand, a tract that is heavy to cherry, sugar maple and red oak in 12 and 14s would be a great retirement investment for a 40 year old.

It is certainly fair for a seller to expect a buyer to pay for the value of his property's merchantable timber, whether or not the buyer plans to gather it for himself. Some sellers underprice their timber value in their asking price; some deliberately overprice it. This chapter discusses how to go about determining that merchantable value. I advise buyers to try to pay little, if anything, for future hardwood value. The further that value lies in the future, the more risk attends to it and the more I rail against paying for it.

How then does an inexperienced land buyer begin to evaluate timber?

The preceding chapter introduced the basic concepts and terms of timber evaluation. The object of a **timber cruise** from a buyer's perspective is to estimate **present timber value (PTV)**, which is the amount of money a timber buyer would pay for the timber being sold. PTV is the forester's estimate of fair market value for the timber he defines as **merchantable**, that is, suitable for immediate sale and saleable. PTV refers only to merchantable timber. A wooded tract may contain much volume that is not merchantable, hence, has no PTV, insofar as the volume is found in small-diameter trees or on acreage that is considered **inoperable**. If a buyer wants to have his newly purchased property clearcut, then PTV amounts to what a forester thinks all the standing timber is likely to bring in the current market. If a buyer wants to sell only certain trees in a **selective cut**, then PTV is what the stumpage buyer will pay for those trees alone. A tree that no one wants to buy is not merchantable. A selective cut is defined by its parameters: it may be trees with a DBH larger than a certain diameter, or trees of certain species that meet a diameter minimum, or trees of a certain quality and diameter, or trees on just one part of a property, among others. Merchantable timber is also referred to as **stumpage value**, or just **stumpage**. The sale process is also called, "**selling timber on the stump**."

Each timber property can have multiple **stumpage scenarios**. Your forester can estimate PTV for a total clearcut as one stumpage scenario, a selective cut that removes everything larger than, say, 6" DBH, a selective cut that removes all hardwood species 16" DBH+ and a selective cut that takes all trees 18" DBH+ plus culls down to 10" DBH (for the purpose of improving the commercial value of the future stand). Another scenario is known locally as a **residential cut** in which the forester marks a relatively small number of large-diameter, high-quality, high-value trees. This minimizes the logged-over look, but it amounts to a more refined version of high-grading. A residential cut generally anticipates conversion of a larger timberland tract into smaller parcels of second-home properties where future timber production is less expected.

Each stumpage scenario will produce a different estimate of sale income, and each involves a different set of consequences for appearance, post-logging uses, opportunity costs and the length of the next cutting cycle.

Cruise methods are similar for both hardwood and softwood (evergreens or conifers) sawtimber, whose market is lumber broadly defined. Higher-quality sawtimber tracts are usually cruised in terms of board-foot volume. Sawtimber tracts that have lower-quality trees are usually cruised in tons. Pulpwood is estimated in terms of tons, cords or cubic feet. A timber tract with timber stands of different qualities may be divided internally and cruised with different measures, depending on each stand's characteristics. Even-age pine plantations will be classified by the age of each stand; older pines, say 20 years and older, will have sawtimber value. A lumber-quality sawtimber tract should in most cases be cruised in terms of diameter classes, species and board-foot volume, not weight. That format gives both the timber seller and buyer the best sense of the wood's lumber potential. The examples that I present below involve hardwood sawtimber estimated in board feet.

A forester will cruise your target property's timber and also refer to his written report estimating volumes and values as a **cruise**. His methodology is to sample the stand systematically and without bias. A cruise has the virtues and risks of any conscientiously done sampling technique. You can assume that a properly done cruise will estimate volume by species and two-inch diameter class within a seven percent +/-range of what a 100-percent marked inventory would show. The seven percent comes from my own experience evaluating cruises; academic research might show a five to ten percent variation. Larger tracts and tracts that have dissimilar stands may have a larger margin of error. The more consistent a property's stand is, the more accurate the cruise since the forester is sampling the same age and type of tree each time he puts in a plot. Sampling accuracy can be increased by taking more plots.

The forester gathers current local stumpage prices by talking with local timber buyers in the target property's area. I have seen cruises in the $50,000 range come within a few hundred dollars of the ultimate sales price. With larger volumes and more species and quality issues, you can anticipate that selling price will vary more from the cruise's estimated value. The most rigorously done cruise should not be assumed to be a perfectly accurate predictor of sale value. But it should be close enough for a land buyer's purposes. Stumpage prices change over time and from season to season. A cruise with species prices that is more than three months old should be recalculated with current prices. A land buyer always prefers that his forester's pre-purchase cruise err on the side of underestimating value.

After confirming the boundaries, the forester superimposes a grid that creates cells of equal size. The forester uses his judgment and observation of the tract to determine how many **cells** he needs and how big the cells need to be to make his sampling representative. Cell size can range from a couple of acres to several hundred acres, depending on tract size. On tracts of 200 acres or less—small tracts to a forester—three acres might be the right cell size.

Once he has his grid laid out, the forester walks to the center of each cell and **takes a plot** by tallying all merchantable trees by species and diameter class within. Each plot is assumed to represent the merchantable timber present in each grid cell. Plot sizes vary, $1/10^{th}$ acre and $1/5^{th}$ acre are typical. The number of plots put in must be sufficient to represent the entire tract. The fewer the number of plots, the more chance for inaccurate extrapolations. An **even-age forest**—planted or not—might require fewer plots than a forest of trees of varying ages. Your forester will be concerned with being efficient (with his time and your money), so he will try to put in just enough plots to be representative. As a general rule, the higher the ratio of plots for every 100 acres, the more accurate the sampling. As the forester puts in his plots, he will keep his eye on the consistency of the stand. If a stand is patchy, he may need to "regrid" and increase the number of plots to pick up the stand's variability. Cruising "small" tracts does not involve more than a day, or two at the most. It is, therefore, a false economy to tell your forester to skimp on plots to save paying for a couple of hours of his time. An acre of woods can easily have $500 to $1,500 or more in merchantable timber, so you want to err on the side of more sampling rather than less.

A tract's merchantable sawtimber is derived by estimating the volume of its merchantable trees using a tree scale and the forester's judgment. Volume is based on a merchantable tree's diameter (either DBH or at the stump), quality, number of logs in its stem and its degree of taper. The forester keeps a tally of the merchantable trees in each plot, disaggregated by species and two-inch diameter class. When he has put in all of his plots, he'll total the volume for each species by diameter class. A typical hardwood sawtimber cruise might organize volumes into the following diameter classes:

<u>Diameter Classes in Inches (DBH)</u>

<10   10-12   12-14   14-16   16-18   18-20   20-22   22-24   24+

Diameter (DBH) is a major factor in determining a tree's value. For reasons having to do with milling lumber efficiently and the value that can be extracted, sawmill buyers want sawtimber logs 18"+ DBH, though they may pay the same high price for 14"+ DBH logs of a few high-value species, such as walnut and black cherry. Sixteens generally bring a full price. With exceptions, sawtimber trees smaller than 16" DBH are often considered by stumpage buyers as **pole timber**, low-quality sawtimber or pulpwood. These types of merchantable trees are valued much lower than sawtimber 16"+ DBH. It is, therefore, important for the land buyer to know how much of a target property's merchantable timber is 18"+ DBH, how much is in the 16-18" classification and how much is smaller than 16". The best money will be found in the 18"+ volumes—at least where I live. Increasingly, mills near me pay the same for 16-18s as 18s+, but you may run into a discount. In New York, I've found mills paying full price for 12+, even 10+, hardwood sawlogs of high-value species.

In addition to diameter, the second main factor in determining the value of a given volume is species. Sawtimber volume in 18"+ classifications of low-value species might bring only $.10 per board foot, or $100 mbf, while a high-value species can bring ten times that unit price.

The third factor is quality. It is not enough to find a tract of woods loaded with large-diameter, high-value species; the trees themselves have to be healthy and well-formed so that they mill into high-value, clear lumber and veneer.

A forester's full cruise analysis might have three parts: 1) estimated merchantable timber volume by species and diameter classes, along with current stumpage prices by species; 2) topographical map of tract showing location of tract boundaries and timber stands, and 3) narrative, which might include his thoughts about sale potential, likely buyers, market conditions, premerchantable volumes, wildlife, erosion potential, boundary problems that he discovered, timber-quality issues and suggestions for his client to consider.

TIMBERING THE JONES FARM

The examples that I show in the following tables illustrate the forester's approach to hardwood sawtimber. TABLE 21-1 shows a tract's volumes, by species and diameter class, based on his plot samples. It presents the forester's aggregation of timber volumes.

Much information is contained in this inventory, and more can be inferred. The cruise involved the Jones farm, which has a few older buildings and an asking price of $189,900. The forester cruised merchantable timber on 100 of the 130 acres in the property. He determined that only 100 acres should be considered **operable acreage**—land having merchantable timber that can be accessed economically and practically. The 30 **inoperable** acres included pasture, crop land, buildings, ponds, wetlands and a steep section that had a few scattered high-value trees but the cost of building a skid road to get them was prohibitive. The topographical map the forester attached to the inventory showed the boundaries of the entire property and the location of the operable acreage.

The forester put in 34 plots, each of which represents a grid cell of about three acres. This ratio of plots to acreage should provide the client with a fairly high degree of confidence in the sampling's accuracy and its representativeness. If the tract's timber is not consistent, he should note that in his narrative.

TABLE 21-1

Timber Cruise Inventory

100 acres/130-acres Jones Farm in Appalachia County
34 plots, Doyle Scale FC 78
10" break
Date: August 1, 2005

	Diameter Class (inches DBH)						Volume (MBF)
HW SPECIES	12-14	14-16	16-18	18-20	20-22	22+	
Northern Red Oak (RO)	10	20	30	27	10	5	102
White Oak (WO)	7	3		1	1		12
Chestnut Oak (CO)	4	4	5	12	20	4	50
Scarlet Oak (SO)	1	1	3	2			7
Hickory (H)		3	2	1			6
Cherry (CH)		5	7	10	6	2	30
Hard Maple (HM)	2	12	12	10	5		41
Red Maple (RM)	3	2	4	6	2	3	20
Misc HW	9	8	10	15	14	10	66
total	**36**	**58**	**74**	**84**	**58**	**24**	**334**
SW SPECIES							
Hemlock (HEM)	7	10	10	7	10	9	53
Spruce (S)	4	6	4	5	8	6	33
total	**11**	**16**	**14**	**12**	**18**	**15**	**86**

Total: 420,000 bf.; 4,200 bf/A
100 acres operable of 130 acres in total tract
Culls: 167 trees, tallied from field notes counted in plots.
MBF = 1,000 board feet or 1000/bf

The forester used the Doyle (tree) Scale, the volume estimator that local timber buyers use. He applied an FC 78 to all trees. This is a taper formula that is used in volume estimates. An FC 100 would indicate no taper from stump to the top of the highest log in the tree. The forester used a "**10" break**." This means that in calculating a tree's volume and log lengths, he stopped where the stem narrowed either to a ten-inch diameter or the first crotch, whichever came first. Had the forester "broken" at a six-inch top diameter, he would be inflating the tract's timber volume by including the small-diameter top logs. Local buyers, the forester knows, don't value logs ten inches in diameter at one end and six inches at the other.

The 100 acres was cruised as one **stand**. A stand is typically an area in which the timber's characteristics—age, species mix, size and quality—are reasonably consistent. A stand need not be a single species. A stand need not be contiguous. A 100-acre tract might have three non-contiguous stands of one timber profile, two stands of a different profile and one stand of a third profile. Had all the softwood been located in one or two spots, the forester would have probably separated the inventory by stands. As it was, the softwoods were scattered throughout the 100 acres. When stands appeal to different markets, the forester may sell the stands in separate sales.

The cruise suggests the stand's **age range** without stating it. Given that so little hardwood volume is larger than 22" DBH, your forester might infer that the land was cut heavily about 75 years earlier. At that time, smaller diameters were left in place. Stump remains give clues as to recent cutting. By knowing the **site index** for this acreage, he will know how tall a northern red oak (NRO)—one of the common species—should be at 50 years. The dominant species on the Jones land is northern red oak with a site index of 85, which would be its predicted height at age 50. Since the forester found large diameter red oaks substantially taller than that, he would guess that the age of the merchantable trees in the stand are between 75 and 100 years. The lack of significant volume in the 22"+ DBH classification confirms this age range. Site index data are found in the **county's soil survey**, available from the local USDA office of the Natural Resources Conservation Service (formerly, the Soil Conservation Service). The county (state) forester and your consultant should be able to estimate a site index even in counties where a soil survey has not been published.

Jones's 100 acres of woodland is more densely forested than many Appalachian tracts on the market. The cruise projects a total of 420,000 bf, or 4,200 bf per operable acre (bf/A) of merchantable timber 12" DBH+. This combines 334,000 bf of hardwoods and 86,000 bf of softwoods. While Douglas fir acreage in the West can easily have 50,000 bf/A, a very respectable volume in the Appalachians is 4,200 bf/A. An Appalachian tract is generally not worth cutting if it cruises out to less than 2,500 bf/A. The exception to that statement would be a tract where most of the volume in a lightly forested tract is found in high-value species. This would be an unusual discovery.

The forester should not have included as merchantable timber in TABLE 21-1 any tree in his plots that he saw being used for dens and certain nests. **Den trees** may contain good sawtimber volume, but they are needed for wildlife habitat. State and/or federal law may require leaving certain trees in which certain species are denning or nesting. With species classified as endangered, both the nest tree and the acreage around it must be left uncut and undisturbed. **Snags** are dead, or mostly dead trees, that provide food and shelter to various creatures. Though unsightly, they should be left standing for that reason. **Seed trees** are healthy, mature well-formed trees of desired (e.g., high-value) species that should be left to reseed a cut area. The forester might decide to leave a particularly well-formed cherry that's 22" DBH even though a buyer will pay a lot for it in hope that its seeds will be the ones to regenerate the newly cut woodland.

PTV is mainly determined on a mixed-hardwood tract, such as the Jones tract, by the way five factors combine:

- volume of merchantable timber (stumpage) across the tract

- amount of volume in sawtimber diameter classes 16-18" DBH and larger

- proportion of sawtimber volume that is found in high-value species

- prices by species that the local market will pay

- quality of stumpage, especially the high-value species

The more volume tract-wide, the more volume that is 16-18" DBH+, the more volume in high-value species, the higher the species price and the better the quality—the more money stumpage buyers will pay the timber owner.

Sawtimber volume is determined by a tree's diameter and the number of logs eight- to 16-feet long that can be cut from its main stem. Sawtimber volume is estimated using a sawtimber **tree scale**, such as the Doyle scale or the International ¼ scale. (You may also hear reference to a "log scale" or a "milling scale." These are used to calculate board feet of lumber from logs before they are milled. The scales that concern a buyer of timberland are sawtimber tree scales that estimate tree volume in the field, not the milling scales.) Smaller-diameter trees in the 8" to 14" DBH classes may or may not have stumpage value, depending on the products that local mills produce. If a sawtimber buyer cannot mill valuable product out of log from a small-diameter tree, it's likely to be left standing or cut for pulp. Whether the smaller-diameter trees have value is a matter of local demand. In Southeast Missouri and northwestern New York, hardwood stumpage is often cut to 8" DBH for milling; along the Virginia-West Virginia border where I live, it's generally not cut below 12 inches. The 47,000 board feet of Jones sawtimber in the 12-14" classification will probably be priced at a discount to the sawtimber that is larger than 14" DBH, because that reflects the local market. The discount may even extend to the volume that is smaller than 16" DBH. Timber near me that is less than 14" DBH is generally either valued as pulpwood or not valued at all by stumpage buyers in their bids, though they may cut and haul it off. For that reason, the forester may tell his client not to include the 12-14s, 14-16s and some of the 16-18s in the sale. Better to leave them in place for the future.

A single 16" DBH 16-foot-long log from a low-value species like black gum on the stump might be valued at $.40 cents as pulp and $10 as size-discounted sawtimber. Once it grows to 18" DBH in, say, eight years, it would bring $20, at its current price and likely more given inflation. This stem has both increased in volume, and the value of the volume is now fully priced. The increase in stumpage value from ingrowth is more dramatic in the higher-value species. So size matters, particularly the growth that shifts a tree from price-discounted sawtimber to fully priced sawtimber.

The stumpage price the landowner receives is also dependent on the species prices at the time of sale. Price depends on the demand and supply for each species; these change according to consumer preferences and other factors. There is a general upward-trending but cyclical pattern to hardwood prices, but within that trend individual species rise and fall in stumpage price. In the mid-1990s, red oak in my area was bringing $600 and more per 1000/bf on the stump; that fell to about $400 per 1000/bf in 2006. Sugar maple rose during the same period from about $400 to as much as $800 per 1000/bf, and then tailed off in 2006-07. Consumers of flooring, cabinetry and furniture preferred sugar maple's white wood for a time. Then the inventory of sugar maple lumber exceeded demand, which softened the price. Stumpage prices track lumber prices for each species.

If you assume that a generic hardwood tree grows in diameter at one-quarter of an inch per year, it would only take 16 years for the discounted 14" log to grow into a fully priced 18" log. A one-log volume that would bring less than 50 cents as pulp would bring $20 to $200 16 years later, depending on species prices. That rate of investment appreciation is spectacular. If you can find a tract with high-value hardwoods in the 12-16" range and can buy it cheaply and can wait, you will make a lot of money on the timber sale 15 to 25 years later. The common investment tactic would be to sell the merchantable trees 16" and larger immediately after purchase to pay off as much of the acquisition cost as possible, then take your long-term profit from the ingrowth in the trees you've left.

When cruise volume is concentrated in smaller diameter classes (say, less than 14" DBH), the forester is probably working with a very young stand that regenerated after a heavy cut, or a poor site index and/or a high degree of crowding. If crowding is an issue, the forester might recommend an immediate **thinning** to remove the small-diameter, low-value hardwood species in order to benefit the remaining high-value hardwood species. Thinning will allow the remaining trees to use the newly freed light, water and soil resources to reach the 16-18" DBH classifications as quickly as possible. The thinning produces a small amount of immediate income for the owner and a greater amount of future income than would be there otherwise. This type of thinning is also called, **timber stand improvement (TSI)**, and may qualify for federal/state cost-share assistance.

In the Jones example, the timber distribution finds the largest hardwood volumes in the 16-18" and 18-20" DBH classes, which are immediately merchantable sawtimber. The 16-18s could either be removed or left for future cutting, depending on the owner's objectives and needs. Good volumes are also found in the 12-16" classifications. These smaller diameters are merchantable in the sense that they could be sold for pulp or as discounted sawtimber. The forester might recommend cutting the low-value species that are less than 16" DBH and leaving the mid-value and high-value species for the future. This would bring in some current income and release the remaining high-value trees from competition. Foresters can work up comparative estimates of what the owner might receive for the 12-16" volume in the current market against what might be gotten at various future dates.

TABLE 21-2, which includes the **price multipliers** for each species that the forester believes reflect the current market, sets out the volume data and values in a format that is typical of a forester's cruise for a landowner (or buyer). If you were to ask a forester to cruise the Jones tract, his report would look something like TABLE 21-2

TABLE 21-2 is a **value analysis** for the type of cutting and sale the forester envisions for this property. The PTV of each species volume is found by multiplying the total volume of that species by its current market price, as determined by the forester.

TABLE 21-2 shows that the Jones tract has 240,000 board feet of 16" DBH and larger hardwood sawtimber worth a projected $79,600 and 59,000 board feet of 16" DBH and larger softwood sawtimber worth a projected $6,475. The two total $86,075. Most merchantable value on the Jones tract is found in cherry and red oak sawtimber.

Most foresters, I think, would recommend a **selective cut** on the Jones farm that removes two types of timber. The forester would first propose to include in the sale all sawtimber 16" DBH and larger, both hardwood and softwood. No sawtimber smaller than 16" would be included in the sale. The small sawtimber has some value, but the forester is recommending that it be left for future harvesting. His price research showed that 16s are not price-discounted as sawtimber, so he includes them in the sale because the buyer wants to pay down the cost of acquisition. All high-value hardwoods smaller than 16" DBH will be left. This can be considered a **sawtimber cut**.

TABLE 21-2

Timber Cruise Valuation

100 acres/130-acres Jones Farm in Appalachia County
34 plots, Doyle Scale FC 78
10" break
Date: August 1, 2005

Large Sawtimber

	DBH 1,000/bf				Total Volume (mbf)	$ per mbf	Estimated Total Value ($)
	16-18	*18-20*	*20-22*	*22+*			
HW SPECIES							
Northern Red Oak (RO)	30	27	10	5	72	400	28,800
White Oak (WO)		1	1		2	250	500
Chestnut Oak (CO)	6	12	20	4	42	150	6,300
Scarlet Oak (SO)	3	2			5	175	875
Hickory (H)	2	1			3	150	450
Cherry (CH)	7	10	6	2	25	950	23,750
Hard Maple (HM)	12	10	5		27	450	12,150
Red Maple (RM)	4	6	2	3	15	125	1875
Misc HW	10	15	14	10	49	100	4,900
total	**74**	**84**	**58**	**24**	**240**		**$79,600**
SW SPECIES							
Hemlock (HEM)	10	7	10	9	36	100	3,600
Spruce (S)	4	5	8	6	23	125	2,875
total	**14**	**12**	**18**	**15**	**59**		**$6,475**

MBF = 1,000 bf
Total Value: $86,075
   HW = $796.00 p/A   Average species price: HW $331.67 /mbf
   SW = $64.75 p/A   SW $109.75 /mbf

Estimated 3 cords per acre @ $5 per cord. Cordage value equals $1,500 (3 x $5 =
$15p/A x 100 = $1,500)

    The second type of recommended timbering would be a pulp cut, which removes all low-value, small-diameter trees both hardwood and softwood that are large enough for a logger to cut economically. The pulp cut would take all of the volume assigned to cord wood, estimated at three cords per acre. This represents about 1,200 bf/A of pulp wood, using a common rule of thumb that 1,000 board feet equals about 2.5 cords. This 1,200 bf/A would be cut from the low-value trees smaller than 16" DBH and from the tops of the sawtimber trees. The pulp cut would leave the low-value species smaller than 6" DBH in place, because no logger wants to bother dropping them, particularly when this chore amounts to free work for the landowner. Loggers may choose to leave all pulp trees standing, regardless of diameter, if market conditions are such that it does not make economic sense for them to spend the time and money to cut them. Similarly, the pulp wood contained in the tops of the sawtimber trees may be left as slash rather than lopped and bucked into pulp lengths, cord wood or firewood.

The pulp estimate of three cords per acre does not include the volume of the cruise's 167 **culls**, which have limited economic value due to disease, breakage, deformities, hollowness and the like. Photographs 21-1, 21-2 and 21-3 show three different culls, each of which is more than 18" DBH but has no commercial value as sawtimber due to poor form (big branches on the butt log or rot). Photograph 21-1 shows a tree with poor form—a large branch coming out of its butt log. The young sawtimber next to it is long, straight and without significant branches.

PHOTOGRAPH 21-1

Cull and Sawtimber

Photograph 21-2 shows a large sugar maple that is made worthless for sawtimber owing to the hydra of big branches low to the ground. The forked cull in Photograph 21-1 could be cut for pulp; the cull in Photograph 21-2 is probably too branchy and time-intensive to cut for pulp.

PHOTOGRAPH 21-2

Sugar Maple Cull

Photograph 21-3 shows a large-diameter tree with extensive rot about 12 feet above the ground. The rot probably extends lower in the stem where it is invisible. Owing to weakness in the upper stem, this tree should be allowed to fall. Although it has pulp value, it is too dangerous to cut, so it has been left. Sometimes, culls can be marketed as pulp or firewood, but a stumpage buyer is not likely to pay anything for them. The trees in Photographs 21-2 and 21-3 have no commercial value despite their diameters.

PHOTOGRAPH 21-3

Large-diameter Cull

On a tract like the Jones's, stumpage buyers would typically bid the value of the sawtimber, bid nothing for the culls and, depending on market conditions, bid either nothing or just a little for the pulp. If the stumpage buyer ultimately decides to remove culls, he will reap a small profit without having had to pay for these trees. If a stumpage seller (landowner) can get the stumpage buyer to have his logger cut the culls, his remaining timber benefits.

The purpose of the two cuts taken together is to leave the new owner with all of the high-value sawtimber smaller than 16" DBH in place for future timbering. All of the small-diameter, *high-value* hardwoods—pole timber (4.6 to 9.5" DBH), small sawtimber (9.6 to 14.5" DBH) and marginal sawtimber between 14.5 and 16" DBH—would be left. The sawtimber cut and the pulp cut remove much of their competition.

If the landowner wants the 167 culls to be cut—which I recommend doing—he should put notice of

430

that in the bid package his forester sends to stumpage buyers and place language in his contract that the stumpage buyer is required to cut the culls. Cutting the culls is uncompensated time from the logger's perspective, so the stumpage buyer may discount his bid a little to account for that expense. The logger working for the stumpage buyer will probably not cut them unless the contract between landowner and stumpage buyer requires it. The landowner may do better to not require the stumpage buyer to drop the culls (given the bid discount) and simply give them to a local fire-wood cutter after the timbering is over. The forester can recommend which approach makes the most sense.

Cutting the pulp and culls is a strategy that will free resources for the high-value sawtimber trees and make it easier for them to establish their seedlings. This promotes the upgrading of the commercial value of the forest's timber over time. Releasing the high-value hardwoods from competition also increases their annual diameter growth rate on the order of moving from 1/4-inch per year to three eighths. Release works best when the beneficiaries are young, 40 to 70 years old; it does not produce substantially higher growth rates in older trees. The fact that the most prevalent merchantable species by volume on this tract are high-value cherry and red oak indicates that the ground is well-suited to these species. Increasing their presence over time appears to be a feasible strategy.

The forester's sawtimber/pulp-cut strategy is a selective harvest that takes the largest (16" DBH plus) sawtimber trees and the pulp/culls. This approach is the opposite of **high-grading**, which only takes the largest, most valuable sawtimber—the **money trees**—and leaves all pulp and culls standing. The forester's approach of combining a 16"+ sawtimber cut with a pulp cut is likely to produce the most present income as possible consistent with preserving future value. Had the forester found that sawtimber in the 12-14 and 14-16 classifications was also fetching the same prices as the 16s and larger, he might have recommended that they be included in the timber sale if the landowner needed the cash.

The forester's cutting strategy for the Jones woods will affect the land's post-timbering appearance. Left will be all the high-value species smaller than 16" DBH, including cherry, sugar maple, red oak and white oak. Gone will be most of the lower-value trees—hemlock, spruce, chestnut oak, red maple, scarlet oak, hickory and the miscellaneous hardwoods (such as basswood, black birch and hophornbeam). Following the timbering, the woods will look more open, given that about 4,200 bf in sawtimber and pulp was removed from each of the 100 operable acres. You will see no tree with a diameter of 16" or more. The top of the forest canopy will be lower since the oldest trees have been cut, but you may not notice that change. A great deal of slash will litter the ground. Deer will flourish in woods cut this way. The slash provides cover. This habitat will usually provide more food for them—and other wildlife—than mature forest. While the Jones woods will look rough owing to the slash and skid roads, the tract's future timber-production value has been greatly improved. The owner can cut the 16" DBH+ trees every 20 to 25 years, and each time he can upgrade the stand for the next cut by dropping the low-value species. The environment has been changed on this tract, but it's not degraded or harmed. The distinction between change and harm is important.

The forester who cruised this property may recommend that the timber be sold in two or even three separate sales—for HW sawtimber, SW sawtimber and pulp. The landowner might benefit financially from dividing the stumpage, but local markets will determine whether that's the best approach. Some stumpage buyers interested only in the sawtimber may subcontract the pulp to a logger who specializes in that. If the timber is sold to more than one buyer, you will have to schedule their **logging windows** (typically 18 months to two years) to avoid two logging outfits working the same tract at the same time. This will stretch the time the Jones property will be tied up in logging activity and delay any reclamation work that you want to do involving cutting slash and dressing roads. While the window runs for a long time, it only takes a few weeks to cut and remove 100,000 board feet. Other things being equal, it's usually best for your woodlot to schedule timber cutting for the late fall and winter months when the sap is down and ground conditions are comparatively firm. Mill prices tend to rise in the winter as well.

As soon as a logger is done, he should release his interest in your timber. This release is a legal document that relinquishes his interest in any remaining sale timber that he bought but chose not to cut. Releases are often recorded. Once the landowner has a release of interest, he can alert the next logger in line. Sequenced logging of this sort is tricky and not common. I think it's better to sell all the timber to one buyer and let him decide whether he wants to subcontract portions. Once the landowner has a release from the stumpage buyer, the remaining trees are once again his to do with as he pleases.

Some foresters include an estimate of the **number of trees per acre** in their cruises. This is useful information if you're considering developing a sugarbush to tap sugar water. In that event, you want to know the number of sugar maples at least 10" DBH, which is the diameter at which one shallow tap can be drilled without harming the tree. As sugar maple gains in diameter, additional and deeper taps, up to four in the largest trees, can be installed. Knowing the number of trees alone, however, does not tell you much about the value of the timber or even the stand's **density**. Two hundred small, junky oak trees per acre are worth little, if anything. Density is a measure of the number of trees per acre. But density has to be considered in terms of average tree size too. Six hundred planted pine saplings at one year old are not dense in the layman's sense. At 20 years old, these 600 trees represent a very dense growth. One hundred HW trees, each 3" DBH, per acre, are far less crowded in terms of competing for available nutrients than are 100 22" DBH trees. When a trees-per-acre calculation is included in a cruise, it is generally limited to trees larger than a certain DBH. Fewer than ten merchantable trees per acre is a sparse stocking rate, and such a tract may have relatively little timber value unless they are large and high-value.

Density, or crowdedness, can be expressed in terms of **percent of crown cover**, that is, the percent of shaded ground beneath the canopy. Or, it can be expressed as **basal area per acre**. If you were to cut all trees on an acre at 4.5 feet above the ground (breast height), the surface area of the stumps taken together represents basal area. As a rule, basal area increases with the stand's average diameter even as the number of trees declines. When stands are crowded—too much basal area—diameter growth will slow and the quality of the timber will be affected. If you are trying to maximize the production of timber value, crowded stands should be thinned—a practice of **timber stand improvement**. Consider an example. A fully stocked stand of northern hardwood all 14" DBH would have 90-95 square feet in basal area per acre. Each 14" DBH tree would contain a little more than one square foot of basal area; a 22" DBH tree would contain 2.6 square feet. For a basal area of 90-95 square feet per acre, 95 14s are needed, but only 37 22s. In terms of stumpage value, the acre of 37 22s is far more valuable than the 95 14s.

A "cruise" that only shows number of trees per acre or basal area per acre does not provide sufficient information to determine the stumpage value of the woodland. Do not buy timberland based on these measures alone.

The Jones cruise provides no information about number of trees, average tree diameter or basal area, so it's difficult to determine the stand's density. Given, however, that there's 4,200 bf/A—a good sawlog volume for the area—you can deduce that the tract is crowded and is ready for some type of cutting. In crowded situations, trees will grow tall without gaining much diameter. Such trees will have very narrow crowns. Woods like this can contain a respectable volume but most of it may be in small DBH classes, say 14" and smaller.

As the forester cruises timber, he will keep his eye open for **quality factors, both bad and good**. He will inform you whether he observed quality discounts in the trees from disease and insects, and damage from wind, ice, frost, lightning, flooding or fire. Other defects that might discount your timber above the norm include excessive crookedness in stems, rot, splitting, crotches, fungus (stains logs), tap holes from maple sap production, skinned off bark from earlier logging, and nails and wire fencing in butt logs.

Disease and insects can kill a tree or a stand of a particular species and/or degrade timber quality to one degree or another. Both conifers and hardwoods are susceptible to various defoliators (e.g., gypsy moth, leafminers, sawflies), bark beetles, wood borers, terminal feeders (which eat buds or roots), sucking insects (aphids, woolly adelgid) as well as diseases—viruses, mistletoe, nematodes, bacteria and parasitic fungi (such as, wilts, e.g., Dutch elm disease), rusts, (e.g., white pine blister) and cankers (e.g., chestnut blight). It's easy for an inexperienced person to see mortality in a forest—you will see dead standing trees. But it's difficult for someone like me to see the first signs and stages of processes whose consequences can range from negligible to catastrophic.

You should have a specific discussion with your forester about long-term risks on a target tract, particularly from insects and diseases that are likely to appear. The southern pine beetle is a scourge of southern pine forests. Gypsy moth has ruined large portions of oak-heavy woods in the east, but it seems to come and go. In California and Oregon, a pathogen, *Phytophthora ramorum*, or "sudden oak death syndrome," has spread to 17 species, including oaks, big leaf maples, redwood and Douglas fir. Hemlock is being lost to the woolly adelgid, and beech and sugar maple are also under attack. Bark beetles are damaging western forests, particularly lodgepole, ponderosa, Douglas fir, and pines, such as sugar and western. These beetles seem to be increasing their range and numbers as winters have grown milder. (Paul R. Epstein and Gary M. Tabor, "Climate Change is Really Bugging Our Forests," <u>Washington Post</u>, September 7, 2003.) Your forester should have a feel for the threats that can occur over the next three to five years. Ask him about the quality negatives that he's observed on the tract. If there's a blinking yellow light in his discussion, your risk of loss is too high to accept. Don't buy, unless you're looking to flip the timber in an immediate lump-sum sale and then the land.

On the positive side, he will look for veneer-quality logs in the high-value sawtimber. Veneer logs are straight, thick and nearly flawless. Hardwood veneer logs are generally sliced into thin sheets the length and width of the log. Logs of softer woods, like pine and poplar, are peeled into long, wide sheets-like unfurling a roll of paper towels. The hardwood veneer is used for surfacing furniture and cabinetry, among other uses. Veneer logs fetch the highest price per unit of measure. Cherry, for example, might bring $5 a log as pulp, $250 a log as sawtimber and $2,000 as veneer. If your forester finds a significant volume of veneer, he may value it separately from the sawtimber of the same species. I've known tracts whose buyers have paid for the acquisition of the land through the immediate sale of just the veneer trees.

A timber cruise is a snapshot estimate of volume and value on a particular day, with current prices. No **risk analysis** is included. A buyer should not forget that all investments can either appreciate or depreciate over time. The years required to allow timber to mature and benefit from ingrowth also involve risks from disease, damage and price variability. Your forester can help you evaluate these natural and market risks. He should also be able to project an appreciated value and then apply a discount formula that fits the type of timber, location and number of years before a projected harvest. In a simple version, a discount formula knocks off a percentage of appreciated value in each future time interval to account for risk. The projected appreciated value might be discounted for the purpose of illustration at 8 percent ten years out, 12 percent at 15 years and 16 percent at 20 years. This method accounts statistically for routine factors that damage trees as well as the total disaster, such as an ice storm that breaks every tree, leaving nothing but a low-income salvage job. A routine cruise would show *merchantable* volumes and projected values, formatted something similar to TABLE 21-2.

TABLE 21-3 estimates the values of the small sawtimber, 12-16" DBH, and the "swing group," 16-18" DBH. A typical cruise would probably not provide this level of detail about the marginally merchantable smaller timber, but it's worth illustrating how these dollars play out.

TABLE 21-3

Small Timber Values

100 acres/130-acres Jones Farm in Appalachia County
34 plots, Doyle Scale FC 78
10" break
Date: August 1, 2005

Marginally Sized Sawtimber DBH

	1					2			1 + 2
	12-14	*14-16*	*12-16 Vol.*	*12-16 $ mbf*	*12-16 $ Value*	*16-18 Vol.*	*16-18 $ mbf*	*16-18 $ Value*	*12-18 Total $ Value*
HW SPECIES					10				
Northern Red Oak (RO)	7	20	30	$75	$2,250	30	$400	$12,000	$14,250
White Oak (WO)	4	3	10	30	300		250		300
Chestnut Oak (CO)	1	4	8	30	240	6	150	900	1,140
Scarlet Oak (SO)		1	2	70	140	3	175	525	665
Hickory (H)		3	3	50	150	2	150	300	450
Cherry (CH)		5	5	200	1,000	7	950	6,650	7,650
Hard Maple (HM)	2	12	14	90	1,260	12	450	5,400	6,660
Red Maple (RM)	3	2	5	50	250	4	125	500	750
Misc HW	9	8	17	40	680	10	100	1,000	1,680
total	**36**	**58**	**94**		**$6,270**	**74**		**$27,275**	**$33,545**
SW SPECIES					7				
Hemlock (HEM)	4	10	17	30	510	10	100	1,000	1,510
Spruce (S)	**11**	6	10	30	300	4	125	500	800
total			**27**		**$810**	**14**		**$1,500**	**$2,310**

Total Value of 12-18" DBH HW and SW: $35,855

HW $335.45 p/A   Average $/mbf: $199.67 ($33,545 / 168,000 bf)
SW $23.10 p/A $56.34   ($2,310 / 41,000 bf)

TABLE 21-3 shows that the 16-18" DBH sawtimber volume, both hardwood and softwood, is 88,000 board feet, or 37 percent of the tract's 240,000 bf total. In terms of value, the 16-18s amount to $28,775, or 33 percent of the $79,600 HW total. The 16-18s would be sold at the same price as stumpage 18" DBH+. That is why this diameter class was included in the sale.

The forester has discovered that local stumpage buyers would not pay the full sawtimber price for the 12-16" DBH trees, even for the cherry. Using discounted prices, he estimates that the 94,000 bf in the 12-16" DBH hardwood to be worth only $6,270, and the 27,000 bf in the 12-16" DBH softwood to be worth $810. Together, the 12-16s sawtimber totals $7,080 for 94,000 bf compared with the projected value of $28,775 for the 88,000 bf of 16-18" DBH sawtimber. The huge difference in price for roughly equivalent volumes demonstrates the **Bingo! effect** that occurs from ingrowth, when the next higher diameter classification shifts unit price out of its (small diameter) discount.

If the 16-18s, the swing group, will bring a full sawtimber price, why not include that volume in the sawtimber sale? First, the owner may not need or want that income increment right away. Second, he may have an anticipated need for it in the future that outweighs any immediate need. Third, trees in this diameter class will gain volume and are a rapidly appreciating asset. Fourth, if they are cut now, the timber's next cut will be extended by another 16 years or more, to wait for the 14s to move up to the 18" class. Finally, the site will look a lot more "logged over" if the trees in the 16-18" class are removed along with all those 18" DBH and larger.

Foresters often use two value measures—**timber value per acre ($/A) and average value per 1,000 board feet ($/mbf)**—that are useful in quick calculations and comparisons. In this example, these value expressions are figured on the tract's 100 operable acres, not straight-through on the 130 acres. Value per acre can be shown as either (or both) timber dollars per tract acre (that is, including all the acreage that's for sale) or timber dollars per operable acre. Value per tract acre (not operable acre) is the more common measure; value per operable acre can confuse an inexperienced buyer to the seller's advantage. When evaluating different timber properties, make sure that your calculations are figured against the same acreage base in all cases.

With HW sawtimber timber 50 years and older, value per tract acre is a quick way of getting a sense of the woodlands' productivity for timber. A high $p/A value usually suggests good site productivity and a favorable concentration of high-value species. The other measure—$/mbf—situates the market value of the tract's timber in the range of species prices. If, for instance, the lowest value sawtimber species are bringing $100/mbf on the stump with the highest at $950/mbf, a tract average of $200/mbf usually indicates that most of its volume is concentrated in low-value species. In the Jones example, the hardwood sawtimber 16" DBH and larger averages out to $796 p/A and $331.67/mbf, indicating a pretty good dollar value per acre and a mid-range average of species value.

A forester generally does not project **future timber value** in a PTV cruise. He might suggest in his narrative the implications for future timber values that follow from alternative timbering strategies involving more-or-less-aggressive immediate cuts. Projecting volume growth by species and diameter class is straight-forward when the forester knows the site indices for the operable acreage and has a timber-cruise baseline, disaggregated by species and two-inch diameter classes. Your forester can also use an **increment borer** (hand auger) to extract a small core of wood—a tree's radius—which reveals its growth rate and soundness. Borings taken from different species provide empirical data for past growth rates for each species from which future growth rates and volumes can be projected. Increment boring is usually not needed to make the rough volume-growth projections that would be useful to most land buyers.

Projecting future species stumpage prices is iffier than projecting volumes. Extension forestry faculty at the land-grant universities usually have access to models that project prices using different assumptions about demand, interest rates and other variables. Doing **future timber analysis** is a common exercise in forestry programs, because it is used so often by industrial owners, pension funds and other investors to evaluate timberland. Your forester—or you—can usually tap into these models at little or no cost. Graduate forestry students are usually happy to run your cruise through their school's model for a modest hourly rate.

Since the cruise gives you a reasonably accurate estimate of present timber value, it may suit your interests to have a future timber analysis done under four sets of assumptions: 1) no immediate timbering; first cut scheduled for a specific future year determined by existing stand characteristics; 2) immediate cut of all sawtimber 16" DBH+ plus pulpwood; 3) immediate cut of all sawtimber 18" DBH+ plus pulpwood; and 4) immediate clearcut (or semi-clearcut of all HW and SW 6" DBH+). Models will show expected returns to you at alternative time intervals out to 100 years and under three simple price assumptions—slow rate of price increase, middle rate and high rate. With this information, you can figure out which cutting strategy nets you the most income over different time frames. The same type of analysis can be done on planted pine plantations. Most modeling does not factor in catastrophic events, such as a forest fire, insect infestations or a ten-year drought. Future value models can punch in a risk discount, and discounting for risk should give you a better projection. I'd recommend doing some form of future timber analysis on the Jones farm because it has good timber dirt and a good stocking of high-value species. The two together means the owner can generate significant future income from properly sequenced HW timber sales.

A forester would charge a couple of hundred dollars to prepare a future timber analysis and forest management plan for the Jones farm once he has done the cruise. If you're either cheap or lazy, here's a knowledgeable shot-in-the-dark way to do your own future analysis. We know the HW site indices on the Jones property are good. Assume for this example that the forester has decided to leave the 16-18" classification out of the sale, because the owner needs less cash immediately and wants more down the road. We can assume that volume in the existing sawtimber classes 12-18" DBH+ will at least double in 20 years given the indices, following an immediate post-purchase sawtimber cut of all 18" DBH+ and a pulpwood cut of low-value species and culls. After release, the remaining HW sawtimber will grow at a rate of at least 1/5 inch DBH per year in all diameter classes. This is a very conservative growth rate for released 12-18" DBH trees, which, on this site, might even double this rate. Also assume a modest 25 percent rise in each species price/mbf over the 20-year period. A two or three percent annual rise might prove to be more realistic, but a conservative assumption of about 1 percent a year will keep us from being too optimistic. TABLE 21-4 projects volumes and values with these assumptions.

The PTV of the 209,000 board feet of hardwood and softwood sawtimber 12-18" DBH that was not cut when you bought the Jones place was $35,855. Under very conservative growth and price assumptions, TABLE 21-4 projects this base to double to 418,000 board feet of both hardwood and softwood in 20 years and be worth $154,001. Volume has doubled but price (unadjusted for inflation) has quadrupled as the volume moved into the preferred DBH classes.

In my layman's opinion, both volume and price could easily be more than twice the rates assumed in the above example—without a stretch. A 1/5 inch per year growth rate could easily increase to 1/4-inch or even 1/3 inch after release.

Moreover, leaving 12-18" trees produces volume faster than in the smaller diameter classes, because the same rate of growth produces comparatively more basal area growth as diameter increases. A

7" DBH tree has a basal area of 38.5 square inches (A =3.1416 x 3.5 x 3.5 = 38.4846".) If this tree's growth rate for one year is 1/4 inch in diameter, its basal area will be 3.1416 x 3.625 x 3.625 =41.2825 square inches. This is a gain of about 2.8 square inches. An 18" DBH tree has a basal area of 254.4696 square inches. When it grows by 1/4-inch in diameter, its area increases to 261.5873 square inches, a gain of 7.1177 square inches. The 1/4-inch diameter increase on a 16-foot-long 7" DBH log would amount to a gain of about two board feet; the same growth on a 16' 18" DBH log would be almost eight board feet. Simply put, volume increases faster on the bigger trees. This growth differential is amplified by the price upgrade when the sawtimber reaches the 16 or 18" ingrowth threshold.

TABLE 21-4

Estimated Volume and Value + 20 Years
(mbf)

	12-14 become 16-18	14-16 become 18-20	16-18 become 20-22	Total Volume mbf	20-year* $/mbf plus 25%	Total value in 20 years
HW SPECIES						
Northern Red Oak (RO)	(10) 20	(20) 40	(30) 60	120	$500.00	$60,000
White Oak (WO)	(7) 14	(3) 6		20	312.50	6,250
Chestnut Oak (CO)	(4) 8	(4) 8	(6) 12	28	187.50	5,250
Scarlet Oak (SO)	(1) 2	(1) 2	(3) 6	10	218.75	2,188
Hickory (H)		(3) 6	(2) 4	10	187.50	1,875
Cherry (CH)		(5) 10	(7) 14	24	1,187.50	28,500
Hard Maple (HM)	(2) 4	(12) 24	(12) 24	52	562.50	29,250
Red Maple (RM)	(3) 6	(2) 4	(4) 8	18	156.25	6,750
Misc HW	(9) 18	(8) 16	(10) 20	54	125.00	6,750
total	**72**	**116**	**148**	**336**		**$142,876**
SW SPECIES						
Hemlock (HEM)	(7) 14	(10) 20	(10) 20	54	125.00	6,750
Spruce (S)	(4) 8	(6) 12	(4) 8	28	156.25	4,375
total	**22**	**32**	**28**	**82**		**$11,125**

Current species prices are: RO $400 mbf; WO $250/mbf; CO 150/mbf;
SO $175/mbf; H $150/mbf; CH $950/mbf; HM $450/mbf; RM $125/mbf;
Misc HW/$100 mbf; HEM $100/mbf; and S $125/mbf

Assuming a 20-year rise in stumpage price of only 25 percent is even more cautious if only because it falls short of the background inflation rate of two or three percent per year. Your forester can suggest an appropriate annual price inflator. The cost to you of waiting 20 years to cut your trees might be thought of in comparison with the return you would have earned had you invested the $35,855 in a stock index fund or sure-fire, can't-miss lottery numbers.

Your forester can also show you historical data that track species prices in your target area and give you an idea about the length of price cycles for locally important species. From 1960 to the mid-1990s, Appalachian HW lumber prices followed an upward trending sawtooth curve with peaks about every four or five years. Since then, however, hard (sugar) maple lumber increased from about $600 to almost $850/mbf green/air dried 4/4 while soft (red) maple went from about $500/mbf to $600/mbf with weakening in between. But red oak dropped $200/mbf, and white oak stayed more or less steady at about $475. These are inflation-adjusted prices for milled lumber, not stumpage. This pattern suggests that hard maple prices will top out and then decline as the oaks come back into favor at their discounted prices. Exactly when that might occur, of course, is unpredictable, but I'd look for hard maple lumber price to soften at $900/mbf. Milled lumber prices determine stumpage prices.

TABLE 21-5 is the buyer's summary of all the financial values that his scoping has produced on the Jones farm, which is priced at $189,900, or $1,461 p/A. The buyer's forester has placed a PTV on the Jones merchantable timber of $94,655, or $728 p/A. If the buyer sold all sawtimber 12" DBH+—a hard cut—the gross sale revenue should be about 50 percent of the asking price.

TABLE 21-5

Summary of All Values

1.	12-16" sawtimber	
	Hardwood	6,270
	Softwood	810
2.	16"+ sawtimber	
	Hardwood	79,600
	Softwood	6,475
3.	Pulpwood	
	3 cords p/A @ $5 per cord	1,500
		$94,655

Merchantable timber = $94,655
    Total = $728 p/A. ($94,655 / 130)

Bare Timberland Value:	$550 p/A = $55,000 ($550 x 100 operable acreage)
Land Value of 30 open acres:	700 p/A = $21,000 est.
Value of old cabin and barn	= $25,000 est.
Timber base	= $94,655

$195,655 Total

Assets:	Liabilities:
Cabin, marginally inhabitable	Cabin, marginally inhabitable
30 acres, good pasture	Moderate slope, no southern exposure
Good access road	No electric to property
No boundary uncertainty	Pasture fence needs to be upgraded
Calls close.	
Year-round spring	
Good timber productivity	

The buyer has also valued the other assets in the Jones property. By doing comparables analysis of recent sales of selectively cut land and small pastures, the buyer has estimated that selectively-cut woodland is worth about $550 p/A and pasture in a 30-acre parcel would bring about $700 p/A. After consulting with a couple of real-estate agents and looking at the tax-assessed values, the buyer has placed a value estimate of $25,000 on the old cabin and barn. Disaggregation shows a gross sale value of all property assets of about $195,655, almost $6,000 more than the asking price. To get there, however, the buyer would have to sell the merchantable sawtimber in the 12-18 classes, which is better left for future harvesting.

To make up this money, the buyer could sell two acres of pasture with their two buildings for about $27,000, leaving 128 acres, or sell the 30 acres including the buildings for $46,000, leaving the 100 acres of woods. If the buyer were to limit the timber sale to 18" DBH+, he would receive $57,300 and $1,500 for the pulpwood. That would be about 31 percent of the asking price. This is tax-free income until the time the new owner chooses to sell the land itself. (See timber-tax discussion in Chapter 24.) The buyer's individual circumstances will determine whether he needs to sell some or all of the timber and/or some of the acreage and improvements to make this deal work.

From an investment point of view, the buyer could consider selling the 30 acres of pasture in ten-acre lots (one of which includes the cabin and barn), the merchantable sawtimber 16 DBH+ and 50 to 60 acres of the woods. That would net out the likely purchase price of the Jones farm and leave the buyer with 40 to 50 acres of woodland (cut to a 16" threshold) for free.

CHAPTER 22: BEWARE THE SELLER'S CRUISE

THERE'S NO BOGUS LIKE SHOW BOGUS

I have discussed the elements of a cruise as a reasonably accurate method of estimating the volume and value of timber stumpage.

Cruises can be "cranked" to show more value than an owner would receive in a competitively bid sale. This is usually done by inflating the volumes above those for which a timber buyer will pay. Cruises can be deflated to show less volume as well, though I've never run across a buyer using a phony, undervalued cruise as a negotiating tool. In theory, a dozen independent foresters should cruise a tract in essentially the same way and come up with roughly the same volumes and values, allowing for a margin of error that's inherent in any extrapolation from sample data. In fact, a dozen foresters could come up with honest answers as well as several that one might rank in order of increasing creativity.

This chapter focuses on a **seller-paid timber cruise** used to help market wooded land to a buyer like you, the type of cruise that can range from dead honest to dead wrong.

Dirt-smart buyers should be alert for a **seller's bogus cruise**, which shows more stumpage volume and value than what the market will buy and pay for. Not all seller-supplied cruises are bogus. Nothing prevents a seller from handing a buyer a good-faith, accurate cruise, especially when it shows a lot of dollars. Buyers must understand, however, that sellers are motivated to invest their sale properties with assets that justify their asking price. A buyer's psychological pocketbook is clearly influenced by a cruise that shows a timber harvest will pay off 60 percent of the asking price as against one that shows only 20 percent.

I've learned that a buyer must know enough about cruising methods to protect himself from a less-than-honorable seller and his forester who inflates merchantable timber. I've seen cruises that double the merchantable timber value without exactly lying to get there. I've seen a cruise emerge from a "sophisticated" computer program that I couldn't evaluate because it provided so much information that the forest was lost for all of the trees. I've also seen a fancy forestry consulting outfit take an outdated cruise done on about 25 percent of a large tract and, without updating and verifying the information on the ground, project the same timber volumes across the entire acreage. This indefensible work resulted in a "timber analysis" given to a buyer that projected about five times the actual amount of stumpage the tract contained. Hundreds of thousands of dollars in anticipated timber value evaporated when the buyer—now owner—had a couple of honest foresters prepare a timber sale.

As you read the following observations keep in mind one simple land-buyer's rule: a scoping buyer is interested in finding out what the market will pay for the target property's (merchantable) stumpage and not a theoretical value for "standing" (merchantable and non-merchantable) timber. If stumpage buyers put no value on a tree, they will not pay anything for it. Honest cruises limit themselves to merchantable timber, that which a stumpage buyer values and will pay for. If you find reference in a seller's cruise to "liquidation value," it probably means a theoretical value based on every wood scrap on the property. Liquidation value is likely to be higher, often much higher, than the **stumpage value of the merchantable timber**, which is the value a buyer wants to know prior to submitting an offer to purchase the seller's property.

Before I begin talking about bogus seller cruises, I want to alert you to an even simpler seller trick: **the bait of big money**. Here's the way the seller works it. The seller tells the buyer that he's never done a cruise on his property, but he thinks that there's at least between "x 1000 board feet and x+y 1000 board feet." He doesn't say how he arrived at that estimate or what definitions of merchantability he used. If the seller is pressed, he'll say something like, "That's just how it looks to me." The buyer multiplies a mid-price for stumpage against the volume number between x and x+y and comes up with "big money," even using these conservative assumptions. The buyer then starts assuming that his calculation represents truth, because he wants "big money" to represent truth. This seller never hands the buyer a phony document. He never hires a less-than-scrupulous forester to inflate cruise values. He simply plants the bait in the buyer's mouth and lets the buyer's own mind direct the swallowing. Using buyer greed is an old seller trick. I've seen it worked on 500 acres as well as a deal where the seller was trawling for more than $100 million.

Hardwood (deciduous trees) and pine (coniferous) tracts are cruised with many of the same measuring and evaluation techniques, but the forester brings different standards to each type. Both types of trees produce pulp and sawtimber. Markets for pulp use more of each tree than mills that produce lumber from sawtimber. For that reason, foresters legitimately count more volume in a pine tree marketed for pulp than a hardwood tree of the same size marketed for sawtimber. Hardwood (tree) tops and low-quality trees are used for pulp as well, but the real value in hardwood timber lies in that portion of each tree— particularly the high-value species—that is good enough for sawtimber or, better yet, veneer. Pine sawtimber brings a higher price than pine pulp. While pine occurs in natural stands and mixed with hardwoods, much pine land now for sale is one-species, even-aged plantations dedicated to producing pulp (fiber) as fast and as cheaply as possible. Companies manufacturing paper and wood products, such as MeadWestvaco, International Paper and Weyerhaeuser, are divesting themselves of millions of acres of planted pine and pine-hardwood tracts.

Owing to their different growth characteristics and markets, hardwood and pine are cruised with different criteria for counting merchantable volume. **The discussion that follows focuses on valuing hardwood, not pine**. Some of the techniques I discuss that are used to overvalue hardwood can be applied for the same purpose in pine valuations. It is, of course, far simpler to estimate volume and value on an acre of even-aged trees of one species than on an acre of mixed species, ages and size. Accordingly, the opportunities for inflating the value of a varied hardwood tract are more numerous.

TRICKS

Here are some of the ways that hardwood cruises can inflate the volumes and/or projected values of timberland.

1. Basic Factors.

Every cruise report should set forth the basic parameters of its methodology and sampling, including:

- the **log scale the forester used**. (Different scales estimate log volumes differently. See below.)

- **number of plots** the forester put in.

- **number of acres** covered by the cruise. (Acres that are inoperable should not be cruised and their merchantable volume should not be counted.)

- **Form Class (FC) used**. Form Class refers to the degree of taper—from stump to top break—the forester used in estimating a tree's log volume. FC 78 is common in Appalachian hardwood.

  Yellow poplar usually merits FC 80. Less taper means more volume counted.

- **top-break diameter**. This refers to the general spot on the upper portion of each tree where the forester stops counting the length of the merchantable log (s) it contains. Foresters are taught to estimate sawtimber log volume in a standing tree up to the first major/natural stem break (e.g., crotch) or to the appropriate diameter "break." If a hardwood tree does not contain a natural break, a forester estimating sawtimber should stop where he judges the stem narrows to about ten inches in diameter. Foresters depend on their experience to tell them how a timber buyer will cut logs from a stem, hence, how he will estimate its volume and value. A forester who does not "see" a tree's volume the way timber buyers do will provide an inflated volume estimate.

Some foresters will include a top-break diameter on their cruise report while others routinely don't. It's important for your forester to use the same top-break diameter that local timber buyers use, otherwise he will be including volume and assigning value to volume that timber buyers will never pay for. On hardwood pulp tracts, it is fair to estimate volume from the stump up to a six-inch diameter in the tree. To a sawtimber buyer, a stem's volume between ten-inches and six inches in diameter has no sawtimber value. The stem above ten inches in diameter can sometimes be sold for pulp, but the price per unit of pulp volume will be no more than a small fraction of the sawtimber price. When a sawtimber buyer bids for your hardwood tract, he may or may not assign a value to the pulp in the tops of the trees he plans to cut for sawtimber. More often than not, such a buyer will leave this **"top log,"** or slash, on the ground. I've sold timber to a sawtimber mill that refused to haul these top logs to a pulp yard less than six miles from my logging site because it was an uneconomical use of the crew's time.

The way a forester can pump sawtimber volume is to **"break the tree too high**." This has the effect of including in sawtimber volume a top log that's only six inches in diameter at its small end. The **phantom volume** in the top log can easily add ten to 20 board feet in each tree. With 1,000 trees so estimated, the seller's cruise will show a phantom 10,000 to 20,000 board feet packaged in with the genuine hardwood sawtimber volume. Timber buyers will not pay you sawtimber price for top-log volume, and often may not pay you anything at all for it. They will not include top-log volume in their own cruise on which they base their bid to you, the owner.

Breaking too high, that is, at six inches in diameter rather than at ten, is an intentional inflation of hardwood volume and, subsequently, value.

Pine, sold for pulp, is properly broken at six or even four inches in the top.

- **Cruise date**. Be wary if the seller's cruise is undated or more than a year or two old. You should be alert to evidence of the seller **"cherry-picking"** (removing) the high-value hardwood trees in the interim, between the cruise date and when you see it.

If you find large, fresh-looking stumps in high-value species scattered around the property, the seller has probably pocketed the best 25 percent of the tract's volume and as much as 50 percent of the value shown on the seller's cruise. A fresh stump is usually light in color rather than a weathered grey; no sprouts will have shot up; its bark will be tight against the wood; and it may still be oozing sap. If you don't know how to identify trees from their bark, ask a knowledgeable person to walk the property with you. If leaves still cling to the top slash, you can identify stump species from them using a tree book.

With older cruises, you can assume volume growth for each year on hardwood tracts of at least two percent on below-average sites, four percent on average sites and six percent on productive sites. That assumption is subject to many field qualifications, such as drought and disease, that inhibit growth. Pine growth ranges from four to ten percent annually.

You should also be aware that five years of volume growth on a hardwood tract starting with an average diameter of five inches still has no merchantable sawtimber value. That same five years of volume growth on a tract where the trees started with an average of 17 inches in diameter can be enormously valuable.

As trees gain in diameter, each yearly increment in diameter growth increases their rate of volume gain. One inch in ring growth increases diameter by two inches. A six-inch diameter tree when it grows to eight inches, increases its cross-sectional area by 22 square inches with a corresponding volume gain. But a 16"-diameter tree when it grows to 18" increases its cross-sectional area by more than 53 square inches, more than double the smaller tree.

If you find a new cruise that projects volume growth, look carefully at the distribution of diameters in the old cruise. You may be looking at an update that shows a lot of volume growth that's concentrated in young timber for which no timber buyer will yet pay.

If a seller's forester wanted to boost volume on the seller's tract, he could manipulate these basic methodology factors to that end. I've seen, for example, a very professional-looking cruise analysis on a large, diverse tract that was based on too few plots to make accurate volume extrapolations. I've also received several older cruises that were never updated to reflect interim cutting.

2. Inflate species price multipliers.

This is easy to implement and may not be easy to catch. To inflate the value of the cruised timber, the forester need only pump the species prices ($/mbf) by five to ten percent to project more timber sales revenue than the landowner would actually receive. Since hardwood species prices vary from area to area and are determined by changing local conditions and market factors, it's easy for a forester to modestly pad the price multipliers without making the fakery obvious. A seller gave me a cruise on about 18,000 acres of Tennessee hardwood and planted pine that boosted price multipliers by about 25 percent. The difference between $100 mbf and $125 mbf might not snag your eye, but it amounted to a tract-wide valuation difference of $2 million, all of which wasn't there.

A seller's forester can limit his price research once he gets the answer he wants. For example, he may call a timber buyer who says, "I had to pay $1,700 for cherry on a sale a few months ago." The forester might end his telephoning there and use $1,700 mbf as his cherry sawtimber multiplier. Had he called the three other local timber buyers, he would have found that cherry on the stump was bringing $950-$1,000 mbf, and that tract a few months ago brought $1,700 mbf because of the unusually high number of cherry veneer logs in the stand. The odds are that the seller's forester knew $1,700 was too high, but chose to remain half-informed. You, as a non-forester, will probably not be able to access local timber buyers to ascertain price multipliers. For that reason alone, you should hire a forester to review any cruise the seller provides that puts dollar values on stumpage.

The simplest way to crank a cruise is to use stumpage price multipliers that are higher than those timber buyers will use. A little cheating—a five percent tweak on cherry, eight percent on red oak and so on—and pretty soon you have a large pile of **phantom value**. A little cheating across the board is more effective than one or two big cheats, because little price boosts are hard to detect while grossly inflated ones are not. Using above-market price multipliers is not as common as other tricks, because your forester can readily verify local stumpage prices with a few phone calls.

Price cheating is almost impossible for a land buyer inexperienced with timber valuations to detect. If a seller categorizes you as a novice, however, you may be given a price-inflated cruise. I was once sent a hand-written "cruise"—no date, no forester named, no diameter classes, no diameter threshold, no acreage definition, no narrative. It showed species, board feet and value by species. I just laughed; it looked like a kitchen-table job done by a fourth-grader. The seller promised that it was "as honest as could be." The price multipliers were double current market. Take a seller's cruise to your consulting forester and ask him to confirm price multipliers as a first step.

I've found most state-employed, county foresters are reluctant to challenge seller cruises, with some notable exceptions. Prices that state and federal agencies get for the sale of public timber are lower than those paid to private landowners, because the public sales require the logger to invest in expensive road-building and reclamation practices. Don't rely on public-sale prices; rely on your forester.

A variation on using inflated price multipliers is for a seller's cruise to include no prices and timber values at all. This forces the buyer to come up with his own price multipliers and overall values, a task that's almost impossible for a non-forester to accomplish with precision.

Mills value stumpage tract by tract, species by species. Timber quality and access vary from tract to tract, and these variations are figured into the buyer's overall bid price. Stumpage bids will vary from buyer to buyer according to the individual needs and costs of each buyer at that particular moment. A 100-acre tract of cherry might be valued by a buyer at $1,600 p/A while he might value another 100-acre tract of cherry 30 miles further from his mill (and lying on a southeast aspect that is accessed by a one-mile-long 4WD road that will require 50 hours of bulldozer work to make it suitable for log trucks) at $1,200 p/A despite having the same volume. The timber quality on the second tract will be lower than the first tract owing to its site index, and the poor access road will increase the buyer's logging cost. Each mill's current stumpage prices will reflect its current inventory of each species, demand for milled products and individual cost of cutting and hauling logs to its facility. A mill short on black cherry and long on orders will pay more for such stumpage than a mill with 500 cherry logs sitting in its yard and no orders for cherry lumber. A mill five miles from the target property can pay a bit more for stumpage than one 100 miles away. A stumpage buyer with a harvest-and-hauling cost of $300 mbf can pay more than one whose cost is $500 mbf. A mill with no market for veneer will pay less for stumpage than one that routinely ships such logs abroad for premium prices.

Stumpage buyers are reluctant to talk to and quote stumpage prices to land buyers and landowners unless it's in the context of a negotiation for a timber sale. It's also difficult for the lay person to understand exactly what a mill manager means when he says "we'd pay $700 for red oak," when his real meaning is that the mill has paid that much for the best quality red oak logs, but his more common bid price is about $500 mbf.

My guess is that the consultants who are not putting prices in their cruises for sellers are doing so to avoid lawsuits over misrepresentation and fraud. A seller's cruise lacking prices tempts the do-it-yourselfer to do it to himself. Resist! Pay a consulting forester to check the seller's cruise and determine current stumpage prices for the seller's tract.

3. Applying Large Sawtimber Price Multipliers to Small Sawtimber Volume to Produce Phantom Value.

This is a common trick. I've seen several forms.

First, the forester may apply the sawtimber price for trees 18" DBH and larger to sawtimber in diameter classes smaller than 16". (The threshold could be 16" or even 14" rather than 18", depending on local markets.) The seller's forester knows, or at least suspects, that the 12-16 sawtimber will be price-discounted in the local market. Depending on the volume in the smaller diameter classes, this calculation can significantly overestimate timber-sale revenue.

The variation on this tactic is to count small sawtimber volume into the merchantable timber base, but use no price multipliers at all in the cruise. The effect is to have the property appear to contain a huge volume of merchantable sawtimber valued at the sawtimber price, when some portion of that volume has only a discounted value.

I was sent a seller's cruise on a 6,000-acre West Virginia tract that showed 12,171,000 bf of merchantable hardwood sawtimber on the Doyle scale. Of that volume, 5,350,000 bf was in the 10-14" DBH categories, too small for a mill to pay for as sawtimber. And another 2,211,000 was in the 16" category; maybe it would be price-discounted, maybe not. High-value species like cherry in smaller sawtimber diameters will often fetch the same price as volume in larger diameters. But this tract had relatively little volume in high-value species, especially high-quality, high-value species. Sixty-two percent of the total stumpage classified as "merchantable" was smaller than 18" DBH. Most of that volume would not bring the sawtimber price bid for 18" DBH+ volume. Of the 3,420,000 bf shown for the most prevalent species, red oak (a high-value species at the time), only 1,208,000 bf was 18" DBH+. The other two thirds was in 10 to 16" diameters. The well-known consulting firm that prepared this cruise noted that timber volumes down to 10" DBH were included for "planning purposes." Fair enough, but all the volume smaller than 14" should have been pulled out of the merchantable category and put into a premerchantable analysis.

A quick reading of those numbers would encourage me to expect a much larger volume of timber than would be immediately saleable. The absence of any price multipliers for each species encouraged a buyer to apply a straight-through price to the aggregated volume of each species, regardless of quality and diameter size. A "guessed-at" straight-through multiplier for both merchantable and premerchantable volume is too gross for your purpose. It's not likely to accurately take into account the distribution of the two volumes that are priced so differently.

Second, the seller's forester can apply the large-diameter sawtimber price multiplier to that volume in the large-diameter trees found in the top log. As noted above, top-log volume has value, if any at all, only as pulp or firewood. It is too small in diameter to be milled cost-effectively for lumber. The most prudent practice in hardwood stumpage is for your forester to assign no dollar value to volume that is above the natural break or above a ten inch diameter, unless the local practice is to salvage these limbs for pulp, chips or firewood. In that event, it's fair to put the current market price on this volume sold for these products, but not as sawtimber.

I was recently handed a cruise that counted as merchantable *sawtimber* that part of the top "with a minimum of 4 inches main bole diameter." I am familiar with timber buying in the area where this property lies, and no timber buyer would pay a nickel for top volume between 10" and 4" in diameter. Any seller's forester who uses a sawtimber price multiplier for top-log volume is showing dollars that will never appear in your pocket.

A third way to produce phantom value is to count all volume in poorly formed and otherwise defective trees or the defective portions of trees, particularly high-value species. Honest foresters don't count poorly formed trees, and they deduct volume contained in the defective portions of a tree's stem. Eliminated is volume that does not meet sawtimber standards owing to severe bends, cankers, hollowness, rot, fire damage and other problems. You might hear this called, "subtracting defect." Take a stem that is 30 feet long and at least 20" in diameter along its length. The forester should include in his cruise the volume in its first 16 feet and the last eight feet, both of which are free of defect. The six feet of stem between these two lengths should not be counted because it contains a deep gash that makes it unsuitable for lumber. This 30-foot stem will cut out into a linear total of 24 feet of logs, not 30. A forester who counts in that six feet of defective stem is creating stumpage value in a log that doesn't exist in the market.

The final example I'll share comes from a tract where the seller's cruise showed $433,000 in total timber value with an asking price on the 886 acres of $350,000. Can't go wrong here, right? Don't write your check yet.

Here are the ringers in this deal. First, the $433,000 represents, the seller said, "total capital value of merchantable timber." Total capital value is the count-anything-with-bark number that a not-overly-honest landowner might use to establish his tax basis in the timber. It does not represent what the landowner would receive from the sale of his genuinely merchantable stumpage. When I read the extremely small print at the bottom of the cruise, I found a very large disclaimer about the seller's expansive notion of total capital value. Total capital value was significantly greater than merchantable stumpage value. Second, the cruise included as "sawtimber," everything 8" DBH and larger. Most of the property's volume was 14" DBH and smaller. Only 25 percent of the total sawtimber volume was 16" DBH and larger. The smaller diameters would not bring the prevailing sawtimber price. Third, the cruise offered a range of sawtimber prices by species—low, high and likely. The "likely" price was multiplied against the total species volume (which includes all the small-diameter volume). If I were to try to apply a single price to sawtimber volume that's mostly 14" DBH and smaller, I would apply a number at the low end of the range, not the middle, as this cruise did. My bottom-line guess is that this cruise showed more than twice the dollars a stumpage seller would pocket from the sale of merchantable stumpage. But it sounded like a hell of a deal when I first heard about it.

4. Inoperable Acreage.

Good timber is often found in places that for various reasons render it without commercial value. **Operable acreage** is land that is legally and physically accessible by locally available conventional logging machines and techniques. In the East, this means self-propelled vehicles with wheels and tracks; it usually does not mean overhead cable systems or helicopters. In swamps, conventional logging may mean "**shovel logging**," which requires cutting pulp-type trees and using them to make a road for a tracked cutting vehicle. These road trees are then salvaged and sold when the logging is done. This is a costlier method of logging, and the trees used for road-building need to be debarked before they are processed further.

Timber buyers will only pay for stumpage that they can cut at a profit. This means stumpage on operable acreage that can be removed with the equipment they normally use.

Inoperable acreage is land on which merchantable timber may exist but it is either legally or physically inaccessible, or uneconomical to harvest because of steep slopes, remoteness or other cost factors. Stumpage buyers will assign no value to otherwise merchantable trees that are so scattered that they're not worth the cost of getting them. A $2,000 cherry will be left standing in the woods if the logger has to spend $2,000 to build a mountainside road to get to it. Stumpage buyers will not pay landowners for trees on inoperable acreage.

Inoperable stumpage would also include merchantable trees that are fully or partially off-limits because they're located in setbacks, streamside buffer zones or designated habitat for endangered or protected species. Land that is considered high-value conservation property and is so classified by public policy may be off-limits to timbering even though it is allowed on paper. Timber on such land should be considered inoperable. The worst example of this I've encountered was a seller with about 8.5 million board feet of koa on 3,000 acres in Hawaii. All of the land was considered "conservation," which allowed timbering, though no timbering permit had been granted to anyone on conservation land for more than ten years. The state forestry official in charge of permitting said that he could not envision a permit being issued.

On one tract of almost 40,000 acres that I came to know, more than 12,000 acres were considered inoperable owing to steepness. A knowledgeable forester assigned no value to their sawtimber and pulp volumes. When a buyer asked a less knowledgeable forester to estimate the value of the tract's merchantable timber, he fully valued the volume found on these 12,000 acres. The land buyer was not pleased when he discovered that he had paid for several million board feet worth nothing to him because they were worth nothing to local stumpage buyers.

On another tract of 5,000 acres in the coastal swamps of eastern North Carolina, a seller's cruise showed about $2.3 million in timber value. Unfortunately, only about $500,000 could be captured through conventional shovel logging. The rest of the value was found in timber growing on land so wet that it could not be harvested economically. Any buyer who believed this seller's cruise was stuck with timber value on inoperable acreage.

I have seen a number of seller-supplied cruises where merchantable timber on inoperable acreage was counted to inflate volume.

5. Failure to disaggregate species by two-inch diameter classes.

Sawtimber value depends in part on diameter size. It is critical that a cruise disaggregate estimated

HW sawtimber volumes by both species and one- or two-inch diameter classes, at least in the 12-and-above diameters. It's acceptable to lump large diameter classes together, as, for example, 22"+, because there's no price discount or premium above a diameter such as that. Disaggregation of volume by diameter and species is important to the land buyer, because it groups timber into readily valued components and allows the drawing of a line between price-discounted premerch and fully priced merchantable stumpage. Cruises that lump all sawtimber, particularly hardwood, into one category, such as "10" DBH and larger," are suspect, because timber buyers will usually apply a price discount on the portion of this stumpage in the smaller diameters.

Similarly, a buyer should doubt the dollar value assigned to all sawtimber volume in an aggregated diameter class of a single species, say, "all sugar maple 12" DBH and larger." It is easy for a compliant forester to help his seller by applying the large-diameter sawtimber price multiplier to the entire group, including all the 12 to 16s. This practice, in my opinion, is deliberate overstatement.

Smaller sawtimber—the premerchantable volume—should be disaggregated into two-inch diameter classes by species to give the buyer a reasonable estimate of the time needed for the volume in each diameter class to grow into a merchantable class and benefit from the associated price increase.

A "cruise" that reports a single gross timber-volume number for a tract as a whole should be suspect, except for even-age stands of one species, such as 50 acres of 25-year-old planted loblolly pine. If a seller hands you a paper showing so many board feet in something called "marketable hardwood," or "hardwood timber," or "standing timber," or "available timber," do not take this number as a valid, trustworthy cruise result. Ask for details and cruise methodology. Ask for a two-inch breakdown of all sawtimber 10" DBH and up by individual species. Don't be surprised if this information "can't" be obtained. If the seller is willing to give you the name of the forester who prepared this number, call and ask for such a breakdown. Do not be surprised if either the seller or the forester stonewalls you. A consulting forester working for you, the buyer, should provide a disaggregated timber inventory on a hardwood stand, not a single number showing gross volume or, worse, an unexplained dollar value.

On pulpwood tracts, volume need not be disaggregated into two-inch diameter classes because a pulpwood buyer is interested in aggregated fiber, not lumber potential.

I have often encountered a seller who tells me that his property contains either so many board feet or "at least" so many dollars in timber. No paper is ever available to support these statements. While it is theoretically possible that such statements are true, it is also theoretically possible for me—a 61 year old with a bum knee—to perform a reverse dunk, the very move I could not hope to do at 19 with two spry knees.

6. Combining Low-Value and High-Value Species of the Same Family.

A forester should separate hardwood sawtimber volumes into botanically distinct species, because stumpage buyers set prices for each species rather than for a tree family. The family of oaks, for example, will include northern red oak at $400-$600 mbf and chestnut oak at $100 mbf. Scarlet oak, pin oak, black oak and the others will fall somewhere in between. A sawtimber cruise that uses one price multiplier against an undifferentiated "Oaks" category where several oak species are present in significant volumes is probably overvaluing the stumpage. Most stumpage buyers in my experience do not value oak sawtimber at a straight-through price unless they're planning on turning the trees into low-value products like pulp or pallets.

A more subtle version of the same trick is to lump together closely related species within the same family, call everything the high-value species and multiply the resulting volume by that price. I've seen this used to combine chestnut oak volume at $100 mbf with white oak volume at $300 mbf, the total volume being multiplied by $300 mbf; scarlet oak at $175 mbf and black oak at $125 mbf with red oak at $400 mbf, the total volume being multiplied by $400 mbf; and soft (red) maple at $125 mbf with hard (sugar) maple at $300 mbf, the total being multiplied by $300 mbf. In each case, the value of the combined total is inflated by using the high-value species price against the lower-value species volumes. This is nothing but fraud.

7. Using the "wrong" scale.

Tree scales are formulas that foresters use to estimate the volume of wood in standing timber. These scales provide fixed volume numbers for inch-by-inch DBH categories on one axis and the number of eight to 16-foot logs in a tree on the other. Where diameter class intersects with log length, a number—volume in board feet—will be found. (Other means are used to calculate volume in tons or cords.) Stumpage buyers usually prefer—and therefore use—a particular scale for specific types of timber in each region. New York, for example, uses three different scales to estimate wood—Scribner, Doyle and International 1/4 inch—depending on the area of the state where the timber is located. Scales "count" tree volume differently, which means that 1,000 board feet under one scale will be valued differently than 1,000 board feet under the other two.

Different scales estimate volume differently because they are constructed for different timber types. One scale, for example, may be most accurate for tall, straight species of fairly uniform diameter, while another may be best suited for trees that taper with height. One scale may be the timber buyer's preference because it undercounts volumes in certain diameter classes while another scale may be the landowner's preferred alternative because it overcounts certain classes. **A forester should use the log scale in his cruise for you that is the one that stumpage buyers in that area will use on the target property's timber.**

Land sellers will sometimes cruise their stumpage with the inflating scale to give a land buyer a rosy sense of its timber value. The bogus seller cruises on hardwood sawtimber that I've seen have used the International Scale where stumpage buyers used nothing but the Doyle Scale. The Doyle is a more conservative and more appropriate scale for hardwood sawtimber. In the smaller diameter classes, the Doyle scale will measure 30 percent less volume than the International; the two scales close toward each other in the 30"+ diameter classes. A tree 24" DBH that contains two usable 16' logs has 370 board feet by the Doyle scale and 441 bf on the International, a 19 percent increase. On tracts where the majority of merchantable sawtimber is in the 16" to 18" and 18" to 20" categories, the International Scale will seriously overestimate stumpage volume that a landowner can sell to buyers using the Doyle. A forester could prepare a "seller's cruise" using the International Scale while knowing that timber buyers will not use it. If the buyer relies on this seller's cruise, he may easily end up with 20 percent less volume for sale than the seller's cruise showed after buying the seller's property.

I've seen the "musical scales" tactic used several times. In one case, a sawmill was selling 12,500 acres of very good hardwood dirt. Most of the acreage had been selectively cut to 16" DBH. The mill's forester handed me a cruise he had prepared using the International Scale. "Do you buy for the mill on the International Scale?" I asked, knowing the answer. "No," he said. Nonetheless, he had deliberately increased the property's timber volume and value. I figured he was showing $2 million that would not be there for my client. If you find a seller using the "wrong" log scale, keep your eyes open for other tricks to pad timber value.

When scoping a seller's cruise, ask your forester to make sure that the seller's forester used the scale that local stumpage buyers use.

8. DBH vs. Point of Severance.

Most of the hardwood sawtimber cruises I've seen use a tree scale in which **diameter at breast height (DBH)** is measured at 4.5 feet above the ground. From that point up, the tree's stem loses the atypical diameter of its splayed base. Volume formulas assume the tree will be cut at about six inches above the ground, measured on the uphill side. The formulas don't force the owner to give 3.5 feet of butt log free to the timber buyer.

The height at which the tree is cut is often referred to as the "**point of severance.**" A cruise whose volumes are tallied from a diameter at the point of severance may include more volume than one using DBH. A timber cruise that includes all merchantable timber 16" DBH and larger will include many fewer trees than one that takes in all trees 16" and larger at the point of severance. The 16"-DBH cruise does not include the small sawtimber trees in the 12 to 16" DBH classes, which represents the future harvest. Because the point of severance can be as close to the ground as a logger can cut, a seller's cruise based on 16" at the point of severance will count the volume in the 12-16 DBH trees that a DBH buyer will not value. Close to ground level 12-16 DBH trees widen for structural support, thus allowing a point-of-severance cruise to count their volume and price it as full-size sawtimber. A 16" cut taken at the point of severance will leave land with much less standing timber and looking far more roughed up.

I know of cases where a stumpage buyer has been known to approach landowners with an offer to buy timber on a 16" point-of-severance basis, during which he says "16 inches and larger" very loudly and "point of severance" next to inaudibly. The landowner is likely to expect that everything 16" *DBH* and larger will be left. Not so. He will find himself owning a third cousin to a clearcut. Most landowners will not know the difference between a 16" DBH cut and a 16" point-of-severance cut even when their hearing is good.

As I was finishing this book, I responded to an ad in the <u>Wall Street Journal</u> for about 7,500 acres in Kentucky with coal, gas and timber. When I phoned the contact person—one of the owners—she never mentioned that the timber was being cut. I went to the virtual room where documents were stored and pulled up the seller's consulting forester's report. He noted that of the 15 million board feet of merchantable sawtimber measuring ten inches and larger, all timber measuring 16 inches and larger *at stump height*—about nine million board feet—had been sold and was under contract until October, 2007. A 16" stump cut translates to about a 12" DBH cut. The forester then goes on to break down the remaining six million board feet, in which he counted *all trees 10 to 14" DBH*. Not so fast, Louie.

If the owner has sold down to about 12" DBH, all the 12 to 14" DBH will be gone. You can't count them as there! Of the six million board feet said to be remaining after the cut, my guess is a buyer would find about one million board feet, all in 10 to 12s DBH. This seller came across as a straight-shooter; she even told me she was. Buyers are frequently disappointed.

The field vernacular for a point-of-severance harvest is a "**stump cut.**" If you are handed a cruise based on point of severance or stump cut, keep in mind that small sawtimber with discounted value is being included as fully valued sawtimber. The principal purpose in my opinion for a seller-supplied cruise to use a stump parameter is to deceive an unsophisticated buyer into thinking that he will get significantly more money for the timber than he actually will. The land buyer will assume that a stumpage buyer will pay a sawtimber price straight through for all volume 16" at the stump when, in fact, the stumpage buyer will discount the volume in the trees smaller than 16" DBH. A seller-supplied stump-cruise is used to justify the seller's high asking price.

9. Using the Wrong Measure of Volume.

Cords and tons are gross measures and are almost always applied against low-value wood used for pulp, chips, or sawtimber used for industrial-type purposes such as railroad ties, pallets, mining props and fence material.

Inherent in timber measured in either cords or tons is the aggregation of the tract's merchantable trees (species, diameter class and quality) into a single volume number (in the case of cords) or a single weight (in the case of tons). That aggregation is exactly the opposite of the disaggregation analysis a forester does when he cruises hardwood sawtimber for the lumber market. A cruise expressed as tons or cords cannot capture the true value of a hardwood-sawtimber tract for lumber, because of the aggregation of high-and low-value sawtimber trees, trees with different diameters, trees with different weights per unit of volume and so on.

A tonnage cruise on a sawtimber tract that uses one, straight-through per-ton price multiplier lends itself to misinterpretation. In some tonnage cruises I've seen, the actual timber value is underestimated. This occurs because quality hardwood sawtimber is priced at the same dollar multiplier as pulp and low-value sawtimber. A forester and I bought a bottom-land hardwood tract in West Tennessee when we discovered that the seller's tonnage cruise masked the real value of the tract when looked at as sawtimber, not pulp. When my partner reworked tonnage into disaggregated sawlog volume in board feet, he found that the timber would more than pay for the purchase.

Where a tonnage cruise uses a single price multiplier, it's easy to inflate value for the gullible land buyer. A cruise that shows 1,000,000 tons on a tract can easily suggest a phantom $500,000 in timber value simply by using a price multiplier of $6 p/t rather than the $5.50 the market will pay.

While cords and tons are perfectly appropriate measures for pulpwood tracts, particularly clearcuts, readers who are scoping most hardwood sawtimber will want a cruise in board feet, organized by species and two-inch diameter class, and priced by species.

10. Volume in Big Trees on High-graded Tracts May Have Little Value.

The high-grading logger cuts only the large-diameter, high-value sawtimber trees, leaving in place most, or all, of the large low-value sawtimber trees and all of the culls. Loggers prefer high-grading because it allows them to net the most money from a timber stand with the least amount of effort in the shortest period of time. The logger removes only the "**money trees**" and leaves the junk. Thirty years after high-grading, you will find a lot of large-diameter, worthless junk. And each time a high-grading logger leaves such trees standing, they use resources that would be more profitably consumed by the small-diameter high-value trees.

When a tract has been repeatedly high-graded, it will appear to the layman's eye as a stand of large-diameter, hardwood sawtimber, and for that reason it must surely have substantial commercial value. Don't be fooled, as I was when I first started looking for timberland. Look carefully at the species of the big trees.

You will find that most are the local low-values; in my area that means gum, black birch, basswood, hickory, chestnut oak and pine. Now look at the large trees again, particularly any high-value species, such as red oak, cherry, walnut, ash and sugar maple. The odds are high that you will find that these trees are culls—trees that are poorly formed; defective from lightning, fire or animals; diseased; hollow or otherwise not worth cutting. You may have to walk around the tree to find the flaw, because one side can be perfect in a worthless tree.

A truly unscrupulous seller will arrange to have his high-graded tract cruised by a not very scrupulous forester who dutifully records all volumes, regardless of quality. This cruise will show significant volumes of sawtimber in large diameter classes. The gross volumes will be accurate but buyers will bid little on this timber, because it has little value to them. An honest forester will not count volume that is defective as sawtimber. At best, it's pulp; at worst, shade.

If a seller gives you a cruise that is formatted into volumes, by species and two-inch diameter classes, see if it shows lots of volume in the large-diameter classes. It's certainly possible that you have found a genuinely valuable timber tract. It's also probable that your seller is showing large volumes in large-diameter, low-value species and culls left from high-grading. A skewed distribution by which almost all of the volume in high-value species turns up in small-diameter classes and most of the volume in large-diameter classes is low-value species tips you that the seller's property has been high-graded several times.

Your forester should be able to look at a seller-supplied cruise and give you a first impression of its reliability based on its format and who did it. (Consulting foresters know who of their peers plays straight all the time and who doesn't.) Cruises of high-graded property usually stand out to the trained eye. In my neighborhood, I'm pretty sure that a tract has been high-graded when the cruise shows disproportionately high volumes of large-diameter (low-value) chestnut oak and hickory.

With high-graded tracts, you are likely to run into either a **hearty verbal testimonial from the seller**—"Buddy, just look at the size of the timber out there; you can believe your own eyes, can't you?" or what I call **"the round-number ringer"**—an unsubstantiated timber value that is both large and suspiciously round, say $100,000, as in, "Buddy, that timber's worth a hundred grand if it's worth fifty cents." I've seen both tactics used on unsuspecting buyers. The buyer's interest lies in spending a few hundred dollars to have his forester take a look at any property with large-diameter trees and a seller's promise of instant riches.

While a high-graded tract has lost much of its timber value, it can be very good for hunting and recreation. Low-value species and culls produce food for wildlife and game. Moreover, high-graded tracts often "look good"—tall trees, big diameters, spreading crowns, clean forest floors. Such tracts can make good buys as long as you don't pay for timber value that isn't there.

11. Counting Pulp Dollars in a Sawtimber Stand.

A stumpage buyer often values a hardwood stand by limiting his estimate of worth to the hardwood sawtimber. Everything else—culls, pulp-value sawtimber, tops and the occasional conifer—are assigned no value, and his bid to the landowner will reflect that. A forester who counts the dollars in this type of volume will be inflating the tract's true market value—unless the stumpage buyers themselves will pay for it. On HW sawtimber tracts where the sawtimber is legitimately valued in the $100,000 to $200,000 range, I've seen pulp—broadly construed—valued at anywhere between $2,500 to $7,500. Sometimes that is a fair market valuation, but only if there's a market for it. Your forester will be able to tell you whether the seller's forester has padded the tract's valuation with pulp volume that stumpage buyers may cut and sell but will not pay for.

12. Data Overkill.

Foresters now have computer programs that can group and analyze field-gathered data in dozens of ways. I've seen at least once instance where the technical virtuosity of the forester's computer program buried the two or three most important bottom-line numbers under pages of printout. Cruise results should be simple and straight forward. An inexperienced land buyer needs to know two facts before making an offer on a wooded tract: 1) how much merchantable timber it contains, and 2) its estimated stumpage value when sold for a lump sum in the local market at current prices. If the seller hands you a cruise that is thick with impenetrable tables that don't lead to answers to the two basic buyer questions, it may be that the seller's forester is **playing hide the ball**. A buyer needs to see the ball whenever a seller is trying to hide it.

13. "Undering."

"Undering" is my word for a forester shorting a timber analysis in some way that works against a buyer. Here are some familiar examples:

a. Putting in too few plots.

The heart of a cruise is the taking of a sufficient number of samples (plots) to generate valid extrapolations for the tract as a whole. A forester must make a preliminary judgment about how many plots are sufficient to sample the tract. The more diverse a tract in age, species and quality, the more plots he might use. On tracts of a couple of hundred acres or less, he might use 20 to 40 plots per 100 acres. On larger tracts that are fairly consistent, he might put in one plot for every 15-20 acres. On very large tracts, I've seen one plot used to represent several hundred acres.

If too few plots are put in, the extrapolations can inflate volume, undercount it or get it right, depending on where the plots "land" in the field. A truly dishonest forester working for the seller would deliberately take plots where the timber was heaviest rather than in a systematic sampling pattern determined by where the lines of a neutral grid intersected. I've found cruises where I thought too few plots were put in to generate valid conclusions, but I've not yet encountered deliberate plot-rigging.

b. Under-updating.

When older cruises are "updated" to help a current sale, it's easy to make a few simple assumptions about growth rates and price multipliers, freshen the dates and present the package as a valid exercise.

Time changes trees, hence, timber values, in both positive and negative ways. An update of a 15-year-old cruise that is done in a computer and never field checked will miss the damage done by fire, insects, storms, timber poaching and a dozen other things that reduce predicted volume and lower timber quality.

There are circumstances when a quick and dirty update is all that is needed, but don't buy timberland with a seller's update as your Bible. It's too easy to **underestimate the field negatives** and, in that manner if no other, overestimate the tract's real volumes.

c. Under-refinement of the timber analysis.

Foresters must choose the level of analysis that gives their clients the truest picture of timber reality. If a forester is trying to inflate timber values for the seller, he can do so by choosing a grosser level of analysis than the one he should use. I've seen this done, for example, when foresters lump all small-diameter hardwood sawtimber into a single category, say 10-16" DBH, which is then multiplied by a single price. The far more accurate predictor is to disaggregate hardwood sawtimber volumes into diameter classes by species and then apply the appropriate multiplier for each species.

The forester finds trustworthy price multipliers through research with local stumpage buyers, which he then assesses in light of his field-based observations of the **quality of the volumes** contained in his cruise. Buyers rank hardwood sawtimber logs on the stump according to their quality. Quality on the stump affects bid price. A forester who wants to increase the value of a seller's timber need only underestimate quality issues in the stand to overvalue the seller's timber.

14. Two Sets of Books.

I have not run into a situation where a forester does an accurate cruise for a seller and a phony one for the seller to hand to a buyer. I have, however, come across properties where a **simplified summary** is given to buyers while the seller retains the more detailed cruise. The simplification uses one or more of the tricks I've described above to show more value than the stumpage warrants.

A simplified summary is an exercise in analytical statistics intended to paint an overly optimistic picture of timber value. But don't assume that every one-page analysis is a fraud. I've seen one page accurately summarize the timber on 18,000 acres. The more reliable suspicion-raiser is a handful of numbers without context, or a couple of fifth-grade multiplication equations with insufficient explanation. If, for instance, a seller's summary consists of "Timber Value: 25,000 tons x $25 per ton = $625,000."— you know nothing at all. You don't know how the tonnage was estimated, where it's located, what species are included, whether the tonnage is based on a clearcut or a diameter threshold, or where the $25-per-ton price came from. In fact, you don't even know whether the tract's "timber value" is gross sale revenue or net after expenses. The seller-supplied timber value may, in other words, be based on delivered price to the mill or logs on a landing, not the stumpage price. If delivered price is $25 p/t and the cut-and-haul cost is $21 p/t, the stumpage price—which is the money that sticks in your pocket—is only $4 p/t. The timber value, that is, stumpage value paid to the landowner, would be $100,000, not $625,000. The seller did not lie to you when he said the timber value was $625,000, he just did not tell you the relevant truth, the truth of the truth.

15. The unsubstantiated seller statement.

I once found a 4,000-acre property that was owned by an investor group, one of whom was a forester. Most of it was wooded. The forester had not cruised the property, but he told me there was "$1,500,000" in timber value. I asked how he had determined that number in the absence of a cruise. "Well," he said, "you have to assume that there's at least $400 to $500 in timber per acre." "Just because," I said. "Right," he answered. "Just because." My friend, a consulting forester, did a walk-through on the best 700 acres of these woods and allowed that a clearcut might produce about $100 per acre in stumpage. This tract had many large-diameter trees with impressive volumes, all of which were worthless because they were culls left standing by repeated high-grading.

I've also run into "deals" where the seller, a knowledgeable timber person, will walk me through the property and put a single dollar number on the timber as he shows me around. My rule in these circumstances is to cut that number in half and then, maybe, I'm in the ballpark.

16. Volume Averaging.

I was sent a cruise summary on 1,600 acres that reported 8,100,000 bf, mostly shown as hardwood sawtimber. For each of 17 species, the summary showed not the total number of trees and total board feet by species, but tract-wide average board feet per tree and an average tree DBH of 14". The summary did not include volumes disaggregated by species and two-inch diameter class. The summary did not state the smallest DBH that was included in the total or the diameter of the top break.

This type of summary looked good at first glance, but wasn't. Volume in an 18" DBH sawtimber tree has value; volume in a 10" DBH tree has little, if any. The average volume of the two is misleading, because all the volume in the smaller classification has value as pulp, not sawtimber. If one 20" DBH tree has 250 bf and 12 10" DBH trees have a total of 1,500 bf, the average volume in each of those 13 trees is 135 bf (1,750 bf / 13 = 135 bf per tree). That average volume number would represent real value if the size distribution was not lopsided. But there is only one tree—the 20"—that has sawtimber value of the 13. There's nothing inaccurate in volume averaging, except that it presents a totally distorted picture of the stumpage value of the tract's trees.

An inventory of a mixed-age, mixed-size stand that expresses volume and DBH as averages should be suspected of trying to pad the value of the timber. It is impossible for a buyer to put one price multiplier against an average volume and produce a reasonably accurate estimate of dollar value on such a tract. In contrast, tract-wide averages on even-age stands of planted pine should be representative and useful for estimating present timber value.

Volume averaging can mislead in another way. Some species, like chestnut oak, achieve large diameters at the expense of quality. Thirty-inch plus diameters in chestnut oak are common, but the butt log in these trees is often hollow or otherwise flawed. Such trees are culls that were left alone when the tract was high-graded. Their value is always chancy, because the timber buyer doesn't know the quality of the butt log until it's cut. Loggers will avoid taking these large trees for pulp because they are too big for the mill's machinery. Any averaging of cull volume with "good" volume inflates the total volume and value of the tract's merchantable timber.

The seller with a genuinely good tract of timber won't show a buyer volume averages and diameter averages. Good timber speaks for itself.

17. High-tech Wizardry.

Large timber tracts are now having their timber valued through high-tech methods, including **infrared aerial photography** and **satellite images**.

I'm seeing infrared used more and more on even-age stands of planted pine. An infrared aerial photograph is taken of the tract, from which tree volume is estimated by the extent and intensity of the red. This technique suggests volume only, and so it is useful on pulpwood tracts. It is not helpful on hardwood sawtimber tracts where the buyer must know volumes by species and diameter class. (An earlier technique used **aerial photographs** to show stand locations and provide a very rough picture of timber volume by extrapolating from crown characteristics. Modern inventory methods are much more accurate. An aerial photograph of woods by itself tells nothing about the property's timber value.)

Satellite photography of woods can produce about the same impressive level of ground-level knowledge that our military gets in its targeting systems. Satellite images provide more information when leaves are off. Both infrared and satellite techniques are used on tracts exceeding several thousand acres. On tracts smaller than 4,000 or 5,000 acres, I would always put a forester on the ground doing a walk-through, if not a conventional cruise. An ATV-mounted forester can get a reasonably good feel for a large tract by chugging through it with periodic walk outs. On larger tracts, I would ask him to recommend the best method of evaluation, given what he was able to see of the tract.

I don't have enough experience with either technique to know how they might be manipulated or their results exaggerated. I'm inclined to trust such techniques on even-age, planted tracts where value is measured in tons of fiber and not as much on hardwood sawtimber tracts where market value depends on volume by diameter class, species and quality.

18. Time and Liquidity.

In my area, it is almost always possible to get an **upfront, lump-sum payment** for timber stumpage when its sale involves less than $500,000. Between $500,000 and $1,000,000, the biggest mills may still be willing to pay a lump sum upfront, though they would prefer to pay in two or three "lifts" as the logging progresses. On very large tracts with timber value in excess of $1 million, the rule of thumb usually is: the larger your stumpage value, the less immediately liquid its full value sold to one buyer. The reader should keep in mind that the dollar numbers in my local "rule" will vary from region to region, but the underlying principle is likely to hold true in most places. Where a timber buyer is willing to pay a lump sum upfront for a very large timber tract, he may discount his offer in light of the time it will take him to cut the tract, carrying costs and market risk. Thus, a tract showing an honest $20 million in merchantable timber might fetch only $15 million in a lump-sum, cash-upfront sale.

Timber sales are almost always marketed to local buyers. The common exception to this statement involves tracts that contain a lot of veneer or high-quality sawtimber that appeal to high-end distant buyers or the export market. The market for most tracts does not reach beyond a three-hour, one-way truck haul. Less haulage time is preferred since it allows the logger to deliver at least two loaded trucks per eight-hour shift. Whoever buys your timber can use only so much of it at a time, and every local market taken as a whole can absorb only so much supply without depressing prices. Consequently, the value of a large tract's timber has to be estimated in terms of local mill capacity, local market factors (supply of stumpage, demand for mill products, prices) and national and international market factors over the time needed to cut it. (Even timber-sale contracts on small tracts of fewer than 200,000 board feet might give the buyer a two-year window to remove the purchased timber. This allows the mill to schedule the logging in light of its cutting crew availability, yard inventory and expected demand for specific products.)

It follows that the larger amount of timber a landowner wants to sell, the fewer buyers there are who will be able to pay a lump sum for it. Smaller stumpage buyers can't afford to tie up their capital over long periods, so they look for small jobs that can be marketed at current prices. On the larger sales, the smaller buyers drop out of the market. On very large volumes, the landowner may have to negotiate a long-term contract with a single buyer whereby he is paid the market price on a **pay-as-cut basis**. A negotiated price with a monopoly is not likely to be what the stumpage owner prefers. One frequently used approach is to market a large volume of timber divided into several small tracts. This marketing tactic gathers in the largest number of potential bidders able to pay an immediate lump sum for each sub-parcel.

Most readers of this book will be interested in land deals where the volume of stumpage timber is less than one million board feet and certainly less than $1 million in timber value. Part of your scoping responsibility with timber is to ask your consulting forester to **determine the immediate liquidity (i.e., an upfront, lump-sum sale) of the target property's timber before submitting a purchase contract for the property**. As timber value exceeds $500,000, it will be increasingly difficult to get paid the full value of the merchantable timber in an upfront cash payment. The consultant is also likely to find that the market gets increasingly less competitive as the value of the timber rises. For these reasons, you should start discounting present timber value in your purchase calculations once the value of the merchantable timber exceeds some locally determined threshold amount. You will need your consulting forester to estimate at what level of value the discounting kicks in and how much the discount factor should be. To complicate things a bit more, he will also need to factor in 1) the increasing value of the stumpage as trees grow, and 2) the increase in timber value from ingrowth.

An honest seller may truthfully tell you that his 10,000 acres contains $10 million in stumpage value. There's no trickery embedded in this seller's cruise. But whether that timber is immediately merchantable for $10 million is a different question. If your consultant's answer is not "within six months of purchase," you must start discounting the $10 million, because it won't show up in your pocket without deductions for time and costs. A buyer of a large tract needs to determine how much of the value shown on the seller's cruise is immediate and how much of it is future.

19. Timber Sales: Competitively Bid vs. Negotiated.

As a general rule, a landowner will get the most money for his timber through a competitively bid sale. In some areas, however, the local practice is to purchase stumpage through two-party negotiation rather than competitive bidding. And some tracts may realistically have no more than one bidder owing to their large volume or the timber's characteristics.

The stumpage value you see on a seller-supplied cruise rarely indicates how the forester arrived at his price multipliers. If the seller's forester assumed competitively bid prices in an area where only negotiated sales occur, the merchantable value will rise beyond what a negotiated sale is likely to bring. Therefore, ask your consulting forester the method by which the property's timber will be sold and whether the seller's cruise used price multipliers that should be discounted for lack of competitive bidding.

20. Non-local price multipliers.

Remember: timber prices are almost always set in the timber's *local* market.

Let's say that you're interested in 100 wooded acres that is situated in Midway, between Richville and Poortown. It is a tract that is "heavy to northern red oak," meaning there's more volume of that species than any other in the merchantable tally. Richville boasts ten modern saw mills and is located within a three-hour radius of excellent stands of high-value hardwoods. It is a very competitive market. Poortown lies 250 miles to the west. Local timber quality there is a bit below average due to rainfall, topography and soils. Poortown has three old mills. Richville mills will pay $600 mbf for local northern red oak on the stump because of its good quality; Poortown mills will not pay more than $400 for the same species from its local area. The Poortown timber is a lower quality, and the markets for its milled lumber reflect that well-known fact.

Your Midway target property is a bit closer to Richville as the crow flies, but driving time is about one-third less to Poortown. Timber from Midway is generally sold to Poortown mills because of its middling quality and travel time.

The seller-supplied cruise, however, uses Richville price multipliers rather than the lower ones from Poortown. The cruise says nothing about the difference in stumpage prices between the two markets. Nor does it indicate which market the seller's forester drew his price multipliers from.

In this example, the use of Richville stumpage prices for the Midway northern red oak instead of the Poortown prices overvalues the volume in this species by 50 percent. The rest of the tract's timber will be similarly overvalued.

21. Hit-a-lick timber inventories.

I don't really know a better way to describe what I've been seeing more and more of lately. On tracts of 1,000 acres and larger, I am being sent an increasing number of timber inventories that are so lacking in detail and so gross in their level of analysis that I routinely assume the real worth to the land buyer is about half the purported volume and value.

I've seen different versions of these hit-a-lick inventories. One of the most common is a cruise that shows gross volumes without any dollar values at all. The gross volumes might be labeled hardwood sawtimber, hardwood pulp, softwood sawtimber and softwood pulp. Without knowing the percentage distribution of species in the sawtimber categories, it's impossible for a buyer to project value. Since it's difficult for a land buyer to find out prices paid by stumpage buyers, he is left with some information and his own active imagination. Don't underestimate the effect of your own hopes when it comes to timber prices. And what better defense does a seller have than to create conditions for a buyer to mislead himself.

A second approach on hardwood tracts is to show volume in board feet without indicating the distribution of volume within diameter classes. This produces confusion since it's impossible to figure out how much of the board foot volume is valuable 16-18" DBH+ sawtimber and how much is in the much less valuable smaller diameters.

A third method are extrapolations of present value using old cruise data and infrared images. The old data are not updated or projected. The buyer is given two seemingly "hard" timber inventories, but neither can support a reasonably accurate estimate of present value. The buyer must get his own forester to walk the tract and provide that estimate.

Some of the most misleading hit-a-lick inventory work I've seen comes packaged in multi-color, three-ring binders that are festooned with maps, charts and tables. These are produced by highly successful TIMOS (timber investment management organizations) and large consulting forestry outfits. Fancy packages can present honest analysis or its opposite. A buyer cannot assume that big names put out work that is trustworthy for a buyer's purposes, though they may. Your own consulting forester can protect your interest in these Las Vegas-style sucker games.

22. Cheating.

A really easy way to inflate volume and value is to lie. A forester working for the seller can pad phantom trees into his plot tallies, say, one or two high-value trees per plot. This can boost tract volume by ten percent or more without leaving a clue. A greedy padding-job will be obvious to your forester, but a sneaky one of ten or 15 percent can only be caught by doing an honest cruise using the exact same grid as the seller's forester.

I've never found a forester cheating like this for a seller, but I have suspected a few seller cruises of benefiting from this practice.

23. "The Combo."

The most common tactic is for a forester working for the seller to employ a combination of volume/price inflating techniques.

It is hard to detect a six percent overestimate here and a five percent overestimate there. The easiest seller cruises to sniff out are those that use the wrong log scale for the timber buyers in that area, those that group the small sawtimber in with the large, and those that apply prices that are far above market. The hard ones to detect are those that cheat around the edges, things like sticking 5,000 bf of red maple in with 60,000 bf of hard maple and calling all 65,000 bf hard maple, or breaking the top at a six-inch diameter and not saying so.

A very simple trick is to project timber on more acres than the seller actually has. The seller owns 450 acres according to the tax maps. He decides to divide it and tells the buyer that he will convey 200 acres. The seller calculates the acreage in the parcel to be sold from the tax maps. His forester—or yours—does a walk-through and determines that there's 3,000 bf per acre of hardwood sawlogs 16" DBH and larger. Multiplication then occurs: 3,000 bf/A x 200 acres = 600,000 bf of hardwood sawlogs. Fortunately, the buyer double checks the acreage using a scaled map and a planimeter or using a computer program with metes and bounds. The actual acreage that the seller will convey is 175 acres, which means 75,000 fewer board feet than anticipated. At an average of \$400/1000bf, that's \$30,000 in timber-sale income the seller led the buyer to think he was acquiring which he wasn't.

No reason exists for a land buyer to become a forestry detective, dedicated to uncovering bogus cruises. You simply need to follow my advice: hire a consulting forester you like and trust, then pay him to give you his honest opinion about a seller's cruise. It doesn't hurt, of course, for you to have read this book.

Almost all of this discussion is based on my experience with hardwood sawtimber tracts in about 15 states east of the Mississippi River. Other places use different log scales. Other places have planted pine plantations rather than natural hardwood stands, or stands of Douglas fir with 40,000 bf or more to each acre, or tree species, such as cherry bark oak and cypress, with which I have no experience. Foresters working for sellers in each area and in each type of timber will undoubtedly have other ways of inflating cruises. Readers should consider my discussion as anecdotal and reflective of my experience. There are tricks that I have yet to see.

Most of those I've mentioned manipulate reality or fudge the truth without engaging in outright lies. Cruises that fabricate volume are rare, though I've seen a couple of doozies. Many seller-supplied cruises include timber volumes—hence, dollar value—that a timber buyer will not pay for. These are intended to induce the buyer to pay the seller his high asking price.

A lot of tricks used to inflate a cruise's volume and value falls between what is sort of ethical and what is sort of not. A forester who slants a cruise toward the interest of his client, the seller, can always wrap himself in plausibility: "Yes, my species price multipliers might be a little high, but those are the prices I was told when I called around. Prices change daily. Mine were in the ballpark at the time." Buyers should remember that ballparks are big places.

Whether or not a particular bag of tricks amounts to fraud in the legal sense would depend on the specifics of what is presented to a buyer and how it is represented. Real-estate law allows for a certain amount of seller "puffing." My opinion, for what it's worth, is that inflating timber volume and value is intended to defraud a buyer. If it's intended to defraud and does so, it's fraud.

Ralph Keyes's, The Post-Truth Era: Dishonesty and Deception in Contemporary Life (New York: St. Martin's Press, 2004) makes the point that members of an in-group have an easier time lying to members of an out-group than to each other. Lying within the group may, in fact, be unacceptable. That is a plausible explanation for the puffing and other deceptions that sellers employ against buyers, particularly buyers they don't know. That is not to say that every local seller tries to deceive every non-local buyer. The facts in my experience do not show that. It is, however, worth a non-local buyer's time to rigorously test statements of fact provided by a local seller, especially with respect to timber values. When your testing confirms a seller's honesty, you have the makings of a purchase.

The best advice I can give an inexperienced buyer is to find a consulting forester whom you like and trust, give him your business and rely on his professional loyalty to you to protect your interests. A consultant working on your behalf can make you a lot of money and prevent you from spending your money unwisely. It's always worth a couple of hundred dollars to have your forester review the work of the seller's forester, and, if necessary, do a walk-through. Your forester will protect your back from consulting foresters working for the seller. Don't cut this corner.

CHAPTER 23: SELLING TIMBER, TOOLS OF THE TRADE

TIMBER FSBO—A BAD IDEA

This book is about how to buy rural property; selling timber occurs after one has bought the land. Still, a land buyer should know a bit in advance about the selling of merchantable timber.

After you take possession of your new property, you should have in hand a timber cruise that your forester has prepared for you as part of your scoping regimen. That cruise establishes the value for tax purposes of the merchantable timber on your land. It is your **timber basis** for the IRS. Chapter 24 discusses timber taxation and the need to establish timber basis and choose a form of ownership at the time of purchase.

As the new landowner, you can sell your **timber as a FSBO (For Sale By Owner)** in one of several ways. I'll explain the steps that a FSBO needs to take, but I don't recommend this route. In any case, I think it's useful to lay out what a FSBO needs to do if only to convince hardcore FSBOs that this is one do-it-yourself deal that should be avoided.

First, you can contact local sawmills and loggers and take out an ad in local papers, announcing that you have timber for sale. You can send your cruise to those who contact you along with a very precise definition of that portion of your timber that you want to sell: let's say, all hardwood and softwood sawtimber 18" DBH and larger and all pulpwood 6" DBH and larger, excluding all cherry, red oak, white oak and hard maple smaller than 18" DBH. Such a cut will produce a more valuable harvest in the future to the degree that high-value species are encouraged and their competition removed.

In choosing this option, you will need to decide on and/or prepare the following for the **timber-sale packet** you send out to interested buyers:

1. **Contract** between you and the timber buyer. A discussion of a timber sale contract appears below.

2. **Establish title to the timber** that you are selling. (Usually done in the contract by the seller [you] warranting that you have clear title to the timber.) By buying the property on which the timber stands, you have title to the timber. You would not have title to the timber if it had been reserved by the seller or locked out by a no-timbering conservation easement.

3. **Mark boundaries on the ground** to reflect your legal ownership. This may be as easy as tying new ribbons on existing fence and marked boundaries. You may need to ask a forester or even a surveyor to "ribbon" the boundaries if they are ambiguous. Boundary marking has to be finished before buyers look at your timber. Do not "ribbon in" land and timber that you do not own. That is called stealing; neighbors frown on it.

4. **Define the timber you are selling and the timber you are not selling. Paint all trees you want to cut.** Spray a dot of bright paint on each tree you are selling at about five feet above the ground and another on its stump at ground level. If you find unpainted stumps during the logging, talk it over with the

logger and insist on an end to this practice as well as payment for the timber involved. Honest loggers don't cut unpainted trees. Put your "cease-and-desist notice" to him in writing.

A true rapscallion will buy the same type and color of paint you've used, remove the tree and then paint the stump that you've not painted. This is intentional theft by any definition. A logger who is a wealth of practical and probably first-hand knowledge about such things told me about this one.

Spray paint for tree marking is available from Forestry Suppliers and similar vendors.

Don't high-grade your own land. Paint pulpwood and low-value species and ask the stumpage buyer to drop them if you don't want to do this yourself. If the stumpage buyer does not cut them, you can sell or give them to local folks who will cut them for firewood.

DO NOT say: "Timber to be sold includes all trees 18" DBH and larger." and assume that is all you need to do. Once a tree is removed, you cannot determine its diameter at what would have been breast height (4.5 feet above the ground). Absent painting, an 18" DBH threshold parameter on paper gives a less-than-honest logger the opportunity to cut trees that are 16 and 17" DBH, even though he has not paid you for them. You will not be able to tell from an unpainted stump whether the DBH was at least 18".

Photograph 23-1 shows the location of two blue dots on a double stump two years after cutting.

PHOTOGRAPH 23-1

Double Painted Stump

Arrows indicate where paint is.

You might consider saying, "Timber to be sold includes all trees at least 20" at the stump." This formula, however, still gives a logger some leeway to cheat if he is so disposed since trees at the stump are rarely perfectly round. If such a logger wanted to cut down to 17 or 18" at the stump, the only way you would catch the theft is by identifying each and every undersized tree that he took. This involves hiring a forester to do a **stump cruise**, which provides an estimate of the volume (by species) and value of the undersized timber the logger took. Rather than fight in court over the findings of a stump cruise, you will do better to paint only the trees you want cut. If you find a stump without a paint dot on its stump, the logger removed that tree without paying you for it.

5. **Decide where you want landings and skid roads to be located**, or leave this to the discretion of the logger, acting within the state's recommended Best Management Practices (BMPs). Since road-building is a major time-and-cost factor to a logger, you need to supply a sketch of your road plan on a topographical map so that buyers will be able to factor the expense of your plan into their bid for your timber. Don't try to work up a road plan on your own. Involve the county forester. If you leave the design of landings and skid roads to the logger, your roads will be built to minimize logging time and cost. This usually means straight and steep. In terms of erosion control and aesthetics, your land benefits from roads that are less steep and less straight. The degree of less straightness needs to be balanced against safety and accessibility. If you're planning to use these roads for 4WD vehicles after the logging, keep in mind that loggers will "design" roads for their bulldozers and skidders that will be too difficult for your type of traffic. Work with the logger to construct roads that meet both his purposes and yours. Once the logging is done, you will value gradual climbs, wide turns and roadbeds that promote drainage by being graded slightly to pitch to the downhill side. It may take a logger a little extra time to build roads this way, and, if so, it's fair to pay him by the hour for the effort he spends on your behalf.

Stream crossings should be put in where banks are shallow to minimize erosion. It's better environmentally to have log trucks crossing a stream than skidders dragging logs through it. The county forester can help you design stream crossings, culvert placement and the landings where logs are stockpiled, sorted, trimmed and loaded onto trucks.

Your road plan should be distributed as part of your sale packet. It should show where you want landings, stream crossings, culverts (including length, diameter and pipe material), turnarounds and any additional grading and excavation.

Be forewarned. Timber buyers and loggers like simplicity, freedom of operation and the absence of landowner interference. If you load them down with a lot of extras, you won't get the best money for your timber, or you will get fewer bidders than you expected.

Most loggers will be familiar with road-building BMPs and do not want to knock heads with the state forestry agency over violations. Your plan is valid to the extent that it is your idea about what you want, but you should be open and willing to negotiate with the stumpage buyer who is likely to know more than you do. Include your plan as a suggestion rather than a requirement.

6. **Identify and mark any trees that you want to save**, particularly those that fit into your cutting criteria. Paint them stump and butt with a different color paint and wrap a plastic ribbon around them. If those signs are ambiguous, spray paint, "No" on the tree and the stump.

In the Contract you provide in the sales packet, make sure to include the following provisions:

7. Establish that the buyer agrees to follow all local, state and federal laws, and that he will comply with all Best Management Practices (BMPs). Some states require BMP compliance; others recommend compliance. Your contract can require compliance in states that don't, but you may trigger grumbling and discounted bids. The logger may have a valid quarrel on particular points in light of the specifics of your property. If you require BMP compliance and then agree to a couple of exceptions, note them in writing and attach the amendment to your timber-sale contract.

8. Establish who will pay for certain expenses attendant to logging, e.g., culverts, permits and gravel/rock at entrance and stream crossings.

9. Set forth liabilities. The logger should be responsible for any injury (to people and livestock) and property damage that arises from his logging operations. He should repair at his expense any damage to your fences and your neighbors' fences, buildings, roads, public property, utility lines, etc. If you clearcut a very steep hillside and flooding occurs, the landowner is likely to be found the guilty party, not the logger.

10. Set forth payment schedule. All money upfront, before any logging begins, is what you want. Include in your contract a provision: "Full payment is due seller when this contract takes effect." The effective date should be the day when the last required signature is added to the contract. If you are doing **shares with the logger**, you will be paid as he delivers your logs to a mill. Do not do shares; see discussion below. If you are being paid in installments, set forth the amount of and date due for each one. If there is a penalty for late payment, make sure to spell out the details in writing.

11. No partnership. Make sure to include a provision that the logger's work on your land for your mutual benefit creates neither a partnership nor a joint liability between you and him.

12. Establish length of logging "window." Loggers prefer to have more time to log rather than less. Winter logging is preferred because the sap is down, making for a better quality log and easier skidding. A two-or three-year window gives the timber buyer a chance to time the market and catch an upswing in prices. A 12- to 18-month window is standard for jobs involving less than 200,000 bf or so.

13. Slash height. Your woodland will shed its cutover look if you require the logger to cut slash to lay within four feet of the ground. Loggers, however, want to leave slash as is because cutting it green is hard, dangerous, time-consuming, unproductive and costly work. Many loggers will refuse to bid a tract that requires them to lop the slash. Others will lower their bid—by a lot. I recommend that you let the logger leave the slash as is. After the timbering is done hire a couple of guys to lop it down on an hourly basis or in return for the firewood if it offends your eye. Sometimes a chipper company will come in after logging and clean up the property.

14. Subcontractors and assigns. Ask the stumpage buyer or logger to whom you sell your timber whether he is planning to subcontract the logging. If so, you want to make sure that the subcontractor has a copy of the timber-sale contract and follows whatever prescriptions you've included. Generally, your interests will be best served if you prohibit subcontracting.

15. Cut all painted culls. The stumpage buyer will remove all painted trees of value to him. If your contract provides that painted culls are to be cut, the stumpage buyer may or may not remove them, depending on whether it's profitable. The logger doesn't have to remove the culls for your remaining trees to get the benefit of reduced competition. You do need, however, to make sure that the logger understands that he is expected to cut all painted trees, including culls. A logger can drop trees faster than you can; even so, you should expect a small discount for the time he spends on this job if he's not removing them.

16. **Clean up**. You want to make sure the logger seeds all skid roads and landings with the appropriate grass mixture. BMPs will suggest other practices that should be applied to reduce environmental impacts after logging. The county forester can tell you what the standard grass mix is and the proper spreading ratio in pounds per acre. If you need a shade-tolerant grass on some roads, you can pay the logger for the difference in seed price. The logger should be expected to remove logging-related trash—oil cans, garbage, etc.—and not drain machine fluids on your ground.

Loggers will leave stubs from logs they've trimmed for length or quality. These will be left in a pile on the landing where the logs were loaded. You can give them away for firewood or burn the pile where it's safe to do so. Loggers don't want to involve themselves in burning stubs or slash.

Photograph 23-2 shows stubs left on a graded and seeded log landing.

PHOTOGRAPH 23-2

Log Landing

17. **Right to Reject**. Include a clear statement in your package that the seller reserves the right to reject any and all bids.

The discussion above assumes that you are a landowner who is selling his timber directly to a stumpage buyer or logger without the assistance of a consulting forester. I advise against selling timber this way, because the buyer, who does such deals on a daily basis, is far smarter about timber deal-making that you and I are together. The **Owner-Buyer Contract** that I've provided at the end of this chapter assumes the involvement of a consulting forester. If you insist on acting as a timber FSBO, the points that I've discussed are basic to a timber-sale contract. I would advise having a local lawyer help draft the contract. Don't sign a contract provided by the stumpage buyer without review by your lawyer.

I advise against being a timber FSBO, because you will be expected to know more than you can know and do things that you've probably never done before. Too many opportunities exist for mistakes. Managing and marketing a timber sale are business activities that require a combination of local experience, personal contacts, a track record that buyers trust and specialized knowledge. Even knowing something about this process, I would not take on this job. Stumpage buyers will be reluctant to bid competitively in a FSBO-orchestrated sale. They will, however, try to negotiate bilaterally for your timber. The odds are high that you will not get the best money for your timber acting as your own agent.

The second way of selling timber *that I advise against* is **working shares with an independent logger**. These deals use different payment formulas. The most common is for the logger to split what he gets as his delivered income with you, 60-40, or 50-50. Another is to guarantee you a certain price per thousand board feet for each species with your share of income depending on the volume he sells. Another is to propose a split of sales revenue after deducting his costs. In theory, working shares appears to be a reasonable approach since you are dividing revenues according to a fixed formula. Working shares involves no work on your part, and you save paying a consulting forester his commission.

If your logger is honorable, as a number are, he will cut exactly what you want, deliver every board foot that he cuts, tally every cent that is received, provide accurate records to you of every transaction and pay you on a timely basis with checks that don't bounce. However, the incentives for a logger working shares to short the landowner are as substantial as the opportunities are numerous. The logger necessarily gathers all sales receipts from the mill, which are typically stuck in his front shirt pocket. Obviously, if he does not report all sales or all sales revenue to you, you will be receiving your rightful share of a wrongful total. It is easy to toss a few receipt tickets into the woodstove at night; you'll never know. If this logger cut and sold 100,000 board feet of cherry from your land but only reports selling 95,000, at $1,000 mbf, he pockets $5,000 that he would otherwise have had to split. If you wave your cruise in his face showing 100,000 bf, he will simply say that a cruise is an estimate and the timber "just didn't cut out that good." Don't count on getting his mill buyers to confirm his sales. Sawmills are very reluctant to get between a logger—with whom they regularly work—and a landowner, particularly a newcomer. You should not expect to be able to get the sawmill to send you copies of the sales tickets your logger hauls from your land. When your logger is selling your timber to more than one mill, which is typical, it's impossible for you to track sales.

A variation on the burned-ticket tactic is even simpler. Instead of hauling all your logs to a mill, he dumps a load or two at the back of his own property or, slyer yet, on the landing of his next job. A few weeks after he's finished your job, he sells your logs for his own account. Even if you were to find his stash, it would be next to impossible for you to prove these logs came from your land.

There's always the possibility of a **piggy-back payment scam** between an unscrupulous mill and an unscrupulous logger. You'll never see the pea in this shell game. It can work like this: The mill is paying about $450 mbf for hard maple, but the mill cuts a receipt to your logger for your maple logs using $375 mbf. That income is then split with you according to your contract. The logger provides you with copies of all scale tickets showing volume (or weight) and receipts. The mill also slips your logger $50 mbf off the books. Two of the three parties win: the mill has bought your maple volume for $25 mbf less than it would otherwise pay. Your logger is now getting as his share $237.50 mbf ($375/2 = $187.50 + $50 =

$237.50) rather than $225 ($450/2 = $225). The $50 he gets off the books will not be declared on his taxes. But you have lost $37.50 mbf. Why would the logger cheat for $37.50? Because over many thousands of board feet, a little cheating adds up to a lot of money, undeclared for taxes. If you get wind of this collusion—a very unlikely possibility—the mill will tell you that it paid $375 mbf for your maple because it found "quality problems" in the logs that were apparent only when they were graded at the mill on delivery. The mill had no choice but to discount the price they paid to your logger. How prevalent is this type of collusion? I can't say.

A third reason to avoid working shares is that it encourages the logger to high-grade your timber. Assume the logger is completely honest. He will do best for himself on your job if he cuts only your most valuable timber. This will not gross the most money, but it will be the most profitable approach from his perspective because he will invest the least amount of time and effort, and incur the least cost. For example, it is clearly in his interest to gross $100,000 by high-grading 100,000 bf of hardwood sawtimber at $1,000 mbf than to gross $105,000 on the sale of 200,000 bf priced at an average of $525 mbf. He and you will get $50,000 each in the first instance, and $52,500 in the second. But the logger will have spent the same amount of time to cut the last $5,000 on 200,000 bf as he did to cut the first $100,000 on the high-graded 100,000 bf. From his perspective, the extra income ($2,500) is gained only by doubling his investment in work, time and expense. From your perspective, you gain $2,500 from the trees you want cut so as to improve your remaining high-value trees by eliminating competition. You might get the logger to drop the trees, but don't expect that he will haul them out for sale.

Don't fall for the line: "I'll just do a selective cut and split the money with you 50-50." That's a high-grading proposition.

Doing shares never gives the landowner a guaranteed amount of money. You are being promised only a fixed percentage of whatever the logger reports as revenue in the sale of your timber to buyers of his choosing. Prices fluctuate at mills, and different mills scale the quality and board feet of arriving timber a little differently. An independent logger faced with the choice of hauling to three mills—the first pays a bit more per 1,000 bf but scales board feet short; the second pays a bit less per 1,000 bf but scales higher; and the third does a little of both—may choose wrong and end up with $500 less per load than had he chosen better. Independent loggers tend to have firm opinions and long memories about timber buyers and mills. The logger you pick may simply like the people at the lower-price mill better than those at the higher-price mill and persist in selling there even though he—and you—make less money.

Even when you have a cruise showing, say, $100,000 worth of hardwood sawtimber 18" DBH, you won't be able to hold a shares logger to guaranteeing you a fixed sum. The logger won't know what your logs are actually worth until he sells them. Uncertainty is always a factor in timber sales—prices fluctuate, standing timber that looks solid may be hollow or have invisible insect damage, the highest-priced mill may be overstocked with the species that you're selling. Working shares is always a roll-of-the-dice arrangement. You're gambling on the logger's integrity, his judgment in marketing your logs, local prices, local inventory surpluses and a dozen other factors. All you have is a fixed percent of some number to be determined by several others, at least one of whom may want to short you every so often.

I am not anti-logger. They work hard at a necessary and dangerous job. I don't begrudge them a living. I understand that every forest product I use first requires a logger to cut a tree. I've done enough woods work to appreciate what that means. The position I assume in this book is to be pro-landowner. And my best advice to landowners is to hire a consulting forester to manage a timber sale rather than work directly on your own with an independent logger.

James Fazio, author of an excellent how-to guide for managing a small woodlot, wrote: "Many people entrust the welfare of their woodlot to a logger on the basis of a handshake. This is as absurd as selling a crop without measuring it. Even with a solid contract there is rarely a perfect marriage between logger and landowner." (James R. Fazio, <u>The Woodland Steward: A Practical Guide to the Management of Small Private Forests</u>, 2nd ed. [Moscow, Idaho, The Woodland Press, 1987], pp. 93-94.)

For these reasons, I advise against both any do-it-yourself, FSBO timber-selling strategy and working shares with a logger. The dirt-smart timber owner tries to strip risk and uncertainty out of the sale of his timber. Direct marketing and working shares is heavy with both. The "savings" you project on a timber sale by not paying a consulting forester is likely to be entirely theoretical. Let me work through the numbers for several ways of selling timber to make my point:

1. Consultant-Managed, Competitively Bid Lump-Sum Sale.

You've paid for a pre-purchase cruise that shows 100,000 bf at $100,000 in stumpage on a $300,000 property. Your forester charges ten percent to manage a **competitively bid marked (painted) sale**. Depending on weather and ground conditions, it can take three to four days for an experienced forester to paint and tally 100,000 bf on the stump. Price research and preparing the bid package (map, inventory, bid form, contract) will take another couple of days. The inventory he distributes is based on the volume he estimates in every tree that he marks for sale, grouped by species and two-inch diameter class.

Let's say the highest bid is exactly $100,000. From this gross of $100,000, you pay your forester ten percent—$10,000. Your pre-tax net income is $90,000. His fee is tax-deductible. Since your pre-purchase cruise valued the stumpage at $100,000, you had no taxable event when you sold it for what you paid for it. The $100,000 is paid to you in a lump sum before any logging starts.

2. 50-50 Split with an Independent Logger.

For you to make $90,000 on a 50-50 split with a logger, he will have to sell your 100,000 bf of stumpage, cut and hauled to a mill as logs, for $180,000. Stumpage price as a percentage of delivered price at the mill varies over time according to species, market conditions, inventories and other factors. Delivered price for hardwood sawtimber is rarely twice stumpage value. (On pulp cuts, however, delivered price can easily exceed stumpage price.) Delivered price in this example might be $130,000 to $160,000, with your share at $65,000 to $80,000 tops. Less than $80,000 is more likely.

3. Negotiated Unilateral Sale to Mill.

If you negotiate unilaterally with a single buyer for this stumpage, my guess is you will be offered $80,000 to $85,000 tops. That's $5,000 to $10,000 less than what the consultant is likely to net for you in a competitive sealed-bid sale. A negotiated sale with an independent logger will net you even less than that, perhaps $70,000 to $75,000.

4. FSBO-Managed Competitively Bid Sale.

This one is hard to estimate, because so many variables are in play. I see no upside on the $90,000. I anticipate buyers reluctant to get involved with an amateur, discounted bids, misunderstandings and contract disputes. Maybe, $60,000 in your pocket.

5. Negotiated Sale with a Custom or "Alternative" Logger.

If you are not interested in getting the best money for your timber, you can research the "alternative-logging" options available in your area.

I've found three types of alternative loggers that you might consider.

There is, first, the **"piddler."** He is a fellow in his 50s or 60s who's been around logging all his life, has some basic equipment and wants to make enough to get by. Left to his own devices, he will generally high-grade a tract, but very slowly. He usually works shares and is happy to have freed himself from the pressure to make as much as possible from each job. He might work by himself or with one other person. I've seen a couple of husband-wife teams make a living working four or five hours a day in good weather.

Second, there are the **loggers with portable sawmills**. One buyer I know buys stumpage and then subs logging and sawing to independent Amish crews. I've also seen a portable mill outfit buy a tract and sub the logging. From an owner's perspective, this amounts to a unilateral negotiated sale.

The third "alternative" I've seen is **horse-logging**, which has environmental benefits. Horse-logging works best financially where the landowner wants to cut a small number of scattered high-value trees rather than large volumes. On 100,000 bf of stumpage, I don't think a horse-logger could submit a competitive bid against a conventional machine logger.

CONSULTANT-MANAGED SALE—SAMPLE CONSULTANT CONTRACT

In almost all circumstances, I would recommend selling timber through a consulting forester who works in the area. It's my experience that a good forester will increase the gross revenue of your timber sale by more than enough to cover the cost of his commission. Your sale expenses—his commission—are tax-deductible, but your time in arranging a sale is not. Moreover, his counsel and presence should leave your property in as good as shape as can be expected at the end of the cutting. The butchered cutover tracts I've seen are almost always done on shares and without a forester helping a buyer.

The key to getting the best money from your sale is competition among buyers. Your sale has to be packaged to make it attractive to at least two or three buyers who want to do essentially the same thing with your logs. Packaging involves including trees that will be valued and excluding some trees that will lead buyers to discount their bids. Your consultant can cover his fee simply by packaging your sale correctly to the local market. Stumpage sales, with the exception of certain high-value logs for the export market, always follow local marketing and contract mores. You will not know these practices, and you probably won't be able to learn them on your own. If you package your timber incorrectly and include unusual or complex language in your contract, you will scare off buyers. Local knowledge and local buyer contacts that are built up over time are your forester's key to maximizing your sale's revenue. If you live four states away from your rural property and hire a forester from where you live to handle your timber sale, he may come in with methods and ideas that are unfamiliar in your timber's local market. You need not hire the forester who lives closest to your property or even one who lives in the same county or state. But you do need to hire a forester who is actively working in your local market with your property's timber types. Stumpage buyers prefer negotiated bilateral sales with landowners, but they will participate in a competitively bid sale managed by a forester whose inventory methods they've come to trust and who manages the sale honestly. A forester who opens bids privately will not be trusted by buyers. Too much incentive exists for the forester to work a sweetheart deal with a preferred buyer. Bids should be opened at the job site, publicly, with bidders in attendance.

Your forester cannot guarantee that your timber will sell for the value he estimates after doing a cruise or even a marked inventory. The buyer he thinks is most likely to bid the highest may not bid at all owing to an unexpected surplus of logs at his mill of the species you're selling. While any particular sale can be depressed by factors operating on individual buyers, your forester should have a track record that shows his pre-sale valuations for landowners are pretty close to the winning sale bids.

Wherever your property is, the steps that a consulting forester will follow in handling your timber sale are linear and familiar to stumpage buyers of all sizes:

1. **Sum up the timber stand**. You should have this done before submitting a purchase offer. If you didn't, you need to decide with your forester's help whether you want to market the sale using a cruise (an estimate), marked inventory (tree-by-tree tally, which is more accurate than a cruise) or as is, letting each buyer submit a bid without any landowner-supplied framework. I advise against the last of these alternatives in almost all circumstances, because it leaves you without any sense of the value of what you're marketing. Where an as-it-is approach can work is with an even-age, one-species tract, all of which would be sold for a single purpose. A forester does not need to cruise or mark a 50-acre tract of 23-year-old loblolly pine (with 500 trees to the acre and an average diameter of 16 inches) whose only market is pulp. He can estimate volume and sales value with a paper and pencil in about five minutes.

2. **Sign a contract with the forester authorizing him to sell your timber for you**. This occurs after you purchase the property, not before. The contract specifies what the forester will do, his compensation and the approximate time-frame. The forester will be acting as your agent in this sale, which means he should have no interest higher than getting you the best money from the most responsible buyer.

3. **Establish the boundaries of the property and flag them on the ground.**

4. **Mark and inventory the sale timber**. If you decide to market the timber through a marked sale (instead of using a cruise), your forester will paint each sale tree stump and butt. As he marks the sawtimber according to your sale criteria, he will tally the number of trees he's painting and group their volumes by species and diameter class.

5. **Prepare a sale packet/bid package/prospectus**, including:

   - **Topographical map** with property boundaries; access to property will be shown or described;

   - **Inventory of sale timber** to be sold. Volumes will be disaggregated by species and diameter class;

   - **Forester's Road plan**, if needed;

- **Schedule**, indicating when the forester is inviting buyers to view the property with him, along with the date and location of the public bid opening. Other visiting arrangements can be made.

- **Bid Format and Submission Date**. Sealed bids are the usual format. The forester will include a bid sheet that requires a buyer's signature. The bid should be put in a sealed envelope. Bids received after the forester's stated deadline will not be accepted. Bids can be mailed to your forester, faxed or submitted in person in a sealed envelope at the bid opening. Bids should always be opened in public where every buyer can see the bids of his competitors.

- **Timber-Sale Contract**, which is the legal document that establishes the terms of the sale between you, the owner of the timber, and the buyer.

- **Notice to all bidders** of the consequences of submitting a bid that the seller accepts which the winner then fails to perfect by not paying his bid amount and/or signing the timber-sale contract.

6. **Coordinate signing of the timber-sale contract and delivery of payment.** Questions and uncertainties will be cleared up at this meeting.

7. **Inspect logging in progress as landowner's representative.** Your forester doesn't oversee or manage the logging, but he should visit every so often. Problems can be worked out on the ground. Your forester will protect you from unpainted trees being cut and BMPs not being followed.

8. **Perform a final inspection just before logger leaves**. Final grading and reseeding should be confirmed, if not already in progress.

Selling through a consulting forester will involve a forest landowner in two separate contracts, one between you and your forester which precedes the other between you and the timber buyer.

The contract between you and your forester that appears below assumes that he has completed a cruise for you, which you relied on in purchasing your property. Your timber-sale contract with him should look something like this:

CONTRACT WITH CONSULTING FORESTER

This Contract is made between John Smith, 111 Universal Drive, Bigcity, New York, 20005, Owner, and William Green, Mountain Forestry Consultants, P.C., 345 Beta St., Woodland, PA, 15555, Agent, for the following professional services with respect to the Owner's property and timber, located on the west side of Rt. 600, three miles north of Woodland, Pa, and more particularly described as 100.00 acres conveyed to Owner by Deed of April 1, 2002, recorded in the Blake County (PA) Courthouse, DB 66, PN 578, whose boundaries are shown on the recorded survey appended as Attachment 1, and more particularly that 96.52 acres of the Owner's 100.00 acres that lie north of Clear Creek and which contain the stand of timber from which its merchantable portion will be sold for a lump sum:

1. Agent affirms that he is a professional forester licensed in Pennsylvania and agrees to the following:

A. That in return for ten (10) percent of the gross selling price of the Owner's Timber-Sale Inventory, payable on the date the Owner receives payment for his Sale Inventory, the Agent will represent the Owner and his interests in performing the following tasks:

1.) Mark with orange ribbon the boundaries of the Owner's stand that is being sold;

2.) Paint stump and butt all trees that Agent and Owner agree are included in the Sale Inventory, according to these criteria:

a. All hardwood sawtimber 18" DBH and larger for the following species:
_____

b. All softwood sawtimber 16" DBH and larger;

c. All hardwood pulp defined as _____; and

d. All softwood pulp defined as _____.

e. All log scales and other parameters used to tally volume shall be those most likely to be used by local timber buyers.

f. Culls shall ___ shall not ___ be marked for cutting.

3.) Tally and group the sawtimber volume in board feet by species and two-inch diameter class; by cords for all pulpwood.

4.) Prepare a Sale Inventory that aggregates sawtimber volumes by species and two-inch diameter class; by cords for pulpwood.

5.) Prepare a Bid Packet for Owner's Sale, which includes:

a. Contract between Owner and Timber Buyer; [This may or may not be included in Bid Packet; see below for one version. Follow the forester's advice on whether or not to include it.]

b. Timber Sale Inventory;

c. Survey of Owner's Property if available;

d. Topographical map of Owner's Property, showing boundary lines, sale stand areas (shaded in blue), Buyer's access point (s) and any no-logging areas (shaded in red);

e. Directions to and road map showing location of property;

f. Schedule of time and dates for property inspection when Agent will be on site;

g. Sealed-bid Schedule—setting forth time/date deadline for receipt of sealed bids; time and location of public opening of all timely bids by Agent;

h. Description of Sealed Bid procedure;

(1.) Date and location of signing of timber-sale contract;

(2.) Forms of acceptable bidding;

(3.) Forms of acceptable payment;

(4.) Time and place of signing of Owner's Contract with Timber Buyer;

(5.) Buyer's payment shall be made directly to Owner at time of signing, unless otherwise provided herein_____.

i. Road Plan, needed____ not needed_____. If needed, Road Plan to be laid out with Owner and implemented with Timber Buyer.

6.) Market Owner's Timber-Sale Inventory to all likely buyers;

7.) Show property on at least one scheduled viewing date and, if necessary, by arrangement;

8.) Conduct sealed-bid auction for Owner's Sale;

9.) Provide Owner with results of sealed-bid auction. If Owner does not accept high bid, Owner and Agent will jointly determine their next steps. If Owner decides that he no longer wants to sell his Sale Inventory through Agent, Owner agrees to pay Agent for his receipted expenses, mileage at $.__ per mile, and time, at the rate of $__ per hour, spent in preparing and marketing Owner's sale through the last consultation with Owner.

10.) Provide periodic inspections of Buyer's logging of Owner's timber, exercising such authority as Agent is provided under Owner's contract with Buyer.

11.) Advise and consult with Owner throughout the process of selling and removing his timber, as needed;

12.) Prepare __ not prepare __ Management Plan for Owner that incorporates Owner's objectives for the Timber Sale and future uses of property.

2. Owner warrants that he has clear title to said property and an unencumbered right to sell any and all of its timber to a Buyer procured by the Agent. Owner further warrants that no liens, easements, claims, reservations or encumbrances, financial or otherwise, restrict his ability to sell this timber through the Agent.

3. Owner agrees to the terms of compensation for the Agent as set forth above.

4. Owner warrants that the boundary lines as set forth on the survey (Attachment 1) are accurate to the best of his knowledge.

5. Owner warrants that he knows of no dispute over the location of any boundary line. [If a dispute does exist that cannot be resolved, the Owner should inform the Agent of that fact and instruct him not to paint trees in the disputed area.]

6. Owner agrees that Agent bears no liability for trees Agent paints in any area the Owner falsely or mistakenly represents as his. Agent bears no liability for the accuracy of deed calls or survey measurements, but does bear responsibility for accurately marking these lines on the ground.

7. Owner agrees to allow Agent access free access to his property during the term of this Contract.

8. Agent may not sign a Timber-Sale Contract on behalf of the Owner, except in the following

circumstances:_____.

     9. No partnership is created by this Agency agreement. Agent is not liable for: 1) fulfilling the obligations of the Owner's Contract with the timber Buyer, 2) failing to fulfill these obligations or 3) satisfying any debts Owner incurs during the Agent's work for him.

     10. Owner agrees that Agent is held harmless for any damage or injury to any property or party that occurs during work on the Owner's property during the term of this Contract, except for those caused by negligent or reckless acts of Agent. Agent agrees that Owner is held harmless for any damage or injury to any property or party of the Agent's during the course of his work for the Owner.

     11. The Contract shall come into effect on the date of the signature of the second signing Party.

     12. The term of this Contract shall run from the date of effect through the date on which the Buyer of the Owner's timber finishes his work, or on any other mutually agreeable date herein set forth _____ .

     13. This Contract is binding on both parties, their heirs, executors and administrators during its term. If the Agent dies or is incapacitated, the Owner may employ another Agent and pay the first Agent, or his estate, and the second Agent in proportion to the work each did.

     14. This Contract may be amended only in writing.

     15. The laws of the Commonwealth of Pennsylvania shall govern this Contract.

     16. Owner and Agent agree to try to resolve any dispute arising between them during the term of this Contract without resort to litigation.

     17. Parties agree ____ not agree ___ to submit any dispute they cannot themselves resolve to binding arbitration by an arbitrator they select from a panel made available through XYZ Association of Arbitrators. Arbitration expenses and fees shall be divided equally.

     18. Notarized signatures are___ are not ____ required.

     19. Facsimile copies with signature and date are____ are not____ acceptable to both Parties.

_____ (Owner) _____ (Agent)
Address   **Address**
Phone   **Phone**
Fax   **Fax**
Date _____   **Date** _____

     Contract language differs from region to region, state to state, timber type to timber type and consultant to consultant. The contract your consultant hands you will not read exactly like the one above, but it should cover most of the same issues. My sample contract is likely to be more detailed and more "lawyered up" than the one your consultant uses. A simpler version may be all that you need. The layers of detail that I added are there if you think you need them. This contract language is owner-oriented. Your consultant may have a contract that is skewed more toward his protection. In that event, you will have to hammer out any differences you think are important. Some owners, perhaps you, prefer language that leaves areas of potential conflict vague or unaddressed. I find security in writing solutions in advance of their emergence as problems. If, however, you insist on a soup-to-nuts contract drafted by the guy who teaches contracts at Yale Law School (who happens to be your old college roommate), you may find that no consultant wants to sign it. Sample consultant contracts are available from forestry departments at land-grant universities, professional forestry societies, forest landowner groups, county foresters and in Beattie *et al.*, Working With Your Woodland, Chapter 3.

The premise of this sample Owner-Consultant contract is that the sale of your timber will result in a lump-sum, full-price payment in advance of any cutting. This is almost always the best method from the landowner's point of view. You may, however, find yourself in a situation where the timber's revenue will be paid in several stages. In that case, you may need to ask your consultant to become more involved in the sale. If you are being paid a percentage of what is being sold at a mill, you may want to ask your forester to monitor the cutting-hauling to assure full payment.

TIMBER-SALE CONTRACT

With your consultant contract in place, you and (mostly) he will jointly prepare a second contract that sets forth the terms of the timber sale between you and the timber buyer, with your forester acting as your agent. I advise against a landowner using a **timber-sale contract** supplied by the stumpage buyer. Your consultant will have a generic contract that he uses, which may or may not be adequate for your purposes. Do not assume that because you earn a living merging and acquiring billion-dollar businesses, that your innate savvy will protect you in a timber sale. In the absence of a carefully thought through contract prepared with the help of a consulting forester, you are likely to be plucked by a logger who thinks an M&A is the almond version of an M&M.

In addition to your consultant's standard timber-sale contract, you can get samples from your county forester, forest landowner groups, forestry extension faculty and in two books, Beattie *et al.*, Working with Your Woodland and Minckler, Woodland Ecology: Environmental Forestry for the Small Owner, 2nd ed. Another publication with much useful contract information is The Forestry Conservation Circular, Vol. 21, No. 5, most recent edition, "Woodlandowner's Guide to Selling Timber and Timber Sale Contracts," prepared by the Department of Natural Resources, Cornell University, Ithaca, NY. See also the Virginia Department of Forestry's, "Selling Timber," at www.dof.state.va.us/mgt/saletimb.htm.

These sample contracts, as well as the one I've drafted, are helpful in orienting you to the contract issues you should consider, but the particulars of your sale—timber type, species mix, volume mix, topography, access, stand density, haulage distance to mill and any post-logging uses you envision—will determine contract language beyond the generic. It may be necessary for you to work with both your consultant and a local lawyer, though the latter will probably be needed more for a final reading and less for a start-from-scratch drafting.

Your forester and your timber-sale contract should protect you against harmful timber-harvesting practices, but not against timber harvesting itself—which is the point of the sale. You cannot expect your land to look the same after logging as before. If you load a contract with restrictions and extras, the best buyer money may not bid at all. You need to find a balance in your thinking and then in the contract between what is fair to ask a stumpage buyer to do (consistent with him making a profit) and what is not. In the contracts I've signed, I've usually wanted the buyer either to remove the "top log" or lop the slash to a four-foot height for aesthetics. Several buyers have refused to do this, though a couple were willing "to work with me" on the slash nearest the roads. These stumpage buyers did not want to cut and haul anything other than the sawtimber logs. The pulp/slash work would have cost them time and probably money. I was persuaded to not include a slash-lopping provision in my contracts.

I now think it's better from a landowner's perspective to not write a top log/lop slash provision into your contract because of the bidding discount you will suffer. The slash will rot down in seven to ten years. You can sell or give it away for firewood. I advise getting the best money from your sale and then dealing with the slash separately if it annoys you.

Every timber-sale contract is a legal document that involves payment, mutual expectations, and issues of liability and responsibility. It should contain the language necessary to protect the interests of the landowner/seller. In the contract I've drafted below, I've placed an * in front of those contract clauses that are more law than forestry. Your local lawyer should pay them particular scrutiny.

This sample timber-sale contract is not one that I suggest you rip and use. Consider it as an exercise to raise issues that you may face in the context of a contract.

A consulting forester with whom I've worked for a number of years reviewed my language and suggested changes that I've placed in italics. He thought some of my language was unnecessary or duplicative of state BMP requirements, or harmful, or so restrictive that stumpage buyers would boycott/bid down the sale. I have placed in brackets my commentary on the language in a particular section and my friend's thoughts. His general point: every ounce of restriction that a contract places on a timber buyer may produce a pound of bid discount. Enough ounces will produce no bids and an aborted sale. This sample contract, then, is a way for you, a landowner, to think about what's important to you and how much it's worth.

TIMBER-SALE CONTRACT

This Contract is made between John Smith, 111 Universal Drive, Bigcity, New York, 20005, herein, Seller, and Big Tree Sawmill, Rt 1, Woodland, PA, 15555, herein, Buyer, for the purchase and sale of the following timber:

1. Seller agrees to sell all trees painted or otherwise marked for sale by William Green, Mountain Forestry Consultants, P.C., 345 Beta St., Woodland, PA, 15555, Agent for the Seller, on the Seller's property located on the west side of Rt. 600, three miles north of Woodland, PA.

The sale property is further defined as a portion of the tract of 100.00 acres conveyed to the Seller by Deed of April 1, 2002, recorded in the Blake County (PA) Court House, DB 66, PN 578, whose boundaries are shown on the recorded survey appended as Attachment 1 and further shown on the topographical map prepared by Agent, appended as Attachment 2.

Of the Seller's 100 acres, 96.52 acres are included in this sale. The sale area is colored blue on the topographical map (Attachment 2), and represents the land of the Seller that lies north of Clear Creek.

Buyer's access to the Seller's property is restricted to the gated road that joins Rt. 600 at the large white oak and which is further identified by three orange ribbons on said oak. No other access to Seller's property is permitted.

Buyer may use that portion of Seller's land that he needs to construct roads, landing areas and the like, subject to state reclamation provisions and this Contract. Agent must approve the design of Buyer-constructed roads and landings before Buyer installs them.

2. "Sale Inventory" represents all merchantable timber to be sold as set forth, a total of 120,685 bf hardwood sawtimber (18" DBH and larger) and 49,940 bf softwood sawtimber (16" DBH and larger) in the following volumes as shown below and on the Seller's Sale Inventory (Attachment 3):

    a. Hardwood sawtimber, 18" DBH and larger

Red Oak	43,565 bf
White Oak	15,610 bf
Scarlet Oak	10,250 bf
Black Oak	5,240 bf
Bear Oak	4,355 bf
Chestnut Oak	3,225 bf
Pin Oak	2,785 bf
Black Cherry	10,475 bf
White Ash	7,995 bf
Hickory	3,445 bf
Hard Maple	6,260 bf
Soft Maple	5,780 bf
Misc.	1,700 bf (includes Cucumber, Basswood, Black Birch)
Total	120,685 bf hardwood sawtimber

    b. Softwood sawtimber 16" DBH and larger, including

White Pine	32,250 bf
E. Hemlock	17,690 bf
Total	49,940 bf

c. Hardwood pulp:	1,150 cords
d. Softwood pulp:	687 cords

[COMMENT: Most contracts specify what is being sold. In this case, my forester believes that it would be a mistake to specify the volumes by species being sold—despite selling the tract as a marked sale—because the owner/seller would be vulnerable to a lawsuit if, for whatever reason, the buyer came to believe that the specified volumes were either not present or not harvestable. Prior to the contract being signed, each buyer will have made his own on-site determination about stumpage volumes and values. The landowner's consultant will have marketed the sale with the disclaimer that no guarantees were being offered by the seller to the buyers, and that each buyer was responsible for his own evaluation of the tract's timber. I agree with the forester on this point. Don't include inventory numbers in your Contract.

"Sale inventory" in Section 2 would be better described simply as "All painted trees with no guarantee of volume, quality or value."

3. All sawtimber and pulpwood trees included in the sale are painted twice with orange dots, one on the stump and one at about 4.5 feet above the ground.

The Buyer shall remove all painted trees during the Contract's term.

[COMMENT: This language requires the removal of all pulpwood logs from trees the forester has painted. A buyer may refuse to bid on the sale because of this requirement. Alternatively, you can require that all painted trees be felled, and leave it to the buyer as to whether or not their logs are removed. You can, of course, say nothing about removal and felling, which is the buyer's preference. If there are 50 pulpwood/cull trees on a tract where, for instance, more than 200 sawtimber trees are being sold, having the buyer cut them is not a deal-killer or much of a discount factor. Having him remove the cull logs, however, could be. Your forester can suggest the best approach. You may do best by removing the pulp/cull cutting requirement and simply pay a neighbor to drop the unwanted trees after the timbering is done.]

No unpainted tree shall be cut, except for trees felled in the building of skid roads *and landings and those inadvertently damaged in the felling of painted trees. Buyer shall pay Seller the stumpage value of all non-painted trees 10"DBH and larger felled as liquidated damages. Agent and Buyer shall jointly determine the value of such trees. Buyer is not liable for any trees that are damaged as a result of his normal work practices that are customary in the industry. Buyer shall make a good-faith effort to protect Seller's unpainted trees during logging activities.

4. Seller does not guarantee sawtimber or pulpwood volumes and quality. Buyer acknowledges that he has had sufficient opportunity prior to signing this Contract to evaluate Seller's timber using his own methods and personnel.

Seller and his Agent bear no liability for any discrepancy between the volumes represented and the volumes cut by Buyer.

* 5. Seller warrants that he has good title to this Sale Inventory and has the right to sell it to the Buyer under the terms of this Contract.

*   Seller further warrants that no liens or encumbrances exist that limit Seller's ability to sell this Inventory. Seller is permitted by the terms of his mortgage on this property with Kountrybanc of Woodland, PA to sell this timber without limitation or reserve.

[COMMENT: It is important for the seller to make whatever arrangements are necessary with his mortgage lender to allow the sale of the timber. A bank might insist that some or all of the timber-sale income be applied to the mortgage principal since the sale of the timber reduces the value of the property that secures the note. A bank might also insist that the timber not be sold unless a minimum price—a reserve— is met.]

* 6. Seller warrants that he will do nothing to restrict Buyer's rights under this Contract during its term.

7. Seller grants to Buyer permission to enter the property at any time during the term of this Contract for the purpose of inspection, assessment, tree removal, clean up, reclamation and any other such work connected to the purposes of this Contract.

* 8. The term of this Contract shall be eighteen (18) ____ twenty-four (24) ____ months from the date on which this Contract becomes effective, which is the date of the last required signature on this document.

* 9. Buyer shall reserve no rights or profit in Seller's timber at the end of this Contract or when he has finished his work, whichever comes first. Upon Contract expiration or the completion of Buyer's work, Buyer's rights under this Contract shall terminate and revert to Seller. Buyer shall then provide Seller with his signed Release of Interest, which includes all standing timber and all logs remaining on the property.

10. Buyer shall pay Seller the lump sum of $____ upon signing this Contract. Payment shall be made by certified funds or other method designated by Seller. This payment represents the full purchase price, unless otherwise provided in an Addendum to this Contract, mutually agreed to.

11. No tree on the Seller's property shall be cut before full payment payment is made to Seller.

12. Seller's Agent shall represent the Seller in managing this Sale, including inspecting the Buyer's timbering and reclamation work.

Agent shall have the right to suspend Buyer's timbering and/or reclamation work without penalty to Seller if, in his opinion, Buyer is failing to perform said work in accordance with the terms of this Contract and/or applicable law and regulation, and/or logging operations are damaging Seller's property beyond reasonable wear and tear. All Parties shall make a good-faith effort to resolve any such stoppage as quickly as possible.

Buyer shall not skid timber, haul logs or perform reclamation work when weather or ground conditions will result in severe rutting, erosion or similarly adverse environmental impact.

[COMMENT: Each forestry consultant will have developed his own timber-sale contract with language that spells out his duties and responsibilities as the seller's agent. Consultants and loggers try to get along, and generally do. A timber buyer who doesn't like the forester representing you is not likely to bid on your sale. I've known foresters who refuse to send sale notices to certain timber buyers because of past difficulties. Your contract should include language of this type, including the right to suspend the logger's operation.

Operating in wet, soft conditions, especially on slopes, will severely disturb your ground. Your consultant can recommend language that is generally accepted in the area to address this concern.]

13. Buyer shall remove each painted sawtimber tree to its lowest merchantable diameter for the products appropriate to each tree.

[COMMENT: The landowner's property will look better and be safer for vehicles if stumps are cut low.]

14. Buyer shall provide phone call ___ written notice ___ to Seller's Agent at least 24____ 48 ____ hours in advance of commencing logging on Seller's property.

[COMMENT: A phone call, rather than written notice, is usually sufficient.]

15. Buyer shall locate and construct skid roads and haulage roads under Agent's direction if no Road Plan is attached to this Contract. Existing roads shall be used wherever possible, unless Agent provides different instructions as part of this bidding process. New roads shall follow contours where possible. All roads—old and new—shall be left at least eight (8) feet wide and no more than twelve (12) feet wide where possible, except in curves and turnouts. Where possible, new roads shall be built in dry areas and avoid wet spots and mud holes.

[COMMENT: My forester thinks I'm crazy. He objects to these guidelines because they are uncommon and subjective. I agree. On the other hand, the landowner's property will be protected from road-building-caused erosion and the roads will be safe for vehicle traffic. On mountain land, you want to avoid to the extent possible straight up-and-down roads and roads dozed through wet spots. An alternative way to handle this would be to have your forester walk the property with the successful buyer and agree on a road plan.]

Seller shall leave roads in condition suitable for a 4WD vehicle. All waterbars and dips left when the logging is completed shall accommodate 4WD traffic, except where BMPs and/or Agent specifically designates otherwise. Buyer shall install waterbars and dips in accordance with BMP standards for road grade.

[COMMENT: Waterbars are one of my favorite hobby horses. I hate them. A waterbar is a trench two or three feet deep and about three feet wide that is excavated at an angle across a skid road to prevent erosion by catching water running down the road's surface and channeling it to the outslope side. A proper waterbar has steep sides, which prevent vehicle traffic. They last a long time, which is their virtue from an erosion-control point of view. A dip is a broad, shallow swag graded into a road that performs the same erosion-control function. I love dips. Your state BMPs may require waterbarring a road that need only be dipped. This is usually one of those cases where a good idea—erosion control—is implemented mindlessly. Your choices are then to 1) live with permanent inaccessibility created by the waterbars; 2) construct detours around the waterbars; or 3) convert the waterbars into dips after the inspector leaves and the logging is done. On ground that I don't want to travel, I've left the waterbars in place. Where I want to use the roads, I've taken the third option. My dipped forest roads are friendly to feet, hooves and tires. If a fire occurs, the local VFD can get to it. Had I not reclaimed the waterbars, my woods would be unusable. In a timber-sale contract, I would ask the logger to put dips in roads that I plan to use and deal with the authorities if they pick a fight. If you convert waterbars to dips, you should have a dozer touch them up every four or five years to maintain their water-carrying capacity.]

Buyer shall leave roads free of rocks and logging debris, including slash. Roads shall be left in a general condition equal to or better than their condition prior to logging.

Buyer shall rough-grade logging roads and landings before seeding with mixture approved by Agent. Areas of road prone to water collection shall be ditched and graded to facilitate drainage. Roads on hillsides shall be graded to the outslope to drain water to the downhill side. Buyer is responsible for installing ditches, culverts and gravel where needed to control erosion in consultation with Agent. No new road shall exceed a gradient of more than ten degrees without the Agent's prior approval. All trees of three (3) inches or more diameter that must be taken down in the construction of roads and landings shall be cut at the stump rather than pushed over.

[COMMENT: My forester objects to the last sentence. Loggers prefer to push trees down rather than cut them when building roads because it's faster. If you don't put this language in your contract, you are likely to find some substantial trees pushed over next to a road or left in a heap. I find pushed-over trees, with their exposed root balls, unsightly and annoying. Since this language could affect a bid, consult with your forester about whether he thinks it's necessary.

I would insist that the logger remove logging slash (tree tops) from roads. This may involve nothing more than dozing them over to the side. If slash is left on your roads, it will make them impassable. You will have to cut and remove the slash by hand or hire a bulldozer to push it away. I've done this work; it is dangerous and miserable. In most cases, loggers can fell trees away from a road or if necessary clean up after themselves. Requiring loggers to leave your roads free of slash and large rocks—and even in as good a condition as they found them—are not unreasonable measures.

Skidding logs kicks up rocks (big) and stones (smaller). The logger's final dressing of the skid roads prior to seeding should remove all of the former and many of the latter. Expect to find stones the size of large grapefruit here and there.

Some states allow loggers to comply with erosion-control BMPs by positioning slash across sloped skid roads. The branches are supposed to trap dirt, diffuse runoff and prevent rutting. This is a cheaper and quicker way of complying than excavating water bars and dips. The technique, in my opinion, doesn't work very well over time because slash rots, leaving roads with no erosion control. The immediate downside is that the landowner's roads cannot be used as long as the slash remains. I learned this lesson the hard way.]

16. Agent shall designate where Buyer is to cross Clear Creek and any other watercourses, and design such crossings with Buyer. Agent and Buyer may___ shall____ consult with the appropriate state forestry official in locating and designing such crossings. If temporary bridges are erected, Buyer shall___ shall not ____ remove them when he is done with logging.

* 17. Buyer shall comply with all state Best Management Practices (BMPs) and logging laws and regulations in effect during the term of this Contract. Buyer bears responsibility for said compliance. Where this Contract requires a higher standard than the BMPs, this Contract shall be followed.

Buyer holds harmless Seller for any failure by Buyer to comply with applicable laws and regulations.

[COMMENT: BMPs vary from state to state. In some states, they're mandatory, and in others they're not. BMP compliance affects a logger's profit, so requiring compliance will increase logging costs in non-mandatory states. The seller should consult with his forester about the pros and cons of requiring compliance in such states.]

18. Buyer is responsible for filing all forms required by law to carry out this Contract and obtaining all permits except those the Owner chooses to obtain, including _____.

Buyer __ Owner __ will notify the local state forestry office prior to commencing any logging activity where such notification is required.

[COMMENT: Some states now require that the local state forestry office—the county forester—be notified prior to logging. Virginia requires the landowner to provide notification; the logger may be the notifying party in other states. Failure to notify results in a penalty. My language places notification responsibility on the logger, but that language may be wrong for your particular state.]

19. Buyer will fulfill his reclamation obligations under the BMPs and this Contract as soon after finishing his timbering as is feasible in light of weather and field conditions, but in no case longer than 180 calendar days from the date his logging crew leaves the property. This obligation remains in effect until it is fulfilled, including beyond the termination date of this agreement.

[COMMENT: The sections that follow spell out specific practices a landowner might want a logger to follow where BMPs are voluntary. The landowner should check with the state forestry department to determine where the language below differs from the state's voluntary BMPs. A far simpler alternative than writing your own BMPs is to require the buyer to follow the state's voluntary BMPs. But occasions can arise where that's not agreeable. The landowner should expect to have his timber discounted for either approach. Certain timber buyers may boycott a stumpage sale where BMP-compliance is required in a non-mandatory voluntary state. If your forester forecasts dire bid results, you may want to opt for having him talk informally with buyers.]

20. Buyer shall incorporate the following practices:

a.) Buyer shall engage in no logging operation of any kind, including use of existing roads and construction of new roads within 50 feet of a pond, lake, wetland or stream without prior authorization of Agent. Agent has designated all no-operation zones on topographical map (Attachment 2).

b.) Buyer may___ may not ____ skid logs through Clear Creek. Slash may not be left in Clear Creek.

c.) Buyer shall __ shall not __ lop all slash to within __ feet of the ground.

[Comment: I recommend against including a slash-lopping requirement in a stumpage contract. Lopping adds cost to the logger without economic benefit. The closer to the ground slash is lopped, the more cost to the logger. If you have no alternative, you might consider a requirement that the logger lop all slash lying within 50 feet of your roads down to five or six feet. If the logger objects to that provision, you might propose that all slash within this corridor be dragged beyond the 50-foot boundary. It takes less time to hook a skidder to a top and drag it off than to work it down with a chainsaw. In any event, do not spring a slash-lopping requirement on the high bidder without advance notice.]

d.) Slash and organic material may not be used as fill for roads and landings, except where permitted by state law and Agent.

e.) Tree tops falling on the property of adjoining landowners shall be pulled back to Seller's property or lopped in place.

f.) Buyer shall leave all landings and roads graded to remove ruts, with 4WD-vehicle-capable waterbars __ dips __, and culverts clean and functioning. All landings and roads shall be seeded with a grass mixture of _____ at a rate determined by the Agent, but not to exceed ____ pounds per acre. Surface area to be seeded shall___ shall not___ be prepared by discing in ____ pounds of lime and _____ pounds of _____ fertilizer per acre. If Seller desires a different mix or a more intensive application rate, he shall provide the necessary materials at his expense or make up the cost difference.

After seeding, Buyer shall ___ shall not___ mulch all landings disturbed by logging.

[COMMENT: Seeding roads and landings is a common practice; mulching is a BMP in some states and not others. Seed selection is site specific. Kentucky 31 fescue is often used on steep slopes in my area, but alternatives are available. I've tried shade-tolerant seed on shady roads with little success. The grass doesn't stand up well to vehicle traffic.]

g.) Buyer shall install and maintain all necessary culverts, bridges and areas where he's applied stone, such as entrances and stream crossings, at his expense, unless otherwise agreed as an appendix to this Contract. Buyer shall leave all such improvements in place upon finishing the job, unless otherwise agreed as an appendix to this Contract.

h.) Buyer shall burn _____, leave _____ all log stubs, trims and unmerchantable logs at landings.

[COMMENT: Buyers and loggers will want to leave in place all stub trimmings and waste logs. Burning is time-consuming and potentially disastrous in dry conditions. Efficient loggers will leave most of their waste in the woods. The landings where logs are gathered and loaded onto trucks often accumulate piles of trimmings. Loggers will object to moving or burning this waste pile. Give the pile away for firewood. Photograph 23-2 shows a stub pile next to a seeded landing about 18 months after logging ended. I gave away this pile for firewood.]

i.) Buyer shall remove all man-made trash generated during the logging operation from Seller's property. Buyer shall remove any temporary structures and all equipment and supplies, unless otherwise provided.

j.) Buyer shall not dump or otherwise leave petroleum products on Seller's property. If a spill occurs, Buyer shall clean up the spillage and reclaim the affected portion of Seller's property.

k.) Buyer shall provide for all erosion-control and reclamation work required by applicable law or this Contract, unless other arrangements are approved by Agent.

l.) Buyer shall maintain adequate drainage on all roads during logging.

m.) Buyer shall leave stumps no higher than 12" from the ground, except where impractical. Buyer shall cut each tree in such a way so as to leave paint mark visible on the stump.

n.) Buyer shall take down and, at his choice, remove any unpainted tree that is broken, badly damaged, bent or leaning as a result of his work. Hung trees shall be felled. Any such tree the Buyer removes shall be paid for at its fair stumpage price, as determined by Agent and Buyer. Buyer shall leave no tree standing that he has partially cut.

o.) Buyer is responsible for repair or replacement of Seller's property (such as fences, gates, bridges, structures) and utility lines/pipes that Buyer damages during his work. Buyer is also responsible for repair or replacement of the property of the Seller's neighbors that Buyer damages during his work.

[COMMENT: If the buyer/logger is not held responsible for such damage, the landowner will be. "Damage" does not mean the normal wear and tear that logging produces. It refers to crushed culverts, broken fences, mashed gates, collapsed bridges and the like. If there is a particularly vulnerable item on your property—such as a low-hanging utility line or a bridge that might weaken under logging traffic—work out in advance who pays for what level of damage. It's normal for the logger to pay for damage he does to a neighbor's fence, trees and other property. You can also establish a no-logging buffer around farm buildings.]

* 21. Buyer agrees to indemnify, defend, and hold harmless Seller from all claims, damages and actions of any kind resulting from the operations of the Buyer, his agents, employees, associates, assigns, subcontractors and third parties associated with his timbering and hauling operation.

Buyer agrees that Seller bears no liability for any property damage experienced by Buyer, his agents, employees, associates, assigns, subcontractors and third parties associated with his timbering and hauling operation.

[COMMENT: You should anticipate resistance to this provision. Your buyer/logger would prefer to have the contract be silent on your potential liability for problems he causes. Accidents and mistakes happen. A motorist who runs into a log spilled on the road in front of your entrance, a real-estate agent visiting your land whose SUV is crushed by a top left hanging in a tree, an equipment fire that starts on your land but burns your neighbor's barn—all can lead to a lawsuit that ensnares you.]

* 22. Buyer agrees to indemnify, defend and hold harmless Seller for any accidents and/or injury to Buyer, his agents, employees, associates, assigns, subcontractors and third parties arising in any way from Buyer's work under this Contract.

[COMMENT: Workers' compensation generally exempts employers from employee personal-injury suits arising from workplace accidents. Some states, however, allow employee suits against employers who have been willfully negligent about working conditions or equipment safety. Language of this sort protects you against a suit brought by an equipment salesman visiting your logger on your property who steps in a naturally

occurring hole and ruins his back. The salesman is a third-party within the meeting of this section. The Buyer should have accident and property insurance to cover these situations, but injured parties often look for a second pocket, such as the landowner's.

Your local lawyer can suggest language to cover 21 and 22 to replace my efforts. See also 28.]

23. Buyer is responsible for the security, safety and maintenance of his equipment and the daily supervision of his employees, associates and subcontractors (if permitted) while working on Seller's property. All Buyer agents, employees, associates, assigns, subcontractors and third parties are bound by the terms of this Contract.

* 24. Buyer shall not sell, assign, subcontract or otherwise convey his interests or rights under this Contract without Seller's written authorization.

[COMMENT: A sawmill that buys your stumpage may use its own employees to timber your land or subcontract the work to an independent. I've also seen occasions where a buyer will sell his interest in a timber tract. It is, therefore, important for the landowner to have yes-or-no control over such actions, and, further, that all parties understand that the terms of this Contract bind everyone in the buyer's chain. There will be certain logging crews that you do not want on your property; your consulting forester should know who they are. A landowner cannot tell the stumpage buyer not to use his own crew, but he should have the right to review and reject, if necessary subcontractors. Talk to your stumpage buyer about the crew he will put on your land.]

* 25. Buyer agrees to supervise his logging crew and assumes responsibility for the crew's compliance with the terms of this Contract.

[Comment: Logging crews—whether employees of the stumpage buyer or subcontractors—may or may not be adequately supervised. I've seen both ends of that spectrum. I have had mostly bad experiences with unsupervised crews. You want to work through one point of contact with the buyer—the person who signs your contract. If the logging crew is not complying with the contract, you need to work it out with the signatory, not the guys running the chainsaws.]

* 26. Buyer agrees to provide his logging crew with a copy of this Contract, or the relevant portions thereof, to facilitate compliance with its terms.

[COMMENT: Loggers rarely see timber-sale contracts. The mill's supervisor or forester should explain its terms to the logging crew. This may or may not be done. I see no harm in asking your timber buyer to show his crew those parts of your contract that affect their behavior. If the buyer refuses to accept this provision, photocopy your contract and hand copies to every logger the first day the crew appears on your land. Explain important provisions in person The contract is notice of what you have a right to expect. Logging crews differ in how they do their jobs and the condition in which they leave the property. Some take great pride in leaving a "clean job." Others leave more than their share of broken and bent trees, tops hung in standing trees, trees needlessly damaged by skidding and equipment, severe ruts and so forth (which "so" can cover a world of unpalatable "forth").]

* 27. Buyer bears risk of loss to all painted trees during the term of this Contract.

[COMMENT: The landowner should not bear any risk of loss once the timber is sold. You are selling your timber "as is" as of the day your timber-sale contract is signed. Once sold, any damage and loss from natural causes fall on the buyer. The buyer may or may not accept risk of loss from vandalism to, or theft of, his painted trees. The language in 26 puts all risk of loss of any kind on the Buyer. If you have agreed to a pay-as-the-cutting-goes arrangement with a logger rather than an all-money-upfront contract, you would bear the cost of such loss because each tree is yours until it is delivered and sold to the mill.]

* 28. Buyer agrees to maintain both workers' compensation insurance and liability insurance to cover this work. Buyer shall provide Seller with a certificate (or copy) of his public-liability insurance policy with minimum limits of $100,000 in the event of death or injury for one individual and $300,000 for more than one individual; and property damage insurance with minimum limits of $25,000 and an aggregate of $50,000 before this Contract takes effect. Buyer shall comply with all applicable *workers' compensation laws, regulations and coverages.

Seller bears no liability and is held harmless for any insurance insufficiency by Buyer during the term of this Contract.

* Buyer shall ___ shall not____ furnish the Seller with a performance bond of $_____ that guarantees his performance of the terms of this Contract.

[COMMENT: Every buyer/logger I've worked with had no problem in providing his workers' compensation and other insurance information. His insurance is your first line of defense. I've never used a performance bond on a timber sale, but you may have circumstances where one would make sense. You should anticipate resistance to a performance bond; in most situations, it won't be necessary.]

* 29. Buyer shall ___ shall not ____ place the sum of $500.00 with the Agent to meet, in whole or part, the cost of damage that Seller's property sustains as a result of any violation of this Contract. Agent shall decide whether damage has occurred and arrange for repair. This sum shall be placed in the Agent's escrow account and returned to Buyer when he completes his work, less any deductions.

[Comment: This is alternative language to the performance bond. It implies that a $500 cap exists on logger liability, though it doesn't include the words, "as liquidated damages," which would cap exposure legally. If you have a routine logging job, neither a performance bond nor a $500 damage escrow is probably necessary. If, on the other hand, a field situation exists that requires delicacy and careful equipment maneuvering, these provisions may be appropriate. Before you include either one, make sure that you, your consultant and the buyer have a common understanding of what constitutes the type of damage that merits compensating you.]

30. Buyer shall notify Seller ___ days in advance before commencing logging operations. Seller shall remove any personal property that might interfere with Buyer's work prior to commencement.

31. The laws of the Commonwealth of Pennsylvania shall govern any dispute arising from this Contract.

* 32. The Parties do _____ do not_____ agree to attempt to resolve any dispute through binding arbitration_____, non-binding mediation _____ or binding mediation_____. If the Parties agree to use any of these methods, they will select an arbitrator/mediator from a panel of three supplied by _____ and agree to divide his costs and fees equally regardless of outcome.

[Comment: I have done arbitration work for more than 20 years. Most arbitrators are quick studies and experienced in understanding unfamiliar work processes. The parties may want to select an arbitrator at the time they are negotiating a contract since that costs nothing except some time. The panel of arbitrators could be supplied by a consulting foresters' association. These individuals will understand the nuances of timber sales, but may have no experience running an arbitration and interpreting a contract in semi-judicial fashion. Arbitration awards should be binding and enforceable. You might do better by selecting a local lawyer who's had some experience as a mediator in domestic-relations or personal-injury cases; experience in contract law is, of course, helpful. If you want a written opinion, I'd limit the writing to ten pages. In most commercial arbitrations, the arbitrator issues an award without explanation.]

33. Parties may amend this Contract at any time by mutual agreement. All amendments shall be in writing.

[COMMENT: Timber buyers and loggers are businessmen who are usually more comfortable with oral understandings than legal writing. If you're working with someone with whom you are comfortable—and you should not be working with someone with whom you are not—don't be surprised if you work out an amendment on the fly and never put it in writing. Oral agreements are binding in a contract such as this, but it's always better to put things, especially changes, on paper.]

* 34. In the event of default by Seller, Buyer is entitled to the prompt return of his full purchase price, plus a twenty (20) percent penalty as liquidated damages. If Buyer defaults, Seller is entitled to his full purchase price, plus a twenty (20) percent penalty as liquidated damages.

[COMMENT: This is a standard liquidated-damages clause that is intended to bind the parties to their contract and cap the penalty if either backs out. You need to be careful that you do not set up an incentive for a timber buyer/logger to frighten you into a default, from which he walks away with all his cash plus 20 percent for his effort. If you allow both parties to walk from the contract with no loss other than a 20 percent penalty, you may be embedding an incentive for the buyer to default if the lumber market takes a nose dive. On the other hand, a landowner can get out of his contract if a last-minute buyer comes up with a price that's more than 20 percent better than the original agreement. A "breach" of contract is a violation of one or more of its agreed terms; a "default" is a failure to perform, a backing out of the agreement altogether. Ask your local lawyer for his opinion on this section.]

* 35. This Contract is binding on the heirs, executors, administrators, successors and assigns of both Parties.

* 36. This Contract comes into effect on the date when the last required signature is affixed.

* 37. Notarized signatures are___ are not ____ required. Facsimile copies with signature and date are ___ are not ___ acceptable to both Parties.

_____ (Seller) _____ (Buyer)
Address   **Address**
Phone   **Phone**
FAX   **FAX**
Date_____   **Date** _____

Timber-sale contracts are necessarily specific both to the landowner's tract and to the geographical area where it's located. Your consulting forester will know the contract mores that will help your sale fit the form and content of what local buyers expect. Remember that the sample contract I've presented above *should be customized.* Your consulting forester and local lawyer will make useful suggestions from their different perspectives.

If the practice in your area is rigged against using upfront, lump-sum competitive bidding, you will have to work within that system. Where bilateral negotiation is the norm, you want to explore whether more than one buyer exists for your stumpage. In that way, you can, at least, pick the buyer who you think will pay you the best money. Where you are forced to be locked into a deal with an independent logger working on pay-as-he-sells shares, you are most exposed to being cheated. In that situation, have your consultant pick the logger and then paint and inventory your timber prior to logging. That work will give you a reasonably accurate idea of what the logger will be cutting and selling. Your consultant may be able to work out a reporting system at local mills where the logger is selling your logs to keep tabs on deliveries and prices. But my experience has been that mills and yards are very reluctant to do this. They do not want to get into the middle of a squabble between landowner and logger.

I've flagged the provisions in the contract that will complicate logging and increase the buyer's cost; these, as I've noted, will discourage bidding and discount bid price. You and your forester need to determine which, if any, of these practices is important enough to you to pay such penalties.

Consultants disagree over whether or not to send out an owner's timber-sale contract with the sale notice. If your contract is loaded with scary, costly provisions, I advise that you include your contract as a matter of fully disclosing the terms of a purchase. If you have some ideas that you might want to include, I wouldn't send out a contract with the sale notice. You will probably be able to work out a satisfactory contract with the high bidder as long as you're willing to be reasonable.

Timber buyers won't hang around physically and legally once they're through logging your property. To avoid situations where you are trying to get them to fix something after they've moved on, ask your consultant to do a walk-through a few days before logging is likely to be finished. He may be able to reach an oral understanding with the crew as to what needs to be done. This may involve highlighting a few sentences in the contract. On more contentious issues, your forester may write up a **punch list** of end-of-the-job things to complete. Where a job is finished in the winter, you and the logger will want to wait until spring to do the final grass seeding. Put any deferred work in writing: **"Final grading and seeding will be completed no later than June 1, 200_."** In wet, muddy conditions, the logger will not be able to dress your roads and landings; that work, too, may have to wait until drier months.

A final point to be made is one regarding which state's laws will govern your timber-sale contract.

"Governance" can be an issue when the owner's timber straddles two states; or where the timber tract lies in one state, and the owner is in a second; or where the property lies in one state, the owner is in a second and the buyer operates his business in a third. If you don't specify which state governs, you will probably find yourself following the laws of the state in which the bulk of the property lies. Other thing being equal, it's in your interest to apply the laws of the owner's state of residence.

I've mentioned the idea of an owner having his timber receive **certification** from an independent third-party, which is an endorsement attesting that the harvesting and reclamation methods used comply with one or another set of environmental protocols. If a landowner insists that a stumpage buyer/logger operate within one of these protocols, he must include notice to that effect in his sales package and contract. Three of the prominent certification programs are: 1) Forest Stewardship Council, whose program is Smartwood in the United States; 2) American Forest and Paper Association, the Sustainable Forestry Initiative; and 3) National Forestry Association's Green Tag Forestry Program for non-industrial private landowners. The owner should limit bidding to buyers and loggers who are either qualified or are willing to become certified prior to starting the owner's job. Your buyer needs to be connected into the markets for certified logs in order to bid appropriately for your stumpage. You want to avoid a situation where your good environmental intentions cost you thousands of dollars.

States regulate logging practices on privately-owned land. Many states now require loggers to pass a certifying exam and have at least one certified individual on site. Logger certification involves first aid, safety equipment and practices, and knowledge of certain legal, commercial and environmental matters. **Best Management Practices (BMPs)** are mainly concerned with controlling erosion and reclaiming logged sites. They concentrate on: 1) road/landing construction; 2) timbering activities; 3) preparing the site for replanting, which can involve mechanical work such as chipping or discing, applications of herbicides and fertilizer, or burning; 4) reclamation of roads, landings and other excavations; and 5) protection of streamside management zones (SMZs).

Where a state requires compliance with its BMPs, the USEPA will have approved them before voluntary compliance was shifted to mandatory. A timber-selling landowner should become familiar with his state's BMPs, whether voluntary or mandatory. They are available from the state's forestry department in print or on the department's website. To get a sense of mandatory BMPs, Virginia's are available at http://state.vipnet.org/dof/wq/bmpguide.htm#intro.htm. Federally mandated BMPs are included there as an appendix. If you want a look at a beefed-up version of one state's BMPs, go to www.wvhighlands.org/Tree Draft.2.htm, which was drafted by the West Virginia Highlands Conservancy.

I've heard a range of stories concerning BMP enforcement in the field: the range goes from "not much" to "too much." Environmentalists may be inclined toward the first opinion and loggers, the second. State inspectors can "write up" a logger for a violation they observe, or a citizen can report a situation to the state forestry department that he believes is either causing a problem or is a violation. Trout Unlimited, for example, often monitors water quality below mining and logging jobs on trout streams. "Trout quarrels" arise over siltation from stream crossings, adequacy of erosion-control measures on logging roads both during and after the cutting, and timbering practices in SMZs. Enforcement is usually an order to the logger to fix the problem; an occasional fine is imposed. Reasonable individuals can reach different conclusions as to whether the enforcement of a particular BMP is reasonable or not. As a forest landowner, you have a right in a mandatory state to have your buyer/logger comply with current BMPs. The effect of BMPs in mandatory states is to have driven out of business or, at least to the commercial margins, the rogue loggers who took a perverse pride in leaving a mess in their wake. In non-mandatory states, the landowner gets to choose the level of protective expectations he wants the logger to apply.

Each state employs foresters—the county forester—who, as part of their duties, inspect logging jobs, usually at least once during the work and then soon after the logger has left. Larger, more complicated jobs and problem loggers may get several in-progress inspections. The inspector has no authority to enforce the landowner's contract with the logger, so do not expect him to. It is next to impossible for an absentee, inexperienced landowner to oversee BMP compliance. Your consulting forester should keep his eye on the timbering and try to resolve BMP issues in the field where possible. Both the landowner and the consulting forester should have a frank conversation early on with the buyer and the logger, if possible, about their expectations. Aim for practical, realistic expectations, and a cooperative, problem-solving relationship with the logging crew. Be as clear as you can about what you want and how you want the site to look when he leaves. But be prepared to compromise with the crew on your ideas. Assume that anything unstated or implied is subject to misunderstanding. Your logger will be far more inclined to help you if you treat him respectfully rather than as a necessary evil.

The visual appearance of woods following logging may or may not indicate harmful environmental impacts. A perfect logging job, with no adverse impacts, may look dreadful. Many logging jobs look bad at first even when they comply with applicable BMPs. Remember that logging changes a woodland's environment, but that change is not necessarily adverse to promoting environmental objectives. Don't judge your land's environmental book by its post-logging cover. Since post-logging visual aesthetics constitute so much of a landowner's objection to logging, you should talk with your forester about which practices you want the logger to follow and to what degree.

The eleven issues/practices that you want to think about are:

1. Lopping of slash

2. Leaving tree tops hanging in standing trees

3. Leaving broken and bent trees standing

4. Leaving a pile of log trimmings at landing

5. Leaving slash in roadways and waterways

6. Ditching uphill side of roads where necessary

7. Grading road with slight pitch to down side to promote water drainage

8. Installing culverts and gravel fords where necessary

9. Leaving roads rutted and subject to erosion

10. Leaving roads ungraded and rocky

11. Waterbars vs. dips.

As noted before, I would not require the stumpage buyer/logger to lop slash, because of the price discount you will suffer on your timber sale. Keep in mind that slash rots. Immediate visual improvement can be achieved by hiring two or three chainsaw operators to do this work *after* the logging is completed. You can pay them by the hour or exchange their labor for the firewood they remove. It should not cost you anything to require that hanging tops be pulled out of standing trees. Leaners and bent trees can be dropped without much work. Log trimmings can be given away for firewood, burned or left alone.

I would, however, insist that the logger remove slash and other debris from roadways and waterways. And in that connection I would ask the logger to not drop trees in skid roads to the extent feasible, because he will then clear the road by bulldozing the slash into large and very unsightly roadside piles.

Logging obviously changes a physical environment, but even clearcutting's changes need not create environmental harm. Logging's principal environmental threat involves siltation of waterways and erosion. The risk of these adverse impacts increases as slopes become steeper and as the logging approaches a total harvest. Clearcuts on steep slopes in wet conditions create the most problems. Clearcuts on flat or gently rolling land are generally managed with little soil loss and erosion.

A great deal of logging can be done with minimal, if any, stream siltation. This is generally accomplished by leaving **buffer zones** on either side of a waterway where no cutting or only reduced cutting is permitted. The specifications for these streamside management zones (SMZs) are state-specific. Zone width should increase with the steepness of the zone's slope toward the stream. Virginia, as one example, recommends a minimum zone of 50 feet on each stream bank; with a 60 percent slope, a 290-foot width is recommended. A zone might be 250 feet wide on one bank and only 75 feet wide on the other, varying with slope. Within an SMZ, Virginia currently allows the removal of no more than 50 percent of its canopy in a given timbering, but the BMPs are not clear as to how much time must pass before 50 percent of that new canopy may be removed.

SMZs used undisturbed buffer ground and vegetation to catch soil and rock before they enter waterways. Proper design of skid roads above a zone should minimize the amount of potential silt the zone has to trap. After logging is done, the skid roads—which are generally the biggest source of siltation problems—should be slightly pitched (3 percent) across their width to allow water to run off to the immediate downhill side. If a road is not graded to slope slightly to the outboard side, water will run down the road itself, eventually cutting in an erosion channel. Flat, level roads collect water. The logger should also be expected to excavate **dips** across the road's width where the grade steepens. These in-road diagonal swales channel water from the road's surface into the forest where it is absorbed.

I object to waterbars as one-size-fits-all, erosion-control devices because they make the roads permanently impassable and unusable. If you are planning to run vehicles, horses, bikes or foot traffic over your woods roads, you want the logger to install dips, not waterbars. This may, however, run afoul of the BMP standards in a mandatory state. If the state forestry inspector insists on waterbars, the logger will have to put them in. At that point, you either lose access to your property or regrade the waterbars with a dozer or by hand.

Crossing streams with logs, logging equipment and trucks can deposit dirt and debris in the waterway. This happens more when ground conditions are muddy and/or ramps must be cut into high stream banks. In most cases, adequately sized culverts and/or **well-graveled fords** minimize the amount of dirt deposited in flowing streams. Crossings should be made at a right angle with the stream's flow, preferably where the channel is narrow and the banks are low. I have seen a small headwaters stream— home to native brook trout—forded with stone and gravel without siltation or harmful effect.

BMPs usually specify how fords are to be designed and constructed. They should not be made of either small logs or "scabs," which are the four bark-bearing sides left after squaring a log. Where possible, it's better to drive trucks through streams than to skid logs through them because less mud and disturbance is created. Logging in wetlands, swamps, floodplains and coastal areas should be done, if at all, with protection of wildlife habitat, plant species and environmental hydrology in mind. Similarly, logging done around high-country lakes and headwater streams must control siltation. Your consulting forester will know what loggers should do to protect your waterways.

You will need one final document to complete your timber sale. The purpose of a **release** is to establish that the stumpage buyer has finished his work whereupon he abandons (releases) his legal interest in your trees and property created by the sale. The release terminates your timber-sale contract and may indicate that both sides complied with its terms to each other's satisfaction.

AGREEMENT AND RELEASE OF INTEREST

This AGREEMENT AND RELEASE made this ___ day of _____, _____ between John Smith of Bigcity, New York, Seller, and Big Tree Sawmill of Woodland, Pennsylvania, Buyer.

WITNESSETH

In accord with the Timber-Sale Contract of _____, 2005 between the Seller and the Buyer, regarding the sale of the Seller's timber located on the west side of Rt. 600, three miles north of Woodland, PA, the Parties agree to the following terms of release.

1. Buyer has completed his harvest of Seller's timber and releases all interest in Seller's trees, logs and property that arose from the Timber-Sale Contract.
2. The Buyer has completed all work required under BMPs, if applicable, and the Timber-Sale Contract to the satisfaction of Seller and his Agent.
3. Seller agrees to release Buyer from all further obligations under their Timber-Sale Contract.

In Witness whereof, the Parties hereto have executed this AGREEMENT AND RELEASE as of the ____ day of _____, _____.

_____   _____
Seller   **Buyer**

CHAPTER 24: TIMBER TAXATION

Let me start with the truth. I am totally witless about federal and state tax laws, regulations, court rulings, agency directives and opinions, let alone the idiosyncrasies of individual IRS agents. I have no advice about taxes other than to pay what your tax-smart CPA tells you to. I am wise enough not to follow my own advice on tax matters were I so foolish as to have any. I am also outraged that Americans are expected to pay their taxes under a system that most of us have no reasonable hope of comprehending.

Diligent readers of this book will recall that Chapter 6 is full of my tax-related opinions, souped up a bit to the level of advice. Now that I have had time to reflect on that indiscretion, I feel obliged to confess my ignorance—before jumping into the same shark-infested pool.

The federal tax code is so massive (60,000+pages), impenetrable, loop-holed, dynamic and arbitrary that the ordinary citizen is less likely to get bitten walking over starving crocodiles every morning than stepping through the jaws of the IRS once a year. The more complicated your return, the more you should not do it yourself. If you call the IRS with a tax question, they often won't answer it. It's the nightmare of being expected to provide the correct answer on a final exam when your teacher refuses to teach you the correct answer during the term. And much of the interpretive information that is provided is incorrect. Every year, I pay the taxes my CPA tells me I owe with only the barest understanding of how these sums are calculated from the receipts and documents I dutifully assemble. For reasons that I can't understand, Americans put up with this bipartisan insult. Americans vote for politicians promising tax breaks and lower tax rates, but we can't seem to mobilize around making the tax-paying process simpler, easier, fairer and less time-consuming. As it is, a taxpayer needs to know tax angles and play them, because that is how the system is organized. It's the legal angles that are threaded through the Code that benefit this organized group and that one; the illegal ones are not what I'm talking about.

Timber taxation fits into this system—if you want the embedded tax benefits available to a landowner, you have to spend time in tax planning and then jump through the hoops. Timber-owners are a special interest when it comes to taxes, a successful special interest.

Timber taxation is a specialty for CPAs, lawyers and investment advisers, not the likes of me. Consult with these professionals about your timber-taxation questions before you buy a single tree. Timber owners and timber sellers benefit from having timber-taxation issues explained to them before they become owners and sellers. Much information can be found at www.timbertax.org; "Forest Landowner's Guide to the Federal Income Tax, USDA, Handbook 718," www.soforext.net/formgnt/aghandbook.html; "Estate Planning for Forest Landowners," www.southernregion.fs.fed.us/spf/coop/taxation/default.htm or www.soforext.net/pdfs/estate.pdf.

An especially helpful booklet appeared in 2005 by Harry L. Haney, Jr., William C. Siegel and Larry M. Bishop, Federal Income Tax on Timber: A Key to Your Most Frequently Asked Questions, R8-TP34, Rev. December, 2005 (USDA, Forest Service Southern Region, 2005); www.srs.usda.gov/pubs/7124. It organizes answers to each timber-tax issue by type (personal use, investment, trade or business), then shows the best tax treatment and exactly which forms and lines you should use.

This chapter is a humble effort—and I know more than any reader how humble it is—to introduce my understanding of the main timber-tax issues, using IRS words where they are comprehensible and my own where they are less so.

SET UP

Timber-taxation issues only affect **timberland.** Timberland is wooded land whose trees have current or future commercial value. Woodland may or may not be timberland, but it's usually in a land-owner's interest to consider his woods as having present commercial value as well as future commercial value for IRS purposes. Of course, not every patch of natural woods should qualify as timberland with commercial value, present or future. Ten stunted oaks behind the old farm house shouldn't qualify as a timberland investment or business. But even small patches of land can be established and managed to produce—or anticipated to produce in the future—some type of commercial wood product—nuts, Christmas trees, seed stock, mistletoe, maple sap, sawtimber, pulp, chips, firewood and so on. And there are non-wood-product uses that fit the woodland environment that can generate income, such as hunting leases, recreational fees for trail usage and camping, among others. Part of your process of considering the value of your new woods is to think through the best way to set up your woodland on paper and on the ground in the most tax-advantaged way.

Let's assume that you have at least a couple of acres of woods; more, of course, is better. If income is never produced or intended to be produced from these woods, you will be able to deduct a proportional share of your mortgage interest and property taxes. That's about it. If you consider these woods primarily for your **personal use**, you may want to cut some timber at some point. You will have additional deductions. If you set up the woods as a noncorporate **investment**, you will get more tax benefits, including itemized deductions that can be taken against any source of income, but only to the extent that the total of these deductions exceeds two percent of your adjusted gross income that year. If you set up the woods as a **trade or business**, you will determine whether this is an activity in which you materially participate or one in which you do not materially participate.

A trade or business is supposed to make money in addition to having a profit motive. It's hard to show gross income from managed timberland each year and even harder to show a profit. Fortunately, you don't have to. **The IRS defines profit to also mean the appreciation in the value of the asset.** As trees grow, their value increases. And in this fashion, you show a non-taxable profit in your timber business each year through the growth of your timber.

There are six tests the IRS uses to determine whether a taxpayer materially participates in a timber trade or business—and you only have to meet one of them. The easiest to meet in my opinion is the one that requires personal participation in the activity to substantially constitute all material participation during the tax year wherein material participation is defined as regular, continuous and substantial involvement. If you find that you devote at least 100 hours during the tax year to your timber business—hours spent traveling to and from the woods, walking through the woods inspecting the trees (for growth, insects, disease, theft), clearing the roads of rocks and tree branches to enhance fire protection, improving the timber stand by cutting low-value species, attending forestry conferences, reading forestry books, keeping forestry accounts, enrolling your woods in the state's managed-timberland, tax-savings program, talking with the county forester, talking with loggers about prices, pruning small branches off high-value saplings to improve their future butt logs, etc.—you should be able to qualify as a material participant. It's arguable—though I've not tried this—that the two weeks you spend deer hunting in your woods should go toward material participation since the purpose of your hunting is to increase natural regeneration by reducing the amount of sapling production lost to winter deer browse. I've asked my neighbor to hunt my woods for that very reason. You lose nothing by making this argument. Your best position tax-wise is to be a material participant in a timber business.

One of your first tax decisions with respect to woodland is to establish your motives and purposes. If you want to make a profit in some way from the trees themselves or their woodland environment during your ownership, then you should consider establishing your woodland as some form of either business or investment. If you don't want to use your trees to try to make money, then you are giving up certain tax benefits. You may still make a profit on your trees without managing them as a business or investment. If, for instance, you sell $100 of firewood from your five-acres of woods, that should be reported as taxable income. And any net profit that you get on the sale of your woodland is likely to be taxable. The National Timber Tax Website organizes a forest landowner's choice of purposes in the following way (see www.timbertax.org):

- o **Personal Use**. Timberland is titled in taxpayer's name. Timber is a capital asset. Taxable gain from sale of stumpage qualifies for capital-gains treatment when held for more than one year; reported on 1040, Schedule D. Timber-management expenses are not deductible and must be capitalized.

- o **Hobby**. Timberland is titled in taxpayer's name. Timber is a capital asset. Taxable gain from sale of stumpage qualifies for capital-gains treatment when held for more than one year; reported on 1040, Schedule D. Timber management expenses are deductible under "hobby loss rule," to the extent of the taxpayer's current timber-related income. Deductions are allowed and are not subject to passive-loss rules.

- o **Investment.** Title in investor's name. Deductible management expenses are reported as miscellaneous itemized deductions on 1040, Schedule A and subject to a two percent floor of adjusted gross income. Stumpage sale gain or loss qualifies for capital-gains treatment when held for more than one year.

- o **Activity Incidental for Farm Business**. Timberland titled with other farm business. Deductible management expenses are reported on 1040, Schedule F if a sole proprietorship. Stumpage qualifies for capital-gains treatment when held for more than one year. Passive-loss rules apply to the farm as a whole.

- o **Activity Incidental to Non-Farm Business**. Timberland titled with other business property. Costs are reported on business return.

- o **Active Timber-Production Business**. Titled in the name of the business. Owners are "active," materially participating in business. Occasional stumpage sales qualify for capital-gains treatment, but ordinary business sales of timber do not.

- o **Passive Timber-Production Business**. Operating losses are restricted by passive-loss rules; otherwise same as Active Timber-Production Business.

- o **Timber Production and Utilization Business**. Timber is produced primarily for in-house use, not outside sale. This applies to sawmills, and presumably the small, portable mills an individual buys, as long as the product is used in-house, that is, for construction of structures on the property. Timber used for fuel on the property might also fit here. (www.timbertax.org/strategies/acquisition.)

Your choice from among these options may be easy or not, depending on your circumstances. Your timber-smart CPA and lawyer should help you understand the benefits and consequences of each option. The most advantageous tax situation is one where you are allowed the maximum deductibility of current costs, fast recovery of capitalized expenditures, capital-gains treatment and active participation. (Self-employment tax does not apply to capital gains.) But these benefits come at a cost—your time, for example, as an active manager, paperwork, an itemized 1040 with schedules and upfront legal expenses. Tax benefits expand as you move from personal or hobby purposes to investment or business status. It is usually in a taxpayer's interest to set up woodland as at least an investment if circumstances permit.

In addition to determining your purpose in the new woodlands, you will need to discuss your **ownership options**—no structure (suitable for land dedicated for personal use), sole proprietorship, partnership, S corporation, limited liability company, corporation, family corporation or trust. An ownership structure of some sort helps to establish an investment or business purpose. Sole proprietors in a trade or business may be subject to self-employment tax on ordinary income, but are not subject to self-employment tax on capital gains. If you sell your timber after one year of owning it, you will get long-term capital-gains treatment and not have to pay self-employment tax. The 2005 self-employment tax was 15.3 percent, with 12.4 percent going for OASDI (old age, survivors and disability insurance) and 2.9 percent for Medicare. OASDI stops being imposed at $90,000 for 2005, but the Medicare hit has no cap.

I have decided not to discuss using timberland as a conventional business, because I don't think it fits the profile of the readers of this book. Therefore, I'm not going to go through thinking about Christmas tree farms, orchards, managed timberland that produces annual income, maple-syrup operations, seed-stock nurseries and other tree-related businesses. If this is your path, see Steven H. Bullard and Thomas J. Straka, Forest Valuation and Investment Analysis, 2nd ed. (Self-published, 1993, ISBN 0-9641291-0-8); William G. Hubbard, Robert C. Abt and Mary L. Duryea, Estimating the Profitability of Your Forestland Enterprise, Circular 836, University of Florida Extension, November, 1989 also at www.sfrc.ufl.edu/Extension/pubtxt/cir836.htm; F. Christian Zinkhan, William R. Sizemore, George H. Mason and Thomas J. Ebner, Timberland Investments: A Portfolio Perspective (Portland, Oregon: Timber Press, 1992); James M. Vardaman, How to Make Money Growing Trees (New York: John Wiley & Sons, 1989); and Laurence C. Walker, Farming the Small Forest: A Guide for the Landowner (San Francisco: Miller Freeman Publications, 1988). Bullard and Straka, Zinkhan *et al.*, and Vardaman are expensive. They can be purchased at Forestry Suppliers, Inc., 1-800-647-5368; FAX 1-800-543-4203; www.forestry-suppliers.com. Books are also available through the Forest Shop at http://forestshop.com. Another source of information on the business and taxation aspects of woodland ownership are the forestry extension professors in each state who hold public seminars on woodland management, taxation and investment strategies. Your consulting forester is a source of first-step information on these subjects.

I've oriented this discussion mainly around the idea of thinking about your woodland as either an investment or an investment-type business in which you materially participate. If you don't qualify as a material participant, you can qualify as a nonmaterial participant. But don't give up on trying to qualify for material participation in your business of managing your timberland (not woods) for profit.

To establish an active timber-investment trade or business, a taxpayer has to meet just one of the following six tests:

1. Taxpayer's participation in the activity must exceed 500 hours during the tax year.

2. Taxpayer's personal participation in the activity substantially constituted all of the material participation during the tax year.

3. Taxpayer's participation in the activity exceeded 100 hours, and no other individual participated more.

4. Taxpayer's aggregate participation in all of the "significant participation activities," including actual timber management, exceeded 500 hours during the tax year. A significant participation activity is one in which participation exceeded 100 hours during the tax year.

5. Taxpayer's material participation has occurred in the activity for any five of the preceding ten tax years.

6. Taxpayer's participation in the activity was on a regular, continuous and substantial basis for at least 100 hours during the tax year based on facts and circumstances; no other individual participated more; and a paid manager was not employed. (See Haney *et al.*, Federal Income Tax, p. 13.)

I think many readers who are looking at wooded properties can qualify as a material participant in a timberland-management business if they plan it out and meet the requirements of at least one of the six tests. I encourage even the most urban-centric buyers to scope wooded property with the idea of purchasing it as an investment or timber-management business rather than for personal, recreational or hobby use. If you're buying woods, it's not that hard to recast them as timberland that you actively manage. There are tax benefits for doing so.

It's not difficult to set up your newly purchased property as either an investment or a timber-management business. The former requires minimal documentation and record-keeping; the latter, which provides additional tax advantages if you qualify as a material participant in this business, requires a business structure, a business-like approach to the investment and business-type record-keeping. In the eyes of the IRS, you can operate a business as a material participant that invests in timberland with one property. That property, of course, has to be genuine timberland, though it need not have merchantable timber at the time of your purchase. To show that you are operating an active business, your CPA may ask that you keep a record of your activities related to your timberland-investment business, including a time log to prove that your participation meets at least one of the IRS's six tests for material participation. The reward for jumping through these hoops is that you can fully deduct management expenses, taxes and interest paid on your timberland business from any other source of your income. If the timber business is managed in conjunction with a farm, deductions over gross income produce a net operating loss, which allows the taxpayer to be eligible for a two-year carry-back to earlier returns or a 20-year carry-forward.

The cruise you commission as part of your scoping will also help you establish a broad commercial—rather than personal—purpose for the IRS. The cruise demonstrates that you were determining the financial value of the timber asset prior to purchase. I think a pre-purchase cruise will also help a taxpayer establish the intent of material participation in a timberland-management business. For the same IRS reason, I advise choosing an ownership structure at the time of purchase that is consistent with managing the property for gain. This can be as simple as filling out a Schedule C in your first ownership year and thereafter, but it may involve setting up a legal ownership entity, such as a limited liability company. A third start-up step for the IRS is to have your consulting forester write a **forest-management**

plan that anticipates future income and demonstrates your commercial motive. You can also consider enrolling your new woodland in the state's timberland-management program, which can discount your property tax, make you eligible for various kinds of financial and non-financial benefits and, again, further substantiate for the IRS your profit-making intentions.

The pre-purchase timber cruise is the first document you will collect in your **timberland records** folder that will help establish your material participation in a timberland business. The forest-management plan is the second. Any expenses you incur related to your purchase should be retained: one copy in your long-term timberland records folder and the other in your folder of receipts for that tax year. Records and receipts help establish that your woods should be at least viewed as an investment. The more business records and documents you have, the easier it is for you to establish that you are actively engaged in the management of the timberland property for profit. Timberland management is the type of business that does not require a high level of activity to sustain itself each year.

On some properties, you can economize by asking your consulting forester to prepare a pre-purchase scoping report based on a thorough **walk-through**, rather than a timber cruise. A walk-though is less accurate than a cruise, but it's often sufficient for you to make a sensible offer. A walk-through will give you a volume break down by species and a dollar value for both sawlogs and pulp. I have had success asking a forester to do a walk-through estimate for all sawlogs 12" DBH and larger by species, using whatever scale local buyers will use. Pulp volume and value appears separately. On 250 acres, a walk-through might take a day with another couple of hours in the courthouse checking boundaries. The write up should take a day or less. A walk-through is usually not good enough to market your timber for its highest possible price or as a database for a management plan. There are circumstances, however, where a walk-through is all you need for a quick timber sale. With a walk-through timber valuation in hand, you can market merchantable timber during escrow contingent on your purchase of the property, with a minimum bid pegged to your walk-through value.

Like all other business and investments, it's necessary for a woodland owner claiming the timber and property as either an investment or business to keep business-like records. Timberland, generally, involves a minimum amount of paperwork each year. In most years, expenditures are few and timber is not sold. But the three-years-profit-out-of-five rule can be met by the IRS policy of allowing profit to be taken to mean appreciation in the value of the timber assets. As an investment, timber generates some expenditures that you can deduct in the year they occur. Other outlays will increase your **basis** in the woodland, which decreases your taxable gain when you sell the property for a profit. As a business, including a timberland-investment business, expenditures will fall into different categories—some can be deducted against income, some depreciated and some taken on the sale of the property. Make sure that you note the date and purpose of each expenditure, and then ask your CPA to sort them properly each year.

If your timber consists of several stands that you manage independently, your CPA will probably set up a **timber account** for each one. This allows you to keep separate income-expenditure records stand-by-stand. On a 100-acre tract that has one stand of merchantable timber and another that has just been clearcut, the money spent on site preparation, herbicides and planting will be allocated to the latter premerch account. Your job is to keep a record of what you do, what expenses you incur and why you are incurring them. Your CPA will take it from there. Record-keeping is discussed in William E. Schlosser, "Financial Record Keeping for Forest Landowners: Developing A Good System," February, 1999, University of Idaho, Extension Forestry; www.ets.uidaho.edu/extforest/feb99.htm.

BASIS AND INCOME

How do you handle **income received from a timber sale** for tax purposes?

If you sell your timber within your first-ownership year, any taxable gain (net sale income – adjusted basis) will be taxed at your ordinary rate. A pre-purchase cruise will establish your basis in the timber that you sold. And the sale should not show much taxable gain, considering the timber sale occurs shortly after you've closed on the property.

If you hold off selling the timber for more than a year and you are materially participating, you must dispose of your timber within the provisions of **Section 631, Gain or Loss in the Case of Timber, Coal, or Domestic Iron Ore**. Under Section 631 (a), cutting of timber is considered a sale or exchange and is eligible for long-term capital-gains treatment. The fair market value, i.e., the taxpayer's basis, of the timber is established as of the first day of the tax year in which such timber is cut. Section 631 (b) figures basis differently and applies to taxpayers who either retain an economic interest in the timber or make an outright sale. Taxable gain under Section 631 (b) for both pay-as-cut and outright sales qualifies for long-term capital-gains treatment.

In all cases, the taxpayer's CPA must calculate the taxpayer's basis in the timber sold, regardless of when the sale occurred or what type of sale it was.

To do this, he organizes your new property into two, or more, **separate accounts**, preferably in your first tax year. One account is for the **land** itself, including costs you've incurred in the purchase of the land itself, non-depreciable improvements to the land and depreciable land improvements—the difference is explained below. A second account is devoted to the costs and income involved in the **timber**. A timber account can include all merchantable timber—that is, the timber you want to sell—and both naturally generated premerchantable timber and planted premerch. Your forester and CPA will help you decide whether each type of timber should have its own timber account. Generally, undeveloped woodland will have only two accounts—land and timber. But you might have basis allocated among as many as seven sub-accounts—forested land, other unimproved land, improved land, timber, premerchantable timber, improvements and mineral rights (such as oil, gas, hard-rock, minerals, clay, sand, topsoil, stone and water). Some of the sub-accounts may be further divided into subassets, each with a separate basis.)

Wooded property used for investment/commercial purposes may come with other types of assets, each capable of having an independent basis, expenses and income. One such account could be set up for **depreciable equipment** used in the timberland investment or business, bought from the property's seller or acquired independently. An equipment account includes all depreciable machinery, tools, vehicles and equipment that have a useful life of more than one year and cost more than $100 each. Separate accounts might be created for **depreciable improvements** (structures), such as a workshop, equipment shed or farmhouse used as a business office. If you're planning to sell a severable asset, your CPA will advise you as to whether you will be better off to separate its basis from other assets or combine it.

The IRS looks at your rural property used as an investment or business as a bundle of separate assets, each of which can independently produce income and involve expenses. These accounts are sometimes referred to as **basis accounts**, but you should understand that calculating basis involves more than just totaling certain costs. Income from the sale of an asset—such as timber, or part of the land, or the minerals—decreases your basis in that account and in the property's entirety as well. So each asset account must keep track over time of both income from any sale and those expenditures that increase basis.

Each asset will also produce a gain or loss when the owner sells it. When an asset is sold, the CPA goes back through your records to determine its original acquisition cost, called **original basis**. If you've increased your investment in the asset during your ownership, you've increased your basis. If, for instance, you spend $10,000 to build woods roads and do timber stand improvements, you will have increased your basis in your timber account by $10,000. You may also have decreased your basis through sales and other activities. Your CPA will add all the allowable increases (certain costs/expenditures) to your original basis, subtract all allowable decreases, and arrive at a number—your **adjusted basis**. By subtracting your adjusted basis from sale income, he will determine whether you had a taxable gain on the sale of an asset, a loss or no taxable gain. If you had a gain, you pay tax on it; if you had no taxable gain, you have no income to pay tax on. If you had a loss, you may be able to use it to reduce your taxable income in other areas. Figuring taxable gain by subtracting adjusted basis from income is the method used when you sell property assets separately, in combination or as an entirety.

If you decide to plant trees, you should be aware that, as of 2005, you can deduct outright the first $10,000 of such expenses in that year and amortize as a deduction all reforestation expenses above $10,000 over 84 months. If you deduct the reforestation cost, it cannot be added to your basis.

Within a timber sub-account, your CPA may establish more finely disaggregated accounts depending on the types of timber on the property, such as:

- o all merchantable timber, which you sell immediately after purchase

- o merchantable sawtimber

- o merchantable pulpwood

- o merchantable timber by specific species, such as paulowina (a very valuable wood)

- o premerchantable timber that has been naturally generated

- o premerchantable timber that has been planted

- o timber dedicated to maple-sap production

- o timber dedicated to production of nuts, seeds or bark

Each such account will follow the same format for keeping track of how the property owner's basis in the asset is changing over time as allowable costs are added and partial sales are subtracted. Adjusted basis is a net figure, after additions to and subtractions from are made. At any given time, it is easy to figure what your adjusted basis is in each sub-account, account and the property as a whole. For simplicity, I will use **timber basis** to represent the total adjusted basis in the property's timber assets and **land basis** to represent the total adjusted basis in the property's land.

For most readers, undeveloped wooded property will be divided into a timber account (with a running adjusted timber basis) and a land account (with a running adjusted land basis). If you buy such a property and neither sell any of its assets nor add to them, your adjusted basis at the time you decide to sell the property as a whole will be your original basis at the time you bought the property. When you have a low basis and a high selling price, your taxable gain—the difference between the two—is high.

Adjusted basis should not be confused with fair market value. Adjusted basis is a number representing the running net of what the owner has put into and taken out of the property from a tax perspective. It has nothing to do with the property's current market value. Confusion can arise on timberland when a buyer uses a cruise to establish both the FMV of the merchantable timber and his original timber basis (cost) at the time of acquisition. When a CPA sets up multiple accounts for a property, he has to divide the original total purchase cost among them, a process called, **allocation**. A timber cruise or an appraisal of equipment can be used to allocate costs to their respective accounts. That allocation of value is really a process of figuring and then apportioning the new owner's cost of acquisition for tax purposes, nothing else.

A buyer should, however, remember that it is usually to his advantage to have an idea of the seller's adjusted basis in a property during negotiations. Knowing a seller's basis will reveal the approximate amount of taxable gain a given price will net for him. From that, a buyer can deduce the seller's after-tax net profit. A buyer may also be able to work down the seller's price if he's able to propose ways, or agree to seller-proposed ways, to reduce the seller's tax hit.

Original land basis is the owner's cost of acquiring the land. The owner's cost of acquisition (basis) can be increased by including certain allowable expenses associated with the acquisition.

If the new owner had an appraisal done as part of his pre-purchase scoping, his original basis is his original actual cost, not the appraisal value. However, appraisals can be used to allocate costs among different accounts. If, for example, the land has a house that the new owner later sells, an appraisal of the house itself done during, just before or just after the new owner purchased the land and house together can establish his original basis in the house alone. Such a property would have two accounts, a land account (basis) and a house account (basis).

A common buyer's strategy is to purchase a large acreage with a house/barn, and then immediately sell the house/barn with five or ten acres as a way to help pay for the retained land. The buyer should have the house/barn appraised at the time of purchase to establish his basis in these improvements and, if possible, receive payment for their sale a year after purchasing them so that he can treat any profit as a capital gain. The higher the appraisal value of the small acreage and improvements, the better it is for the buyer tax-wise. When selling an asset from a property, the more basis that can be allocated to the sale asset, the less taxable gain will result. Less taxable gain means less tax to be paid on income from the sale.

Land basis may or may not be the same as **bare land value**, which is one of the assets you try to estimate when figuring a fair-market-value purchase price. Remember that land basis is essentially a cost calculation for tax purposes. Bare land value is a market value, not a cost; it's the amount of money you think the land is worth to you, and, possibly, the amount of money you think another buyer would actually pay you for the land, severed from all other assets, were you to sell it, by itself, immediately after buying the property. Thought about in two different ways, it is likely that the first value of bare land will not be the same as the second. None of the factors that increase or decrease your estimate of the value of the bare land in either instance play a role in calculating land basis.

Where timberland is divided for tax purposes into a timber account and a land account, the IRS requires that the land be assigned some minimum value, which could be either a percentage of the purchase price or a specific number, such as $300 per acre. A tract you bought for $500 per acre, which your forester cruised out prior to purchase at $1,000 in present timber value per acre, might be allocated at $300 per acre in original land basis and $200 in original timber basis even though you sold the timber for $1,000 per acre three days after buying the tract. Your total original basis (adjusted for miscellaneous acquisition expenditures) in the property cannot exceed your original cost (adjusted for those expenditures). The forester's cruise "appraised" the value of the timber, not your cost to buy it. There always has to be a land basis in timberland, allocated as some portion of the original property cost, even where the value of the timber exceeds the property's purchase price. Your taxable gain on this timber sale—assuming no acquisition adjustments—would be $800 per acre ($1,000 income -$200 basis = $800 per acre taxable gain). **Timber basis** is what you paid for the timber in tax terms, not what you sold it for. If you're going to have a big gain on a timber sale involving recently purchased property, it's likely that you will come out ahead by selling after holding for more than one year to get the capital-gains rate.

A pre-purchase timber cruise is an estimate of value that can be used to establish your cost basis in your property's timber. Say that you buy 100 acres for $1,000 per acre, and your forester cruised the merchantable timber before purchase at $600 per acre. Your CPA will allocate your cost basis, i.e., timber basis, at $600 per acre and your land basis at $400 per acre, using the cruise to show the cost of the timber at time of purchase. If you sell the timber for $600 per acre, you've sold it for what you paid for it, hence no taxable gain was realized. If you sell the timber for less than $600 per acre, you have a loss; if you get more than $600 per acre, you have a taxable gain. If you don't have a cruise done around the time of the property's purchase, your CPA has to come up with a reasonable allocation of cost (basis) between land and timber when you do sell the timber. A consulting forester can work backward to estimate the cost of your property's stumpage at the time of purchase, but a buyer/taxpayer is advantaged by having the timber evaluated prior to submitting a purchase offer.

The timber-selling taxpayer's interest usually lies in having his timber basis calculated as high as possible when he's keeping the property from which he's selling the timber. For that reason, many buyers have a cruise done immediately *after* purchase rather than before, and ask the forester to push the timber value as high as possible to shelter timber-sale income from taxation. A buyer who cruises after purchase, however, loses the edge he would otherwise have in knowing the timber value before submitting an offer to the property seller. I suppose an individual could pay for two cruises by different foresters—one before purchase, and the other after for tax purposes. I've never heard of this being done, but I suppose someone who plays this game with the IRS would not boast about it. I doubt that you will find a consulting forester who will give you an honest cruise before purchase and an inflated one after

If you've acquired woodland through inheritance, gift or exchange, you will need to establish a property basis—both timber basis and land basis—at the time of your acquisition. A timber cruise can establish your timber basis at the time you buy woodland or inherit it. If you receive the woodland as a gift, you assume the donor's basis, not the basis at the time of the gift. The donor's basis may possibly be adjusted for gift taxes paid. With an exchange, you will carry into the new woodland your adjusted basis from the property you exchanged out of. Your CPA may be able to value the woodland property as an entirety using comparables. The timber basis can then be subtracted from the entirety appraisal to produce a land basis. Your interest at the time you acquire the property through means other than purchase is to have the timber and the land valued as high as possible to lower future taxable gain. If your intention is to sell the timber but keep the property, your interest usually lies in having as much of the property's total basis as possible allocated to timber.

Recent changes in estate taxation increased the amount a taxpayer's estate can exempt from federal estate taxes. The exempted amount rises from $1 million in 2002 to $1.5 million in 2004, to $2 million in 2006, to $3.5 million in 2009, to full exemption (no dollar cap) in 2010, then back to $1 million in 2011. This scheme is so arbitrary that it will likely be modified during the years it's in effect. Still, all of us will have to do estate planning in light of these rules as well as the high probability that they will be changed. If they are not changed, those readers who are really rich should try to die in 2010 if they like their heirs; if they hate them, die on January 1, 2011. Aside from your own estate lawyer and CPA, you might want to contact attorney Stephen J. Small at the Landowner Planning Center, 75 Federal Street, Suite 1100, Boston, MA, 02110-1911; 617-357-4012, ext. 264; FAX 617-357-1857; www.stevesmall.com. Small, a former IRS lawyer, is experienced in using conservation easements in estate planning, and he has written two helpful books: Preserving Family Lands: Book I: Essential Tax Strategies for the Landowner; and Book II: More Planning Strategies for the Future. Another resource is William C. Siegel, a lawyer and forest resource consultant, in River Ridge, Louisiana who has written widely on timber taxation and pens a column, "Taxing Matters," in RMS Timber Landowner Report, POB 380757, Birmingham, AL, 205-991-9516; FAX 205-991-2807; www.resourcemgt.com; e-mail: rms@resourcemgt.com. Siegel can be reached at 504-737-0583 or e-mail: wcsieg@aol.com.

Your **original timber basis** can and, usually does, change over time to the extent that you add allowable costs to the running basis balance and subtract allowable basis that you've captured from timber sales. If you've planted timber and made no sales, it's possible that you will find that your current (adjusted) timber basis exceeds your original basis. That will change once you sell timber and recalculate your running timber basis. Depending on what you've done after purchasing a property, your adjusted basis in the property may be greater than, less than or the same as your original basis.

Once you've established your original timber basis at the time you acquire the property, you will use it against the income you get from a timber sale. Take the example of a purchase of undeveloped woodland at $1,000 per acre where your CPA allocates $500 per acre to land basis and $500 per acre to timber basis. If you sell the timber for $500 per acre, your new timber basis after the sale is $0 per acre. You pay no federal income tax on that timber sale, because you sold the timber for exactly the amount of its value (and what it cost you) at the time of acquisition based on your consultant's timber cruise. Since you've used up your entire timber basis, the only basis you have remaining in the property is your $500 per acre land basis. And if you do nothing to increase your timber basis after your first timber sale, your next sale of timber will be figured against a timber basis of $0 per acre. Accordingly, all your net income from that second timber sale would be taxable.

What happens if, after selling the timber, you decide to sell the land? In the example above, you used up all of your $500 per acre timber basis, leaving you with a $500 land basis as the only remaining basis in the property. If nothing changes and you sell the property for $2,000 per acre in two years, you will have a taxable gain of $1,500 per acre ($2,000 income -$500 basis = $1,500 taxable gain), taxed at your capital-gains rate.

It should be apparent that you and your CPA should look for ways to pack in as much timber basis as possible prior to a timber sale. The cost of a pre-purchase cruise is added to the original timber basis. The cost of a survey will probably be allocated between the timber basis and the land basis, but if the survey is done solely to facilitate the timber sale, it's arguable that all of its cost should be assigned to the timber basis. (Remember that arguments that make sense to me will probably carry no weight with the IRS.)

Even woodland that is without current merchantable timber value should carry as much timber basis as your CPA feels is defensible. That timber basis, for which you've paid, is found in the property's premerchantable timber plus whatever basis you've added to the timber in allowable costs.

If you buy woodland that has no timber value, either merchantable or premerchantable and your plan is to create timber value in the future, the cost of site preparation (herbicides, cleaning up slash, road development) and planting seedlings can begin building your timber basis. Reforestation, as mentioned above, can be deducted instead of added to basis. Certain land-improvement costs, such as building a bridge to be used by the logger, will probably be divided between your timber basis and your land basis. If you are setting up timber sub-accounts, you may need a forester's help in allocating start-up costs among them.

This discussion is limited to trees used for producing timber on the stump. Other types of trees with other purposes may or will have different IRS rules. You need to establish the appropriate basis accounts for planted crop trees (fruits, citrus, nuts), Christmas tree plantations, non-planted crop trees (such as paw-paws and butternut whose fruit or seeds are sold), nursery stock and seedlings, among others.

After selling your timber, you need to figure your taxable gain or tax loss on the sale. You start by determining your **adjusted timber basis in the year of your sale**. This is your original timber basis at the time of the property's purchase plus the net of all your adjustments to that basis from that time through the sale. You increase your purchase-time timber basis primarily through capital improvements. You decrease your timber basis through depreciation of capital improvements, amortization, depletion and sales. (You can't depreciate land or timber.) You can deduct all permissible timber-selling expenses, such as the cost of a cruise and marking, your consultant's sale-management commission, legal fees, surveying fees, advertising and the like. You don't add these sale-related expenses to your basis. The **up-dated adjusted timber basis** is the number you subtract from gross timber-sale income (less permissible deductions) to determine your **taxable gain**.

If your up-dated adjusted timber basis exceeds the amount you received from your timber sale, you have a **tax loss** even though you're holding cash in your hand. If your up-dated adjusted timber basis at the time of the sale is $500 per acre and you receive $400 per acre in timber sale income, you have $400 per acre in your hand tax-free (because it is covered by your $500 per acre basis) and $100 per acre in tax loss.

Calculating and adjusting your timber resource basis over time is referred to as, **depletion**. The cruise you did at the time of purchase establishes your **timber depletion base**, which is the volume, diameter classes and species of your stumpage. Your timber base at any given time is figured in terms of a **depletion unit**, which is basis/cost (dollars) per unit of timber volume (board feet, cords, tons). If you have $15,000 in adjusted timber basis and have 3,000 merchantable cords of wood in your timber base, each depletion unit (cord) is valued at $5 ($15,000 / 3,000 = $5). As your timber depletion base changes over time through sales, so does your timber basis. When you sell your timber in certain ways, you can take a **depletion deduction**, which is calculated this way: adjusted basis divided by total timber volume just before the sale multiplied by timber volume sold.

Depletion of your timber base does not produce the same level of tax benefits that depletion of oil or natural gas does. Since timber is a renewable resource, cutting it produces a time-limited depletion, not a permanent one. Still, you can claim a deduction for depletion of your timber if you cut the timber yourself for sale or have someone cut it for you, but not if you sell standing timber on the stump. You cannot claim a depletion allowance when you cut your timber for personal use. Let your CPA determine whether you're eligible for depletion benefits and what they might be.

Timber can experience **non-sale losses** as it matures. Trees grow in size and value and, at the same time, they suffer mortality from natural forces as well as diminished value from fire, wind breakage, drought, disease, insects and the like. The **normal, background-type loss** that occurs from Nature's variability—a tree falling over; woodpeckers ruining a tree—is **not deductible.** A **casualty loss** is a loss from a naturally occurring physical event that happens suddenly, unexpectedly or in an unusual manner. Such events include timber damage from windstorm, wild fire (not arson), hurricanes, volcanoes, hail, ice storms and plane crashes. The IRS seeks "suddenness" in casualty loss, which means drought and most disease and insect losses are not deductible. Casualty loss must be more than a diminution in value (such as loss from breakage); the event must eliminate the timber's value suddenly. Casualty loss deductibility is handled differently according to the type of timberland owner you are. A casualty loss may be deducted up to the amount of the lost timber's adjusted basis, and other limits apply to this type of loss.

If you own the timberland as an investment or business, you can deduct a **noncasualty loss** when the level of loss is beyond what is considered normal and the cause is out of the ordinary (i.e., unusual and unexpected). In some circumstances, you could claim that loss from drought or disease was a deductible noncasualty loss.

Loss from timber theft is also deductible in the year it is discovered. Theft loss can be deducted up to the adjusted basis in the timber stolen.

When figuring loss, you have to count in salvage proceeds, insurance payments and, in the case of theft, any money you get as reimbursement. Since the rules and forms vary, it is best to work with a CPA who is up to speed on recent IRS rulings. Determining whether a loss qualifies as a casualty loss and then calculating its value will involve a CPA and a forester. Don't try this yourself. A good discussion is found in Melvin J. Baughman's, Income Tax Guide for Woodland Owners, rev. 1999 at www.extension.umn.edu/ distribution/naturalresources/DD3934.html. Since tax law and interpretations change, you have to get timely information when you have a question. The National Timber Tax Website provides up-dated information.

When your CPA divides your rural property into various accounts (and, if necessary, sub-accounts), he is setting up a plan for handling the ordinary and necessary expenses you incur in each one. Expenses, depending on their nature, can be 1) **deducted** (expensed) **against income** in the year that you incur them, 2) **capitalized** (depreciated, amortized, allocated to basis, depleted, sold, or otherwise disposed) or 3) **deducted from sale proceeds**. To be able to do each of these things when appropriate, you must have your timberland property set up as an investment or a business, which means the activity you engage in must be carried out with the intention to profit, if only eventually. Holding woodland for personal pleasure/recreation or as a hobby gives you access to many fewer tax benefits involving deductions and capitalized expenses.

IRS looks at a combination of factors to test your profit motivation, including how you carry out your timberland activity; your expertise; amount of time you devote to the activity; appreciation of assets; success in making a profit; your taxpayer history of income and loss; your overall financial status; and, finally, how much recreation or personal pleasure is involved in the "investment/business." (IRC Section 212 pertains to investment; Section 162 for business.) If questioned, you have the burden of persuasion and proof. Timberland investment/business by its nature is a very long-term venture so you will not have to show a cash profit every year or at any particular future moment. Profit in timberland is also established by appreciation in the value of the timber through growth.

Current expenses and depreciable assets may be allocated among your accounts. If, for example, you use your tractor about 60 percent for farming that is intended to make a profit, 30 percent in timberland intended to make a profit and 10 percent in personal non-profit work, such as tilling your garden, your CPA will allocate the tractor's purchase price and certain maintenance costs as 60 percent to your farm account and 30 percent to your timber account. The 10 percent of the tractor's time that you use for personal chores is lost for depreciation purposes, because that share of your tractor is not used in a trade or business.

Equipment, depreciable in whole or shared with another account, that can be related to your timberland investment/business can include a tractor with a bushhog, hydraulic log splitter (used for a business purpose, such as firewood sales), chipper, bulldozer, walk-behind trail mower, tractor winch, farm truck, chainsaw, 4WD ATV and the computer you use to manage your timberland. Such items are called **capital assets**. They have to be valued at more than $100 and have a usable life of more than one year. Once you establish the original basis of the equipment, you depreciate it on your yearly tax forms according to a specific term of years. Depreciation allows you to recover the cost of acquisition over a period of years.

You can also depreciate the cost of an existing building or the construction of a new one that you use to store/maintain timberland-related equipment, tools and supplies.

Just as you cannot operate a hobby farm and get farm-related tax benefits, so too you cannot run a **hobby woodlot** and get timber-related benefits. The stuff you buy should have some reasonable connection to your for-profit timberland activity. You might have a hard time persuading an IRS auditor that you should be allowed to fully depreciate a $75,000 bulldozer, $25,000 tractor, $30,000 pick-up truck and a $400 chainsaw for use on a three-acre "timber tract" in your backyard. To make that level of investment fly against this undersized tract, you would have to show that the work you are doing with it can arguably justify that level of investment. If you were planting Paulownia—a high-value species—you might be able to sell the IRS on it even though the time horizon before your profit may be 60 years away. You can argue that the three acres requires intensive mechanical work to prepare the site—stump and slash removal (dozer/saws), road work (dozer), environmental protection (dozer/saws), ground preparation (tractor with implements), maintenance (tractor), regular application of inputs ("inputs" is a great IRS word) such as herbicide, fertilizer, pesticide, seedlings, all of which require a truck) and so forth. You should expect that the IRS auditor will visit the three acres to see whether you've done all the work you've described. Less extreme examples will, of course, raise fewer eyebrows.

My own experience with being audited is that **paper persuades and a field trip settles any questions**. I had one of the audits from hell where an auditor sat in my dining room for two days going through every check, receipt and scrap of paper I had collected for three tax years. One question involved why I had such high expenses for fencing. I explained that I had installed a rotational grazing system for the cattle that required division of the pasture into small paddocks. By rotating a gang of cattle from fresh field to fresh field every couple of days, I could about double the number of pounds of gain my farm produced each grazing season. The auditor was stilled puzzled. So I walked her out back and through the fields and gates, through the muck and manure. No problem.

In justifying your timberland as an investment/business, you should show an auditor your cruise at the time of purchase (which establishes your timber basis and your timber-depletion base), forest-management plan and simple business plan for your timberland (showing number/species of trees planted, if any, likely year of harvest, projected revenues and costs). Then walk the auditor, if it comes to that, through the three acres, showing where you have used the dozer, tractor, truck and saw. Even though cheaper alternatives for accomplishing this work would have been available to you, the IRS does not require that you use them. The IRS does not care that you are investing your capital inefficiently, or that you could have hired the work for $5,000, or that you could have spent half the money by buying used, smaller models. The Agency mainly cares that you show them you have thought seriously about making a future profit. Your plans and your intentions, rather than your long-term success, are what will be examined for the obvious reason: you can't show long-term success (or failure) in timber until the long term arrives. In this regard, timberland can cover the purchase of machines and equipment by projecting a very large cash profit many decades in the future; timber can be better than farming in this respect.

I am not recommending that you cheat on your taxes. Your profit purpose has to be authentic, and you have to do the work. But I am also observing that timberland can expand the elasticity of your tax situation if you do the proper legal, forestry and tax planning, have the right intentions and follow through.

Remember that depreciation helps you on your annual taxes for each year of its multi-year schedule, but 25 percent of the total amount you depreciate on residential and nonresidential property is added back when you sell the depreciated asset, thus increasing your taxable gain. The recapture tax does not apply to depreciated equipment.

Land and certain land improvements, such as earthen work of a permanent character, are not depreciable. Other non-depreciable land improvements include land leveling, excavating roadbeds of permanent roads and earthen impoundments, such as berms and dikes. Land assets that are depreciable include bridges, culverts, graveling, fences, non-permanent structures, temporary roads and firebreaks. For land assets to be depreciable and for other property, such as equipment, vehicles and tools used on the timberland to be depreciable, you must hold the property as either a business or as an investment, not for pleasure, personal or hobby use.

Non-depreciable equipment (with a less than one-year usable life) might include a used chainsaw, hand tools, gas can, protective chaps and helmet with hearing protectors. Certain equipment might be depreciable or might not—like a chainsaw or gate—depending on size, number, cost, life expectancy and your CPA's judgment. Such items should be deducted.

You can depreciate certain **maintenance and repair costs** on depreciable equipment, but not all such costs. If the expense adds to the life of the equipment, or significantly increases its value, you can depreciate it. Basis in such a machine is increased when maintenance and repair costs are depreciable.

The **costs of consumables and other supplies** are not depreciable. They are deducted from your annual gross income. These timberland-related costs can include gas and oil, herbicide, nails, posted signs, chains and locks, gates, grass seed, software, books and subscriptions to forestry publications.

Payment of management and operating expenses, including overhead, related to your timberland investment or business is deductible. This can include things such as travel to a timber-taxation conference, conference fees, conference food/lodging; travel to look at potential timberland investments; certain educational expenses; travel to meet potential buyers of your stumpage; property taxes; timberland-related phone, fax, internet and postage; proportional shares of insurance, utilities, vehicle costs, rent, office maintenance and equipment; research supplies, books, timber pricing services and other-related expenses.

Your timberland investment/business may also be eligible for all or some of the **home-office** deductions if you dedicate a room of your residence to that activity. You cannot make use of the home-office benefit if you have set up your timberland as a hobby or for personal recreation. Home-office status is a big, flapping red flag to the IRS computers, but don't be scared away from taking legitimate deductions. I've had a home office for more than 20 years without a problem.

You have tax benefits from the cost of hiring **equipment time and operator** for your timber investment/business, but how your CPA handles them can depend on what the time was used for. If you hired a bulldozer to build permanent roads through your timberland, the IRS would consider that a depreciable purpose. The same dozer building ponds for fire protection might be depreciable. The dozer time devoted to maintaining or improving roads is probably a deduction. When you give $25 to your neighbor to take down a tree that's too big and tricky for you to try with the penknife-size, ring-a-ding-ding chainsaw your wife gave you for your first Christmas as a timber owner, that's a deductible rather than depreciable expense. The same is true for the neighbor you hire to mow your woods trails, with his equipment or yours. Hired spot labor is deductible, except when it's spent on depreciable assets, in which case, it's a depreciable cost.

Also deductible annually are any fees you pay to your forester, lawyer or CPA who provide timberland-related advice and services.

All costs you incur in **planting, or reforestation by natural or artificial seeding, can be amortized**, a process, like depreciation, of recovering your basis over a period of years as the asset is used up, worn out or sold. This includes all timber-establishment costs—site preparation, seedlings, equipment used in preparation and planting, hired labor and post-planting work until the trees can survive on their own. Currently, the first $10,000 of reforestation costs can be deducted outright in the year incurred and expenses above that can be amortized/deducted over 84 months.

You cannot capitalize your own labor or pay yourself a wage that you deduct. While you may feel it is unfair that you cannot pay yourself for timberland work, you will not win this fight with an auditor. You may, however, be able to set up your timberland and farm businesses as a limited liability company or other organized entity, which then pays you as an independent contractor to perform certain part-time work. In any event, you must capitalize pay to family members and in some cases your spouse.

You should keep a record of all timber-sale expenses you pay, such as forester commission, legal fees, CPA fees, purchases related to getting the timber out, such as a culvert and so on. Such one-time expenses should be deducted from timber-sale income. These sale-specific expenses are in addition to and separate from your routine timberland expenses noted above.

You may also incur some **post-sale expenses** related to extra reclamation, additional excavation, planting of seedlings, herbicide application, site preparation, fire-pond development, more erosion-control work in the roads, slash clean up and so on. Post-sale expenses are not usually added in with sale expenses, though some exceptions might exist. They should be deductible.

I've discussed in Chapters 6 and 33, the federally funded, state-administered **cost-share** programs that help a landowner pay for conservation, reforestation, timber stand improvements and environmental protections on his property. Some of this money (such as the Conservation Reserve Program) is required to be reported as part of your ordinary gross income; other money, such as that for the Forest Land Enhancement Program (FLEP), Wetlands Reserve Program (WRP), Environmental Quality Incentives Program (EQIP) and the Wildlife Habitat Incentives Program (WHIP) can be excluded from gross income, fully or partially. Different cost shares are handled differently; and the rules can change from Congressional tax bill to Congressional tax bill. Let your CPA sort this out.

Your timberland may also generate income and expenses from **non-timber-sale activities**, such as 1) annual rental income from a hunting or recreation lease; 2) income from renting your sugar maples for sap production; 3) sale of maple sap you collect; and 4) sale of occasional products like nuts, firewood, locust fence posts, mistletoe or ginseng. These would be handled as either ordinary rental income or sale income.

Form T (Timber), Forest Industries Schedules, is the attachment that you use for timberland acquisitions, sales and expenses. It has the following schedules that you may or may not need to complete, depending on your circumstances: A, Maps; B, Acquisitions; C, Profit or Loss from Land and Timber Sales; D, Losses; E. Reforestation and Timber Stand Activities; F, Capital Returnable Through Depletion; G, Land Ownership; H, Road Construction Cost; and I, Drainage Structures. If you make an isolated timber sale and are a small woodlot owner, you need to complete only Schedules C and F. Haney *et al.*, Federal Income Tax, provides an excellent guide to how to report timber-related income and expenses and which form to use.

A lot of information is available on timber taxation. (A lot of information appears to be necessary.) Start with the USDA's, Forest Owners' Guide to Timber Investments, The Federal Income Tax, and Tax Recordkeeping, Forest Service, Agriculture Handbook 718, most recent edition. This is obtainable from the U.S. Government Printing Office or your local USDA Forest Service Office or at www.timbertax.org/ research/aghndbk/aghndbk.asp?id=research&topic=aghndbk. The **National Timber Tax Website** at www.timbertax.org is a fountainhead of information on the subject, including links to all relevant federal regulations, at www.timbertax.org/research/regulations/regulations.asp?id=research&topic=regs. Visit the Purdue University website at www.fnr.purdue.edu/ttax; Baughman's, Income Tax Guide for Woodland Owners, rev. 1999, University of Minnesota Extension Service at www.extension.umn.edu/ distribution/_naturalresources/DD3934.html. Good references can be found at www.nyfoa.org/ NYFOACasualtyTaxIntro.html. The Journal of Agricultural Taxation & Law carries the most articles on the subject. Additional information can be obtained from the Forest Industries Council on Taxation (FICT), 1111 19th St., N.W., Suite 800, Washington, D.C. 20036; 202-463-2757; FAX, 202-463-2057. General sources for taxation and investment information include The American Agricultural Law Association's www.aglaw-assn.org/biblio/22%20%20%Forestry.htm; and www.na.fs.fed.us/pubs/ misc/ir/irtoc.htm, the USFS's "Guide to Internet Resources." Attorney William C. Siegel, who specializes in forestry taxation and was referenced above, may be contacted at 504-737-0583; e-mail: wcsieg@aol.com. The Haney *et al.*, Federal Income Tax, is current as of 2005, comprehensive and well-organized.

All of this discussion applies to the federal tax code as of 2005. The Breaux-Mack Commission proposed a sweeping simplification of the tax system in the fall of that year. Mortgage-interest deductibility would be reduced significantly, and many deductions removed. The Bush White House did not endorse these proposals. A land buyer, particularly one considering farm and timber assets, must consult with his CPA prior to making an offer to determine the then-current tax rules that will be applied to his purchase.

CONSERVATION EASEMENTS AND TAXES

More common than the sale of a conservation easement is its **donation by the landowner to a public agency or 501 (c) (3) charitable organization,** such as a land trust, conservation group or a landowners' association of neighbors set up to hold such easements on their own land. The holder of the easement must have the capacity to enforce the easement over time. Not all rural land automatically qualifies under state laws and IRS regulations for the substantial income-tax and estate-tax benefits a donor can get for contributing one or more of his rights in his land. Among the rights often contributed, in whole or part, are the right to develop for commercial or residential purposes, right to timber, right to mine and quarry, right to install a wind farm, etc. To get the tax benefits, the conservation easement—what you are giving—has to have both an authentic market value and a clear environmental benefit. You are giving away something of value, leaving your property, theoretically, that much less valuable than before. An appraiser determines the value of the right (s) you've chosen to donate.

Your land needs to be located where some significant public or environmental benefit will be achieved by restricting one or more future uses of the property through the easement. An easement that preserves open space on an inaccessible patch of remote mountainside is not likely to qualify under the IRS rules, because the development right you're giving away has no value on that property. Similarly, a donation of a restriction that has no market value will not wash. The organizations that accept these donations, such as land trusts, should not be in the business of scamming the IRS. You should assume that the easement's valuation has to be based in reality. Timber easements, whereby the landowner donates his right to cut timber on his property, or limits this right, are often overvalued by a compliant forester who inflates the donation's value. The IRS may not pick up some inflation, but egregious inflation will probably catch their eye.

Donation of a qualifying easement brings the donor four different tax benefits. First, the donation is a charitable contribution whose value may be deducted from your income for federal and state income taxes. The full value of your donation is multiplied by your federal income tax rate and state rate combined to determine the value of your deduction. If you—an individual—have held your property for more than one year, your deduction is limited to 30 percent of what amounts to your adjusted gross income in the year you make the donation. If, on the other hand, you take your deduction in the first ownership year using your basis in the land, you can deduct up to 50 percent of your adjusted gross income. If you are inclined to place a conservation easement on your land, consider doing it soon after you purchase the property to take advantage of the extra benefit. You can carry any unused deduction forward for five years, giving you a total of six years to use the entire deduction. Second, the easement reduces your estate's value, which can help lower or even eliminate estate tax, depending on your individual circumstances. Third, the executor of your estate can exclude from your estate 40 percent of the value of the land carrying your easement after subtracting the value of the easement up to $500,000, using Section 2031 (c) of the American Farm and Ranch Protection Act. Fourth, a number of states allow land with such an easement to be assessed in light of the value of that easement being severed, which will produce lower property taxes.

The rules for using these tax benefits are more complicated than these few sentences suggest. I have relied on several publications written by attorney C. Timothy Lindstrom, who is director of The Jackson Hole Land Trust, POB 2897, 5455 East Broadway, Suite 228, Jackson, WY 83001; 307-733-4707; tim@jhlandtrust.org. My brief discussion is based on Linstrom's, A Simplified Guide to the Tax Benefits of Donating A Conservation Easement (available from the Jackson Hole Land Trust); "Tax Advantages of Conservation Easement Donation," November, 1998 and "Conservation Easements in Virginia," 1999; The Conservation Easement Handbook, The Federal Tax Law of Conservation Easements and other information published by the Land Trust Alliance, 1319 F Street, N.W., Suite 501, Washington, DC, 20004. State and sub-state land trusts are now common. They can be accessed by doing a search on www.google.com, using "land trust, state or city." The Land Trust Alliance and The Nature Conservancy (TNC) can also provide information on "qualified organizations" in your area that are set up to accept these easements. Tim Linstrom is willing to chat briefly with interested callers and takes on paying clients. Steve Small, cited above, specializes in conservation easements.

While the tax benefits of conservation easements are huge, you should approach donation or sale cautiously and with great thoughtfulness. First, a valuable right today is likely to be much more valuable in the future. The tax benefit you get is based on current value. Today's $100,000 no-cut-timber right could easily be worth ten times that in ten years. What do you need more and when do you need it: tax benefits now or cash later? Life is so uncertain that I would hesitate to sever an asset that might at some future point rescue me from my habit of shooting my own financial foot. Second, the value of any no-cut timber easement will depend on when, in the growth cycle, you grant it. A no-cut easement immediately following a clearcut would, I think, have little value. The same easement given on a stand of cherry in its 80th year, would be worth much money. A ten- or 15-year difference can multiply value many times over if the first year of that span occurs when the trees are still considered too small for sawtimber but the last year captures the **ingrowth effect**. A no-cut easement could have additional value where the timber is around, but not part of, habitat for a federally endangered species. Third, most conservation easements are donated in perpetuity, which means forever. Fourth, you may have a problem selling a valuable tract once you've peeled off a right that makes it valuable. One hundred acres of woods surrounded by suburbs has scant market value if you've donated its timber and development rights. Who, you should ask yourself, will want to buy it so that it can be kept untouched? This is not a brief against conservation easements. It is simply a few words to make you understand that these vows, unlike those of marriage, cannot be broken.

If you're considering an easement, think of ways to limit its scope while achieving your objectives. You can, for example, donate a no-development right while keeping the right to build a house or two if the acreage is sufficiently large. You might donate an easement that prohibits clearcutting, but allows cutting of mature timber at least 20 years after the previous cut. You can also put a full no-cut easement on one part of your land, but not on the rest. Do not donate an easement that allows public access to your land unless that is what you and your immediate heirs want. You might also investigate a time-limited easement, say one that runs for 20 years, or one that is in effect during the life time of the donor.

As a rule, I would advise against putting a no-cut timber easement on your property.

STATE AND LOCAL TIMBER TAXES

Timberland is subject to **local and state taxes**. The principal local tax is likely to be the county's **property tax**, which can take several forms. Some states also tax income earned on the sale of timber. The National Timber Tax Website provides information on forest property taxes each state uses, along with a general discussion of their differences. Each state adopts a property tax format, which is administered through a local jurisdiction—such as city, county, township or parish. Differences in timberland taxes— property and/or sale—can be significant from state to state. See www.timbertax.org/state_laws/ quickreference.asp?id=statelaws&topic=reference. In most states, standing timber is not taxed, either by custom or law. California is one exception, imposing a 2.9 percent tax on timber every 60 years.

The Website's property-tax data, when I reviewed them, were based on a 1996 publication by Sun Joseph Chang. Sun lists **five types of state forest-property-taxation systems**: 1) *ad valorem* **property tax**, by which tax is collected on the basis of the value of the land and the trees; 2) **productivity tax**, by which the annual tax is based on the capitalized value of either the gross or net mean annual revenue from the timberland; 3) **site value tax**, by which only the land is taxed; 4) **flat property tax**, by which the same amount of money is collected per acre of timberland no matter the timber's current value; and 5) **exemption** states where some or all of the timber value is exempt from property tax, or the tax is qualified or discounted in some way. When scoping timberland property, keep in mind that some states tax timber production. That will lower income from any sale of timber immediately following purchase. The National Timber Tax website at www.timbertax.org provides the following analysis of state timber-tax systems, which differs from Sun's typography:

TABLE 24-1

STATE TAX LAWS

State Taw Laws > Quick Reference: Forest Property Taxation Systems in the United States

Ad valorem property tax (Current Use) - A tax, duty, or fee which varies based on the value of the products, services, or property on which it is levied.

Flat property tax - under this system the same amount of money per acre is collected on any acre of timberland regardless of its value.

Site Map

Yield Tax - is a tax on the value of the harvested timber. The tax is collected after the timber is harvested.

Severance Tax - is a flat tax on a specific unit of volume harvested (i.e., board feet, cubic feet, cords, tonnage etc.). The tax is collected after the timber is harvested.

State	Ad Valorem	Flat	Exemption	Severance Tax	Yield Tax
Alabama	X			X	
Alaska			X		
Arizona		X		X	
Arkansas	X			X	
California	X			X	
Colorado	X				
Connecticut	X^1				
Delaware	X		X		
Florida	X				
Georgia	X			X	
Hawaii	X^2				
Idaho	X				X
Illinois	X				X
Indiana	X	X			
Iowa	X		X		
Kansas	X^2				
Kentucky	X				
Louisiana	X				
Maine	X^1				
Maryland	X				
Massachusetts		X^4			X
Michigan		X			X
Minnesota		X^3			
Mississippi	X				

512

State					
Missouri		X			X
Montana	X			X	
Nebraska	X				
Nevada	X				
New Hampshire		X			X
New Jersey	X				
New Mexico	X				X
New York	X	X^3			X
N. Carolina	X			X	
N. Dakota		X			
Ohio	X	X^3			
Oklahoma	X^2				
Oregon	X^1				
Pennsylvania	X^1				
Rhode Island	X		X		
S. Carolina	X				
S. Dakota	X^2				
Tennessee	X				
Texas	X				
Utah	X				
Vermont	X				
Virginia	X^5			X	
Washington	X^1				
W. Virginia	X				X
Wisconsin		X			X
Wyoming	X				

X^1 Current use based on forest productivity

X^2 Current use based on agricultural productivity

X^3 Reduction in Fair Market Value (FMV)

X^4 Reduction in FMV for land classified as forestland or recreational lands; Flat tax for land classified as agricultural & horticultural land.

X^5 Current use based on site productivity

Source: http://www.timbertax.org/statetaxes/quickreference.asp

10/5/2005

The quickest way to obtain current property tax information in the jurisdiction of your target property is to visit the local (tax) **assessor's office**. Here you will find the **tax-assessed value** of the property, which comes from the jurisdiction's periodic **reassessment** of all property within its borders. The property's tax-assessed value will be divided into categories: the land itself, according to its class (e.g., residential, agricultural, timberland), improvements (structures that are permanently attached to the land, such as a house or barn), minerals and, where applicable, possibly water rights. Such assets, including standing timber, are considered **real property**. (A right, benefit or interest that runs with the land—such as a life estate—is also considered real property.) The tax-appraisal value is supposed to represent current **fair market value (FMV)**. The values you find in the county records may represent 100 percent of FMV, or something less, depending on the state's policy. West Virginia, for example, values land for tax purposes at 60 percent of FMV; some towns in New York use 94 percent. (For convenience, I will use "county" to represent the appropriate jurisdiction for the target property.) Tax-assessed values, tax rates, current taxes and related information are collected in the jurisdiction's **Land Book**, copies of which are usually available in several county offices. Your jurisdiction may have another name for this comprehensive compilation of property information. It also may be fully accessible by computer and no longer kept in hard copy. Whatever the format and name, this information is public record and should be freely available.

The quickest and easiest way of getting a ballpark sense of the fair market value—likely sale price—of a target property is to phone the tax assessor and ask a generalized question that fits your target. Don't ask, "Whadda you think the Fred Smith place is worth?" Ask, "What is unimproved timberland in the 200 to 300-acre range selling for per acre in the southeast end of the county?" If you decide to base your offer on that general opinion, don't quote the assessor to the seller. Attribute the opinion to "knowledgeable sources," if you're asked.

In the assessor's office and the Land Book, you should find the following:

- target property's **acreage** (as carried on the tax rolls; this figure may or may not be the same as the deeded acreage; it is often inaccurate)

- most recent **tax-appraisal values for its land, improvements and minerals**

- information as to **what percentage of fair market value** the tax-appraised value represents (This can be 100 percent or less.)

- **property classification** to which your property has been assigned

- whether this county has adopted **use-value taxation (land use)** and whether the target property is so classified (See below.)

- whether any **special taxes, levies, fees or charges** apply to this property

- **tax rates** that apply to the property's land, minerals and improvements

- **dollar amount of current taxes** by land, minerals and improvements

- **date** when property taxes are **due**

- **discounts**, if any, for early payment; **penalties** for late payment

- **exemptions and breaks**, e.g., seniors, resident homeowners, etc.

- information on **other taxes** the jurisdiction imposes, such as a machinery and equipment tax, farm-machinery tax, business or occupation tax, self-employment tax, special taxes/levies or fees (sewer and water districts, trash disposal, road taxes, school construction etc.) and personal property taxes (vehicles, boats, motorcycles etc., which are assets that do not fit the definition of real property). You may have to visit other offices as well to get a complete picture of the full load. Personal property, which is property other than real property, is usually taxed, though jurisdictions may be more or less inclusive as to the types of personal property they tax. Some items, such as vehicles, may be taxed both locally and at the state level.

In terms of timberland, it is important to remember that standing timber—timber on the stump—is considered real property that conveys when you buy the land, unless the owner explicitly retains ownership or reserves an interest in it. But cut timber—logs or trees on the ground—is personal property. Thus, an unscrupulous owner might take advantage of an inexperienced buyer by cutting the 50 best cherry sawtimber trees between the day the buyer submits a contract and when the owner accepts it, 15 days later. The 50+ logs are worth $35,000 and become the owner's personal property as soon as they are on the ground. The unfortunate buyer failed to include a provision in his purchase contract that linked his offer to the owner leaving the timber unchanged as of the offer's submission date, not its acceptance date. The buyer should also include language that prohibits timbering between the date of contract submission and closing. This is scummy behavior, but the owner has a breastwork of law to hide behind.

A word about **minerals**. Minerals are usually taxed both as property and as they are produced. If the property's minerals have not been severed from the surface, then the landowner owns the subsurface minerals and is responsible for their taxes. If the mineral rights have been sold outright, the owner of the target property is not responsible for any taxation on minerals. If, as is far more common, the mineral rights have been leased to another party, the owner of the minerals is responsible for the property tax. Who is responsible for payment of the production tax as the minerals are produced? The answer will depend both on state law and on the terms of the lease agreement the owner (lessor) has negotiated with the lessee, the outfit that's leased the owner's minerals. (The lessee may, in turn, assign his lease rights to a production company who will do the actual mining or drilling.) The lease may specify how the lessor (owner) and lessee will divide the tax hit. This language can be written as the parties agreeing to pay 1) the state severance/production/yield tax in equal shares, fifty-fifty; or 2) in the same proportion as they have agreed to divide (gross or net) production revenue, e.g., seven-eighths to the lessee, one-eighth to the owner. If the lease does not specify how the production tax is to be apportioned, assume that the lessor, you, are liable for the production tax until you are explicitly told differently by your CPA or tax attorney. Ask this question as part of your pre-purchase scoping so that you are not surprised by a post-purchase wake-up call.

The major property tax break in rural areas is **use-value taxation systems**, which are now in place in every state, though not in every county in every state. Commonly called **land use**, these programs allow counties to tax agricultural, open and/or timberland at the value for which the land is currently used rather than at a higher and better use which is the fair market value. Use value is the expected selling price of the property with the restriction that it can be used only for its current use or a similar use. The purpose of land use is to help owners hold their property for these lower-value uses, such as agriculture or woodland, instead of converting it to commercial or residential development. Conservation easements that sever or limit development rights are designed to keep such land in its current use. Land-use land is appraised at the FMV of its current use, not its FMV as its highest possible use, which produces a big tax savings for the owner. If a landowner decides to withdraw land-use property from the land-use program, he usually has to pay some portion of his past tax savings, plus interest, as a **rollback tax**. Not all rural counties employ land use. Where it has not been adopted, individual property may still be eligible for land-use treatment if the state provides this status for managed timberland and land in **agricultural and forestal districts**. The rules and formulas governing these calculations are complicated and state-specific. Check with the county or regional office of the state forestry agency regarding the tax break for managed timber lands; the assessor should be able to provide information on agricultural and forestall districts.

Most states extend a **use-valuation** approach to timberland that is similar to the agricultural use or land-use tax break for valuing agricultural land. The way this is handled varies. Some states classify all timberland as agricultural land, which then makes it eligible for a use valuation. Others extend use valuation to timberland that is part of an owner-occupied farm, but not to non-occupied land. In a few states, timberland can get use-valuation status if it is enrolled in the state's managed-forest program, which usually requires a forester-written plan for the owner's timber property. State policies on use-valuation for timberland is in E.B. Kelley, "Recent Developments in Forest Taxation Policy: A Comparative Overview of Selected Major Timber-Producing States," 1998 at www.cnr.umn.edu/FR/publications/proceedings/ improving_forestproductivity/papers/KELLEY~1.PDF.

Do not be surprised if a county classifies wooded land in several ways, each of which has a different tax rate. Wooded land that is part of an occupied farm residence may enjoy a much lower rate than wooded land that is not. Residential status may have been established years ago, so even if you are a new absentee landowner, you may still benefit from it. In such cases, you, as the new owner, want to do nothing that provokes a review: some counties are vigilant, while others are not.

Wooded land with some version of land-use status is taxed more lightly than the same land without. Ask local officials about how agricultural, undeveloped and timberland are taxed. Ask whether there are different classifications of timberland, depending on ownership or the productivity of the land for growing timber. Ask if the tax rate is fixed, regardless of stumpage value. Ask, finally, about the current and future status of the target property. If your property is in a state that imposes a **tax on yield or timber-sale income,** you will need to figure that into your offering price.

You will also want to do a little **future analysis** when it comes to local taxes. If you think the county is a backwater, you will probably assume that the property tax burden will continue to be comparatively low, consistent with the minimum public services available. I urge caution about making such straight-line extrapolations. Demands for services can change quickly, and for different reasons. State and federal programs often do not adequately fund the new standards they impose on localities; the phrase that drives local officials nuts is "unfunded mandates." Requirements related to water supply, waste-water treatment, education, corrections and the like can force localities to raise taxes to fund worthy improvements. A low-tax community with inadequate services may be on the cusp of raising its property tax. Big projects—second-home developments, resorts and so on—can also inflate property values and taxes. You must look in the local newspaper and ask around to determine whether you are about to be blindsided. If the county has land use, you can assume it will continue to have it. If it does not have land use, I would assume that it will not adopt it in the future. Our most rural/agricultural counties often don't adopt land use because their populations are so overwhelmingly farm-based that there are too few non-farmers to carry the tax burden that land use would shift away from farmland. In this case, farmers might lower their property tax but they would have to pick up the local tax needed in some other way. If the county is developing as an outer-ring suburb, anticipate higher local taxes. Ask whether any new levies or special assessments are in the works. Check the zoning office to see whether the target property is located in a designated growth area under the local comprehensive plan. If so, you can expect residential and/or commercial development—and higher taxes. But your target property will be worth more. Finally, ask how the county treats recently sold property for taxes. If you pay far more for your property than the tax-appraised value, it's a good bet that the next county-wide reappraisal will increase your property's valuation. Make sure to ask when the next county-wide reappraisal will take place. It's actually a pretty good bet that your property's valuation will increase in every subsequent county-wide reappraisal. If you see selling prices rising, property taxes will follow.

Jurisdictions reappraise their property for tax purposes every few years, according to their state's requirements. This is referred to as the county's **reappraisal** or **reassessment**. The purpose of the reappraisal is to determine the current fair market value for every piece of real property in the jurisdiction. You must assume that your property will be reappraised at higher value in each round, unless it's located where market prices are falling. My property value more than doubled between five-year assessments—and I think that it is still undervalued in light of the market.

Property tax is levied by a local jurisdiction according to its state's rules. The local **tax rate** is often expressed in dollars per $100 of assessed value. It may also be referred to as the **millage rate**, where so many mills, each of which is equal to $1/10^{th}$ of one cent, are levied per dollar of assessed value. If your 100 acres of undeveloped land is appraised for tax purposes at $150,000 and the tax rate is $1.65 per $100 of tax-appraised/tax-assessed value, the current annual property tax would be $2,475 ($150,000 value / 100 = 1,500 x $1.65 = $2,475). The bottom line in understanding your property tax burden is the dollar amount of the annual payment, which is the product of your tax rate and the property's tax-assessed value.

Appraisal values for similar agricultural, undeveloped and wooded properties are likely to differ within a county according to their slightly different uses, locations and possibly zoning status. Sometimes, it's impossible to figure out why pasture or woodland on one side of a fence is appraised differently than pasture or woodland on the other side. Each jurisdiction provides an appeal process by which you can challenge your reappraisal. You will need to make your case before an official board of "review and equalization." This is done by assembling information on nearby comparables the reassessment appraiser valued lower than your property. You can also present recent-sale comparables. I have seen landowners win appeals on house values, but not on land, particularly undeveloped land.

Each state has its own reappraisal system that counties follow. **Land tables** are constructed, using recent selling prices and other data, to provide values for different land types. Digital cameras are now used to build data banks on improvements. Agricultural land is usually grouped/graded into one of several classes—cropland, pasture, woodland, range and so on. Agricultural land may be valued according to rental rates rather than selling prices. Timberland, apart from that associated with agricultural land, is also subject to categorization by type, purpose, location and/or size. My experience is that tax appraisers do not try to determine the merchantable timber value on the land they classify as timberland. Instead, they use the appropriate land tables that are developed at the county level. In many counties, this results in a single appraisal value, say $400 per acre, applied to all timberland, whether it has just been clearcut or contains $2,500 per acre in merchantable timber.

Your **local tax burden** is the sum of all local taxes that you will be expected to pay as the new owner of a target property. Local tax burden is always somewhat greater than the property tax alone. You will discover much tax-burden variation among counties within a state, depending on their degree of urbanization-suburbanization, but not that much variation between like counties in the same state. Local taxes and particularly the property tax reflect each county's expenditures for local services. Counties that share a basic profile—rural, low-population, low development potential, similar topography—should be roughly comparable in spending, taxing and regulating. You should find the local tax burden, particularly property taxes, declining as you move further away from suburbs into increasingly rural, small-population counties. My experience is that rural counties provide the basic package of public services, but not much over that unless they are a hot second-home market for urban buyers. Basic services translate into a low tax burden. Rural counties also try to keep property taxes low as a way to help farmers, the elderly on fixed incomes and local families with limited earnings. When reappraisal values are announced, rural counties will often lower their tax rates to keep the tax burden about the same as before (with a little increase, of course).

Timberland owners need to be aware that some states impose a tax on the sale of timber. This may be called a **severance tax, yield tax, excise tax or production tax**. Several states—Washington, California and Louisiana—combine an *ad valorem* tax on property with what I will refer to as a production tax, which is generally calculated on gross sales revenue. However, California levies a 2.9 percent tax once every 60 years against the value of standing timber. California also extends a use-value tax break for managed timberland in timberland production zones that results in lower valuations and lower taxes. (See John W. LeBlanc, "How Much Will I Owe in State Taxes: The Yield Tax and Timber Production Zones," Working in the Woods: A Guide for California's Forest Landowners, University of California, Natural Resources Cooperative Extension, undated, at www.cnr.berkeley.edu/departments/espm/extension/ YIELDTAX.HTM.) Georgia taxes timberland owned by large landowners annually at its full FMV in its highest and best use, and also taxes production. Georgia continues to be a major timber-producing state.

When comparing different target properties, it's often useful to compare their current **per-acre total tax burdens**. If similar type land is taxed differently from one to another, you might start asking why. Land carrying a higher tax burden may be, simply put, "better land" in terms of its productivity and location. You can also compare the per-acre tax-appraised value of your target property's timberland, pasture and cropland with the same types of land held by its neighbors. If your target property's lands are significantly out of whack with those of your neighbors, it may reflect some fact on the ground or, alternatively, a difference in ownership history. Properties that have been sold repeatedly and recently are likely to have higher tax-appraisal valuations than those that have not.

Kelley, *op. cit.*, estimated the **per-acre tax burden** (both land tax and production tax where imposed) on very large timberland owners in about a dozen major timber-producing states. The lowest burden was calculated for eastern Oregon, at a little more than $1 per acre. Oklahoma, Alabama, Idaho, North Carolina, Minnesota, West Virginia and Arkansas were less than $3 per acre. Mississippi, eastern Washington and inland California were between $3 and $5 per acre. Georgia and western Oregon were at $8; coastal California was at $9; and western Washington was almost $25. The West Coast rates reflect the incredibly high volumes and values that appear in these forests. The key assumption in Kelley's work was that the owner had an annual harvest requirement of 20 million board feet.

Tax considerations are always a factor when evaluating investments. But both local and federal tax policies are broadly favorable to timberland investment. I've never seen a timberland purchase fall through because of its tax burden, except in New York, where the local property and school taxes are very high.

CHAPTER 25: COUNTRY LAWYERS AND COUNTRY REAL-ESTATE LAW

Buying rural property always requires that the buyer have some knowledge of the legal framework in which such transactions occur, common problems of ownership and conveyance and, finally, the procedural steps he is expected to take to complete a purchase. I've touched on these points in other chapters. The discussion that follows is not meant to substitute for competent legal advice. Consider these next chapters not as a law-school text on real estate but as practical lessons learned on the campus of rural give and take. **Don't try to buy rural land without competent local counsel.**

FINDING A COUNTRY LAWYER

Every buyer needs an experienced, local dirt lawyer. He should be your advocate and source of guidance. He will know the state's code (laws), which governs land transactions, and he will have access to relevant case law (legal decisions). He will also know the local players—zoning official, real-estate agents, bankers/lenders, farmers, USDA employees, soil engineers, excavators, surveyors, consulting foresters, home inspectors, well drillers, septic-system cleaners and so on. A lawyer in your target county is local; the further away your lawyer is from local, the less he will know about the local players.

Your lawyer may know, or at least know of, the seller. Any knowledge of the seller's financial circumstances, motives for selling and negotiating personality are invaluable to you. If you have specific questions about the seller, your lawyer's network of friends and contacts can probably come up with reasonably accurate answers. Your lawyer may be able to get sensitive information for you because he works with local folks every day and knows how to approach such matters better than you do. He will know the individuals in each county office who get things done and those who can't, don't or won't. Following his advice—"Go here, not there."—will save you time and money.

The time to find local counsel is after you've chosen your target county but _before_ you approach any seller. I would even advise securing a relationship with a local lawyer before you start driving around with real-estate agents or on your own. Pay for an hour or two of his time to learn about the county's politics, economics and personalities. You may want to introduce yourself to the county through your lawyer. You want his advice regarding your buying objectives and local fair-market values. Lawyers often know about property that's coming on the market, as well as land that's not listed but is for sale privately or about to come on the market. He'll also know of property that's had a troubled legal history. He should have opinions about which properties are over-priced. Land that has been sold and resold several times within the last five years is often priced above market. He may also be able to steer you away from areas in the county that may not suit your objectives, such as places whose dirt is hard to perc, as well as spots that may be close to a planned development. Make sure that the lawyer knows from the outset that you will pay him for his time. Don't mutter and scrimp over these dollars. Consider them the cheapest degree you've ever paid for.

How do you find a dirt-smart lawyer in a place where you are walking in cold? The local bar association can provide names. The legal reference, <u>Martindale-Hubbell,</u> is available in larger libraries. It will give you a sense of the size of the firm and its self-professed areas of competence. Buy a copy of the local phone directory. Start your screening by eliminating lawyers who don't include "real estate" in their directory advertisements. Ask people you know and whose judgment you trust. I once found a dirt lawyer in Cody, Wyoming by asking a friend in Pennsylvania who had graduated from the University of Wyoming's law school for a contact; he called his former roommate, now a Wyoming judge, who gave him the name.

Country lawyers are usually general practitioners out of financial necessity, but some specialize more than others in real estate. You can narrow the field by walking into the county clerk's office where deeds are recorded and digging through recent land transactions. Deeds are usually prepared on a lawyer's stationery. That ten-minute research should supply the names of several lawyers who are doing most of local real-estate work. In and of itself, that information doesn't highlight the best lawyer for you, but it can introduce you to your main choices.

New, out-of-county buyers are always told to "ask around" for a lawyer. This hit-and-miss technique can work as long as you test those whose opinions you've gotten. Don't just request a lawyer's name. Ask your source why he prefers this one over the others. What's the source's personal experience with the lawyer? Are they related? You have to get a fix on the source before you can trust his opinion. It won't hurt to ask for legal references from the county's zoning officer, one or more local lenders and recent out-of-county buyers. If you know a local resident, start there. Don't ask the seller.

The danger that lurks in asking for a reference is that you may feel that you are then locked into the recommended person. Another lawyer may be a better fit for you after interviewing both. Thank the source of the recommendation for his effort and tell him that you'll be interviewing several possibilities. Try to keep your source from becoming invested in your decision.

Rural lawyers, particularly sole practitioners, have been slower to establish Internet websites than their city counterparts. Since everybody in the county knows who the local lawyers are, there's little reason to bother with a website. An out-of-county buyer can easily do an Internet search for local lawyers by typing into a search engine, "lawyer, county name, state"; or "lawyer, zipcode." Listing websites such as www.findlaw.com, will produce lawyers in larger cities and those with websites and profiles. But when I typed in "lawyer, Highland County, VA" and "lawyer, 24465," the closest hits were lawyers 45 miles distant. Three lawyers practice full-time in Highland County, one of whom is my wife. None have a website, and none showed up on the any of the legal websites I tried. If these websites don't work for you, go to the website of the state bar, which is the licensing and administrative organization for lawyers in the state, and the state's bar association, which is a due-paying organization of state lawyers. One or both should have a referral service, by which you can find a real-estate lawyer in your target county. I finally discovered a listing for two of the three Highland County lawyers on the website of the Highland County Chamber of Commerce in the Business Directory under Attorneys. The third lawyer in the county apparently chooses not to be a Chamber member.

The more rural the county, the smaller its population and the fewer its lawyers. In the smallest communities, you might find only two or three. Other things being equal, it's better to pick from the target county's lawyers rather than pull one from the next county over. Leave your Big City lawyer at home, particularly if he does nothing but appellate work before the U.S. Supreme Court, is president of the American Bar Association and teaches at Harvard Law School. He will not have the ground-truth knowledge and information of a local dirt lawyer, even a mediocre one. Two of the best land deals I ever negotiated involved very expensive, out-of-county, Big-City lawyers representing the sellers. They knew absolutely nothing about how to evaluate undeveloped rural land for their clients.

A rural county usually has a cluster of lawyers around its court house. You will find several sole practitioners and a couple of partnerships. At least one of the bigger firms will be run by an older, "connected" white male. He is likely to have his finger in a real-estate project or two and will represent some of the major local economic interests. He might sit on the board of a local bank or provide part-time counsel to the county. He's a product of one of the state's law schools and has chosen to be a big fish in a small pond. This generic guy, in my experience, places his interests before those of any new client. If, however, you look like a fat pigeon—someone who is wealthy or prominent by local standards—this fellow may be your best choice, because he will curry favor in hope of future business. If, on the other hand, you have a low profile, I'd recommend a different choice.

Lawyers, like all of us, are inclined to find formulas and stick with them. Real-estate work lends itself to using a standard contract form (each word of which has been tested), standard title-search procedure and standard way of handling buyers. The buyer's lawyer should always be responsible for checking the seller's title, and he may perform other tasks as well including handling escrow, finding financing and managing the closing. Experienced dirt lawyers do their title work the same way every time to protect themselves and their clients from errors of both omission and commission. This may be good enough, but you will go far to protect your interests if you can gently persuade your lawyer to work on your behalf beyond his customary standard. Since you are an out-of-county buyer, you will tell him that you need more advice and different advice than is his norm. For instance, you say, you would prefer to use something other than the standard purchase contract because, as he knows, it favors sellers. This is particularly true of the boiler-plate language found in contracts used by real-estate brokers (who are, as a rule, working for the seller.) You will be asking this lawyer to do a little bit more advising, both legal and non-legal, owing to your inexperience in the county. I've found that if you put your needs and expectations on the table during your first meeting, lawyers can adjust their services. I caution, however, against coming across as excessively needy or compulsively nerdy.

Finally, you need to be frank in saying to him that you intend to be a little more involved than most clients without—emphasize this—being a pest. Lawyers hate clients who call them every ten minutes with a "quick legal question," change their contract terms a dozen times and then squabble over every billed minute. You want to be helpful by researching the non-legal aspects of your target property; you don't want to do legal work for your lawyer. You can share information that has legal implications, raise points about the property of which he may or may not be aware and ask questions. You need to respect the line between being helpful and being controlling and neurotic. It's fine to provide thoughts about direction, but avoid telling your lawyer how to be a lawyer.

If you get the feeling that the local lawyer you're interviewing sees you as a nuisance, either change your approach or start fresh with your next choice. I recommend doing the former before doing the latter. If you sense that the lawyer you're interviewing is not very flexible and doesn't want to do anything different, keep looking. You're trying to find the lawyer who will work with you as well as for you.

I find that treating a lawyer as a colleague in a joint project works best for me. Some out-of-town buyers treat local lawyers as servants. This doesn't wear well. I've also seen buyers be cowed by their own lawyers. This, too, is not the right relationship. I can't offer a one-size-fits-all relationship for buyers and local lawyers, but I would encourage you to respect your lawyer's professional knowledge without kowtowing to it. Get his fee money figured out at the start, and don't quibble. If something goes haywire, you want this lawyer on your side.

I look for a well-organized, efficient lawyer with at least ten years of local experience. I look for evidence of a real-estate practice. Maps and surveys scattered around an office are good signs. I like relatively neat, organized offices with a touch of local art, but I don't trust desks that are free of paper. A bit of legal clutter indicates to me that work is being done. I avoid pretentious offices with needlessly expensive décor—the lawyer is likely to be the same. Lawyers whose hourly rates are in the middle of the local pack are best bets. They're not too fancy to work hard for you, and they're not likely to bill you for the time they "spend on your case" while taking a shower.

I like rational, analytical lawyers. I avoid the bullies and screamers. They may work for you, but their bullying and screaming are tactics they've devised to disguise their intellectual weaknesses. I also avoid any lawyer who cannot write a letter without grammatical errors.

I prefer working with women. My experience, admittedly limited, is that male country lawyers sometimes tend to be disorganized, or not very serious about being a lawyer, or not particularly conscientious about working for new clients, or a little loopy, or burned out, or fast and loose, or infected with contorted legalese, or otherwise unsuitable. I look for a female lawyer at least in her mid-30s who has run her own practice for a while and has family responsibilities. I ask about her educational background, local ties and current real-estate practice. I'm looking for thoroughness and judgment. I want someone who's analytical and protective of my interests. I ask her to tell me in advance when she might have a conflict representing me with a particular seller. I want to feel intellectually and emotionally comfortable with her as a lawyer. I have found that female country lawyers work a bit harder for their clients and, generally speaking, are at least as good if not better than their male counterparts. Exceptions to all of the above generalizations exist, and every reader should keep an open mind. Crummy lawyers exist, both male and female, both urban and rural. My experience is that the out-of-county buyer, male and female, has better odds of finding a good fit with a female attorney. (This has a little to do with the fact that my wife is a country dirt lawyer—but not that much.)

I also have decent experiences with male urban refugees who went back to the land 30 years or so ago. They have blown through their hippie days and are now semi-respectable members of the local establishment. They tend to have fancier law degrees than the home-grown lawyers, but may not be as locally smart. I've also found I like ex-student trouble makers and those who take on public-interest cases—environmental issues, indigent clients and court-appointed work—from a feeling of political ethics and professional obligation. For me, they tend to be easier to connect with than the "straight" local lawyers who are occasionally unreasonably suspicious of "outsiders," even their own clients. I've found such "marginal" lawyers more trustworthy and better suited to me than the good ole boys, though I've worked successfully with the latter. But this preference reflects who I am. If you're a Marine, look for a fellow vet. If you graduated from a certain college, look for an alumnus. If you're a Mason or a bird watcher, look for those connections.

Check out the stuff hanging on the office walls and cluttering her work space. It always gives you a clue about how the lawyer sees herself. My wife, for example, has hung the Brownie Pledge in needlepoint at the entrance to her private office and paintings of her horses inside. (She has a wallet-size photo of me that she hides behind a potted plant on an inaccessible bookshelf.)

Dirt lawyers may affect the persona of the "country lawyer." They put on this exaggerated display of being unsophisticated and "just folks" for the same reason a mother bird feigns being wounded—to draw the attention of a predator from her valuables. Certain lawyers like to be underestimated, and others may be testing you. The best way for a potential client to handle this in his own lawyer is to pretend it doesn't exist, and sooner or later it won't. I also tend to go along with it, as if the two of us are conspirators on an inside joke. The danger in the "country lawyer" routine is that your lawyer will underestimate you if you buy into his schtick. When opposing lawyers start sugaring their approach with down-home self-deprecation, it's time for Code Red: you're about to be knifed. I'm also wary of the country gentleman routine, which I've seen combine manners and pedigree for the purpose of masking piracy.

It is important that you start your lawyer's billable clock when you walk into her office. You're interviewing, that's true, but you're also soliciting advice that will help orient you. Country lawyers will begrudge giving free time to a Big-City land buyer who blows down Main Street in a $75,000 Mercedes and then whines about paying $125 for an hour's advice. Buying property is usually the least expensive piece of legal work you can get, because only a few hours of lawyer time will be involved in a routine transaction. At 2006 hourly rates in my area, such a closing costs the buyer $500. A complicated and troublesome closing might cost $1,000, but that's an exception. It can cost you about the same in legal fees to buy $500,000 in land as it would to have your lawyer represent you in a $250 dispute in small claims court. The hour or two of local legal advice you pay for before you start looking at property can help you avoid the complications that cost big dollars down the road.

You should also ask your lawyer how you will be billed. Some lawyers may charge a fixed fee for representing a real-estate buyer. Others will quote a buyer a likely cost range, say $500 to $1000. Most, I think, bill their time at an hourly rate, logged in six-minute increments. Simple purchases involve an hour or so in the courthouse, several hours at closing and time spent talking with you and others involved in the transaction, such as lenders, real-estate agents, appraisers, surveyors and inspectors. Complications and unforeseen problems will increase billed time. Coordination also consumes time. Closings now can involve as many as 100 pages of documents that your lawyer may have to assemble and present to you. While the number of billed hours in your purchase can't be predicted, your lawyer should be able to estimate its likely range of costs, especially if he knows the property. He can also give you a heads-up about factors and circumstances that might arise that will increase your bill.

Some lawyers may ask a client, especially a new one, for an upfront retainer that assures them of at least partial payment. This is more common in lawsuits than in real-estate purchases, because your lawyer will be paid from your funds at closing. You should hand your lawyer a check for the time spent with you during your first advisory conversation. This establishes a professional relationship and builds confidence. As part of your first conversation, also discuss your expectations about access and communications. It's fair to expect your calls of a general nature to be returned in a day or two and urgent calls sooner. E-mail may be a comfortable channel for both of you. Before you leave, hand your lawyer a contact sheet that lists your name, address, phone, cell, fax, e-mail, Social Security number, lender contact information, contact information for spouse and any other items that he's likely to need.

Apart from general questions and information, I would advise discussing the following with any lawyer you interview:

- Local zoning regs—get a sense of what the various zoning designations allow and what is involved in obtaining a use variance or change in zoning status for your target property if that's a necessary part of your plan;

- Procedures for new construction and remodeling—what permits are needed; will septic system need to be inspected/upgraded; which contractors are best suited for the project;

- Recommendations for local professional help, such as surveyor, home inspector, CPA who does farms and timberland, etc.;

- His local lender preferences—ask why one is preferred over the others;

- Negotiating—if you don't want to dicker with the seller or the seller's agent, ask your lawyer to help, or even do it for you;

- Navigation—lawyers are good at pointing clients in the right directions; it may be cheaper for you to track down certain information than to pay a lawyer or paralegal; in any event, self-help produces increased land literacy; but don't get too much in the middle of your lawyer's work;

- Backstopping—if you and your lawyer are comfortable with having you do certain research tasks, make sure he backstops and double checks your work; your lawyer should do your title search, though there's no reason why you can't dig out some of the deedwork as part of your scoping;

- Research—ask your lawyer to flag potential issues/problems that might not be part of a routine title search, e.g., water issues, ownership of subsurface minerals and lease status; questionable access, etc., as well as things he recommends that you investigate on your own;

- Purchase Contract—you can use a standard purchase contract that your lawyer may have in hand or one that you and your lawyer write together. I prefer the second option, but it depends on the lawyer and the circumstances of the purchase. Ask whether he is comfortable with having you participate in writing a contract. Ask yourself, first, whether this is something that you want to do.

The danger in "helping" your lawyer is that you will wear out your welcome, even one that you're paying for. If you think you have something to offer in this regard, then propose it. But don't feel obligated simply because you've read this book. If you tend to do-it-yourself projects, try not to drive everybody nuts, including yourself.

If you are uninformed about your target county, I recommend that you ask your local lawyer—whom you've chosen before you ever start your property search—to help you. Take an ad out in the local paper that states you're a land buyer looking for a property with the features you've decided on. Have landowners send replies to a local post office box that you open for this purpose. Ask for a brief written description of the property; tax map, survey and/or topo with boundaries; photos if available; size, price and contact information. Ask your lawyer to pick up your mail and rank the responses in terms of what he thinks best fit the objectives you've discussed with him. He will weed out the problems, scams and properties priced for the out-of-town billionaire.

You may be tempted to work into your purchase a fixed-price title search outfit to save yourself a hundred bucks on legal charges. These will be found in larger cities, but they may do work in rural areas. Instead, I encourage you to use a local lawyer who will either do the work herself or use her experienced real-estate paralegal who has worked for her for a number of years. The generic title-search firms provide a generic title search, which will work in the majority of cases. What the generic title search will not pick up is the local knowledge about the property that your local lawyer is likely to have. It's the unrecorded ground truth, the word-of-mouth wisdom, that can save you.

The final step in the process of purchasing land is the **closing**, or **settlement**, where buyer money is exchanged for seller documents and possession. In some places, you'll hear about "**closing escrow**," where "**escrow**" refers to the time between when the buyer's contract takes effect—with earnest money held in escrow on behalf of the purchase—and when the purchase is completed. Most property is purchased with the involvement of an **escrow agent**, whose job is to hold money and documents as a neutral party. A third-party—other than one of the lawyers working for the seller or the buyers—is often retained to serve as the escrow agent. Experienced buyers often prefer to have their lawyer act as the escrow agent for the purchase, because they feel their deposit is safest there.

The **settlement agent**—the person who manages the closing—may be the escrow agent too, or he may be a real-estate broker, lawyer, or a representative of a title company. The settlement agent's job is to get all of the paperwork and money in order, explain the transaction, get signatures where needed to complete the transaction, then route each item to its proper destination. It's not unusual in rural areas for one of the lawyers to handle both settlement and escrow while also representing either buyer or seller. Closings can get complicated, and your lawyer should be present, especially if you're not.

At the heart of the closing is the **settlement statement** (also called a **HUD-1**), which is the transaction's balance sheet. It shows debits and credits for each side, a debit being an item that a buyer or seller is paying out (fees for home inspection, mortgage points, legal fees, commission) and a credit is money coming to a buyer or seller. As a buyer, you will need to refer to your settlement statement when you do your 1040 deductions for the purchase year. It also will be used to establish your original **basis** in the property when you sell it and need to calculate taxable gain. Keep one copy of your settlement statement in your tax records for the year of purchase and another copy in your property folder.

A settlement statement can make a buyer feel as if he is sitting on a carnival dunking stool with Sandy Koufax throwing at the bull's-eye. Each time you look at the document, you're getting soaked for something else. Buyers need to understand that property sales always require that a buyer pay more than the agreed purchase price. The add-ons are items such as taxes, professional fees, loan fees and sale-related charges. The time to defend yourself against garbage fees and inflated charges is when you are first negotiating with lenders and those whom you hire to provide you with advice or work. Whether you are an experienced buyer or not, have your local lawyer walk you though the expenses you are likely to owe at settlement **before** you get to closing. While exact dollars are difficult to project on all items, a buyer should not be surprised by debits and credits on his side of the settlement statement. Big, bad surprises can derail a closing. Be forewarned: A buyer can easily pay five percent or more above the purchase price, the bulk of it in financing fees.

You will also be expected to sign a number of fine-print documents at closing. It is next to impossible to read and comprehend these documents when a half-dozen stakeholders are staring at you in a pressure-packed conference room. Ask your lawyer to show you these documents well in advance. Read them! Once you've signed a document, it will be construed to mean that you have read and understood it even if you never have and wouldn't understand it even if you had. Everyone benefits from a settlement that goes without a hitch. Previewing your documents with your lawyer and anticipating your expenses will further this shared interest.

The key closing documents are the **settlement statement, deed of trust, promissory note and deed**. Both the deed of trust and the deed will be recorded in the county clerk's office: keep copies at home as well. The **deed of trust**—also called a **trust deed**—is your mortgage document. It creates a **lien** on the property you're buying for the benefit of your lender. (If you have no lender, you have no mortgage or deed of trust.)

A **lien** gives your lender the right to have your debt paid from the sale of the property. When property alone secures the borrower's debt, the arrangement is called a **purchase money mortgage**. The buyer should resist signing a personal guarantee of real-estate debt. A lien can be called even when you are current on your note payments. Lenders may define a default as breaking a promise to the lender, failure to perform promptly, false statements, the borrower's death or insolvency, an attempt by a creditor or public agency to take property on which the lender has a lien, events of this type affecting a co-signer, and whenever the lender "…in good faith believes itself insecure." The **promissory note** sets forth the terms of your borrowing with the lender, to which you will be held. This note spells out the amount financed, interest rate, repayment schedule and all the rules the lender imposes. The buyer does not own the property free and clear until all notes secured by the property are paid in full and released by the lender.

The **deed** is the document that conveys title to the property from seller to buyer. It is very important for the property's **legal description** in the deed to be accurate and be exactly the same as the legal description in the seller's chain of title. Inadvertent description errors can be corrected later on, but errors that are defects can be barbed hooks, and, once embedded, may be removable only with much pain.

Well in advance of closing, discuss with your lawyer **how you want to take title**. This decision has both legal and tax implications. An individual has the choice of taking title in his own name or through an entity the individual owns, in whole or part, such as a limited liability company (LLC) or corporation. Lenders may not lend money to an LLC. The LLC members must personally guarantee the note or take title in their names then transfer title to the LLC. Lenders may also be sticky about financing purchases for a living trust. (Robert J. Bruss, "Real Estate Mailbag," Washington Post, July 6, 2003.) A married couple has several options, including an entity, or as husband and wife where the surviving spouse becomes the owner of the common property (**tenancy by the entirety**), or as **tenants in common** where each has an undivided interest in the property as a whole, with or without the right of survivorship, among other rights. State law governs forms of ownership, so it is important to have clear objectives and an equally clear understanding of the implications for taxes and inheritance of each option in the state where you are holding title.

The form of ownership you choose should be consistent with your ownership goals. I've advised in other sections of this book for buyers to consider ways to organize rural property as an investment or a business if, for no other reason, than the tax advantages. Consider this: the 2003 tax law allowed small businesses—such as one set up for land investment—to expense up to $100,000 in equipment costs in the year they were incurred. Farm equipment, logging equipment, ATVs, and pick-up trucks and SUVs weighing more than 6,000 pounds used in business qualified. For equipment placed into service after May 5, 2003 and before January 1, 2005, a first-year "bonus" depreciation write-off of 50 percent existed, up from 30 percent. The buyer's form of ownership should match his objectives in buying the land, and the time to decide both is in advance of purchase with proper legal and tax-planning counsel.

A buyer should retain at least one copy of every document he signs at a property closing. Put them in a 9"x14" accordion-type folder with a tie hood so nothing slips out. You should have a similar file for your scoping documents—home inspection, termite report, survey or topographic map with boundaries, timber cruise, appraisal, field notes, permits, regulations, title report, correspondence, certificate of occupancy and the like. Put every communication with the seller, his agents and your lawyer in writing— and keep a copy. You might want to start a third file dedicated to financing and lender documents, and a fourth file for insurance documents, including house/farm, title insurance, liability and so on.

I would keep copies of your basic **start-up documents**—appraisals, timber cruises, settlement statement, communications from your lawyer, receipts for major items, loan documents, deed, etc.— forever. You will need some for tax purposes, such as calculating your original basis. While the IRS's statute of limitations for audits requires the taxpayer to keep records for only three years, no such time cap exists if the IRS accuses you of fraud. The IRS can, therefore, ask for a 20-year-old settlement statement or other documents establishing basis when they think you're cheating on capital gains arising from a property sale. Other documents—like an appraisal or timber cruise—can establish FMVs that you can show a purchaser when you want to sell. Both lenders and insurance companies change their documents from time to time, so it can be helpful to have the originals in your possession. Your estate administrator will also welcome a rudimentary level of organization and document retention.

Find a local lawyer in whom you have confidence and then understand the legal aspects of the buying process before you enter it—that's how you get started.

THE LEGAL FRAMEWORK

State law governs the purchase and sale of **real property**, which includes all the rights, interests and benefits of real-estate ownership. The law governing real property differs from state to state, sometimes significantly, as with theories of water rights. Common to all states is the idea that land is purchased and sold through a **written contract of sale** between buyer and seller in which ownership/title is conveyed in return for some type of "**consideration**," usually cash. Real estate is not governed by the **Uniform Commercial Code**, now adopted wholly or partially by all states. The UCC provides uniform laws for commercial transactions, including all **personal (chattel) property**. Each state has a supreme court that has interpreted its laws—the body of which is called "**case law**." If you find yourself in a real-estate dispute, a county judge will adjudicate your case according to his reading of the relevant state statutes and case law. Suing can be expensive and aggravating, and appealing decisions is even worse. Courtroom justice can be a crapshoot, especially if you're new to the county and come across as arrogant, greedy, a smarty pants, rich or just different. Dirt-smart buyers should try to stay out of local courts, especially as a first step into a new community.

Federal laws and regulations bear on various aspects of land buying. Your financing is shaped by the Fair Credit Reporting Act, Truth-in-Lending Act (whose Regulation Z requires lenders to tell borrowers the true cost of obtaining credit on personal loans of $25,000 or less, or when a loan is secured by a residence) and various federal mortgage loan and loan-guarantee programs. Federal law and regulation also provide a framework for environmental protection, anti-discrimination (Fair Housing Act) and myriad programs affecting farms. Apart from the federal financing programs in the Department of Housing and Urban Development, Veterans Administration and Department of Agriculture, today's rural land buyer may find himself involved with agencies of the Departments of Agriculture and Interior, Army Corps of Engineers (wetlands and streams) and the Environmental Protection Agency. State and regional agencies (e.g., inspection/enforcement offices related to animal health, water quality, logging, water impoundments, new road entrances and wildlife management; irrigation and water districts; conservation districts) may find their way into your new life. Most of this infrastructure of statute and regulation did not exist 50 years ago. You will inevitably touch it if you borrow institutional money or use a federal mortgage program. (Each touch requires that you sign something that's as long as the Bible and reproduced in half the size of unreadable fine print.) It is reasonably safe to assume that use of your land for anything other than the lowest-impact activities—such as camping and hiking—will eventually brush you against some public agency and its regulations.

Ignoring the framework of laws that surround property ownership doesn't exempt you from compliance. In addition, ignorance can be costly. Before buying rural land or a farm, you should become conversationally familiar with current Internal Revenue Service (IRS) policies on:

- capital-gains tax rates and how to qualify for this treatment when you sell rural land; as of 2005, there were three capital-gains rates, 5% and 15% depending on income level, and 25% on certain real-estate sales where depreciation was taken

- advantages of itemizing on your 1040 (mortgage interest and property taxes are currently deductible on a vacation home or personal recreation land if you itemize, but not if you don't)

- farms/rural property set up as an investment or profit-making business, rather than for lifestyle or hobby purposes

- mortgage-interest deductibility for land investments and second homes

- types of land-related expenses that can be taken in the year you incur them

- types of costs and incomes that change your **basis** in the property

- types of improvements and equipment that can and must be depreciated

- conservation easements

- timber-taxation strategies if you're buying timberland

- farm-taxation strategies if you're buying farmland

- mineral-taxation strategies if you're buying land with minerals

Each of these topics can make you money or cost you money, depending on your knowledge and actions. Current IRS policies are discussed in other chapters. Many of the most critical tax decisions you make with your new property are made at the time of purchase.

While a miasma of legal, tax and regulatory complexity can loom in front of you, the buying of land—like getting married—is usually quite simple. You need the following elements:

- A seller with **clear title** to the property. A seller with a defective title is more than willing to sell to you, but you don't need this headache.

- A _**written agreement**_—**purchase contract**—between buyer and seller that sets forth:

   What is being sold—deed description, number of acres;

   Selling price;

   Terms and conditions;

A schedule for getting the deal done, setting out who is expected to do what by when, and how various costs are to be apportioned; and

Signed and dated by both buyer and seller. Signature notarization is preferred, but not necessary.

- **Financial arrangement** providing the buyer with the means to pay for the property that is acceptable to the seller;

- **Closing**, or settlement, date at which time the buyer acquires the property in return for his consideration (money) and/or promises to repay a lender's note. (It is worth understanding that a buyer does not acquire the deed and unfettered ownership until he has removed all property-secured mortgage notes. During the interval, the actual deed would be held in escrow by a trustee or by the seller himself if he is financing the sale. When you own property **free and clear**, it means that it carries no mortgage debt.)

These basic elements of a real-estate deal can require the services or opinions of lawyers, lender (s), appraiser, real-estate broker(s) or agents (one to four), home inspector, surveyor, insurance agent, forester, soil engineer, termite inspector, zoning official, building inspector, government farm officials, CPA and neighbors. Most of this crowd will be bringing a framework of law and regulation to your purchase. They should know more about what they're doing for you than you do.

Each of these individuals will have a relationship to the buyer and the purchase process. These relationships are governed by laws and regulations that are mostly invisible until something goes wrong.

For instance—the home inspector visits the seller's farmhouse in May, tries the furnace and reports that it is in working order. Between that inspection and when you turn it on for the first time in November, two months after your closing, the fuel-oil pump stops functioning and the cost of repair is $1,500. Is the home inspector responsible? Was there a material defect in the pump that the seller knew but did not disclose? Can you prove the inspector missed something that he should have found? What laws might have been broken? What legal remedies are available?

Dozens of things can go screwy in buying property because buying property puts hundreds of potentially screwy things in play. Each screw up takes place within the law and gets you thinking about lawyers, lawsuits, justice and money. This is a heady brew, and I urge you to think about other ways of resolving a dispute over a fuel pump besides a lawsuit. When all is said and done, a fuel pump is a fuel pump, but a lawsuit is a protracted agony.

To simplify matters, you can group your new associates into three categories from your legal perspective:

1. Those with whom a buyer contracts for a service that they provide, such as a lawyer, buyer broker (who represents you), CPA, forester, home inspector, surveyor, soil engineer and so on.

Some of these individuals will bill you on an hourly basis for their time, plus expenses. Others will charge a fixed fee for their service, which is usually the case with home inspectors. Surveyors often bill on a cents-per-linear-foot basis. Their foot-rate for interior lines is likely to be less than their foot-rate for boundary lines, though they may have to shoot the boundaries before they can shoot lines for internal divisions. If you're asking a surveyor to research your boundary lines or check acreage and closure, he'll probably bill at an hourly rate, because it's difficult to estimate the time needed to solve a complication.

A buyer-broker is a special case. He may be paid either from the commission the seller pays the listing broker or from the buyer's funds.

Whether or not you have a written contract with these individuals, you will have an understanding and agreement with them that they will perform some service or work for you in return for which you will pay them. Unwritten understandings of this sort are usually construed as **constructive contracts**, that is, an agreement amounting to a legal contract. To avoid squabbles, make sure you understand what you are asking each vendor to do, what work he will do to meet your request and how he will bill you.

You have a right to expect that such individuals make a good-faith effort to provide you with accurate information and services that meet the standards of their profession or trade. They shouldn't miss something obvious or important, or make a careless mistake that costs you money. Lawyers carry malpractice insurance, and some other professionals carry **Errors and Omissions (E&O) insurance.**

If a mistake is made, you will have to decide whether it is worth the time, expense and emotional strain to seek a remedy. The best strategy all things considered may be to say nothing and fix the problem yourself. Sometimes you can negotiate a settlement with the individual who did the flawed work, assuming the individual either agrees with your analysis or figures its cheaper to settle than to fight.

Suing is almost always the least promising way of settling a dispute for at least three reasons: first, its outcome is unpredictable; second, it is expensive; and third, it is not much fun. Lawsuits do not necessarily produce justice. I have seen judges rule without regard to equity and justice, disregarding where the weight of the law fell. I've also seen excellent work from the same individuals. I admire folks who get into court fights over principle, but judges may not share your interest in having the system do what's right. If you can't work out something with the other side, suggest **mediation**, in which a neutral third-party helps the disputants reach a compromise settlement. Mediation can be set up either as a format by which the parties are bound to the result or not.

In the matter of the bad fuel-oil pump in the farmhouse, it's doubtful that you can get compensation from either the inspector or the seller. Both will deny knowledge of any problem, and both can be telling the absolute truth. Had you discovered the problem within a week or two of taking possession, you would have a stronger claim against both of them. Two months, however, is probably too long. Everyone has had experience with a machine that works perfectly today and is totally inoperable tomorrow. Lesson: if you don't do a walk-through just before closing during which you test all systems (which you should), do your testing within a day or two of taking possession.

If the home inspector failed to inspect the furnace, you may have a claim against him. Your position is weakened if you accepted his report as presented, which indicated by the absence of checks in appropriate boxes that he had not inspected the furnace. Often it costs more to sue and win than it does to forget about it.

2. Those with whom a buyer's relationship is essentially that of cooperative adversaries, such as with your seller and lender. In each case, the land buyer enters into an elaborate written contract, specifying what each party will do and when they will do it. You have a right to expect the seller to disclose the property's **material defects,** which can be thought of as deficiencies of various kinds that a reasonable person would consider to be of such size or seriousness that they bear on—are "material" to—the basic soundness of what the buyer is purchasing, and, therefore, are material to the sale itself.

Sellers will sometimes place language in their bid package or a purchase-offer contract they prepare that says the buyer is expected to perform his own **due diligence** on the property and its assets. Due diligence refers to a buyer's investigation and research into a property that satisfies whatever are his standards of competency and thoroughness. I've used the word, "scoping," instead.

Contract language that states the buyer is expected to perform his own due diligence is a pre-emptive effort to shift liability for future problems onto the buyer. The seller gives himself the basis for arguing that the buyer did not do adequate due diligence, otherwise he would have discovered the bad pump, which, of course, was perfectly fine the last time the seller used it. The seller could also argue that the buyer knew the pump was bad (as a result of his due diligence) when he made his offer and is now trying to force the cost of an anticipated repair onto the seller.

Buyers should always perform thorough due diligence, especially when the seller has inserted a due-diligence clause in the contract. When facing such a clause, the buyer should get in writing, if possible, what exactly the seller thinks due diligence covers and what types of liability he thinks it excludes.

If you think the seller is using due-diligence to rig up a last-minute parachute for himself, you can add your own language behind his:

> **Buyer agrees to perform due diligence on Seller's property, but his effort does not relieve Seller of his obligations to disclose all material defects of which he is aware and bear any liability arising from the warranties this Contract includes.**

While consumer law has gotten away from *Caveat emptor!*—Let the buyer beware!—due-diligence language and "**permitted title exceptions**" struggle to make it rise again. The latter is the seller's statement to the buyer in a purchase contract that he will convey good title, *except for* those items (exceptions) where he doesn't want to, or can't. Permitted exceptions give the seller a way to sell property with a defective title or other problems. I've encountered permitted exceptions a number of times. Sometimes the seller includes this language because he doesn't want to spend the time to determine whether he has a problem. Other times, however, he knows of a title problem and wants to get out of cleaning it up. Remember the seller is the one giving himself this permission; you need not agree.

I think any buyer will do well to act as if *Caveat emptor!* still rules. To protect the buyer, the buyer's side needs to inform the seller that state law requires him to disclose fully known defects and problems in his property. *Caveat vendor!* –Let the seller beware!— is much more current law: the seller will be held legally accountable for defects, significant problems and deficiencies in the property of which he is aware or about which it is reasonable to assume he should have been aware. Let your lawyer make these positions known to the seller's lawyer. Brokers are required to disclose defects that they know about. Make sure that you ask the seller's broker/agent to disclose all defects in writing well in advance of submitting an offer.

While current law appears to be more on the side of the buyer on disclosure issues, the cost of enforcing disclosure falls on the buyer. Sellers, in other words, still wiggle off the hook of their own making. For this reason, disclosure is most effectively enforced during negotiations where the threat of enforcement carries weight with the seller.

Despite the law and the buyer's best efforts, a seller may eventually fail to disclose a situation that will adversely affect the buyer's use and enjoyment of the property. In court, the aggrieved buyer must prove that the seller either knew of the problem, or that it is reasonable to suppose that he should have known of it. These standards of proof are often hard to meet. To avoid these messes with a seller you think is playing hide the ball, insert a "**disclosure clause**" in your purchase offer:

> **Seller warrants that he has disclosed all material defects of which he is aware in the property's title, improvements, assets, resources, access, boundaries, rights and interests. Such defects include, but are not limited to, conditions, situations, facts, deficiencies, uncertainties, disputes, claims and unresolved issues that would negatively affect the Buyer's use, possession and enjoyment of the property.**

This language is a big, fat Seller Beware! Lawyers will roll their eyes. Let them roll. You want this seller to do what he's supposed to do, and this is the way to get him to do it. If the seller refuses to sign, it's possible that you've smoked him out.

This language covers material defects that are both **latent** (hard to see) and **manifest** (visible but perhaps not understandable).

3. Those who seemed programmed to get in the way of making a deal. This could be anybody, including you, by your attitudes and behavior. The two usual suspects are the seller who blows up a decent deal in hope that a better one will walk through his front door the next day and the seller's real-estate agent who holds a TNT in miscommunication.

Once the seller signs a purchase contract, the purchase should go through assuming all contingencies are satisfied or voided before closing. If the seller backs out on an oral agreement to sell before he signs your written purchase contract, you have no contract, hence no remedy in court. (A few exceptions may exist in certain circumstances, but don't count on exceptions to win in the absence of a written contract.).

Purchase contracts are usually written in a way that gives the buyer several contingencies to get out of doing the deal. But, as a rule, few sellers work into their contracts similar ways to extricate themselves. While real-estate agents in my experience can muddle up a purchase and often fail to do what they are supposed to do, the buyer usually has little legal recourse for their lack of competence, laziness and poor judgment.

I was interested in a 50-acre timber tract north of Lake Placid, New York in the spring of 2006. It was priced at $30,000, a little high but in the ballpark. So I started scoping. I found the following:

The property had no physical or legal access; it was completely landlocked;

No metes and bounds were available;

At least one boundary line was in dispute;

The seller's deed provided for ownership of 100 acres—an error. Once the seller took possession of the property, he came to realize that he had purchased only 50 acres. The seller did not have title clear of a defect, i.e., he lacked a merchantable title.

The seller would not draw boundaries on a topo map to orient me;

The seller's deed contained the word "warranty," but it appeared to me to be something less than a general warranty deed. Given all the title and legal problems, I wanted the seller to be held to the seller's obligations under a general warranty deed. The seller wanted to get out of this mess by pawning off the property with what amounted to not much more than a quitclaim; and

The seller would not tell me whether he had title insurance; I was reasonably sure that he did not have a policy and that none could be obtained.

I began negotiations with the one neighbor who could provide access to a public road. The neighbor and the seller did not get along. The seller's real-estate agent then told me that she had advised the seller to consider only a no-contingency contract. The seller wanted to survey the property at a cost of $8,000, thinking that it would make the property more marketable. If an access easement could be worked out with the neighbor, the survey would not be necessary because I was prepared to sell the timbered land to the neighbor at a discount in return for being allowed to haul out the timber. I told the agent to relay this information and ask the seller to wait for two weeks to let me see what I could do with the easement. She responded by telling me that she had advised her client to pay for the survey. This was the same agent who had been unable to orient herself on a tax map, insisting that north was west until I asked her to look at the directional arrow at the bottom of the tax map in the portion marked "Legend." Her sales tactic was to try to stampede me into a purchase while playing hide the ball. Her other job, I was told, was bartending.

As you scope property, you will find yourself digging a metaphorical hole. As you work, the sides of the hole should become firmer with each piece of information you strike. At some point, you will find a solid bottom. The process is one of growing more and more confident of the hole's dimensions and stability. The Lake Placid 50-acre hole kept getting mushier and mushier. The more I found out, the more I knew that none of the sides were stable. I was digging in sand. I felt like Alice in her rabbit hole, guided by the seller's real-estate agent who consistently misread both me and the facts in front of her. A brighter agent would have helped make this deal.

Buyers are usually on their own when dealing with both seller and real-estate brokers. The latter are almost always representing the seller, even when you are "working with" one who drives you around on Sunday afternoons. Such brokers/agents will be paid by the seller and are legally obliged to represent his interests, not yours. The only exceptions are where a broker/agent signs a **dual agency agreement** with both seller and buyer in which he works for both sides or where a buyer signs a **buyer-broker agreement** with a broker/agent who is then obliged to work exclusively for the buyer. A buyer can easily find himself making a written offer on a standard seller-oriented contract surrounded by two or more broker/agents, all of whom are working for the seller.

You can even up the sides by doing the following:

- **Never submit a standard seller-oriented contract without your local lawyer being there when you fill out its terms. Never!** Consult with him on language and contingencies. This is your most important hour of his time.

- **Contain the confusion.** Put everything in writing. Copy all written work to the appropriate parties. Be clear, explicit and simple in telling brokers/agents what information you want and what, if anything, you want them to do to get the deal to work. Don't let problems slide. Buying land is like tacking down a piece of linoleum that wants to curl up on all edges. You have to nail down every corner, otherwise one will trip you. Organize the process. Keep an accordion file devoted to the purchase. Separate tasks. Make a timeline, so that you know at a glance each deadline.

- **Know what you want to do before the time when you are asked to do it.** Buyers are usually expected to make a lot of decisions all at once without being able to think through the legal ramifications of the language they're signing. If you want to include contingencies, have them written out before submitting them to the buyer. Avoid situations where you have to think up "legal" language off the top of your head, under pressure. If you've prepared a contract with your lawyer ahead of time, don't change it or delete language without consulting with him in private.

HELPING HANDS: BUYER-BROKER, FINDER, LAND CONSULTANT

It is amazing—almost inconceivable—that most real estate is sold to buyers working with real-estate professionals representing sellers. Put another way, most buyers are on their own until they sign a purchase-offer contract. This is crazy. Buyers should pay for loyal professional advice from the beginning of their property search. Why? Because it will either save money or make it. The less the buyer knows about an area, the more valuable this advice is likely to be.

One way to get help is to retain a **buyer-broker** who works for the buyer's interests. This individual is a licensed real-estate professional who may choose to represent buyers exclusively or both buyers and sellers. The buyer pays his buyer-broker a percentage commission figured against the selling price from his own funds. The buyer signs a **buyer-agency agreement** with the brokerage setting forth the terms of their understanding. If the target property is listed with a cooperating broker, your buyer-broker can be paid from the seller-paid commission, depending on your agreement. If the target property is not being represented in this way or is being sold by a FSBO, the buyer pays his buyer-broker directly.

Real-estate agents/brokers are permitted to work for both buyer and seller as long as the arrangement is disclosed and approved by both parties. Dual arrangements can benefit the buyer when the seller is paying for it, but I'm generally suspicious of these work-for-both-sides deals, because I think they mainly serve the wallets of the broker/agent. But I have seen circumstances where they work without favoritism or harm. Dual agency on a purchase may produce a total commission paid to the dual agent that is higher than what the agent would receive were he to be paid by either buyer or seller, but not both.

I would trust a buyer-broker (also called, a buyer-agent) who represents buyers exclusively, or even principally. These individuals make their living by providing good service to buyers. They shouldn't let their buyer clients get into harmful legal and financial situations. They have no financial loyalty to sellers as a group, or any particular seller. If you retain a buyer-broker who will not be paid from the seller-paid commission, you will be buying his undivided loyalty. Four percent of the gross sales price is a fair fee for a buyer-broker whom the buyer is paying. In any case, try to find a buyer-broker who does nothing but work for buyers. There are now about 2,500 affiliated with the National Association of Exclusive Buyer Agents, 1-800-986-2322; www.naeba.org.

I'm wary of a generalist agent/broker who tells a buyer, something like, "I swing both ways." This individual, I fear, is mainly working for himself. Even when he signs with you as a buyer-broker, his long-term interest and the bulk of his business lies mainly with sellers.

Realtors—a real-estate agent or broker who is a member of the National Association of Realtors—can become an **Accredited Land Consultant (ALC)** by completing an education program through the Association's Realtors Land Institute. This program provides background in land issues, including finance and marketing. An agent who is an ALC should know more about the subjects in this book than an agent who isn't. An ALC who is a buyer-broker and only works for buyers can be a great find for you.

A buyer-broker will help you find properties. He will check the Multiple Listing Service (MLS) for prospects in your target area that match your search criteria. He'll show you properties. A broker representing the seller does all this for a buyer too. A buyer-broker becomes valuable to a buyer to the extent that he helps a buyer with scoping. This can be a time-consuming task, so you will need to obtain an understanding of exactly what services and information the buyer-broker will provide for you. At the very least, ask him to help with the scoping that will be difficult for an out-of-town buyer to do. This can involve information that is not on the public record but is available through discussions with older members of the community and neighbors. It can mean asking questions in the right way. It can mean having a local person ask a question. It can mean telling a buyer where to go and how to do things.

You may be able to obtain a buyer-broker by asking a local agent to act as one for you, though I recommend focusing on agents who have a record of working for buyers. Another place to look is www.rebac.net, the website for the Real Estate Buyer's Agent Council, whose members are called Accredited Buyer's Agents.

Finders are not licensed for their work. In many cases, a finder is acting *ad hoc*. He may be a lawyer, surveyor, forester, excavator, contractor or friend of a friend who knows of a property and informs a buyer of its availability. A finder should work directly and exclusively for a buyer, not through a real-estate agent or broker. Licensed brokers/agents do not share their commissions with finders, and, in some states, may not be allowed to do so. A buyer who wants to use a finder must work out a consulting contract with him directly—and probably on the buyer's initiative. Finders are not allowed to provide brokerage services and should disclose to their clients that they are not brokers if that is the case. A finder's job is to identify target properties for a buyer, and generally nothing else. Finders are generally paid a percentage fee of the gross selling price at closing. Finders usually get one to four percent for a successful effort, depending on the particulars.

A non-resident buyer must find a local finder—a person who may not have ever thought of himself as a buyer's finder. If you take out a "Land-Wanted" ad in the local classifieds, include notice that you're willing to pay a one percent finder's fee for any property brought to you by the finder which you did not already know about and which you subsequently buy. You must be scrupulously honest about dealing with finders. If you already know about a property when the finder first starts telling you about it, stop him and say that it is known to you. Do not cheat a finder by pretending to have knowledge which, in fact, the finder is introducing to you *de novo*. On the other hand, you want to protect yourself against a seller who tells his cousin to answer your ad with reference to the seller's property. In that case, you're paying a fee for a lead that the seller would have otherwise provided on his own.

If you buy land found by a finder, you should be prepared to have your local lawyer help you with the purchase contract. Finders should not perform such tasks.

A **land consultant** may or may not be trained in real estate or investments. I am not aware of licensing requirements. I describe myself as a land consultant. Apart from having taken a real-estate course and losing money in the stock market, I have no specific training for what I do. I have background in a number of fields that I've found useful in helping buyers find and scope properties—journalism and research skills are the two that come into play most often. I'm good at seeing connections and putting things together—I don't know what field that is, but it's probably common to many professions. I'm very good at asking questions and finding out stuff. The grander term for those activities I've called, scoping, which also involves analyzing situations and writing summary memos. I am not a licensed broker or agent. I disclose this to my clients and state in writing that I do not provide brokerage services. Buyers also ask me to find property that fits their investment criteria.

A land consultant should work for the client's best interest and not his own. He should avoid becoming invested in having his client make a purchase that generates a fee but is not good for the client paying him that fee. It is essential that buyers enforce this rule with any investment consultants they interview. A land consultant will have a buyer sign a contract that holds the consultant harmless for the uses to which the client puts the consultant's work. Were it otherwise, the consultant would be forced into a position of back-stopping any loss the client might suffer after a purchase. The consultant should obviously do his best work in scoping a property. Nonetheless, nothing protects a buyer as much as his own due diligence on all aspects of a purchase, including scoping his consultants.

I work two tracks: first, I will be asked to scope a property that a client thinks is a possible acquisition. This work has taken me from a golf resort in Alabama to 600,000 acres of timberland in Ontario—and many properties in between. I charge an hourly rate.

The second track combines a preliminary screening of a property with a particular client in mind. I try to find a good fit with a client's individual objectives and financial capabilities. I will screen a target enough to think that it has possibilities. When the client wants me to investigate further, I reach an understanding about what tasks I'm expected to do. I put this understanding into a contract with the client before I start scoping. I will then research the target and write an evaluation. I will flag risks, problems, uncertainties and particularly things that a buyer can't determine prior to purchase. I will offer opinions about the value of the property's assets, profit potential and marketing strategies where that is appropriate. I often discuss strategies and tactics for buying, including the benefits of managed-timberland programs, conservation easements and other approaches that help a seller with taxes. I will frequently recommend hiring consultants where specific evaluations are needed. I'll also offer an opinion about what the client might consider paying for the property in light of the client's objectives. And not infrequently, I'll suggest that the client consult with his lawyer about specific issues and contingency language of the type found in this book. The level of due diligence the client employs beyond my work depends entirely on the assets and problems identified in the target property. I know something about minerals, timber and farms, but I don't consider myself an expert; I always note for the client where I've pushed my knowledge and expertise to its boundary. I continue to be available as the client learns more about the property. I often advise clients to not purchase a property that we've researched because of a problem turned up during the scoping. This means that I earn nothing from my work, but it protects my client. When agents/brokers are working for the seller, they are not supposed to offer such advice to a buyer because their fiduciary obligation is to the seller.

My rule of thumb is simple: I want repeat business. To that end, I try as hard as I can to make sure I find deals that work well for my clients.

CHAPTER 26: COMMON MESSES

OWNERSHIP AND ACREAGE ISSUES

In other chapters, I've touched on the many little matches that can burn a buyer. Here are the ones related to ownership and acreage that I've seen most often.

BUYERS WANT 100 PERCENT OF EVERYTHING

Rural land in the United States is usually sold by the acre, which is 43,560 square feet, or the area in a square, 208.71 feet on each side. (A "state acre" is 40,000 square feet; a football field, goal line to goal line, is 48,000 square feet.)

Acreage is determined by calculating the number of acres contained within a property's legal boundaries. Boundary lines are always measured and described as if they existed on a level plane, never as running with the land's ups and downs. Hilly land will always contain more than one square acre of land for every one square acre to be conveyed.

My concern is that a buyer not acquire less acreage than what he believes he is buying. The process of determining ownership and acreage can be easy as pie or a mess.

The initial piece of the puzzle the buyer needs to understand is **the nature of the seller's ownership in the property**. The seller may be ready to convey to you his full ownership in the property's acreage, but he may not fully own the entire property or he may not own all the rights in the property.

Ideally, the seller should own 100 percent of all rights and interests in the land he's selling. The real world is often different.

Ownership of rural land is often **fractionalized through inheritance**. Part of the **title search** that a buyer hires a lawyer to do is to make sure that the seller owns 100 percent of the property. Occasionally, a title search will turn up a long-forgotten orphan fraction, a $1/32^{nd}$ or a $1/64^{th}$, that is now several generations distant from the original division. Your seller doesn't own this orphan fraction. The seller may be able to buy this share from its rightful owner. The seller can also propose that he and the fraction owner divide the land in a mutually agreeable way, whereupon the seller sells you his somewhat diminished share. If the fractional owner refuses to sell or divide, the seller can file a **partition suit** that forces the sale of all shares in the entirety. You could then buy the property at that public auction. To the extent that the auction is competitive, you may end up paying more than the original asking price. The sellers will split the net proceeds after paying off their mortgage debt, if any, plus legal and auction expenses.

If you find yourself faced with a group of sellers each of whom owns a fractional share of the entirety, you have to be certain that the group is agreed on selling at the price you've been quoted. Insist on having one of the sellers be authorized by the others to act as their agent, so that you need to negotiate with only one individual. Be prepared for your negotiated price to be rejected by one hold out. This is often a ploy to get more money from a buyer. When you negotiate your money with the sellers' agent, tell him that it's a final offer, because you have placed your negotiating faith in his promise to you that he is the authorized agent of all the sellers. Once you say, take it or leave it, you must be prepared to walk away. Sellers in this circumstance are likely to come back to you in a week or two, "after the holdout has had time to reconsider your offer."

When the owner of the long-forgotten or disputed fraction can't be located, the seller should file a **suit to quiet title**, an action that allows anyone with an ownership claim to submit it to the court or lose his right in the property forever. Such suits are often used to free the seller's title from old or bogus claims arising from distant divisions, dower's rights (a widow's claim on the real property of her deceased husband), squatting and other adverse actions against the property. Buyers should insist on the seller doing what's necessary to convey a clear title.

The other way to look at the seller's ownership is to determine whether he owns and is conveying **all the rights of ownership** in the property.

Ideally, the seller owns a **fee simple absolute estate**, which may be referred to as **ownership in fee** or **fee-simple ownership**. This type of ownership means the seller possesses all of the rights in the land that an owner can have. This means he has unrestricted control, possession, use and enjoyment of all of the property's rights and assets, limited only by public authority and recorded easements. Fee-simple ownership should mean that the property is free of all life estates, easements, leases and interests that others hold in the seller's land. Many fee-simple owners don't own their entire property in absolute. A simple road easement that allows a neighbor to use a road on the seller's property alters absolute ownership.

The buyer is interested in getting all of the rights and interests he needs, even if that bundle is something less than fee simple absolute. Sellers use the terms, fee and fee simple, to mean whatever they want it to mean. When a seller says he owns the property in fee simple, you should write a **fee-simple section** into your purchase offer, such as:

> **Seller agrees to convey said property in fee simple to Buyer, subject only to easements and other documents of record in _____ County, _____. The Parties understand and agree that fee simple includes all mineral and water rights; all solar and air rights; all timber, recreational and agricultural rights; and all other rights customarily included in fee-simple ownership.**

> **Seller agrees to convey the property free of all life estates, unrecorded easements and deeds, leases and reservations of interest or profit.**

> **Seller shall disclose to Buyer all matters, including all unrecorded easements, deeds, contracts, arrangements, permissions and understandings, that limit in any way the conveyance of this property in fee simple, or its full use and enjoyment by the Buyer, excluding only easements and other documents of record.**

> **Seller's disclosures shall be in writing and delivered to Buyer within ten calendar days of this Contract taking effect.**

> **All exceptions and disclosures must be acceptable to the Buyer. If any exception or disclosure is not acceptable, Buyer may void this Contract without penalty or further obligation. The Escrow Agent shall then return Buyer's deposit in full and in a timely manner.**

I've included specific language in this fee-simple clause that goes beyond the typical boilerplate you'll find in a standard purchase contract. Lawyers will object that a buyer does not need this elaboration; usually, you shouldn't. But where you and your lawyer suspect that a seller cannot convey his property in fee simple, you need to know what's missing, both recorded (which you should be able to find) and unrecorded (which can hit you blindside). Buyers need to discount their offers to owners who cannot convey a complete set of property rights, or move on to a less complicated purchase.

One wrinkle on fee ownership that I've seen is a **subject-to clause** that the seller insists on inserting into any buyer-submitted purchase contract. The seller in this case sends to every buyer a sample purchase contract *that he will accept*, which includes the following:

> **Seller shall convey an insurable title, qualified by the usual standard preprinted exceptions, to Buyer by General Warranty Deed in fee simple, free from all liens, excepting taxes not yet due and payable, but subject to all matters of public record.**

The buyer can read the "preprinted exceptions," which may or may not be significant.

The reverse in this language is that the seller is promising to convey the property in fee simple, but subject to matters of public record which, in this example, meant, something quite a bit less than fee simple. When I found this language, "all matters of public record" meant that my buyer would not get the mineral rights on approximately 75,000 acres nor would he have hunting rights on approximately 10,000 acres that had been granted to a state agency. Both severances were matters of public record. If a buyer had not done a **title search prior to submitting a purchase contract**, this language would have forced him to accept the property less both severances. If I had not done the Courthouse scoping, the buyer would have made an offer assuming fee-simple ownership. He would have been forced by this contract language to buy the property less two valuable rights that he wanted. At the very least, he would have ended up paying more for the property than he should have paid.

In this instance, the seller found a way to avoid saying in his sale prospectus and in his proposed contract that mineral rights and hunting rights were not included in the sale.

In my experience, simply stating in your purchase contract that "Buyer's offer is for the Seller's land in fee simple." is insufficient protection. I've done that, only to find sellers failing to disclose missing pieces of their ownership. Their defense is that they misunderstood the meaning of fee simple. Since the time and cost of suing the seller was more than what was at stake, I accepted the drubbing with mutters. Had I used the more elaborate and redundant language of the fee-simple section above, I think I would have forced full disclosure.

A quick look at the deedwork should uncover the **recorded** limitations on the seller's rights in the property. The deed itself should make reference to these limitations. But that is not always the case. The deed into your seller may not include references to all recorded documents affecting the property—both easements and limitations that others hold against the property and easements and rights that the seller's property holds against others. I looked at a 230-acre tract in western Maryland recently whose deed made no mention of a recorded ingress-and-egress easement over an adjoining neighbor that provided the only access to the property.

The best title search will not turn up **unrecorded** deeds, leases, contracts for sale, life estates, gifts and easements; oral understandings and permissions; claims against the property by adverse possession and prescription; disputed boundary lines; unrecorded notes that use the property as security; and liens, litigation and judgments that are in the works but have yet to be recorded. Such items can short a buyer of purchased acreage, limit enjoyment and use of the property, or reduce the value of the property's assets. That is why it's important for your contract to ask the seller to disclose unrecorded items that affect ownership and acreage.

Here is one example. The seller sells the timber rights—that is, the right to cut sawtimber-sized trees for 12 months—but this sale contract is not recorded. The seller then sells the land to an absentee buyer without disclosing the timber sale. The logger appears in February, six months after the buyer has closed. The logger finishes his work in a month and leaves. The new owner appears with his family on a sunny day in May and is overcome with shock and awe. The seller, meanwhile, has retired to a 100-foot-long RV with no fixed address. The logger informs the new owner that the seller told him that he had orally disclosed the reservation and had secured the buyer's oral approval at that time. The logger makes a point of then saying that in his opinion the seller, were he ever to be located, would so testify in court while standing on something holy from each of the world's more than 600 religions. The new owner is screwed. Even if he manages to get something for the timber, which is unlikely, he's left with a cutover tract that he no longer wants.

Had this buyer included a fee-simple clause similar to the one above (which requires seller disclosure of unrecorded contracts), he would have protected his interests. An honest seller will not take offense at this language. If the unscrupulous seller did not disclose the timber sale in writing as required by the fee-simple language, the seller could not hide behind an "I-said/you-heard" defense, which boils down to the seller's recollection of his word against the buyer's. This is a suit worth filing against the seller, because the buyer has the paper to win it. Whether the buyer can collect his money is, sadly, another question. The best reason for including fee-simple language is that it forces the marginally honest/crooked seller to disclose a quagmire before you get stuck in it. It won't help when the seller is out to scam a buyer intentionally.

Here are several other examples of complications that lack of recordation and oral understandings can cause for a buyer.

1. A buyer purchases a farm and five years later a neighbor informs him that the seller, recently deceased, had orally given him six veneer-grade cherry trees at the back of the farm in return for having built a long section of fence. The neighbor now wants to cut the trees, which are worth about $7,500. The neighbor wants the current owner to "honor" the previous owner's "contract," about which he knew nothing. The new owner loses whichever way he resolves this. He can pay the neighbor $7,500; he can allow the neighbor to cut the trees; he can ignore the neighbor's claim (which should be placed against the seller's estate, not the current owner). If he refuses to pay or give the neighbor the trees, the neighbor bears him ill will, perhaps forever. This dispute is not between the current owner and the neighbor legally, but it is practically.

I think the best way to handle this problem is to explain to the neighbor that the seller never disclosed the tree-for-fencing deal when the buyer bought the farm, either orally or in writing. Then explain that the neighbor should send the former owner's estate a bill for $7,500. The new owner should tell the neighbor that he will write a letter in support of this claim, attesting that the fence was built and that the deceased owner never informed him of the neighbor's claim on the trees. If the neighbor is being honest about his claim, he should understand your dilemma and accept your decision. If he's just trying to pick your pocket for an easy $7,500, you've avoided helping him.

2. A buyer purchases a farm that contains three or four acres of blackberry thicket. A neighbor informs the new owner that the seller always allowed him—and his very extended family—to pick berries. The seller, of course, never said anything about this permission. Not wanting to be hateful and selfish, the new owner agrees to continue this arrangement, only to find the bushes picked clean when he and his family arrive with buckets ready. This is a case of permission rather than prescriptive use: the neighbor has no legal right to use the blackberry thicket or hold the new owner to the old owner's practices. A permission ends when the owner who gave it sells the property. But once the new owner mumbles his own begrudging permission, he will incur a double dose of hard feelings if he subsequently retracts it. If the seller is available, you might first check with him about the validity of the neighbor's "claim." It may be that the seller hated blackberries and placed no value on giving them to the neighbor. It may be that the seller once gave the neighbor permission, only to find the bushes stripped. If you want your blackberries for yourself, you will need to choose from four options: 1) just say no politely and explain that you intend to strip the bushes yourself; 2) offer to make the patch available after you've taken whatever you want; 3) offer to split the patch if that suits your needs; or 4) propose a trial arrangement of some sort for one year with no promises implied after that.

3. Mr. A purchases a wooded tract with a road running through it from front to back. There's a small, second home cabin in the middle of the property that he wants to use on pretty weekends and during hunting season. The cabin fronts this lovely road. The elderly seller had not used the cabin for many years due to poor health. At the back of the tract, the road forks: one branch enters National Forest land, the other leads to an adjoining 50 acres owned by Mr. B. Neither the National Forest nor Mr. B have a recorded easement that allows use of Mr. A's road. But Mr. B does have a recorded access easement to get to his property that crosses property owned by Mr. C.

Mr. B says that he has always used Mr. A's road, because his deeded right of way is undeveloped and the cost of constructing a road is high. Many years ago, a previous owner of Mr. A's land informed Mr. B that he didn't like Mr. B using the road and told him to stop. But no one ever put up a locked gate or took any action against Mr. B's continued use. The seller never told Mr. A anything about Mr. B's use of the road, and Mr. A never observed Mr. B using it during his visits. Mr. A wants Mr. B to stop using his road. If, however, Mr. B's practice fits that state's criteria for an **easement by prescription**, he has the legal right to use Mr. A's road though nothing was ever recorded. To establish this type of claim, Mr. B's use had to have gone on continuously for a statute-set number of years and meet the other standards, such as Mr. B's use of the road had to be open, notorious, continuous and adverse (that is, against the wishes and interests of Mr. A, the property's owner).

Since Mr. B owns an access easement over Mr. C, he can not claim continued use of Mr. A's road as an **easement by necessity**, which allows an owner of landlocked property to acquire an ingress-egress easement to a public road. (If Mr. B wanted an electric line run to his place, he would have to negotiate a utility easement with the landowners whose property the line would cross. He could not claim an electric easement by necessity.) Mr. A may or may not be able to keep Mr. B from using the road, depending on the facts of Mr. B's prescriptive-use claim.

The unfortunate Mr. A also discovers in his first ownership year that his road is inundated with 4WD pickup trucks and ATVs during hunting season. Hunters are driving from the public highway into the National Forest over his road because it is the easiest access for miles around. Mr. A places a heavy cable and lock across his road each day of the two-week November deer season, only to find it cut repeatedly. When he physically stops hunters in front of his cabin, they claim they have always used this road just like Mr. B does—and continue on. If Mr. A prevails legally, his cabin is a sitting duck for retribution. If he does nothing, he puts up with trespassers. I know of a landowner who was forced to sell his land because he could not keep hunters from crossing it to get to National Forest land. A partial solution to Mr. A's problem lies in persuading the National Forest to install a locked gate where Mr. A's road enters federal land. Excavations on each side of these stout metal gates prevent circumvention. The National Forest's network of roads would be blocked from vehicle traffic coming to it over Mr. A's road, but hunters may still choose to drive to that point over Mr. A. If the Forest is unwilling to install a gate, Mr. A will have to build something similar where his road joins the highway, post his property, take an ad out in the local paper providing notice against trespass and use of his road, excavate waterbars and, if necessary, press charges.

Every land buyer should become familiar with two legal doctrines—**adverse possession and prescription**. **Adverse possession** is the acquisition, i.e., ownership, of land through its protracted, actual, continuous and unauthorized *occupation* when its true owner knows of the occupation, opposes it, but does nothing to evict the adverse occupier during the statutory time period that varies from state to state, from five to 30 years. Some states require that the party claiming ownership by adverse possession must have paid the property tax on the disputed acreage. Virginia does not require tax payment, but it does require that the party asserting possession (ownership) by adversity must show "**color of title**," that is, a plausible argument and facts supporting his claim.

Prescription is a method by which a party can acquire title to the land of another, i.e., ownership, by protracted and unauthorized *use* that is open, notorious, adverse to the rightful owner and continuous for the statutory period of time. The difference between them is that adverse possession requires occupation while prescription requires use but not full-time occupation. A party that uses a road on another's property against the owner's wishes can acquire a **prescriptive easement** to continued use of that road if his use meets all of the state's statutory requirements. A prescriptive easement gives its holder continued use of a road on another owner's land, but not its ownership.

4. You discover after buying a farm that a 500-foot-long fence line doesn't follow the boundary line that your surveyor just marked. Your neighbor has fenced in about five acres that your survey and deed calls indicate belong to you. Your seller says "they've been fussing about that line for years, but I never paid it any attention since they never moved the line onto me." The neighbor claims he built the new fence five years ago exactly along the run of the old fence. When you bought the farm, the acreage you bought was calculated from the deed calls, which means that you paid for five acres that you don't occupy or use, and may or may not own. You did not have the surveyor check whether the deed calls matched the functional boundary lines on the ground. The legal issue in this case is whether the neighbor can meet all the state's tests for **adverse possession**. The land is worth $20,000. The seller, of course, told you nothing about a disputed fence line. In fact, the seller thought the fence line was in the right place. So you go to court.

The neighbor gets on the stand and knows all about adverse possession. He ticks off each of the state's tests that he's met. And then to clinch the deal he testifies about his Granddad—now deceased— who "was told by the seller himself that he didn't object if we wanted to leave that old line where it was, and I was standing there 40 years ago when he said it." The neighbor's testimony undermines his adversity argument. Adverse possession must be established against the wishes of the owner, not with his consent. Further, the seller was not aware that the fence line was wrong; he thought it ran along the boundary. Therefore, he did not know of the neighbor's possession of his property, so the neighbor's adversity claims fails on a second test. And if the seller had agreed to leave the line where it was, then he gave the neighbor's granddad permission to use *his* five acres. If the neighbor had oral permission to use it, the

Court should consider the arrangement to be a **license**—a personal privilege for one person to enter another's land for a particular purpose, in this case, pasturing cattle. A license can be ended at any time by the party that gave it in the first place. Licenses do not run with the land. An oral or informal license would end with the death of either party or when the land is sold. The neighbor loses the five acres that he never had a right to possess or use.

It's obviously better to discover the mismatch between the deed calls and the fence line before you submit your offer. Once you've purchased the property, you've probably acquired the seller's position in the dispute, for better or worse. If your contract asked that the seller disclose all boundary disputes and he didn't, you may be able to get your $20,000 from him if you were to lose this case.

5. To get to the seller's 100 acres, you have to cross land owned by A. Troll. A leaf-strewn road shaded by an overarching canopy of mature sugar maples takes you from the state-maintained road into the seller's property, about 1/2 mile away. Mr. Troll, the seller of the 100 acres, drives you in over this deal-clinching driveway. You check the deed and find specific reference to a 24-foot wide ingress-and-egress right of way (ROW) easement crossing Mr. Troll. You value the driveway access as being worth at least $10,000. You buy the 100 acres from a grinning Mr. Troll. The next day you find that Mr. Troll has chained off the wonderful driveway leading to your land. When you confront him, he smiles and tells you to read your deed. You finally discover that your deeded ROW is not the driveway. In fact, your ROW is no road at all. It will cost you at least $20,000 to construct a road over your ROW, which you finally locate in an inhospitable gully filled with quicksand and boulders the size of beer trucks. Though Mr. Troll now says he doesn't want the likes of you using his fine driveway, he allows, with great reluctance, that he will sell you a 24-foot-wide ROW over it for $10,000—to be neighborly. You're skewered. Mr. Troll, the seller, never said that his driveway was your deeded ROW—and you never asked. Mr. Troll has now bitten you for an extra $10,000 on top of the $10,000 extra you paid him for the driveway access that you assumed was your ROW.

Always locate a ROW easement on the ground as part of your pre-purchase scoping. Its location will be fixed either by deed or survey. If you have to cross the land of another to get to your seller's land, always insist that the seller convey a recorded ROW easement (deeded easement) that shows and/or states its location, along with any restrictions on its use. Then locate the ROW/easement location on the ground so that you avoid being captured by Mr. Troll and his far-flung relations. Always nail down the legal basis for access if the seller's property does not have **frontage** on a public road. Insert language into your purchase contract that makes your offer contingent on having access that is legal, unambiguous, physically usable, of sufficient width for your purposes, uncontested and permissible by public authority (usually the State's Highway/Road Department issues a permit for a new entrance). If your land does not have electricity, you should make sure that you can run an electric line in this ROW.

If you are buying land where the seller tells you that you have access by prescriptive use, adverse possession, necessity, implication or permission, place a contingency in your offer that requires him to secure access to a degree acceptable to you and your lawyer. Individual circumstances will dictate the level of security you will need.

Permission from the landowner whose land your access road crosses is not good enough, because permission can be withdrawn at any time. Permission is not an easement. Be particularly careful when buying land from large paper companies, utilities and land companies. They've often acquired their holdings decades earlier and may not have good access easements. An unrestricted easement that is recorded prior to your purchase is preferred. While you have an absolute right to get to landlocked property, you don't have a right to get there by the most convenient and cheapest route. If you have to build a road from scratch over a ROW, discount your offering price.

The best position for a buyer in every purchase is to have an existing entrance on owned frontage along a maintained public road. Next best is a recorded ROW easement over an adequate access road to an existing entrance on a maintained public road.

If you are buying land with frontage but without a developed entrance on the public road, you need to make sure that you have sufficient **sight clearance** in both directions from your proposed entrance so that you can obtain a permit to install your entrance. In Virginia, for example, a new entrance now needs 100 feet of sight clearance in both directions for every ten miles per hour of speed limit: thus, a 50-mph zone requires 500 feet of clear sight in both directions from the proposed driveway's centerline. This is a safety-enhancing regulation that can catch an unknowing buyer. Existing entrances are grandfathered, regardless of their hazardousness. The local office of the state highway department will know the applicable standards and may be persuaded to measure free of charge. New entrances usually require a permit.

In sum, when submitting a purchase contract, a buyer should make sure that the seller understands that he is to convey to the buyer, subject to items of record: 1) 100 percent ownership of the property; 2) the full set of fee-simple rights in the property, unless otherwise disclosed and agreed to; 3) all that he owns in the property with nothing reserved or omitted; and 4) full disclosure or any unrecorded claim, boundary dispute, access issue and the like that might in any way negatively affect the buyer's full use, possession and enjoyment of all the rights in the property. While a title search occurs after your contract is accepted, it's in the buyer's interest to check out enough of the seller's deedwork to understand all the recorded limits on the property and the location of any easements before submitting an offer. See Chapter 27 for additional discussion of ownership issues.

LEGAL DESCRIPTIONS

Once you have determined the nature of the seller's ownership, you then must **make sure the property is described legally** in such a way that the acreage you will receive at closing is the same as that which you are paying for. Acreage to be conveyed from seller to buyer should be described in the deed that transfers the property. The same description—or a reference to its exact statement in a previously recorded document, such as an earlier deed—should be included in your purchase contract.

Don't buy land that is not legally described in a recorded document in the property's chain of title. Don't buy land that cannot be described with specificity.

It is not enough, however, to insert a reference in your purchase contract to an earlier recorded description, because such descriptions can range from erroneous and vague to Mary-Poppins practically perfect in every way. States, to my knowledge, do not require that deed descriptions be checked for closure and accurate acreage when property is sold. I know of no state that requires a survey as a condition of land sale. To make matters even more interesting, vague descriptions can be accurate in terms of acreage and precise descriptions can include an error.

A special level of acreage uncertainty is reached when the seller's deed was not recorded, recorded improperly, or an **"off-conveyance"** from the seller's property was not recorded. An "off-conveyance" refs to a piece of the whole being separated by sale, gift or exchange. An unrecorded deed binds only the parties who made it. If you buy 100 acres, of which 12 had been previously sold to a neighbor through an unrecorded deed and you had no knowledge of this transaction at the time of your purchase, your interest in and claim to the disputed 12 acres is superior to the neighbor's. You should win a lawsuit on these facts. But do not be surprised to find the seller testifying that he orally informed you of the unrecorded deed. If your purchase contract specified that you were making an offer for 100 acres, you should prevail against the seller's testimony. But if your contract includes a boundary description (that you did not check for acreage) that amounts to 88 acres, not 100, or refers only to the seller's property, you will lose. Unrecorded sales will not turn up in a title search. You increase your chances of discovering one and protecting your interests in any future lawsuit when you include something like my fee-simple language above that requires the seller to **disclose any "unrecorded easements and deeds."**

Property deed descriptions can be set forth in a proper format with elaborate detail and still contain errors that add to or subtract from the actual acreage being conveyed. These problems are discussed below.

A property's deed description, even when dead-on accurate, does not mean the seller holds **clear title** to the property accurately described. Don't assume that once you confirm the seller's acreage as advertised, it means that the seller has good title to that acreage. You've simply determined that the acreage the seller claims to own is accurate. The title-search question for your lawyer is: Does the seller have good title to this acreage?

Confirming deed acreage starts with a plotting of the calls, described in Chapter 17. The title search should show that the seller has a clear chain of title for the specific number of acres described in the seller's deed. Keep in mind that the acreage in the chain of title may contain an error; and also remember that the title history may not reflect acreage in the field that the seller will convey. Again, **the buyer's job is to make sure that each layer of analysis—deeded acreage, acreage in the chain of title, acreage on the ground—all agree on the same acreage number.** And, again, it's better to do most, if not all, of this research before you submit an offer, because your offering price will reflect what you've found. If you don't do the necessary research before making an offer, place a contingency in your contract that allows you, the buyer, to void your offer without penalty if the seller is unable to convey the amount of acreage under contract, legally and physically, to your satisfaction.

A **title search** is a backtracking process in which the researcher follows the acreage's legal ownership back in time through deeds, wills and other records. Establishing **clear title** to the seller's 100 acres does not guarantee that the seller's property actually contains 100 acres. Your lawyer can certify good title to inaccurate acreage through no error of his own or lack of diligent effort. The buyer in this case has no claim—cause of action—against the lawyer who performed a competent title search. An acreage error can be passed along from title search to title search with each lawyer confirming the erroneous antecedent acreage figure. While the lawyer's title search tracks a specific acreage, he's checking for ownership of that acreage, not whether that acreage number is correct in the passed-down calls and on the ground. He will pick up gross errors in acreage, something like a sale of ten acres 30 years ago that was not deducted from the root property that he's now searching. The acreage errors that are not obvious are found only when a surveyor checks the calls for closure and acreage and then confirms the calls for closure and acreage on the ground.

Each state determines how far back title is to be searched. In Virginia, it is the custom, not the law, that the search be taken back 60 years. If you're buying property that has not been sold once or twice within the last 50 years, I'd take the title back through at least three or four sales to make sure the ownership line of the deeded acreage is, at least, consistent over a longer period. A buyer can always ask his lawyer to take the title back beyond the period set by custom or law.

Title insurance, which insures a property owner against certain adverse claims and errors, should cover a new owner from the day the property was first titled until he disposes of it. Title policies exclude certain acts from their coverage, such as public regulations affecting the use of the property, takings under eminent domain and adverse developments (defects, claims, encumbrances) that the new owner was aware of but did not disclose to the insurance company. Policies usually do not cover unrecorded easements, acreage discrepancies and boundary conflicts that a correct survey would disclose. If you buy without a survey and later discover an acreage shortage, your title insurance won't make you whole. What is protected is the policyholder's title to the property; his title free of any defect, lien or encumbrance other than those of record and listed in the policy; his right to ingress and egress; and the marketability of his title. I've bought rural property without title insurance, following the advice of local lawyers who said it wasn't necessary in their county. I would do so again only if I were confident about the items that insurance covers.

It is easy for errors in calls and acreage to creep into documents, particularly lengthy deed descriptions that were copied and recopied by hand or typewriter. I found one deed, for example, that had been properly searched for title back more than 60 years. In each change of ownership in the twentieth century, the property was described in typewritten deeds as containing, "100 acres." However, when this parcel was originally sold from a large tract in the early 19th Century, the original handwritten deed described it as "108 acres." Sometime after that, a now-long-deceased lawyer misread a handwritten "8" for an "0" and wrote the deed for "100 acres," leaving it eight acres short on paper but not on the ground. The error was not caught until a surveyor plotted the deed's calls on his software.

When deeds were transcribed as land was sold and resold, it was easy for a lawyer or secretary to drop, transpose, miswrite, miscopy and otherwise mess up numbers and compass directions. The farm where I live is divided by a state road: the deed I received when I bought it in 1983 had a 20-acre chunk on the wrong side. My lawyer, then in his late 70s, also represented the seller in our transaction—a fact I learned when I walked into his office for the closing. No one caught his mistake at closing, and I was then too stupid to take the time to read the deed before I signed all the papers. He had inadvertently written 20 acres "west of SR 640" instead of "east of SR 640." Since the error harmed no one, a simple **deed of correction** was done several years later after I took the time to read our deed. A deed of correction is also referred to as a **correction deed** and **deed of confirmation**. Its purpose is to correct spelling mistakes, typographical errors and other misstatements. The point I'm making is simple: legal descriptions should be verified, both in title and on the ground.

And, perhaps, I'm drawing an additional point from my own lack of diligence. Make sure that *you* read and understand your deed description and other documents before you sign them. By the time you get to your lawyer's office for closing, you should have read the deed several times, at least once in conjunction with a topo in the field.

If you ask your lawyer to do a complete title history back to the first records, he will prepare an **abstract of title**—a written chronology and narrative of the property's history of record showing surveys, mortgages, liens, estates, easements, court rulings and the like. Doing an abstract of title is more likely to uncover errors of the type described above than the conventional time-limited title search. Title insurance requires a lawyer to prepare an abstract of title. Since title searches are only looking at the relatively recent chain of title—and things that adverse the seller's title—the standard title-search report will usually contain a boilerplate disclaimer that neither acreage nor boundaries are confirmed by that search. Once again clear title does not validate or establish actual acreage in the field. A run-of-the-mill title search may reveal an acreage problem; an abstract of title will show you how the problem came to be.

The next step in confirming acreage on paper is to determine whether a **recorded survey** exists for the target property. **Recordation** refers to entering a drawing of the property's boundaries into the county's deed books, noting time and date. Recording a survey provides notice to the general public that the owner of the surveyed land claims certain boundaries and location. Recording, however, does not establish the validity of the survey's measurements or validate the deed's acreage claim. It does, on the other hand, place the holder of the recorded survey in an advantageous position in the event of a challenge to his boundaries or acreage. The survey's measurements have to be based on calls in a deed, presumably a deed of record.

A survey may be found, once recorded, either immediately following the deed in the deed book or in a separate book devoted to surveys and plats. In the latter case, the clerk should note on the deed the location of the survey in the survey book, by book number and page. Make sure the recorded survey carries the surveyor's signature, state license number and date of completion. The recordation date and time will also appear on the survey document. Remember recordation does not guarantee a survey's accuracy.

Property can be, and is, sold without a survey being recorded by either buyer or seller. But the calls in the seller's deed had to come from somewhere, from some earlier survey, for the seller's land to have been "deeded off." Dig back enough and you will find a first deed description and survey, though they may be primitive. Somewhere in the chain, there should be surveyed calls that constitute the current description. And that's the set on which the seller's title rests. As you backtrack the seller's deed, you will often find gifts and sales of land that reduce the original tract. Some of these off-conveyances provide a legal description of the parcel that was severed, and some provide a description less than a set of calls. When the seller's acreage is the remainder of a tract that's been whittled, hire a surveyor to check acreage and boundaries.

The seller may have, or know of, an **unrecorded survey** on his property. This is not common, but it's not unknown. Why would a landowner not record a survey that he possesses? The obvious answer is probably right: the survey shows something the seller does not want to be known. If you get wind of an unrecorded survey, make the effort to find out what that something is. You may be able to do this without seeing the unrecorded survey through diligent sleuthing with neighbors and local surveyors. If you know the seller has an unrecorded survey and you think it's necessary to see it, you can always insert an **unrecorded survey contingency** in your purchase contract:

> **Buyer's offer is contingent on the Seller providing him with a copy of any unrecorded survey of Seller's property. Buyer may modify or withdraw his offer without penalty if this survey reveals information that is, in Buyer's opinion, unacceptable.**

If you can't figure out the problem and the seller refuses to produce the survey, I would not submit an offer.

When the seller cannot or does not provide a survey, a buyer has four other information sources to check before giving up hope. First, surveyors often collect old local surveys and documents in the course of their work. Retired surveyors may give their files to one of their occupational heirs. Ask them for help. One of the local surveyors may have the unrecorded survey of the seller's land or an unrecorded survey of adjoining land. Second, some counties employ a full- or part-time surveyor; ask him. If your seller's land is part of a larger tract with shaky calls, the county's surveyor may have had to plot out the original deed, from which your seller's land came. Third, check the neighbors' deeds to see whether they have recorded surveys that show the common boundaries with your seller's property. Their deed calls should match exactly the seller's deed calls where the two properties join and share a line. A discrepancy between your seller's calls and a neighbor's may indicate where a closure or acreage error is in your seller's deed. Lawyers and surveyors often search the deed work for adjoining landowners to clear up problems in a seller's deed. If you can find no deed calls at all for the seller's property, you will have to use the calls from the neighboring deeds and piece the target's boundaries together. Let a surveyor do this work for you. Finally, if the target property has ever been leased for minerals, the lessee—the company that's leased the minerals from the owner—may have worked up a map or survey and may share its information with you.

If you commission a survey that shows you have a questionable claim to say 25 acres of the 250 that you just bought from the seller, you can choose either to record your new survey or not. Recordation will support your claim to 225 acres within your survey boundaries if that's an issue, but it will weaken your argument for the other 25. It's obviously in your self-interest to record a survey that shows your new property contains 250 acres, especially if your neighbor is using 25 of them. Your lawyer can advise you on whether or not to record.

Different surveyors working from the same records can—and, occasionally, do—come to different conclusions about a boundary line.

One survey surprise is an **overlap**, in which the seller's survey (or your new survey) includes land that a neighbor's survey shows as his. Overlaps tend to involve an acre or two at most, but not always. Overlaps can be found on the ground, in the paperwork, or in both places. Surveyors should note on a newly drawn survey where they have found one. If the overlap is inconsequential, I'd suggest either ignoring it or, when each side has a defensible claim, working out an equitable division, swap or sale. Court victories in such disputes may cost the winner more than the contested terrain is worth. Where the overlap involves land with significant value, you have no choice but to look for resolution. Surveyors representing each party may be able to correct the error, or, failing that, suggest a compromise. If you and the neighbor can't figure it out, you have four choices: forget about it, mediation, arbitration or litigation. It's always better to discover an overlap before you submit a purchase offer. That allows you to place a contingency in your contract that requires the seller to solve the problem with the neighbor, subject to your approval.

ACREAGE DISCREPANCIES

Non-alignment situations—where the boundary lines in the deed, survey or topo don't match the boundary lines on the ground—often present themselves as an encroachment by a functioning fence line. If, for instance, your topo map (using the deed calls) shows a boundary running along a hard-to-access ridge but you find a well-maintained fence at the base of the ridge (and none at the top where it should be), either the paper boundaries are wrong or the fence is—and there's always the third option, that both are. But the likeliest explanation is that it was too hard to build the fence along the real boundary, so it was built where it was feasible, whether or not by mutual agreement.

A fence encroachment means that a buyer may be buying land that the seller may or may not own when the seller is encroaching on the neighbor. Or, the buyer may be facing a claim to the seller's land that the neighbor may or may not own. A fence encroachment, in and of itself, does *not establish* legal ownership to the fenced-in land. It does, however, give the buyer notice that he needs to determine the seriousness and source of the problem. A fence encroachment, even with a small amount of land involved, is one loose end that can quickly turn into a biting snake. People are touchy and self-righteous about their property; I know I am.

The smallest non-alignments can create large, long-lasting grievances between neighbors. If your new land is the victim of even a long-ago willful encroachment, it's hard not to think of your current neighbor as a complicit beneficiary. At the very least, you may harbor undeclared hard feelings and end up with less functional acreage than you thought you had purchased. Don't assume that a friendly approach to your new neighbor will result in quick-and-easy justice for you, the newcomer. It's far more likely to poison the well of local opinion regarding your "arrogant" demand for change. When you discover a non-alignment that benefits your seller, you will take over his position. Don't be surprised when the neighbor appears asking you for justice. Keeping silent about a non-alignment that seemingly brings you free acreage does not strengthen any legitimate claim you have to ownership. It may simply paint you as dishonest. For these reasons, the best path I think is to **disclose any non-alignment or acreage discrepancy your scoping discovers to the seller in writing and have him to sort it out as a condition of your purchase**.

Know going into this discussion that both the seller and the neighbor may be genuinely ignorant of what you have uncovered. Neither is likely to be pleased by the prospect of having to work a deal with each other because you want them to. Your seller is going to be especially miffed if the encroachment benefits him and you're asking him to give up sale money for your benefit. Your leverage with the seller is to tell him that you will alert the neighbor if he refuses. And your leverage with both the seller and the neighbor is to say that they are both under the obligation to disclose this problem to every buyer of both properties in the future. So they may as well work it out now, for you.

"Ground shrink" is a term hunters use to describe a deer that scoped out at 250 pounds standing at a distance but weighs only 150 on the ground after the shot. Ground shrink is always blamed for the loss of the other 100 pounds, which, of course, never existed, except in the hunter's excited imagination.

Land buyers want to avoid ground shrink, where the buyer has bought "x" number of acres in an impulsive, non-researched rush, only to find upon completing the purchase that he owns something less than "x."

Here's a typical ground-shrink dilemma.

More or less. The seller's deed says he owns "100 acres, more or less." You offer him $100,000, which he accepts. Just before closing, you learn that he has only 90 acres. Can you void the contract? Probably not. Can you force him to take $90,000? Probably not. In both cases, the "more or less" probably covers him. What if you can prove beyond any doubt that the seller knew the property was short ten acres, and still advertised the land as being 100 acres, more or less, which is the precise language found in his deed? Sorry, you're probably still out of luck, though you may have an argument based on failure to disclose a material defect. "More or less" allows him to sell you less than 100 acres. If you didn't turn up the ten-acre shortage before closing, most courts, I think, will find that failure was caused by the buyer's failure to perform his own due diligence,

You would, on the other hand, have a right to void your contract if the seller advertised the property to be sold as containing "100 acres," rather than "100 acres, more or less."

You would not have a right to void if the seller advertised "100 acres, tax-map acreage," which means only that the seller is paying tax on 100 acres as it appears on the county's tax rolls. Tax-map acreage does not establish that a seller either owns that amount or can convey that amount.

When a seller advertises 100 acres, more or less, the buyer can stipulate in his purchase contract that his offer is based on "**$1,000 per acre conveyed and not $100,000 in gross.**" That language would allow the buyer to void his offer if the seller can't convey the full 100 acres, and, if needed, provide the basis of a post-sale lawsuit against the seller. As an alternative, the buyer could insert into his contract, "**$1,000 per acre, established by survey or other means acceptable to the Buyer, and conveyed.**"

What happens in this example of a ten-acre shortfall when the buyer offers "$1,000 per acre" and the seller's deed conveys 100 acres, more or less? The buyer discovers the shortfall prior to closing and wants to pay $90,000. The seller says 100 acres, more or less, means that $1,000 should be multiplied by 100, not 90, because the buyer is buying the deeded acreage, not what's on the ground. In fact, the seller argues, the buyer is getting exactly what the deed provides, 100 acres more or less. Were this to come to court, I think judges would not be of one mind. My hope is that a judge would find that the buyer's contract language trumps the seller's deeded-acreage argument, because it is more specific and both parties agreed to it. But my record of predicting judicial behavior is abysmal. I have seen judges act arbitrarily and without regard to where the weight of both facts and law fell. The buyer in this example will do better to resolve this dispute as part of his purchase, rather than bring a lawsuit whose expenses are likely to exceed the money at issue. All things considered, the buyer would do well to settle on buying the 90 acres he wants for a split-the-difference $95,000, or $1,055 per acre.

Ground-shrink disputes often involve the "more or less" qualification in a deed. This phrase and concept, I think, was intended to cover the minor, inescapable errors that were inherent in the old survey methods and instruments. To what degree "more or less" can be stretched to cover major mistakes is, a matter of local judicial interpretation and the facts specific to each dispute. The buyer's argument is strengthened if he can prove that the seller knew of a large shortfall and failed to disclose it. The size of the shortfall may also swing a judge to one side or the other. The buyer should argue that the seller's failure to disclose and the $10,000 he wants to reap from this concealment amounts to a deliberate "unjust enrichment." The legal predisposition is to support the seller in such disputes because the buyer had the opportunity and means to verify acreage prior to purchase. The facts in this example lend themselves to a split-the-baby ruling, similar to the $95,000-for-90-acres compromise mentioned above.

I am not arguing against buying property whose deed carries the "more-or-less" qualification, because many safe-to-buy properties do. I am arguing that buyers must protect themselves by verifying acreage prior to submitting an offer.

I have been involved with two instances of 300-acre properties with "more-or-less" language that were badly off: one was 90 acres more than what the seller and his deed were conveying; the other was 100 acres less. I also bought a property with a deed providing for "447 acres, more or less" that upon a post-purchase survey at my expense turned out to be only 425 acres. The seller knew of the shortfall and did not disclose it. My preliminary scoping suggested that the property would be short 15 acres, plus or minus. This purchase turned out to be as good an investment as I ever made. Another example is a tract—sold as 30 acres, more or less—that contained only 20; the buyer, who did no scoping or deed plotting, was stuck. I've scoped at least a dozen properties during the last five years that diverged on the ground from the deed by more than five acres.

If you find yourself with a "more-or-less" deed, have a surveyor plot the acreage for you. When you face a shortage, you have to make a decision about how to proceed. You can, of course, abandon the property altogether. Or, you can submit a dollar-per-acre-conveyed offer along with a copy of your surveyor's mapping and acreage calculation. This should be accompanied by words to the effect that the seller now has an obligation to disclose the acreage shortage to any buyer following you. Or, you say nothing about the shortage and make an offer that includes a **minimum-acreage contingency**, such as:

Buyer's offer is contingent on Seller being able to convey 100 acres, legally and physically. If the Seller is unable to so convey at least 99.50 acres to the Buyer's satisfaction, Buyer may amend or void this Contract at his discretion and without penalty.

Buyer will determine acreage at his expense and within thirty (30) days of the effective date of this Contract.

This approach—not disclosing what you already know—allows the seller to become invested in a sale to you. When you show him the bad news, you've set the stage for an acceptable compromise. A fourth alternative is to include an **acreage-slide formula** in your contract by which the buyer agrees to pay increasingly more per acre as the number of acres the seller can convey falls and increasingly less per acre as the number of acres the seller can convey rises, acreage to be determined by means acceptable to both parties and jointly paid for.

Less is Not Always More. What do you do when your seller occupies less land than his deed provides because a neighbor has fenced some in?

During your pre-purchase scoping, you discover that your seller's deeded 100 acres is 25 acres short on the ground. A neighbor's fence encloses this parcel. Your seller believes that the fence line is on the deeded boundary. This is too large a matter for you to forget or forgive. If you're paying for 100 acres, you don't want to end up with 75.

You have to show the fence encroachment to the seller. You are the bearer of very bad news so be prepared for anger and rejection. His first defense is that you are wrong. Since you only have a plot of his boundaries and not a survey, he will feel justified in quarreling with you. He will argue that his land contains more than the 100 acres in the deed owing to its rolling topography. (This, as you know, is true, but irrelevant.) He'll argue that he's selling "what you can see with your own two eyes." (No, he's not.) Then he'll say that he priced the property "as it lays," so your piece of paper means nothing in terms of price. (How it lays or doesn't lay has nothing to do with how much acreage it contains legally.) He will be reluctant to open this can of worms with his neighbor, because every solution promises to cost him in time, money and aggravation. Although 25 acres is at stake, the seller's not sure that he can, if it comes down to it, prevail in a lawsuit. Let him blow off steam and then come back a week or two later after he's had a chance to check your information and talk to a lawyer. He will soon realize that he's now supposed to disclose this 25-acre "latent defect" to all buyers as long as it's not resolved. If the seller chooses to stonewall you, walk away. If you buy the property, you buy the problem. And since you are aware of it, you have no cause of action against the seller after buying it. Any solution will, therefore, cost *you* money, time and aggravation—and there's no guarantee that you will get the acreage.

Let's assume that you've raised the issue of the 25 acres before submitting an offer, and have gotten nowhere. You might consider two approaches to force the seller to respond. First, you could make an offer based on 100 acres that is contingent on the seller being able to convey 100 acres, both in deed and on the ground. The seller has the burden of resolving the shortage to your satisfaction if he wants your money. If your offer is close to full price for 100 acres, you've given him an incentive to do so. Your offer has also made the shortfall public knowledge if a broker is involved.

The second approach is to make a fair offer for 75 acres without mentioning the 25-acre problem. This assumes that you really want the land as it is. You may be able to get some or all of the 25 acres eventually, but that speculation and likely expense is not a factor in your offer. You offer less money because you're bargaining over 75 acres on the ground, not the 100 in the deed. Point out that your offer is higher on a per-acre basis, assuming that it is. You can also offer to pay the seller for the disputed 25 acres whenever a suit that he brings at his expense is successful. If your seller balks, mention that he'll never sell 75 acres at a 100-acre price unless he deliberately conceals the shortfall. Introduce the word, "fraud," into the conversation. The way you get this seller to accept the reasonableness of a price reduction is to show him gently that his alternatives are worse. Ease him into understanding that a sale to you is likely to be his best money all things considered, even though he will realize less than he expected initially. Make sure to mention that most buyers will sue a seller over acreage that is 25 percent less than promised. So it's better to sell the property as 75 acres now, than to trick another buyer into a "100-acre" purchase, which will cost the seller the expense of defending his unethical action and is likely to forfeit the amount gained to boot.

What should you do if your pre-purchase scoping shows that a seller will convey to you by deed less land than you will own on the ground? You would be getting more land than you're bargaining for and paying for. This non-alignment is not caused by a fence encroachment, but by a deed error of which you know and the seller doesn't. I've encountered this issue on a 385-acre tract on the ground that was being sold as a 295-acre tract, based on the seller's deed. This seller had inherited the property years earlier and had made no effort to check the acreage.

What to do? I would first consider who the seller is. If he is a competent, knowledgeable individual who's either too lazy or cheap to find out how much land he's selling, I see nothing wrong in taking advantage of his lack of due diligence on his own behalf. One way to proceed is to offer this seller his full asking price. That's what I did. The seller eagerly accepted, thinking that he had lucked into a fool for a buyer. A slyer alternative is to offer five or ten percent less than the asking price and make the seller work for the deal. I didn't try this, because I didn't want to jeopardize getting the land under contract. I do not think a buyer is under any obligation to a competent seller—who is capable of becoming knowledgeable— to disclose information that the buyer acquires at his expense and which benefits him at the seller's expense. Remember this is information that the seller could have and should have developed on his own.

If, on the other hand, your seller can not be reasonably expected to understand the selling process and reasonably defend his interests, I would either walk away from the property or disclose the information as I submitted an offer. P.J. Proudhon, the 19th Century French anarchist, said: "Property is theft." A buyer taking advantage of an unsophisticated or powerless seller is one such example.

An ethical line exists between taking unfair advantage and making a bargain purchase. Dirt-smart buyers should appreciate the difference and keep to the right side of the line.

I've had two clients over the years who have introduced themselves to me by saying that they were "thieves" and only interested in land that they could "steal." In both instances, I initially supplied a more generous interpretation of their intentions: "You're looking for an investment without risk, land that you can buy with the sale of the timber covering the full acquisition cost. Right?" Wrong. They *were* thieves, not investors. And they stole a lot of my time. I don't see how a person can be a thief in one area of his life without being a thief in others. Perhaps, I'm ethically dense. Thieves succeed every so often, but I've seen them get taken just as frequently. Thieves undermine themselves through greed. It's best to think of yourself as a land investor, guided by an interest in stripping risk out of a purchase and making a reasonable profit.

What should you do when you discover after a purchase that your seller occupied more acreage on the ground than he had title to?

Against my advice, you did not have the deed's calls plotted before purchasing 100 acres. You are thinking of selling a portion to pay down some of the debt, so you commission a post-purchase boundary survey. The surveyor reports that you, indeed, own 100 acres as provided in your deed. But he also found that the seller occupied and used about 25 acres of a neighbor's land that was fenced into your new property years ago without dispute. The surveyor informs you that your deed provides no right to these 25 acres.

If you pull down the surveyor's ribbons and don't record the survey, you are hiding the truth. This doesn't strengthen your claim to the land once it's discovered, because adverse possession requires that your occupation be open and notorious. But there is an interesting twist to this set of facts. Your functioning fence line is clearly open and notorious, though the neighbor is unaware that it is wrong. Must your real boundary line be marked on the ground to show the neighbor where the common line really lies? I don't know. But what is clear is that you won't win an adverse-possession claim for the 25 acres unless the neighbor knows or has public notice (via recordation) that you are occupying land that is his.

You consider not recording your survey. If your neighbor never sees it, you hope that you might avoid a dispute and continue to occupy and use the 25 acres without a legal right to do so. Then you realize you have to pull down the new ribbons that your surveyor just put up. If the neighbor sees the ribbons far inside your side of the existing fence, he's likely to figure out where your common boundary lies. Your plan to sell some of your new acreage is now squirreled up, because you can't guarantee good title to the 25 acres.

Recording your survey, however, provides public notice that you don't own the 25 acres if someone takes the time to copy your survey and match it against the presumed boundary on the ground. If no one checks—which is likely—your public notice is made, but bears no adverse consequence. You should understand, however, that you're taking a step toward establishing ownership of land that you do not own. Your case for title by adverse possession may start either from the date on which the fence was erected or the date on which you record the survey. Gaining title/ownership might be as much as 30 years in the future and require a lawsuit. If you wait six months or more after purchase before recording your survey, you've made it harder for your neighbor to find it in the records. A standard title search of *his* property will probably not dig out your recorded survey—but it could, depending on the diligence of the researcher. Since there's nothing wrong with his deeded acreage, the title search on his land will probably not reveal his fenced-out loss of 25 acres on the ground. Your occupation will reveal itself if the neighbor's land is surveyed or field-checked against the deed's calls.

Sooner or later, someone on the neighbor's side will discover your occupation. If you claim you never knew about it, the facts leaking out are likely to show that you're not telling the truth. You can argue that you did not understand the ground implications of the survey that you recorded. Landowners often do not make the connection between survey and ground truth. But a surveyor should make note of a very large discrepancy on his survey, unless you persuade him not to. I will simply note the obvious: people have different levels of tolerance for their own intentional dishonesty.

If you suspect this situation, you could instruct your surveyor not to mark the boundaries on the ground, or not to mark the boundary where the encroachment occurs. Your surveyor may or may not cooperate with you once he discovers the 25-acre encroachment. Your neighbor's chances of discovering the error are reduced, but your ability to sell that 25 acres is not enhanced. This type of deception will blow up in your face eventually.

If you leave the ribbons up and record your survey, the neighbor has nobody to blame but himself for not becoming aware of the boundary. If he sleeps on his rights after recordation, he weakens his claim to the land. Recordation provides public notice of your adverse possession of his land whether or not he ever sees the survey in the courthouse. The longer this clock runs without his alarm going off, the longer he sleeps on his rights, the stronger your claim is. The **doctrine of laches** (pronounced, "latches") is the idea in law that an individual who believes he is wronged must assert his position in a timely fashion. Failure to advance a timely claim is grounds for dismissal. But remember: you are trying to take land legally that does not belong to you legally at the time you are trying to take it.

Your choice is to reveal the problem and deal with it openly with your neighbor, or conceal it in hope that he never figures it out. Honesty may result in your "loss" in whole or part of the 25 acres. Dishonesty may result in your continued occupation of his 25 acres. It may result in your legal ownership of the land. It may have other results on the order of "What goes around, comes around."

There's another way for you to look at this problem. You did not pay your seller for the 25 extra acres; you only paid him for the deed-based 100 acres. Therefore, it costs you nothing to "give" them back to your neighbor. An act of this sort is not being an urban patsy. It's no different than returning a wallet that you find on the sidewalk. It's a good way to move in to your new community.

ACREAGE-VERIFICATION CONTINGENCIES

Placing a **deeded-acreage-verification contingency in your purchase offer** is a fast, cheap way of protecting your interest in obtaining the acreage the seller is marketing. The contingency makes your purchase depend on having a surveyor of your choice run the calls through his deed-mapping program, which will either confirm the seller's calls and acreage or identify an error or uncertainty. *The plotting does not verify the seller's acreage on the ground, however. For that, you need the surveyor to field-check the calls.* If an acreage error in the deed is explainable or small, you can accept it without haggling. This should build good will that you may have to spend on more contentious issues. If the error is substantial, this contingency allows you to either walk away from the contract without penalty or renegotiate in light of the acreage problem.

Here is generic deeded-acreage-verification contingency that you can use if you have reason to suspect the deeded acreage *exceeds* the seller's acreage on the ground:

> **Buyer's offer is contingent on receiving a satisfactory acreage-verification report within _____ calendar days of the effective date of this Contract. This report shall be prepared at Buyer's expense by a licensed land surveyor of Buyer's choice. The report**

shall determine the accuracy of Seller's deeded acreage.

If these results are unacceptable to the Buyer, he may either amend or void this Contract without penalty by written notice to Seller. In the event of an amended offer, Seller is free to accept, reject or propose alternative terms.

You can adapt the language in this contingency to provide for a verification of acreage and boundaries *on the ground.* Simply revise the last sentence in the first paragraph to read: **The report shall determine the accuracy of Seller's acreage and boundaries, both in the deed and on the ground.**

The cost of verifying deeded acreage is often no more than an hour of a surveyor's time at his computer. The cost will rise if he has to work back through the chain of titles to locate the root of an error. This is not a survey contingency; you are not obligating yourself to pay for a field survey. You can anticipate surveying costs for field-checking acreage; some errors can be found by having a surveyor walk the lines with the calls in hand.

Once you have a signed purchase contract with a seller, you have negotiating leverage in the event of an acreage issue. He now has knowledge of a material defect, which he needs to disclose to any other buyer. If he tries to finesse the problem by including a **permitted title exception** involving acreage, it's a red flag to other buyers, at least the ones who are not buying on impulse and certainly those who have read this book. Moreover, the seller has invested time and energy in working a contract with you; there's no percentage for him to repeat the process with someone new with little expectation of a better outcome.

A buyer faces a different decision when his scoping suggests that the seller's deeded acreage is less than what the seller will convey on the ground. If the cause of this windfall for the buyer is some error in the calls, I don't think I would bring it up. It's the seller's obligation to know how much acreage he's selling. If he thinks he's selling 100 acres and the deed's calls plot out to 125, pay him for the 100 acres. On the other hand, if the extra 25 acres will be conveyed by the seller's adverse occupation or use of neighboring land, I would certainly bring it to the seller's attention.

Another variation of an acreage problem is one where you suspect a discrepancy of some significance, probably requiring survey work, but you're not sure of its size. In this case, you can propose that both parties arrange for and share the costs of verifying boundaries and acreage. You can also couple that with an **acreage slide.**

Buyer's contingent offering price is $100,000, based on Seller's representation that the property contains 100 acres.

The Parties agree to select a mutually acceptable surveyor to confirm acreage and boundaries, and they further agree to share equally the cost of this work.

Buyer is offering $1,000 per acre conveyed in the deed and on the ground rather than a lump sum of $100,000. Buyer's final offering price will be determined by multiplying $1,000 per acre by the number of acres the surveyor determines to be in the property, subject to the following formula:

The offering price of $1,000 per acre will stand for any surveyor-certified acreage within 3.000 acres of 100 acres.

If the certified acreage is determined to be between 90.000 and 97.000 acres, the offering price will be increased to $1,050 per acre.

If the certified acreage is determined to be between 103.000 and 110.000 acres, the offering price will be lowered to $950 per acre.

If the certified acreage is less than 90.000 acres or more than 110.000 acres, the Buyer reserves the right to withdraw this offer and submit a replacement.

An acreage slide is fair in concept to both sides. It will work when you are dealing with a reasonable and, preferably, motivated, seller. Whatever the findings, the Parties are obligating themselves to carry the deal through, except when a large discrepancy is found.

Acreage slides can work tricks on your pocketbook when a big dollar difference kicks in for the next increment of acreage change. For that reason, the fairest slides are those that adjust price to acreage in small increments. If, for instance, you increase your price $50 per acre for the first three acres under 100 acres and then $50 per acre more for the next three acres, you would pay $101,850 for 97 acres and $105,600 for 96 acres. You avoid these jumps by figuring a different price per acre for each total acreage.

Consider one other way an acreage slide can bite you. Take the example of a 25-acre shortfall in a 100-acre tract. You, the buyer, will be expected to increase your **per-acre price multiplier** from, say, $1,000 per acre to say, $1,100 per acre, for a total of $82,500 (75 x $1,100 = $82,500). If you gain 25 acres, you agree to drop your per-acre price to $900, a total of $112,500 (125 x $900 = $12,500). This appears at first glance to be an acreage slide that adjusts the *per-acre price* by ten percent in either direction with equitable and equivalent results. But note that you are buying the next 25 acres for $12,500, or $500 per acre, whereas you're giving up 25 acres for $17,500 at $700 per acre. A true ten-percent slide would be figured on the gross purchase price of $100,000, not the per-acre price. Figured on the gross purchase price, a ten-percent slide on the agreed purchase price would amount to a flat $10,000 for 25 acres in either direction. Each acre is now valued at $400, whether it's a gain or a loss to the buyer. This formula, however, does not reflect market reality by which larger acreages sell for fewer dollars per acres and smaller acreages sell for more per acre.

Buyers and sellers can disagree as to which slide formula is fair to both sides. I want readers to be aware that different formulas produce different results, some of which may not be obvious. Make sure that you understand the dollar arithmetic for both buyer and seller any time an acreage slide is proposed.

As a buyer, I prefer to use an acreage-certification contingency that covers both the deeded acreage and a field-check, if necessary. I pay for this work and have no obligation to share its results with the seller. If results favor the buyer, he can proceed at the price offered; if the results favor the seller, the buyer can use them to reopen negotiations or walk away. Most sellers agree to an acreage contingency that the buyer pays for; it never seems to occur to them that it's possible that they may be conveying more acreage than is shown in their deed.

The following generic acreage contingency will protect a buyer in most circumstances:

Buyer's offer is contingent on obtaining acceptable results from a surveyor's report regarding the property's boundaries and acreage, in the deed and on the ground. Buyer shall arrange for this work at his expense.

Buyer shall complete this work within 60 days of the effective date of this Contract. He must notify Seller in writing within ___ calendar days of receiving these results whether or not they are acceptable. Absent such notice, this contingency shall become void.

If results are not acceptable to Buyer, he may void this Contract without penalty and his deposit shall be promptly returned in full in a timely manner.

THE SPECIAL CASE OF LEASES

Acreage for sale, especially in the West, can involve a seller-held lease to private or public land and/or water. Seller-owned acreage is referred to as **deeded acreage**; seller-leased acreage is referred to as **lease acreage**. The seller can transfer the lease acreage to the buyer in several ways, including the assignment of the seller's interest in the lease; seller sale to the buyer of such interest; or even a risk-reward sharing arrangement by which the seller continues to pay a share of the lease's rent in return for a percentage share of future profits.

Be careful with leases. The deeded acreage you are about to buy may be **operationally dependent** either on a lease or a use easement that can be cancelled arbitrarily. Operational dependency means that the deeded land more or less requires access to, or the use of, the leased resources to function as an economically viable unit. The leased land may, for example, be the best, or only, source of livestock water in dry weather or the strongest patch of August grass which the deeded acreage must have to carry cattle through until September's last flush of growth.

Use of federal land and resources is subject to the vagaries of Congressional and Presidential policies. Buyers should not expect unfettered continued use of public land for grazing where endangered, threatened or sensitive (ETS) species exist or where grazing has caused substantial land-degradation or water-pollution problems. Leasing public land is cheap and cost-effective from the lessee's (tenant) perspective, which is why farmers and ranchers want to continue doing it. From the public's point of view, it can be environmentally expensive. Federal land leasing is, therefore, likely to be subject to future rent increases, greater regulatory constraints and uncertainty. While the profitability of a small deed and a large public lease may work well on paper, you can find yourself leaning on a lease that gets caught in a protracted regulatory fight which will, at the very least, raise your costs. Sooner or later, livestock farmers should expect federal agencies to lower allowable stocking rates, tighten regulations related to the pollution of surface waters and ETS protection, and raise leasing fees.

Leased land almost always involves different types of risk, each ranging from pretty small to very high. Risk can take the form of higher rent; new requirements for tenant-paid land improvements or different practices; and, in the worst case, loss of the lease. Risk is often expressed as the product of probability times consequences, with the highest risk being associated with a catastrophic event that's expected to happen. That's a useful way of assessing risk associated with leased land.

A common situation is a "small" farm being dependent on a large leased acreage. I would avoid buying land that needs lease acreage to function profitably, except if you are looking for a second home and have no interest in farming the lease. Your interest in the lease can be turned into cash by selling or subletting it to a new tenant. An undersized farm can also work for a buyer who is looking to change the operation to make a profit on the deeded acreage alone. Buyers like these should look for ways to cash out lease acreage.

A buyer's opportunity arises when a seller preemptively discounts his asking/selling price because he sees no use for his lease-dependent deeded land other than for that which he has used it for—and not very successfully. If a buyer has figured out a different use, he will benefit from the seller's self-inflicted price discount *as long as the new use works*. New wine in a seller's old bottle works only when the new vinter knows what he's doing. If you have no experience in the new idea to which you are committing your life, you are taking on a high risk of failure. Don't be seduced into a particular property because you are entranced with a nifty outside-the-box idea. It may be outside the box because it can't fit inside.

The first acreage considerations, then, are to determine whether the deeded acreage comes with and is dependent on leased land and/or water. As a general rule, a buyer can expect that the seller and his agent will reveal the existence of such leases. (On the other hand, I've found sellers and agents may or may not reveal that mineral rights have been either leased or severed.) If the seller owns a **water right,** make sure that it is included in what you're buying. If the seller has leased a needed water right to a neighbor prior to your purchase, don't buy his land. Do not assume that you will be able to obtain water rights in arid country. Where a target property depends on irrigation or off-site water for livestock, make sure that water supply is part of your deal.

If you want to be safe, you can insert a **lease-and-severance disclosure section** in your purchase offer:

> **Seller agrees to disclose to Buyer all leases of whatever kind affecting the property, both pending and in effect, recorded and otherwise, whether Seller is landlord (lessor) or tenant (lessee), including, but not limited to, leases related to minerals, timber, water, air, land, crops, hunting, fishing, improvements, recreational use and gathering.**

> **Seller agrees to disclose all severances, reservations of and limitations on interests or rights in the property, both pending and in effect, recorded and otherwise, including, but not limited to, minerals, timber, water, air, land, crops, hunting, fishing, improvements, recreational use and gathering.**

> **Seller shall provide Buyer with photocopies of all such leases and severances within five business days of this Contract taking effect. Buyer may withdraw this Contract without penalty if Seller fails to comply with this section or if the disclosures are unacceptable to Buyer.**

Almost every lawyer who reads this language will tell you that it is onerous, too detailed, cumbersome and redundant. I agree. Boilerplate in the standard contract will protect a buyer, they will say.

Language, such as I've proposed, is intended both to educate the seller about your expectations and protect your interests in the event of willful or unintended failures to disclose. Since most real-estate contracts are either written by the seller's lawyer or are pre-printed forms used by real-estate brokers representing the seller's interest, they neither educate the seller about what the buyer expects nor protect the buyer's interests sufficiently.

Real-estate contracts are not "**adhesion contracts**," which are contracts that offer consumers take-it-or-leave-it terms. The buyer can add language to a pre-printed contract, but the large blocks of small print often intimidate buyers into leaving those sections alone.

Think I'm being nerdy? I found for a developer a wooded 800-acre tract with extensive river frontage. Despite the presence of an active single-track rail line through its middle, the land could be developed for second homes. A contract was offered and accepted. The buyer then happened on the fact that the seller had reserved the timber. My client tried to buy the timber reservation without success. The deal collapsed. I am now noticing that this tract is being marketed by the same broker with the notation, "Timber reserved." Stuff like this happens. An honest seller will not be put off by disclosure language on leases and severance, because it requires nothing more of him than to disclose what he's already prepared to disclose. A seller who wants to hide something from you is likely to feign offense. That's good, not bad. You want to pop every jack-in-the-box at least once before you give it to your kids.

And, finally, speaking of surprises. I once leased a farm for summer grazing during a severe drought. I put my cattle on and a few weeks later I drove up with a fresh supply of mineral salt. I noticed three or four horses that had not been there before. When I asked the owner about the horses, she said she had leased the farm to their owner after she had signed the lease with me. She saw nothing wrong with the arrangement inasmuch as "horses are not cattle." Given my circumstances, I came to the conclusion that it was best to not point out that both horses and cattle eat the same grass. I let the double lease go without comment. On the off chance that other landlords might reason that grass eaten by a steer differs in some way from grass eaten by a horse, I advise including the words **"lease the landlord's premises exclusively to the tenant"** in your contract. If the landlord wants to reserve some portion of his land for his own use, he will include that exception in the lease.

CHAPTER 27: TRICKS OF THE SELLER'S TRADE: LEGAL, NOT LEGAL AND OTHERWISE

The ingenuity of human greed, especially over small sums, is always entertaining to observe.

Sometimes, it's infuriating and occasionally it's the cause of despair for our species. The buying and selling of land is as good a stage as any on which to observe actors playing small.

Here are some scenes I've seen in the theater of the deal.

1. General Warranty Deed. A general warranty deed is what a buyer wants.

A general warranty deed binds the seller (grantor) to six types of covenants and warranties about his ownership and title that go back to the origins of the property. A **special warranty deed** limits these promises to the buyer (grantee) to the seller's period of ownership.

The six covenants are:

1. **Covenant of seisin**: Seller promises that he owns the property.

2. **Covenant of the right to convey**: Seller promises that he has the legal right to convey the property that he owns. The right to convey is often combined with, or read into, the covenant of seisin, though there are circumstances where a seller, such as a trustee, may hold title to a property but be prohibited from selling it.

3. **Covenant against encumbrance**: Seller promises that his deed at the time he conveys title to the buyer is free of all liens and encumbrances except those set forth in the deed.

    One encumbrance that should be recorded is an access easement that allows the seller's neighbor to drive over the seller's property to get to his property. This easement **runs with the seller's land and is a right held by the neighbor**. The neighbor in this case holds an **appurtenant easement**, that is, a right of way annexed to his property. The seller's land over which the neighbor's easement runs is called the **servient tenement**; the neighbor's land that benefits is called the **dominant tenement**. Other common recorded easements are those held by utilities and public highway departments.

    This covenant is supposed to protect the buyer from encumbrances, such as mortgages, liens, easements, restrictive covenants and reservations of interests in minerals, timber, crops and improvements. It should also protect the buyer from unrecorded encumbrances, such as a claim of adverse possession or prescriptive use. Sellers may breach this warranty in my experience, if only because they don't know what a general warranty deed requires of them. And there are sellers who know and don't give a flip. Sellers often do not disclose unrecorded claims, disputed areas and encroachments. After the sale, these sellers want nothing more than to walk away from unresolved troubles running with their recently sold property. The buyer can sue the seller for his expenses in removing an encumbrance. But it is often not worth the effort to fight both the individual claiming something against the property and the seller who won't pick up the phone.

    To protect yourself, you can insert language into your purchase contract that makes this covenant explicit for the seller:

> **Seller warrants that he will convey the property to Buyer free of all encumbrances, except those that are stated in the deed. Encumbrances include, but are not limited to, liens, mortgages, leases, judgments, lack of—or restrictions on—ingress and egress, encroachments, unrecorded easements, life estates, restrictive covenants, boundary disputes, claims of prescriptive use or adverse possession, understandings, agreements, promises, permissions, licenses, allowances, reservations of profit or interest, and any other arrangement that might diminish the Property's value and Buyer's possession, use and enjoyment of it.**

While a lawyer will argue that this language is too specific and there is too much of it, take comfort in the fact that you are giving clear notice to the seller that you expect him to deliver both a clean title and a property free of surprises. If the seller objects to this language, the buyer needs to find out what specifically he objects to, because that is where the trouble lurks. The buyer's response is ask the seller's lawyer to explain the terms of a general warranty deed to the seller.

4. **Covenant of quiet enjoyment:** The seller guarantees that the title he gives to the buyer will be superior to any third-party claim of ownership. The seller is liable for damages if his title is found to be inferior.

5. **Covenant of further assurance:** The seller promises to get whatever legal instrument (deed, release, waiver) is needed to make the title good. Not all states read this covenant into a general warranty deed.

6. **Covenant of warranty forever (covenant of general warranty):** The seller promises to defend the title against "lawful claims" and compensate the buyer for any loss arising from the failure of the title.

All of these protections are embedded in the phrase, "general warranty deed," though state law determines the exact content of a general warranty deed used within its jurisdiction. It is, therefore, worth asking your local lawyer to tell you what such a deed both means and includes in your target property's state.

Equally important is the time dimension of the seller's warranties. Under a general warranty deed, the seller is making these promises to the buyer back to the property's origins. The seller is promising to defend the buyer's title against his own actions that may have clouded the title as well as any such actions taken by all of his predecessors in title. The other time consideration is that the covenants of seisin, conveyance and encumbrance are present promises; the others—general warranty (forever), quiet enjoyment and further assurances—are **future promises**. I recommend that buyers think about asking sellers for other future promises to support seller-provided disclosures and warranties.

Other types of deeds provide the buyer with less protection. A **special warranty deed,** or **limited warranty deed**, has the seller making good on the covenants only for the period of his ownership. Here's an example of a buyer needing to understand the difference between a special and a general warranty deed.

A seller offered about 12,000 acres of timberland in five separate tracts. He included a purchase contract in his bidding package that contained the following language:

Warranties of Title: Seller is the owner of the Property (exclusive of mineral interests) and will convey title to the Purchaser by Special Warranty Deed, warranting title against damages or losses resulting from claims of parties claiming by, through, or under the Seller, but not otherwise.

That's what I expected from a Special Warranty Deed. On top of the time limitation, the seller then gave himself "**Permitted Title Exceptions**," which included, among other items, the following:

Such matters as would be disclosed by a current survey or inspection of the Property including, without limitation, all encroachments, overlaps, boundary line disputes, shortages in area, cemeteries…and other similar matters not of record.

Any access related exceptions or any loss or claim due to lack of access to any portion of the Property.

Rights and claims of parties in possession of the Property.

Licenses and easements not of record.

A buyer of this property might end up owning 1,000 acres, not 12,000, and he would have no grounds to challenge the shortage in area. A general warranty deed would not be compatible with all of these permitted title exceptions; a special warranty deed can accommodate them.

Another contract I was sent in 2003 used the identical exception language and then added more exceptions related to all riparian rights, all mineral rights, all rules and regulations of any governmental authority and all "…other matters, recorded or otherwise, which would not materially affect the use of the Property for its intended purposes." This Seller was willing to convey title, but was unwilling to make it good or defend it against almost every imaginable problem. The Seller had trouble finding a buyer, for good reason.

Sellers who convey with a deed less than a general warranty along with permitted title exceptions are putting the buyer at risk in many ways. As a rule, I would advise against buying a property whose owner proposes a sale where he wants to be let off every hook that he thinks will snag his buyer.

If, however you insist on pursuing a property like this, insert into your purchase contract a **disclosure contingency** that requires the seller to inform you in writing about all that he knows or should reasonably know about each permitted title exception he demands. Thus, if the seller wants to back out matters of access from his title, your contingency will force him to reveal what is bad about his access. Disclosure does not fix the access problem and may not obligate the seller to do anything. Disclosure increases your knowledge, which increases your security to the extent that you can cost out the price of a remedy. A property discounted by title exceptions should be discounted in price. A disclosure requirement should be coupled with a provision that allows a buyer to void or amend his offer if the results of the disclosure are unacceptable.

Fiduciaries, such as trustees and executors, and corporations, often use special warranty deeds, because they can't make promises about what occurred before they came into temporary possession. Corporations use them to limit their liability. You can easily check to see whether the title going into the seller was a general or special warranty deed.

If it was a general going in and a special coming to you, you are fairly well covered, as long as you're careful about researching what happened during the seller's ownership. If the seller can't give you a reasonable explanation of why he's conveying with a special warranty deed, I'd look for a problem in the title and/or on the ground. The buyer may be able to purchase **title insurance** to supplement a special warranty deed.

A **bargain-and-sale deed** gives the buyer no express covenants or warranties against liens and encumbrances. This instrument might also be referred to as a **statutory warranty deed**. Such a deed implies that the seller holds title and possession, but it's an implication not a warranty. These deeds usually use the phrase "grant, bargain and sell" or "grant and release." They can be beefed up to a special warranty deed if the seller (grantor) adds a **covenant against grantor's acts**. Such deeds are in common use, but must be thoroughly researched because they put the buyer at risk. Be very careful with them. See if you can get title insurance. When a seller offers a bargain-and-sale deed, a buyer can counter by asking to append to the contract and deed all covenants that are typically included in a general warranty deed. This puts the seller on the spot, if only to get him to disclose what a buyer might need to know. And after all, the buyer is asking for nothing more than normal guarantees when he asks for a general warranty deed.

A **quitclaim deed** conveys whatever interest the seller possesses in the title, such as that interest is. The seller is not promising either that he owns the property or that he is conveying title to the buyer. The buyer is getting none of the covenants. Don't buy property with a quitclaim unless you and your lawyer are absolutely certain about what you are doing and why.

To prevent a seller from unloading a problem property onto an unsuspecting buyer, include the following sentence in your purchase contract: **"Seller shall convey marketable title to this property in fee simple with a General Warranty Deed."** If the seller balks at meeting these three ordinary standards, make sure that he explains why he can't. Then make sure that you and your lawyer can live with a purchase that lacks them.

2. A second trap involves two, two-letter words, **"As is."**

When the seller advertises his property "as is," what does it mean? My guess is that most *sellers* believe that "as is" means, "Buyer Beware!"—that the seller is selling what a buyer can see as well as all problems, visible or not.

I bought an "as is" 1957 tractor, in the late 1980s, which I still have. Its transmission was worn in third gear such that it slipped into neutral when the tractor was going down a hill with a load behind. The seller made no mention of this defect, and I did not discover it when I took a modest test drive around his flat barnyard. About a week after I had the tractor home, I was using it to haul two five year olds in my cart down a sloping pasture when third gear popped out. The tractor's brakes turned out to be not so good as well. We rode the runaway at increasing speed onto the flat, turning just in front of a fence line and road ditch. The kids thought I was a swell daddy for bouncing them around like exploding popcorn. My "as is" tractor brought three of us to within a few feet of death or serious injury.

Many buyers also believe that "as is" means "Buyer Beware!" and take your chances. Real-estate columnist Robert J. Bruss, however, correctly pointed out that while "as is" means the seller will not remedy any defect or condition, he still has the obligation to disclose any defect or problem known to him. (Robert J. Bruss, "'As is': Is seller absolved?," Richmond Times-Dispatch, January 26, 2003; www.bobbruss.com, or http://inman.com/bruss/. Informative reports on buying and selling property are available through Mr. Bruss's web site.)

The "as is" country property I've seen generally involves land with a handyman's special house or land with a hidden defect, such as problematic access. The "as is" condition is rarely identified. You may think the "as is" applies to the wretched farm house when the seller is really trying to unload a farm whose water system goes dry for three months every summer. The wretched farm house distracts you from looking deeper into the property. If you don't insist on the seller disclosing all defects and problems, he may not.

Auctioneers often sell rural land, "**as is, where is**," a phrase that certainly provides a buyer with another layer of warning, though I doubt it adds or subtracts anything legally from the seller's duty to disclose specific problems. When I've sold land "as is, where is" through an auction, what I meant to communicate was that I would put no money into improving the property for the buyer's benefit and would accept no contingencies on the sale.

Protect yourself from as-is sellers with a **disclosure contingency**:

> **Buyer's offer is contingent on Seller disclosing all latent or material defects in the property, its improvements, title and legal status that would in any way adversely impact or otherwise limit Buyer's possession, use and enjoyment of all of the Property and all of its rights and interests.**

> **Defects shall be construed to include items needing repair or replacement and conditions (including, but not limited to, physical, environmental, structural and legal), both visible and invisible.**

This language does not ask the seller to fix anything, only to disclose everything. Don't be bashful about asking in writing what "as is" specifically covers. Look the seller in the eye and say: "Before I put an offer in front of you, I want you to tell me in writing everything that needs to be repaired or replaced, everything that I need to do to make the place safe and in compliance, everything that might lead to a dispute between you and me or between me and my new neighbors." A seller who might feel alright about concealing something from you in the contract's legal briars might be incapable of lying to your face. Give the "as is" seller a chance to tell you the truth.

Most disclosure language appears to me to be limited to "*latent* material defects," which would probably be construed as significant items that are concealed, and possibly defects that are in the process of becoming either significant or manifest. I would have disclosure cover all defects, both latent (concealed) and visible, both latent (not yet at the point of a full-blown problem) and manifested as significant. Inexperienced buyers cannot be counted on to understand the visible, manifest defects their eyes see. Put the burden of explanation on the seller and don't assume that you can interpret what can be seen.

3. Seller owns less than 100 percent of property. Buyers assume that sellers own 100 percent of the property they're selling. Sometimes, this assumption is wrong. Sometimes, sellers don't know that they don't own all of their property, and sometimes they do.

What I mean by 100 percent ownership in this example is 100 percent of all of what might be called "shares" in the seller's property. If you think of the seller's property as a stock company with 100 shares, the seller should own 100 percent of every share, and the company should own 100 percent of all of the property's assets.

With real estate, those 100 shares may have been divided among several owners, often through several generations of inheritance where property is split equally among each generation of children. Your seller may own 95 shares, with the other five being divided equally among ten individuals, each of whom owns one-half of one share. A buyer does not want to pay a seller for 100 shares and wind up with 95 and ten partners. A title search is supposed to identify such situations.

In real estate, "shares" are referred to as "**ownership interests**." Mr. Smith may own a $1/8^{th}$ interest in your target property while the other $7/8^{ths}$ belong to the seller, his brother. Such divisions are enlivened when Mr. Smith's $1/8^{th}$ is divided equally and passed to his five children, each of whom now owns $1/5^{th}$ of a $1/8^{th}$ interest. Generational equity begets difficulties. When a lawyer finds it impossible to track down or clear up the last fractional interest, he will usually recommend a **suit to quiet title**, which asks all owners to show the court the nature of their claims.

If you find a seller who says he's willing to convey all of the **"Seller's rights, title and interest in the property**," proceed with caution. A buyer does not want that phrase used in the purchase contract or in the deed, because it can be construed to mean 100 percent of *whatever* rights, title and interest the seller has, which may be less than 100 percent. If no covenant or warranty language follows this sentence, the seller is providing title without any promise to the buyer that the title is good. Such an instrument—lacking warranties against liens and encumbrances, and clear title—is a **bargain-and-sale deed**. A deed of this type can, however, carry such warranties.

I have seen the predicament of **fractional ownership** occur in two ways. First, I've found a seller who simply did not know that he did not own all $100/100^{ths}$ interests. This happens with property that has been divided amongst several generations of children. This inheritance pattern is common in rural areas where land was a family's chief estate asset, and parents in each generation wanted to be fair to each of their children.

The second set of circumstances is deliberately deceptive: the seller knows he does not own 100 percent but does not disclose this to the buyer. If the buyer's lawyer finds the problem in his title search, the seller may be pushed into acquiring the outstanding interest, or the sale proceeds can be proportionately divided if the sellers agree to that, or the buyer's deal falls apart.

If the buyer completes the purchase without becoming aware of the seller's short ownership, one of several things may follow. Nothing: the minority interest never turns into a problem or claim. Or, the owner of the fractional interest appears with a demand for money from the new owner, i.e., the buyer. The new owner may be able to go back against the seller for compensation. If the fractional owner and the new owner (buyer) can't resolve the dispute, either can bring a **partition suit**, in which the court orders a public sale with the net proceeds divided proportionally. Nothing prevents one or the other owner from buying the property in full through this means. Anyone else, however, can bid more, leaving both factional owners without the property but dividing the net proceeds. Or, a **suit (action) to quiet title** can be brought by either claimant to ownership, which forces a judge to decide who owns what. Suits to quiet title are often used where a gap is found in the chain of title, or a **cloud on the title** arises from an easement, occupation (squatting) or **dower's rights** (a widow's legal interest in the real property of her deceased husband). Such suits are also used to establish the legitimacy of everyone's ownership claims, and lack thereof. Finally, a deal can be negotiated among the parties where one of the owners buys a **quitclaim deed** from the other(s), in which the latter conveys whatever his interest may be in the property.

Where a legitimate ownership interest materializes, the new owner/buyer can initiate action against the seller who can be asked to make up for damages the buyer suffers from the seller's conveyance of a defective title. This action is based on the seller having promised that he was conveying a **marketable title** and **general warranty deed** to the buyer. The buyer might also look at the malpractice insurance of the lawyer who performed his title search. The new owner's title insurance may fix some, if not all, of the problem. A good chance exists that this buyer ends up in a courtroom.

The **concept of title** in real estate covers both the bundle of rights in a property and the idea of ownership. A buyer's purchase offer that includes the words **fee simple** and **marketable title** should protect a buyer on both counts. Marketable title should be construed as meaning title to **all interests** in the property, but a seller may argue that the buyer knew he was only buying title to 17/18^{ths} interests (95 of the 100 shares) with the remaining 1/18th unaccounted for.

Prevention is cheaper than cure. Prevent a seller from hiding behind his statement of what he believed the buyer understood by including language in your contract that specifically requires the seller to convey **all interests in all the rights and assets in all the property** that are being conveyed.

> **Seller shall convey to Buyer at closing all ownership interests in all rights and assets in the entire Property, consisting of ___ acres. Seller shall convey the Property in fee simple with marketable title and a General Warranty Deed, subject only to limitations of record.**

> **If Seller is unable to warranty and convey anything less than a full and complete set of rights, interests, title and ownership in the Property, Buyer may void this Contract without penalty, and his deposit shall be returned in full within five business days.**

> **Seller is liable for all costs and damages borne by Buyer in the event that Seller fails to comply fully with these obligations.**

If you want to flush out a seller whom you suspect of knowingly trying to sell you less than 100 percent ownership interest or property with less than 100 percent of all rights and assets include language like this. See Chapter 26 for additional discussion.

These short-ownership situations are not uncommon. I know of one experienced buyer who offered $2,000 per acre for an 80-acre farm that he could see was "covered up with timber" properly estimated at about $400,000. A great buy—except that a good portion of the best timber was on an adjoining property despite a fence line that made it appear that it was included in the 80 acres. After hiring a consulting forester I recommended, the timber value on the seller's 80 acres was established at $159,000. And, then the seller, it turned out, only owned 6/7th of the ownership interests though she let the buyer assume he was buying all interests in the property. A good lawyer—my wife—discovered the orphan 1/7th interest in the title search, which was held by an individual in another state who had no idea that he owned an interest in West Virginia property.

Some years ago, I bought a farm from 17 fractious heirs, divided into three groups—siblings of the decedent and children of the decedent's two families. (The decedent had divorced his first wife, married his secretary and had a second family. The heirs of the first family did not care for those of the second, in part because the property of the second-family heirs had come to their father from the mother of the first family's heirs.) One sibling considered himself first among equals, and he was angry about selling the property and the share-and-share-alike division his brother-in-law's will set forth.

In such a situation, the sellers are supposed to agree on a sale price before putting their property on the market. One person—the executor of the estate or a lawyer representing all heirs—should be authorized to handle the sale and negotiate on behalf of the group. The typical procedure is that all ownership interests need to agree for the buyer's offer to be accepted. Occasionally, the group decides to allow their agent to negotiate and bind them all, as long as a predetermined minimum price is met.

Buyers need to be wary in such circumstances. I've seen the "**hold-out seller**" appear, the one who wants more money than all the others. Sometimes this is genuine, but often it's not. The seller's agent keeps blaming each new bite out of your wallet on this "unreasonable" soul who is impossible to please. My advice is: don't play the game. Make your best dollar offer, and once the agent informally accepts it, don't budge. The exception would be if you made a low-ball offer and want the property. Then expect a lot of offer-counter-offer bargaining.

Since the 17 heirs were in a precarious internal balance, I assumed that I would have to pay the minimum price they had established. I tried an offer below that, which did not fly. I wanted to make the deal as quickly as I could before stronger money showed up. Dividing these sellers was not in my interest. The time for a buyer to try to divide sellers is when their set price is unrealistically high. I paid the minimum price and have always considered myself fortunate.

On a different tract, I made a full-price offer to the family member who represented herself to me as the designated agent of nine equal interests, all of whom, she said, were agreed on a price of $1,000 per acre. I scoped the property and determined that it was under-priced. So I offered her the full price for all the shares. After placing her signature—representing her share—on my purchase contract, she informed me that one of the other heirs had just bought six of the remaining interests, leaving one outstanding. Interesting news, I thought, given that I had been told that she was representing all interests. My offer per share was about half again better than what the inside buyer had paid. I found myself with two shares under contract and a simple purchase growing more and more tangled.

The insider filed a lawsuit against my two sellers that challenged the validity of their ownership. I thought this far-fetched, since he had acknowledged their ownership when he tried to buy both shares. It struck me as legal bullying. He had money to scare them, and they didn't have enough money to not be scared. Although my contract said the sellers would defend their title, I decided to pay a lawyer to defend their ownership because they were ready to cave. I stayed in this test of wills, because I knew the real value of the property. At worst, there would be a partition suit, from which I would make a profit. I didn't see a downside; my wife thought I was nuts. The insider's suit was so weak that he eventually abandoned it. His lawyer then threatened me with a partition suit. I felt like B'rer Rabbit being threatened with the briar patch. "Fine with me," I said, "but before your client shoots himself in the foot, you might want to know what I think the property is worth." "Oh, we know all about it," he sneered. "Well, I'll just send you some information anyway and maybe we can work something out." I then faxed my timber cruise and other materials, showing the timber alone was worth twice the selling price that I had agreed to. The blowhard lawyer shut up, and the insider soon purchased my shares after I tacked on a profit. I was willing to accept the results of a partition suit, because I knew that many stumpage buyers would be interested in buying this land with its timber. But I was also willing to keep things simple and make a deal. It made sense to me to give the insider a shot at solving his problem, which, to his credit, he did.

Estate land that is gummy with intra-family squabbles may have to be approached as a problem in dysfunctional-family analysis. Fifty-year-old grievances that began when one heir was eight and another 12 often explain why the former eight year old now refuses to do the sensible thing recommended by the former 12 year old. A buyer can make the situation worse by throwing money at the sellers if resolving one holdout creates demands for more money from all the others. If the buyer can extend time to the sellers to sort it out among themselves, old patterns of dominance may once again prevail. Non-involved agents of the sellers—executor or lawyer—may be helpful. If your lawyer can work with the seller's lawyer that may prove to be the key. Try not to get in the middle of these fights and try not to gang up on the hold out. You want to acquire this property by being the solution to the sellers' chaos, not its perpetrator.

4. Acreage Tricks. I've discussed acreage booby-traps in other chapters. Apart from errors in deeds and on the ground that are unknown to the seller, there are sellers who try to take advantage of unwary buyers. There is, for example, the seller who uses a tax map to establish the acreage he's selling when he knows the tax-map acreage exceeds what his title will convey. I've also cautioned about the perils of buying acreage, **more or less**.

A similar caution should be issued regarding rural acreage to be conveyed "**in gross**," which is "more or less" in bigger clothes. "In gross" means the buyer is not buying a certain number of acres and is not making an offer of so many dollars per acre. Rather, the buyer is essentially buying what the seller has as an entirety whatever that may be. Some lawyers will argue that the buyer is better protected with "in gross" language than I have represented it. But I don't think most courts will provide a remedy to a buyer who buys 100 acres in gross, which is then surveyed after the sale at 95 acres, even if the deed states 100 acres.

A buyer will not persuade a seller to delete acreage "in gross" from sale documents when the seller is knowingly including the phrase to disguise an acreage shortage. Consider the phrase a flag to have a surveyor run the deed's calls through his mapping program.

5. Jacking Up the Price. Buyers assume that once a seller either advertises his asking price as a FSBO or establishes his listing price with a broker, that a cap has been placed on the property's price. Not so. A FSBO can reject a full-price offer at will and without explanation. When a FSBO senses a buyer is able and willing to pay more, the buyer may find even a full-price offer countered with a higher asking price. Similarly, a seller is not required by law to sell for the asking price he's set through a broker. A seller would, however, be obliged to pay the broker's commission on a full-price offer free of all contingencies. Since few full-price offers are free of all contingencies, sellers can reject most offers without penalty. I've seen prices increased by local sellers against non-local buyers who they viewed as "rich." I've never seen it used by a local seller against a local buyer.

If you sense that a seller is gaming you, stop playing. Restate your offer and without verbalizing the thought, it becomes a take-it-or-leave-it proposition.

If you are genuinely "rich" and want the property, pay the extorted difference and laugh it off over drinks. But the better tactic is to have your local lawyer negotiate on your behalf while you remain anonymous until closing.

As a general rule, I would advise buyers to stick with any offer, full-price or less, they feel is justified by the property's assets and their own finances. Price negotiations are usually controlled by buyers, even though it seldom feels that way. Be disciplined; don't offer more than it's worth and don't pay more than you can afford.

A genuinely slimy trick is for the seller to low-ball his asking price in a classic bait-and-switch move. The buyer invests emotionally and financially in preparing an offer only to have the seller bump the price up a couple of times. Since the law views an advertised price only as an invitation to buyers, you can't hold the seller to it. These sellers hope that a low-ball asking price will lure buyers into a bidding war where the switch is made as the bait is forgotten. A favorite way of doing this is for the seller to tell the buyer that he, the seller, would gladly sell for the original asking price but his spouse, or kids, or siblings, or widowed mother, or lonely Bassett Hound just can't let the place go for that little.

A seller playing low ball may be truly desperate to sell or, more commonly, just the opposite. The desperate tend to price high and come down due to the weight of their circumstances. Professional land buyers always hope to find a desperate seller who must sell fast and cheap.

A variation on the low-ball asking price is the seller who announces an increase in the asking price soon after the buyer arrives on the property. I've had this trick pulled on me twice, in both cases by wealthy sellers. I've also seen it used when the seller's real-estate agent was writing up my purchase offer after the seller and I had agreed on a price over the phone. The best counter is to stop dead in your tracks. Announce that you're going out for coffee and you'll stop by on your way home to see whether the seller has returned to the agreed price. If the seller doesn't budge, go home. Your phone is likely to ring in a few days. If you split this difference, however, the seller has won something extra from your wallet that he doesn't deserve. This lesson cost me $3,500; my professor was a grandmother, wearing an apron and brogans.

In one case, a family—a father and two sons—seemed to be selling about 40,000 acres of hardwood timberland and a sawmill. As my client and I stepped out of our car, their broker whispered to me that the price of the mill had just been raised by about $3 million. Once inside, I learned that the company owned about 12,500 acres, not 40,000 plus. The non-owned acres were subject to long-term timber leases that landowners could cancel. And then the company's forester handed me a cruise of the 12,500 acres using a tree scale that inflated the merchantable volume by about 25 percent, which he admitted when I helpfully pointed it out.

I've seen a country seller pull something out of the deal at the last minute to sweeten his own pot. This seller had about 95 percent of the sale property on one side of a road. He tried to keep the other five percent after a price agreement was reached. I've also seen sellers try to reserve a last-minute interest in timber, minerals and rental income.

In hot real-estate markets, desperate buyers will sometimes submit offers that exceed the asking price or allow themselves to be run up in price. The fortunate seller benefits from too many buyers pursuing too few properties. In the country, I've seen this market principle materialize more commonly as several buyers pursuing a particular property that has some especially value combination of assets which makes it desirable. It's the same principle that allows the owner of a certain 1955 Chevy with certain assets to price his car twice that of other 55s. Since any particular parcel of country property is almost always a discretionary purchase as either an investment or a second home, don't step onto the hot-market escalator of rising offers. Suitable alternatives are almost always available; they just have to be found.

Low interest rates tend to inflate asking prices. Buyers need to keep in mind that buying an over-priced property with a low interest rate is not generally a good deal. If a choice has to be made, I think it's better to buy a discounted property at a high interest rate and then refinance when rates drop.

6. Seller does not live up to contract. I divide this familiar situation into two groups: chips and big deals.

Chips. Some wrongs—and all insignificant ones—are best forgotten. My wife says I preach this better than I practice it. She's right, of course. I chew on slights that are decades old. But I know that chips—when everything is said and done—are just chips. Chips should not hang a good buy. Here are a few examples.

It is common practice for property taxes to be **pro rated** between buyer and seller for the sale year, using the date of closing as the dividing line for each share. I had a contract with a seller that provided for proration of property taxes in this fashion. The seller signed the purchase offer. At closing, the seller did not appear. His lawyer—the settlement agent—informed me the seller had decided that I should pay all the property tax for the year. I confidently pointed out to him the language in the contract providing for proration and even used my index finger to point to the seller's signature. The lawyer shrugged. A stick up! Fortunately, not every molecule in my brain was seeing red. The large property at stake was being bought at an excellent price, and the tax in question amounted to a couple of hundred dollars. The seller was just this kind of guy—small smart, big dumb. I could have insisted that the settlement agent apply the contract's terms exactly as they were written. Had he refused, I knew that I would win somewhere down the legal line. But the principle involved in winning this chip wasn't worth the expense and aggravation. More important, fussing would have jeopardized the entire deal. Having spent inordinate amounts of my life making grand stands for great principles over small matters, I considered benign indifference a matter of maturing wisdom. I smiled as I thought, a chip is, after all, a chip. I'm not mature enough to have forgotten about it in case you haven't noticed.

In another case, a seller had agreed to not cut any timber on his property, beginning on the date on which the contract came into effect. During the next few months, the seller's tenant on the property continued to cut trees for firewood despite being asked—then told—not to. The tenant knew he was expected to leave a few days before closing. He had stopped paying rent seven or eight months earlier and his firewood cutting was, I guessed, a juvenile show of thumbing his nose and saving face. Not much money was being burned in the tenant's woodstoves, so I pressed it just a bit. The non-rent-paying tenant accused me of depriving him and his family of winter heat. That he was a logger and could cut firewood on the job didn't count on his abacus. So I stopped after I realized that he needed to show public defiance more than I needed to win the point.

One chip that often disappears is an item of the seller's personal property the buyer expects to remain and for which he has paid when buying the property. Washers and dryers, barn refrigerators, materials—such things have a way of not being there when the buyer takes possession. Obviously, the buyer is in an unassailable position if a specific item is written into the purchase contract as conveying with the property sale. A wronged buyer can walk away from the purchase over a missing chip, but that rarely makes sense. (Sellers understand this.) I have found sellers saying that they did not understand that the item was included in the sale despite it being specifically written into the contract. Often, the choice facing the buyer is between being taken advantage of a little and being seen by the community as a legal hammer bringing in lawyers to bang the last penny out of a local seller. Sellers offer last-minute quibbles over chips when the buyer is getting a good deal on the property, and the sellers can't do much to rebalance that. A seller getting the worst of a deal feels justified in evening the score, psychologically.

The cost and time of going to court to be compensated for a chip are never worth it.

And some chips make for funny stories. Like the house purchase I once made where the seller took every light bulb.

Where the buyer has not specified in the contract those items of the seller's personal property that he has purchased, some may vanish. The seller has a powerful incentive to throw in deal sweeteners when his land is over-priced, and that incentive disappears once the contract is carried out. I've found four tactics that discourage disappearance: 1) write each item into the contract using language that describes location, amount and condition; 2) take a photo of each item and attach it to the contract, 3) take dated notes of when and where buyer and seller agreed on each item; and 4) tag the item: "Conveys to Buyer." I've seen sellers substitute bad lumber for good lumber, non-working appliances for functioning ones and cheap stuff for good stuff. I've also seen paid-for tools, farm equipment, stored hay and consumables (paint, fencing materials) wander off prior to possession. It's almost impossible to win these disputes unless you've documented each item with one or more of these four prevention measures.

It's often convenient for a non-resident buyer, particularly one who lives at a distance, to store stuff on the seller's property prior to closing. Most of the time this works without a problem. However, the buyer must realize that the seller bears no liability if the buyer's items disappear. A vacant property is an invitation to light-fingered passersby. And then there are the phantoms. A seller told me that two small antiques I had purchased and left in an obscure closet with her permission were stolen from her empty house just before closing. No neighbor could remember a house burglary ever happening in this community, certainly not in houses that have just been emptied and cleaned. No, I was told when I asked, the seller had not filed a police report. I didn't miss the put-upon air at the effrontery of my question. After a while, I blamed myself for having left them in the seller's house. Too much temptation.

I think the best rule is: don't tempt sellers with chips, theirs or yours.

Far more common than the once-in-a-blue-moon-theft story, is the failure of the seller's memory regarding your chip: "Gee, I just don't remember that as being part of our agreement." If you've done one or more of the four preventive actions, you can refresh his recollection. If he sticks to his failed memory in the face of your proof, you may have to concede the chip—but make sure to get one back in exactly the same way. Failed memory can afflict both seller and buyer.

A buyer might be interested in some of the seller's farm goods, which can be anything from a butchered hog in your new freezer to 300 bales of alfalfa in the barn. Livestock is personal, not real, property, so farm animals do not convey in a farm purchase, unless specifically included in your contract. Cattle don't run with the land.

Crops growing in the field are considered real property. Harvested crops stored on the seller's farm are his personal property and will not convey unless specifically included in the contract. Cut crops in the field—like recently mowed hay—is personal, not real property; the seller owns it. Standing timber will convey as real property, but downed timber and wood piles will not because they are personal property. I've known a seller to cut several valuable trees during escrow, so that they became his personal property…and ran with him, not the land. The buyer could not prove that these trees were cut after his purchase contract was in effect. This theft amounted to about $3,500.

Big Deals. If you think through the issues and write your purchase contract properly, the seller should not be able to snooker you out of any Big Deal.

When a big event has occurred in the escrow period between when your purchase contract came into effect and closing—fire destroys a barn, a vicious tree-killing insect takes up residence in the timber, an access problem blindsides you—you can delay closing by mutual consent. The seller should always bear the risk of loss from natural disaster and fire during the escrow period. Where the barn is insured, your goal would be to get the amount of money needed to replace it. If the insurance money is short of that amount, ask the seller to either make up the difference or lower his selling price. If you place a contract on a wooded tract in early April before the leaves are out and find that by the end of August when you are scheduled to close that something is defoliating and killing all the oaks, you should not be expected to perform since the seller is not delivering the property in essentially the same condition, less normal wear and tear, as it existed when the contract came into effect. The buyer should not bear this cost.

Often, the best way to handle last-minute problems of this sort is for the seller to put a portion of the sale revenue he gets from the buyer in a special **escrow account** until the matter is sorted out. The buyer's lawyer should hold this money in his trust account. If the seller makes the problem go away, he gets the escrowed cash. An escrow can compensate the buyer for the changed condition in the property. Depending on the final disbursement of the seller's escrowed money, recorded documents and tax computations may require amendment. Escrowing money from the sale can be used on both chips—if you really insist—and big deals, assuming the seller agrees. It lets the deal go through and provides an incentive for the seller to resolve the dispute. In the worst circumstances—say, the charming *ante-bellum* house that you had planned to convert into a B&B burns to the ground—you can void the contract, because the lost item is essentially irreplaceable. Your contract allows you to do this because it provides that the condition of the property should be the same on the day of closing as it was on the day the contract took effect.

Buyers face a difficult choice if some Big Deal disappears before closing. If the deal favors the buyer, I might go ahead with the closing after giving notice that you reserve your right to seek a remedy for the missing value. With your sales money in his pocket, the seller may see the logic of buying his way out of a scrape of his own making. Some Big Deals are obviously deal-killers.

7. Backup Contracts and Piggy-back Buyers. When a buyer has a purchase contract in place, he should be concerned when the seller accepts a backup contract for more money and/or better terms. This seller now has an incentive to find a way to scrub your contract. To avoid a buyer-initiated lawsuit, a seller has to be very crafty in contriving to entice the buyer in first position to void his contract.

I've never seen a contract where a seller inserts a contingency that allows him—the seller—to void the deal in the event that a better offer comes along. But I don't see anything "illegal" about a buyer and a seller agreeing to such language.

I have seen a seller make it difficult for a buyer to perform after he had a better offer come in. The seller may, for example, not provide information to the buyer, or he may create difficulties for the buyer in gaining access to the property. If a buyer in these circumstances fails to comply with every deadline and procedure in the contract, the seller can use technical failure to justify voiding the contract. I have not seen a case where a seller arranges for an accomplice to submit a bogus backup contract as leverage for getting the buyer to increase his already accepted offer. Anything, of course, is possible. The buyer protects his contract through full and timely compliance, and then performance. A buyer should work closely with his lawyer to make sure all deadlines and other contract breakers are satisfied.

I had a client some years ago who submitted a bid on more than 10,000 acres of timberland. The seller inserted language into the contract that allowed the seller to pay for an appraisal after the contract came into effect. If the appraisal came in at some percentage higher than the contract price, the seller reserved the right to void the purchase. I advised my client against agreeing to this provision, because it was such an obvious ploy—it was so obvious that even I could figure it out—to boost the sales price once the buyer was invested in the purchase. The appraisal, paid for by the seller, came in above the cap and the seller bumped up the buyer by almost $1 million. I advised my client to walk away. He didn't, and he lost money in the deal. Don't sign a contract with a seller-appraisal contingency.

I once faced a piggy-back-buyer situation. A large farm was being sold through sealed bids with a published minimum bid. A fellow I knew had observed me scoping the property. A week or so before the bids were due he called to scope me. His unstated thought was: If Seltzer is going to bid on it, I could bid $5,000 more and get a good deal. I certainly did not want to help my competition. Nor did I want to share the fruits of my year-long research with him. Since he had more money that I had, I knew he would be a stronger buyer. I didn't want to make him angry—leading to a bid; and I didn't want to motivate him to submit a bid by sharing the real value of the property that I had discovered. Since he trusted my research and judgment, he was playing with the idea of riding my expressed interest against me. He would know I was concealing the truth had I told him the property was without virtues. My best defense I figured was to try to freeze him in place by feeding him some good news, some bad and a lot of uncertainties. He never submitted a bid.

It is not uncommon for buyers to run into each other as they look at a property. Nor is it uncommon for buyers to determine what each other might know. If you tell another buyer something useful about the target property, you should assume that he will use it for his own interests. It's best to be cordial and as selectively informative as a President's press secretary.

There's one situation where you can profit from finding another buyer. If you've scoped a property and determined it's not for you, it might be suitable for someone you know. In this case, it's fair for you to ask for a one or two percent **finder's fee** from that buyer for introducing him to the property and giving him the benefit of your research. The fee is payable only if your buyer purchases the property. The buyer owes you the fee because he has benefited from the information that you gave him and upon which he acted. This legal principle is called, ***quantum meruit***. Acting as a finder is not acting as a real-estate broker, for which you need to be licensed. It's always best to draw up a finder's fee agreement between you and your buyer.

8. Access Maintenance. The seller has divided his property into six, 100-acre parcels, configured side by side in a line. The seller has constructed a so-so, gravel road about 12-feet wide on the longest boundary line of his original 600 acres. Access roads to each lot come off this common road, which ends at Lot Six, the one you want to buy. The seller has recorded a right-of-way (ROW) easement that gives each Lot owner access to the common access road, which, the easement states, 'the Lot Owners shall maintain." The access road is 6,000-feet long from the gate on the public road to the back boundary of the property's 600 acres where you—Lot Six—want your driveway, because that places it as far from Lot Five as possible. Everyone agrees that the cost of the improvements is $6,000.

Lot Six—you—are buying a mess, left there intentionally by the seller. Your first question involves upgrading the common road to 16 feet wide and improving its quality. Let's assume that all six lot owners agree on the benefits of upgrading and improving. Should the $6,000 estimated cost be split six ways equally? No, no, says Lot One; I only use 200 feet of the common road before my driveway turns off. I should pay $200, which represents my portion of the common road, figured on $1 of cost per linear foot. While I have 1,000 feet of frontage on the common access road, I only use 200 feet for ingress and egress. Lot Six uses all 6,000 feet for access," Lot One points out, "so maybe he should pay $6,000."

Different formulas are available to allocate these costs fairly. The seller, foreseeing the squabbling arising from six lot owners, has bailed on a solution in favor of letting the lots slug it out after he's gone. Each lot buyer would be treated better if the seller had devised an equitable formula that is disclosed when buyers visit the property.

Here is the formula I suggest:

The first $1,000 for the first 1,000 feet should be split equally among the six lot owners.

The second $1,000 for the second 1,000 feet should be split equally among Lots Two through Six.

The third $1,000 for the third 1,000 feet should be split equally among Lots Three through Six.

The fourth $1,000 for the fourth 1,000 feet should be split equally among Lots Four through Six.

The fifth $1,000 for the fifth 1,000 feet should be split equally between Lots Five and Six.

The final $1,000 for the final 1,000 feet should be paid exclusively by Lot Six.

The actual money would look like this for Lot Six's share:

1/6 of 1st $1,000 for Lot One's 1000 feet =	$ 166.67
1/5 of 2nd $1,000 for Lot Two's 1,000 feet =	200.00
1/4 of 3rd $1,000 for Lot Three's 1,000 feet =	250.00
1/3 of 4th $1,000 for Lot Four's 1,000 feet =	333.33
1/2 of 5th $1,000 for Lot Five's 1,000 feet =	500.00
1/1 of 6th $1,000 for Lot Six's 1,000 feet =	1,000.00
Lot Six Total	$2,450.00 (41%)

Lot Six is paying for remoteness. The danger to everyone in the seller's language is that it fails to specify how costs are to be allocated and maintenance decisions made. I have seen the absence of a maintenance formula spark a war among neighbors sharing a homeowners'-association road.

9. **Seller Provides False Information**. You arrange a face-to-face meeting with the seller prior to submitting an offer. During the pleasant conversation in the seller's living room, you ask the following questions:

Are there any disputed boundaries? Answer: No.

Is there an approved septic system? Answer: Yes.

Have you promised anything off the property that would otherwise convey? Answer: No.

Does the roof leak? Answer: No.

Does the flat bottomland next to the river ever flood? Answer: Not that I recollect.

Is the spring water to the house safe to drink? Answer: I've been drinking it all my life.

The seller has answered each of these questions falsely, knowingly. Can you win in court on any of them? Probably not. Let's look at each one.

Approved septic system. The seller has lied. The seller has nothing more than a four-inch-diameter pipe that empties into a large covered hole in porous ground. This cesspool was installed in the 1940s before the county required septic systems and permits. It is not an approved septic system. It is one step up from a straight pipe into the creek. While its use may be grandfathered, if you want to add a bath or a bedroom, the county health department is likely to require installing a real septic system that complies with current standards. Is the seller liable for the cost of the new system? Can you prove that he lied, and, even so, is that enough to win? The seller's defense is that he thought he was telling you the truth inasmuch as the party that he bought the farm from ten years ago told him that the house had an approved septic system. "Never had a bit of trouble with it," he said, "so I never had reason to check about approval." The cesspool functions well, and there's no record of it ever being serviced by a local plumber or septic-cleaning service.

I doubt that you can prove that the seller committed fraud, that is, a deliberate lie. Do you win the cost of an approved septic system for your extra bedroom or new bathroom? That's doubtful. As long as you keep within the grandfathered use, the grandfathered system probably won't be challenged even though it won't meet current standards. (There will be exceptions to that generalization.) Once you undertake an upgrade, like a new bedroom or a bathroom, then it's your responsibility to upgrade the support systems. Even if the seller lied when he told you that he thought the house had an approved system, the mistake doesn't harm you if you continue the use of the property as it was when you took possession. Further, if the seller erred honestly, your pre-purchase due diligence (scoping) should have included a visit to the county office where septic permits and applications are kept. Your negligence and laziness, the seller will argue, explains why you didn't find out the truth. Cost of installing a new system: $3,500 to $25,000, depending on soil conditions and local standards. You might get a judge to split the cost of a new system if you can prove beyond a reasonable doubt that the seller knew of the condition and intentionally misled you. But that is very difficult to prove.

You could have inserted a **septic-system contingency** in your purchase offer that gives you the right to inspect the system and void your offer if the findings are unsatisfactory.

Promise Off the Property. The seller's barn is serviced by a ten-ton-capacity metal, silo-style grain tank and an electric auger unloader. The tank's legs are bolted to four 55-gallon, concrete-filled drums that are completely buried in the ground. The unloader is a 100-foot-long pipe that encloses a motor-driven auger. It has drop tubes every 20 feet inside the barn for unloading the grain, which drops into feed trays. The pipe is attached to the exposed roof rafters using metal strapping and heavy bolts. The tank and auger were used to feed corn to cattle.

You don't think you'll use this equipment, because you are planning to convert the seller's Vermont dairy farm to an organic rose garden, from which you plan to sell only the inner petals of the rare albinos. You've done no marketing study, but you're sure this idea will make you as rich as Bill Gates, because you like roses. You see no use for the tank and unloader. You have no interest in climbing the tank's ladder and looking inside.

You don't do a walk-through inspection prior to closing. Upon visiting your new farm the day after closing you notice the tank and auger are missing. You make inquiries and determine to your surprise that a neighbor in the dairy business will pay you $1,800 for "that rig if you get it back in decent shape." Eighteen hundred dollars will get you started in the albino rose business.

You also learn that the seller says he had promised this equipment to his cousin who lives about 250 miles away.

The seller's tank and unloader are considered real, rather than personal, property because they are physically attached to the land and building respectively. All real property should convey, unless specifically excluded; all personal property doesn't convey unless specifically included.

Of course, the seller failed to exclude this real property from his sale to you. The cousin now claims that it had always been *his* tank and *his* auger, which he had simply loaned to the seller some years ago. The cousin has no receipt of purchase, but does threaten to produce his pellucid 112-year-old grandfather who will recall the entire arrangement as if it were still 1960 when the deal, he says, was struck; the cousin will serve as translator because the grandfather had a stroke in the 1970s and has been unable to speak or write since. The seller, his recollections now refreshed, confirms the cousin's story. The seller, further, says he always told you the truth: that nothing that belonged to him had been promised off the purchase prior to your possession. (The seller should be splitting hairs at Yale Law School not feeding cows.)

The grain tank is considered real property, because, like a house, its foundation becomes part of the ground. The unloader was personal property until the seller attached it to the barn, which made it part of the barn, an improvement. At that point, it became a **fixture**, that is, personal property that has become real property by becoming permanently attached to real property. Both items should convey. While both can be detached, the nature of their attachment is far more permanent than temporary. Nonetheless, the seller's story about this equipment being loaned to him by the cousin is probably good enough to get a local judge to go along with it, even without the receipts or tax returns that might verify their claim.

You protect yourself from these shenanigans by being both very broad and very specific in your purchase contract concerning what you are buying. For illustration purposes, you might consider language of this type:

> **Seller shall convey to the buyer his farm of 100.00 acres, as conveyed to him on March 14, 1992, Deed Book 73, Page 106, in fee simple, including all real property, all subsurface minerals and all other interests and rights in the property, and all improvements and fixtures, including but not limited to, all buildings, structures, facilities, barns, sheds, windows, doors (including remote control to garage door), garages, woodsheds, windmills, antennae, outbuildings, grain tanks/unloaders, bridges, culverts, fences, gates, satellite dishes, roads, water resources and systems, pumps, electrical boxes and lines, standing and downed timber, and roadside mailbox and post. All fixtures and attachments convey except for:**

_____

_____

_____

_____

> **The following items of personal property shall convey:**

_____

_____

In addition, Seller, per agreement, shall convey to Buyer the pile of road gravel next to his barn, the stacked firewood next to his house and the 700 linear feet of two-inch-diameter PVC water pipe stored in his barn.

Here are a couple of variations on the tank-and-auger story.

The weekend after closing, the cousin appears with a flatbed truck and begins to dismantle the tank and auger. He tells you the loan story. You try to reach the seller, but can't. The cousin, backed by four burly sons, continues to work. What do you do? Call the sheriff? Call your lawyer? Stop them at gunpoint?

A call to your lawyer first and then the sheriff might work. You want to halt the removal and give yourself the time and a legal venue to figure things out. If the cousin hauls off the equipment, you will have a hard time getting it back in usable condition. Perhaps you can videotape your peaceful opposition to the removal in which you make clear that you consider it your property, and it's being taken against your will. You will undoubtedly lose a fistfight with Daddy and his four big boys.

The seller appears two weeks after closing with cousin, four burly sons and truck, and begins to take down tank and auger. You say, "Stop! What's going on here?" Seller says, "What's the problem? I'm taking the tank and auger that I had orally reserved when we were negotiating four months ago." You, despite being a Mensa member and having total recall of every one of the 10,688 bridge hands you've played during the last three decades, have no recollection of this conversation. Seller produces wife from cab of truck who confirms that she heard her husband say exactly what he now says he said.

"Otherwise," she says, "why would we be here? We're not thieves." Who's not? you ask silently. "Me and…him," she adds.

Give it up. You won't win in court. Your word against theirs; one against six.

You can protect yourself by writing language into your contract that excludes all **sidebar agreements, written and oral**. This is referred to as the **Entire Agreement** section; it is usually standard:

This Contract, including any attachments initialed and dated by the Parties, shall constitute the entire agreement between them. It shall supersede any other written or oral agreement between them. This Contract can only be modified in writing that is initialed and dated by both Parties.

Be careful with Entire Agreement language, since it cuts both ways. If you have made beneficial arrangements that fall within its scope, the Entire Agreement language will end them.

Roof Leaks. Three weeks after you move in, a heavy rain falls. This is the first rain since you've taken possession. You place a five-gallon bucket under a leak in the back closet. The bucket happens to be in the closet's darkest corner. You now notice old water stains on the closet's ceiling. You talk to the seller. "Wasn't leaking when I owned it. Must have just started," he says. You say, "What about all the signs of old leakage on the ceiling?" "Oh that," the seller says, "was years ago. I just never repainted the ceiling after I fixed it. Never took that old bucket out of there, I guess."

You, or the house inspector in your employ, should have noticed the water stains prior to placing a purchase contract in front of the seller. The price of being non-observant and doing inspections without a flashlight is $1,000.

Most properties have little dings like a leaky roof that hide from buyers. They're either tucked out of the way or are so out in the open that they're not noticed—leaky basement pipes, painted-shut windows, warped doors that can't close tightly, dead electrical outlets, semi-operational equipment like a basement sump pump that you look at when the basement is Sahara dry and a ten-ton-capacity access bridge that won't handle the 30-ton logging trucks that are needed to haul timber from the property.

It's hard for the buyer to prove that the roof wasn't in fine shape at closing. Usually, each nickel and dime is not worth the aggravation of a fight, even though loose change adds up to dollars. It does not make sense to spend a dollar to win a nickel.

Prevention, of course, is your most economical defense. Rural property may look simple to evaluate, far less complicated than a suburban house, but it is not. And its scoping frequently requires consultants with whom the typical suburban buyer is not familiar—forester, soils engineer, farm consultant, minerals consultant, water engineer, excavator, farm-equipment appraiser, septic-system inspector and so on. These experts are in addition to the routine home-inspection and termite report you should have in both suburb and country. And while your bug guy is poking and prodding, ask him to look for other bogies— powder post beetles, carpenter ants, fire ants, winter flies, black widow spiders and any similarly unattractive guests.

The expensive overlooked problems in rural property tend to be outside the house—water systems that go dry or need to be rebuilt, septic systems that don't function well or are undersized, old barns that cannot be cheaply adapted to your new purposes, electrical and plumbing systems that need to be totally replaced, livestock ponds that leak, fences that need to be rebuilt, outbuildings with problems (rotting floors, leaky roofs, collapsing foundations), undersized or weak bridges, pasture that can support fewer animals than before due to overgrazing or climate change and so on.

Invisible liabilities are almost always the ones that pinch the buyer of rural property the hardest. Lack of mineral ownership is an obvious one. Others include the severance of some other property right, such as, the sale of air rights on the back ridge to a wind-farm developer; a neighbor's right to deprive the target property of water; underground pollution that affects water quality; an acreage shortage or boundary dispute; insect infestation or disease in the timber; termites in the barn (which is rarely looked at in the required termite inspection of the residence); and nuisances created by neighbors that don't reveal themselves during your visits. (Remember, for example, that Laura Cunningham bought her place in the country without "seeing" that her property was situated next door to an over-lighted, noisy community college campus.) Keep your eyes open for the invisibles.

With working farms, I would hire an independent **farm consultant** for help in evaluating the property's assets in terms of your plans. This person might be a retired agricultural extension agent, a full-time consultant or just a person with a lot of experience. You may need to combine the latter with an individual who provides the latest business analysis, depending on your plans. Your local lawyer may be able to recommend a retiree with the farm and building experience you need. Dollars paid to such consultants are the most cost-effective investments you can make.

You can also protect your interests by inserting "**warranty language**" in your purchase contract, such as:

Seller warrants that all mechanical, electrical, plumbing (including water supply, water purifiers and septic/sewerage systems), heating and air conditioning (including attic fans, ventilators and humidifiers), and structural components of all buildings, structures and other improvements, together with all fixtures and personal property that will convey under this Contract, will be in good, safe working order and not require repair as of closing. Exceptions to this warranty include by mutual agreement of the Parties the following:

_____

_____

_____

_____

You can specify individual systems and items for warranty to the degree you think necessary. For example, if the property has a water impoundment (lake with a man-made dam), make sure the seller has a current inspection and state permit. Swimming pools, spas, electric garage doors, working fireplaces, woodstoves, built-in appliances—one or more may deserve to be singled out. With a woodstove, for example, its installation needs to be in compliance with the current standards imposed by the fire-insurance carrier you plan to use. That means it has to be set up at least 16 or 20 inches from adjacent combustible walls, on an approved fireproof pad that extends a certain distance beyond the stove. If you're worried about the seller's roof, include no-roof-leak language.

You generally want the seller to promise good working order as of closing, not as of when the purchase contract takes effect, which might be three months earlier. Put another way, you want working order and property condition to be the same at closing as they were when the contract took effect. Stuff can happen between the two dates.

One 1,500-acre purchase I worked on involved a contract that came into effect two years before closing occurred. The buyer needed to get the property rezoned so he placed a contingency in his contract that made closing contingent on getting all necessary approvals—a complicated process that ultimately required him to spend $400,000 on archeological investigations alone. This property included a beach along a river that the buyer valued highly in his development plans. If something occurred during escrow that diminished the value of that beach—erosion from a hurricane, an oil-tanker spill—the buyer had contract language to protect his financial interest in the property as it was when he and the seller reached a meeting of the minds on their contract.

Warranty language establishes the buyer's expectations about property conditions and reflects what the parties have agreed to, insofar as the seller warrants (promises) to deliver the property at closing in the same condition, less normal wear and tear, as it existed when the contract was signed. Exceptions to warranty language can be noted in the contract by specifying items that are excluded from the seller's promise. An item in "as-is" condition means its condition at the time the contract takes effect, not "as-is" at the time of closing.

The necessary companion protection with warranties is to write in a **walk-through** provision in the purchase contract that allows you to visit the seller's property just before closing; test all systems to make sure they are in working order; confirm that whatever the seller promised to do, if anything, during escrow as part of your contract, has been done; and check that everything you are buying is still on the property and in essentially the same condition as when you signed your contract. Your walk-through, or **final inspection**, is usually scheduled for within 48 to 72 hours of closing. If you are working with a FSBO, make sure he is present for the walk-through. Otherwise, the seller's broker/agent typically accompanies the buyer.

Many, if not most, real-estate brokers advise their sellers to stay away from the buyer on his final walk-through. They want to be the communication channel between the two. Since rural property is more complicated than urban/suburban housing, I urge non-local buyers, novices in particular, to do at least one pre-purchase **walk-around with the seller** who, after all, will be far more knowledgeable about his property's assets and liabilities than even the most conscientious agent. If the seller walked you through when you were "just looking," you have a base of agreement as to what was what, then. Don't let his real-estate agent talk you out of having the seller walk you around on a final inspection. If nothing has changed, you will find nothing wrong. When a disagreement materializes, try to approach it as a joint problem with a common history to be solved rather than the first in a series of grievous wrongs inflicted on an innocent. If the seller has made a mistake, give him room to correct it. If the seller is trying to take a second bite out of your lunch, let him do it if it's small enough; resist if he's stealing your meal; or bite back.

If you determine that something is not there, not the same or not in working order during your walk-through, try to resolve it quickly. If the issue is a chip, forget about it. If it is significant, you have leverage—your willingness to void the purchase—and the seller has incentive to make it right. The seller is near enough to closing to smell your cash. This is your most advantageous negotiating moment. If you void your contract, the seller may sue you for performance, depending on the circumstances. At that point, you either work out something with the seller or convince a judge that you were justified in voiding your contract. Voiding a contract is a serious act because of its risks and potential expense. Don't do this without first consulting your lawyer. It is not worth losing a farm over a roof leak.

A familiar walk-through drama occurs when a buyer picks a number of nits to extort a price reduction from an anxious seller. I advise against taking this last bite out of the seller's apple. First, it's not honest bargaining. Second, it's a transparent tactic. News of your clumsy, cheap "cleverness" will precede you in your new community. Third, you risk losing the deal. I have seen people act against their rational economic self-interest time and again to make a point if only to themselves. In your eyes or mine, that point may be off-center or just plain counter productive. But in their eyes, a principle is being stood for by acting economically "irrationally." Push too far with nibbles and nits, and the seller might blow up the deal despite his compelling motivation to sell. My belief is that buyers "make their money on purchases" through diligent research and thoughtful planning, not through last-minute shakedowns.

Does the flat land by the river flood? Of course it does. Every water channel will overflow its banks given sufficient rainfall. Flashfloods in semi-deserts are notorious killers. Key Run, the creek behind my farmhouse, is dry nine months of every year; I've also seen this "intermittent stream" cover the entire bottom to a depth of four feet four times in 20 years. Flooding creates flat bottom land by depositing dirt eroded from ground higher in the watershed. If your target property has a creek with bottom land, assume flood potential whether or not the seller recollects any high water. Check the floodplain maps available from the Federal Emergency Management Administration (FEMA) and the U.S. Army Corps of Engineers. Avoid land that is listed as flooding more frequently than every 100 years if possible. Ask neighbors. A seller's opinion or his honest recollection doesn't bind the seller in court; neither opinion nor memory amount to warranty.

The failure of sellers to recollect adverse events may be a new field for academic research. One seller will forget that he only owned a one-third interest in the land he was selling. Another will forget an agreement on a selling price. Buyers tend to lose in these episodes, because they are trying to be accommodating and cooperative. Where you are sure that the seller is doing nothing more than trying to hurt you with his failure-to-recollect tactic, don't participate in your own wounding.

Drinkable Spring Water: That the seller and his family—all of whom drink household water drawn from a spring—say they have never been sick, proves not much about this water's **potability** (drinkability). They may blame their chronic diarrhea on the "weak stomachs" that seem to run in their family, not the bacteria-contaminated water they've drunk for three generations. People can become acclimated to some contaminants and bacteria over time, which is why, I suppose, Montezuma wreaks more gastric vengeance on tourists than natives. Your city stomach is used to chlorinated or bottled water that contains no fecal bacteria, which is associated with mammalian waste. (The level of *Escherichia coli*, or *E. coli*, is the common indicator.) In this instance, the seller suspected his water might be a little gamey, but had no evidence that it was harmful.

If farmhouse water is drawn from a well, spring, lake, stream or cistern, place a **"water-quality contingency"** in your contract:

> **Buyer's offer is contingent upon obtaining acceptable results from a water test Buyer arranges for and conducts at his own expense. Water must meet minimum safety and quality standards, as set forth by local sanitarian or other public health official. In the event that results are below these standards, Seller shall, at his expense, take steps necessary to upgrade water to meet these standards. Buyer shall take a second test at his expense. If results are still unsatisfactory, Buyer may void this contract at his choosing or reopen negotiations with Seller.**

Under no circumstances should a buyer allow the seller to take the sample (hold a sterilized bottle under a flame-sterilized kitchen tap) on his own and send it to the laboratory. It's too easy for an unscrupulous seller to mix Evian from the supermarket into the sample.

"Fixing" a spring system with a high coliform count can involve nothing more than dumping a gallon of bleach into the water source and running the house tap until the water tastes clean of chorine, at which point a sample is taken. This "fix" may produce an acceptable sample without fixing the cause of the problem, which is something like livestock being pastured too close to the spring or septic-system effluent getting into it. The real fix may require rebuilding the fence line so that animals are kept further back or relocating a drainfield. Proper fixes tend to cost more than quick ones, which is one of humanity's long-standing grievances. A usually less desirable option is to install a home-chlorination unit that mixes a bleach solution with the incoming water, and the blend is pumped through the house. Drinking clean spring water is one of life's pleasures; drinking chlorinated water in the country is one of life's grumbles.

CHAPTER 28: BARGAINING CULTURES AND RESOLVING PROPERTY DISPUTES

Every community has a bargaining culture that shapes the conduct of negotiations, suggests which tactics are acceptable and which aren't, and regulates what words and signals mean or don't mean. After more than two decades of living in a rural county with 2,500 residents, I'm just getting the hang of my **local bargaining culture**. In work that I've done in other rural areas East of the Mississippi, I've found basic similarities.

If you come from a bargaining culture where yes means yes and you propose to buy land in a culture where yes means a contingent maybe, miscommunication and fouled understandings are inevitable.

A familiar example is the fixed-price construction contract, where you and a contractor agree on a single sum in advance that is supposed to cover all contractor costs and profit. In the contractor's mind, he may come from a bargaining background that will hold to a fixed price as long as it is profitable. When his fixed price turns out to produce breakeven, or worse, he asks for an extra payment or two. Sometimes paying money above a fixed price is justified, and at other times, you're working with a contractor who bid low to get your business and figured he could wring more dollars out of you down the road. All of this is made more complicated when different individuals acting within a bargaining culture interpret its code differently, or follow it, or ignore it. Maybe the entire notion of a bargaining culture has no practical relevance. I'm willing to concede the point without much argument, because I've seen shifty individuals come out of honest and straight-up rural bargaining cultures such as the one where I live.

I try to factor into land bargaining a limited sense of how the seller's local bargaining culture shapes his perceptions and ways of communicating. I try to use words and tactics that I think the seller's heard and seen before from buyers. I listen intently for cue words that I've heard before, from which I infer movement or heels being dug in. Admittedly, this may amount to no more than hunch and guess. I can usually establish an approximate "bargaining fix" that suggests how I should approach negotiations. Having said all that, it's equally important to keep in mind that rural sellers are not a single group from a single bargaining culture. Even individuals from one group bargain differently with different people.

Let me say this in another way: I negotiate differently, and communicate differently, with an Ivy League lawyer selling land than with a local graduate of the hard-knocks school (who is likely to be the better bargainer). For that matter, I have bargained differently with a Harvard-trained lawyer than with a 1960s graduate of the University of Virginia's Law School. I bargain differently with wheeler-dealers than with small landowners. I bargain differently with environmentalists than I do with business interests. (I have found dishonorable individuals in both groups. The business guys are simply after money; the environmentalists believe their morally superior goals justify ethically inferior behavior. It's a recurrent source of disappointment.) I don't try to affect the culture of the seller by pretending I'm someone that I'm not. It's hard to say empirically whether my approach achieves better results than alternatives.

When you find yourself dealing with a seller who gives his word and would keep it even when it's against his self-interest, you have lucked out. Bargaining may be hard with such a person, but a deal struck is a deal made. You need to be the mirror image of such a seller.

Don't be surprised to find a seller whose bargaining style is to slide around like an eel in a barrel of crude oil. These individuals think they are being clever negotiators by dragging out bargaining and "revisiting" agreed-on terms. Smart they may be, but the outcome of such tactics may not produce more money or a better deal. It can just as readily produce a buyer who walks away in disgust before a contract is signed.

Then there is the seller who combines the two: you will be able to count on some of his yeses, but not others. This individual may be deliberately dishonest or simply slipshod. You have to convert this person's commitments to paper asap.

Bargaining involves testing each other's reliability. By agreeing and testing on small, preliminary points, you can get some sense of the seller's style. It's always useful to learn what you can of the bargaining culture from your local lawyer and, more importantly, get his read on the seller's bargaining history and style.

The danger in thinking of negotiating through the lens of cultural styles is to fall into the quicksand of stereotypes. Individuals who share ethnicity, or religion, or regional identification, or class, or occupation, or social status, or educational background or gender preference don't necessarily share a way of negotiating. But individuals who fit a multi-factor profile often, but not always, do. Sellers who live in the country don't fit a single multi-factor profile. They don't all bargain the same way because of one shared characteristic: rural residence. Some are honest sellers; others aren't, as is the case across the board with individuals in every group. You can use the idea of bargaining culture to sharpen your communication skills. Owing to individual variability, it's a sometimes useful predictor of behavior, but not always.

I find much negotiating insight in Peter Wink's, Negotiate Your Way to Riches: How to Convince Others to Give You What You Want (New York: Barnes & Noble, 2003). Despite the distasteful title, Wink presents a sensible framework for approaching negotiations based on research, effective communication, shared problem-solving and fair dealing. The principles he uses can readily be applied to negotiations over land.

I have found that rural people prefer oral agreements to written ones. When you come from a bargaining culture that always uses written documents and the seller comes from an oral bargaining culture, your document will be viewed with suspicion. A pervasive history of legal land swindling exists in America. Much of it involved paper in the form of legal documents that took advantage of the party less legally literate. Mineral buyers came into the Appalachian coalfields after the Civil War and bought billions of tons of high-quality coal reserves for pennies per ton using a deed that allowed the mineral owner and his leaseholder to use the surface in any way necessary for extraction. Often, they employed "native" lawyers as their fronts. Mining, at the time, meant underground mining. A century later it often meant surface mining where the leaseholder cut the timber and then stripped away the dirt and rock to get at the coal. The old deeds legally wrecked many a mountain farm. A communal memory exists in rural areas regarding outsiders with "lawed-up" paper and cash money. Rural populism fed on tales of carpetbaggers, land buyers, railroads and bankers acquiring resources with outside cash and the help of government.

Walking into a seller's farm kitchen with a purchase contract drawn up on 14-inch Big City law-firm stationery with 30-line-long, one-sentence paragraphs that include three "except that's," will get you nowhere. And properly so. Your goal is to have a meeting of the minds, not effect a land swindle. You should give the seller a contract as simple as you can make it while protecting your interests. Write it clearly, using short declarative sentences and familiar words. Your intent is to have both of you understand what is being signed.

While it's fine to bargain orally with a seller, you should assume that any oral agreement you reach on the sale of real estate binds neither of you and is not legally enforceable. For that reason, a buyer should submit a purchase offer in writing with all terms and contingencies included. Explain to the seller that oral agreements are not binding, which is why you're sticking paper under his nose. Once your negotiation succeeds, get it down on paper immediately, with both parties signing and dating the document. When you're working through a real-estate agent, your written offer will be presented to the seller without you being present. This format is awkward and often gets in the way of a deal, but a buyer is rarely allowed to present his contract directly to a seller when an agent representing the seller is involved.

If, as part of your pre-purchase scoping, you find yourself walking the property with the seller and agreeing on matters as you move about, write them on a legal pad attached to a clipboard that you just happen to be carrying. Both of you should initial each agreement with a date. This document might cover items such as:

Property definition—acreage to be determined by _____. Back fence needs repair. That fence is neighbor's section. Seller will ask neighbor to have this section replaced by next spring. No guarantees. Three 16-foot-long, 12"-diameter metal culverts next to creek convey. Seller reserves cattle scale; does not convey. Seller to remove by closing. Seller retains 100 percent interest in all crops that he's planted, but agrees to pay $25 per acre on 53 acres of planted corn for this retained interest. All crops to be harvested by December 1 of this year. Seller will seed back 20 acres with cover crop by October 15 at his expense. New barn roofing materials stored in barn to convey. 50 panels of sheet metal, nails and 10 gallons of red roof paint. Agreed on contract price: $275,000. $4,000 security deposit. 60-day due-diligence contingency, results acceptable to buyer. Closing within ten calendar days after contingency is removed.

Have your lawyer incorporate these notes into the purchase contract he prepares. Tell him to use plain English and simple sentences wherever possible. I would append a photocopy of your original field notes to your contract. Some "boilerplate" can be translated into plain language to everyone's benefit with no loss of legal meaning. Other sections can be lifted verbatim from any standard contract. A contract drawn by a local lawyer—even the buyer's—will go much further with a local seller than one cooked up by a new associate in the 500-partner law firm you use in Big City. It will work better in most cases than the standard real-estate contract, which favors sellers. Never approach kitchen-table bargaining with a fancy brief case, tie, cufflinks and $1,000 Italian loafers. Keep your hands on the table, not in your pockets. Don't take the seller's pen.

As to eye contact. Conventional wisdom has it that the absence of constant eye contact indicates a shifty bargaining partner. I've found the opposite to be true. Swindlers and thieves, even the pettiest ones, have mastered continuous eye contact. I disregard it. I look much more toward a total package of behavior: body language, voice inflection, choice of words, how points are stated, hand movement, intentional tactics and so on.

When a buyer comes into a new place, he has no lines into the local word-of-mouth communication network on which the community depends. He can't extract information from this system, and he has no ready means of feeding it either credible information or his spin on an argument. The seller becomes the only source of community information on the stranger who's just rolled into town with a checkbook. The buyer's seller-reported behavior is fresh meat to the local lions. Your vehicle will be noted, along with accent, dress, vocabulary, restaurant orders, questions, marital status, appearance and suspected origins. The community will be trying to classify the newcomer into a sociological type with which it already has some experience. You cannot protect yourself from what the seller feeds into the local network about you. It does not matter that the seller is the sleaziest slime ball in the county, and every local knows it. Even those who distrust the seller may extend to him a presumption of credibility about a buyer of whom they know nothing at all. No independent and competing source of information is available about the buyer. If the seller spreads the word that the buyer nickel-and-dimed him, or didn't keep his word, or acted unreasonably (however defined), the buyer will move into the community burdened with bad press whether or not the specific charge is true. Some people won't talk to you on that basis alone—and you will never know why. (They may be kin to the seller, which you may or may not learn.) Others will try to get the better of you to prove some point to themselves. Still others will consider the source of the gossip and pay no attention to it, preferring to make their own judgments on their first-hand experience with you. Your goal is to have current residents deal with you on the basis of their first-hand knowledge which shows that you are decent and honest. (If you are not decent and honest, you deserve what you get.)

For these reasons, I advise buyers to establish independent communication contacts with members of your target community <u>before</u> you look at your first property. Visit the county casually before you start serious land-looking. Eat at local restaurants; tip 15 percent, neither more nor less. Buy stuff at local stores, while striking up introductory conversations. Subscribe to the local paper in person, not by mail. Chat with the paper's editor. Open an account at a local bank. Buy a county phone book. Have casual conversations with as many folks as possible, while always introducing yourself to the extent possible as having a connection to a local person or neighborhood. Include on your list the librarian, county clerk, sheriff, EMTs, firemen, county dump operator, store keepers, Chamber of Commerce director and others who work in the town nearest your target property and in the county seat. Get a haircut in the local barbershop. If you are a member of an organization or fraternal order—Lions, Elks, VFW, Ruritans, Masons, AARP, etc.—contact the local chapter and go to a meeting. If you are a church member, attend services and introduce yourself to the minister and congregation. Put something into the collection plate. You can't help but learn about a community new to you through this low-key, self-introduction process. Of equal importance, you are building a track record with information gatekeepers on your terms. It won't prevent a seller from bad-mouthing you, but it will broaden your base of support and provide others with independent assessments.

Unequal access to the local communication network puts a strain on a buyer. The buyer doesn't want to quibble over every dollar and in so doing assure himself of bad local press from the seller. On the other hand, no buyer should be a negotiating patsy by giving in on every seller demand. The best way to handle this is to make sure that the seller sees that you're willing to give on some things in return for take on others—and that you expect the same from him. Assume that you will be negotiating with your mirror image until the seller demonstrates that you aren't.

This doesn't mean you should be unskilled or naïve in bargaining. A buyer should enter land negotiations with a pile of **throwaway chips** that he can give up without much loss. Throwaways might include some (not all) warranty language in the purchase contract, or fence/buildings you'd like the seller to repair prior to closing, or farm gates that you like to have him replace, or a situation you'd like the seller to clear up that can be lived with, or an upgrade on an access ROW (from an 18-foot-wide easement to 24 feet that would be nice but isn't truly needed). Concede these chips as needed for things that are important to you. Trading is usually done on the basis of equal values, but getting something more important by giving something less important may often be a matter of perspective. You can also give a lot of chips for one big something. And you always can gain leverage in negotiations by giving away seller-perceived leverage.

Tactical "giving in" can show the seller you're willing to work with him for the deal, not that you're a pushover. Keep in mind that a willing and able buyer with a reasonable attitude is the solution to a seller's need to sell. Think of yourself in this way, and you will empower yourself in negotiations.

A hard-ball, take-it-or-leave-it offer will guarantee you bad word-of-mouth, especially if it works, which I suspect it won't. Whatever the bargaining culture, such offers work mainly with sellers whose backs are against the wall, but not even then. I urge readers not to play the game the way Michael Scanlon, the conduit between crooked influence-peddler Jack Abramoff and Congressman Tom DeLay, described his advice to DeLay during the Clinton impeachment: "'This whole thing about not kicking someone when they are down is B.S.,' Mr. Scanlon once wrote to Mr. Rudy [a DeLay and Scanlon associate] in an email published in The Breach, a book by Peter Baker about the impeachment. 'Not only do you kick him—you kick him until he passes out—then beat him over the head with a baseball bat—then roll him up in an old rug—and throw him off a cliff into the pound surf below!!!!!'" (Brody Mullins, "Behind Unraveling of DeLay's Team, A Jilted Fiancee, Wall Street Journal, March 31, 2006.) I've seen land buyers act like this; I hope not to see another.

In some situations, you might benefit from asking a seller whether he'd prefer that you submit your best offer or a lower one that is negotiable. This is a simple way to establish the ground rules of your negotiations; I've found that it works. Do not, however, raise your best offer if that is what the seller chooses. If you submit a best-money offer, give the seller no more than 24 hours to respond.

The bargaining rapport and momentum that you establish on peripheral issues will provide a path for your negotiations on more substantive issues where you give up something you want for something you want more. I've found rural sellers to be comfortable with give and take in various forms. I've found that folding myself into a give-and-take bargaining system is usually acceptable to these sellers. It's a fair system when both sides are knowledgeable. In this type of give and take, buyers often can succeed more by listening harder and talking softer.

Take, for example, Yankee buyers South of the Maryland border. (The same example could be drawn from the downstate Big City buyer in the rural upstate.) Country sellers may both fear and despise such buyers. Urban Yankees, in particular, sound smarter (though they're not), act dumber (often true) and appear richer (sometimes true, sometimes not) than they are. They are usually more comfortable with a high-speed, secular, professional business culture than the rural seller. Urban anybodies—Northern or Southern—may now be lumped together by rural sellers and considered a Yankee type. Yankees are, of course, distrusted for these reasons as well as our funny accent, aggressiveness and the guilt we bear for winning the War of the Northern Aggression. Any seller who enters negotiations believing the buyer is both smart and dumb can easily get crosswise in his own assumptions. A buyer wants to avoid fitting into the seller's cultural preconceptions, especially when they're accurate. If you feel that you would not negotiate well with a seller, have your local lawyer do it for you.

I've found variations of the Yankee-Dixie dynamic in the West ("amenity buyers" vs. ranch sellers), the Northeast (city buyers vs. native Yankee sellers), West Virginia (outsider buyers vs. West Virginia sellers) and even within certain counties.

Urban buyers are also the country seller's most coveted market, because it is assumed such buyers have more money than sense. First-generation country residents—urban folks who retired to the country or younger bail outs—also prefer to sell to the "surgeon from Denver" or the prominent Manhattan editor. Me too; every seller should do better with a wealthy buyer. You may find, consequently, that if you are so categorized, negotiating with a dollar-blinded seller feels like a street shakedown with the seller's attitude summarized as, "Give it up."

What can an urban buyer who fits the country seller's preconceptions do to protect his pocketbook? First, don't be stupid. Don't look at country property no matter how expensive from the leather-clad bucket seat of a show-room-new $100,000 Hummer or a $250,000 Lamborghini. Don't flash diamonds the size of cow flops. Don't brag about your job, your important friends and the appreciation rate of your portfolio. Look and act average, while *silently* projecting the ability to make this purchase at the right price. Second, scope the property. If money is no object, your scoping is looking for the hidden legal and physical liabilities that will turn the purchase into a nightmare. Third, bargain. I don't care whether you can buy the seller's property 25 times over with your pocket change. Your willingness to bargain gives respect to the seller, which improves the buying process for you. Finally, let your local lawyer do the heavy lifting. He will carry off the purchase on your behalf better than you will.

A dispute arises with the seller: what do you, the out-of-county buyer, do?

If it's a chip, forget about it. Winning a chip from a local seller almost always costs the newcomer-buyer more over his long run than the chip is worth. The cost is paid in stories about your poor behavior if nothing else.

When the dispute is over something more substantial—involving, for example, at least two percent of your purchase price—a buyer might feel more comfortable in asking his local lawyer to negotiate with the seller's lawyer. Let lawyer haggle with lawyer, which they do all the time. At most, this task will cost you a couple of hours of your lawyer's time.

If the dispute is of such magnitude that it's a deal-breaker, I'd first try local lawyer to local lawyer negotiations. If that fails, I'd have your lawyer suggest **third-party mediation** of the dispute to the seller's lawyer. Mediation is a method of resolving disputes in which the parties hire an independent neutral to help them reach a compromise. The mediator has no power to impose a settlement. His role is to keep negotiations moving, present different ways of solving issues and help the parties write a settlement that everyone signs. Mediation fails when this process—usually a day or less—produces no acceptable settlement. Mediation works in a majority of cases. But it requires good-faith bargaining on both sides. A party who refuses to bargain stops mediation cold. The disputants' incentive to resolve their problem through mediation is their knowledge that mediation allows them to control their settlement and that litigation is always a more costly, more time-consuming and less predictable option. Since both buyer and seller want the purchase to go through, they share an interest in having mediation succeed. One of the ground rules for mediation is that both parties have at the negotiations an individual authorized to make a deal then and there.

In selecting a mediator, the parties must agree on a person who has no interest in the outcome, is not biased for or against either party and has experience in both mediation work and real-estate issues. Community mediation centers can recommend trained mediators. Dispute-resolution organizations can also provide referrals. These include the Society for the Promotion of Alternative Dispute Resolution, American Arbitration Association and several for-profit mediation vendors. The local bar association might recommend names of lawyers who do mediations. Choose someone who has been trained in mediation techniques and has experience in real estate. Mediators whose experience is with personal-injury cases or divorces may have the mediation skills, but not sufficient background in real estate. If your dispute concerns a particular area of expertise, such as the valuation of timber or a farm business, you may want to provide the mediator with a consultant who is present during the mediation session and helps the mediator propose alternative solutions. The mediator and the costs of mediation are divided equally between the parties. Some mediation issues benefit from having lawyers present for both sides, but I have seen lawyers derail mediated settlements in favor of litigation. I have also seen a lawyer use a mediation session for discovery, that is, to find out what the other side was going to present as evidence in the litigation he was planning. When the issues and resolution have tax consequences for one or both parties, share the cost of a CPA presence at the mediation.

If mediation fails, you have four choices: 1) ask the two lawyers to give it a last try between themselves; 2) concede defeat; 3) **arbitration**, in which the parties must agree to submit their dispute to a third-party neutral who has full authority to issue a binding decision; and 4) litigation. I'd always try option one, since you have little to lose and everything to gain.

I've worked as an arbitrator for 20 years, primarily dealing with workplace grievances arising within a contract between a union and employer. I've also done a few commercial mediations. Each process works, though each works best in different circumstances. When the parties are genuinely locked up, arbitration is the better choice because it guarantees a settlement. Arbitration is a cheaper, faster option than litigation. Arbitrators are not, of course, of one mind. In any given case, my guess is that 20 arbitrators would reach ten different conclusions. Fifteen would side with one party, with varying levels of agreement and award. Maybe five of the 20 would rule for the other party, with their own variations on agreement and award. The split among arbitrators is determined by how they view the facts, law and case presentation. Where one party is obviously in the right, 20 of 20 arbitrators should rule that way, but that might slip to 95 out of 100. Most cases, however, present arbitrators with degrees of rightness on each side. This explains why arbitrators would split among themselves on a particular case as well as why arbitrators split their own decisions, giving something to each party. Some arbitrators decide cases on the basis of which party made the better presentation; others look more for the truth. Arbitrators also differ in the degree of their participation in the hearing: some ask no questions; others ask questions limited to clarification; still others ask substantive questions that are intended to reveal what happened and the degree of reliability of the information presented.

Arbitrations resemble court hearings with the arbitrator as the judge. Each side presents its case with documents and witnesses. Cross-examination occurs. The arbitrator is expected to be fair and neutral. Rules of evidence are not applied, other than those consistent with basic fairness and due process. Arbitrators may be asked to make a win-lose decision in which one side totally prevails over the other. As chancy as it is, I favor letting an arbitrator reach whatever decision he thinks is best. That is neither more nor less risky than submitting the case to a judge. Where buyer and seller are in dispute before the purchase contract has been carried out, an arbitrator might be asked to devise a reasonable compromise. I recommend that buyers be represented by counsel in any arbitration. I also recommend that the parties authorize the arbitrator to write a short opinion that presents his view of the issues and the reasons for his position on each one. Otherwise, the parties are left with a legally binding award and no explanation of how the arbitrator got there.

One example will suffice. A developer bought at an "as-is" auction a 124-acre tract of undeveloped land along a Virginia creek for $2.25 million and a buyer's premium of $225,000. After signing the contract but before closing, the developer discovered an active bald eagle's nest on the property, which limited its development potential. The developer said that he had asked about the presence of bald eagles; the seller said the developer had the knowledge and means to discover the nest on his own. The arbitrator ruled the contract valid and directed the developer to perform. The developer appealed and the arbitrator's decision was upheld by a county circuit court judge in 2006. ("Arbitrator enforces sale of Stafford property," <u>Virginia Lawyers Weekly</u>, March 27, 2006.)

I would do everything possible to keep buyer-seller disputes out of court. While arbitration involves elements of a crapshoot, judges are no different and juries can be worse. Justice is not guaranteed in either arbitration or court. Litigation may not produce a reasonable result, and may produce a deferred result where the losing side appeals. Judges and arbitrators as individuals differ in ability, dedication and perspectives; even good ones blow decisions. I've seen excellent work from rural county judges, as well as a decision so pre-determined that it still makes me talk to myself. I've seen usually competent judges and arbitrators render decisions that are half thought through and not very defensible. Where judges are elected, the out-of-county buyer must consider the local politics of his dispute. Where judges are appointed, a buyer has to fear the arbitrary or quirky individual with a sinecure who doesn't much care any more about the reasonableness of his decisions. In some communities, local judges and local juries will be predisposed to rule in favor of the local seller they know over the Big City buyer they don't know. If you come across as arrogant, stay out of local courts because you risk getting a comeuppance based on who you are not what your case is. Rural judges and juries in my experience favor the side—client and lawyer—they like more often than not. If you are likeable, you have a chance. Your local lawyer should make the call as to whether litigation gives you a shot at fairness in the local court.

I'll add one final point. I have on occasion used something that might be called an **informative non-threat** to persuade a party to work with me. I'm not a lawyer, but I've married two and have been around legal stuff as an arbitrator and land buyer. I've had on occasion predicted how a court might rule in an effort to persuade a party to resolve a common problem with me. I was, for example, interested in buying a small timber tract that had a great deal of timber value. It had not been cut for years, because it was completely landlocked, physically and legally. The landlocked timber parcel had only one way to access a public road—all other ways were blocked by public land. I wrote to the owner of the land lying between the road and the landlocked parcel, observing that in my opinion a court would grant an easement by necessity to the landlocked parcel over him, which would cost each of us about $10,000 to fight it out were it to come to that, which, I said, I certainly hoped it wouldn't. I proposed selling him the landlocked parcel at a steep discount after I cut the timber in return for using his land to get the timber to the public road. I both wrote and said that I was not threatening him with a lawsuit, but I did want him to understand my sense of the situation. He saw it in essentially the same way. Had I threatened him with a lawsuit, I think he would have called my bluff—and won. I did not want the headache of a suit. But by laying honest cards out on an honest table, he and I could play an honest hand with each other.

CHAPTER 29: WRITING A PURCHASE-OFFER CONTRACT: STRATEGIES AND TACTICS

MAKE THE MOST OF YOUR CONTRACT OFFER

Purchase (offer) contracts on rural land present buyers with opportunities both to accomplish certain bargaining objectives and protect their interests. The contract itself should be used to further both ends.

The standard contract that real-estate agents use advantage sellers, if only to the extent that protections for buyers have to be added or written in as modifications to the boilerplate. These contracts are not neutral; they protect the seller without the seller doing anything while forcing the buyer to actively rebalance the contract. I prefer to use a contract that I write, incorporating the boilerplate protections for the seller while adding those a buyer needs. I don't try to skew the contract unfairly in my favor. I write the contract to advance objectives related to the purchase that are tangential to the basic functions of a purchase contract.

Your offer to purchase gives you a one-time opportunity to acquire both vital information about the property and warranties (promises) from the seller. Lawyers will disagree with broadening the functions of the offering contract, but I have found that my way serves a buyer better than using the standard form. One danger in following my advice is that a buyer will write a contract that is too complicated or too one-sided for the seller's taste.

Any contract a buyer—lawyer or not—writes should be done with the active assistance of the lawyer you're using in the target-property's county. Thus, writing your own contract may come down to talking out issues with your lawyer who then does the writing. Do not write a real-estate contract on your own. The harm that you might do to yourself outweighs the benefits.

I use purchase contracts to accomplish some, or all, of the following objectives, depending on the property:

Get information from the seller that he alone possesses, such as knowledge of an unrecorded easement, an erroneous fence line that benefits the seller's property, farm-business financial records, tax schedules, insurance values, participation (and obligations) in government cost-share programs and crop subsidies and so on.

Get the seller to disclose legal and physical problems with the property, which your scoping might not otherwise reveal, e.g., a covered hazardous-waste dump, an unknown archeological site that would foul up a building project, presence of an ETS species or a water supply that is based only on permission.

Have the seller do something to make the deal go through, such as repair electrical service to the barn or remove fallen trees from access road.

Allow the buyer to perform certain on-site investigations, such as sampling for water quality, radon, asbestos or mold; doing a timber cruise; having a structural engineer examine a bridge or a dam; or taking percolation tests in anticipation of a new septic system.

When these investigations are structured as contract **contingencies**, the buyer must include language in each contingency that permits him to be the sole judge as to whether or not the results are satisfactory. If **results-acceptable-to-the-buyer** language is not part of each contingency, the buyer cannot void his contract and get the return of his deposit when results are not acceptable. When results are adverse, the buyer should be able to void his contract or offer to resume negotiations with the seller based on new information. A "contingency" that simply permits the buyer to seek financing or take a water sample does not allow the buyer to get out of the deal if he fails to get financing or does not like the results of the water sample. A contract contingency that benefits the buyer is one that makes the deal's completion depend on getting satisfactory results.

Allow the buyer to perform certain work on the property in advance of closing, such as marking timber in anticipation of a sale, surveying or excavating. Seller should approve all such work as part of the contract, and the buyer needs to understand that he will not benefit from his expenditures if the purchase does not close.

Educate the seller as to what the buyer expects of him and his property. This is done through 1) **warranties that survive the contract**, 2) disclosures and 3) conditions of sale. Warranties that survive the contract are also referred to as warranties that survive escrow.

Notify the seller that he will be expected to stand behind warranties that survive the contract.

Identify and clean up loose ends that a title search is not likely to find, such as unrecorded contracts and easements, encroachments, boundary disputes, licenses (permission to use the land or its assets) and pending actions that might adversely affect the buyer's use and enjoyment (such as seller's inside knowledge that his across-the-road neighbor is planning to build the largest hog farm on the East Coast).

Provide the seller with opportunities to refuse certain language and demands as a way to secure others of more importance to buyer.

Provide sufficient complexity to allow bargaining within the framework of the contract if buyer thinks negotiating is advisable. A buyer can concede throwaways, contingencies, repairs and some disclosures for seller concessions.

Provide the buyer with time to put in place post-purchase plans for property. This usually involves doing work in advance of selling some of the land or a severable asset.

Strip risk from a purchase by making it contingent on buyer securing all approvals he deems necessary to implement a post-purchase plan. This is commonly used by buyers who want to divide a large property or turn it to some purpose that requires rezoning or a conditional-use permit.

A purchase contract should be seen as involving three sequences.

The first is an offer from the buyer to purchase property on terms he proposes. Those terms involve getting the seller to disclose information, allowing the buyer to do certain things, making the offer contingent on results acceptable to the buyer and agreeing on price and other sale conditions.

The second phase—**escrow**—begins once the contract is signed by both parties and comes into effect. Escrow is the time when all of the agreed work by both buyer and seller that was set forth in the accepted offer is done. Escrow is usually scheduled for 45 to 90 calendar days, but I've seen open-ended escrows used by buyers whose offer is contingent on getting the property rezoned.

The third phase begins after closing and the buyer takes possession. The several future warranties included in a general warranty deed and whatever warranties the buyer stipulated would survive the contract are now available for protecting the buyer. The contract offer is the one chance the buyer has to get his seller to both promise something and live up to it.

Many lawyers will look disapprovingly at my discussion of contracts and the sample language I've included. They'll say: "Too much extraneous stuff; keep it simple." Every buyer knows without having to be told that a full-price, all-cash offer free of contingencies, disclosures and title search will "win" the property of almost every seller. That level of simplicity—what the seller's real-estate agent calls a "clean contract"—can get the buyer into trouble after the deal is done. And if the seller is not on the warranty hook after closing, he's off the hook—and you've taken his place. I'm not recommending that every buyer write his own contract, and I'm certainly against readers festooning every contract with every contingency I've described in this book. You need to balance a contract with words that cover the needs your scoping has identified with fair play for the seller. The buyer needs to find that level of detail and self-protection that lies between too much and not enough—the place determined by the individual characteristics of each deal and the needs of the seller.

I do not advise inexperienced buyers either to write their own contracts or use the sample contract in this chapter *verbatim*. I advise, instead, that readers become familiar with contract concepts and the language that expresses them. In consultation with your local lawyer, lift and adapt whatever language that helps. If you have cold feet, use the standard contract *your* lawyer would use when working for a buyer and add any additional language you and he feel is appropriate. Do not, however, use your lawyer's standard contract if it's the same as the standard contract used by sellers—which is likely to be the case. That standard contract is likely to be no different than the real-estate broker's standard contract.

The following discussion focuses on ways that contract language and tactics can help a buyer get better terms, safer terms and pay less.

INFORMATION

Sellers and real-estate brokers vary in their willingness to inform buyers about items of importance. When a seller fully complies with a state's disclosure requirements, many pieces of information may still not be made available. Use your contract to ask for information from the seller.

I looked at 170 acres in 2005 that was accessed by way of a 2.5-mile-long driveway, about two miles of which were private road that crossed and served four property owners. My target property had a deeded right to use this road, but the easement said nothing as to the width of the easement, who was responsible for the road's maintenance (a not inconsiderable expense) and whether the easement was unrestricted in terms of the types and number of vehicles that could use the road. The absence of written restrictions should be interpreted as the intentional absence of restrictions, but the other property owners might complain about its use by logging trucks and cement mixers. [A buyer could put in his contract a provision that requires the seller to secure written advance approval of the buyer's easement plans from the other owners as a condition of sale.] The right to use this road was located in an antecedent deed, an owner or two back, and no reference to it was included in the seller's own deed of record. I sensed that the seller was reluctant to use this access road for anything more than an occasional safari ride in with his pick-up truck. The neighbors, I guessed, opposed any other usage and were willing to fight in court over more traffic and heavier vehicles. The seller did not say this to me outright, but I felt confident in making those inferences from the non-answer answers he provided. I never got to a contract with this seller. My pre-offer discussion of an access contingency was enough for me to learn that this deal was more headache than I wanted.

A few months later I was working on a 1,000-acre property in New York's Adirondack Park, which fronted a large reservoir and appeared to have an unrestricted, deeded, ROW easement that the owner never used. He canoes in, I was told, several miles each way when he visited, which wasn't often. The property had merchantable timber value, but I was not interested in trying to find a logger who wanted to truck logs across frozen water to a state-owned public boat landing even if the state environmental regulators approved that idea. Use of the four-mile-long ROW was the key to this property, but the key wouldn't turn the lock's tumbler. Relations between the seller and the property owners over whom his easement crossed were so hostile that any effort to use the easement—certainly by logging trucks—would initiate a legal war. The prize wasn't worth the blood. Again, the discussion of potential contract language prior to submitting a contract with an access guarantee in it led to information that forced me to scratch this one off my list.

A buyer's contract should always require that the seller deliver **marketable title** at closing. A marketable title is one that has no serious defects, does not depend on problematic questions of law or fact to prove its legitimacy, does not leave the buyer open to litigation, does not threaten the buyer's quiet enjoyment of the property and allows the new owner to sell or mortgage the property. Marketable title does not guarantee acreage; it refers to ownership of what the seller is selling. A marketable title can have certain defects that might impose limits and restrictions on ownership. These should be turned up in either the buyer's **title search**, whereby the buyer's lawyer investigates all public records for title defects for a certain number of years back, or an **abstract of title**, which is the lawyer's narrative report of all the items found in the record. A title search usually occurs after contingencies are removed. A **preliminary title search** generally takes place after the seller accepts the buyer's contract. I feel more comfortable with a preliminary title search occurring during scoping, before the offer is submitted. If a problem is turned up, the buyer can then include in his contract a provision for the seller to cure the found defect. Nothing is lost by having the buyer request that the seller disclose any defect in title.

When a seller has evidence of title, it shows proof of his ownership. But a deed, in and of itself, does not establish ownership. The seller's deed must be combined with evidence of ownership as recorded in a chain of title leading up to the seller's ownership. This is done through the buyer's lawyer (or licensed abstractor or title company) issuing a **certificate of title** (which is research-based opinion that the seller's title is marketable and no claims against the seller's ownership are found in the public record), title insurance or a Torrens certificate (a title system used in some states). A certificate of title does not guarantee the seller's ownership, however. It will not pick up unrecorded liens and claims against the property, as well as hidden defects, such as fraud, incorrect marital information and forgeries. For that reason, the buyer needs to ask the seller to disclose what he knows about defects in his ownership (title). It's one more step a buyer should take to protect his interests. If a buyer has doubts about the seller's title, he can make his offer contingent on obtaining title insurance and acceptable results from an abstract of title.

CONTINGENCIES

The tactical use of **contract contingencies** is one way of accomplishing many of the objectives I listed at the beginning of this chapter.

A contingency provides for either something to be done to the buyer's satisfaction and/or something to occur before the contract becomes binding on the parties. The buyer can use unacceptability as grounds for either voiding his offer without penalty or resuming negotiations within the existing offer. A purchase contract with a **results-acceptable-to-the-buyer contingency** gives the buyer a legal out if that need arises. The non-specific language of results acceptable to buyer is better than a contingency where, for instance, the offer is made to depend on specified financing terms, such as a 25-year mortgage at no more than seven percent with no more than three points. The buyer may find himself not wanting to do the deal even when he arranges financing that fits the specific requirements of his offer. Results-acceptable-to-buyer language gives the buyer an emergency all-purpose release if one is needed. Results-acceptable-to-the-buyer contingencies are much more useful to buyers and, therefore, may be harder to get sellers to accept. This type of contingency never incorporates specific terms. The buyer says to the seller: the results of my efforts to fulfill my obligations under this contract need to work for me; I can't anticipate what those results will be at this time because there are things I still don't know; I'll perform on the contract if I get results—financing, information, etc.—that in my opinion meet my needs. If a contingency produces unacceptable results, the buyer can terminate the contract offer without penalty or do a final round of negotiation with the seller in light of the new information.

Used judiciously and prudently, contingencies can be made a part of a buyer's negotiating strategy to:

- protect the buyer from booby-traps that he did not find in his pre-purchase scoping;

- get the property under contract quickly with a no-penalty escape;

- force disclosure of seller-controlled information;

- provide time and opportunity within an incentive-loaded framework for the parties to solve a problem within a buyer-friendly context;

- build momentum toward closing as each contingency is resolved;

- negotiate changes in price and terms when new information is uncovered;

- buy time without paying for it;

- pressure a seller into concessions by stretching his time frame and getting him invested in working with you; and

- give the buyer leverage by being able to terminate his offer without financial penalty when results of a contingency investigation don't suit him.

These are powerful points of leverage and should not be used frivolously.

Every contingency represents a loose end that needs to be either resolved to the buyer's satisfaction or withdrawn by the buyer for the sale to close. Contingencies present both parties with the possibility of additional negotiating where results are either marginally acceptable or marginally unacceptable to the buyer. This grey area of marginal acceptability/unacceptability usually takes the form of information that either increases the anticipated expense of the buyer's purchase or decreases the estimated value of a property's assets. When a buyer uses an unacceptable result to suggest reopening negotiations, the seller is no longer bound to anything in the contract. It may be fair for the seller to give something to the buyer to help him with the less-than-pleasing result while taking more of some other thing. If a seller comes to think that a buyer is gaming him with contingencies, it's likely to blow up the deal. Contingencies can be used to straighten out the smallest details as well as matters that will make the deal or break it. Buyers should not use contingencies gratuitously. They should be inserted when needed and written with great deliberateness.

While contingencies are protective, they cannot take the place of thorough pre-offer scoping. The reason, of course, is that the buyer's contract offer must include a price, which should be one the buyer can comfortably afford and is justified by the value of the property's assets. *You determine your price and calculate assets before you submit your offer, based on what you discovered during your scoping.* You can fine-tune an offer with grey-area bargaining once the results are in hand, but I would not put too many oxen loads on that burro. A seller may be willing to reopen your offer on one or possibly two items (including price), but I would assume that two items is the outside limit with all but the most desperate of sellers.

A buyer will sometimes find a seller who announces that he will consider no contract that contains any contingency. That may be a tactic to prevent a buyer from discovering what the seller is hoping to hide. Rather than confront this seller directly, a buyer can offer a **three-price contract** and a 90-day closing. During escrow, the buyer continues his scoping. If a lot of discounting factors are found, his lowest price becomes his offer; if some discounting factors appear, his offer is then his middle price; and if the property comes up clean, then he commits to his highest offering price. A three-price offer, however, does not give the buyer the opportunity to void the contract if something unacceptable is discovered. Submit such an offer only with the consent of your local lawyer—and even then be careful.

I've found that when a seller does not want to allow the buyer to thoroughly research his property, he's trying to hide something big and bad. Why else would he refuse to let you smell his cantaloupe?

A contingency can save you from disaster. One of my clients made an offer on about 1,000 acres of Virginia timberland that bordered a river. The seller was a sawmill; the buyer was a developer. The contract contained a results-acceptable-to-the-buyer timber-evaluation contingency. The timber value turned out to be just fine; the problem with it was that the owner had secretly sold it. His broker was innocently marketing the land as if the timber were part of the purchase. The seller might have argued in his court defense that he had orally informed the buyer that the timber did not convey. From what I understood of the facts, the seller simply hid the timber sale. When the buyer discovered the backdoor deal, he tried to buy out the timber contract without success. He then used the timber contingency—results acceptable to the buyer—to cancel his offer and get his deposit back without further entanglement.

The danger in learning about contract tactics and contingencies is that readers will approach every land sale over-armed for their need and, as a result, play it too clever by half. The buyer wants to buy the seller's property, not scare him away or humiliate him with contract virtuosity. **The best purchase contract is as short, clean and simple as is needed.** One results-acceptable-to-the-buyer contingency is sufficient protection; two is aiming a pistol at your foot; and three is pulling the trigger. A land buyer should not see himself as trying to trick the seller. Trickery gets you into trouble. Buyer tactics discussed here are available to block seller tactics that are adverse to the buyer's interests. Think of it as a ju-jitsu defense where the buyer turns his opponent's aggressiveness to his own ends. If you start throwing a bunch of legal bean balls at a seller, he'll take his bat and go home. As a buyer, you've become more trouble than your offer is worth.

Many real-estate contracts include a **financing contingency**, which makes the purchase depend on the buyer's arranging institutional financing, usually a specific dollar amount at no more than a specified rate and terms. If the buyer is unable to secure acceptable financing within a certain number of days, his contract offer becomes void without penalty. If he gets acceptable financing, the purchase goes through. Take my advice: don't offer a financing contingency pegged to a specific rate and term, and try to have the seller agree to give you an unspecified reasonable amount of time to arrange financing, not to exceed two or three months. You justify this open-ended language to the seller by saying that you want to maximize your chances of getting the deal done. If you are forced into using a specific rate and term, always make sure to provide a cap on points or closing costs. If your contingency simply states five percent interest, the seller may be able to find a lender who is offering a five percent rate that carries a load of points and an unfavorable adjustable term.

When institutional financing is not forthcoming, a buyer can propose **seller financing** as a replacement, which brings advantages and disadvantages to both sides. I advise against rigging an institutional-financing contingency so that it will fail in order to force a seller into financing your purchase. As soon as you miss the deadline on a single payment, the seller can get even—and more—by declaring the note in default and repossessing his property along with whatever cash of yours he has in hand.

Familiar contingencies provide for a **house inspection, termite inspection, urea-formaldehyde (found in old insulation) test, mold test, radon test and indoor-air-pollution tests**. Most termite-inspection contingencies require the seller to treat the infestation; he voids the contract by refusing. Fixing other problems found in various tests and inspections is a matter of negotiation.

Mold was the subject of some 10,000 lawsuits in 2003. It tends to be a problem in air-tight, energy-efficient houses in warm, wet climates. (Associated Press, "Mold-based lawsuits on the rise," Richmond Times-Dispatch, July 27, 2003.) Mold—one of many types of fungus—requires moisture and food—cellulose, wood, soap scum, dust. It's found in damp basements, bathrooms (unventilated), attics, air-conditioning ducts and around leaks in pipes or outside walls. Old farmhouses, especially those lacking basements, may be less likely to have mold, radon and indoor-air pollution, because they have leaky windows and doors and no wall insulation—all of which promote higher indoor-outdoor air-exchange rates. This leakiness, which increases heating/cooling bills, allows indoor-air pollutants to move outside. Modern housing is more heat-efficient, but the tightness created by insulation and energy-efficient windows and doors creates air-pollution sumps. These can be mitigated by installing in-line filters on forced-air heating systems. Systems using radiators and electric baseboard heaters need stand-alone room air purifiers. Dehumidifers help with mold. (See Mary Beth Breckenridge, Knight Ridder, "Mold Enters Quietly, But It Makes Its Presence Known," Washington Post, March 25, 2006.) Mold is not necessarily harmful. Whether its presence kills a purchase, depends on its type, extent and estimated cost of remediation.

Two common country contingencies involve an **acceptable water sample** and a **septic-system investigation**. The latter can make a purchase be contingent on obtaining buyer-acceptable results in locating a site for a new system or determining that the existing system is in working order and of acceptable size and design for the buyer's purpose. On old household-water systems, the buyer should make sure that the sample is tested for **lead** (in addition to bacteria, chemical pollutants, hardness, suspended solids, etc.), which can leach from old lead pipes or lead-based solder that is now banned.

On houses built before 1978, sellers are required to disclose any knowledge of **lead-based paint** and provide the buyer with a booklet, "Protect Your Family from Lead in Your Home." The buyer may have the house inspected at his expense for such paint within ten days of the contract coming into effect. Lead was used as a pigment and a drying agent in alkyd oil-based paint for home interiors and exteriors. It is estimated that about 75 percent of pre-1978 private housing has some lead-based paint. Fixes include removal, which is expensive, and repainting (i.e., painting over), which is less. Testing will determine the level of hazard, if any. Flaking and peeling lead-based paint is extremely hazardous, especially to small children. Stripping and sanding such paint elevates the likelihood of ingesting or breathing lead particulate. If you suspect a problem, insert a **lead-testing contingency** with results acceptable to buyer. The lead-disclosure statement is not a contingency that allows the buyer to void the contract; it simply discloses what the seller claims to be his knowledge of the hazard.

On rural property, a buyer should use contingencies to deepen his knowledge of a property's assets and liabilities when there's insufficient time to do the necessary scoping prior to submitting a purchase offer. Occasions arise when it's more important for a buyer to get a contract in place as soon as possible than to scope every detail to absolute certainty. A contingency protects the buyer's back in fast contracts. If, for example, you are targeting a working farm with other buyers circling, you might propose a contingency that asks the seller to show you his profit-and-loss statements, Schedule Fs and net-worth statements for the last five years, with results acceptable to the buyer. You can offer a bit more than you would otherwise and prepare to back out or renegotiate price if the seller's numbers are lower than you anticipated. When a seller balks at disclosing information required by a contingency, he's showing you more than anything he may be telling you.

You may want to use a **timber-evaluation contingency** for wooded acreage. Your offer is contingent on the seller's agreement to allow your forester to perform an evaluation (walk-through or cruise, the choice is your forester's) of the property's timber, with results acceptable to you. Budget a window of 60 calendar days for this work. Foresters can generally get to a new client within that period of time. More time should be allowed for very large properties. Consult with your forester before writing your contingency's term. Any contingency that includes a term gives you that amount of time to continue scoping other aspects of the property at no cost or risk to you. *As a rule, a smart buyer will have his forester do a walk-through or cruise before submitting a contract offer, not as a contingency within a contract where price is already agreed to.*

If you've determined the value of the seller's timber—or any other asset—prior to making an offer, you can propose a contingency with the idea of negotiating it away in return for some seller concession. A concession of this type appears to the seller as if you are giving up a lot and assuming a big financial exposure, when, in fact, you're giving up nothing and assuming no risk at all. This can be quite effective with one or two contingencies. The buyer needs to be convincing and bargain with a poker face.

A generic form of scoping contingency is one that land investors use: it's a **90-day study contingency**, with results acceptable to the buyer. Study contingencies are often used when a buyer wants to get a contract in place before other buyers submit theirs. They're also used when a buyer doesn't know enough to feel confident in his price, or he doesn't know what he doesn't know and hopes that he can find out what he doesn't know over a couple of months. From the buyer's perspective, a study contingency creates a 90-day option to buy, but it's more advantageous than a normal option because it allows the buyer, first, to reopen the contract's purchase price if the study results don't please him, and, second, to not lose any money if he fails to perform. Sellers of large tracts are accustomed to study contingencies. If you find your seller rejecting a 90-day study contingency, you can substitute a 90-day timber-evaluation contingency or a 90-day environmental-assessment contingency, both of which are the same wolves in different sheepskins. Thirty- and 60-day study periods are appropriate for small acreages.

You can propose a **clean-it-up contingency** for specific messes—e.g., where the seller's access is unclear or in active dispute, a disgruntled tenant has left after wrecking the house, or a boundary dispute exists that you do not want to inherit. You probably want to call it something other than a clean-it-up contingency, but you should be clear about its purpose with the seller who in all likelihood will be expected to do something he probably would prefer to pass on to you.

An **environmental contingency** is appropriate where the buyer suspects a problem, such as a leaking, buried fuel tank; hazardous materials (a pile of disintegrating asbestos shingles dumped out back; disintegrating metal drums of creosote or agricultural chemicals); presence of wetlands or endangered, threatened and sensitive (ETS) species; restrictions on water use and the like. Working farms often have large fuel tanks on the premises. In the past, these tanks were usually buried. Today, they are more commonly installed on the surface in cast-concrete vaults. Farms and residences have generally been exempt from federal regulation of tanks when they hold less than 1,100 gallons of fuel oil for noncommercial purposes as well as heating oil used on site. But abandoned tanks can leak residues and require some degree of remediation. If you suspect contamination, ask the seller to disclose what he knows and then write a contingency that allows an inspection with results acceptable to the buyer. On large tracts, an environmental contingency usually calls for a Phase I Environmental Analysis—sufficient scoping to alert you to the type of problems found on the property and a preliminary assessment of their hazardousness and remedies.

If you are intending to sell a portion of the target property, divide it for future sale, or do any construction, you are likely to find yourself requesting plan approval from the local zoning authority, building inspector, architectural review board or one or more environmental agencies, such as the county health department or a state office. Plans that raise zoning/rezoning issues, conditional uses and exceptions to the local plan bring public scrutiny and often opposition. Public hearings are scheduled, and plans require approval by public boards. An applicant has no guarantee that his proposal will be approved as submitted or approved at all. Whenever your immediate post-purchase plans involve a permit, rezoning, conditional-use permit (which is authorization for the applicant to engage in a use of his property that is inconsistent with existing zoning but may be allowed if the "general welfare" is advanced), it is imperative that you include in your contract a clause that makes your **purchase contingent on receiving all necessary permits and approvals in a form acceptable to buyer**. This is usually handled by having the owner/seller apply for the permits that are then conveyed with the property. Have your local lawyer work out this language.

One other type of contingency exists that a buyer may use. It is not part of the buyer's purchase contract with the seller. It is a **contingent sale contract** that the buyer negotiates with those who want to buy all or part of the seller's property once the buyer closes with the seller. A contingent contract obligates the investor-buyer to sell something to the next buyer at a certain price and terms only if he purchases the entirety.

Negotiating by manipulating contingencies should be used sparingly, if at all. Bogus contingencies will be seen as such by most sellers. When a seller reaches a certain point of unease with a buyer's genuineness and good faith, he's more likely to stop negotiating than to be backed into a deal holding his nose.

I usually write contingencies using the phrase, **"with results acceptable to the buyer."** That reserves to the buyer full control over his performance on the contract's initial terms and gives him an unchallengeable, penalty-free exit if he needs it. I resist putting fixed numbers into contingencies, with the exception of a specific number of days for its term.

However, I have employed fixed-number contingencies when my pre-offer scoping made me confident of their results. The circumstances would be an offer where I'm sure of two contingency results, but not of a third. I want the seller to become increasingly invested in my offer, so I use two contingencies whose results I know will be acceptable. The third contingency—results acceptable to buyer—may come in positive or negative. In the first case, I can close the deal. In the second, I hope the seller will help me solve the unacceptable result now that we are this far along.

You may find it advisable to insert a one-time, no-additional-deposit **time extension** on a contingency that the buyer activates through written notification. I'd cap the extension at no more than 30 calendar days. The most common rationale for writing in extension language is that certain investigations may be hard to schedule and even harder to predict their duration. Archeological and environmental studies often open new doors of investigation that take a long time to shut.

I've seen a number of inexperienced buyers insert a **non-contingent non-contingency** into their contracts. Real-estate professionals working for the seller may "help" with its wording. These non-contingencies read something like this: "Buyer reserves the right to have Seller's house inspected and a radon test performed at his expense within 30 days." Such language only gives the buyer the right to have this work performed on his nickel within that period of time. It does not make the buyer's purchase contingent on obtaining acceptable results. This buyer can't void his contract without penalty even when the inspection results are horrendous. Buyer performance is still required at the contract price. Don't use non-contingent non-contingencies, except as chips, which means you are willing to cut them from your offer to get the seller to sign.

It's sometimes beneficial for a buyer to have a **general bail-out contingency**, though it's never called that. This is a contingency that a buyer uses to get out of a purchase if he needs to. It can be related to any plausible condition on the property, as long as the words say that buyer determines the acceptability of results and no penalty is imposed for voiding the contract where results are deemed unacceptable. Don't tie a bail out to specified results or specific numbers. A general bail-out contingency should be time-capped and buyer-paid to make it palatable to the seller. Don't propose an appraisal contingency as your bail out, because sellers will resist a deal dependent on the buyer getting a satisfactory appraisal from a buyer-paid appraiser. This type of contingency protects you for the period of its term, not longer.

A timber-evaluation (not cruise—too specific, too costly) or soils-evaluation contingency can be used this way. A timber-evaluation contingency might look like this:

> **Buyer's offer is contingent on obtaining results acceptable to the buyer from a timber evaluation that he arranges with a forester of his choice and at his own expense and concludes within sixty (60) calendar days of this Contract taking effect. Buyer shall perform on this Contract if he deems results acceptable, and shall provide timely written notice to Seller of such acceptability. If Buyer deems results to be unacceptable, he shall provide timely written notice to Seller of such unacceptability. In that event, Buyer's earnest money/security deposit shall be returned to him in full within five (5) calendar days of receipt of notification, and this Contract becomes void without penalty to Buyer or further obligation from Seller.**

A bail-out contingency is an emergency parachute that gives you the right to walk away from your offer within its term. If you remove this contingency, you will be expected to buy the property. If you insert a bail-out contingency, you will be required to do whatever it is you say you want that time to do. You must do that work before voiding the contract. A study-period contingency is, for this reason, a good choice, since its work and costs can be negligible. Still, you have to do something. You can't bail out without at least paying for your parachute.

A results-acceptable-to-the-buyer contingency steers the buyer into a five-branch decision tree. The first is that the results are acceptable, allowing the purchase to be completed with no change to the original terms. The second is that the results are so unacceptable that the buyer immediately voids the contract and gets his full deposit back. The third is that the results are marginally unacceptable, but the buyer goes through with the deal anyway. The fourth branch is one where the results are unacceptable and the buyer approaches the buyer to reopen the negotiations based on the new information. The last of these is available to the buyer without having to write it into the contingency language itself. The fifth branch—which I advise against taking—is the case where the results are acceptable, but the buyer pretends that they are not to effect one final cut in price. Some buyers bargain this way; I don't recommend it.

Contingencies are usually assumed to disappear at the end of their term if the buyer does nothing to alert the seller that he is invoking their escape language. That means you will be expected to perform on the contract if you do not explicitly invoke the contingency's termination and escape in writing. A buyer cannot use a contingency to void his purchase offer after the contingency deadline has passed. You should consider a contingency to be self-liquidating if you do not invoke its escape protections in writing within its time limit. A self-liquidating contingency is one that removes itself, which means that your offer is no longer contingent and will proceed to closing.

Where results are unacceptable, notify the seller that you're voiding the contract at least a day in advance of the contingency's termination. You can use an e-mail or a fax as long as you also send a letter that gets there no later than the deadline date. Get a return receipt. Don't cut contingency escapes close or scrimp on postage. If you miss the deadline, you can be held to performance. Once a buyer removes all contingencies or allows them to liquidate themselves, all parties should expect the purchase to go through as set forth originally, or with whatever modifications the parties might have added during escrow. Going through with the contract is called, **performance**.

Once a buyer's contingencies expire (liquidate themselves by not being invoked), are removed or are declared satisfied, the seller expects performance. Where a buyer doesn't close, the seller may sue for **specific performance**, which means the buyer will be forced to go through with the purchase as set forth in the contract offer.

ALL-CASH OFFER WITH NO FINANCING CONTINGENCY

Sellers like brief, straight-forward, short-escrow, uncomplicated, all-cash purchase contracts. They hate contingencies, and most won't do seller-financing propositions, because they need their cash out of the property immediately. Buyers can accommodate some or all of these seller wants in certain circumstances—in return for a price discount or **boot**. (Boot is a generic term for other stuff that a buyer or seller incorporates into a deal in addition to the simple sale of property for cash. Seller boot might be agricultural equipment, materials, labor or all manner of personal property. Buyer's boot can be anything of value that the seller agrees to accept. Boot is included to even out a deal or sweeten the pot, depending on your perspective. Boot is often used to even 1031 tax-deferred exchanges.) A buyer should understand that when he has arranged financing and makes up the difference with cash, he is submitting a no-strings, all-cash offer to the seller. Every buyer should describe such a no-contingency offer—as NO STRINGS, ALL CASH—at least five times in the seller's presence as explanation for his discounted price. An all-cash, no-contingency is a bird in the hand to a seller.

Only if I've done my scoping thoroughly would I consider making an offer without a contingency of some sort. If a contract does not carry a financing contingency, the buyer will be expected to perform whether or not institutional financing is available on acceptable terms. Freeing a contract of a financing contingency and some type of bail-out contingency is needlessly risky in many cases. Sellers don't usually quibble over a financing contingency, so you're really only asking for one contingency. If you have your money worked out in advance and you've done your scoping, you might consider a contingency-free offer in return for better price or terms.

What is an all-cash offer free of financing contingency worth to a seller? It depends on the seller's circumstances, particularly his urgency to make a deal with *you*. A buyer can use the carrot of an all-cash offer free of financing contingency in negotiating. Don't toss it in as a freebie; it's worth something—maybe a lot—to the seller. I'd assume it's worth at least one or two percent off your best negotiated price. An all-cash offer free of contingencies could be worth as much as five percent off the seller's lowest price in some situations. If the seller is unwilling to budge from his low (last) position, work with his number as you start adding contingencies, complications and sweeteners you want. A seller often realizes that simplicity and certainty offset a lower price.

The best negotiating approach is to separate and individualize items conceded and sought. That approach allows you to judge how the seller values each one. You can then combine items from both sides of the table in whichever way works. Always trade something for something. An all-cash offer unencumbered with contingencies is a close-to-guaranteed, go-through offer to the seller; get its value in return. Don't offer to eliminate the financing contingency and come up with an all-cash offer as your beginning position. Approach it like this: "If I were able to make you an all-cash offer, how much of a reduction in price would that be worth to you? And if I were able to assume the risk of an offer free of a financing contingency, what would that be worth to you?" If his first response is negative, don't make your offer all cash and don't eliminate contingencies. Keep negotiating. The more tentative his stubbornness makes you, the more he will come to value the possibility of all cash and no contingency. Patience.

SELLER CONTINGENCY

I've run into a seller contingency once. The seller had agreed to the buyer's purchase contract and price, subject to an appraisal that the seller would arrange. If the appraisal value came in at more than 103 percent of the contract price, the seller reserved the right to cancel the contract. The deal, in other words, was contingent on the seller's appraiser submitting an appraisal value that worked against the seller's interest. I told my client to reject this contingency, because I figured the seller would get the appraisal he was paying for. Were the appraisal to come in at less than 103 percent, the seller could simply accept the results and go through with the deal on the agreed terms. The seller, however, sensed that he could get more out of this buyer. The appraisal came in about $1 million more than the contract price, about 105 percent of the original. Against my advice, my client agreed to pay the appraisal price—and then lost his security when he couldn't flip the property during escrow. Subsequently, another buyer came along, paid the appraisal price and struggled to resell at a profit.

Buyers should reject a seller-contingency ploy out of hand. Facing such a seller, the buyer can respond in one of two ways:

1. "Sure," the buyer says, "I (the buyer) will arrange and pay for the appraisal, and we'll go with whatever the appraisal value is as our agreed selling price." The buyer is likely to get the appraisal value he pays for, just as the seller will get what he pays for.

2. Buyer says to seller: "You know the value of your property better than any appraiser. Let's move along or forget about appraisals. Your appraiser will give you what you want, and mine will give me what I want. They're just a waste of our money."

The second response is used if the first fails. There are other responses, but they all tend to suck a buyer into playing this seller-rigged game. I see no purpose for a seller contingency in a purchase contract other than to take a second bite out of the buyer's pocketbook.

A variation on this trick is a seller who has an appraisal in hand, which he doesn't reveal, and confides to the buyer, "I'll sell it to you for the appraisal price." I ran into a Denver developer with a 9,000-acre ranch (9,000 deeded, about 40,000+ on public lease) in Wyoming who proposed this through his broker. The seller was sitting on a jacked-up appraisal, the actual value of which he would disclose only after my buyer agreed to this way of determining selling price. I didn't laugh aloud, but a ploy as clumsy as this surely deserved a Kramdenesque har-de-har-har.

A purchase contract is, in one sense, a set of seller contingencies that expect the buyer to accomplish certain tasks during escrow. These typically include arranging his financing so that the buyer can pay the price he's offered the seller, carry out whatever investigations the buyer has insisted on, waive or satisfy the buyer's own contingencies and complete the buyer's side of the legal work. The seller's sale, in other words, is contingent on the buyer getting these jobs done. I would be wary of a seller contingency that gives the seller room to reopen the buyer's contract in any way during escrow. The appraisal contingency is one such device. Others might involve an independent evaluation of timber or minerals with a reservation allowing the seller to increase the agreed purchase price or void the deal; a contingency that allows the seller to sell or remove certain assets during escrow with price revisions; a contingency that allows the seller to increase the contract price if a higher offer comes in during escrow; and, finally, a seller bail-out contingency that gives the seller the right to void the contract, with or without cause.

EQUITABLE TITLE

The buyer can make use of the escrow time, typically 30 to 90 days, to perform certain work to benefit his impending possession. This work is distinct from that which the buyer does to satisfy his contingencies. *A buyer should consider doing such work only if he is certain that he will complete the purchase.*

During the escrow period, the seller continues to hold title and ownership. Title conveys to the buyer on the day he pays the seller at which time the seller delivers the deed (which may then be held by a trustee if an institutional loan using the property as security is involved) and the buyer accepts the deed. A buyer with a mortgage acquires full ownership only upon removing the debt (lien) from the property. The

602

day on which closing occurs is usually the day on which documents are recorded with the county clerk.

The buyer holds a legal interest in the property during escrow that is called, **equitable title**. (When a seller is fully financing a sale of his own property though an installment land contract, the buyer holds equitable title in the property he's possessing until he completes the purchase.) A buyer with equitable title has the right to obtain absolute ownership during the time the seller holds legal title by completing the purchase. In states following the **title theory of mortgages**, the buyer with a mortgage holds nothing but equitable title until the mortgage is paid. In those states, equitable title gives the borrower possession and use of the property. In states where the **lien theory** is followed, the mortgage borrower (mortgagor) holds both legal and equitable title with the mortgage lender (mortgagee) holding a lien on the property. Equitable title begins once a buyer removes all contigencies.

The set of buyer rights under equitable title during escrow varies from state to state. The buyer, for example, may be able to insure assets on the seller's property. Within these rights, work done on the property by the buyer at his expense during escrow can save him time and money once he takes possession. If escrow occurs during good weather and closing is scheduled for the beginning of bad weather, a buyer may want to do good-weather work during escrow rather than postpone those jobs for a year. Work done under equitable title should not surprise a seller, but the legal concept can be invoked when necessary to help in persuading a seller to allow the buyer to do reasonable tasks during escrow.

When a buyer wants to do work on the property during escrow, I advise him to write these tasks into the purchase offer and discuss the work directly with the seller. A buyer's purchase contract might provide for the buyer doing one or more of the following tasks during escrow:

- Cruise and paint merchantable timber; allow timber buyers to visit the property and evaluate timber. (This will allow the buyer to sell the timber shortly after closing.);

- Survey and mark lines on the ground in anticipation of selling part of the property soon after closing;

- Allow prospective buyers for the newly surveyed parcel(s) to visit the seller's property in the company of the buyer. (This doesn't work very well when the buyer is trying to sell the seller's owner-occupied house.) The buyer can then negotiate contingent contracts—contracts of sale contingent on his purchase of the property from the seller—with these buyers. Do not under any circumstances sign a contract to sell a lot from an impending purchase without making that lot sale contingent on your purchasing the property;

- Arrange for the local utility to design and cost out power access to the the property; determine whether neighbors will grant easements;

- Arrange for septic-system site tests. Both percolation and soil-color methods require digging holes with backhoes and then filling them (The number of holes dug depends on how many are required to find a spot that satisfies the standard.);

- Allow engineer and contractor access to property to design new septic system;

- Allow access to seller's property/house by buyer's architect and contractor to develop construction/remodeling plans;

- Allow testing of water quantity and quality;

- Allow farm consultants to visit the property, test soil and water, and evaluate operation;

603

- Where farm equipment is part of the purchase, allow access of mechanics to test and evaluate equipment;

- Allow buyer to do farm-related work, such as pruning orchard or vineyard, controlled burning of undergrowth to increase certain types of game forage, mechanical cutting of unwanted brush (e.g., multiflora rose), planting of seedlings, application of fertilizer and other season-dependent treatments to cropland or pasture;

- Allow the buyer to store materiel and equipment in designated places; and

- Conduct agreed-on excavations, such as road grading and pond construction.

Within a purchase contract, the buyer's right to possession and full use of the seller's property is deferred until closing. Equitable title does not change this. However, equitable title does provide a framework for securing the seller's consent to do tasks of minimal intrusiveness. More intrusive tasks, such as excavations and controlled burns, are probably beyond the buyer's rights under equitable title, though the seller may raise no objection as long as it costs him nothing and his property benefits.

The buyer must understand that any activity he undertakes during escrow that improves the seller's property will not be compensated if he fails to perform. Buyers should secure seller consent to any activity that alters the seller's property, rather than rely on their rights under equitable title. When I've wanted to do something during escrow, I've talked it over with the seller and, assuming he agrees, spelled it out in the contract. I don't try to use equitable title as a club to beat out permission to use the seller's land. But I do explain that I'm not asking for anything that is legally unreasonable.

In 2005, I was helping a client who was pursuing a 3,000-acre property in the Adirondack Park that was owned by a prominent record producer and his wife, an equally prominent singer. My client wanted to cut some of the merchantable hardwood sawtimber immediately after completing the purchase. The best stumpage bids for that timber would be found in the fall for winter cutting. It was, therefore, advisable to have his forester mark the timber during escrow, so that the sale could take place as early into the winter as possible. The problem was that the sellers might not do the deal if they understood the buyer wanted to cut some of *his* newly purchased trees. Rather than invoke equitable title, my client did not bring up the idea of marking trees during escrow, equitable title or not. In this case, the seller had the wherewithal to kill a deal were he offended and not worry too much about paying the penalty for doing so. Better, then, to wait and not put the purchase at risk.

Equitable title gives a buyer with an **installment land contract** the right to possess, use and alter the seller's property. But that is a different application of equitable title than its use during escrow.

Buyers of urban/suburban residential property are always told to put no money into the seller's property before closing. The logic of this advice is clear: if the buyer fails to perform, he loses the money spent on improving the seller's property. The same risk comes with buying rural property, but the context can be much more personal and less formal, depending on the rural seller.

As a seller, I would not object to most escrow work a buyer wanted as long as I bore no responsibility to compensate him if the purchase fell through. I would not go along with work that would disturb my occupation during escrow or work that would change the property in a way that I would not want to live with in case of failure to perform. That leaves a lot of room, especially with rural property that a seller does not occupy. I think you will find most rural sellers willing to "work with" a buyer on escrow work, particularly tasks that are dependent on a season or ground conditions. The rural seller will understand the reasonableness of such requests.

A buyer may be able to use an escrow investment to act as a proxy for earnest money. A buyer who puts $10,000 into improving an access road during escrow is offering the seller more security in getting performance than $7,500 escrowed as earnest money. The **investment proxy** becomes even more persuasive to the seller when he understands that a buyer's failure to perform will limit the seller's recovery to the earnest money because the buyer—as all buyers should—will package a **liquidated damages** clause with any cash security deposit. This language limits the buyer's financial exposure from a bail out to his cash deposit. A buyer can also argue to the seller that his road investment should shave a thousand or two off the purchase price, because the seller is getting an improvement he will value in the event that the buyer fails to perform. These tactics work when the buyer's proposed investments during escrow match what the seller would want to do were he keeping the property or making it more marketable. Depending on the buyer's intentions and subsequent use of the new property, tax benefits can be available for certain expenses. The buyer must remember, of course, that the $10,000 in new road will not be available to pay for the land purchase, which is the destination of escrowed earnest money.

Some escrow investments may lend themselves to a **buy-back provision** in the purchase contract. This comes into play only when the buyer is unable to complete the purchase. Here's one example where a buy-back might work. It is fairly common for access to property to involve a seller-owned bridge. No one likes to rebuild bridges, even simple ones. It's hard work, usually expensive, and may cut the road link to the outside for several days or more. If both buyer and seller agree that the access bridge needs to be replaced, the buyer might agree to pay for the construction with the proviso that if he fails to perform for any reason, the seller agrees to reimburse him for all receipted expenses, or, if not that, some percentage. The cost bears on the buyer, but the inconvenience is borne by the seller. A buyer can get favorable terms if he agrees to couple this investment with some security deposit.

LONGER RATHER THAN SHORTER ESCROW

Sellers like to close in 30 days. They want their money sooner rather than later. They don't want the buyer thinking about the purchase for longer than is necessary. They don't want "buyer's remorse" or cold feet to set in. The shorter the escrow, the more secure a seller is likely to feel.

Conversely, buyers usually benefit from a longer escrow period. They need time to carry out whatever inspections and contingency evaluations they've written into the contract. A longer closing provides the opportunity for important information to turn up and for issues to be resolved. Where a buyer is planning sell a portion of the property soon after closing, a longer escrow gives him more time to market the lot(s) without paying interest on the purchase. Buyers benefit from a late-starting mortgage clock. And there's always the "woodwork" factor, as in once a contract is in place, you just never know what's going to come out.

If a buyer has done his pre-purchase scoping, he can consider giving up a longer escrow for something taken off the purchase price. I stress the "if" in that sentence. The danger in a short escrow is that the buyer's pre-offer scoping has missed something important that would turn up in a normal escrow term. First-time rural buyers should stay away from short escrows as a price-reduction tactic. As your experience grows, keep the idea in your tool kit.

WARRANTIES TO SURVIVE THE CONTRACT

In both a General Warranty Deed and a Special Warranty Deed, the seller gives the buyer three warranties—promises—that bind the seller to him in the future. These are: 1) the covenant of warranty forever or general warranty, in which the seller promises to defend the title against lawful claims and compensate the buyer for any loss from a successful claim to superior title; 2) covenant of quiet enjoyment, in which the seller promises that no claim of superior title will disturb the buyer's possession and enjoyment of the property; and 3) covenant of further assurances, in which the seller promises to execute any additional documents needed to perfect the title conveyed. The difference between the two types of deeds is that the seller's promises under a General Warranty Deed covers the property from its origins, whereas the seller's promise under the Special Warranty Deed is limited to his time of ownership. These are the only three covenants from the seller that survive the purchase contract unless additional language is included.

A seller often makes representations about his property and promises of one sort or another to encourage a buyer to proceed with a purchase. *For these statements to bind a seller after the sale*, the buyer's contract must include language, seller's "**warranties to survive closing**." The more specific these warranties are, the more enforceable they will be.

A standard real-estate contract will include language about "warranties that survive closing." This boilerplate usually has the seller promising that he has paid in full all construction/repair expenses that were undertaken within 120 days of closing; that the information in a listing agreement, if any, regarding connection to public sewerage or septic tank is correct to the best of his knowledge; that the seller has disclosed all material latent defects on the property that are known to the seller; and that the seller has disclosed any information that he possesses that materially and adversely affects the consideration to be paid by the Buyer. The seller is only warranting his disclosure of defects he knows or information he possesses. If he doesn't know something and doesn't possess information about a defect, he has no obligation to disclose anything. This is a reasonable standard when dealing with a good-faith buyer with nothing to hide, but it's less effective with a seller who wants to avoid disclosure.

The boilerplate warranty on disclosure relies on the seller's judgment as to what he thinks a material latent defect is; what he thinks he knows about such defects; and what information he believes he possesses (however, he defines possession) about what he thinks might materially and adversely affect the Buyer's "consideration" however the seller chooses to define that term. Whatever protection the boilerplate language provides in theory will be defined in practice when the buyer has to prove that a seller-known defect was not disclosed. Nonetheless, the boilerplate is better than nothing. If a seller-written contract fails to include it, the seller's promises about disclosure terminate with the close of escrow.

SELLER DISCLOSURE AND WARRANTY SURVIVAL: GET AS MUCH AS YOU CAN

Readers who have purchased houses should be familiar with the **standard disclosure forms** now in fairly common use. These forms are state-specific and vary in the questions asked of sellers and level of detail requested. Some states use an **environmental disclosure form** that asks sellers to disclose what they know about various hazards. Institutional lenders may require an environmental review or seller disclosure. Insurance companies may perform their own review of a property—screening for asbestos, PCBs, radon,

USTs, waste sites, urea, lead paint, and air and water pollutants.

A buyer should always ask a FSBO or a seller's agent to see the seller's completed state-required disclosure forms before he submits a purchase offer.

Some standard real-estate disclosure forms give the seller a choice between completing the disclosure form and signing a **disclaimer** that says the seller is making no statement about the property's condition. Disclaimer amounts to a seller offering his property "as-is" while getting out of any obligation to disclose known problems. Disclaimers are a red-flag warning to buyers.

If either the disclosure form is less than adequate for your purposes or the seller signs the disclaimer, you should consider inserting a **disclosure contingency** into your purchase offer with a warranty that survives closing. This contingency should include broad disclosure language as well as a list of items, including defects, that you want the seller to think about in terms of disclosure, rather than leaving his thoughts to his own judgment.

Defects common to houses in both rural and urban/suburban areas include:

- Wet basement
- Crawlspace—unheated, not enough headroom, uninsulated, pipes subject to freezing
- Problems with sewerage/septic system—backups, undersized
- Water problems—pressure, quality, quantity, leaky pipes
- Radon gas in basement
- Infestation of wood-destroying insects—termites, beetles, ants
- Infestations of other creatures—bats, squirrels, bugs, rodents, snakes
- Mold
- Lead hazards—lead-based paint, lead solder in water pipes
- Urea-formaldehyde-based insulation (referred to as Urea-formaldehyde Foam Insulation [UFFI], which emits a gas that irritates some individuals.)
- Cracks, deterioration or shifts in foundations and concrete slabs
- Roof problems—leaks, gutters, water getting into eaves
- Asbestos—shingles, siding, hot-pipe insulation
- Inadequate draw in chimney flue; fire hazard in fireplace or chimney
- Inadequate ventilation in garages
- Inadequate mechanical ventilation in bathrooms and kitchens, or for furnaces
- Water pipes that tend to freeze
- Inoperable windows; warped doors
- Poor quality construction materials—composition board instead of plywood; cheap windows, doors, cabinets

- Old electrical system—lack of three-hole outlets; less than 200 amp service; old/unsafe wiring; no Ground Fault Indicators (GFIs) in bathrooms, kitchens; no wired smoke detectors

Defects common in farms and undeveloped rural property and other items about which you should seek disclosure, include:

- Unrecorded easements, licenses (permissions), life estates, rental agreements, donations, leases, reservations of interest, etc.

- Severance—minerals, water, other assets

- Boundary disputes, acreage discrepancies/shortages, encroachments

- Pollution from neighbors—water, light, noise, odors, visual, etc.

- Pollution on property—water (chemicals, fertilizer, hardness, softness, acidic, iron, sulfur, petroleum), dumps; underground storage (fuel) tanks; PCBs, invasive weeds

- Unauthorized use of property—chronic trespass problem; dumping; dogs running about; hunters

- Adverse potential—any situations that might qualify as adverse possession or adverse use; prescriptive use; easement by necessity

- Environmental restrictions—floodplain, wetlands, presence of ETS species, conservation easements, earthquake, windstorm, hurricane, wind-driven rain, coastal flooding/storm surge, drought, lightning strikes, pests/disease in crops and/or timber, land enrolled in federal conservation programs, non-native weeds (kudzu, multiflora rose, Spotted Knapweed, Leafy Spurge, etc.)

- Physical conditions in land—arid/wet, water supply/quality, sinkholes, soils unsuitable for buyer's plans, septic sites won't perc, surface subsidence from underground mining; over-grazing; erosion

- Land-use restrictions—zoning restrictions

- Access problems—physical, legal

- Fencing issues—bad sections of fence that buyer will need to repair/replace; fencing inappropriate to buyer's plans; gates need to be replaced

- Operability and safety of farm infrastructure, equipment and machinery that will convey

- Soundness of farm buildings—roofs, electrical systems and foundations

The seller and/or his broker will say that the standard contract covers disclosure of each and every item above with boilerplate language such as the following:

Seller warrants that he has disclosed to Buyer and Brokers all material latent defects concerning the Premises that are known to Seller. Seller further warrants that he has disclosed to all parties any information, excluding opinions of value, that he possesses which materially and adversely affects the consideration to be paid by Buyer. (Arizona Association of Realtors "Residential Real Estate Purchase Contract and

Receipt for Deposit," included in Galaty, *et. al*, <u>Modern Real Estate Practice</u>, 13th ed., p. 149.)

The devil in this excerpt lies both in the details that are provided and those that are not. This language lacks specificity from the buyer's perspective. While the seller is asked to disclose all defects that he judges to be both material and latent, what about defects that the seller judges not material and/or not latent? It is arguable that a material defect that is out in the open, such as a floodplain, overgrazing, erosion or a pine stand showing pine beetle infestation, is not latent and therefore need not be disclosed. It's far better to let the buyer judge whether a defect is worthy of mention than to leave it up to the seller. This standard language will give rise to differences of opinion, both large and small. An obvious defect, such as a sound but undersized bridge or a boundary encroachment that would be revealed in a survey if the buyer pays for one, may or may not need to be disclosed. What happens if the seller claims that he did not know of a material latent defect at the time of the contract? In many situations, he'll be able to shed liability. What happens if the seller claims he disclosed something orally and the buyer claims no such disclosure occurred?

Finally, why is the seller exempted from having to disclose defects and adverse information that he should reasonably know about? As a result of the corporate scandals in the early 2000s, Stephen M. Cutler, director of the Securities and Exchange Commission's enforcement division announced: "'If you [corporations, financial/accounting firms] know or have reason to know that you are helping a company mislead its investors, you are in violation of the federal securities laws.'" (Jerry Knight, "SEC: Look Out, Aiders and Abettors," <u>Washington Post</u>, August 4, 2003.) If a buyer does not hold a seller to this same standard, the seller can hide behind professed ignorance of the condition. This standard is less than the covenants of warranty forever and quiet enjoyment, which protect the buyer whether or not the seller knows about them at sale time.

I would consider holding the seller responsible for conditions about which it is reasonable to expect him to know, even though he may not. The justification for such a seemingly overly rigorous standard is simple: the buyer should not be expected to bear a future burden for the seller's present ignorance, deliberate or otherwise. This is exactly the standard that sellers are held to in a General Warranty Deed. The seller's lack of knowledge about a title defect or an encroachment doesn't exempt him from future responsibility and financial liability, at least in theory. The seller will object to this language. He may be trying to conceal a defect that he knows about but is not revealing. Or he may simply be objecting to the open-endedness of this language, an understandable position. You will have to determine how important this type of warranty is to you in relation to the property and the seller's capabilities.

State law governs most aspects of the seller's obligation (and that of his real-estate agent if one is involved) to disclose *latent* problems. The law assumes the buyer can discover on his own, or with the help of those he hires, manifest problems. Rural property often contains defects and adverse conditions that are perfectly visible to an inexperienced buyer, who, for that reason, will not understand the implications, hazards and remedial costs of what he sees. This happened to Jeanne Marie Laskas in western Pennsylvania when she saw the seller's pastures loaded with multiflora rose without understanding how this infestation reduced the land available for grazing, lowered the value of the land and would cost her thousands of dollars to bulldoze them out. When I was first starting out, I saw a sinkhole without understanding what it revealed about the porous limestone beneath it. I've seen a floodplain without comprehending its danger to a barn. I've seen a pasture filled with Viper's Bugloss without knowing what it was revealing about the soil underneath my feet or the (poor) quality of the grazing it would support. My own list of defects-seen-but-not-processed is not endless, but it does go on.

I've run into my share of material, latent problems that were never disclosed. One example represents the class. I was interested in buying a 425-acre tract that a real-estate agent said contained one million board feet of hardwood sawtimber. I knew the agent was knowledgeable about timber, so I put some preliminary faith in his judgment. The land lay on the West Virginia side of the Tug Fork River opposite Kentucky, about 35 minutes south of Huntington. It was a convenient commute over a good road. West Virginia has a disclosure form; neither the seller nor the agent disclosed anything. My partner, a consulting forester, smelled a rat long before I found it. "Fire damage," he said, when I told him where the land was. "Either from the railroad traffic or people setting fires. Sometimes you can see it; sometimes not. Depends how far back it occurred. Fire damage will ruin a butt log." So I called the county forester. "Yeah, I know the place," he said laughing. "I've been in this job 24 years. That hollow has been burned at least 15 of those years. The last time was two years ago. I'm in there almost every year, putting out arsons. I wouldn't give you $30,000 for that place [the sales price in 1989]." It was priced at $215,000. Assuming, for the sake of argument, that this property contained one million board feet of hardwood sawtimber, that level of fire damage would make almost all of that volume worthless. Is fire damage not a material, latent defect? Apparently, it wasn't—in the eyes of the seller and his agent.

While many states require sellers to sign property disclosure forms, the specifics of what is expected to be disclosed may not always clear to the seller. This grey area gets bigger when dealing with rural land and rural sellers, particularly those who assume the buyer will comprehend the significance of obvious conditions, such as mortality in certain tree species in the seller's forest or a seasonally swampy field the buyer visits in the dry season that cannot be used for a residence or a septic system. Disclosure laws may not provide sufficient guidance concerning how significant a defect must be before the seller is expected to reveal it. Is the disclosure requirement limited to current problems or does it reach back for the length of the seller's ownership…and beyond? The absence of a current problem in a condition that routinely recurs every ten years should be disclosed, but may not be. What about latent problems the seller thinks could become manifest in the future? And what about conditions that exist in the neighborhood but not on the property itself, such as low-flying military jets practicing maneuvers over sparsely populated rural areas; or a mat of habitat-destroying, propeller-fouling hydrilla (*Hydrilla verticilata*, the most challenging aquatic weed in much of the U.S.) next to the seller's lakefront house; or a Saturday-only, dirt-bike race track on the neighboring farm?

Before meeting with the seller or submitting a contract, work up a list of potential defects to submit to him, first for discussion, possibly as disclosure inclusions in your contract. These would be general possibilities, as well as items that you noticed on your visits. You can append a winnowed list of disclosure items to your contract and request that the seller disclose any information he has on any of the items on the list, *and any other item*, that would adversely affect your occupation, use and enjoyment of the property. Your list, you tell the seller, is not meant to be exhaustive. It's representative and illustrative of defects, broadly conceived. You want him to disclose any problems that you have not listed that would adversely affect you. If a "reasonable person" would consider something such a defect, tell the seller to disclose it. The buyer needs to give the seller a chance to disclose "**any other condition or fact that would adversely affect the buyer's possession, use and enjoyment of the property,**" both in conversation and in his contract. Work through each item with the seller. Keep a copy of your list with his responses. Note the date of your discussion on the list. Provide a copy of the list with your notes to the seller.

You need to be tactful and polite in this process. You're not trying to incriminate the seller or place him under Gestapo-like interrogation. Your tone in talking about your concerns can establish a working relationship even when your questions are pointed.

If the seller gets testy or stonewalls when you ask for full and specific disclosure, he may be concealing something that's important to your plans. Your objective is to get him to disclose prior to submitting your offer. This allows you to discuss remedies and shape your offering price. Failure of the seller to disclose defects and, more broadly, adverse items known to him, gives the buyer grounds for a post-purchase lawsuit if that becomes necessary. But post-purchase lawsuits are a buyer's least-preferred option.

When you encounter a situation where you need the type of disclosure that conventional research and standard disclosure forms are not yielding, try something different. Once you have the property under contract with at least one 45-day contingency (results acceptable to the buyer) included, take out an ad in the local newspaper for two or three weeks, such as the one below:

NOTICE OF PENDING PURCHASE

I have a contract to buy John Blow's 105 acres on Honest Eddie's Road in Highhope County. It's tax map A-1-10 in the Big Spring District, DB 98, PN 45. The property lies three miles north of Smitty's sawmill on the left.

I would appreciate learning as much about this property as possible during the next three weeks, by October 30th. Please send me any information that you think is relevant to my purchase, such as unrecorded easements or rights of way; leases or rental arrangements; boundary disputes; access problems; uncertainty over water supply or water rights; sale of any of the property's assets, such as timber or minerals; possession or use of this property without the owner's permission, and so on.

If anyone has a claim against this property, now is the time to make me aware of it. I will protect your identity and privacy.

Please send your letter to me:

Mr. Innocent Buystander
Big City, USA

I have never had to do this myself, but I would consider it in the appropriate circumstances. Make sure that you take the ad out after you have the seller's signature on your purchase offer contract. You also need to have a contingency included; otherwise, you can't void the contract without penalty. You must receive the information at least a week or so before your contingency expires, to give you time to investigate. I see nothing wrong, legally or ethically, in doing this, but I would run the idea by my local lawyer before going ahead. You should anticipate some ill-feeling from the seller, which you should weigh into your decision. You may want to show the seller your proposed ad after he signs your contract so that he's not totally blindsided. Where a seller signs a disclaimer, I would not hesitate to take out an advertisement of this sort. This ad would smoke out a **right of first refusal** held by a neighbor and properly set forth in his deed but not in the seller's. I know of one example when a seller signed a contract with an out-of-town buyer even though he knew that his neighbor held a valid right of first refusal. By chance, the neighbor ran into the seller's lawyer at a social event just in time.

The buyer wants two things from the seller. First, he wants full disclosure prior to submitting an offer, and, second, he wants every seller's promise of no problem to survive closing. This is no different from the seller's perspective than what is implied in the standard disclosure form, namely, that the buyer can sue the seller for remedy if the seller fails to disclose a problem that he was required to reveal under state law.

What I am proposing is that the buyer may need to enlarge the normal items of required disclosure, make the items specific by listing them and make the seller's post-purchase warranties explicit.

Buyers should understand that misrepresentation/disclosure suits are expensive and difficult to win. Sellers defend by saying that they did not need to disclose problems about which they did not know; or conditions they had fixed; or problems the buyer should have seen and understood on his own; or something that the seller failed to understand was a latent defect at the time of the sale; or some small defect that inexplicably became big only after the sale; or conditions that the buyer's due diligence, including a home inspection, should have revealed. To prevail, the buyer must prove that the seller had knowledge of a problem, and then intentionally misrepresented it to the buyer either by saying nothing or by saying something that was misleading. The buyer may have to prove that the seller did not orally inform him of the defect. The buyer also has to prove that he suffered monetary damages as a result of the seller's actions. If the seller signed the disclaimer, a lawsuit becomes even harder to win.

An excellent article on this subject offered a rule of thumb in the Washington metropolitan area: aggrieved buyers should forget about claims for damages of less than $20,000. (Daniela Deane, "Truth or Consequences: How Much to Tell Buyers is Tricky Terrain for Sellers," Washington Post, July 5, 2003.) The misrepresentation issues most frequently cited in the Washington area involved wet basements, termites, roof leaks, sewers, wells and septic tanks. Since lawyer time in the country is less expensive, the 2006 rural threshold might be that buyers pass on misrepresentation suits of less than $7,500. The deciding variable regarding to sue or not may be whether your local lawyer thinks the local court will award you attorney's fees in addition to direct damages. To win in a financial sense, the buyer has to prove fraud, then prove damages (i.e., what the seller's fraudulent behavior cost the buyer), then persuade the judge that the damages are as much as is claimed, then convince the same judge that the seller should pay the buyer's lawyer's fees as part of the award. If attorney's fees are not granted, the money you win as compensation may not break you even on the suit.

In theory, where a seller agrees that his warranties survive closing it should mean that the seller stands ready to compensate the buyer for any covered loss during the buyer's ownership without a lawsuit. The covenants included in a General Warranty Deed generally last only for the buyer's term. The succeeding owner (you) assume these liabilities for the next owner, your buyer. Warranties, outside of the deed, should have **time caps** to be fair to both parties. Appliances (personal property) that convey might carry a six-month cap; house systems, one year and so on. Some warranties and time caps on warranties can be bargaining chips. Do not time-cap any covenants and warranties in the seller's deed.

So what happens in the real world when you think a warranty covers a problem that arises a couple of years after you take possession? It depends, of course, on the facts, law and individuals. The seller may no longer be alive or accessible. The seller may not be financially able to defend his warranty to you or compensate you for damages. If the cost of fixing the problem is less than your attorney's projected fees, you might be wise to do nothing to enforce your warranty. Extended title insurance might help on some claims. Warranties, I think, are most enforceable the closer in time they are to when they were given. That's not fair, and it's not the law, but that, I think, will be the practical application in most cases. Your best chance of winning lies with a warranty dispute that happens within your first year of ownership.

Warranties, even those clad in the stoutest iron, can be unenforceable. But the minimum value of writing in warranties to survive closing is to scare the seller into dealing honestly with you and revealing problems about which he knows. And that is worth a lot to a buyer, particularly when he is able to use the anticipated cost of remedying disclosed problems to reduce the purchase price.

Here is language for a disclosure-and-warranty contingency that you might discuss with your local lawyer:

> **Buyer's offer is contingent on Seller disclosing to Buyer in writing within 20 calendar days of this Contract taking effect all conditions in the Property, latent or manifest, including, but not limited to, those involving title, ownership, rights, interests, warranties, assets, boundaries, easements, encroachments, encumbrances, access, improvements, environmental hazards and conditions, natural resources, law and regulation that could in the mind of a reasonable individual adversely affect the Buyer's occupation, use and enjoyment of the Property.**

> **Buyer may void this Contract without penalty if Seller either fails to comply with this disclosure requirement or if any disclosure is unacceptable to him. If the Buyer voids this Contract, his security deposit shall be returned in full within five (5) business days of providing the Seller written notice.**

> **Failure to disclose said conditions of which Seller knows or should reasonably know does not exempt Seller from his responsibilities after closing. Seller shall bear the responsibility and liability for those conditions that adversely affect the Buyer's possession, use and enjoyment of the property, which conditions pre-dated closing, and were either known or should have reasonably been known by the Seller. "Conditions" are to be broadly construed and would include facts, disputes, claims, defects, issues of reliability and capacity in systems, lack of service capability (cell phones, electricity, sewage, trash pick up, etc.), annoyances, trespass, restrictions on property use and so forth.**

> **Seller and Buyer shall discuss each disclosure and decide whether a remedy is needed and how the cost of any such remedy shall be apportioned.**

> **All warranties from Seller under this Contract, including, but not limited to those in the General Warranty Deed, shall survive closing.**

The question of how long any particular warranty survives is not specified. A court would apply a reasonableness rule when warranty length is a matter of judgment rather than law. The parties can establish whatever time caps or dollar caps they agree are fair and reasonable. If you find this language cumbersome, you might write a simpler section and append a list of things you want the seller to consider for possible disclosure.

In sum, the buyer protects himself against seller misrepresentations and failure to disclose by: 1) thorough pre-offer scoping; 2) understanding the strengths and weaknesses of the standard disclosure statement; 3) including contract contingencies that allow additional investigations; 4) inserting a disclosure-and-warranty contingency in the purchase contract; and 5) providing in the purchase contract that the seller's warranties, regarding disclosure and other matters, survive closing.

SECURITY DEPOSITS: THEIR USES

The buyer normally gives an escrow agent a **security deposit** (also referred to as **earnest money, hand money, consideration** or **good-faith deposit**) at the time he submits his purchase offer to the seller.

The escrow agent should be someone on the buyer's side of the transaction, such as the local lawyer the buyer is using. Don't use the seller's lawyer as the escrow agent if you can avoid it. You may run into difficulty in retrieving your deposit if you have to void the contract in adversarial circumstances. Where the buyer is working through a real-estate broker, the deposit would routinely be held in the brokerage's escrow/trust account. The buyer can insist that the deposit be held by his lawyer instead, which may or may not succeed. The alternative is to deposit the earnest money with a neutral escrow agent—recommended by the buyer's lawyer. A real-estate broker who is working for the seller is not exactly neutral from the buyer's perspective. If you don't want the seller's broker to hold your deposit, simply submit a purchase contract through your lawyer and deposit your money in his trust account. If you are using a standard real-estate contract, you will have to do a small bit of editing in its text to accomplish this. **Never give your deposit directly to the seller, especially to a FSBO!** Never give your deposit to anyone without getting a receipt in return and/or a paper trail documenting it. Never put your deposit in anything other than an escrow, or trust, account, held by a lawyer, escrow agent or licensed broker.

The buyer's deposit is intended to show and secure his willingness to perform on the contract. It is supposed to prove to the seller that the buyer is serious. The deposit is the buyer's money that is at risk in an offer. (But this risk is minimal if the buyer uses contingencies with results acceptable to the buyer.) If the buyer fails to perform on the purchase for any reason once all contingencies are resolved, compensation to the seller should be limited in the buyer's contract to the escrowed deposit, a concept known as **liquidated damages**. The buyer gets his full deposit back if he voids the contract because the contingency results are unacceptable. The buyer's money is not at risk in any way until after the buyer removes all contingencies, that is, accepts results, resolves a contingency issue with the seller or allows the contingency to expire without invoking it.

Sellers prefer larger rather than smaller deposits, because they think it increases both the likelihood of performance and provides more compensation if the buyer fails to perform. I have my doubts. If a buyer decides that he is unable to perform after removing his contingencies, the size of the deposit won't persuade him to go through with the deal. Larger deposits do provide the seller with more compensation, but they also increase the likelihood of costly, lose-lose litigations when a deal falls apart. A shrewd seller might propose to a buyer that he will accept a one percent earnest-money deposit instead of the normal three percent if the buyer will increase his offering price by $1,000.

Real-estate agents (working for the seller) often advise a buyer to make a deposit of sufficient size to make it worth the seller's time to sign his contract—the bigger, the better. In some cases, this may help a buyer, such as when several buyers are submitting contracts at about the same time. But I'm skeptical of the argument in most cases. I think selling price and, then, terms drive sellers, not the size of a deposit. Your signed contract will discourage other buyers from coming forward with backup offers. It's that discouragement effect for which your deposit should compensate the seller, because that's his risk. The valuation of that risk depends on the specifics of the property and the local market. In a hot seller's market, there is arguably no risk to the seller. If you're proposing a shorter-than-typical escrow, give the seller a smaller-than-typical deposit.

A buyer who has done his pre-purchase scoping can feel confident in putting down a larger rather than smaller deposit if only because his contract will contain contingencies that, if exercised, void the contract and activate return of his earnest money without penalty. Buyers can negotiate concessions in price and terms in return for larger deposits. Larger deposits—even with contingencies—can bring a seller to your contract. You can always propose a large increase in your deposit in return for the seller agreeing to disclose-and-warranty language. If the seller agrees, you will have much more confidence in your purchase, which allows you to increase your deposit.

The other way to think about a security deposit is to offer it to the seller in two stages. The first deposit—a token—is made when the buyer submits his contract. The second—a larger one—is due when the buyer removes all contingencies, indicating that he will perform. The first stage of a contract may be larded with contingencies, which the buyer uses to justify a two-step deposit.

The buyer accomplishes several goals in a **two-step deposit**. First, he minimizes the amount of his money that's at risk during the early phase of the contract when the chance of a deal blowing up can be high. Contingencies protect this money in the early phase. Second, he retains his money a little longer, earning a bit of interest. Third, he gives the seller a real incentive to help him resolve problems that arise during the contingency investigations. Finally, he builds a process of working together with the seller.

Security money in escrow may earn interest for the buyer in some states. In others, escrow interest is taken and used to fund public goods, such as legal services. In states that allow the buyer to keep the interest, the amount that accrues over the two or three months of a typical escrow at passbook rates is small. Conceding this interest to the seller has psychological and negotiating value.

Earnest money goes to the seller at closing once all the buyer's contingencies are satisfied or removed and all terms have been met on both sides. Accordingly, a buyer who deposits $2,500 as earnest money in a non-interest-bearing escrow for a $100,000 purchase, has to come up with $97,500 at closing, in addition to closing costs.

Sometimes, a buyer will tag his deposit with a "subject to" condition, such as, the deposit or the purchase is subject to approval of a relative. It's hard for me to imagine why a seller would sign a contract with such an "escape clause," but some do. This is too tricky for my tool kit.

If the buyer fails to perform on the contract for reasons outside the various contingencies his contract includes, the seller can **sue for specific performance** to force the buyer to do the deal on the terms offered and accepted. Such a suit can be a disaster for the buyer. The usual reasons for a buyer's failure to perform involve an unexpected change in personal or financial circumstances, or last-minute surprise information that fundamentally alters the buyer's interest in a purchase. But the buyer is exposed to the seller's demand for performance only if he has failed to include a **liquidated-damages section** in this contract. This language limits the buyer's exposure for bailing out to his deposit:

> **The Parties agree that Buyer will relinquish his deposit to Seller as liquidated damages in the event that Buyer fails to perform on this Contract once all contingencies are satisfied or removed. This payment shall be Seller's sole remedy for Buyer's failure to perform. Any fees due real-estate brokers shall be paid from this deposit.**

Liquidated-damages language gives the seller quick and litigation-free compensation for the buyer's breach. The seller gives up a theoretical and a lot of hard-to-get money (performance) for a small but guaranteed amount of cash (deposit, possibly less some or all of a broker's fee). Liquidated damages shields both buyer and seller from having to go through a contentious and expensive lawsuit over performance. If your contract does not contain a liquidated-damages section, the seller will get your deposit and then sue you for performance.

There is one other security-money tactic that you might find an occasion to use. Most buyers try to put in as little security money as they can, because they fear its loss. As I've shown above, a properly worded contingency—with results acceptable to the buyer—will protect your deposit. Go at the seller from a different direction: if his asking price is $100,000, offer him $60,000 to $70,000 with a deposit of $25,000. Your message is that you are a serious buyer, but your scoping has proved that his asking price is demonstrably above market. Couple this with a results-acceptable-to-the-buyer contingency, of course. And then offer to increase the deposit by $10,000 once you remove all contingencies. This may help you with a seller who knowingly has inflated his asking price. This tactic is strengthened when the tax-assessed value of the property is in the $60,000 to $70,000 range, and you base your offering price on that publicly available number.

I know an investor who prefers optioning land to buying and taking title. His business is to option land and then get a significant portion resold before his option runs out. If he doesn't get a sufficient portion under contract (contingent, of course, on his purchase of the land), he loses his option money. An **option to purchase** allows its holder to buy the land at a set price for some period of time—the option period. Option agreements expire if they are not exercised. The option buyer gives his "option money" to the seller in return for this right to purchase at the agreed price during the option period. Option money may be larger than a deposit if it ties up the seller's property for a long period of time. The option period can start either before or after the buyer has done his due diligence and has removed contingencies. The seller keeps the buyer's option money if the buyer fails to exercise his option and make the purchase by a specific date. Option money is typically between two and three percent of the purchase price on smaller deals and less on large deals. This investor's game is high-stakes gambling, and I do not advise readers to try it. The longer the option period, the better are the chances to make the deal work. My acquaintance always tries to get a six-month option, or longer.

One tactic I've learned from him is that it's usually handy to include an **extension clause** in a purchase contract or an option contract that allows the buyer to lengthen the closing by another 30 to 60 days in return for increasing the amount of the deposit. Time is bought by upping the buyer's ante. If you anticipate needing extra time to complete pre-closing investigations or allow for the contingent sale of a few lots from the target property, put an extension in your contract. If you don't have a buyer-activated extension opener in the contract, the seller may not agree to give you more time. Use an extension when the odds of a deal working out for you are strongly in your favor. Don't play "in for a dime, in for a dollar" unless you're prepared to lose your dollar. If an extension will help you strip risk out of the purchase, then it's worthy of serious consideration. The cost of extending a contract that you know you're going to complete is cheaper—far cheaper—to you than closing and paying a month or two of mortgage interest.

Earnest money—your deposit—is not funny money. It's your cash, and you can lose it if your contract doesn't protect it. I've seen deposits of between $2,000 and $325,000 lost when buyers couldn't perform. However, when a contract is properly written with a results-acceptable-to-the-buyer contingency, your deposit is not at risk until you remove the contingency.

DEPOSITS: SIZE MAY OR MAY NOT MATTER

An earnest-money deposit must be at least a dollar, but its actual size is a matter of negotiation between buyer and seller. How big should it be?

Sellers generally believe that a buyer is more likely to go through with a purchase if a big deposit is escrowed. Under a liquidated-damages clause, the buyer's failure to perform brings the deposit to the seller. The deposit may or may not be reduced by broker fees, depending on contract language and circumstances. The seller's logic—larger deposit levers the buyer toward performance—only works with a buyer who has removed all contingencies or accepted their results. During the time when contingencies are operating, the size of a deposit does not work against a buyer because he can get it back without penalty. A buyer should be 100 percent committed to performance before removing the last of his contingencies.

However, even in the most carefully thought out deal, a buyer's circumstances can suddenly change for the worse. A buyer may find himself facing a choice between losing his deposit or performing on a contract that he no longer wants. Buyers in this bind are of two sorts: those who want to perform but unexpectedly find themselves unable to do so and those who can perform but no longer want do so. The seller's logic—size of deposit matters—does not apply to the unable because, by definition, the purchase is now beyond his means. His impending breach is a matter of necessity, not discretion. He will lose his deposit as liquidated damages; a larger deposit doesn't force him into performance. Buyers who can perform but no longer want to might be influenced by deposit size, but I doubt that will occur in most situations because of the seriousness of the adverse surprise that has turned around their buy decision. Accordingly, I think the seller's belief—large deposit is incentive to perform—is largely specious, because it applies to so few cases. If a seller demands a large deposit, I would walk him through this analysis in an effort to loosen his grip on a false premise. If he's not persuaded, write into your contract a provision that increases the size of your liquidated-damages obligation if you fail to perform after all contingencies are removed or satisfied.

Where a contract does not contain a liquidated-damages clause, the size of the deposit may be functionally irrelevant to getting the buyer to perform. Absent such a clause, a buyer is open to being sued for performance if he doesn't want to perform. The size of the deposit has no bearing on the buyer's behavior since he is on the hook for the entire amount. A buyer without a liquidated-damages clause must begin negotiations with the seller to buy his way out of performance, making the best deal he can.

From a buyer's perspective, I would not hesitate to increase a deposit in exchange for some seller concession as long as the buyer has at least one contingency—with results acceptable to buyer—in place. That's a smart use of deposit money.

The buyer's deposit, regardless or size, is at risk of loss only after the buyer removes all contingencies. Therefore, it's often sensible to offer a very small deposit—say $500 or $1,000—as a good-faith gesture and then agree to a substantial increase once all contingencies are resolved. At that point, the buyer should feel comfortable about performing and all of the financing will be in place. Sellers, I think, will be inclined to go along with a two-step deposit once the buyer lays out these arguments and agrees to make the second deposit larger than might be expected. In effect, this approach allows the buyer to purchase an option to buy at no cost and no risk, which the buyer converts into a binding contract with the second deposit.

Take these tactics one step further. Offer the seller a very small deposit…along with a closing within one week of your removal/satisfaction with your last contingency. The seller should understand that he has no sale until the buyer removes all contingencies, regardless of the size of escrowed deposit. On a 90-day escrow, all contingencies might be resolved in the first 45 days. While there are reasons to close at the end of 90 days, the last 45 days are risky to both parties. It should be worth something to the seller to not have to sweat out those last escrow weeks. Increase the seller's security in your purchase by giving up that time, unless, of course, you need it for some reason. A shorter escrow will cost a buyer something, because you will be starting to pay mortgage interest six weeks earlier. So you need to judge whether the concession you're getting from the seller is worth the price you'll pay.

Submitting a contract with a low-ball deposit will work only when you explain to the seller your reasons for doing so and explain that he really doesn't have much of an interest in a larger sum. If you simply submit a contract with a low-ball deposit, the seller will question your intentions and capabilities. A small deposit with a short closing should push the parties to work together to get contingency issues resolved. The seller should be helpful because he will see that his money is a lot closer to his hand in a 45-day closing than in a 90. Since the contingencies keep the buyer's deposit out of the seller's grasp for the length of the contingency period, the seller should realize that insisting on a large deposit doesn't get him real security.

In my experience, a short closing is worth something to the seller. It's far better than language that provides for a "closing within 90 days, or sooner by mutual agreement," which gives the seller nothing for certain. In practice, the buyer often has no incentive to close sooner. The "or sooner" bait simply increases the seller's crankiness as he sweats out the last half of escrow. Sellers won't concede anything for "or sooner."

As I wrote this in the spring of 2006, I was toying with submitting a purchase offer on a timber tract with a **jumbo deposit**, perhaps 30 to 50 percent of the purchase price. The seller was uncooperative and refused to supply any information about his property. His real-estate agent has announced that he will accept no contingencies, despite the property being landlocked with uncertain acreage. The only reason to be interested in this piece is that its merchantable timber value is about double the seller's asking price. If my scoping cleared up all the uncertainties, a big deposit might have squashed seller roadblocks, eliminate competition and justify a slightly lower offer. But maybe not. I wasn't quite there.

And in the end, I never got there. A neighbor got in line first.

TIME I: TIME IS NOT OF THE ESSENCE

Most standard real-estate contracts include a section: "Time is of the essence." What does that mean to the buyer?

It means the seller can void the contract if the buyer does not act on its provisions and contingencies by their specific written deadlines. Since most—and often all—such deadlines fall on the buyer, the seller wants "time is of the essence" in the contract so the buyer does not intentionally dawdle. When a buyer agrees to this language, he may ultimately face a choice: either go ahead with the purchase even if one or more of his contingencies cannot be resolved within its specified deadline or lose the contract altogether. Sellers who have an acceptable **backup contract** in hand may not or may not agree to give their first buyer an extension. A seller in that situation judges which of the two buyers is most likely to perform and at what selling price.

It's fair for a seller to expect the buyer to move forward on the contract in a timely fashion. Both parties share a common interest in performance. Buyers should assure sellers of their good-faith intention to perform while resisting, if possible, the draconian straitjacket of "time is of the essence." The buyer might propose that his contingencies be worded with some wiggle room:

> **This _____ contingency will be removed or invoked no later than 45 days from the date this Contract takes effect. Buyer may extend this deadline by five (5) business days on his own initiative and without penalty. Seller may grant Buyer additional time upon Buyer's request.**

Where a seller has bargained hard for a short closing, he will be reluctant to agree to extensions. In such circumstances, the buyer should assess the seller's options. If the seller has an equal to or better alternative than to grant the buyer's request, he's likely to refuse.

I have used "time is of the essence" and a short closing on several occasions to prevent a seller from coming down with seller's remorse. I do this only when I am absolutely sure that I have scoped the property thoroughly and negotiated favorable terms. As a rule, I would not include a "time is of the essence" provision since it rarely functions in a way that benefits buyers.

TIME II: FIRST RESPONSE

A critical consideration for the buyer is **how much response time to give to the seller** when submitting a purchase contract.

Real-estate agents working for the seller may suggest as much as two weeks. Where the seller is out of town, or hard to reach, or involves several parties, a week is fair. But I think being time-short rather than time-long is generally in the buyer's best interest, especially when other buyers are preparing offers. I have seen offers appear within a three-day window that are just slightly better than the one submitted. Sellers are not above using one buyer's offer to extract slightly better terms from a competitor.

In most circumstances, the buyer should make his offer good for no more than 24 hours. This will not prevent a cagey real-estate agent from having another client slip in his offer, but it will make it harder. A 24-hour window works well during the week, but not when it's submitted between Friday and Sunday. Submit your offer Monday through Thursday if possible.

If the reader thinks I'm paranoid about real-estate agents, I offer this anecdote. Some 1,500 acres was for sale at $1.3 million through a United Country broker in West Virginia. When I visited the property on behalf of a client, the seller's broker told me another offer was coming in. He had not mentioned that on the phone. He volunteered that it was not a full-price offer. My client quickly made a full-price offer with a couple of reasonable contingencies, but he gave the seller and his broker too much response time. The broker announced that the other buyer had suddenly submitted a full-price offer with no contingencies, which the seller had accepted. This broker, who was working for the seller, told the other buyer about the terms of our offer. One mistake we made was in giving the seller more than 24 hours. The second was in not including a **strict confidentiality provision** in the contract that prohibited both seller and his broker from revealing the terms of our offer. The other buyer, incidentally, should feel miffed too. This broker used our offer as leverage to get him to raise his and strip it of contingencies, which put him at risk. A broker working for the seller has no obligation to preserve the confidentiality of a buyer's offer from what I can determine. A buyer can, of course, insist on confidentiality and demand that the broker sign such a provision. Keeping your offer open for as short a period as possible will lessen the chance of a broker playing this game.

If you find yourself in this situation, write a confidentiality statement into your offer that prohibits the seller's broker from sharing the terms of your offer with anyone other than the seller.

Broker agrees to keep the price, terms and conditions of the Buyer's offer confidential and shall not disclose them—or allow them to be disclosed—to any party other than Seller.

Broker's dated signature in the margin of this Contact indicates his acceptance of this provision.

Anticipate that the broker will object to signing this restriction. Tell him to get the seller's approval if he thinks he needs it. If the broker continues to fidget and stonewall, you may have uncovered his plan to work you against another buyer. If that is your hunch, make your offer good for no more than a few hours. You can always extend it.

WHEN A BUYER LAYS A TRAP

A few buyers I know offer sellers contracts with a time-related, spring-loaded trap. It goes like this. The buyer gives the seller 24 or 48 hours to reject in writing the contract offer. If the seller does not do so, the buyer's contract asserts that the contract shall be deemed accepted by the seller.

This is a self-defeating approach, because it undercuts the trust and mutual problem-solving that a buyer should be promoting. Moreover, I doubt that the buyer could persuade a judge to enforce a purchase in circumstances where no meeting of the minds existed and no contract was signed.

NEGOTIATION WITHIN THE CONTRACT

Purchase contracts are not symmetrical. Buyers usually have to do more than a few things before closing while sellers may have to do nothing but sweat out the buyer's efforts. If the buyer does not obtain acceptable results in all of his contingencies, his contract should allow him to void his offer without penalty and have his earnest money returned in full.

While voiding his contract is one choice, the buyer has another option available when contingency results adversely impact the buyer's pre-offer estimate of property value. The buyer realizes that he has offered too much, now that he has the results in hand. The buyer should take the new information to the seller and ask for one of two responses—either remedy the problem if it's remediable, or, alternatively, agree to a lower purchase price to reflect the new information and the buyer's willingness to accept the property "as is." When a buyer proposes to negotiate a modification to the purchase contract arising from a contingency, the seller faces an identical choice: say no, whereupon the contract becomes void, or negotiate in an effort to salvage a deal.

Once the buyer notifies the seller in writing that results are unacceptable, he should make sure that the seller agrees that the contract's time limits are suspended until the parties decide what they want to do. When negotiations produce a resolution within the time window of the contingency, the buyer is not at risk. If, on the other hand, informal negotiations extend beyond the contingency's time frame, the seller may claim at some arbitrary point that he now expects full performance given that the contingency deadline has passed. Even though the buyer has told the seller that results are unacceptable, he has not formally voided the contract. So it can be argued that the contract is still in effect with a running clock. The seller can argue that the buyer told him that results were unacceptable, but did not notify him that he was voiding the contract on that basis. This is less than honorable behavior—and may be part of an effort to hammer the buyer into going through with the contract in some form or another. The buyer should protect himself against this tactic by having the seller sign an amendment to the contract, extending the contingency deadline to allow for additional negotiations. If the seller does not grant an extension, the buyer can agree to go ahead with the contract or immediately terminate his offer in writing.

Whether a buyer can get a seller to negotiate with him depends on the type of problem that the contingency turned up, its seriousness and cost and, finally, the other options available to the seller. A buyer who tries to hammer the seller with new information into a huge price discount will be turned down. A smaller bite can work, but not always. I've seen excessive demands push a rural seller into walking away from negotiations when his pride trumps his economic self-interest. It's one thing to horse-trade, but it's quite another for a rural seller to feel that he is being gamed by the "city" buyer. The seller must feel that the buyer is being genuine, reasonable and fair in his requests, not greedy or bullying. The buyer should approach the seller with a willingness to concede something in return for the seller's willingness to help out on the contingency results. This is a delicate time for both buyer and seller. It requires a buyer to bring reasonableness and tact to the table.

Having made the above point, I should add that a buyer who has done his pre-offer scoping should not be surprised by a contingency result. The point of scoping is to eliminate surprises and accurately value property prior to making an offer.

Good scoping gives a buyer a chance to game a seller with a non-surprise surprise result, which is used to force a price discount from a seller now invested in the buyer's offer. There may be sellers who deserve this, and there may be buyers who can bring it off without blowing up the deal. I've not tried it myself, and I don't think I would feel quite right about it.

A NON-DEAL DEAL: SELLER'S REMORSE

A type of seller exists who thinks a better offer will materialize from somewhere the moment he signs your purchase contract. He reasons that if you are willing to buy his property for $100,000, somebody "out there" will pay $110,000. A sale at $100,000 is, therefore, too cheap; I'm losing money, he thinks. This is seller's remorse, and it can occur whether the seller is right or wrong about his new intuition, and whether or not he's making a considerable profit on the $100,000 sale. The buyer has no contractual obligation to better his offer, but some circumstances may warrant a voluntary buyer concession to grease the skids even when the buyer need not do so.

Feigned seller's remorse is a tactic I've seen a seller use to create conditions within the contract that are adverse to the buyer in hope he will increase the contract price. Sellers have many ways to gum up a contract after signing it. They can be unhelpful in providing access—keys to locks on gates and house visits not being accommodated; FSBOs failing to show up at arranged meetings; a large freshly cut tree suddenly sprawls across a woods road, blocking access. They can stall and stonewall the buyer's requests for information. They can claim they can't find information they had led you to believe was available. They can refuse to discuss any contract revisions when a buyer's contingency results reveal an unexpected surprise. This seller is playing a risky game, because he may lose you—a buyer under contract—through his artifice to avoid remedying a contingency result or his interest in picking out a bit more money from the buyer's pocketbook.

When the buyer feels that the seller is faking remorse, it's best to stick with the original offer. Any willingness to negotiate is likely to harm the buyer's current position. This is a bluff worth calling. But like all called bluffs, you may lose the hand.

Signs of seller remorse, genuine or phony, are always easy to recognize. The seller starts whining about how good a deal the buyer "was given." The seller discovers new information showing one asset or another to be worth more than he previously communicated. The seller starts complaining about how the sale will work a hardship on him. He says a better offer has just come through as a backup contract and waves paper under the buyer's nose. (The buyer will not know whether this backup is genuine or a dummy submitted by the seller's third cousin, currently collecting seashells on Grand Cayman Island in lieu of making license plates under state supervision.) Some sellers like to play this kind of poker.

But most don't play a serious game with a real-estate contract, because they don't want to lose the sale, even when it's not quite what they wanted. Buyers can usually count on the seller's self-interest in making the sale overriding the inevitable second thoughts. Don't hesitate to remind the remorseful seller of the old homily: a bird in hand is worth two in the bush. And keep in mind that your contract does not require you to do anything more than fulfill the terms of your offer: you don't have to pander to the seller's insecurities. But a buyer may have to test the authenticity of the seller's remorse. If he's feigning for tactical reasons, hold your ground or give him a face-saving throwaway. If he genuinely wants to get out of the contract, meet all deadlines and perform.

If a seller stonewalls your effort to renegotiate after your house-inspection contingency reveals a latent $50,000 roof problem that your pre-offer scoping failed to detect, remind the seller that he will now have to disclose the bad roof to every buyer coming after you. Signing a disclaimer may or may not allow a seller to avoid disclosure of a now-documented defect, depending on state law. Once you put disclosure into the mix, the seller may decide that he'll net no more money from the backup contract than he would from you. You may have to exert pressure by writing a letter to both seller and his broker that discusses the hidden roof problem. Attach the inspection report. You may even have to send a copy to the state agency that handles real-estate disclosure issues. Buyer disclosure can trump seller remorse.

All this advice changes if the seller has a genuine **backup contract** in hand that's better than yours. As long as the buyer removes contingencies or accepts their results in writing within the deadlines and satisfies all other terms, the purchase should go through. But sellers may start throwing monkey wrenches into the gears. This buyer needs to recognize that this seller has no incentive to negotiate over contingency results. You may have to buy the property "as is" on the contract's terms or abandon the purchase.

ANNOYANCE, NUISANCE AND TRESPASS

I have never seen a purchase contract ask the seller to disclose problems related to annoyance, nuisance and trespass. I think it's a good idea whose time should come.

A nuisance in the law is thought of as an activity by one property owner that unreasonably annoys or seriously affects the use and enjoyment of the property of reasonable others. A public or private nuisance does not exist until a court says so. The court can then order a remedy. Absent a finding of nuisance, the condition is an annoyance that neighbors have to endure. Annoyances/nuisances can be noise, pollution, odors, wood smoke from an outdoor wood-burning furnace, safety hazards, bright lights, headlights in your window, visual obstructions (that ruin a view), commercial activities or social activities.

Rural property is often burdened with annoyances that are not obvious to the first-time visitor—a kennel of dogs next door who sleep during the day and bark at night, extra-bright "security" lights, late-night socializing, pungent but episodic odors, chemical fumes, late-night chainsaw testing, teenagers on ATVs and dirt bikes, unauthorized trash dumping (visible in winter, but not in summer), early morning wake ups, the seller's driveway that is used as the community turn-around, a colony of fighting cocks crowing their challenges 24/7, target practice with automatic weapons and unscheduled varmint shooting.

Certain buyer-perceived "nuisances" may be no more than routine life in the country. Such things are to be anticipated and accommodated. Farms, it must be remembered, are large, mechanized workplaces, not oil paintings. Farmers manure their fields in the spring. Calves bawl for three or four days when they are weaned. Rifle-firing hunters roam woods and fields. Logging trucks and tractors are inevitably noisy. Such things are normal rural background. They are to be expected. A court has to decide whether any particular activity rises to the level of nuisance. Routine, necessary rural activities won't. If you object to this "background," you might want to rethink a country purchase.

Even large properties of several hundred acres or more can be affected by neighboring noise and eyesores. As I write this paragraph, several large landowners in my county are objecting to the plans of an adjoining neighbor to lease his land for a wind farm. The neighbors object to seeing 400-foot-tall wind turbines from their front porch, among other reasons. They believe the turbines will be an eyesore and lower their property values. Each buyer has to decide what type and scale of rural activity he can and cannot put up with. Offenses that would not meet a court's test of nuisance can still drive you batty. The one thing worse in an owner's mind than an annoyance is an annoyance that a court has declared is not a nuisance.

Whether a court finds an annoyance to be a nuisance usually depends on the specifics of the case. Activities that are out of normal scale, or highly concentrated, or atypical, or abnormally burdensome, or totally unanticipated will be hardest to defend. Were I to buy a cottage on one acre surrounded by working dairy farms with nearby waste lagoons, I would have to put up with the constant smell of fresh manure. A local judge would not rule that the pre-existing dairy farms were a nuisance to me. He would say that the annoyance was obvious, and I bought the place with an open nose. In situations where an annoyance does not rise to a legal nuisance, you are stuck with it. My guess is that local judges will not find pre-existing conditions a nuisance, and I will extend that guess to say that local judges will be predisposed to favor locals over newcomers in these disputes—and properly so.

If you are a princess who is rendered sleepless by a pea under your mattress, you should be very cautious about buying property in an environment that's new to you. The occasional down-the-road shot at a garden-raiding woodchuck will set you to phoning the sheriff. If you are offended by a neighbor's level of disorderliness (which is different than your own), you will be offended each time you drive by his disconnected downspout. Parts cars drive some neighbors nuts. I try to keep in mind a distinction between (offensive) things that are normal and typical for the property's neighborhood and things that are abnormal, atypical and out of scale. That allows me to live with certain annoyances that are part and parcel of where

623

I've chosen to buy property. Since rural areas are normally quiet and peaceful, noise and disturbances acquire more power over newcomers who think nothing of living in a downtown area roiled by sirens and a dozen other routine assaults on their senses. In the spring, my wife has occasionally shouted from the depths of her early-morning blankets: "Shut up, birds!" Each buyer needs to decide his tolerance for the target-property's rural neighborhood. If an annoyance is open to view prior to purchase, you are likely to be expected to live with it afterwards. But a princess may never learn to sleep on a pea, no matter the number of mattresses. If you decide that you are a princess, find yourself a castle in a kingdom that has outlawed peas.

Annoyances that have been declared nuisances by a court can be modified or even stopped. Annoyances that don't rise to nuisance will continue. Most annoyances never get challenged in court, which means the put-upon party learns to put up with being put upon. It's difficult for a newcomer to challenge a rural neighborhood's equilibrium by proclaiming that his long-residing neighbor's behavior is a nuisance. If everyone else has put up with the neighbor's behavior for years, why shouldn't the newcomer fit in by putting up with it too? No one likes to be told, particularly by someone just moving in, that what he's been doing for years is objectionable and should end on the newcomer's say so. The newcomer who assumes that all of his new neighbors will join him in asking the offending neighbor to change his ways is fooling himself. The in-coming buyer might win a nuisance suit against the neighbor, but it will come at a high price that will be paid repeatedly in the years ahead. If the outsider wins in court, his victory will not be seen as a community benefit even though it is. It will be seen as a city-person throwing his weight around.

Rural people tend to be more accepting of the bothersome quirks of their neighbors than city newcomers, even when they have no bothersome quirks of their own. This is consistent with their high degree of tolerance for live-and-let-live eccentricity among people they know well. They are far less tolerant of the same eccentricities occurring in remote places (like Manhattan) and among people they don't know. Newcomers with their city peculiarities benefit from this willingness to accept differences as soon as their rural community incorporates them as familiar. When a newcomer stirs up a claim of nuisance no matter how justified, it jeopardizes the *laissez-faire* ethic that tends to benefit everyone, often the newcomer himself most of all.

The buyer's best protection against annoyance and nuisance is to scope for them in every possible manifestation prior to making an offer. This means you should try to visit the property on a normal weekday, in the evening and on a weekend. The seller may or may not be helpful, given that you are asking him to reveal a condition that might dissuade you from purchasing his property. Casual conversations with neighbors may be the best source of information; ask each neighbor about the other neighbors.

Consider including an **annoyance disclosure** in your purchase contract. Don't call it a nuisance disclosure, because nuisance, legally speaking, is confined to those annoyances that a court has already ruled are nuisances. A seller could deny his property was affected by a nuisance when it was surrounded by multiple annoyances that had never been litigated. **Ask the seller to reveal any neighborhood conditions or activities that a reasonable person might consider intrusive or annoying, and which might negatively affect the buyer's possession, use and enjoyment of the property.** This should, at least, open a discussion with the seller as to what you are concerned about. I would explain the difference between annoyance and nuisance, and, further, tell him that you want to fit into the neighborhood as much as possible. If nothing else, you want to know what to expect, and what level of annoyance acceptance is likely to be expected of you.

I encourage buyers not to become their new neighborhood's self-righteous, self-appointed enforcer of correct behavior. Sooner or later, everyone around you, including you, will do something of questionable legality or taste. Temper your beliefs on these matters with patience and a strong dose of tolerance. These qualities will come around to you in return.

Trespass is a common problem with rural land. It comes in two general forms: trespass by those who have been trespassing in one way or another for years, and one-time trespass usually by strangers. The first type is more common and difficult to handle. It may be neighbors, nearby landowners, local folks or non-residents who regularly visit your property. They may be hunters, berrypickers, firewood cutters, teenagers, "cut-throughers," "mounties" (ATVs, snowmobiles, horse riders, 4WD off-roaders, dirt bikers, boaters or RV campers), swimmers, trash dumpers or fishermen. Non-local trespassers tend to be birders, hikers, hunters/fishermen, mountain bikers and ATV riders. The trespass can be seasonal or constant, blatant or sneaky, benign or amazingly invasive. Trespass by non-local parties is usually easier to control through **posting the property** with signs prohibiting trespass. Posting and newspaper ads will help with local folks, but word of mouth is best. Don't be surprised to have some trespassers proclaim a right to use your property against your wishes based on history, permission or inventive legal theories devised on the spot by instant experts in English common law.

And there is always the situationally blind trespasser. I was visiting a friend's land near Greenfield, Massachusetts many years ago when I ran into one. My friend had been having trouble with hunters coming onto her land without permission and hunting birds in her swamp. She posted her property, particularly around the beaver pond. As I was leaving one afternoon, I noticed a truck parked at the end of her swamp road. I drove down, got out and walked in about 30 feet. A fully decked out hunter was standing with shotgun ready, taking aim. I politely pointed out that he was standing next to—not under, not close to—a newly mounted yellow posted sign tacked to a tree. The sign was not more than six inches from his rear gunsight. I explained the landowner's position and asked him to turn his head about one degree to the right, toward the sign. "Never saw it," he said. Given that he was armed and I was not—except with my first wife, a passive-aggressive pacifist and Yale law student—I did not laugh. "Anyway, I'm not hunting, just looking," he allowed, as the bird flapped away. I asked this non-hunting hunter to leave…and left before he mistook me for a bear in season.

There's only one way to stop trespass: the owner must take whatever steps he needs to take in the circumstances to stop it. The landowner must be clear, firm and consistent. To the extent possible, denial of access should be business, not personal. You should not negotiate with trespassers; any negotiation comes out of your side. You can listen and then explain, but don't negotiate. If necessary call the sheriff and get a restraining order. Such measures should be taken only as a last resort.

Ask your seller to **disclose any trespass** in your purchase contract. Trespass is not likely to be construed as an "encroachment" or an "encumbrance," so you need to include a specific trespass disclosure. Neighbors will probably know of trespass patterns on the seller's property, though it may turn out you're asking them to squeal on themselves. The point of your trespass disclosure and a warranty that no trespass has occurred is not so much to get the seller on the hook if a problem turns up, but more to get him to reveal the problem before you buy it.

When the seller discloses a trespass, he and the buyer can then devise a plan to: 1) provide public notice prohibiting trespass through newspaper advertisements, posting signs and personal contact; 2) undertake prevention measures, such as stout chains with locks and locked gates; and 3) enforce the no-trespass policy by notifying the sheriff's office and the local game warden of your posting, having your lawyer send warning letters to habitual offenders, and bringing charges as a last resort. Solving trespass is likely to be easier if the seller initiates notice to chronic trespassers before closing. These situations can bruise feelings on all sides, so move with thoughtfulness rather than self-righteousness.

The buyer's purchase offer might include language on annoyance, nuisance and trespass such as the following:

> **Seller agrees to disclose situations and patterns of annoyance, nuisance and trespass on and around the Property that might adversely affect the Buyer's possession, use and enjoyment of it.**
>
> **With annoyance and nuisance, Seller agrees to discuss each situation with the Buyer within seven (7) calendar days of this Contract taking effect. Seller further agrees to implement a control plan that the Parties negotiate.**
>
> **In the event of trespass, Seller agrees to provide names of individuals known to him who are engaging in trespass. The Parties agree that they will negotiate a plan of action for each trespasser.**
>
> **If the Buyer is not satisfied with the implementation of this section or the situations as disclosed, or otherwise known to him, he may void this Contract without penalty within 30 days of its coming into effect, whereupon his deposit shall be returned to him in a timely fashion.**

A special case of "trespass" arises from animals owned by one party finding their way onto another's property. Bulls seeking cows are often the culprits. A bull with his nose open will go through the best, stoutest, highest and newest fence on my farm. If you are running pure-bred cows and the neighbor's mongrel bull comes over, you have a right to be upset. Your breeding program and farm income are diminished. Most neighbors, you will find, will try to keep their stock at home. Absentee owners may be less cooperative. You will need to take legal action if this situation becomes chronic, with demonstrable financial impacts.

LEASE-PURCHASE OPTION

The idea of a purchase contingent on buyer satisfaction with the property can be taken down a different road: the **lease-purchase option**. There's no more thorough investigation available than a year-long, on-site colonoscopy of the seller's property. It's also a low-risk, not-too-expensive way to see if country living on this piece of land fits.

A lease-purchase option may or may not establish a future selling price between the parties. The right to buy at a set price during the term of the lease, or at its end, is typically part of an option. If it isn't, your year-long rental can at least give you an inside track if your tenant-landlord relationship has been positive. The option could include a **right of first offer**, that is, the tenant/buyer has the right to submit an offer before the seller puts the property back on the market. In the absence of a fixed, future selling price, the buyer can anticipate that the seller will argue that his property has appreciated, thus justifying a price higher than a year earlier. From the buyer's perspective, you may have more money after a year's rental, and you should certainly have more knowledge about the property that may, perhaps, be used to whittle the price. If you think you're going to buy when the lease expires, propose to the seller that in lieu of all or part of your rent you put rent dollars and/or labor into property improvements. But if you do that, make sure to agree on a purchase price in advance, otherwise you will end up paying for the improvements that you made.

I would use a lease-purchase option on rural property more as a deep investigative tool than as a negotiating tactic over price. It gives you time to scope the property and experience it. It gives you a way into a property as well as a way out. If you're subject to impulse buying, a lease-purchase option satisfies your impulsiveness without permanent harm, since the most you can lose is a year's rent. Make sure that your lease-purchase contract contains a **right to assign** your interest. That gives you the option of selling your arrangement to a third-party who is bound by the terms you negotiated. With a lease-purchase contract that sets a future selling price, you may be able to sell it for more than what the seller is owed, thus producing a profit.

Your local lawyer should draft the lease-purchase option agreement. He needs to make sure the seller has clear title before you sign. The seller should be required to produce evidence of ownership or offer a warranty as part of the lease that he possesses clear title and the unencumbered right to transfer title. When the purchase is effected, it should include updated seller warranties on title. You and your lawyer should also be comfortable with language regarding missed/late rental payments, grounds for the landlord/owner terminating the lease, circumstances where you lose your option money and property maintenance responsibilities. You need to protect yourself against a landlord/owner who wants to terminate the option agreement over an insignificant issue to pocket your option money without further obligation. (See Kenneth R. Harney, "The Nation's Housing," "Danger Lurks In Lease-Option Deals," <u>Washington Post</u>, December 17, 2005.)

BUY A LAWSUIT

There are times—though not many—when you might want to get into a messy deal. If the mess can be cleaned up for a known and acceptable amount of money, over a period of time that can be reasonably estimated, and a large pot of money/value can be realized for your effort, consider buying a property that requires a lawsuit. Messes always discount sales price.

A common messy situation involves a **suit to quiet title** and a **partition suit**. The first is used when your title search reveals the fact of, or the possibility of, another ownership claim in the property (land, minerals, rights, interests) the seller will convey. In land purchases, the buyer wants fee-simple ownership of the property, which includes all ownership interests in all of the property's assets, interests and rights. In some cases, when your deedwork reveals that another party may, or does, hold an ownership interest in one of the target property's assets, a suit to quiet title gives that person an opportunity to come forward and establish his claim. This type of suit is not usually very expensive. It may result in no one coming forward to assert a claim, or someone asserting a claim that the court rejects, or someone with a claim the court upholds. Two of these three outcomes solve the mess to the buyer's benefit. Where a valid claim exists, it's usually a (small) fractional claim. Since the buyer has no standing before purchase to bring a partition suit, it's up to the seller. You can, of course, buy the property and then live with the situation as is, or try to buy the minority interest, or propose a physical division of the property, or file a **partition suit** that asks the court to order the sale of the land with the net proceeds to be divided proportionately between the owners. Bringing a partition suit is not very expensive. But the cost of implementing an auction sale can result in a ten or 15 percent whack out of the gross selling revenues. The sellers may also have to pay for other expenses, such as an appraisal, survey, consultant opinions and lawyer time. In the end, you will receive cash for your ownership interest. You get the property itself only if you are the high bidder. Partition suits are the least preferred option if you want the property, because it can significantly increase your total acquisition cost and open you to being outbid.

Landlocked properties present an investor with both risk and reward. The current owner may not be able to negotiate a ROW easement with his neighbors owing to a history of squabbling. He may also be unable to afford bringing a lawsuit. If you're scoping and review by your lawyer indicates that the seller would win a lawsuit, I would approach the neighbors. You may be able to succeed where the current owner never will. Negotiate a ROW easement that is contingent on your purchase of the seller's property. You can trade part of the seller's land for the ROW or, if it's a timber tract, sell the land after timbering at a steep discount to the neighbor who lets you "haul out over him."

I would enter a legal mess with the greatest caution. It can easily consume far more time and money than you anticipated, which is why they're messes. Lawsuits, even easy ones, are emotionally intense, and when they've passed, like Southern history, they're still not past. A court's ruling may not always decide the issue on the ground. I know one land buyer who purchased a large tract at a very good price, knowing that his legal access was muddled. He believed he had access over a particular road, but the judge disagreed. The access the judge awarded to him was on firmer legal ground, but impractical on real dirt. Eventually he had to buy a right of way over the first road. Gaining access to his property took, money, aggravation, a court suit and five years. The suit consumed the first couple of years and then negotiating with the winners consumed the rest. Had he done better scoping, he would have been better able to forecast his troubles. He assumed that the judge would grant his request for the most practical entrance, even though it was not as legally defensible as at least one of the others. Had he asked a local lawyer about this case, he would have been warned against proceeding on his hopes. He might have done better had he had his local lawyer approach the owners of the road he wanted to use. Had his original purchase price not been steeply discounted, this investment would have been a disaster. As it was, the investment worked for him despite the protracted time and considerable expense. Had he wanted the property for something other than a long-term investment, he would have been stuck for five years.

A buyer is sometimes asked by a seller holding a minority interest in a property to buy him out. Often, he fears the majority seller whose fighting capabilities exceed his. Or, he may not be sure of the validity of his own ownership. I have turned down such proposals because the effort to resolve the mess seemed large and uncertain in terms of the gain that might be realized. A minority seller must discount his asking price to make it worth your while to take his place. When work and payoff are in more favorable alignment, I would consider jumping in. But where the likely benefit is not worth at least twice the anticipated cost in terms of time, expense and aggravation, I would avoid buying a lawsuit.

And if you do buy one, keep in mind that you did so for financial gain, not principle. I advise buyers not to fight for principle alone in a land squabble. Having done it once, I found it to be a dreadful experience. Fighting over money is when all is said and done, just fighting over money. But losing on principle—when you're right—really hurts.

CHAPTER 30: SOME IDEAS ORGANIZED AS A PURCHASE-OFFER CONTRACT

The "contract" that follows is a sample of possible approaches, presented as a contract might organize them. I didn't write a model contract because one size never fits all.

State laws vary, and every purchase presents its own combination of things you need to worry about and things you don't, based on your pre-offer scoping. Even basic contract features will vary—how property is described, deed types, mortgage and trustee arrangements, etc. States may require specific provisions and specific language in real-estate contracts. It is, therefore, helpful to have a copy of the local broker's contract in front of you for purposes of comparison and adaptation. Ask a local broker for a copy of this standard contract; you certainly want to read it at your leisure before you sign one.

I advise against a buyer writing his own contract from scratch. Yet, I also think it's essential for every buyer to be conversant with contract ideas and language so that he can work with his local lawyer to craft a contract that fits his specific needs and circumstances. After scoping, you may decide to use the standard contract with only one or two changes, which you can write in on that form. If you do decide to write a contract from scratch with your lawyer, keep the language simple and clear. Lawyers often write badly, and even good lawyers tend to write in a lawyerly style that can be difficult to understand.

Your interest in a purchase will be subverted if you hand a seller a semi-comprehensible contract. Please don't toss in every contingency and provision I've included in this book. Don't include every contingency that you can think up on your own. Offer a seller a contract that protects your interests with economy of concept and language. The more incomprehensible a contract, the more legal pretzel twisting it contains, the more one-sided it is, the more reluctant your seller will be to sign.

The "contract" that follows is not meant to be a contract. Don't rip and use it.

A standard real-estate contract will follow the format I've used, more or less. I've added language for illustrative purposes that a standard contract will not contain. Think of this as an exercise in thinking through how various elements of contract ideas and language might fit together. In other chapters, I've written examples of contingencies and other contract language that you can discuss with your lawyer where they might be needed. Real-estate forms of all kinds can be obtained from Professional Publishing Co. of Novato, California at www.TrueForms.com.

I have deliberately included more language than would normally be needed for illustration purposes. This contract exercise is more elaborate than buyers will normally need. I have included different ways of getting at similar points as a way of presenting choices.

Individual circumstances will dictate when a buyer should insert specific contingencies and other protections. Remember, clear and simple is more likely to fly with a seller than convoluted and complicated.

DO NOT USE THIS CONTRACT VERBATIM. Use it to organize your thoughts about how to make an offer. Any contract that you offer a seller should be reviewed by your local lawyer prior to doing so.

REAL-ESTATE SALES CONTRACT

This Contract of Sale and Agreement, made and entered between _____ (name and address of Seller [s]), herein Seller, and _____(name and address of Buyer [s]), herein Buyer, on the ___ day of _____, 2___, provides as follows:

1. PREMISES AND DISCLOSURES.

A. Seller shall sell and convey and Buyer shall purchase on the terms and conditions herein set forth all interests, assets and rights in Seller's real property, together with all improvements thereon, including but not limited to, all standing and fallen timber; all natural resources, surface and subsurface; all water rights; all appurtenances to the property, including, but not limited to, rights of way (recorded and unrecorded), easements, prescriptions and permissions; all gates, fences, culverts, roads, bridges and stores of gravel and soil; and all other rights and privileges of ownership, lying and being situate near _____, Virginia in _____ County, more particularly described as _____ acres, conveyed to Seller by Deed of _____, [date] in Deed Book __, Page ____, in the _____ County Clerk's Office, and being the same property as shown on the _____ County Tax Maps as Parcels ___ and ___ in the _____ District, and being the same property as shown by a recorded survey of August 6, 1999, Map Book ____, Page ____, prepared by John Johnson, a surveyor licensed in the Commonwealth of Virginia.

B. Seller warrants that he is lawfully seised of this property in fee simple. Seller shall convey all assets of, and rights and interests in, the property in fee simple with marketable title free of encumbrance and limitation, except for those of record in the Clerk's office and those disclosed in writing to Buyer that are accepted by Buyer in writing prior to this Contract taking effect. Buyer retains the right to withdraw or modify this Contract in light of Seller disclosure regarding any encumbrance or limitation. This Contract shall not come into effect until Buyer accepts in writing any such disclosure.

C. Encumbrance and limitation are defined to include, but are not limited to, unrecorded rights of way and easements; claims of possession and/or use against the property; claims of prescription, implication or necessity against the property; permissions to access or otherwise use the property; retentions of profit and/or interest in the property; liens of any kind against the property; zoning and/or other regulatory restrictions on the property; any environmental condition or status (such as presence of wetlands; endangered, threatened or sensitive species; migratory bird habitat; floodplain; public conservation plan; buried fuel tank; sites or sources of ground and/or water contamination and/or pollution; sensitive or restricted surface waters; old mines and pending plans to mine or extract other minerals, including oil or gas; subsidence hazards from underground excavations; karst topography; caves; geologic faults; earthquake zone; hurricane/tornado/hailstorm belt, etc.); claims on behalf of or against the property involving water, irrigation, springs, pollution, water impoundments, surface and subsurface water, and water rights; non-compliance with local, state and/or federal laws and regulations; and any other condition or situation that would adversely affect the Buyer's possession, use and enjoyment of the property and/or its value.

D. Seller shall convey the property with a General Warranty Deed and English Covenants of Title that include the six customary warranties: seisin, conveyance, against encumbrances, quiet enjoyment, general warranty (forever) and further assurances. [*English Covenants of Title are invoked in the Commonwealth of Virginia; some General Warranty Deeds do not include all six covenants, depending on the state.*]

E. Seller warrants that the conveyance shall be without encumbrance (other than those disclosed or of record), lien, limitation, discount, lease, easement, reduction or reservation of interest or profit, excepting those of record in the Clerk's Office of _____ County or disclosed and accepted by Buyer in the manner described in 1.B., above.

F. Parties agree that the Seller is selling this property "as is, where is" as of the date that this Contract takes effect_____ is submitted_____. Any change in the condition or status of the property beyond reasonable wear and tear as of Closing may, at Buyer's option, lead to his voiding of this Contract without penalty or its renegotiation on mutually agreeable terms.

G. Seller warrants that the property shall be free of any material defect, latent or otherwise, as of Closing that would adversely affect Buyer's possession, use and enjoyment of the Property and/or its value, except for defects disclosed by Seller in writing and accepted by Buyer in writing prior to this Contract taking effect. Buyer reserves the right to void this Contract without penalty and, at his choice, submit a revised offer or none at all when he determines that any defect is unacceptable.

H. Defect shall be construed broadly to mean a condition, status, situation, problem, complication, uncertainty and the like, including but not limited to, unrecorded rights of way and easements; claims of possession and/or use against the property; claims of prescription, implication, or necessity against the property; permissions to access or otherwise use the property; retentions of profit and/or interest in the property; unrecorded liens and estates of any kind in or against the property; zoning and/or other regulatory restrictions on the property; conditions of annoyance or nuisance around the property, such as offensive and/or unreasonable odors, noise, light, disturbance of view, activities, behavior and so forth; trespass occurring on the property; environmental condition or status (such as presence of wetlands; endangered, threatened or sensitive species; migratory bird habitat; floodplain; public conservation plan; underground storage tanks; sources of ground and/or water contamination and/or pollution; sensitive or restricted surface waters; ground or geologic faults or instability; excavations beneath the surface or otherwise concealed; reclaimed excavations and/or mines; plans to mine or extract other materials and/or minerals, including oil or gas, on or around the property; subsidence hazards from underground excavations; karst topography; caves; earthquake zone; hurricane/tornado/hailstorm belt, etc.); unrecorded claims on behalf of or against the property involving water, irrigation, springs, pollution, water impounds, surface and subsurface water, and water rights; non-compliance with local, state and/or federal laws and regulations; and any other condition or situation that would in the judgment of a reasonable individual adversely affect the Buyer's possession, use and enjoyment of the property and/or its value.

I. The property and Seller are subject to the Seller disclosure provisions in this Contract as set forth herein and all those required by local, state and federal law.

J. Seller warrants that no timber cutting or surface-disturbing activities of any kind shall occur on the property after the date this Contract takes effect. If any such cutting or surface-disturbing activity does occur, the Buyer may void this Contract without penalty, or, alternatively at his option, resolve the matter through negotiations.

K. Seller warrants that he will not enter into any agreement for the sale, lease, option, exchange, severance, reservation or exploitation of the timber, minerals, water rights, hunting (game) rights and other wildlife rights, access rights, recreation rights and all other property rights and resources once this Contract takes effect, except with the prior written authorization of the Buyer. Buyer reserves the right to reject any such agreement without penalty and without affecting this Contract. Where an agreement is acceptable to both Seller and Buyer, they agree to pro rate income from this agreement with _____ percent to the Seller and _____ percent to Buyer from the date this Contract takes effect until the date of Closing at which time all income accrues to Buyer.

L. If any such agreement is in effect prior to the effective date of this Contract, Seller shall disclose all terms of each such agreement in writing prior to the date on which this Contract takes effect. Buyer reserves right to withdraw or modify his offer without penalty in light of any such agreement whose terms Buyer deems unacceptable. Buyer shall notify Seller of his response to such disclosure in writing.

M. Seller shall provide the Buyer with copies of all leases (including mineral leases), rental agreements, easements, estates running with the property, reservations of interest or profit and any other limiting agreement prior to accepting this Contract, excepting those documents that are of record with the Clerk of _____ County. Seller shall at the same time provide Buyer with information setting forth his understanding of any oral agreements, licenses or permissions the Seller gave to other Parties that affect the property to be conveyed.

N. Seller shall disclose in writing prior to acceptance of this Contract all boundary disputes; any boundary lines on the property that are marked and/or run differently than their presentation in Seller's Deed and/or in Seller's survey; unresolved ownership claims against the property; adverse possessions, uses and claims against the property; any easements—or claims of—easements in gross, by necessity, implication or prescription of which he is aware.

O. Seller shall disclose in writing prior to acceptance of this Contract any incidents of which he is aware of trespass whether or not declared so by a court of law; unauthorized use of the property for camping, picnicking, trash dumping, hunting, fishing, trapping, timber cutting and firewood cutting; unauthorized use of the property by private vehicles (such as motorcycles, snowmobiles, ATVs, 4WD vehicles, boats and air-borne craft), commercial vehicles and public vehicles; unauthorized use by horse riders, hikers, bird watchers, swimmers and skiers; unauthorized use of the property by livestock; unauthorized tapping, exploiting or gathering of resources (including, but not limited to, water, coal, minerals, soils, rock, oil, gas, ginseng, plants, crops, wildlife, mushrooms, nuts, roots, mistletoe, berries and the like); and incidents of theft or attempted theft, whether or not reported to law-enforcement authorities.

P. Seller shall notify in writing any individual known to him engaging in such unauthorized uses, above, that he is to cease and desist immediately, unless otherwise directed in writing by Buyer.

Seller _____ shall _____ shall not post his property prior to Closing. Buyer shall pay for the posting materials if the Parties agree to posting prior to Closing. Seller shall make good-faith effort to help Buyer end any such activities that Buyer determines are adverse to his possession, use and enjoyment of the property and/or its value.

Q. Seller shall disclose in writing prior to acceptance of this Contract any environmental condition of which he has knowledge that would adversely affect the Buyer's possession, use and enjoyment of the property and/or its value, resources and assets. Environmental "condition" is to be construed broadly, to include, but is not limited to, the presence of state and/or federal endangered, threatened or sensitive flora and fauna and/or their habitat; wetlands; protected streams and/or restricted waterways; flooding and/or floodplains; pollution of surface and/or underground waters; acid-mine drainage; surface subsidence and/or instability; landslide potential; karst topography; soil conditions unsuited to building, agriculture and septic fields; earthquake; severe weather (windstorms, hail, tornado, hurricane, ice and snow, early frost, lack of precipitation, high heat); infestations of insects (e.g., fire ants, termites, gypsy moth, wood-destroying beetles and/or ants, Africanized bees), birds, bats, snakes, and other aquatic and land fauna; infestation of nuisance flora (e.g., toxic plants, multiflora rose, kudzu); and the presence of diseases, insects and conditions that adversely affect crops and/or timber.

R. Seller shall disclose in writing prior to acceptance of this Contract information of which he is aware regarding the property's compliance status with state and federal environmental and safety regulations including, but not limited to, surface and underground mining for coal and other minerals; exploration and production for oil and natural gas; water and air quality; forest management and stewardship plans; buried fuel tanks; disposal sites for garbage and/or toxic/hazardous waste, including agricultural chemicals; water impoundments; and the installation of unapproved septic and/or wastewater systems. Copies of Seller permits, inspection reports, notices of non-compliance, and planning documents for any environmental condition or land use (including reclamation, conservation, forest-management plans and the like) shall be furnished to Buyer at such time.

S. Seller shall ____ shall not ____ provide Buyer with current tax-assessed values for the property's land, improvements, timber, minerals, water and any other assets and resources. Seller shall inform Buyer of any information he has regarding current and/or proposed reassessments and proposed local or state tax policies that would affect the property. [*This information is public record. Let the seller persuade you to delete it.*]

T. Seller shall disclose in writing prior to acceptance of this Contract any matters of land use, regulation, zoning, planning, and condemnation by public authority that affect property, whether in effect or proposed. Seller shall ____ shall not ____ provide the current zoning status of the property and its status under whatever local comprehensive plans are in effect. [*Also in public record.*]

U. Seller shall disclose in writing prior to acceptance of this Contract any instances or patterns of annoyance involving the property of which he is aware, including, but not limited to, unauthorized trash dumping; vehicles using the entrance drive for turning; bright lights, loud noise, dust/dirt, and/or offensive odors originating off the property; low-flying aircraft; and early-morning/late-night activities, among others.

V. Seller shall disclose in writing prior to acceptance of this Contract information of which he is aware regarding any Party having, exercising or claiming access to, or through, this property by right of way, easement, prescription, implication, necessity, adverse use, permission, license or otherwise. Seller need not provide information that is recorded in the Clerk's office in _____ County.

W. Buyer may void this Contract without penalty if Seller is unable to convey 100 percent of ownership interests in all of the property assets, rights and interests. Buyer, at his option, may submit an amended and revised Contract to reflect Seller's true position in the property.

X. Seller shall disclose in writing prior to acceptance of this Contract any arrangement whereby Seller, or any previous owners of this property, sold, purchased, leased, rented, optioned, granted, or been granted water or water rights for or from this property.

Z. This property has_____ has not _____ used irrigated water during the last ten years.

AA. This property has _____ has not _____ purchased water during the last ten years.

BB. If the property has needed, used, sold and/or purchased water, Seller shall provide Buyer with copies of all documents related to such activities.

CC. Seller shall provide the following:

(1). This property is _____ is not _____ currently classified in a land-use (farm use) valuation category for tax purposes.

(2). This property is _____ is not _____ currently enrolled in a public forest management/stewardship program.

(3). This property is _____ is not _____ subject to a conservation easement of any kind, whether of record or not.

(4). This property is _____ is not _____ currently enrolled in a state and/or federal agricultural program. Seller shall attach information regarding each such program, including obligations running with the property, plans, payments and taxability of such payments.

DD. Failure of Seller to disclose and/or inform Buyer of such information of which he is aware in regard to the above shall be sufficient grounds for Buyer, at his option, to withdraw this Contract prior to acceptance or void this Contract once it has taken effect.

EE. Buyer may withdraw or void this Contract without penalty if either Seller fails to disclose as provided or the results of such information and disclosure are unacceptable to Buyer. Upon withdrawal or voiding of this Contract in these circumstances, Buyer shall have all security deposits returned in full and in a timely manner. Buyer shall have no further obligation to Seller.

FF. Buyer at his option may, alternatively, propose to Seller negotiations to resolve items or information and disclosure. Seller at his option may accept or reject Buyer's offer to negotiate. Depending on the results of these efforts, Buyer may submit a substitute Contract for Seller's consideration.

GG. If Seller fails to disclose a condition of the type set forth above, Seller shall bear full liability for all subsequent costs of remedy incurred by Buyer.

HH. Upon voiding of this Contract, Buyer shall have his security deposit returned in full within five business days of providing Seller written notification of the termination of this Contract. "Without penalty," as used in this Contract, shall be construed to mean full return of the Buyer's security deposit as provided in the preceding sentence.

II. All warranties to survive Closing.

2. PRICE.

A. The exact purchase price for this property shall be calculated by multiplying $_____ per acre by the number of acres and fraction thereof contained within the boundaries as established by _____ survey of record, or _____ deed description, or _____ tax maps, or _____ survey done at the expense of Buyer, or _____ other means acceptable to Buyer and Seller. Any expense incurred in establishing acreage shall ____ shall not____ be divided between Seller and Buyer in the following manner: ____% Buyer; ____ % Seller.

B. Buyer shall deliver a first security deposit of 0.75 percent of the gross sales price of $_____, as calculated above, to the Buyer's attorney _____, with this Contract. Buyer's attorney shall serve as Escrow Agent for the Parties. Escrow Agent shall hold this deposit in accordance with the escrow provisions of the Commonwealth of Virginia. It shall be deposited in the Escrow Agent's escrow account at the following financial institution: _____. Buyer shall deliver his deposit in cash, wire transfer or certified check. Buyer's attorney shall provide receipt to both Parties.

C. Buyer shall deliver in the same manner a second security deposit of 5.25 percent of the gross sales price on the day he notifies Seller in writing that all disclosures and contingencies have been accepted or withdrawn.

D. Both security deposits shall be applied to the sale of the property, unless otherwise agreed.

E. The balance of the purchase price shall be paid in cash, wire transfer or certified check or other means acceptable to the Parties at Closing.

F. Buyer's security deposits are subject to the prorations set forth in **Section 9.**

3. TERMS.

A. Seller acknowledges that Buyer has deposited in escrow for all Parties the sum of $_____ with _____, Escrow Agent and attorney for the Buyer. This sum is the first good-faith deposit toward the purchase of the property described above.

B. Interest shall ____ or shall not___ accrue to Seller____ or Buyer ____as provided by the law in the Commonwealth of Virginia on all deposits.

C. In the event Seller cannot provide a marketable title in fee simple to the property described above and a General Warranty Deed with English Covenants of Title and fulfill all other terms of this Contract, this Contract shall be terminated. Buyer shall notify Seller and Escrow Agent of termination in writing. Escrow Agent shall then return all monies deposited as security deposit in full to Buyer within five calendar days and without penalty.

D. The purchase price shall be paid as follows: The escrowed deposits together with the balance of the purchase price shall be given by Buyer, or his designated representative, to Seller, or his designated representative, at Closing.

E. Seller agrees_____ does not agree _____ to pay _____ percentage of the financing charges incurred by Buyer to secure a mortgage on this property.

F. Buyer's possession shall begin at settlement on the date of Closing.

G. Recordation of the Deed shall take place in _____ County, Virginia on the date of Closing, or other date agreeable to the Parties.

H. The Closing shall take place at the office of _____, or at another location the Parties designate at a mutually agreed time.

4. EFFECT AND DURATION.

A. This Contract shall take effect on the day the Parties agree in writing on its provisions in their entirety, as evidenced by the last required signature or dated set of initials. The Contract takes effect at 5 p.m. on that day, unless otherwise agreed.

B. This Contract shall be in effect until Closing, which is scheduled for _____ (month, day, year), or no more than _____ calendar days from the date that Buyer notifies Seller in writing that all contingencies are withdrawn or satisfied, whichever is later.

C. The Parties may extend their Contract escrow by mutual agreement in writing.

5. DEED.

A. Seller shall convey the property by General Warranty Deed with English Covenants of Title, free of liens, covenants, reservations, restrictions, tenancies, estates, encumbrances and arrangements other than those recorded in the Clerk's office in _____ County, Virginia or disclosed by Seller and accepted by Buyer in writing, as provided above.

6. TITLE.

A. Buyer shall take title in the name (s) of _____.

B. Buyer may assign, transfer, convey, option, gift, or sell his interest in this Contract prior to closing at his option without penalty. Any such act shall not diminish or alter any provision in this Contract or the Buyer's obligations to fulfill its terms, including price. Buyer shall notify Seller in writing prior to invoking this provision.

7. TITLE REPORT.

A. Buyer does_____ does not_____ require a preliminary title report _____ and/or abstract of title _____. If Buyer does require such document (s), he shall make arrangements for this work at his expense, to be completed within thirty (30) calendar days of the date this Contract takes effect.

B. If the title report reveals a defect, the Buyer may void this Contract without penalty. Seller shall be provided a reasonable amount of time, not to exceed _____ calendar days from receiving written notification from Buyer, to cure his title to Buyer's satisfaction before Buyer may void this Contract.

8. TITLE INSURANCE.

A. Buyer does _____ does not _____ require a Standard _____ Extended _____ Title Insurance Policy. If Buyer requires such a policy, he shall arrange for it in a timely manner at his expense.

9. PRORATIONS AND COSTS.

A. The Parties agree to pro rate property taxes, assessments, fees and other state and local taxes for the current year from the date of Closing, with the Seller paying his proportional share through that date and the Buyer assuming all such liability as of the following day. Seller bears sole responsibility for bringing all such accounts current from prior years.

B. Rental and/or royalty income shall be pro rated in the same manner.

C. Seller agrees to pay the expense of preparing the deed and any taxes due from grantor/Seller.

D. Buyer agrees to pay for a title examination, costs associated with activities described in **Section 8**, title insurance and the fees of his attorney.

E. The Parties agree to pro rate all other settlement costs from the day of Closing, including but not limited to, homeowners-association fees, utility bills and irrigation fees.

F. Buyer agrees to purchase from Seller all heating oil, propane gas and gasoline in tanks on the Property. The supplier of each fuel shall estimate the stored quantity as of the date of Closing and Buyer shall pay the Seller for each volume multiplied by current delivered price as of the date of this estimate.

G. Parties agree that Buyer _____ Seller _____ shall pay the costs of recording the Buyer's Deed.

H. Parties agree _____ do not agree _____ to pro rate other income, such as government cost-shares, agricultural production payments, etc. If the Parties do not agree on proration, they shall attach to this Contract an Addendum setting forth their plan for dividing such income.

10. BUYER'S RIGHT OF VISITATION AND IMPROVEMENT.

A. The Buyer, his Agents, Employees, Contractors, Surveyors, Foresters, Associates and Others acting on his behalf or in the furtherance of his interests in this property and in this Contract may visit the property at any time between the effective date of this Contract and Closing. The Parties agree to work out a visitation-notification and access procedure. Seller agrees to allow the Buyer, his Agents, Employees, Contractors, Surveyors, Foresters, Associates and Others acting on his behalf or in the furtherance of his interests in this property and this Contract to perform any of the following work and tasks during this period at Buyer's expense:

(1) Survey perimeter boundaries, to be marked on the ground where needed;

(2) Survey of interior divisions for three 25-acre lots on west side of property and interior road, to be marked on the ground;

(3) Cruise of the property's timber by consulting forester; no increment boring;

(4) Painting of the property's merchantable timber inventory by consulting forester, using blue paint dots stump and butt;

(5) Improvements to existing entrance road, including widening to 16 feet with a two-foot-wide apron on either side; grading, ditching, installing rock and gravel where needed; and installing one 36"-diameter, 20-foot-long metal culvert in stream.

Merchantable trees cut in the process of making road improvements shall be gathered as logs at a landing near the gate and not sold prior to Closing. In the event of default or failure to perform, these logs remain the property of Seller; otherwise they belong to Buyer;

(6) Securing appropriate utility easement and installing underground lines to new house site by pond, located on the drawing attached to this Contract;

(7) Sampling of soil and water resources;

(8) Taking soil samples by hand auger or backhoe in anticipation of application for three (3) septic permits;

(9) Showing the property to prospective buyers; and

(10) Other_____.

Seller shall maintain existing roads in current condition during the time this Contract is in effect.

B. Seller shall provide Buyer with key (s) to locked gates for these purposes. Gates shall be left locked at the end of each visit or day, unless otherwise agreed.

C. Seller agrees to apply for _____ rezoning, _____ permit or _____ variance on behalf of Buyer. Closing shall take place within ten (10) calendar days of Seller getting appropriate approval. Buyer shall pay all costs incurred in obtaining the approval he requires. All approvals shall run with the property and convey to Buyer. Failure to obtain the necessary approvals in a form acceptable to Buyer shall be grounds for Buyer to terminate this Contract without penalty.

D. Seller bears no responsibility for or liability for any personal property, materiel, supplies, tools, equipment, machinery and the like that Buyer, and those associated with Buyer in any way, use or leave on the property, except for those instances of damage from fire, vandalism, accident and theft and the like that are covered under Seller's insurance policies. Where the Seller's policy covers such damage, Seller shall submit a claim and pay the Buyer and/or his associates the award, less the amount of the Seller-paid deductible.

E. Seller agrees to keep his current property-protection and liability insurance policies in effect until Closing. If Seller has no such insurance, he shall secure adequate coverage for the escrow period.

11. FAILURE TO PERFORM.

A. Once all contingencies are removed or deemed acceptable by Buyer and he notifies Seller of same in writing, any Buyer failure to perform on this Contract shall result in the forfeit of Buyer's deposits and all of the documents and physical improvements to property as produced under Section 10 as liquidated damages and a reasonable estimate of Seller's damages from said lack of performance. This sum, together with the documents, improvements and materials below, shall be Seller's sole remedy as to damages for any failure to perform

B. All culverts, bridges, rock, gravel, fences, gates, utilities, and other materials and supplies Buyer has on property at the time of his failure to perform become Seller's property at no cost to him as of the date of Buyer's failure to perform.

12. INSURANCE AND RISK OF LOSS.

A. Risk of loss from all naturally occurring acts, such as fire, ice, wind and flood remains with Seller until Closing.

B. Seller agrees to secure a farm homeowner's policy to cover the duration of this Contract which will provide sufficient funds to fully replace Seller's farmhouse, three major barns, machinery shed and silo.

C. Seller does ____ does not____ have an accident liability policy in place.

D. Buyer holds Seller harmless and without liability of any kind for any accidents, personal injury and/or damage, including fire damage, to property of any persons visiting, inspecting, analyzing and/or working on this property in connection with Buyer's activities permitted under this Contract, including, but not limited to, activities listed in **Section 10**. Those subject to this language are the Buyer, his Friends, Visitors, Associates, Prospective Buyers of Timber and/or Land, Representatives, Agents, Prospective Representatives and Agents, Employees, Contractors and their Subcontractors, Surveyors, Foresters, Public Officials invited to the Property by the Buyer and Others acting on his behalf or in the furtherance of his interests in this property and this Contract.

E. If any Buyer activity, or individual associated with Buyer as set forth above, causes any damage, including fire damage, to Seller's property and Buyer fails to perform, Buyer shall compensate Seller for the cost of repairing the damage or the fair market value of the loss.

13. DAMAGE.

A. If the property's natural resources are materially damaged from a naturally occurring event or activity, such as flood, casualty, fire, wind and infestation/disease during escrow, Buyer may terminate this Contract without penalty. Material damage shall be construed to mean more than $1,000 in loss, as estimated by the Parties jointly, or, if there is no agreement, by a qualified professional chosen by the Parties whose fee shall be divided equally between them. The Parties may renegotiate the terms of their

Contract in light of a material loss.

B. If the property is damaged in any manner from fire or other acts related to the presence or activity of Buyer, his Friends, Visitors, Associates, Prospective Buyers of Timber and/or Land, Representatives, Agents, Prospective Representatives and Agents, Employees, Contractors and their Subcontractors, Surveyors, Foresters, Public Officials invited to the Property by Buyer and Others acting on his behalf or in the furtherance of his interests in this property and this Contract, Buyer is not relieved of his obligations to perform under this Contract, according to the terms as set forth herein.

14. CONTINGENCIES:

The Buyer's offer is contingent on the following items being resolved to his satisfaction:

A. Seller must be able to provide clear, marketable title; undivided and full ownership in fee simple, subject to easements of record and disclosures accepted by Buyer as set forth above; and a General Warranty Deed to the Property described and conveyed and all its rights, resources and assets.

B. Results of a timber evaluation, paid for by Buyer, must be acceptable to Buyer;

C. Seller shall provide Buyer a deeded right of way of at least 16 feet in width or other arrangement satisfactory to Buyer allowing vehicular access from State Route 3 over the road currently being used.

D. Buyer's offer is contingent on the Property being free of any environmental encumbrance, pollution from off-site sources and/or liability.

E. Buyer's offer is _____ is not _____ contingent on obtaining a satisfactory percolation test at a site of his choosing and at his expense. If Buyer's offer is contingent on such a test, Buyer shall have _____ calendar days from the date on which this Contract takes effect to arrange for and receive results from such a test. Buyer shall notify Seller within three (3) calendar days of receiving results whether the results are or are not acceptable. Seller shall make the property available for such testing at mutually agreeable times. Buyer shall replace and regrade excavations made on the property.

F. Buyer's offer is _____ is not _____ contingent on obtaining a septic permit at his expense for either _____ bedrooms or _____ square feet of residential area. If Buyer's offer is contingent on such a permit being obtained, Buyer shall make a good-faith effort to obtain such a permit within _____ calendar days of this Contract taking effect, or as soon thereafter as possible. The permit shall be issued to the Seller's property and convey to the Buyer at Closing.

G. Buyer's offer is _____ is not _____ contingent on performing a septic-system inspection at his expense within _____ calendar days. Buyer may void or modify this Contract if the inspection results are unsatisfactory.

H. Buyer's offer is _____ is not _____ contingent on the sale, settlement, lease or exchange of other real property owned or controlled by Buyer.

I. Buyer's offer is _____ is not _____ contingent on obtaining acceptable financing from an institutional lender.

J. Seller is ____ is not ____ asked to finance any part of this purchase. If Seller is being asked to finance a part of this purchase, the Buyer's proposal is appended to this Contract.

K. All contingency results must be acceptable to Buyer. If these contingencies are not met or resolved to Buyer's satisfaction, Buyer may terminate this offer without penalty and his security deposit shall be returned in full in a timely manner.

15. FEES.

A. A brokerage fee of _____ percent is due to _____ _____ at closing from Seller's funds. Additional terms of this brokerage fee are appended to this Contract.

A fee of ____ percent is due to _____ at closing from Buyer's funds for consulting. Additional terms of this fee are appended to this Contract. Fees owed shall be paid by the Escrow Agent at closing.

B. Broker and Seller agree to keep the price, terms and conditions of Buyer's offer completely confidential and shall not disclose them or allow them to be disclosed to any other party, including other buyers.

16. PROPERTY OWNERS' ASSOCIATION DISCLOSURE.

A. Seller represents that this property is not located within a development that is subject to the Virginia Property Owners' Association Act.

17. AMENDMENT.

A. This Contract may only be amended in writing. Signed and dated facsimile documents are ____ are not ____ an acceptable means of amendment.

18. NOTICE.

A. Whenever notice is to be given under the terms of this Contract, such notice shall be deemed to have been given when enclosed in an envelope having proper postage, addressed to the receiving Party and deposited as Certified Mail at a U.S. Post Office. The date at which such notice shall be deemed to have been given shall be the date of the envelope's postmark.

B. The Parties agree ____ not agree ____ to substitute a private overnight mail carrier, either UPS or Federal Express, for the U.S. Post Office. Date of notice shall in this case be the pick-up date from the point of origin as evidenced by receipts.

C. The Parties agree ____ not agree ____ to substitute facsimile documents for mailed original documents under both **A.** and **B.** above. Such documents shall be signed and dated by the Party giving notice. Date of notice shall in this case be the transmission date from the point of origin. Sender shall include transmission date on his facsimile cover sheet. The receiving Party shall acknowledge time and date of receipt by signed and dated return facsimile document.

19. GOVERNANCE.

A. The laws of the Commonwealth of Virginia shall govern this Contract.

20. MECHANIC'S LIEN NOTICE.

A. The law related to Mechanic's Lien Notice in the Commonwealth of Virginia shall apply.

B. Seller shall deliver to Buyer at closing an affidavit, on a form acceptable to Buyer's lender, if applicable, signed by Seller that no labor or materials have been furnished to the property within the statutory period for the filing of mechanic's or materialmen's liens against the property. If labor or materials have been furnished during the statutory period at Seller's behest, Seller shall deliver to Buyer an affidavit signed by Seller and the person (s) furnishing the labor or materials that such costs have been paid.

C. Buyer is responsible for prompt payment to those providing labor, services, and materials at his behest on, or related to, Seller's property between the effective date of this Contract and closing. This includes, but is not limited to, those activities listed in **10. A.** Liens of any kind filed against the property for such activities during this time are the sole responsibility of Buyer. Seller is not liable for the payment or resolution of such expenses and liens.

21. RESOLUTION OF DISPUTES.

A. The Parties, Broker and consultant agree to submit any disputes or claims arising out of this Contract to non-binding mediation before binding arbitration or litigation. Non-binding mediation by a third-party neutral does not obligate either Party to agree to a settlement arising from this process unless that settlement is accepted by both Parties, in which case it becomes binding. If non-binding mediation fails to bring forth a settlement, the Parties are free to transfer their dispute to binding arbitration by mutual agreement or litigation. The Parties shall choose a mediator, and if necessary, an arbitrator, from panels of qualified commercial neutrals experienced in real estate provided by the _____.
The costs of such services shall be divided equally between, or among, the Parties in dispute.

22. ENTIRE AGREEMENT.

A. This Contract, including any attachments initialed and dated by the Parties, shall constitute the entire agreement between them. It shall supersede all other written or oral agreements between them. This Contract can only be modified in writing that is initialed and dated by both Parties.

23. WALK-THROUGH.

A. Buyer shall have the right and opportunity to walk through the property within 48 hours of the scheduled Closing.

B. If the Buyer observes any change in the property's condition, apart from normal wear and tear, from the day on which this Contract took effect that he finds unacceptable, the Parties agree to attempt to resolve the issue prior to Closing. The terms of any resolution shall be appended to this Contract.

C. If the Parties are unable to resolve the issue, Buyer may void this Contract without penalty.

24. MISCELLANEOUS.

A. This Contract may be signed in one or more counterparts, each of which shall be deemed to be an original document. All such documents together shall constitute one and the same document.

B. For the purpose of computing the duration of this Contract, the first day shall be the day this Contract comes into effect by the dated signature of the last required Party. All time periods shall begin at 5 p.m. on the day specified in this Contract. Each time period shall run for the specified period of days, ending at 5 p.m. on the termination day as provided.

C. This Contract shall be binding on the Parties, and it shall bind and inure to the benefit of their heirs, agents, personal representatives, successors and assigns.

D. If handwritten or typed terms conflict with or are inconsistent with the printed terms of this Contract, the more recent shall control.

25. ACCEPTANCE.

A. This Contract shall constitute an offer to enter into a bilateral contract with Seller upon the dated signature of the Buyer.

B. Buyer's offer shall become null and void as of _____ (time) on _____ (day/month), 2____, if not accepted by Seller. Changes, counter-offers, and amendment are permitted until that time and date without a binding Contract coming into effect. Buyer at his choice may extend the offering period at his option in writing.

C. The Parties do _____ do not _____ require signature notarization on this document.

WITNESS the following duly authorized signatures.

Sellers accept this offer at 5 p.m. on _____ day of _____, 2____.

SELLER	DATE	BUYER	DATE
ADDRESS		ADDRESS	
PHONE		PHONE	
FAX		FAX	

Escrow Agent, _____, acknowledges receipt of $_____ from Buyer as security deposit.

CHAPTER 31: THINKING ABOUT DIRT MONEY

RESEARCH AND FUTURES ANALYSIS

Buying property usually involves spending your own money. This is unfortunate.

In the real-estate aisle of your local book store, you will find numerous guru books promising that you can buy property for free, and, if not that, with no money down, and, if not that, with just a little something in the deal. Each of these books—and the initially free seminars that often trail them—has some useful information. Their systems, however, may or may not work, and may or may not be unethical or illegal. (John T. Reed is the anti-guru guru whom I endorse. He evaluates all of the get-rich-quick gurus at www.johntreed.com/Reedgururating.html. His own invaluable website is www.johntreed.com/.) I recommend reading the short-cut boys with Reed in one hand and a three-bin sorter in the other: 1) information that appears useful and legal; 2) information that does not; and 3) stuff in the middle, about which you might want to learn more.

The key to making money in country real estate is research.

If your scoping has discovered a property whose purchase price is less than its break-up value, you should be able to borrow close to 100 percent of the purchase price and immediately sell enough of the property or assets to repay some, if not all, of your short-term note. This leaves you with a core holding in the property free and clear. There's no trick to this flip, other than to find a property that can be parted out quickly for more than you've paid for it. Your research has to be based on facts and analysis that a lender knows is credible. If you bring a longer term perspective than that of a flipper, your profit comes from appreciation rather than dismemberment. Your research is no less rigorous, however; it does have different questions, depending on your objectives. Research—pre-purchase scoping—allows you to buy at the right price, given your goals, which, in turn, allows you to get your investment onto a profit track. There's no trick to research, just diligence and effort applied to questions you know you need answers to.

Real-estate investment is a subject that can be learned. That is, after all, what this book is about. Like every investment, rural land carries risk. In my experience, a patient, persistent buyer can strip much, even most, risk out of a land investment. I could never write that sentence about common stocks.

I urge readers to become familiar with the vernacular literature on buying real estate. Robert J. Bruss recommends these: William Nickerson, How I Turned $1,000 into Five Million in Real Estate in My Spare Time (New York: Simon & Schuster, 1984); Robert G. Allen, Nothing Down for the 90s: How to Buy Real Estate With Little or No money Down, or latest edition (New York: Simon & Schuster, 1990); Robert Shemin, Unlimited Riches: Making Your Fortune in Real Estate Investing (New York: John Wiley & Sons, 2002); William Bronchick and Robert Dahlstrom, Flipping Properties: Generate Instant Cash Profits in Real Estate (Chicago: Dearborn, 2001); and David Schumacher, Buy and Hold 2004-2005: 7 Steps to a Real Estate Fortune, rev. ed., (Schumacher Enterprises, 2004). Robert Irwin has written a "Tips and Traps" series of books on buying and selling real estate that I've found very practical. My all-time favorite—because it got me started—is George Bockl, How to Use Leverage to Make Money in Local Real Estate (Englewood Cliffs, N.J.: Prentice-Hall, 1965). I bought George Bockl for a buck at a library book sale, and it changed my life. I'd also advise reading Julie Garton-Good, All About Mortgages: Insider Tips to Finance or Refinance Your Home, 2nd ed. (Chicago: Dearborn, 1999); Peter G. Miller, <u>Successful Real Estate Investing: A Practical Guide to Profits for the Small Investor </u>(New York: HarperPerennial, 1995); William Benke and Joseph M. Fowler, <u>All About Real Estate Investing From the Inside Out </u>(Chicago: Irwin, 1995); Gerri Willis, <u>The SmartMoney Guide to Real Estate Investing </u>(New York: John Wiley & Sons, 2003); and Andrew McLean, Gary W. Eldred and Andrew James McLean, <u>Investing in Real Estate</u>, 3rd ed. (New York: John Wiley & Sons, 2001). All of these books focus on investing in urban/suburban real estate, a similar but different game than what you're thinking about.

I've bought rural land with no money several times. They were 100 percent lender-financed, using the value of the merchantable timber as extra security and as a near-instant pay down of the note. The lender, in other words, had my consulting forester's timber cruise showing the merchantable value that was likely to materialize within a month or two of the deal being done as well as his own sense of the land's FMV as bare dirt. The timber's sale value was projected to cover the acquisition cost, or very close to it. A client recently bought a large wooded tract for about $5.5 million. The merchantable timber cruised out at about $4 million and the sale of the compound, lake and 600 acres (about 20 percent of the entirety) would net him another $4 million. The quick sale of the timber would come close to paying off his debt on this investment. Consequently, the lender's exposure in these loans was minimal, given that most, if not all of the debt, would be repaid within a couple of months.

I would not have been able to make a self-financing timber deal work without knowing how to scope property and having a competent consultant forester estimate the timber's merchantable value as part of that scoping. Lenders in rural areas will understand how these deals work; lenders who don't have this experience will be reluctant to get their feet wet. I've uncovered a few deals where the immediate timber sale more than paid for the acquisition cost.

Self-financing timber deals are hard to find, especially for an inexperienced buyer. But deals that combine the sale of several assets—some timber, an unwanted main house, a bit of acreage to a neighbor, a hunting lease to cover the property taxes—are readily available to anyone willing to part with some assets to pay for others. For these deals to work most advantageously, you have to buy more property than you want, and those assets that you want to sell should be of the type that have a ready market. If you are a non-resident, first-time buyer with no knowledge of a particular community, don't weigh down your first "deal" by trying to buy something for nothing. Don't throw every curve-ball California-acquisition technique that you've read about at a guy whose back is bent from 50 years of honest work. That stuff will confuse the seller into not responding to your offer. Just try to protect your interests through scoping and buy at a reasonable price. Keep your mistakes small. Prudent investing in land never involves rolling the dice on anything. Make a good deal for yourself honestly. Swindling is not recommended.

The "system," though I don't call it one, that I've set forth in this book is based on learning how to ask questions about a property and its seller, obtain reasonably reliable answers and then combine the acquired information into an offer that keeps the buyer's risk to a minimum. This is the process of **dirt-smart scoping**, which will save you money in the property's acquisition, expose you to as few risks as possible and make you money on its sale. These are not tricks or schemes. I have never dazzled a seller with my negotiating wizardry or cheated anyone. Being dirt smart is simply a matter of being a good investigator who doesn't push the facts he acquires farther than they take him on their own.

The investment strategy that I advocate in this book is research: know as much as you can about the target property and the seller prior to purchase and fit your buying strategy to the property itself. Save money through knowledge and thoughtful planning.

The real-estate investment books show you how to use financial leverage, whereby a small amount of money puts into play a much larger amount of borrowed capital that is forecast to produce a large profit on the small amount with which you started the deal. If you are absolutely sure that you can cover the debt payments under all circumstances, it generally pays to borrow as much as you can, given the current tax break on interest for mortgages and investments. The more you borrow, the more highly leveraged your deal. But the key to making money is buying at the right price after you know the property's value, not the degree of leverage you are able to arrange. A no-cash purchase—a 100-percent leveraged acquisition—can go splat; I've been there once. Leverage is one tool in rural real-estate investing that can help you, but it is of less importance than property research and planning. Leverage can get you into deep trouble; research and planning keeps you out of what heady leverage can get you into.

It's easy to think that buying a house is the ordinary American's best real-estate investment, if only because it forces savings. That's certainly true when property is appreciating at ten percent a year over the term of the mortgage. But let's think about appreciation and leverage in more normal terms. On a $100,000 home, you put in ten percent—$10,000—as a cash down payment, which allows you to leverage $90,000 in mortgage money. You might have another $6,000 out of pocket in various charges and fees. You keep the house for 30 years, paying off the $90,000 in a 30-year, nine percent note in 360 identical monthly payments of $724.17, for a total of $260,701.20. You've paid $170,701.20 in interest on the $90,000 in principal. Inflation has helped you as the years went by allowing you to pay a fixed sum with dollars that are less valuable and easier to earn. (That, of course, is one reason why lenders front-load interest on mortgages. Front-loading has you paying most of the interest in more valuable dollars and most of the principal in dollars eroded by inflation.) You also get to deduct interest payments from your gross income, which means roughly that for every three to five dollars in interest paid to the lender you will pay one dollar less in federal tax. (The tax benefit varies according to your income and tax rate, year to year. There is a $100,000 cap on the interest deduction, which means that you can't deduct interest paid on a home mortgage over that amount.) Now let's assume that your home has appreciated in value over 30 years, so that you net $250,000 from its sale. How do the numbers work:

	Cash In	Cash Out
Down payment	$10,000	
Fees/charges	6,000	
Principal	90,000	
Interest	170,700	
Interest deduction		$57,000
Net Gain on Sale		250,000
Tax on Profit		0
	$276,700	$307,000

Over 30 years, you've made about $30,300 above what you paid in; that's about an 11% gain on your total cash paid over time. Looked at from a leverage perspective, you made $30,300 in profit on an initial cash investment of $16,000 over 30 years while living in your investment. If you adjust the value of these dollars over 30 years to account for inflation, you've lost money. Your $30,300 in profit won't buy what your upfront $16,000 would have bought 30 years earlier. You've also paid property taxes, insurance and maintenance. Think of that as rent—the amount of money that you have to pay for living somewhere. Keep the rent expense out of the investment analysis; if you put it in, the profit disappears. The $16,000 in upfront cash got this "investment" rolling, but your payment of interest and principal over the years reduced leveraging's benefits. The $6,000 I've allocated as a cost to get a mortgage is about what you'd pay at a big bank. As an investment, you would do better at the end of 30 years to have invested your $16,000 in CDs.

You can argue to yourself that you've leveraged $16,000 to make $307,000, but it's more honest to say that you've leveraged $276,000 to generate $307,000 after 30 years. Which is okay, but not so great. It helps that you don't have to pay tax on this amount of gain from the sale of a principal residence—at least that's the rule as of 2006.

The numbers will obviously improve if your house benefits from a much higher appreciation rate. It follows, then, that the long-term benefits of leveraging depend largely on the property's appreciation.

Now let's see how leveraging works when you invest in property for more than a year (but not much longer than that) to get the capital-gains rate on taxable gain. A one-year-plus holding period qualifies for the capital-gains rate, which is now 15 percent or less on taxable gain, depending on your income level. Investors usually try to hold for at least a year for this reason. For middle- and upper-income taxpayers, the capital-gains rate is less than the rate applied to their wage or salary (ordinary) income. A short-horizon investment strategy also limits the cascade of interest you pay over a long-term note. If you invest with leveraged money and resell after one year, you will be repaying what basically amounts to an interest-only loan. Unfortunately, the upfront cost of a one-year mortgage or a 30-year mortgage is the same. For that reason, a short-term investor in land is usually better to take a commercial loan (with a higher rate, but much smaller upfront charges, if any) than a mortgage of whatever kind.

A very short digression is in order. **Long-term capital gains** is profit made on an investment—things like real estate or stocks—that are held for more than one year. For most investors, this type of profit is now generally taxed at a lower rate than ordinary income, such as wages or salaries. The Jobs and Growth Tax Relief Reconciliation Act of 2003 lowered the long-term capital-gains tax rates from 20 percent to 15 percent, and from ten percent to 5 percent, depending on your income. The top four ordinary income rates are all higher than 15%. If you flip property in less than a year, you will pay tax at your ordinary rate, which can be ten percent, 15, 25, 28, 33 or 35, depending on your income and your filing status. With investors in the upper four ordinary-income brackets, the long-term capital-gains rate of 15 percent will save them between ten and 20 percent on federal tax owed. In many if not most situations, it is to the taxpayer's advantage to set the closing on the flip of an asset for at least a year and a day past his own closing. It can be more profitable to carry the property for the year and pay interest on the debt if it allows the taxpayer to qualify for the 15 percent capital-gains rate on profit from the sale. If, of course, you're selling the severable asset for about what you paid for it, then you will have little taxable gain and the cost of carrying for a year will exceed the break on tax rates. These capital-gains rates are set to expire in 2008, and Congress is currently debating extending them. If nothing happens, the pre-2003 rates will reappear on January 1, 2009. Extension is likely for 2009 through 2010.

There are two other long-term capital-gains rates that you should be aware of. A 25-percent rate applies to part of the gain from selling depreciated real estate. This category of real estate is known as **Section 1250 property.** (See Chapter 3 in IRS Publication 544, Sales and Other Dispositions of Assets.) You would pay 25 percent on the amount you depreciated as "recapture," then your capital-gains rate on your taxable gain. Timber sales do not involve depreciation. If you split off 15 acres from the 100 you just purchased, there is no depreciation involved. A 28-percent rate applies to gain realized from the sale of small-business stock held for more than five years after you exclude one-half of your gain from income.

The 28-percent rate also applies to the sale of collectibles, such as art, antiques, gems, coins, precious metals and stamps. These rates existed before the 2003 legislation and were continued.

When planning a purchase of rural property coupled with the sale of some of its assets, you need to determine whether you net more after taxes by flipping within the first year or waiting for the long-term capital-gains rate to apply. End of digression.

Let's rework the house example to fit the purchase of a $100,000 piece of rural property that you finance at nine percent over 30 years. Nine percent is above market as I write in 2006; so the actual dollars in these examples will be lower when you plug in mortgage money at, say, six percent. Lenders may charge a higher rate when the borrower's purpose is to buy a second home in the country. And rates go up if the borrower is buying undeveloped (raw) land with no improvements. You might choose to amortize the loan over 30 years to keep your monthly payments as low as possible. The longer the amortization, the more you're leveraging a small amount of money to acquire a property. **You must be sure that your mortgage agreement *allows you to prepay some or all of the principal at any time without penalty.*** You sell the property a year and a day after you purchased it for $110,000, a ten-percent appreciation. You don't use a broker to sell the property and you make no improvements to it. This is not considered your principal residence, and you sell it a year after buying it to get the 15 percent capital-gains rate. Here's how these numbers look:

	Cash In	Cash Out
Down Payment	$10,000	
Fees/charges	6,000	
Principal	592	
Interest	8,125 (e)	
Interest deduction		$2,681
Gain on Sale		10,000
Tax on Profit (15%)		(1,500)
	$24,717	$11,181

(I've not added certain costs to each column, such as property tax on the cash in and selling fees on the cash out. I've also not recast the loan as a no-fee/charge commercial note, which is what I would recommend doing in this example.)

You've leveraged $16,000 in cash to acquire a $100,000 property, which you sold for a $10,000 net gain after a year. Leveraging looks good this way. But let's look again.

This investment shows a loss of almost $13,536 after taxes, even though it looked like you "made" $10,000 on the flip. You had $24,717 invested over a year, and you cashed out for $11,181.

To make this investment work with borrowed money, the rate of appreciation over the time you hold the property must be much higher, or the selling price, regardless of appreciation, must be higher. It's hard to make a real profit on a short-term flip with borrowed money when appreciation is the only factor working in your favor. Leveraging alone does not produce a profit. Leveraging, on the other hand, does allow you to get in the game where profit can be made on a big-ticket item bought right and sold right. In the right circumstances, a ten percent profit on a $100,000 property purchase using $10,000 as a down payment will exceed a ten percent profit on the $10,000 invested in stocks. But you cannot assume this will occur automatically without projecting realistic numbers over the term of your investment.

How can this investor increase his profit in this example?

1. If the investor takes $100,000 out of his savings and borrows nothing, he'll make a $10,000 gross profit and pay $1,500 in capital-gains tax. That's an 8.5 percent profit on the use of his money. His Cash In is $100,000 but he saves $14,717 in fees, principal and interest. But most of us don't want to use our cash this way; and even more of us don't have the full purchase price in cash. His 8.5 percent profit is lowered by the amount of money he would have earned on the $100,000 invested for a year in something else.

2. A fully leveraged deal doesn't help. If the investor is able to borrow $100,000, his monthly payment at nine percent on a 30-year schedule is $804.63, for a total one-year P&I expense of $9,655.56. About $700 of that sum went to principal, and $8,955.56 to interest. Roughly $3,000 came back as a mortgage interest deduction. The investor still has $6,000 in buying costs. When each column is totaled, the investor loses about $3,000. Leveraging even with a ten percent appreciation rate doesn't make the numbers work. The $6,000 cost of getting the loan and the $9,656 in P&I exceed the $3,000 in deduction plus the $10,000 in gain, less the 15 percent in tax ($1,500). Leveraging makes the short-term flip worse than the conventional loan when structured over 30 years.

Both examples above, 1 and 2, work a bit better if the investor takes a six-month or one-year adjustable-rate mortgage at 7 percent instead of nine. That would save a good bit of interest. Finding a lender that charges fewer points and fees would knock down the $6,000 loan-origination cost.

3. The two locally owned banks in my county charge higher interest rates on mortgages than the big banks, but neither charges much to originate the loan. The numbers in a short-term investment can turn positive when the cost of getting borrowed money drops to $500. Therefore, if you're looking to flip, find this type of lender. You might also check out borrowing from a local community credit union. A commercial loan for land, or even a personal loan, carries a higher rate, but avoids the front-end mortgage costs.

4. Reduce your borrowing. A short-term flip works best in generating profit to the extent that you can use cash and borrow as little as necessary. The comparison that you must do before making this investment is whether the profit you project (together with the investments risks) promises a sufficiently greater reward considering risk than leaving your cash where it is.

5. Keep carrying costs down. Holding a house for a year involves insurance, maintenance and significant property taxes. Holding unimproved rural land for a year involves paying low property taxes and perhaps nothing else. Cosmetic improvements to a home will pay for themselves and then some, but major jobs—especially hidden ones like rewiring, replumbing and fixing a foundation—won't. Cosmetic improvements to undeveloped land such as $1,000 in grading and seeding an access road or mowing the interior roads do pay for themselves and more. Flipped investments, as a rule, work best when the improvements are limited to low-dollar cosmetics. Unimproved land can often generate enough income through a hunting lease to cover the property taxes.

6. If the seller finances the purchase, you save the $6,000 in fees/charges and perhaps some interest. But you still end up losing money.

7. The real way to make this type of flip work is to **part out** the property as your investment strategy. A 100-acre property bought for $100,000 can be divided into four 25-acre parcels and sold for a total of $150,000, because smaller acreages always fetch higher per-acre prices than larger acreages. Division might require a total of $10,000 in road work and surveying. You might spend another $5,000 for marketing. But the profit rises from $10,000 to $35,000, even after these expenditures. (Of course, you need to be able to come up with the additional $15,000 to get that next $35,000 in gross profit.) Parting out automatically boosts the per-acre price of the land and allows each small parcel to gain more value even if the appreciation rate is the same. The land is not depreciated so the long-term capital-gains rate of, say, 15 percent, will apply.

You can also part out assets in advance of division. If you sell the merchantable timber for $50,000, then divide into four cutover lots that sell for a total of $125,000, you're even better off. A timber job of this sort is called a "residential cut." It leaves timber untouched around the four house sites and removes high-value species. Lopping the slash improves aesthetics before resale.

Profiting from a rural land investment usually involves combining a number of elements discussed above. Leveraging through borrowing is one. Selling merchantable timber immediately after purchase for the pre-purchase cruise value is a second. Selling some other severable assets is a third. Buying the entirety at the right price is an obvious fourth. Calculating the most tax-advantaged way of timing your sales is the fifth. Finally, holding for more years rather than fewer allows appreciation to work for you.

Buying a second home in the country or investing in rural property should be approached with an accountant's eye right from the start. A buyer's wants and emotions cannot be allowed to trump his own pocketbook. So before you scope your first acre, and even before you get in the car to spend a sunny Saturday afternoon with a real-estate agent, draft a **goals-and-money plan**. This is a document that puts in writing (don't skip this step) your generic ability to acquire property of the type you're seeking. The document becomes property-specific once you've found one that you think will work. Then it becomes a **target property**. I urge you to think of your money plan in terms of your goals. You will find that modifying goals can either increase or decrease the money you need to buy the property. For example, if you want to buy woodlands and your initial goal is to not intervene in their management in any way, you will have to pay for the tract without any help from the land itself. If, on the other hand, you want to buy woodlands and your goal is to have the timber pay for a portion of its price—after which you decide to follow a hands-off policy—your purchase will be a lot easier to manage financially but harder aesthetically in the short run.

You can brainstorm goals at whatever level that you think is operational. That can include everything from maximizing the property's contribution to fighting global warming on one hand to squeezing the last dollar out of the property as soon as possible on the other. Here are some ideas about *possible* first-draft, property-buying goals in relation to purchase money. Your job is winnow your list of goals into an internally consistent set in terms of the level of contribution, if any, you want the property to make to the purchase.

Ask: Is this goal consistent with having property help pay for itself?

First-draft Property Goals	Can Property help pay for itself?		
	Yes	No	If yes, how?

Family recreation opportunity
Long-term appreciation as investment
Place to relax—no work, maintenance
Possible retirement home
Hunting property—leave undeveloped;
     place for camper desirable
Flip—turn as much profit asap and get out
Conserve environment for specific objectives
     e.g., enhance bird habitat or game
     habitat, promote diversification of
     plant species, no human interference
     in natural processes
Build second home
Accrue retirement capital

Most land-buying goals, like many aspects of buying and selling, can be combined in various ways and are subject to adaptation and balanced compromises. In this case, it's a matter of negotiating with yourself. Welcome this internal bargaining, because it's beneficial. It focuses your thinking and forces you to research your ideas in light of the property's specifics.

I started this discussion about money by asking you to think through your goals for the property. Only after you have done that, should you move into the more conventional considerations of money, such as how much cash can you put into the purchase. I've asked you to think about how the property can help pay for itself, because your answers to that question in terms of each goal directly affects how much cash you need to put into the purchase, how much money you need to borrow and for how long, what level of income the property might generate, how you might cover P&I payments and so on.

Apart from asking questions about how you will pay for the property, discussed in the following chapters, one of your initial financial questions about any land purchase is **how liquid is it**? Rural property is not illiquid, but it's far more illiquid than stocks or cash. A liquidity "analysis" will give you a sense—but no certainty—as to how long it will take you to sell the property if you have to.

If you project your cash flow to be variable or uncertain in the future, you probably don't want to buy discretionary property with substantial financing (leveraging) if you anticipate that it will take a year or more to sell at an acceptable price. The monthly mortgage payments can drain your cash and even produce a foreclosure. If the property is odd owing to location, size, shape or other factors, it's likely to be less liquid than properties comparable in price and acreage.

A **liquidity analysis** starts with determining the recent sales prices of properties that are roughly comparable to your target property. (You should be doing this anyway as part of your scoping.) This information should be available in, or calculable from, recent deeds. If not, talk with a couple of local real-estate brokers as well as the county clerk and assessor. Your task is to determine approximate selling prices as well as the amount of time each property was on the market before being sold. It's also helpful to get an idea of the spread between asking price and selling price of each comparable; asking prices for listed properties should be available from brokers. Then you want to ask the brokers their opinion as to how much time might have been shaved from the time it took to sell each comparable for each, say, five percent, off the asking price. You might find, for example, that the brokers think, as a general current rule, that a five percent discount on asking price might have produced a sale three months earlier. This is a very coarse opinion-analysis, but it's probably worth something for your purpose.

Assuming, then, that market conditions and interest rates will be roughly the same as current conditions three years into the future, you can make a few reasonable liquidity projections. Take the price you are willing to pay as FMV for the target property. Project appreciation of this FMV year by year, compounded, at what you anticipate the appreciation rate of the target property will be. The brokers can help you estimate the recent appreciation rate for properties comparable to your target property. Then take the brokers' consensus opinion about average time on the market for your type of property, say, one year, and discount your appreciated FMV projection by whatever the brokers estimate to be the local price discount-to-time ratio. If, in other words, your ratio is 5:3 (five percent discount in asking price to three fewer months on the market), you can project that a 20 percent discount in your future FMV/asking price will produce a very quick sale, a 15 percent discount will produce a sale in six months, a ten percent discount will produce a sale in nine months and a five percent discount will produce a sale in 12 months. A 20 percent discount on FMV does not mean you lose money on the sale. How much you make or not make depends on the appreciation rate you use and how quickly you need to sell. There's lots of slop in this "methodology," but it will give you a reasonable guess at how much time it will take you to sell your target property at a particular price at various points over the next year. Projecting appreciation rates and assuming steady market factors much beyond three years gets increasingly chancy.

Property values can go down. Most readers will be familiar with stories of booms and busts in urban residential real estate. Property can become illiquid in a down turn though the degree of illiquidity is driven by price. I've not seen rural property in most areas go down in price. I have seen appreciation go through periods of fast increase, slow increase and in-between increase—but the trend has always been up. The exception has been in certain West Virginia counties that have lost significant population; there, I've seen house prices weaken, but prices for undeveloped land continue to increase. The general trend in rural land has been one of appreciation—at least from what I've seen.

An owner can increase the liquidity of rural property by division. Cut a large tract into smaller parcels, each of which is priced at market. The smaller tracts are affordable to a larger market, and the total sales revenue obtained should exceed that gained from a single entirety sale. Make sure to incorporate your cost of sales—broker fees, taxes, etc.—in your calculations. Successive sales of divided land also keep your lender feeling secure to the extent that you use a portion of the net proceeds to repay proportionately your mortgage principal.

A second quick digression. I've emphasized that you consider yourself an investor in rural real estate. An investor gets the benefit of long-term capital-gains rates on property sales. If, however, the IRS classifies you as a **real-estate dealer**, your properties are considered inventory, rather than investments, and your gain is taxed at your ordinary rate. The line between investor and dealer is murky. Courts have used nine tests to determine the difference, among the most important are the purpose for which the taxpayer held the property just before its sale, the extent to which it was subdivided, how much improvement was made to the property, and the amount of time and effort the taxpayer devoted to selling the properties. Your pre-purchase investment plan should be oriented around your new property as an investment, rather than a dealer-like buy, divide and flip. Selling merchantable timber and several severable assets as a strategy for keeping the core property should not classify you as a dealer. As part of your scoping and pre-purchase planning, work with your CPA to make sure that your intentions and plan stay within the confines of investment. Your investment should be made and held for "productive use," not trade or business. (Dealers also have to pay self-employment tax and cannot do installment sales where gain is deferred until the money is received.)

You can also assume with some, but not all, rural properties that growing demand over time will increase its liquidity. But market liquidity is a function of demand, supply and price. If demand is strong and supply is adequate, a price way above FMV will produce an illiquid property. You can take comfort by knowing that you can affect your property's liquidity insofar as you set its price. You can always sell property quickly by pricing it below market, but you have to evaluate that emergency tactic in light of your need for net sale income sufficient to pay off any debt. The flexibility you have in pricing is determined by the level of debt you need to repay and the amount of equity you've built up. The lower your debt, the lower you can price the property and get it sold quickly.

Two other considerations when selling property are the direct costs of selling (broker fee, taxes, legal fees, etc.) and the amount of federal income tax you owe on your taxable gain. The first of these questions is fairly easy to project; your CPA or lawyer can estimate these costs with reasonable accuracy for three to five years, at least. You can always expect these charges to rise over time.

The tax-hit question involves the specifics of the property, your length of ownership, your applicable tax rate and how your original basis in the property has been adjusted over time. I would ask a tax accountant to work up a **tax forecast** before you agree on terms with your buyer. The tax forecast will start with your anticipated cost of acquisition (basis) and incorporate projected changes in light of your plans for the property, such as sale of assets and investment. Your CPA will have to estimate your selling price and the applicable tax rate. A tax forecast is a very small expense that can save you thousands of future tax dollars by showing you your future tax hit in light of your alternative plans for the property and form of ownership. The form of your ownership—personal property, sole proprietorship, corporation, trust, limited liability company, etc.—should fit your objectives, both toward the property and in terms of minimizing future tax obligations. Your CPA should also factor in state tax considerations where they apply.

The first steps, then, in working up a financial plan for the purchase of the property are to think through your goals, the money you will need in light of those goals, where it's going to come from consistent with those goals and, finally, a couple of likely future scenarios, involving hypothetical sales at different points in the future in different circumstances, including an emergency bail-out plan. The plan will change, and should change. Most of the issues won't.

Do Not Skip thinking about and doing something about the questions just discussed as part of your scoping. Add your own.

Do not skip writing them out as a plan!

If you are unwilling to take the time and effort to do this little bit of work, which requires a small amount of your time and perhaps a few hours of CPA and lawyer time, don't buy country land. Failure to start a land purchase right increases the risk of poor results down the road.

HOW ABOUT A TRIAL RENTAL?

For those who prefer to toe-dip before jumping in, **consider renting your target property with an option to buy**. I recommend renting for at least one year if you are hesitant to buy. (You may be able to combine this with a lease-purchase option discussed in Chapter 29.) Renting gives you the opportunity to be on the land at least a couple of times in each season for a couple of days each time. You may run into some highly informative bad weather. If you can live with the target property in miserable conditions, it should suit you at all other times. (Bad weather is also the best time to visit target properties or negotiate a purchase. Nothing beats haggling over price with a seller while standing in *his* mud, with rain blowing in *his* face.)

You will not *know* your target land after a one-year rental; that takes at least ten years. But you should know a lot more about it than when you started if only from what you learn when you take a home-made pie over to each neighbor as a way to introduce yourself. (Store-bought pies are tacky, no matter how expensive.) Consider your tenancy as a year-long engagement that may or may not lead to a wedding. Take Louis Agassiz's instruction to his students, "Look at your fish." as your own. Observe like a science student. Learn what you can. Identify what you don't know. And at the end of the year speculate knowledgeably about what it is that you don't know you don't know.

The cost of renting will depend, of course, on the target property's assets, asking price, the seller's carrying costs and your expenses outside of the lease. Farmhouses tend to rent for at least 50 percent less for the equivalent floor space than urban/suburban houses, and sometimes the rural discount is much larger. Old farmhouses are the cheapest rental deals—and serve your part-time needs. Expect quirks with old wood-frame structures—windows that rattle in the wind, possums that visit your front porch, odd noises in the attic and plumbing from a Rube-Goldberg manual. Don't expect much maintenance from your landlord if he senses that you're a buyer. Such relics are just fine for renting on a try-out basis, and you will get a first-hand lesson in what needs to be done to meet your needs as an owner. "New farmhouses" are usually brick ramblers, log cabins or second homes. If a relatively high-rent house runs with the target property, you might be able to swing a deal whereby you rent a spot for your tent/camper and allow the owner to rent the house and farmland to another party. That puts you on the property for next to nothing possibly within a lease-option contract. If he balks, consider renting the entire farm with a provision that allows you to sublet the house. The ball, on which you want to keep your eye, is big and moving slowly: **get access to the land for a while, for cheap, while postponing any sale**. Done wisely, a buyer can option a property in this fashion for far less than through a conventional option.

A seller whose only carrying costs are routine maintenance and property taxes is a likely rent-option owner as long as he does not need his equity out of the property for some pressing purpose. Offer to pay the property taxes, for starters—and that alone might be a fair rent. You can also offer to provide labor in lieu of rent. Since the seller will be far smarter than you about the **misery content of any farm labor** you are negotiating, I'd be very careful about such a swap. Do not agree, for example, to "help with the hay" in lieu of rent. The seller may quite rightly take this to mean that you will be on hand six days a week from June 15 to October 1 as needed. (You, on the other hand, are thinking that this will involve no more than two or three hours on two or three pleasant Saturday afternoons during which time you drive his tractor with a beer in hand.) "Hay help" generally gets the hard jobs. I know of one such swap that involved putting up more than 10,000 "square" bales of hay—with the tenant stacking 50-pound bales on a moving wagon and then restacking them in the barn's mow. This had him lifting and toting one million pounds of hay over several months in return for some machine work.

Assuming that you've done your pre-purchase scoping before renting, you should have a reasonably accurate idea of the seller's carrying costs and his income from the property. You can propose a straight cash rental, maybe two or three percent of the asking price for property with a livable house. On undeveloped land that is suitable for your camper/RV/tent, you might offer one year of property tax payment plus something extra. The extra might be one to four of his mortgage payments (which he will pay tax on because it's rent and you will get no interest deduction) or some percentage of his asking price, say, 3/4 to 1 1/2 percent. You can also propose a rental credit formula that kicks in if you exercise an option to buy. Obviously, the higher the credit, the more money you save. When negotiating, remember that rental income and capital gains are taxable revenues to the seller, and likely at different rates. He may pay at 30+ percent (his rate on ordinary income) on rental income and 15 percent on the long-term capital gains from the sale of the property. He will, therefore, have more money left in his after-tax pocket from a sale dollar than from a rental dollar. Accordingly, you might discount the rent a bit in return for upping the deferred sale price. Don't get too fancy with this, though. If the seller's after-tax net is important to the property's sale, he'll take you up on your flexibility. Your CPA can project alternative tax differences for the seller that will help you in your negotiations.

You may encounter a seller who agrees to **rent** to you for a year on the basis of **cash-only payments**. Such a seller may or may not declare cash income on his tax return, but probably not. He will be unlikely to agree to sign a rental agreement with you or a lease with an option to buy, because he doesn't want to create a paper trail. In return for cash, he might knock 15 percent or more off the property's fair rent. You can live without a written rental agreement, paying monthly, since you are really just trying on the property for size. But you take on many risks without a written lease—who pays for the grease-fire damage that your guest starts in the landlord's antique kitchen woodstove; do you need to pay him for the firewood you cut on his land; when the toilet backs up because the septic tank is full, who pays to empty it.

The other risk in cash deals comes from the IRS. A lot of cash transactions in the country are done to allow the person who receives the cash to avoid declaring it and paying tax on it. Since the payer—you—may be in a position to deduct certain types of expenses paid in cash, the lack of receipts may cost you additional tax dollars if you're audited and can't produce paper supporting the expense. Apart from that penalty, if you have knowledge of the seller's fraudulent purpose in requesting cash, you are aiding his tax deception. Pay by check or get a receipt, you'll sleep easier. If the seller/landlord insists on cash without receipt, find another place. And if you do pay cash, keep a record of each payment with its purpose to support a deduction. If you're set up as a land investor or business, it may be possible to deduct some, or all, of the rent to the extent that it was incurred pursuant to making an investment or business-related purchase. Clear this plan with your CPA.

Buyers/renters—you—sometimes offer to pay rent in cash to sellers/landlords. This can be perfectly innocent where, for instance, you claim no tax benefit for your rental expense. On the other hand, you may be offering cash—less than he's asking in rent—to lure him into not declaring the income on his taxes. If he accepts your low-ball, cash offer, you both gain: you by paying less, he by netting out more from cheating the government. As long as you don't collude in planning the seller's tax strategy, I suppose your cash-offer strategy is legal enough. The tax fraud rests on the seller as long as you don't know about it, or the IRS can't prove that you should have reasonably known about it. If, with the advice of your CPA or lawyer, you propose a low-ball, cash offer, withdraw it immediately if the seller starts talking about his taxes. At the level of ethics, a buyer/renter of this sort does not walk way with clean hands.

There is one other variation of the buyer's cash offer that I should mention. I've occasionally heard about land purchases where the buyer and seller agree on a low-ball official purchase price that is used in all the legal documents, with a back-door cash payment that leaves no paper trail. The cash helps the seller reduce his taxable gain. The lower price helps the buyer and reduces the hit of recordation taxes and broker commissions. In states that require deeds to include the full purchase price, this practice is fraudulent. Even where no requirement exists to include the full purchase price in the sale documents, a phony figure cheats on recordation taxes. I've found buyers of large tracts in both Virginia and Tennessee shorting the recorded number to save on taxes. A buyer who conceals part of his purchase price may run into trouble establishing his actual basis when he goes to sell. If you engage in paying back-door cash on the purchase of land, you are being foolish and, often, criminal. Don't play this game.

COUNTRY MONEY IS DIFFERENT FROM CITY MONEY

Buying rural property will differ from your experience in buying urban or suburban property. Several of these differences affect the buyer's money—how much you pay the seller; how much you borrow from and repay the lender; where you get the money; how much you pay in local property taxes; and how much tax you pay on both your annual *itemized* 1040 and on taxable gain when you sell. What you buy and how you plan for your country property directly affects the income, if any, that it generates and your tax obligations.

The two most familiar tax benefits of real-estate ownership are the mortgage-interest deduction and the tax-exclusion on the sale of a principal residence. Both carry dollar caps, above which they don't apply. Other tax breaks—expensing of business-related costs, capitalization of other costs, deferment of capital-gains tax, depreciation, conservation easements, 1031 exchange and the like—can be batched together for your benefit. Interest on a first mortgage (debt up to $1 million) is deductible; up to $100,000 in interest can be deductible on a second mortgage or home-equity line on the same property. Mortals, mere and otherwise, are not likely to know the labyrinthine ins and outs of our changing tax code. So at some point in your pre-purchase scoping, you should hire a dirt-smart CPA and a lawyer to structure your purchase, ownership and management with tax considerations in mind.

One of the first differences you are likely to encounter involves your relationship with the seller. You will in all likelihood meet directly with the rural seller either before you make an offer or soon thereafter, even when a real-estate broker is involved. It is usually in the buyer's interest to meet the seller inasmuch as a broker, no matter how willing and able, does not know as much about the land or farm as the owner. The broker representing the seller may or may not disclose relevant information to you. A buyer's broker, one who's working for the buyer exclusively, may not know the right questions to ask even though he's supposed to. When all is said and done, the buyer has to take responsibility for the quality of his pre-purchase due diligence. In almost every case, I would recommend at least two meetings with the seller.

The first is a best-behavior, get-acquainted session. Tell the seller something about yourself and your intentions for his property as a way of starting this conversation. Don't fudge. Your first words to the seller will be what he holds you to. Gently ask general questions and write down the owner's answers. Ask whether there are any boundary disputes, unrecorded agreements and claims against the property. Ask how the owner uses the land—which field is good pasture, which is best for the locally grown crop, which might be suited for something you want to do, such as plant a small fruit orchard or vineyard. Ask about water—quality and reliability—and soils. Probe for troublesome issues, such as boundary disputes, without being accusatory. Plead ignorance and ask for his help, invoking the Golden Rule. Try not to be aggressive, know-it-all, urban-neurotic, big-wordy (a sesquipedalian), urban stupid, piously Green, shocked (that a cattle-raising farmer sells his cattle to meateaters) or slippery. Don't affect a local accent; don't chew grass. Don't share your opinions about why farm animals are mistreated, guns should be beaten into plowshares and loggers should be retrained for cell-phone repair. Don't drive into the seller's front yard in the biggest, shiniest, yellowest Hummer you can buy. Similarly, don't wheel up to the seller's farmhouse in an urban trophy car that hangs up in his driveway athwart a cow flop. If you have access to a moderately old, moderately styled, moderately priced pick-up truck, drive that. Don't drop big-shot names, tell how important you are or reveal how much money you make. Don't ask where the closest "decent" wine shop is. Don't lard your conversation with any of the following: Latin legalisms (such as *per se*, *ad hominem* and *sui generis*—all of which I've heard buyers use); Yiddish (Don't ask if the neighbor is a mensch or a schmuck.); French (The seller's farmhouse may indeed have a je-ne-sais-quoi quality, but the seller may not appreciate the comment just the same because it sounds a lot like that new, pesticide-impervious Formosan termite the county extension agent told him about last week.); Valley Girl/1960s Hippie; or your office-dot-com blah blah. Be friendly, interested and bland without being condescending. Keep opinions about politics, religion, ethnicity, race, animal rights, bovine flatulence, exotic vegetables, tobacco use, guns, hunting, rednecks, hillbillies, local yokels, tacky Christmas decorations and pink-painted rooms to yourself. If the seller's house is lovingly planted in forsythia, don't yuk it up over the "vomit of spring." Ease into a conversation where the seller explains about his land and why he's selling.

The second time you meet the owner will be after you've done your scoping. Come to his house bearing normal American food—a pie is always good, or a signature item from your hometown that will be familiar to the seller. Don't give the seller a gift of booze, dope or the dish of the day, such as leaf litter from Amazonia harvested sustainably by right-on indigenous peoples. Ask specific questions about things only the owner can answer. You want to pin down answers, but you don't want to pin him. You want to obtain information in a way that doesn't threaten the owner or challenge his honesty. You want to create an atmosphere of mutual problem-solving: "I'll help pay to get the barn roof fixed by closing, if you get the well pump repaired by then, ok?" Remember that you want to buy the seller's place, not prove that you're smarter than he is. Lawyers are especially bad at this type of information-gathering.

In this second conversation, you may want to raise money issues. Doing this hypothetically—"What if I offered you $100,000 (instead of the $150,000 being asked)?"—is a common tactic, but I advise against it. Hypothetical offers are worthless to a seller because an oral agreement on real estate is not legally enforceable. You'll hear this invoked as the state's statute of frauds, which requires that certain types of contracts—such as real-estate offers, deeds and leases longer than a year—be in writing so that they can be enforced. If, in other words, the seller orally accepted your $100,000 offer—"I'll take it. We have a deal."—he, the seller, can't enforce that in court, and neither can you. You may not have a deal despite both of you agreeing that you do. (Exceptions exist to the statue of frauds.) It doesn't matter whether you shake hands or swear on Bibles. Real-estate agreements are binding when they are written, dated, reasonably specific and signed by buyer and seller. (A contract should, of course, reflect a meeting of the minds.) So the seller's reply to every oral offer should always be: "Put any offer you might want to make in writing, including dollars and all terms." Hypothetical offers are usually no more than tire-kicking—non-serious, low-ball offers from buyers who are looking for a distressed seller forced to accept humiliation. From a buyer's perspective, there's nothing wrong in being a tire kicker. But don't be surprised when a seller invites you to leave as soon as you've kicked his.

I recommend raising the set of money issues all at once, putting them on the table and watching which ones the seller is willing to work on with you and how he goes about it. Such issues beyond price and terms—seller financing, asset sales, 1031 exchange, tax implications—are discussed below.

Putting together a workable money package is no different than working a jigsaw puzzle. In both cases, it's most efficient to spread everything out. Keep in mind that every puzzle is solvable, though you may not be the solution to this seller's puzzle. Unlike a jigsaw puzzle, you may do better with certain sellers to work from a whole solution back toward troublesome parts instead of starting with the pieces that are easiest to figure. The way to do this is to discuss a possible range of prices acceptable to you, depending on how the difficult issues are resolved (that is, what is done and who pays for doing them). With other sellers, however, you may need to work in baby steps toward a deal, starting with the easiest issues.

Before you open negotiations, have in mind the elements of the deal that you want. Identify a general range of acceptable prices, terms, throw-ins, throwaways and so on. Put your whole offer on the table at once. Don't bog down fighting over price. Movement—even little agreements—creates momentum toward a deal.

An old real-estate adage goes: "I'll agree to any price the seller puts on his property, if he'll agree to my terms." If the seller's asking price of $200,000 is $50,000 over all the comparables and he knows it, propose agreeing to his price so long as he finances the entire $200,000 at one percent over 40 years, with a one-time balloon payment of the entire principal at the end of the term. Do this with a twinkle in your eye: you want the seller to know that you're kidding around because he started it. If the seller wants more than you want to pay, work down the price through terms, throw-ins and seller financing. Be ready to give up all of these negotiated advantages in return for what you really want—a lower price. If you fall into pounding one another over price, price and nothing but price, you may never get to a deal. Sellers are looking to hear something close to their number; give them an offer that will sound right with terms that favor you by a lot. See if that doesn't get things off dead center. There are times when inductive negotiating—from the particulars to the whole deal—can work, but my experience is that the buyer should approach the seller using deductive negotiating—which is based on having a general sense of your final number and final terms and then tying up loose ends as part of that general understanding.

Remember that the right price from your perspective depends partly on the nature of the deal's loose ends. Where, for instance, you have identified a specific problem, such as a neighbor claiming access to his property over the seller's land, you will need to determine the seller's position and, if possible, agree on a method of resolving the dispute. That type of problem is common. Its impact can be negligible—the neighbor uses the road a few times a year—or a daily nuisance that will drive you bonkers. Therefore, as part of spreading the deal's pieces on the table, make sure to pitch in everything that your scoping has turned up that could cost you money, time or enjoyment. Do this directly with the seller, preferably while sitting at his kitchen table.

I usually write a letter to the seller, explaining how I arrived at my offering price. I include this letter with a purchase contract. I think I am more effective in putting my arguments forward in writing than orally. A letter also allows you to get everything out, the way you want it out.

You will also notice that there is a more **informal sales process** in rural areas. The paperwork may be a bit simpler; fewer people and organizations are likely to be involved; everything is personal. Your new local banker might want to rent your pasture; your local lawyer might want to sell you hay. **Don't let informality substitute for scoping**, no matter how friendly your new friends are. You may be told that you don't need to worry about mineral ownership, title insurance, testing the water, etc., because "we just never do much of that out here." That's not good enough. Worry about something if you think it's necessary.

You have to determine when your scoping is legitimate as against when it crosses into compulsive

658

nerdiness. I've seen deals blow up when buyers rag sellers on detail after detail with no judgment applied as to which detail is truly important and which is not. A real-estate broker recently told me not to worry about the fact that a 170-acre parcel was accessed by a two-mile-long road for which he knew of no recorded easement. You don't need a deeded right of way, he told me, because "you have a prescriptive easement." A prescriptive easement is not established legally simply by using a road over someone's property. It must meet state-specific tests. If use is based on permission, it is not a prescriptive easement. Permission ends with a sale or the death of either party. That means a new owner has no right to use the road. Permission can be withdrawn at any time and without cause. A prescriptive easement, finally, needs to be established in court "against" each landowner over whom the road crosses if it is challenged. A real-estate broker's opinion establishes nothing in the eyes of the law. Fortunately, an earlier deed was finally found that did provide an access easement.

The borrowing aspect of buying rural land can be, and often is, different than the elaborate process you go through in the city. There, you would shop for the best loan terms with little regard for which financial institution is closest to you, or has the most borrower-friendly board, or is most open to working with newcomers to the neighborhood. These factors, alone or in combination, may drive your decision in the country. It's useful to check out the differences in loan packages between locally owned banks (possibly state-chartered) in your target county and the local offices of the big regional banks. I discuss these alternatives below. The key point to understand is that locally owned lenders are likely to have more flexibility on mortgage terms in their communities, particularly when they keep the loan, than the big banks, which more often than not will insist on the borrower meeting rigid loan requirements that will allow them to sell the loan in the secondary market soon after it is made. Flexibility, of course, comes with a price. You may get better terms (no fees, no points, even 100 percent financing) from the local lender, but at a much higher interest rate than the big bank. Generally speaking, if you're looking to pay back the note quickly, take the local lender's terms; if you're going to keep the note for ten or more years, take the lower interest rate.

Rural property lends itself to classification as an investment or business for IRS purposes. Even if your first intentions are purely recreational for the targeted 150 acres of woodland, I urge you to discuss setting up the ownership and tax management as an investment using the timber—whatever its present value—as the door in. You will be able to write off mortgage interest, as well as expense certain costs and depreciate certain improvements. Many rural counties, especially those feeling development pressure, give a break on property taxes to farmers and others with undeveloped property called **land use**. It may be easier to qualify for this lower property tax rate if your land is set up as a farm or timberland investment. Ask if the county in which your target property lies has land-use taxation, and, if so, whether the seller's property is "currently in land use." It's far easier to continue land-use than to get your property reclassified.

If the property has a house or your intention is to build a house, consult with your local CPA before purchasing the property. As a taxpayer, you get certain tax benefits from a second home, and even more if you rent it for a minimum number of weeks each year. Rental property can also be depreciated. Depending on your plans, it may be worth considering renting out the house and buying a small trailer or RV for your own use while on site.

Every taxpayer can currently take advantage of the tax exclusion of $250,000, single filer/ $500,000, joint filer of taxable gain (profit) on the sale of his **principal residence**. Simply put, if you file a return by yourself, you don't have to pay federal income tax on the first $250,000 in profit that you make when you sell your home. If you file with a spouse, the two of you don't have to pay taxes on $500,000 from such a sale. Generally speaking, your principal residence is one where you have lived for any two out of the last five years prior to sale, spending the majority of each of those two years there. The years don't have to be consecutive. A *second home* in the country is not your principal residence. Therefore, gain on its sale is not eligible for the exclusion, nor is it eligible for a 1031 tax-deferred exchange because it is not held for investment or use in your trade or business. But you might choose to configure your life so that you meet the residency requirement and other qualifications to allow you to turn a second home into a principal residence prior to sale. The IRS would look to confirm a principal-residence claim by checking your addresses for voting registration, utility bills, driver's license and the like. I don't know how prevalent such scrutiny is. You can use this exclusion on your principal residence every two years. During a five-year period, you can, it appears, qualify two residences as a "principal residence," with both getting the big tax break. No exclusion of this sort exists on rural property that is not used as your principal residence.

You may be able to get a partial exclusion if you have to sell before you meet the two-year, principal-residence requirement. If you lived in your second home as your principal residence for just one year, you could exclude $125,000 in profit if you meet certain tests. Accordingly, if you made a $100,000 profit (taxable gain) on the sale at the end of your one year, you would owe no tax on that gain because you could legitimately exclude $125,000. Current IRS rules limit the circumstances in which you can get the partial exclusion on home sales forced by health reasons (related to a disease, illness or injury to an owner or co-owner); change in your place of employment (the new workplace has to be at least 50 miles farther from the old home than the old workplace was) or "unforeseen circumstances." The last would include circumstances involving death, divorce, job loss, change in job status that leaves the owner unable to pay the mortgage or living expenses, multiple births and condemnation of the property. These rules do not exclude other unforeseen circumstances, but you will need to make that case. The partial exclusion can be used to get a refund for prior years if your forced sale qualifies. I'd advise against using "unforeseen circumstances" to obtain the partial exclusion on your own intuition of IRS intent: run your circumstances past your CPA first. (Kenneth R. Harney, "IRS loosens rules about home sales," Richmond Times-Dispatch, December 29, 2002.)

While you should be aware of the tax benefits available to you in the principal-residence game, most readers will ultimately benefit the most from setting up a rural property purchase as an investment, investment business (though not as a real-estate dealer) or, possibly, as another type of business where the land purchase is a necessary part. (This need not foreclose your opportunity to use the rural house as a principal residence at some future point.) You may want to organize only some of your new property as an investment or business. The tax code is far more helpful to those purposes than to buying and using land for personal recreation. While a farm classification opens its own set of tax benefits, you need not meet the IRS farm tests to rent your open land for grazing or "organize" your woods as a timber investment or timber-investment business. Even inaccessible, undeveloped land can be rented for hunting or hiking. Crop land can always earn money. If your new property can generate income, consider the advantages of doing so in light of the tax benefits that result. As a personal playground, your rural property provides you with minimum tax benefits—mortgage interest and property taxes, mainly. The same ground organized as an investment allows you to take these items as well as all investment-related expenses (from a lock on the gate to a culvert in a road) and depreciation on existing and new improvements (from battle-scarred tractors to outbuildings). As a business, rural property losses can offset gains from other sources of income. Whether you set up your new property as a personal asset, investment or business, you can still donate or sell conservation easements on the land if that severance fits your overall plan for the property. Conservation easements, however, benefit individual taxpayers more than corporations, so that may be a factor in how you take ownership. **Your CPA will help you understand the tax implications of each ownership option and property plan during your scoping.**

Another money difference between city and country property involves the owner's annual carrying costs. You would, of course, be able to determine your annual mortgage payment, insurance and property taxes in each case with a high degree of accuracy. Rural property tax, particularly if you have land use on your rural property, should be very low, in both absolute and comparative terms. You might pay $4,000 in property tax on a modest suburban lot and its 2,400-square-foot suburban house and half that on a 150-acre farm with a similar house.

You should also price out **homeowners' insurance** and **private mortgage insurance (PMI)**. Conventional homeowner's insurance on farms—a farm policy covers a lot of things, but probably doesn't protect against damage from floods, forest fire, electricity surges to appliances with chips, among others. You should ask whether all of the outbuildings are covered and what your liability coverage is for visitors drowning in your swimming hole, falling from your barn loft and rolling your tractor. One type of PMI protects you: you buy a policy that protects your property in the event that you are unable to make payments. The other type of PMI protects your institutional lender when you borrow more than 80 percent of the property's value.

If the property has functioning utilities, ask the seller for a year's bills so that you can project your basic service costs. Make sure that you determine how much use the seller made of the property in the winter (heat) and summer (possibly AC). If there is no electricity on the property, get a free estimate from the local power company of the cost to run a line to where you want it along with assurances from neighbors that they will agree to a utility easement across them to you. Try to negotiate the location of utility easements with the neighbor and the power-company engineers on site at the same time. Utility engineers prefer to run straight lines regardless of how they affect your neighbors who are under no requirement to agree to anything. Neighbors may only agree to an underground installation, which is usually more expensive than pole service. The three utilities with which I've dealt allow the new, remotely located homeowner to spread the installation cost over a number of years and apply some of the monthly usage charges against that sum. In the country, you should expect to pay a trash fee and local taxes on farm equipment and vehicles.

Sewerage can be a capital expense in the country whereas in places served by public systems you may be charged only a nominal amount for hooking on or opening a new account, followed by periodic usage charges. If you find yourself scoping a country house that does not pipe grey water (sink, shower, washing machine) *and* black water (toilet) into an **approved sewage system**, you may be required to install one following your purchase.

If there is no sanitarian-approved sewage treatment system in place where you need it, you may be able to install a conventional septic system (for $3,000 to $5,000) if the ground is suitable. This is determined by a water percolation test in some states or a soil-color test administered by the sanitarian or a soils engineer in others. If your dirt doesn't "perc," you can construct an engineered system for $15,000 to $20,000. In some circumstances, it may be possible to substitute a self-contained chemical or composting toilet for a drain-field-type system. If you are thinking about such alternatives, check with your county sanitarian before submitting a purchase contract to determine which, if any, alternatives are acceptable and their likely cost.

Jurisdictions differ widely over what they require in terms of wastewater treatment. One West Virginia county that I contacted recently required no sewerage system as long as the remote cabin had no inside running water. If a line from a spring was run to the kitchen sink, however, a gravel-lined ditch would need to be constructed to accept its grey water. If a shower and toilet were installed, then an approved septic system was expected. At least one state, North Carolina, now requires all residences whose waste waters are not connected to an approved system to put one in. Localities may have different rules for full-time residences and part-time hunting camps. You cannot assume that a current sewerage arrangement will be grandfathered for the new owner. The rule is: ask specific questions of the proper official during scoping. If you're going to get hit with a $20,000 sewerage-system-installation bill immediately after taking possession, you need to know that before you submit your offer.

A major difference between city and country real estate lies in routine maintenance costs. Country property can be maintenance free when you're working with undeveloped land. But even these properties can involve unanticipated expenses, such as fence replacement, aerial spraying to protect trees from insects and flood clean up. Improvements (structures, residences, facilities, roads, bridges, etc.) on country property always require upkeep, though deferring upkeep is common enough. Some upkeep can be deferred, though roof leaks and failing bridge girders cannot. Self-initiated safety investments take on more prominence in the country. In town, your investment choice might be between spending $30,000 on a prettier kitchen or a prettier bathroom. In the country, your first investments are likely to go to rewire the house for safety and rebuild the cattle guard (bridge) that gives you access to the state-maintained road. On the whole, skilled and unskilled labor is much cheaper in the country, which means that all such work is proportionately cheaper. This also holds true for excavation, tree trimming, auto mechanics, shop work and the like. Materials, if procured locally, are likely to be higher than at your suburban Home Depot.

Therefore, as part of your pre-purchase scoping it's important to gather as much information as you can about what the new place will require for safety-related improvements and then move to costing changes related to immediate other needs related to convenience and functionality. Following that, list things that are deferrable needs and discretionary expenses. Each item in the safety and immediate-need category should be a bargaining chip in your negotiations with the seller.

CHAPTER 32: BORROWING MONEY

SYSTEM OVERVIEW

Since institutional lenders, such as banks, are often involved in rural property purchases, it's useful to know some of the basic concepts, vocabulary and procedures they use. A borrower cannot avoid becoming conversant with these matters, if only because the choices each borrower must make to pick a loan require it.

Realize going in that taking out a mortgage is a process that is often opaque. It is made more impenetrable by unfamiliar words that have legal and financial meanings as well as acronyms that rival those of the Pentagon. Membership-owned credit unions are, in my experience, the most consumer-friendly mortgage lenders. They usually have the best loan packages, and they should be completely open about charges and profit spreads. Their institutional purpose is not to wrest the most profit out of each loan, so they don't try to trick and stick their borrowers. But a credit union may not be available to you in your target area.

Even with the most scrupulous lender, each borrower needs to develop at least a background familiarity with how money is borrowed—its benefits, risks, choices, standard formulas, vocabulary and procedures. I recommend the following sources: Jack Guttentag, The Mortgage Encyclopedia: An Authoritative Guide to Mortgage Programs, Practices, Prices, and Pitfalls (New York: McGraw-Hill, 2004); Randy Johnson, How to Save Thousands of Dollars on your Home Mortgage (New York: John Wiley & Sons, 1998); Julie Garton-Good, All About Mortgages: Insider Tips to Finance or Refinance Your Home, 2nd ed. (Chicago: Dearborn, 1999); www.bankrate.com; www.nfsn.com; www.hsh.com; www.mortgage-x.com; and www.mtgprofessor.com.

Figuring out the best mortgage for you is far more involved than finding the lowest interest rate. In fact, the lowest rate can be nothing more than sucker bait for a hugely disadvantageous loan package. The key question you have to answer is how long you anticipate owning the property. If you anticipate either owning it for less than five years or being able to pay down a large chunk of the principal within that time, find a mortgage with the least amount of upfront fees, points and other closing costs. Make sure your mortgage allows you to pre-pay at any time some or all of the principal without penalty. (If you pre-pay principal, make sure to note on your check the exact amount you are applying to principal pre-payment or write a separate principal-only check.) Most borrowers—some 95 percent—pay off their mortgages before the full term expires. (Johnson, Save Thousands, p. 131.) Since interest is **front-loaded**—that is, the borrower's monthly payment goes mainly for interest in his first payment and mainly for principal in his final one—and given the upfront charges you've had to pay to get the loan, the quicker your pay off, the higher the interest rate you will have paid on the borrowed money. In return, you pay far less interest (total dollars), which is a great reason to pay off debt sooner rather than later. If you plan to hold the country property over a 20- or 30-year term, you're best off shopping for the lowest *fixed* interest rate—which stays the same over the loan's entire term—even if you have to pay the lender a bit more upfront to get that rate.

In mortgage shopping, a complicated array of loan choices are available, which combine an interest-rate formula and a set of closing charges (upfront fees, points and other costs) that produce a target yield—that is, gross profit—for the lender over the term. Consumer Reports refers to these choices as a "bewildering assortment…all of them designed to help Americans get into a house with a minimal amount of cash and low monthly payments." (Consumer Reports, "Your Home: how to protect your biggest investment," May, 2005.) Rates and charges change with the length of the term, but the lender's target yield is roughly the same whatever the combination. You won't get a lender to agree to terms that drop him below his target yield, but you may be able to get him down from way above his target. Play one lender against the others to get the best deal. A lender may cut his mark up a bit to get your business, but be aware that the lender most willing to cut may have started above the others. Evaluate lender offers from your perspective, not the lender's. Every loan package you are offered should produce a profit for the lender, but the benefits of each offer from your perspective can range widely, depending on the terms you agree to and how long you hold the mortgage.

You also need to understand that benefits for you may involve high risk for you: **adjustable-rate mortgages (ARMs)** are riskier than fixed rates, and interest-only ARMs are riskier still. When risk converts to reality, you can lose your property. It's fair for your lender to make a profit on his business dealings with you. Your job is not to strip his profit out of the deal, but to estimate to the best of your ability which combination of interest rate, charges, risks and terms is likely to cost you the least and work best for you given your plans for holding the property. A win for the borrower does not require a loss for the lender.

Most property is bought in a standard format: the buyer comes up with a cash **down payment** and borrows the rest from an institutional lender, such as a bank, savings and loan or credit union. The borrowed money takes the form of a **mortgage**, which is a **lien** that uses the property as security for the debt the buyer has just taken on. The property's market value—what you just paid for it—will exceed the mortgage amount in most cases. (Loans are also made in certain circumstances that require no down payment, which means the loan covers 100 percent of the purchase price or even 125 percent. Such notes carry higher interest rates. They can make sense in markets where land prices are appreciating rapidly and the borrower has a strong income flow, but they are very risky.)

One of the many decisions a lender makes on each loan is how much of the borrower's cash it wants to be sunk in a particular property. This decision takes the form of a **loan-to-value (LTV) ratio**, which expresses as a percent the amount of money the lender will offer (loan) in terms of the property's "value." The common LTV ratios are 80 percent and 90 percent, that is, the bank lends to the borrower 80 percent of the property's current value, as the lender defines it. On large land deals, however, I've encountered banks that would lend only 50 or 60 percent of value, packaged as an interest-only commercial note. A lender might use a 90 percent LTV ratio of an appraisal value for a property with a quality improvement (usable house) and 80 percent or less for a totally unimproved property. What the lender won't lend, the borrower must produce from other sources. An 80 percent LTV ratio means the borrower must come up with 20 percent of the value—as determined by the lender—usually in addition to closing costs. The lender decides which definition of "value" he wants to use. It may be the property's appraisal number (which should be fair market value), or the contract price, or the lesser of the two. *If the appraisal price is less than your contract purchase price, an 80 percent LTV ratio based on appraisal price means that you will have to produce more than 20 percent of your purchase price from your other resources.* Lenders have historically preferred a higher percentage of borrower cash in the property, that is, a lower LTV ratio. But that's changing. Many offer 90 percent LTV loans and even 100 percent LTV loans—at higher interest rates, with higher points and a strong borrower.

Some states have lenders holding mortgage liens directly, while others use a trustee to hold the note, in which case the mortgage is called a **deed of trust**. A mortgage lien of either type is a claim by a creditor—in this case the lender from whom you've borrowed—to control the property you've just bought to meet your debt/liability. If the borrower does not make his mortgage payments, the creditor who holds the lien can seize the property and sell it. The trustees or the creditor directly hold legal title until either the debt is paid in full or a default occurs, in which case a foreclosure is declared and the property sold to benefit the lender. (See Benny L. Kass, "Housing Counsel: Deed of Trust Gives Lender Broad Power Over the Home You Buy," <u>Washington Post</u>, February 5, 2005.) While the borrower—you—possesses the property, uses it and improves it, the lender retains the power, though seldom exercised, to either prevent you from doing what you want with his **security interest** or establish certain guidelines that you must follow to do what you want.

If, for example, you want to sell a portion of the land that you've just mortgaged and put the cash in your pocket, you will need to clear it with the lender since the sale of that acreage will reduce his collateral securing the entire debt. The lender must agree to issue a **release** on the partial sale before you can sell. A lender may insist that you pay down your mortgage by a proportional amount before you put sale dollar one in your own wallet. The amount a lender will ask you to pay toward your mortgage from a partial sale will depend on how much equity you have in the root property, how much the property has appreciated since you first borrowed the money and how much of the property you will have left to secure the remaining note. The lender may also insist that you receive a minimum amount of money from the partial sale. This is known as imposing a **reserve price** on your sale. The lender will not release that portion of the property for sale unless your buyer meets the lender's reserve price. If you plan to sell either timber or a lot from the rural property you are about to purchase, discuss your idea with your lender so that you will know in advance how he will respond.

If you fail to meet the terms of your mortgage, which is called a **default**, the holder of the lien can sell your property that's serving as collateral/security in an effort to get his money. **Foreclosure** is the legal process by which the property securing borrowed money is sold to satisfy a debt. A borrower in foreclosure can be charged for the lender's expenses in cashing out the property. If the foreclosure sale does not net enough money to cover the loan principal, expenses and accrued interest, the lender may be able to get a **deficiency judgment** against the borrower to make up the difference. This will be ugly. If a foreclosure sale covers all claims, anything left goes to the borrower. Foreclosure, default and bankruptcy require a borrower to get help from a lawyer. If you have personally guaranteed the note in addition to placing the property as collateral, the lender will expect you to make up any shortfall. But mortgaged property is generally secured only by the real estate, the common exception being business deals involving property. With most real-estate mortgages, your risk is generally limited to the loss of the property serving as collateral (which includes the cash you have invested in the property), since a foreclosure sale generally produces enough income to cover most, if not all, of the debt. If you find a mortgage structured as a **recourse loan**—that is, one under which the lender can get at your other assets when a foreclosure sale does not cover your note—don't be shy in striking that language. A borrower, pinched in default, should have his lawyer try to arrange with the lender for the borrower to give a **deed in lieu of foreclosure** to the lender. The borrower loses the property and his invested cash (equity), but the lender agrees not to foreclose and take other assets. You want to avoid default and foreclosure.

The foreclosure rate historically tracked the economy. But another factor that should have driven up the foreclosure rate in the middle of the 21st Century's first decade is the willingness of lenders and borrowers to get into riskier loans with each other. For their part, lenders offered the bait of no-interest and adjustable-rate loans to get borrowers on the treadmill. Refinancing was easy. The Internet offered quick, low-interest loans, even to, or especially to, borrowers with marginal financials. And borrowers took the bait, because they saw home and property ownership as a constantly appreciating asset. In one sense, borrowers are right: property, generally, appreciates over the long term, which makes it less risky than investment alternatives. But it is the most risky investment in another sense, since three or four missed monthly payments can lead to the loss of the entire appreciated asset, including all the equity the borrower has in it, and additional costs. Michael Powell of The Washington Post reported that 63 percent of new mortgages in 2005 were interest-only or those with adjustable rates. (Michael Powell, "U.S. housing boom a bust for many," www.washingtonpost.com, May 29, 2005). One third of the home mortgages in the Washington, D.C. area and 54 percent in the District of Columbia were **interest-only** (IO) loans during the first six months of 2005. (Albert B. Crenshaw, "Interest Only, Except for the Risk," Washington Post, June 12, 2005.) Where borrowers and lenders agree to a loan that situates the borrower right at the edge of his ability to repay, both sides are hoping that his financials don't change for the worse. A spell of unemployment, an illness, car crash, any unexpected event that negatively affects the borrower's cash flow or savings—can lead to foreclosure for such individuals. Powell reported that "...more than 8 percent of homeowners spend at least half of their income on their mortgage," which is way above the standard income-to-mortgage formulas.

Having said all that, the foreclosure rate in mid-2005 was about one percent of all outstanding mortgages, compared with 1.2 percent in mid-2004 and about 1.16 percent in 1998. (Kenneth Harney, "Late-mortgage-payment data may surprise you," Richmond Times-Dispatch, September 25, 2005; 1998 percentage from the Mortgage Bankers Association.) That amounts to about 400,000 foreclosures at mid-2005 on 40 million current home loans. The nation-wide average late-mortgage-payment rate is 4.3 percent. (See also Terry Savage, "The hazards of some home-equity loans," March 12, 2003 at: http://moneycentral.msn.com/content/Banking?Homefinancing/P37886.asp.)

If risk is up, why is the foreclosure rate steady to down? Harney writes:

Foreclosure rates in general are lower in 2005 than they have been in prior decades in part because Fannie Mae, Freddie Mac, the Federal Housing Administration and most major lenders now use sophisticated 'loss-mitigation' techniques to keep even the most seriously delinquent borrowers in their homes. The techniques include restructuring loan terms, deferring late balances to the end of the loan and sometimes even lowering interest rates.

This suggests to me that foreclosures would have increased had not these institutions found it wiser to lower the foreclosure rate by nursing along troubled loans. A more lenient set of rules disguises the real increase in penalty that borrowers bear from assuming "easy" loans of higher risk. If the old rules (less the new loss-mitigation techniques) were still being applied, the foreclosure rate would probably be rising. As it is, an apples-to-oranges comparison proves nothing save that we are looking at different fruits. My guess is that the foreclosure rate will rise if only because both lenders and borrowers are now operating under a false sense of borrower capacity to handle the riskier loans.

In April, 2006, the Wall Street Journal reported a shift in trends. Both foreclosures and delinquencies were up. Mortgage loans in some stage of foreclosure had risen by 117,000 in February, an increase of 68 percent over February, 2005. Late payments ran at about three percent for poor credit risks and at about .76 percent for better risks, both up from a year earlier. Two factors were cited as driving the shift—economic distress (unemployment) and a cooling off of home appreciation. The Midwest—Indiana, Ohio and Michigan, in particular—showed especially high rates of foreclosures and delinquencies. In December, 2006, the Journal reported that about 80,000 subprime mortgages—almost four percent of that type—were behind in payments, and "there are signs [delinquencies] are spreading to other parts of the mortgage market." (Ruth Simon and James R. Hagerty, "More Borrowers With Risky Loans Are Falling Behind," <u>Wall Street Journal</u>, December 5, 2006.) I've not found data on foreclosures and delinquencies on second homes or unimproved rural property, but I think it's fair to assume that most borrowers will sacrifice those assets before they'll abandon their principal home.

If you find yourself in this type of jam, approach the lender or the mortgage company that services your loan in a straight-forward manner, explain the circumstances and provide a realistic overview of your resources. Harney believes that mortgage holders are willing to help borrowers for reasons of self-interest, namely that "...they lose tens of thousands of dollars on average with every foreclosure..." and for reasons of social policy. (Kenneth Harney, "The Nation's Housing," "Many options available to head off foreclosure," <u>Richmond Times-Dispatch</u>, December 25, 2005.) These foreclosure-avoidance options include: "forbearance" arrangements by which the borrower is allowed to pay less each month, or even nothing; "reinstatements" that allow the borrower's account to be brought into balance at some specified future point; "repayment" plans that allow the borrower to catch up on missed payments by adding on to future monthly payments; and "loan modifications" that recast the terms of the note, e.g., converting an ARM to a fixed-rate mortgage or lengthening the term. A Freddie Mac study in 2004 found that repayment plans—where a portion of the past-due money is tacked on to each monthly payment over a fixed time period—lowered the home-loss chances for 80 percent of all borrowers. www.freddiemac.com provides detailed information about foreclosure-avoidance options.

Many lenders will consider trying to develop a **work-out plan** with you rather than categorize your loan as **non-performing** or take back the property. With most institutional lenders, you'll have a month or two of leeway in the event that a payment is delayed. But don't expect more than 60 days, and don't expect 60 days more than once or twice. Use this time to put a plan into place; this is not a grace period that can be invoked at your discretion. Lenders are lazy. They don't want to foreclose for their money; they want placid payers and no problems. But foreclose they will; some more precipitously and self-righteously than others. The one time I found myself in this situation, the lender did nothing but demand all of the money owed immediately. Had this lender been willing to give me two or three years in a restructured note, I could have paid off all the obligations without going through a fire sale.

When a foreclosure occurs, the borrower has an **equitable right of redemption in most states**. This allows the borrower (or some other party with a legal interest in the property, such as a creditor with a junior lien) to pay off the amount in default and costs. This renews the debt under the same terms as before. Some states also have a **statutory right of redemption**, which allows the borrower a period in which to reacquire his property *after* the foreclosure sale—at great expense. If you find yourself struggling in these waters, approach the mortgage holder after getting legal advice. If you ignore your missed payments and stonewall the bank's calls, you will be foreclosed.

The point I'm making is simple: while the purchase of rural property is readily financed and should, if properly scoped, prove to be a profitable investment, no one should place himself at financial risk to acquire this asset (or any other) simply because borrowed money is available.

Most buyers find themselves involved in two types of initial money-borrowing decisions when buying rural property. The first is a decision about the **package of financing** the buyer needs to effect the purchase. The package usually involves several sources of money, though it may be as simple as the buyer withdrawing the full purchase price from his passbook savings. In this unusual case, the buyer is borrowing the full purchase price from himself—losing earned interest, but saving paid interest. If your money is sitting in a one-percent savings account, you are borrowing from yourself at a very favorable rate, that is, the one percent of taxable interest your money would have earned. Generally, a buyer looks to piece together the purchase-price package.

The package's biggest component is usually the loan that originates from an institutional lender as a **property-secured note**—the lien described above. The seller may also finance a portion of the sale in the form of a note that is in second (junior) position after the institutional lender. A **second mortgage** note can involve another institutional lender, the seller or an individual. In a foreclosure, creditors are paid in accordance with their seniority ranking.

Most of the time, the buyer is expected by the lender to pay the seller ten to 20 percent of the purchase price as a down payment. This money provides security to the lender in case of default and represents the buyer's beginning **equity**, which is at risk of loss if he defaults. A lender can adjust the down-payment percentage, up or down, depending on the mortgage terms, purchase price, appraisal value, financial position of the borrower and whether the borrower plans to sell some of the property's assets quickly to reduce his debt principal. Where the property securing the note is substantially more valuable than the loan involved in its purchase, a borrower may be able to negotiate a loan covering 100 percent of the purchase price with minimal risk. Rural property containing significant merchantable timber can be financed this way.

Down payment can also take the form of a gift (e.g., a parent gives cash on behalf of an adult child purchasing property), or land (where a lot has been owned for a long time, some lenders will allow the owner to use its appreciated value as down payment when the owner is ready to build; the difference between the appraised value of the lot plus completed house and the house's construction cost is the amount of down payment the lender will assign to land in a note secured by both lot and house), or a gift from the seller (who raises the price by the amount of the gift which lets the buyer into the deal with less cash and more debt; this must be done openly and transparently, and the appraisal value has to cover the higher purchase price) or borrower-owned securities (e.g., stocks) deposited with the lender. (See Guttentag, Mortgage Encyclopedia, pp. 51-57.) Borrowers are usually expected to contribute at least three percent of their down payment, but no down-payment loans can be gotten in the right conditions.

First-time buyers sometimes confuse the **earnest money** they submit with their purchase contract with down payment. Earnest money (security money, deposit) is the cash a buyer offers to the seller when he submits his contract. It's usually on the order of one to five percent of the offering price. Earnest money is held in escrow pending completion of the purchase. It usually is folded into the buyer's down payment at closing.

The buyer's down payment, combined with the principal he retires, combined with any additional investment he puts into the property—represents his evolving **equity** in the property. The process of paying down debt and increasing the owner's stake in the property is called **equity build up**. The more equity an owner has in his property, the more secure the institutional lender feels and the less likely he should be to pull the plug over a couple of missed payments. An unscrupulous lender with a 20 percent down payment in a property and a couple of years into the note might be very quick to foreclose on a very marketable place because of the high profit that will result. That is my fear with Internet lenders, though I have no first-hand experience to feed my suspicion.

Equity build up along with appreciation over time allows the owner to borrow additional money using the original property as security.

A **home-equity loan** borrows against the owner's increased equity and the property's appreciated value. You can borrow your down payment for country property from yourself this way as long as your overall debt-to-income ratio does not exceed the lender's standards. Such a loan is a second mortgage on your principal residence. As a **home-equity loan**, it's a fixed amount with a fixed interest rate; as a **home-equity line of credit (HELOC)**, the amount you borrow can go up to the limit set by the lender, but it is a variable-rate loan with no cap on interest rates.

You can also raise a down payment for country property by **refinancing** your principal residence. Borrowers refinance mortgages when current interest rates are at least two points lower than their mortgage rate. Large loans can benefit from refinancing with a rate reduction smaller than two points, but the question in all instances is how long it will take for the costs you incur in refinancing to be recouped in savings. If the new interest rate is a lot lower than your current rate that **break-even point** comes sooner; if the new rate is not much lower, it takes a lot longer.

A refinancing replaces your existing first mortgage on a property with a new first mortgage. You pay off the old note and take on a new one under new terms. You can replace your current lender with a different one as well.

When equity has built up and the principal residence has appreciated, a borrower can refinance at a lower interest rate and pull some cash out of the deal for down payment on country property (or anything else). The cash you extract is money on which you still pay interest.

Refinancing for a reduced interest burden involves comparing the costs of your existing mortgage over a period of time against a refinanced note (with its costs) over the same period. Guttentag's Web site—www.mtgprofessor.com—provides these comparisons. Refinancing can help a borrower or hurt him, depending on the new terms, their cost and how long he holds the property. When you refinance to get a lower interest rate, you have to weigh into your calculations the upfront costs of refinancing and the total interest that you will pay over the term of the note. The best deal for refinancing is to be able to do so without incurring any costs. You may be able to modify your existing note at not much cost with your current lender if he gets the idea that you're shopping to refinance. But where the lender only services your mortgage, rather than owns it, this can prove difficult. Guttentag suggests requesting a **payoff statement** from your current lender, which is a heads up that you're looking to refinance. It's then in your lender's interest to keep your business.

In refinancing, you also need to estimate your **break-even point**, that is, the date in the future when the costs you incur to refinance match the benefit in savings from the lower interest rate. Break-even points depend on the interest rates, term of the note and the amount of refinancing costs. Guttentag provides tables for refinancing break-even points. (Guttentag, Mortgage Encyclopedia, pp. 251 ff.) The less you have to pay in refinancing costs and the greater the spread between your existing interest rate and your lower, refinanced rate, the shorter is your break-even point. If, for example, you refinance a new loan over 30 years, with one point and pay other costs that amount to two percent of the loan amount, your break-even month is 83 (of 360) if you get a one percent interest rate reduction; month 48 for a two percent reduction and month 22 for a three percent reduction. Cutting the other costs from two percent to one percent of the loan amount lowers the break-even period to 49 months for a one percent rate reduction, 22 months for a two percent reduction, and 14 months for a three percent reduction. If you refinance at a lower rate and a shorter term, that is helpful; if you lengthen the term, you can end up paying more interest, though in smaller monthly payments. A recent study of 3,785 fixed-rate mortgages between 1996 and 2003 found that only 1.4 percent of borrowers carried their mortgages long enough to break even against their upfront points. The lesson seems to be for most of us: take the higher fixed interest rate with fewer points, because we pay off the loan early. (Ron Lieber, "Deciphering Mortgage Points," Wall Street Journal, December 23-24, 2006.)

Generally, the interest rate has to be about three points lower than your current rate for refinancing to be beneficial, but it also depends on the amount of points and costs you have to pay and the length of time you hold the property. A new rate two points lower with low costs can also work. Remember that every time you refinance, you start paying the full term on the new note with front-loaded interest. The deductibility of interest will help on your taxes, but this is not reason enough to refinance. You may also be able to rid yourself of **private mortgage insurance**, the non-deductible monthly premium charged to borrowers with less than 20 percent down payment.

Serial refinancing can pull cash out of a property, but you may find that your principal is never reduced by very much. Your equity build up in a serially refinanced property comes almost entirely from appreciation, not from principal repayment. And you turn that type of equity into cash only when you sell. If you keep refinancing for the same term (30 years) every few years, your total cost of borrowing can be more than if you had stuck with the original higher rate, owing to charges you pay each time. But whether refinancing makes sense depends on the specific loan terms you get in relation to your existing note and how long you keep the property. Weston points out that you can end up paying more total interest over your term by refinancing from 8 percent to 5.5 percent if its length is extended by ten years. (See Liz Pulliam Weston, "Beware the hidden costs of refinancing," March 12, 2003 at: http://moneycentral.msn.com/ content/Banking/Homefinancing/P42715.asp.)

Apart from thinking about a package of financing options, the buyer's second decision involves **fitting the available sources of money to his package of needs**. In its simplest form, the borrower needs to choose one lender from among many. But a dirt-smart buyer can have other sources of money available to buy rural property beyond a bank loan. Rural property, for instance, often lends itself to **partial self-financing**, whereby some of the purchase price can be quickly recouped from the property itself through the sale of an asset. I discuss non-bank sources of money below.

Underwriting is the term used to describe the many-stepped process that a lender goes through with a borrower in determining how large a loan the lender will offer and on what terms. The borrower initiates the process by approaching a lender with information about himself and, eventually, a target property. The lender evaluates and investigates both the borrower and the property. The lender may decide not to extend mortgage credit at all, or offer loans whose terms range from harsh to favorable from the borrower's perspective. Once a loan is underwritten, the lender may keep it or sell it. The borrower has no say in that decision. It's worth asking the lender you're working with whether his institution plans to sell your loan. Loans that a lender sells will have to fit standard formulas; you may do better with a lender who won't sell your note. If your loan is a little out of the ordinary, ask your lender whether he can **keep it in his portfolio**; this gives the lender a bit more flexibility in making a loan that fits your circumstances.

Where your package of financing includes an institutional lender, such as a bank or savings and loan, your first step will be to **prepare your financial profile**. Your profile consists of a number of documents that you package for the lender's consideration. I discuss these below.

A key part of your financial profile is your **credit report and your credit score**. The former is a selective history of your bill paying, focusing on mortgages, car loans, credit cards and the like; the latter rates you numerically as a credit risk based on the report. You do not provide the lender with this report, though you pay for it. Your report is routinely accessed when you apply for a credit card, mortgage or loan, and with increasing frequency with rental housing, insurance and employment. The report captures all of your credit payments—credit cards, mortgages, student loans, car loans, consumer loans, etc.—and any problems you may have had, such as defaults, bankruptcies, late payments, court judgments, check bouncing, tax liens and so on. (Bankruptcies are required to be removed from your report after ten years, most other blemishes after seven.) In addition to your payment history, a credit report will assess your current borrowing capacity.

You have rights under the federal Fair and Accurate Credit Transactions Act to obtain a free copy of your credit report. The three major credit bureaus that produce reports are: **Equifax**, Disclosure Department, POB 740241, Atlanta, GA 30374, 1-800-685-1111, www.equifax.com; **Experian**, POB 2002, Allen, TX 75013, 1-888-397-3742, www.experian.com; and **TransUnion**, Consumer Disclosure Center, POB 1000, Chester, PA 19022, 1-800-916-8800, www.transunion.com.

You can theoretically access a free report from www.annualcreditreport.com; also at POB 105281, Atlanta, GA 30348; 1-877-322-8228. I found access impossible with TransUnion when I tried, because the Website demanded that I provide account numbers for accounts I do not have. TransUnion did not include my mortgage lender's account. Consumer Reports had exactly the same experience, describing the free credit report process as an "online maze…that can make it seemingly impossible to get your personal information." (Consumer Reports, "Credit Scores: What you don't know can be held against you," August, 2005.) Consumer Reports suggest that consumers go to www.myfico.com and order the $44.85 package, and then correct the errors in each of the three reports. www.bankrate.com offers a number of articles on credit reports and credit-rating scores.

Credit reports will be used in most cases to evaluate your ability to carry new debt. These reports are notoriously inaccurate, errors usually weighing against the borrower. Consumer Reports wrote that 25 percent of credit reports "…had errors serious enough to cause consumers to be turned down for a loan or a job, according to a 2004 survey by the U.S. Public Interest Research Group." The less creditworthy your report says you are, the more money you will have to pay in fees and interest rate to get a mortgage or a loan. The Consumer Federation of America reported in December, 2002 that as many as 40 million consumers are at risk of paying higher interest rates than their true circumstances merit owing to errors of missing information in their reports. (See Kenneth R. Harney, "Study shows credit scoring shortcomings," Richmond Times-Dispatch, December 22, 2002.)

What you will not find in most credit reports is your **credit-rating score**, or **FICO**. This number reflects the assessment of a computer model at Fair, Issac and Co. (FICO) as to your credit worthiness, based on your credit history involving delinquent payments, the extent to which you use credit, the length of your history (age of credit file), the number of times credit is applied for and the mix of credit you have. (See, Michael D. Larson, "Credit scores can make or break borrowers," www.bankrate.com/brm/news/pf/19981204.asp; and Pat Curry, "Consumers want access to those powerful, secret credit scores," www.bankrate.com/brm/news/mtg/20000508.asp?.)

The FICO score runs from about 300 to 850, with 660 and above, good; 620-660, a bit chancy; and below 620, rocky. Above 720 (the U.S. median) is golden; below, you won't get the absolute best deals. Credit providers and mortgage lenders use FICO scores to screen applicants and offer terms to each one based on risk and profitability. It appears that it's difficult to improve your FICO score quickly, though you should establish a record of making prompt installment payments and clean up errors on your credit report. <u>Consumer Reports</u> suggests carrying at least five credit cards (which gives you a lot of credit), but don't use much of it because you gain FICO points by using a small percentage of your available credit. The scoring system itself tends to most hurt young borrowers, first-timers, minorities, the elderly, folks who have errors in their credit reports and individuals who hate credit cards. Lenders, of course, have no particular interest in doing anything about this scandal, since they benefit by charging higher interest rates to worthy borrowers with less-than-worthy FICO scores.

Thirty-one percent of the Consumer Federation of America's 500,000-plus sample, cited above, showed at least a 50-point difference between credit reports, and five percent showed a variation of 100 points. A 50-point difference, Harney pointed out, could mean a difference between a 6.01 percent interest rate on a 30-year fixed note and a 7.70 percent rate, about $4,500 per year. The average variation among the reports was 43 points—enough to cost you more than $100,000 in interest over a mortgage's 30-year life. For this reason alone, **you should correct omissions of favorable information and errors on your three credit reports well before approaching an institutional lender**.

The three major credit bureaus—Equifax, Experian and TransUnion—proposed in the spring of 2006 to replace using FICO scores with a system they call, VantageScore, which is a program that unifies the scoring and makes it consistent across the bureaus. Scores now can vary from one bureau to another, and lenders may seek three bureau scores for a borrower and take the middle one. The VantageScore runs from 501 to 990, with 900 to 990 representing an A, 801 to 900 a B and so forth. The proposed system does not address the main problems with these systems, which are that they give false results if borrower information is not up to date, incorrect or missing. VantageScore was not widely used as of the beginning of 2007.

When asking for a report use a consistent identifying name. Communicate with the credit bureaus in dated writing when you have a correction or dispute; keep copies of your correspondence. Check on your credit reports before you apply for any mortgage loan. If you are rejected, ask the lender in writing for the specific reasons and then go about correcting your credit reports if that is where your problem lies.

As part of putting together your financial profile, get your three credit reports and correct in writing all errors and old information six months before you apply to an institutional lender for a mortgage. Make a paper trail. Supply each bureau with the documents needed to support your position. Keep copies of everything. Assume that it will take three or four months to straighten things out. Don't walk into a bank without having checked your credit reports, because the bank most assuredly will. In addition to reviewing your credit reports, you will be using this pre-purchase time to put together the rest of your financial profile, as discussed below. (See Dani Arthur, "5 steps to do-it-yourself credit repair," www.bankrate.com/brm/news/cc/20011008b.asp?keyword=CREDITCARDS.)

My inclination is to provide a lender with more information instead of the least I can get away with. That includes complete 1040s for the last two years, possibly a list of savings/checking accounts and information on life-insurance policies, retirement accounts, stocks, real estate and so on. I also provide the names and contact information for the professionals who've worked on the property I want to buy, such as the forester, surveyor, lawyer who's done title work on it in the past, soils consultant, appraiser familiar with the property, etc. If there's something quirky about my income for the last couple of years, I explain and offer my best guess as to my future income. Where references are requested, I'll give my CPA/tax preparer, lawyer, business associates and others who know my circumstances and financial character. The more confidence I can build with a lender, the better deal I'm likely to get.

Self-employed people often bear an extra burden with lenders if their cash flow varies from month to month, or year to year. In that case, the borrower needs to show long-term trends and substantiate current and future prospects. This can be hard. I once had a credit union turn me down for a mortgage because they would only accept 1040s as evidence of income. When I submitted cancelled checks for income received and confirming bank-deposit records in the current year (when a 1040 could not obviously exist), I was told this evidence of self-employment income proved nothing.

As you prepare your financial profile for evaluation, you will, in turn, be evaluating the institutional lenders available to you and the loan packages (rates, fees, formats and other terms) each offers. You can start your screening by comparing advertised terms that are being offered—interest rates, (packaged either as a **fixed rate** over a certain number of years or a **variable rate** that changes at predetermined times), upfront fees and charges, and other terms. You will quickly discover that you can compare one type of loan from one lender with exactly the same type of loan from other lenders, but it's very difficult to compare the cost of an adjustable-rate mortgage to a fixed-rate mortgage even when they're amortized over identical terms, because you can't anticipate what your interest charges will be on the ARM. Monthly ARM mortgage payments are fixed for certain periods of time. A fixed-rate mortgage sets the payment when the loan is originated, and it never varies. An ARM payment will change every time the interest rate is adjusted, unless the new interest rate is identical with the old one. Each monthly payment with any loan contains a changing ratio of interest to principal; your first monthly payment is almost entirely interest, and your last is almost entirely principal. The total amount of interest you will pay over the life of your loan depends on the interest rate you are charged and either the **term (length)** of the loan if you hold it for the full term or how long you keep the loan before paying it off. The lower the interest rate and the longer the term, the lower your monthly payment. But the longer the term and the longer you hold the note, the more total interest you will pay.

You should ask around locally about each lender's reputation. Banks don't differ much in their procedures and terms, but they can be quite different in their flexibility and, for lack of a better word, "warmth" toward customers. What you want is a lender who will not spring his trap door if you're late on a payment and will offer some time if you run into cash-flow trouble. Lenders don't like to repossess property, but all do. Some lenders will be very quick to foreclose, particularly on notes that are well into their terms with a lot of equity build up. The deeper into the term, the less interest is being paid, which can provide a financial incentive for foreclosure. Banks project a neighborly image, but they have the ability to pound you into the dirt. While banks suffer some financial and image damage over each foreclosure, my feeling is that they fully understand that the occasional repossession keeps the fear of their hammer right in the middle of their borrowers' brains.

As a newcomer, small rural lenders may treat you either with more deference or less than community natives. You might seek out other out-of-town folks who have bought property recently and get their opinions. I admit this is a slap-dash methodology, but you might gain the anecdotal insight you need to choose the friendliest lender. I would make a point of meeting some of the lender's board, particularly its leadership. A friend on the board even a new one can't hurt though don't count on much help if you ever need it. Banks are not social workers; helping borrowers through jams is not their nature.

Banks want to *feel* "secure" about their loans. Normally, they provide mortgage money using only the purchased property as collateral with a ten to 30 percent down payment. The amount of down payment is one of those requirements that can be negotiated if you show reasons why the lender should feel just as secure with less down payment. The greater your equity build up, the more secure your lender will feel, because his chance of losing money is decreasing. A history of regular payments doesn't count for much when your lender finds you in default. Your lender's feeling of security can be based on your last, full monthly payment. Don't expect loyalty, though lender self-interest might provide some relief by way of loss-mitigation techniques.

Most mortgage notes contain a **demand clause**, which allows the lender to call your note—that is, demand full payment of all principal and interest due—when the lender no longer feels secure. The document—a "Promissory Note"—that I've signed says a "default" occurs when, among other things, any of the following occurs:

- Borrower fails to make any payment when due under this Note.

- The death of the borrower. [Having life insurance that more than covers mortgage principal calms jittery lenders. The face amount of the insurance also improves net worth on the borrower's annual financial statement.]

- A material adverse change occurs in borrower's financial condition, or lender believes the prospect of payment or performance of this note is impaired. [Lender does not have to define what it considers to be an adverse change or tell the borrower why it believes the prospect of payment is impaired.]

- *Lender in good faith believes itself insecure*.

If you are ever faced with a lender calling the note for reasons of insecurity, don't waste time and money fighting it. The presence of a demand clause means you will lose. Move the note to another lender as quickly as you can.

COSTS OF BORROWING

A typical mortgage loan is burdened with three types of fees/costs: 1) government-imposed fees, such as a tax (deed stamps) and recording fee; 2) lender-imposed fees, including points, loan-origination fees, processing fees, garbage fees (see below), etc.; and 3) third-party fees, for services such as an appraisal, home inspection, title search, soils report, percolation tests, termite inspection and so on. You cannot negotiate with the government to lower its fees though you may be able to negotiate with the seller as to who pays how much of them. You can negotiate with the lender on his fees/costs, and you can ask the seller to pay some portion of them. You can price-shop on third-party fees that you commission, and you can negotiate with the seller over allocation on some of them. You can also complain to the lender about third-party services he "provides" for you, particularly where the costs are jacked up. The borrower needs to understand from the start that certain charges are fair, such as those for a credit report, appraisal, title policy, recording fee and, where applicable, a state registration fee. On some of these legitimate fees, the borrower needs to be on the look-out for gratuitous inflation. On illegitimate fees—processing fee, underwriting fee, warehousing fee, loan-originating fee, document preparation fee, application review fee and the like—the borrower needs to fight tooth and nail.

Each one percent of interest is called a **point**. A borrower pays a lender cash upfront to cover each point the lender charges to make the loan. You will find that lenders use a system where they offer borrowers lower interest rates in return for more points paid at the time the loan is made. On a typical fixed-rate loan with a 30-year term, a borrower might pay 2.75 points for a 5.375 percent rate, .0125 points (1/8th) for 5.875 percent, and get a 2.0 percent rebate for 6.375 percent. (A rebate—or negative points—is cash the borrower does not have to pay to get the loan, but it means a high interest cost if you hold the loan for 30 years.) The difference between a 30-year fixed-rate loan at 5.5 percent with no points on $100,000 in principal and 6.5 percent with no points is more than $23,000 in interest over the full term. If you're going to hold the note for a long time, pay higher points in exchange for a lower fixed interest rate. But if you're going for a short term or plan to pay it off well before 30 years, pay fewer points and take a higher rate. Your key variable in this decision is how long you will hold the note. www.mrtgprofessor.com provides calculators that allow you to figure which combination of points and interest-rate costs the least, given your projected timeframe. However, no one, not even the insightful professor, can help you predict how long you will hold a note; that's up to you and your crystal ball.

The borrower usually has the ability to bargain for a lower rate by paying more points. Lenders are not required to bargain, and no federal rule exists that governs the process. But Bruss believes that for "…each one-point loan fee paid, you should receive at least a one-eighth percent reduction in your loan's interest rate for the life of the mortgage." (Robert J. Bruss, "Which Home Mortgage Fees Are Proper?," The (Staunton) News-Leader, June 18, 2006.)

Many institutional lenders tack on **points**. Some points may also be referred to as "discount points," though from the borrower's perspective they should be called "extra points" paid by the borrower. Each **discount point** represents one percent of the loan amount. This point is pre-paid interest. If you agree to pay a **one percent discount fee** (that is, one discount point) to the lender, you will receive $99,000 on a $100,000 loan, but you will pay interest on the full $100,000—thereby, increasing your effective interest rate. (In your mortgage shopping, you may also hear the term "**basis point**," which represents 1/100th of one percent of interest. Thus, a 6.75 percent mortgage interest rate represents 675 basis points.) If the lender says he is charging you "a point" to originate the loan, it is one percent of the amount he's willing to lend you. You will then pay that one percent to the lender at the time the loan is made, and it is on top of the interest you will pay each month. This $100,000 loan would cost you $1,000 cash at closing, plus all other front-loaded charges and costs. The more points of any kind that a lender forces you to pay, the more the loan costs you to start your borrowing. Paying high points can make sense if you get a very low fixed interest rate that you hold for a long time.

In most cases, the points you pay at closing are tax-deductible over the course of the loan, not in the year in which you pay them. You should check with your CPA about which of your projected loan costs are immediately deductible and which are taken over the life of the loan.

Lenders will also often charge **fees for processing your loan**. In effect, you are being charged twice to get a loan: first, the lender is charging you an upfront processing fee to process your loan application; and second, the lender is charging you a rate of interest that covers his cost of overhead and loan processing. Fight processing fees.

It is common for a lender to charge a **loan-origination fee**, which generally amounts to one to two percentage points. A fee is a set dollar amount, however; it is not a percentage of the principal. A loan-origination fee is not pre-paid interest. It is a charge to cover the costs of generating the loan, including staff salary and overhead. A loan-origination fee can be a fair charge or foul, depending on what other costs the lender is imposing. Just remember, the more money a lender squeezes from a borrower upfront, the lower the lender's risk and the more profit he's likely to make.

You may also hear about a **pre-approval fee**, which is money you are expected to pay to have the lender evaluate your credit-worthiness. Even credit card companies don't try this one.

Also be alert to a **cancellation fee**, which may be imposed at various points during the underwriting if you don't go through with the loan.

You may also encounter an **assumption fee** if you are taking over a loan from the seller. An assumption fee should be resisted since the lender has already evaluated the property for the seller who has been making payments. How much can it cost a lender to change the name on a note? The lender will get a current appraisal on your nickel so his risk in lending on the property will not increase. Nonetheless, you may get nowhere with the lender on this fee.

Don't agree to a **pre-payment fee (penalty)** that falls on you for paying off any portion of your principal or your entire note before the full term. Such fees range from one percent of the balance to "…as much as all the interest due for the first ten years of the loan." (Galaty *et al.*, <u>Modern Real Estate Practice</u>, p. 212.) When the federal government insures or guarantees a mortgage, pre-payment fees are prohibited. Front-loading interest means the lender makes an above-rate of return on all early pay offs during the first half or more of a mortgage's term. The lender does not lose on pre-payment; in fact, he wins—just as you do. If the seller's note has a pre-payment penalty attached, it is his obligation, not yours, to pay it. But don't be surprised if the seller's pre-payment fee, in whole or part, wanders over to the buyer's side of the settlement sheet. You are perfectly within your rights to "wander" it back where it belongs.

You may also be charged specific, line-item fees, such as for a bank-required appraisal. If you are financially strong and borrowing a lot, grumble and complain; negotiating may save you some money. If you've had an appraisal done as part of your scoping, submit that to the lender and refuse to pay for a duplicate. If your appraiser is on the lender's "approved list" of appraisers, you should win; if not, you won't. Before hiring an appraiser as part of your scoping, check with the lender you think you will use to find out whether your choice is approved. Hire an approved appraiser.

In the loan business, a distinction is drawn between institutional lenders who are considered fair in their dealings with consumers of credit and those that practice "**predatory lending**." I've always been a bit skeptical of this division, given that the good guys engage in some of the same practices as the bad guys. I won't write that all lenders are in the predation business since several have treated me fairly and decently. I've found community credit unions often offer better loan packages than banks and S&Ls.

Mortgage brokers find loans for borrowers from various lenders. They do not lend their own money. The borrower pays a fee when he accepts a loan the broker has found. The fee is usually disguised as an undisclosed mark up above what the mortgage broker has found as terms from a lender. A two percent mark up on a $150,000 loan is common; a lower mark up is applied as the loan amount increases. Mortgage brokers may find a better deal than any the borrower finds for himself, even after his fee is included. A 2005 study by Gregory Elliehausen of Georgetown University found that total costs on broker-originated first mortgages for subprime borrowers (subprime equals credit problems) were 1.13 percentage points lower than loans originated by employees of lenders, and 1.98 percentage points lower on second mortgages. (Kenneth Harney, "Brokers get some respect in new study," <u>Richmond Times-Dispatch</u>, April 17, 2005.) You want to make sure that the mortgage broker is not receiving a fee from the lender outside of closing. If you find the phrase—**Premium Yield Adjustment/POC**—on your settlement statement, it means the broker is expecting another fee in your deal—Paid Outside Of Closing (POC). The broker gets this fee for steering you, the borrower, into a loan with a higher interest rate than you would otherwise receive.

Since most mortgage brokers do not reveal their fees (mark ups), it's impossible for a consumer to know the size of the fees that competing brokers are charging. A more consumer-friendly system is being organized by Jack Guttentag for what he calls, "**upfront mortgage brokers**." Such brokers disclose the amount they are charging for their service before you agree to retain them. Guttentag provides a list of upfront brokers at www.mtgprofessor.com.) See also www.bankrate.com/brm/news/mortgages/ 20021024a.asp?prodtype=mtg; this article discusses the practices of mortgage brokers who are not upfront.

Mortgage bankers make and service loans; they also sell loans they originate. Cast your net broadly when looking for the best loan package, and remember that you will throw all your catch back into the sea, save for one.

The nature of the lender-borrower relationship is clearly one in which every dollar that is put into your lender's pocket comes directly out of yours. "Money-lending" has an off-putting quality about it, but "banking" is accorded prestige. While the definition of predatory lending is unclear because the suspect practices vary from state to state, the following are those that appear to be most commonly included:

1. Interest rates that are noticeably above others in the area.

2. Adds points to the loan without reducing the interest rate.

3. Adds fees and costs, particularly padded fees and costs.

4. Demands an upfront application fee to look at your material. Don't use a lender that demands a fee for processing your application. Such fees, ranging from about $100 to several hundred dollars, are rip-offs.

5. Requires the borrower to buy unnecessary items, such as a pre-paid, one-premium, credit-life insurance policy whose cost is sometimes added to the loan principal so that the borrower pays interest on it.

6. Offers a loan based solely on the borrower's equity in the property (e.g., a down payment) and not on the borrower's repayment capacity. If you are not asked to demonstrate your income, be suspicious. This lender is signaling that he's likely to foreclose at the first excuse.

7. Large penalty, which may be called a "fee," for pre-payment of the loan.

8. Upfront fees that total more than three percent of the loan amount. "…most lenders say the total for origination fees and closing costs shouldn't add up to more than 3% of the loan amount, not counting 'points,' assuming the borrowers have reasonably good credit." (Patrick Barta, "Swimming With the Home-Loan Sharks," Wall Street Journal Sunday in Richmond Times-Dispatch, February 9, 2003.).

9. Be very careful with loans that tag on one large "balloon payment" at the end of your term. A balloon means that you have that amount of principal still to repay. Balloons are big lump sums. If you don't have the money, you'll have to renew the note at current rates or move the note to another lender.

Some mortgages refinance the remaining principal periodically at current interest rates with no danger or additional fees. But predatory lenders will add fees each time you refinance through them. Borrowers are often lured into predatory balloon loans by short-term **teaser** interest rates. Frequent balloon payments, or multiple refinancing, is also known as "flipping." Each flip is accompanied by additional fees and costs. Each refinance starts the interest front-loading fresh. The effect can be that the borrower spends his life paying a lot of interest and very little principal even when the interest rate is declining.

10. Outright falsification of loan documents. Consumer advisers say to fill in all blanks on loan applications, because blanks that have been left open have been known to have been completed by the lender—and not as a favor.

11. Promise of a guaranteed loan. A lender, credit-assistance business or mortgage broker who advertises or promises that you will get a mortgage regardless of your credit history is not your new best friend. Think about it. Why would anyone lend you money if there's a high likelihood that you will be unable to repay? Could it be that he hopes you are unable to repay? To get such a loan a borrower will have to cough up lots of upfront fees and have a lot of equity in the purchase going in. Foreclosures on such borrowers make a lot of money at the borrower's expense.

12. Closing-costs runaround. Lenders are required to give an applicant/borrower a **good-faith estimate of closing costs** no later than three business days after receiving a mortgage application. This can take the form of a single dollar amount or a range. A loan officer should be able to give a borrower a reasonably accurate estimate of the official good-faith estimate at the time the borrower orally outlines his financial profile and describes the target property. If the loan officer won't give a ballpark estimate during that interview, ask him to provide a list of the lender's standard charges. If these appear padded, be prepared to slide down a slippery slope. If you don't get the good-faith estimate by the fourth day, the lender is likely to prove slicker than the slope itself.

The federal Real Estate Settlement Procedures Act (RESPA) governs closing-cost procedures, including the good-faith estimate. But some types of mortgage lending are not covered. RESPA covers mortgage loans made by federally insured lenders, loans insured by the Federal Housing Administration (FHA) or guaranteed by the Veterans Administration, and those to be resold on the secondary mortgage market. It applies to first-position (lien) residential mortgage money applied to one- to four-family dwellings, for either investment or occupancy. RESPA does not apply to seller financing, an installment contract and a buyer's assumption of the seller's note, except where the lender charges more than $50 as an assumption fee. RESPA applies to second mortgages and home-equity lines.

13. One-stop shopping. A borrower may find himself working with a multi-faceted, real-estate firm, known as a Controlled Business Arrangement (CBA). The same company provides the borrower with a broker through whom to work, lender, title insurance provider, home inspector and so on. This is a closed loop once you're in it; closed loops can have another name as well, noose. The potential for borrower abuse is great. The borrower is supposed to be made aware of a CBA, whereupon he can contact other providers at his option. Any particular CBA can provide good service that is fairly and competitively priced, but you may benefit from additional research.

A variation on this idea is the lender who leads borrowers to a particular lawyer or appraiser. A clear conflict of interest exists when a lender steers customers to the law firm of the one lawyer on its board of directors. If you ask a lender to recommend local professionals, you should get at least two names, and preferably three. Sweetheart arrangements are indicated when you ask for the "names of some local lawyers," and are given one name. In a dispute, the odds are that the lawyer to whom you have been steered will side with the business-generating lender, not you, his one-deal client from somewhere else. A very common sweetheart arrangement is one between a real-estate brokerage and a title (insurance) agency, or a lawyer and a title agency. In such cases, as much as 80 percent of the buyer-paid title premium can go to the title agency where it is split with whoever—broker or lawyer—steered the buyer to that agency. The actual cost of the policy is 20 percent of the premium. Ask the title agency to show you how much of your premium is going to policy and how much to fees.

14. Negative amortization. This is the situation where the borrower makes monthly payments, but the loan is structured in such a way that he ends up owing more principal at the end of the note than when he started. This often happens through repeated refinancings. Make sure to get an amortization schedule from the lender, which shows exactly where you are in terms of principal and interest for each month of your term.

15. Deals that are too good to be true, e.g., "No money down/no fee." Would you lend money to a stranger on those terms? Read the fine print. (These practices are discussed in Barta's "Swimming"; Fannie Mae Foundation, "Borrowing Basics: What You Don't Know Can Hurt You," 2001, pp. 2-3; 1-800-541-6300; www.fanniemaefoundation.org; and www.aarp.org/consumerprotect-homeloans.)

A useful legal discussion of predatory lending, including an analysis of mortgage documents, can be found in the National Consumer Law Center's, STOP Predatory Lending: A Guide for Legal Advocates, available from the NCLC, 77 Summer Street, 10th Floor, Boston, MA 02110-1006; 617-542-9595; FAX 617-542-8028; www.nclc.org/initiatives. Additional information can be found at http://twincityhomeloans.com/protect.htm and http://helpdesk.uvic.ca/technote/1998/tn98012.html. At this writing, the federal Office of the Comptroller of the Currency (OCC), which regulates federally chartered banks, is considering issuing national guidelines on predatory lending. The bank lobby favors these guidelines because several states, particularly Georgia, have enacted much tougher rules. The Georgia law allows a borrower to sue both the original underwriter and any subsequent buyer of a loan that fits the definition of predatory. Georgia places no limits on punitive damages. It appears that the banks will win this contest, which will result in weak national guidelines. (Anitha Reddy, "U.S. Advises Banks to Stop Predatory Lending," Washington Post, February 22, 2003.).

The cost to you of borrowing with a mortgage is the total amount of money you have to pay the lender, both at the start and over the time you carry the note. This will include the total of interest paid; one-time front-end points, fees and charges; penalties that you are likely to incur; and **private mortgage insurance (PMI)** premiums that you may be required to pay to protect your lender.

Lenders differ in how they combine their various bites out of a borrower's pocketbook. Locally owned banks in my very rural area don't charge any points or loan-origination fees, but always impose an interest rate higher than the lenders who do. It is typical for a major regional/national lender to have upfront points, fees, charges and costs that add three to six percent (or more) to the principal you are borrowing. Borrowers usually pay these sums, included in **closing costs** or **settlement costs,** at closing (settlement) when the buyer's package of monies is exchanged for possession of the seller's property. Closing costs may include loan-origination fees, points (sometimes called discount points or financing points), attorney fees, document-preparation fees, inspections, title and/or settlement services, transfer and recordation taxes, title insurance, survey fee, inspection fees, appraisal fee and PMI, among others. The lender gets points and origination fees. The former is charged as a percent of the loan and the latter as a fixed amount. Some, but not all, lenders charge a loan-origination fee. The Fannie Mae Foundation says that loan fees by themselves—points and origination fees together—should not exceed 5 percent of the loan amount unless you are [intentionally] paying more for a lower interest rate." (Fannie Mae Foundation, "Borrowing Basics: What You Don't Know Can Hurt You," 2001, pp. 6-7). Five percent is on the high side in my experience. Loans with reasonable interest rates—though not the rock-bottom rates—should be available with a hit of two percent or less for points and origination fee combined.

The lender may also impose other fees presented as dollar amounts on the settlement statement, such as "processing," tax service, wire transfer, document preparation, courier, postage, "lender inspection" and so on. Ask each lender you interview to give you a rough estimate of these dollar fees when you're comparing loan packages.

A **Good Faith Estimate (GFE) of settlement costs** is supposed to be given to a borrower within three days of his mortgage application. But you should ask for a general (non-binding) approximation of the lender's total settlement costs when you're shopping for the best loan package, that is, before you formally apply. A lender won't guarantee either estimate, but it's worth haggling over a cap on settlement charges during your shopping phase. Simply say that you don't want to pay more than X dollars in such settlement costs packaged with Y rate and Z terms—and then ask him to work his side to help you get there.

Aside from the fees you pay to the lender, you will pay settlement fees to third parties at closing, each of whom will have done something that is needed, such as a termite inspection or an appraisal. Some third-party fees cannot be readily predicted by lenders, such as title and settlement services, which vary with each deal.

As a rule, buyers do not borrow their closing costs from their lender, though some types of costs can be handled that way. If you pack closing costs into your loan, you increase the amount you're borrowing and the interest you will pay. There are circumstances when this is a sensible strategy. A borrower has to figure how much cash he will need at closing as part of the process of his self-evaluation of how much debt he can afford.

The last financial factor to consider on loan packages is the tax deductibility of various items. Interest and property taxes are tax deductible on home/second-home mortgages, subject to certain limits. Points and origination fees are also deductible on home mortgages, but lender fees and other settlement costs are not. If, on the other hand, you are taking out a mortgage on country property as an investment or for a business purpose, then everything should be tax-deductible. Since your mortgage's interest is front-loaded, your benefit from its deductibility is disproportionately high at the beginning of the note's term and disproportionately low at its end. The degree of your tax benefit depends on your income level and the amount of your annual interest payment. Most middle-income taxpayers will be able to deduct all the mortgage interest paid from their gross income. (See discussion below.)

My experience is that credit unions and locally owned, small rural banks impose lower closing costs than the big banks.

There is no single upfront-costs-to-interest-rate formula that is always best for every borrower in all circumstances, because the final cost of every loan to every borrower depends on the individual's circumstances and how long the loan is held. Certainly, low costs with a low interest rate is a good initial target, except when it's bait to get you into an adjustable-rate mortgage with unfavorable terms. If you start with a higher interest rate and low closing costs, you can wait for an interest-rate dip and then refinance. Closing costs are dollars lost forever. You can erode some of the pain of high interest rates by pre-paying principal as long as your lender allows pre-payment without penalty. As I write in 2006, the mortgage rate has been eight percent or less for a decade—relatively low historically. A fixed-rate mortgage for 30 years at five or six percent is a good deal, assuming, of course, you can make the payments. (A no-interest, no-cost mortgage is a bad deal if you can't.)

The interest rates offered by lenders reflect interest rates in the national economy, which are set by financial markets, speculation and politics. The mortgage interest rate—the interest on a 30-year fixed-rate mortgage—tracks the ten-year Treasury yield and the yield on 30-year Treasury bonds. The mortgage interest rate has been running about 1.4 points higher than the ten-year Treasury yield for about 18 months. In June, 2005, the ten-year Treasury yield was about 4.26 percent and the mortgage interest rate (on a 30-year fixed-rate note) was 5.65 percent. When demand increases for bonds in financial markets, their prices rise and their yields go down. In bond terms, yield represents the interest rate paid on a bond after taking purchase price into account. When yields on bonds and Treasuries fall, mortgage interest rates should rise. But in 2004 to mid-2005, this expected relationship did not materialize. In fact, the opposite occurred: the ten-year Treasury yield slid and so did the mortgage interest rate. And the mortgage rate declined at the same time the Federal Reserve was raising its Federal Funds interest rate, which, according to conventional wisdom, should have had the effect of boosting the mortgage interest rate. Countervailing factors were at work. I include this contrarian information to caution readers about trying to be too clever by half in predicting interest-rate trends. Anytime you can borrow for 30 years for less than seven percent with two points or less, that's a package worth considering.

Buyers of country property should ask lenders specifically about a **land loan**, in addition to fixed-rate mortgages and ARMs. Community-minded lenders in rural areas may offer one, because they want to encourage the purchase of unimproved land for agriculture, timber production and subsequent construction. If your target property has a house (improvement) on it, it may not qualify for a land loan. A second complicating factor is that your lender may try to shift your land-acquisition loan to a business loan (with a higher interest rate) if you are setting up the property as an investment or business. It's worth asking about land loans because their terms are usually borrower-friendly. The community credit union I belong to offered the following types of loans in May, 2005 that could be used for buying country property:

ARM (1 year/80% LTV)	30 year term	4.26% (for 1 year)
ARM (1 year-90% LTV)	30-year term	4.76% (for 1 year)
ARM (3 year-80% LTV)	30-year term	5.51% (for 3 years)
ARM (3 year-90% LTV)	30-year term	6.01% (for 3 years)
ARM (5/1 year-90% LTV)	30-year term	5.26% (for five years)
ARM (5/1 year-100% LTV)	30-year term	6.51% (for five years)
ARM (7/1 year-90% LTV)	30-year term	5.76% (for seven years)
Land Loan (80% LTV)	20-year term	4.51% (for 20 years)
Land Loan (90% LTV)	20-year term	5.01% (for 20 years)

A 5/1 ARM means that the starting interest rate is fixed for five years, after which it is adjusted at one-year intervals. All the ARMs carried a minimum interest-rate "floor" of 1.5 percent. I found it interesting that this credit union no longer offered the standard 30-year fixed-rate mortgage. The longest fixed-rate "products" were the 20-year land loans at rates between about 0.5 percent and one percent below the then-current 5.65 percent mortgage rate on a 30-year fixed bank mortgage. The credit union charged neither points nor an origination fee. Closing costs were reasonable. The land loan was my best deal, and the credit union was the best lender I found when I shopped for one.

You may also benefit during your lender shopping from asking whether each lender might make an exception or modification to its offered terms. You might, for example, ask the lender to set up a 30-year amortization schedule rather than the offered 20. If that sticks, propose a 30-year schedule for the first five years after which the monthly payment is increased to pay off the note in 20 years. Or you might propose paying an extra point or two to get a lower interest rate on a fixed-rate loan, which makes sense if you know that you will hold the note for 20 or 30 years.

No deal is any good if you can't afford it. Remember that ARMs are crapshoots. If you start an ARM when interest rates are historically low, the odds are that your rate will rise. Nonetheless, the percentage of new home loans using ARMs is now almost 50 percent. Interest-only ARMs, whose monthly payments don't include principal, are even riskier. Lenders have been willing to make borrowing easier in an appreciating real-estate market because of competition among them and because foreclosure protects their money. Every borrower needs to be alert for the scam outfits who offer *really* easy terms with payment plans that beckon from the outer limit of your ability to pay. These thieves want the borrower to default so that they can foreclose, sell the property and grab the borrower's equity as ill-gotten profit. The rip-off now has a name, **equity stripping**. Never stretch your ability to pay a mortgage to buy country property no matter how good the deal is.

Interest-only loans are increasingly popular, but they involve far more risk of borrower failure if income doesn't rise. An IO gives the borrower a fixed monthly payment for a certain period, say five years, that only pays the lender interest. With a 30-year amortization schedule, the last 25 years is set up to repay both principal and interest with a new fixed monthly payment. The rescheduled monthly payment will be higher than the first, because all of the principal will be packaged into a repayment plan set up for 25 years, rather than 30. Crenshaw provided the following example: a $300,000 loan at five percent would have a $1,250 monthly payment for its first five years and a $1,754 payment for the next 25 years. (Crenshaw, "Interest Only," Washington Post, June 15, 2005.) If the borrower's income has not risen sufficiently, default follows. An IO can work to the borrower's benefit on second-home and country property, particularly where the borrower plans to sell an asset to pay down acquisition debt or the borrower has the means to pay off the note by the end of the IO's first phase.

While you are evaluating lenders, you should already have evaluated yourself as your lender will. This self-evaluation will give you a rough idea in advance of how much additional debt the lender thinks you can carry. Use the same two guidelines a lender will apply. First, the lender will follow the rule that your monthly housing cost (mortgage, property taxes, insurance and homeowner-association fees if applicable) should not exceed 28 percent of your monthly, pre-tax gross income. Second, the lender will say that all of your long-term monthly debt (housing costs plus car payments, student loans and other installment debt) should not exceed 36 percent of your monthly, pre-tax gross income. These rules are applied to your recent income history, which may or may not predict your income prospects. If your income is going up on a predictable basis, you might consider arguing for a larger loan. If the lender is keeping the loan in his own portfolio, he may have more flexibility than if he intends to sell it. If, on the other hand, you are either self-employed or otherwise decoupled from a regular paycheck, the lender will insist on compliance with his guidelines.

TABLE 32-1 plots interest rates against income to show the loan amount an individual is likely to be offered. This TABLE assumes that the interest rate is fixed for the entire loan term and that borrower income remains the same. It was constructed using a 25 percent rule, rather than 28 percent, to account for taxes, insurance and other costs the borrower has to pay. The dollar amounts in TABLE 32-1 represent the maximum loan amount you should consider assuming at each interest rate for your income level.

TABLE 32-2 provides a quick-and-simple reference for determining a borrower's monthly payment of principal and interest for a 30-year, fixed-rate mortgage at different interest rates for various amounts of principal.

TABLE 32-1

Feasible Mortgage Amounts, By Interest Rate and Annual Income

INTEREST RATES	ANNUAL INCOME											
	$15,000	$20,000	$25,000	$30,000	$35,000	$40,000	$45,000	$50,000	$55,000	$60,000	$65,000	$70,000
5.5%	$55,000	$73,400	$91,700	$110,100	$128,400	$146,800	$165,100	$183,500	$201,800	$220,200	$238,500	$256,800
6.0%	52,100	69,500	86,900	104,200	121,600	139,000	156,400	173,700	191,100	208,500	225,900	243,200
6.5%	49,400	65,900	82,400	98,800	115,300	131,800	148,300	164,800	181,300	197,700	214,200	230,700
7.0%	47,000	62,600	78,300	93,900	109,600	125,300	140,900	156,600	172,300	187,900	203,600	219,200
7.5%	44,600	59,600	74,500	89,400	104,300	119,200	134,100	149,000	163,900	178,800	193,700	208,600
8.0%	42,600	56,700	70,900	85,100	99,300	113,500	127,700	141,900	156,100	170,300	184,500	198,700
8.5%	40,600	54,100	67,700	81,200	94,800	108,300	121,900	135,400	149,000	162,500	176,100	189,600
9.0%	38,800	51,700	64,700	77,700	90,600	103,500	116,500	129,400	142,400	155,300	168,200	181,200
9.5%	37,200	49,500	61,900	74,300	86,700	99,100	111,400	123,800	136,200	148,600	161,000	173,400

■ *Interest Rate*   □ *Annual Income*   □ *Mortgage Amount*

Assumes a 30-year, fixed-rate mortgage. This TABLE uses a 25 percent ratio of mortgage debt to income, with an additional three percent allocated for taxes and insurance. The typical lender ratio is 28 percent.

SOURCE: Fannie Mae Foundation, "Opening the Door to a Home of Your Own," 2001, p. 16.

TABLE 32-2

Monthly Mortgage Payments, By Interest Rate and Loan Amount

LOAN AMOUNT	INTEREST RATES								
	5.5%	6%	6.5%	7%	7.5%	8%	8.5%	9%	9.5%
$20,000	$114	$120	$126	$133	$140	$147	$154	$161	$168
25,000	142	150	158	166	175	183	192	201	210
30,000	170	180	190	200	210	220	231	241	252
35,000	199	210	221	233	245	257	269	282	294
40,000	227	240	253	266	280	294	308	322	336
45,000	256	270	284	299	315	330	346	362	378
50,000	284	300	316	333	350	367	384	402	420
55,000	312	330	348	366	385	404	423	443	462
60,000	341	360	380	399	420	440	461	483	505
65,000	369	390	411	432	454	477	500	523	547
70,000	397	420	442	466	489	514	538	563	589
75,000	426	450	474	499	524	550	577	603	631
80,000	454	480	506	532	559	587	615	644	673
85,000	483	510	537	566	594	624	654	684	715
90,000	511	540	569	599	629	660	692	724	757
95,000	539	570	600	632	664	697	730	764	799
100,000	568	600	632	665	699	734	769	805	841

▨ *Loan Amount*   □ *Interest Rate*   □ *Monthly Payment*

Assumes a 30-year, fixed-rate mortgage. Monthly payments do not include Taxes and homeowner's insurance.

SOURCE: Fannie Mae Foundation, "Opening the Door to a Home of Your Own," 2001, p. 12.

More sophisticated **loan calculators** are available in book form and on the Internet. (See Delphi Information Sciences Corporation, The Loan Calculator: Monthly Amortization Loan Schedule [Chicago: Contemporary Books, Inc., current edition]; Robert de Heer, Realty Bluebook: Financial Tables [Chicago: Real Estate Education Company, 1995, or current edition]; www.eloan.com; www.LendingTree.com; www.mrtgprofessor.com; and www.moneycentral.com, among others.)

You can calculate monthly payment amounts for common interest rates and terms, using the mortgage factor table below.

TABLE 32-3

Monthly Mortgage Payment Estimator

<table>
<tr><td rowspan="2">How To Use This Chart</td><td rowspan="2">Rate</td><td>Term</td><td>Term</td><td>Term</td><td>Term</td><td>Term</td></tr>
<tr><td>10 Years</td><td>15 Years</td><td>20 Years</td><td>25 Years</td><td>30 Years</td></tr>
<tr><td rowspan="40">To use this chart, start by finding the appropriate interest rate. Then follow that row over to the column for the appropriate loan term. This number is the interest rate factor required each month to amortize a $1,000 loan. To calculate the principal and interest (PI) payment, multiply the interest rate factor by the number of 1,000s in the total loan.

For example, if the interest rate is 10 percent for a term of 30 years, the interest rate factor is 8.78. If the total loan is $100,000, the loan contains 100 1,000s. Therefore

100 × 8.78 = $878 PI
only

To estimate a mortgage loan amount using the amortization chart, divide the PI payment by the appropriate interest rate factor. Using the same facts as in the first example:

$878 ÷ 8.78 = $100
1,000's, or $100,000</td><td>4</td><td>10.13</td><td>7.40</td><td>6.06</td><td>5.28</td><td>4.78</td></tr>
<tr><td>4⅛</td><td>10.19</td><td>7.46</td><td>6.13</td><td>5.35</td><td>4.85</td></tr>
<tr><td>4¼</td><td>10.25</td><td>7.53</td><td>6.20</td><td>5.42</td><td>4.92</td></tr>
<tr><td>4⅜</td><td>10.31</td><td>7.59</td><td>6.26</td><td>5.49</td><td>5.00</td></tr>
<tr><td>4½</td><td>10.37</td><td>7.65</td><td>6.33</td><td>5.56</td><td>5.07</td></tr>
<tr><td>4⅝</td><td>10.43</td><td>7.72</td><td>6.40</td><td>5.63</td><td>5.15</td></tr>
<tr><td>4¾</td><td>10.49</td><td>7.78</td><td>6.47</td><td>5.71</td><td>5.22</td></tr>
<tr><td>4⅞</td><td>10.55</td><td>7.85</td><td>6.54</td><td>5.78</td><td>5.30</td></tr>
<tr><td>5</td><td>10.61</td><td>7.91</td><td>6.60</td><td>5.85</td><td>5.37</td></tr>
<tr><td>5⅛</td><td>10.67</td><td>7.98</td><td>6.67</td><td>5.92</td><td>5.45</td></tr>
<tr><td>5¼</td><td>10.73</td><td>8.04</td><td>6.74</td><td>6.00</td><td>5.53</td></tr>
<tr><td>5⅜</td><td>10.80</td><td>8.11</td><td>6.81</td><td>6.07</td><td>5.60</td></tr>
<tr><td>5½</td><td>10.86</td><td>8.18</td><td>6.88</td><td>6.15</td><td>5.68</td></tr>
<tr><td>5⅝</td><td>10.92</td><td>8.24</td><td>6.95</td><td>6.22</td><td>5.76</td></tr>
<tr><td>5¾</td><td>10.98</td><td>8.31</td><td>7.03</td><td>6.30</td><td>5.84</td></tr>
<tr><td>5⅞</td><td>11.04</td><td>8.38</td><td>7.10</td><td>6.37</td><td>5.92</td></tr>
<tr><td>6</td><td>11.10</td><td>8.44</td><td>7.16</td><td>6.44</td><td>6.00</td></tr>
<tr><td>6⅛</td><td>11.16</td><td>8.51</td><td>7.24</td><td>6.52</td><td>6.08</td></tr>
<tr><td>6¼</td><td>11.23</td><td>8.57</td><td>7.31</td><td>6.60</td><td>6.16</td></tr>
<tr><td>6⅜</td><td>11.29</td><td>8.64</td><td>7.38</td><td>6.67</td><td>6.24</td></tr>
<tr><td>6½</td><td>11.35</td><td>8.71</td><td>7.46</td><td>6.75</td><td>6.32</td></tr>
<tr><td>6⅝</td><td>11.42</td><td>8.78</td><td>7.53</td><td>6.83</td><td>6.40</td></tr>
<tr><td>6¾</td><td>11.48</td><td>8.85</td><td>7.60</td><td>6.91</td><td>6.49</td></tr>
<tr><td>6⅞</td><td>11.55</td><td>8.92</td><td>7.68</td><td>6.99</td><td>6.57</td></tr>
<tr><td>7</td><td>11.61</td><td>8.98</td><td>7.75</td><td>7.06</td><td>6.65</td></tr>
<tr><td>7⅛</td><td>11.68</td><td>9.06</td><td>7.83</td><td>7.15</td><td>6.74</td></tr>
<tr><td>7¼</td><td>11.74</td><td>9.12</td><td>7.90</td><td>7.22</td><td>6.82</td></tr>
<tr><td>7⅜</td><td>11.81</td><td>9.20</td><td>7.98</td><td>7.31</td><td>6.91</td></tr>
<tr><td>7½</td><td>11.87</td><td>9.27</td><td>8.05</td><td>7.38</td><td>6.99</td></tr>
<tr><td>7⅝</td><td>11.94</td><td>9.34</td><td>8.13</td><td>7.47</td><td>7.08</td></tr>
<tr><td>7¾</td><td>12.00</td><td>9.41</td><td>8.20</td><td>7.55</td><td>7.16</td></tr>
<tr><td>7⅞</td><td>12.07</td><td>9.48</td><td>8.29</td><td>7.64</td><td>7.25</td></tr>
<tr><td>8</td><td>12.14</td><td>9.56</td><td>8.37</td><td>7.72</td><td>7.34</td></tr>
<tr><td>8⅛</td><td>12.20</td><td>9.63</td><td>8.45</td><td>7.81</td><td>7.43</td></tr>
<tr><td>8¼</td><td>12.27</td><td>9.71</td><td>8.53</td><td>7.89</td><td>7.52</td></tr>
<tr><td>8⅜</td><td>12.34</td><td>9.78</td><td>8.60</td><td>7.97</td><td>7.61</td></tr>
<tr><td>8½</td><td>12.40</td><td>9.85</td><td>8.68</td><td>8.06</td><td>7.69</td></tr>
<tr><td>8⅝</td><td>12.47</td><td>9.93</td><td>8.76</td><td>8.14</td><td>7.78</td></tr>
<tr><td>8¾</td><td>12.54</td><td>10.00</td><td>8.84</td><td>8.23</td><td>7.87</td></tr>
<tr><td>8⅞</td><td>12.61</td><td>10.07</td><td>8.92</td><td>8.31</td><td>7.96</td></tr>
<tr><td>9</td><td>12.67</td><td>10.15</td><td>9.00</td><td>8.40</td><td>8.05</td></tr>
<tr><td>9⅛</td><td>12.74</td><td>10.22</td><td>9.08</td><td>8.48</td><td>8.14</td></tr>
<tr><td>9¼</td><td>12.81</td><td>10.30</td><td>9.16</td><td>8.57</td><td>8.23</td></tr>
<tr><td>9⅜</td><td>12.88</td><td>10.37</td><td>9.24</td><td>8.66</td><td>8.32</td></tr>
<tr><td>9½</td><td>12.94</td><td>10.45</td><td>9.33</td><td>8.74</td><td>8.41</td></tr>
<tr><td>9⅝</td><td>13.01</td><td>10.52</td><td>9.41</td><td>8.83</td><td>8.50</td></tr>
<tr><td>9¾</td><td>13.08</td><td>10.60</td><td>9.49</td><td>8.92</td><td>8.60</td></tr>
<tr><td>9⅞</td><td>13.15</td><td>10.67</td><td>9.57</td><td>9.00</td><td>8.69</td></tr>
<tr><td>10</td><td>13.22</td><td>10.75</td><td>9.66</td><td>9.09</td><td>8.78</td></tr>
<tr><td>10⅛</td><td>13.29</td><td>10.83</td><td>9.74</td><td>9.18</td><td>8.87</td></tr>
<tr><td>10¼</td><td>13.36</td><td>10.90</td><td>9.82</td><td>9.27</td><td>8.97</td></tr>
<tr><td>10⅜</td><td>13.43</td><td>10.98</td><td>9.90</td><td>9.36</td><td>9.06</td></tr>
<tr><td>10½</td><td>13.50</td><td>11.06</td><td>9.99</td><td>9.45</td><td>9.15</td></tr>
<tr><td>10⅝</td><td>13.57</td><td>11.14</td><td>10.07</td><td>9.54</td><td>9.25</td></tr>
<tr><td>10¾</td><td>13.64</td><td>11.21</td><td>10.16</td><td>9.63</td><td>9.34</td></tr>
</table>

Monthly mortgage payments includes principal and interest. Does not include other expenses, such as taxes and insurance.

SOURCE: Fillmore W. Galaty, Wellington J. Allaway and Robert C. Kyle, Modern Real Estate Practice, 15th ed. (Chicago, IL: Dearborn Financial Publishing Co./Real Estate Education Company, 2000, p. 231.).

Remember the true cost of your loan includes closing costs; whether these costs are paid upfront or folded into your borrowing; the degree of benefit that you get from the tax deductibility of interest and other costs; and whether you will be expected to pay continuing charges, or premiums, during the term of the loan for, say, mortgage insurance. Any calculation that you use to predict your tax benefit, however, will have to make large assumptions over small to large periods of time regarding future interest rates; your income each year; the absence of economic bad fortune in your life over the term of the loan; your anticipated length of holding the note before paying it off; and federal tax policy. You can make things simple by assuming that for every three dollars in paid home-mortgage interest, you will pay one less dollar in federal income tax each year (subject to two or three dozen qualifications and exceptions that may apply) in the higher tax brackets.

Internet sites that provide mortgage calculators, loan comparisons and useful information include: www.interest.com; www.usatoday.com/money/calculator.htm; www.LendingTree.com; and www.mrtgprofessor.com.

Many loans are now set up as **adjustable-rate mortgages (ARMs)**. They offer a fixed interest rate for, say, one to five years, at which time the rate is reset according to a formula pegged to a pre-determined financial **index,** such as the interest rate on a certain type of Treasury bill (T-bill) plus the lender's **margin**, usually two to three points. At the end of each adjustment period, which can range from a month to ten years, the interest rate is recalculated in light of whatever index your loan is tracking. The lender's margin should stay the same. ARMs, thus, give you a fixed interest rate at the start for some amount of time, and then a fluctuating interest rate for the rest of the term or until you pay it off. Your monthly payment is, accordingly, fixed at the start, after which it can be changed in line with the loan's index. In effect, an ARM is a system of scheduled refinancings of the declining balance of the note at set intervals based on then-current interest rates. But an ARM "refinancing" doesn't cost you anything each time you do it, because the schedule is set up at the time you take out the loan and you pay its costs then. Like fixed-rate mortgages, you choose the length (term) of the loan with an ARM: shorter terms should, in most cases, mean higher monthly payments but less total interest paid; longer terms should have the opposite effect. Since ARMs will undoubtedly carry different interest rates over the loan's term, you cannot compare an ARM's total interest cost to the total interest cost of a fixed-rate loan (which you can calculate precisely).

ARMs always start you off at an interest rate below the typical fixed rate for a 30-year mortgage. Whether an ARM is a better deal than a fixed-rate loan depends on how long you carry the mortgage and the trend in your index. ARMs often carry very low "**teaser rates**" that last for six months to a year, whereupon they are converted to the higher "contract interest rate." A teaser rate is a baited hook, with you as the fish. But a low starting rate that is fixed for a year or two can work to your benefit in buying a rural property whose principal you pay down quickly through the sale of some of its assets. A buyer with this in mind must make sure that the ARM allows him to pre-pay some or all of the loan principal without penalty.

Borrowers should avoid ARMs where the interest rate is adjusted frequently. When an adjustment formula starts adding interest into the principal balance, the borrower ends up paying interest on interest. A financing arrangement whose loan balance is increasing rather than decreasing over the term and whose monthly payments are less than the true amortized amounts, is called **negative amortization**. ARMs can create conditions leading to negative amortization as when the interest rate adjusts more frequently than the borrower's payment or when the index rises faster than the borrower's payment. In these circumstances, the ARM's "locked in" monthly payment for the first years of the note conceals the fact that the interest rate is adjusting upwards monthly, or semi-annually or annually during that period, thus adding unpaid interest into the balance owed. In the worst case with a monthly adjustable and a rapidly rising interest rate, your monthly payment can be less than the interest due that month. Federal law requires that lenders disclose certain information regarding a loan that contains this potential. The only certain way to protect yourself against an ARM or other loan with terms that allow negative amortization is to get written assurance from the lender that it does not. Staple it to your loan documents, and don't lose it. Loan documents are dense and complicated. Don't hesitate to ask your local lawyer to explain each bank's proposal.

It is important to research lenders and their loan terms with care. Don't just compare interest rates. Dig into the details. It is often the case that a lender advertising the lowest interest rate is not the best overall deal. The lender may impose conditions on his lowest rate that only some properties and borrowers can meet. The low rate may be packaged with terms that make the deal unfavorable. The low rate may be limited to borrowers with near-perfect credit scores. The low rate may also carry an assortment of fees and charges that raise your cost of borrowing substantially. If you decide that you can handle an ARM, look at the three-, five- and seven-year packages. Your choice will be shaped by where on the interest-rate-curve the Federal Reserve is when you start the note. A fixed-rate loan always benefits a borrower with rising income, and the fixed monthly payment allows inflation to make it easier for your pocketbook to pay back the note.

If you've decided that you want a fixed interest rate for 20 or 30 years and you hope to be able to pay off the debt in 15, you might have something like the following conversation—conducted with genuine politeness—with the lenders you're interviewing. You will adapt this script to your individual circumstances and the lender's general policies, which should be available on its website.

> I'm shopping around for a loan. I plan to have a talk just like this with Banker B and Banker C this week or next. I want to get a pretty good idea of the best deal you [Banker A] can offer me.
>
> I want to borrow $100,000 for __ years at a fixed interest rate to purchase property that will be your only security. The property is located in ____ County. I'm setting this up as an investment for tax purposes. I'm doing my research on the property now, and I will share with you what I find about the value of its assets and any liabilities or uncertainties. It is ___ is not ____ unimproved land. [If it's improved, state what improvements are on the property. If it's unimproved, state the nature of its physical access and whether or not it's currently serviced by utilities.] The land is currently used for _____, and its tax-assessed value is $_____.
>
> Here is a brief overview of my financials. [Hand him a two-page, typewritten summary of your financial profile on your letterhead.]
>
> > Your name and contact information. Age. SS number. Education. [If you and spouse are applying jointly, include spouse information]
> >
> > Place of employment. Years there. Other major employment experience.
> >
> > Adjusted Gross income [Line 35] from your last two 1040s.
> >
> > Current monthly income, including sources. [Include "est." after figure]
> >
> > Short net worth statement, listing all major assets, all major debts
> >
> > Estimate of future gross income, monthly/annually for next five years
> >
> > Very short explanation of any unusual circumstances bearing on your ability to pay, such as, kids about to go to expensive college, or illness in the family

Equally short explanation of any past payment problems.

Credit report and FICO, if you have them.

The asking price is $110,000, and I plan to make a cash down payment of ten percent of the purchase price.

What is the lowest interest rate you are currently offering on a 90 percent LTV over your longest term? What points and origination fees, if any, do you want to impose on such a loan? How much will it cost me to buy down the rate on this loan to the lowest fixed rate I can get from you?

I want you to help me get into this loan with the least cost at your lowest interest rate.

What is the longest term you routinely offer? Can I get a longer term approved, if I want it?

This property will not be my principal residence now, but it could be in the future. I'm looking for a mortgage, not a personal or business loan.

What debt-to-income requirements must I meet?

Please itemize all charges (types, not dollar amounts) that will be imposed on me. Leave nothing out.

On a $100,000 loan, give me a ballpark estimate of what these closing costs will come to. I realize that this is not a number that will bind you.

Please add up my total cost of borrowing $100,000, including all estimated closing costs, over the term of this loan.

Are you willing to offer me better terms on such a loan than Bank B and Bank C to get my business?

Would you also be interested in financing a house on this land down the road?

I want a loan that does not carry any pre-payment penalties or charges.

The script that you prepare for your initial round of lender shopping will vary according to the particulars of the property and what terms you want. Ask your local lawyer to help you prepare for this negotiation. It may even be to your benefit to have him come along with you.

I've oriented this introductory script around a fixed-rate loan rather than an ARM to encourage you to shop lenders using a comparable loan product each has. Be prepared for a response that inundates you with choices. Don't get sucked into the option miasma where confusion is supposed to govern your judgment. Keep your proposed loan as simple as possible. You will be operating on the assumption that the lender who offers you the best deal on the simplest loan will offer you (at least) a competitive deal on the riskier options. That assumption may not be true, but it's as good a starting point as any.

This script approach is the way I shop for a new Toyota truck from three Toyota dealers. Give each one the exact specifications of the vehicle you want and get each dealer to quote his best price—everything included—for that exact model. Many lenders like many car dealers may try to tack on fees (profit) after quoting you an everything-included price. Resist. When a loan officer quotes you specific loan terms, you should confirm that he is legally authorized to commit the institution. Car salesmen are not "agents" of the dealership and cannot commit the dealership to a deal. The car deal must be done with the sales manager. If you find yourself facing a loan manager renegotiating terms that you've agreed on with the loan officer, walk away from it. You're probably being hustled.

INTEREST RATES

Much of your lender shopping and lender negotiating will involve looking for the lowest **interest rate**. Lenders offer their lowest mortgage rates to borrowers willing to borrow for the shortest terms with adjustable interest. An adjustable-rate mortgage (ARM) that is adjusted every year should carry the lowest interest rate the lender offers, because the lender is offering a low starting out rate to get you into a loan where all risk of interest variability over the loan's term is shifted onto you. This can, however, be a great deal if you are able to pay off the ARM at the end of the first rate-adjustment period. ARM loans are amortized over whatever term you and the lender agree on. The rate is changed at the end of the year (or adjustment period) to reflect changes in the lender's cost of money. Remember that interest rate is only one part of *your* cost of borrowing over the time you have the loan out. If you're looking for a fixed-rate over a specific term, it's easy to compare lenders on the basis of rate and costs. ARMs can be compared on the specifics of each lender's package, but the best you can do is project hypothetical total interest costs based on different assumed future interest rates.

Interest rates vary with the amount of time you want it to be fixed. You will not get to choose how the bank computes interest—and there's the rub.

Institutional lenders say they charge "**simple interest**." Simple interest is calculated with the formula of I = PRT, where I is interest, P is principal, R is rate and T is time. Simple interest could look like this on a $50,000 loan at seven percent for one year:

> I = PRT
> I = $50,000 x .07 x 1
> I = $3,500

This is a fair calculation if you have one payment that you make at the end of the year since you will have the bank's money for the entire 365 days. This is how a seller-held second mortgage is usually figured. If you are making monthly payments of both principal and interest, you should be paying simple interest on the declining balance of the principal. If you are not, you are paying more than seven percent. While banks charge mortgage interest on the declining balance, they rig the process in their favor by front-loading interest. This is not negotiable with your loan officer.

All institutional mortgage notes **front-load interest payments**. Front-loading means that each of your fixed-sum, monthly payments contains a changing ratio of interest to principal, with almost all of your first monthly payment being interest and almost all of your last payment being principal. FIGURE 32-1 provides an approximate trend of the changing ratio of principal to interest payment each year over a 30-year, fixed-payment (or level payment) term. Note that it's not until the 25th year, that the borrower is paying more principal than interest. If you have a 30-year term and you pre-pay the entire note after ten years, you will still owe the lender almost all of the original principal. The interest rate that you've agreed to is true only when the note is paid out over the full term. If you pay on a shortened term, you will end up paying a higher interest rate because of front-loaded interest scheduling. As it is, if you pay the note at 30 years as scheduled, you will end up paying about $3 in interest (depending on the interest rate) for every dollar in original principal. As you might expect, lenders don't feature this aspect of consumer borrowing in their advertising.

FIGURE 32-1

Front-loaded Interest Repayment Schedule

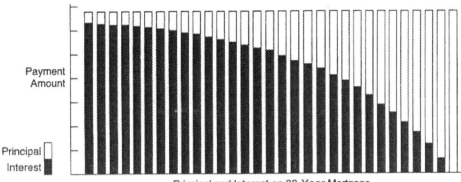

Principal and Interest on 30-Year Mortgage

Calculated on a 30-year, fixed-rate (level-payment) amortization schedule.

SOURCE: Fillmore W. Galaty, Wellington J. Allaway and Robert C. Kyle, Modern Real Estate Practice, 15th ed. (Chicago, IL: Dearborn Financial Publishing Co./Real Estate Education Company, 2000, p. 229.).

You should consider one other wrinkle with front-loaded interest: **balance owed as a ratio of original amount borrowed**. As you know, the amount of principal owed to the lender declines each year during the term of a note. But the rate of decline is faster the lower your interest rate. TABLE 32-4 shows these ratios for six interest rates on a 25-year, fixed-payment note.

TABLE 32-4

Balance Owed as a Ratio of Original Amount for Six Interest Rates on a 25-Year Note

Age

(Years)	5%	6%	7%	8%	9%	10%
1	.979	.982	.985	.987	.989	.990
5	.886	.899	.911	.923	.932	.941
10	.739	.762	.786	.807	.826	.845
15	.550	.578	.608	.635	.659	.686
20	.308	.330	.356	.380	.399	.425
24	.066	.070	.080	.087	.088	.100

SOURCE: William Benke and Joseph M. Fowler, All About Real Estate Investing from the Inside Out (Chicago: Irwin, 1995, p. 190. TABLE 32-4 is excerpted from Appendix A, pp. 183-190.)

At the end of year one, the five percent borrower owes 97.9% of the principal while the ten percent borrower owes 99 percent. At the end of the 24th year, the five percent borrower owes 6.6 percent of the original principal while the ten percent borrower will pay off ten percent of the original loan amount in his last year. The lender's way of calculating front-loaded interest makes it harder for the high-interest-rate borrower to build up equity—just in case you didn't know. And as the term of a note increases, it takes the borrower longer to build up equity at every interest rate; the higher the rate, the harder it is. The borrower gets to 50 percent of principal repaid on a ten-year note at five percent in year five, at ten percent interest in year six. On a 20-year note, the five percent borrower gets to 50 percent principal repaid in year 12; the ten percent interest rate gets there in year 15. On a 30-year note, the five percent borrower gets to 50 percent principal repaid in year 20; the ten percent borrower gets there three years later. The obvious reason for borrowers to search out the lowest fixed-interest rate is to pay as little total interest as possible; now you know a couple of other reasons as well.

One interest trick that you might run into is the **add-on rate**. Some real-estate lenders use it. The lender calculates the interest due on the total principal for the entire term, then adds this sum to the principal owed for you to repay over the loan's term before calculating your fixed monthly payment. The effect of an add-on rate is to almost double the advertised simple interest rate you're being charged. Be particularly watchful for add-on rates with private mortgage companies and with home-improvement loans. Internet lenders might use it too. Lenders sucker borrowers in to add-ons with obviously low advertised rates.

Buyers should determine what is the **truer rate of interest being charged**. The truer rate of interest in my mind is the total cost of borrowing the lender's money expressed as an annual percentage rate. The truer interest rate will be higher than either the **nominal rate** or the **simple interest rate** the lender advertises. Your total cost of borrowing will include the one-time fees and charges that you pay as closing costs, on which you don't pay interest. The truer rate of interest should reflect the cost of borrowing from a lender when all fees and charges are added to the nominal rate, and recalculated as a single percentage rate. This methodology overstates your interest rate, because it includes charges on which you won't actually pay interest. But the approach should end up giving you a valid way of ranking interest-rate offers, despite the built-in inaccuracy. A lender's nominal (advertised) rate will not include the one-time, upfront fees and charges that are imposed as part of your closing costs. You may be able to get each lender to do a truer rate calculation for you, but don't be surprised if you have to do it yourself. I discuss APR (annual percentage rate) below. Your truer interest rate along with the amount of time you have the loan until it is paid off determines your total cost of borrowing.

Most borrowers start their comparison shopping for mortgages by looking at interest rates. The alternative recommended by several consumer-oriented professionals is to start by examining lender closing costs. The latter comparison is difficult at best, and "'...the good-faith estimate is often not sufficiently close to the mark so consumers know what the closing costs will actually be,'" said Allen Fishbein, director of housing policy at the Consumer Federation of America in 2004 after the U.S. Department of Housing and Urban Development refused to reform the disclosure process to provide borrowers with clear, comparable information about closing fees. (Andrea Coombes, "Closing-cost maze: You're on your own," CBS Market Watch, <u>Richmond Times-Dispatch</u>, May 30, 2004.) The good-faith estimate given three days after application is not set in stone, because some costs vary with the actual closing date. Non-lender fees, such as the recording fee and tax, vary with the selling price. Where problems arise in the title search, other costs will increase. It is unreasonable for a borrower to expect that a good-faith estimate will remain unchanged over two or three months, given the uncertainties of getting a purchase to closing. But the lender's fees that appear on the settlement statement should be reasonably close to those the lender estimated in good faith. You can use the good-faith estimate or even the preliminary estimate that lenders may give prior to application for the purpose of calculating your true interest rate.

Lenders are expected to disclose to borrowers the **annual percentage rate (APR)** of interest that they will be charged. This is a central component of a truer rate, as I'm using the idea, but it's not the complete story. One might assume that a borrower could feel confident in comparing one lender's APR with all others, secure in the knowledge that an apple is being compared with other apples. Lenders are not required to factor into their APR certain **"garbage fees,"** including, but not limited to, charges for postage, courier service, review of documents, administration fee, preparation fee, notary fee and other overhead items. I've also read about a warehousing fee, sub-escrow fee, lender-review fee and "miscellaneous fee." I anxiously await a lender adding in fees for loan approval, director compensation and office Christmas party. Lenders rework their fees from time to time, changing names and adding new ones. A first-time borrower might challenge a "miscellaneous fee," but not something as important-sounding as a "sub-escrow fee." Garbage fees and phony costs cut into borrowers twice. First, they are paying for lender overhead that should already be figured into the interest rate and other fees. And second, lenders pad these fees which they shouldn't be charging in the first place. The amount of garbage fees will vary from lender to lender, which can make a decision based on an APR to APR comparison misleading. Not all lenders, of course, charge garbage fees or pad the fees they do charge.

Three federal appeals courts have ruled that the federal Department of Housing and Urban Development cannot prevent lenders, title companies, mortgage brokers, escrow agents and others that facilitate real-estate settlements from **marking up fees** far beyond their actual costs. (Kenneth R. Harney, "Another court rebuffs HUD's junk fee rules," Richmond Times-Dispatch, February 2, 2003.) The appeals courts upheld a $55 courier-service fee to the borrower that cost the lender $15; $350 for a part-computer, part-drive-by appraisal that cost less than $50; and a $65 credit-check fee that cost only $9. These anti-consumer decisions cover 15 states, and the Supreme Court is likely to uphold this line of argument unless Congress specifically empowers HUD to limit fee padding. The 15 states, as I write in mid-2005, that allow lenders to mark up loan charges without limit are Maryland, Virginia, North and South Carolina, West Virginia, Illinois, Iowa, Wisconsin, Indiana, Minnesota, Missouri, Arkansas, Nebraska and North and South Dakota. The no-mark-up states are Florida, Georgia, Alabama, New York, Connecticut, Vermont and New Jersey. The situation is in limbo in most other places until Congress or the U.S. Supreme Court decides the issue, which has split appellate courts. In the 15 no-limit states, mark-up fees can cost a borrower hundreds of dollars for nothing. The federal government's position has been that mark ups without additional services should be prohibited.

One alternative to dancing with the fee thieves is to find a so-called **"zero-cost mortgage,"** in which all lender fees are bundled into the interest rate, except for title-insurance. The lender does not offer the borrower a package of lender fees, points and other costs inasmuch as the package is incorporated into the rate. This differs from the fixed-fee cost packages that Ditech.com and ABN-AMRO Mortgage Corp. offer. Bank of America is offering a zero-cost primary mortgage for home buyers; it should be arguable that its "Mortgage Rewards" program be available for rural second homes as well as rural property. If you are a Bank of America customer, you may be able to save as much 40 percent on closing costs through this program. (Kenneth Harney, "Fee simple: Mortgage giant streamlines a loan," Richmond Times-Dispatch, May 8, 2005.)

Most ripped-off borrowers grumble and pay, inasmuch as it's a one-time rip-off and the cost of suing is not worth the effort and money at issue. They walk out of their closing feeling cheated and violated, and rightly so. The individual's only chance to contain this thievery in the no-limit states (4th, 7th and 8th federal appeals circuits) is to force lenders to reveal the costs they pay for services, such as appraisals, overnighting mail, documents, credit checks, electronic house evaluations, etc., against the amounts they will charge you to pay for these services. This needs to be done when lenders are competing for your business. If these costs suggest padding, ask your friendly loan officer in a no-limit state when he is in his friendly mode (that is, when he's trying to get your business) if he has any problem with allowing you to pay the actual cost of each required service plus a ten percent mark up. A fee-padding lender will be reluctant to agree to a reduction in his padded fees, but a ten percent sweetener might work. Shame, I think, is your only realistic leverage, but don't count on it working. Ask the loan officer why the lender should pad a cost that you are fully paying. Don't personalize this discussion or be hostile. Frame your questions in terms of simply trying to learn what that lender will charge you *altogether* to borrow money, and why.

I would ask the lender for a full disclosure of **all fees and estimated settlement costs** during your first or second interview with a loan officer. Together, fees and costs averaged $3,562 on a $180,000 mortgage in 2004 according to a www.Bankrate.com survey. (Consumer Reports, "Your Home: How to protect your biggest investment," May, 2005). This is your most opportune moment to use the leverage of your potential business to free your loan from the lender's add-ons and padding. Consumer Reports recommends that a borrower "compare, haggle, challenge." Ask for the **preliminary estimate** while you're sitting in front of the loan officer; tell him you understand that it's approximate, a reasonable approximation that should be pretty close all the same. At that time, ask him to estimate your true interest rate based on all fees/costs on which you will be paying interest. Whether or not you get an answer, you will at least have put a shot across the lender's bow that you will be scrutinizing his offered loan package and shopping for the best one. More likely than not, you will end up comparing loan terms from each lender in two tiers: APR against APR, and all other costs against all other costs.

Even though most APRs don't include all costs, they are the handiest way to start comparing interest rates from various lenders. (Remember that the APR alone is only part of what determines a loan's cost to a borrower over the term and what the true interest rate is.) Each lender's APR will be a bit higher than the nominal (advertised) rate, because it includes pre-paid finance charges. These have the effect of reducing the principal that you're borrowing, which, in turns, boosts your APR over the nominal rate. But your truer rate—sometimes defined as a borrower's **effective interest rate;** the rate you actually pay—folds in all of the lender's charges that you pay to get the mortgage. That rate you have to figure yourself, from loan to loan and lender to lender.

Every APR that you are shown, in addition, is calculated over the full term of the note. If you pay off before the term, as almost all mortgage holders do, your true/effective interest rate will be higher than the stated APR. Johnson shows that a nominal interest rate of exactly ten percent with the borrower paying one percent in pre-paid finance charges amounts to a projected APR of 10.123 percent—the publicized APR—only over the full 30 years. If the borrower holds the note for five years, the effective interest rate is 10.2 percent; four years, 10.25 percent; three years, 10.33 percent; two years, 10.5 percent; and one year, 11 percent. (Johnson, Save Thousands, pp. 132-133.) If pre-paid finance charges are identical among the lenders you're interviewing, then comparing APRs is a good starting point. But APRs alone do not provide sufficient information about the cost of borrowing for valid comparisons. The true/effective interest rate of each lender's loan package (interest rate plus all costs, fees, charges, etc.), not the nominal interest rate or the APR, is what you want to calculate. And that true/effective interest rate requires that you use the number of months you expect to hold the loan, because term length changes the rate you wind up paying.

You can now see that projections are murky on both sides of the lender-borrower relationship when a borrower is trying to make a true-rate calculation to obtain the cheapest loan cost. Lenders are not likely to give you a true rate, because they don't want you to know it. The only lender whose self-interest is advanced by full disclosure and comparison shopping is the one offering the lowest true rate. All the others are higher; hence, they're likely to be less helpful. But on the borrower's side, it may be impossible to predict when you will pay off the loan. And if you can't do that, you can't figure your true rate for comparisons among lenders.

If you find yourself in this familiar muddy muddle, do the best you can. Get from each lender a reasonable estimate of all the costs of the loan, then compute your truer rate from each lender over a fixed term of your choosing. Your CPA can do these calculations for you. If you're working with an ARM or a no-interest loan, you can't project your truer interest rate, because it's impossible to predict the rates you will be charged at each adjustment period. So work up a worst-case future where your interest rate is increased one half of one percent each year over the 15 years you expect to be in the loan, a middle case where the rate goes up by one quarter of one percent each year, and an optimistic case where the rate rises one tenth of one percent each year. Your chances are greater for paying higher interest rates over an ARM's term if you start the loan when interest rates are historically low, and vice versa.

It's fair for you to ask each loan officer you interview to calculate your total cost of borrowing and your true/effective interest rate (based on that total cost) over both the full term of the note and the period that you estimate you will hold it. Don't be surprised if he says he can't—a revealing admission, if nothing else. He may say "it's against policy" to do these calculations, or that too many costs are unknown for him to project an accurate estimate. Push him a bit. Make him feel a bit guilty and defensive in hope that you can get disclosure on other information you're requesting. It will help to have had your CPA do these estimated calculations before you start interviewing lenders.

You should ask every mortgage lender to print out for you an **amortization schedule** for the **loan terms** you are considering. These would be based on the length of the term in number of months and interest rate if it is fixed. The **amortization print out** should show the break down of how each of your fixed monthly payments is divided between interest and principal. From the amortization schedule, you will be able to determine how much principal remains to be paid at any month during the term of your fixed-rate mortgage. The sooner you can pay off principal, the less interest you will pay. That is why many real-estate writers advise borrowers to make one extra principal-only payment every year if possible. (This principal-only payment must be clearly designated as "principal only," otherwise the bank may use it for interest. And your note must permit pre-payment without penalty.) Such a strategy gets you out of a 30-year mortgage at about 22 years, with a goodly saving in interest. Be aware that the amortization schedule you are handed will use an interest rate that does not include points and fees that you will be charged. Your actual cost of borrowing will be higher than the amortization schedule's interest rate. Amortize, incidentally, contains the root "mort"—familiar to us in words such as "mortality," "mortician" and "mortgage." Amortize means "to kill slowly over time." Make sure that it is your debt that is killed slowly and not you by paying more than you can afford.

Adjustable-rate mortgages (ARMs) are not generally not considered a predatory-lending practice, but they can be foreclosure traps waiting to be sprung. An adjustable-rate mortgage changes the interest rate on your remaining loan balance at scheduled times in the future. What adjusts is the amount of money that you pay during the next payment period, and the period after that. Your interest rate will be revisited at the beginning of each payment period in relationship to whichever financial benchmark your lender is using. In the worst case, the total cost of paying back your loan over its amortized term can double. Special caution must be exercised when you take out an ARM during a period of low interest rates. The up-down cycle of interest rates will be working against you; anticipate paying higher rates deeper into the term. Always insist on having the lender show you the worst case for you under his ARM—the fully indexed rate. If you cannot afford that rate, don't borrow the money.

ARMs change your interest rate according to some public economic or money-related index, such as the one- or five-year Treasury Bill (T-Bill) Rate or the Federal Reserve Discount Rate. The lender will adjust your rate periodically and automatically according to a set schedule that you choose when you first borrow the money. The months/years between resettings is called the "adjustment interval." If you are comparing ARMs among lenders, your best bet for a long-term note is to take the one whose interest rate is tied to the **slowest-moving index**, except, of course, if the starting rate is above the stratosphere. If you have to jump in at 16 percent, which some did in the early 1980s, you had to assume that rates would go down. In that case, a fast-moving index and a short adjustment interval would have helped, and a 30-year fixed rate would have been ruinous over the full term. Refinancing a high fixed-rate is the borrower's best option, but refinancing usually involves additional, upfront costs. The six-month T-bill index and the one-year Treasury securities index are the fastest roller-coasters in this park. If interest rates are high and likely to decline, you could shop for one of them on a note of a couple of years. The three-year Treasury securities index is the usual borrower choice when rates are likely to rise. The longer Treasury indexes—five and ten years—are the slowest moving; if you're getting in when interest rates are low, consider them. The National Mortgage (NACR) Interest Rate Index moves slowly, because it is an average rate charged on previously occupied homes. The Eleventh District Cost of Funds Index and the London Interbank Offered Rate (LIBOR) also move slowly.

The lender's ARM rate will be set according to his chosen index rate plus the lender-added **margin** or "**spread**," which is a fixed percentage or ratio established at the time you agreed to borrow the money. The lender's cost of money approximates the index rate, and the margin represents the lender's business costs and profit. The formula that you are offered might be something like the "prime (interest) rate + two points." That formula covers the lender's cost of money and his spread. If prime is five percent, you will pay the lender seven percent during the next period on your principal. The smaller the lender's margin, the less you pay over the life of your loan. The lender's margin should not change during the entire term of the loan. If you take out an ARM with a 30-year amortization schedule, your index never changes; your lender's formula never changes; your formula never changes; but your monthly payment will go up and down according to the interest rate of your index when adjustments are made.

There are three types of **caps** (or ceilings) that you should look for with ARMs. A **periodic cap**, or **rate cap**, imposes a limit on the interest rate to which an ARM can rise over a period of time. A commonly used periodic cap is two percent, which means the lender can't raise your interest rate more than two percent in any one adjustment period. A **payment cap** imposes a ceiling on the amount you will be expected to pay in any one mortgage payment. A **life-time cap** means the lender can't raise your interest rate by more than a certain specified number of percentage points over the term of the loan. This is often packaged as something like a "2-and-6 cap," under which the maximum upward rate adjustment during any one period is a two percentage point increase (e.g., from a three percent interest rate to a five percent rate) and the maximum rate increase over the life of the loan is nine percent. Using these numbers, the worst case for this ARM is that you pay a nine percent rate over most of the loan. If you're planning to pay off a note quickly, look for a low interest rate ARM with as few fees and points as you can find. When considering ARMs, compare the cap packages from each lender.

Beware of **teaser interest rates** in bait-and-switch ARMs. A teaser rate is one that is two or three points below the prevailing range of rates that most lenders are offering. It is fixed for a few months or a year, then "upgrades" to an adjustable rate, often with one or more high caps. The purpose of a teaser rate is to get you into what will soon amount to a very favorable, low-risk, high-profit loan for the lender. The bait is the below-market rate for the introductory period; the switch is into a variable rate in which you bear all the risk and cost.

A final word on interest rates. Institutional lenders are smart about loan terms, particularly interest rates. It is how they make a lot of their money. They are way smarter than I am, and probably smarter about their business than you. Their objectives are to make money from each mortgage loan with as little work as possible and to strip as much risk out of their lending as they can. You can reasonably expect of yourself to weed out the worst deals. But it's difficult to find the single best deal if only because you cannot predict your own future.

You can start sorting through lenders by finding the loan packages with the fewest of your dollars required in upfront fees, points and costs. Then compare the total cost of interest over the term of the loan, if you want a fixed rate. If you're shopping for an ARM, you have more variables to compare—rates, caps, adjustment periods and so on. Make sure that the property alone is securing the loan and that no pre-payment penalty exists. Have your short list of possible lenders give you good-faith estimates of their closing costs in writing. Ask to see a **remaining balance** table, which shows how much principal remains to be paid at your rate for various years during the note's term. You can get this table for both fixed-rate loans and ARMs, but the interest you will pay on the ARM cannot be predicted. You still may not be able to compare apples with apples, but these requests will at least get you into the produce section.

When you have advanced your conversation with your top pick to the point where you ask for the **full disclosure statement** (mortgage lenders are required to provide certain disclosures within three days after application which describe closing costs, origination fees, "effective interest rate" and whether or not the lender might sell your loan), also ask for a copy of the note you will be expected to sign. Read this document. If particular language troubles you, ask the loan officer to explain how the lender applies those words. I doubt that you can get troublesome language deleted, but at least you can get a sense of how and when it is used against borrowers. You may want to have a lawyer review the loan documents if they scare you. Mortgaging your life is a scary proposition, and the risk of calamity—along with its awful pain—is on you, not the lender.

If you are proposing to have the seller finance a portion of the purchase through a second mortgage, you will need to negotiate loan terms and particularly the interest rate with him. When a seller finances all or part of a purchase, the note is often called a **purchase-money mortgage**.

Be careful that both you and the seller have the same idea about the amount of interest you will be paying. Let's say the seller agrees to take back a second mortgage at seven percent interest. What does that mean? Is it seven percent on the original principal you're borrowing from the seller, or seven percent on the declining balance? If you have three payments on a three-year $45,000 second, your schedule could look like this:

Seven Percent Interest Paid on Original Balance

Principal = $45,000
Payment 1: $15,000 plus 7 percent of $45,000 = $3,150
Payment 2: $15,000 plus 7 percent of $45,000 = $3,150
Payment 3: $15,000 plus 7 percent of $45,000 = $3,150
Total: $45,000 principal, plus $9,450 in interest = $54,450.

This format amounts to an interest payment of 21 percent of the principal.

The alternative is this:

Seven Percent Interest Paid on Declining Balance

Principal = $45,000
Payment 1: $15,000 plus 7 percent of $45,000 = $3,150
Payment 2: $15,000 plus 7 percent of $30,000 = $2,100
Payment 3: $15,000 plus 7 percent of $15,000 = $1,050
Total: $45,000 plus $6,300 in interest = $51,300.

This format amounts to an interest payment of 14 percent. Interest is usually paid on the declining balance, as in this example.

It's possible that you can negotiate a seven percent note for three years where you pay only $3,150 in interest (that is, seven percent of $45,000) at the end of three years, along with all $45,000 in principal. That would be a very good deal. You could work the same interest payment while making three equal installment payments of $15,000 each in principal.

In sum, buyers should look for a loan with the **lowest truest interest rate**, consistent with a borrower's other objectives and needs. A low interest rate that is fixed for a long time is usually best for most borrowers as long as it carries no penalty for pre-payment of principal or early pay off. A long term—20 years or more—means a low monthly payment. The longer the term, the more total interest a borrower will pay.

PITCHING AND HITTING

Once you narrow the field to a couple of lenders, you might want to submit a full **financial profile** with each loan application. This profile expands the summary that you gave the loan officer when you were interviewing. Your profile puts you in front of the lender voluntarily and in your own format. It is your first step toward having a lender **pre-approve you for the maximum amount that he is willing to lend you at a specific rate and set of terms**. The lender will probably ask you to fill out his own form. Nonetheless, you establish confidence in your application and credibility by submitting an accurate profile of your own design before being asked. Don't be obscure or dishonest. After reviewing your application, the lender will tell you the amount of mortgage for which you are pre-approved. **Pre-approval is what you ultimately seek, not pre-qualification**. Pre-approval means you will get the money; pre-qualifying is less certain. Pre-qualification gives the borrower a ballpark idea of what the lender may lend, based on the information submitted. It does not bind the lender to give a particular amount, or even anything at all. Negotiating for a pre-qualification amount is not dissimilar to negotiating with a dealer's salesperson over the price of a car—in both cases, the number may or may not mean something. In your shopping for a lender, pre-qualification gets you started, which is good enough during your lender-selection phase.

Your financial profile should set forth in sufficient detail your ability to borrow the sum you want. "Ability to borrow" means the ability to repay the note over its term. You don't want to try to borrow more than your financials show that you can feasibly repay. "Stretching" of that sort gives lenders the willies and compromises the credibility you're trying to establish. Worse, if the lender gives you more than you can handle, it puts you at a high risk of loss. Review your profile as a lender would. You want to make it easy for the lender to verify your statements. Therefore, provide copies of account statements, pay stubs, 1040s and other documents. Provide all relevant financial and employment information, including:

1. Contact information and profile.

    a. Name, address, phone, fax and e-mail of the applicant (s). (Be consistent in using your name. Don't be R. Frederick Balderdash, III on your SS card, Frederick Balderdash on your credit cards, and Fast Freddy Balderdash on your checks. If you have multiple names, so to speak, note them on your profile.)

    b. Social security number of applicant (s).

    c. Name, address, phone of employer. If self-employed, state place of business, nature of business and how many years so employed.

    d. Age, marital status, number and age of financially-dependent children.

    e. Brief history: place of birth, education, short employment history, military service, licenses (work-related).

    f. Credit report, FICO score, if you have them.

    g. Immigrant status and nationality, if relevant.

2. Summary statement of your net worth (which is all your debts subtracted from all of your assets). Group your assets and itemize them:

1 Assets	2 FMV	Net Worth, Date 3 Debt	(2-3) Net Worth

Real Property
  Personal residence
  Rental property
  Non-rental Investment property

Personal Property
  Vehicles
  Boats/Planes
  Household (lump sum)
  Special stuff—artwork, jewelry

Financial resources
  Stocks/bonds/future contracts/options/CDs
  Cash
  Savings accounts
  Checking accounts
  Retirement accounts/Social Security
  Life insurance/annuities
  Receivables
  Other

Other
  Personal loans
  College loans
  Business loans
  Credit card debt (other than current)
  Tax obligations (out of the ordinary)*
  Alimony/child support
  Future income expected
    Trust fund
    Inheritance
    Don't include hoped-for winnings in the lottery.

  * If you are self-employed and have set up a dedicated tax-escrow
    savings account, don't count that as a liquid asset. It's obligated.

A net-worth statement for assets carrying debt is set up in three columns. The first column is Fair Market Value (FMV) of the asset. Assets should be included at their gross fair market value. On items like real estate, pencil in your best estimate of current market value. Higher values are better than lower values as long as the higher value is credible and established in a defensible way. A more conservative approach would be to use the tax-assessed values of your property, which are, generally, lower than current FMV. If you have current appraisals, include them. Don't inflate asset values, especially items such as cars that the lender can check in his Blue Book. If you have separate appraisals to show the value of discrete assets that are part of your real estate—such as a building or merchantable timber—append them.

The second column is Debts where they apply to an Asset, such as a mortgage on property, or where they are unsecured. It might also mean a reservation of interest/profit in part or all of your asset held by another.

The third column is Net Worth, that is, the difference between each asset's FMV and the amount of outstanding principal in its Debt. You do not include interest owed as part of your debt; only remaining principal. Unsecured debt, such as credit cards or personal loans, are also subtracted from your asset values. Your net worth is the sum of the third column. When your debt exceeds your asset values, you have a negative net worth—not good.

For a bank loan, you don't need to have your assets and real property professionally appraised for your net-worth statement. But you should be clear and honest. Don't fail to mention debt. Make a reasonable estimate of FMVs whose logic and basis you can defend if asked.

I suggest including other assets that are not normally requested, such as expected inheritance and money owed (receivables). They help you make your case.

3. **Last two years of your IRS 1040s.** Use more years if you are self-employed or had big fluctuations in income or adjusted gross income. Explain anomalies. Lenders like to see rising income each year.

4. **Current monthly balance sheet.** Show all income sources/gross amounts.

Income (est. for current year, not last tax year)

Wages/salary, or self-employment earnings
Interest
Dividend
Royalty
Rent
Pension/social security/disability
Revenue anticipated from something big, e.g., sale of something,
court award, pension start

Expenses

Household (estimate total food, clothing, utilities, repairs)
Current rent/mortgage payment
Property tax
Loan payments, e.g., car, college
Credit card
Tuition
Alimony/child support
Vehicles—gas, insurance, maintenance
Insurance—health, life, homeowner, other
Health care/medicines, not covered by insurance if out of the ordinary
Other

5. **Estimated future annual gross income for next three years**.

6. **Account numbers and contact information**: Include mortgages with other lenders, credit cards, checking, savings, retirement, stocks/bonds, CDs

7. **Items of public record**, summaries of consent agreements, divorce settlements, judgments, etc. that affect your cash flow.

8. **Any other items that materially affect your ability to meet a mortgage payment,** including costs of treating serious disease, special child-related or parent-related expenses, anticipated changes in your cash flow or expenses, etc.

9. **Mortgage history with other lenders**. Include names of recent lenders, approximate dates, location of property, amount. If you don't have these records, provide a one-sentence summary of what you recall about each mortgage.

10. **Current mortgage record.** Include name of lender, amount, terms, number of the note and the amount of interest paid annually. Do not count on your current mortgage lender to provide another lender with accurate information. Do not assume that a lender will be able to figure out a mortgage interest payment from your 1040, particularly a complicated one.

11. **Your (corrected) credit report/score that you've purchased.**
(www.mifico.com for $44.85 in 2005.)

This financial profile provides more information than most lenders ask for. Even if you have a shaky financial history, it's better in my opinion to put it on the table voluntarily and in advance of your lender digging it up. Your profile allows you to inject into your conversation the ideas of future income and future financial stability—assuming, of course, that these ideas work to your advantage. (If they don't, you probably shouldn't be thinking about taking out a mortgage.) It takes some effort to pull together your financial profile, much of which you will have to do anyway as part of the lender's application that you will be required to complete.

If a conventional lender won't give you a conventional loan—fixed for at least 20 years or something like a five- to seven-year ARM on reasonable terms   for rural property, then you should forget conventionality. You're asking for more mortgage than you can handle, or your past has caught up with you. In this situation, find a property where you can sell part of it quickly, using the net proceeds to pay down the loan. You may need to arrange a release with the lender. Make sure to get a professional evaluation of the asset's value prior to purchase, which you will have to do anyway to qualify the property for a lender. To the extent that you sell post-purchase for the established value pre-purchase, you minimize taxable gain and tax owed on the immediate sale. The tax obligation shifts down the road. This **buy-whole-sell-part strategy** changes your loan request. It can reduce your mortgage principal by 10 to 90 percent depending on how much you sell. You can sell during your escrow on a contingent basis. You can assign part of your interest in the purchase to your buyer. It also changes the borrowing time frame. You now want a 100 percent LTV loan for no more than six months, after which you want a different loan for a much smaller amount over a much longer period. Many ways exist to configure this two-step borrowing plan. In both steps, the lender should feel very secure.

Institutional lenders use a cookie-cutter procedure for determining the amount of money they will lend. They focus on your historic cash flow and its reliability. They review the amount and cost of debt you're already carrying to figure how much more you can reasonably carry based mainly on your past. They also look at your assets beyond the property itself to measure your ability to meet your obligations if your normal cash flow is interrupted by unemployment or illness. Most readers who are looking for country property will already be carrying a mortgage on their principal residence. That's good; new lenders like borrowers who make payments on time to other lenders. It's evidence that "your mind is right," in the way the prison-camp boss wanted Cool Hand Luke to meet his obligations without complaint. If the cookie-cutter formulas don't quite get you into the loan that you want, ask the lender to tell you his specific concerns. Use your purchase to help buy your purchase. That helps lenders make the loan.

Banks and other institutional lenders will subject your numbers to a percentage analysis, which they often refer to as a "**qualifying ratio**." The details of this calculation are not important for this discussion, but the idea is. The lender will determine your gross monthly income and then multiply that number by a percentage that the bank has determined is the amount of debt you can handle in relation to the debt you are already carrying. On a principal residence, most lenders will allow you to borrow up to 28 percent of your monthly income for this expense; and allow 36 percent for your total long-term debt. If you have a lot of cash, or easily cashed out assets, and the rural property is a relatively minor addition to your assets, you have room to negotiate. You are particularly strong if your recent history shows steady income growth, which has the effect of lowering the percent of income you spend on debt service. A low percent is a low ratio; low ratios are good for your application since they indicate room for additional debt. Banks turn down borrowers on the basis of high ratios, not because of their concern for you, but because of their concern for their money. Lending money is not "A Wonderful Life," and your banker is not Jimmy Stewart, complete with hems and haws.

The lender assembles a picture of your financial past and present. From those patterns, the lender sort of projects your future and takes into account uncertainties. Many futures are not very predictable based on the past. You are likely to be as good a predictor of your future as any bank formula. There is always room for discussion of this type when you think your income and/or net worth are likely to increase over time.

Once the lender reviews your profile, he'll assign you a ratio and, assuming everything is okay, pre-approve you for a loan amount with terms. At that point, you need to ask whether your approved loan amount will be reduced if you modify your offer to the seller, say by decreasing your down payment (which preserves your cash) and having the seller take back a second for the difference (which increases your debt). Get such matters straight with your lender before you start negotiating with the seller. Once you have an approved loan amount, you don't need to max it out on a purchase. Carrying less debt is always easier than carrying more.

Debt is the foundation of our consumer economy. It's easy to forget that debt is neither benign nor passive. It has to be fed each month, and if you don't, it will gobble you up in one bite. I encourage middle-income readers to finance country property by selling some of its assets rather than stretching to buy with maxed-out debt. The least amount of debt in your life, the better. Mortgages are often structured over 20 to 30 years. Who can predict what will happen to you during that time? Debt assumes financial stability. But everyone is subject to illness, unemployment, financial reverses, unforeseen expenses, divorce, death and dozens of other unpredictable events that destabilize personal finances. Many, if not most, Americans, are one big illness away from financial disaster. Having been burned by debt and one such disaster, I suggest considering buying more country property than you need and quickly selling one or more assets to reduce the debt as much as you can. You will almost always sell a parted-out asset for more than you paid for it when it was part of an entire package. This strategy can reduce your debt by a significant amount while allowing you to retain the core of your target property, comfortably financed. If you want to build wealth, this is as safe a way as I know to do it.

Once you have worked up a financial profile and gotten pre-approved, the next step—after finding the target property—is to **pitch your deal to your chosen lender**.

Pitching property is no different than pitching any other proposal. You have to show how the deal will work from the bank's perspective. Get all the relevant property data that you have gathered from your pre-purchase scoping. Put them in a tabbed portfolio or loose-leaf binder. Once again, I'm proposing to give the lender more than he's likely to ask for; and again, you're doing it out of self-interest. The items will be part of what you're gathering in your scoping, so little effort is required to make copies for your lender. More information improves your pitch, which unlike in baseball, you want your lender to hit out of the park. So free your property pitch from curves and sinkers. When a borrower is asking for some exception to the lender's policies, it helps to be as forthright and comprehensive about the property—warts and all—as is consistent with the lender's attention span. Consider the following items for submission:

1. Short narrative description of the property, including the obvious—road location, acres, improvements, current uses, types of land, water resources, minerals, timber, etc.

2. Current deed into the seller.

3. Copy of any recorded easement that materially affects the value or use of the property. You don't need to include vanilla utility easements.

4. Survey if available; tax map if not.

5. Topographical map with boundaries drawn.

6. The legal description that was used to draw the boundaries on the topographical map. (Should be in the deedwork's back trail if it's not in the seller's deed.)

7. Note whether the deed's calls close and whether the acreage in the deed matches what your surveyor has calculated as that which is in the deed. Note boundary problems, if any.

8. Note any recorded items that bear on the value of the property, such as the severance of mineral rights, life estate, reserved interest or profit in the land or timber. Also note current zoning/land-use classifications of property.

9. Tax information.

    a. Tax-assessed value of land, improvements and minerals.

    b. Annual property tax.

    c. Is the property either in land use or enrolled in a tax-break-giving timber management program with the state?

    d. Is there a conservation easement in place? This should reduce the property tax, but it reduces market value by the easement's estimated value. I recommend against buying rural land with conservation easements in place, unless the property is price discounted and the easement is what you want.

10. Photos of improvements, land, assets.

11. Cash-flow analysis if the property generates income from leases, sales, etc.

12. Your plan for purchasing the property.

    a. Amount of cash down payment.

    b. Sale of sub-asset, such as timber, minerals, acreage or improvement if that's part of your plan.

    c. Seller's second, if applicable.

    d. Other sources of money toward the purchase, such as gift from parent, sale of conservation easement

    e. Anticipated amount of lender's money you will need.

    f. Project amount of money the property will generate that you will use for mortgage repayment.

    g. Show sources of income for remainder of monthly payment.

    h. Short discussion of cash reserves available to meet payments in the event of a change in circumstances.

13. Your plan for managing the property.

    If you want to have the property generate income, explain your idea with some rough numbers. Indicate what portion of anticipated income will apply to the lender's debt service and your overall debt service. If you are buying an operating farm, you should submit a CPA-prepared set of financial projections. If you are planning to sell timber or other asset, submit a cruise or an FMV appraisal value along with an estimated net from the sale. Indicate how much of the net after-tax income you will apply to the mortgage principal.

14. Your pitch.

Put in a short narrative paragraph about the type of loan you want; its term; amount of cash down payment you want to invest; LTV ratio you prefer, definition of "value" you prefer (appraisal value or purchase price); total amount of points, fees and other closing costs you are willing to pay; security in addition to the property and so on. Be aggressive in putting forth your opening position, but reasonably so. You can stretch a lender in several directions, but you can't break him. You want the lender to negotiate a few things with you, not run from the office when you appear. So peg your pitch to the type of loans/terms that his website indicates he offers.

Your lender will evaluate your target property to determine 1) whether the amount of the loan you want can be comfortably covered by its liquidation value, and 2) your ability to pay it off without a problem. A pre-approved amount does not mean that you can borrow that sum against any property you want to buy. The property's liquidation value has to exceed the lender's exposure (money lent to you) by whatever the lender determines is its comfort level.

APPRAISALS AND BORROWING

The lender's review of your target property starts with a buyer-paid **appraisal**, which is an estimate of its current **fair market value (FMV)** by an independent third-party, the appraiser. You may have already paid for an appraisal as part of your pre-purchase scoping; submit that and argue no need exists for you to pay for a second. (If you pay for an appraisal during scoping, make sure that it is done by an appraiser on your lender's approved list. Otherwise, it won't be accepted.) Appraisers say that an appraisal is an "estimate of value," i.e., a reasoned estimate. (William L. Ventolo, Jr. and Martha R. Williams, Fundamentals of Real Estate Appraisal, 7th Edition [Chicago: Dearborn Financial Publishing/Real Estate Education Company, 1998, p. 19.]) Robert J. Bruss, the knowledgeable real-estate columnist, believes that an "...appraisal is a guess of a property's probable market value." The process, he writes, is an art, not a science. (Robert J. Bruss, "Real Estate Mailbag," Washington Post, January 25, 2003.) When done honestly and without bias in either direction (toward buyer or the lender), my experience with rural appraisals is that they provide an FMV number that is within 15 or 20 percent of current market value, and often within ten percent. When done to satisfy the party paying for the appraisal, they can be off by 25 percent or more.

Appraisers use one of three methods for determining the FMV of real property: 1) cost method, which estimates the dollars needed to replace a property; 2) income method, which compares the net income a target property is generating for the seller with income-generating properties of the same type; and 3) comparable sales approach, or **comparables (aka "comps")**, which derives an FMV for the target property by finding recent sales of roughly similar properties and tweaking their characteristics to match those of the target property. The tweaking adds or subtracts dollars to account for differences between the comps and the property that is being appraised. Determining FMV using comps is the way most country property is appraised. Large, working farms might be appraised on an income basis, because they are more a business than a property purchase from the lender's perspective. Most, if not all, institutional lenders now require a third-party appraisal as one step in determining how much money they will lend to you. Local bankers will have personal experience with local property that will allow them to double-check the appraiser's FMV. Often, a lender will have financed the same property for a previous buyer. If there's a problem with access, soils or boundaries, a local banker may know about it.

Appraisals currently run about $300 and up, depending on the area. Lenders require one, and the borrower pays it as a closing fee. A lender may mark up the appraisal cost in some states and pass it through. When you're working with an existing residence, you may be able to lower the appraisal cost by insisting on a "**collateral valuation insurance**" **(CVI)**, which uses a combination of electronic databases, drive-by visual exterior inspection and insurance for the lender. CVI costs about one-half of the standard appraisal since it requires far less appraiser time. But it may not be available in your target area, and it may not be applicable to undeveloped land. A CVI is worth asking about, particularly during your scoping when you should be getting an appraisal to both inform and enhance your negotiating.

With an appraisal in hand, the lender then applies his loan-to-value (LTV) ratio, which is the amount of money he will lend to you as a percentage of either the appraisal value or your purchase price—*whichever is lowest.* You will be told that the LTV percentages are set in institutional stone. In my area, those stated percentages are a maximum loan of 90 percent on land with improvements and 75 to 80 percent on undeveloped land. But I have seen stone-set percentages fall, even vanish, in light of a property's specific characteristics, price and the borrower's plans. Lenders will give buyers more, if they're going to get a chunk of principal back reasonably soon after closing. Remember that the lender chooses the lowest of the two numbers in front of him—your purchase price or the appraisal value. Lenders force the lower number on the borrower to protect their money by levering more of the borrower's into the deal.

And so we come to the familiar buyer's crack. Your purchase-offer price of $500,000 has been accepted. You assume the local branch of Big Friendly Bank will lend you 90 percent of that price, or $450,000. This means that you have to come up with $50,000 as down payment, plus maybe $25,000 more in closing costs. Then the appraisal comes in for $450,000. The appraiser, you find out, does a lot of work for Big Friendly. The bank says it will lend you 90 percent of the appraisal value ($450,000), that is, $405,000. This means that you have to find $95,000 in down payment and $25,000, in closing costs, not $50,000 and $25,000. In the event of default, Big Friendly is in a far less risky position, because you have more cash equity in at the start. Maybe the lender's policy helps by preventing you from borrowing beyond your effective payment capacity. But maybe it leads you to stretch your resources to come up with the unexpected difference. The $25,000 in closing costs at this point in the process is a hard number; any room to negotiate with the lender is probably passed. The real-estate agents involved might help out by cutting their commissions; it's worth asking.

This is an interesting situation. The buyer has offered $500,000. Is that not ground-truth evidence of market value? Is the buyer's offer above fair market value? Alternatively, it may be that the appraiser has lowered his appraisal value to protect the lender and guarantee future business for himself. When you apply to an institutional lender for a loan and "agree" to have an appraisal done, you are forced to pay for an appraisal that is being done for the bank, not you. Banks often won't even show you the appraisal you've paid for. If you want to see it, you may have to ask for it in writing. I don't think I've ever seen a property appraisal for a bank or the Federal Land Bank, a principal lender for rural property, that came in above the buyer's offering price, though nothing prevents that from occurring. I've seen a number of appraisals that come in for less. I've drawn my own conclusion; maybe I'm wrong.

So what should you do?

Challenge the $450,000 appraisal. It is obviously quite possible that the $450,000 appraisal is a better reflection of fair market value *based on comparables* than your well-researched offer of $500,000. But if you've done your scoping and know the real value of the property, take your information and analysis to the lender and show him why your estimate of value—based on the market value of the property's assets disaggregated or whatever method you used—is a truer indication of the property's total FMV than a cookie-cutter appraisal, done by an approved appraiser who may be trying to maintain favorable relations with the bank. Explain why your offer of $500,000 is at, or below, the true FMV of the property—which it should be if you've taken my advice. Insist that the bank's appraiser redo his appraisal in light of the information you've developed on your own. You can also attack the comparability of the three properties the appraiser used as comps. If your research has turned up more relevant comps—more recent sales; closer fit; nearer to the target property—than those used by the appraiser put them in front of the lender. If you have commissioned an appraisal as part of your pre-purchase scoping that has produced a value of $500,000, or higher, submit that to the lender. I think it's a good idea to give your lender a copy of your scoping appraisal when you apply for the loan. I would not tell your appraiser which bank you're applying to. You're trying to get an appraisal that is a true FMV estimate and one that fits your needs; don't confuse the appraiser with thoughts about his own self-interest. If you have a scoping appraisal from an unapproved appraiser, then you need to demand a meeting at the bank where both appraisers appear and argue their cases. You will frequently develop information during scoping that affects FMV which an appraiser never seeks to discover. Use it now to establish the superior FMV credibility of your offering price to the appraiser's valuation. You can also offer to split the cost of a third appraisal, the result of which either, by mutual agreement, trumps the first two or is used to calculate a value that is the average of the three appraisals. While you may be incensed about having to pay for more than one appraisal, spending $1,500 for three appraisals to save $50,000 in upfront cash makes sense to me. You may also want to point out that an appraisal value is tied to past prices. In an appreciating market, comps that are even a few months old, can produce a value for your target property that is out of date.

Conventional wisdom is that appraisers and banks work more often to get borrowers into loans pegged to the property's selling price, which overvalues the property securing the note, and thereby get a borrower on the mortgage hook for more than the property is worth. I've seen this happen with cash-heavy, non-resident buyers. Early in 2003, the Federal Housing Administration proposed a plan whereby the mortgage lender would be equally responsible with the appraiser for appraisal errors. Mel R. Martinez, Secretary of Housing and Urban Development, said: "'[Some] lenders tacitly require appraisers to make the appraisal computations match the sales price to ensure that a home sale and mortgage loan closes for the appraiser to obtain additional business,' [and]...other lenders collude with appraisers, he adds, to fraudulently create property 'flips'—rapid-fire resales of homes with inflated valuations—that harm consumers and the FHA insurance fund." (Kenneth Harney, "Appraisal rules aimed at lenders," Richmond Times-Dispatch, January 19, 2003.)

In my geographically limited experience, I've sensed collusion from time to time between lender and appraiser going toward *undervaluing* the property to protect the bank by squeezing the borrower for more down payment. I had this game run on me years ago before I knew what was going on: I bridged the gap between what the lender wanted to lend based on his appraisal and the purchase price with a three-year second mortgage from the seller. Robert J. Bruss concludes that "...appraisals remain the weakest link in the home mortgage process." (Bruss, Washington Post, January 25, 2003.)

The advice to be drawn from these impressions such as they are is this: Be aware that your price expectations and the lender's expectations can influence some appraisers. If you want a "high" appraisal, let that be known. If you want an appraisal at the purchase price, let that be known. If you intend to back out of a deal if the appraisal does not meet the purchase price, let that be known.

The way to protect yourself against lender-oriented appraisers who are deliberately discounting the target property's value is to place an **appraisal contingency** in your purchase contract:

> **Buyer's offer is contingent on Buyer's lender receiving and accepting a property appraisal from a qualified appraiser approved by lender within ___ days of this Contract taking effect that establishes the fair market value of Seller's property at no less than the purchase price agreed to in this Contract.**

> **Buyer may void this Contract without penalty in the event that the lender's appraisal is less than the Buyer's price accepted by Seller.**

I find it useful in many instances to have the buyer commission his own appraisal in advance of approaching both the seller with an offer and the institutional lender with a pitch for a loan. Approach your appraiser after doing some of your scoping so that you can share your findings with him. Give him your expectation about the property's value and the reasons justifying it. If you've paid for a timber cruise or an independent valuation of farm assets, give these documents to the appraiser. If you want a high valuation, make sure to have him take into account all assets on the property, including the ones you've valued separately.

This **full-factor appraisal** requires a different format than the conventional comparables approach. Most of the land appraisals I've seen do not adjust the target property's value according to separate valuations of timber and other less-obvious assets. Appraisers adjust price for acreage, percent open vs. wooded, style of house, square footage of house and so on, but not for the value of certain assets, such as timber and minerals. Most appraisers don't know how to evaluate those components. Accordingly, an appraiser does not factor in the value of merchantable timber on wooded property. He sets the property's worth according to wooded comps regardless of how much or how little merchantable timber both the comps and the target property contain. This is nonsensical, since the three wooded comps might have no immediate timber value and the target property of approximately the same acreage might contain $250,000, or vice versa. Small farms and part-time farm operations might be used as comps for a target property whose real market value is much higher as a second home to an urban buyer. If a land appraiser says he can't change his comparables format, accept his position and then ask him to file an appendix to his appraisal that includes your independent valuations. You then take his appraisal and add on the values of assets the appraiser did not include. (This, of course, assumes that you're trying to get the appraisal up. If you want to lower the appraisal, share all the negatives that you've found during your scoping.)

Keep in mind that a comparables analysis involves adjusting judgments about each comp in terms of judgments about the target property. Appraisers have guidelines for making adjustments between properties for house-related items like finished area (square feet), basements, finished attics, garages and the like. But comparisons between land-related items, such as soil quality, water, topography, access, floodplain, fence condition, farm infrastructure and many other variables that actually determine land FMV, are rarely done, or done well. While it's relatively straight forward to do a comparables analysis for 500 acres of Illinois crop land, it's harder to find comparables for a 500-acre mountain farm in Virginia with 75 acres in pasture, 175 acres in bottomland and 250 acres in hardwood timber of mixed ages with a house and four significant outbuildings. While the appraiser is expected to produce a single "hard" number as his FMV for the target property, much of his approach is not "hard." This gives you a way to introduce hard evidence into his semi-subjective analysis. The appraiser should have choices among the comps he uses, what asset factors to value and by how much, and what liability factors to include as a discount. The more your target property is one of a kind, the more leeway he has in choosing his appraisal number.

The point here is an unfortunate one: appraisals can be influenced and should be in some cases. Appraisers can be corrupted by their self-interest enough to hurt a buyer. A seller can buy an inflated appraisal; a buyer can buy a deflated appraisal. And a lender can set up certain expectations for appraisers on his approved list. Given the opportunities for others in the buying process to influence appraisal value, I can only advise buyers to defend their interests.

Kenneth Harney wrote about the key role of appraisals and appraisers for sellers in a weakening market. (Kenneth Harney, "The Nation's Housing," "In a sagging market, the appraiser's word is key," Richmond Times-Dispatch, January 1, 2006.) He quoted Tom Berge, head of a California appraisal firm, who said that he "ignores pressure by lenders or realty agents to 'hit the number' on the sales contract." Berge's advice to sellers, buyers, lenders and realty agents about how to influence the final appraisal number ethically and legally is this: "'If you want me to adjust [the number], go out and get me better comps....'" In the best of circumstances, all parties would find the three property sales that are closest in all respects to the property being appraised—and all adjustments will be the same. But in most circumstances, the comps used are chosen somewhat subjectively, leaving room for other comps to be used with equal justification.

Your first objective in using your scoping appraisal is to bring an above-market-price seller down to earth. Your second objective is to protect yourself from a low-ball bank appraisal that seeks to wring more down payment out of you. Your third objective is to be able to offset a bogus seller's appraisal. Both the seller and the bank may want to dismiss your appraiser's FMV number. With both of them, force a discussion on the details of the process and the specifics of the property. You have nothing to lose with either party. If the seller has not paid for his own appraisal (which is likely), your appraisal is one of three pieces of fair-market-value information available for negotiations: 1) your appraisal; 2) a realtor-provided competitive market analysis (CMA), which is a comparables analysis; and 3) current tax-assessed value. Both your appraisal and the tax-assessed value should help you in your negotiations with the seller. Both will be done by a neutral, third-party professional who has no self-interest (presumably) in the results of his work. If the seller is working through a real-estate broker, the CMA can be marginalized as a self-interested exercise intended to get an above-market price.

If your scoping appraisal is substantially below the seller's asking price, share the information with the seller and use it to work him down to a more realistic price. If you can negotiate a price with the seller that's in line with the appraisal, hand the appraisal to the bank during your first meeting as part of your property-information package. If you can't get the seller to come into line with the appraisal, then ask yourself how much of a premium you're willing to pay for this particular property. You can always ask the seller to take back a second mortgage on terms that are very favorable to you: say, five years at two percent, interest-only annual payments with a balloon of principal at the end of the term. You're still overpaying, but the burden is a little lighter. If the seller's price is significantly above market and he figures that the next buyer will be no more nor less of a fool than you, he should come into line. There are, of course, sellers who deliberately price their property high above market and simply wait until someone comes along who is able and willing to pay the premium, fool or not.

On-the-ground appraisals for conventional rural property currently cost between $300 and $400 in my county. That's likely to be on the low side for many places. A **drive-by appraisal** with some comparables analysis—which is what you can get without the seller's cooperation—costs about $200. You may need to give the institutional lender an on-the-ground appraisal, but a drive-by will suffice for negotiating with the seller. Drive-bys can be combined with electronic appraisal techniques in some areas.

Look for an appraiser who is certified by the National Association of Real Estate Appraisers. If you've done some price research, tell him what you've found in terms of tax-assessed comps and asking-price comps. Give him an idea of what you think the ballpark purchase price might be if you're confident in your analysis. If not, keep quiet. Your appraiser should help you out a bit without any obvious pressure from you. If you're looking for a figure on the high side, you can give him a comparables analysis of current asking prices that a real-estate broker can run for you.

TAX BENEFITS AND MORTGAGE-INTEREST DEDUCTIBILITY

The tax benefits of owning real property are significant. The precise package of benefits available to you depends on whether the property is your primary residence, second home (that you use exclusively and personally), full-time rental property, vacation rental property (that you use no more than the IRS-allowable days), land that has usable or saleable assets (pasture, house, timber, minerals, water rights, etc.), the nature of your plans for the property—personal use, investment, business, a combination—and how you organize your plans legally and implement them subsequently. Your individual package of tax benefits arising from any particular parcel of rural land depends on how you, your lawyer and your CPA combine these various options. At the risk of sounding like a jaded taxpayer, it appears to me that tax benefits rise with the level of complexity you choose—in the property itself (the more differentiated the property's assets, the more benefits are likely to be available), your plans and your type of ownership organization.

Underlying the United States real-estate market is the **deductibility of mortgage interest**. On your principal residence, you are currently allowed to deduct the interest you pay up to $1 million in mortgage debt. You cannot deduct up to $1 million in interest; rather you can deduct the interest paid on up to $1 million in mortgage loans. To qualify for deductibility, the mortgage must be secured by the house. A mortgage from a friend, relation or seller also qualifies as long as it's so secured. The $1 million cap on mortgage debt applies to the buying, building or improvement of your principal residence and/or second home.

Mortgage interest is known as a **below-the-line deduction**, because the amount of interest is subtracted from your 1040's adjusted gross income (AGI). An **above-the-line deduction** is subtracted from your gross income and is part of the subtraction process that produces your AGI. Below-the-line deductions spare the taxpayer more in taxes than the same amount applied above the line.

Mortgage interest can be deducted for a primary residence, second home, unimproved rural land and investment/business property. (See IRS Publication 550, Investment Income and Expenses and Publication 936, Home Mortgage Interest Deduction.) But you need to set up your taxes appropriately, and you need to itemize deductions on your tax returns.

On a primary residence and *one* second home (in the country or anywhere else, including a yacht that provides basic living accommodations), mortgage interest is generally deductible, not to exceed a total of $1 million in debt each year, when the mortgage was taken out after October 13, 1987. There are some qualifications to this general statement that Publication 936 explains. Mortgage interest is deductible only when the home is collateral for the debt. If mortgage money is not used for buying, building or improving a "qualified residence," primary and secondary, you can't take the home-mortgage deduction for that interest. "Grandfathered debt," a mortgage taken out before October 13, 1987 that was secured by a qualified home, is deductible without having to meet the buy-build-improve rule. A qualified home will include all the land that goes with it. Your deduction is limited to one second home. *If you set up your rural property as an investment, you can deduct mortgage interest and other expenses only if you file an itemized return.* (Only about one-third—46 million of 130 million returns—itemize.) Unimproved land will be considered an investment property if you do not begin construction of a home/second home that you can occupy within 24 months of purchase.

Mortgage interest on home-equity loans taken against a "qualified residence" (essentially your principal residence) for the purposes cited above is deductible below the line as long as the debt does not exceed $100,000. Interest paid on a home-equity loan is deductible, up to $100,000 in debt on top of the $1 million in debt for mortgage-interest.

A second home that you rent out can qualify for the mortgage-interest deduction if you use it as a residence for either more than 14 days that year or more than ten percent of the number of rented-out days that year, whichever is longer. You don't have to live in your second home to have it qualify for the deduction.

If your second home does not qualify for the home-mortgage interest deduction, you may be able to set it up as a rental unit, investment or business and obtain the appropriate tax benefits, including depreciation. The deductibility of interest directly reduces the cost you pay to buy country property, so check with your tax adviser before borrowing for this purchase.

The simplest purchase—buying a full-time personal residence in the country—gives you the deduction of local property taxes and mortgage interest from your taxable income, subject to IRS limitations. You can deduct *all* mortgage interest you pay if you 1) took out the mortgage on or before October 13, 1987; 2) took out the mortgage after that date but these mortgages and any grandfathered debt equal $1 million or less; or 3) took out a mortgage after that date that you used for something other than buying, building or improving your home; and these mortgages totaled $100,000 or less and the mortgage total on the home does not exceed its fair market value. Those who don't fit into these categories, can deduct interest on up to $1,000,000 in mortgage debt a year. If you have a second home in the country, the interest on that mortgage debt qualifies for deductibility as long as the taxpayer's total mortgage debt does not exceed $1 million. (The IRS has exceptions to this rule if you rent your second home.)

In addition to mortgage interest, you can deduct the **real-estate tax** you pay on your rural property if you itemize. In the year of your purchase, you can deduct the share of the property's taxes you paid, as shown on your settlement statement, or HUD-1.

Finally, on your principal residence, you can deduct **points** related to your mortgage loan for the tax year in which you purchased the home. Or you can amortize these points over the term of the loan. That choice is yours. (Points may also be called loan-origination fee or loan-discount fee.) The points must be related to the buyer's purchase, construction or improvement of the qualified residence. The buyer is also generally able to deduct points that are paid by the seller on his behalf. If you refinance your principal residence, you have to amortize the points over the loan's term. With a second home or land purchase, the buyer has the same choice of deducting or amortizing points. The IRS imposes a reasonableness standard concerning the amount of points a buyer can deduct or amortize. Ten or more points are probably beyond what the IRS would consider reasonable; six or fewer is probably okay. Consult with your CPA before agreeing to five or more points, just to be certain.

The IRS imposes no interest-deductibility cap on land bought for investment or business. Mortgage interest paid on land purchased for business or investment is deducted above the line. Mortgage interest paid on rental property is similarly an above-the-line deduction.

Many of your closing costs are not deductible. The tax that you pay to record your deed—called a recordation tax, transfer tax or deed stamps—is not deductible. Neither are the cost of title insurance, credit-report fee, appraisal fee and private mortgage insurance. Your CPA or lawyer will be able to tell you in advance of closing which of your closing costs are deductible. (See Kay Bell, "First-time home buyers' guide to taxes," www.Bankrate.com, April 13, 2006.)

As I write this in 2006, the Bush Administration's tax policies, the war in Iraq and the Katrina/Rita/Wilma clean up have created record annual budget deficits. The Administration would like to cut taxes more and certainly not increase them. But doing so would enlarge the budget deficits that are being offset by increased borrowing. Reducing tax benefits may be one approach to increasing revenues without raising tax rates. (Cutting federal programs would offset some of the debt-financed spending.) A Bush-appointed panel, chaired by former Florida Senator Connie Mack, ranked the mortgage-interest deduction as the second most costly for 2006 ($76 billion est.) after the business deduction for providing employees with health benefits ($126 billion est.). The capital-gains tax break on the sale of a *principal residence* (joint filers can exclude from tax $500,000 in gain; individuals, up to $250,000; *this break does not apply to second homes*) was the third largest, $36.3 billion, and the deduction for state and local property taxes was the fourth, $14.8 billion. (The Associated Press, "Group studies tax breaks," The [Staunton] News Leader, April 25, 2005.) The President, it was reported, asked the panel—President's Advisory Panel on Federal Tax Reform—to preserve tax breaks that promoted home ownership and charitable giving.

The panel recommended in late 2005 that the mortgage-interest deduction for both a second home and a home-equity loan be eliminated. Also under consideration was the idea that the mortgage-interest deduction on a principal residence be limited up to 15 percent of interest paid with caps equal to the Federal Housing Administration's loan limits in the homeowner's area—currently $172,000 to $312,000. (David Brunori, "Bush's Tax Panel Has a Crazy Idea. Let's Go For It." Washington Post, October 23, 2005.) The elimination of second-home interest and home-equity interest will fall on many more taxpayers than putting a $300,000 interest cap on principal-residence interest. The Administration did not endorse the Mack Commission recommendations. They are, however, out there, and land buyers should keep an eye peeled for changes in interest and expenses deductibility brought into the IRS code piecemeal.

If the budget deficits continue to grow, pressure to reduce property-related tax benefits will grow. This uncertainty is yet one more reason to set up your rural property purchase as an investment or business rather than as a second home.

CHAPTER 33: SOURCES OF DIRT-SMART MONEY

Dozens of ways exist to finance real-estate purchases. Some are more risky to the buyer than others. Some involve falsification and/or concealment, both of which I advise against. The real-estate books I've mentioned in other chapters discuss many techniques that are applicable to rural land. It's worth reading several to have a general sense of what tools are available, and, more importantly, which ones you feel comfortable working into a rural land purchase.

Financing brings out greed. I've seen buyers push their financing packages beyond anything they need in pursuit of finding the last dollar of **OPM—other people's money**. That isn't necessary, and, ultimately, it's probably not in your best interest. You want a good deal, a deal that works for you by stripping risk out of the purchase through scoping and promises a healthy profit. That's enough. If you've bought at the right price in relation to the property's value, you've secured a profit for your anticipated length of ownership. Applying a house-of-cards-financing scheme to avoid putting your own cash into the purchase is more than likely to jeopardize either your deal or your financial security.

If you are a beginner at buying land follow this rule: the simpler a deal, the more likely it won't go wrong anywhere along the line from purchase to disposition. Your buyer's pitch to the seller should be clear, understandable and feasible; the same must be true of your post-purchase plan. I've seen good buys squirreled up by a many-phased, post-purchase plan that is too intricate for the buyer to implement. The more dependent each layer of profit is on the one preceding it, the more precarious the profitability of the purchase will be. Financing is, in a sense, a buyer's first step toward simplicity or complexity. I'm sure that simple deals can be based on complicated financing arrangements, but my brain is disposed toward linear consistency, from scoping through liquidation.

The money sources I discuss below include both the familiar and the not so familiar. If you are wealthy enough to buy real simplicity, put down a big cash payment and borrow the rest from the largest bank in the target property's county seat. Simplicity getting in, however, does not eliminate the risk of a flawed purchase. Usable cash does not lift the obligation you have to yourself to protect it through scoping.

13 PLACES TO START

Purchase money in one or another form can be found from one or more of the following sources, singly or in combination:

1. Your own resources
2. Sale of one or more "severable" assets from the target property
3. Neighbors
4. The seller
5. Co-investors/partners
6. Locally owned local lenders
7. Regionally owned local lenders

8. Non-local lenders

9. Life insurance companies

10. Internet

11. Government agencies

12. 1031 Like-Kind (Starker) Exchange

13. Conservation easements

All of us faced with the purchase of property must decide how much of our own kaboodle we want to put in and how much we want to borrow. The more cash in upfront, the less we need to borrow, the lower our monthly payments, the less interest we have to pay and, perhaps, the more secure we feel in light of life's pending bummers that eventually befall all of us. But it can be either hard or expensive to get cash out of property, which is one reason to borrow OPM.

For every upfront dollar invested in a down payment, the buyer incurs both a **direct cost** and an **opportunity cost**. The direct cost can be considered as the amount of his down payment plus his **transaction costs** in buying the property—points and fees charged by the lender; recordation and other taxes; scoping costs and miscellaneous professional fees. The buyer also has the direct cost over time of paying his mortgage interest and principal along with property-maintenance charges. In return, the buyer gets the use of the property and its appreciation in value.

The property buyer also incurs **opportunity costs**, which are the opportunities the buyer might have pursued with his direct-cost dollars had he not made the purchase. The dollar spent for dirt cannot be spent to buy stocks, bonds or a Ferrari. Any dollar placed in a real-estate investment can lose value over time. That goes for stocks, bonds and Ferraris as well. The possibility of loss in any investment is a risk, not a direct cost or an opportunity cost. Real-estate risk is contained, though never totally eliminated, through research, analysis and planning. The costs of buying property are contained by: 1) buying within your means, 2) understanding the true value of the property before acquiring it and 3) predicting with some reasonable accuracy its appreciation at the anticipated date of sale.

Most land buyers want to put in as little of their own cash as possible. Using Other People's Money is usually necessary. The buyer uses a little of his own cash to **leverage** the borrowing of a much larger sum. Leverage is debt, which must be repaid. It is OPM on which you pay interest. OPM is not free money. Leverage can get you into and out of a deal cleanly and profitably; it can also lead to default and bankruptcy. The Crash of 1929 wiped out my grandfather and thousands of other paper millionaires when the perceived value of his highly leveraged properties nose-dived and the banks called their notes. It took him years to pay back his creditors. He was never wealthy again, even on paper. Leverage works to your benefit as long as you can make the monthly payments on your debt. As soon as you can't, leverage starts working against you. Think of a person using a fulcrum and a lever to lift a large boulder off the ground and over his head. As long as sufficient forced is applied down, the boulder stays up. When force stops being applied, the boulder's full weight falls straight down. That is how leverage works for and against you.

Real-estate writers always advise readers to use other people's money to finance purchases. Taking out a mortgage is the simplest and most familiar form of this practice. The borrower is using the lender's money to acquire an asset that's likely to appreciate over time. Keep in mind, however, that the structure of that repayment has you, first, paying back far more than you borrowed, and, second, exposed to losing the entire asset plus whatever you've paid in interest and principal. **For those reasons, I advise to look for ways that you can use both your current assets and a portion of the rural asset you're about to buy to come up with the cash you need to buy.** I don't rule out borrowing.

If you like to live on the edge of disaster, write me off as an old fuddy-duddy. If the absolute worst that can happen in a default on a purchase of country property is the loss of the property itself and your sunk cash, that's an acceptable level of risk, assuming that the probability of default is low. If the probability is not low, don't buy. If you risk losing other significant assets, then don't get into the deal.

I offer one exception to this rule. If you are looking at rural property exclusively as an **investment flip**, you will want to narrow your search to properties with an **immediate cash-out profile and use as much OPM as possible**. You may take out an ARM or an interest-only mortgage on a 30-year term to finance the deal, but your plan is to pay off the entire note as you sell the property's assets. A successful flip, however, depends on the flip yielding more money than you have in both the front-side of the deal (purchase) and its back-side (the cost of resale, as an entirety or in parts). The danger in using OPM for flips is that the resale takes longer and you net less than you've anticipated.

I would attach four caveats to using OPM in highly leveraged purchases of rural land, and all have to do with melt-down scenarios, such as a foreclosure. First, make sure that the property alone secures your mortgage. If a **non-recourse loan** cannot be arranged, you must be very confident that any forced sale of the property will cover the note. Don't personally guarantee OPM. Second, don't tie the leveraged rural property into your core assets, such as your principal residence, with a mortgage that covers both. Third, be psychologically ready to lose the rural land to save your primary butt. Don't liquidate every cash asset you have to hold on to it if that will leave you cash poor and land rich. Finally, I would use OPM to buy rural property that did not exceed the value of my principal residence. Your first rural venture might be limited to 50 percent or less of the value of your principal residence unless you have extensive cash or other assets to see you through a pinch. This rule of thumb will allow you to sleep at night.

Buyers correctly assume that inflation and normal growth in their earnings will make it easier for them to pay off a loan with fixed terms over time. Counting on background inflation over time to help pay a long-term note works as long as macro-economic factors, such as economic growth and interest rates, are reasonably favorable. A recession/depression can catch an otherwise sound investment in a triple bind of no buyers for your property, falling values and a cash drain on all your other assets. If you can't sell your land investment when you need to, you either have to continue to carry it or lose it. Time and inflation can work against a buyer if his earnings don't rise. Buying rural land with a 30-year mortgage does not lock you into prison for 30 years. Rather, it locks you into paying back the principal borrowed and interest accrued to date, with the balance of the principal to be paid by the sale of the property itself if you can't carry it.

Buyers try put in as little of their own cash because they've read or heard that rural land and undeveloped land are **illiquid**. Is it hard to sell rural property? In my experience, rural land is illiquid in four types of circumstances: 1) where the property has one or more major negatives, such as no legally established access; 2) where the property has been dedicated and configured for an activity that is increasingly out of favor, such as farms that can grow tobacco but nothing else; 3) when it's priced above market and the seller won't budge; or 4) when it lies in a **zone of repugnance**.

This last phrase needs a bit of explanation. Cattle will not graze where they have recently fouled the grass. Beef-cattle academics call the area, under and immediately around a cow flop, "a zone of repugnance." Certain areas of our country have been either so beaten up or are so inhospitable that not many people live there and even fewer want to move there. Fairly or not, they are seen from the outside as zones of repugnance. In such places, land will be illiquid, even at knock-down prices. I should add that some old zones of repugnance, such as some played-out Western mining towns, can be turned into recreational cash cows. A "nice" community can have a zone of repugnance, such as a 5,000-head feedlot on one side of town or a noisy mill. Places for sale nearby will have a limited, illiquid market.

While I do not agree that rural land is inherently illiquid, it may not be immediately saleable at your preferred price. Average land for sale at market price should sell, though it may take six months or a year. In the best circumstances, it will take between 30 and 90 days to get to closing. And if the buyer's contingencies are not satisfied, the contract will be terminated, which means the owner must start from scratch. Land cannot be converted to cash with the same-day convenience of a drive-through ATM. If you are an absentee owner, a land sale can take longer, especially if you are selling it yourself.

Still, I think it's generally wrong to assume that an owner will have a long, hard ordeal selling run-of-the-mill rural land for current market value. The degree of liquidity, that is, the time needed to sell a property at approximately fair market value, is often determined by how much above FMV the owner sets his asking price and how determinedly he doesn't budge. While the owner may be under financial pressure to get as much for the property as possible, it remains his choice as to how to balance asking price and selling price against time on the market. The cost of holding tight to an above-market price is often not worth it when sales are slow. Fear of illiquidity is not in my opinion a good reason for limiting the amount of cash you put into the purchase of rural land.

When your circumstances are such that using OPM to buy discretionary rural property is a feasible approach subject to the caveats I've expressed, then I would advise proceeding if you are confident that the property will sell within six months at a price that will cover the note and sale expenses. A six-month time frame means you might have to sell it below FMV—and still have enough to pay your debt. These parameters change, of course, if you have sufficient cash assets to replace the income you normally will be spending to pay the country note. Go into an OPM-based purchase with a clear idea of how you will handle a worst-case scenario. (Don't cheat on the definition of "worst"; assume a real catastrophe.) A large mortgage on a property other than your primary residence can drain your cash resources in a time of financial crisis without contributing anything to getting you through the squeeze. Your worst-case planning has to include letting the rural property go before it drags you under.

Consider these sources for dirt money.

1. Your own resources.

Most lenders require at least ten percent down on rural land that has a house or other improvement and at least 20 percent on undeveloped rural land. Out-of-pocket cash need not be your first choice for this money. What other sources might be available for a required down payment?

First, sell stuff. Raise down payment by cleaning out your attic, garage and basement. Sell stocks (equities) that are losing money and which you've grown to hate. Sell one or more of your less-than-needed possessions—the Mercedes that's capable of 150 mph at one gallon per mile, the sailboat that leaks no matter how many times you pay for repair or the RV that hasn't moved since Nixon walked on the beach in wingtips.

Second, borrow some cash. Borrow from relatives. Borrow against life insurance. Borrow from a credit union or take out a personal note for the down payment. You may be able to borrow against your primary residence, but that is a sleep-loss tactic. If you borrow your down payment and transaction costs, you do not want to push your debt to the edge of your carrying capacity. Leave yourself plenty of room to muddle through the losing crapshoots of life. The best borrowing strategy is from friends or relatives who won't need a specific payback date. Borrow sensibly—not from your kid's college savings, not from a loan shark or credit card, not from your tax-escrow account, not more than you need and can pay back with no sweat. All things considered, borrowing down payment is the least preferred option.

Third, trim current expenses and save the difference to accumulate a down payment. How much do you really want this country property? Do you want it enough to eat out less, buy cheaper clothes, drive an older car?

Fourth, get money from your family. Money from family can take many forms: a formal loan, complete with signed note; an informal loan that you are expected to repay when you have it; an informal loan that you are not really expected to repay; a co-investment, whereby a family member joins in the purchase with you; an investment with family members (by way of a corporation, partnership or limited liability company) that holds title and manages the investment according to a plan that is agreed to prior to purchase; and a gift of cash, kind, income flow or saleable asset. You might propose waiving some portion of your inheritance in return for cash now if that's agreeable to parents and siblings. A gift is best, and, indeed, it was $3,500 from my mother that allowed me to buy my first piece of rural America—a half share in 60 acres about 40 minutes north of Amherst, Massachusetts in 1970.

Both the money source and recipient should check out the tax consequences of various arrangements and amounts. As of 2006, a donor can give a **gift** of $12,000 tax free each year to an individual; above that a gift tax applies, subject to other factors. (See www.irs.gov; Publication 950: Introduction to Estate and Gift Taxes.) Each parent can give $12,000 annually to a child, tax free. This exclusion may be increased in the future. The recipient pays no federal tax on the receipt of a cash gift. A loan is not a taxable event on either end. However, a loan that is never paid off and was never expected to be paid will, if examined by the IRS, be considered a gift. A **gift of property** requires that the recipient assumes the giver's adjusted cost basis in the property. (It is tax-smarter for a recipient to inherit property than have it come as a gift, because the recipient's basis in the inherited property is figured at the time of the decedent's death, not the decedent's adjusted basis from when he bought it. The recipient's basis at the time of death is known as a "**stepped-up basis**." Inheritance is not conveniently scheduled, so you may have to make do with a gift.) If you are fortunate enough to have access to gift help in one form or another, run the options through the CPA who does the giver's taxes. He can estimate the tax consequences for both donor and recipient.

Fifth, rework debt to free cash.

When interest rates are low, you can **refinance** the debt on your appreciated primary residence and use the cash—on which you will pay interest—for down payment on additional property. This is a fairly common way to find down payment. It results in a fully financed purchase of the second property, with all of the virtues and risks that entails. (See Kenneth R. Harney, "Acute Cases of Refi Fever," Washington Post, August 24, 2002.) The five features you're looking for in a refinancing are: 1) significantly lower interest rate, 2) as little refinancing cost as possible, 3) less total interest paid over term; 4) relatively short break-even point; and 5) a total debt load that you can handle in emergencies. Be careful with refis that you are not hit with both a pre-pay penalty along with upfront costs.

A typical refi with cash out might look like this. Assume that you have $100,000 remaining on your home mortgage at 8 percent fixed rate with an amortization term of 30 years. Your monthly principal and interest mortgage payment is $734. If you refinance that $100,000 at 6 percent for 20 years, your monthly P&I payment would be $716. If you refinanced $110,000 at 5.75 percent for 20 years, your monthly payment would be $703, leaving $10,000 available for a down payment. But keep in mind the risk of this strategy. Those who refinance to pull cash out of their homes default at a higher rate than those who refinance either the original principal amount or the remaining principal. The more borrowed, the greater the default likelihood. "Fannie Mae says a borrower who takes a new loan that is 20 percent larger than the balance due on the old loan is three times more likely to default than a borrower whose cash out is 3 percent or less of the old balance." (Jeff Brown, "Cash-out deals tempting many: Refinancings may lead to more debt," Richmond Times-Dispatch, November 6, 2002.)

If you are refinancing a primary residence for more than the principal so as to pull cash out for a down payment, expect to pay upfront costs. Lenders who have not sold your note on your primary residence should be able to refinance the remaining balance at low cost. But the lender who sold your note on the secondary market is collecting only a 0.25 percent fee for servicing your loan. That $250 a year on a $100,000 loan does not get the borrower much refinancing help in many lender offices. (See Robert J. Bruss, "Real Estate Mailbag," Washington Post, August 24, 2002.)

Even where you can get a low-cost refi from the lender, be aware that state-imposed transaction costs vary from state to state, e.g., $1,207 in North Carolina to $3,001 in Florida on a $150,000 refi with a 70 percent loan-to-value (LTV) ratio, according to a Quicken-Loan Inc. study. These costs would include, where applicable, document (deed) stamps, transfer tax, title fee, among others. (See Kenneth R. Harvey, "Rates make it hard to stay out of market," Richmond Times-Dispatch, March 16, 2003.)

A second option is to use a **home-equity loan** to raise cash for a down payment. A home-equity loan is for a fixed amount, and can be used for the homeowner's choice of purpose. The loan is a lien against the property that secures it. A home-equity loan leaves the original mortgage in place. It is a new debt, secured by your primary residence. Interest is usually a variable rate, such as the **prime rate** plus two points. (A bank's prime rate is its base rate that it extends to its most creditworthy commercial customers. In practice, large banks tend toward adopting the same prime rate, which reflects their cost of borrowing short-term as set by the Federal Reserve's interest rates.) Home-equity interest rates tend to be higher than other interest rates a lender offers. If you fail to meet the payments on the home-equity loan, the lender can come after your primary residence, which is his security for the loan. (His security for the home-equity loan is not your second home in the country.) Lenders typically add fees and charges for these loans.

A third option is to establish a **home-equity line of credit (HELOC)**. A HELOC makes cash available to a homeowner at a variable interest rate, using the primary residence as security. The homeowner can choose to borrow the available money at any time. The line will be set up as a second mortgage on the primary residence. The lender will make available up to 70 or even 80 percent of the home's appraisal value, less the principal remaining on the first mortgage. HELOCs are available for as much as 125 percent of appraisal value less the value of the first mortgage, but such loans would, in the event of default, require the homeowner to come up with more than the primary residence is worth to keep it. A HELOC with the same lender can be done with low transaction costs. HELOC interest rates are lower than those on credit cards, but higher than most mortgage rates. Mortgage interest on home-equity loans and HELOCs is tax-deductible up to $100,000 for any purpose, and for over $100,000 if the money is used to buy investments (e.g., timberland, farmland) or for business reasons. (Holden Lewis, "Trading mortgage for a loan on equity," <u>Richmond Times-Dispatch,</u> from <u>www.bankrate.com</u>, March 9, 2003.)

A fourth option is take out a **second mortgage** on your principal residence. Your first mortgage is left untouched and in first position. Your second mortgage is also secured by your residence. Whoever holds the first mortgage has first claim on your house in a default. A home-equity loan is one type of second mortgage.

These sources are also discussed in Chapter 32, with an emphasis on their risks.

Sixth, try to get a rental payment upfront. Many rural properties have rentable assets—pasture for grazing; flat land for row crops; woods and fields for hunting; water for fishing; trails for horses, snowmobiles and ATVs; facilities for storage; and tenant houses for renters. To the extent you can, get as much of any rental payment upfront so that you can use it to help purchase the property. This money won't come to you prior to purchase for use as your down payment, but it might be scheduled for soon after closing so that you can repay borrowed down-payment money. You might discount the first year's rent for an upfront payment of the full year's payment. Rental income is subject to taxation.

Seventh, take advantage of an assumable mortgage. An "assumable" is a seller's mortgage obligation that allows the buyer to take the seller's place. A buyer would like to take over an assumable that has better terms than are currently being offered. The additional advantage to the buyer is that the lender's fees imposed are substantially less than those on new loans and refinancings. Loans originating with the Federal Housing Administration, Veterans Administration and some ARMs are likely candidates for assumable mortgages. The buyer will usually need to qualify with the lender to assume the seller's position. Most mortgage notes no longer allow assumption, because lenders make more money on new loans.

Assumptions help buyers. Sellers need to exercise caution in allowing a buyer to assume their notes because such mortgages usually keep the seller liable in some way for the debt. A **mortgage assignment** substitutes the buyer for the seller's obligation to pay the note. If the buyer defaults on an assigned mortgage, the seller is liable for paying the note's outstanding balance. A "**subject to**" assumption places the seller in a position of being responsible for paying both the note's balance and any deficiency following a foreclosure sale. A **novation** frees the seller from all obligations on the note the buyer has assumed.

Eighth, take over seller-owed, non-mortgage debt. The seller may be in trouble with back taxes owed, liens on the property and consumer debt. If your cash is short but your cash flow is strong and getting stronger, you may be able to persuade the seller to reduce his asking price in return for paying some portion of his debt. Creditors should welcome the idea of substituting a stronger financial profile for the seller's. You might also propose to the creditors that they write off some of the debt in return for getting you on their obligations. Talk to your lawyer and CPA about this.

2. Sell some of the property's "severable" assets

Rural property often includes one or two severable assets that can be sold without unduly diminishing the core reasons that you wanted to buy the property in the first place. I mean by "severable," an asset that can be sold generally within one year of purchase for more than you paid for it.

Severable assets can include merchantable timber, houses, mineral rights, small lots with road frontage, back acreage, agricultural equipment, personal property that came with the sale (tractors, farm machinery, tools, wood stoves, fuel tanks, materiel) and abandoned buildings (especially log cabins). I have used timber cruises to arrange 100-percent-financed purchases from a local bank on the understanding that I would use the net proceeds from the lump-sum timber sale that I would arrange soon after purchase to pay down the loan. The bank ended up with far more than the normal 20 percent in down payment and almost zero risk. I bought the properties with nothing out of pocket. You can work the same tactic with other assets. The more severable assets your target property has—things that can be sold without degrading the core asset that you want to keep—the more that property can pay for itself.

It will be to your advantage to have the value of any severable asset you're planning to sell appraised by a qualified, independent third-party prior to your purchase of the entire property. That appraisal, valuation or timber cruise can then be used to establish your original **tax basis** in the specific asset. In simple terms, your "**adjusted basis**" is what you have net in an asset when you sell it, after deductions from and additions to basis are calculated. If you immediately sell an asset for the same money as your pre-purchase valuation, you will show no taxable gain, hence no current tax obligation at your regular rate on the sale. A transaction of this sort changes the way your accountant allocates your total basis among the remaining assets. The sale of this asset decreases your basis in the remaining property. This tactic defers your tax obligation, it does not eliminate it. (If the property goes into your estate, the deferred tax may never be paid if your estate falls beneath the tax-free cap.) As a rule, the higher your basis in an asset/property when you go to sell it the better, because it means your taxable gain—the difference between what you net on the sale of the asset/property and what you have in it—is less. When you sell the remaining entirety, your basis will be lowered in proportion to and how you handled your post-purchase asset sales. The lowered basis left in your timberland as a result of the post-purchase sale of timber (which reduces basis) means that your taxable gain on your last sale—the property itself—will be higher. Estate planning, however, can protect both the tax-deferment and, by bequeathing the property to heirs rather than selling it, eliminate or reduce taxation altogether. Different types of **trusts** are also available to minimize current and future tax burdens; talk to your lawyer and CPA about these options. And, if the country property becomes your principal residence for two years out of five prior to its sale, you will be able to exclude from taxation as much as $250,000 (individual) and $500,000 (joint) of profit on its sale. Your CPA and lawyer can advise you on strategies to minimize your future tax obligations.

Another strategy that you can apply to severable assets is to arrange for their sale as part of your purchase. The seller of the target property will be selling to at least two buyers: you, the principal buyer, and the asset buyers whom you are coordinating. A lender or a seller financing the sale may count some or all of the income you receive from the immediate sale of the asset as amounting to down payment if you put it against your note. If you are working with an institutional lender, you may have to take title to the seller's entirety and then sell the asset. But this is usually not necessary. You line up your buyers with a **contingent sales contract** between you and them, then sell them the assets they want contingent on your buying the entirety from your seller. This approach involves a **simultaneous closing** by which you buy the whole from the seller and at the same time sell an asset to your buyer. I did this on a 425-acre farm, selling the house and 30 acres for just under 30 percent of the total purchase price. You can avoid paying some transaction costs, like recordation fees and property transfer taxes, to the extent that you arrange before closing to have separate deeds to you and your **piggy-back partners** for whichever assets they're buying.

A variation on this tactic is to persuade the seller to sell you only that combination of his property's assets you want. This reduces the money that you have to front and borrow as well as eliminates the risks and headaches that can be involved in selling unwanted assets. The common downside of trying to persuade a seller to part out his own property to your advantage is that he will increase the per-acre price to you for the smaller parcel. And if what you want is the choice piece, be prepared to pay top dollar. It's worth trying to persuade the seller that he will net more money by following your parting-out strategy than by selling the entirety, which means, you argue, that he doesn't need to raise your per-acre price. Most sellers don't want to bother with parting-out their property. It's been my experience that a buyer has trouble convincing a seller to sell him only what he wants. If you do buy more than what you want, I think you will find that your unwanted assets can often be sold at a profit, though it may take some time.

It's important to think through your plan to sell some assets of your newly acquired property before you buy it. First, this will help you project costs and income. Second, you need to start very low-key testing with potential buyers as you are moving toward a purchase. Your quiet marketing should be designed to avoid stimulating other entirety buyers. Once you have a signed purchase contract, you can market hard during your escrow period with the idea of scheduling a simultaneous closing. Third, you will need to make certain that any mortgage note you sign allows you to sell a portion of the collateralized property. Your note-holder needs to agree to release what you want to sell, and, in return, you will usually have to pay off a proportional part of your note. Make sure that your lender does not have a pre-pay penalty in your mortgage document, which would penalize your sale of severable assets. Fourth, you need to project the tax consequences of your parting-out strategy. How your CPA allocates original basis among the various assets will affect your tax obligations. If you can sell an asset soon after closing, but schedule the majority of your payment for one calendar year later, you will get capital-gains treatment on that delayed profit to the extent that it's not tax-deferred. Most taxpayers benefit from paying their capital-gains rate on income rather than their regular rate, when it is higher.

The other way to think about lender releases is to arrange with your lender at the start to pay off your new property, parcel by parcel. This allows you to free your core "keeper" asset (s) from debt relatively quickly. One or more of those assets can then be sold or refinanced with cash sticking in your pocket. A **partial release** allows you to pay down your debt so that you free an asset for your unencumbered use fairly quickly. Lenders should like this strategy, because their time exposure is short and the repayment is pegged largely to sales, not borrower cash flow.

Here is an example of how an entirety purchase can be paid for by the sale of severable assets. Take a 200-acre farm near, but not on, a developed lake, with the following asset mix:

1. 100 acres of merchantable timber with an immediate cash value for the standing timber and an independent value for the cutover land (bare land value);

2. 30 acres of open pasture, with road frontage and two house sites;

3. 20 acres of relatively level, tillable ground with high agricultural value. Also very developable owing to long road frontage;

4. 30 acres of marginally productive open land that is sometimes used as hayfield, sometimes as pasture, sometimes as cornfield. Has road frontage; and

5. Two-story farm house with assorted outbuildings and livestock pens, and 20 acres.

The asking price is $230,000. Proximity to the lake adds market value to the lots. The investor's objective is to have his investment pay for the 100 acres of timberland, which he wants to add to his estate. He values these five assets separately and sells them quickly. His investment strategy is: 1) sell the merchantable sawtimber 16" DBH and larger and keep the cutover land; 2) sell the 30 acres as two 15-acre lots, each with a nice house site; 3) sell the 20 acres of valuable agricultural land to a local farmer for agricultural use, or to a house builder, or as two ten-acre lots; 4) sell the 30 acres of marginally productive agricultural land to a local farmer or as a lot; and 5) sell the house, barn and 20 acres to a second-home buyer, possibly with the 30 acres of marginal land. This investor has chosen to keep the productive timberland as his core long-term investment and is flipping off all other assets to pay for that acreage. The investor could choose to follow the same strategy to retain any other asset, though the numbers will work differently. A common example for a second-home buyer is to sell most of the land to pay for the farmhouse and 20 acres.

This strategy is no different from that used in **merger and acquisitions (M&As)** to pay for corporate raider B's purchase of conglomerate A by shedding A's saleable assets and keeping those B wants. The economic logic is this: the sum of the pieces sold individually will exceed the investor's purchase price for the whole. The difference between what the investor nets after taxes on his sales and his costs for acquisition and resale is his profit. If the investor plans to part out all assets in a flip, he should borrow most, if not all, of the entire amount of the acquisition and other costs, using the pre-purchase valuations of each separate asset as security for his business plan and debt. A **parting-out strategy** will not work if your seller has priced his land to you at its "parted-out" value, and, you, the buyer, foolishly pay his retail price. Nor will it work if you overvalue the selling price of the parts. Time always has a money value in such deals, and the longer a highly leveraged investment is carried, the harder it is to make a profit. On the other hand, time usually increases the value of each country part.

Here's a simplified picture of how the numbers might work. The seller's asking price is $230,000, to which the investor/buyer agrees. Prior to placing his full-price purchase offer with the seller, he has a timber cruise in hand, along with an FMV appraisal of each asset. His plan is to sell all the assets except for the 100 acres of cutover timberland. Using the timber cruise and a two-page business plan that shows his pre-purchase asset valuations (column II, in TABLE 33-1 below), he is able to secure 100 percent financing. He pays down the note with every asset sale until it's completely retired.

The investor uses the 120 days of escrow between when his purchase contract takes effect and when he closes with the seller to complete the following tasks: 1) introduce his division plan to local authorities and revise, if necessary; 2) survey the property for division; 3) retain a consulting forester to mark the timber for a competitively bid sale to be conducted one month after the closing; 4) test the soil for perc sites; and 5) market the assets to appropriate buyers, e.g., local farmers, local residents, and non-local lot buyers. The last of these tasks can take the form of a sale contingent on the investor's purchase. Property division can be simple—or expensive, complicated and uncertain. If you're working with a difficult property, you have to insert a **division-approval contingency** in your purchase offer that makes your purchase contingent on obtaining to your satisfaction all necessary permits and approvals to implement your post-purchase plans. Your closing occurs within two weeks of obtaining the final permit or approval. The costs of applying for and securing these permits is yours, but they will be secured in the name of the seller and then conveyed along with the property. Any activity such as surveying or marking timber during escrow should be introduced to the seller as part of your offer. The buyer should have the seller agree in writing to each and every activity the buyer wants to do during escrow, none of which harm the seller's land. In many states, the buyer should be allowed to do such tasks during escrow as a matter of equitable title once contigencies are removed, but I advise buyers to notify sellers through their purchase offer of their intentions. A good part of the investor's work can be finished during the seller's ownership in this manner.

I've simplified the example by assigning a straight-through price to all land, even though the parcels of acreage to be sold will be priced differently according to their retail value in the marketplace. I've allocated values at the time of purchase as $60,000 for all improvements and $850 per acre for the land, $230,000 in all. I've also simplified the investor's costs by not including any upfront charges he incurs in scoping and purchasing the property.

TABLE 33-1

Cash-Out Investment Analysis

	I Cost	II Investor's Pre-Purchase Valuation	III Actual Net Sale Value	IV Investor's Retained Value or Cash
1. 100 acres. Sell timber	$85,000 (Land + timber)	$140,000 (Timber only)	$90,000*	$40,000 (RV)**
100 acres cutover	-	35,000		35,000 (RV)
2. 30 acres of open	25,500	75,000	65,000	39,500 (Cash)

3. 20 acres of
    developable
    land
	17,000	55,000	50,000	33,000 (Cash)

4. 30 acres of marginal land	25,500	30,000	25,500	-0-
5. House/20 acres pasture.	77,000	150,000	155,000	78,000 (Cash)
	$230,000	$485,000	$385,500	$75,000 RV + $150,500 Cash

* Net sale value is the buyer's remaining money after deducting his expenses in selling each part. These expenses would include attorney fees, consulting forester fee for managing the timber sale, surveying, interest, closing costs, interest, etc.

**The buyer sold a selective harvest of the standing timber at the time of purchase, say all trees with stems 16" DBH and larger. That left a number of premerchantable trees standing whose estimated present value is $40,000.

This investor finances the entire purchase of $230,000. After selling all the assets he is able to sell, he nets $385,500. He pays off his note and $25,000 in interest, a total of $255,000. His pre-tax cash in hand is $150,500 from the asset sale. He also keeps 100 acres of cutover timberland that has a retained value of $40,000 in the premerch timber less than 16" DBH and $35,000 in the land. The 100 acres is now owned free of a mortgage. On the cash, he will owe federal income tax at his regular rate or his capital-gains rate, depending on when he sold each asset. He will have deductions for interest and other costs. He can defer paying income tax on the timber sale, because he sold the timber for his pre-purchase valuation, which created no taxable event.

It was not OPM that made this deal work so well. It was, rather, the buyer's careful and accurate pre-purchase scoping that allowed him to see that the seller's wholesale price on the property was way below the retail price of its separate assets. The seller priced his property as a farm, not as a collection of assets near a lake. The advantage to this buyer of using OPM was that it left his own cash free to cover other costs, emergencies and the dollar cost of delays. This investor used his own resources—mainly his brain—to finance this purchase.

3. Neighbors

While the Old Testament instructs us not to covet our neighbor's assets, I have found such coveting is as common in the countryside as everywhere else. It's actually quite understandable. Farms—and often other types of rural land—depend on having in place an integrated system that works efficiently. The best 500 acres of Iowa dirt is not worth much if it can only be accessed by a mile-long easement that is restricted to equipment no wider than six feet. Every good property works physically, legally, environmentally and in terms of its resource mix. Where one or more components is less than optimum, the property as a whole works below its optimum. A neighbor, therefore, may need one of your seller's components more than your seller does. And for reasons that can range from rational to petty, your seller has always refused to sell this something to this neighbor. The odds are high that at least one of your neighbors both covets and has the money to buy one of the asset components that you are about to purchase. This sale alone can produce your down payment—without substantially reducing the core asset you want to keep.

You do need to be careful in distinguishing between a severable asset that does not substantially diminish the ability of your new land to do what you want it to do and an asset that does. An inexperienced buyer should not assume that he knows the difference. I would proceed cautiously, asking your seller what he thinks of the sale to the covetous neighbor; also ask the county extension agent and other neighbors. You do not want to sell your only barn or the one livestock pond on the farm. As long as the sale of the component is marginal to your use of the core property, it can be sold. The covetous neighbor will be smarter than you about the value of the asset he seeks; don't sell quickly when someone waves quick cash under your nose.

4. The Seller

The rural seller is an obvious source of cash.

When a seller fully finances a buyer's purchase, he does not reach into his pocket and give cash to the buyer the way a bank does. Rather, he retains ownership of the property and allows the buyer to pay him the agreed price over time with interest. When the buyer has paid the note completely, the seller conveys the title to him. While the buyer is paying the seller, he holds **equitable title** in the seller's property, which allows him to possess and use the property. The buyer should not be allowed under the terms of this agreement to damage the seller's property. The seller holds a first and primary mortgage in such circumstances, which means he is due his payment before any other party whose loan is secured by the property. This might also be referred to as the "seller taking back a first trust." (See Benny L. Kass, "Housing Counsel: In Matters of Trusts, Sellers Shouldn't Make Deals on Faith," Washington Post, May 10, 2003.)

A common format for this arrangement is the **installment land contract** (also referred to as a "land contract," "land installment contract," "contract for deed" and "installment contract"). This type of purchase contract provides that the seller retains legal title to the property that you, the buyer, are allowed to possess and use. The property is the seller's security in the event that you default on the agreed payment schedule of interest and principal. The buyer receives a deed from the seller upon his last payment and the fulfillment of all other contract provisions. A seller-financed sale contract should specifically provide that the buyer is permitted to possess and use the seller's property without restriction, except for activities that reduce the value of the property as collateral. You and the seller should have a meeting of the minds about which activities will be permitted and which won't. If you want to cut timber on the property, your installment land contract should be written in such a way that you are permitted to do so. If there are rent, lease income or production royalties from minerals, the contract should reflect how these are to be handled and monies to be apportioned. The seller may insist that some or all of the proceeds be applied to your debt. If you want to build a house, you will have to make an arrangement that works for both of you; otherwise, all improvements you make to the property will run with the land in the event of your default. One way to handle this situation is to arrange with the seller that your note with him runs in two stages: the first is for, say, 25 acres, on which you build your house; the second is for the remainder of the property. In that fashion, you pay for the 25 acres first so that they and your new house are not exposed to the seller if you fail subsequently to pay for the rest of the land.

A seller-financed purchase generates money to the buyer through savings. First, the buyer is spared paying all points, fees and charges that a lender would normally impose. This alone can keep five percent of the purchase price in the buyer's pocket. Second, interest charged the buyer is not front-loaded and should be calculated on the declining balance. The interest rate should be a truer rate, lower than the same rate from a bank. A buyer should pay less total interest to a seller at any given rate than he would pay at that rate to an institutional lender over the same period. Third, a buyer may be able to get a discount on price by structuring the seller-financed payments over several years to advantage the seller's after-tax net income each year. Fourth, if you're doing a seller-financed purchase when interest rates are low, have the seller carry the note on a fixed rate rather than on an adjustable basis. Fifth, the seller may agree to a proposal that requires either no down payment or less than an institutional lender. Finally, you may be able to establish a below-market rate with a seller, something that's never possible with an institutional lender. Seller financing, obviously, is an option only with sellers who don't need to cash out the full sale price at closing.

It is essential for the buyer to record the installment land contract. Indeed, some states require recordation. The county office where this occurs might be called the Clerk's Office, Deed Registrar or County Recorder. Recordation prevents the seller from mortgaging the property or selling it out from under you.

In such a contract, nothing prevents the seller from encumbering his property with liens that can remain in place after the buyer makes his last balloon payment and title transfers. The seller must remove any existing mortgage and liens before transferring title. This requirement should be written into your seller-financing document. Better yet, your agreement should prohibit the seller from placing liens on the property during your period of equitable title.

If you are considering such a contract, make sure that you have a thorough title search and get title insurance. Your purchase contract should include language that requires the seller to prove that he has marketable title. (In reality, your lawyer may have to determine whether the seller has good title.) Don't do a land contract without having a smart lawyer reading every line *as you are negotiating*, not after.

A note between buyer and seller for all or part of the selling price is often referred to as a **purchase-money mortgage**. The seller accepts a note on his own land for all or part of the purchase price, using the property as collateral. If the buyer fails to make payments, the seller retakes possession of his property. The note may also be called a **mortgage** or a **deed of trust**.

A land contract should include a 60-day grace period that allows the buyer to cure a missed payment. If you do default, you lose all the payments you paid to the seller as **liquidated damages**; you should not owe the seller money beyond what you have paid. You will lose the property as well.

If the seller is totally financing the sale, he may ask that you provide additional collateral in addition to the property itself. This would cover his foreclosure and remarketing costs if you were to default soon after taking possession. I would resist adding collateral to the seller's land, except if he's allowing you to finance 100 percent of the purchase. If you do increase collateral, negotiate a **release schedule** that frees the add-on security when you reach and satisfy a certain scheduled payment. Make sure to record the release documents.

Why would a seller become his buyer's banker? First, this arrangement may be the only way to sell a unique property or one that is over-priced. Second, there may be tax strategies involved. The seller may want to reduce his tax hit by spreading income from the sale over several tax years. Third, holding title to his own property while a buyer makes interest-bearing payments does not put the seller at very much risk. If the buyer defaults, the seller still owns the property plus whatever improvements the buyer made. The seller keeps all the principal and interest the buyer has paid. The risk to the seller involves damage to his property or the sale of its timber that is not used to repay the note. Fourth, it's not a bad investment. The seller may figure that a note paying an interest rate above what he could get on a three-year CD and is secured by his own appreciating property is a better investment than his alternatives. Fifth, the seller may be more interested in predictable future payments than in a lump sum that he has to invest. Finally, the seller may know of some complication running with his property that, if discovered, would complicate a conventional sale. Seller financing may keep the cover on this defect or allow it to be resolved in the future.

The major reason why sellers don't do seller-financing all the time is simple: most need to get all their cash at closing. Only sellers who don't need to cash out completely can fully finance a purchase. Sellers will weigh the risk of default buyer to buyer, and the burden of remarketing according to the individual property.

The most common form of seller-financing is for the **seller to take back a second mortgage** to help the buyer piece together a workable money package. A **seller's second** is usually for less money than the first mortgage. When a seller partly finances the buyer's purchase with a second mortgage behind a lender's first, title is held either by the lender holding the **first mortgage** or in trust. In either case, the buyer gets title (ownership) when he finishes paying both mortgages. In the event of a default, the seller is in second position—after the institutional lender—in getting his loan repaid from a sale of his property.

Being in second position is also referred to as the seller agreeing to **subordinate** his loan to the one held by the primary lender. When a buyer defaults on either the first or second mortgage, foreclosure ensues. If the buyer defaults on the first mortgage, the holder of the second gets whatever is left after the first mortgage and the costs of foreclosure and resale are paid. If the buyer defaults on the second mortgage, the seller can force the sale of the property. But the holder of the first mortgage would be paid first, with anything left going to the seller. A seller with a second mortgage will not get his land back in the event of default unless he negotiates a buy-back with the lender or is the high bidder at the foreclosure sale. The seller holding a second could, therefore, wind up without the payment due him and without his property in the absolute worst case. A seller offering a second to a buyer tries to minimize his risk by carrying a note for no more than two to five years.

Institutional lenders rarely object to a seller holding a second mortgage, because they end up lending less on the property and feeling more secure about their exposure. The lender's first mortgage becomes increasingly secure as the buyer pays down his second. Once the seller's second is paid off, it will be the buyer's equity rather than the lender's principal that will be hit hardest by a default. Further, the holder of the first mortgage has no responsibility to protect the holder of the second. To the degree that the lender's risk is pushed onto the second-holding seller, the lender is in a win-win situation—a profitable loan with little, if any risk, from a default.

If you choose to work with some form of seller financing, you need to make sure that you understand who has the title to the property during the time of your indebtedness; what circumstances allow the seller to call the note, that is, payment of the entire amount; and precisely what happens once you make your last payment to the seller. On the day you complete paying off a second mortgage, you should have the seller sign a **certificate of satisfaction** and record it that day. (In states using a deed of trust or title theory of mortgage, this document is called a **deed of reconveyance**.) This document shows that you have paid your obligation to the full satisfaction of the note holder, and that his lien is removed from your property. When you pay off the first mortgage, you or the trustee holding the note, will record a similar document. Only at that point will you own the property free and clear, with the original deed and satisfied lien notes in your possession.

Seller-financed notes rarely front-load interest. But be advised that the term **"simple interest"** can have different interpretations. (See discussion under "Interest Rates" in Chapter 32.) I believe the best policy is for the buyer and seller to agree at the time the note is negotiated as to how interest is to be calculated, when exactly interest (and principal) is to be paid, how much exactly each interest payment will be, and exactly how payments will be delivered from buyer to seller. I would also insist on a **no-penalty, pre-payment option** that allows the buyer to pay off the entire note early. The seller-financing document should be drafted by a lawyer, preferably yours. It should set out what happens when the buyer is either late with a payment or misses one entirely. The parties should agree on a correction period—15 to 30 business days, for example—during which the buyer can make good a missed payment without penalty. It's also reasonable to limit the number of such no-penalty periods to no more than, say, two over a five-year term. If the buyer is late more than twice, the seller can impose a penalty. The trigger for default should be simple and unambiguous. Default procedures will depend on whether the buyer has improved the property through the construction of a house, for example or taken value from the property. I'm always inclined to work out **anticipated-catastrophe language**, such as for default, in advance when everyone is being nice as pie, or at least fairly cooperative. Most seller-financed documents I have seen, primarily seller-held seconds, leave a lot to everyone's imagination. As an out-of-town buyer, don't sign a seller-financing document without first running it by your local lawyer.

I should point out a "found-money-for-the-buyer tactic" that you might find a seller proposing. Many older rural landowners have their life's work and capital tied up in their property, buildings and equipment. Depending on their individual circumstances, a large property sale could mean a large tax payment. Where equipment and improvements (buildings, silos, farm structures, etc.) have been depreciated, a portion of that depreciation will be recaptured upon their sale, which increases the tax owed. Such a seller may advertise as a FSBO and offer you a noticeably below-market price for what he calls **"an all-cash deal."** The specifics of such a proposition will vary but its essence is that you are being asked to agree to buy his land in a fashion that will not be honestly reported on his 1040 or settlement statement and which will leave as little paper trail as possible. This may involve falsifying documents, or not recording the deed of sale, or delaying recordation of the deed until after his estate is settled, or not using a lawyer (who is required to file certain IRS forms for every property transaction), or not claiming sale expenses on your own 1040. I don't mean to suggest that all sellers, or even most sellers, in this circumstance will offer you a proposition of this sort. But someone might, and he'll call it "seller financing." **DO NOT PARTICIPATE IN SUCH CONSPIRACIES.** You will likely get caught. Sooner or later, you will have problems in your record of ownership, and that can lead to headaches in disposing of the property. Such a seller will always have something on you. You will be co-conspirators in a scheme to defraud the IRS and your local/state taxing authorities. Having said all that about a slippery seller, let me add that it is just as scummy to offer an aged, vulnerable seller a pay-in-cash deal at a low-ball price to lure him into tax fraud.

In addition to seller-financing arrangements, a buyer can propose to a seller a sale using a **wraparound purchase money mortgage** where circumstances are favorable. A "wrap" is subordinate to the seller's own mortgage, but it draws into its terms the seller's note. If the seller's mortgage includes an **acceleration clause**, which provides that the note's unpaid balance is due immediately if the seller fails to meet his payments or property taxes, then a wraparound cannot be used. The wrap's advantage to the buyer is that his down payment on the entire property is limited to the cash required for the wrap. In the right conditions a comparatively small wrap can leverage the purchase of a large property as long as the buyer can handle the monthly mortgage payment on the combined notes. Since the wrap is smaller than a primary mortgage, all the fees and points the seller would normally pay are scaled down. The buyer gets title to the property, and the seller gets cash. But the seller remains liable for payment of the original note, so buyer and seller continue to be involved with each other. A wrap, in this way, is not an **assumption**, by which the buyer takes over the responsibility for the seller's original note. A wrap allows the buyer to acquire an over-priced property on terms that make it favorable. Do not write a wrap note yourself! It requires a skillful lawyer, and it must include protections for both buyer and seller. The buyer, for example, must be protected against the seller's failure to keep up payments on the original note (for which the buyer is providing him funds each month).

A seller can help a buyer through a **buydown**. This is a seller-made, lump-sum payment to the buyer's lender to reduce the buyer's interest rate. The seller is, in effect, paying the lender a point or two to increase the lender's yield. On a 30-year note, the general guideline is that six points reduce the interest rate by one percent. A buydown does not give cash to the buyer, but it reduces his total interest cost. A note for $100,000 at ten percent for 30 years involves a monthly payment of $877.58, or a total P&I of $315,929. The same $100,000 at 9 percent for 30 years has a payment of $804.63, or $289,667. The $6,000 buydown at the beginning of the note saves the buyer $26,262 over the full term. Time-limited buydowns might be arranged where the buyer repays the seller at a future date. Rules for buydowns are set up for some programs, such as those through Fannie Mae, VA and FHA.

The seller can also pick up a greater share of the settlement costs as a way of helping a buyer reduce his need for cash. **Seller contributions** can include the payment of discount points, routine closing costs, mortgage insurance, moving costs, property tax, among others. When a seller pays certain points for a buyer, the buyer may deduct them.

The seller can also help you with a down payment by selling you certain items of personal property for you to cash out and use for that purpose. (Better yet, the seller could give you such items for resale.) You might, for example, offer to buy all of his farm equipment "for one money." This can be attractive if the farmer does not want to go through the emotional travail of watching his stuff auctioned and paying the auctioneer ten percent plus costs for doing so. If you're willing to spend the time selling the seller's assets, you may be able to generate enough after-tax cash to cover an appreciable portion of your down payment.

Finally, a seller can help you by agreeing to **reserve some asset** from his sale to you that he can sell to another party. This might be a tenant house or acreage. The idea is that the seller can sell two things— the big thing to you and the small thing to someone else—for more money than he can sell the two things together to you. You now need less down payment to buy the property that you want than before. You've also avoided the cost and hassle of selling the smaller property.

5. Co-investors and partners

Rural property lends itself to "going in on it together." One hundred acres of woods or a farmhouse and acreage are easily shared with friends, either sequentially (as in a time share) or simultaneously. A number of legal structures are available by which buyers can organize shared property ownership. The advantage of a partner to a cash-strapped buyer is that your down payment and mortgage obligations are cut in proportion to his financial contribution. There are, as you might expect, down sides to sharing. You may also persuade a partner that he should pay disproportionately more in down payment as compensation for having you find the property and do all of the scoping.

I've been involved in three joint purchases. All used **tenants (tenancy) in common**, by which there was one title to the property and each of the owners had an undivided interest in the property as a whole. If four buyers each put up 25 percent of the cash to buy a property, as tenants in common each owner would have an equal ownership interest in the entire property. Each owner's interest is inheritable, and each owner can sue for partition of the property if things don't work. Another ownership format is **joint tenants (tenancy)**, by which upon the death of one owner the other owners inherit his share in the whole. Thus, upon the death of a quarter interest, the remaining three owners automatically assume that interest with each now owning one-third of the whole. The last surviving owner gets 100 percent of the property. Joint tenants must own equal shares; tenants in common can own unequal shares. Joint tenancy avoids **probate**, which is the legal process by which a court determines the assets of the decedent's estate and who owns what. Heirs want to avoid probate because it can be lengthy and costly. But joint tenancy means that the longest lived wins the property lottery at the expense of the other joint tenants, and, more accurately, their estates and heirs.

Two of my three tenants-in-common land purchases ended sourly, mainly, I think, because of divorce, relocation and changed circumstances of all involved. In one case, I had to sell a highly-appreciated interest in land on which I did not live to a partner without much money. My partner who lived on the property wanted to preserve the status quo at best, and, alternatively, pay less than FMV to buy me out. We had a hard time agreeing on how much the property, less his improvements, had appreciated. Appraisers we hired did not estimate timber value on the 100 acres of woods. Had we not finally reached a buy-out number, my circumstances would have forced me to bring a **partition suit**, by which a court would have supervised the property's sale and the distribution of its proceeds. In the other purchase, the two remaining partners of the original four decided to sell the property together following divorces, but had a hard time determining the value of a house I had built. The third example, done 20-25 years after the first two, has been problem free, because both owners see the property as a long-term timberland investment. While I would be inclined to use this mortgage-free property in a 1031 exchange to increase the value of our shared asset, I'm not opposed to keeping it for our daughters as their joint inheritance. It helps, of course, to have paid for this property with a selective timber cut two years after purchase, with cash left over.

The lesson I draw is that partnerships among older, more settled individuals who share goals are likely to work better than partnerships among younger adults who can be more subject to changes in relationships, careers and needs. Key to making these "go-in-together deals" work are pre-existing friendships that have weathered a bump or two, shared objectives and flexibility to adapt to the inevitable changes in individual circumstances. The other factor that benefits a partnership is having each member hold sufficient net worth and represent enough financial stability to exempt the shared property from anyone's emergency need to cash it out. If one member is pinched, the partners should be able to buy his share.

The wildcard in partnering is how you and your partners behave toward each other over time. If you've ever acted selfishly in such an arrangement or had others disappoint you, you know that individuals do not always act nobly and honestly. Therefore, I advise entering any partnership with exits clearly marked and understood. Nothing helps more than a written plan signed by all partners that spells out shared objectives, how to change those objectives and what to do when the partners disagree.

For the purpose of coming up with cash for a down payment, you can consider a more business-like "partnership." Contract for the property in its entirety, then sell a piece or a share in the whole to a friend for a profit, which becomes your down payment. Do a simultaneous closing so that you can give the down payment to the seller at settlement. Calculate your tax consequences before agreeing on numbers. There should be limits to your mark up, which will be determined by the degree of closeness in your relationship, both present and anticipated. If you're selling the "partner" a piece off the entirety, you're not partners in the future, except to the extent that you socialize and borrow each other's stuff. If, on the other hand, he comes in as a tenant in common or as a joint tenant, then you want to be as fair as you can. Ten to 20 percent profit on what you sell seems reasonable if you were the one who found the property and did the legwork. You may want to give each other a **first right of refusal** if either decides to sell.

Other shared-ownership formats are available, including corporations, limited liability companies, partnerships, among others. Each offers a different set of implications for debt liability and tax obligations.

All **partnering arrangements** work better when everyone agrees at the outset on the long-term objectives of the ownership, its term and what happens when one or more of the principals wants to get out. Once everyone agrees on the objectives, put them in writing. At minimum, the group should see the rural property as an investment first rather than as an affirmation of lifestyle values. Emotions quickly get incorporated into "my land, my trees, my picnic spot, my spiritual center." It's fine to have feelings for your shared property, but try to keep those feelings secondary to a certain business-oriented objectivity. Rural land bought as an investment can be managed with collective objectivity, rather than owned as a shared family pet or an axis of psychic security. It is, however, difficult to get lifestyle oriented partners thinking this way about lifestyle property. The problem I've found with my own **lifestyle land partnerships** is that lifestyles change, attitudes about many things evolve and money becomes needed.

Shared-interest partnerships—such as a group of hunters buying hunting land—seem to last better than shared lifestyle partnerships.

Parents, of course, can be the best partners a child can find for a land deal if only because they're likely to be more forgiving than other lenders. One way to pay them back for purchase cash is to promise them a **future right (reservation)**—say, a right to cut merchantable timber in 15 years when they are looking for retirement money or the right to sell a piece of the property when needed. If a parental gift exceeds the annual tax-free cap on gifts, a tax hit will follow.

An individual can gift up to $12,000 to any number of individuals each year without being bitten by the federal gift tax. Each parent, in other words, can gift $12,000 to a child and his spouse tax-free each year, for a total of $48,000. One $48,000 gift can be given in December and the next $48,000 can be gifted in January, a month later. When a taxpayer's lifetime gift cap of $1 million is exceeded, a 47 percent tax is imposed. The recipient pays no tax, however. One alternative—or supplement—to a gift is a loan. Parents can make below-market-rate loans, but the IRS will force the parents to pay tax on "imputed interest" on what is known as the applicable federal rate. If a loan is made, the child should record it so that he can deduct the interest payments to his parents. (Colleen DeBasie, "Helping a Home Buyer Can Trigger Taxes," Wall Street Journal, April 10, 2005.)

6. Locally owned local lenders

I've mentioned institutional lenders, such as banks, in discussing mortgages and interest rates. For the purpose of finding money for rural property, I'll distinguish between locally owned lenders in your target county and the local branch offices of regional/national banks.

Many rural counties still have at least one more-or-less locally owned bank along with the branch offices of larger banks. The locally owned bank may be state chartered and regulated. State banking rules are likely to be fewer and less intrusive than federal rules. Consumers/borrowers are likely to have fewer protections. In Virginia, for example, state bankers have no state code of ethics they're expected to follow.

The larger the bank the more tied to procedure and numerical measures it's likely to be in making loans. This is not necessarily harmful to a buyer's interest. Coming from a city or a suburb, you're likely to be familiar with big-bank rigmarole and their formulas. Your "**financials**" will have already been gathered and scrutinized if you've borrowed the mortgage money for your principal residence from such institutions. The high-income urban buyer looks good to rural banks of both kinds. Such individuals often benefit from the disparity between high-paying city jobs and low-paying country jobs. But if you're an out-of-county buyer with "a problem," you may find that the loan officers at the rural branch banks may not have much discretion on applications that don't fit within their cookie cutter. Their LTV ratios are probably immutable, and I would expect no negotiation on fees and points, which they will pronounce are set by policy.

Locally owned banks, in contrast, may be expected to exercise some flexibility on individual applications. Many continue to hold most home-mortgage loans in their own portfolios, which allows them to make loans that don't conform to the standards of the secondary mortgage market. They should have a good idea of the foreclosure value of your local property, even if they don't know much about you. As a stranger appearing on its doorstep asking for money, a local bank will review your financials and apply its formulas. Don't be surprised if the bank makes a few inquiries with whomever you've dealt with locally—real-estate agent, surveyor, forester, lawyer, perhaps even the waitress who served you lunch (who may be the bank president's cousin).

A local bank is likely to charge a higher interest rate than the local offices of the big banks. But I've seen four practices that offset that interest premium: 1) if the locally owned bank charges fees and points at all, they are likely to be substantially lower; 2) it's likely to accept deals where you use something on the property to help with the purchase, such as using a timber sale to generate a down payment; 3) it's not likely to sell a non-conforming note, which gives them a bit more flexibility; and 4) they push paper faster and probably require less of it. A higher interest rate with low upfront costs will work much better for a borrower who plans to pay off a long-term debt within five or so years.

One down side to using a local banker of whichever kind is that folks in the community may come to know your business. The price you paid will in most states be public record, stated in the deed or calculable from taxes paid at closing. The new tax-appraised value when it appears should reflect your purchase price. And, people talk.

After you've been around a while, you will undoubtedly have rubbed some folks the right way and others differently. Local bank boards sometimes make decisions based on personality, friendship and kinship. A bank with a mortgage wields awesome power over an individual, particularly one who's in financial trouble. If you've made the wrong enemy, don't be surprised by active pay back. Small places have large virtues, but affairs within them can be conducted on the basis of personal likes and dislikes. Some in your new community, like any other place, will view your position as a zero-sum game, with every dollar you gain as a dollar out of their pocket and every dollar you lose as a dollar they win. You may find that certain individuals in your new community are hostile to "outsiders." This attitude may or may not be reasonable and justified. You may run into individuals who don't want your business, don't want you to compete with them, don't want your advice and don't want you to succeed. You will also find local individuals with exactly the opposite views. Small places harbor a diversity of local opinions, though that may not be obvious to a newcomer. Having said all that, it is advisable to get to know the directors of the bank that holds your note. This may not help you in a crunch, but it can't hurt. (If, on the other hand, you are an insufferable, arrogant know-it-all, you might do better to apply online.)

Locally owned rural banks tend to be very profitable. The exception would be a bank in a chronically depressed area or in a place that was undercut by a cataclysmic financial disaster. Bank holding companies are always looking to buy small independents, whereupon they are made into branches even though the faces may remain the same. Banks mainly get in trouble from **insider loans** to their officers and directors that are not repaid. Both big banks and small banks are susceptible, because boards do not like to deal harshly with their own. If you pick up information that a local bank is being run as a cookie jar, avoid it. Many rural banks in farm country are susceptible to farming-related troubles affecting the bulk of their borrowers. A bank's failure, however, should not materially hurt a borrower. If stock in a well-run local bank comes up for sale, buy some. It should prove a wise investment on its own merits, as well as help you as a borrower.

The situation that you truly want to avoid is one where the self-interest of a bank's board member conflicts with your own. This can be especially troublesome when you are in a jam on the bank's loan. In my experience, board members of small, local banks do not recuse themselves from bank loans and decisions that benefit their non-bank private interests, but that may be atypical. Whether you, a newcomer and new borrower, are treated fairly in this situation depends entirely on the individual bank. I've seen local banks be helpful with their non-local borrowers as well as go out of their way to hurt those on the ropes. If you are thinking about starting a new business in town, or buying out an old one, it is critical for you to determine whether your plans run counter to the interests of those on the board of your lender.

Other local mortgage lenders include **savings institutions, credit unions** and **private mortgage brokers.**

A **savings institution** can be a savings bank, savings and loan association (S&L) or mutual savings bank. Such organizations are profit-making lenders that concentrate on long-term loans for single-family, owner-occupied housing. An application for rural undeveloped land that is some distance from your principal residence will raise a flag at an urban savings bank. Still, it's worth making a phone call. If your target county has a savings institution, pay it a visit.

Credit unions are membership-based, non-profit lenders that are specifically organized to lend money to their members. Membership is confined to a particular subset population with a common bond—employees of a specific company, residents of a particular area, members of a particular group and so on. Credit unions are organized as cooperatives and are tax exempt; some are federally chartered while others operate with state charters. Owing to their ownership structure and tax-exempt status, credit unions should be able to lend money at better rates and terms than conventional lenders. Their lending guidelines and formulas may be no different than any other lender's. But the range and type of loans is likely to be narrower than that of a bank.

In November, 2002, the National Credit Union Administration (NCUA) proposed new regulations that would expand the ability of federally regulated credit unions to operate. More people would be allowed to form and join credit unions. Banks opposed these changes. The new regulations allow credit unions to increase their presence and share of loans. You should look for a county-based or multi-county credit union as a lender. (Albert B. Crenshaw, "Cash Flow," Washington Post, December 8, 2002; see also www.ncua.gov. The NCUA charters and supervises all federal credit unions and insures savings in federal and most state-chartered credit unions.) In 2006, banks were asking Congress to remove the tax-exempt status of credit unions. Some credit unions are converting to banks. (Bernard Wysocki, Jr., "Bankers Struggle To Contain Growth Of Credit Unions," Wall Street Journal, March 7, 2006.) Credit union financial reports are publicly available.

Mortgage brokers, or mortgage companies, are private, profit-making businesses that match a borrower with a lender. They make their money by charging a fee. A mortgage broker does not hold your note; he arranges the placement of your note. Mortgage brokers work with a variety of institutional lenders. While they prefer that your loan profile fit the conventional template every bank prefers, a broker can earn his fee by finding a lender for an individual with a non-conventional financial profile. Brokers should shop your loan for the best overall deal for you, and that can be better than the package you negotiate directly with the corner bank. Mortgage brokers are actively involved in urban/suburban mortgages; I've not seen an equal presence in rural areas and on land loans. Mortgage brokers are commonly criticized for getting their clients into loans with unfavorable terms and tacking on junk fees.

7. Local lenders owned by regional/national banks

Apart from a locally owned bank, you are likely to find **branches of national or regional banks** in rural areas. Such branches make mortgage loans according to guidelines established at headquarters. Do not expect much flexibility. They may be leery of lending on unimproved land that cannot be connected to big public or private water and sewerage systems, because such properties may be hard to sell in the event of a foreclosure.

I would approach these banks with all the information they need to analyze your property and financial capabilities. The more you can focus the bank officer on your data and your forthright presentation, the easier it will be for the bank to get to know you first as an individual and then as a customer. In other words, make your financial profile—its numbers and format—fit the bank's expectations, particularly when you don't exactly. It will help if one of the lender's current customers introduces you to the the loan officer, directly or off-handedly. Approach this process as one in which both you and the loan officer want to find that common ground on which your relationship can stand. Make it easy for the loan officer's supervisor to say yes to your application.

It is always possible that you will find a loan officer hostile to your application because of who you are. The federal **Equal Credit Opportunity Act (ECOA)** prohibits lenders and others who arrange credit from discriminating against credit applicants on the basis of race, color, religion, national origin, sex, marital status, age and dependence on public assistance. If the lender doesn't like your opinions, manners, speech, grammar, regional origins, educational attainment or profession, you are not protected. The ECOA requires that lenders inform rejected applicants in writing within 30 days of the principal reasons for rejection or termination of credit. The borrower can also get a copy of the property appraisal if he's paid for it. Discrimination is difficult to prove in mortgage credit cases because it's easily disguised, and part of every application involves the subjective weighing of many factors in the applicant's presentation. If a lender wants to discriminate against an individual, he might simply offer only 70 percent of the purchase price rather than the 80 percent the applicant needs. The discrimination that I've seen is banks occasionally helping or hurting individuals based on kinship and financial interests. If you find yourself with a discrimination claim that you believe meets the test of being beyond a reasonable doubt, you can bring suit or file a complaint. Don't be surprised if your claim is hard to prove beyond a reasonable doubt. It's a bad idea to announce your presence in a new community by filing a lawsuit—even if you're dead right. Consider taking your business elsewhere and rising above the lender's slight.

8. Non-local lenders

One group of non-local lenders is the set of institutional lenders available to you in the community where you live and work. If you have a well-established relationship with one or more of these lenders, you may be able to take out a mortgage for distant property. But the further the distance, the more remote the property, the less it is developed with utilities and improvements and the more out of the ordinary it is—the more trouble you will have getting a stand-alone mortgage for it. In such cases, you can propose financing through your principal residence, using a home-equity loan, refi or line of credit. Lenders often have self-imposed geographic restrictions and property standards that eliminate some rural properties from consideration. The non-local lender may not finance a mortgage on distant property, but money may be available to help with a down payment.

An urban/suburban mortgage broker will probably be not much help on a distant country property, but it's worth a try if you've worked a mortgage through him in the past. Mortgage brokers generally work with borrowers on *residential loans in their local area* that can be sold on the secondary market to buyers, such as Federal National Mortgage Association (Fannie Mae), Government National Mortgage Association (Ginnie Mae) or Federal Home Loan Mortgage Association (Freddie Mac). Such loans must conform to certain guidelines, and are, therefore, called **conforming loans.** A loan for undeveloped land 100 miles away would not conform and would not be easily placed. But...a mortgage broker in your hometown may know a broker who knows a broker near your target property—so it's worth a local phone call. A broker in a town or city that is the financial center of a rural area may be able to work with an out-of-town buyer on country property.

9. Life-Insurance Companies

Life-insurance companies hold about 12 percent of all U.S. farm mortgage debt, covering about 14,800 loans and amounting to $11.8 billion. Although some 20 companies are involved, six—AEGON USA, Citigroup Investments AgriFinance, Lend Lease Agri-Business, Metropolitan Life, MONY Life Insurance and Prudential—account for about 90 percent of these farm mortgages. These companies finance large working farms with demonstrated cash flow sufficient to cover their payments. The Pacific Coast, Florida and Texas account for almost 57 percent of the total dollar volume in mortgages held by life-insurance companies. These companies will not lend on a rural second home or to individuals interested in purchasing undeveloped rural land for recreation. If your focus is on buying a real working farm as a business or investment, you can check with local life-insurance lenders. (USDA, Economic Research Service, "Agricultural Income and Finance: Situation and Outlook Report," AIS-76, February, 2001, p. 23; 1-800-999-6779 to order.)

Several insurance companies both lend money to large customers to buy big tracts of timberland, farmland and land suitable for development and manage such investments themselves for their own clients, such as endowments, trusts and individuals. Certain companies—including John Hancock, Travelers and Metropolitan Life—have lent money to "high-net-worth" individuals to finance the purchase of timberland for investment purposes. They will evaluate the merchantable timber and the value of the bare dirt along with the plans and creditworthiness of the borrower. Insurance companies look for an LTV of about 60 percent. (See Liane Luke, "Timberland Financing: A Relationship Business," Growth Magazine, Summer 2002.) These companies also sell large tracts from time to time, either directly or through a broker.

10. Internet

I have no first-hand experience borrowing from Internet lenders, such as www.ditech.com, the GMAC subsidiary, which advertises on television. I suppose these lenders work best with conforming loans where everything is straight-forward and saleable on the secondary market. This would, I think, rule out undeveloped land, second homes and farm businesses. The Internet loans I've heard about in my area require a residence on a lot of no more than five acres. My wife, a lawyer who does country real-estate work, has run into procedural screw ups with Internet financing on several occasions. These usually involved timing and forms. Internet lenders have a hard time getting their paperwork done in a timely fashion, which forces the closing attorney into a last-minute scramble. These lenders will e-mail a 90-page loan package to the attorney on the morning of the closing and expect everything to get sorted properly in an hour or two. The Internet lenders also seem to be hard to reach by 20th Century technology, such as the telephone.

The Internet provides a number of mortgage-information sites that do not make loans, such as www.bankrate.com and www.HSH.com. You can also find sites of individual lenders, including the largest banks, but I have found several large bank sites nearly impossible to use for as simple a task as acquiring a physical phone number and street address. The www.nolo.com article, "Online Mortgage Shopping," 2003 notes: "…any of the direct lender sites offer general consumer information, but it's impossible on the Web to compare rates among them. These lenders rarely provide complete product price information including points, fees, lock periods and the like."

Sites like www.LendingTree.com and www.RealEstate.com ask the borrower to complete an application, which is then submitted to lenders for possible bid.

A third type of site is used for comparison-shopping. Here you enter basic information on the target property and the applicant and then obtain general loan terms from a number of lenders. From those, the borrower can choose one or more and submit an application. If there are wrinkles in your financial profile or the property itself, plan on talking to the lender through something other than a keyboard.

The danger in online mortgage applications is exposing your financial data—credit card numbers, bank account numbers, etc.—to unknown individuals. This can lead to identity theft. I advise against responding in any way to a mortgage offer coming to your e-mail account as spam. This is called "**phishing**," the object of which is to get you to provide personal financial information. A known scam involves **mortgage aid**, where the e-mail scammer offers to help a troubled borrower get out of debt within 12 months, or so. The scammer may ask the victim to provide a copy of his deed or make payments directly to the scammer. Don't. The scammers keep the payments and may file for bankruptcy in the victim's name, without the victim knowing about it.

A second problem appears to be that a buyer with a pre-approval letter from an Internet lender may not actually be pre-approved for anything. Kenneth Harney reported the findings of an opinion survey of 1,717 real-estate agents and brokers across the country by Campbell Communications in which 39 percent of all pre-approvals extended by Internet lenders were either faulty or invalid. Almost 30 percent of mortgage-broker pre-approvals and about 20 percent of national-lender pre-approvals were similarly flawed. (Kenneth Harney, "The Nation's Housing," "'Preapproval' letter can deliver some headaches," Richmond Times-Dispatch, July 10, 2005.) A buyer who receives pre-approval without first submitting financial documents or without having the lender verify his credit and financial statements gets into a jam of this type. A non-verified pre-approval leads the buyer into submitting and/or signing a contract that he may not be able to finance.

The www.nolo.com article provides cautions and good advice on using Internet lending. (See http://www.nolo.com/lawcenter/ency/article.cfm/objectID/DB153289-50E8-4632- AA3CE.

Every lender—your corner bank to an e-mail lender—has the power to wreck you once he gets your financial information and then your note. Consumers cannot guarantee that the local bank teller with the nice smile is not stealing your identity. But the odds of that type of nightmare appear to me much higher on the Internet sites. A borrower has some protection with a local lender who wants to protect its reputation for community-mindedness and fair-dealing. An Internet lender has no such concerns. With an Internet lender, you could be dealing with an organization that is entirely legitimate, a total scam or anywhere in between.

11. Government agencies

The federal government is deeply involved in the lands, finances and management of rural America, including providing mortgage money and loan guarantees for the purchase of property.

Interior's Bureau of Land Management (BLM) alone owns about 264 million acres, about one-eighth of the United States. BLM sells timber, issues livestock-grazing permits and leases minerals—all of which may affect a new nearby landowner and the price he just paid. Much western ranch land is sold with deeded acreage the seller owns and BLM acreage that is leased. Where BLM has designated its land as part of its National Landscape Conservation System, traditional uses are being curtailed. A ranch buyer should be particularly concerned about water issues and overgrazing of BLM leased lands.

The National Park Service manages about 84 million acres, the U.S. Fish and Wildlife Service about 93 million acres and the U.S. Forest Service, about 192 million acres. Proximity to public land brings both benefits and liabilities to adjacent private landowners, which I've discussed in other chapters. **Inholdings**—land surrounded by public land—are prized and can usually be sold to the public agency at appraisal value depending on the availability of funds. Some states appropriate money for acquisitions of private land to add to their holdings. New York, for example, buys private land within the Adirondack Park.

The federal government plays a direct role in rural finance through its various programs of support. Certain sectors of agriculture receive direct support payments, while all of agriculture benefits from federally funded research and marketing efforts. The 1996 Farm Act provided about $15.9 billion in production flexibility payments during the 1998-2000 period. Another $5.8 billion ($5.4 billion in direct payments) was tacked on in 1998. Another $4 billion was added in 2001. Additional billions were added in these years for marketing-loss relief, disaster relief, emergency assistance, production losses, etc. In 2000, the Agricultural Risk Protection Act authorized $15.1 billion for federal farm assistance with about $6.7 billion in direct payments to farmers. Such payments in 2000 were $22.1 billion. In 1990-1997, farmers received about $8.8 billion a year in direct payments. In 1998-2001, that average rose to $17.3 billion annually. (USDA, ERS, "Agricultural Income," p. 7.) Then in 2002, Congress passed a $414 billion, multi-year farm bill. The next farm bill is scheduled for 2007. At the end of 2005, discussion was reported in the media about Washington cutting farm programs.

The economic effect of this yearly infusion of cash into farm counties is to maintain production at high levels and provide further repayment capacity for the $181 billion in farm business debt, about 54 percent of which is agricultural real estate and the remainder non-real-estate farm loans. The USDA's ERS survey reported: "Total direct government payments are expected to account for almost half of reported net farm income and about 39 percent of net cash income." (*Ibid.*, p. 30.) Owing to these payments, agricultural banks show low delinquency in farm loans, low charge offs (losses), zero failures in 2000 and good profitability despite weak farm prices and demand problems in certain sectors, such as tobacco and beef.

While farming and debt often go hand in hand, it surprised me that about 58 percent of America's 2.148 million farms reported no debt outstanding in 1999. (*Ibid.*, p. 44.) What explains almost 60 percent of U.S. farms having no debt, and the rest carrying a huge amount? My guess is that it's related to the fact that 57 percent of all farm households are classified as either retirement (297,566) or residential/lifestyle (931,561) in that year. (*Ibid.*, p. 34.) Such small farmers are likely to have paid off their mortgages with non-farm income while engaging in the small-scale agriculture associated with retirement and lifestyle.

Federal cash to farmers has another effect. It maintains the value of agricultural land in the face of real-estate market pressures. At the beginning of 2000, agricultural real estate nationally averaged $1,050 per acre. This figure compares favorably with the low-year value of $599 (not adjusted for inflation) in 1987 when overproduction and low prices devastated farmers. Average acreage price in 2000 ranged from $2,470 in the Northeast (Maryland to Maine) to $440 in the Rockies. Agricultural land continues to appreciate even in the face of weak commodity prices and chronic oversupply of agricultural products, partly related to federal payments. This type of support allows a farmer to build wealth through his land even when his farm business is marginal. The other factor, of course, that drives rural land prices is demand from second-home and relocating retirement buyers

The buyer of rural land needs to understand the political basis of some of its value and the

736

derivative risks. If Washington reduces the flow of cash, agricultural land values can erode. Were agriculture to have its subsidies deeply curtailed for many years, many sectors of the agricultural economy would not show a net profit. A harsh consolidation would occur. Marginal farmland would erode in value as production was cut to boost prices. Non-agricultural rural land would probably erode in value too with, I think, the exception of timberland. Privately owned timberland should continue to rise in value as more and more public land is backed out of timbering and demand for wood products continues to show strength.

Buyers should also be aware that the political stability of federal payments to rural and farm sectors fluctuates. If, accordingly, crop payments come with the seller's property and that income helps secure a mortgage, you should try to obtain a general forecast regarding the reliability of these payments out to the mid-term future. I'd start with the experts at the state land-grant universities who specialize in the particular crops your target farm produces. While the farm lobbies are powerful far beyond the numbers of farmers, certain sectors, notably tobacco, have been pruned. Dwight Watson, the North Carolina farmer who stalled traffic in Washington D.C. for two days by parking himself and his John Deere tractor in a decorative pond the day before America invaded Iraq in March, 2003 to protest the halving of the tobacco subsidy, showed how dependent a farm sector can become on federal monies.

The other factor in rural land appreciation has nothing to do with agriculture. Where rural land lends itself to second homes, individually and in developments, land prices are driven by urban cash and urban demand. These buyers want mainly to live in the country for lifestyle reasons, not to work the land. USDA's ERS estimates that ten to 20 percent of U.S. farmland is "subject to" urban influences. Second-home buyers in the West are known as "amenity buyers" when local real-estate brokers are being polite.

I live about a 4 1/2-hour drive from the White House and three hours west of Richmond, Virginia in an Appalachian mountain county that has 2,500 people. Our closest direct "urban influence" is an hour's drive over four mountains to a city of 25,000 on Interstate 81. But our land market is driven almost entirely by second-home buyers from the Richmond-Baltimore corridor. In my sheep-and-cattle county, a farmer can no longer buy pasture for his stock because the lowest price—$2,000+ per acre—is too high for him to pay it off through farming. Poor pasture is now bringing $3,000 to $5,000 an acre in 20-acre lots. Consequently, lifestyle farmers have replaced make-a-living farmers as buyers for local farms. Farming as a livelihood is almost incapable of providing a reasonable living. We have more than 1,000 farms, but fewer than 25 full-time farmers, and the majority of those are contract poultry growers. The vast majority of the 1,000-plus farms are not farming dependent: they run enough livestock to keep the grass down, or lease the pasture, or are operated as part-time (after work) businesses, or maintain a barnyard that is part Old MacDonald and part California exotica. We are a rural county that's becoming ever less dependent on farming and ever more dependent on the aesthetics of "farminess." Much of our agricultural production is now done as a sideline, or out of habit, or for the tax benefits or as a matter of lifestyle. Almost all farmland purchases are by non-farmer, urban, non-residents—a mix of home-schoolers, preservationists, retirees and Big City refugees. Friends in Florida agriculture have told me that ordinary citrus land is bringing as much as $25,000 per acre if it's developable. This source of demand—people like you and me—is driving up agricultural land prices in pretty places—the Delmarva Peninsula, New England, southern Appalachia, parts of the Rockies, many parts of the South and on the West Coast.

In places where this type of market is operating, a borrower and his lender should feel very secure about the value of rural-land collateral. A higher-value market is replacing a lower-value market, which lifts every property value. Land prices continue to rise each time a property is sold. This underlying movement should help a land buyer use his current urban property to finance a rural acquisition. If you are looking for property where federal agricultural payments are a presence and urban demand is driving land

737

prices, you're in a pretty good spot.

The three major lenders to farmers are: commercial banks with about 41.3 percent of all farm debt (real estate and non-real estate), federal **Farm Credit Administration (FCA)** with 26.1 percent, and individuals and others with 22.2 percent. Looking at real estate alone, commercial banks hold about 18 percent of the total farm debt, FCA about 17.5 percent, individuals and others about ten percent, life insurance companies about 6.5 percent and the USDA's **Farm Service Agency (FSA)** about 2 percent. The FSA holds a direct loan portfolio and also guarantees farm loans, including certain types of land acquisitions. The federal players in rural mortgage money are the FCA, also known as the **Federal Land Bank**; various programs within the FSA, which focus on loans for emergencies, beginning farmers (ten years of experience or fewer) and farmers socially disadvantaged by way of race, ethnicity or gender; and the **Rural Housing Service**, which provides loans, grants and loan guarantees to low- and moderate-income individuals.

A few federal housing programs may also fit your profile and needs, though they are not directed at rural housing. The Department of Housing and Urban Development (HUD) operates the **Federal Housing Administration (FHA)**, which promotes home-ownership through guaranteeing single-family home mortgages made through FHA-approved lending institutions. The FHA website is helpful: www.hud.gov/offices/hsg/index.cfm. FHA does not make direct mortgage loans. By insuring the loan, the FHA makes the private lender more secure, and, in effect, replaces much of the normal cash down payment. FHA helps low- and moderate-income borrowers whom private lenders would ignore. These borrowers, in turn, must jump certain qualification hurdles: an upfront premium must be paid that is usually factored into the financing; a monthly or annual premium may also be charged; the house must meet certain standards; an FHA-approved appraiser must appraise the property; among others. The lender may charge the borrower discount points on top of a loan-origination fee. A dollar cap is imposed that limits the FHA-insured loan on a single-family residence; in 2003 that cap was $154,896 in most areas though in high-cost locales, like New York/Long Island, it was $280,000.

Title II, Section 203 (b) of the National Housing Act is the most frequently used FHA program. Its purpose is to help qualifying individuals purchase or refinance a principal residence. It provides borrowers with guarantees for fixed-rate loans for ten to 30 years; the rates are competitive; and as much as 97 percent of the *FHA-appraised* value can be borrowed. FHA also operates a guarantee program for mobile homes and home improvements.

FHA has a loan-guarantee program for **Outlying Areas, Section 203 (i)**, for low- and moderate-income individuals in certain "underserved places where mortgages are hard to get." (See: www.hud.gov/progdesc/sin14121.cfm.) The guarantee can apply to the purchase of proposed, under-construction, or existing farm housing or single-family housing on 2 1/2 acres or more adjacent to an all-weather public road. This is a little-used program, but it could help folks who fit the criteria. The website above links to information and regulations.

The **Veterans Administration** (VA) provides loan guarantees to qualifying vets for the purchase of homes, farms, manufactured housing and lots; and the construction of new housing as well as improvements. You may also hear VA loans referred to as "GI loans." The VA does not make direct loans to vets. VA loans (i.e., the VA's guarantee of such a loan that is made by a private lending institution) can be made on no down-payment purchases. The lender can lend up to four times the veteran's "entitlement," which currently amounts to a loan cap of about $240,000. Both the veteran and the property must meet agency eligibility standards. The VA's appraisal process may hang a purchase to the extent that the VA insists the seller correct conditions before the loan guarantee is made. In this circumstance, the seller might pay for the repairs and then raise his price to the veteran to cover the expense. The VA's terms—competitive interest rates, low down payment and other benefits—are borrower-friendly, but there are fees imposed, both by the VA and the lender. If your rural property involves a house that you intend to occupy at least half the year, check out the VA program. Vacation homes, however, won't qualify; nor will purchase of land for investment. If the VA borrower defaults on the mortgage, the VA pays off the lender, leaving the borrower to repay the VA. Borrowers can access the VA through a private lender, real-estate agent or directly through one of nine regional loan centers. Contact information is available on the VA's website: www.homeloans.va.gov/.

If you're interested in working with either the FHA or VA programs, you can get **free pre-purchase counseling** at www.hud.gov/offices/hsg/sfh/hccl/hccprof14.cfm, or 1-800-217-6970.

You will hear about other national mortgage players—Fannie Mae (formerly the Federal National Mortgage Association or FNMA), Ginnie Mae (formerly the Government National Mortgage Association or GNMA), Freddie Mac (Federal Home Loan Mortgage Corporation or FHLMC) and Farmer Mac. These organizations are either federal agencies or quasi-governmental organizations that together make up the country's secondary mortgage market. They don't make direct loans to buyers of land or homes.

Farmer Mac refers to the Federal Agricultural Mortgage Corporation, set up in 1987 by the Agricultural Credit Act as a separate agency within the Farm Credit Administration system. (www.farmermac.com). Farmer Mac is a government-sponsored, though not government-funded, enterprise that provides a secondary market for agricultural real-estate and rural-housing loans. It also buys the guaranteed portions of farmownership and operating loans along with USDA loans made to rural businesses and communities. You and your lender may want to qualify your loan for a Farmer Mac **loan pool** whose requirements include, among others, the loan must be secured by a first lien on agricultural real estate (land, improvements affixed to land, rural housing); the loan must be less than or equal to 70 percent of the property's fair market value; the loan must be for less than $5 million when secured by more than 1,000 acres, and not greater than $22.5 million for loans secured by 1,000 acres or less; and after the loan is in place, the borrower's total assets must be at least twice his total debt. In return, a Farmer Mac loan can offer a borrower a fixed, favorable interest rate.

FCA, FSA and individual states offer programs whereby borrowers can access mortgage money for agricultural and non-agricultural rural property. Such programs provide direct loans and loan guarantees for rural land, rural housing and agricultural enterprises to qualified borrowers. FCA had long-term real-estate loans of more than $35 billion in 2000. FSA direct mortgage lending was about $250 million that year, with more than $1 billion in guarantees for funds coming from private-sector lenders.

If you're looking to buy farmland as an investment, or undeveloped rural land for recreation or appreciation, a locally owned bank and the FCA will be the institutional lenders most likely to work with you.

The Farm Credit Administration (FCA), also known as the Federal Land Bank and the Farm Credit System (FCS), provides direct loans for certain types of property purchases in rural areas. (FCA, 1501 Farm Credit Drive, McLean, Virginia, 22102-5090; 703-883-4000; www.fca.gov/; e-mail: info-line@fca.gov.) These loans are directed to: 1) individuals who want to buy and occupy a single-family residence in the country, and 2) farmers (and others engaged in agricultural production either full- or part-time) to buy farmland and farm equipment. "Farmers" are defined to include those in the timber business, commercial fishermen, ranchers, nursery operators and others who produce an agricultural product. Even if you live in Manhattan, you may be able to qualify for such a farm loan if you can show that you will operate your new farm as a business or a woodland tract for timber production.

The Land Bank will not help you finance a vacation home on rural recreation land. But, the Bank has **forestland loans** available to buy undeveloped timberland (for timber production) on which you can build a second home. The trick is to qualify the woodland as being used for the production of timber, which can be satisfied by an initial cruise and a consultant-prepared timber management plan. The value of the merchantable timber as established by the cruise acts as the Bank's collateral in addition to the land's bare-dirt value. If you don't want to cut the merchantable timber, you may want to consider working out a long-term plan with your forestry consultant who will recommend that you do little to your timber for the term of your note. As an alternative, you could undertake a **timber-stand improvement** immediately (which cuts or removes low-value trees so that the high-value trees have additional resources) and then not cut your increasingly valuable forest. The Land Bank will lend on agricultural land of all types, including producing farms that you use as a second home, referred to as multiple-use. If your second-home farm is set up as a farm (IRS Schedule F) or investment to produce some agricultural product—cattle, timber, crops, orchard products, honey and so on—you should consider the Land Bank programs. You don't have to produce the product yourself; a renter can produce the product.

FCA operates through user-owned regional cooperatives that require each borrower to buy shares in the local land bank (association), proportional to the size of the loan. The five to ten percent of your borrowing that is dedicated to stock purchase provides part of the association's loan capital. Each regional land bank is run independently. Depending on that association's financial performance, dividends may be issued on your stock. Your stock may also be awarded a "patronage refund." When you pay off the note, the balance of your stock is returned at its current value. It's hard to compare the local association's loan package with a local bank's because of the former's dividend/patronage feature and the unpredictability of those returns over time. While you may front more cash to get a Land Bank loan, you should get it back with interest in most cases.

The FCA will lend up to 85 percent of a property's appraised value. If the financing is guaranteed by another federal or state program, a borrower can get up to 97 percent financing. Most Land Bank loans are made to individuals with a net worth of less than $100,000. FCA loans make up almost a quarter of the country's farm-property loans. Get material on the Bank's programs from the local land-bank association, which may be listed in the telephone directory as either "federal land bank" or "farm credit." The county's cooperative extension agent should be able to provide local contact information. The Land Bank system is independent of the USDA's Farm Service Agency.

The USDA's Farm Service Agency (FSA) is the principal entrance into the world of federal agricultural programs (www.fsa.usda.gov). You will find FSA offices in rural areas, though a local office may cover more than one county. The Agency's website gives local office contact information. Walk through the door and start asking questions.

FSA provides direct loans for farmownership of up to $200,000 to purchase land, construct buildings and other facilities, and undertake soil and water conservation. Borrowers must meet certain eligibility requirements. The Agency also provides direct down-payment loans to beginning farmers and direct operating loans of up to $200,000. FSA also provides a loan-guarantee program for farmownership (up to $762,000, adjusted annually) and farm operation. With the direct loans, the borrower has to show that other lenders won't provide a mortgage; similarly, a borrower who wants a guarantee must show he can't obtain credit without one (See www.fsa.usda.gov/dafl/directloans.htm and www.fsa.usda.gov/dafl/Guaranteed.htm).

The other USDA portal is the **Natural Resources Conservation Service (NRCS)**, which administers an assortment of programs intended to conserve soils, water quality and supply; reduce erosion; and otherwise benefit land used for agricultural purposes. NRCS funds conservation-enhancing practices, such as tree planting and spring development, but does not provide money to purchase land. The local FSA office will put you in touch with the NRCS programs.

The **Rural Housing Service (RHS)** is the USDA agency that succeeded the Farmers Home Administration (FmHA), but it is not part of either the FSA or the NRCS. To access the RHS, which has no field staff, you have to contact the USDA's local Rural Development staff through the local FSA office. The RHS website is: www.rurdev.usda.gov/rhs/Individual/ind_splash.htm. Most of the RHS programs are directed to low- and very low-income individuals, and involve direct home-ownership loans, home-repair loans and grants, rent subsidies and other services. The RHS's Section 502 direct-loan program provided more than $1 billion in direct loans and $3 billion in loan guarantees for its target population, which is, generally, families with income below 80 percent of the median income in their communities. The Section 502 loan-guarantee program will finance 100 percent to eligible individuals.

Foreclosed USDA farms and houses can be accessed at www.resales.usda.gov.

I used my local Farm Credit Association (Land Bank/FCS) when I bought the farm where I've lived since 1983. At that time, I did not know how to shop for a loan. The appraiser chosen by the FCA came in at about $127,000 on a purchase price of $143,500. The seller eagerly agreed to take back a three-year second for $30,000 to make the deal go through, with $113,500 in FCA financing. I should have done some renegotiating with the seller over purchase price, given the gap between the lender's FMV appraisal at $127,000 and the purchase price of $143,500. But I did not have an appraisal contingency—performance on the contract being dependent on the appraisal value at least equaling the purchase price—in my contract. I've subsequently seen other FCA appraisals come in below contract prices, which forces the buyer to come up with more cash or work in a seller second. I refinanced the FCA loan with a local bank five or six years later when interest rates were considerably lower. I advance no claim that the local land bank jiggered appraisals intentionally, since I have no way of knowing what its internal policies are. I would consider FCA financing as one option of several when buying rural land. If you are working with the FCA, I'd advise that you talk with the FCA-approved appraiser before he visits your target property. You are aware that he has a business relationship with the FCA. The least you should insist on is honesty, fairness and professionalism.

Various states help low- and moderate-income individuals acquire single-family housing in rural areas. Private non-profit housing organizations also help with lot purchase and house construction. You will have to dig out the names of the programs and the agencies by interminable telephone or Internet work. For state agencies, start looking under "rural development," "housing," "farming" and "mortgage." HUD's website provides links to state programs: www.hud.gov/buying/localbuying.cfm. For private programs, start with Habitat for Humanity in the target county, the county's local economic development office and any county office with "housing," "farming" or "development" in its name. You can also learn about rural housing through the National Housing Law Project, 614 Grand Ave., Suite 320, Oakland, CA 94610; 510-251-9400; 510-451-2300 FAX; www.nhlp.org/html.

12. 1031 Like-Kind (Starker) Exchange

The Internal Revenue Code's (IRC), Section 1031, allows a taxpayer to exchange one kind of property for a "**like-kind**" property *of equal or greater value* without creating a taxable event. The properties need to be like in type, but not identical. You can't exchange a car for a lot, but you can exchange a rental house for undeveloped land, or an apartment building for a farm, because all four are real property. The property that the taxpayer exchanges (from) must be "held for productive use in trade or business or for investment." This excludes exchanging out of your principal residence and into a farm held as an investment, but you could exchange out of an urban rental property that you own or a vacation home that you rent out a sufficient number of days each year into timberland or undeveloped pasture held for investment. You cannot exchange out of a property that you hold primarily for sale or that you've acquired for the purpose of making a like-kind exchange. Stocks, bonds, notes and certain other securities and interests cannot be exchanged. Personal property can be exchanged for personal property, but the items have to be of the same type—a car for a car, but not a car for equipment.

This technique is often referred to as a **Starker exchange**, named for the taxpayer who exchanged title to his timberland for a contractual promise from Crown-Zellerbach to acquire like-kind property designated by him at a future date. The company paid Starker no cash at the time he conveyed title and carried its obligation to him as a credit on its books. When Crown-Zellerbach acquired the properties that Starker wanted, their titles were transferred to him. This was a delayed exchange, which the U.S. Supreme Court upheld in *T.J. Starker vs. U.S.*, 432 F. Supp 864 (D.OR. 1977) aff'd, rev'd & rem'd 602 F. 2d 1341 (9th Cir., 1979).

A like-kind exchange is not a *sale*, where you, the seller/taxpayer, walk away with a cash gain on which you pay tax. (If you do get some cash out of an exchange, you have to pay tax on it.) In an exchange, your taxable gain is retained in the like-kind property that you've exchanged into, and your tax obligation on that gain is deferred until you sell. Tax deferred is tax eroded. A dollar in tax owed today will cost you less than 50 cents in 20 years or so, owing to inflation. Like-kind exchanges protect profit. If the sale of your property won't generate taxable gain, you have no reason to do an exchange.

If the exchanged-into property passes into your estate, much, if not all, of the deferred tax obligation can be erased, depending on the size of your estate and applicable tax policy in the year of your death. The value of the exchanged-into property—as well as all other assets of the decedent—is calculated on the day of death, not the date of the property's purchase by the decedent. Heirs inherit this **stepped-up basis** in the exchanged property. **"Basis"** is the owner's financial interest in a property for IRS purposes, used to calculate gain or loss on a sale. An owner's basis starts with the property's original cost. **Adjusted basis** reflects additions and subtractions to the owner's starting basis over his term of ownership. Depreciation lowers basis; new investment increases it. A stepped-up basis through inheritance allows the heir to sell the asset with taxable gain figured on the value of the property at the time of inheritance. This can result in a tax-free, or at least a tax-diminished, sale when the heir flips this inherited exchanged property.

A 1031 exchange works for a seller who does not need cash from the sale of his property. If you sell because you need cash, don't involve yourself in an exchange. The exchanger must keep all the cash equity built up in the just-sold property going forward into the property that he acquires through the exchange. You can't cash out partially, except by a pre-exchange refinancing. Because the exchange defers tax on gain until the last exchanged-into property is sold for cash, it is an excellent way of building wealth. You buy a property, allow it to appreciate, exchange, defer tax, allow that property to appreciate, exchange, defer tax, and so on. When all is said and done, the most you will likely owe is the then-current capital-gains tax applied to taxable gain figured against your adjusted basis. You can pull cash out of exchange properties by borrowing against them. Various ways exist to soften any final tax burden, involving estates, trusts, gifts, charitable donations and the like.

1031 exchanges can be worked into your purchase of rural property. In its simplest two-party form, you would exchange an apartment building you own for rental income in Big City worth $500,000 for a 200-acre farm in Blue Sky County, also worth $500,000. No money changes hands; no taxable gain is recognized by either party.

A far more common format is a **three-party exchange** that involves a buyer for your (the taxpayer's) property and an escrow agent. Here's how it works. You, the taxpayer, sell your rental building to Mr. Buyer who deposits $500,000 into an escrow account. The holder of the escrow account, called the "qualified intermediary," is a neutral player who manages the escrow's mechanics for a fee. He will provide the paperwork, including the "exchange agreement," which spells out how everything is to work. You, the taxpayer/seller, do not get Mr. Buyer's $500,000 from the escrow account—ever. When the escrow opens, you put the deed to your rental building into it. You are conveying your deed into the escrow. Mr. Farmowner also puts his deed to the 200 acres you want into the same escrow. At that point, there are two deeds and $500,000 in the escrow pot. Then the escrow agent gives 1) $500,000 to Mr. Farmowner to complete your purchase of his 200 acres, 2) the deed to your rental goes to Mr. Buyer, and 3) the deed to Mr. Farmowner's farm comes to you. Your basis in the 200 acres starts with whatever your final adjusted basis was in the rental property you sold. But you pay no tax on any gain, because you've never realized any taxable gain on the property sold. A three-party exchange of this sort has no effect on Mr. Farmowner who gets his $500,000 or Mr. Buyer who gets your rental apartment property. Mr. Farmowner may owe tax on his gain from the sale, but the gain that you've realized over the time you've owned your rental is tax-deferred. Diagram 33-1 below shows the flow of money and paper into and out of the escrow pot.

Exchanges in real life, of course, involve complications—mortgage payoffs, unequal values of the like-kind properties being exchanged; appraisals; basis; and **boot,** which is the cash or personal property that one party puts in to bring his property up to the value of the property that he wants to exchange into. Boot is usually cash, but it can be other things that qualify under the IRS rules. If your rental is worth $450,000, you might put in $50,000 to make the exchange for the 200 acres even. You would pay no tax on the boot. You, the taxpayer/exchanger must never be in receipt of the cash from your sale, collect interest from that cash, or control the cash in the escrow. Where mortgages are involved, the party whose mortgage principal is reduced through the exchange pays tax on that reduction.

Since the exchange must comply with the federal rules, it is important to use a qualified intermediary who knows them and walks you through each step. Time limits, for instance, are critical. The taxpayer who is doing the exchange has 45 days from the date he relinquishes his property to identify the property he wants to exchange into. And the exchange must usually be completed within 180 days of the date of relinquishment. You can exchange one property for several as long as all other requirements are satisfied.

DIAGRAM 33-1

1031 Exchange Flow

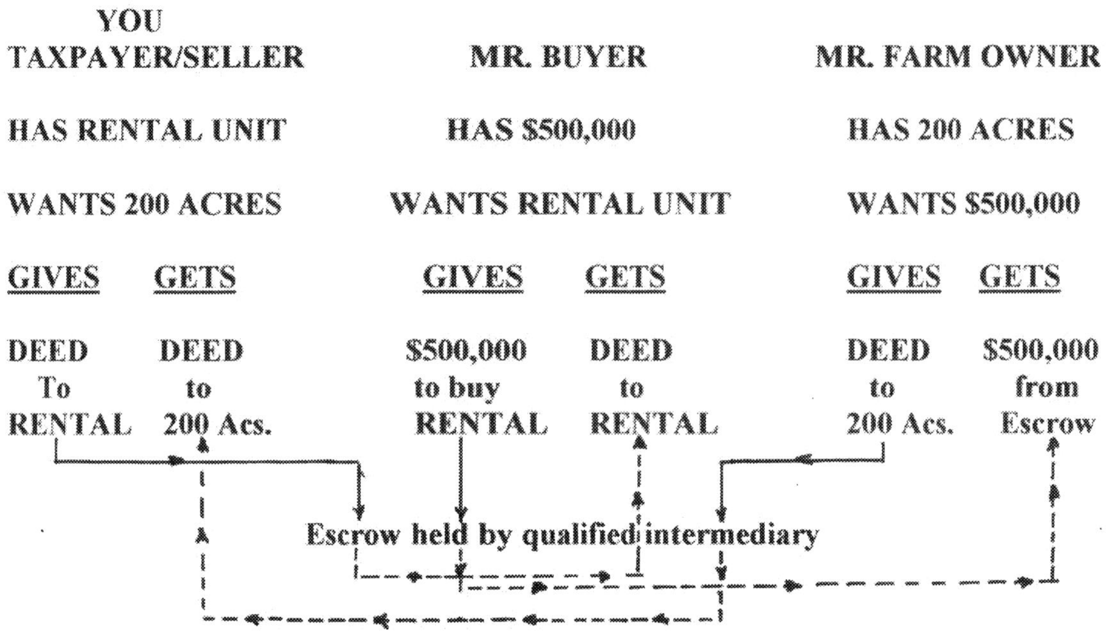

YOU TAXPAYER/SELLER	MR. BUYER	MR. FARM OWNER
HAS RENTAL UNIT	HAS $500,000	HAS 200 ACRES
WANTS 200 ACRES	WANTS RENTAL UNIT	WANTS $500,000

GIVES	GETS	GIVES	GETS	GIVES	GETS
DEED To RENTAL	DEED to 200 Acs.	$500,000 to buy RENTAL	DEED to RENTAL	DEED to 200 Acs.	$500,000 from Escrow

Escrow held by qualified intermediary

A land buyer may also have occasion to consider a **reverse like-kind exchange**. In simple terms, a reverse exchange occurs when you have identified the rural property that you want to exchange into in advance of finding a buyer for the property that you want to sell and exchange out of. This situation arises when you fear the country property you want may sell before you can get your exchange lined up. In that case, you can arrange with an "accommodator" to buy the property you want and hold it for you until you find a buyer. Once you have a buyer, you transfer your property to the accommodator who sells it to the buyer. The accommodator then transfers title to the rural property to you. The IRS refers to this as a "qualified exchange accommodation arrangement." Time limits and other requirements are imposed. A reverse exchange, where the taxpayer acquires the replacement property before divesting himself of property he is selling, has not been approved by the IRS. Nonetheless, if done carefully, it appears, at least to a tax illiterate like me, to be workable. (See Max Hansen, "What is a 1031 Exchange?" www.bozeman~montana~real~estate.net/1031~exchange.htm; and "Unusual Like-Kind Exchanges," Small Business Taxes & Management, August 1, 2000; www.smbiz.com/sbw1080.html; and "FAQ The 'How To' of Real Property Exchanges," undated; http://freec.net/FAQ.html.)

Here are some general ways to weave a three-party 1031 exchange into your effort to obtain rural property:

Exchange your non-residence, second-home property for rural property;

Exchange an investment property for a rural investment property;

Exchange a business with a building/land for a farm business;

Exchange a vehicle you own for farm vehicle;

Exchange equipment you own for farm equipment;

744

Exchange a conservation easement for farmland or timberland; (See IRS, Letter Ruling No. 9621012, February 16, 1996.)

Exchange an urban lot for timber or mineral rights.

An experienced dirt lawyer in the county where you're buying should know how to advise you on doing an exchange. If a question arises, I would run to a CPA who knows the 1031 regs since an ounce of prevention is worth ten pounds of legal briefs in search of a cure. "Qualified intermediaries" are also found on the Internet.

13. Conservation Easements

From a buyer's perspective, a **conservation easement** that benefits the buyer is a tax break that can protect income and assets. But a conservation easement that the seller has imposed is a tax break that's already been taken and which, in many cases, will diminish the value of a target property in perpetuity.

A conservation easement separates some property right that has value from the property. The separated right is given to a certain-type of organization that owns and manages it from then on. The separated right must involve a legitimate conservation purpose. If you buy 100 acres and want to build houses on 60 acres, but leave the ugly back 40 alone, the ugly 40 won't qualify as a conservation value worthy of protection based on ugliness and your need for a tax break. If, on the other hand, the ugly 40 is important wetlands, donating a no-development/no-disturbance easement would probably qualify. The size of the tax break depends on the appraised value of the donation. It can be used to protect the gain you made from the sale of a property whose proceeds you used to buy the country place on which you placed the donated easement. You will be able to use the break against current income in future tax years until it is gone. You should also have the tax-appraised value of your country property lowered in proportion to the value of the easement that you've given away, hence a lower property-tax bill. Individual states also offer tax benefits for these easements. Finally, you can reduce the value of your estate through a conservation easement on property in your estate, thus reducing anticipated estate tax.

A conservation easement is not a free lunch. A conservation easement imposes some type of restriction on a valuable use of the owner's land usually *in perpetuity* for the purpose of promoting one or more conservation objectives. The restriction might prohibit activity, forgo an activity or require an activity. A typical easement on farmland near metropolitan areas is a full prohibition on residential and commercial development to preserve open space.

A less onerous easement—and one with proportionately less monetary value to the donor/taxpayer—is a cap on residential density. On a 1,000-acre farm near Big City, for instance, the easement might limit residential construction to no more than one home per 25 acres instead of no homes on 1,000 acres. A partial restriction of this type may be able to give the landowner the amount of tax benefits he wants while protecting his land to an acceptable level. Another type of easement might define acceptable and unacceptable uses for the land. The owner might, for example, place an easement on his land that prohibits all mineral development or all timber harvesting; or limit one or both activities in areas that are environmentally sensitive.

Each conservation easement is written to fit the particular needs of the owner and the characteristics of his land. Organizations like The Nature Conservancy (TNC) and land trusts are very interested in accepting easements on environmentally significant land, such as wetlands, the headwaters of certain watersheds and habitat for endangered species. Local and regional land trusts will work with small properties, as long as the land covered by the easement and the use-right that is donated has some conservation importance. Tax-exempt conservation organizations will not accept an easement over environmentally insignificant land. Conservation organizations emphasize different objectives, so you may find yourself talking with a state wildlife agency, a local land trust or a branch of a national organization. Informative gateway websites include The Nature Conservancy (http://nature.org/, (refers to state and local affiliates); The Conservation Fund (http://www.conservationfund.org/); The Trust for Public Land (http://www.tpl.org/); and the Land Trust Alliance (http://www.lta.org/).

While there are circumstances where a conservation organization will either buy environmentally important land or buy a conservation easement, the more widespread practice is for individual landowners to donate an easement to such an organization and take the tax benefits. Once the easement is donated, the conservation organization is responsible for managing it and assuring the landowner's compliance with its terms. The organization may charge the donor/taxpayer a one-time fee to cover the anticipated future costs of managing the easement, but this practice is more common with very large tracts. The easement is recorded and runs with the land so that all subsequent owners are bound by it. Some easements can be bought back if they are drafted with such a provision originally. Public access is not required to property bearing a conservation easement, though some form of public access to private land may be one of the elements voluntarily incorporated into an easement.

The dollar value of any particular conservation easement is determined through an appraisal by a neutral professional. What is being estimated is the current fair market value of the easement, i.e., the right in the property that the landowner is proposing to donate. If, for example, you are fortunate enough to own a 500-acre farm 15 miles from the U.S. Capitol, your **development rights** in that land are worth millions. Preserving some or all of your farm as open space or limiting development density are sound conservation objectives. An appraiser would compare your property to others of similar size and type in the area that have been sold recently to developers. Let's assume that comparables sold for $25,000 per acre and the appraiser determines that the land less all development rights with continued use as farmland is worth $4,000 per acre. Accordingly, the value of the donated development rights is $21,000 per acre, or $10.5 million.

The tax benefits to the donor vary according to the individual's circumstances. **You should have a competent CPA/lawyer who does a lot of work with conservation easements in the state where the property is located and the state where you live run the numbers for each conservation-easement option you are considering _before_ you make any choice and _before_ you make an offer to purchase.** I advise clients to have these conservation-easement options calculated as part of their property scoping so that the buyer knows in advance of purchase his range of probable tax benefits, if any.

As of 2005 in the example above, the $10.5 million value can be taken against up to 30 percent of an individual's gross income with certain adjustments (called a "contribution base") during the donation year. Any unused portion can be taken during the next five years. The landowner in this case could subtract $1.75 million a year from his gross income (with certain adjustments) for six years, as long as the amount of the deduction never exceeded 30 percent of his gross income with adjustments in any year. If the donor takes the deduction using his "adjusted basis" in the property—which is usually the case with buyers who immediately donate an easement as part of their purchase strategy and "adjusted basis" essentially amounts to the recent purchase price—the deduction can rise to 50 percent of adjusted gross income. In both cases, any unused portion of the deduction can be carried over for a maximum of five years following the donation year. The deduction benefits vary according to who is making the donation—an individual can use the 30 percent standard, but corporations can use only ten percent. This difference may determine whether a buyer organizes his ownership as an individual investment, corporation or limited liability company, among other choices. An easement's value may be deducted up to 50 percent of an individual donor's income in certain circumstances, which includes the first year following the property's purchase. Competent, seasoned professional help is required to obtain the maximum tax benefit. Even more generous time-frames and deductions were put into place in 2006, extending the carry-forward period for deductions to 15 years and raising the deduction caps.

Current information on conservation easements is available from "qualified organizations" themselves, including local, state and federal agencies along with private organizations, such as land trusts. These organizations, however, may be reluctant to provide tax counsel. To get started, read Section 170 (h) of the Internal Revenue Code along with relevant regulations. An excellent guide to this subject is: C. Timothy Linstrom, Esq., "A Simplified Guide to The Tax Benefits of Donating A Conservation Easement," October, 2001, which is available from the author at The Jackson Hole Land Trust, PO Box 2897, 555 East Broadway, Suite 228, Jackson, WY 83001; 307-733-4707; tim@jhlandtrust.org. The legal guru of conservation easements is Stephen J. Small, a lawyer who helped draft the statute and then wrote the 170 (h) regulations. He's written several books on the subject and now has a private practice specializing in conservation easements. (See Stephen J. Small, 75 Federal St., Suite 1100, Boston, MA 02110; 617-357-4012; www.stevesmall.com; e-mail stevesmall@stevesmall.com.)

States also offer varying tax benefits for donors of conservation easements. North Carolina, for example, offers a tax credit for up to 25 percent of the fair market value of the "donated property interest" (i.e., value of the easement) with a maximum credit of $250,000 for individuals and $500,000 for corporations. (See The Conservation Trust for North Carolina, www.ctnc.org.) Virginia allows its taxpayers to apply one-half of their easement's appraised value against their state income tax bill. This credit can be used over five years; it can also be sold. (Lawrence Latane, III, "Easements protect land from development," Richmond Times-Dispatch, March 16, 2003.) Tim Linstrom surveyed the tax benefits in all 50 states in "State Tax Incentives for Conservation Easements Can Benefit Everyone," Journal of MultiState Taxation and Incentives, November/December, 2002. The local "qualified organization" that would accept your donated easement can explain current state policy.

Two other tax benefits attach to a conservation easement. First, since the landowner is giving up something of value in his property, his local property-tax burden should be proportionally reduced. Localities will have different ways of discounting their tax-appraised values, so your scoping should include a visit to the local assessor to determine your likely benefit in advance once you have a good idea of the easement's appraisal value. Second, for estate purposes, a conservation easement reduces the value of the decedent's real property on which it falls, thereby enabling the estate to pay less tax. This may or may not benefit your particular estate depending on its total value, estate components, and federal and state tax policies in the year of your death. The other estate benefit is the exclusion of 40 percent of the land's value after the easement's value is subtracted. A number of qualifications and limitations apply to this "40 percent exclusion" so it's essential that you talk to a knowledgeable CPA or lawyer before assuming that your estate will enjoy the full 40 percent exclusion on a specific property.

The dirt-smart buyer should evaluate his target property for conservation-easement potential. Every easement must promote some environmental or conservation objective. Depending on the individual property, such objectives could include one or more of the following donations, among others:

- development rights to preserve open space
- partial development rights (limits residential-development density or limits development to certain portions of the property)

- rights to change current uses

- right to explore for/extract subsurface minerals

- right to cut timber, in whole or in part

- right to erect wind turbines on ridges or other sensitive areas

- right to farmland that has significant environmental values (such as, habitat for critical species)

- rights to engage in certain high-impact, industrial-type farming activities, (such as a feedlot or confined livestock facilities) or commercial activity (such as landfill)

- right to use water from critical source (such as river or aquifer) whose water is also needed to support habitat

In each case, the value of an easement right is determined by a qualified appraiser and the organization that is the intended recipient. The IRS imposes certain standards that the appraisal must fit. A common source of getting in trouble with these easements is to have a compliant appraiser inflate the value of the right being donated. While appraising a right in a property is always going to be somewhat subjective, it is not a bottomless cookie jar. A bit of puffing is likely to slip by; greed probably won't. The receiving organization does not want to have its tax-exempt status challenged on the grounds that it is being used by tax scammers.

To maximize your tax benefits and minimize future IRS problems, develop a plan for a conservation easement on a target property before submitting an offer and with the assistance of an experienced CPA and lawyer. Your easement idea must meet the IRS's standards, and you must have the numbers (of your tax benefits) run in advance of negotiating a purchase price. You need professional help to do this. (Do I need to repeat this?) The local organization should have a list of experienced appraisers, CPAs and lawyers.

Conservation easements can protect a buyer's profit in flipping a target property, as well as profit from the taxpayer's other activities. They don't directly generate money to buy, but they can increase after-tax net income. A buyer has to run sale numbers on a flip with alternative easement scenarios to see, which, if any, are of benefit. Without an easement, a buyer who flips can expect higher gross income, but less net after-tax; with an easement, there will be lower gross sale income but possibly more after tax. When buying property that carries a conservation easement, remember you are buying less than the whole package of rights. The property should be priced below how it would be priced in tact.

Life is always easier when you have cash. It certainly helps when buying land. There's nothing wrong with putting 30 percent down in cash and borrowing the rest from the first bank that gives you two balloons and a lollipop. That's easy. If you're not cash-lucky, consider some of the ways I've presented to piece together a purchase using the cash you can comfortably spare, different types of debt, the resources of the property itself and the federal tax code. Think of patching together a financing package, a technique that works as well on a $25,000 two-acre lot as on a $10 million purchase of 10,000 acres. Patching purchase money together from five or six sources takes time and persistence, but it can save you thousands of dollars. Not having cash is a problem that can almost always be solved as long as you acquire the information you need to develop a feasible plan before you submit an offer. But no plan should stretch your ability to pay off mortgage debt.

CHAPTER 34: A FINAL PLEA

As I was writing, I heard a report that 90 percent of house buyers make a yes/no decision within the first 30 minutes of their first visit. And about the same percentage of big life decisions are made on the basis of emotions, what feels right.

Given this evidence, the best advice I can offer is this: don't communicate your intention to buy to the seller or his agent during your first visit or immediately thereafter.

Take the questions and methods I've discussed and start scoping the property you've already chosen to buy. But leave yourself room for an analytical out. If your head can't solve the property's problems and issues during your scoping, buying certainly won't. Keep looking. Most problems have solutions, fortunately, but some are too expensive to consider seriously.

Scoping a property that you must have will help you in at least two ways: first, you'll know what you're getting into before you get there, which can help you negotiate solutions with the seller; and second, you'll know what you're getting into before you get there whether or not you can negotiate solutions with the seller.

Knowledge is worth the time spent and expense of acquiring it.

CHAPTER 35: AFTERWORD

I provide three types of consulting services to land buyers.

First, I provide telephone consultations charged at $125 per hour. My number is: 540-474-3297.

I do not accept credit cards. They add cost to my service and detract from the trust I promote with my clients.

Send me a check for $62.50, which covers my time in setting up your account and provides you with 30 minutes of assistance. Call me five days after putting your check in the mail. Time beyond the first 30 minutes is billed to you at my hourly rate. Payment is due at the end of each session.

Focus your questions as much as possible. Put them in writing. I am not a lawyer or a CPA, so specific questions in those fields are better directed to those practitioners. I have a network of contacts around the country, which may be useful to you.

Second, you can mail me a summary of your situation and follow it up with a phone consultation. Include your address, phone, fax and e-mail. I'll get back to you as soon as I can.

I charge a flat $50 to read your initial contact information and think about it. Enclose a check for that amount, made out to Curtis Seltzer. After that it's $125 per hour. I've found over the years that clients are best served by taking the time to put their story in writing rather than tell it to me cold. Keep your narrative to three or four pages.

Send this to:

Curtis Seltzer

1467 Wimer Mountain Road

Blue Grass, VA 24413-2307

Third, I am available to find property on a fee basis. My fee is a percentage of the gross sales price, to be paid by the settlement agent from the buyer's funds at closing. The amount of the fee depends on the size and value of the property purchased along with other factors. The larger the property, the lower the percentage. You and I will sign a contract that sets forth my duties and your obligations.

This is a finder's service. A small amount of consulting will be thrown in for free. But after that, say an hour, I will charge the hourly rate. You owe me the fee only if you buy a property that I introduce to you, but you owe me the hourly rate for discussions beyond the basic introduction.

Scoping is charged at the hourly rate. If you want me to visit the property with you, I will charge the hourly rate, plus expenses.

If you're interested in working with me as a consultant-finder, write me a short letter that outlines what you're looking for, where, why and your price range. I don't charge for reading these proposals. I'll talk with you and send a contract if we decide to work together.

I'm not a real-estate agent or broker, and I do not provide clients with brokerage services. I am paid by the buyer, not the seller.

MONEY-BACK GUARANTEE

If you feel after reading
How To Be a DIRT-SMART Buyer of Country Property
that you did not get $34.95 worth of information
or, at least, 750 pages of sleep therapy, send me the umarked copy
with your receipt and I will reimburse you.

Positive comments are welcome – especially from those who don't
owe me money and family relations with different last names.

I may post comments on my website, www.curtis-seltzer.com.

Snide, nitpicky and hateful observations will be posted on my office
wall where they will do the most good.

curtisseltzer@htcnet.org